2000

CHARACTERS IN 19th-CENTURY LITERATURE

CHARACTERS IN
19th-CENTURY LITERATURE

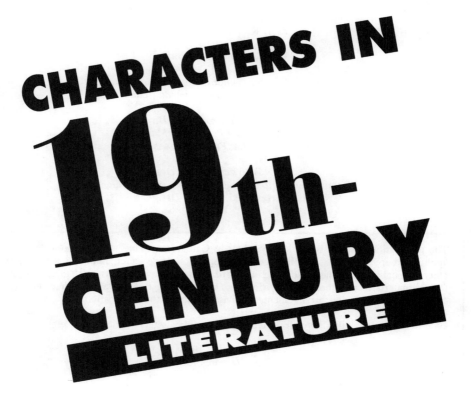

Kelly King Howes

 Gale Research Inc.

DETROIT • WASHINGTON, D.C. • LONDON

Kelly King Howes, *Editor*

Gale Research Inc. Staff

Lawrence W. Baker, *Senior Developmental Editor*
Carol DeKane Nagel, *Developmental Editor*

Mary Beth Trimper, *Production Director*
Evi Seoud, *Assistant Production Manager*
Mary Winterhalter, *Production Assistant*

Cindy Baldwin, *Art Director*
Arthur Chartow, *Technical Design Services Manager*
Mary Krzewinski, *Graphic Designer*

This book is printed on acid-free paper that meets the minimum requirements of American National Standard for Information Sciences—Permanence Paper for Printed Library Materials, ANSI Z39.48-1984.

ISBN 0-8103-8398-5

Printed in the United States of America

Published simultaneously in the United Kingdom
by Gale Research International Limited
(An affiliated company of Gale Research Inc.)

To my grandmother,
Katherine Jane Kelly Cleary

Contents

Preface   ix

Preface

Characters perform necessary functions in works of fiction and drama. They advance plots, voice themes, and embody authors' ideas and dreams. Yet to readers, characters are more than technical elements—they supply a lifeline into literature. In addition to its lush language and imagery, compelling themes, and fascinating depictions of human life a century ago, nineteenth-century literature is a rich repository of unforgettable characters. Elizabeth Bennett, Captain Ahab, Natty Bumppo, the Mad Hatter, Mr. Micawber—these are not just names but beloved or comical or awe-inspiring acquaintances who seem nearly as real as the people around us. One of the purposes of *Characters in 19th-Century Literature* is to show how the works featured here afford readers both the pleasure of escape from the modern world and the exhilaration of discovering again and again that so many human questions and concerns were as important one hundred years ago as they are today.

The Scope of the Work

The essays in *Characters in 19th-Century Literature* elucidate the function and significance of more than 2200 characters from nearly 200 works of 100 of the nineteenth century's major novelists, dramatists, and short story writers. Readers will find that, in general, a writer's most representative and widely discussed works are featured. *CNCL* is modeled after *Characters in 20th-Century Literature,* published by Gale Research in 1990, which included in its scope authors now living or who have died since 1899. Thus some authors whose works were produced in the latter years of the nineteenth century (such as Mark Twain, Thomas Hardy, and Leo Tolstoy) appear in both *CNCL* and *CTCL,* with the *CNCL* entries supplementing those in the previous volume. In the case of Stephen Crane, for instance, both volumes cover *The Red Badge of Courage,* but *CNCL* also features Crane's other novel, *Maggie, Girl of the Streets,* and three of his acclaimed short stories. In addition to authors who died in the early years of the twentieth century, several who began their careers in the eighteenth century and lived into the nineteenth (including Johann Wolfgang von Goethe and Susanna Haswell Rowson) have been included in *CNCL,* based on the influence or importance of their work to nineteenth-century literature.

A special effort has been made to cover lesser-known women writers and others from a wide spectrum of ethnic backgrounds. Thus *CNCL* focuses not only on such acknowledged masters as Charles Dickens and Jane Austen but on African-American novelists Harriet Wilson and William Wells Brown, Scottish novelist Margaret Oliphant, and Brazilian novelist Joaquim Machado de Assis.

The Organization of the Work

The book is arranged alphabetically by author. Each author entry begins with the following elements: the author's name, birth and death dates, nationality, and principal genres. The author's works are chronologically arranged, and the title heading offers the full title (including original-language title, where necessary), genre, and date of publication. The essay on each work begins with a brief plot synopsis followed by descriptions of characters and analysis of how they illustrate the author's central themes and aesthetics. Major characters are elucidated in some depth, while attention to minor characters is commensurate with their significance. *CNCL* is designed to help students and general readers understand authors' ethical or philosophical points of view and discover trends or patterns in his or her major works, as well as ways in which the works were affected by—or themselves influenced—the historical context in which they appeared.

All characters' names when first mentioned in the character profiles are boldfaced for easy reference. If a character is known by more than one name—for example, "Tony Jobling" and "Weevle" in Dickens's *Bleak House*—both are included, boldfaced, and indexed. Essays vary in length, reflecting the magnitude, complexity, and importance of individual works. A list of critical essays and articles for further reading concludes each author entry. This section includes references to several literary series published by Gale Research, including *Nineteenth-Century Literature Criticism, Twentieth-Century Literary Criticism, Short Story Criticism,* and *Dictionary of Literary Biography.* The book concludes with an index to characters and titles. If a character is designated with a generic term such as "the Devil," the character name is followed by the title of the work in which that character appears.

The final list of authors for *CNCL* was compiled with the invaluable assistance of an advisory board comprised of respected librarians and teachers, whose professional perspectives and guidance ensured that the book would best serve its intended audience. Advisors included: Ted Balcom, Candy Carter, Sara Karow, Kathy Martin, Mike Printz, Pam Spencer, Hilda Weisburg, and Brooke Workman. In addition, curriculum guides from selected school districts (urban, suburban, and rural) and two studies on secondary school reading lists (sponsored by the State University of New York at Albany and by the New England Association of Teachers of English) were consulted to determine which nineteenth-century works teachers are currently using in the classroom.

Acknowledgments

I would like to thank Dedria Bryfonski, Chris Nasso, and Amy Marcaccio of New Publications Development at Gale for entrusting me with this project; Dan Marowski of the Literary Criticism series for his encouragement and guidance; my developmental editor, Carol DeKane Nagel, for her dedication, professionalism, and moral support; my copyeditor, Fran Freiman Locher, for her conscientious work; the editors of *Nineteenth-Century Literature Criticism,* particularly Paula Kepos, for their help in honing the author list; and especially Margaret Rose King for research assistance. It is not possible to adequately thank my husband, Robert Craig Howes, Jr., for his unflagging good humor, tolerance, and encouragement, but I do.

William Harrison Ainsworth

1805-1882

English novelist, short story writer, poet, balladist, and editor.

Jack Sheppard (novel, 1839)

Plot: The novel takes place in and around London in the first quarter of the eighteenth century. As it opens, carpenter Owen Wood is paying a condolence call on Joan Sheppard, whose husband Tom has been hanged for stealing from Wood. Joan lives in poverty in the criminal-infested Old Mint district. She tells Wood of an ominous prophesy that her son Jack will meet the same fate as his father, but she refuses Wood's offer to take the baby away to a better life. Wood then encounters a mob of men led by Sir Rowland Trenchard and accompanied by the "thief-taker" (similar to a modern-day bounty hunter) Jonathan Wild; they are pursuing a man named Darrell. Later that night, during a great storm, Wood rescues a baby that the fleeing Darrell had been carrying when he drowned in the Thames River. Wood names the baby Thames Darrell and raises him. Twelve years later Wood has brought Jack Sheppard into his shop as an apprentice; Jack is lazy, however, while Thames is an industrious worker. The two boys, along with Wood's daughter Winnifred (also twelve years old), are good friends. Meanwhile, Wild has been plotting to ensnare Jack and hang him just as he hanged Tom Sheppard. He also discovers that Thames is the son of Sir Rowland's sister Lady Alvira, whose husband Darrell had drowned that stormy night and who had subsequently been forced against her will to marry her cousin, Sir Cecil Trafford. Sir Rowland stands to inherit all of his sister's property if she has no heir, so Wild offers to help him by removing Thames from the scene. He also claims to know where to find Sir Rowland's other sister, Constance, who as a baby was stolen by gypsies. Wild and Sir Rowland falsely accuse Jack and Thames of stealing, but they manage to escape from jail. Wild manages to have Thames forcibly sent off to sea with the Dutch sea captain, Van Galgebrok, while Jack quickly becomes a full-fledged criminal, spending his time in the seedy Old Mint district. His mother tries to persuade him to return to an honest life but he spurns her, and she is ridiculed by his companions. Wild, now plotting against Sir Rowland because he hopes to acquire the estate of Sir Montacute Trenchard (Thames's grandfather) as well, has Sir Rowland arrested and jailed for treason. Wild also gives Jack Owen Wood's master key, which he had picked up the night of the great storm twelve years earlier. Jack breaks into Wood's house and is caught, but he again escapes from prison. Visiting his mother, Jack affirms his love for her but claims he will never give up his criminal ways.

Nine years later, Jack is a celebrated thief and jailbreaker. Wood has become a wealthy man. Joan Sheppard has been driven mad by worry over her son and has been committed to Bedlam, the notoriously squalid insane asylum. Sir Rowland is released from prison, and Thames—who managed to escape with his life after being thrown overboard from Van Galgebrok's ship—has made his way to France and is serving under Philip of Orleans. Jack

1

learns that his mother is actually Sir Rowland's sister and demands that Wild give him his rightful share of her property. Wild refuses. After breaking their ties with Wild, Jack and Blueskin (Wild's former henchman) again try to rob the Wood house. Mrs. Wood resists them and is murdered by Blueskin. Jack visits his mother at Bedlam and her sanity is restored by a blow from Wild, who has followed Jack there. Wild now informs Sir Rowland of Joan Sheppard's real identity then kills Sir Rowland and tries to force Joan to marry him so that he will gain her property. She kills herself rather than marry Wild. Jack has since been imprisoned but he escapes in order to attend his mother's funeral, where he is again apprehended. Meanwhile, Thames has returned to England and learned that his father Darrell was in reality a French nobleman, the Marquis de Chatillon. He inherits the Trenchard estates and marries Winnifred Wood. Jack is finally executed for his crimes, and Wild eventually meets the same fate.

Characters: *Jack Sheppard* is usually associated with the Newgate novels, a genre of nineteenth-century English works that feature sympathetically portrayed criminal heroes and underworld settings. Published serially and immensely popular with the general public, *Jack Sheppard* was criticized by early reviewers for its focus on a flagrantly immoral person whose behavior was not adequately censured. Although the criminal characters are eventually punished for their evil deeds, the novel lacks the didactic tone of such works as Charles Dickens's *Oliver Twist,* which also chronicled the life and personalities of London's seedy underworld. Although Ainsworth's characters are often described as flat and unrealistic—"the merest cardboard puppets," as critic Francis Gribble called them—he is praised for his attempt to probe the darker side of human nature and for the accurate descriptions and riveting action that mark *Jack Sheppard.*

The character of **Jack Sheppard** is based on an actual seventeenth-century thief and jailbreaker who, according to the celebrated novelist William Makepeace Thackeray, is in the novel "metamorphosed from a vulgar ruffian into a melodramatic hero with all the melodramatic virtues and splendours about him." Ainsworth's Jack is physically dashing and agile as well as intelligent and resourceful, qualities that account for his great success in thievery and escaping from prisons. The revelation that he is actually a bearer of aristocratic blood—through his mother, who is in reality Sir Rowland's sister—seems to be offered as an explanation of Jack's more noble attributes, which, because of the environment in which he was raised, have been overshadowed by his coarser impulses. Though Jack does enter into criminality wholeheartedly and commits many heinous deeds, it is always evident that he is at heart a good person who has been molded by forces outside his control. His basic goodness is particularly evidenced by his loyalty to his mother, for whom he professes undying love but with whose wishes for his reform he will not comply. Jack does, however, die repentant and full of remorse for his crimes.

Thames Darrell is presented as the antithesis of Jack Sheppard: he is virtuousness personified, the romantic hero of conventional literature. That Jack and Thames come from similar backgrounds (both of their fathers were killed and their mothers mistreated) makes Thames's role as a foil to Jack even more pronounced. He has reacted to his disadvantages with industriousness and avoidance of evil, while Jack has responded to his own situation by turning to crime. In the end, Thames is rewarded with marriage to Winnifred. Thames also provides an example of Ainsworth's frequent use of mistaken identities; it is finally revealed that his father was a French aristocrat—another similarity with Jack, whose mother was actually descended from the noble.

The "thief-taker" **Jonathan Wild,** like Jack Sheppard, is based on a historical figure of the same name, though Ainsworth has embellished his character to make him the epitome of corruption. While Sir Rowland demonstrates the aristocracy's capacity for evil, Wild comes from a much lower social strata but is at least as evil (if not more so) than his higher-born crony. He is conniving and vengeful; he not only has not forgotten that Joan Sheppard once spurned his love but has cold-heartedly plotted to wreak his revenge in the most protracted, hurtful way possible—by corrupting first her husband and then her son and seeing both executed. Wild's lust for power is such that he wants to gain control of the entire underworld. His violence and brutality are demonstrated when he beats Sir Rowland nearly to death and then stomps on his fingers as he clings desperately to the rim of the well into which Wild has thrown him—a gruesome, graphic scene often cited to illustrate the violence of Ainsworth's work.

The remaining characters in *Jack Sheppard* do not stand up to detailed analysis. Jack's mother **Joan Sheppard** is a sensitive woman whose obvious refinement even in the most dismal and reduced of circumstances foretells the later disclosure of her noble birth. Thus she provides an example of Ainsworth's often employed—and much faulted—device of mistaken identity, for she is in reality Constance Trenchard, stolen at birth by gypsies. Joan's sojourn at the famous insane asylum Bedlam also allows Ainsworth to include a hair-raising description of that notorious place. **Sir Rowland Trenchard** is primarily a stock villain, evil and calculating, who meets the ignominious end he clearly deserves. **Owen Wood,** the carpenter who adopts Thames and apprentices both him and Jack in his shop, is hapless and kindhearted, while **Mrs. Wood** is a shrewish, domineering woman who disapproves of her husband's kindness to Jack and whose prediction that he'll amount to nothing helps push Jack toward a life of crime. **Winnifred Wood,** offered as Thames's reward for being so virtuous, is a conventional heroine—beautiful and chaste. **Blueskin** is first Wild's and later Jack's henchman; his brutal murder of Mrs. Wood demonstrates his capacity for violence but he also serves to show that Jack does inspire loyalty. **Bess** and **Poll,** the two prostitutes who encourage Jack to defy his mother, help to flesh out Ainsworth's vivid portrait of London's criminal realm; they provide a hint of carnality that probably added to the book's sensationalist appeal. **Van Galgebrok** is the shady Dutch seaman and conjuror who prophesies when Jack is a baby that he will meet a bad end; he is later employed by Wild to dispose of Thames.

Further Reading

Dictionary of Literary Biography, Vol. 21. Detroit: Gale.

Ellis, S. M. *William Harrison Ainsworth and His Friends.* 2 vols. London: John Lane the Bodley Head, 1911.

Gribble, Francis. "Harrison Ainsworth." *Fortnightly Review* LXXXIII, No. CCCCLIX (1 March 1905): 533-42.

Hollingsworth, Keith. "The First Newgate Novels, 1820-1834" and "The Newgate Novel and the Moral Argument, 1837-1840." In *The Newgate Novel, 1830-1847: Bulwer, Ainsworth, Dickens, & Thackeray,* pp. 65-110, 111-66. Detroit: Wayne State University Press, 1963.

Ligocki, Llewellyn. "Ainsworth's Historical Accuracy Reconsidered." *Albion* 4, No. 1 (Spring 1972): 23-8.

Nineteenth Century Literature Criticism, Vol. 13. Detroit: Gale.

Thackeray, William Makepeace. "William Ainsworth and 'Jack Sheppard.'" *Fraser's Magazine* XXI, No. CXXII (February 1840): 227-45.

Worth, George J. *William Harrison Ainsworth.* New York: Twayne Publishers, 1972.

Pedro Antonio de Alarcón
1833-1891

Spanish novelist, novella and short story writer, poet, dramatist, travel writer, and critic.

The Three-Cornered Hat (*El sombrero de tres picos;* novel, 1874)

Plot: Much of the novel's action takes place at an old flour mill in a village in Spain's Andalusian (southern) region. Many of the town's most prominent citizens meet under the mill's grape arbor to eat, talk, and admire Frasquita, the beautiful wife of mill owner Lucas. A frequent visitor is the town's *corregidor,* or mayor, Don Eugenio, who falls in love with the happily married Frasquita. After his attempt to seduce her fails, Eugenio plots revenge. He lures Lucas away from home one night, but Lucas has suspicions about the mayor's real intentions and warns Frasquita to bolt the door. When Eugenio arrives at the mill, Frasquita repels his advances. After he falls into the millpond, however, she has Eugenio put to bed while she searches for Lucas. Meanwhile, Lucas has managed to sneak back home undetected, only to find Eugenio in his bed. Thinking that his wife has been unfaithful, Lucas plots his own revenge: he dresses in Eugenio's clothing and pays a call on Dona Mercedes, the mayor's wife. Frasquita, unable to find Lucas, returns to the mill just in time to see Eugenio leaving in the miller's clothes. Both head for the mayor's house, where Lucas is found hiding under Dona Mercedes's bed. The wives are furious, but the confusion is finally straightened out. Lucas begs Frasquita to forgive him for mistrusting her, and the two live happily together into old age. Eugenio is permanently scorned by his wife and never visits the mill again.

Characters: Considered Alarcón's finest achievement, *The Three-Cornered Hat* combines elements of the romantic literary tradition dominant in the early nineteenth century with the realism that emerged in the late nineteenth and early twentieth centuries. The story is based on an oral folk tale that Alarcón remembered from his childhood; his witty, lively recounting reveals his delight in Spanish characters and customs. Critics have noted that the characters seem merely incidental—that they conform to types based on their roles in the story. Still, Alarcón is praised for his use of naturalistic dialogue, colorful descriptions, and brisk pacing.

The characters in *The Three-Cornered Hat* who uphold the typically Spanish virtues of chastity, honor, and decency are rewarded, while the one who represents the sins of lust and egotism is punished. **Lucas,** the miller whose wife is the object of the mayor's desire, is friendly and good hearted. Though he is ugly and has a slightly humped back **Frasquita** loves him, and he is not jealous despite the admiration she attracts from other men. Lucas reveals his sense of humor in his successful plot to thwart Don Eugenio's first attempt to seduce Frasquita. She, like her husband, enjoys a good joke and is willing to play innocently along with the mayor in order to humiliate him—by knocking his chair over in a flurry of pretended confusion. While Frasquita proves her faithfulness to Lucas by fending off the mayor's later seduction attempt, Lucas shows that he is capable of misjudgment and suspicion when he believes that Frasquita has succumbed to Eugenio's advances. In the end, though, all is explained and forgiven and the couple continues along as before—happy, prosperous, and popular with the townsfolk who gather at the mill.

Don Eugenio does not meet such a happy fate. An older man with a wrinkled face, no teeth, and a large hump on his back, he is as ugly as Lucas but lacks the miller's inner goodness. Eugenio creates an image of self-importance partly through his dramatic costume—the big, black hat that gives the novel its title, a red cape, white stockings, and buckled shoes. As an egotistical government official who expects subservience from everyone, the mayor has been said to represent the jaded modernism that Alarcón rejected in favor of a more simple, traditional, and inherently moralistic outlook. Lust and vulgarity were thought to result from the influence of the French on Spanish culture, and those negative qualities are conquered in *The Three-Cornered Hat* by Spanish faithfulness and chastity. Ironically, the married Eugenio sets out to gain the sexual favors of another man's wife; in the end, however, he not only falls short of that goal but is banished from his own wife's (**Dona Mercedes**) bedroom. In addition, he loses the respect of the villagers, for he never joins them under the grape arbor again.

Further Reading

Atkinson, William C. "Pedro Antonio de Alarcón." *Bulletin of Spanish Studies* X, No. 39 (July 1933): 136-41.

Colford, William E. Introduction to *The Three-Cornered Hat*, pp. i-xiii, by Pedro Antonio de Alarcón, translated by Harriet de Onis. Hauppauge, N.Y.: Barron's Educational Series, 1958.

Dendle, Brian J. "The Religious Problem in the Spanish Novel: Pedro Antonio de Alarcón." In *The Spanish Novel of Religious Thesis, 1876-1936,* pp. 21-6. Princeton: Princeton University Press, 1968.

Nineteenth Century Literature Criticism, Vol. 1. Detroit: Gale.

Winslow, Richard W. "The Distinction of Structure in Alarcón's 'El sombrero de tres picos' and 'El capitan veneno.'" *Hispania* XLVI, No. 4 (December 1963): 715-21.

Leopoldo Alas
1852-1901

Spanish novelist, short story writer, dramatist, critic, essayist, and journalist.

La Regenta (novel, 1884-85)

Plot: Set in the fictional town of Vetusta in nineteenth-century Spain, the novel centers on a young woman named Ana Ozores. Essentially orphaned as a child—her mother died and her father primarily left her in the care of a cruel governess—she was raised by her two equally unkind, unmarried aunts after her father's death when she was fourteen. Ana's aunts were eager to marry their pretty niece to a wealthy man, and she subsequently wed Don Victor Quintana, a respectable judge who was much older than his new wife. Ana, who would like to be a mother but remains childless, is lonely and bored with life among the gossipy, relentlessly materialistic residents of Vetusta. She turns to religion for solace, seeking the guidance of Fermin DePas, the most powerful priest in the city. Like Ana, he is in desperate need of affection and feels oppressed by the vulgarity of those around him. He eventually falls in love with Ana, though he initially channels his feelings into his efforts to increase her spirituality. Ana, however, feels attracted not to DePas but to a man notorious in Vetusta for his amorous conquests: Alvaro Mesia, a frequent visitor in her home and supposedly a friend of her husband. Torn between her spiritual yearnings and the physical desire that draws her toward Mesia, Ana falls seriously ill. Although Victor is concerned about his wife's condition, he does not comprehend its true cause. After her recovery, Ana spends a happy period of platonic harmony with DePas that is shattered when the priest reveals his love for her. Ana is initially repulsed by this declaration and then feels compassion for DePas, but she does not return his love. Instead, she succumbs to the advances of Alvaro and is soon embroiled in a passionate affair with him.

Desperately jealous, DePas seeks revenge against Ana by plotting with her maid, Petra, to expose the liaison. Petra sets Victor's clock ahead one hour so that he rises earlier than usual and sees Alvaro leaving Ana's room; he immediately challenges his wife's lover to a duel. Although Victor comes to realize that such an action is outmoded and foolish, he goes through with the duel and is killed by Alvaro, who subsequently flees Vetusta. The townspeople now turn on Ana, whom they had previously admired, and condemn her for her immorality. Abandoned and isolated, Ana goes to the cathedral to find some comfort in faith and to beg DePas to forgive her. He coldly rejects her. Ana faints, and while she is lying on the floor of the dark cathedral, an unsavory young acolyte takes advantage of her vulnerability and kisses her; she wakes with a strong feeling of repulsion.

Characters: Widely recognized as one of the greatest works of nineteenth-century Spanish literature, *La Regenta* is noted for its wealth of realistic detail, its biting criticism of social and religious hypocrisy, and the psychological depth of its characterizations. Influenced by the realistic and naturalistic movements in literature—particularly as practiced by the French novelists Emile Zola and Gustave Flaubert—Alas combines a sarcastic and critical attitude toward small-town narrow-mindedness with sympathy for his primary characters and a mild humor not found in the more pessimistic works of his French counterparts.

The central figure of *La Regenta,* **Ana Ozores,** is often compared to the title character of Flaubert's 1856 novel *Madame Bovary* because she is emotional and introspective and struggles with the conflict between the life she has idealistically envisioned and that which she actually leads. She is a beautiful woman but her beauty was used as a lure for marriageable men by her calculating aunts, who also instilled in her a lingering guilt when they severely chastised her for spending a night in a boat with a young boy, because strong surf prevented their landing. Both Ana's upbringing and her elderly husband's impotence contribute to her repressed sexuality; her physical need is compounded by her desire for affection and her vaguely mystical yearnings. Refined and idealistic, she feels out of place among the avaricious, licentious people with whom she must associate. She can resign herself to marital faithfulness (and accept the sexual starvation it entails), sublimate her own personality in religion by following DePas, or seek sexual fulfillment with Alvaro. In focusing on Ana's choice and its consequences, Alas compellingly portrays the human need for physical and emotional companionship with others as well as for spiritual union with God. In the end Alas exposes the frailty of the human situation and the failure of love to liberate people when he depicts Ana alone and despairing. Alas has been universally praised for creating in Ana a well-rounded character who is neither totally victimized nor entirely blameless; though subject to vanity and unrealistic romantic longings, she is basically well-intentioned and is to some extent the product of her lonely childhood and unfulfilling marriage. Some critics identify such characteristics as her occasional masochism, her mystical tendencies, her strong need for affection, her pride, her individuality, and her romantic idealism as traditionally Spanish qualities.

Scholars also laud Alas for his portrayal of **Fermin DePas,** the priest who serves as Ana's confessor and eventually falls in love with her. Strong both physically and intellectually, DePas has raised himself to his current position of influence through hard work and determination, pushed along every step of the way by his domineering mother. Although he is proud of his accomplishment and even hungry for more power, DePas feels lonely and isolated in the limited confines of his small town. His reasons for pursuing Ana are various: he wants to help her reach a higher level of spirituality but he also wants to dominate her, and there is also a sexual element in his attentions that he reveals when he declares his love for her. While a few critics have described DePas as hypocritical for concealing his lust for power and sex behind fervent piety, others characterize him as a complex character who combines both good and bad qualities. Like Ana, he exemplifies the individual trapped in a confining social role and experiencing a conflict between what he aspires to be and what he actually is. In the end DePas succumbs to his feelings of frustration and jealousy and contributes to the downfall of the woman he loves, finally rejecting her with a cold cruelty that runs directly counter to the precepts of his professed faith.

Don Victor Quintana, Ana's kind and generous but elderly husband, plays an important role in the story because he represents the conjugal duty that is one of the forces with which Ana struggles. Although sloppy in appearance, sexually impotent, boring, and incapable of truly understanding his wife's needs or wishes, Victor is basically a decent person—he might even be seen as the most sympathetic character in the novel. An amateur botanist and inventor and an ardent hunter, Victor is nevertheless ill-equipped as a husband for a sensitive and intelligent young woman; in fact, the marriage was not his idea but that of his friend Frigilis, who exerts undue influence over him. Victor never suspects Ana's infidelity before he is forced to confront it, and he is naively proud with the friendly attentions of the man who later betrays him, Alvaro. Fond of the romantic works of the seventeenth-century Spanish dramatist Pedro Calderon, Victor responds to the discovery of his wife's affair as a romantic hero would—by challenging her lover to a duel. He realizes too late how ridiculous it is to adhere to exaggerated ideals of honor and to adapt theatrical practices to everyday life.

Ana's dashing lover **Alvaro Mesia,** known as the Don Juan of Vetusta, is an experienced seducer who heartlessly manipulates women to attain their sexual favors. While DePas may be said to represent the false religious ideals of his society, Alvaro embodies its most flagrant immorality and corruption in his quest for self-gratification. Alvaro pursues Ana relentlessly and finally breaks down her resistance; she does find sexual satisfaction with him. After the duel in which he kills Victor, however, Alvaro reveals his cowardice by fleeing from Vetusta. Not a particularly well-rounded character, he serves as a necessary component of the love triangle chronicled in *La Regenta*.

The remaining characters in the novel, though not depicted with much psychological depth, advance the plot and also personify some of Alas's major concerns. Ana's maid, **Petra,** conspires with DePas to expose her employer's infidelity, because she hopes that the priest will assist her in making a profitable marriage; her conniving has been seen as a rebellion of the servant class against the aristocracy. **Dona Paula,** DePas's mother, is a strong-willed, domineering woman who is partially responsible for her son's accomplishments. She compensates for her own insecure social position by ensuring that he attains power and prestige, but she has raised him without affection. **Frigilis,** Victor's best friend, arranged the marriage between Ana and Victor. Although he is basically a compassionate person, Victor submits too easily, perhaps, to his friend's will. Both men are enthusiastically interested in inventions, a manifestation of the materialism and reliance on emerging technology to solve humanity's problems that was gaining momentum in the mid-nineteenth century. Among the other secular residents of Vetusta are the **Marques de Vagellana,** who typifies the hypocrisy of Ana's society when he calls her affair "nauseating" despite his own brood of illegitimate children; and **Obdulia,** a sexually aggressive and voracious widow with whom many of the supposedly morally upright male townsfolk have had affairs.

Celedonio, the effeminate and oily young acolyte who kisses Ana at the end of *La Regenta,* embodies the clerical hypocrisy that Alas condemned and provides an example of the inappropriate juxtaposition of religion and sex that is one of the novel's central themes. By contrast, **Bishop Camoiran** is a somewhat more sympathetic though flawed character: he is pious and kindly but too weak to stand up to DePas's domination. Critics have noted that

Alas's flagrant scorn for corrupt or unworthy church officials signifies not a lack of belief in the Catholic faith but a concern for the church's survival.

Further Reading

Durand, Frank. "Characterization in *La Regenta:* Point of View and Theme." *Bulletin of Hispanic Studies* XLI (1964): 86-100.

Rutherford, John. *Leopoldo Alas: "La Regenta."* London: Grant & Cutler, 1974.

Sanches, Elizabeth Doremus. "'La Regenta' as Spatial-Form Narrative: A Twentieth-Century Perspective." *Modern Language Notes* 103 (March 1988): 335.

Schyfter, Sara E. "'La loca, la tonta, la literata': Woman's Destiny in Clarín's *La Regenta.*" In *Theory and Practice of Feminist Literary Criticism,* edited by Gabriela Mora and Karen S. Van Hooft, pp. 229-41. Ypsilanti, Mich.: Bilingual Press, 1982.

Twentieth-Century Literary Criticism, Vol. 29. Detroit: Gale.

Valis, Noël M. *The Decadent Vision in Leopoldo Alas.* Baton Rouge: Louisiana State University Press, 1981.

Louisa May Alcott

1832-1888

American novelist, short story and fairy tale writer, poet, essayist, editor, and dramatist.

Little Women; or, Meg, Jo, Beth, and Amy (novel, 1868-69)

Plot: *Little Women* focuses on the March girls—motherly Meg, tomboyish Jo, gentle Beth, and artistic Amy—who live with their mother (whom they call "Marmee") in a small house in Concord, Massachusetts. In the mansion next door reside the wealthy Mr. Lawrence and his nephew Theodore, nicknamed "Laurie." When the novel opens, the girls' father is away serving as a chaplain in the Civil War. It is Christmastime, and Marmee has given her daughters a dollar to spend on presents for themselves. Instead, they buy gifts for her; they then decide to give their delicious breakfast to a poor German family living in their town. Later, Mr. Lawrence sends the Marches a Christmas feast that includes ice cream and bon bons. At a New Year's dance, Jo meets Laurie, who has long wished to make the family's acquaintance. He becomes a frequent visitor in the March household. Almost a year later, in November, word comes that Mr. March is ill. Jo sells her beautiful long hair so that Marmee can go to nurse him. While she is away, Beth contracts scarlet fever and nearly dies. Marmee is called back, but by then Beth has recovered. The family receives a joyful surprise on Christmas Day, when Mr. March returns. The book's second part, called "Good Wives," was published a year after the first. As it begins, Laurie's tutor, John Brooke, has fallen in love with Meg and they are married. Jo, who is now selling stories to newspapers to supplement the household income, is mortified when the family's Aunt March asks the much more ladylike Amy to accompany her to Europe. Jo goes to New York to work as a governess for Mrs. Kirke, who runs a boarding house, and befriends one of the boarders, kind Professor Bhaer. When Jo returns home to care for Beth, whose health has taken another turn for the worse, Laurie asks her to marry him. Jo refuses him, declaring that she will never marry. After Beth dies that spring, Jo feels very lonely, though she is somewhat cheered by Meg's children, twins Daisy and Demi. Meanwhile, Laurie has traveled to Europe, where he and Amy see each other often. The two surprise the Marches by announcing on their return that they are married. On his way to a new teaching post in the Midwest, Professor Bhaer visits Jo at home. When he learns of Jo's sadness over his impending departure, the professor asks her to marry him, and she accepts. When Aunt March dies and leaves her home, Plumfield, to Jo, the Bhaers open a school there. The novel ends with Marmee surrounded by her family on her sixtieth birthday and wishing that her present happiness will continue throughout her childrens' lives.

Characters: Alcott's autobiographical novel has been loved by readers of all ages for more than one hundred years. She has often been praised for creating realistic characters who sometimes speak ungrammatically and behave badly. Although she defied the prevailing rules for children's literature in the nineteenth century by creating these flawed though likeable characters, readers could identify more with them than with the angelic, adult-like children common in the literature of the period. Alcott's episodic portrayal of nineteenth-century family life has struck some critics as overly sentimental and moralistic, but others describe her work as far less moralistic than much of the literature of the time and type.

Little Women centers on the efforts of each of the four March sisters to overcome, in the manner of Christian in John Bunyan's seventeenth century allegorical novel *The Pilgrim's Progress,* her particular "burden" or weakness. At the end of the first half of *Little Women,* each of the girls has improved, though none has attained perfection. In the second section, the girls' characters develop further as they grow old enough to work, travel, and marry.

Spirited, tomboyish **Jo March**—the second oldest sister—is based on Alcott herself and is considered, not surprisingly, her most successful character. Jo likes to write and devises plays for the sisters to perform; later she helps support the family by selling her stories to newspapers. She is adventurous and spirited, and she finds a kindred soul in Laurie, who becomes her close friend. The "burden" that Jo must overcome is her temper, the violence of which is demonstrated when she almost allows Amy—who has destroyed one of Jo's manuscripts—to drown. Readers and scholars alike have found Jo a delightfully unconventional figure in her determination to pursue her writing avocation and in her disdain for girlish manners, clothes, and conversation. In a 1968 review, Elizabeth Janeway noted that Jo is "the one young woman in nineteenth century fiction who maintains her individual independence . . . and who gets away with it." Despite her unconventional bent, Jo is devoted to her warm family circle and resents—at least initially—the intervention of such outsiders as John Brooke, who will take Meg away by marrying her. Her deep loneliness after Beth's death is another indicator of her attachment to her family. Jo plans to remain unmarried, refusing even the hand of the charming Laurie—an action of which many romantically minded readers disapproved. In an apparent compromise to their wishes, Alcott does have Jo marry Professor Bhaer, a decidedly unromantic figure but Jo's friend and intellectual equal. Some scholars have interpreted Jo's marriage as a disappointing concession to the Victorian notion that a woman's true worth is as a wife and mother. Others, however, note that Jo does continue with her writing and also finds meaningful work and satisfaction as headmistress of Plumfield School.

Meg March, the oldest sister, is sixteen when *Little Women* begins. Pretty and plump, her weakness is her vanity. While serving as a governess to the wealthy Moffat family, she develops a yearning for the kind of luxury she is exposed to in their home. But Meg eventually overcomes her desire for stylish clothing and invitations to elegant balls, and is reconciled to a life of modest circumstances and domesticity. She marries John Brooke, and seems destined for a happy though undistinguished life caring for him and their children. Meg is based on Alcott's oldest sister Anna, who married a man named John Pratt and had two sons.

Beth March, the demure homebody who seems to have no faults at all, claims that her burden is "dishes and dusters, and envying girls with nice pianos, and being afraid of people." More than any of the sisters, Beth is devoted to her home, where she is lovingly sheltered. Many critics have noted that Beth is portrayed as too good and fragile a creature for the real world, so it seems inevitable that she will finally die. Alcott has been commended for the subtle poignancy and lack of melodrama in Beth's death scene; the restraint evident there was rare in an age of drippingly sentimental fiction. Again, Alcott based the character on her own sister, Elizabeth, who also died while still a teenager.

Curly-haired **Amy March,** the youngest sister, is depicted as a somewhat over-indulged girl who must learn to be more thoughtful of others. She is artistic and has rather grandiose dreams about being a famous painter and living in Europe—dreams she is fated to abandon when she settles into a relatively unglamorous, if wealthy, life as Laurie's wife. Amy's tendency to dramatize ordinary events provides some humorous moments, such as her account of the pickled lime incident. The sometimes problematic relationship between Jo and Amy—exemplified by Amy's burning of Jo's manuscript and her being chosen to go to Europe with Aunt March—may reflect Alcott's own mixed feelings about May, the baby of the Alcott family and, like Amy, an artist.

The girls' beloved mother, **Marmee,** is the emotional mainstay of the March family. She represents the Victorian ideal of motherhood in her strength, wisdom, and unbending love. Selflessly devoted to her family, Marmee serves not only as a source of knowledge for her daughters but as their sympathetic confessor and confidante, and she inspires them to better themselves. After they have presented her with Christmas gifts bought with money they might have spent on themselves, Marmee urges them toward even greater generosity by suggesting that they give their delicious breakfast to their less privileged neighbors. Though some critics have faulted Alcott for portraying Marmee as too good to be true, others note that she reveals her imperfection when she tells Jo that she too has a violent temper that she has not always been able to control. She successfully runs the March household while her husband is away—like Alcott's own mother during the long absences of Bronson Alcott.

The girls' father is a much less developed character, never even appearing until the middle the book and playing a muted rule thereafter. It is clear that **Mr. March** is a man with humanitarian and religious instincts, for he is serving as a chaplain for the Civil War troops (Alcott herself served briefly as a Civil War nurse). He is much loved and revered and provides the girls with inspiration to overcome their weaknesses, congratulating them when they do. Scholars have noted that the distant Mr. March resembles Bronson Alcott, who also spent long periods away from his admiring family and whose unorthodox lifestyle made their finances precarious.

Theodore "Laurie" Lawrence is the charming next-door neighbor who becomes a valued member of the March family circle, eventually joining it formally when he marries Amy. Described as a romantically handsome boy with curly hair, Laurie is Jo's age and her equal in high spirits and adventurousness. In addition to being wealthy and good-looking, he is entertaining, affectionate, and generous—if occasionally irresponsible—and generations of female readers have considered him a remarkably good "catch." Some even protest that Jo is wrong to turn down his marriage proposal. But Jo claims that the two are not meant for each other, and that she expects never to marry. Alcott vowed that she would never satisfy her readers' longing to see Jo and Laurie paired off, so it is not surprising that Jo eventually marries a man utterly unlike her old friend. Some critics have viewed Laurie's union with Amy as markedly second-rate, a simple transference of his feelings for Jo to her conveniently available sister.

Professor Bhaer befriends lonely Jo when she moves to New York and eventually wins her heart. The scene in which he proposes to Jo as the two, burdened with packages and standing under an umbrella in the rain, has been praised for its tender realism. Yet Professor Bhaer seems an unlikely object for her affections—a virtually penniless, middle-aged professor of German heritage and fatherly aspect—but she values his intellect and kindness. Although he doesn't approve of the sensational stories Jo writes for newspaper publication, the professor appreciates her intelligence and thus seems an appropriate, supportive partner for her. Although Jo makes a concession to traditional domesticity by marrying, her husband does not demand that she play a particularly domestic role. She continues to work, for instance, as an educator and writer.

The minor characters in *Little Women* include **Aunt March,** an irascible old lady who tests the girls' determination to remain amiable but who reveals her goodheartedness when she wills her mansion to Jo. **Mr. Lawrence,** Laurie's uncle and the Marches' neighbor, is a man of inherent integrity who is indulgent of his nephew and very kind to the girls; his generosities include the delightful Christmas feast he sends to the family, a piano for Beth, and the use of his library for Jo. It is thought that Alcott based the character of Mr. Lawrence on Ralph Waldo Emerson, the acclaimed American writer and thinker who was her father's close friend and the family's neighbor when they lived in Concord. Likewise, Meg's husband **John Brooke** was also modeled after a real person: John Pratt, the husband of Alcott's oldest sister Anna. In *Little Men,* he will be eulogized as having led a "busy, quiet, humble life" and winning many friends along the way.

Little Men: Life at Plumfield with Jo's Boys (novel, 1871)

Plot: This novel provides an account of Plumfield, the school established by Jo and her husband, Professor Bhaer. Plumfield is patterned on the same educational principals espoused by Alcott's father, renowned social theorist Bronson Alcott, particularly the idea that education should nourish not only the mind but the body and spirit. Thus the students at Plumfield not only study traditional subjects but tend garden plots, play games, and take nature walks after church on Sunday. Also emphasized are a sympathy for youthful high spirits (evidenced, for instance, by sanctioned weekly pillow fights), the concept of equal educational opportunities for both sexes and all races, and the absence of corporal punishment. The novel features the same cast as *Little Women,* in addition to some new characters who are students at Plumfield—Tommy Bangs, Nat Blake, Nan Harding, and Dan Kean—the March grandchildren, and a few other minor student figures. Each of the central characters represents one personal failing with which he or she struggles during the course of one year. The story ends at Thanksgiving with a harvest festival celebrating the conquests each has made over his or her fault.

Characters: Though neither *Little Men* nor *Jo's Boy's* is considered as accomplished a novel as *Little Women,* both answered the clamoring of readers for more books about the March family. *Little Men* is much more didactic than its predecessor; it clearly is meant to demonstrate the value of Bronson Alcott's educational theories. Critics have claimed that the characters are not particularly well developed and seem more incidental than those in *Little Women.* Nevertheless, Alcott was lauded for again creating—in contrast to accepted practice in juvenile literature of the time—children who are neither uniformly angelic nor totally bad. The cast includes the March grandchildren: **Daisy Brooke,** as domestic as her mother Meg and utterly devoted to her sometimes abusive brother; **Demi Brooke,** a bookish boy who is curious about how things work; Jo's sons **Teddy Bhaer,** a cuddly, loving, and loveable baby, and **Rob Bhaer,** energetic and impetuous, like his mother; and Laurie and Amy's daughter **Bess Lawrence,** a little blonde beauty adored by all the boys at Plumfield.

Much of the book's action centers on four newly introduced characters and their pranks, misdeeds, and eventual redemption. **Tommy Bangs** is a jokester and budding arsonist; **Nat Blake** is a former street musician who has been known to tell an occasional lie; **Nan**

Harding is an energetic tomboy who competes successfully with boys both on the playing field and in the classroom; and the wild **Dan Kean** fights, gambles, and swears—he is finally expelled from Plumfield but returns chastened and promising to reform. Several minor characters are also featured in *Little Men,* though they have generally been considered stock figures without much thematic importance: the professor's nephews, **Emil and Franz Bhaer;** overweight **Stuffy Cole;** undistinguished **Dolly Pettingill;** clumsy **Ned Barker; Billy Ward,** made mentally deficient by having been pushed too hard intellectually when very young; and **Dick Brown,** a hunchback. Through all of the young people who inhabit *Little Men,* the book espouses the idea that, as noted in an 1871 review in *Harper's Magazine,* "personal sympathy with children, in all their life, even in their pranks and mischief, is the first condition of acquiring influence over them."

Jo's Boys and How They Turned Out (novel, 1886)

Plot: This novel concludes the March family saga. Jo has become a successful novelist in addition to her role as headmistress of Plumfield School. Lawrence College (endowed by the wealthy Mr. Lawrence introduced in *Little Women*) has been established next door to Plumfield and many of the young students from *Little Men* now attend it. *Jo's Boys* illustrates the success of the educational system promoted in the previous book as the children grow into adults and study, marry, and enter the work force. Significantly, both boys and girls establish careers, reflecting Alcott's advocacy of women's rights. Three of the boys who were central to *Little Men*—Nat Blake, Dan Kean, and Professor Bhaer's nephew Emil—also play important roles in *Jo's Boys.* Each has an educative adventure and finally returns to Plumfield. In addition, an interesting new character is introduced: Meg and John Brooke's third child, Josie, a spirited and intelligent girl who insists on equality with boys.

Characters: Written fifteen years after *Little Men, Jo's Boys* is Alcott's farewell to the audience that had so loved the March family. The book was reportedly difficult for Alcott to write, due both to her failing health and to the emotional pain of dredging up memories of people now dead in order to recreate them in fiction. The schoolchildren of *Little Men* are now young men and women and are embarking on such adult pursuits as college, work, marriage, and travel. **Demi Brooke** has become apprenticed to a printer, and **Daisy Brooke**—ever docile and domestic—finally achieves a happy union with a much-improved **Nat Blake. Teddy Bhaer** is still lovable despite the temper he has inherited from his mother, and he surprises Jo (and the reader) by ending up a clergyman. Each of the book's three main characters—Nat Blake, **Emil Bhaer,** and **Dan Kean**—has a trying adventure in the world outside Plumfield, but each survives and returns. Nat goes to Europe to pursue a musical career; he gets into financial trouble when he consorts with a high-living crowd. Emil serves as an officer on a ship that capsizes, but he manages to display his true leadership ability by taking charge of the dire situation. Dan, still emanating what several critics have described as a dangerous sexuality, heads west into the American frontier. He is unfairly imprisoned when he kills a man in self-defense, but—after being injured in an accident—he does return to Plumfield. His ultimate fate, however, is to go back to the West to work as a missionary among the Indians.

One of the most notable aspects of *Jo's Boys* is its unabashedly feminist tone. Alcott seems to have put aside the restraint that marks the other March family novels—all of which contain hints of the author's belief in equality for women. The three main female characters are all successful in their chosen careers: **Nan Harding** is a respected physician who seems to fulfil the promise of a happy unmarried life *almost* achieved by Jo; **Bess Lawrence** is an artist; and **Josie Brooke** is a playful, competitive, bright girl who demands equality with her cousin Teddy and who will eventually achieve a successful career as an actress. Financially secure and solidly established in her literary reputation, Alcott could afford—in this final salute to the March family—to overtly express the feminist convictions her work had always implied.

Further Reading

Brophy, Brigid. "A Masterpiece, and Dreadful." *New York Times Book Review* (10 January 1965): 44.

Dictionary of Literary Biography, Vols. 1, 42. Detroit: Gale.

Elbert, Sarah. *A Hunger for Home: Louisa May Alcott and Little Women.* Philadelphia: Temple University Press, 1984.

Janeway, Elizabeth. "Meg, Jo, Beth, Amy, and Louisa." *The New York Times Book Review* (September 29, 1968): 42, 44, 46.

MacDonald, Ruth K. *Louisa May Alcott.* Boston: Twayne Publishers, 1983.

Nineteenth Century Literature Criticism, Vol. 6. Detroit: Gale.

Review of "Little Men." *Harper's New Monthly Magazine* XLIII, No. CCLV (August 1871): 458.

Stern, Madeleine B. *Critical Essays on Louisa May Alcott.* Boston: G.K. Hall and Co., 1984.

Horatio Alger, Jr.
1832-1899
American novelist, short story writer,
poet, biographer, and essayist.

Ragged Dick(novel, 1868)

Plot: *Ragged Dick* is set in New York City in the last quarter of the nineteenth century. As it opens, the title character wakes up after sleeping outside in a box and goes to work as a bootblack (shoe shine boy). He wears old, ragged clothes, but reveals a plucky spirit as he jokes with his customers. Dick meets a well-to-do businessman, Mr. Whitney, and offers to give the man's nephew Frank a tour of the city. First the Whitneys offer Dick a new set of clothes and the chance to take a bath, and afterward he hardly recognizes himself. Dick and Frank range across the city, viewing such sights as Central Park, City Hall, Broadway, Fifth Avenue, Wall Street, and various famous hotels. Along the way Dick shows Frank how to avoid being swindled, and they ride on a horse-car (a trolley pulled by horses), take a ferry ride to Brooklyn, and come to the aid of a country man who has been cheated of his savings. On their return to the Whitneys' hotel, Mr. Whitney advises Dick to try to make something of himself and gives him a five dollar bill. Inspired by this encounter, Dick determines to raise himself up in the world, beginning by renting a room in a shabby boardinghouse on Mott Street. Feeling more and more ambitious, Dick opens a bank account, then arranges for another street boy, Henry Fosdick, to share his apartment in exchange for tutoring. Dick learns his lessons quickly. The two boys attend church at the invitation of a sympathetic businessman, Mr. Greyson, and eat dinner at the man's home. Dick is now avoiding his old pursuits of gambling, smoking, and attending shows at the Bowery Theater. After an initially discouraging search for a clerk job, Fosdick is chosen over the conceited Roderick Crawford to work in a hat shop.

The story now jumps nine months: Dick has saved $117 and has learned all that Fosdick can teach him. After he offers some money to a friend in trouble, Dick discovers that his bankbook is missing. The thief, fellow boarder Jim Travis, is quickly identified and Dick assists in his capture. Dick would now like to get a job as an office or shop clerk but is unsuccessful in finding one. While riding the ferry to Brooklyn, he saves the life of a small boy who has fallen overboard, nearly drowning himself in the process. The boy's grateful father, James Rockwell, offers Dick a job, and he and Fosdick make plans to move to better quarters. The story ends with the promise of more adventures to be related in successive books.

Characters: Alger wrote more than one hundred works of juvenile fiction. His immense popularity in the late nineteenth century made his name synonymous with the American dream of success through hard work and personal merit, of a rise from ''rags to riches'' that is within the grasp of every citizen. *Ragged Dick* has been called Alger's most popular novel, and in its style, themes, and characters serves as an archetypal model for his many successive books.

Most critics acknowledge that Alger's works display little literary merit but serve instead as interesting documents of American ideals and sentiment in the later nineteenth century. **Ragged Dick** is usually described as Alger's most appealing and most successful character, and his qualities typify those of other Algerian heroes. Dick is an orphaned street boy in his mid-teens who supports himself by blacking boots, sleeps wherever he can, and wears ill-fitting, dirty, torn clothing. Despite his destitution, however, Dick has an inherently noble nature—he is honest, cheerful, bright, and hard-working. He speaks in a slangy street tongue and is adept with wisecracks. Although he indulges in such vices as smoking, gambling, and attending shows at the Old Bowery Theater, Dick would never steal and he is generous to his fellow street boys—especially those who are younger or weaker or lack his own energy. After Dick meets the Whitneys, his long-harbored desire to attain respectability grows stronger, and he sets out on a course of self-improvement that includes dressing neatly, living in a fixed home, becoming educated, saving money, and going to church. Through such imminently improvable subjects as Ragged Dick—who will eventually refer to himself, if somewhat facetiously, as Richard Hunter, Esquire—Alger promotes the value of hard work, education, honesty, cleanliness, abstention from drinking and smoking, and being a dependable, obedient employee. Though critics have traditionally viewed Alger as an enthusiastic proponent of capitalism, more recent scholars have asserted that the goal of Alger's heroes is never great wealth but rather modest respectability; hence Dick aspires only to the lowly income of a clerk. Thus Alger reflects a middle-class ethic nostalgically rooted in the years preceding the industrialized age in which he was actually living. Although Alger is popularly thought to promote the idea that individual effort will be rewarded, luck plays an important role in *Ragged Dick* and other Alger novels as well. For instance, Dick's attempts to gain a better job are unsuccessful until he happens to save the drowning child—then he is rewarded for his courage. Nevertheless, Dick is portrayed as a very deserving recipient of such a reward, and one who is bound to make the best of this unforeseen opportunity.

Dick's fellow bootblack, roommate, and tutor **Henry Fosdick** is typical of the many secondary heroes in Alger's books. He is virtuous, principled (unlike Dick, he has never frequented the Bowery), and intelligent, but he lacks Dick's self-confidence and energy. A fairly recent arrival on the street, Fosdick differs from the other boys in his gentleness and timidity. His former existence—a relatively prosperous, nurturing family life—was upset by his father's death and the swindling of the family's savings. The arrangement Fosdick makes with Dick—to share his learning in exchange for room and board—provides both boys with a sense of home and companionship that they could not have found during their precarious and essentially lonely life on the streets. Ever supportive, helpful, and grateful, Fosdick serves as an amiable foil to the more resourceful Dick.

Two other street boys play significant roles in *Ragged Dick*. Though not as intelligent as Fosdick, **Johnny Nolan** is similar to that character in his marked inferiority to Dick, and, like Fosdick, he provides opportunities for Dick to display his virtues. Near the beginning of the story, for instance, Dick buys Johnny breakfast when the younger boy is out of money. Alger describes Johnny as good-natured but lacking ambition and "that . . . natural sharpness for which Dick was extinguished." After Dick has attained a higher level of accomplishment himself, he resolves to help Johnny whenever he can; he promises to buy his friend a new bootblacking box and brush and to refer his old customers to Johnny. Another of the street boys, **Mickey Malone,** is a stereotypically Irish character described as "a stout, red-haired, freckle-faced boy of fourteen." A great bully who leads a gang of young ruffians, Mickey he grows increasingly hostile toward Dick because he is jealous of the improvements Dick has made in his life. He lacks not only the ambition but the intelligence to overcome his environment, and he has even served some time in prison. In later books in the six-volume Ragged Dick series, Mickey is reformed—though he never attains Dick's level of nobility. Some scholars have faulted Alger's portrayal of Mickey and other members of immigrant groups (especially Irish, Germans, and Italians) as stereotypical; though they may display positive qualities, these characters are almost always shown as inherently inferior.

Similarly, the wealthier characters in *Ragged Dick* tend to conform to types. **Mr. Whitney,** Frank's uncle and the source of the five dollars that begin Dick's bank account, is an educated, sympathetic older man who understands Dick's situation because he himself began as a printer's apprentice. He dispenses such wise gems of advice as "All labor is respectable, lad," encouraging Dick to raise himself up through studiousness and frugality. Described by scholar Alan Trachtenberg as "the voice of bourgeois confidence," Mr. Whitney represents Alger's ideal of gentility. It is significant that he is a member of the merchant class which had, by the time *Ragged Dick* was written, already faded from dominance as America became industrialized and great fortunes were made by such industrialists as Carnegie and Rockefeller. **Frank Whitney,** the privileged boy whom Dick escorts around New York City, provides an occasion to include such attractions as Central Park (then under construction) and Wall Street, thus giving countless young readers their first glimpse of life in the big city. Frank is a kind, educated boy capable of appreciating Dick's merits—particularly his plucky and spirited humor—and of wishing for a better life for his friend. Frank serves as a link between Dick's world and a more genteel life, and both boys learn valuable lessons from each other. Frank represents an ideal, particularly in terms of his schooling, to which Dick aspires, and Frank values Dick for his knowledge of the city and street culture, his wit, and his sincerity.

The minor characters in *Ragged Dick* include the quintessentially upstanding citizen, **Mr. Greyson; James Rockwell,** another wealthy benefactor type; and **Roderick Crawford,** the young aristocrat who competes with Fosdick for the hat store job. Crawford, who also appears in succeeding Ragged Dick novels, is typical of Alger's rich villains (and particularly of their sons) in his snobbery, meanness, and indolence. Dick's landlady **Mrs. Mooney** is another stereotypically Irish character—though poor and slatternly, she is basically honest and warm-hearted. **Jim Travis,** whose "sallow complexion" and "bloodshot eyes" mark him as an obvious villain, is too lazy to get the money he needs by respectable means and is quick to stoop to thievery.

Further Reading

Alger, Horatio, Jr. "Writing Stories for Boys—IV." *The Writer* IX, No. 3 (March 1896): 36-7.

Cowley, Malcolm. "The Real Horatio Alger Story." In *A Many-Windowed House: Collected Essays on American Writers and American Writing,* pp. 76-88, edited by Henry Dan Piper. Carbondale, Ill.: Southern Illinois University Press, 1970.

Dictionary of Literary Biography, Vol. 42. Detroit: Gale.

Gardner, Ralph D. *Horatio Alger, or the American Hero Era.* Mendota, Ill.: Wayside Press, 1964.

Nineteenth Century Literature Criticism, Vol. 8. Detroit: Gale.

Scharnhorst, Gary. *Horatio Alger, Jr.* Boston: Twayne, 1980.

Tebbel, John. *From Rags to Riches: Horatio Alger, Jr. and the American Dream.* New York: Macmillan, 1963.

Trachtenberg, Alan. Introduction to *Ragged Dick; or, Life in New York Among the Bootblacks* by Horatio Alger, Jr. New York: Penguin (Signet Classic), 1990.

Jane Austen
1775-1817
English novelist and poet.

Sense and Sensibility (novel, 1811)

Plot: After the death of their father, Elinor and Marianne Dashwood move with their mother to a cottage on Barton Park estate, owned by Sir John Middleton. The girls' half-brother, John Dashwood, has inherited his father's estate, while his wife Fanny convinces him to refrain from helping his stepmother and stepsisters financially. Fanny also notices with displeasure her brother Edward Ferrars's growing interest in Elinor. Elinor, Marianne, and Mrs. Dashwood become acquainted with Sir John's friend, Colonel Brandon, a pleasant thirty-five-year-old man who grows fond of Marianne. She, however, feels that Brandon is too old for her, and falls in love instead with the dashing John Willoughby, who is visiting some nearby relatives. When Brandon is called away from the neighborhood unexpectedly, it is rumored that he has an illegitimate daughter hidden away somewhere. Willoughby also leaves the neighborhood suddenly, never having proposed to Marianne and unable to make a suitable explanation for his departure. Edward Ferrars visits the Dashwoods at their cottage and Elinor is disappointed that he no longer appears particularly interested in her. Elinor and Marianne meet two visitors in the neighborhood, Miss Lucy Steele and her sister Anne, who prove to be markedly ignorant and vulgar girls. Lucy confides to Elinor the unwelcome information that she has been engaged to Edward for four years, but that the couple—because the occupationless Edward has no money of his own—has had to hide their attachment until his mother consents to the marriage. Though deeply chagrined, Elinor agrees to help them if she can.

When Elinor and Marianne travel to London with Mrs. Jennings, Marianne writes several times to Willoughby to announce her presence, but he never responds. When she meets him at a party, he is accompanied by another girl and behaves toward Marianne in a polite but detached manner. The next day Marianne receives a letter from Willoughby in which he expresses regret if she has misconstrued his intentions, and announces that he is engaged to another. Marianne's friends are angry with Willoughby for deceiving her but she defends him despite her sorrow. Brandon, who is now also in London, explains to Elinor why he left so abruptly: his young ward—not his daughter but the child of his brother's divorced wife—had been seduced by Willoughby, who then abandoned her. Marianne is severely upset by this account of her former suitor. After the Steele sisters arrive in London, Mrs. Ferrars learns of Edward's engagement and immediately transfers his inheritance to his brother Robert. Edward decides to study for the ministry, and Elinor and Brandon arrange for him to serve as curate of Brandon's estate after he has taken religious orders. This will allow him, eventually, to marry Lucy. While Elinor and Marianne have stopped for a brief visit at a country estate on their way home from London, the still emotionally distraught Marianne falls ill. Willoughby calls on them when he hears that she is ailing, and tells Elinor that his family—disgusted by his escapade with Brandon's ward—has cut off his allowance, necessitating his marriage to a wealthy young woman. He asks Elinor to explain his situation to Marianne and to tell her that he still loves her. After Marianne recovers and the sisters return home, Elinor relays Willoughby's story. Though still saddened by the situation, Marianne is no longer in love with him. Edward Ferrars visits the Dashwoods unexpectedly, revealing that Lucy, whose real object was the Ferrars inheritance, has married Robert. Edward is now free to propose to Elinor, and she accepts. He returns to London to ask his mother's forgiveness; because she has since disinherited her other son she is willing to listen to Edward and consents to the marriage when her attempts to dissuade him from marrying Elinor fail. Brandon continues to gently press his suit with Marianne, and she finally realizes that she loves him. They marry, and both couples live happy and prosperous lives.

Characters: Although generally considered her least accomplished novel, *Sense and Sensibility* features many of the concerns and techniques Austen more skillfully executes in later works. The novel is structured in the manner of the antithetical novels popular in the eighteenth century, with Elinor and Marianne representing the opposing values of calm reason and impetuous emotion. Within this thematic framework, the novel explores social manners, mores, and interactions in an upper-middle-class English setting.

The action of *Sense and Sensibility* is primarily viewed through the eyes of **Elinor Dashwood**. Elinor, characterized as possessing ''strength of understanding'' and ''coolness of judgment,'' is a remarkably mature, steady nineteen-year-old who provides a reasoning balance to the melodramatic excesses of her sister and mother. Despite her placid exterior, however, it is always clear that Elinor is capable of deep feeling. She hides her emotions out of a sense of responsibility, though. For instance, she reacts coolly to Edward's rejection in order to spare her family and friends the anxiety they would surely have felt over her distress. Clear in judgment and perception while those around her stumble, Elinor is a figure of stability who is isolated by but finally rewarded for her inherently superior qualities. Many critics have described her as too statically representative of the title's ''sense,'' claiming that she never quite comes to life and is too faultless to be embraced or believed. As a teller of ''polite lies'' who maintains the correct social order by her proper conduct, Elinor is often said to embody a rather narrow-minded adherence to convention. Yet some scholars have pointed out that Elinor's decorousness expresses not so much the claims of society over the individual as a profound and laudable regard for those around her.

As the novel's representative of ''sensibility,'' **Marianne Dashwood** helps to illuminate some of its most important themes. While not completely bereft of sense, she is willfully impulsive and romantic and feels that emotions should always be openly expressed. Although she claims to value sincerity and spontaneity, Marianne displays attitudes that are actually quite rigid. ''At my time of life,'' she confidently says, ''opinions are tolerably fixed. It is not likely that I should now see or hear anything to change them.'' Such a statement from a seventeen-year-old girl foreshadows the comeuppance Austen duly provides. Marianne consistently judges others by her own preconceived notions of what constitutes admirable behavior. Her inability to see others clearly is evinced by her preferring the dashing Willoughby to the conventional Brandon. Unlike Elinor, Marianne has much to learn. In the course of her education she will cause her loved ones great worry and will nearly kill herself with the physical manifestations of the melodramatic, imprudent heartbreak in which she insistently indulges. Marianne's outpouring of passion—though not necessarily the passion itself—is portrayed as dangerous and selfish. While some critics have characterized her eventual union with the unromantic Brandon as a sign that Marianne has attained maturity, it might also be interpreted as punishment for her socially unacceptable behavior.

The girls' mother, **Mrs. Dashwood,** is a warmhearted but impractical woman who has obviously passed her self-indulgent impulsiveness along to Marianne. Elinor must compensate for the maturity her mother lacks and serve as an advisor to someone from whom she might have hoped to receive guidance and help. Thus Mrs. Dashwood is an example of the inadequate parents who people Austen's fiction: usually well-meaning, they force their more sensible and sensitive children to fend for themselves. **John Dashwood,** Elinor and Marianne's half-brother, cold-heartedly ignores his father's directive to provide well for them. The conversation he has with his wife **Fanny,** in which she encourages him to neglect his obligations, is often cited as a bitterly funny spectacle of selfishness. She reflects and reinforces her husband's heartlessness as well as her mother's admiration for wealth and social position.

Edward Ferrars is the unobtrusive hero of *Sense and Sensibility.* His awkward position as the secret fiance of Lucy Steele makes it impossible for him to spend much time with Elinor, thus he does not play a major role in the novel. Quiet and serious—in keeping with his clerical ambitions—and intelligent and reasonably motivated to pursue his chosen vocation, Edward is a disappointment to his more socially ambitious mother and sister, who are horrified to learn of his engagement to Lucy and discourage his interest in Elinor as well. Though initially unimpressive in appearance and personality, Edward grows more admirable as he reveals himself to Elinor, who is able to perceive his finer qualities.

John Willoughby, the villain of *Sense and Sensibility,* is handsome, charming, and wealthy. But beneath that agreeable exterior he is unscrupulous and dissolute, and capable of not only trifling with Marianne's feelings but of seducing (and thereby ruining) another innocent young girl. Such vulgarities as his ridiculing Colonel Brandon to Marianne and Elinor prove that he is not the upstanding young aristocrat he pretends to be, yet Marianne, characteristically, is blind to these signs. Willoughby will be well punished for his villainy, however, trapped in a loveless marriage of his own design. He does display his humanity when he appears at Cleveland Park during Marianne's illness and declares to Elinor that he does sincerely love Marianne and regrets the pain he has caused her.

Edward and Fanny's mother, **Mrs. Ferrars,** is an arrogant, ill-natured, and colossally domineering woman who freely uses money to manipulate her children. After disinheriting both Edward and Robert, however, she finds herself alarmingly lacking in sons and is forced, ironically, to capitulate to Edward's desire to marry Elinor. **Robert Ferrars** has generally been considered a faceless figure who merely helps the plot progress by providing a way to dispose of Lucy Steele. Like his mother, he is insensitive and mercenary.

Colonel Brandon, on the other hand, is quiet, intelligent, gentlemanly, and of great integrity, but his thirty-five years—and the fact that he wears practical flannel waistcoats—make him seem hopelessly old to Marianne. He plays a functional role in the story by revealing Willoughby's past to Elinor, although the history he relates and his connection with Marianne's suitor have struck some critics as too convenient to be believable. Several scholars have noted that while Brandon clearly stands as a force of sense in the novel, he also embodies some romantic elements. For instance, he has a decidedly dramatic past, having nearly eloped with his first love, who then married his brother against her will. Furthermore, he challenges Willoughby to a duel to defend the ruined honor of his young ward.

Lucy Steele is one of Austen's most disagreeable characters—a decidedly vulgar, obnoxious, scheming girl whose motives turn out to be mercenary. She is hypocritical in her cloying expression of sentiment toward Edward, whom she does not really love. Lucy is also characterized by her overt flattery of the aristocratic Middletons, her malicious trampling of Elinor's feelings, and her unloving relationship with her sister. Lucy's sister **Anne,** who is obsessed with clothing and "beaux," has been described by W.A. Craik as "the most vulgar and most stupid person Jane Austen ever uses . . . but she is funny as well as necessary." Her inconsiderate eavesdropping on her sister and Edward's conversation reveals the true nature of their relationship.

Minor characters in *Sense and Sensibility* include **Sir John Middleton,** the kind and wealthy neighbor whose main interest is hunting and who provides the necessary connection with the Steeles, and his wife **Lady Middleton,** an insipid but fairly pleasant woman whose admiration of Fanny Dashwood indicates her lack of sense. The occasionally vulgar but inherently good-hearted **Mrs. Jennings** is the neighborhood matchmaker and Lady Middleton's mother. **Mrs. Palmer**—Lady Middleton's sister—is good-natured but brainless, while **Mr. Palmer** has a sensible but cold and sarcastic nature.

Pride and Prejudice (novel, 1813)

Plot: Set in the English countryside in the early 1800s, this novel centers on the upper-middle-class Bennett family, who live at Longbourne manor. The story opens with the arrival in the neighborhood of a rich young bachelor, Charles Bingley, who is renting a nearby mansion. Mrs. Bennett hopes that Bingley will want to marry one of her five daughters—Jane, Elizabeth, Mary, Catherine (Kitty), or Lydia. The customarily disdainful Mr. Bennett, however, declines any such speculation. The Bennetts meet Bingley, his two sisters, and his friend Fitzwilliam Darcy at a ball. Darcy behaves in a markedly aloof, haughty manner and Elizabeth even hears him make a disparaging comment about her lack of any beauty sufficient to attract him. The Bennetts and Bingleys have frequent social encounters, and an attraction grows between Jane and Charles Bingley despite the disdain his sisters and Darcy show for some of the other members of Jane's family—such as her mother, who often makes inappropriate comments, or her flirtatious sister Lydia. In spite of himself, Darcy begins to admire the spirited Elizabeth, but she retains her initial prejudice against him. Her negative impression is reinforced when Wickham, a young military officer stationed nearby, tells her that Darcy has cheated him out of an inheritance promised him by Darcy's father. When the Bingley party returns to London unexpectedly, Elizabeth suspects that Darcy and Bingley's sisters are conspiring to keep Bingley away from Jane. The Bennett's pompous cousin, Reverend William Collins—who, because of the family's lack of male heirs, will inherit their estate—arrives for a visit, intending to secure Longbourne for the Bennetts by marrying one of their daughters. After Elizabeth rejects him, he proposes to her close friend Charlotte Lucas, who shocks Elizabeth by accepting him. Elizabeth and Wickham carry on a brief flirtation, but he soon begins to court a wealthier woman.

Elizabeth visits Charlotte and her new husband in Kent. There she meets Collins's benefactor, and Darcy's aunt, Lady Catherine de Bourgh. Darcy is also staying in Kent, and after a few social encounters with Elizabeth he surprises her with a marriage proposal. Still convinced of Darcy's excessive pride and insensitivity and angry at his suggestion that he has had to overcome his disapproval of her family, Elizabeth rejects him. She soon receives a letter from Darcy in which he responds to her criticisms; he maintains his objections to her family's improprieties but reveals that he did, in fact, treat Wickham fairly and that Wickham had tried to elope with Darcy's young sister. Elizabeth's prejudice against Darcy is further weakened when, traveling through Derbyshire with her aunt and uncle Gardiner, she visits Darcy's estate and unexpectedly encounters him there. She is impressed with his considerate behavior and with his home.

Elizabeth's visit is disrupted by the news that   Lydia has eloped with Wickham and may be living with him in London. After Wickham finally agrees to marry Lydia, Elizabeth learns that it was Darcy who located the pair and provided the money necessary to bring about the marriage. Lady Catherine visits Elizabeth and demands that she agree never to marry Darcy, but Elizabeth refuses to make such a promise. Darcy hears of this exchange and proposes to Elizabeth again. She accepts, and Jane and Charles Bingley also become engaged. All live happily thereafter.

Characters: Jane Austen's most popular novel, *Pride and Prejudice* features some of the most memorable characters in literature, through whom Austen demonstrates her gift for comedy, her understanding of human nature, and her ability to subtly manipulate point of view.

Austen herself found **Elizabeth Bennett,** the novel's spirited heroine, "as delightful a creature as ever appeared in print." Seen mostly through Elizabeth's eyes, the story chronicles her progression to maturity and self-knowledge. Austen's description of Elizabeth's physical appearance is vague: she has "fine eyes" and a "light, pleasing" figure; although she is not beautiful, her sparkling personality animates her looks. She is intelligent and perceptive as well, and has a satirical sense of humor. Because she is surrounded by people whose judgment is faulty, she tends to trust her own too much. As the novel progresses, however, she learns that even her superior judgment is not infallible and she proves that she is open to change and growth when she conquers her prejudice against Darcy. Austen has long been praised for creating this character who, operating within the severely circumscribed social context of an upper-class nineteenth-century woman, displays a remarkable degree of integrity and individuality; her adamant refusal to bend to Lady Catherine's demand that she not marry Darcy is often cited as evidence of her strength of character. In choosing Darcy as her life's partner, Elizabeth demonstrates that she requires an honest, equal relationship with a man who values her singular, spirited personality.

Fitzwilliam Darcy is generally thought to deserve the regard he eventually wins from Elizabeth Bennett—particularly because, like her, he demonstrates a capacity for change when he overcomes his pride. Described as a handsome, aristocratic man of impressive wealth, Darcy carries himself in a haughty manner borne partly of his genuine feeling of superiority and partly of his naturally reserved, taciturn personality. Some critics have noted that the snobbery Darcy reveals in his comments about Elizabeth at the ball—"She is tolerable, but not handsome enough to tempt *me*"—comes close to the more obvious vulgarity routinely dispensed by his aunt, Lady Catherine, whose arrogance will later embarrass him. The difference is that Darcy's pride—if sometimes excessive—is tempered with a sense of his own position and responsibility. His housekeeper, for instance, who might have more occasion than anyone to feel the pinch of his self-importance, describes Darcy as the kindest of masters. Darcy's disapproval of Elizabeth's family is due more to their undeniable improprieties than to their lack of social credentials. Nevertheless, he is forced to reevaluate his own behavior and attitudes when Elizabeth spurns his first proposal and reacts so angrily to his condescending manner. Although a few critics have claimed that Darcy is a flat, conventional figure who serves primarily as a necessary love interest for Elizabeth, most consider him an appropriate counterpart in the ideal alliance their marriage represents.

Austen describes **Mrs. Bennett** as "a woman of mean understanding, little information, and uncertain temper." In addition to providing a wealth of memorable comic moments, this silly, son-in-law-hunting woman whose outrageously inappropriate statements exasperate her two oldest daughters serves a practical role as the most flagrant example of Elizabeth's undesirable family connections. Yet Mrs. Bennett's lack of understanding, self-pity, and frequent improprieties are distinctly human attributes; indeed, in an 1870 review of *Pride and Prejudice,* the critic George Saintsbury remarked that it is "not easy to say whether she is more exquisitely amusing or more horribly true." The novelist Fay Weldon has pointed out that, despite her flaws, Mrs. Bennett is the only character in the novel who, in her obsession with providing secure futures for her five practically penniless daughters, seems aware of the harsh realities of her time and social milieu.

Mr. Bennett is an intelligent man who often uses his considerable wit to make sarcastic observations about the people and situations around him, providing some of the novel's funniest moments. Although fond of his two eldest daughters, Mr. Bennett openly mocks his wife and other children, a habit that Elizabeth comes to perceive as wrong. Having chosen his wife on the basis of her physical attractiveness and amiability but soon realizing the limits of her sense and intellect, Mr. Bennett retreated into his study and there he remains, sarcastic and detached from everyone except his favorite, Elizabeth. By observing her father and the results of his poor marital choice, Elizabeth realizes the cost of an ill-considered marriage and subsequently makes a wiser, more informed match. Mr. Bennett is something of an eccentric—an individualistic scorner of society's conventions—but in the end the freedom he claims is revealed as irresponsibility: ignoring Elizabeth's warning and allowing Lydia to visit Bath alone, Mr. Bennett precipitates her disastrous elopement. His seemingly harmless indolence is thus shown as damaging to those dependent on him for guidance.

Critics have suggested that Austen modeled Elizabeth's serene, sweet-tempered sister **Jane Bennett** after her own beloved, supportive sister Cassandra. Jane is Elizabeth's closet confidante; she offers not only a willing receptivity to Elizabeth's opinions and reflections but, occasionally, an alternative perspective on them. Unlike Elizabeth, she has a placid demeanor (which causes Darcy to mistakenly think that she is not in love with Bingley). Jane also differs from Elizabeth in that she is prejudiced *in favor* of people rather than against them; she will never believe the worst of anyone without conclusive proof. Her relationship with Bingley runs more smoothly than does Elizabeth's with Darcy—at least until outsiders intervene—but also seems to lack the depth that these more troubled lovers achieve.

Elizabeth's other sisters are not portrayed in as flattering a light. **Mary Bennett** compensates for being the plainest of the five with a pompous intellectuality that is often ludicrous. **Lydia Bennett,** the frivolous fifteen-year-old flirt who almost visits ruin upon herself and causes the family so much shame and heartache, never seems to realize the error of her ways. **Kitty Bennett** serves primarily as Lydia's less energetic sidekick.

Although the long-winded clergyman **William Collins** is a purely farcical figure presented for the reader's enjoyment, he also plays a practical role in the plot by providing a link between Elizabeth's family at Longbourne and Darcy's aunt, Lady Catherine at Rosings. Simultaneously pompous and obsequious, Collins is a self-important bore. His verbose and spectacularly passionless proposal to Elizabeth constitutes what is perhaps the finest comic scene in the novel. Austen reveals some sympathy for Collins, however, when she suggests that his curious combination of abject humility and pompousness is the result of an unhappy upbringing.

The woman who does marry Collins is Elizabeth's best friend, **Charlotte Lucas,** an intelligent, practical, and plain twenty-seven-year-old who is willing to overlook Collins defects in exchange for the security he offers. Elizabeth is appalled at this development and feels estranged from her friend. Austen writes that marriage is "the only honourable provision for well-educated young women of small fortune''; thus Charlotte provides a sobering reminder of the limited opportunities available to women in the nineteenth century. Nevertheless, in choosing to bend entirely to the demands of her social context and to abandon the possibility of an equal partnership Charlotte stands in contrast to Elizabeth; her relationship with Collins helps to illuminate the value of Elizabeth's with Darcy.

Charles Bingley is the handsome, wealthy young bachelor whose arrival in the neighborhood causes a stir. His pleasant, friendly, unaffected manners make him popular with everyone—and especially with Jane Bennett. Despite his own feelings for Jane, however, Bingley allows Darcy and his sisters to separate him from her. Elizabeth views this as weakness, though Darcy will later contend that it reveals Bingley's great modesty. Bingley and Jane are both attractive and amiable but, although they are genuinely fond of each other, their relationship seems to lack self-confidence and deeper insight, unlike the alliance between Darcy and Elizabeth. Bingley's sisters, **Mrs. Hurst** and **Caroline Bingley,** are portrayed as cold, calculating creatures who are quite shallow beneath their sophisticated veneer. In her attempt to impress Darcy, whom she wishes to marry, Caroline tries to disparage Elizabeth and the other Bennetts. Her efforts have the opposite effect.

George Wickham, the charming militia officer who initially gains Elizabeth's regard but eventually seduces her sister, is the villain of *Pride and Prejudice.* His good looks and lively personality mask his inner corruption, and his hypocrisy teaches Elizabeth that appearances can be deceiving. Though it has been observed that Wickham is a somewhat flat, stereotyped villain, he plays a significant role in the story not only by furnishing an occasion for Elizabeth to learn more about herself but by providing an opportunity for Darcy to demonstrate his regard for Elizabeth when he rescues her sister from ruin.

Lady Catherine de Bourgh, the tyrannical grande dame who resides at Rosings and who feels she has a perfect right to run the lives of everyone she knows, is one of Austen's most skillfully drawn comic characters. She is an aristocrat by birth, but her insistent meddling and often ludicrous arrogance make her as vulgar as the lower-born Mrs. Bennett. Pride is an important part of her makeup, as it is of Darcy's, but her pride is unsubstantiated by any true superiority. Lady Catherine is essential to the plot because, in interfering with the romance blossoming between Elizabeth and Darcy, she unintentionally brings them closer and precipitates their understanding each other. This irony is noticed by Elizabeth, who says, ''Lady Catherine has been of infinite use, which ought to make her happy, for she loves to be of use.''

The minor characters in *Pride and Prejudice* also contribute to the novel's unity. **Mr. and Mrs. Gardiner,** Elizabeth's kind and sensible aunt and uncle, provide a model of a happy marriage and family life which contrasts with that of Mr. and Mrs. Bennett, and as such they represent to Darcy a more flattering view of Elizabeth's family. Similarly, Darcy's shy sister **Georgiana Darcy** helps to reveal an unsuspected side of Darcy when Elizabeth notices his tenderness toward her; Darcy also shows his esteem for Elizabeth by encouraging her acquaintance with his sister. **Colonel Fitzwilliam**—to whom Darcy refers Elizabeth for verification of the claims he makes in his letter explaining his previous ties with Wickham— is portrayed as an upright, trustworthy man, and thus Elizabeth knows that what Darcy has told her is true.

Mansfield Park (novel, 1814)

Plot: Fanny Price is the daughter of a woman who married a rather dissolute lieutenant in the British navy; the Prices are hard pressed to support their nine children. At the instigation of Fanny's mother's sister, Mrs. Norris, a third sister and her husband—Lady Bertram and Sir Thomas Bertram—offer to take Fanny into their home. Arriving at Mansfield Park from working-class Portsmouth, the shy ten-year-old is initially overwhelmed by her four rich cousins. Only Edmund, who will later study to become a clergyman, is really kind to her. The others—Tom, Maria, and Julia—pay little attention to Fanny, and Aunt Norris is always reminding her of her inferior status. Five years later, Sir Thomas leaves home to oversee some business in the West Indies, taking with him his irresponsible son Tom. While they are away, Maria becomes engaged to Mr. Rushworth, a young man of great wealth but little intelligence. A new rector and his wife, Dr. and Mrs. Grant, arrive in the neighborhood and soon Mrs. Grant's brother and sister, Henry and Mary Crawford, come for a visit. Both Bertram girls are taken with the suave Henry, but since Maria is engaged it is assumed that Henry will be matched with Julia. Edmund is attracted to Mary, a circumstance which saddens Fanny, who not only has long loved Edmund but who perceives Mary's shallowness. Fanny also notices with disapproval that Henry and Maria are carrying on an inappropriate flirtation. Tom returns from Antigua ahead of his father, bringing with him his fun-loving friend, Mr. Yates. Yates suggests that the young people stage a play called "Lovers' Vows." Fanny objects, knowing that Sir Thomas shares the disapproval of amateur theatrics typical of his generation and social milieu, but even Edmund goes along with the idea. Rehearsals are well underway when Sir Thomas returns unexpectedly, calling an immediate halt to the theatrical plans. Henry leaves rather abruptly for Bath, greatly disappointing Maria because she fully intended to break off her engagement with Rushworth if Henry proposed to her. Determined not to let Henry know that he has hurt her, Maria marries Rushworth and the two travel to Brighton with Julia in tow. Upon his return, Henry begins a callous flirtation with Fanny, then surprises himself by falling in love with her. When Fanny rejects his proposal—despite her gratitude that he has arranged a promotion for her beloved sailor brother, William—Sir Thomas is very angry, convinced that Fanny has thrown away a chance to make a brilliant marriage. Meanwhile, Edmund is in love with Mary but is discouraged because she ridicules his clerical vocation. Nevertheless, Edmund thinks Mary has been influenced by the corrupt people among whom she was raised and hopes to change her mind. Fanny returns to Portsmouth to spend some time with her family, and finds them in a highly disordered state. The length of her stay is repeatedly extended, but events at Mansfield Park precipitate her return: Tom becomes gravely ill and is near death, then the news comes that Maria has left her husband and run away with Crawford and that Julia has eloped with Yates. Fanny is warmly welcomed back to Mansfield Park, for Sir Thomas now understands her rejection of Henry Crawford, and—full of regret for his detachment during his own children's upbringing—appreciates Fanny's virtues more than ever. Fanny's sister Susan accompanies her to Mansfield Park and proves a welcome and tolerant companion for Lady Bertram. Tom recovers from his illness with a character improved by his brush with death, and Julia and her new husband settle down into a fairly stable domesticity. After her eventual parting with Henry, Maria is sent to live away from the family and is joined (to everyone's delight) by Aunt Norris. Edmund is shocked by Mary's casual attitude toward his sisters' behavior and becomes disenchanted with her. Waiting in the wings is Fanny, whose love he finally returns. They are married and move to the parsonage near Mansfield Park.

Characters: *Mansfield Park* seems more concerned with social and moral edification than any of Austen's other novels, with virtue finally rewarded and vice punished. Thus many critics have characterized it as promoting conventional values and mores.

Fanny Price, one of several Cinderella figures found in Austen's fiction, suffers in solitude the neglect of those around her despite her inherent superiority. Shy, humble Fanny comes to Mansfield Park as a waif-like young girl and finds in Mrs. Norris the consummate evil stepmother. Fanny is allocated a distant attic room where she sits alone, often without even a fire to keep herself warm. Despite these somewhat pitiable circumstances, Fanny grows into a morally upright, serious, intelligent young lady who behaves correctly while others founder and is eventually recognized and embraced by those who initially overlooked her. Fanny is considered Austen's least appealing heroine because of her extreme virtuousness and insipidity; she takes no decisive action except that of resistance (such as when she turns down Crawford's marriage proposal), and is physically weak as well. Yet some critics have noted that Fanny's humanity may be detected in such emotions as her fear and loneliness as an uprooted ten-year-old, her glowing love for her brother William, and her jealousy of Mary Crawford. In the end, Fanny is rewarded with marriage to Edmund, who has been characterized as an equally stiff, uncompelling character. Critics have frequently noted that Austen devotes hardly any space to the courtship between Edmund and Fanny, suggesting that even she was not as interested in their union as in the more colorful events that preceded it.

Austen's reverence for men of religious integrity is evident in her depiction of the young cleric, **Edmund Bertram.** The quiet and serious Edmund finds himself in love with Mary Crawford, a girl who considers the clerical profession insufficiently glamorous and distinguished. Fanny perceives that Edmund is noble and virtuous, although these qualities are never overtly demonstrated. He is undoubtedly kind to Fanny after her arrival as a child at Mansfield Park and, later, when she is a rather frail young lady, arranges for her to build up her health with horseback riding. Edmund proves his fallibility in allowing himself to be swept along with the enthusiasm for "Lovers' Vows" despite his better judgment, in deceiving himself about Mary's real character, and in encouraging Fanny to marry Crawford mainly because it will facilitate his own union with Mary. That Edmund would be taken in by Mary is not surprising, for Mary is depicted as bright and charming (almost in spite of Austen's intentions) while Fanny is a self-effacing and meek homebody. But Edmund will come to value the latter's virtue over the former's glamour, and will learn that his earlier conviction in the permanence of first love will give way to the possibility of a second, superior attachment.

Edmund's father, **Sir Thomas Bertram,** is described by critic W. A. Craik as embodying "the best principles and authority of his society." He is a stiffly correct, dignified, solemn man who lives by rigid preconceptions about the world. The inadequacy of these preconceptions is demonstrated when the children he has raised so detachedly and presumably correctly disappoint him grievously. That Sir Thomas is basically a kind person is never in question, despite the awe he inspires in his timid niece. Fanny grows fonder of her uncle after his return from the West Indies, when he appears weary, weathered, relieved to be back home with his family. It is the mutual respect and affection that had been steadily growing since Sir Thomas's return that makes Fanny's rebellion against his wish that she marry Crawford so painful to her. Sir Thomas shows that he is capable of personal growth when he realizes both his own mistakes and Fanny's worth, embracing her as the kind of daughter he would most wish to have.

Lady Bertram, who was in her youth the most beautiful of the three Ward sisters, is spoiled, self-indulgent, and indolent; she spends her time reclining in her drawing room and lavishes affection only on her pet dog. She takes no apparent interest in guiding her children's values or behavior; they are left entirely under Mrs. Norris's direction when Sir Thomas is away. Although insensitive to Fanny's true worth and feelings, Lady Bertram is at least kind to her niece—sincerely valuing her company and the little tasks Fanny does for her—and thus provides an antidote to Mrs. Norris's cruelty.

Though not depicted with much humor, **Mrs. Norris** is the most farcical character in *Mansfield Park.* Her stinginess, overbearing manner, and admiration for the undeserving Bertram children at Fanny's expense are well-pronounced. She is a meddler who revels in arranging others' lives, though she must be given some credit for instigating Fanny's ultimately advantageous installation at Mansfield Park. She is also partly responsible for the fate of the Bertram daughters, for she has overvalued and indulged them while she constantly needled and manipulated submissive Fanny. Mrs. Norris has real influence over an important figure in the action—Sir Thomas. She will prove herself unworthy of that influence, however, when she mismanages the Bertram household during Sir Thomas's absence, encouraging Maria's disastrous marriage and failing to perceive the impropriety of the theatrical proceedings. There is some justice in the fact that Mrs. Norris and Maria are ultimately isolated from the rest of the family together, however severe the banishment may seem to modern readers.

All of the Bertram children except Edmund display the selfishness, vanity, and lack of values that are portrayed as resulting from a proper but remote and indulgent upbringing. **Maria** and **Julia Bertram** are elegant and well-mannered, but, educated only in etiquette, they lack the insight and awareness of others that would make them useful, happy people. Thus Maria marries Rushworth partly because it is the approved course of action and will bring her wealth and status, and partly to spite Crawford. Her father senses her lack of esteem for Rushworth and offers her a means of escape, but Maria shows no inclination to break off the engagement. Such callousness toward love and marriage will, of course, lead to her downfall when she comes under Crawford's influence again and runs away with him. Although the extreme reaction to Maria's misbehavior, which blights her remaining life, may seem overblown to modern readers, it does illustrate the mores of the society Austen was depicting. Though just as spoiled as her sister, Julia is a less brilliant character and her fate is less tragic. She elopes with Yates primarily to resist the further restraint she thinks Maria's flight will bring upon herself. It is suggested that Julia's marriage is not the unmitigated disaster her father had suspected it would be.

Tom Bertram is the type of dissolute elder son who appears often in Austen's fiction: a worldly, self-indulgent young man who irresponsibly squanders his family's resources. Indeed, Tom's carelessness results in his father's having to leave England to raise money in the West Indies. The young man's repentance after his near-fatal illness is somewhat abrupt, but not necessarily unlikely. Although Tom is initially a pleasure-seeker like Crawford, he serves as a foil to that character because he is ultimately shown as less reprehensible.

Henry Crawford is in some ways a typical Austen villain: wealthy, handsome, worldly, and superficially charming. But several critics have noted that Austen comes dangerously close to making Crawford more the hero of *Mansfield Park* than Edmund in that the latter is relatively dull. From the start Crawford is portrayed as a vain rake who amuses himself by making young women fall in love with him and who is unconcerned about the damage his cruelly disengaged flirting may cause. He is surprised to find himself in love with Fanny, whom he intended to ensnare only temporarily in his customary manner. Her sincerity, moral uprightness, and innocence redirect Crawford, and he is in turn very nearly successful in persuading her to love him. Austen makes it clear that if Edmund and Mary had married and Crawford had kept up his assault on Fanny's heart, he would have won her. But Crawford's inherent weakness will finally triumph over Fanny's favorable influence, and when he is away from her for an extended period he falls back into his former debauchery. Because he is a ''man of sense,'' Crawford will regret his own wickedness. Along with his sister, Crawford provides an additional example of the importance of upbringing in the formation of character.

Like her brother, **Mary Crawford** nearly gains the reader's approval despite her obvious defects. She is charming, beautiful, witty, and vivacious—all qualities that Fanny lacks. She is also sophisticated, cynical, and quite confident in her own judgment, which is repeatedly shown to be faulty. Mary's fault is in basing her judgment on public opinion: she remarks that ''where an opinion is general, it is usually correct.'' Disdaining the clerical profession, which she finds boring and lacking in sophistication, she attempts to convince Edmund to choose some more prestigious occupation. Although she does love Edmund (and that is in her favor, for he is worthy of love), she cannot quite see herself as a clergyman's wife. Mary may be acting in a purely self-interested way in cultivating Fanny's friendship—knowing

25

that Fanny and Edmund are close—yet she is also genuinely kind to Fanny. She comforts her after one of Mrs. Norris's insults, and she tells Fanny that if she and her brother marry it is Henry who will benefit more—that is, from exposure to Fanny's virtues. However, it is Mary's inability to perceive the evil in the Bertram sisters' behavior that finally alert Edmund to her defects. Critics usually see Mary not as a completely sly figure but as a character with both good and bad traits whose faults finally triumph.

The portrayal of Fanny's family at Portsmouth is significant in that it introduces a social setting different from that on which Austen usually focuses. A military family, the Prices are members of a lower social class than the Bertrams. The disorder of their home and the dirty, noisy urban setting contrast with the elegant, sedate surroundings of Mansfield Park. **Mrs. Price** is the Ward sister who made the worst choice of husbands; she is similar in character to Lady Bertram, but her natural indolence appears more as slatternliness. She is unable to run an orderly household and supervise nine children. Though apparently fond of Fanny, she clearly favors her sons—particularly William—and the fact that Fanny visits only once in so many years also indicates that she and her mother do not play particularly important roles in each other's lives. Fanny's father, **Lieutenant Price,** is a gruff and vulgar man who provides a strong contrast to the dignified Sir Thomas. Though not unkind to Fanny, he is most interested in nautical matters and thus, like his wife, tends to focus on his sailor son William.

Two of Fanny's siblings are depicted as exceptions, along with Fanny, to the general Price family tendency toward squalor. **William** is a pleasant, handsome, and capable young man of whom Fanny is immensely fond and proud. Though not particularly cultured, William is naturally virtuous and serves as a loyal friend and confidante to his adoring sister. Crawford soon perceives that the quickest route to Fanny's heart is through William, and he facilitates the young man's naval promotion. Fanny's sister **Susan** is also a good-natured young girl, apparently unspoiled by her Portsmouth upbringing. She is highly susceptible to Fanny's positive influence and thus promises to improve even more in character after she moves to Mansfield Park. In addition, she is not as sensitive as her sister and will make a smoother transition into her new life, proving an excellent replacement for Fanny as Lady Bertram's companion.

Other characters in *Mansfield Park* include the two young men who marry the Bertram sisters, **Mr. Rushworth** and **Mr. Yates.** The very wealthy and very ignorant Rushworth is both comical and pitiful in the face of Maria's obvious preference for Crawford. Yates is fashionable, fun-loving, and shallow, but his crudeness and frivolity do not prove particularly harmful. He plays a practical role in the plot by introducing the idea of producing ''Lovers' Vows'' and by providing a means for Julia to scandalize her family. Equally useful are the Grants, who bring the Crawfords into the neighborhood. **Dr. Grant,** the local rector, contrasts with the kind of clergyman Edmund promises to be in that Dr. Grant seems more interested in what he will eat next than in spiritual concerns. **Mrs. Grant** is a fairly amiable woman who seems more aware than Mary of the harm their brother might do with his flirtations.

Emma (novel, 1816)

Plot: *Emma,* which takes place in the village of Highbury in early- nineteenth-century Surrey, England, focuses on the intelligent, wealthy, and beautiful Emma Woodhouse. After her companion and governess, Miss Taylor, marries the Woodhouse's neighbor Mr. Weston, Emma is left alone at Hartfield manor with her kind but worrisome father. She befriends Harriet Smith, a seventeen-year-old girl of uncertain parentage who is attending the local school and whom Emma decides should be elevated to a higher social station than the one she currently occupies. She persuades the ever-deferring Harriet to reject the marriage proposal of the respectable farmer Robert Martin and to pin her hopes on the young clergyman, Mr. Elton. Emma scorns the warning of her sister's brother-in-law (and the Woodhouses' neighbor) Mr. Knightley that her friendship with Harriet benefits neither. She is chagrined when Mr. Elton proposes to her instead of to Harriet, and she rejects him.

When the beautiful and accomplished Jane Fairfax, the niece of Emma's neighbor Miss Bates, arrives in the neighborhood for an extended visit, Emma is cool to her because, she says, Jane is too reserved. The much-anticipated visit of Mr. Weston's son from his first marriage, Frank Churchill, finally takes place. A flirtation quickly develops between the handsome, personable young man and Emma; he also visits the Bates household and reveals that he and Jane Fairfax have been previously acquainted. Frank leaves for London just as it seems he might be about to propose to Emma; because Emma had planned to refuse him, however, she is not disappointed. Mr. Elton returns to Highbury with his new wife, a vulgar and pretentious woman. Harriet begins to think romantically of Mr. Knightley and tells Emma she has detected some interest on his part, but Emma assumes that she is talking about Frank Churchill, with whom Emma has been plotting to match Harriet. When the death of his domineering grandmother makes it possible for Frank to marry whom he wants, he reveals that he and Jane have been secretly engaged for some time. Concerned that this news will hurt Harriet, Emma learns that it is actually Mr. Knightley who interests her friend. With this discovery comes Emma's realization that she herself is in love with Mr. Knightley. Presently, Mr. Knightley proposes to Emma, she accepts, and they agree to live at Hartfield with Mr. Woodhouse after their marriage. Robert Martin again asks Harriet for her hand, and the two are married.

Characters: Widely considered Austen's most masterful work, *Emma* features some of her most insightful and compassionate characterizations. Austen's prediction that *Emma*'s title character would be "a heroine who no one but myself will much like" proved erroneous, for **Emma Woodhouse**—despite her weaknesses—is one of Austen's best and most beloved creations. The twenty-one-year-old Emma has never had much to "distress or vex her"; in fact, she has been overindulged all her life by an adoring father and a soft-hearted governess. Her sense of self-worth is inflated to the point of outright conceit. She is a snob who thinks herself superior to most in "connections [and] in mind." A self-appointed matchmaker, Emma considers herself eminently qualified to meddle in others' lives— particularly in that of her submissive protegee, Harriet Smith—and to make conjectures about people according to her own imaginative whims. The novel chronicles Emma's progress to maturity, and by the end she is wiser and more sensitive to others, having learned that other people exist separately from her and have their own agendas and desires. The novel is narrated entirely by Emma, yet through Austen's masterful presentation the reader is aware of more than Emma herself is. Thus Emma's tendency to overlook the truth and her snobbish, self-satisfied attitude are all evident, as well as her vitality, her genuine affection for those closest to her, and her appealing (if dangerous) insistence that life be interesting and entertaining. Emma is wrong about so many things—her thwarting the marriage of Harriet and Robert Martin, her misreading of Frank Churchill's intentions, her dislike of Jane Fairfax, her not even realizing that she is in love with Mr. Knightley—yet her errors neither do any permanent damage nor lessen her appeal.

It is **George Knightley**—Emma's neighbor and advisor and her sister's brother-in-law— whom our heroine finally realizes she must marry. A thirty-seven-year-old man of impressive looks and stature as well as intelligence and sense, Knightley is the one of very few people in Emma's life who seems aware of her faults as well as her attributes. He has known Emma since she was a small child and is very fond of her, but he sees her as she really is and feels free to openly criticize her; he tells her, for instance, that he disapproves of her condescending relationship with Harriet and her interference in the girl's romance with Robert Martin. Though his calm maturity makes him a somewhat unromantic hero,

Knightley is quite likable and reveals that he is not immune from human weakness when he succumbs to feeling jealous of the younger, more sparkling Frank Churchill. Knightley consistently provides a check on Emma's misbehavior, often encouraging her to see the error of her ways; beneath his occasional censure, however, he is Emma's steadfast friend and admirer, as well as her future husband.

Emma's kindhearted and indulgent father is a fine comic character. **Mr. Woodhouse**'s obsession with his own health and that of his family and friends results in constant worry over such matters as whether Jane Fairfax changed her stockings after a walk in the rain. He is an indolent man who rarely exerts himself except to take an occasional short walk and is satisfied with the familiar; he often expresses disapproval of people marrying, for instance. Though not particularly intelligent, Woodhouse has a warm heart and friendly manners that recommend him to his neighbors. He also provides many occasions for his daughter to patiently tolerate her father's foibles, thus demonstrating the basic goodness of her own heart. It has also been noted that in spite of his general lack of perceptiveness about people, Woodhouse sometimes makes prophetic observations—as when he goes against popular opinion to observe that Frank Churchill is "very thoughtless."

It is primarily through the pretty, sweet-tempered **Harriet Smith,** who allows Emma to direct her life, that Emma comes to see the folly of her machinations. Emma thinks that Harriet's good nature and appearance are enough to endear her to any man, and she sees the uncertainty of Harriet's parentage as a romantic mystery rather than as an embarrassment. For her own part, Harriet's modest intellect and admiration for the more accomplished Emma lead her to form four romantic attachments in one year. Her comical collection of "Most Precious Treasures"—consisting of a piece of a bandage and a pencil stub discarded by Mr. Elton—exhibit, as she herself admits, her lack of sophistication. Harriet's deference appeals to Emma's most reprehensible qualities, her vanity and her snobbery, but Harriet also serves as a major source of self-knowledge when Emma sees how disastrously she has meddled in her young friend's life.

Frank Churchill, whose arrival in Highbury is long and eagerly anticipated, proves to be different things to different people. To his father and to Emma, he is a thoroughly charming, handsome young man whose occasional lapses in protocol or feeling are attributable to high spirits—and are thus forgivable. To Knightley, jealous because Emma is so taken with Frank, he is a "trifling, silly fellow." Likewise, Emma's father considers Frank the kind of inconsiderate person who—oblivious to drafts—is always leaving doors open behind him. Yet Frank shares with Emma an appreciable desire to enjoy life and does love the deserving Jane Fairfax. While it is true that the necessity of concealing his alliance with Jane might justify some of his behavior, he acts thoughtlessly when he encourages Emma to think that Jane had been involved with a married man. It is suggested, however, that life with Jane will lessen Frank's irresponsibility while leaving his ebullience intact.

Jane Fairfax, the secret object of Frank Churchill's affections, is a beautiful, intelligent, and talented young woman. Unlike Harriet, Jane is Emma's equal or possibly even her superior, and thus Emma perceives her as a threat and does not pursue her friendship. The reserve that Emma cites as Jane's unforgivable flaw is revealed in the end as justifiable in light of her need to conceal her engagement; thus Emma is again forced to confront her own capacity for misjudgment. Because Jane is destined, due to her lack of wealth and family connections, for the isolated and demeaning life of a governess, she brings to the novel a hint of the harsher world that exists outside of comfortable Highbury and of the fate of a nineteenth-century woman in her particular circumstances. Many scholars have noted that Austen never divulges Jane's thoughts and feelings, perhaps because doing so would detract from the novel's more unfinished, more flawed heroine.

The garrulous **Miss Bates** is one of Austen's funniest creations. Talking steadily along almost all of the time, she wanders from topic to topic, connecting thoughts randomly and going into great detail about the most trivial matters. Although she is a source of annoyance to most of her friends, she is also a kind soul who exhibits, as described in an 1870 article in *Blackwood's Edinburgh Magazine,* "the natural excellence that lies under a ludicrous exterior." Miss Bates is useful to the story's progression in several ways: her rambling conversation often includes information the reader needs to follow the plot and she is an instrument in Emma's education when Emma is rude to her (during the Box Hill expedition) and later repents. In addition, Miss Bates provides an admirable example of a woman who, though unmarried, unmoneyed, and middle-aged, seems happy with her life. Her mother, **Mrs. Bates,** is primarily a background figure—a deaf, smiling old lady who is seldom seen but often referred to by Miss Bates, and who keeps Mr. Woodhouse company while the young people amuse themselves.

Emma's former governess and beloved companion, **Mrs. Weston,** is a steady, reliable woman whose soft-heartedness toward her young charge may have contributed to Emma's inflated opinion of herself. Although Mr. Woodhouse always refers to her as "poor Mrs. Weston" because she has left the cozy hearthside at Hartfield for her own home, in marriage she actually achieves a measure of security and fulfillment she did not possess before. Although she misreads Frank's intentions toward Emma, Mrs. Weston generally exhibits good judgment and encourages Emma to greater self-awareness. **Mr. Weston** is easy-going and indiscriminately friendly (in Emma's opinion) and does not seem to notice his son's fault. Though he is affectionate, he perhaps does feel as deeply as his wife because he recovers much more quickly than she from the disappointment of Frank's canceling his first planned visit to Highbury.

Mr. Elton is Highbury's handsome young rector whose attentions to Emma she misinterprets as regard for Harriet. Elton reveals his vulgarity when he drunkenly makes his marriage proposal to Emma, which alerts her to the fact that he is interested in marrying a wealthy woman. He will continue to display his lack of integrity when, after his marriage, he continually snubs Emma and heartlessly insults Harriet at a ball. **Mrs. Elton,** the former Augusta Hawkins, is a fitting partner for him. An inherently vulgar woman who considers herself a flower of high society, she is always reminding everyone of her wealth, connections, and personal "resources." With her constant references to her well-married sister Selina, who lives at palatial Maple Grove estate, she provides an exaggerated version of the same snobbery Emma exhibits. The only truly farcical (and thus perhaps flat) character in the novel, Mrs. Elton introduces some comic relief in the middle of a complicated plot.

John Knightley, Mr. Knightley's brother and Emma's brother-in-law, is not popular with Emma because he feels free to criticize her. Although he is often moody and ill-tempered, John is shown to be a good father who would rather stay at home with his family than make social visits. He is also a somewhat insightful person, for it is he who first detects Mr. Elton's interest in Emma. Emma's sister **Isabella Knightley** is devoted to her husband and children, and Emma wishes she could emulate her sister's tolerant, affectionate nature. The Knightley children provide occasion for both Emma and Mr. Knightley to demonstrate their capacity for love.

As in Austen's other novels, *Emma* contains some characters who serve primarily as background figures and, though they're important to the story, rarely or never appear. The upright farmer **Robert Martin,** whose intelligence and hard work Mr. Knightley praises, is one such figure; the reader is relieved when he finally wins Harriet's hand. Others include the physician **Mr. Perry,** whose medical advice Mr. Woodhouse swears by, and his wife; **Mr. and Mrs. Coles,** whose dinner party Emma disdains until she learns she is not invited; **the Sucklings,** Mrs. Elton's much-touted relatives; and **the Churchills,** who, upset over

Jane's lack of wealth and stature, provide the reason the young couple must conceal their engagement.

Northanger Abbey (novel, 1818)

Plot: The novel centers on Catherine Morland, a young English fancier of the lurid gothic novels that were especially popular in the late eighteenth and early nineteenth centuries. Catherine travels from her quiet village of Fullerton to the resort town of Bath to enjoy the social life there as the guest of her wealthy neighbors, the Allens. There she befriends the worldly Isabella Thorpe and her brother John, who happens to be a college friend of Catherine's brother James. She also meets a girl named Eleanor Tilney and is particularly interested in her handsome brother Henry. While Isabella and James become engaged and Catherine spurns John's advances, Isabella and the two young men repeatedly try to thwart Catherine's budding friendship with the Tilneys. When James temporarily leaves Bath, Isabella flirts shamelessly with the Tilneys' older brother, a dashing captain in the army. Eleanor and her father, General Tilney, invite Catherine to visit their country home, Northanger Abbey. She is thrilled at the prospect of seeing the kind of gloomy gothic abbey she has read about in novels, but the actual dwelling is elegant and modernized. Nevertheless, when she learns that Mrs. Tilney died suddenly several years earlier, Catherine envisions mysterious circumstances—even suspecting that the moody General Tilney murdered his wife. Henry, however, assures her the death was natural and encourages to curb her overactive imagination.

Catherine receives a letter from her brother revealing his knowledge of Isabella's behavior in his absence. Isabella also writes to Catherine to ask her to facilitate a reconciliation between the two now-parted lovers, but Catherine refuses. General Tilney leaves home for a business trip to London, but returns suddenly and insists that Catherine immediately depart. A mortified Eleanor cannot explain her father's action. Though Catherine worries, on returning to Fullerton, that she'll never see Henry again, he soon arrives at her home. He tells her that his father had acted graciously toward Catherine at the beginning because he had heard from John Thorpe, who hoped to marry Catherine himself, that she was wealthy. The general's goodwill ended when John—angry over Catherine's rejection and the breakup of Isabella's engagement—told him that Catherine was penniless. Henry now proposes to Catherine, she accepts, and he returns to Northanger Abbey to try to persuade his father to allow the marriage. Conveniently for the two lovers, Eleanor's marriage to a wealthy aristocrat puts General Tilney in a generous mood—and the three thousand pounds that Catherine will bring to the match is also in her favor. With the consent of all their parents, then, Catherine and Henry are married.

Characters: *Northanger Abbey* is an entertaining parody of such popular gothic novels as Ann Radcliffe's *The Mysteries of Udolpho* (1794), but it also features finely drawn characters who help illuminate the deeper theme of what constitutes moral social behavior. Critics describe the novel as both a polished burlesque of the kinds of fiction that preceded Austen's and a work that stands up very well on its own merits.

Although she is the central character of *Northanger Abbey,* **Catherine Morland,** Austen writes, was not "born to be a heroine." She is the ordinary, middle-class daughter of a clergyman, one of ten children. As a child she was thin, plain, and something of a tomboy; at seventeen she often looks rather pretty and she's interested in dancing and curling her hair. Though affectionate and open, she is not particularly accomplished at music or drawing. And she is a voracious reader—especially of terror-filled fiction—who must learn to discriminate between the realm of romantic heroes and faultless, fainting heroines and the less melodramatic but (as Catherine comes to see) ultimately more interesting world around her. *Northanger Abbey* tells the story of Catherine's struggle toward a mature, insightful understanding of herself and others—a process helped along by Henry Tilney but primarily through her own basically sound judgment. Catherine is usually viewed as a charming girl whose ignorance and adherence to novelistic and societal conventions are symptoms of immaturity rather than serious character flaws. Her frankness endears her to Henry Tilney, and her willingness to grow and change as she learns that there is more to life and to people than she had expected endears her to the reader. Several critics have noted that while Catherine seems at first a mere antiheroine meant to parody such visions of perfection as the smoothly accomplished protagonist of Charlotte Smith's 1788 novel *Emmeline, the Orphan of the Castle,* she has acquired by the end of *Northanger Abbey* a full, rounded personality of her own. Still far from flawless at the novel's close, Catherine leaves one with the impression that her newly developed awareness, her natural spontaneity and enthusiasm, and her marriage with the delightful Henry Tilney equip her well for adult life.

Henry Tilney is a witty, good-hearted young clergyman. He initially likes Catherine because she so obviously likes him, but he eventually develops a deeper appreciation of her affectionate nature and simple, direct manner. Henry is intelligent and sophisticated, though he lacks the distasteful worldliness of his father and brother. Henry teases Catherine about her probable desire to live like a fictional heroine, but his main role in the novel (besides serving as Catherine's love interest) is to help in Catherine's education. He repeatedly shows her how her distorted perceptions have led her astray. For instance, when he discovers Catherine's suspicions about the death of his mother, he encourages her to trust her observations, to rely on her own good sense, and to consider what other people's real motives might—or might not—be. He is an imaginative, often playful person who demonstrates that life in the real world can be infinitely fascinating. "It is through Henry's many-faceted charms," critic Susan Morgan has noted, "that Austen makes her claim to Catherine and the reader for the value of life over fiction."

Although none of the other members of the Tilney family is portrayed in as much depth as Henry, each has his or her role to play. In her intelligence and sincerity, **Eleanor** provides a contrast to Isabella Thorpe, and is obviously a much more suitable friend for Catherine. The suave, worldly **Captain Tilney** is closer in nature to his father than his brother; his careless flirtation with Isabella (during which he is never in any real danger of attachment) provides an occasion for Catherine to learn the truth about the girl whom she previously admired and who almost became her sister-in-law. **General Tilney** is the closest character to a villain in *Northanger Abbey* and, indeed, Catherine thinks he resembles the infamous and wicked Montoni in *The Mysteries of Udolpho.* In the end, though, the general's villainy is shown to have more to do with arrogance, vanity, and greed than with any evil deeds. Some critics have claimed that General Tilney's eccentric behavior in abruptly banishing Catherine from his home is unconvincing; the act merely expedites (and somewhat flimsily) the plot's progression. Still, he is a useful instrument in Catherine's development, for he demonstrates to her that she is more likely to encounter and suffer from ordinary cruelty and insincerity than the extravagant horrors she has read about in novels.

Catherine's attractive, stylishly dressed friend **Isabella Thorpe** is at heart a self-centered, cold, vulgar young woman. With her speech full of exaggerated endearments, she seems to personify the kind of overwrought sentimentality common in the fiction Austen is lampooning. Like her brother, Isabella thinks nothing of lying to promote her own ends. In her essentially jaded outlook, she provides a strong contrast to Catherine's pleasant naivete, enthusiasm, and basic honesty. It is partly through Isabella that Catherine learns that people are not always what they seem, and in finally rejecting Isabella she demonstrates her capacity for proper judgment. **John Thorpe,** too, consistently displays his vulgarity in his exaggerated, boastful talk that centers on his own self-perceived merits. He lies easily, and is as money-hungry as his sister. His acquaintance with General Tilney is revealed early in the story, foreshadowing the latter's lack of integrity.

Mrs. Allen is a character similar to Miss Bates in *Emma,* though less worthy. She keeps up a steady stream of vacuous chatter—mostly about her main interest, clothing—and confuses the trivial for the serious in her conversation. She often provides unconscious commentary on the action as well. Mrs. Allen is ironically ill-suited as a chaperon for young Catherine, for she has hardly evolved past the interests of a young girl herself. **Mr. Allen** shows more sense—in fact, the narrator wonders why such an intelligent man would have married such a silly woman—but he is only peripherally involved in Catherine's supervision. Catherine's mother, **Mrs. Morland,** is another basically sensible, plainspoken person whose influence on her daughter, it is suggested, has been limited by the necessity of her looking after nine other children. She sometimes makes unexpectedly insightful observations; for instance, on Catherine's arrival back in Fullerton she tells her daughter that it was probably not so bad for her to have to journey alone from Northanger Abbey in a public coach: "[You] must have had to have your wits about you." That period of solitary travel, in a mood of shame and confusion, was indeed a sobering and educative experience for Catherine.

Persuasion (novel, 1818)

Plot: Sir Walter Elliott, a vain and conceited man, lives at Kellynch Hall with his two daughters, the attractive but cold-hearted Elizabeth (her father's favorite), and gentle, intelligent Anne, who is habitually neglected and undervalued by her family. A third daughter, Mary, is married to Charles Musgrove and lives nearby at Uppercross. Because Sir Walter has been living beyond his means, he is forced to rent out his beloved home and move to more modest quarters. He takes a smaller but still posh house in the resort town of Bath, and Admiral Croft and his wife lease Kellynch Hall. Mrs. Croft is the sister of Frederick Wentworth, who was Anne Elliott's suitor eight years earlier. Because her father and Lady Russell, a close family friend, disapproved of the match due to the young man's lack of connections and wealth, Anne broke off the engagement. Wentworth has become a prosperous captain in the navy and Anne, who is now 27, still loves him. Sir Walter and Elizabeth leave for Bath with Mrs. Clay—the daughter of Sir Walter's agent—whom Anne suspects of pretending friendship with Elizabeth in order to lure Sir Walter into marriage. While staying with the Musgroves, Anne becomes better acquainted with Charles's two sisters, Henrietta and Louisa. She also comes into frequent contact with Captain Wentworth when he visits his sister at Kellynch Hall; Anne finds him as attractive as ever, but he treats her coldly. It soon appears that Wentworth is interested in Louisa Musgrove. During a visit by the whole group to Wentworth's friends, Captain Harville and his wife, in the coastal city of Lyme, Louisa is injured while Wentworth is helping her to jump down from a stone embankment near the shore. He feels responsible for the accident. Anne's calm and competent resourcefulness in the emergency impress and comfort Wentworth, but it seems more likely than ever now that he will marry Louisa.

When Anne joins her sister and father in Bath, she learns that they have seen the girls' cousin, William Elliott, who is in line to inherit Kellynch Hall. Several years earlier he had offended Sir Walter by marrying a rich woman instead of Elizabeth. The now widowed Elliott has apologized for the estrangement and has been welcomed back. Anne, who had seen Elliott in Lyme, suspects that his real motive is to ingratiate himself with Elizabeth again and marry her, while Lady Russell thinks he is interested in Anne. When the surprising news of Louisa's engagement to Captain Benwick (the Harvilles' widowed friend) arrives, Anne is pleased but wonders how Wentworth feels about this development. Later she notices that Wentworth seems jealous of Elliott's attentions to her. Anne, who has already rejected a proposal from Elliott, learns the truth about him from her old school friend, the widowed and impoverished Mrs. Smith. Elliott was a friend of her dead husband, and had helped to bring about Mr. Smith's financial ruin. Mrs. Smith tells Anne that Elliott's real motive in befriending his relatives is to prevent a marriage between Mrs. Clay and Sir

Walter, thereby preventing the birth of a male heir who would usurp Elliott's inheritance. By now Wentworth has learned to value Anne as much or more than he did eight years before, and he becomes convinced that she too still loves him. He writes her an emotional letter declaring his love, and the two are soon united. Both Musgrove sisters also marry, while Mrs. Clay goes to London to live as William Elliott's mistress.

Characters: Many critics believe that *Persuasion,* Austen's last completed novel, marks a transition in her work from the mindset of the eighteenth century to the romantic influences of the nineteenth. It begins eight years after the happy endings recorded in all of Austen's previous novels and signifies a shift to a more mature and reflective protagonist. The story's power has been well described by critic Reginald Farrer, who notes that "though *Persuasion* moves very quietly . . . in drawing rooms and country lanes, it is yet among the most emotional novels in our literature."

Though Austen seems fond of all of her heroines, twenty-seven-year-old **Anne Elliott**— intelligent, principled, and sensitive—has often been perceived as closest to her heart and representative of her own world view. Through Anne we see what happens when the idyllic conclusion so standard in Austen's other novels, in which the deserving young woman almost loses but finally wins the deserving young man, is thwarted and the disappointed heroine must live (for eight years, at least) solitarily on. And Anne Elliott's solitude is complete, for she has no dear sister or friend to confide in, and her virtues go unnoticed by those around her. A Cinderella figure (like several other prominent figures in Austen's fiction) surrounded by neglectful, unperceptive people, Anne does eventually attain the handsome prince. Although she is fully aware of and accepts responsibility for her faulty decision not to marry Frederick Wentworth initially, she knows that she was not wrong to heed the advice of the trusted Lady Russell: the mistake was made by Lady Russell. Thus Anne's sense of regret is tempered with the self-knowledge and self-respect that make her a particularly mature heroine. In addition to being elegant, gentle, and well-mannered, Anne shows herself capable of effectively carrying out such practical matters as making the arrangements for the family to leave Kellynch Hall or nursing her sick nephew. Most important, of course, is her calmness and efficiency after Louisa's accident, when not even the experienced Captain Wentworth can keep a cool head; it is this incident that reminds Wentworth of his original love for Anne. Through Anne and her long and painful but ultimately rewarding journey to happiness, Austen presents the possibility of love's renewal.

Unlike the heroine of *Persuasion,* its hero is in need of education. Stung by Anne's rejection, **Frederick Wentworth** has been unable to recover from his anger and consequently perceives Anne as diminished in attractiveness when he meets her eight years later at his sister's home. He has a warm, enthusiastic nature, and because he acts decisively and confidently himself he finds it hard to understand Anne's susceptibility to persuasion. Wentworth maintains that although he has not yet seen Anne's equal in any other woman, she no longer has any power over him, a view that will be revealed as erroneous when Anne does begin to regain his affection. He learns to value the very quality he had once interpreted as weakness—persuadability—as a laudable receptiveness to change and growth. The engagement scene which brings together the two long-familiar, long-separated lovers who can now approach their relationship with the deeper appreciation that comes with maturity has often been praised for its emotional power.

Anne's father, **Sir Walter Elliott,** is bitingly portrayed as a man whose bottomless vanity and pride make him blind to the value of people—like his own daughter—who possess true integrity. Thus it was partly his negative opinion of Wentworth which, eight years earlier, had caused Anne to spurn her worthy suitor. Sir Walter's foolish mismanagement of his wealth has been said to signify a shift in Austen's fiction: the weakening of the stable social order portrayed in her other novels is indicated both by the necessity of letting Kellynch Hall and by the favorable portrayal of the navy men and their families, who represent a lower social level. The upright, admirable qualities of the gentry that Austen presented in her previous novels seem to be replaced with meanness, irresponsibility, and shallow values in *Persuasion.* Sir Walter exhibits this superficiality when he states that he objects to the military profession because it brings "persons of obscure birth into undue distinction" and that it prematurely ages men. Like her father, **Elizabeth Elliott** values wealth and attractiveness above integrity. She is depicted as handsome but unfeeling, and is certainly not a supportive sister. Elizabeth views marriage as a way to gain material advantage and not as anything in which love plays a part. The youngest Elliott daughter, **Mary Musgrove,** is selfish but not as cold-hearted as Elizabeth. Though unreasonable and constantly detecting injury against herself where none has occurred, Mary is capable of amiability. Her marriage to the jovial sportsman **Charles Musgrove** (who, interestingly, had expressed a rare appreciation of Anne by proposing to her before he married his wife) is not necessarily unhappy—Anne observes that although the two are admittedly limited in their perceptions, they have achieved a kind of accord.

The villain of *Persuasion* is the Elliotts' cousin, **William Elliott.** Though not especially handsome, Elliott's power lies in his wealth, charm, and smoothly proper manners. Underneath this admirable facade, of course, is a coldly calculating, self-interested, corrupt nature. Having once spurned his relatives to serve himself by marrying a rich woman, Elliott returns to their good graces not because he regrets the estrangement but in order to continue promoting his own interests. Elliott does do some good in the story, for his admiration of Anne calls Wentworth's attention to her subtle beauty that is not as faded as he had thought. Anne, of course, is never actually susceptible to Elliott's charms and rejects his proposal before she even knows the story of his treachery. Lady Russell, however, is taken in by Elliott and praises him to Anne, providing an ironic reverberation of the persuasion theme (this time she'll be unsuccessful in persuading Anne). Several critics have complained that Elliott's final flight to London to live with Mrs. Clay seems an unlikely development contrived purely to tie up the novel's loose ends and to give it a moralistic conclusion.

The persuasive **Lady Russell,** though responsible for separating Anne and her lover, is not presented in a completely unflattering light. A widowed old friend of the family, she has taken the place of Anne's dead mother. She is basically a respectable person with good principles, though she overvalues wealth and rank and is insensitive to the feelings of others. Although she wrongly advises Anne to marry Elliott, part of the reason she does so is out of a sincere desire to see Anne permanently established at Kellynch Hall in the position of the original Mrs. Elliott, whom she evidently loved. Lady Russell also proves her worth in the practical assistance she offers Sir Walter in recovering from his financial difficulties.

Admiral and Mrs. Croft provide a convenient means for Frederick Wentworth to reappear in Anne's neighborhood and life, but they are even more important in the novel for what they represent. Though somewhat comically portrayed (particularly in the admiral's frequent use of nautical terms), the Crofts are a happily married couple who seem to have achieved a laudable equality and mutual respect in their relationship. Admiral Croft is kindly but plainspoken, and Mrs. Croft is cheerful, vigorous, and practical, furnishing a balance to her husband's frankness in her greater perceptiveness. They provide Anne with a favorable example of the kind of life a naval officer and his family might expect to lead. In a similar role are Captain Wentworth's friends, **Captain and Mrs. Harville,** a naval couple whose love has endured through the hardships of illness and poverty, and who are portrayed as admirable despite their lower social status. Also helping to flesh out the novel's theme of happy married love are Charles Musgrove's parents, **Mr. and Mrs. Musgrove,** who, despite their limited sense, share a cheerful union.

Of **Louisa** and **Henrietta Musgrove,** Admiral Croft says, "very nice young ladies they both are; I hardly know one from the other." The reader might agree, for neither character is particularly well developed. Louisa plays a fairly important role in briefly attracting Captain Wentworth, who seemed headed toward proposing to her before the accident at Lyme not only revealed her true nature but put her in Captain Benwick's range. Both Louisa and Henrietta are blooming young girls whose fresh looks and vigor provide a contrast to Anne. In insisting on being ''jumped down'' from the stone wall against Wentworth's advice, Louisa displays an unreasonable wilfulness that shows up poorly against Anne's susceptibility to persuasion. Henrietta Musgrove does little else than marry her cousin **Charles Hayter,** but in doing so she reinforces the idea that a longstanding relationship with a familiar person can lead to happiness. Anne envies the Musgrove sisters for their good-natured relationship with each other, for she and Elizabeth have never approached a similar closeness.

Both **Mrs. Clay** and **Mrs. Smith,** though representing opposite poles of respectability, have been described as incidental characters used primarily to move the plot along. Mrs. Clay is a schemer who hopes to insinuate her way into Sir Walter's heart by becoming Elizabeth's confidante and flatterer. In the end, Mrs. Clay reveals her inner corruption by running away to London as William Elliott's mistress. Mrs. Smith, on the other hand, is a virtuous woman whose troubles—she is impoverished and ill—are not her own fault. She is depicted as sensible and agreeable, adjusting cheerfully to misfortune, but she is also alarmingly fond of gossip. Scholars have contended that Mrs. Smith is too abruptly introduced and then discarded, and that the circumstance of her previous acquaintance with both Anne and Elliott is too coincidental.

Remaining characters with significance in *Persuasion* include **Mr. Shepherd,** the father of Mrs. Clay, and Sir Walter's agent, a calculating, clever man who says what he knows Sir Walter wants to hear; and **Captain Benwick,** the melancholy widower who is a friend of the Harvilles and who, despite his romantic devotion to his dead fiancee, first finds Anne attractive and then falls in love with Louisa Musgrove.

Further Reading

Amis, Martin. ''Miss Jane's Prime.'' *Atlantic Monthly* 265 (February 1990): 100.

Bloom, Harold, ed. *Modern Critical Views: Jane Austen.* New York: Chelsea House, 1986.

Brown, Julia Prewitt. ''The Feminist Depreciation of Austen: A Polemical Reading.'' *Novel: A Forum on Fiction* 23 (Spring 1990): 303.

Craik, W.A. *Jane Austen: The Six Novels.* London: Methuen & Co., Ltd., 1965.

Honan, Park. *Jane Austen: Her Life.* New York: St. Martin's Press, 1987.

Morgan, Susan. *In the Meantime: Character and Perception in Jane Austen's Fiction.* Chicago: University of Chicago Press, 1980.

Nineteenth Century Literature Criticism, Vols. 1, 13, 19. Detroit: Gale.

Oliphant, Margaret. ''Miss Austen and Miss Mitford.'' *Blackwood's Edinburgh Magazine* CVII, No. DCLIII (March 1870): 290-313.

Paris, Bernard J. *Character and Conflict in Jane Austen's Novels: A Psychological Approach.* Detroit: Wayne State University Press, 1978.

Saintsbury, George. ''Miss Austen: 'Pride and Prejudice.''' In *Prefaces and Essays,* pp. 194-209. New York: Macmillan and Co., Limited, 1933.

Trilling, Lionel. ''Mansfield Park.'' In *The Opposing Self.* New York: Viking Press, 1955.

Weldon, Fay. *Letters to Alice on First Reading Jane Austen.* New York: Taplinger Publishing Co., 1985.

Honoré de Balzac

1799-1850

French novelist, short story and novella writer, dramatist, essayist, and editor.

Pére Goriot (*Le pere goriot: Histoire parisienne;* novel, 1837)

Plot: Set in Paris in 1819, the novel begins in a boarding house owned by Madame Vauquer. Located in Rue Nueve Ste. Marceau, an impoverished district, the tenement is ostensibly "respectable" but has a shabby, dirty interior. Eight boarders live in the Maison Vauquer, one of whom, Monsieur Goriot, is frequently the butt of the others' jokes and derision. He was well-dressed and confident when he arrived at the boarding house six years earlier, but he has since become increasingly dilapidated in appearance and manner. He is sometimes visited by two beautiful, apparently wealthy women who are thought to be his lovers but are, in fact, his daughters. Eugene Rastignac is another boarder, a poor law student from the country. Eager to enter the elegant Parisian society centered in the Faubourg Ste. Germain, he secures an invitation to visit a distant relative, the Viscountess de Beauseant. With her introduction, Eugene calls on the lovely Countess Anastasie de Restaud. She spurns him, however, when he mentions his connection to Goriot, whom he saw leaving her house. He learns that Goriot is Anastasie's father, and that he had risen from humble beginnings to make a fortune as a noodle and flour maker after the 1789 French revolution. He thus provided both daughters with generous dowries that allowed them to marry rich, influential men, who subsequently banished Goriot from their homes. Eugene gradually grows aware of the many sacrifices and humiliations Goriot has borne for his daughters' sake, and he begins to admire him for his unflagging devotion.

With Madame de Beauseant's encouragement, Eugene then pursues Goriot's other daughter, Delphine de Nucingen. Realizing that he lacks the funds necessary to court such a woman, Eugene borrows 1200 francs from his family. Another of the Maison Vauquer boarders, Monsieur Vautrin, proposes that Eugene engage the affections of the already infatuated Victorine Taillefer, who also lives at the boarding house and who is the rejected illegitimate daughter of a wealthy man. Vautrin promises to have Victorine's brother—who currently stands to inherit their father's fortune—killed, in exchange for a share of the wealth Eugene will gain as Victorine's husband when Monsieur Taillefer inevitably recognizes his daughter. Eugene refuses Vautrin's offer, but when Vautrin later sees the young man flirting with Victorine he goes ahead with the plan. Just as the news comes that Victorine's brother is dead and her father has summoned her, Vautrin is exposed as a notorious criminal and arrested. Meanwhile, Eugene has begun a love affair with Delphine, and the delighted Goriot uses the last of his money to furnish a glamorous apartment for the two. But both daughters soon experience financial crises, and, for the first time, their father is unable to help them. The stress of this failure brings on Goriot's death. Neither of his daughters is with him at his deathbed (both are attending Madame de Beauseant's ball), though Delphine arrives after he has lost consciousness. Goriot is buried at the expense of Eugene and the medical student Bianchon; only Eugene and a servant are present at the burial. Eugene weeps for Goriot, then cynically vows to conquer Parisian society.

Characters: *Pére Goriot* may be the most celebrated novel in Balzac's breathtaking body of work, which he called *La comédie humaine* ("The Human Comedy"). In almost one hundred novels, Balzac attempted to portray the whole spectrum of French life in all of its colorful diversity—rich and poor, city and country, male and female, good and evil. Though sometimes faulted for the effusive details and occasional sloppiness that marks his writing and for overemphasizing the darker side of human nature, Balzac is revered for the imaginative scope of his fictional vision and for the authentic, vividly drawn characters that bring so much meaning and depth to his work. *Père Goriot* was the first novel in ''The Human Comedy'' to include the recurring characters for which the series is noted; this technique is employed as a unifying device between books, and it also allows for deeper psychological exploration of the characters' development.

The title character of *Père Goriot* is often cited as one of the best examples of Balzac's monomaniacal figures. **Pére Goriot**'s accumulation of wealth, which allowed him to ensconce his daughters in the Parisian aristocracy, illustrates the social consequences of the tumultuous post-revolutionary period in France. Likewise, the fact that the husbands of Goriot's daughters have forbidden him to enter their homes indicates that a notion of class hierarchy still had a strong hold on French society. The psychological aspects of Goriot's character, though, are even more compelling than the historical. He loves his daughters fanatically despite their neglect, and it is this overwhelming passion that drives him. Critics have often noted that the intensity of his feeling sometimes seems close to romantic love. Goriot's income is much reduced by his daughters' marriages to prominent men, and he is further impoverished over the years by their requests for more money. As Goriot's finances decline, so does his appearance and confidence; he becomes a confused, tattered shadow of the cheerful, dapper man he was when he first arrived at the Maison Vauquer. Consumed by his paternal affection and unable to see beyond it, Goriot is eagerly grateful for the least attention from his daughters—he feels rewarded, for instance, by a slight smile from one of them when she drives by in her elegant carriage. While most critics acknowledge that Goriot, like other monomaniacal figures in Balzac's fiction, is defined exclusively by his one obsession and is thus a somewhat flat character, Balzac has been universally praised for his detailed, insightful portrayal of this father's devotion. Few readers could deny the power and pathos of the scene in which, attended only by the sympathetic Eugene and Bianchon, the mortally ill Goriot alternately curses his absent daughters and professes his great love for them. Despite the monetary and emotional wealth he has lavished on Anastasie and Delphine—and perhaps because of it—Goriot dies in a poverty of both material circumstance and inner feeling.

Eugene Rastignac is also an important figure in *Père Goriot,* for the novel chronicles his passage from innocence to knowledge. Eugene is a poor law student from a formerly noble but now impoverished family that must make sacrifices to finance his studies. Eugene is a handsome young man with pale skin, black hair, and he reveals his natural elegance when he dresses for an evening out. Although he is naive and socially clumsy at first, Eugene develops graceful manners and an increasingly cynical attitude through his exposure to Parisian society. He chooses to make his mark via social conquests—by alliance with wealthy women eager for the attentions of a good-looking, charming, and devoted young man—rather than through the more arduous course of a law career or through the criminal alternative that Vautrin suggests. Although Eugene begins as a basically good person—he sincerely loves his mother and sisters and he becomes Goriot's devoted friend and surrogate son—his growing disillusionment with the people and situations around him tarnishes his youthful innocence. Eugene's dismay over Goriot's dismal fate leads to his final resolution to triumph over the brutal society with which he has aligned himself. He is an important example of Balzac's use of recurring characters: designated Eugene Massiac in early drafts of the novel, he was renamed Eugene Rastignac to correspond with a minor character in Balzac's earlier work, *The Wild Ass's Skin* (*La peau de chagrin*). The Eugene in that novel is a jaded aristocrat, and in novels subsequent to *Père Goriot* Eugene's further descent into corruption as he becomes a wealthy, ruthless financier is chronicled.

Monsieur Vautrin, the sharp-tongued boarder who describes himself as a former merchant, turns out to be the infamous criminal **Jacques Collin.** Before his exposure, Vautrin maintains an aura of secret knowledge through his reserve, his elegant manners, and his penetrating glances. Vautrin combines physical strength and vitality with an intuitive intelligence. He reveals to Eugene his cynical, opportunistic, and ultimately corrupt view of life when he sketches out a bleak picture of Eugene's future if he pursues only honest means of achievement. Vautrin thoroughly rejects the limitations of society and of law in favor of manipulating others to further his own interests. He scorns society while Madame de Beauseant embodies it; yet the plans that each formulates for Eugene are immoral—although only Vautrin's is blatantly criminal. Vautrin will continue to represent an ubiquitous force of evil in "The Human Comedy"; his criminal career is recounted in several subsequent novels.

Balzac's portrayal of the other residents of the Maison Vauquer contributes significantly to *Pére Goriot*'s panoramic view of Parisian life. These characters represent the underside of the huge and varied metropolis and provide a dramatic contrast to the glamorous existence Eugene discovers in the Faubourg Ste. Germain. **Madame Vauquer** embodies the spirit of the squalid boarding house she operates; Balzac's room-by-room description of that dismal place segues into an introduction to its proprietress. She is a fat, sloppily dressed, sly, older woman whose manners toward her boarders improve as the amount they pay for their room and board increases. Thus her matrimonial intentions toward the seemingly well-off Goriot when he first moved into the house dissolved over the years into disgust and mockery as his poverty became more obvious.

Mademoiselle Michonneau, a bony, vaguely sinister spinster, proves her greediness when she betrays Vautrin/Collin to the police because of the reward they offer. Her ravaged face bears a suggestion of former beauty, and it is intimated that she has a firsthand knowledge of corruption. When Mademoiselle Michonneau is forced to leave the Maison Vauquer by the other boarders, who are disgusted by her treachery toward Vautrin, her only ally is **Monsieur Poiret.** He is an elderly, decrepit, former government worker whose willingness to help turn Vautrin over to the police is rooted in his blind allegiance to authority. Another elderly boarder is **Madame Couture,** the kind and pious distant relative who serves as **Victorine Taillefer**'s guardian. Poor but respectable, Madame Couture is loyal and well-intentioned toward her young charge and greatly resents the behavior of Victorine's father. Victorine is portrayed as a frail, sickly girl whose prettiness is masked by her shoddy clothing. She is passive in the face of her father's rejection and does not seem to hold it against him, even though it relegates her to a disadvantaged and melancholy state. Victorine's love for Eugene transforms her into a vision of innocent happiness that provides a contrast to the more worldly, sensual passion of Eugene's aristocratic lover, Delphine. **Bianchon,** like Eugene, is a poor student, but he embraces the idea of eventually leaving Paris and living a quiet provincial life as a country doctor. Though he claims to be interested in Goriot's illness for scientific reasons, Bianchon reveals his compassionate nature while treating the dying man. He remarks that Goriot's physical disintegration shows the connection between emotional and physical well-being, a concept that interested Balzac. Bianchon makes many more appearances throughout "The Human Comedy," and it is rumored (though not confirmed) that Balzac called out for him on his own deathbed.

Their social position made possible by their father's wealth and sacrifice, Goriot's overindulged daughters acquired the shallow morality and greed for luxury that permeate the Parisian realm they inhabit. At the beginning of *Pére Goriot,* **Anastasie de Restaud** is the more fashionable of the sisters because she became a countess by marrying a member of the aristocracy, while Delphine's husband is a banker only recently elevated to the status of baron. Anastasie, dark-haired and beautiful, is involved in an affair with another aristocrat, the irresponsible Maxime de Tailles. Even more than her sister, Anastasie is ashamed of her father; when Eugene naively mentions Goriot while visiting her he is barred from entering her home again. And it is Anastasie's request for twelve thousand francs to save her lover from financial ruin that helps precipitate Goriot's death—his inability to help her ultimately kills him. Anastasie is not in attendance at her father's deathbed because she is arguing with her husband (who has forced her to admit that he is the real father of only one of their children), and she chooses to make a dramatic appearance at Madame de Restaud's ball—wearing the heirloom diamond necklace she is rumored to have pawned to help Maxime. Anastasie never appears at the Maison Vauquer during her father's last hours, nor does she attend his funeral. Her obsessive love for the unworthy Maxime de Tailles resembles that of Goriot for his daughters. In the end, it is obvious that Goriot's efforts to furnish Anastasie with a pampered and happy life have only led to deceit, anger, and sadness.

Delphine de Nucingen is portrayed as a somewhat more considerate daughter than Anastasie, though she shares with her sister a desire to gratify her own desires at any cost. She would like to advance her position in society, particularly so that she will gain equality with the more fashionably placed Anastasie. Unhappily married, Delphine responds eagerly to Eugene's advances and becomes—in typical Goriot fashion—his passionately devoted lover. Eugene is able to influence her to be kinder to her father, but her determination to make a dazzling show at Madame de Beauseant's ball overcomes all other considerations. She is dancing there as her father is dying. This demonstration of self-centeredness and ambition disheartens Eugene, particularly when Delphine chooses to sleep late the morning after the ball rather than attend her father. She does finally arrive at the Maison Vauquer, but Goriot is already unconscious. Like Anastasie, she sends only her empty carriage to her father's funeral.

It is through the poised, elegant **Viscountess de Beauseant** that Eugene gains access to the fashionable drawing rooms of Paris. A distant relative of Eugene's formerly noble family, Madame de Beauseant symbolizes the centuries-old French aristocracy that—despite the intended leveling of the 1789 revolution—again gained favor during Napoleon's reign. When Eugene first meets her, Madame de Beauseant is in the middle of a romantic crisis: she is about to lose her lover, the Marquis d'Adjuda-Pinto, who has decided to make an advantageous marriage. Madame de Beauseant advises Eugene to make his way in the world by charming a wealthy woman, and promises to sponsor him in this goal by allowing him to invite the socially ambitious Delphine de Nucingen to a ball at the viscountess's home. She tells Eugene to avoid love and sentiment if he wishes to succeed—ironic advice, since it is the dashing of her own sincere love for the Marquis which causes her withdrawal from society. Heartbroken and humiliated by her lover's betrayal, Madame de Beauseant keeps up a proud, apparently unconcerned appearance before the cruelly curious onlookers at the ball (all of whom know what has happened to her) then isolates herself forever by leaving Paris. The story of the viscountess's later life in exile in Normandy is recounted in an earlier novella, *La femme abandonnee.*

In addition to Madame de Beauseant, several other wealthy inhabitants of the Faubourg Ste. Germain make appearances throughout "The Human Comedy." The **Duchess de Langeais** acts unkindly at the beginning of *Père Goriot* by pointedly informing the viscountess of the Marquis's marriage, but she eventually makes a gesture of friendship when she recognizes that both women have suffered the same fate. Madame de Langeais also serves a practical function when she relates Goriot's history to Eugene. Like the viscountess, the duchess is featured in an earlier novella: *La Duchesse de Langeais.* Other characters in *Père Goriot* which recur throughout "The Human Comedy" include Delphine's husband, the shifty **Baron de Nucingen; Gondureau,** the detective who arrests Vautrin; and **Gobseck,** the moneylender to whom Goriot sells his valuables to raise money for his daughters.

Eugénie Grandet (novel, 1837)

Plot: The novel takes place in the small town of Saumur, located in France's wine producing district. Monsieur Felix Grandet is a former cooper (barrel maker) who made a fortune after the Revolution by buying up land once owned by the church and by marrying the daughter of a wealthy merchant. As the novel opens, in 1819, Grandet is a very rich man who owns many acres of vineyards and grazing lands as well as several farms and an old abbey. He has become more miserly as his wealth has increased. The family lives frugally and without many basic comforts. Grandet has one daughter, Eugénie, whose valuable hand is sought by the scions of two local families: Monsieur Cruchot de Bonfons, a judge and the son of a notary, and Adolphe des Grassins, the son of a banker. On Eugénie's twenty-third birthday the two families arrive at the Grandet's house to offer congratulations. Also arriving that evening is Charles Grandet, the son of Grandet's brother. Accustomed to a glamorous life in Paris, Charles is contemptuous of his provincial relatives. He brings with him a letter from his father to his uncle which announces the former is financially ruined and intends to commit suicide. Charles hears the news the next day and is grief-stricken. Madame Grandet, Eugénie, and the family's servant Nanon sympathize with the young man and Eugénie begins to fall in love with her handsome, sophisticated cousin. When she reads a letter that Charles has written to his married Parisian lover, Annette, explaining his newly penniless state, Eugénie give Charles her valuable collection of coins even though she knows that her father will be furious. He accepts the gift (worth six thousand francs) and begins to prepare for his departure for the Indies (Indonesia), where he will seek his fortune. Charles and Eugénie share some moments of innocent passion and vow to love each other forever; Eugénie promises to wait faithfully for Charles to return. Meanwhile, Grandet arranges to save his brother's estate from bankruptcy, but at great advantage to himself and without completely paying off all of his brother's debts. He sends Monsieur des Grassins and Adolphe to Paris to assist in his affairs. Grandet is enraged when he discovers that Eugénie's coins are gone and confines her to her room. Madame Grandet, who has grown increasingly ill and now seems near death, pleads for a reconciliation between Grandet and their daughter before she dies. Grandet agrees because he is afraid that Eugénie will demand her share of her mother's dowry. After Madame Grandet dies, he persuades Eugénie to sign away her right to the money.

Seven years later, no word has come from Charles. Grandet dies, but not before telling Eugénie to take good care of the family's money. Eugénie is now a wealthy woman with a fortune of seven million francs, but she continues to live a lonely, simple life and gives much of her money to charity. Charles finally returns to Paris; he has become rich through the slave trade. He writes to Eugénie, telling her that he plans to gain a title through a loveless marriage with an aristocratic young woman. Though devastated by this development, Eugénie provides the money Charles needs to pay off his father's remaining debtors, thus allowing him to marry. Eugénie herself marries Judge Cruchot, though in name only, and her husband dies after only a few years. Eugénie continues to live alone, giving generously to charity but denying herself many comforts despite her wealth, to the end of her life.

Characters: *Eugénie Grandet* is one of the most celebrated novels in "The Human Comedy." The novel differs from many of Balzac's other works in its depiction of only one setting—the provincial household of a miser—and in its restraint. Though less detailed and eventful than other components of "The Human Comedy," *Eugénie Grandet* is valued for the peek into small-town French life it provides and for the compelling characters it introduces.

Although Felix Grandet might be fairly termed the central figure of *Eugénie Grandet,* the novel's title character is its most sympathetic. **Eugénie Grandet** is twenty-three as the story begins. She is a tall, healthy country girl with almost masculine but appealing looks. Having lived all her life in the sheltered household of a notorious miser, she is innocent of the world's pleasures as well as its evils and is not even aware that her father is wealthy. When her glamorous cousin Charles arrives, Eugénie is awakened to a broader perspective and sees both her own surroundings and life's possibilities in a new light. Her love for Charles arouses both her kindness and generosity—as she sympathizes with his grief and tries to comfort him—as well as a previously unknown defiance, as she dares to give Charles her valuable coins. Eugénie is supremely faithful, both to her parents and church and to the lover who, after an uncommunicative absence of seven years, marries someone else. In the end, Eugénie—whom Balzac portrays as ideally suited for marriage and childbearing—accepts with pious resignation a stark, loveless existence in the big, empty house of her childhood. It is obvious that, despite her charitable gestures, Grandet's parsimony has infected his daughter as well. She continues to do without not only luxuries but the basic comforts he had always denied her. Eugénie's fate exemplifies Balzac's belief in *determinism,* the theory that the combination of genetic heredity and environmental influences inescapably determines what we become. (Determinism was one of the main tenets of the nineteenth-century school of realistic fiction, which Balzac is credited with precipitating.) Thus Eugénie becomes a rich but unhappy woman—a tragedy made even more poignant by the knowledge of what she *might* have become.

Like Balzac's earlier creation, Pére Goriot, **Felix Grandet** is a monomaniacal character, obsessed with one interest at the exclusion of all others. Grandet's passion is for money, which he loves for its own sake rather than for what it can buy. He delights in the very look and feel of money; he derives great pleasure, for instance, in his yearly examination of Eugénie's coin collection. Greed and the corruptive power of money are common threads that run through much of Balzac's work, and Grandet more than any other character represents the embodiment of avarice. He is a shrewd, unscrupulous businessman who will stop at nothing to gain a profit; he has no other philosophy, interests, or emotions. Scholars often describe Grandet as a one-sided character with whom no one could sympathize, yet all acknowledge that Balzac's portrayal of Grandet's one quality is remarkably vivid. Although never a party to Grandet's inner thoughts, the reader learns about him through the author's skillful depiction of his actions, conversation, and even facial expressions. Grandet's resentment of any ''extravagance''—such as allowing the fire to be lit before the middle of November—blights the lives of his wife and daughter. He is genuinely surprised that Charles is more upset over his father's death than over the loss of his fortune. Even Grandet's apparent kindnesses, like the reconciliation with Eugénie that he affects when his wife is close to death, are coldly calculated to serve his own ends. Grandet's own death scene appropriately consummates his avaricious life: his eyes light up at the sight of the priest's gold vessels, and his grasping gesture toward one of them finally brings on his death.

Madame Grandet is as much a victim of her husband's miserliness as is her daughter. She endures the deprivation imposed by her husband with the submissive piety taught by her church and never contradicts Grandet or asks for more than what he begrudgingly gives her. She truly loves Eugénie and sympathizes with her feelings for Charles. There is tragic irony in the fact that Madame Grandet, finally made fatally ill by her husband's neglect, dies believing that he has forgiven Eugénie and that the two are reconciled.

On his arrival in Saumur, **Charles Grandet** is an elegantly dressed, handsome young man who emanates Parisian sophistication and feels superior to his country cousins. Spoiled by indulgent parents and accustomed to luxury, Charles has known nothing but pleasure. Despite his apparent shallowness, Charles is plunged into real grief by the news of his father's death. This outpouring of sorrow is part of what makes Eugénie—already dazzled by Charles's looks and air—fall in love with him. Touched by her innocence, purity, and generosity, Charles responds to and returns Eugénie's love. But the memory of their tender moments in the Grandet's garden do not have as permanent an appeal for him as they do for Eugénie. His character deteriorates when he is exposed to, among other corrupting influences, the slave trade and the fortune he amasses (financed, initially, by Eugénie's money). On his return to Paris, he writes Eugénie a cruel letter trivializing their young passion then cynically marries another woman for selfish reasons. Ironically, the young man on whom Eugénie has lavished all of her love has proved himself singularly unworthy of it.

Nanon, the Grandet's faithful family servant, is portrayed as a constant source of strength and unyielding loyalty—especially to Eugénie, who by the story's end considers Nanon her only friend. The large, masculine, unattractive Nanon was hired by Grandet when no other employer wanted her, and she remains grateful to him despite her knowledge of his failings. Nanon is perhaps the only character in the novel who is not afraid to tell Grandet what she thinks, and he respects her—as far as he is able to respect anyone—for the thrift and efficiency with which she runs the household. Nanon sides with Madame Grandet and Eugénie against Grandet when he banishes Eugénie to her room with a diet of only bread and water; Nanon brings Eugénie food and lets her out to visit her dying mother whenever Grandet is away. In the end, Nanon is rewarded for her virtues and is probably the happiest character in the book: she finds satisfaction in her marriage with the gamekeeper, **Antoine Cornoiller,** with whom she competently oversees the affairs of the Grandet estate.

The two families that compete for the privilege of marrying their offspring to the rich Eugénie Grandet are the Cruchots and the des Grassins. Both represent further expressions of the quest for money; their apparently fond attentions to Eugénie are calculated to impress her father and thus improve their chances of success. **Monsieur Cruchot de Bonfons** is a notary and one of the few residents of Saumur who is aware of the true extent of Grandet's fortune. His nephew is a self-important judge who aspires to increase his already substantial wealth by marrying Eugénie. She does eventually agree to the marriage—though it is a marriage of form only—but ironically, **Judge Cruchot** will have only three years in which to enjoy the long-sought fruits of his greed. The equally avaricious des Grassins clan includes **Madame des Grassins,** a calculating woman with ambitions for her worthless son; **Monsieur des Grassins,** a banker who goes to Paris to arrange Grandet's affairs and likes the exciting night life there so much that he never returns; and the son, **Adolphe,** a pleasure-seeking spendthrift who joins his father in his Parisian revels. Balzac's portrayal of the two families, with their artificial sentiment masking their basic greed and lack of morality, provides further evidence of his interest in the corruption that results from the lust for money.

Further Reading

Dargan, Edwin Preston. *Honoré de Balzac: A Force of Nature.* Chicago: University of Chicago Press, 1932.

Festa-McCormick, Diana. *Honoré de Balzac.* Boston: Twayne, 1979.

James, Henry. "The Lesson of Balzac." *In The Question of Our Speech: The Lesson of Balzac; Two Lectures,* pp. 55-116. Boston, New York: Houghton, Mifflin, 1905.

Kanes, Martin, ed. *Critical Essays on Honoré de Balzac.* Boston: G. K. Hall, 1990.

Marceau, Felicien. *Balzac and His World,* translated by Derek Coltman. New York: Orion, 1966.

McCarthy, Mary Susan. *Balzac and His Reader: A Study of the Creation of Meaning in "La comédie humaine."* Columbia: University of Missouri Press, 1982.

Nineteenth Century Literature Criticism, Vol. 5. Detroit: Gale.

Pugh, Anthony. *Balzac's Recurring Characters.* Toronto and Buffalo: University of Toronto Press, 1974.

Pritchett, V. S. *Balzac.* New York: Knopf, 1973.

Short Story Criticism, Vol. 5. Detroit: Gale.

Henri Becque
1837-1899
French dramatist, critic, and journalist.

The Vultures (*Les corbeaux;* drama, 1882)

Plot: The play centers on the Vignorons, a middle-class family of nineteenth-century France. In the opening scene, the Vignorons are preparing to celebrate the engagement of third daughter Blanche to a young aristocrat named George Saint-Genis. But the family's joy is spoiled by the news of Monsieur Vignoron's sudden death. Soon Madame Vignoron and her children are preyed upon by her husband's partner, the miserly and immoral Teissier, his sly lawyer Bourdon, and a host of other conniving business associates and creditors. The family's financial burden becomes more and more troublesome, and the naive Madame Vignoron is unable to extricate herself from the rapacious clutches of the "vultures" who surround her. Her daughters' attempts to help are equally ineffective (the one son, Gaston, chooses the self-centered solution of joining the army). The oldest daughter, Judith, learns that she had been deluded by her music teacher as to her talent and that the theatrical career she had planned is impossible. Meanwhile, Blanche's engagement has been dissolved by her fiance's mother, Madame Saint-Genis, since the girl can no longer furnish the generous dowry that had made the match desirable. Blanche's consequent distress is such that she begins to sink into madness. Finally, the youngest of the Vignoron daughters, Marie, agrees to marry the repellent Teissier in order to save her family from ruin. The play ends with Teissier sending away one of the dishonest creditors and making the much-quoted, thoroughly ironic observation, "Child, since your father died you've been surrounded by a lot of vultures."

Characters: Becque is considered an important originator of the naturalistic movement in French drama. His work differs from the drippingly sentimental melodramas popular at the time in its realistic settings and characters and the brutal honesty with which it presents social mores and behavior. He is often given credit for introducing a new genre termed *comedie rosse* (bitter, nasty, or tough comedy), which is dominated by a cynical tone and a sometimes painful realism. *The Vultures* employs a "slice-of-life" technique that features a plot trimmed of all but essential dialogue and characters who illustrate the play's themes through their actions and unintentionally revealing comments. Becque is frequently compared to the great seventeenth-century French dramatist Moliere in his creation of comically ironic figures whose dominant traits are disapprovingly lampooned.

Becque's portrayal of the Vignoron family, though basically sympathetic, is significant in its emphasis on their weaknesses. They are not meant to represent an ideal, but instead are lifelike characters who can be weak, troubled, and uncertain and who do not always see what appears to be obvious. The head of the family, **Monsieur Vignoron,** makes only a brief appearance in the first act; it is his death that sets the play in motion. He is portrayed as a good-natured man who is a loving father and husband and an honest, hardworking businessman. But he is also naive enough to have the shifty Teissier as his business partner and he is typically middle-class in his cultural shallowness. **Madame Vignoron** is even more naive than her husband and is thus subject to the dishonest manipulation of his associates. Her naivete is exemplified by her frequent repetition of the claim "As long as I am alive, the factory will not be sold," for in reality she is powerless to alter the course of events. She also shares with Monsieur Vignoron a devotion to her family and a certain bourgeois mentality. Nevertheless, Madame Vignoron provides a strong contrast to Madame Saint-Genis, whose concern is not for her son's happiness but for the financial gain his marriage will bring the family. In praising Becque's portrayal of Madame Vignoron, Arnold Bennett observed that "he exposes every foolishness of the ruined widow; he never spares her for an instant; and yet one's sympathy is not alienated."

At the beginning of *The Vultures,* **Judith Vignoron** is a dreamy girl who is immersed in her love of music; her teacher has convinced her that she has a great deal of talent. After her father's death she considers embarking on a theatrical career in order to help her family but learns that Monsieur Merckens had been flattering her merely so that she would continue to pay for music lessons. With the destruction of her illusions about her own ability comes the realization that the mores and values of her society are insubstantial. Once she has made this futile attempt to offer aid to her family, Judith becomes passive and helpless, and even her plea to Marie to resist marrying Teissier is too weak to be effective. **Marie Vignoron** is the most sympathetically portrayed of the sisters; she is thoughtful, intelligent, and sensible and the others look to her for guidance. She shows strength of character not only in her sacrifice of personal happiness for the good of her family but in refusing to become Teissier's mistress—she insists that he marry her. There is irony in the fact that the only way Marie can save her family from the vultures is by joining their ranks through marriage to one of them; thus she claims she is ashamed to take this step but would feel guilty if she did not. Marie's family loyalty is contrasted with Teissier's lack of any similar sentiment—he has abandoned his parents because of their demands for money, though he admits they are starving.

Blanche Vignoron begins as a romantic, sensitive girl who is very much in love with her fiance. The fact that she has already submitted to George's advances and lost her virginity diminishes her purity in the world's eyes, though Becque does not present her as immoral—it is those around her who display their baseness. Madame Saint-Genis calls Blanche a "fallen woman" during their final confrontation, refusing to allow the marriage that would save Blanche from guilt because the girl can no longer bring her son a good income. As a result, Blanche's spirit crumbles under the weight of shame and regret, and she begins to lose her mind—thus becoming an additional burden to her family rather than an asset. **Gaston Vignoron** does not play a very significant role in the play. He is portrayed as an irresponsible young man who has been spoiled by his adoring father and who responds to his family's distress by escaping into the army. Becque was forced to strike Gaston's essentially good-natured impersonation of his father—which happens just before the news of his death arrives—from the opening night performance of the play; the producers apparently considered this behavior too heartless for audiences to accept.

Another member of the Vignoron household who deserves mention is **Rosalie,** the family's devoted servant. She seems more perceptive than anyone else because she immediately recognizes the dishonest interventions of Monsieur Vignoron's business associates and foresees the results. It is Rosalie who observes that these men are like vultures who will only leave behind what they cannot carry away. She remains utterly faithful to the Vignorons, however, sharing their misery and trying to offer them comfort. Rosalie has been compared to other similarly good-hearted servants in literature and has been said to evince Becque's belief in the possibility and value of such virtue.

The most distinctive of the "vulture" characters is **Monsieur Teissier,** a miserly, unscrupulous, sixty-year-old financier who takes a purely utilitarian view of life and business. He lacks any virtue and is always eager to find loopholes in the law or weaknesses in others in order to turn a profit. Although Teissier might be described as lecherous in his desire for the attractive Marie, he actually admires her common sense and stability more than her looks; the most important inquiry he has about her is whether she has a good head for figures. It has been noted that, like other unsavory characters in *The Vultures,* Teissier does not comprehend the immorality of his behavior; as far as he is concerned, he is a fine and upstanding person. The reader clearly sees that he is not. This discrepancy gives Teissier an ironic aspect that has generated comparisons with the character of Harpagon in Moliere's play *The Miser* (*L'Avare,* 1668).

The other vultures include Vignoron's sly, conniving lawyer **Monsieur Bourdon,** who finds ways of bending the law to his own selfish advantage; **Monsieur Merckens,** the cynical music teacher who only praises his student's ability when she has the money to pay for lessons; and the creditors, vulgar and self-serving **Monsieur Lafort** and **Monsieur Dubois,** who is rude to Marie but servile when Teissier appears. Also aligned with the vultures of the world is **Madame Saint-Genis,** a domineering woman who arranges her son's life to suit her own greedy purposes. **George Saint-Genis** is depicted as a foppishly attired and mannered young man who, though of aristocratic lineage, has no fortune of his own and who shows neither decency nor backbone in his relationships with Blanche and his mother.

Further Reading

Bennett, Arnold. ''Henry Becque,'' first published in 1910. In *Books and Persons: Being Comments on a Past Epoch, 1908-1911,* pp. 255-62. Doran, 1917.

Gassner, John, ed. ''Realism and Naturalism: Henry Becque.'' In *A Treasury of the Theatre, Vol II: Modern European Drama from Henrik Ibsen to Jean-Paul Sartre,* rev. ed., pp. 95-7. New York: Simon and Schuster, 1963.

Huneker, James. ''Henry Becque.'' In *Iconoclasts: A Book of Dramatists,* pp. 163-81. New York: Scribner's, 1905.

Hyslop, Lois Boe. *Henry Becque.* New York: Twayne, 1972.

Nineteenth Century Literature Criticism, Vol. 3. Detroit: Gale.

Smith, Hugh Allison. ''Henri Becque and the Theatre Libre.'' In *Main Currents of Modern French Drama,* pp. 189-207. New York: Holt, Rinehart, and Winston, 1925.

Wooten, Carl W. '''The Vultures': Becque's Realistic Comedy of Manners.'' *Modern Drama* 4, No. 1 (May 1961): 72-9.

Edward Bellamy
1850-1898
American novelist, short story writer, essayist, and editor.

Looking Backward: 2000-1887 (novel, 1888)

Plot: The novel begins in Boston in 1887. Wealthy young Julian West suffers from insomnia that is aggravated both by his own anxieties and by the city's excessive noise. He is engaged to the lovely Edith Barrett, but the wedding has been repeatedly postponed because labor strikes have delayed the construction of Julian's new house. After a pleasant evening with Edith and her family, Julian retires to the soundproof room he has built in his cellar, and, with the assistance of the mesmerist (hypnotist) Dr. Peabody, falls into a hypnotic trance. When he wakes, he finds himself in the presence of a man he does not know. He learns that 113 years have passed, and he is in the home Dr. Leete, a retired physician. Julian's house had burned down that night over a century ago, but the concrete-enforced bunker survived and was only recently discovered. Miraculously preserved, Julian is still the same man he was when he went to sleep, but his city—and indeed, the world—has changed drastically. In a series of pleasant, casual talks, Dr. Leete describes society as it now exists. The tumultuous labor unrest and other evils of the late nineteenth century led to a mass conversion to the idea of cooperation for the common good. The peaceful revolution resulted in a system called "Nationalism," involving the consolidation of individual businesses and services into one huge governing organization that oversees all industry. The totally egalitarian system features education for all citizens through age twenty-one, after which they work as menial laborers for three years then may either enter professional schools or join the "Industrial Army" in jobs that suit their abilities and desires. All workers earn the same amount of money, and all retire at age forty-five. Education and health care are provided free of charge, there is virtually no crime, and the city is clean, quiet, and attractive. The government is run by wise older workers who have proven their commitment to the cooperative society, while such tedious domestic tasks as washing and cooking are handled by communal laundries and kitchens. Music is piped into each home through telephonic devices, libraries still carry the novels of Charles Dickens and other classic works, and censorship does not exist, as Dr. Leete's daughter Edith explains. Dr. Leete proposes that Julian accept a position as a college lecturer in history as soon as he becomes acclimated to his new surroundings.

Julian falls in love with Edith Leete and asks her to marry him. She accepts, revealing that she is a descendent of Edith Barrett and that she has already come to love him through his letters to his former fiancee. Suddenly, Julian sits up in bed and finds himself back in the nineteenth century. Walking around the city, he notices for the first time the suffering around him. He feels horrified and guilty and attempts unsuccessfully to convert others to his vision of the year 2000. It is with great relief that Julian wakes again in Dr. Leete's house, realizing that his return to the nineteenth century was just a dream. He and Edith continue to plan a happy life together in the twenty-first century.

Characters: Much to its author's surprise, *Looking Backward* became enormously popular soon after its publication. By combining his conception of a utopian society based on socialist principals with traditional American values such as the reverence for technology, Bellamy achieved a work of broad appeal. Many scholars have noted that crafting the story as a romance with a confused hero who finally wins the love of a beautiful girl made the book particularly accessible. Indeed, Bellamy himself spoke of having "sugar-coated" his ideas about political and social reform in a pleasing, novelistic format. While divided on whether the characters in *Looking Backward* are uninteresting and stereotypical or help to illustrate Bellamy's ideas, most agree with Granville Hicks that "readers picked up the book as seekers of amusement and laid it down converts."

Through the character of **Julian West,** the narrator of *Looking Backward,* Bellamy personalizes what otherwise might be a dry theoretical treatise. The young, wealthy resident of nineteenth-century Boston is described as a typical New England aristocrat who lives indolently on inherited income. Before the trance that marks his passage into the year 2000, Julian's outlook is characterized by fear, pessimism, and alienation from society and from himself. In his dismay over increasing labor unrest and the encroachment of factories and slums into his own neighborhood, Julian typifies the late-nineteenth-century American who was distrustful of rapid industrialization and urbanization. Thus Julian, as critics have noted, represents just the sort of average person Bellamy would wish to convert to his ideas. Frustrated by both the postponement of his wedding and his inability to sleep, Julian retreats at night into an insulated vault that may be viewed as a tomb-like symbol of his spiritual deadness and rejection of the world, or as a womb from which he is reborn into a new life. After waking from his century-long sleep, Julian undergoes a gradual process of recognition as he learns about the changes that have taken place in the world. While initially overwhelming and confusing, Julian's period of initiation leads to his acceptance and appreciation of his new existence. His conversion is completed by his nightmare of return to the nineteenth century.

In a 1975 review of *Looking Backward,* Tom H. Towers described the book as ''a romance of the loss and restoration of individual selfhood.'' Other scholars, however, have faulted Bellamy's depiction of Julian and the other characters in the novel, agreeing with Walter Fuller Harris that they are all ''shadowy men and women in the background standing and sitting like the dummies in shop windows.'' But some critics contend that *Looking Backward,* like other utopian novels, does not require complex characterization because what happens to the characters is more important than their personal qualities. Several scholars have noted that Julian's two personas—manifested before and after his trance—exemplify the current of duality that runs through the novel (other examples include Edith Barrett/Edith Leete, nineteenth-twentieth—century Boston, past/future, and poverty/progress). As Julian recounts his story, he remembers recognizing ''that I was two persons, that my identity was double.'' In moving from an individualistic to a collectivist outlook, Julian manages to shed his nineteenth-century self and adopt a more impersonal self that is better suited to the world he now inhabits.

Dr. Leete is Julian's host and guide through the Boston of the year 2000; he and Julian carry on a relaxed, Socratic-style dialogue that conveys Bellamy's ideas in simple, practical prose. Like the character of Virgil in Dante's classic fourteenth century poem *The Inferno,* Dr. Leete leads Julian through paradise—the paradise of the future. Presented as a model of the new, improved Boston citizen, Dr. Leete is portrayed as an eminently civilized man of reason and benevolence. It is significant that Dr. Leete is a physician, for he helps heal the psychological turmoil that Julian experiences as he adjusts to a new life. He is friendly, but there is also an air of detachment in his analytically toned discussions with Julian. Critics have noted that the Leetes's family life runs perfectly smoothly and seems to lack any kind of passionate expression; extremes of human feeling—like other, more obviously negative aspects of human nature—have been overcome in favor of a highly rational approach.

Julian's nineteenth-century fiancee, **Edith Barrett,** is only present in the first few chapters of *Looking Backward* and is not described in depth. She too is a member of a wealthy Boston family. Both ''beautiful and graceful,'' according to Julian, Edith is far too delicate a creature to bring to the increasingly seedy neighborhood in which he lives—hence his need to build an elegant new home before the two can marry. **Edith Leete** is also beautiful (the most beautiful girl Julian has ever seen, he claims) but, unlike the women of a century earlier, she exhibits a healthy vitality as well as softness and delicacy. Scholars have noted that although Edith is supposed to represent a model woman of the year 2000, she displays the traditional feminine traits valued in the nineteenth century. She is warm and nurturing; her presence comforts Julian in his moments of doubt and confusion, and she seems eager to perform that role. Women in this new society have been freed from housework and are encouraged to pursue their own careers (though never competing with men for jobs); yet Edith defers to her father when the discussion turns to such ''masculine'' subjects as economics or politics. Women are now free to propose to men they wish to marry; nevertheless, Edith waits for Julian to ask for her hand even though she admits to a long-standing love for him that began when she read his letters to his nineteenth-century fiancee. It is partly through this connection with Julian's previous life that Edith helps to ease his transition from one world to the other, and he transfers his affections fairly easily from one lovely Edith to another. The typically Victorian, sentimental portrayal of the romance helped to make *Looking Backward* especially accessible to its original audience; the novel's conventional female characters were perhaps essential to that effect.

Further Reading

Bowman, Sylvia E. *Edward Bellamy*. Boston: Twayne, 1986.

Dictionary of Literary Biography, Vol. 12. Detroit: Gale.

Hicks, Granville. "Struggle and Flight." In *The Great Tradition: An Interpretation of American Literature since the Civil War,* pp. 131-63. New York: Macmillan, 1935.

Howells, William Dean. "Edward Bellamy." In *Criticism and Fiction and Other Essays,* pp. 246-55, edited by Clara Marburg Kirk and Rudolph Kirk. New York: New York University Press, 1959.

Nineteenth Century Literature Criticism, Vol. 4. Detroit: Gale.

Patai, Daphne. *Looking Backward, 1988-1888: Essays on Edward Bellamy*. Amherst: University of Massachusetts Press, 1988.

Taylor, Walter Fuller. "Edward Bellamy." In *The Economic Novel in America,* pp. 184-213. Chapel Hill: University of North Carolina Press, 1942.

Towers, Tom H. "The Insomnia of Julian West." *American Literature* XLVII, No. 1 (March 1975): 52-63.

Robert Montgomery Bird
1806-1854
American novelist, playwright, short story writer, poet, and essayist.

The Gladiator (drama, 1831)

Plot: Set in the days of the early Roman empire, the play is based on the actual figure of Spartacus whose experiences were recounted by Plutarch, a Greek biographer of the first century A.D. Spartacus is a native of Thrace who has been captured by the Romans and forced to serve as a gladiator; he is already well known for his fighting skills. One of Rome's best gladiators, Pharsarius, has been planning a massive slave revolt while the generals and soldiers are out of the city. He decides to delay his plan, however, in order to fight the renowned Thracian. Spartacus agrees to the fight, hoping to win freedom for his enslaved wife and child. When the two gladiators meet in the ring, they realize they are brothers. They refuse to fight, and go on to instigate an uprising. When they have nearly conquered the city, Pharsarius is bent on all-out destruction while Spartacus wishes merely to return with his family to Thrace. Then Pharsarius attempts to seduce Julia, the captive daughter of a Roman official, and Spartacus saves her. Because the other gladiators are now split in loyalty between Spartacus and Pharsarius, the Romans are able to defeat them. As a result of Pharsarius's treachery, Spartacus's wife and child are killed. Though the Romans offer to spare his life out of gratitude for his saving Julia's honor, Spartacus chooses to die in the ring.

Characters: *The Gladiator* was one of the most popular American plays of the nineteenth century. American poet Walt Whitman wrote in 1846 that the play was "calculated to make the hearts of the masses swell responsively to all those nobler manlier aspirations in behalf of mortal freedom,'' yet Bird himself did not support emancipation of the slaves in his own country. Although it is sometimes called a one-character play—only Spartacus is anything more than flat and conventional—*The Gladiator* has been praised for its poetry, passion, and glorification of noble ideals.

The central character of *The Gladiator* is **Spartacus,** the strong, courageous, honorable Thracian who has won acclaim for his fighting skills and eventually leads the fight for freedom against Greek tyranny. He is an idealized figure typical of classical drama who combines physical prowess with courage, passion, and simple kindness. A rough, unpolished man of humble origin who is nevertheless noble, Spartacus represents the glorification of the common man that is an important part of the mythology of freedom and democracy. As an honorable figure who is yet a member of an oppressed race, Spartacus embodies the concept that no one race is superior to another and that slavery is evil. This was a controversial position at a time when slavery was still legal in the United States. Some scholars have described Spartacus as a notably unrealistic character in his uniform goodness and nobility and his assured response to every dilemma that confronts him. Yet this melodramatic figure—particularly as portrayed by the famous actor Edwin Forrest, whose style was ideally suited to Spartacus—was embraced by nineteenth-century audiences as a personification of American ideals.

The only other character of any note in *The Gladiator* is **Pharsarius,** Spartacus's fellow gladiator and brother as well as his collaborator in attempting to overthrow Greek domination. Pharsarius is depicted as rash and somewhat inept; he is corrupted by the success he achieves and goes too far in his bid for more power. He dies recognizing the folly of his actions.

Nick of the Woods; or, The Jibbenainosay (novel, 1837)

Plot: The story takes place on the Kentucky frontier in 1782. Two Virginians, Captain Roland Forrester and his cousin Edith, arrive at Bruce's Station with other immigrants. Both are orphans who were raised by their wealthy uncle, Major Roland Forrester. His original will favored an illegitimate daughter, but when she was reported dead he informed Roland and Edith that they would inherit his money; Roland subsequently forfeited his portion when he fought on the American side in the Revolutionary War. When Major Forrester died, his shifty lawyer Richard Braxley claimed to have in his possession a will naming the illegitimate daughter as beneficiary, and he said that she would soon appear. Roland and Edith had left for Kentucky to make a new life; they hope to marry some day. They are befriended by the commander of the station, Colonel Bruce, and his family. Telie Doe, the daughter of a man who had deserted his people to join an Indian tribe, lives with the Bruces.

News arrives that the Jibbenainosay has struck again. This is a mysterious and violent figure whose name means "Spirit-that-walks" to the Indians and is called Nick of the Woods by the English. He brutally kills Indians by smashing their skulls, then slashing crosses in their chests. Bringing the news is Roaring Ralph Stockpole, a boisterous braggart who is, to everyone's surprise, bested in a contest of strength by the gentle, peace-loving Quaker trapper, Nathan Slaughter (ironically known as Bloody Nathan). That night, Telie asks Edith to let her travel on with her and her cousin, but Edith refuses. The next morning, it is discovered that Roaring Ralph has stolen Roland's prize horse. Although the horse is returned, Roland and Edith are delayed. Left with no one to guide them, they accept Telie's offer to join their party and show them the way. While heading for the upper ford of the river, they encounter Ralph, who has been strung up on a tree and left to hang for his horse thievery, then the settler Pardon Dodge, who tells them that Indians are on the warpath up ahead. They start to look for the lower ford but become lost. Unexpectedly they come upon another of the Jibbenainosay's victims but see no one around except harmless Nathan Slaughter.

While the group is spending the night in a deserted cabin, they are attacked by hostile Shawnees whom they eventually repulse. Nathan leaves to find help while the others venture across the swollen river; Pardon Dodge is lost and presumed drowned. During another encounter with the Indians, Edith and Roland are captured but Ralph escapes. A band of frontiersmen led by Tom Bruce, son of Captain Bruce, attempts to rescue the two cousins but does not succeed, and Tom is mortally wounded. Roland learns that one of his captors is the white renegade Abel Doe. While camped, the Indians are attacked by some unknown force and Roland blacks out; when he awakes, only Nathan is with him. Nathan tells him that he overheard Doe talking to a white man about the price for capturing Roland and Edith; Roland surmises that the man is Braxley. The two head for the Indian village to rescue Edith, saving Ralph from Indian captors on the way. While sneaking around the village looking for Edith, Nathan hears Braxley telling Doe that he has a second will of Major Forrester's that leaves the entire fortune to Edith. Braxley intends to marry Edith and thus obtain her wealth. Continuing his search, Nathan finds Wenonga sprawled drunk on the ground. He is about to kill the Indian when he hears Edith's voice and goes to rescue her; he manages to surprise Braxley and overpower him, then ties him up and escapes with Edith. Meanwhile, Ralph has made an attempt to steal some horses from the Indians but inadvertently releases the whole herd into the camp, leading to the group's capture. While angrily defying Wenonga, Nathan has an epileptic seizure that the chief interprets as a sign that Nathan is a great medicine man. The next day, Doe goes to Roland and informs him that he is in possession, unbeknownst to Braxley, of the second will; he offers to help Roland escape if he will agree to marry Telie. Roland refuses, and Doe also refuses Roland's offer of half the fortune if he will rescue Edith. That night, Nathan tricks Wenonga into freeing him from his bonds, then announces that he is the Jibbenainosay. He kills the chief, who had murdered Nathan's wife and children years before and thus inspired his subsequent deeds of vengeance. Retrieving the scalps of his family members, Nathan escapes. The next day, Roland and Ralph are about to be burned alive by the Indians when a band of Kentuckians arrives and frees them. Braxley, however, manages to ride off with Edith. Nathan reappears on the scene and helps the white settlers win the battle, but in the process Tom Bruce is killed. Pardon Dodge arrives with Edith in tow; he had survived his dousing in the river and had encountered and killed Braxley. The mortally wounded Doe gives Major Forrester's second will to Roland, who promises to look after Telie. Roland and Edith return to Virginia, and Nathan is never heard from again.

Characters: *Nick of the Woods* is frequently contrasted to the frontier novels of James Fenimore Cooper. In its realistic depiction of the settling of the Kentucky wilderness and its unflattering portrayal of Native Americans, who were the area's original inhabitants, the novel employs some qualities of the romantic genre—such as the retelling of history and the use of a highly conventional hero and heroine—but is permeated with the unromantic view that nature brings out not the best in people but the worst. As such, those who live closest to nature, the Indians, are the most brutal and even take pleasure in brutality. Popular at the time of its publication for its fast-paced action and sensational scenes of war and bloodshed, *Nick of the Woods* interests modern scholars as a literary document of the American attitude toward westward expansion.

The gentle Quaker **Nathan Slaughter,** who is revealed to be the fabled **Jibbenainosay** or **Nick of the Woods,** appears to be mild and pious but harbors a ferocious capacity for violence that erupts when he encounters an Indian. Although this quality is foreshadowed when he beats Roaring Ralph in a contest of strength, none of those who know Nathan suspect the truth about him. Despite his familiarity with the nonviolent ideal of the Quaker faith, Nathan is unable to reconcile his religious training to the brutal murder of his wife and children. He himself seems hardly aware of his own actions while he is wreaking vengeance against the Indians, for which critic Vernon Louis Parrington describes him as "one of the most striking and fearful figures in our early fiction." The story's author, Bird, was a physician who was particularly interested in abnormal psychology, and the concept of the split personality is evident in his portrayal of Nathan's dual nature. Peace-loving and gentle before each murder he commits and remorseful afterward, he is only able to break the pattern of violence when he has killed Wenonga, the Indian responsible for his family's deaths. Then he becomes an ordinary frontiersman again. Nathan is often compared to Cooper's more famous character Natty Bumppo, for both are essentially solitary men who have chosen life in the wilderness over confined civilization. An important difference is that Natty relates with friendship and mutual respect to several Indians, while Nathan's dealings with Indians are uniformly antagonistic.

Another memorable character in *Nick of the Woods* is **Roaring Ralph Stackpole,** the "ring-tailed squealer" who serves as the quintessential frontiersman in his bravado and pluckiness. Although he is a notorious braggart and even a horse thief, Ralph is essentially good-hearted, loyal, and brave in defending his friends. Much praised for his vivid, comic portrait of Ralph, Bird seems to have modeled him after colorful individuals whom he met during his own travels through the western United States and whose distinctive dialect is reproduced in Ralph's speech. Scholars have identified this character as a forerunner of those later created by such writers as Mark Twain as they sketched their own visions of life on the American frontier.

Chief **Wenonga** of the marauding Shawnee tribe is also a significant character in the novel, not only for the part he plays in the plot but because he represents Bird's conception of the Native American. He is a dirty, drunken, bloodthirsty savage who finds it both easy and enjoyable to scalp and murder white men, women, and children. The implication is that such noble qualities as decency, kindness, and honor occur only in "civilized" people. Though early reviewers praised Bird for presenting Indians in a more realistic light than that offered by Cooper, modern critics have seen in Bird's portrayal of Wenonga and other Indians a justification of westward expansion underway in nineteenth-century America and of any mistreatment of Indians that that effort might entail. These scholars maintain that the downfall of such brutal people was considered inevitable and even desirable as civilization made its way into the far reaches of the continent; they note that white frontiersman also resorted to brutal, violent behavior and killed and scalped Indians.

The other characters in *Nick of the Woods* may generally be categorized as stock figures present primarily to flesh out the story. Twenty-three-year-old **Captain Roland Forrester,** a veteran of the American Revolution, is a fairly conventional hero of great courage and gentlemanliness. Nevertheless, he is not perfect: he is somewhat snobbish and tends to rely too heavily on the genteel concept of honor; a more pragmatic approach seems to be called for in this wild country. In the end he returns to the civilized world of Virginia, proof perhaps that such a refined person is ill-suited to the demands of the frontier. The beautiful **Edith Forrester** is even more conventionally portrayed—her role is primarily to be kidnapped by various villains and then rescued by valiant men. **Telie Doe** is a somewhat more interesting character who combines reticence with courage; critic Curtis Dahl describes her as "the most humanly appealing person in the novel." Although she is in a humbled, downtrodden, and dependent position, she remains steadfastly loyal to her friends and inherently noble. The latter quality is perhaps implicitly explained by the fact, revealed near the end of the story, that she is the long-lost illegitimate daughter of Major Forrester.

Richard Braxley serves as the traditional villain of melodramatic literature: greedy, heartless, and conniving. Some critics have noted the implausibility of Braxley's carrying the second will with him into the wilderness, where he can be separated from it so easily. Despite his alliance with the unsavory Indians, the traitorous **Abel Doe** is not as completely villainous as Braxley, particularly in his concern for his daughter's welfare. Other characters in the novel include **Colonel Bruce,** the roughhewn but friendly, gregarious commander of Fort Bruce, who embodies some of the more likable qualities of the frontier personality; his talkative and hospitable wife **Mrs. Bruce**; and his son **Tom Bruce,** a courageous young man who is eager to prove himself by fighting the Indians but who loses his life in the process. **Pardon Dodge** is initially a rather timid person but gains courage near the end of the story when he rescues Edith and shoots Braxley.

Further Reading

Dahl, Curtis. *Robert Montgomery Bird.* Boston: Twayne, 1963.

Lewis, R.W.B. "The Hero in Space: Brown, Cooper, Bird." In *The American Adam: Innocence, Tragedy and Tradition in the Nineteenth Century,* pp. 90-109. Chicago: University of Chicago Press, 1955.

Nineteenth Century Literature Criticism, Vol. 1. Detroit: Gale.

Parrington, Vernon Louis. "The Old Capital." In *Main Currents in American Thought: An Interpretation of American Literature from the Beginnings to 1920,* Vol. 2, *The Romantic Revolution in America, 1800-1860,* pp. 85-92. New York: Harcourt, 1930, 1958.

Whitman, Walt. "'The Gladiator'—Mr. Forrest—Acting." 1846. Reprinted in *The American Theatre: As Seen by Its Critics, 1752-1934,* edited by Montrose J. Moses and John Mason Brown, pp. 69-70. New York: Norton, 1934.

Anne Brontë
1820-1849
English novelist, poet, and hymn-writer.

Agnes Grey: An Autobiography (novel, 1847)

Plot: The title character of the novel, which is set in the nineteenth century in the north of England, is the daughter of a poor parson whose wife defied her family and gave up her inheritance to marry him. When Mr. Grey loses his own patrimony through a disastrous speculation, the family is left penniless. Though Agnes and her sister Mary have led sheltered, studious lives, both feel obligated to help augment the family income: Mary offers to try to sell her paintings and Agnes decides to become a governess. Her first assignment is with the Bloomfield family at Wellwood Hall. She quickly learns that the children are incorrigible and the parents unpleasant. Mrs. Bloomfield is cold to Agnes and supremely indulgent of her children, while her husband is an overly strict disciplinarian who blames Agnes when the children misbehave. Agnes finds it impossible to control—much less teach—her charges, and her objection to a particularly cruel prank by Tom (encouraged by his equally unsavory Uncle Robson) results in her dismissal.

After a few months with her family, Agnes is hired as governess to the Murrays, who live at Horton Lodge. Though richer and more sophisticated than the Bloomfields and somewhat more respectful to Agnes, they are not much more admirable than her previous employers. Agnes's attempts to instruct sixteen-year-old Rosalie, a pretty flirt who is obsessed with making an advantageous marriage, and fourteen-year-old Matilda, who is interested only in horses, meet with general politeness but no real receptivity. After a year, Agnes returns home to attend her sister's wedding. On her return to Horton Lodge, Agnes finds Rosalie flirting shamelessly with every man around and coldly calculating her marital possibilities. A new curate, Edward Weston, arrives in the neighborhood and proves vastly superior in manner, sincerity, and piety to the pompous rector, Mr. Hatfield. Agnes and Weston grow attracted to each other, often meeting when both pay charitable visits to an impoverished old widow, Nancy Brown. After rejecting a proposal from Mr. Hatfield and unsuccessfully attempting to attract Mr. Weston, Rosalie marries the richest man in the neighborhood, Sir Thomas Ashby.

When her father suddenly dies, Agnes is called home. She and her mother decide to start a school for girls in another town, and Agnes does not see Mr. Weston again for a long time. Although the school is successful, Agnes's spirits are low. Rosalie invites her to visit Ashby Park, where she learns that her former charge's marriage to the cantankerous and boorish Sir Thomas is unhappy. After returning home, Agnes happens upon Mr. Weston, who has recently taken a clerical post in a nearby town. He begins to call frequently on Agnes, and he eventually proposes. The two are married and live a modest but happy and pious life together.

Characters: Long overshadowed by her more talented and famous sisters, Charlotte and Emily, Anne Brontë nevertheless continues to attract the attention and admiration of both readers and scholars. *Agnes Grey*—the first novel written by any of the Brontës and perhaps the inspiration for her sisters' literary careers—is a simply written yet sharply observed account of the experiences of a nineteenth-century English governess. It provides an interesting portrait not only of what that particular life was like, but of general social behavior and mores of the period. Though few critics would agree with George Moore that *Agnes Grey* is "the most perfect prose narrative in English literature," many praise the novel's unadorned narrative style, subtle moral tone, and quiet humor.

Agnes Grey is an honest, upright, religious young woman of plain appearance and unassuming manner through whom Brontë sets the novel's moral tone. Though Agnes is innocently optimistic as she enters into her first assignment, she is by the end of the novel a sadder and wiser woman, educated in the wicked ways of the real world. A perceptive observer of other people's misbehavior, she is finally rewarded (if modestly) for her virtue with marriage to the equally fine and principled Edward Weston. Although some have seen her as priggish or self-righteous, Agnes is generally perceived as a humble sort of heroine who wins the reader's respect and attention without alienating him or her by her excessive goodness. Brontë describes Agnes's day-to-day experiences as a governess—often humiliating and almost always isolating—in meticulous detail. While some claim that in its portrayal of a tedious profession the book becomes tedious itself, others laud the realism that was no doubt enhanced by Brontë's own experiences as a governess.

Brontë's portrayal of the Grey family, though not extensive, is significant because it provides the background and basis of Agnes's character. Her parents married for love despite the censure of Mrs. Grey's family and created a warm, emotionally secure nest for their children. Thus they provide a sharp contrast to the morally bankrupt though financially well-off families Agnes encounters in the outside world. **Mrs. Grey** in particular is portrayed as an ideal mother in her stability, wisdom, and affectionate nature—an especially interesting depiction in view of the fact that Brontë never knew her own mother, who died when she was very young, and was raised by a rather stiff though kindly aunt. Despite making an unwise business decision, **Mr. Grey** is a sympathetic character, for he makes the speculation in order to materially benefit his family and is utterly devastated by the ruinous outcome. His status as a poor but sincere clergyman lays the groundwork for Agnes's later admiration for Edward Weston and also calls attention to Brontë's consistent portrayal of the poor and working class as virtuous and the bourgeoisie and aristocracy as shallow and immoral. Agnes's artistic sister **Mary Grey** is as selfless as she, for she offers to earn money for the family by selling her paintings; like Agnes, she marries an honest clergyman.

The few chapters devoted to Agnes's first employers, the Bloomfields, were described by critic W. A. Craik as "hair-raising." Other scholars too have remarked on Brontë's vivid portrayal of the outrageously ill-behaved Bloomfield children and their unlikable parents. **Tom Bloomfield** is a vicious seven-year-old who delights in tearing the legs and wings off baby birds; six-year-old **Mary Ann Bloomfield** is ignorant, affected, and bad-tempered; four-year-old **Fanny Bloomfield** is a liar who spits at people who cross her. Even the toddler **Harriet Bloomfield** is unpleasantly fat. As Agnes is the product of a caring upbringing by intelligent parents, the Bloomfield children reflect the faults of their mother and father. **Mrs. Bloomfield** indulges both herself and her obnoxious offspring; she considers Tom's cruelty toward animals a perfectly acceptable pastime for a young boy. **Mr. Bloomfield** is a stern boor who bullies his wife and takes no personal responsibility for his children's behavior, preferring to blame Agnes for their wickedness. The peripheral members of the Bloomfield family are just as unsavory: **the grandmother** pretends to sympathize with Agnes but derides her behind her back, and **Uncle Robson** encourages his nephew not only to torture small creatures but to drink alcohol. This relatively brief but memorable glimpse at the Bloomfields sets the stage for a more detailed look at the Murrays.

The residents of Horton Lodge include Mr. and Mrs. Murray and their four children. **Mr. Murray** is a tall, heavy man with red cheeks and nose; a stereotype of the sporting gentleman farmer, he is prone to boisterous swearing. He is an unconcerned parent who encourages his daughter Matilda in her interest in hunting and her habit of cursing. **Mrs. Murray,** occupied primarily with socializing and her appearance, also indulges her children's whims. Her primary goal is to see her daughters advantageously married. Though not overtly hostile to Agnes, there is no question that she considers the governess her inferior. When Agnes's father dies, for instance, Mrs. Murray advises her not to pine but to feel grateful for the patronage of her social betters. The two younger Murray children— mischievous, lying **Charles** and tough, boisterous **John**—are portrayed as impervious to Agnes's influence. Gawky, horse-loving, foul-mouthed **Matilda Murray** mainly provides an unsophisticated contrast to her older sister.

Pretty, coquettish **Rosalie Murray,** whom Brontë uses brilliantly to illustrate the inevitable result of a careless upbringing and subsequent irresponsible behavior, is a shallow, vain, heartless flirt whose inadequate education has imbued her with only the ability to act charming. She has no real sense of right and wrong and is, as Brontë notes, "swallowed up in the all-absorbing ambition to attract and dazzle the other sex." Yet Agnes likes Rosalie in some ways, for she is basically intelligent and does feel affectionate toward her governess. Agnes, in turn, attempts to teach the young girl a more moral approach to her life but ultimately fails. It is the sense of wasted potential that makes Rosalie's character tragic and which lends the book some of its bleak tone. Further, Brontë provides an unsentimental, realistic portrayal of Rosalie's disastrous marriage to a wealthy but thoroughly unpleasant man. Even the baby which arrives in due time is no comfort to the disappointed Rosalie, who considers it an encumbrance and an eventual rival for attention.

Craik described **Edward Weston** as "possibly the shadowiest hero ever invented by a woman novelist"; indeed, Brontë's portrayal of him is vague. He is a scion of virtue and piety whose goodness and sincerity strongly contrast the artificial values of most of the characters in the novel except Agnes and her family. Weston is far from being a romantic hero; not handsome but sensible and principled, he provides Agnes with a welcome haven from the distasteful people who surround her. Weston's kindness and moral rectitude are further demonstrated by his considerate visits to Nancy Brown.

Weston's superior in position—though not character—is the neighborhood's vicar, **Mr. Hatfield.** He is an insincere churchman who betrays his vanity more than his spirituality in his performances at the pulpit. Interested only in his rich parishioners, Hatfield sees no reason to be kind to Nancy Brown. There is some justice in Rosalie's rejection of his marriage proposal after she shamelessly leads him on. His outraged reaction to her audacity in refusing him further illustrates his self-importance and insensitivity.

Nancy Brown plays a minor but significant role in the novel by providing a reason for Agnes and Weston to become acquainted. Because she has wavered in her faith and has been confined by rheumatism to her cottage, she has been visited by both of the neighborhood clergymen, though she much prefers Weston. She relates anecdotes to Agnes which illustrate the quality of Weston's nature; her lengthy comparison between him and Hatfield strongly points to the virtue of the former and the shallowness of the latter.

The Tenant of Wildfell Hall (novel, 1848)

Plot: The novel is presented as a series of letters from country gentleman Gilbert Markham to his brother-in-law, Mr. Halford. The story Markham relates turns on the arrival in the neighborhood twenty years earlier of Mrs. Helen Graham, who became a tenant at Wildfell Hall. A young and beautiful woman, she aroused speculation because of her desire for seclusion and her extreme protectiveness toward her young son, Arthur. It was also rumored that she was having an affair with her landlord, Frederick Lawrence. On first meeting Mrs. Graham, Markham learned that she was a talented landscape painter. During their long walks together, he fell in love with her, but she insisted that their relationship remain platonic. Markham began to suspect that the rumors about the young woman were true, and during an encounter with Lawrence he struck and severely injured the other man. Then Mrs. Graham invited Markham to read her journal, begun six years earlier. As a young girl she had fallen in love with the dashing Arthur Huntingdon and had married him despite her family's disapproval. It soon became apparent that Huntingdon was an unprincipled, irresponsible alcoholic who was ill-suited for domestic life. He spent long periods away from home, and enmity grew between him and his wife. When a baby was born several years later, Helen hoped Huntingdon would settle down, but his behavior only worsened. After discovering that he was having an affair with Lady Annabella Lowborough, the wife of one of his friends, Helen made plans to escape to a hiding place where she and her son would be safe. Huntingdon, however, learned of her scheme when he read her journal and tightened his control over her. When he brought another mistress into their home—ostensibly to serve as a governess for little Arthur—Helen decided to leave, though she had no money. This time she was successful. The journal ends at her arrival at Wildfell Hall.

After reading her journal Markham hastened to propose to Helen again, but she still refused his offer. Having realized that Frederick Lawrence was not Helen's lover but her brother, Markham apologized for attacking him and the two are reconciled. When Huntingdon is injured in a fall, Helen felt obligated to return to his estate, Grassdale, to nurse him. But after drinking a bottle of wine against the advice of his doctor, Huntingdon died, and Helen went to live with her aunt. After a year had passed, Markham visited her there and again proposed to her. The two were soon married.

Characters: *The Tenant of Wildfell Hall* is generally considered a more accomplished novel than *Agnes Grey* because it features a more complex structure and a greater number of characters, settings, and events and because it demonstrates Brontë's growing command of dramatic effect and invention. Though it has a didactic intent—to illustrate the tragic consequences of a dissolute lifestyle, of which Brontë had firsthand knowledge through her brother Branwell—*The Tenant of Wildfell Hall* avoids preachiness. Some early reviewers considered Brontë's realistic portrayal of the scenes of drunkenness and gambling too coarse, but she insisted that she meant not to titillate but to tell the truth. While a few critics have found the novel's tale-within-a-tale format unwieldy, others laud Brontë for her skill in handling separate narrative perspectives. In its intimations of physical violence and its portrayal of turbulent relationships between men and women, *The Tenant of Wildfell Hall* suggests the influence of Brontë's sister Emily, whose *Wuthering Heights* had been published the previous year.

The novel's heroine is **Helen Graham/Huntingdon,** whose initial aura of mystery and apparent coldness dissolve when, through the journal that she shares with Markham, she tells her story. As a girl, Helen had spurned the advances of the suitably named **Mr. Boarham** and the lecherous **Mr. Wilmot** in favor of dashing Arthur Huntingdon. Though she knew something of his rakish background and had been warned against marrying him by her aunt, Helen was confident that the love and domestic comfort she would offer him would influence him to change. In her journey from innocence to experience, Helen realizes the depth of her mistake in marrying Huntingdon, as well as the extent of her husband's corruption. Many readers and scholars have found Helen an admirable character not only because of her resolution and courage but because she is elegant, intelligent, self-assured, and lacking in self-pity. The story of Helen's confinement in a disastrous marriage to a tyrannical husband invites feminist interpretation, for it demonstrates the subjugation of the nineteenth-century woman; when she finally leaves Huntingdon, Helen is not legally entitled to retain any wealth that was hers before her marriage. Her final escape is motivated by her concern for her son, whose corruption by his carousing father she fears. The happiness Helen eventually finds in her second marriage is tempered by a lingering sense of failure because she was unable to improve Huntingdon—thus the novel retains a bleak tone despite its happy ending. Though her account is framed at beginning and end by the voice and perspective of Gilbert Markham, it is Helen who provides the novel's guiding standard of moral behavior.

Brontë's vivid portrayal of the profligate **Arthur Huntingdon** is usually attributed to her intimate knowledge of such men, for her brother Branwell's life and talents were destroyed by his addiction to alcohol and laudanum (a sedative made from opium) and he brought much suffering to his family. It is through Huntingdon's deeds and the effect they have on his loved ones that Brontë makes her plea for morality and sobriety. Although he truly loves his wife at the beginning of their marriage, the self-indulgent Huntingdon finds domestic life boring and spends longer and longer periods in London, where he presumably partakes of alcohol, gambling, and affairs with other women. He also brings his vices into his own home, subjecting Helen and little Arthur to scenes of gross depravity. Particularly reprehensible are his liaisons with Annabella Lowborough and with the young woman he introduces as a governess for his son. Huntingdon's blatant sexual misbehavior is accompanied by a contradictory insistence that his wife remain faithful (even though, during a drunken bout, he offers Helen to any man who wants her), and Brontë condemns this double standard. Huntingdon's physical attractiveness (at least before his final illness) and charisma are well-evidenced, and the fact that he is actually a leader of his fellow carousers and a corrupter of his friends attests to his charisma. While many critics would agree with W. A. Craik that Huntingdon is "a frighteningly convincing and original creation," some have pointed out that Brontë's utterly unsympathetic portrayal detracts from his believability. While Helen is all-suffering and all-forgiving, Huntingdon is bitter and petulant to the end, even complaining on his deathbed that Helen has come to his side only "to gain a higher seat in heaven for yourself, and scoop a deeper pit for me."

The sensible but passionate **Gilbert Markham** is revealed through his own account of his acquaintance with Helen Huntingdon and what he learns about her life. He is the son of a fairly well-to-do, though not wealthy, farmer; he hints that he has had to regretfully stifle artistic aspirations in order to take up his father's profession. Markham is well regarded in the neighborhood and is the object of at least one young lady's designs before he meets Helen. Some scholars have seen Markham as a somewhat incidental character whose purpose is as a narrator: his honesty and uprightness make him unquestionably reliable. Further, the sequence of events in which he nearly kills Frederick Lawrence with his whip and then easily makes peace with the other man has been viewed as unrealistic. Nonetheless, Markham's role seems intentionally secondary to Helen's: his being a less compelling character allows the reader to focus on what happens to her.

Markham's family and neighbors help to create the more modest, countrified social milieu into which Helen—who has an aristocratic background—moves and eventually marries. **Mrs. Markham** is a doting mother and a friendly woman who is popular with her neighbors; she initially mistrusts Helen but is eventually won over by the young woman's virtue and her son's persuasion. **Fergus Markham** is a somewhat sulky, lazy young man who is constantly making jokes; he will eventually be improved by a wise marriage. **Rose Markham** is a pretty young woman with a good heart—she does not believe the malicious gossip about the new tenant at Wildfell Hall; her marriage to Mr. Halford will eventually provide the context for Markham's letter-writing. The Millward family is also prominent in the neighborhood: **Reverend Michael Millward** is a self-righteous, elderly vicar who immediately believes the rumors about Helen and lectures her on her behavior. By contrast, his quiet daughter **Mary Millward** is a generous and helpful person who is unappreciated by almost everybody. **Eliza Millward** is the pretty, charming, playful young woman who captured Markham's attention before he met Helen; she spreads rumors about her rival out of jealousy. The Wilson family is comprised of the gossiping **Mrs. Wilson,** the rough-edged farmer **Robert Wilson,** reserved and studious **Richard Wilson** (who will eventually marry Mary Millward), and the elegant, educated, and haughty **Jane Wilson** (whose designs on Frederick Lawrence will be shattered when he marries another woman).

The people who share the Huntingdons' life at Grasslands serve as foils to the relationship between Helen and her first husband. **Ralph Hattersley** and **Lord Lowborough** carouse with Huntingdon, though neither is as truly corrupt as he. Hattersley is married to a virtuous, submissive woman, **Milicent Hargrave Hattersley,** who loves him but whom he treats cruelly. Chastened by what happens to Huntingdon, he will become a good husband and father. Lowborough's similar reformation is brought on by his shock and dismay over his wife's affair with Huntingdon; he will divorce her and marry an upstanding, good-hearted woman. **Annabella Wilmot Lowborough** is a thoroughly corrupt person who not only never regrets her faithlessness to her own husband but torments Helen with her obvious pleasure in being Huntingdon's mistress. She was Helen's rival for Arthur's affection before their marriage, and she herself married not for love but for the prestige it brought her. She will elope with a third man, the reader is told, and will meet an impoverished and ignominious end. **Mrs. Hargrave,** the mother of Milicent, Esther, and Walter, is a domineering and materialistic woman who pressures her children to make advantageous marriages. **Esther Hargrave,** however, defiantly resists her mother's influence and marries the man she loves (Frederick Lawrence). **Walter Hargrave** is a friend of Huntingdon but is a little more temperate in his habits; he continually tries to gain Helen's affections when he sees how cruelly and neglectfully her husband treats her. He offers her not illicit love but marriage if she will divorce Arthur. **Frederick Lawrence,** Helen's brother, is a somewhat sketchily depicted character. He is reserved, self-contained, and generally virtuous and serves as a link between Markham's world and Helen's; he also keeps Markham informed of Helen's activities after she returns to Grasslands to nurse Huntingdon.

Other characters in *The Tenant of Wildfell Hall* include young **Arthur Huntingdon, Jr.,** an energetic and affectionate little boy who likes Markham enough to serve as an important bridge between him and Helen. Before Helen took him away from Grasslands, little Arthur had begun to exhibit his father's influence by taking sips of alcohol and cursing. **Rachel** is the faithful servant who helps Helen in her escape from Huntingdon and who maintains a protective attitude toward her mistress after their arrival at Wildfell Hall. **Mrs. Peggy Maxwell** is the aunt who raised Helen, who warned her about Huntingdon before their marriage, and with whom Helen lives after his death. **Alice Myers** is Huntingdon's unpleasant mistress, whom he brings to Grasslands to serve as his son's governess.

Further Reading

"Acton Bell's 'Tenant of Wildfell Hall.'" *The Spectator* No. 1045 (8 July 1848): 662-63.

Craik, W. A. "''Agnes Grey''" and "''The Tenant of Wildfell Hall.''" In *The Brontë Novels,* pp. 202-27, 228-53. London: Methuen, 1968.

Dictionary of Literary Biography, Vol. 21. Detroit: Gale.

Evans, Barbara, and Gareth Lloyd Evans. *The Scribner Companion to the Brontës.* New York: Scribner's, 1982.

Eagleton, Terry. "Anne Brontë." In *Myths of Power: A Marxist Study of the Brontës,* pp. 123-28. London: Macmillan, 1975.

Liddell, Robert. *Twin Spirits: The Novels of Emily and Anne Brontë.* London: Owen, 1990.

Moore, George. "Conversation with Edmond Gosse." In *Conversations in Ebury Street,* pp. 211-23. 1924. Reprint. Chatto & Windus, 1969.

Nineteenth Century Literature Criticism, Vol. 4. Detroit: Gale.

Pinion, F. B. *A Brontë Companion: Literary Assessment, Background, and Reference.* New York: Barnes & Noble, 1975.

Charlotte Brontë
1816-1855
English novelist and poet.

Jane Eyre: An Autobiography (novel, 1847)

Plot: The novel takes place in northern England around the year 1800. The title character is a penniless orphan girl who at the beginning of the story is under the care of her widowed aunt, Mrs. Reed. Mistreated and neglected in favor of the three spoiled Reed children, Jane is eventually sent to a charitable institution called Lowood School. Despite the poor living conditions at the school, Jane finds friends there and is a good student. She continues at Lowood as a teacher until accepting a governess position at Thornfield, a country estate. Her sole charge is Adele Varens, the illegitimate child of the absent Mr. Edward Rochester. While walking in the surrounding countryside one day, Jane meets the master of Thornfield accidentally when he is thrown from his horse. She likes Mr. Rochester despite his somber looks and brusque manner, and he approves of her as well. A series of mysterious circumstances—including the sound of maniacal feminine laughter, the setting afire of Mr. Rochester's bed, and the arrival late one night of a stranger who is subsequently wounded—lead Jane to the knowledge that a disturbed woman is living on the mansion's locked third floor. Meanwhile, the mutual regard between Jane and Mr. Rochester blossoms into love, and they become engaged. The night before their wedding, the mad inhabitant of the third floor appears in Jane's room. Mr. Rochester tells Jane that the woman is the household's unsavory seamstress, Grace Poole. Moments before Jane and Mr. Rochester are to be married, it is revealed that Thornfield's madwoman is Bertha Mason, whom Mr. Rochester had married in the West Indies fifteen years earlier.

Leaving Mr. Rochester and Thornfield, Jane finds herself destitute and friendless. She is taken in by the Reverend St. John Rivers and his sisters, calls herself Jane Elliott, and becomes a teacher. Rivers proposes to Jane, offering her not love but admiration and a place by his side in a missionary post; the prospect of a loveless marriage does not appeal to Jane. She subsequently dreams that Mr. Rochester is calling her name and returns to Thornfield to find the mansion burned to the ground and Bertha Mason dead. Mr. Rochester, who lost his sight and one of his hands in the fire that destroyed Thornfield, is living alone on a farm. Jane joins him there, the two are reunited in love, and they are married. Mr. Rochester's sight gradually returns, so he is able to see the child born to Jane several years later.

Characters: Acknowledged as a masterpiece of English literature, *Jane Eyre* explores a consistent Brontë theme—the conflict between passion and reason—through the unique relationship of its two memorable protagonists. The novel, though sometimes faulted for its melodramatic moments, is praised as penetratingly insightful and its heroine is considered a major achievement in characterization.

Through the character of **Jane Eyre,** Brontë employs a distinctive and effective first-person narration that brings emotional power and directness to the story. Jane is an intelligent and independent woman whose plain exterior belies the passion and intensity of her personality. She bears little resemblance to the traditional Victorian ideal of womanhood, which decreed that a woman must be endowed with beauty rather than intelligence and be submissive rather than self-sufficient. Like other Brontë heroines, Jane has no close family connections to support her either financially or emotionally; she survives—even thrives—on her own. Some early reviewers were offended by what they viewed as Jane's coarseness and vulgarity. For instance, though she chooses not to become Rochester's mistress, she can imagine the pleasures she might experience in that role. Nevertheless, eminent English novelist William Makepeace Thackeray called her "nobly planned," and nearly all subsequent critics have agreed. In taking the course that she does—leaving Mr. Rochester despite her love for him because she will not accept the illicit arrangement that his legal ties with Bertha Mason necessitates—Jane displays a remarkable degree of moral fortitude. Similarly, Jane resists the arrangement—albeit quite legal—proposed by St. John Rivers because she cannot value a loveless relationship. In recent years, the character of Jane Eyre has inspired feminist interpretation: not only her independent nature but her insistence on equality in her relationship with Rochester are seen as highly unconventional for a nineteenth-century female.

Edward Rochester, like Jane Eyre, is a highly unconventional figure. He has often been described as embodying the romantic qualities of individuality and passionate expression, and in his emotional and essentially isolated nature often resembles the Byronic (referring to the renowned poet, George Gordon, Lord Byron) heroes of late-eighteenth- and early-nineteenth-century romantic literature. The origin of Rochester's character has also been tied to a tempestuous figure, the Duke of Zamorna, who plays an important role in the juvenile literature created by Brontë and her siblings. A rough-edged, moody, sometimes violent man who says what he feels, Rochester welcomes Jane's strong-mindedness and delights in her singularity; proposing marriage to her he says, "My bride is here, because my equal, and my likeness." Critics have applied differing interpretations to the accident which maims Rochester. Some see it as a symbolic castration that puts Jane decidedly in control of the relationship; others view it as an experience necessary in the humbling of an egotistical man; still others see it as a method of exorcising the sins of the past (for in addition to attempting to commit bigamy, Rochester has fathered a child by a former mistress). In any case, Rochester's injuries have an equalizing effect on his relationship with Jane and allow him to recognize the depth of her love for him when she is willing to accept him in his diminished state.

Critics initially overlooked the character of **Bertha Mason,** the unfortunate wife of Rochester who, due to her insanity, is confined to Thornfield's third floor. Though Jane, when she finally sees Bertha, describes her as "tall, dark, and majestic," she is generally characterized as terrifying and destructive. Critic Eric Solomon acknowledges Bertha's demonic aspect when noting that she "represents the flames of hellfire that have already scorched Rochester," and, indeed, she will be destroyed by fire and will almost cause Rochester's destruction as well. Recent interpretations of this somewhat Gothic, melodramatic character have focused on her animalistic nature. She has been said to embody the consequences of unbridled sexuality, a danger that Jane must try to avoid. She also has been seen as Jane's darker double, reflecting the anger and terror that Jane has experienced in her own life (such as when Aunt Reed punished her by locking her in a room by herself). In her critically acclaimed novel *The Wide Sargasso Sea,* Jean Rhys creates a compelling vision of Bertha's early life in the West Indies and suggests that she was driven insane by her sexually repressed English husband.

The characters in Jane's early life are seen through the eyes of a small, lonely, often frightened girl and thus seem to simply embody either goodness or wickedness. **Aunt Reed** is an outright terror, a relentlessly mean and tyrannical woman who provides none of the maternal nurturing her orphaned niece might crave. Her children are equally distasteful: **John Reed,** purely physical and male, delights in tormenting his sisters and cousin and will eventually commit suicide; **Eliza** is insensitive and **Georgiana** outrageously vain. The Reed family allows Jane to demonstrate her power to overcome the obstacles of an unhappy childhood and also contrasts with the more pleasant Rivers family that will play a part in her later life.

Another villainous figure of authority is **Mr. Brocklehurst,** the strict, rigid clergyman who runs Lowood School and self-righteously deprives its inmates of a healthful atmosphere. He is a comically grotesque and hypocritical figure who insists, for instance, that the students be dressed in the most severe clothing while his wife and daughters are adorned in silk and velvet. At the other end of the spectrum is the saintly **Miss Maria Temple,** a kindhearted and dedicated teacher who sincerely wants to improve her students' lives. It is she who helps Jane attain a position as a teacher at Lowood after her graduation. Jane's friend **Helen Burns** is a highly intelligent girl who is harassed by her teachers because she is often slovenly and tardy. She is submissive in the face of abuse and eventually succumbs to the school's harsh conditions. Helen may have been patterned after Brontë's own beloved sister Maria, who also perished while living at a boarding school.

Among the people Jane meets while living at Thornfield are the calm, pleasant housekeeper, **Mrs. Fairfax,** and **Adele Varens**—Jane's reason for being there. Adele also provides an opportunity for Rochester's basic honorableness to be shown, as he treats his illegitimate child very decently in keeping and educating her in his own home. Rochester's elevated social strata is best represented by **Lady Ingram,** a self-satisfied, arrogant woman whose daughter Blanche is rumored to be engaged to Rochester. **Blanche Ingram** is as pretentious and sentimental as Jane is frank and down-to-earth. Rochester uses her to make Jane jealous, and his ploy is successful: fearing that the two may indeed be engaged, Jane realizes how much she herself feels for Rochester. **Grace Poole** is the unattractive, tippling seamstress who is actually employed to take care of Bertha Mason. Also encountered at Thornfield is **Mr. Mason,** Bertha's brother, who is injured while visiting her and later performs the practical function of halting the marriage between Jane and Rochester and revealing the latter's secret.

St. John Rivers is portrayed as a handsome, disciplined, upright clergyman who is also egotistical and ambitious. He is not at all the kind of person to be attracted to Jane or to appreciate her real worth and thus constitutes a perfect foil to Rochester. He offers Jane a platonic marriage. The kind but vacuous and beautiful **Rosamunde Oliver,** in whose school Jane works as a teacher, is a much more appropriate mate for St. John. **Diana and Mary Rivers**—though depicted with little to distinguish between them—are good friends to Jane and provide an ideal of energetic, learned, and admirable but unconventional womanhood to which she can aspire.

Shirley (novel, 1849)

Plot: Set in the northern Yorkshire region of England, the novel opens in the early 1800s, soon after a cotton mill owner named Robert Moore has begun introducing machinery into his operation—a development which, implemented on a broad scale throughout the region, has led to reduced wages and unemployment. One night, angry workers destroy more equipment while it is being transported to the mill. The next day, young Caroline Helstone arrives at the Moore home for her French lesson with Robert's sister Hortense (the Moores are half English and half Belgian); Robert is too preoccupied to notice Caroline's obvious regard for him. Caroline is later dismayed when, due to a disagreement between her guardian-uncle, Matthewson Helstone, and Robert, she is forbidden from visiting the Moores. But a new arrival in the neighborhood soon brightens her outlook: the wealthy, beautiful, and charming Shirley Keeldar comes to take possession of her long-empty mansion, Fieldhead. Shirley is outgoing, spirited, and soon popular with everyone and she forms a special friendship with the much shyer Caroline. Robert also enjoys Shirley's company and the two engage in political discussions; a disheartened Caroline grows even quieter when she notices their attraction to each other. Caroline decides to forget her apparently futile love for Robert by engrossing herself in charitable work, determining that she will become an old maid like Miss Ainsley, who selflessly works for the benefit of others.

Robert continues to install new machinery in his mill while the widespread labor unrest continues. Shirley donates money to assist unemployed workers. One night, a gang of rioting workers bursts through the mill gates. Robert and his friends—including Helstone and fellow mill owner Mr. Yorke—are prepared for the attack and exchange gunfire with the rioters. They turn the men away, and Robert subsequently leaves the neighborhood to search for the leaders of the gang. Caroline becomes so depressed that she is unable to eat and takes to her bed. She is lovingly nursed back to health by Mrs. Pryor, Shirley's former governess and current companion, who reveals that she is actually Caroline's mother, the former Agnes Helstone. She had sent Caroline to live with her uncle in order to protect her from the influence of her errant father. Meanwhile, Shirley's aunt and uncle, the Sympsons, arrive for a visit and seem determined to arrange a suitable marriage for their niece. They promote several suitors, including Sir Philip Nunnely, whose proposal Shirley rejects. Robert Moore also asks Shirley to marry him, but she refuses because she knows that he does not really love her. However, Louis Moore, the Sympsons's son's tutor (who is also Robert's brother), wins Shirley's hand despite his lower station in society—a circumstance that infuriates the Sympsons.

While pursuing the leaders of the rioters who attacked his mill, Robert is shot and badly hurt. Caroline visits him frequently while he is in seclusion convalescing, and he is gradually awakened to his love for her. The two are engaged and plan a double wedding with Shirley and Louis.

Characters: *Shirley* is considered Brontë's least successful novel. It was written during a period of intense loss, during and after the illnesses and deaths of three of her siblings, and some critics have suggested that the author was distracted by her grief. For the first and only time, Brontë made use of an omniscient narrator and as a result this novel lacks the singular power and unified tone of her successful first-person narratives in *Jane Eyre* and *Villette*. Brontë wove into this dual love story an account of the 1811-1812 riots in Yorkshire, which were prompted by a trade embargo between England and France and by increased mechanization of industry and the consequent loss of jobs.

One of the most frequently voiced complaints about *Shirley* is that its title character does not make an appearance until the novel is well underway, thus lessening her impact as an object of interest to the reader. The wealthy, intelligent, beautiful **Shirley Keeldar** is an unconventional Victorian woman, for she is highly independent and wary of marriage because she does not want to become a submissive wife. In fact, early reviewers disapproved of Shirley's aggressiveness and lack of feminine grace, finding her too opinionated and plainspoken, even to the point of occasional rudeness. Yet she proves that she has a warm heart and a social conscience when she takes practical steps to relieve the suffering of the unemployed workers in her community. Her wealth allows her to challenge the limits her society places on women, but she finds that her money also makes her a valuable prize over which men will compete when she would rather be approached on an equal footing. It has often been reported that Brontë instilled in Shirley's character her sister Emily's love of nature and deeply perceptive but stoical approach to life. Yet Brontë also appears to use Shirley as a mouthpiece to express her own views on such subjects as religion and class conflicts. Many readers and critics are disappointed with Shirley's eventual marriage to the uninteresting Louis Moore.

Caroline Helstone is a somewhat more lifelike character than Shirley. She is pretty, sweet, and intelligent but very reserved. Thus while Robert and Shirley are carrying on a lively political discourse she fades into the background; while they are grow fonder of each other she turns away. She takes a stoical approach to what she perceives as her fate—a loveless future. The character of Caroline illustrates the limited opportunities available to the nineteenth-century woman: if she did not marry, she must—that is, if she had means of support—content herself with the life of a spinster. If she had to support herself, she could take the isolating and often degrading course of becoming a governess. With only these choices open to her, Caroline decides to become a useful (if lonely) unmarried woman like Miss Ainsley. However, the sensitive Caroline—possibly modeled after Brontë's sweet, mild sister Anne or her friend Ellen Nussey—is unable to suppress her emotions and, overcome by despair, grows seriously ill. Many critics have noted that the conflict between passion and reason is a persistent theme in Brontë's work; Caroline in this novel represents feeling, Shirley reason.

Robert Moore is portrayed as an ambitious, practical businessman whose loving, thought-ful side is only fleetingly seen—at least initially—in his interactions with his sister and with Caroline. It is partly through him that Brontë plays out the book's sociological theme, for Robert represents the viewpoint of management in the labor dispute that occurs in the community. Robert differs from Mr. Helstone and Mr. Yorke in opposing the trade embargo that had been necessitated by the Napoleonic War, but his reasons are more selfish than political: he resents the embargo's damaging effect on his business. Selfish motives are also behind his proposing to Shirley: he desires not her but the money she could provide to safeguard his business. Through the course of the book, Robert becomes aware of the suffering that has been caused by his callous and self-interested actions; he sees that the industrialization of his business has human consequences and he determines to cease ignoring them. Despite his faults, Robert is shown to be ultimately open-minded, intelligent, and compassionate, and his eventual realization that he loves Caroline is also in his favor.

Brontë has been widely faulted for her depiction of **Louis Moore,** the man who eventually wins Shirley's heart. Introduced very late in the novel, Louis is not portrayed in much detail. He is quiet, intelligent, and indistinct. Forced by the depletion of his family fortune to become a tutor, he exhibits a self-sufficiency that allows him to survive under adverse circumstances. Thus he finally reveals his love for Shirley despite the difference in their social positions and his own lack of wealth. His ability to captivate the vivacious Shirley Keeldar has been called unconvincing.

Mr. Matthewson Helstone, Caroline's guardian and the rector of Briarfield parish, is portrayed as an unsympathetic man who would be better suited to the military profession than the clerical, for he seems to relish his role in helping Robert oppose the rioting workers. A dynamic and self-centered man, he is incapable of understanding his passive, sensitive niece. In his youth he had married the object of Mr. Yorke's ardor, **Mary Cave,** but he had not particularly cherished his wife. Indeed, he had reportedly neglected her, just as he neglects (at least emotionally) Caroline. His view that marriage is to be avoided reflects his low opinion of women and his own incapacity to connect deeply with other people.

The resurfacing of Caroline's long-lost mother, **Mrs. Pryor** (originally **Agnes Helstone**), has been considered a rather awkward coincidence, but it does allow Brontë to include a bitter description of a governess's life. Like her daughter, Mrs. Pryor is pleasant and reserved, and she was obviously once pretty. The disastrous union she made with Caroline's profligate father, **James Helstone,** apparently to escape from her humiliating role as a governess, has given her a cynical view of marriage.

A different kind of marriage than that experienced by Caroline's mother is exemplified by Mr. and Mrs. Yorke, both of whom display the typical Yorkshire quality of forthrightness. **Mrs. Hester Yorke,** a practical, often abrasive mother of six children, scorns Caroline's romantic view of love and marriage. **Mr. Hiram Yorke,** who once ardently loved the beautiful Mary Cave, now perceives his youthful emotions as illusory and seems to have achieved a fairly comfortable union with his wife. A mill owner, Mr. Yorke is portrayed as a highly experienced, intelligent, somewhat stubborn man of basic integrity.

The three alarmingly unspiritual curates provide a little comedy in an otherwise somber book. As the daughter of a clergyman, Brontë had extensive knowledge of various types of clerics obviously thought that many were ineffective and ill-suited to their profession. The realism of *Shirley*'s three curates is attested to by the fact that their real-life models were immediately identified by those who knew them. **Mr. Joseph Donne,** a self-indulgent, arrogant bigot, will eventually be redeemed by marriage to a more principled woman. The ineffectual **Mr. David Sweeting,** the least offensive of the three, will also make a good marriage. **Mr. Peter Malone,** stereotypically Irish in his boisterousness and propensity for alcohol, displays his shallow values when he advocates, in a discussion with Robert, the advisability of marrying for money.

Among the other characters in the novel are Shirley's relatives, the Sympsons. **Mr. Sympson** is a tyrannical, domineering representative of conventional society; the well-bred **Mrs. Sympson** shares her husband's values. Yet Shirley is quite fond of their crippled son, **Henry Sympson.** Also significant are the three elderly single women, **Miss Ainsley, Miss Mann,** and **Miss Hall,** who illustrate the bleak and lonely future that may be Caroline's; **Sir Philip Nunnely,** the wealthy writer of inept poetry who tries to win Shirley's hand; **the Hardmans,** Mrs. Pryor's memorably snobbish employers, whom she describes while telling Caroline about her life as a governess; and **Michael Hartley,** the crazed and drunken weaver who shoots Robert.

Villette (novel, 1853)

Plot: The novel is narrated by Lucy Snowe, who is reflecting on her past life. As a young, orphaned girl, she paid twice-yearly visits to her godmother, Mrs. Bretton, and her teenaged son John Graham Bretton. Once a little girl named Polly Home came to stay with the Brettons while her father traveled in Europe. Terribly lonely for her father at first, Polly developed a tender, strangely maternal devotion to Graham, ignoring Lucy's attempts to be friendly. After the Brettons moved away, Lucy lost touch with them. The adult Lucy worked as a companion to several elderly women, but felt the need for a change and decided to move to France. She is hired to teach English at a boarding school run by Madame Beck, a somewhat sly but practical woman who keeps order in her school by spying and secret searches. Yet Lucy develops a measure of respect for the capable Madame Beck. Among Lucy's fellow teachers is the brilliant but eccentric Monsieur Paul Emanuel, who frequently instructs, corrects, and challenges her intellectually. Lucy realizes that the young, handsome Dr. John who comes to care for the Beck children is Graham Bretton, but he does not recognize her and she keeps her knowledge a secret—even (at least until later) from the reader. The pretty but self-centered student Ginevra Fanshawe, whom Lucy had met on the boat from England and with whom she had formed a mocking friendship, discusses with Lucy her own admirers: the lovesick suitor she calls Isidore, and the aristocratic dandy Colonel de Hamal (whom Ginevra prefers). Lucy later learns that Dr. John is Isidore, and he confesses to her that he does love Ginevra and hopes to marry her.

Lucy is left alone at the school during a vacation and becomes severely depressed, particularly after being visited by the apparition of a nun that she has previously seen. She wanders through the streets of Villette and finally goes to confession in a Catholic church despite her strong aversion to that religion. On her way home she faints, and when she wakes she is in a room whose furnishings she recognizes. It happens to be the home of Mrs. Bretton; Dr. John has been attending her through her illness, and now recognizes her. After her return to the school, Lucy visits the Brettons often and grows more attracted to Dr. John. Meanwhile, Monsieur Emanuel's remarks concerning the relationship become sarcastic. At a concert, Dr. John notices Ginevra mimicking his mother and, abruptly awakened to her faults, is no longer infatuated with her. While leaving another concert, Dr. John saves a delicate young girl from the crushing crowd. On bringing her into his home, he finds that she is Paulina de Bassompierre, the Polly Home who stayed with the Brettons when she was a small girl and whose father subsequently adopted an aristocratic French name. As Lucy watches dejectedly from the shadows, Dr. John falls in love with Paulina, who still adores him. Lucy's work, however, grows more satisfying as Madame Beck gives her more latitude and Monsieur Emanuel encourages and stimulates her both intellectually and emotionally. However, Lucy is again troubled by the mysterious appearance of the nun. When Madame Beck sends Lucy on an errand to the home of Madame Walravens, she learns the story of Monsieur Emanuel's past: as a young man he had loved a girl named Justine Marie, but her family forbade them to marry and she subsequently died. Out of respect for her memory he now supports her remaining relatives—Madame Walravens and Father Silas, the same priest who had heard Lucy's confession and wanted to convert her to Catholicism. Father Silas, Monsieur Emanuel's spiritual advisor, now fears Lucy will lead Emanuel away from his faith.

Lucy has become increasingly attached to Monsieur Emanuel, so she is distressed to learn that he is leaving for the West Indies to discharge some financial obligations. The jealous Madame Beck, who is a relative of Monsieur Emanuel and does not consider Lucy an appropriate partner for him, prevents the two from talking. Meanwhile, Ginevra elopes with Colonel de Hamal, revealing in a letter that it was he who posed as the ghostly nun in order to visit Ginevra at the school. Finally, Monsieur Emanuel manages to arrange a meeting with Lucy. He reveals that he has arranged for the establishment of a school which Lucy will operate in his absence; on his return after three years, he will be free to marry her. The novel ends with a strong intimation that Monsieur Emanuel perished in a storm at sea while on his way home.

Characters: Although some readers and critics consider *Villette* a more accomplished novel than Brontë's popular *Jane Eyre, Villette*'s mature heroine is not as immediately appealing as Jane Eyre. Nevertheless, an early reviewer noted in *The Athenaeum* that "a burning heart glows throughout it." Many details of *Villette*'s setting and several of its characters are rooted in the reality of Brontë's experiences at the *Pensionnat Heger* in Brussels, Belgium, where she was a student and teacher.

Like Jane Eyre, **Lucy Snowe** is an orphaned, homeless, plain-looking girl who, having to fend for herself, proves her self-sufficiency—as well as her courage—by moving to a foreign country and finding a job there. Intelligent, hard-working, and principled, she is also profoundly lonely and she suppresses her own feelings, hopes, and desires. Brontë told her publisher that she gave Lucy the last name "Snowe" because "she has about her an external coldness." Most of Lucy's friends perceive only this unflappable exterior—Dr. John calls her his "inoffensive shadow" and Ginevra finds her caustic and cynical. Her calm exterior, however, belies a passionate nature which, as the book progresses, she will gradually learn to express more openly. At the beginning of *Villette,* Lucy is a spectator; eventually, and primarily through her relationship with Paul Emanuel (who singularly is aware of her emotional depths and who finds her "adventurous, undocile, and audacious"), she becomes a participant in life—and thus less detached as a narrator. Several critics have noted that Lucy is a less reliable narrator than Jane Eyre—some of her views, such as her extreme aversion to Catholicism, are presented with a touch of irony that suggests she does not always see clearly or perceive correctly. Hence the superficial love she develops for handsome Dr. John is presented as a mere prelude to the profound, true connection she will make with Paul Emanuel, a man whose warmth and intellectual vigor make him an ideal partner for Lucy. She claims that the three years she spends operating her school and waiting for him to return are the happiest of her life, for she has both a satisfying occupation and the knowledge that she is loved. It is possible to interpret the ending, which strongly suggests that Paul Emanuel never returned, as somberly indicating that Lucy will never attain complete happiness, or as showing that she is now equipped to live a full, rewarding life regardless of her circumstances.

Monsieur Paul Emanuel is one of the most interesting and appealing characters in Brontë's fiction. This eccentric and often-contradictory teacher of literature is both noble and flawed. He is a hot-tempered and irascible man and both delights and terrifies his students. Occasionally arrogant, overbearing, and petty, he is also intellectually brilliant and completely honest. He demonstrates his nobility by his longtime support of the family of his dead fiancee. His ability to see beneath the surface of things and people leads him to realize that lonely, reserved Lucy has a passionate soul; he further encourages her to express that side of herself. He insists, for instance, that she take part in the play that the students perform, an experience that both excites and frightens her, and he constantly tries to provoke responses from her. Emanuel is presented as an antithesis to Dr. John, and it is proof of Brontë's skill that the reader begins to perceive his superiority even before Lucy—who, after all, is telling the story—does. The character of Emanuel is generally acknowledged to be based on Monsieur Heger, the married Belgian director of the Pensionnat Heger with whom Brontë was said to have been in love,

When first introduced in the story, **John Graham Bretton (Dr. John;** also called **Isidore** by Ginevra), is a mischievous, carefree sixteen-year-old who views Polly's devotion to him with a combination of amused tolerance and indifference. (That indifference will change to love when he meets the still-devoted Polly later in life.) As an adult he is handsome, kind, and generous and is popular with everyone he meets—particularly women, for he wins the regard not only of Lucy and Paulina but of Madame Beck, who eventually realizes she is too old to attract him. Because Dr. John is such a conventional hero in his good looks, charm, and pleasing manners, some reviewers have considered him a flat character. However, the superficiality and self-delusion he betrays in his infatuation with the obviously undeserving Ginevra Fanshawe as well as his undervaluing Lucy make him an effective foil to Paul Emanuel. It has been reported that Brontë modeled Dr. John after her publisher, the attractive and energetic George Smith, with whom she seems to have had a somewhat flirtatious but unromantic relationship.

The all-seeing ruler of the "Pensionnat de Demoiselles," **Madame Modeste Maria Beck,** is a somewhat stout but healthy-looking and neat middle-aged woman who is supremely self-possessed. Lucy quickly sees that Madame Beck maintains control over her school through a sneaky system of surveillance, and she develops a certain respect for her employer. Later, of course, Madame Beck will become a real menace and antagonist when she tries to protect her fellow Catholic and kinsman Paul Emanuel from Lucy's influence. Possibly based on the real-life Madame Heger, the jealous wife of the man Brontë supposedly loved, Madame Beck serves a useful role in the plot by providing a test for the love between Lucy and Monsieur Emanuel—an obstacle they must, and do, overcome. The Beck children, used mainly to flesh out the atmosphere of the pensionnat and to help the story move along, include **Desiree,** a mean and spoiled girl, honest and gay **Fifine,** and **Georgette,** whose broken arm brings Dr. John to the school.

Pretty, vain **Ginevra Fanshawe** serves the practical purpose of telling Lucy about Madame Beck's school, but she also provides a vivid example of the superficial nature that may be masked by an attractive exterior. There is great irony in the fact that Ginevra—who, according to nineteenth-century critic Susan M. Waring, is "tiny of soul . . . [and] infinitesimal of heart"—receives all of the blessings of life solely because she is beautiful and wealthy, while plain, impoverished Lucy remains in the shadows. Lucy almost seems to enjoy that contrast, though, and carries on a sarcastic relationship with Ginevra. Ginevra is essential to the story in several ways: she provides a link to the English society of Villette and with Lucy's English past; she contrasts strongly with Paulina, who is much more deserving of Dr. John's love; and she embodies markedly false social values, particularly in preferring the shallow Colonel de Hamal to Dr. John.

As a little girl, **Polly Home** (later **Paulina de Bassompierre**) is characterized by her extreme petiteness and contradictorily mature demeanor. She is capable, even at that early stage, of remarkably strong attachments. Though she seems to transfer her great love for her father to Graham while she is apart from her father, she remains devoted to both even after their situations have changed. As a grown woman, Paulina is beautiful, poised, intelligent, and still diminutive. Critics have claimed that Paulina never really attains the status of a fully developed or interesting character, but she does help to illuminate Lucy's much different personality.

Paulina's agreeable father, **Mr. Home,** or the **Count de Bassompierre,** is a remarkable devoted father whose adoration of his daughter is reportedly the result of his beautiful young wife's having neglected him in favor of social pursuits. Along with Mrs. Bretton, Mr. Home serves as a poignant reminder to Lucy of the parental love she has never experienced. **Mrs. Louisa Bretton,** who is said to resemble the mother of Brontë's publisher George Smith, is a good, vivacious, still-attractive woman who adores her son. It is because he sees Ginevra mocking his kind mother that Dr. John falls out of love with her.

As in all of Brontë's novels, the minor characters are not as skillfully fleshed out as the principal figures, but they do provide atmosphere and serve practical roles in the plot. **Miss Marchmont** is the elderly, wealthy, crippled spinster for whom Lucy worked before she came to France; she is morose and irascible, though she is kind to Lucy, and she chose to retreat from life after losing her lover when she was young. **Madame Walravens** is a grotesque, hunchbacked old woman—only three feet tall—whose granddaughter Justine Marie was in love with Paul Emanuel. **Mademoiselle Justine Marie Sauver** is Paul Emanuel's ward and the niece of his dead fiancee; Lucy mistakes her for his lover when she sees them together at the town's carnival. **Father Silas** is the Catholic priest whom Lucy suspects of wishing to gain converts to his religion. **Colonel de Hamal,** Ginevra's beloved, with whom she eventually elopes, is a dandified young aristocrat who is unprincipled enough to masquerade as a ghostly nun in order to make covert visits to his schoolgirl lover. Also part of Villette's gentrified set is **Mrs. Cholmondely,** Ginevra's fashionable chaperon. **Mademoiselle Zelie St. Pierre** is an untrustworthy teacher at the pensionnat; **Fraulein Anna Braun** is the hearty, alarmingly demonstrative but basically good-hearted woman who gives Lucy and Paulina German lessons. Students at the school include **Blanche, Virginie, Angelique,** and **Dolores;** they provide Lucy with opportunities to demonstrate her disciplinary skills. **Rosine** is a pretty, dimwitted servant at the school who is terrified of Monsieur Emanuel. **Mrs. Svini** (the French transliteration of "Sweeney") is the intemperate Irish governess whom Lucy replaces upon her arrival at the school. **The nun,** while not an actual character and labeled by some critics as a superfluous Gothic device, plays a significant role in the story by the response she provokes in Lucy: Lucy allows the apparition to unhinge her, suggesting that she is not as emotionally stable as she seems.

Further Reading

Allott, Miriam, ed. *The Brontës: The Critical Heritage.* London: Routledge & Kegan Paul, 1974.

Bloom, Harold, ed. *The Brontës.* New York: Chelsea House, 1987.

Dictionary of Literary Biography, Vol. 21. Detroit: Gale.

Evans, Barbara, and Gareth Lloyd Evans. *The Scribner Companion to the Brontës.* New York: Scribner's, 1982.

Gaskell, Elizabeth C. *The Life of Charlotte Brontë.* 1857. Reprint. New York: Dutton, 1957.

Gilbert, Sandra M., and Susan Gubar. "A Dialogue of Self and Soul: Plain Jane's Progress." In *Madwoman in the Attic: The Woman Writer and the Nineteenth Century Literary Imagination.* New Haven: Yale University Press, 1979.

Knies, Earl A. *The Art of Charlotte Brontë.* Columbus: Ohio State University Press, 1969.

Nineteenth Century Literature Criticism, Vols. 3, 8. Detroit: Gale.

Pinion, F. B. *A Brontë Companion: Literary Assessment, Background, and Reference.* New York: Barnes & Noble, 1975.

Rich, Adrienne. "'Jane Eyre': The Temptations of a Motherless Woman." In *On Lies, Secrets, and Silences: Selected Prose, 1966-1978.* New York: W. W. Norton, 1979.

Solomon, Eric. "'Jane Eyre': Fire and Water." *College English* 25, No. 3 (December, 1963): 215-17.

Tayler, Irene. *Holy Ghosts: The Male Muses of Emily and Charlotte Brontë.* New York: Columbia University Press, 1990.

Thurman, Judith. "Reader, I Married Him (The Brontës)." *New Yorker* 65 (20 March 1989): 109.

"Villette." *The Athenaeum* No. 1320 (12 February 1853): 186-88.

Waring, Susan M. "Charlotte Brontë's Lucy Snowe." *Harper's New Monthly Magazine* XXXII, No. CLXXXIX (February 1866): 368-71.

Emily Brontë
1818-1848
English novelist and poet.

Wuthering Heights (novel, 1847)

Plot: The novel takes place in the north of England during the last quarter of the eighteenth century and first few years of the nineteenth. The initial narrator, Lockwood, has moved to a new home called Thrushcross Grange and is intrigued by his landlord, Heathcliff, who lives at nearby Wuthering Heights. Heathcliff's daughter-in-law Catherine lives with him, and Lockwood also meets there a crude youth named Hareton and a gloomy servant named Joseph. When he is unable to return home from a visit to Wuthering Heights due to a snowstorm, Lockwood spends the night there. He dreams that a girl named Catherine Linton—whose name he read in a diary left in the room in which he is sleeping—is at the window begging to be let in. His screams wake Heathcliff, who runs to the window and calls for "Cathy." On his return to Thrushcross Grange, Lockwood asks his housekeeper, Ellen "Nelly" Dean, to tell the story of the family at Wuthering Heights. Nelly (who will narrate the majority of the novel) relates that about thirty years earlier, Mr. and Mrs. Earnshaw, their daughter Cathy, and son Hindley had lived at Wuthering Heights. Mr. Earnshaw had returned from a trip to Liverpool with an abandoned, dirty waif whom the family named Heathcliff. Cathy was very fond of the child, but Hindley was jealous of the attention his father paid Heathcliff and the two boys bickered often. After Mrs. Earnshaw died, Hindley went away to college while Cathy and Heathcliff grew even closer. After the death of Mr. Earnshaw, Hindley had returned with his wife Frances. Still resentful of Heathcliff, Hindley treated him like a menial servant. Frances died after giving birth to a son, Hareton, and the embittered Hindley began to drink heavily and to be even more abusive toward Heathcliff.

Cathy and Heathcliff were virtually inseparable, running wild together over the moors around their home. Once, while the two were spying on the Linton family at Thrushcross Grange, Cathy was injured and had to stay with the Lintons for five days. Soon the Linton children, Edgar and Isabella, were frequent visitors at Wuthering Heights and Cathy began to imitate their more refined manners. Heathcliff overheard Cathy confiding to Nelly that Edgar had proposed to her and that it would be degrading for her to marry Heathcliff in his subservient position; he ran away before she added that she loved Heathcliff deeply. Heathcliff consequently disappeared, leaving Cathy in great distress.

Three years later, Cathy and Edgar Linton were married and lived happily together until the return of Heathcliff caused tension between them. Cathy was overjoyed to see her friend, who was now well-dressed and seemingly prosperous. However, Heathcliff began to ingratiate himself with the dissipated Hindley, frequently gambling with him in order to gain power over his old tormentor. He also made Isabella fall in love with him and eloped with her, precipitating a mental and physical breakdown in Cathy. When Isabella and Heathcliff returned two months later, he treated his new wife—whom he had married purely out of vengeance—cruelly. Heathcliff arranged to meet Cathy, who was now near death, while Edgar was at church. In a powerful exchange, the two expressed both their love and their sorrow, breaking their passionate embrace only after Edgar had entered the room. Cathy died giving birth to a premature baby who was named after her mother. Heathcliff seemed deranged with grief, smashing his head repeatedly against a tree and calling out for Cathy to stay with him. Tired of her abusive marriage, Isabella left for London, where she gave birth to Heathcliff's son, Linton. After gambling away Wuthering Heights to the conniving Heathcliff, Hindley died and Hareton was left in Heathcliff's care.

Thirteen years later, Isabella died in London and Heathcliff demanded that his son Linton come to live with him at Wuthering Heights. Heathcliff wanted Linton to marry the young Catherine, thereby gaining ownership of Thrushcross Grange for himself. Despite the strong disapproval of both the gravely ill Edgar and Nelly, the two young people did correspond and met occasionally. Now the story is brought up to the present. Heathcliff kidnaps Nelly and Catherine and tells Catherine she cannot see her dying father unless she marries Linton. She does so, and because Edgar Linton dies before he can change his will, Thrushcross Grange is inherited—through Catherine, whose property by law becomes her husband's— by Linton Heathcliff. The sickly young man soon dies, leaving Catherine a widow. As Lockwood has seen, she lives at Wuthering Heights with Heathcliff and the uncouth Hareton, sullen and unhappy.

Lockwood leaves the neighborhood, and returns after a year to find an altered atmosphere at Wuthering Heights. He learns that Heathcliff has died after noting a resemblance in the relationship between the now congenial Hareton and Catherine to his own with Cathy during their youth. While Catherine has been teaching Hareton to read, the two have fallen in love and made plans to marry. They will move to Thrushcross Grange, away from the stormy memories of Wuthering Heights. Lockwood hears that the ghosts of Cathy and Heathcliff have been seen walking over the moors together, and the novel ends with him reflecting over the three side-by-side graves of the two lovers and Edgar Linton.

Characters: Emily Brontë's novel is universally acknowledged as a remarkable achievement and a landmark work of English fiction. In depicting the tempestuous, doomed love of Heathcliff and Cathy, Brontë employed a complex and carefully plotted narrative structure; richly wrought images of weather, landscape, animals, and the supernatural; and unforgettable characters whose emotions are deeply and humanly felt. Although early reviewers were shocked by the coarseness they perceived in *Wuthering Heights,* the novel has since generated voluminous and mostly admiring critical response. However, Brontë's judgment of her characters—whether she affirms the stormy emotional energy represented by Heathcliff and Wuthering Heights or the calm refinement embraced by Cathy when she moves to Thrushcross Grange—has never been decisively determined. Most scholars agree that that ambiguity is part of what makes *Wuthering Heights* great. This powerful, memorable novel ends, according to Barbara and Gareth Lloyd Evans, "by triumphantly asserting the quite unequivocal naked power of human love."

Heathcliff is the dominant character in *Wuthering Heights*—it is his energy that illuminates the story and precipitates the action. The dark-haired, dark-skinned, gypsy-like boy of unknown birth (some have suggested that he may be Mr. Earnshaw's illegitimate son, but this has never been conclusively demonstrated) is transplanted from a Liverpool slum to a respectable upper-middle-class English country home—a circumstance some have seen as emblematic of class struggle, particularly in view of the rejection Heathcliff later undergoes by both Hindley and the Lintons. Though Heathcliff quickly becomes Cathy's soulmate, Hindley hates him for the partiality and consideration that Mr. Earnshaw shows him. When Hindley becomes the head of the household after his father's death, he has the power to degrade Heathcliff, subjugating him to the status of a servant. Naturally passionate, proud, and volatile, Heathcliff is warped by this cruel treatment; he is even more disturbed by the loss of Cathy to the weak, elegant Edgar Linton. After his return from making his fortune (it is never specified exactly what Heathcliff has done to effect this change in his circumstances) he goes about systematically wreaking vengeance on those who have hurt him in the past. He cheats Hindley, his drunken nemesis, out of Wuthering Heights; enrages Edgar by marrying Isabella (whom he subsequently mistreats); subjects Hareton and then his own son Linton to degradation and fear similar to what he himself experienced as a young man; and forces his beloved Cathy's daughter into an unwanted marriage and the loss of her rightful home. Although it seems impossible to evoke pity for such a character, Brontë does elicit the reader's sympathy—particularly by conveying his great loss at Cathy's death. Heathcliff has been compared to the melodramatic villains of Gothic fiction for his dark, stormy aspect and uncontrollable, vicious temper; he has also been commonly viewed as a Byronic (referring to the influential Romantic poet, Lord Byron) figure of great passion who suffers in isolation. Yet he has also been called a tragic hero comparable to those created by Shakespeare (particularly King Lear, who was also isolated and driven to madness by the loss of love) and Milton, particularly his compelling Satan in his epic seventeenth-century poem *Paradise Lost*. Indeed, Heathcliff is surrounded by devil imagery throughout the novel, beginning with his arrival as a small child: "it's as dark almost as if it came from the devil," says Mr. Earnshaw as he introduces his family to the orphan he's befriended. Although some scholars have found Heathcliff thoroughly hateful and vengeful—never relenting in his cruelty even to the innocent offspring of his enemies—others point to those moments when he does reveal a spark of humanity: he saves Hareton's life when Hindley has dropped him over a banister, and he binds the wound that he himself has brutally inflicted upon Hindley. Constantly associated with the wind-torn landscape and rough weather of Wuthering Heights, Heathcliff seems equally ravaged by the force of his own emotions. Unlike Cathy, though, he is not bodily devastated by grief and frustration; instead, he thrives physically. In the end, he is defeated by life's relentless tendency to mend itself; despite his machinations, Hareton and Catherine recreate the love—though in a much milder form—that once existed between himself and Cathy.

Catherine "Cathy" Earnshaw is a spirited, beautiful, headstrong young woman who delights in running over the moors with her beloved Heathcliff and rebelling with him against the self-righteous strictures of the servant Joseph. She has grown up "half savage and hardy and free," and in the freedom that she and Heathcliff forge for themselves they are often said to represent the force of nature and nonconformity in opposition to civilization or society. Significantly, Cathy once dreamed that she had gone to heaven and found it lacking, so the angels deposited her, much to her joy, back on the earth; thus she affirms that paradise is to be found in life and in her union with Heathcliff. This union is both spiritual and natural (though not particularly sexual, as many critics have noted). In explaining her bond with Heathcliff to Nelly, Cathy says, "I *am* Heathcliff—he's always, always in my mind—not as a pleasure, any more than I am always a pleasure to myself—but as my own being. . . ." Her love for Edgar is more conventional, for he is an attractive and kind young man who can provide her with a comfortable, refined lifestyle. Though she claims that in marrying Edgar she will benefit Heathcliff—because she plans to use her husband's money to raise her friend out of her brother's power—her choice has been interpreted as essentially selfish. In fact, Cathy demonstrates her self-centeredness after her marriage when she happily maintains her relationship with Heathcliff after his return—despite Edgar's obvious anguish—and even allows him to humiliate her husband in front of her. Although she may not be a completely likeable character, it is difficult not to acknowledge Cathy's power, especially in the influence she retains over Heathcliff even after her death. In choosing Edgar over Heathcliff, Cathy wrenched herself in two, and she found the resulting frustration unbearable. Heathcliff's consequent departure, before she has married Edgar, brought about her illness, and the strong emotions that followed his return precipitated her death. Some recent interpretations of Cathy's character have had a feminist bent; Sandra Gilbert and Susan Gubar, for instance, suggest that in leaving the Edenic world of her childhood for the adult realm of marriage and Thrushcross Grange, Cathy was destroyed by society's demand for compliance with conventional standards of femininity.

The two narrators of *Wuthering Heights,* though minor characters themselves, are important in the novel's overall effect. Both **Lockwood** and **Ellen "Nelly" Dean** remain detached from the deeper meaning of the action, but in that detachment they increase the emotional profundity of what happens. Lockwood—whose name suggests a locked or closed mind— is a conventional person who is curious about the events surrounding Wuthering Heights and Thrushcross Grange but lacks the perception to fully realize the true meaning of what he sees and hears. For example, Lockwood initially thinks Heathcliff is a "capital fellow," despite the fact that Heathcliff has cursed him under his breath during their first meeting. Lockwood's primary purpose in the book seems to be to vary its narrative perspective, allowing Brontë to relate her story in an indirect but telling way. Like Lockwood, Nelly represents a profoundly conventional viewpoint. Though honest and loyal, she too lacks the insight to make any real sense of the events she's witnessed. Her responses are those of a naive human being unaware of ulterior motives or connections. When Cathy explains her feeling of deep union with Heathcliff, Nelly says that she was "out of patience with her folly," suggesting that she attaches no great meaning to what Cathy has said. Her ordinary reality makes the emotions smoldering beneath the surface of events even more dramatic. As an integral part of both the Earnshaw and the Linton families for several generations, she is a constant presence, and serves as a sounding board at times and as an intermediary at others. Though some critics have pointed out some incongruities in Nelly's character— most notably her extreme literacy—most would agree with Carl R. Woodring that "in Nelly, Emily Brontë ingeniously produced the exactly needed combination of servant, companion, and saucy antagonist."

Hindley Earnshaw's character reveals a passion that is apparently a family trait, and like his sister Cathy, he will eventually be destroyed by his emotions. He reacts to the arrival of Heathcliff with a jealousy that can never be assuaged and is expressed in cruelty toward its root. After the death of his wife, Frances, whom he apparently loved deeply (Cathy complains about their constant kissing and cooing), Hindley sinks despairingly into excessive drinking and gambling, neglecting his son Hareton and the sister who is still under his guardianship, and subjecting Heathcliff to even greater abuse. When Heathcliff returns after a three-year absence, Hindley is a confirmed drunkard who is, ironically, willing to befriend Heathcliff now that he has money to gamble with. Heathcliff sees Hindley as the real cause of his separation from Cathy, because Cathy considered the subjugated Heathcliff as too lowly for her to marry, so he is eager to take his revenge on Hindley. In the end, Hindley loses Wuthering Heights to the same person he had been so jealous of as a boy—but he is portrayed so unsympathetically that it is difficult to pity him.

Edgar and Isabella Linton occupy a higher social position than the occupants of Wuthering Heights. In contrast to Heathcliff, **Edgar Linton** is polished, cultured, and refined—if somewhat spoiled and weak. In addition, he is good-looking and kind to Cathy, so it is not surprising that she is attracted to him. His own love for Cathy is different from that of Heathcliff; it is more ordinary and even more physical. He is patient with Cathy and seems steadfastly devoted to her despite her behavior. Though not a particularly well-developed character, Edgar is worthy of admiration in the courage he shows when—despite his weakling image—he punches the much bigger Heathcliff in the throat. **Isabella Linton** is perhaps even less developed than her brother, serving primarily as a vehicle through which Heathcliff seeks revenge on Edgar and Cathy. She is a spoiled young woman who drastically deludes herself about Heathcliff's love for her despite Cathy's warning that she is being used. Before making her eventual escape to London, Isabella responds to Heathcliff's ill treatment with passive despair, allowing her appearance to deteriorate into slatternliness. However, she does display some of the same latent courage her brother shows when she finally rebels against Heathcliff and leaves Wuthering Heights.

Linton Heathcliff, the son of Isabella and Heathcliff, has been called the least likable character in the book. Spoiled by his mother during his isolated upbringing, Linton is weak-willed, petulant, and sickly and subject to temperamental rages and petty tyranny over the sympathetic Catherine. Linton's primary purpose, however, is to provide a means for Heathcliff not only to acquire Thrushcross Grange but to diabolically recreate the Cathy-Heathcliff-Edgar love triangle of the previous generation. Several critics have noted that Brontë's depiction of the legal consequences of Catherine's marriage to Linton—with her property transferred, by law, automatically to her husband and then to her father-in-law after Linton's death—is accurate.

Catherine Heathcliff, the daughter of Cathy and Edgar who marries Linton Heathcliff, is like her mother in her beauty and spiritedness, but she is not bound to meet the same fate as Cathy. Though she is a somewhat spoiled young girl, she is capable of real pity for Linton as well as love for her father and, eventually, for Hareton. Because she lacks Cathy's wildness and makes a suitable, markedly untempestuous union with Hareton, Catherine might be identified more with the staid, civilized values of Thrushcross Grange. Similarly, **Hareton Earnshaw** has been raised by the violent and brutal Heathcliff but seems to need only brief exposure to Catherine's kindness and refinement to become the honest, warm and intelligent young man he was always meant to be. Although depicted as crude and oafish at the beginning, Hareton's desire to learn to read suggests the possibility of redemption. His eventual ability to read the name of his ancestor—Hareton Earnshaw—carved into the doorway of Wuthering Heights provides a sense of continuity with the past, but in his relationship with Catherine and planned move to Thrushcross Grange there is also an intimation of hope for the future.

The morose, superstitious servant **Joseph,** who serves at Wuthering Heights throughout the story and will remain there after all of its other occupants have gone—is described by Nelly as "the wearisomest, self-righteous pharisee that ever ransacked a Bible to rake the promises to himself, and fling the curses on his neighbors." He continually rails against the behavior of others in a bigoted, surly manner, thus serving as an ironic representative of authority and religion against which Cathy and Heathcliff frequently rebel. Despite his unpleasant nature, the grotesque Joseph provides some moments of humor in the story— although Brontë's transcription of his heavy Yorkshire accent is sometimes hard to follow.

Minor characters in *Wuthering Heights* include **Mr. and Mrs. Earnshaw** (Mr. Earnshaw's main role is in bringing home Heathcliff, for such ambiguous reasons, from Liverpool); **Mr. and Mrs. Linton,** who both fall ill and die soon after Cathy has spent five weeks recovering from her own illness at Thrushcross Grange; **Zillah,** a servant at Wuthering Heights who never seems to notice that anything is amiss there; **Frances Earnshaw,** the unfortunate wife of Hindley who dies of consumption after giving birth to Hareton; and **Dr. Kenneth,** who is in attendance at most of the illnesses throughout the novel.

Further Reading

Bloom, Harold, ed. *The Brontës.* New York: Chelsea House, 1987.

Davies, Stevie. *Emily Brontë: The Artist as a Free Woman.* Manchester, England: Carcanet, 1983.

Dictionary of Literary Biography, Vols. 21, 32. Detroit: Gale.

Eagleton, Terry. "Wuthering Heights." In *Myths of Power: A Marxist Study of the Brontës,* pp. 97-121. New York: Barnes & Noble, 1975.

Evans, Barbara, and Gareth Lloyd Evans. *The Scribner Companion to the Brontës.* New York: Scribner's, 1982.

Gerín, Winifred. *Emily Brontë: A Biography.* Oxford: Clarendon Press, 1971.

Gilbert, Sandra M., and Susan Gubar. "Looking Oppositely: Emily Brontë's Bible of Hell." In *The Madwoman in the Attic: The Woman Writer and the Nineteenth-Century Literary Imagination,* pp. 248-308. New Haven: Yale University Press, 1979.

Nineteenth-Century Literature Criticism, Vol. 16. Detroit: Gale.

Oates, Joyce Carol. "The Magnanimity of 'Wuthering Heights.'" *Critical Inquiry* 9, No. 2 (December 1982): 435-49.

Pinion, F. B. *A Brontë Companion: Literary Assessment, Background, and Reference.* New York: Barnes & Noble, 1975.

Pritchett, V. S. Review of "Wuthering Heights." *The New Statesman and Nation* 31, No. 800 (22 June 1946): 453.

Sinclair, May. *The Three Brontës.* 1912. Reprint. Port Washington, N.Y.: Kennikat Press, 1967.

Whipple, E. P. "Novels of the Season." *The North American Review* 67, No. 141 (October 1848): 354-69.

Winnifreth, Tom. "Wuthering Heights." In *The Brontës,* pp. 46-65. New York: Macmillan, 1977.

Woodring, Carl R. "The Narrators of 'Wuthering Heights.'" *Nineteenth-Century Fiction* 11, No. 4 (March 1957): 298-305.

William Wells Brown
1816(?)-1884

African-American novelist, dramatist, historian, and memoirist.

Clotel; or, The President's Daughter: A Narrative of Slave Life in the United States (novel, 1853)

Plot: The story begins in Richmond, Virginia, where an African-American slave woman named Currer lives as the property of John Graves. Her two daughters, Clotel and Althesa, were fathered by Currer's former owner, President Thomas Jefferson. When Graves dies, Currer and Althesa are acquired by a slave speculator named Dick Walker, and Clotel is purchased by young Horace Green, a white aristocrat who had met the beautiful girl at a quadroon (mixed-race) ball. Taken to Natchez, Mississippi, Currer and Althesa are bought by a Methodist minister, Reverend Peck, whose daughter, Georgiana, is opposed to slavery. Later, Althesa is sold to a man from Vermont who does not approve of slavery but who needs cheap domestic help. Althesa falls in love with her owner's friend and boarder, the young physician Dr. Henry Morton, who buys Althesa and marries her. The couple, who become the parents of two daughters, attempt to acquire Currer from Peck but are unsuccessful; after his death, Peck's daughter sets his slaves free and sends them north, but Currer has already died. Meanwhile Clotel and her owner and lover, Green, have established a romantically idyllic home in Richmond, where Clotel gives birth to their daughter, Mary. When Horace decides to enter politics, he marries the daughter of a powerful local politician. His new wife is enraged to discover her husband's relationship with Clotel and Mary, and she insists that Clotel be sold to speculator Walker. She takes Mary into her own home as a servant but treats her cruelly. Clotel is transported to Vicksburg, Mississippi, and sold, but she escapes from her new owner, disguising herself as a young white man and traveling with a slave named William, who poses as her servant. Eventually William leaves her to make his way to Canada, and Clotel proceeds to Richmond to find her daughter. Before she can do so, however, she is captured and imprisoned in Washington, D.C.; although she escapes, she becomes trapped on a bridge over the Potomac River and dies after jumping into the water.

Althesa and her family have moved to Louisiana, where they die of yellow fever. Because Morton had never actually purchased Althesa's freedom, their marriage was considered illegal and thus their daughters are still slaves. Each is acquired by an evil owner—one an old lecher and the other a young drunk—and each soon dies, one by suicide and the other of a broken heart after her owner kills her lover. In Richmond Mary's lover, George Greene, has been arrested for his involvement in the bloody insurrection orchestrated by Nat Turner. Mary helps him to escape. She is then taken to New Orleans but eventually escapes and goes to France, where she marries the dashing Frenchman who had helped her flee the United States. George, meanwhile, makes his way to England and becomes a successful business-man. While visiting France he encounters Mary, whose husband has since died, and the two are married.

Characters: Brown is considered the first African-American novelist and dramatist. The son of a slave and her white owner, he was born on a Kentucky plantation, escaping at twenty to freedom in Cincinnati, Ohio. He later became a renowned abolitionist lecturer, historian, and essayist and also published an account of his own life as a slave. In fact many of the scenes and details of *Clotel* are drawn from Brown's own experiences as well as other slaves' narratives and articles published in abolitionist journals. It is generally agreed that Brown, though a gifted speech writer, lacked the command of the novelist's craft necessary to create a successful work of fiction. *Clotel* is overly melodramatic (as was much of American fiction in the mid-nineteenth century) and poorly structured, and its characters are stiff and lifeless. In addition *Clotel* is heavily didactic; Brown clearly wrote the novel to advance his anti-slavery beliefs. The revised edition published in America in 1864 is less polemical and, as many scholars note, makes no mention of Thomas Jefferson as Clotel's father—an aspect of the first version thought likely to offend American readers. Despite its weaknesses, *Clotel* is remarkable for its realistic depiction of the conditions and dilemmas experienced by African-Americans in several different regions of the country in the nineteenth century.

Brown's portrayal of the novel's protagonist, **Clotel,** as the daughter of President Thomas Jefferson by his African-American house slave was apparently based on a rumor spread by famous abolitionist William Lloyd Garrison, that Jefferson had fathered several children by a slave woman and that one had been offered for sale in New Orleans for a thousand dollars. By making Clotel the offspring of such a beloved and important figure, Brown hoped to dramatize the horror and irony of slavery. The publishers of the novel's American edition did not believe that their readers would accept such a premise, however, and all references to Jefferson were removed. Critics note that the beautiful, very light-skinned Clotel is modeled in the tradition of the tragic mulatto whose almost completely Caucasian appearance intensifies the injustice of his or her subjugation. Clotel has been compared to the heroine of Lydia Maria Childs's earlier, highly sentimental anti-slavery novel *The Quadroons,* although Clotel differs from her predecessor in the ingenuity and courage she displays in her daring escape from captivity. Clotel's status as the illegitimate daughter of a white owner illustrates the sexual domination of white men over black women, and the heartbreaking separations from her family members—first from her mother and sister and later from her daughter—that she endures are also portrayed as typical events in slaves' lives. Clotel is a markedly romantic heroine not only in her great beauty and inherent dignity but in her courageous response to oppression and the tragic death she finally meets. It has been noted that Clotel is a character with whom few blacks of the period could have identified and that Brown intentionally depicted her in a manner that would appeal to a white audience, thus gaining support for the anti-slavery cause. Scholars agree that, despite the general failure of her characterization, Clotel is an important figure in African-American fiction. In later versions of the novel Clotel's daughter, Mary, becomes Clotelle, thus giving the title character a longer and ultimately successful, happy future.

The novel's secondary characters are interesting mainly for the aspects of society they represent. Clotel's mother **Currer** (renamed **Agnes** in later editions) may be identified as the stereotypically strong matriarch of a fatherless African-American family. Brown has been faulted for failing to develop the early importance of this figure, who finally fades into obscurity and dies. Currer's other daughter, **Althesa** (subsequently called **Isabel**), marries a white man who, by failing to buy her freedom and thus condemning their daughters to slavery after his death, demonstrates the harm perpetrated even by the most well-intentioned whites. Similarly, **Horace Green,** the young white man who buys Clotel, establishes her in a comfortable home, and fathers her child, later reveals his true priorities when he marries a white woman in order to further his political career, an action that ultimately separates the woman he supposedly loved from her (and his own) daughter. Horace is called **Henry Linwood** in later versions of *Clotel.* The slave speculator who initially buys Currer and her two daughters after the death of their master, **John Graves,** is **Dick Walker** (later named **Dick Jennings**). Walker is based on the identically named speculator for whom Brown had once worked as a servant and who, like his fictional counterpart, habitually advertised his scheduled stops in the New Orleans newspapers, lied about his slaves' ages in order to increase his profits, and owned a slave named **Pompey** who was commissioned to either pluck the grey hairs from slaves' heads or brush them with a blacking solution to make them appear younger.

The **Reverend Peck** (renamed **James Wilson**), who buys Currer and Althesa in Mississippi, is a Methodist minister who was born in the North but married a southern heiress. Despite his religious calling, he not only owns slaves but also treats them as harshly than any of his slave-owning neighbors. This character seems intended to demonstrate the hypocritical capitulation to slavery to which even the supposedly religious were subject, as well as the economic temptation that cheap slave labor represented to many northerners. However Peck's daughter, **Georgiana,** opposes slavery, and when her father dies she frees her father's slaves and sends them to (relative) safety in the North.

Mary is the daughter of Clotel and her lover and owner, Horace Green. The new **Mrs. Green** is horrified to learn of her husband's arrangement with his slave and, after selling Clotel, moves Mary into her household as a servant so that she may continuously humiliate and torment her. Mary has obviously inherited her mother's resourcefulness and courage, for she succeeds in helping her imprisoned lover to escape and later escapes herself from captivity in New Orleans. In a particularly melodramatic turn of events, Mary is finally reunited with her lover after moving to France and—her French husband conveniently dead—she marries him. Mary's lover and eventual husband **George Green** is described in the first version of *Clotel* as light-skinned and small in stature; in later editions he is large, strong, and coal-black in color and his name is **Jerome.** Obviously intelligent and educated, George ultimately becomes a successful businessman in England. He is reading *The Life and Pontificate of Leo the Tenth,* a book about a reputedly part-African pope that influenced Brown's thinking, when he happens to encounter Mary in a French cemetery.

Another significant character in *Clotel* is **William,** the slave who poses as Clotel's servant when she makes her successful escape attempt and who finally flees to Canada. Their daring scheme was based on a similar feat executed by former slaves Ellen and William Craft, with whom Brown often appeared on the abolitionist lecture circuit.

Further Reading

Andrews, William L. "The Novelization of Voice in Early African American Narrative." *PMLA: Publications of the Modern Language Association* 105, No. 1 (January 1990): 23-34.

Bone, Robert. "Novels of the Talented Tenth: Abolitionist Novels." In *The Negro Novel in America,* rev. ed., pp. 30-2. New Haven: Yale University Press, 1968.

Bontemps, Arna. "The Negro Contribution to American Letters." In *The American Negro Reference Book,* edited by John P. Davis, pp. 850-78. Englewood Cliffs, N.J.: Prentice-Hall, 1966.

Campbell, Jane. "Celebrations of Escape and Revolt: William Wells Brown's *Clotel* and Arna Bontemps's *Black Thunder.*" In *Mythic Black Fiction: The Transmittal of History,* pp. 1-17. Knoxville: University of Tennessee Press, 1989.

Farrison, William E. *William Wells Brown: Author and Reformer.* Chicago: University of Chicago Press, 1969.

Jackson, Blyden. "The First Negro Novelist." In *A History of Afro-American Literature,* Vol. 1, *The Long Beginning, 1746-1895,* pp. 326-342. Baton Rouge: Louisiana State University Press, 1989.

Nineteenth-Century Literature Criticism, Vol. 2. Detroit: Gale.

Fanny Burney
1752-1840
English novelist, dramatist, diarist, and letter writer.

Evelina; or, A Young Lady's Entrance into the World (novel, 1778)

Plot: This novel is presented in the form of letters written by seventeen-year-old Evelina Anville—primarily to her guardian, the Reverend Arthur Villars. Evelina and her mother, who had died soon after her daughter's birth, had been deserted by Evelina's profligate father, Sir John Belmont. Evelina was raised by Mr. Villars at his home, Berry Hill, in the Dorsetshire region of England. Evelina is invited to visit London with the friendly, kind Mrs. Mirvan, but Mr. Villars fears the influence of that city on his innocent ward and refuses to let her go. He does, however, allow Evelina to visit Mrs. Mirvan's mother, Lady Howard, at Howard Grove, and finally agrees to let Evelina travel from there to London with Mrs. Mirvan and her daughter Maria, with whom Evelina has formed a close friendship. In London, Evelina enters the exciting, glamorous life of the wealthy and socially prominent. She meets charming Lord Orville, and the two young people are immediately attracted to each other. However, Evelina is disturbed by several social gaffes she commits out of ignorance and by the unwanted attentions of Sir Clement Willoughby. Evelina also happens to meet her maternal grandmother, Madame Duval, who has returned to England after twenty years in Paris. Evelina finds her grandmother—as well as the other relations with whom she becomes acquainted—exceedingly vulgar and ill-mannered, and she is embarrassed by their behavior before her sophisticated friends.

Evelina now leaves London for Howard Grove. With Madame Duval's encouragement, Lady Howard schemes to make Sir John Belmont acknowledge Evelina as his daughter. Mr.

Villars disapproves of the plan, and indeed, Sir John refuses to admit his connection with Evelina. Madame Duval would like to present Evelina to Sir John in person, but Mr. Villars will not allow it. He does, however, give Evelina permission to return to London with her grandmother. Evelina has an unhappy and embarrassing visit there, due to the indiscretions of her relatives. She meets a young Scottish poet named Mr. Macartney and prevents him from committing suicide, giving him some money to help with his financial problems. Madame Duval plots to marry Evelina to her boorish grandnephew, Tom Branghton (whose vulgar family causes Evelina many distressing moments, particularly when they act in too familiar a manner with Lord Orville). Evelina finally returns to Berry Hill, where she writes to Maria Mirvan and describes her activities in London. Having written to Lord Orville to acknowledge the rudeness of her relatives, Evelina receives a highly insulting reply. Shocked and upset, she becomes ill. Journeying to the resort town of Bristol with her neighbor, Mrs. Selwyn, Evelina encounters many of her well-heeled London friends. Lord Orville acts very courteously toward her so she decides to overlook his offensive letter (later it will be revealed that Sir Clement had forged the letter, as well as one had Lord Orville received, in order to sabotage their romance). Mr. Macartney appears on the scene unexpectedly, embarrassing her and causing her to worry that they will be suspected of having an affair. Another new arrival is Miss Belmont, rumored to be Sir John's daughter. Then Mr. Macartney reveals that he may be the illegitimate son of Sir John, which would make Evelina his half-sister. In order to defend Evelina's honor now that a young woman claiming to be Sir John's daughter has appeared, Mr. Villars is ready to force the other man to confirm Evelina's parentage. However, the confusion is soon unraveled: the Miss Belmont who had appeared at Bristol and who had been raised by Sir John as his daughter was actually Polly Green, the daughter of a nurse who had substituted her own baby for Evelina when she heard that Mr. Villars had refused to send the child to her father. Sir John now gladly accepts Evelina as his real daughter, and also acknowledges that Mr. Macartney is his son. Polly marries the young poet, and Evelina finally wins the heart and hand of her beloved, Lord Orville.

Characters: Fanny Burney was an early practitioner of the English novel of manners and a predecessor to Jane Austen, whose domestic comedies were similarly focused on the social and moral development of young women of the upper middle class. Influenced by the seventeenth-century allegorical novels of such authors as Henry Fielding and Tobias Smollett, *Evelina* is a freshly narrated, transparently autobiographical coming-of-age novel that provides a closely observed portrait of late-eighteenth- and early-nineteenth-century British society (both upper and middle class). Acclaimed upon its publication as a remarkable achievement—Burney was only seventeen when she wrote it—*Evelina* continues to be read and appreciated, particularly for its memorable heroine.

Burney describes **Evelina Anville** as possessing "a virtuous mind, a cultivated understanding, and a feeling heart," as well as "ignorance of the forms, and inexperience . . . in the manners of the world." Evelina is beautiful, clever, and gay, and the book chronicles her transformation from the naive and socially awkward girl who makes her first journey to London to the wiser and more sophisticated young woman who wins the heart of the gallant Lord Orville. All of the novel's characters and situations are seen through her eyes as she learns to survive in the sometimes treacherous world of English high society. While making it clear that Evelina is an unaffected, intelligent young woman who can tell the difference between real value and pretense, Burney uses her character to promote the values of feminine virtue, propriety, and conformity. Indeed, from beginning to end of the novel, Evelina is under the direction and guidance—though she is sometimes temporarily supervised by variously reliable chaperons—of an authoritative male whom she obeys unquestioningly, starting with her guardian Mr. Villars and ending with her fiance Lord Orville.

The **Reverend Arthur Villars** has raised his young ward with great care and protectiveness, and his devotion to Evelina is clear. Beyond these qualities, though, the reader learns little of his character. His letters to Evelina number only fifteen of the total eighty four of which the book is comprised; he serves primarily as the recipient of her letters. Villars is the main voice of moral authority in Evelina's life, dispensing wise advice and counseling her on correct social behavior. For her part, Evelina accepts his guidance obediently, even, for example, giving up the idea of romance with Lord Orville when Villars tell her that this wealthy young man could not possibly love her.

The other important man in Evelina's life is the handsome, sophisticated **Lord Orville,** the object of her girlish ardor who will eventually become her husband. He is presented as the ideal male figure: strong, well-bred, and intelligent (the word "noble" is often used to describe his behavior), and in his urbanity he provides a model of correct social behavior that benefits Evelina by example. Lord Orville is the quintessential aristocrat who lacks any hint of the common vices of his class, such as drinking or gambling, and whose jealousy when Evelina is pursued by other admirers is forgivable. Although Evelina's conquest of Lord Orville might be interpreted as proof that even a young woman of modest background can win a prince, it is also significant that, by the end of the novel, Evelina is an heiress and thus a socially appropriate partner for Lord Orville.

Prominent among Evelina's other suitors is the obnoxious and conniving **Sir Clement Willoughby.** Insensitive and impertinent in pursuing Evelina, he keeps her out unnecessarily late after offering her a ride home from the opera, which causes her to incur a scolding from her guardian. Sir Clement is quite clever and witty and thus is able to ingratiate himself with almost everybody, though Evelina is quick to see through his shallow charm. He proves wickedly deceitful when he forges letters to Evelina and Lord Orville in order to disrupt their relationship, and Evelina is not inclined to excuse him when he finally begs forgiveness for this action.

Other members of the elegant London and Bristol milieus in which Evelina finds herself include Lord Orville's sister, Lady Louisa, and her fiance Lord Merton. Said to be modeled after Lydia Languish in Richard Sheridan's eighteenth-century drama, *The Rivals,* **Lady Louisa** is arrogant and insincere, approving of her brother's romance with Evelina only after she learns the young woman will inherit a fortune. **Lord Merton** is equally distasteful, flirting shamelessly with Evelina whenever Lady Louisa is not present. **Mr. Lovel** is another of Evelina's unsuccessful suitors; he is stereotypically foppish and ostentatious and makes frequent references to Evelina's humble origins.

While Burney's depiction of aristocratic characters has been termed weak, she is more often praised for her portrayal of Evelina's middle-class relatives. Evelina's grandmother, **Madame Duval,** a former English barmaid who has fashioned a flimsy French identity for herself by living in Paris for twenty years, is a vulgar, blunt, ill-mannered woman who causes her granddaughter much chagrin. Her habit of using double negatives and also multiple superlatives (such as "most impudentest"), which she attributes to her long exposure to the French language, is actually evidence of her affectedness. Because she is so outspoken and severe, when Captain Mirvan and Sir Clement play a cruel practical joke on her the reader does not sympathize with her plight. Madame Duval's nephew **Mr. Branghton,** a shopkeeper and boardinghouse operator, and his family are no more flatteringly portrayed than Evelina's grandmother. They are vulgar, quarrelsome, and unselfconsciously aggressive in their pursuit of social status. **Tom Branghton** uses his connection with Evelina to try to gain favor with Lord Orville, while his sisters **Biddy** and **Polly** act ridiculously proud and conceited. The Branghton's attendance at the opera provides Burney with an opportunity not only to describe that setting in detail but to demonstrate, through realistic dialect and slang, the Branghton's ignorance and tactlessness. Their friend **Mr. Smith** is a little more refined but also boorish; he is the middle-class counterpart to the Evelina's aristocratic suitor Sir Clement. His verbose and pretentious proposal to Evelina is one of the novel's funniest scenes. Samuel Johnson felt that Mr. Smith was a fine comic character: "such a varnish of low politeness! such a struggle to appear a gentleman! Madam, there is no such character better drawn anywhere!"

The Mirvan family provides Evelina with a link to London. **Captain Mirvan** is a seafaring man in the tradition of Tobias Smollett's famous nautical character, Commodore Hawser Trunnion—he speaks in a salty sea lingo even though he is living a landlocked life. Captain Mirvan is coarse, surly, and mean and appreciates a good laugh at someone else's expense, but he is basically honest and good-hearted. He serves as a foil to Madame Duval: his scorn for everything not British and her contempt for the English make for continual squabbling. **Mrs. Mirvan,** by contrast, is well-mannered and amiable, and **Maria Mirvan,** Evelina's closest female confidante, serves a practical role as a letter recipient. **Lady Howard,** Mrs. Mirvan's mother, is significant primarily for her success in convincing Villars to allow Evelina to go to London. Evelina's neighbor **Mrs. Selwyn** is also instrumental, for she takes Evelina to Bristol and also determines to help her establish her connection to Sir John. Mrs. Selwyn is a domineering, outspoken woman with a sharp tongue; Evelina comments on her "want of gentleness." Several critics have seen this character as an embodiment of the unattractiveness of women who adopt masculine qualities such as the aggressiveness Mrs. Selwyn possesses in abundance.

The young, indolent Scottish poet **Mr. Macartney** plays a practical role in the plot by putting a conventional stumbling block in Evelina and Lord Orville's path to love. In his melancholy manner and suicidal tendencies, Macartney fits the romantic stereotype of the poet. That he is viewed as Evelina's suitor—at least by Lord Orville—when in fact he is her brother adds a hint of incest to the story that echoes the incestuous circumstances in Henry Fielding's 1749 novel *Tom Jones.* The girl he eventually marries, **Polly Green,** who has been raised as **Miss Belmont,** is not portrayed in much detail. The other characters treat her kindly after the truth is revealed, because she had no conscious part in the deception. **Sir John Belmont,** who was also unaware of the deception, initially rejected Evelina's claim because he thought Polly Green was his daughter. Although apparently an unsavory and selfish person in his youth, he seems to have reformed and he repentantly opens his arms to Evelina in a weepy scene that modern readers tend to find overly sentimental.

Further Reading

Adelstein, Michael E. *Fanny Burney.* New York: Twayne Publishers, 1968.

Agress, Lynne. "Wives and Servants: Proper Conduct for One's Proper Place." In *The Feminine Irony: Women on Women in Early-Nineteenth-Century English Literature,* pp. 114-45. Rutherford, N.J.: Fairleigh Dickinson University Press, 1978.

Bloom, Lillian D., and Edward A. Bloom. "Fanny Burney's Novels: The Retreat from Wonder." *Novel: A Forum on Fiction* 12, No. 3 (Spring 1979): 215-35.

Dictionary of Literary Biography, Vol. 39. Detroit: Gale.

Hemlow, Joyce. *The History of Fanny Burney.* Oxford: Clarendon Press, 1958.

Howells, W. D. "Frances Burney's 'Evelina.'" In *Heroines of Fiction,* Vol. 1, pp. 13-23. New York: Harper, 1901.

Johnson, Samuel. Letter to Fanny Burney. In *Diary and Letters of Madame D'Arblay,* Vol. 1, edited by Charlotte Barrett and Austin Dobson, p. 72. London: Macmillan, 1904.

Nineteenth Century Literature Criticism, Vol. 12. Detroit: Gale.

Spacks, Patricia Meyer. "Dynamics of Fear: Fanny Burney." In *Imagining a Self: Autobiography and Novel in Eighteenth-Century England,* pp. 158-92. Cambridge, Mass.: Harvard University Press, 1976.

Samuel Butler

1835-1902

English novelist, essayist, biographer, and poet.

Erewhon; or, Over the Range (novel, 1872)

Plot: A young Englishman named Higgs, who works as a sheep farmer in an unspecified British colony, travels into a forbidden region located beyond a treacherous mountain range; he is accompanied by his native guide Chowbok. Higgs finds a pass through the mountains and, after the frightened departure of Chowbok, finally reaches a wide plain upon which he sees a group of statues that emit weird sounds as the wind blows around them. Higgs is discovered by some inhabitants of the area (all of whom are exceptionally attractive), who take him to a town. There he is given a thorough medical examination, and his watch is taken from him; later he learns that such devices are in this country—called Erewhon—found only in museums. Higgs is put in jail, where he learns about the language and customs of Erewhon from the jailer's comely daughter, Yram. One custom is that of treating illness as a crime, while crime is considered an illness: sick people are punished while criminals are given medical treatment. Higgs learns that he will have to appear before Erewhon's king and queen, and that he will stay with a man named Nosnibor, who is recovering from having embezzled money from a widow (the widow, however, will be punished for having allowed the crime to happen). While living with Nosnibor, Higgs often visits the Erewhonian court and becomes a popular figure because of his rare blond hair and good health. The people share their history with Higgs, informing him, for instance, that they became vegetarians many years ago, when a prophet decreed that it was wrong to eat meat. Then a later prophet proved that it was no less wrong to eat vegetables, and as a result the Erewhonians nearly starved. In addition, all machines were banned in Erewhon because a scientist asserted that they could eventually overrun the population. The economy of Erewhon is based on a system of Musical Banks in which coins are exchanged for music (a monetary system is used only for trade and is not as respected as the Musical Banks). The official religion involves the worship of idols representing such qualities as love, fear, and wisdom, while the religion that is actually practiced revolves around a goddess called Ydgrun who demands social conformity from her followers.

Higgs falls in love with Nosnibor's beautiful daughter, Arowhena, but his host is angry because Erewhon custom decrees that the older daughter, Zulora, be married first. As a result of their argument, Higgs moves out of Nosnibor's house but continues to see Arowhena often. He is given a tour of the country's University of Unreason by a new friend, Thims. The university teaches only hypothetical and unpractical subjects, focusing on obsolete languages (just as the nineteenth-century English educational system emphasized Latin and Greek). Higgs is also told that a man's worth in Erewhon is determined by the amount of money he possesses. Suspicion against Higgs is beginning to grow because of his relationship with Arowhena and his having possessed a watch, so he decides it is time to leave Erewhon. He is permitted to construct a balloon which he says will allow him to speak with the god of the air. Having hidden Arowhena aboard the balloon, Higgs floats away from Erewhon and over the mountain range, finally landing in the ocean. The couple is picked up by a Spanish ship and returned to England, where they marry and settle. Higgs is surprised when he sees his native guide Chowbok in England, posing as a missionary named Reverend William Habbakuk. Higgs still hopes to return to Erewhon and is telling his story in order to raise financial support for his journey.

Characters: Frequently compared to Jonathan Swift's *Gulliver's Travels* (1726), *Erewhon* satirizes Victorian England through the reversed morality and inverted values of Erewhon (an anagram for "nowhere"). The novel's characters are primarily used to illustrate Butler's rebellious attitude and ideas, which include the possibility of humanity's enslavement by mechanization, the commercialization of religion, and the opposing concepts of Darwinism (which suggests that behavior is determined by heredity and environment) and free will.

The novel's narrator is the young, adventurous Englishman **Higgs** (though his name is not actually revealed until the book's sequel, *Erewhon Revisited*). His limited perspective and true nature are gradually revealed through his actions and observations. Although Higgs does not always seem to understand the broader implications of the new world he discovers, he is not necessarily the naive narrator usually found in satirical works. Instead, he is sharp and cunning and takes advantage of his hosts' benevolence for as long as it lasts, managing to escape just when it seems at an end. He appears to be a pious follower of the Christian religion, but Butler's perception of the hypocrisy beneath much of Christianity is made evident through Higgs's contradictory behavior. His primary motivation is greed—he initially ventures into Erewhon in search of riches, and he refuses to disclose its location after his return to prevent other speculators from getting back there before he does. He even suggests that the Erewhonians could be enslaved and converted to Christianity, thus justifying an inhumane but profitable practice by claiming to have the victims' salvation at heart. It is also revealed in the novel's sequel that Higgs impregnated the attractive jailer's daughter, Yram, during the period when she was educating him about Erewhon (in *Erewhon Revisited,* he meets the son she bore). Through this profoundly conventional, smug, and commercially minded character, Butler reveals his opinion of many of his society's most deeply embedded ideals.

The setting for *Erewhon* is thought to be modeled after New Zealand, where Butler spent several years as a sheep farmer after his graduation from Cambridge. Higgs's native guide **Chowbok** (whose real name is **Kahabuka**) might be interpreted as a member of the Maori tribe, New Zealand's indigenous people. Chowbok, an older man with a fondness for liquor, issues an ominous warning of what Higgs will find if he ventures "over the range," imitating the noise that Higgs later hears coming from the statues at the entrance to Erewhon (the mouths of the statues are carved with holes to make a strange sound when the wind passes through). Chowbok proves an unreliable guide, fleeing before Higgs reaches his destination. His later appearance as a pillar of religion, the **Reverend William Habbakuk,** is presented as ironic, and yet Higgs seems to accept it and even takes credit for his former guide's conversion to Christianity.

Residents of Erewhon encountered by Higgs include **Senoj Nosnibor** (an anagram for Jones Robinson), the embezzler who is recovering from his crime and who instructs Higgs about Erewhonian customs; and his daughter **Arowhena,** the lovely girl with whom Higgs falls in love and whom he brings back to England and marries—it is suggested that she joins the Anglican church after their marriage but still retains some of her old beliefs. **Zulora** is Nosnibor's eldest daughter; she has a desire as well as, according to Erewhonian custom, a right to marry before her younger sister. The jailer's daughter **Yram** (Mary) teaches Higgs about her country's language and traditions; the novel's sequel revealed that she gave birth to Higgs's son.

Higgs's friend **Thims** (Smith), who works as a cashier at one of the Musical Banks, guides him through the University of Unreason, where students are taught nothing that will ever be of any practical use. Instead they study only theoretical sciences and obsolete languages, satirizing the English educational system, which Butler felt did its students a disservice by ignoring their practical needs. At the university Higgs also reads the *Book of the Machine,* a treatise suggesting that machines represent a further stage in evolutionary development and could become intelligent enough to conquer humanity. This section is often cited as evidence of Butler's strong interest in Darwin's evolutionary theory; it asks, among other things, whether machines are organic or organisms machines.

Other significant characters in *Erewhon* include **the Straighteners,** who are employed to treat those suffering from various crimes (like the man who embezzled a large sum of money from a widow). Often compared to the psychiatrists of the twentieth century—and considered a brilliant anticipation of the modern concept that criminal behavior is rooted in environmental and psychological factors—the Straighteners treat criminals through confession and discussion of their deeds as well as chastisement. **Ydgrun** is the goddess whom the Erewhonians unofficially worship. Her name is an anagram of Grundy, referring to Mrs. Grundy, the fictional character who first appeared in English playwright Tom Morton's play "Speed the Plough" (1800) and who has since come to represent the community standards with which the majority of people feel obliged to comply. The Ydgrun faith is based on social conformity and the worship of public opinion rather than individually achieved ideals, thus revealing Butler's scorn for the enforced conformity of organized religion.

The Way of All Flesh (novel, 1903)

Plot: Though primarily focused on Ernest Pontifex, the story begins several generations earlier with his great-grandfather John Pontifex, a good-natured carpenter who likes art and music. He and his wife have a son, George, who eventually becomes wealthy as a publisher of religious books. George decides that his second son, Theobald, should become a clergyman and threatens to disinherit him when the boy protests. So Theobald does become a minister, and marries a young girl named Christina Allaby, who has won the privilege in a card game with her two equally eligible sisters. They settle in the town of Battersby and have three children—Ernest, Joseph, and Charlotte—whom they raise with strict discipline and frequent beatings. After an unhappy childhood, the weak and gloomy Ernest is sent to Roughborough School, presided over by its rigid, tyrannical headmaster, Dr. Skinner. Ernest's misery during this period is somewhat relieved by his kind aunt, Alethea, who moves to Roughborough so that she can determine (unknown to her nephew) if she should leave her considerable wealth to Ernest when she dies. She nurtures Ernest's creativity, encouraging him to take carpentry lessons so that he can build an organ. When Alethea dies, she leaves her money in the care of her friend Edward Overton, with the understanding that Ernest should receive his inheritance on his twenty-eighth birthday.

Ernest attends Cambridge to prepare for the ministry and moves to London after his ordination. He naively allows his friend and fellow clergyman Nicholas Pryor access to an inheritance he had received from his grandfather, but instead of investing the money Pryor flees with it. Ernest feels ill-suited for a life in the ministry. He solicits the favors of a woman he mistakes for a prostitute, and is arrested and sentenced to a six-month prison term. When released, Ernest breaks his ties with his family and turns to Overton for guidance and advice. While walking along a city street, Ernest chances upon the Pontifex's former maid, Ellen, who had been fired when she became pregnant. The sympathetic Ernest decided to marry her and, with Overton's help (despite his disapproval of the match), they establish a second-hand clothing and book shop. Although his wife's alcoholism and obnoxious behavior soon make the marriage unbearable for Ernest, two children are born and he feels obligated to stay with Ellen. But then Ernest happens to meet John, the Pontifex's former coachman, who admits that he is the father of Ellen's first, illegitimate child. John reveals that the two had actually married after Ellen's dismissal from the Pontifex household. Ernest is now free to leave Ellen; he arranges for her to receive a weekly allowance, and sends his children to live in the country with a happy, loving family because he fears his father's influence if he raises them himself. Ernest becomes a writer of philosophical articles and, on his twenty-eighth birthday, receives the generous legacy from Alethea that allows him to travel through Europe for a year before returning to England to continue his writing career. After his death, Ernest's story is told by Overton, who is well acquainted with Ernest and the Pontifex family history.

Characters: Butler's autobiographical novel depicts the oppressiveness, cruelty, and hypocrisy Butler felt were regularly practiced in Victorian families. Considered an indictment of social and religious conventions of the time, the novel reveals Butler's belief in the Darwinian concept that personality is shaped by heredity and environment. Yet Butler rejects the inevitability implicit in the evolutionary theory by suggesting that his central character has transcended the limits of his background to create for himself a healthy and freely chosen way of life.

In his role as a weak, despairing character victimized by others and eventually rebelling against convention, **Ernest Pontifex** has been seen as a precursor of such twentieth-century antiheroes as Stephen Daedalus in James Joyce's *Portrait of the Artist as a Young Man* or Paul Morel in D.H. Lawrence's *Sons and Lovers.* Like Butler, Ernest is the son of a clergyman who receives harsh and demeaning treatment as a child; he is told that he is a bad and ungrateful boy and deserves to be beaten. Physically weak and pitifully unhappy, Ernest is unsuccessful in school and in his later career as a minister. His naivete plagues him both when he allows himself to be cheated of his inheritance and when he makes sexual advances to the wrong woman. Each stage of his development seems to confirm his isolation from others, but he does not begin to understand the reasons for his isolation until he has had the clarifying experience of imprisonment. There he finally faces the truth that his upbringing has made him what he is, and that he must now begin to reshape his life according to his own ideals. His desire to reject his family's values leads him to marry a woman from a lower social class—a mistake from which he is miraculously (and, according to some critics, implausibly) rescued. In the end, Ernest becomes a thoughtful writer who, like the author who created him, lives a quiet, bachelor existence and enjoys the music of Handel. Most critics concur that Butler's portrayal of Ernest is more successful during the first part of the book, when he is weak and pitiful, than at the end, when he becomes rather self-satisfied and priggish. Furthermore, the circumstance of Ernest's generous inheritance from Alethea, which allows him to lead a worry-free life, has been seen as weakening the novel's message of self-regeneration. While some scholars also fault Ernest for abandoning his two children to be raised by strangers, others consider it a brave and practical act that acknowledges the influence of heredity and proves Ernest's determination to spare his own children the kind of upbringing he himself suffered.

Ernest's great-grandfather, old **John Pontifex,** is an unassuming and hardworking carpenter who loves music and art. He has a variety of talents but is unselfconscious and modest, and he treats his son and grandson gently. **Mrs. Pontifex,** however, is a domineering, humorless, ambitious woman who, some critics feel, introduced into the Pontifex family the unpleasant traits that would dominate the next few generations. Their son **George Pontifex** earns his fortune by publishing religious books—an irony in view of his decidedly unchristian behavior. He is an egotistical bully who browbeats his children into doing his bidding, forcing his son Theobald to become a clergyman against his inclination and thus contributing to his son's warped personality and his grandson's later unhappiness. Whereas his artisan father took his place in an essentially rural community, George represents the burgeoning commercialism and urbanism of English society as well as the typically Victorian notion that children ultimately benefit from severe punishment.

Theobald Pontifex is thought to be a merciless portrait of Butler's father, who was a well-respected clergyman and the patriarch of a typical Victorian family. Although Theobald is depicted as mean, conceited, vindictive, and brutal—he whips his little boy for saying "tum" instead of "come," for instance—Butler is careful to include information about his background that helps to illuminate his behavior as an adult. Browbeaten by his father into becoming a clergyman against his will, he is full of suppressed anger, which he takes out on his own children. He perpetuates the pattern of tyranny by insisting that Ernest become a minister. Respected by the outside world for his piety and position, Theobald can interpret Ernest's arrest and imprisonment as nothing less than a catastrophe, while in fact the experience has a liberating effect on his son. Theobald will end as a lonely old man, and the fact that the reader can pity him for this despite his savagery and insensitivity toward his children testifies to Butler's skill in creating a rounded character.

Like her husband, **Christina Pontifex** is portrayed as a victim of circumstances. The fact that she "wins" her husband in a card game is both comic and tragic, for this marriage based on a combination of chance and necessity will not bring real happiness to either partner despite the image of domestic harmony that they will present to the world. Submissive and pious, faithfully mirroring Theobald's concerns and ideals, Christina nourishes herself on daydreams. Although she seems to mean well and is kinder than her husband, Christina too can be cruel to her children, as when she passes along to Theobald a secret with which Ernest has entrusted her and for which he will be severely punished. Many critics have praised Butler for his thoughtful portrait of Christina, whose character English novelist Virginia Woolf called "rich and solid, because all the clergyman's wives whom Butler had ever known were put into her stew."

Edward Overton is the Pontifex family friend who narrates *The Way of All Flesh*. Although he is of the same generation as Theobald, he is a different kind of man altogether and one who proves much more desirable as a father figure for Ernest. He is employed as a seasoned, skeptical, and genteel mouthpiece for many of Butler's views, and like the author he lives an orderly bachelor's life. Overton agrees with Ernest's eventual conclusion that the traditional family unit is outdated and destructive, and it is implied that in this union of two like minds a new kind of family has been formed. Although Overton is a wealthy man, he does not belong to an elevated social class—in fact he is classless, a position that Ernest too comes to inhabit. Some critics have described as implausible the idea that, under Overton's supervision and wise investments, Ernest's fortune is five times larger by the time he inherits it. Overton's theorizing about the Pontifex family and compassion for all of its members has been seen as either too complacent or as admirable and condoned by Butler.

Ernest's aunt, **Alethea Pontifex,** provides evidence, along with old John Pontifex, that the family is not entirely comprised of unpleasant and warped personalities. She is an understanding and broad-minded person who treats her nephew with kindness and encourages him to pursue his own interests rather than what his father has decreed he should do. As generous and sympathetic as Theobald and Christina are mean and insensitive, Alethea is sincerely interested in Ernest, perceives his good qualities, and bequeaths her fortune to him. Some scholars believe that the character of Alethea was modeled after Eliza Mary Ann Savage, a sympathetic friend who encouraged and helped Butler through many years of his career.

The other characters in *The Way of the Flesh* are less developed. **Ellen** is the alcoholic former maid whom Ernest marries; she represents the lower class that Ernest feels compelled to enter. The fact that Ellen was already married to the Pontifex's former coachman, **John,** giving Ernest an easy way out of their union, has been described as too convenient to be believable. The shifty minister, **Nicholas Pryor,** who cheats Ernest out of the money he inherits from his grandfather, comprises another unflattering portrait of the clergy. Ernest's siblings, **Joey** and **Charlotte Pontifex,** obviously take after their parents. Joey seems likely to follow in his father's footsteps as a cold-hearted clergyman, and Charlotte (said to be based on Butler's sisters, Harriet and May) is an unattractive and mean-spirited spinster. **Dr. Skinner,** the tyrannical headmaster of the aptly named Roughborough School, is a somewhat comical character in his exaggeratedly superior manner.

Further Reading

Dupee, F. W. "Butler's Way." *New York Review of Books* 9, No. 3 (24 August 1967): 26-31.

Holt, Lee E. *Samuel Butler,* rev. ed. Boston: Twayne, 1989.

Howard, Daniel F. Introduction to *Ernest Pontifex; or, The Way of All Flesh,* by Samuel Butler, edited by Daniel F. Howard, pp. v-xxi. 1964. Reprint. London: Methuen, 1965.

Jedrzejewski, Jan. "Samuel Butler's Treatment of Christianity in 'Erewhon' and 'Erewhon Revisited.'" *English Literature in Transition: 1880-1920* 31, No. 4 (1988): 415-36.

Pritchett, V. S. "A Victorian Son." In *The Living Novel,* pp. 109-15. Reynal & Hitchcock, 1947.

Twentieth Century Literary Criticism, Vols. 1, 33. Detroit: Gale.

Woolf, Virginia. "The Way of All Flesh." *Times Literary Supplement* No. 910 (26 June 1919): 347.

Fernán Caballero
1796-1877
Spanish novelist, novella, short story, and sketch writer, and essayist.

The Sea Gull (*La gaviota;* novel, 1849)

Plot: The novel begins in 1836 aboard an English ship bound for Spain. German physician Fritz Stein meets a Spanish aristocrat, the Duke of Almansa, to whom he explains that he plans to serve as a medical officer with the Spanish army; he hopes to lessen the suffering of the wounded soldiers. Two years later, Stein has become disillusioned and physically exhausted by his war experiences. He was discharged from the army for treating an enemy soldier, and he has now traveled into the countryside. After climbing to the top of a hill from which he has a spectacular view of the surrounding landscape, Stein faints and is rescued by several local residents, including the good-hearted Brother Gabriel and Aunt Maria, a kind peasant woman. Stein's new friends nurse him back to health, and when he has recovered he begins to explore the village of Villamar. His depression is eased by the beautiful scenery around him and by the people he meets, whose colorful customs interest him. As a result, Stein feels no inclination to leave. In order to repay his hosts for their kindness, he treats a consumptive schoolgirl named Marisalada, the daughter of fisherman Pedro Santaló. During the course of the next three years, Stein falls in love with Marisalada, who soon recovers from her illness and to whom he gives music lessons. Though somewhat unruly and arrogant in her behavior, the girl is a talented singer. Aunt Maria encourages Stein to court Marisalada, and, despite his misgivings about their age difference (he is now twenty-nine while she is only sixteen), proposes marriage. Marisalada accepts, though without much enthusiasm or apparent affection for Stein.

The next three years are happy ones for Stein, who is devoted to his young wife. The Duke of Almansa is injured when he falls from a horse while passing near the village; he is so grateful for Stein's expert treatment of his wounds that he offers to take the physician and his talented wife to Seville, where her gifts will be appreciated and where Stein may establish a more lucrative medical practice. Marisalada is ecstatic at the prospect of moving to the city, but Stein is reluctant and sad to leave Villamar.

After the Steins have settled in their new home in Seville, the Duke takes the couple to a bullfight. Stein is repulsed by the brutality of this traditional Spanish spectacle, and he leaves to view some of the landmarks of Seville. Marisalada, however, is enthralled with the bullfight and particularly with a handsome and dashing young toreador named Pepe Vera. The Steins attend a series of parties in which they mingle with the city's aristocracy and participate in numerous discussions. The action then shifts to Madrid, where Marisalada pursues her successful singing career and also enters into an adulterous affair with Vera. She earns a bad reputation because of her rudeness to the devoted Duke and her discourteous behavior in the homes of her aristocratic friends. Meanwhile, Aunt Maria's grandson Momo has been sent to Madrid to inform Marisalada that her father is dying. After a series of misadventures in the city due to his lack of sophistication, Momo sees Marisalada performing on stage. Her character is killed, and Momo assumes that Marisalada herself is now dead and reports this development to the waiting residents of Villamar. Pedro Santaló dies without seeing his daughter.

Vera treats the lovesick Marisalada cruelly and her health begins to decline due to a rigorous life of singing engagements and parties. Stein finally learns of Marisalada's infidelity and plans to leave her; the Duke also realizes that his devotion to the young singer has caused him to neglect his own wife, and he takes his family away from the city. Vera insists that the ailing Marisalada attend his bullfight, and she does so in order to prevent his former lover from taking her place. Vera is fatally gored by a bull, and Marisalada now finds herself alone and destitute. She is assisted, however, by a kind nun whom she had previously berated. Six months later, those present at a gathering at the Countess of Algar's house discuss Marisalada, agreeing that she brought on her own downfall through her arrogance and thoughtless behavior. One of the guests reports that Stein has died of yellow fever in Cuba while treating other sufferers of that disease; a letter is read aloud in which Stein offers Marisalada his forgiveness. The novel's final chapter, set in 1848, reveals that Marisalada has returned in disgrace to Villamar and married her old suitor Ramón Peréz, the son of the local barber. Her voice gone, her strength dissipated by a brood of children and a boorish husband, she clings to her memories of former glory and is continually taunted by Momo, who delights in reminding her of her failure.

Characters: Caballero is considered an important contributor to the development of realism in Spanish literature, which had, prior to the mid-nineteenth century, been dominated by romanticism. A strong believer in traditional, conservative Spanish values—particularly the importance of the Catholic faith—she advocated the realistic depiction of Spain's people and customs. Thus she is seen as a major proponent of the *costumbriso* novel, which called for a faithful rendering of Spanish personalities, scenery, and folklore. Despite the occasional intrusions of Caballero's moralistic asides on religion, *The Sea Gull* serves as a significant example of the increasingly realistic nineteenth-century Spanish novel.

Marisalada is given the nickname "the sea gull" by Momo, Aunt Maria's grandson, in reference to her considerable singing ability. She is the daughter of a poor fisherman who adores her and over-indulges her; thus, she grows into a willful and haughty woman.

Marisalada's personality features a combination of opposing elements: she is both passionate and sullen, both primal—particularly in her love for the arrogant bullfighter, Vera—and sophisticated—entering into a glamorous aristocratic life and conducting a singing career. While she resigns herself to marriage with Stein (presumably in order to escape her father's grasp and because others think she should), she is most eager to leave Villamar to seek a more glamorous existence. Marisalada subsequently reveals the passionate, irrational, and sexual side of her nature when she falls in love with Vera, whose *machismo* apparently appeals to her more than Stein's decency. The interesting question of why the conservative Caballero was willing to broach the topic of adultery in her novel is at least partially answered by the fact that both adulterers are punished—Vera with death and Marisalada with societal disgrace and marriage to a boor. The novel is notably realistic in its portrayal of Marisalada's dismal later life rather than of the dramatic death that might have been her fate in a romantic novel. The steep price she pays for her disdain and cruelty includes losing not only her husband and lover but also her voice, which had brought her so much satisfaction. Further, Momo taunts Marisalada mercilessly by assuring her that she is still a sea gull and always will be one; but now this appellation acquires its traditional Spanish, degrading meaning of a loud, vulgar woman. Most critics have found Marisalada an unsympathetic character, although some have noted that she exhibits an admirable independence and vitality. It is generally agreed that Caballero condemns Marisalada's arrogance and misbehavior.

The highly sympathetic character of **Fritz Stein** may have been modeled after Caballero's father, a German with a deep appreciation of Spanish folklore and customs who married a Spanish woman. As the novel opens, Stein is a somewhat melancholy twenty-four-year-old physician with a strong humanitarian instinct. Although he is bitter and disillusioned after his experience in the war, Stein finds himself rejuvenated through his exposure to the landscape and people of the Spanish countryside. Ironically, he eventually grows even more appreciative of this colorful and unspoiled environment than his Spanish wife. Although in general Caballero feared the influence of liberal, progressive Europeans on Spain's traditional ways, Stein is portrayed as a foreigner with the unique ability to appreciate the Spanish for their true worth and with no desire to modernize them. In his love of music and nature, his tendency toward melancholy and sentiment (tears come easily to his eyes), and his idealism, Stein has been identified as a representative of the German strain of nineteenth-century romanticism. Some scholars describe Stein as an unconvincingly perfect character who always behaves admirably. Even after his devotion to Marisalada has been exposed as misguided, for instance, his commitment to serving humanity remains strong; he is aiding those stricken with yellow fever when he himself contracts the disease and dies.

Caballero created two sets of minor characters to illustrate the two worlds, rural and urban, depicted in *The Sea Gull*. It is generally thought that the residents of Villamar are more colorfully and skillfully portrayed than those of Seville; even though Caballero had personal experience of both realms of Spanish life, she presented the countryside as the center of Spain's most valuable traditions. The good and generous **Brother Gabriel**, for instance, is a positive representative of the Catholic religion, which Caballero considered a mainstay of Spanish civilization. Because he has been the subject of anti-clericalism and because his monastery was increasingly neglected and finally abandoned, Brother Gabriel illustrates the movement away from Catholicism that the author regretted. **Don Modesto Guerrero,** the commander of Fort St. Christopher, embodies another important aspect of Spain's history and pride—its military might. The fact that the noble and brave Guerrero is dead by the end of the novel suggests that he too has become an anachronism. **Aunt Maria** is a traditional Spanish peasant woman: warm, generous, capable, and maternal. Another important aspect of her character is her knowledge of folklore; she helps to pass along this important oral tradition to future generations. Other Villamarians include **Ramón Peréz,** the barber's son and local Don Juan with whom Marisalada flirts as a young girl and whom she eventually marries, and **Pedro Santaló,** Marisalada's indulgent and neglected father, whose death scene has been cited as a melodramatic moment in an otherwise realistic novel.

One inhabitant who plays a somewhat more prominent role than the others is Aunt Maria's grandson, **Momo.** Ugly, belligerent, and ill-mannered, Momo is nevertheless used as the mouthpiece for Caballero's moralistic views when he condemns Marisalada for her misdeeds. Momo also provides some comic touches, such as when he travels to Seville and displays his ignorance of city ways, later reporting incorrectly that Marisalada has been killed. Because of his unpleasant nature and coarse humor, Momo provides an antidote to Stein's sentimentality, and it has been noted that he is the only one of the rural characters who is not ideally portrayed.

Although the urban characters in *The Sea Gull* are considered less interesting than their village counterparts, they do provide a contrast that helps to illuminate Caballero's ideas. The **Duke of Almansa** is an exception to the generally unflattering portrayals of the aristocratic characters. A warm and generous man who becomes utterly devoted to Marisalada and tries to nurture her talent, he embodies all the best qualities of the Spanish character. The author may have drawn on her own experience as a member of the Spanish aristocracy (while she was married to the Marqués de Arco-Hermoso) in creating the **Countess of Algar,** the hostess of many sophisticated gatherings in Seville. Although the conversation at these parties tends toward a polished frivolity that some reviewers have found tedious, such topics as the foreign perception of Spain, the rift between liberalism and conservatism in Spanish politics, and the direction which should be taken in Spanish literature are discussed, allowing Caballero to present her own views. One lively participant in these discussions is **Rafael,** who helps to articulate the new trend toward realism in the fiction of Spain. Other aristocratic characters include **General Santa Maria,** a representative of Spanish chauvinism, and the snobbish **Eloisa.**

In Seville and later in Madrid, Marisalada also encounters the bullfighter **Pepe Vera,** who becomes her lover. Though handsome, manly, and presumably brave, Vera is at heart a cruel man whose fate seems justified, particularly in view of the fact that Caballero abhorred the tradition of the bullfight and wished to reveal its brutality and destructiveness. **Lucia del Santo** is Vera's bitter former lover; she provokes Marisalada's jealousy and also informs Stein that his wife has been unfaithful.

Further Reading

"A Spanish and a Danish Novel." *Fraser's Magazine* LXXVI, No. CCCCLII (August 1867): 190-203.

Klibbe, Lawrence H. *Fernán Caballero.* New York: Twayne, 1973.

Nineteenth Century Literature Criticism, Vol. 10. Detroit: Gale.

Qualia, Charles B. "'La Gaviota' One Hundred Years After." *Hispania* XXXIV, No. 1 (February 1951): 63-7.

Walton, L.B. "A Brief Survey of Spanish Fiction prior to the Appearance of 'La fontana de oro.'" In *Perez Galdos and the Spanish Novel of the Nineteenth Century,* pp. 1-27. London: J.M. Dent, 1927.

Lewis Carroll
1832-1898

English novelist, satirist, poet, and essayist.

Alice's Adventures in Wonderland (novel, 1865)

Plot: The story takes place in England during the latter half of the nineteenth century. While reading outdoors with her sister, seven-year-old Alice sees a White Rabbit hurry by, muttering about being late. She follows him into a hole, at the bottom of which he disappears down a corridor. Alice is faced with several doors. She drinks from a bottle and grows small enough to enter a tiny garden she has seen through one door, but now she is too small to reach the key. Eating a piece of cake, Alice grows huge and begins to cry. The White Rabbit reappears, exclaiming that the Duchess will be angry if he keeps her waiting. When Alice picks up the fan and gloves that the rabbit has dropped, she becomes small again and falls into a pool made of her own tears. There she meets a mouse, whom she unintentionally frightens with a story about her cat, Dinah. Soon many creatures are around Alice in the pool, including the Dodo, who suggests a Caucus Race so that all of the animals may run themselves dry. When Alice mentions her cat again, she is left alone.

After entering the White Rabbit's house in order to retrieve for him another fan and set of gloves, Alice drinks from a bottle again and grows so large that she must put her leg up the chimney and arm out the window. After eating more cake she shrinks to normal size and runs into the woods. There she meets a blue caterpillar resting on a large mushroom and smoking a hookah (a water pipe); he speaks rudely to Alice and makes her recite the poem "You Are Old, Father William." Next Alice comes to the Duchess's house, where a footman who looks like a fish is presenting to a footman who looks like a frog an invitation for the Duchess to play croquet with the Queen. Alice finds a chaotic scene inside: the Cook is stirring an extremely peppery soup, there is pepper in the air, and everyone is sneezing except the Cook and the grinning Cheshire Cat who sits on the hearth. Alice takes the Duchess's wailing baby outside, but it turns into a pig and trots away. After demonstrating his amazing ability to appear and disappear at will, the Cheshire Cat suggests that Alice visit the March Hare and Mad Hatter. He finally fades away from view, though his grin stays visible longer than the rest of him. Alice attends a strange, disorderly Mad Tea Party, at which she meets the March Hare, the Mad Hatter, and the Dormouse. The other guests confuse her with their odd, insulting conversation and behavior.

Leaving the party, Alice enters a garden in which three gardeners are trying to paint all of the white roses red before the Queen of Hearts arrives and discovers the mistake they made when planting the flowers. The gardeners are caught by the queen and sentenced to have their heads chopped off, but Alice rescues them by hiding them in a large flower pot. The croquet match soon begins, with flamingoes serving as mallets and hedgehogs as balls; Alice finds the game ruleless and frustrating. Then the queen takes Alice to the seaside to meet the Gryphon, who leads her to the Mock Turtle. With the Gryphon chiming in occasionally, the Mock Turtle tells Alice his life story and sings a song. The news arrives that a trial is taking place because a thief has stolen some tarts. The trial is presided over by the King and Queen of Hearts and attended by all of the creatures Alice has met in Wonderland. Alice is ordered to serve as a witness; her claim that she knows nothing about the crime enrages the queen, who orders that Alice's head be chopped off. As all of the trial participants rush toward Alice, she yells that they are nothing but a pack of cards. She finds herself back with her sister, who is brushing leaves away from her face.

Characters: Carroll's highly imaginative tale of Alice's journey through Wonderland was intended to entertain children, and it has done so admirably over the years while also inspiring an abundance of critical interpretations. Some scholars see *Alice* as pure and delightful nonsense, but others extract from it a wide variety of thematic meanings and concerns, including the ambiguities of language and communication, the anxiety caused by growing up and impending sexuality, the eternal conflict between children and adults, and the absurdities of Victorian morality. Thus the characters who inhabit Wonderland may be appreciated for their uniqueness or examined for deeper significance.

Lewis Carroll (the pen name of Oxford University mathematics professor Charles Dodgson) is said to have written the first of his two Alice books at the urging of young Alice Liddell (the daughter of an Oxford dean), with whom he had become friends and for whom—during a summer boat excursion—he had made up a fantastic story of a little girl in Wonderland. One of the most famous and memorable children in literature, **Alice** is seven years old when the story takes place. She is an intelligent, sensible, and curious girl who reacts with admirable patience and calmness to the many strange events and people she encounters. Nevertheless, Alice differs from other heroines of Victorian children's literature because she is neither completely angelic nor utterly naughty. While generally open to new experiences and courteous to others, she can also be priggish or unpleasantly aggressive. The fact that Alice does not learn anything or alter her behavior as a result of her adventures indicates the book's lack of didactic intention—also unusual during the period in which it was written. Alice is often said to embody the innocence and fresh outlook of childhood, while the characters she meets caricature adults with their tyrannical, pretentious, and often wildly illogical actions and conversation. In the end Alice exposes her new acquaintances for what they are—a pack of cards—and is instantly transported back to her own world. This circumstance may be interpreted as a rejection of the chaos that dominates Wonderland and by extension the adult world, or as an inevitable step in Alice's growing up—she must leave the fanciful realm of childhood for bland, stodgy maturity. Many critics have noted in *Alice* indications that Carroll, in his fondness for little girls and nostalgia toward childhood, connected the approach of adulthood—and in particular of sexuality—with death. Regardless of the many possible interpretations of Alice's character, generations of readers have found her a charming and rational guide through Wonderland.

The **White Rabbit** is the first character Alice encounters in Wonderland—in fact, he precipitates her arrival there by enticing her to follow him into the rabbit hole. He is a dapper creature who wears a waistcoat and frequently consults his pocket watch; he is very anxious and expresses worry over the possibility of being late. The White Rabbit reveals his aristocratic notions both in his ordering Alice about when he mistakes her for his servant and in the way he treats the King and Queen of Hearts. He appears by their side at the croquet game, smiling at everything they say and generally fawning on them. Critics have characterized the White Rabbit as a parody of an adult who is simultaneously pretentious and obsequious.

While the shrunken Alice is swimming in the pool of her own tears that she wept while she was huge, she meets several creatures. The most significant of these are the **Mouse**, whose tale takes the shape of his own tail (an example of emblematic verse, which typographically imitates the shape of its subject); and the **Dodo**, who suggests the Caucus Race as a way for the animals to dry themselves. The Dodo is generally considered a gentle parody of Carroll himself because of his instructive tone: "I'm older than you, and must know better." He tells Alice that the best way to explain a Caucus Race is just to do it; thus he provides an example of the inadequacy of language to explain everything. The pool-of-tears scene, in which a variety of animals rises dripping from the pool, is also significant for its suggestion of Darwinian theory; the Dodo, appropriately, is an extinct animal.

After her experience in the White Rabbit's House—in which poor **Bill, the Lizard** is chosen to go down the chimney to force Alice out and is rewarded with a kick that sends him up into the air again—Alice meets the blue **Caterpillar.** His first question is "Who are YOU?" which brings up the difficulty of identity that is a dominant theme throughout the book. The caterpillar rudely pesters Alice with questions and scorns her answers; he is easily offended and irritable. Some critics have seen in his hookah smoking and magic mushroom (which alters Alice's size when she takes bites of it) intimations of drug use. The caterpillar insists that Alice recite the poem "You Are Old, Father William," thus introducing Carroll's brilliant parody of "The Old Man's Comforts and How He Gained Them," a didactic poem by the English poet Robert Southey (1774-1843).

Arriving at the Duchess's house, Alice sees the **Fish Footman** and the **Frog Footman,** who seem utterly oblivious to the chaotic scene going on in the house even when one of them is nearly hit by a flying plate. Inside reigns the **Duchess,** one of Carroll's most celebrated characters. She is an alarming creation (particularly as depicted by the book's original illustrator, Sir John Tenniel)—ugly, sadistic, aggressive, and ridiculously moralistic. She constantly spouts platitudes having no bearing on the matters at hand; her motto is that "Everything's got a moral, if only you can find it." The Duchess's violent manner with her baby—she blares a lullaby at him ("Speak roughly to your little boy. . .") and jostles him mercilessly—has been viewed as a grotesque parody of the image of the Madonna and Child. Alice is alarmed by the Duchess's overly friendly behavior when they meet again at the croquet game; some scholars have perceived in the Duchess's walking close to Alice and poking her chin into Alice's shoulder a sinister suggestion of sexual aggressiveness that reflects Carroll's uneasiness about sexuality.

Also part of the madcap scene in the Duchess's house are the diabolical **Cook,** who extravagantly dumps pepper into the soup and throws pots and pans at the Duchess; and the **Duchess's baby,** a squalling, squirming infant who eventually turns into a pig (that he is apparently a male baby is often noted—Carroll's dislike of boys was well known). But perhaps the most famous character Alice encounters there is the strangely smiling **Cheshire Cat.** The expression "grin like a Cheshire Cat" was commonly used during Carroll's day and is said to derive either from the inn signs of England's Cheshire county, which often featured a grinning lion, or from that region's cheeses, which were often molded in the shape of smiling cats. In any case, it is Wonderland's long-clawed, excessively toothed Cheshire Cat who confirms for Alice that "We're all mad here"—he is the only character who acknowledges that fact. Critics have interpreted the Cheshire Cat as an embodiment of existentialism (because he tells Alice that if she doesn't know where she wants to go it doesn't matter where she goes), or of the intellectual detachment of those who place themselves on a higher, more ethereal plane than others.

The Mad Tea Party is one of the most famous scenes in *Alice's Adventures in Wonderland.* Its host, the **March Hare,** collaborates with the Mad Hatter in treating Alice rudely: he offers Alice wine when in fact there is no wine, and he participates in proclaiming her stupid. "Mad as a March hare" was a common expression in Victorian England, referring to the time of year when hares mate; the Mad Hatter states that the March Hare is not as crazy now (the story takes place in the month of May) as he was back in March. In Tenniel's illustrations, the **Mad Hatter** wears a large top hat with a price tag in its brim. Hatmakers in nineteenth-century England were actually known to go mad, their insanity brought on by exposure to the mercury then used in curing felt. The Mad Hatter is blunt, outspoken (immediately informing Alice, for instance, that she needs a haircut), and utterly irrational. His madness is typified by the riddle he poses to Alice—"Why is a raven like a writing-desk?"—for which even he has no answer. Both the March Hare and the Mad Hatter demonstrate the arbitrary nature of language as they tease and confuse Alice, and the fact that their tea party is perpetual because it is always six o'clock there reinforces the general disorder of Wonderland. **The Dormouse** (a common animal in Britain, more like a squirrel than a mouse) is a sleepy creature who dozes off in the middle of his story about the three sisters who live at the bottom of a treacle (molasses) well. His behavior seems to enrage his two companions, who eventually attempt to stuff him into the teapot.

Alice encounters the imperious **Queen of Hearts,** an animated playing card, for the first time at the croquet game. In recounting his adaptation of *Alice's Adventures in Wonderland* for the stage, Carroll wrote that he saw the queen as the "embodiment of ungovernable passion—a blind and aimless fury." Indeed, the queen is exceedingly ill-tempered and irrationally cruel, ordering the execution of anybody who crosses her in even the most benign way. Her distorted viewpoint is displayed at the trial, when she proclaims, "Sentence first—verdict afterwards." The Queen's demands of "Off with his head!" are never carried out, however, because the mild-mannered, kindly **King of Hearts** pardons all of the transgressors behind her back. The King is a timid fellow dominated by his wife; he is very alarmed at the presence of the Cheshire Cat, and he serves as an uneasy judge at the trial of the **Knave** (also called Jack) **of Hearts,** the shy poet accused of stealing tarts.

Two other important characters in *Alice's Adventures in Wonderland* are the Gryphon and the Mock Turtle. The **Gryphon** is based on the mythical half-man, half-animal creature found throughout literature—though nowhere else is he portrayed quite as he is in this story. He seems to represent a tiresome adult in the unpleasant, officious way in which he orders Alice around and in his shallow sentimentality as he and the Mock Turtle recall their school days. Critic Martin Gardner claims that both characters satirize the "sentimental college alumnus" typical of Oxford University. The constantly weeping **Mock Turtle** gets his name from the soup that is an imitation (usually made with veal) of green turtle soup, and the delightful song he sings about "Beautiful Soup" (a parody of a popular song of the period called "Beautiful Star") is one of the book's highlights. The Mock Turtle makes many puns while recounting his life story, explaining, for instance, that he studied "reeling and writhing" (reading and writing) in school as well as "laughing and grief" (Latin and Greek).

Other characters in the story include the three quarrelsome and bumbling playing-card gardeners (who are, appropriately, spades): **Five, Two,** and **Seven. Dinah** is Alice's beloved cat, who generates a less than enthusiastic response in Wonderland when mentioned by Alice. At the end of the book, **Alice's sister** continues to muse about the younger girl's adventures even after Alice has run off; she espouses the sentimental hope that Alice will retain the innocent joy of childhood even after she becomes an adult.

Through the Looking Glass, and What Alice Found There (novel, 1871)

Plot: While playing with her black kitten, seven-and-a-half-year-old Alice imagines that she can go through the mirror to the world behind the looking glass. She finds herself in a double of the room she has left, except that all of the inanimate objects are alive, including the chess game. When Alice moves the game's White Queen, that figure screams in fright; the White King is also alarmed, but neither seems aware of Alice. She floats downstairs and into the garden, where several flowers—Tiger Lily, Rose, and Violet—inform her that the Red Queen is the only other person around. Alice is surprised to see that the queen, whom she subsequently meets, is bigger than herself. As Alice approaches the queen, she finds herself back at the house and thus learns that everything in this unusual place must be done backward; she must walk backward, then, to reach the queen.

The Red Queen takes Alice to a hill that overlooks a landscape arranged like a chessboard with hedges and brooks dividing the columns and rows; Alice says she would like to play chess there. The queen tells Alice she will be the White Queen's pawn and takes her to the second square, from which she is to begin. They both start to run but don't get anywhere, and

Alice learns from the queen that in order to move one must run twice as fast as one can. Alice starts down a hill and finds herself aboard a train inhabited by insect creatures. She lacks a ticket, and the insects treat her unkindly. The train jumps over a stream and heads straight up into the air. Then Alice is sitting under a tree talking to the pleasant, chicken-sized Gnat, who tells her about the other insects before fading away from view. Next Alice encounters two funny, fat little men called Tweedledum and Tweedledee, whose statements always have double meanings. They recite a poem about a Walrus and a Carpenter and tell Alice that she is only part of the Red King's dream—if he wakes up, they claim, she will disappear. Alice begins to cry. The Tweedles get into an argument over a broken rattle and are preparing for a battle when they are frightened off by a crow.

Now Alice meets the strange, scatterbrained White Queen, who exists in a backwards state—she remembers things, for instance, before they actually happen. She and Alice end up in a little shop, and, after finding herself in a rowboat with the queen (who earlier had turned into a sheep), Alice buys an egg that grows into Humpty Dumpty. He lectures Alice about words and explains the meaning of the Red King's poem "Jabberwocky." On leaving the shop, Alice encounters a group of soldiers who keep falling off their horses; these were sent, she learns, by the White King, with whom she watches a fight between the Unicorn and the Lion. Afterward, Alice is serving a self-cutting cake at a party when the Red Knight and the White Knight both arrive, each claiming her as his prisoner. Like the other soldiers, they continually fall off their horses. Finally the Red Knight leaves, and the kind White Knight tells Alice she will be a queen when she crosses the next stream; he promises to show her how to reach it. When Alice crosses the brook, she immediately realizes that she has a crown on her head. The Red Queen and White Queen appear and initially chide Alice for thinking that she too is a queen, but after they have given her a test they begin to call her "Your Majesty" and discuss a party that Alice will give. Entering a door marked "Queen Alice," Alice finds all of the characters she has encountered behind the looking glass assembled for a fantastic party. So many weird things happen that Alice grows frustrated and jerks the tablecloth off the table, then begins to shake the Red Queen. She soon finds that the queen has turned into her black kitten and that she is back in her own world.

Characters: This sequel to *Alice's Adventures in Wonderland* tends to appeal to adults even more than its predecessor. It is more sophisticated in its presentation of problems of logic and perception, employing the game of chess and an indoor, late autumn setting rather than Wonderland's game of cards and springtime setting. Carroll is praised for his clever use of mirror imagery—inversions, doublings, and opposites are found throughout the book—and for his creation of many vivid characters who are, as expressed by critic Guy Boas, "not merely of the author's imagination, but a permanent stimulus to imagination in others."

Although the sequel was written six years after the first *Alice* book, the title character has aged only six months since her last adventure. **Alice** is still an intelligent, rational, patient, and curious girl who must still put up with rude and overbearing adult-like creatures. Whereas previously Alice played croquet with a pack of cards, she becomes in *Through the Looking Glass* a white pawn in a huge game of chess. As opposed to the chaotic world of Wonderland, the land of Looking Glass is strictly ordered and Alice's movements are determined by the rules of chess. Thus as a pawn she may move only one square at a time, and her ability to communicate and perceive is limited to whoever or whatever is in the squares directly adjoining hers. Many critics have seen in the giant chessboard a metaphor for life and in Alice's role a metaphor for either the human condition in general or the subjugated position of children, who are moved around like chess pieces by adults. The question of identity which played a part in *Alice's Adventures in Wonderland* is also important here, as Alice struggles with such dilemmas as whether a person's name reflects their real being or their being is determined by the name they are given. For instance, the beautiful fawn that Alice befriends is not afraid of her until he learns that she is "a human

93

child"—the name by which he now knows her causes him to fear her. At the end of the game, Alice reaches the eighth and last row of the chessboard, to be crowned a queen and finally to checkmate the Red King and win the game. Many scholars have interpreted Alice's passage across the last brook and coronation as queen her passage into adulthood; in bidding farewell to the White Knight, then, she bids farewell to her childhood. This moment has also been seen as Carroll's farewell to Alice Liddell, the little girl who provided the inspiration for the character of Alice and who was then growing into young womanhood.

Upon her arrival in Looking-Glass House, Alice encounters the animated chess pieces the **White Queen** and the **White King.** For the moment they are still only as large as normal chess pieces. The White Queen does not realize that Alice has picked her up and moved her, but assumes that the change in position was caused by a volcano—thus demonstrating her limited perception. After more contact with the White Queen Alice learns that she is slow, vague, and careless; she misses an early chance, for instance, to checkmate the Red King. The White Queen explains to Alice the unique Looking Glass concept of living backward in time: she feels pain before she pricks her finger, for example, and explains that the King's messenger is thrown in jail before he has committed the crime. Alice spends only a short period with the White King, joining him to watch the fight between the Lion and Unicorn. He provides some comic turns of language with his tendency to take words completely literally; he tells Alice that when he says "There's nothing like eating hay when you're faint," he means not that there is nothing better, just that no other experience is similar to that one.

The next representative of chess royalty that Alice meets is the **Red Queen.** Compared to the White Queen, the Red Queen is cold, calm, strict, and precise. She is somewhat reminiscent of the Queen of Hearts in *Alice's Adventures in Wonderland*—particularly when she imperiously proclaims, "Queens never make bargains"—but she is much more agreeable than that tyrannical character. The Red Queen shows Alice where to begin the game and reacts pleasantly when she says that she would like to become a queen; critic Judith Bloomingdale describes her as serving as "the governess-like mentor" of Alice's journey. The **Red King,** by contrast, sleeps throughout the game and is primarily used as a symbol of one of the novel's philosophical concerns. Tweedledee and Tweedledum inform Alice that she exists only as part of the Red King's dream, and that if he wakes up she will vanish like the snuffed flame of a candle. Many scholars have likened this concept to the philosophy of Bishop Berkeley (1685-1753), who claimed that reality has no existence except in the mind of God; thus the Red King stands for God, and Alice's existence hinges on his perception of her. When her adventure is over, Alice wonders whether it was she or the Red King who dreamed it—the latter possibility suggests an infinite, dream-within-a-dream regression that heightens the novel's sense of inversion.

The **Gnat,** whom Alice meets on a bizarre train from one square to the next, is one of two characters (the other is the White Knight) in *Through the Looking Glass* thought to represent the author because he persists in trying to get her attention. The Gnat is as big as a chicken but has a tiny voice in which he tells Alice stories about the other insects. He tries to make jokes, but his attempts at humor only make him cry; he says that he wishes Alice would tell the jokes instead—then they would be funny.

Tweedledee and **Tweedledum** are two of several well-known characters from nursery rhymes that Carroll incorporates into the story. Such a use of fairy tale figures was rare in Victorian children's literature, which was generally didactic and firmly grounded in reality. The Tweedles fit well into the book's mirror motif because they are mirror images of each other, even shaking hands with their right and left hands. In addition, Tweedledee's favorite expression is "Contrariwise!" and the twins always speak in ambiguities. The Tweedles upset Alice by suggesting that she is merely a character in the Red King's dream and may vanish at any moment, and they even question whether the tears that she claims verify her reality are real tears. They also recite the charming and famous poem "The Walrus and the Carpenter." Tweedledee and Tweedledum are destined to fight over the broken rattle because the nursery rhyme decrees that they will, and that the crow flying overhead will frighten them away; thus some critics have seen the twins as representing the concept of determinism, which postulates that behavior is predetermined and not subject to free will.

Another famous character from nursery rhyme who appears in *Through the Looking-Glass* is **Humpty Dumpty,** the oversized, animated egg who waits on top of a wall for his inevitable fall. Through Humpty Dumpty, Carroll explores the arbitrary nature of language and also pokes fun at the academic world. Humpty maintains an authoritarian air, claiming that words mean whatever he decides they should; for instance, he tells Alice that "glory" means "a nice knock-down argument." He goes on to assert that while other words are arbitrarily assigned, proper nouns describe what they name—thus his own name, Humpty Dumpty, describes the shape of his body. Critics have called his famous explication of the nonsensical poem "Jabberwocky" a brilliant anticipation of modern literary criticism. Humpty Dumpty interprets everything said to him as a riddle that he is well equipped to solve and also claims that he can explain poems that have not yet been written. Although he is proficient in linguistics, Humpty Dumpty reveals that mathematics is his weakness; he is unable to subtract 1 from 365.

After vanquishing the **Red Knight,** the **White Knight** tells Alice that he will take her to the brook she must cross to become a queen. But as they walk along together, the Knight continually falls off his horse—this erratic movement is designed to imitate the actual move of the Knight chess piece, which proceeds two spaces in any direction and then one space to either side. The Knight is a dreamy, kindly character who is generally considered a parody of Carroll, both in his appearance (he has shaggy hair and a gentle face) and in his relationship with Alice. Like Carroll, the White Knight likes to invent things, although his inventions always have a touch of absurdity. For instance, he has made anklets for his horse to protect against shark bites, and the box he has fashioned for storing his belongings is hung upside-down so that everything falls out. Scholars have interpreted the White Knight in several ways: as a parody of the traditional gallant white knight of literature, as a kind of Christ figure, and as a diligent Victorian scientist. It is often noted that the White Knight is the only character in the novel who seems really fond of Alice, and his sadness in leaving her may reflect Carroll's own sadness in seeing Alice Liddell grow up.

Other characters in *Through the Looking Glass* include the **Lion** and the **Unicorn,** whose battle in the novel reflects their perpetual rivalry in traditional nursery rhyme; Alice's cat **Dinah** (also mentioned in *Alice's Adventures in Wonderland*), and her two kittens, the mischievous **Black Kitten** and the milder **White Kitten,** who correspond to the story's two queens; and the three unexpectedly rude, animated flowers in the garden of Looking-Glass House: **Tiger-Lily, Rose,** and **Violet.**

Further Reading

Blake, Kathleen. *Play, Games, and Sport: The Literary Works of Lewis Carroll.* Ithaca, N.Y.: Cornell University Press, 1974.

Bloom, Harold, ed. *Lewis Carroll.* New York: Chelsea House, 1987.

Dictionary of Literary Biography, Vol. 18. Detroit: Gale.

Gardner, Martin. *The Annotated Alice: "Alice's Adventures in Wonderland" and "Through the Looking Glass,"* by Lewis Carroll. New York: Bramhall House, 1960.

Kelly, Richard. *Lewis Carroll.* Boston: Twayne, 1977.

Nineteenth-Century Literature Criticism, Vol. 2. Detroit: Gale.

Philips, Robert, ed. *Aspects of Alice: Lewis Carroll's Dreamchild as Seen through the Critics' Looking-Glasses,* 1865-1971. Vanguard Press, 1971.

Van Doren, Mark, Porter, Katherine Anne, and Russell, Bertrand. "Lewis Carroll: *Alice in Wonderland.*" In *The New Invitation to Learning,* edited by Mark Van Doren, pp. 206-20. New York: Random House, 1942.

François René de Chateaubriand
1768-1848

French novelist, essayist, translator, and biographer.

Atala; or, The Amours of Two Indians, in the Wilds of America (Atala; ou, Les amours de deux sauvages dans le désert; novel, 1801)

Plot: The story takes place in the early eighteenth century in the wilderness of Louisiana and Florida. René is a young Frenchman who wishes to become a member of the Natchez Indian tribe. His mentor is the blind, elderly, wise Chactas. As the two are waiting for a hunting expedition to begin, Chactas tells René the story of his youthful love affair with a beautiful Indian girl named Atala. When he was seventeen years old, Chactas had been captured by hostile Spaniards, who had also murdered his father. Taken to the Florida settlement of St. Augustine, he met a kind old man named Lopez, who took the boy in and educated him in the ways of European civilization. Several years later, however, Chactas decided to return to his own people, and with Lopez's reluctant blessing he went off into the woods to find them. He soon lost his way and was taken hostage by an enemy tribe, who brought him to their camp to await his death by burning. There he was visited by a young woman named Atala, who told him she was the daughter of the chief and that her mother was dead. Atala was disappointed to learn that Chactas was not a Christian but an adherent of the traditional Indian religion. She continued to visit him, however, and finally managed to free him. Chactas refused to leave, declaring that he wished to stay with Atala forever; Atala replied with anguish that their religious differences would forever keep them apart. She finally replaced Chactas's bindings, but every night she released him and the two wandered through the forest together. Despite their mutual desire, their ever-deepening love remained chaste.

Eventually the two lovers were discovered, and Chactas was put under heavier guard. The tribe finally reached the place where Chactas was to be executed, and many Indians gathered to witness the spectacle. Atala again managed to free Chactas and the two escaped, making their way through the wilderness. Atala told Chactas that, despite her love for him, she could not marry him because her faith forbid it; she also confessed that she was not the daughter of the chief but the illegitimate daughter of a white man, who happened to be Chactas's old friend Lopez. The two young lovers eventually encountered an old missionary, Father Aubrey, who gave them shelter and promised to instruct Chactas in Christianity. He introduced them to his peaceful community of Indians who had accepted the Christian faith, and Chactas began to feel the stirrings of religious faith in his heart. One day Father Aubrey and Chactas discovered that Atala had become very ill, and they now learned her secret. Hoping to protect her daughter from a fate like her own, Atala's dying mother had made her vow to remain a virgin for the rest of her life. Father Aubrey informed the young couple that Atala's vow was not irrevocable, but this revelation came too late: in despair of ever being able to marry Chactas, Atala had taken poison. After she had received Chactas's promise that he would become a Christian so that they might meet after death, Atala died. Chactas then resumed his wandering and, many years later, officially became a Christian.

In a prologue to the story, René's daughter reveals to a curious stranger that Chactas and Father Aubrey had been killed by enemies but were now together with Atala in heaven.

Characters: *Atala* was one of the most popular novels of the early nineteenth century, and is considered an important work of the romantic movement in literature. Combining an emphasis on ordered form that evokes the earlier classical period with a romantic focus on emotion, Chateaubriand created a vividly impressionistic work that contains some of the most lyrical, descriptive prose in French literature. Set in the primitive, exotic landscape of the American wilderness, *Atala* centers on the nineteenth-century European ideal of the Noble Savage—the personality uncorrupted by society and infused with nature's purity.

René is the young Frenchman to whom the story of the two Indian lovers is told. The somewhat melancholy René has become disillusioned with European civilization and is enthralled with the beauty of the wild American continent; he wishes to break with his "civilized" past and join the Natchez Indian tribe. Although René plays a relatively minor part in *Atala,* his character is developed further in a later work, *René,* which was included in Chateaubriand's long essay *The Genius of Christianity* (1802). In this work, René is portrayed as a typically romantic or Byronic (in reference to the English poet George Gordon, Lord Byron) hero in alienation, hopelessness, and tendency toward excessive introspection. Like the author who created him, René has a strong and possibly incestuous attachment to his sister. The version of René found in *Atala* also resembles Chateaubriand, whose travels through the American frontier in the late eighteenth century influenced his outlook.

Since the publication of *Atala,* many critics have commented that its idealized Indian characters bear little resemblance to actual native Americans of the period, in contrast to the perhaps sentimentalized but much more realistic Indians found in the later novels of the American author James Fenimore Cooper. Yet Chateaubriand's defenders contend that his novel was intended to create an impression rather than render life realistically. The wise, elderly Natchez chief **Chactas,** who relates the story of his love for Atala to René, is an example of Chateaubriand's idealized Indian characters; writing in the *Foreign Quarterly Review* in 1832, a critic described him as an "exemplification of the sentimental philosophism of Europe travestied in a savage garb." Though raised among his own people, Chactas was taken in as a young man by a Spanish settler who exposed the boy to European civilization, a circumstance meant to account for his sophisticated, refined speech. He has even been to France but prefers the simplicity and natural splendor of the wilderness; the romantics considered nature superior to the well-ordered gardens and pretensions of Europe. Also typically romantic is the passion that develops between Chactas and Atala, an individual love that ends tragically. Chactas's eventual conversion to Christianity, which results from his exposure to the benevolent Father Aubrey and his peaceful community of civilized though still primitively pure natives, suggests that a harmonious melding of nature and civilization is Chateaubriand's ideal.

The novel's title character is **Atala,** the beautiful Indian maiden with whom Chactas falls in love. Unlike her lover, Atala is a Christian; through her now-dead mother's influence she abandoned the beliefs of her own people for the faith of America's European settlers. Because she is golden-haired and pale-skinned and has a refined manner of speech, Atala, like Chactas, is often identified as an unrealistic character. Yet critics contend that Chateaubriand encourages the reader to suspend judgment about whether the characters are lifelike and to focus instead on the impression they make. Atala's naturally loving nature and physical passion for Chactas cause her to suffer from a kind of romantic agony, for she thinks that she will never be able to marry him. She believes the chastity vow she made while her mother was dying is irrevocable and finally commits suicide, a tragic outcome that Chateaubriand attributes to excessive religious zeal. Some critics view Atala's devotion to her vow as a contrast to the popular notion that Christianity had a positive, civilizing influence as depicted in Father Aubrey's community. Some early reviewers also rejected the idea that by refusing to give up her virginity Atala caused her own downfall. Chateaubriand's portrayal of Atala's death, combining the lush beauty of the surroundings with the pathos of lost love and life, has been widely praised.

Father Aubrey is the dedicated missionary who befriends Chactas and Atala after their escape from Atala's tribe. He is a good, selfless man of God who claims that his difficult work among savages in an untamed wilderness is a privilege rather than a duty. In the kindness and tolerance with which he treats the young couple, Father Aubrey embodies the Christian ideal of compassion, and his peaceful little settlement illustrates the concept of Christianity as civilizing. This utopian community is quintessentially romantic because it is populated by "Noble Savages"—people untouched by the corrupting influence of society, primitive but pure and living in harmony with their natural surroundings. Father Aubrey introduces Chactas to the Christian faith, and helps to further illuminate one of the novel's concerns: the struggle between individual rights and emotions and the responsibility to maintain an ordered society.

The only other significant character in *Atala* is **Lopez,** the kind Spaniard who takes in and educates Chactas after he is brought as a prisoner to St. Augustine. He treats Chactas as his own son and is reluctant to allow him to return to his people. In a typical romantic coincidence, Atala is Lopez's daughter, providing the two young lovers with a vaguely familial link.

Further Reading

Brady, Charles A. "From Broceliande to the Forest Primeval: The New-World Quest of the Chevalier Chateaubriand." *Emerson Society Quarterly* 42 (1968): 17-31.

France, Anatole. "Chateaubriand." In *The Latin Genius,* translated by Wilfrid S. Jackson, pp. 230-53. New York: Gabriel Wells, 1924.

Lister, T. H. "Chateaubriand's 'Works.'" *Foreign Quarterly Review* X, No. XX (October 1832): 297-334.

Maurois, André. *Chateaubriand: Poet, Statesman, Lover,* translated by Vera Fraser. New York: Harper, 1938.

Nineteenth Century Literature Criticism, Vol. 3. Detroit: Gale.

Porter, Charles A. *Chateaubriand: Composition, Imagination & Poetry.* Saratoga, Calif.: Anma Libri, 1978.

Switzer, Richard. *Chateaubriand.* New York: Twayne, 1971.

Anton Chekhov
1860-1904
Russian dramatist and short story writer.

"The Duel" (short story, 1891)

Plot: Ivan Laevsky and his married lover Nadyezhda Fyodorovna have left St. Petersburg and settled in a small town on the Black Sea, where they plan to establish a farm. Both have found the new life unsatisfying, though neither has shared his or her disillusionment with the other. Laevsky, employed not as a farmer but by the Ministry of Finance in an essentially inactive position, has decided that he no longer loves Nadyezhda. He dreams of fleeing from her, but he cannot afford to leave. Meanwhile, Laevsky tells his friend, the good-natured Army doctor Alexandr Samolyenko, Nadyezhda's husband has died, which makes the situation even more awkward because he fears that when he tells her the news she will expect him to marry her. Meanwhile, Nadyezhda has had a brief affair with the town's police captain, Ilya Kirilin, with whom she has become bored. She actually welcomes Laevsky's coldness toward her because it alleviates somewhat the guilt she feels over her infidelity. Nadyezhda has also accumulated some debts with the local merchant, Achmianov, about which she has avoided telling Laevsky. During a community picnic in the nearby countryside, Laevsky fantasizes about leaving while Nadyezhda considers starting an affair with the shopkeeper's son—both as an adventure and as a possible means of discharging her debt. And Kirilin makes it clear that he still desires Nadyezhda. After the picnic, Laevsky informs Nadyezhda that her husband has died, then he leaves their apartment and visits Samolyenko to ask for a loan so that he can return to St. Petersburg. Samolyenko borrows the money from Kolya Von Koren, a coldhearted zoologist who has expressed great scorn for Laevsky because of his inactivity and immoral behavior. Laevsky is angry when he learns that Samolyenko approached Von Koren for the money. He gets into a violent argument with Von Koren, who interprets one of his enraged statements as a challenge to a duel. That night, Laevsky discovers Nadyezhda in bed with Kirilin, who has blackmailed her in order to attain her sexual favors. Instead of provoking his hatred, the incident makes Laevsky realize that he does love Nadyezhda after all. He is filled with regret for his past behavior and with a strong desire to live. During the duel, Laevsky fires his shot harmlessly into the air, while Von Koren's aim is thrown off by a sudden shout from the town's young deacon, who has been hiding in the bushes nearby. The shot merely grazes Laevsky's neck, so both combatants emerge from the duel with their lives. Three months later, Laevsky has married Nadyezhda and is working diligently to pay off their debts. At the urging of Samolyenko, Von Koren admits to Laevsky that he had misjudged him and the two are reconciled before Von Koren's departure from the town.

Characters: Written during the later, more philosophically contemplative period of Anton Chekhov's career, "The Duel" features isolated characters who struggle toward hope and direction and whose inner thoughts and feelings comprise the bulk of the story. The skillful evocation of mood, the narrative balance and control, and the emphasis on the emotional dilemmas of realistic characters evident in "The Duel" exemplify Chekhov's innovativeness and careful crafting, which significantly influenced short story writers of the twentieth century.

Chekhov typically presented slices of reality through characters with distinct individual personalities rather than through figures meant to represent particular authorial viewpoints. The confused, directionless **Ivan Laevsky** is one such character—a flawed person with whom it is still possible to sympathize. An intellectual who has been unable to commit himself to anything, Laevsky has fled to the Black Sea in the hope of achieving the kind of redemption through manual labor that the renowned Russian author Leo Tolstoy promoted. Instead, Laevsky continues to live aimlessly, employed in a pointless job with the Ministry of Finance and bored with his lover. He is a rather pathetic figure with his torn slippers and constant nail-biting, and in his fantasies about a different, more meaningful life in a large city anticipates the characters in Chekhov's 1901 drama *The Three Sisters*. He often compares himself to such indecisive or desperate literary figures as Shakespeare's Hamlet and Tolstoy's Anna Karenina; in fact, Laevsky is well aware of his own defects and criticizes himself more harshly than even Von Koren can. Laevsky is an example of the "superfluous man" so common in nineteenth-century Russian literature: sensitive, alienated, and overcome by ennui, he seems incapable of positive action. Yet his discovery of Nadyezhda's infidelity and the prospect of the absurd duel—none of the participants can even remember the correct rules for staging a duel—serve to jar him out of his stupor. Just as the possibility of death is directly before him, Laevsky wants to live. In the story's final scene, a newly married and industrious Laevsky watches the boat carrying Von Koren maneuver away on choppy seas, and he compares its motion back and forth to humanity's search for truth—"two paces forward and one back." Laevsky is typical of many other Chekhovian characters in his resolve to continue struggling forward in pursuit of meaning, if not of happiness.

Like her lover, **Nadyezhda Fyodorovna** embarked on her new life with romantic visions of what that life would be like. Subject to the same disillusionment, inactivity, and ennui experienced by Laevsky, she is no more fulfilled than before she escaped with him; she confides to townswoman Marya Konstantinovna that she feels she has not yet lived. Out of boredom Nadyezhda has contracted nagging debts with the local shopkeeper and begun an affair with a man who initially interested her but of whom she quickly tired. Alternately gay and languid, vain and self-critical, Nadyezhda is tormented by conflicting feelings and impulses. While she pities Laevsky and regrets her infidelity, she experiences waves of desire which make her vulnerable to temptation. In portraying this interesting female character, Chekhov demonstrates an honesty and sensitivity toward sex that was rare in the nineteenth century; the modern novelist Eudora Welty praised him for having "treated with candor and seriousness a young woman of compelling sexuality."

The idealistic, judgmental zoologist **Kolya Von Koren** is a coldhearted, anti-individualistic man of science, a character type often found in Chekhov's work. An adherent to Darwin's theory of the survival of the fittest, Von Koren believes that those who represent destructive forces in society should be eliminated so that the future will be free from corruption. Yet Von Koren himself is ridiculously vain as well as arrogant and power-hungry; Laevsky suggests that he has come to this small town in order to seem more important than he really is. Responsible and hardworking, he is disgusted by Laevsky's indolence and also feels a puritanical revulsion to his illicit relationship with Nadyezhda. Von Koren's apology to Laevsky might be seen as either admirable and humbling or as a forced gesture that lacks sincerity and thus points to Von Koren's shallowness.

Alexandr Samolyenko is also a scientist, but he has retained a deep humanity that redeems him. Chekhov was himself a physician, and his writings are full of doctors who—though sometimes weary and discouraged—usually embody an optimistic and forward-looking view. Samolyenko is kindhearted, self-sacrificing, and much liked by all who know him. He is also somewhat comical in his sentimentality, naivete, and insistence on being addressed as "Your Excellency"—qualities that make him all the more human and thus more likeable. The principle which guides Samolyenko's behavior is tolerance for the opinions and weaknesses of others, and he tries to influence his friends to adopt a similar attitude, as demonstrated in his conversations with Von Koren and Laevsky when each derides the other, and in his attempts to conciliate their rift.

Other significant characters in ''The Duel'' include **Marya Konstantinovna,** the townswoman who reluctantly befriends the two lovers and then melodramatically lectures Nadyezhda about her shameless behavior; **Ilya Kirilin,** the tall, handsome, and arrogant police captain who forces Nadyezhda to sleep with him two more times or he will cause a public scandal; and young **Achmianov,** the shopkeeper's son, whose jealousy leads him to expose Nadyezhda and Kirilin to Laevsky.

The Sea Gull (drama, 1896)

Plot: The play takes place at the estate of retired judge Peter Sorin. His sister Irina Arkadina, an actress, is visiting with her lover, the successful writer Boris Trigorin. Irina's twenty-five-year-old son Konstantin Trepliov, also a writer, lives on the estate with his uncle. Also present are Eugene Dorn, a middle-aged doctor, and Ilia Shamrayov, Sorin's estate manager, along with his wife Paulina and his melancholy daughter Masha. Simon Medviedenko, a teacher, is in love with Masha, who in turn is in love with Konstantin, who loves Nina Zarietchnaya, an aspiring young actress. Konstantin has written a play and stages it for his mother's benefit during her visit; Nina is featured in a major role. During the performance, Irina refuses to take her son's play seriously and keeps interrupting. Nina is impressed by Trigorin's reputation and becomes infatuated with him. Konstantin, depressed by his inability to inspire love in either his mother or Nina, shoots a sea gull and brings it to Nina, claiming that he will soon take his own life as well. Overhearing this exchange, Trigorin sees in it material for a story; he tells Nina that the incident illustrates how human beings can be casually destructive, and that he sees her as a sea gull endangered by callous men. Nina and Trigorin begin an affair, and she joins him in Moscow. Konstantin shoots himself but is only superficially wounded, and he and his mother soon resume their bickering.

The play's final act takes place four years later. Sorin is now very ill, and Trigorin and Irina have come to visit him at the estate. Despairing of ever winning Konstantin's love, Masha had married Medviedenko and had borne a child; she is still in love with Konstantin, however, and neglects her family. Konstantin has had some of his work published but is still unhappy. Nina had become pregnant but lost the baby after being abandoned by Trigorin; she is now pursuing her acting career in various provincial towns. Nina returns to the estate and speaks with Konstantin, who still loves her. She is the only character who has changed in any way; she has learned to endure life's hardships and to continue living with hope for the future. Despite her continuing feelings for Trigorin, she leaves the estate to accept a position with a mediocre theatrical company in a small town. Konstantin now feels utterly desolate and lonely, and, while the others are playing cards, kills himself.

Characters: Despite the highly unfavorable reception it received from its opening night audience, *The Sea Gull* has since been acclaimed as an important and innovative work of nineteenth-century drama. Chekhov created deeply human characters who effectively illustrate the play's major themes, which include the role of the artist, the human response to loss and disillusionment, and the necessity of meaningful work and faith in the future. Through its naturalistic dialogue, its emphasis on emotion rather than action—what happens offstage affects the characters more than the action itself—and its compassionate reflection of life's complexity and absurdity, *The Sea Gull* anticipated many concerns that would dominate drama in the twentieth century.

If *The Sea Gull* is indeed an indictment of the theatrical milieu of Chekhov's time—as its first audience considered it—the character of **Irina Arkadina** embodies many of the qualities Chekhov condemned. She is concerned primarily with surfaces, and her interest in her art has more to do with its glamour and excitement than with its meaning or lasting value. Irina wants to remain the young, beautiful actress she once was, and thus she is jealous of Nina because she is at the beginning of her life and career and she is cold to her brother because of his illness and impending death. Most importantly, she can only treat her son—who serves as a constant reminder of her age—with hostility. She is opposed to him professionally as well, for he is attempting to overturn the theatrical traditions she represents. Thus she openly scorns and dismisses Konstantin's play, despite his obvious need for her approval; her cruelty toward him is a significant part of what drives him to suicide. Yet Irina is a pathetic figure in her profound insecurity about aging and death and her inability to connect meaningfully with others. The play closes with the implication that she—blithely playing cards as the curtain falls—will be devastated by the news of her son's suicide.

Through the unhappy and frustrated young writer **Konstantin Trepliov** Chekhov explores the idea of creativity and the struggle to become an artist. As exemplified by the mystical and melodramatic play he presents at the estate, Konstantin is an advocate of new forms of expression; in fact, he has been seen as representing the symbolist movement, which emphasized exoticism, aesthetics, and an impressionistic writing style, dominant in Russian literature in the late-nineteenth and early-twentieth centuries. Critics have debated whether Chekhov condemned or approved Konstantin's attempts to innovate: some maintain that the struggle to create new forms is presented favorably despite the failure of Konstantin's play, while others claim that Chekhov stressed Konstantin's lack of solid ideas or meaningful content. The use of the play-within-a-play device in *The Sea Gull,* in addition to Konstantin's troubled relationship with his mother, have led many scholars to identify him with the title character of Shakespeare's classic drama *Hamlet.* Konstantin is frustrated by his inability to live up to his ideals of either art or love (for he has unrealistic expectations for his personal relationships as well as his writing, romanticizing his relationship with Nina and viewing Irina as the young, loving mother she once was) and is unable to reconcile himself to the reality of his life. "Like so many Chekhovian heroes," wrote critic Robert Louis Jackson, "his tragedy consists in his inability to rise to the level of tragedy." Thus he may be contrasted to Nina, who faces her own misfortune, limitations, and potential with courage and determination.

Nina Zarietchnaya is the primary embodiment of the sea gull for which the play is named. Trigorin, ever the compulsive writer, perceives   Nina's encounter with Konstantin—in which he drops a dead sea gull at her feet—as material for a story, and he envisions her as a free-flying bird which may at any time be casually shot down by some callous, indifferent hunter. Yet Trigorin's apparently sympathetic view of Nina is ironic in view of his role in the tragedy that befalls her. Confused by the choices before her and enthralled by Trigorin, Nina becomes his mistress and bears his child; later she also bears the death of the baby and his desertion of her. Her return to the estate could be interpreted as a move to shed finally and completely her identification with the fallen sea gull, or as a brief stop on her flight toward the future. In either case, she will not be beaten by what has happened to her. Although she has not realized her potential and may never realize it at all, Nina has decided that the struggle to achieve is more important than success and fame. She loves acting for its own sake and has faith in her "calling," so she will pursue her career even if it means performing with second-rate companies in provincial towns. Although it is also possible to interpret Nina's action as a capitulation to the lifestyle and shallow attitude represented by Irina Arkadina, most critics have characterized Nina as embodying the endurance and fortitude that is such a dominant theme in Chekhov's work.

Despite the cruelty of his seduction and desertion of Nina, **Boris Trigorin** is too human a figure to earn the reader's unqualified hatred. Like Konstantin, he is evidence of Chekhov's interest in creativity and the artist's place in society. Trigorin is a successful author who has won the world's approval by creating art that imitates life as it is rather than as it might or should be, which is Konstantin's approach. Thus he may be said to represent the concrete style that was giving way, at the time of the play's writing, to innovative new forms like symbolism. In consistently depicting in his work the trivial and the ordinary, Trigorin—despite his fame—has failed to produce art of real value or timelessness, and he seems hardly more satisfied than Konstantin, who is still struggling to achieve his own identity. Trigorin claims that the writer has no choice but to draw from his own life when plying his trade, so it may be that his affair with Nina is an attempt to embrace experience. But his essential weakness is shown by his abandonment of Nina and return to Irina. Some critics have noted the resemblance between Trigorin and the play's author, for Chekhov too was driven by his compulsion to write, had a fondness for fishing, and was a shy and polite person. However, like all of Chekhov's characters, Trigorin has a personality of his own and cannot be said to entirely represent Chekhov's own viewpoint or self-perception.

Peter Sorin is the good-humored but disillusioned estate owner whose home provides the play's setting. He is profoundly bored, and has found at the end of his life that he has failed to realize the dreams of his youth. Ineffective in overseeing his estate, he defers instead to his ambitious manager, **Ilia Shamrayov.** Shamrayov is a surly and crafty man who is dissatisfied with his lower social status and would like to elevate himself. Thus he flatters Irina while running the estate with a tyrannical hand. His wife **Paulina Shamrayov** is also bored and dissatisfied with her life; in love with Eugene Dorn, she finds him unwilling to make any changes in their situation. Their daughter **Masha** has one of *The Sea Gull*'s most memorable lines: when asked why she always wears black, she replies, "I am in mourning for my life." This comment has been interpreted as both tragic and ironically humorous; Chekhov insisted that the play—despite its gloominess—was a comedy, thus Masha's melancholy might be interpreted as ridiculous, as might her argument with Medviedenko as to which of them is most miserable. Masha is weighed down by her unrequited love for Konstantin and her dissatisfying marriage to a dull husband and she makes no effort to overcome her troubles, providing an illuminating contrast to the more determined Nina.

Simon Medviedenko is one of several boring but steadfast schoolteacher characters in Chekhov's work, men whose intellect is of a weak, uncreative kind that Chekhov seemed to find distasteful. Likewise, **Eugene Dorn** takes his place alongside other doctor figures in Chekhov's plays—and indeed, the fact that Chekhov himself was a physician makes these characters particularly interesting. Dorn, however, is not a well-developed character. Bowed down by a long, wearying practice in which he has helped others but has remained virtually penniless, Dorn affects an attitude of indifference, playing the role of the caring but distant observer of those around him. Indeed, he reacts calmly at his discovery of Konstantin's body.

Uncle Vanya (drama, 1899)

Plot: Retired professor and scholar Alexandr Serebryakov has returned to his country estate with his second wife, beautiful young Elena. His daughter Sonya and Ivan Voynitsky—called Vanya—the brother of his first wife, have been managing the estate for many years in a frugal, efficient, and productive manner. They now find their lives disrupted because they learn that the man for whose benefit they have worked is not the brilliant writer they thought he was; instead, they discover, he is ill-tempered, gouty, and self-centered. Vanya in particular feels cheated. He falls in love with Elena, who also manages to captivate the weary, disillusioned Mihail Astrov, a doctor and friend of the family. Plain, hardworking Sonya has quietly loved the doctor for many years and is saddened by his obvious regard for Elena. Elena, however, befriends Sonya and confides her indifferent feelings toward life. Serebryakov calls a family meeting and announces that he intends to sell the estate so that he can afford to live in the city. Vanya is furious, for he feels that this would lay to waste the twenty-five years that he and Sonya have spent in devotion to the estate. Serebryakov abandons the plan and tries to make amends with Vanya, but Vanya responds by trying twice to shoot him—missing both times.

After all of the family members have reconciled, Serebryakov and Elena go back to Moscow and life on the estate returns to its old routine. However, Vanya is now disillusioned and Sonya has realized the futility of her love for the doctor, who now visits less frequently. In a final speech, Sonya voices the necessity of endurance, and expresses the hope that their continuing dedication to their work will eventually bring them rest.

Characters: Like Chekhov's other plays, *Uncle Vanya* emphasizes what has been called "indirect action" over direct action and explores the human response to disillusionment. The play's characters are isolated and incapable of communicating deeply with each other, and their desire to change their lives is frustrated. However, *Uncle Vanya* is permeated with the same underlying, indestructible hope that is present in his other plays.

The bitter disappointment felt by **Ivan Voynitsky** or **Uncle Vanya** is at the center of the play. He has spent the better part of his life living a meager, uncomfortable existence so that Serebryakov could carry on his important work in comfort; Vanya was comforted to think that by his work and sacrifices he was contributing to the creation of something great. Realizing that Serebryakov is a man of only commonplace ability—and feeling that he himself might have accomplished something with his own intellect—Vanya despairs, and, marooned at the edge of old age, he feels betrayed. His initial response is rebellion, signified by his falling in love with Elena, his turning to drink, and, finally, his attempts to murder Serebryakov (these failed attempts may indicate that Vanya is not a murderer at heart). Left alone with Sonya again on the estate, Vanya returns to his old routine, but without the consolation of believing that he is working for something worthwhile. What his fate will be—whether he will sink deeper into despair or join his niece in looking forward to a better future, even if it is in the afterlife—is left ambiguous.

Alexandr Serebryakov is the pompous, irascible professor whose return to his country estate upsets so many other lives. His career has been spent writing books about art, but he has produced nothing of lasting value. It becomes painfully obvious to those who have sacrificed for his sake that he is not the success he seemed. Although his failed career might be expected to provoke a sympathetic response, Serebryakov negates that possibility with his whining and conceit. He maintains that he deserves to be pampered by others and to be disagreeable if he wishes, and he carelessly disturbs the routine of the estate with his demands and the odd hours he keeps. Although in the end Serebryakov concedes to his brother-in-law's desire that he not sell the estate, the decision requires little sacrifice on his part, for he merely returns to his old life—living in the city and receiving money from Vanya and Sonya. Although his young wife Elena is disappointed with her husband, they are in one way an appropriate pair—neither participates actively or creatively in life and in fact they detract from the lives of others. Serebryakov also serves a functional role in the plot by providing for the arrival/departure pattern that Chekhov often employs as a framework for his plays.

Chekhov has been praised for creating in **Mihail Astrov** a "thoroughly convincing human being," as Donald Rayfield has written. Like Vanya, Astrov has worked hard and idealistically for many years and now wonders what he has accomplished. Though discouraged and weary, Astrov has a great enthusiasm for the planting of trees. This pursuit has a particularly symbolic aspect, for Astrov sees in the preservation of existing forests and creation of new ones a concrete way to ensure a brighter future. To plant a tree is an act of faith which carries with it no immediate gratification but reflects the tree-planter's concern for generations not yet living. Astrov's interest in trees and hope for the future reflects the duality of his nature: he is both a cynic and an optimist. He claims that his feelings have become deadened by his long years of tedious work, yet he is able to fall in love not with the good and long-suffering Sonya but with Elena. In fact, his visits to the estate—previously monthly—become daily, and he neglects both his medical practice and his forests in order to be near Elena. Yet in the end her value is revealed as illusory, and Astrov returns to his old ways and to a loveless but useful life.

Elena Andreyevna, the professor's beautiful young wife, is capable of stealing men's hearts but not of injecting meaning into her own life. She married her husband in the belief that he was a genius and bound for great accomplishments, and though she has since been disillusioned she remains faithful to him. This might be seen as evidence of a laudable loyalty or indicative of her general inertia, but in any case, Elena is a negative force in *Uncle Vanya* because she is not only profoundly bored and directionless herself but infects others with her indolence. By distracting Astrov from his more worthy pursuits, by increasing Vanya's antagonism toward Serebryakov, and by wrecking Sonya's happy illusions when she forces Astrov to admit that he doesn't love her, Elena proves a destructive element in the lives of those around her as well. She provides a strong example of Chekhov's belief in the necessity of creative, satisfying work for a full life.

By contrast, **Sonya Alexandrovna** lacks Elena's physical beauty but has always worked hard and unselfishly. She is good-hearted and innocent, and her unrequited love for Astrov makes her a particularly poignant figure. For a long time she has been able to convince herself that Astrov returned her feelings, but Elena's callous confrontation of the doctor on the matter—ostensibly undertaken for Sonya's benefit—shatters that illusion forever. Nonetheless, Sonya struggles on determinedly without knowing whether she will ever attain happiness. She is the play's mouthpiece for the idea of endurance and of salvation through work, and at the end of the play she delivers the pivotal line "We shall rest!" She tells Vanya that they must go on working as they always have, for in the future—perhaps after death—they may attain the relief they crave.

Other characters in *Uncle Vanya* include **Marina,** the old family nurse who represents stability, comfort, and tradition—unlike the others, she values the monotony of life on the estate and considers it preferable to change; Vanya's widowed mother **Marya Voynitsky,** who lacks her son's sensitivity and intelligence and who spends her time reading pamphlets about feminism and dreaming of a better future; and **Ilia Telegin,** nicknamed **Waffles** for his pockmarked face, a friend of the family and a farcical character who considers himself proudly resigned to his fate but is actually oblivious and stupid.

The Three Sisters (drama, 1901)

Plot: The play centers on the three Prozorov sisters—Olga, an unmarried teacher; Masha, the wife of schoolmaster Fyodor Kuligin; and Irina, a young girl—as well as their brother, Andrey. Eleven years earlier, their father's military career (he was a brigadier general in the army) had necessitated the family's move from Moscow to a small provincial town. The sisters long to escape their stifling existence for a new, meaningful life in Moscow and frequently dream of moving back there. Olga would like to be married, while Masha is disillusioned with her husband, and Irina wants to find satisfying work. Andrey aspires to become a professor at a university in the city. The action begins on Irina's name-day, when several guests arrive for a celebration. Ivan Tchebutykin, an old and incompetent army doctor and a friend of the family, brings a present for Irina. Alexandr Vershinin, the newly arrived commander of the military garrison in the town, also visits. He is an old friend of their dead father. The sisters envy his former life in Moscow, but he claims to be content with the small town. At the end of the first act, Andrey proposes to his sweetheart, Natasha, and she accepts.

During the play's final acts, Andrey and Natasha are married and have two children, but Natasha treats her husband cruelly. He has taken a dull government job and spends his time playing cards. Andrey is the only one who does not realize that his wife is having an affair with a local government official, Protopopov. Vershinin and Masha fall in love, but he will never leave his wife and children. Baron Tuzenbakh, a lieutenant in the army, has long been in love with Irina but she is not attracted to him; she dreams of meeting her husband in Moscow. Captain Vassily Solyony also courts Irina. It gradually becomes obvious that the Prozorovs will never leave their current situation. When the military battery moves away, Masha must part with Vershinin and dejectedly returns to her weak but still devoted husband. Irina, who has been unable to find fulfilling work, agrees to marry Tuzenbakh because it seems to be her only means of escape. A jealous Solyony, however, kills Irina's fiance in a duel. Olga's life also remains the same, although she is made headmistress of her school and is even more overworked. Andrey is left to care for his children while Natasha spends time with her lover. Their dreams shattered, the three sisters attempt to cope with their lives and still look to the future for improvement.

Characters: The only one of Chekhov's four greatest plays that he termed a drama rather than a comedy, *The Three Sisters* is an exploration of desire, frustration, ennui, and endurance. Set in a dull provincial town that provides an effective contrast with the exciting, idealized Moscow of the main characters' dreams, the play offers a biting commentary on the rise of the middle class in turn-of-the-century Russia and its bourgeois values and cultural pretensions.

Olga Prozorov, the oldest of the three sisters, is an industrious, successful teacher who nevertheless feels profoundly dissatisfied. Overworked and unhappy, she suffers from headaches that are the physical manifestation of her inner turmoil. Like her sisters, she cries "To Moscow!" with the belief that an escape from the stifling atmosphere of the small town into the unlimited possibilities of the big city will save her. When the play ends, she not only has not moved to Moscow, but has been pushed out of her home (by Natasha) into a dismal flat and has been promoted to headmistress at her school—an ironic honor in that she had dreaded the idea of a promotion and is now even more burdened with responsibility. Yet Olga expresses to her sisters the hope that somehow, in some way, future generations will benefit from and appreciate their efforts to make the world a better place.

Masha Prozorov married a man whom she was convinced was very intelligent and she has been disappointed to learn that he is actually stodgy and unimaginative. She is bored and depressed and always wears black as a symbol of her inner desolation. Once an accomplished pianist, Masha claims that she has forgotten how to play—more evidence of the ennui that has enveloped and paralyzed her and her siblings. In a significant discussion with Vershinin and Tuzenbakh, Masha expresses the view that a person must continue to strive to discover the reason for his or her existence and must have faith that this knowledge is attainable. Attracted to the intelligent Vershinin, who—like many military characters in Chekhov's work—has brought an element of culture to the town, Masha seems to hope that their affair will bring her some fulfillment. However, Vershinin is tied to his wife and children and is eventually transferred to another town, so the possibility of redemption through love is crushed. Masha returns to her still-devoted husband, and, despite her emotional devastation, seems determined to endure her life as it is rather than as she hoped it would be.

Through the youngest daughter, **Irina Prozorov,** Chekhov articulates the importance of striving for a better life. Irina believes that she will find fulfillment through work, but the jobs she takes—as a telegraph operator and on the town council—soon bore her. Just as Masha has forgotten how to play the piano, Irina has forgotten what Italian she once knew, and she always feels tired; thus ennui takes both a mental and physical toll. Although she always dreamed of meeting a husband after the move to Moscow, Irina agrees to marry the decidedly unromantic Tuzenbakh as a desperate effort to effect a change in her life. When he is killed, even this pathetic course will be denied her. Nevertheless, Irina embodies not only a great yearning but a great stamina. As the play ends, she is determined to find some mode of existence which will benefit others and to look toward the future for the answers to her longings.

While each of his sisters displays to greater or lesser degrees an indomitable spirit, **Andrey Prozorov** is too weak to overcome the circumstances which engulf him. At the beginning of the play, he is planning to become a university professor and plays the violin. Then, in an apparent attempt to fit into the provincial milieu in which he lives, Andrey marries the middle-class, domineering Natasha and eventually accepts a menial position with the town council. By the end of the play, he is completely ineffectual, ill-tempered, and defeated. His wife mocks him by having an affair with his boss and he spends his time playing cards rather than the violin. Whereas his sisters retain some hope for the future, Andrey is last seen wheeling a baby carriage as his wife cavorts with her lover. Critics have noted that *The Three Sisters* provides a good example of the contrast between Chekhov's strong, hopeful female characters and his weak, resigned male characters, with Andrey serving as an apt illustration of the latter.

Chekhov's portrayal of Andrey's wife **Natasha Prozorov** has been described as a particularly malevolent depiction of a pretentious bourgeois with no redeeming qualities. It is primarily through Natasha that Chekhov delivers his indictment of the Russian middle class, for she is vulgar, rude, and selfish and she serves as an antithesis to the sophistication to which the Prozorovs aspire. A native of the provincial town in which they all live, she is as maliciously practical as her husband and his sisters are intellectual, but her attempts to seem cultured (such as her clumsy use of French phrases and her pointed mistreatment of the servants) betray her ill-breeding. After marrying Andrey she becomes increasingly tyrannical, and she eventually overruns the Prozorov household. Olga and Irina are forced to move out to make room for Natasha's expanding family, compounding their spiritual isolation with a disruption of their physical surroundings. Natasha is also overtly immoral, carrying on her affair with Protopopov in front of her husband.

Alexandr Vershinin is the army commander who befriends the Prozorovs when he is assigned to the garrison in their town (he is also an old friend of their father). Like many military characters in Chekhov's work, he is a refined, intelligent man who brings a breath of culture to the stifling atmosphere of the isolated community. Although he is basically unhappy—he is burdened with a wife who undergoes periods of insanity and his love affair with Masha must come to an end—Vershinin maintains an optimistic outlook. During his talk with Masha and Tuzenbakh, Vershinin poses the question of what the world will be like in two or three hundred years. He believes that it will be a better place, and that if people must sacrifice their happiness now it is because future generations will benefit from the sacrifice. Scholars have often contended that Vershinin's view reflects Chekhov's own feelings and essentially optimistic perspective.

The military physician **Ivan Chebutykin** is also a part of the Prozorov's small enclave of cultured people. He is a longtime friend of the family—he was once in love with their dead mother—and now serves as something of a father figure to them. Chebutykin is an ineffective doctor who was very disturbed when he caused the death of a patient, and he deals with his disillusionment by drinking heavily and by denying reality. He is known for his repeated muttering of a phrase variously translated as "It doesn't matter!" or "What's the difference?" He spends much of his time reading the newspaper, and often injects headlines or other random phrases from his reading into conversation; this habit is often cited as an example of Chekhov's use of trivial details to create a mood of ordinary human life and discourse. Having assumed the role of detached observer, Chebutykin reacts in an unnaturally casual way to the death of Tuzenbakh and is humming a song as he tells Irina that her fiance has been killed.

In order to escape from her tedious existence, even if only marginally, Irina agrees to marry **Baron Tuzenbakh,** a rather slow-witted man who lacks good looks and charm. In his discussion with Vershinin and Masha about the shape the future will take, Tuzenbakh expresses the view that nothing will ever change—that people will always complain about their lives while fearing their deaths, and that since there is really no way to know why one is alive there is no need to think about it. Tuzenbakh's decision to leave the army and go to work in a brickyard reflects his desire to find salvation in hard, manual labor, but he differs from Irina in that he sees work as an escape from thinking rather than as a route to fulfillment. His fellow army officer and eventual murderer, **Vassily Solyony,** seems to be shy and harmless—though he does have a sarcastic wit—but proves cruel and selfish in his refusal to allow Natasha to marry the man she chooses. He has ironically vowed that he will have no "happy rival," and he takes drastic measures to ensure that this is so.

Masha's spineless husband **Fyodor Kuligin** is a teacher who represents provincial, uncreative learnedness. Despite his insensitivity, Kuligin's situation as a cuckolded husband and his continuing devotion to his wife make him a pathetic figure.

Minor characters in *The Three Sisters* include **Protopopov,** Andrey's employer and Natasha's lover, who is never seen on the stage and thus heightens the sense of indirect action so common in Chekhov's plays; **Ferapont,** the senile messenger who delivers documents to Andrey; and **Anfisa,** the longtime family servant who represents stability and the past.

The Cherry Orchard (drama, 1904)

Plot: Madame Lyubov Ranevsky has returned to her country estate after five years in Paris, where she fled with her lover to escape from her grief over the death of her young son. She is now nearly penniless and must decide what to do with her estate and its magnificent cherry orchard. Madame Ranevsky's family and friends include her deluded brother Leonid Gaev; her adopted daughter Varya, who has managed the estate for her and is in love with Lopakhin, a former peasant who has become a wealthy merchant; her seventeen-year-old daughter Anya; the idealistic student Peter Trofimov, who is in love with Anya; and the family's servants—governess Charlotta, clerk Yepihodov, maid Dunyasha, footman Fiers, and Fiers's grandson Yasha, also a footman. Lopakhin proposes that the orchard be destroyed so that cottages may be built on the land and rented out, thus ensuring a good, steady income. Madame Ranevsky will not consider the plan because the orchard has played an important role in her life since childhood and she cannot bear to part with it. Several other schemes for saving the estate are discussed—such as obtaining money from relatives or marrying Anya to a rich man—but none proves feasible. The family seems incapable of resolving the question of how to save their estate while Madame Ranevsky continues to squander what little money she has.

The practical, ambitious Lopakhin is puzzled by the attitude of Madame Ranevsky and her relatives. He muses that the cherry orchard, which represents childhood memories and a happy life to them, must have been a symbol of oppression to generations of serfs. Trofimov also holds this view of the situation and expresses it to Anya. Finally, at a ball hosted—inappropriately, in view of her situation—by Madame Ranevsky, Lopakhin announces that he has bought the estate at auction and intends to proceed with his plan for leveling the orchard. As the disheartened Madame Ranevsky and her family leave their home for the last time, the sounds of trees being felled are heard in the background.

Characters: Chekhov's most famous play, *The Cherry Orchard* is usually classified as a "tragicomedy" because it combines trivial and absurd dialogue and activity with the sensitively delineated themes of change, loss, the difficulty of communication, and the struggle to endure. While some critics—particularly those of modern Soviet Russia—have characterized *The Cherry Orchard* as an indictment of the old Russian landowning class, others detect in it a deep ambiguity and humanity that makes specific conclusions difficult.

The play chronicles the effects on a particular family of the passing of the Russian feudal system (which featured large country estates owned by the gentry and worked by peasants or serfs) and the rise of the middle class. **Madame Lyubov Ranevsky** is a representative of the Russian aristocracy which, at the end of the nineteenth century, was beginning to fade from dominance. The threatened loss of her estate thus signifies an even greater loss—of her place in society, of her memories, of her identity. She associates the cherry orchard with the happiness and security of her childhood, before she had to grapple with such adult realities as the death of a child or the lack of adequate finances. Faced with inevitable change, Madame Ranevsky shows that she is incapable of adapting: she gives money away to a beggar and hosts an elegant ball when she needs every penny to hold onto her home. Thus she allows her estate and beloved cherry orchard to fall into another's hands. Madame Ranevsky provides for the pattern of arrival and departure which gives the play its framework; although she arrives in a flurry of excitement and nostalgia, her leave-taking is full of melancholy and disillusionment.

Madame Ranevsky's brother **Leonid Gaev** is also a holdover from a life that is quickly passing as Russian society changes. Like his sister, he cannot bear to lose the cherry orchard because of all it signifies—a brighter, more carefree past. He is also as impractical as Madame Ranevsky and he lacks the willpower and backbone to adapt to a new situation as well. All of his grand plans for saving the estate come to nothing, and he spends his time playing billiards. Gaev is a somewhat comical figure as he tries to relay his ideas with a piece of candy in his mouth that distorts his words. Even this image has its poignant side, however, for Gaev, unable to adequately express his feelings, illustrates the difficulty of meaningful communication between people. In his indolence and ineffectiveness, he provides a strong contrast to the capable, shrewd Lopakhin.

Ermolai Lopakhin is a member of Russia's rapidly growing middle class. A wealthy merchant whose father was a serf, he views the past with little nostalgia and lives entirely in the present. When he looks at the cherry orchard he sees not golden memories but gold—the profit it can bring—and the faces of the serfs for whom the orchard served as a symbol of their subjugation. Lopakhin's natural inclination to act decisively and to work hard makes it difficult for him to understand his aristocratic neighbors. He is not necessarily malicious— he acts out of kindness when he suggests that Madame Ranevsky build cottages on the orchard land and he does give her the chance to do so before he buys the land himself—but he is opportunistic. He cares more about making money than he does about Varya, who loves him, and he finds that although he would like to improve himself he is too tired at night to read. Although Lopakhin could be interpreted as an insensitive manipulator, he might also be viewed as the only character in the play who is capable of acting in accordance with his principles.

Varya is Madame Ranevsky's adopted daughter, and her uncertain parentage means that she is clearly aligned with neither the aristocracy nor the middle class. Like other of Chekhov's spiritually desolate female characters, Varya always wears black. She has been running the estate in Madame Ranevsky's absence and is exhausted by worries about money, the servants, and her own future. Although she is tempted to escape from life's demands by entering a convent, Varya chooses instead to find her salvation in work, and in this way she resembles those other significant characters in Chekhov's work who respond to misfortune by trying to move forward. The change that will come to all of the characters in *The Cherry Orchard* with the sale of the estate will for Varya be quite concrete and dismal: she will become a housekeeper at a nearby estate.

Anya Ranevsky, seventeen years old, wears white clothing signifying her purity and openness to a new life. Her youthful innocence and energy equip her well for the changes she will face—she is the only member of her family who seems to look forward to the future. Although she loves the estate and cherry orchard, she is not particularly sorry to lose them, for she believes with Trofimov that all Russia will now be her orchard. Anya's sweetheart and the former tutor of Madame Ranevsky's dead little boy, **Peter Trofimov,** is another representative of youth and enthusiasm. An idealist and political radical whose views have led to his expulsion from school, he looks forward to a brighter future and a new egalitarian social order. Not surprisingly, he was readily adopted as a hero by the critics who wrote about *The Cherry Orchard* after Russia's 1917 communist revolution. Yet many scholars see Trofimov as plainly unheroic, for he makes speeches but rarely acts, he promotes an ideal of human concern but lacks real understanding of those around him, and he disdains the ordinary physical love offered by Anya in favor of an abstract, sanitized sentiment. Still, Trofimov is an enthusiastic young man who has his eyes on the future and plans to work for the benefit of future generations, and this attitude is one of which Chekhov is thought to have approved.

Among the other characters in the play are the family's neighbor and fellow landowner, **Boris Pishchik,** who trusts in fate to resolve his financial problems and eventually allows his land to be ravaged for the mineral deposits that are found there (he does not share Madame Ranevsky's reverence for the past); and **Charlotta,** the governess of uncertain heritage and undelineated class whose solemn performance of magic tricks adds a somewhat bizarre comic touch to the play. **Simeon Epihodov** is the ineffectual, fatalistic clerk whose mismanagement of the estate contributes to the family's dilemma; his tendency to deliver risqué malapropisms ("Allow me to copulate to you") provides some comic relief. Epihodov eventually marries the woman he loves, the maid Dunyasha, who is herself in love with Yasha. **Dunyasha** dreams of becoming an elegant lady and parodies Madame Ranevsky; she must give up her illusions when the estate is sold and she marries not the dashing, insensitive Yasha but the dull Epihodov. **Fiers** is the family's faithful, nostalgic old servant; at the end of the play he provides one of its most memorable moments: forgotten by the entire family and locked in the empty mansion, he observes that "Life has slipped away as if I haven't lived." **Yasha** is a footman like his grandfather Fiers, but he is eager to move up in the world. Thus he is happy when the estate is sold because it means he will travel to Paris with Madame Ranevsky. Callous and self-centered, he is unconcerned about how he treats Fiers or Dunyasha.

Further Reading

Baricelli, J. P., ed. *Chekhov's Great Plays: A Critical Anthology.* New York: New York University Press, 1985.

Clyman, Toby, ed. *A Chekhov Companion.* Westport: Greenwood Press, 1985.

Debreczeny, Paul, and Thomas Eeckman, eds. *Chekhov's Art of Writing: A Collection of Critical Essays.* Columbus, Oh.: Slavica, 1977.

De Maegd-Soep, Carolina. *Chekhov and Women: Women in the Life and Work of Chekhov.* Columbus, Oh.: Slavica, 1987.

Hahn, Beverly. *Chekhov: A Study of the Major Stories and Plays.* Cambridge: Cambridge University Press, 1977.

Jackson, Robert Louis, ed. *Chekhov: A Collection of Critical Essays.* Englewood Cliffs, N.J.: Prentice-Hall, 1967.

Kirk, Irina. *Anton Chekhov.* New York: Twayne, 1981.

Nabokov, Vladimir. "Anton Chekhov." In *Lectures on Russian Literature,* edited by Fredson Bowers, pp. 245-95. New York: Harcourt Brace Jovanovich, 1981.

Pritchett, V. S. *Chekhov: A Spirit Set Free.* New York: Random House, 1988.

Rayfield, Donald. *Chekhov: The Evolution of His Art.* New York: Barnes & Noble, 1975.

Short Story Criticism, Vol. 2. Detroit: Gale.

Twentieth Century Literary Criticism, Vols. 3, 10, 31. Detroit: Gale.

Wellek, Rene, and Nonna P., eds. *Chekhov: New Perspectives.* Englewood Cliffs, N.J.: Prentice-Hall, 1984.

Nikolay Gavrilovich Chernyshevsky
1828-1889
Russian novelist, critic, essayist, translator, and editor.

What Is to Be Done?: Tales about New People (*Chto delat';* novel, 1863)

Plot: The first section of the novel takes place in St. Petersburg, Russia, in 1856. The employees of a hotel are upset because a traveler who has spent the night there does not answer his door. When the door is broken down, a suicide note is found in the room. Later, a bullet-riddled cap is found in a canal near a bridge on which shots had been heard the previous night. In the second section, a young woman named Vera Pavlovna receives a letter from the man who committed suicide; she breaks into sobs and a pale young man arrives and tries to comfort her. He eventually leaves, presumably forever. Next comes a "Preface" in which the author announces that the novel's subject is love; he derides his own abilities but asks for the reader's indulgence. The main story now begins, with a description of Vera's miserable childhood: her father is an ineffectual, minor government official and her mother a coarse, drunken shopkeeper who also rents rooms to illicit lovers. Vera is often exposed to depravity and subjected to the cruel jibes of her mother. When Vera is sixteen, her mother arranges for Vera to marry a wealthy but stupid young man. One of her friends suggests that the marriage would allow Vera to escape from her difficult home life and then manipulate her dull husband. Vera rejects such an arrangement and then befriends an idealistic medical student named Lopukhov. She soon dreams she is released from confinement in a dark cellar and cured of paralysis by a female figure, identified as Love of Mankind, who charges Vera with performing the same liberating function for other girls. In order to help Vera escape from her mother, Lopukhov proposes that the two enter into a "legal marriage," which would involve their living together and sharing resources but no romantic or sexual relationship. Although she is aware that there can be no turning back from such a legal bond (since divorce was virtually impossible in Russia at that time), Vera agrees to the marriage but insists on supporting herself by giving piano lessons; the two move into an apartment where they maintain separate bedrooms and enjoy a peaceful existence.

After an evening of conversation with Lopukhov and his intellectual friends, Vera has a dream in which many elements are intertwined: the concept of well-irrigated soil as a metaphor for the constant motion and labor necessary for growth, her mother accusing her of abandoning her parents, and, finally, the reappearance of the female figure from her first dream. The woman explains that evil people sometimes do good unintentionally—Vera's mother gave her life, for instance—and she predicts that the wicked will eventually realize that it is in their best interest to become good and change their ways.

Vera opens a dressmaking business and hires several seamstresses, organizing the operation as a cooperative based on fair wages and profit sharing. The operation is highly successful and eventually expands to include a communal house and a school for the workers.

While nursing Lopukhov through an illness, Vera and her husband's friend and fellow medical student, Kirsanov, fall in love; they attempt to hide this knowledge from both Lopukhov and themselves. Vera, however, has a third dream about the female figure, but this time she appears as a rather lurid opera singer who produces a diary in which are written Vera's real thoughts about her lack of love for the man she married and her desire for freedom. Upon waking, Vera runs to Lopukhov's room and tearfully confesses the content of her dream, after which their marriage is apparently consummated. Nevertheless Vera and Kirsanov become involved again, and Lopukhov confronts Kirsanov about the matter. He invites his friend to continue to visit their home, implying that he does not object to Kirsanov having an affair with his wife. Kirsanov refuses, because he feels that such an arrangement would harm Vera by bringing disapproval upon her, and that it would be better to wait for society to change. Lopukhov solves this ethical dilemma by faking his suicide and immigrating to America. A grief-stricken Vera tells Kirsanov they must part forever.

Then a nobleman turned professional revolutionary named Rakhmetov arrives and gives Vera a letter from Lopukhov explaining the faked suicide; he also urges her to feel no qualms about marrying Kirsanov. Vera does marry Kirsanov and goes back to work at the cooperative, later deciding to prove the fitness of women for any profession by studying to become a doctor. Several years later, Lopukhov returns to St. Petersburg, disguised as an American of French-Canadian heritage. He marries an emancipated young woman and the couple eventually develops a harmonious, jealousy-free friendship with Vera and Kirsanov.

Characters: Written while the author was imprisoned for his participation in revolutionary activities, *What Is to Be Done?* was conceived as a rejoinder to the unflattering portrayal of radical intellectuals presented in Ivan Turgenev's 1862 novel *Fathers and Sons.* Thoroughly permeated with the revolutionary socialism that Chernyshevsky and other members of Russia's intelligentsia advocated, the novel demonstrated the author's belief in the utilitarian theory of art. By writing it as a "love" story, with characters who undergo personal rather than overtly political dilemmas, Chernyshevsky was able to dupe the Tsarist censors who suppressed openly radical manuscripts. Though many critics have faulted the novel's strongly didactic tone and rather flat characterizations, *What Is to Be Done?* inspired and influenced many subsequent generations of Russian intellectuals, who would eventually try to bring about the socialist society they envisioned through the 1917 revolution.

One of the novel's most compelling aspects is its bold advocacy of feminism and focus on the legal and social tyranny to which nineteenth-century Russian women were subjected. Chernyshevsky concentrated his ideas about the emancipation of women in the character of **Vera Pavlovna,** who forms one corner of the love triangle upon which the novel centers. Vera suffers through a miserable childhood—presented as typical of Russian families— with a weak father and a horrid mother who not only withholds maternal love from her daughter but aggressively insults and torments her. Although Vera is a pretty girl, her mother destroys her confidence and self-esteem by repeatedly asserting that her complexion is unattractively dark. As a result of years of ill treatment, Vera becomes highly sensitive and also highly resistant to manipulation by others—hence her refusal to accept a conventional marriage, despite the practical freedom from her mother that it offers. The legal and social injustice of marriage is demonstrated by the fact that even Vera's union with the benevolent Lopukhin is permanently binding; when she falls in love with her husband's friend, she is faced with the choice of denying her feelings or committing adultery and risking societal condemnation. Chernyshevsky's portrayal of this dilemma may be interpreted as a plea for more liberal divorce laws. Vera's role as director of the dressmaking cooperative, described in a long and particularly didactic section of the novel, illustrates both the desirability of socialism and the fitness of women for taking an active role in all aspects of society. Vera successfully combines work and family—she and Kirsanov have a son after their eventual marriage—and later challenges the popular image of women as weak, overly emotional, and unstable by becoming a doctor.

Vera's three dreams chart her innermost thoughts as well as some of the book's dominant concerns: the first signifies the imprisonment and paralysis of her early life and her desire for escape as well as the general need for the emancipation of women. The second presents the socialist vision of a new society in which even formerly evil people are transformed. The third demonstrates the importance of emotional and sexual fulfillment. Some critics have noted that Chernyshevksy's innovative use of dreams in structuring the story anticipates the dreams of Raskolnikov in Fedor Mikhailovich Dostoyevsky's 1866 novel, *Crime and Punishment.*

The novel's subtitle, "Tales about the New People," refers to Chernyshevsky's concept of the "new man," his code name for the revolutionary individuals he attempted to positively portray. One of the "new men" presented in *What Is to Be Done?* is the generally admirable **Lopukhov**, whose choice of a medical career indicates his simultaneous allegiance to humanitarianism and to the rational realm of science. Lopukhov's willingness to enter into a marriage that does not involve sex or childbearing is distinctly un-Christian and marks him as a radical intellectual who values reason above tradition. Critic Francis B. Randall describes Lopukhov as the "ideal negative husband" (i.e., the husband in name only) because his independent, even solitary personality makes him ill-suited to conventional marriage. When he discovers that his wife and his friend have fallen in love, he reacts not with jealousy but with tolerance, encouraging Kirsanov to continue the affair and asserting that to repress natural desires is unhealthy and even dangerous. He does not press Kirsanov to pursue the arrangement when Kirsanov objects that it would be unjust to risk Vera's reputation. The ethical problem embodied in the love triangle seems unsolvable, so Lopukhov takes the melodramatic step of faking his suicide and leaving Russia so Vera and Kirsanov will be free to marry; some critics have characterized the false suicide as a too-easy solution. Though the marriage would have been viewed by many of its first readers as technically illegal as well as sinful, Chernyshevsky seems to approve of it. When Lopukhov, after his return to Russia, is considering marrying a young woman, he proposes that they have sexual relations in order to test their attraction to each other; he obviously does not want to risk a dilemma like the one he experienced with Vera. The couple decides, however, that the social risk is too great for such a step, and they marry in a conventional way. While early readers might have seen the amiable friendship attained by the two couples (none of whom seems to harbor any jealousy or feel that their honor has been damaged) as unlikely, such behavior is not difficult for modern readers to accept.

Lopukhov's fellow medical student and friend **Kirsanov** is an equally admirable young man; he is perhaps more outgoing than his friend. There is also a character named Kirsanov in Turgenev's *Fathers and Sons,* and scholars contend that Chernyshevsky chose the name intentionally so that his own character would overshadow the previous one and bring a more positive portrait of a "new man" to the fore. Through Kirsanov the problem of emotional needs is introduced into the plot, for the highly rational, essentially asexual arrangement of Vera and Lopukhov is disrupted when Kirsanov arrives and he and Vera fall in love. His theoretical argument with Lopukhov about the situation has been termed implausible by some critics, who claim that such a discussion would be much more difficult and emotionally charged than the one depicted in the novel. Nevertheless, the conversation illustrates a major problem faced by many of the young radicals who found themselves opposed to the Czarist regime and unsure how far to take their ideals: is it right to act against societal strictures when to do so threatens not only oneself but those one cares for? Kirsanov claims that although criticism of Vera for engaging in an adulterous union would be stupid, it would be cruel to subject her to it; he proposes simply waiting for the new, more reasonable society that must eventually arise. Kirsanov becomes a medical professor and forges a remarkably equal, supportive relationship with his wife.

The iron-willed, self-disciplined **Rakhmetov**—who plays a small but very important role in the novel—has been described by critic Mark Slonim as "the first revolutionary socialist in Russian fiction." Because of censorship, it was not possible for the author to overtly identify him as a revolutionary, but there are oblique hints that he spends his time disseminating propaganda and organizing among the peasants. Rakhmetov is a member of an aristocratic family descended from the Tartars, the Central Asian people who invaded Russia in the thirteenth century; this heritage has apparently resulted in his remarkable determination and endurance. As a teenager he deliberately built up his physical strength through diet, exercise, and hard labor, and he later traveled through Europe gathering knowledge from every country he visited. He has become a kind of superman: strong, utterly rational, honest, and often making earnest pronouncements that expose the truth. Many critics have commented on the ascetic quality of Rakhmetov's commitment to social change; like a monk, he has denied himself such material and physical pleasures as a bed to sleep on, alcohol, and sex, and he has given away all of his wealth. He once even spent a night on a bed of nails in order to both demonstrate his sincerity and steel himself for the possible rigors of an "underground" life. Rakhmetov has shaped himself into an effective instrument to help bring about revolution. The primary criticism leveled against him by scholars is that he is flat and implausible: self-assured to the point of arrogance, utterly incorruptible, never hesitant or unsuccessful in what he attempts, he seems more propagandistic than real.

Other characters in *What Is to Be Done?* include **Vera's mother and father.** Chernyshevsky's portrait of the weak, ineffectual father, a minor government official, might have been an additional stab at Turgenev, who held a similar post for a brief period. The mother runs a second-hand shop and frequently serves as a fence for stolen goods; she also rents rooms to wealthy couples engaging in illicit affairs. The author's portrayal of this coarse, drunken, cruel woman and the effect she has on her long-suffering daughter is generally considered quite convincing.

Further Reading

Barstow, Jane. "Dostoevsky's 'Notes from Underground' versus Chernyshevsky's 'What Is to Be Done?'" *College Literature* V, No. 1 (Winter 1978): 24-33.

Nineteenth Century Literature Criticism, Vol. 1. Detroit: Gale.

Paperno, Irina. *Chernyshevsky and the Age of Realism: A Study in the Semiotics of Behavior.* Stanford, Calif.: Stanford University Press, 1988.

Pereira, N. G. O. *The Thought and Teachings of N. G. Cernysevskij.* The Hague: Mouton, 1975.

Randall, Francis B. *N.G. Chernyshevskii.* New York: Twayne, 1967.

Slonim, Mark. "The Critics and the Nihilists." In *The Epic of Russian Literature: From Its Origins through Tolstoy,* pp. 203-18. New York: Oxford University Press, 1950.

Charles Waddell Chesnutt
1858-1932

African-American short story writer, novelist, biographer, and journalist.

The Conjure Woman (short stories, 1899)

Plot: The book is comprised of seven loosely connected stories framed by the narration of John, a grape farmer from Ohio who moves to North Carolina because its milder climate will benefit the health of his wife, Annie. The white couple learns about the history and culture of their new home through tales told by Uncle Julius, an elderly former slave who has for many years lived on the old, deserted plantation they buy. They hear the first story, "The Goophered Grapevine," during their first visit to the plantation, which features a long-untended vineyard. Uncle Julius advises them not to buy the property because the vineyard is "goophered," or bewitched. Before the Civil War, the plantation owner received a substantial income from the grapes, but he was unable to stop his slaves from pilfering the fruit. Therefore he commissioned Aunt Peggy, a "conjure woman" with prodigious magical skills, to put a goopher on the vineyard; she did so, decreeing that any slave who ate the grapes would die within a year. Those who defied the goopher did indeed soon die. When a new slave named Henry arrived and ate some grapes before anyone could tell him about the curse, Aunt Peggy made a counter-goopher that allowed him to live. His life-cycle, however, began to imitate that of the grapes: during the spring he became young and strong, while in the fall he weakened and shriveled up. The plantation owner took advantage of this strange circumstance by selling Henry every spring for a good price and buying him back at a pittance in the fall, thus realizing a substantial profit. The master was later financially ruined, however, when he accepted the guidance of a conniving "expert" and cut his vines back so much that they all died; the slave whose condition mirrored that of the vines also died. Although Uncle Julius warns John and Annie that the conjure is still on the vineyard, they buy the plantation, and John later learns that Uncle Julius had been selling the grapes himself while living in his cabin on the property. John hires the old man as his coachman.

The couple hears the story of "Po' Sandy" when John decides to tear down an old schoolhouse to obtain wood to build Annie a new kitchen. Uncle Julius warns that the schoolhouse was goophered during the time of slavery by a conjure woman named Tenie whose husband Sandy, a strong and able man, was often sent away to work on other plantations. To keep him near her permanently, Tenie turned Sandy into a tree in the daytime, turning him back into a man at nightfall when he would slip into their cabin. One day she was sent away to help at another plantation before she had a chance to turn Sandy back into a man; while she was gone the master had the tree cut down to build a new kitchen. The resulting building was said from then on to be haunted by Sandy, and Uncle Julius advises John not to use the goophered wood. John then learns that Uncle Julius wants to use the schoolhouse for his church meetings; apparently Sandy's ghost will not affect the services and might even be comforted by them. John and Annie buy new wood for the kitchen. When John considers purchasing a mule, Uncle Julius tells him about "The Conjurer's Revenge," which involves a slave named Primus who was turned into a mule by an angry conjure man from whom he had stolen a pig; the curse was eventually taken back but Primus was left with a club foot as a remnant of his term as a mule. Uncle Julius says that most mules are conjured and suggests that John buy a particular horse instead; he does so and Uncle Julius is soon seen wearing a new suit, suggesting that he was a party to the sale of the horse; the animal dies three months later.

John hires Uncle Julius's grandson Tom but fires him after he proves lazy and careless. Later, after witnessing a man beating a horse, Uncle Julius tells the story of "Mars Jeem's Nightmare," in which a particularly unkind and neglectful master is transformed into a slave by a conjure woman and experiences firsthand the cruelties of the overseer he hired to manage his slaves. Turned back into a white man, Mars Jeem reverses his former practices and everyone lives happily and prosperously thereafter. Inspired by the story to give Tom a second chance, and in spite of John's misgivings, Annie rehires Tom and the boy becomes a more diligent worker. When Annie experiences a period of deep depression, Uncle Julius relates the tale of "Sis Becky's Pickaninny" to comfort her. Becky was traded by her master, Colonel Pendleton, for a racehorse, but her baby, Little Mose, was not part of the bargain. She was devastated by her separation from her child, so Aunt Peggy turned the baby into a hummingbird, and later a mockingbird, and sent him to soothe his mother with his singing. When he grew up, Little Mose became an accomplished singer and a successful blacksmith who was able to buy both his mother and himself out of slavery. Uncle Julius tells the much-comforted Annie that Becky could have avoided her trouble if she had carried a rabbit's foot with her, and later John finds a rabbit's foot among Annie's possessions. As John is about to clear some land on the plantation, Uncle Julius shares the story of "The Gray Wolf's Ha'nt": that particular piece of land is haunted by the spirit of a slave named Dan who was turned into a gray wolf by the conjuring father of a free black man whom Dan had accidentally killed. The man also turned Dan's wife into a cat and tricked Dan into killing her. The gray wolf's spirit does not, however, impede Uncle Julius from gathering honey from a beehive located on the land.

Annie's sister Mabel becomes engaged to a local man, Malcolm Murchison, but the two lovers quarrel one day. Uncle Julius, while driving Annie and Mabel in the carriage, remembers the story of "Hot Foot Hannibal." The title character was a house slave upon whom Aunt Peggy put a goopher so that another slave named Chloe—with whom Hannibal was supposed to be matched—would be free to marry her lover, Jeff. As a result of the goopher, Hannibal fell into disfavor with the master and was sent to work in the fields, but he managed to wreak revenge on the lovers by planting a false story about Jeff's visits to another woman. After the jealous Chloe spurned her lover for his infidelity, she learned that he had actually been faithful to her, and she subsequently died. Uncle Julius has taken an unusually long route and stops in a spot remarkably close to where Mabel's fiance happens to be standing. The two lovers are reunited; Malcolm later tries to hire Uncle Julius but the old man stays with John and Annie.

Characters: Chesnutt is considered one of the first American writers—and notably the first African-American writer—to examine honestly and vividly the realities of plantation life during the years before and after the Civil War, and to portray with skill and power the ways in which slaves used imagination to affirm their dignity and survive under demeaning and harsh circumstances. While similar in some ways to the Uncle Remus tales written by Joel Chandler Harris—especially in the use of an elderly black narrator and of African-American dialect—the stories in *The Conjure Woman* are seen as demythologizing the benevolent, pastoral portrait of slavery and of antebellum Southern life presented by Harris. While Chesnutt's characters are sometimes described as thin and conventional, they serve as compelling embodiments of particular human viewpoints and motivations.

The memorable character **Uncle Julius McAdoo,** the former slave who tells the tales in *The Conjure Woman,* is often compared to the storyteller Uncle Remus. Several critics, however, have identified important differences between the two. Although he is loyal to his employers and basically respectful, Uncle Julius is not the traditional, faithful black retainer. Through his colorful, entertaining stories, Uncle Julius both educates his white employers and subtly manipulates—as when he convinces John not to tear down the schoolhouse that he wants to use for religious services. In his venerable, low-key voice and faithfully rendered southern black dialect, Uncle Julius illustrates the horror and tragedy of slavery and the imaginative strength that allowed blacks to survive it. To a certain degree Uncle Julius exhibits the ingratiating manner of such black characters as Uncle Remus, whose portrayal has been called demeaning to African-Americans because of his simplicity and submissiveness. Yet through his ironic and revealing storytelling, Uncle Julius actually wields a measure of personal power and sustains a strong individual identity. By the end of *The Conjure Woman* his employers, who thought they were doing Uncle Julius a favor by allowing him to remain on the plantation and giving him a job, need him much more than he needs them. His ability to illuminate the truths of the past and of the human heart make him valuable not only to John and Annie but to the reader, whose awareness of African-American experience and history is enhanced by his imaginative skills.

The Conjure Woman faithfully portrays the locale in which it is set, and one of the necessities in such "local color" fiction is an outsider in need of education about his new home. This role is fulfilled by **John,** whose narration frames the stories told by Uncle Julius. As a white Ohioan, John arrives in North Carolina with the typically liberal, anti-slavery viewpoint of many northerners. Despite his basic decency and apparent lack of prejudice, however, John has a patronizing and superior attitude toward the elderly black man whom he finds living on the plantation and whom he employs. Preoccupied with practical responsibilities and concerns, John interprets Uncle Julius's stories as merely entertaining and perceives in them only the narrator's self-interest (e.g., his desire to retain access to the profitable grapevines or beehive). Critics describe John as personifying the limited ability of many whites—even those who seem most sympathetic—to comprehend the realities of black life both during and after slavery. John speaks in a florid, legalistic manner that contrasts strongly with Uncle Julius's dialect, and he is extremely skeptical of the magic that permeates the former slave's stories. While he recognizes Uncle Julius's storytelling skill and value as a local historian, John fails to detect the serious purpose that underlies his tales. When, for instance, Annie reacts empathetically to the story of Tenie and Sandy, John asks how she can believe that a man could be turned into a tree—thus revealing his inability to comprehend the story's deeper message of human love and the losses engendered under slavery.

By contrast, John's wife, **Annie,** brings to Uncle Julius's stories a much higher level of comprehension. She instinctively understands that there is more than just their literal meaning; she can disregard the unlikely phenomenon of conjuring and see that they reveal conditions under slavery and the coping techniques employed by the slaves. Upon hearing the story of Tenie and Sandy, for instance, Annie focuses not on the likelihood of Sandy's actually being turned into a tree but on the tragedy of families separated from each other and the treatment of human beings as property; she exclaims, "What a system it was, under which such things were possible!" Significantly, the deep melancholy she experiences is alleviated when Uncle Julius tells her a story of even greater suffering and how it was overcome. When Annie accepts the rabbit's foot from the old man, she indicates her understanding of the power of the imagination as a healing force.

Although there are several other conjurers mentioned in the stories, the conjure woman of the book's title is **Aunt Peggy,** who makes several appearances. In her ability to dispense goophers and thus influence the course of events, Aunt Peggy wields substantial power, though she is still subject to white domination. She is not a slave but a free black, and her powers are valued and called upon not only by other blacks but by white people (from whom she insists on payment). Nevertheless, she has no influence over such occurrences as Becky's being traded for a racehorse, though she can alleviate Becky's suffering by turning her baby into a bird and sending him to sing for his mother. Aunt Peggy embodies the mysteries of the natural world with which blacks are portrayed as closely interacting, and she also brings into the context of American slavery an ancient art that originated in Africa.

117

A variety of other characters inhabit the stories in *The Conjure Woman,* though none are portrayed in any great detail. In "The Goophered Grapevine," **Mars (Master) Dugal** is the shrewd, stingy plantation owner who initially requests the spell on the grapevine, exploits his slave **Henry**'s unusual condition to gain a profit, and is ultimately ruined by his own greed. Thus he seems to represent the capitalistic forces that were ultimately brought down by their dependence on slavery. **Sandy** and **Tenie** are the primary characters in "Po' Sandy," the latter a hard worker whose master unwittingly kills him by chopping him down while he is in the form of a tree, the former a conjure woman whose attempt to keep her mate near her is tragically thwarted. Conjuring is thus presented as a means of preserving cherished emotions and relationships as well as establishing a personal identity, and it is sometimes inadequate in the face of white domination. Uncle Julius's initially lazy but eventually more industrious grandson **Tom** is a central figure in "Mars Jeem's Nightmare," as is **Mars "Jeem" McLean,** a harsh master who learns to treat his slaves more humanely. Beneath the surface of "The Conjurer's Revenge," in which the slave **Primus** is transformed into a mule, is the traditional use of the mule as a symbol for slavery and the clubfoot as an indication of the way it permanently handicaps human beings. Similarly, the crime of slavery is mimicked in "The Gray Wolf's Ha'nt" when one man takes control of another's body; in addition, **Dan**'s inability to perceive that the cat he chases and kills is actually his wife points to the importance of looking beneath surfaces for the true meanings of things.

"Sis' Becky's Pickaninny," perhaps the most moving of the stories, compellingly presents the grief experienced by blacks whose families were torn apart by slavery. **Becky**'s son, **Little Mose,** who comforts his mother through song and eventually makes her a free woman, demonstrates the importance of music for solace, strength, and expression in the lives of slaves and a reminder that freedom was their constant goal. **Colonel Pendleton,** the white master who callously trades Becky for a racehorse, demonstrates an inhumane, utilitarian outlook that causes great suffering. "Hot-Foot Hannibal," considered by some critics the weakest of the tales, is the only one featuring the treachery of the slaves themselves rather than the cruelty or insensitivity of the white owner. The tragic end of the love affair between **Jeff** and **Chloe,** brought about by the jealous and vindictive **Hannibal,** causes Annie's sister **Mabel** to regret her quarrel with her fiance **Malcolm Murchison.**

Further Reading

Andrews, William L. *The Literary Career of Charles Waddell Chesnutt.* Baton Rouge: Louisiana State University Press, 1980.

Bobb, Valerie. "Subversion and Repatriation in *The Conjure Woman.*" *Southern Quarterly* XXV, No. 2 (Winter 1987): 66-75.

Callahan, John F. "The Spoken in the Written Word: African-American Tales and the Middle Passage from 'Uncle Remus: His Songs and Sayings' to 'The Conjure Woman.'" In *In the American Grain: The Pursuit of Voice in Twentieth-Century Black Fiction,* pp. 25-61. Champaign: University of Illinois Press, 1988.

Fienberg, Lorne. "Charles W. Chesnutt and Uncle Julius: Black Storytellers at the Crossroads." *Studies in American Fiction* 15, No. 2 (Autumn 1987): 161-73.

Keller, Frances Richardson. *An American Crusade: The Life of Charles Waddell Chesnutt.* Provo, Utah: Brigham Young University Press, 1978.

Morgan, Florence A.H. Review of *The Conjure Woman,* by Charles W. Chesnutt. *The Bookman* IX, No. 3 (May 1899): 372-73.

Render, Sylvia Lyons. *Charles W. Chesnutt.* Boston: Twayne, 1980.

Short Story Criticism, Vol. 7. Detroit: Gale.

Wilkie Collins

1824-1889

English novelist, short story writer, and dramatist.

The Woman in White (novel, 1860)

Plot: The novel takes place in the mid-nineteenth century in the Cumberland district of England. Walter Hartright is a young artist who has been employed as a drawing instructor to the two nieces of Frederick Fairlie, Laura Fairlie and her half-sister, Marian Halcombe. Just before he is to travel to Limmeridge House to begin his new position, Walter encounters a mysterious young woman dressed in white who seems to have some connection with the Fairlie family. She barely escapes capture by a man who says he is searching for a white-clothed, female escapee from an insane asylum. The next day, Walter meets his two students—unattractive but intelligent and pleasant Marian, and the beautiful heiress Laura. Hearing the story of the woman in white, Marian decides that she must be Anne Catherick, who, some years earlier, had gained her now dead mother's attention and help because of her resemblance to Laura. After spending several months at Limmeridge, Walter falls in love with Laura, but he learns that she promised her father on his deathbed that she would marry the aristocratic Sir Percival Glyde. The woman in white makes a brief appearance near the estate, calling doubt on Sir Percival's character. On his arrival at Limmeridge, Sir Percival explains that the woman is the disturbed daughter of a family servant whom he has, with her mother's blessing, committed to an insane asylum. Laura and Sir Percival are married, and a dejected Walter joins an expedition to Central America.

When the Glydes return from their honeymoon, Laura is obviously unhappy and the atmosphere at their home, Blackwater Park, is foreboding. Laura's aunt Eleanor arrives unexpectedly for a visit with her fat but suave Italian husband, Count Fosco, and it becomes apparent that Sir Percival has some sort of financial relationship with the count. After a suspicious Laura refuses to sign a document that she is not allowed to read, Marian overhears Count Fosco and Sir Percival discussing how to deprive Laura of her fortune. When Sir Percival learns that the woman in white is in the area—she and Laura have already had a chance encounter in which she hinted at the existence of some secret about Sir Percival's life—he locks Laura and Marian in their rooms. Marian manages to escape and learns that Sir Percival and the Count's plan to obtain Laura's wealth now includes murder; subsequently, however, Marian develops pneumonia and Laura also becomes ill.

After Laura has recovered, she is told that Marian is in London (actually Marian is still imprisoned in the house); when Laura travels there, Count Fosco drugs her and has her committed to an insane asylum under the name of Anne Catherick. Meanwhile, Anne Catherick—the woman in white—dies while confined by Sir Percival and he has her buried as Laura, Lady Glyde. Marian refuses to believe that Laura is dead and eventually discovers her in the asylum. She helps Laura escape and they return to Limmeridge, but Frederick Fairlie refuses to believe that the young woman before him is really his niece. Marian and Laura meet Walter, who has returned to visit Laura's grave, and he sets out to help them. He manages to uncover Sir Percival's secret: his parents were never legally married and thus he has no right to his title. While attempting to thwart the discovery of this information by burning the church records that prove it, Sir Percival burns down the church and is himself killed in the fire. Walter also learns that Anne Catherick was the illegitimate daughter of Laura's father, thus explaining their resemblance. In order to make Count Fosco admit in writing to his part in the conspiracy and thus establish Laura's real identity, Walter enlists the help of his friend, the Italian Professor Pesca, who recognizes the count as a traitor to the secret Italian political organization to which both men belong. After confessing to the substitution plot, Count Fosco leaves England and is subsequently killed by the group he betrayed. Walter and Laura marry and, after proving to Frederick Fairlie that Laura is his heir, they leave Limmeridge (eventually their son will inherit the estate). Marian lives with the Hartrights for the rest of her life.

Characters: Considered Collins's most popular work, *The Woman in White* is a skillfully structured and innovative example of the intrigue-filled novels of "sensation" that were popular in the last half of the nineteenth century. Influenced both by an actual eighteenth-century French criminal case and Collins's own dramatic meeting with the woman who would become his longtime mistress, Caroline Graves, the novel features narration by several different characters who provide their own subjective interpretations of events.

The novel's hero—or closest approximation, at least, to a conventional hero—is **Walter Hartright,** the young drawing instructor whose dedication to restoring Laura Fairlie's rightful identity leads to the mystery's resolution. Although he does not strike most reviewers as a particularly interesting character, Walter is intelligent and courageous and applies himself with dedication to the task before him. He has been said to embody distinctly middle class, British values such as loyalty, reason, hard work, and tenacity, as opposed to the indolence and corruption demonstrated by the story's upper class characters. For this reason, and because he takes a stand in favor of morality, Walter was a figure calculated to appeal to Victorian readers.

Collins's characterization of the two primary female characters in *The Woman in White*—Laura Fairlie and Marian Halcombe—provides a compelling glimpse into his attitudes. **Laura Fairlie** is the stereotypical heroine of conventional fiction: blonde, beautiful, and passive. She is frail and dutiful, deferring to her dead father's wish that she marry the unpleasant (and ultimately corrupt) Sir Percival Glyde. The extreme vulnerability of her position—her wealth becomes her husband's upon her marriage, and she no longer has any legal claim to it—demonstrates Collins's sensitivity to the subjugated position of women in Victorian society. (He is often credited with upholding the rights of the downtrodden, whether their condition was due to their sex or their economic status.) Laura's half-sister **Marian Halcombe** is one of Collins's most acclaimed creations. Her physical unattractiveness (she has a swarthy complexion, the suggestion of a mustache, a protruding jaw, and coarse black hair) is countered by her virtues: she is loyal, courageous, perceptive, and resourceful. Marian provides a direct contrast to the conventional femininity that Laura represents, for she is a strong, assertive woman who says exactly what she means. Thus Marian is often cited as exemplifying Collins's innovativeness as an author as well as his rejection of many traditional Victorian attitudes. This intelligent character, whose affection for her sister and respect for the truth leads her to oppose the evil plans of Count Fosco and Sir Percival, even gains the admiration of her enemy, and Fosco's ability to appreciate Marian's finer qualities adds depth to his character as well.

Count Isidore Ottavio Baldassore Fosco is one of the most notorious villains in nineteenth-century literature and a precursor of many subsequent fictional characters. His huge physique, in combination with his charming manners and inner wickedness, make him an original and captivating figure. Fosco is an intelligent, witty, articulate, and cultured man whose size does not impede his strange attractiveness to women—even the wise and virtuous Marian Halcombe finds him frighteningly appealing. Collins infused complexity into Fosco's character by giving him several humanizing qualities, such as his tenderness toward animals (he allows his pet white mice to crawl all over him) and his admiration for Marian. Somehow, the gentleness and refinement that are part of Fosco's personality make his essential wickedness and greed—for money and power as well as food—even more pronounced and compelling.

Sir Percival Glyde is depicted as a foil to Count Fosco. Equally evil, he lacks the Count's suaveness and humanizing qualities. He is surly and unpleasant, treating his lovely young wife with contempt and eventually attempting to acquire her fortune by dastardly means. Overcome by debts and desperate to hide the fraud by which he acquired his aristocratic title and status, Glyde joins the Count in the conspiracy that ultimately leads to his downfall. Unlike his Italian counterpart, he is a weak and unintelligent villain whose botched attempt to rescue himself by burning the church records which document his illegitimate birth typifies his lack of skill—he is incapable of successfully executing even such a simple deed as that would seem to be.

Although **Anne Catherick** is the woman in white and thus the novel's title character, she is not portrayed in much detail. She is important more as an impetus to the action and as a symbol than as a fleshed-out figure in the story. Her dramatic appearance at the beginning of the book, in addition to her other unexpected appearances throughout the story, help to establish a mood of intrigue and danger. Her white clothing directly reflects her essential innocence—Walter initially suspects, for instance, that she may have been seduced by Sir Percival but learns that this is not so. Like Laura Fairlie, Anne Catherick serves as an example of Collins's interest in the rights of society's oppressed: her dilemma demonstrates the plight of those who were committed to insane asylums against their will and with little legal recourse.

Although **Frederick Fairlie,** Laura and Marian's uncle and Walter's employer, is not an outright villain he is not sympathetically portrayed. He is a self-centered, indolent hypochondriac who lives in seclusion and whose emotional isolation from others prevents him from recognizing that Laura is indeed still alive and before him. Yet it might also be noted that Fairlie's distasteful personality is necessary to the story, for if he had been a more normal person he would probably have protected Laura from those who preyed upon her. **Mrs. Catherick,** Anne's mother, is a similarly inadequate and selfish guardian more concerned with her own interests than with protecting her daughter. Although she pretends, like the other wicked characters in *The Woman in White,* to be perfectly respectable, she is inwardly corrupt; she has collaborated with Sir Percival in hiding the truth about his parentage. Mrs. Catherick does play a practical role in the plot by revealing that Anne and Laura had the same father, **Philip Fairlie.**

Two minor characters who play significant roles in the novel are **Eleanor Fairlie Fosco,** Laura's aunt and the wife of the count; and Walter Hartright's Italian friend, **Professor Pesca.** Countess Fosco was once a gay denizen of British high society, but her marriage caused her family and friends to reject her. She is now a cold, jaded woman who is utterly subservient to her husband—thus providing another example of the subjugated role of married women in the nineteenth century. Pesca, a man of stereotypical Mediterranean volubility, is important to the plot both because he gets Walter his job with the Fairlies (in repayment for Walter having once saved him from drowning) and because he later provides a link with the Italian political society of which Fosco is also a member, revealing Fosco's shameful secret and precipitating his downfall.

The Moonstone (novel, 1868)

Plot: Set during the first half of the nineteenth century, the novel centers on the sacred moonstone, a valuable diamond that was originally part of the statue of the moon-god in an Indian religious shrine. The gem was stolen by an Englishman, John Herncastle, and subsequently pursued by three Hindus who have sworn to return it to its rightful place. Securing the gem in a bank vault, Herncastle left it to his niece, Rachel Verinder. After Herncastle's death, Rachel's cousin Franklin Blake is charged with delivering the moonstone to her home in time for her birthday celebration. After his arrival at the country estate, he and Rachel start to fall in love, despite the efforts of Godfrey Ablewhite—a handsome philanthropist from London—to gain Rachel's affections. Those gathered at Rachel's birthday party also include the Verinders's lawyer, Mr. Bruff, and the local physician, Dr. Candy. The three Hindus appear during the celebration, disguised as jugglers, but another guest, Mr. Murthwaite—who has traveled extensively in Asia—sends them away. That night, the moonstone is stolen from Rachel's room and the police are called. The Hindus are able to prove that they were not the culprits. Then the renowned Scotland Yard detective, Sergeant Cuff, arrives and quickly points out that the fresh paint from the door of Rachel's room must have come off on the thief's clothing. Rachel, however, refuses to allow a search and effectively calls an end to any further investigation. Cuff suspects that Rachel herself has staged the theft with the assistance of the maid, Rosanna Spearman, who has a history of criminal activity. But Rosanna later kills herself by jumping into quicksand, leaving behind a letter for Franklin Blake, who has already left England.

Rachel agrees to marry Ablewhite but breaks the engagement when she learns of his interest in her fortune. Returning to England a year later, Franklin hears about Rosanna's letter from the Verinders's faithful servant, Gabriel Betteridge. The letter declares Rosanna's hopeless love for Franklin and her knowledge of his theft of the moonstone, and it leads to the discovery of a box which contains Franklin's paint-stained nightgown. Returning to London, the confused Franklin talks to Bruff about the mysterious circumstances of the theft. The lawyer tells him that the gem is now in a bank vault, deposited there by a pawnbroker named Mr. Luker. Believing that Franklin and Rachel are still in love, Bruff arranges a meeting between them at which Rachel reveals that she saw Franklin come into her room and steal the moonstone. Because she loved him and assumed he needed money she had halted the investigation; she was convinced that Franklin did not return her love. Franklin swears that he has no memory of his actions that night, and in order to resolve the mystery he returns to the country estate. There he learns from Ezra Jennings, Dr. Candy's assistant, that because he had insulted the medical profession in a discussion with Dr. Candy on the night of Rachel's party, the physician had secretly given him a dose of laudanum (opium). With Bruff and Rachel in attendance, Franklin recreates the circumstances of that evening: he takes the drug and again steals a stone—this one a substitute—from Rachel's room, but falls asleep before revealing what he did with the real moonstone.

Sergeant Cuff now returns to the case. Bruff's office clerk is told to follow the pawnbroker when he goes to the bank to redeem the gem. It is then determined that Luker has given the moonstone to a bearded man who appears to be a sailor and who takes a room in a seaside inn. Arriving at the inn, Franklin and Cuff find the man dead and, removing his false beard, discover that he is Godfrey Ablewhite. They surmise that after stealing the gem from Rachel's room, a drugged Franklin had given it to Ablewhite with instructions to place it in a bank vault, but that Ablewhite—realizing that Franklin would have no memory of his actions—had instead kept the gem for himself. Before he could escape with the moonstone, the Hindus had killed him and taken the diamond. With all of the obstacles to their union now removed, Franklin and Rachel are married. Years later, Murthwaite reports that he has witnessed a religious ceremony in India at which the statue of the moon-god was unveiled with the sacred moonstone returned to its customary position. He also saw the three Hindus fading into the gathered crowd of worshippers.

Characters: This novel, which the renowned poet T. S. Eliot called "the first, longest, and best of English detective novels," was wildly popular soon after it was published and remains acclaimed for its crucial influence on later detective novels. Techniques employed in the novel that have since become conventions include the shifting of suspicion among an assemblage of characters and the sharing of clues with the reader (known as "fair play"). Collins's stated purpose in *The Moonstone* was to "trace the influence of character on circumstance"; consequently, the vagaries of the unconscious mind and the limits of individual perception are major themes.

With his creation of the knowledgeable but unassuming Scotland Yard detective **Sergeant Cuff,** Collins established a character type that has since dominated this genre of fiction. Even the much more famous sleuth Sherlock Holmes owes something to his predecessor, who is similarly lean and hatchet-faced. Collins describes Cuff as "grizzled, elderly," and dressed in black—"[He] might have been a parson, or an undertaker—or anything else you like, except what he really was." Cuff is an amiable, experienced man with an astute perception of human nature and a dry sense of humor. His fondness for growing roses contributes to his humanity, as does his fallibility. As many critics have noted, Cuff does not actually solve the mystery of the moonstone, and even falsely accuses Rachel of the theft. He is also absent during much of the novel, reappearing as a narrator just in time for the denouement. Although Cuff is assuredly a skillful detective who combines scientific investigative techniques with an awareness of human psychology, he is not necessarily brilliant. Nevertheless, several of Cuff's methods—including the scientific reconstruction of the crime and the summary explanation in front of the assembled suspects—became standard fare in subsequent detective novels.

Another of the book's narrators, **Franklin Blake,** is not a detective by profession but proves crucial to the crime's resolution, thus establishing the tradition of the amateur sleuth who proves at least as adept as the celebrated professional. Franklin also has the unique distinction of being both the novel's hero and its culprit: in unconsciously attempting to protect Rachel from the harm that possession of the moonstone might bring, he steals it from her room and thus is a primary contributor to all of the subsequent trouble. Franklin is a lively young man with a genial, engaging personality who combines cosmopolitan experience (he was educated in Europe, and it is suggested that he is quite worldly) with the typical English virtues of honesty and tenacity. The circumstance of Franklin's unconscious thievery allows Collins to enter the realm of human psychology, thereby lending the novel greater depth and originality.

Although it is **Rachel Verinder** who has captured Franklin's heart and whose interest he seeks to protect, she is not depicted as the demure and fainting heroine of conventional fiction—nor is she frail and dutiful like Laura Fairlie in Collins's earlier novel, *The Woman in White.* The old servant, Gabriel Betteridge, says that Rachel "always went on a way of her own, sufficient for herself in the joys and sorrows of her life." Indeed, Rachel's secretiveness is exemplified by her refusal to expose her knowledge of the real thief. She is vivacious, independent, and intelligent, and virtuous without seeming unnatural. In fact, Rachel responds quite naturally (if not admirably) to her disappointment when she believes that neither Franklin nor Godfrey Ablewhite sincerely loves her: she becomes sullen and ill-tempered.

Rachel's ironically named fiance **Godfrey Ablewhite** is similar to other villains in Collins's fiction in that he hides a corrupt nature behind a respectable facade. Handsome and smooth-tongued, his charity work is merely a cover for his true wickedness. Ablewhite is deeply in debt and thus wants to marry Rachel for her fortune (luckily, she discovers his real intentions in time); his financial problems also influence him to keep the moonstone for himself, an act that ultimately leads to his death. Ablewhite provides an example of Collins's unsympathetic portrayal of members of the English aristocracy—his sympathies are obviously with the lower classes, especially those who are powerless to change their situations.

Gabriel Betteredge narrates one of the chapters of *The Moonstone* and is often cited as a particularly successful character in the novel. Critic Kenneth Robinson describes him as combining "the functions of Greek chorus and amateur detective" (the latter role is verified by Betteredge himself when he claims to have caught "the infernal detective fever"). An elderly and devoted servant to the Verinders, Betteredge takes a negative view of marriage and of the aristocracy, scorning the indolence of the gentry. His use of his beloved *Robinson Crusoe* (the eighteenth-century novel by Daniel Defoe) as a source of general information and a guide to morality lends humor to the novel and has been said to spoof those pious people who constantly apply passages from the Bible to their daily lives. As both a participant in and observer of the action, Betteredge provides a unique perspective and also helps to demonstrate the subjectivity of individual perception, a concept that Collins is often credited with developing. And as an inhabitant of the realm of servants, Betteredge exemplifies Collins's interest in that realm and consistent compassion for his society's lower classes.

Another character and narrator who brings some comedy into the novel is the spinster evangelist, **Drusilla Clack,** the Verinder's poor relation. She is a religious fanatic who sees sin everywhere and zealously attempts to convert the sinners around her by distributing devotional tracts. The fact that Miss Clack worships Ablewhite foreshadows the eventual exposure of his unworthiness. Collins's portrayal of Miss Clack has been termed somewhat heavy-handed by a few critics—due perhaps to his real distaste for such ostentatiously religious people—although the noted novelist V. S. Pritchett claimed that he had "hit upon a wonderful type."

Dr. Candy's assistant, **Ezra Jennings,** who helps Franklin discover the mystery behind his behavior the night of the crime, is one of the novel's most interesting and often noted characters. Born in the West Indies of mixed blood, Jennings is something of an outcast in English society. His strange appearance and secretiveness initially result in his being a prime suspect for the theft of the diamond, but he is revealed to be not only innocent of the crime but essentially good and helpful. The reader eventually learns that Jennings has been suffering for many years with a painful illness which led to his use of, and then addiction to, laudanum. The fact that Collins suffered from an excruciating case of gout and himself used opium to ease his pain—eventually becoming addicted—lends both authenticity and poignancy to Jennings's account of the drug's effects.

Collins is also praised for his portrayal of the Verinders's maid, **Rosanna Spearman,** whose letter to Franklin Blake comprises one of the novel's sections. The daughter of a prostitute, she is a former thief and inmate of a women's prison, now employed by Lady Verinder. Rosanna's lower social status and unattractive appearance make her love for Franklin a hopeless one, and critics have admired Collins's sensitive portrayal of her pathetic but dignified passion. Rosanna demonstrates her devotion to Franklin by trying to help him when she believes he has stolen the moonstone, hiding his stained nightgown before she takes her own life. Her suicide in the "Shivering Sands" has been called both melodramatic in its use of quicksand and an effective and moving scene.

The **three Hindu worshippers** of the moonstone who travel to England to retrieve the gem are significant in several ways. Superficially, they create an aura of exoticism and intrigue, but they might also be seen as heroic figures devoted to their religion and persistent in their quest, whereas many of the English characters behave in a bungling or valueless manner. Collins often infused his fiction with social commentary, and several critics have suggested that Collins's portrayal of the Hindus in this novel as morally superior to the British colonials evidences his belief in the idea of Indian independence.

The Verinder family's lawyer, **Mr. Bruff,** is one of the novel's narrators and a participant in unraveling the mystery. He is an elderly man—he has been with the family for three generations—and a trusted friend, becoming Rachel's guardian after her mother's death. He guesses why Rachel has become embittered and is wise enough to bring her into contact with Franklin again to resolve their misunderstanding. Other significant characters in *The Moonstone* include **Superintendent Seegrave,** the pompous, incompetent local policeman who initially investigates the crime and who is described by critic Audrey Peterson as heading "a long line of inept plodders serving as foils to great detectives in literature"; **Lady Julia Verinder,** Rachel's mother, whose kindness is attested to by her compassionate treatment of Rosanna Spearman; **Dr. Candy,** who takes revenge on Franklin for his unflattering remarks about the medical profession by secretly dosing him with opium; and **Mr. Murthwaite,** who provides a link with India through his travel experiences and scholarship, and who relates the final disposition of the moonstone. **Septimus Luker** is the London pawnbroker in whose possession the gem rests for a time; **Lucy Yolland** is the ugly, clubfooted, and loyal friend of Rosanna who keeps her letter safe; and **Octavius Guy** is the clerk from Mr. Bruff's office who follows Ablewhite to his lodging.

Further Reading

Dictionary of Literary Biography, Vols. 18, 70. Detroit: Gale.

Eliot, T. S. "Wilkie Collins and Dickens." *Times Literary Supplement* No. 1331 (4 August 1927): 525-26.

Frick, Patricia Miller. "Wilkie Collins's 'Little Jewel': The Meaning of 'The Moonstone.'" *Philological Quarterly* 63, No. 3 (Summer 1984): 313-21.

Lonoff, Sue. *Wilkie Collins and His Victorian Readers: A Study in the Rhetoric of Authorship.* New York: AMS Press, 1982.

Nineteenth Century Literature Criticism, Vol. 1, 18. Detroit: Gale.

Page, Norman, ed. *Wilkie Collins: The Critical Heritage.* London: Routledge & Kegan Paul, 1974.

Peterson, Audrey. "Wilkie Collins and the Mystery Novel." In *Victorian Masters of Mystery: From Wilkie Collins to Conan Doyle,* pp. 11-69. New York: Frederick Ungar, 1984.

Pritchett, V.S. "The Roots of Detection." In *Books in General,* pp. 179-84. London: Chatto & Windus, 1953.

Reed, John R. "English Imperialism and the Unacknowledged Crime of 'The Moonstone.'" *Clio* 2, No. 3 (June 1973): 281-90.

A review of "The Moonstone." *The London Times* (October 3, 1868): 4.

Benjamin Constant

1767-1830

French novelist, essayist, journalist, autobiographer, and translator.

Adolphe (novel, 1815)

Plot: The story begins in Germany, where the young protagonist has finished his studies at the University of Göttingen. Adolphe's somewhat cold, remote father, a government official, hopes that his son will enter a government position after a short period of travel. The young man has been influenced by his constrained relationship with his father as well as by a brilliant and unconventional older woman with whom he engaged in long, analytical conversations. Adolphe now joins the aristocratic society of a small German principality. His new friends are eventually put off by his artificial gaiety as well as his disdain for convention and the mediocrity he finds in their company. When one of his friends manages to seduce a fairly interesting woman, Adolphe focuses on Ellénore, the longtime mistress of Count P——; she has remained devoted to the count for ten years, bearing him two illegitimate children, and has finally won a certain degree of acceptance in his social circle. Although Ellénore initially resists Adolphe's overtures, she finally gives in to him, and the two fall in love. They are happy for a time, but Adolphe soon feels hemmed in by the relationship. He tires of the deceptions necessary to carry on the affair and of Ellénore's domineering manner, but he knows that her own position is dangerously compromised. After a serious argument between the two lovers and their subsequent reconciliation, Ellénore is even more anxiously ardent, and she breaks off her relationship with the count. This sacrifice disturbs Adolphe, but he is unable to object. When he leaves the town for his own home, he feels regret instead of relief and continues his relationship with Ellénore through letters. Ellénore announces that she plans to join Adolphe at his home and is angered when he tries to dissuade her; she arrives even sooner as a result and Adolphe shows his embarrassment. A violent disagreement erupts between the two.

Adolphe learns that his father disapproves of his son's liaison and has tried to force Ellénore to leave. Resentful at what he sees as his father's capitulation to the values of a corrupt society, Adolphe flees with Ellénore to Bohemia and behaves lovingly toward her. She, however, accuses him of pitying rather than loving her. Though Adolphe resolves not to cause Ellénore any more suffering and tries to feign happiness, he is soon overcome by the same desire for escape that he had previously experienced. Count P—— offers to take Ellénore into his care again, so Adolphe tells her that he does not love her, hoping that she will return to the count; Ellénore's deeply grieved reaction, however, forces him to retract his statement. Then Ellénore learns that her father, who many years before had been ruined by political turmoil in his native Poland, had regained his fortune but has since died and left all of his wealth to Ellénore. The two travel to Poland, where their now consistently unhappy relationship continues. Adolphe receives a letter from his father suggesting that he should now be free to leave Ellénore; he advises Adolphe to visit Baron T——, an old friend of Adolphe's father and a German ambassador to Poland. The baron tries to encourage Adolphe to leave Ellénore, showing him how such a relationship could affect his future. This plunges Adolphe into even more mental turmoil. He fails to make a clean break with Ellénore, but allows the baron to send her some hurtful letters. Ellénore becomes very sick and finally dies. Though free from his tie to her, Adolphe feels only great despair and emptiness.

Characters: Based in part on Constant's own love affair with French writer Madame de Staël, *Adolphe* transcends the limits of autobiography to comprise a universally compelling portrait of a human dilemma. Written in spare, economical prose, the novel features an insightful psychological depiction of its title character and illuminates the complexities of his need for and response to love. In focusing on the weaker, indecisive qualities of the human psyche through the eyes of a guilt-ridden, conflicted protagonist, *Adolphe* is often described as anticipating the concerns of twentieth-century fiction and has even been called one of the first truly modern novels.

One of the most modern aspects of *Adolphe* is its decidedly unheroic protagonist, who in fact more closely resembles the anti-heroes that would become predominant in the novels of the twentieth century. An innovative element in Constant's portrayal is that **Adolphe's** background is emphasized as psychologically important in his behavior as an adult. Raised by an undemonstrative but notably indulgent father and influenced by his relationship with an intelligent older woman who encouraged him to reject convention and mediocrity, Adolphe disdains the society he enters after leaving college. His desire for passion and love leads him to initiate a liaison with an older woman, the fiery yet troubled Ellénore. Once he has won her love, Adolphe feels trapped, but his timid and indecisive nature prevents him from ending the relationship.

Critics have noted that Adolphe embodies both negative and positive qualities. Conceited, weak, deceitful, and resentful, he is also compassionate and loyal, and he makes no attempt to seek pity or to pretend that he is an admirable person. Even as he continues his relationship with Ellénore, Adolphe is acutely aware of her suffering and does not wish to increase it. Thus he impresses the reader as an essentially human character whose desires and weaknesses are recognizable—particularly his tendency to rationalize his own behavior. Because the entire story is told from the perspective of the obviously fallible Adolphe, he has been identified as one of literature's first unreliable narrators, a device which became more popular as the nineteenth century progressed. Although Adolphe scorns social conventions, he wants to succeed socially and knows that his connection to Ellénore prevents this. At the same time, he feels that his personal integrity will be damaged if he abandons her. Unable to choose the best course, Adolphe takes no real course at all, and finally Ellénore's death provides an opportunity for change. Ironically, though, the final tragedy generates no change in Adolphe's nature, as might have been the case for a more traditional hero of fiction. Instead, he feels helpless and deflated, a "child of the age of disillusionment" (referring to the less optimistic, less idealistic period that followed the French Revolution of the late eighteenth century), as George Brandes proposed in his 1872 review.

Although some scholars have described the other characters in *Adolphe* as mere stick figures present only to illuminate the protagonist, others contend that a few of them are interesting in their own right. One such character is **Ellénore,** the other participant in the disastrous love affair chronicled in the novel. She is an older woman with a troubled past: daughter of a family ruined by political turmoil in her home country, Poland, she has since led a life on the fringe of acceptability as the mistress of a count and mother of two illegitimate children. No longer as ostracized, Ellénore still feels isolated. She is not at all the stereotypical female character found in the literature of the period; instead of sweet and submissive, she is passionate, willful, and energetic. It is thought that Constant modeled Ellénore after Madame de Staël, but Ellénore is of ordinary intellect, which comprises an important difference. Though not brilliant, Ellénore is perceptive, and she quickly becomes aware that Adolphe's feelings for her have changed to pity. Ellénore is particularly noted for her pride and her devotion. Pride makes her position difficult, for she truly desires acceptance and suffers the disapproval of those around her. Her devotion is evident in her long relationship with Count P—— and in her consuming love for her children; eventually this devotion will be channeled to Adolphe. Ellénore initially resists Adolphe's attention but after she accepts it she becomes immersed in joy. When she begins to fear its loss, she grows demanding, possessive, and even shrewish, and she eventually dies unhappily. Constant has been praised for depicting in Ellénore the emotional turmoil of a mature and vital woman.

Another significant character in *Adolphe* is **Adolphe's father.** His inarticulate and outwardly cold nature hides a deep affection for his son, in whom he has nurtured high expectations. The timidity he has in common with Adolphe has created a strained atmosphere between them, but he treats his son indulgently, which may have contributed to Adolphe's immaturity and indecisiveness. Constant uses the father as an aid in his psychological penetration of the title character. In addition, in disapproving of Ellénore and trying to end her relationship with Adolphe, the father represents the broader society against which Adolphe rebels.

Although responsible for the socially compromised position that Ellénore holds at the beginning of the novel, **Count P——** has made her somewhat acceptable to his friends and associates. He does appreciate her sacrifice and her devotion, but after ten years his cold, matter-of-fact appreciation does not show up well against the passion that Adolphe offers. **Baron T——,** the man charged by Adolphe's father with persuading him to abandon Ellénore, is a diplomatic, clever manipulator who arranges a dinner party to show how such a liaison will effect Adolphe's future, which reinforces Adolphe's own doubts about the relationship. The baron also serves to relay the feelings of Adolphe's more reticent father.

Further Reading

Brandes, George. "Constant: 'On Religion'—'Adolphe.'" In *Main Currents in Nineteenth-Century Literature: The Emigrant Literature,* Vol. 1, translated by Diana White and Mary Morison, pp. 63-88. 1901. Reprint. Heinemann, 1923.

Fairlie, Alison. "The Art of Constant's 'Adolphe': II. Creation of Character." In *Imagination and Language: Collected Essays on Constant, Baudelaire, Nerval, and Flaubert,* edited by Malcolm Bowie, pp. 28-31. Cambridge: Cambridge University Press, 1981.

Nineteenth-Century Literature Criticism, Vol. 6. Detroit: Gale.

Wegimont, Marie A. "Constant's 'Adolphe.'" *Explicator* 48, No. 3 (Spring 1990): 182-83.

Wood, Dennis, ed. *Constant: Adolphe.* Cambridge: Cambridge University Press, 1987.

James Fenimore Cooper
1789-1851
American novelist, satirist, essayist, historian, and travel writer.

The Last of the Mohicans (novel, 1826)

Plot: The novel takes place in northern New York in 1757, during the middle years of the French and Indian Wars, in which the British fought the French and their Indian allies for territory that is now the northeastern United States. Half-sisters Cora and Alice Munro are traveling from Fort Edward to Fort William Henry, where their father Colonel Munro is the commanding officer. They are escorted by Major Duncan Heyward; David Gamut, a choirmaster from Connecticut, is also part of their group. Instead of following the relatively safe military road that runs between the two forts, they take a shortcut recommended by Magua, an outcast of the Huron tribe (aligned with the French), who is enlisted to guide them. The group encounters frontier scout Nathaniel "Natty" Bumppo—called Hawkeye by his Indian friends—along with his faithful and noble Indian companion Chingachgook and his son Uncas, who comprise the last remnants of the once mighty Mohican tribe, and learn that they have been traveling in a circle and are not far from their starting point. Natty suspects Magua of treachery, but the Indian manages to escape. Natty agrees to guide the group to the fort. That night, while they are sheltering in a cave, they are attacked by hostile Indians led by Magua and seem to face certain capture. Natty, Chingachgook, and Uncas leave the others in the cave and slip away, planning to rescue them later. After Heyward, Gamut, and the Munro sisters are captured, Heyward tries to convince Magua to betray his cohorts and deliver the group to Colonel Munro, but Magua agrees to the plan only if Cora will promise to marry him. She refuses, and Magua is enraged. Natty and his friends eventually lead an attack on the Indians and drive them off, and the group proceeds toward the fort. As they near it, they are stopped by a French sentinel, whom Chingachgook kills and scalps. The fort is besieged by French troops under the command of General Montcalm, but they are able to enter it undetected. After five days of fighting, Natty is sent back to Fort Edward with a message from Munro requesting help from the other fort's commander, General Webb. The request is refused, so Munro is forced to surrender to the French. Those inside the fort are allowed a safe passage away, but as they are leaving they are attacked by the Indians who had been fighting alongside the French. In the midst of the slaughter Magua kidnaps Alice, and Cora and Gamut follow him into the woods.

Natty, Heyward, Munro, Chingachgook, and Uncas track their missing friends and finally locate their trail. They find Gamut wandering alone in the forest—he has been left alone by the Hurons because they interpreted his habit of sporadically breaking into song as insanity. He tells them that Alice is still held captive by the Hurons, while Cora is with the more peaceful Delawares. Through a cleverly executed plan of exchanged identities, Heyward and Natty rescue both Alice and Uncas (who had subsequently been captured) and they flee to safety with the Delawares. The next day, Magua and his warriors arrive at the Delaware camp in search of their former captives. The Delaware chief, Tamenund, agrees that Magua's wish to make Cora his wife gives him a legitimate claim to her. In accordance with Indian custom, Magua—with Cora in tow—is allowed to leave, but Uncas, who is in love with Cora, warns him that he and his friends will soon start in pursuit. In a final, bloody battle, Magua stabs and kills Uncas and is in turn shot by Natty; Cora is also killed. A sorrowful Munro returns to his own territory with Heyward and Alice, who plan to marry. Natty returns to the forest with a grieving Chingachgook, to whom he has pledged undying friendship.

Characters: Considered the first American novelist, Cooper is credited with chronicling in his romanticized stories of frontier life a period of great change in American history. While his minor characters strike many readers and scholars as one-dimensional, Cooper is universally praised for creating the unique and distinctly American figure Nathaniel "Natty" Bumppo—variously called "Hawkeye," "Deerslayer," "Pathfinder," and "La Longue Carabine" in the series of five Leatherstocking Tales that chronicle his life. Though perhaps weakened by inconsistent characterizations, implausibility, and dull passages, these books have thrilled generations of readers with their exciting action and descriptions of natural splendor, and have fascinated critics with their focus on the tension between nature and civilization and wilderness and settlement that was so intrinsic to America's westward expansion.

The great French novelist Honoré de Balzac described **Natty Bumppo** as a character "born between the savage and the civilized states of man, who will live as long as literature endures." The product of a fairly ordinary white Christian education followed by exposure to the Delaware Indians among whom he has since lived, Natty embodies a synthesis of traditional, "civilized" values and the natural ways of the wilderness. He is a frontier scout, hunter, and trapper whose skills are legendary: he earned the appellation "Hawkeye" for his precise marksmanship, and he repeatedly proves his competence in the skills necessary for survival in the forest and on the lakes. In this second novel of the Leatherstocking series, Natty is in his early thirties. Portrayed as a skinny, grizzled, rather grotesque man in his seventies in the earlier *The Pioneers* (1823), Natty is now in his prime as the quintessential hero of early America—capable, self-reliant, brave, and possessed of a remarkable moral uprightness and code of honor that guides all of his behavior. Natty maintains a strict standard of integrity in all of his actions and relationships—loyal to his friends, he is also respectful of his enemies, and he avoids unnecessary conflict or bloodshed. His lifelong friendship with Chingachgook evidences his ability to value people for their inner nobility, though some critics have maintained that Cooper is suggesting through this interracial

129

relationship not that the white and Indian races are equal (Natty often remarks on the purity and superiority of his white blood) but that cooperation is essential to the survival of both. Though Natty can sometimes be superstitious, ignorant, and tiresomely verbose, his admirable qualities are more memorable, and he is especially noted for his reverent attitude toward the magnificent environment in which he lives. In addition to his practical interest in the ecology of the wilderness (which anticipates the concerns of the twentieth century), Natty has formulated out of his awe for nature a personal religious faith that is notably pantheistic—he sees God in all around him rather than just within the confines of a church. In *The Last of the Mohicans,* this approach is contrasted to the rigid, narrowminded Calvinism—represented by David Gamut—that has influenced American life and thought. In addition to being on a superficial level an unusual and highly entertaining figure, Natty Bumppo has been characterized as, according to Edwin Fussell, "that new man, the generic American, the metaphor of the Western frontier fleshed out as a human being."

Major Duncan Heyward, the British officer who at the beginning of the novel is charged with delivering the Munro sisters safely to their father, is depicted rather flatly as a standard romantic hero. He is handsome, brave, intelligent, and gallant and eventually wins the hand of the character who most thoroughly embodies the traditional feminine qualities of virtue and beauty, Alice Munro. Like that of the other British officers in the novel, Heyward's relative ineffectiveness in this unfamiliar American environment contrasts strongly with Natty's skillfulness and savvy. Though very competent in the warfare of his own world, Heyward must learn to adapt to the different conditions and style of the frontier. He makes a foolish decision in allowing Magua (whose treachery is immediately apparent to Natty) to guide the group, thus endangering the lives with which he has been entrusted. This circumstance is often cited as the novel's most flagrant example of implausibility—why would the group depart from a safe route on the advice of the obviously unreliable Magua? Still, Heyward does display a capacity for unconventional behavior when he disguises himself as Natty and penetrates the Huron encampment. Significantly, though, he returns to civilization at the end of the novel, while Natty ventures back into the wilderness with Chingachgook.

Though **Cora** and **Alice Munro** share with Cooper's other females a notable lack of depth, they provide an interesting illustration of his persistent pattern in portraying women as representing either dark or light aspects of femininity. Cora is a dark-haired beauty with a bold, spirited nature. The fact that she is the distant descendant, through her West Indian Creole mother, of a black slave and that she and Uncas fall in love has caused some scholars to detect in the novel the theme of miscegenation (the intermingling of races through marriage). While some critics maintain that Cooper avoids this controversial issue by having both Cora and Uncas die at the end of the story, others contend that he was a strong advocate of racial purity and the deaths are necessary to reinforce this stance. Despite her stated aversion to the evil Magua, Cora is obviously fascinated by his athletic form; her trace of black blood may have been included in order to account for her unusually passionate, even sensuous, nature. Critics have noted that in addition to her heritage of mixed race, Cora has a personality in which male and female traits are combined: she is remarkably capable, courageous, and calm under pressure. By contrast, Alice is the kind of woman who faints in trying situations. She represents the light side of the dichotomy, both in her blonde prettiness and in her passivity and weakness. Alice is a stereotypically helpless girl like those who were common in the sentimental fiction of the early nineteenth century, and she brings out the gallant Heyward's protective instincts. Young—even childlike—and guileless, she lacks Cora's passion and vitality, even to the point of seeming asexual.

The New England singing master **David Gamut** is mild-mannered and physically clumsy, and his habit of bursting unexpectedly into song demonstrates his social ineptitude (though it also saves him from harm by the Indians, who think he is crazy). He is a talkative bore whose attempts at humor have annoyed many readers; in an 1826 critique in the *North American Review,* Gamut was called "the most stupid, senseless, useless, and unmeaning monster we remember ever to have met with." In his conventional religiousness, Gamut provides a contrast to Natty's nature-centered, wide-ranging view of God and faith. Gamut represents some of the least attractive qualities of the civilization that encroaches upon Natty's unspoiled natural world.

One of the most notable qualities in Cooper's fiction is his portrayal of such noble Indian characters as **Chingachgook** and **Uncas.** Some early critics disapproved of Cooper's flattering depiction of these figures, claiming that such a view of savage people was unrealistic. While some modern scholars contend that these portraits, despite their sympathetic quality, enforced demeaning stereotypes, others have seen them as expressing Cooper's condemnation of the unjust dispossession of native Americans that was occurring as the boundaries of American civilization moved westward. Natty's close friend Chingachgook is a chief of the now almost extinct Mohican tribe (which later became part of the Delaware tribe) who is even more adept at forest skills than Natty. Called "the Great Serpent" by his people, he is dignified, morally upright, and honorable in his relations with others. Despite his integrity, though, it is always clear that Chingachgook adheres more to the savagery of the wild than to the values of white civilization. For instance, he is willing to leave the women undefended in the cave in order to save himself because he—as a warrier and a chief—is more valuable than any females; he also kills and scalps the French sentinel who stops the group for no other reason than that the man represents the enemy (they have already been allowed to pass). Natty, by contrast, only kills when he has no other alternative.

Chingachgook's son Uncas is the last scion of the ancient race of Mohicans and thus is the figure referred to in the book's title. He has been said to represent the highest point of development in the Indian character both in his appearance and in his nature. Handsome, physically strong, and classically proportioned (as noted by the Munro sisters), like his father he is skillful, intelligent, and dignified. Fussell called him "the ultimate hero" of *The Last of the Mohicans.*

Sullen, brutal, and conniving **Magua** represents the more stereotypical variety of Indian character which dominated the popular imagination well into the twentieth century. A renegade of his own tribe, the Hurons, Magua is a self-centered figure who will stop at nothing to achieve his own ends. Though he is similar to Uncas in his physical prowess, attractiveness, and courage, Magua lacks the other's inherent integrity. Both men love Cora, for instance, but Magua's feelings for her are overtly carnal while Uncas's are pure and honorable. Magua also displays a fierce pride that makes him eager for revenge after Colonel Munro orders him whipped for drunkenness—the circumstance which led to his initial treachery toward the group of white travelers.

Three white men also play significant roles in *The Last of the Mohicans.* **Colonel Munro,** the affectionate father of Alice and Cora and the commander of Fort William Henry, is a native of Scotland and a military man still bound to traditional ideas of warfare. He feels betrayed when General Webb refuses to come to his aid and depressed by his helplessness is attempting to defend the fort. This circumstance, combined with the death of his daughter Cora, leaves him a spiritually broken man. **General Webb,** the commander of Fort Edward, embodies the ineptitude of the British command in America that would eventually result in their losing the Revolutionary War. Faced an utterly unfamiliar terrain and methods of warfare, Webb is afraid to act and thus precipitates the downfall of Fort William Henry. The **Marquis de Montcalm** is the French general who leads the assault on the fort. He is portrayed unsympathetically as a shrewd hypocrite who pretends to know less English than he does in order to gain advantage and who allows his Indian allies to slaughter the British refugees to whom he had earlier—and sanctimoniously—granted safe passage.

Another notable minor character in *The Last of the Mohicans* is **Tamenund,** the Indian chief who allows Magua to leave the Delaware encampment with Cora. Based on an actual prophet and chief of the Delaware tribe, Tamenund is a voice of wisdom in the novel who speaks eloquently of the coming downfall of the Indians as the white man continues to push his way west.

The Pathfinder; or, The Inland Sea (novel, 1840)

Plot: The story takes place in Ontario in 1756. As it opens, Mabel Dunham is traveling through the frontier to remote Fort Oswego with her uncle, the Atlantic seaman Charles Cap, to meet her father, Sergeant Tom Dunham. The party is accompanied by an Indian guide named Arrowhead and his wife, Dew-of-June. Reaching the Oswego River, they meet the frontier guide Natty Bumppo (known to the English as "Pathfinder" for his scouting abilities and to the Delaware Indians, with whom he lives, as "Hawkeye" for his marksmanship) and Jasper Western, a Great Lakes sailor and frontiersman. As Natty is leading the group down the river, his noble friend Chingachgook, a Mohican Indian chief, warns him that there are hostile Indians in the area. All survive an encounter with these Indians, but Arrowhead and his wife disappear. Mabel and her friends reach the fort safely. Sergeant Dunham hopes that his daughter and Natty will marry; another officer at the fort, Lieutenant Muir, however, is in love with Mabel, while she has fallen in love with Jasper. Natty allows Jasper to best him in a test of shooting ability (though he could have won easily, he honors his friend's wish to impress Mabel). Dunham leads a group of soldiers on an expedition to the Thousand Islands, located in Lake Ontario. Because the fort's commander, Captain Duncan, has received a letter accusing Jasper of spying, he is kept under strict surveillance during the voyage, which is undertaken on a ship called the *Scud,* which Jasper had previously piloted. After a suspicious encounter with Arrowhead and Dew-of-June, who flee from the ship in a canoe, Jasper is ordered to remain below decks and Cap takes over at the helm. When a big storm blows up, however, the oceangoing Cap almost allows the ship to founder, and Jasper comes on deck and saves it from destruction. Back at the fort, Natty proposes to Mabel but she tearfully refuses him, despite her knowledge of her father's wishes. She also spurns Lieutenant Muir's advances. When Dunham leaves the fort on another expedition, Muir and five other men are left behind to defend it. Mabel learns from Dew-of-June that a group of Indians led by a white man plan to attack, but her warnings are ignored by Muir and another officer, Corporal McNab. The eventual ambush is led by Arrowhead. McNab is killed and Cap and Muir captured, while the rest—including Natty and Chingachgook—take refuge in and fight from the block-house. When Dunham and his soldiers return, they too are attacked and many are lost; Dunham is mortally wounded but reaches the blockhouse. As the fight draws to a close, Muir is killed by Arrowhead, whom Chingachgook then chases and kills. Upon his capture, Captain Sanglier—the white leader of the Indian attackers—reveals that Muir was a spy employed by the French. On his deathbed, Dunham mistakes Jasper for Natty and joins his hand with Mabel's, blessing their union before he dies. Natty—whom Mabel earlier had promised to marry after all if he would save her father—releases Mabel from her obligation so that she may marry Jasper. Natty then vanishes into the woods and is never seen again by Jasper and his wife, though Mabel occasionally receives anonymous gifts of fur. The Westerns eventually leave the frontier for New York City.

Characters: *The Pathfinder* is the fourth novel in Cooper's Leatherstocking series. While the previous installment in the series, *The Prairie* (1827), chronicles the old age and death of Natty Bumppo on the western plains of American, this novel depicts Natty in his prime, returning for its setting to northern New York and the context of the French and Indian War used in *The Last of the Mohicans.* Considered by many as one of Cooper's two most accomplished novels (the other is *The Deerslayer,* 1841), *The Pathfinder* presents the frontier scout as a notably mythic figure and explores the consequences of American expansion across the continent. As in the other Leatherstocking Tales, the conflict between the wilderness and encroaching civilization is shown as inevitable and potentially devastating.

Nathaniel "Natty" Bumppo, the wilderness scout nicknamed "Pathfinder" by the English for his extraordinary abilities in the forest, continues to embody the admirable qualities established in the earlier novels: he is skillful, brave, self-reliant, intuitively intelligent, and thoroughly moral. Because Natty's attributes are innate rather acquired through wealth or education, he represents a distinctly American ideal of accomplishment and nobility; he is, as stated by Edwin Fussell, "America as America ought to be." Critics have also characterized Natty as an Adamic figure, not only because he resides at the earliest stage of development of the American character and in the paradisical American wilderness, but because he is both innocent and knowledgeable (thus resembling Adam both before and after his fall from grace). In *The Pathfinder,* Natty's innocence is threatened when he falls in love with Mabel Dunham and almost marries her, and the fact that this is only one of two such instances in his life is often noted by scholars. Like many of the American heroes who have followed him, Natty is an essentially solitary figure. His closest friendship is with his fellow woodsman and reverer of nature, Chingachgook. Thus many critics have seen Natty's parting with Mabel as inevitable and even—despite his apparent chagrin when she rejects him—what he actually wanted to happen. Given an opportunity to escape the loneliness of his rugged life and to adopt (at least to some extent) the trappings of civilization as represented by a wife and home, Natty chooses instead to return alone to the forest.

Jasper Western is the novel's romantic hero, the man who does win Mabel's heart and eventually marries her. He is a freshwater sailor—as opposed to the seagoing Charles Cap—and is highly experienced and skilled on the Great Lakes. Jasper's friendship with Natty is an immediate indicator of his virtue, and indeed he proves a capable, loyal, upright person who acts honorably even when he is falsely accused of treason. Although he was ignominiously banished from the deck of the *Scud* as a probable traitor, he willingly returns to the helm to save the ship from destruction and also participates in fighting the hostile Hurons. Jasper is portrayed as a much more appropriate choice than Natty as a partner for Mabel; although Natty and Jasper both have integrity, Jasper is educated, refined, young, and handsome and it is no surprise that Mabel prefers him to the rangy, unpolished, and middle-aged frontiersman her father would like her to marry. Eventually, Jasper and his new wife leave the wilderness for New York City, where Jasper becomes a merchant. This might be interpreted as a regrettable concession to civilization that Natty is lucky to avoid or as an inevitable and not necessarily condemned response to marriage and family. Near the end of *The Pathfinder,* Jasper and Mabel are compared to Adam and Eve, and as such they seem to comprise an image of a young America ready to embark on a new life.

As the nineteenth-century American poet James Russell Lowell wittily described Cooper's female characters: "And the women he draws from one model don't vary, / All sappy as maples and flat as a prairie." Many readers and critics would agree. **Mabel Dunham,** who aptly fits the poet's assessment, is a young, pretty, warm, and honest creature who is sought after by several of the novel's male characters. Despite the shallowness of her portrayal, Mabel is significant in view of her effect on Natty, who comes as close as he ever will to attaching himself to a woman. Devoted to her father, Mabel faces the difficult choice of marrying in accordance with his wishes or according to the inclination of her own heart. Her position is also complicated by her uncertain social position—she is too educated and refined to marry an ordinary soldier, but her father's lower rank precludes her marrying an officer. This situation demonstrates Cooper's awareness of social classification in American society, though most scholars claim that he does not necessarily censure such stratification. Jasper is obviously the best suited of Mabel's suitors; Arrowhead is an Indian (and a disreputable one at that); Lieutenant Muir is not only much married but a dishonorable man; and Natty (whom Mabel sincerely admires) is too rough hewn to be matched with a delicate young lady. Nevertheless, after initially rejecting Natty's proposal, Mabel agrees to marry him if he will rescue her father, revealing the depth of her filial loyalty.

Sergeant Thomas Dunham, Mabel's father, has been a good friend of Natty for twenty years. In choosing his old comrade as a mate for his daughter he implies that she needs a husband who will resemble a father. Though he tells Mabel that she may marry whom she wishes, he makes it abundantly clear that she will break his heart if Natty is not her choice, thus ensuring her compliance with his desire. Like other British military figures in Cooper's fiction, Dunham reveals an unfortunate reliance on European convention and an inability to adapt his behavior to unfamiliar surroundings. For instance, he allows himself to distrust Jasper despite his knowledge of the young man's true character, simply because his commanding officer has received an accusing letter about him. He also unnecessarily subjects his troops to an Indian ambush when they are returning from an expedition, resulting in the loss of many soldiers' lives, including his own.

Mabel's crusty sailor uncle, **Charles Cap,** also relies too heavily on his previous experience and refuses to bend to the demands of entirely different circumstances. Skillful and experienced at ocean sailing, Cap will not admit that maneuvering a ship on the Great Lakes requires any special ability or technique, and he nearly wrecks the *Scud.* Cap is sometimes compared to Commodore Hawser Trunnion, a comical nautical character in Tobias Smollett's eighteenth-century novel *The Adventures of Peregrine Pickle.*

Natty's devoted friend **Chingachgook,** a noble chief of the almost extinct Mohican tribe, is a constant presence throughout the Leatherstocking Tales and the primary example of Cooper's sympathetic, romantic portrayal of Indian characters. Called "The Great Serpent" by his people, Chingachgook is a highly skilled, dignified figure despite his somewhat savage ways; as D.H. Lawrence said of the native Americans in Cooper's work, "the Indians are gentlemen through and through, though they may take an occasional scalp." Illustrating the other side of the Indian character is **Arrowhead,** a Tuscarora who is ambitious, audacious, and treacherous and who is eventually killed—perhaps symbolically—by Chingachgook. Like Magua in *The Last of the Mohicans,* Arrowhead is an outcast of his own tribe who is willing to pursue any means to achieve his own interests, and, also like Magua, he pays for this behavior with his life. Interestingly, Arrowhead's subjugation of his wife resembles Sergeant Dunham's treatment of his own daughter, though the Indian's death-threatening tactics are fiercer if no more effective. Arrowhead's wife, **Dew-of-June,** is a gentle and completely submissive woman. Although she has the decency to warn Mabel of the coming attack, she ultimately remains loyal to her husband. In fact, Dew-of-June's identity is so completely submerged in Arrowhead's that when he is killed she also dies.

Among the officers of Fort Oswego is the commander, **Major Duncan,** whose Old World perspective is revealed as faulty when he suspects the honorable Jasper Western of spying for the French when the real culprit is Duncan's old schoolmate, Lieutenant Muir. Duncan provides yet another example of the ineffectiveness of the British command, whose inflexibility, Cooper suggests, led to their defeat on the American continent. **Lieutenant Davy Muir,** the middle-aged and thrice-married quartermaster who courts Mabel, is at heart a corrupt man. Because of his resentment over his inferior rank, he becomes a spy for the French and then accuses Jasper of treason. Like Arrowhead, he has abandoned integrity to satisfy his own greed, so it is appropriate that in the end he is killed by Arrowhead. **Corporal McNab** is the stubborn officer who refuses to heed Mabel's warning about a probable Indian attack, and he is lecturing her on Scottish military strategy when he is shot and killed by the ambushing braves; again, a British officer has relied too heavily on European convention while ignoring frontier reality. The cold-blooded and selfish **Captain Sanglier,** the French leader of the marauding Hurons, seems to have developed some of the coarser traits of his Indian companions, and has undoubtedly been tainted by his proximity to such traitorous characters as Lieutenant Muir. In an otherwise glowing review of Cooper's work, the French novelist Honoré de Balzac took exception to his unflattering portrayal of this French officer.

The Deerslayer; or, The First War Path (novel, 1841)

Plot: The novel is set in northern New York in 1740, a decade prior to the French and Indian War. The young woodsman and scout Nathaniel "Natty" Bumppo travels to Lake Glimmerglass with his fellow frontiersman Hurry Harry March along a route made dangerous by the escalating warfare between the British and the French. There Natty plans to meet his friend, the young Mohican chief Chingachgook, with whom he will join to fight their common enemy, the Hurons, a tribe allied with the French. Hurry intends to warn his old friend Tom Hutter about the danger of Indian raids. Hutter lives with his two daughters, beautiful Judith (whom Hurry plans to marry) and sweet but imbecilic Hetty, in a cabin built on stilts in the middle of the lake; he uses a large scow referred to as "the ark" for travel. Natty, Hurry, and the Hutters narrowly escape an attack by the Indians, fleeing on the ark. But Hurry and Hutter notice a Huron encampment and decide to raid it and scalp as many Indians as they can—they will be paid a bounty for each scalp by the British. They are captured while Natty, unaware, waits for them in a canoe offshore. The next morning, Natty kills an Indian in order to save a canoe that has drifted away from him; his dying foe gives him the name "Hawkeye" in recognition of his shooting skill. Natty returns to the nearby fort where Hutter's daughters are staying and informs them of the other men's capture. Chingachgook has now also arrived, and he tells Natty that he wants to rescue his sweetheart, Wah-Ta!-Wah, who has been kidnapped by the Hurons. Meanwhile, Hetty has set off in a canoe by herself for the encampment, hoping to rescue her father. Wah-Ta!-Wah finds Hetty and takes her to the camp, where she is not harmed because the Indians believe that the mentally deficient are protected by the Great Spirit. When a Huron brave brings Hetty back to the cabin, where Natty is stationed with Chingachgook, Natty proposes that the Indians exchange the two captive men for some ivory chess pieces found in Hutter's sea chest. The offer is accepted and the men released. Chingachgook and Natty plan to meet Wah-Ta!-Wah at a prearranged spot; when she is unable to slip out of the encampment they make a daring attempt to rescue her. The two lovers escape, but Natty is captured. The next morning, Hutter and his friends are ambushed as they are returning to the cabin; Chingachgook saves Hurry from drowning and the two girls escape in a canoe, but Hutter is killed. After they bury Hutter in the lake, Hurry asks Judith to marry him. She rejects his proposal. Natty arrives at the cabin, explaining that he has been allowed to leave the Huron encampment temporarily in order to strike a bargain for his release—he will be freed if Wah-Ta!-Wah and Judith agree to marry Huron warriors. They refuse, so Natty must return to the encampment. Before he does, he and Judith discover that Tom Hutter was not Judith's real father, but a former pirate who had married her abandoned mother when Judith and Hetty were babies. A disheartened Judith hints strongly that she would like to become Natty's wife, but he says that she is too good for him. The next day, Natty is about to be put to death by his captors when Chingachgook springs into the camp and releases him, followed by the arrival of troops brought by Hurry. The Hurons are defeated, though Hetty is accidentally killed in the process. Judith returns to the fort, while Natty goes back to the forest with his Delaware friends. After fifteen years have passed, Natty and Chingachgook, along with the Indian's son Uncas, visit Lake Glimmerglass again to find the area still apparently untouched by humans.

Characters: The final book in the Leatherstocking series, *The Deerslayer* is first in line chronologically because it tells the story of Natty Bumppo's early life. The novel is distinguished from the other Leatherstocking Tales by its strong religious tone, relayed through Natty's awestruck reverence for the natural splendor that surrounds him and his belief that God is present everywhere. While the previous novels had chronicled the encroachment of civilization across the American continent, Cooper returns to an idealized vision of the frontier and of its most vivid representative, Natty Bumppo.

In the first book of the Leatherstocking series, **Nathaniel "Natty" Bumppo** is a grizzled frontier scout of seventy, and subsequent novels recount his life at various other ages. But in *The Deerslayer,* Natty is in his twenties and still at the beginning of his colorful life as a hunter, trapper, and wilderness guide. Educated by Moravians (a Christian sect which emphasizes conduct over doctrine) and later adopted by Delaware Indians, among whom he has since lived, Natty is called "Deerslayer" in honor of his prodigious skill with a rifle. He embodies the same admirable qualities as a young man that are present in the more mature versions of his character—simplicity, honesty, courage, skill, honor, and (despite his basic illiteracy) innate intelligence. Natty believes that every person has a "gift" to express or offer, and he respects others for their uniqueness. Though not a churchgoer, Natty lives by a pantheistic faith that features a perception of God in all things and particularly in nature. The episode in which Natty spars with the Indian brave and finally kills him is significant in several ways: the subdued battle that ends in the warrior's death has a ritualistic quality and thus might be seen as Natty's initiation into manhood; it also exemplifies the respectful way he treats others, including his enemies. *The Deerslayer* is also distinguished by its inclusion of a female character who is interested in Natty, Judith Hutter. However (unlike his near-miss with Mabel Durham in *The Pathfinder*), Natty is never in any danger of succumbing to Judith's charms, and thus maintains the celibacy that seems to be an essential part of his nature.

Hurry Harry March provides a strong contrast to Natty Bumppo. He is a big, powerful, good-looking frontiersman with a boisterous, bragging nature. Many critics have seen in Hurry a manifestation of the worst qualities of the American character: he is money-hungry, restless, self-rationalizing, careless, and scornful of other races. He lacks Natty's reverence for nature; instead, he exploits his environment for his own gain. In brutally killing and scalping Indians—including women and children—for the bounties their scalps will bring, Hurry demonstrates not only his greed but an alarming absence of morality. Likewise, his desire to marry Judith is based entirely on her appearance and not on the substance of her character. Judith's father **Tom Hutter** resembles Hurry in his avariciousness and brutality, so it is not surprising to learn that he is a former pirate who fled to the northern woods to escape hanging. Whereas Natty avoids violence if possible, Hutter seems to pursue it, enthusiastically joining Hurry in ambushing an Indian encampment. Living away from the strictures of civilization has led to the degeneration of his character, while Natty's has been elevated by his exposure to the wilderness. It seems fitting that, in the end, Hutter dies an agonizing death and loses his own scalp after depriving so many others of theirs.

Tom Hutter's two daughters bear a close resemblance to the Munro sisters of *The Last of the Mohicans.* **Judith Hutter** is a dark beauty whose virtue has been tainted by her seduction by a callous British officer. She is coquettish and vain, but, like Cora Munro, also clever and spirited; Chingachgook gives her the nickname "Wild Rose" in honor of her tempestuous beauty. Judith finds Natty's honesty and straightforwardness attractive and is willing to give up her social ambitions to marry him and live away from civilization. Knowing this match would be inappropriate, Natty declines it. It is suggested that Judith ultimately becomes the mistress of the disreputable Captain Warley—a fate which seems predestined because Judith's mother was also seduced (and later abandoned) by a British officer. **Hetty Hutter** is called appropriately called "Drooping Lily" by Chingachgook. She represents the light side of Cooper's typical dark/light female dichotomy. Blonde, frail, and innocent, she is also mentally deficient and thus supremely trusting. It is significant that the guileless Hetty, with her positive view of human nature, is not allowed to survive.

Natty's closest friend is the noble Mohican chief **Chingachgook,** whose nickname "The Great Serpent" honors his "wisdom, and prudence, and cunning." Friends throughout their lives, the two young men are, in *The Deerslayer,* on their first warpath together as they join forces to fight a common enemy. Like Natty, Chingachgook is adept in wilderness skills and lives by a strict code of honor. Some critics have perceived Chingachgook, who represents a people threatened by the encroachment of American civilization and who dwells of the paradisiacal American forest, as symbolizing—in the words of Leslie A. Fiedler— "whatever in the American psyche has been starved to death, whatever genteel Anglo-Saxondom has most ferociously repressed."

Minor characters in *The Deerslayer* include **Captain Warley,** the officer who is responsible for Judith's fall from virtue. Cooper's portrayal of this worldly, heedless, immoral officer is no more flattering than most of his other depictions of British military men; Warley, for instance, sponsors a needlessly brutal attack on the Indian camp. **Rivenoak** is the chief of the Hurons and thus an enemy; nevertheless, he has integrity and Natty calls him an "oncommon man." **Le Loup Cervier** is the young warrior whom Natty kills and who gives him the appellation "Hawkeye"; their match is notably honorable and marked by mutual respect. **Wah-Ta!-Wah,** Chingachgook's beloved, is known as the most sought-after girl in her tribe, indicating that she is a fitting partner for the noble young chief.

Further Reading

Balzac, Honoré de. "Literary Notices: 'The Pathfinder: Or the Inland Sea.'" *The Knicker-bocker* XVII, No. 1 (January 1841): 72-7.

Baym, Nina. "The Women of Cooper's Leatherstocking Tales." *American Quarterly* XXIII, No. 5 (December 1971): 696-709.

"Cooper's Novels." *North American Review* (n.s.) 23, No. 41 (July 1826): 150-97.

Dictionary of Literary Biography, Vol. 3. Detroit: Gale.

Fiedler, Leslie A. "James Fenimore Cooper and the Historical Romance." In *Love and Death in the American Novel,* pp. 162-214. Stein and Day, 1966.

Franklin, Wayne. *The New World of James Fenimore Cooper.* Chicago: University of Chicago Press, 1982.

Fussell, Edwin. "The Leatherstocking Tales of James Fenimore Cooper." In *Frontier: American Literature and the American West.* Princeton, N.J.: Princeton University Press, 1965.

Lawrence, D. H. "Fenimore Cooper's Leatherstocking Novels." In *Studies in Classic American Literature,* pp. 47-64. 1924. Reprint. Viking Press, 1964.

Lowell, James Russell. *A Fable for Critics: A Glance at a Few of Our Literary Progenies.* G.P. Putnam, 1848.

Nineteenth Century Literature Criticism, Vols. 1, 27. Detroit: Gale.

Oliver, Lawrence J. "'Their Foot Shall Slide in Due Time': Cooper's Calvinist Motif." *Nineteenth-Century Literature* 42 (March 1988): 432.

Twain, Mark. "Fenimore Cooper's Literary Offenses." *North American Review* 151, No. 464 (July 1895): 1-12.

Stephen Crane

1871-1900

American novelist, short story writer, poet, and journalist.

Maggie: A Girl of the Streets (novel, 1893)

Plot: The novel takes place in the late nineteenth century in the Bowery, a slum section of New York City. Maggie Johnson is a young woman who has grown up in impoverishment and neglect. When her alcoholic father dies, Maggie and her one surviving brother, Jimmy, are left in the care of their quarrelsome, drunken mother. Somehow Maggie's character remains uncorrupted. Jimmy works to support the family and falls prey to drinking, fighting, and affairs with many women; he fathers numerous children but scoffs at their mothers' pleas for financial help. Maggie chooses a job in a factory over a life of prostitution—these are the only options available to a young woman in her circumstances. She falls in love with her brother's friend Pete, a dashing bartender who introduces her to a night life more exciting than what she has known. Maggie initially resists Pete's sexual advances, but she eventually succumbs and then goes to live with him. When Pete grows tired of Maggie and rejects her, she returns home, but her mother denounces Maggie's loss of virtue and bars her from the house. After an inconclusive fistfight with Pete, Jimmy joins his mother in condemning Maggie.

Now destitute, Maggie again approaches Pete for help, but he sends her away. She sees that to survive she will have to take up prostitution. Maggie does not have much success in her new occupation, however, and one night, while walking through the waterfront district, she throws herself into the river and drowns. On learning of Maggie's death, her mother cries that she forgives her wayward daughter.

Characters: *Maggie, A Girl of the Streets* is often identified as one of the first and most influential naturalistic novels in American literature. Naturalism became a prevalent force in the late nineteenth and early twentieth centuries; it was influenced by the Darwinian theory of scientific determinism, which emphasized the importance of biology and environment in shaping people's live. Written in the impressionistic style that characterizes all of Crane's work, *Maggie* features an authentically depicted setting in the brutal streets of New York; a significant lack of moralizing; and realistic, unexceptional characters who are seemingly trapped in their desolate lives.

Despite her upbringing in a deprived and sordid environment, **Maggie Johnson** has remained pure and virtuous. She is a pretty, well-meaning girl whom Crane describes as having "blossomed in a mud puddle." Maggie is also naive and vulnerable, and she lacks the self-esteem that might have helped her perceive the truth about Pete before it was too late. Because her life has been devoid of any beauty or even ordinary affection and decency, Maggie is dazzled by Pete's attentions and by the night life to which he exposes her. Modern critics have lauded Crane for his frank approach to sexual matters (though the same quality drew the censure of nineteenth-century reviewers) and his compassionate approach to the issue of the "fallen woman." While other authors of the time portrayed prostitutes as either morally corrupt and deserving of their degradation or as ultimately reforming, Crane created a girl whose descent into prostitution resulted from her unlucky circumstances and her own naivete rather than from moral deficiency. Through Maggie, who finds escape only in death, Crane illustrated the helplessness of the human condition and the absence of definite answers to human dilemmas—themes that would mark his later, more critically acclaimed works as well.

Maggie's brother **Jimmie Johnson** is introduced when he is still a little boy, humiliated by his playmates and struggling to maintain his dignity. His evolution into an egotistical bully with an inflated sense of his own daring is portrayed as an adaptive reaction to circumstance. Forced to go to work early to support his family, Jimmie is a poorly paid truck driver who takes out his frustration on those around him. Like Maggie, Jimmie has little chance of escaping from the destructive cycle in which he has always lived. Raised in violence, anger, and neglect, he grows up to brawl in barrooms, ignore the women he has used and the children he has fathered, and condemn his sister for her alliance with a man much like himself.

Though he has a smoother exterior than Jimmie, **Pete** is no less callous. Arrogant and slick, he swaggers confidently through the Bowery. Maggie is susceptible to Pete's charms and sees him as a shining knight sent to rescue her. But Pete is no knight; he is not even a decent person: he quickly tires of the young girl whose life he has irreparably altered, and he discards her. But while he can go on just as before, Maggie is ruined—illustrating the cruel double standard for the sexual behavior of men and women that prevailed in this period (as well as later).

Mary Johnson, the alcoholic, nightmarish mother of Maggie and Jimmie, is depicted as a big, powerful, slovenly woman with a nagging, fractious nature. Circumstances have driven her to rely on liquor to provide temporary solace, and she ceaselessly harangues and neglects her family. Mary's false, melodramatic grief over the news of Maggie's death is often characterized as a bitter parody of motherhood—Mary describes herself as self-sacrificing and well-intentioned and claims that she will forgive her daughter, when in fact she gave Maggie neither love or guidance, and is herself in need of forgiveness. **Mr. Johnson** is also an alcoholic and an inadequate parent. Compared to his wife, he is weak and resigned, lapsing into sullenness between the tumultuous fights that frightened their children and drew the neighbors' derision.

Though she makes only a few brief appearances, **Nell** is another significant character in *Maggie, A Girl of the Streets.* The bold, attractive woman who lures Pete away from Maggie, she is a strong contrast to Maggie's passivity and vulnerability; Nell is ruthless and tough and exhibits a strong survival instinct. Also a prostitute, she conducts her business shrewdly, evaluating and manipulating her customers. Though Nell may lack Maggie's essential innocence, her self-sufficiency promises to keep her alive for a long time.

The Red Badge of Courage (novel, 1895)

Plot: Set during the American Civil War, the novel centers on a young farm boy named Henry Fleming whose dreams of glorious battle led him to sign up in the Union Army, against his mother's wishes. With his regiment at an unspecified location (probably near Chancellorsville, Virginia, where a famous battle took place in May 1863), he waits for his first encounter with the enemy. He wonders if he will behave bravely when the fighting starts. Henry initially fires his gun mechanically but panics when, after a short lull, the Confederates launch a surprise attack. He flees from the battle into the nearby woods, where he realizes his cowardice. After seeing a dead soldier's decomposing corpse in a clearing, Henry leaves the forest and meets a group of men, many of them wounded. His friend Jim Conklin (also called the Tall Soldier) is among them; Jim has been mortally wounded and soon dies. Another ragged soldier asks Henry where he is wounded, causing Henry extreme embarrassment. As he nears his old regiment, a line of retreating men runs past him; when he asks one soldier why they are running the man hits him over the head with his rifle. Now wounded and confused, Henry is led back toward his regiment by an unidentified "Cheery Soldier" and finally meets another soldier he knows, the formerly boastful but now strangely quiet Wilson (also called the Loud Soldier). Henry reports that he has been shot and the others tend respectfully to his wound and encourage him to sleep. His consciousness of his cowardice and the fact that he did not receive the wound in valorous battle begins to recede.

When another battle begins, Henry participates energetically, firing his rifle continuously even after the fighting has stopped. Realizing that the enemy has fled, Henry is pleased with himself—even more so when the regiment's lieutenant compliments his fighting skills. Wilson and Henry overhear some officers insulting the overall performance of the regiment and making a pessimistic forecast for the remainder of the day's battle. But the men fight bravely, and Henry rescues the regimental flag from the fallen flag bearer. Afterward the regiment is criticized for falling short of its objective, but the colonel praises Henry's performance. His conviction that he has acquired courage and reached manhood is strengthened during the last engagement chronicled in the novel, when Henry successfully leads a charge against the Confederates.

Characters: *The Red Badge of Courage* is Crane's most famous work and one of the most significant novels in American literature. Crane combined vivid imagery, realistic detail, and an objective narrative perspective with the impressionistically rendered, subjective viewpoint of the main character to create a work of unique power. Simultaneously proclaimed as representing the literary schools of realism, naturalism, and symbolism, the novel treats such themes as the conflict between illusion and reality, the interplay of courage and fear, and the absence of God and meaning in the universe. This is also the first novel to depict modern warfare and the psychological effects of battle on the individual participant.

Referred to throughout the novel as "the youth," **Henry Fleming** is a naive young farm boy whose dreams of glorious battle in the manner of the Greek warriors he has read about are shattered by the confusion and panic of his regiment's first confrontation with the enemy. Fleeing from the battle into the woods, Henry seeks there some kind of confirmation that his actions were justified, but he encounters only the indifference of nature to humanity (made gruesomely manifest in the image of the dead soldier with ants crawling across his decomposing face). Henry feels the sting of his own cowardice, but after he receives his wound—his "red badge of courage"—this sting begins to recede and he can almost believe that he acted bravely. With Henry's second performance in the field, when he holds his ground and fights gamely, his pride begins to swell and he is pleased to be called a "wild cat" of war by the superior officer. By the end of the novel he has achieved self-confidence and marches briskly toward the future with his fellow soldiers. While some scholars believe that the novel chronicles Henry's initiation into manhood, others contend that the ending is actually ironic, and that Henry has turned away from the possibility of self-knowledge in favor of a shallow egoism, allowing him to fight a war whose causes and meanings he only vaguely understands. Regardless of the possible readings, Crane is universally praised for his insightful, compelling depiction of the psychological reactions of a young participant in the American Civil War.

Like Henry, **Wilson** (also called the **Loud Soldier**) is an untried Union recruit anxious to take part in his first battle. He differs from the protagonist, however, by bragging and refusing to admit the possibility of cowardice. He reveals an awakening fear, however, just before the first battle begins when he hands Henry a packet of letters to be delivered to his family; he admits that he does not expect to survive this experience. Although Wilson's experiences while Henry was running away and hiding in the forest are not specified, it is obvious that the battle has had a profound effect on him. He is no longer bombastic but quiet and serious, lending aid to his fellow soldiers and taking a prominent position in later confrontations. Wilson now embodies the concept of Brotherhood—often identified as one of Crane's concerns—in his devotion to his regiment; Henry's focus, by contrast (at least until he becomes aware of his own capacity for courage) is more individualistic.

Jim Conklin (the **Tall Soldier**) is more realistic about battle than either Henry or Wilson. He states there would be no shame in running away from the fight if his fellow soldiers were doing the same thing; if they held fast, however, he would stay with them. Jim's outlook combines both pragmatism and loyalty to the group. His dramatic death affects Henry strongly, highlighting his own cowardice. Telling Henry that his greatest fear is that he will fall down in the road and be run over by a wagon and repelling Henry's and the Tattered Soldier's attempts to help him, Jim manages to stagger into a field, where he finally dies. The curious, almost ceremonial dignity of this scene of courage has impressed many critics.

Also portrayed as courageous—though not in any conventional way—is the **Tattered Soldier**, who speaks gently to Henry and tries to engage him in conversation, even though he has been gravely wounded and will soon die. However, obsessed with his own cowardice and eager to escape the memory, Henry callously leaves the Tattered Soldier to die a solitary death.

Several other characters play significant though minor roles in *The Red Badge of Courage.* **Henry's mother** is portrayed as a highly religious woman who does not approve of the war and discourages Henry from joining the army. Henry has envisioned a dramatic and tearful farewell scene like those he has read about in books, and he is disappointed when his mother acts in a rather impersonal manner, hardly looking up from milking a cow to say goodbye to him. Henry initially identifies nature as a female figure that, like his mother, disapproves of the fighting and wants him to escape. The **Cheery Soldier** is Henry's unidentified, strangely lighthearted guide back to his regiment; this mysterious person has been seen as an allegorical figure akin to the ancient gods and goddesses who lent their help to the heroes of myth. **Lieutenant Hasbrouck** is depicted as an ideal military man, encouraging his soldiers to behave correctly in battle and praising them for their bravery. Likewise, **Colonel MacChesnay** compliments Henry's performance, even though he himself has been criticized by the general for not pushing the regiment to achieve a full victory.

"The Blue Hotel" (short story, 1898)

Plot: The story takes place in late-nineteenth-century Fort Rompers, Nebraska, where three travelers arrive on a train: the nervous Swede from New York, a cowboy from the Dakotas named Bill, and the easterner Mr. Blanc. They are greeted by Pat Scully, the Irishman who operates the blue-painted Palace Hotel. Arriving at the hotel, the guests see Scully's son, Johnnie, playing cards with an old farmer. As a blizzard rages outside, the three men settle into their rooms and then return for the noon meal. The Swede behaves strangely, referring nervously to the dangers often encountered in western towns. He starts to play cards with Johnnie, Bill, and Mr. Blanc. When he suggests that many men must have been killed in this room, the others disagree, and he responds by defensively stating that he does not want to fight. The Swede returns to his room and begins to pack his bags, but Scully cajoles him into staying, giving him whiskey and showing him pictures of his family before leading him back downstairs, where the others have been discussing the Swede's peculiarity. During supper, the Swede continues to act erratically—gay one moment and belligerent the next. He finally accuses Johnnie of cheating during the card game and challenges him to a fight; the much bigger Swede quickly overpowers and humiliates his opponent. Still feeling threatened, the Swede goes to a saloon and drinks more whiskey. He offers to buy drinks for four men sitting at a table but they turn down his offer; angered, the Swede provokes one of them, a gambler who subsequently stabs and kills him. Meeting several months later, Mr. Blanc and the cowboy relate that the gambler received a three-year prison sentence. Bill blames the Swede for causing his own downfall by falsely accusing Johnnie of cheating, but the easterner admits that he also saw Johnnie cheating and now regrets his silence. When Mr. Blanc goes on to imply that all of those present were participants in the crime, the cowboy protests: "Well, I didn't do anythin', did I?"

Characters: Set in the rapidly changing western United States through which Crane himself had traveled, *The Blue Hotel* demonstrates how its central character's illusions about that region and refusal to develop a broader view lead to his downfall. The story is heavily ironic, portraying through realistic detail and characters the ultimately ambiguous nature of courage, fear, and violence, and the "conceit of man" in attempting to attach meaning to a an indifferent, incomprehensible universe.

Crane describes **the Swede,** a native of the more civilized eastern states, as "shaky and quick-eyed." His conviction that western towns are inherently violent and lawless and its inhabitants bloodthirsty is apparently rooted, as suggested by Mr. Blanc, in the lurid dime store western novels that were popular in the late nineteenth century. If he were willing to look around him, the Swede would see that he is in no danger, but he is fixed in his preconceptions, and his perspective is limited by them. The blinding snowstorm which rages outside while the story's action is taking place is often described as symbolizing this narrow outlook; the Swede even tells the bartender, "I like this weather . . . . It suits me." He acts nervously and suspiciously and then masks his fear with arrogance and false bravado, annoying the people who would otherwise have been happy to befriend or at least tolerate him. Like the blue heron whose color the hotel mimics, the Swede feels compelled to declare his position (Johnnie calls him a "wild loony"), and he goes even further, forcing others to conform to his distorted view. He almost insists that he be killed and his prophecy be fulfilled—thus questioning whether human beings are trapped in a hostile environment or by their own erroneous ideas about their environment. After being stabbed, the Swede lies with his dying eyes staring toward the sign on the cash register that reads, "This registers the amount of your purchase." This ironic detail may be a sign that the Swede has purchased his own death, or it may be a more general symbol of nature's indifference to the plight of human beings.

The hospitable proprietor of the blue hotel is **Pat Scully,** a friendly businessman eager to keep his guests happy. He is a representative of the new West, which is becoming more like the East as civilization encroaches and less like the wild frontier depicted in dime novels. Scully offers the Swede comfort and friendship but his viewpoint is limited; he wants to keep his customers more than he wants to understand the other man's dilemma. Some critics interpret the fact that Scully considers himself an ideal host and entrepreneur and has painted his hotel an obtrusive blue, so that it stands out even in a snowstorm, as another symbol of man's desire to assert himself against the indifferent universe.

Mr. Blanc is an easterner like the Swede, but he lacks the other's illusions about the West. Representative of the older American civilization—which is increasingly more evident in this formerly "wild" region—Mr. Blanc is quiet and rational. He suggests that because he did not take a moral stance by revealing his knowledge of Johnnie's cheating, he (and, by extension, the other card players) is implicated in the Swede's death. While some scholars feel that this indicates that the author believed in the notion of ethical responsibility, others feel that Crane is actually mocking Mr. Blanc for trying to make sense of an essentially unexplainable occurrence.

Bill provides another example of a limited and passive viewpoint when he vehemently denies Mr. Blanc's suggestion that they are all collaborators in the Swede's death. **Johnnie Scully** is primarily a plot mechanism, providing an impetus for the expression of the Swede's aggressive impulses. Likewise **the gambler** is primarily the means by which the

Swede attains his own death, though some critics doubt that such mild provocation would cause a stabbing.

"The Bride Comes to Yellow Sky" (short story, 1898)

Plot: Jack Potter is a marshal in the small, late-nineteenth-century town of Yellow Sky, Texas. He has gone to San Antonio to be married and is now returning on a Pullman train with his new (and unnamed) wife. The train is luxurious, making the couple feel self-conscious and embarrassed by their lack of sophistication; the condescending porter and waiter contribute to their discomfort. Jack grows more nervous as they approach Yellow Sky; he feels that he has let down his community by getting married, and he dreads their reaction to the unexpected news. When they arrive, the still self-conscious couple hurries toward their home. Meanwhile a group of men are drinking in the town's Weary Gentleman saloon. A "drummer" (salesman) from the East is telling a story that is interrupted by news that Scratchy Wilson is on one of his characteristic drunken rampages. Scratchy is the sole remaining member of a gang that once headquartered near Yellow Sky, and he has had many confrontations with Jack. Shooting off his gun and shouting epithets, he goes to Jack's house in search of a fight. Jack and his wife encounter Scratchy as they arrive at the house, and Scratchy accuses Jack of trying to catch him unaware by approaching from behind. Scratchy is surprised to find that Jack is unarmed and even more astonished when he learns that the marshal is now married. Confused and deflated, Scratchy leaves without any further action.

Characters: This story, set in what was once the unsettled frontier but which has become increasingly civilized, dramatizes in a humorous, ironic way the passing of a much sentimentalized era in American history. While some scholars contend that the story is purely comic and should be read primarily as entertainment, others perceive in it a skillful blending of pathos and comedy, highlighting the clash between illusion and reality.

The marshal of Yellow Sky is **Jack Potter,** a conscientious man who takes his job seriously—too seriously, perhaps. He assumes that the townsfolk consider his role central to their safe existence and that they will feel he has let them down when they learn that he has married. But in fact, the residents of Yellow Sky are threatened by nothing more serious than the anachronistic Scratchy Wilson on one of his occasional and relatively harmless drunken binges. The community is no longer as remote as it once was—in fact it is easily accessible by the elegantly appointed Pullman train—and neither is it visited by the drama and violence of the frontier days. Like Scratchy, Jack is a relic of a time passed, but his marriage marks his relinquishment of his mythic role as the solitary western marshal.

Jack's wife is given no name, signifying for many critics her role as a faceless representative of the institution of marriage, just one of many vestiges of eastern civilization that have made their way to Yellow Sky. As she and Jack travel westward on the elegant train, she displays a shyness, clumsiness, and lack of sophistication that is noted by the other travelers, who immediately recognize her lower-class status. Indeed, she is a rather pathetic figure in her lack of youth and beauty and in how the porter and waiter intimidate her on the train. Crane uses a mock heroic style to describe the wife's fascinated horror on seeing the gun-toting Scratchy: she was "a slave to hideous rites, gazing at the apparitional snake."

It is primarily through the character of the aging cowboy **Scratchy Wilson** that Crane imbues the story with both tragedy and comedy. Scratchy is a perfectly nice person when he is sober, but he turns belligerent and uncouth when drunk. Although the townsfolk tend to lock themselves indoors when he is on one of his rampages, he never actually shoots at anything alive or valuable, so he is not a serious threat to the community's safety. In fact, as his name indicates, Scratchy is more of an annoyance than a danger. Although he plays the part of an old-style frontier character, the truth is that his flannel shirt was made in an eastern factory and his boots are the same kind coveted by schoolboys. Although old, he has a simple, childish nature that resists adulthood; ironically he begs Jack Potter not to treat him like ''no kid.'' His role as the mythic western cowboy and rogue has changed, just as Jack's role has changed, but he has no new role to assume and thus seems particularly pathetic as he trudges away at the end of the story.

The drummer is one of several men drinking in the saloon when Scratchy begins his rampage. Like other similar characters in Crane's fiction, he is a sober and rational (though perhaps overly talkative) representative of the East and is innocent of frontier ways; he is surprised to learn that such anachronistic characters as Scratchy still exist. The drummer plays a practical role in the plot because he is an outsider who needs to be educated about Yellow Sky, thereby providing a reason to include an explanation of Scratchy's background and nature.

"The Open Boat" (short story, 1898)

Plot: Most of the story's action takes place in the Atlantic ocean off the coast of Florida. Four survivors of a shipwreck—including the ship's captain, cook, and oiler as well as a newspaper correspondent—are adrift in a small dinghy. As the sun rises on the first day of their dilemma, they battle the fierce January waves in an effort to reach a lighthouse and lifesaving station the cook has heard about. The captain was injured during the sinking and is lying in the bow; he offers directions as the oiler and correspondent row. Finally the men spot the lighthouse on the horizon and fashion a makeshift sail from the captain's overcoat. They make some progress until the wind dies and they must resume rowing. When the boat draws close enough for the men to see the beach, they realize that it is empty and that it harbors no lifesaving station. They finally spot a man on the beach, but he responds to their frantic waving and yelling with ambiguous gestures that suggest he does not realize they are in distress.

During a frightening night in which the oiler and correspondent take turns rowing, the correspondent sees a shark in the water while the others are asleep. Sensing the sea's great and oblivious power, he reflects on how unjust it would be to die after so much effort. The next day the men attempt to maneuver the boat close to shore through the savage surf. Eventually they are forced to jump into the sea, and the oiler immediately starts to swim strongly toward the beach while the others struggle and cling to the overturned boat. A man on the beach rushes into the sea to help them. The correspondent, captain, and cook are pulled safely to shore but the oiler—the most powerful of them all—drowns. With the approach of night, the three survivors stand looking out to sea as if they now know how to interpret it.

Characters: The story is based on Crane's own experience when, as a young reporter, he was aboard a Cuba-bound ship that sank off the coast of Florida. The four men in ''The Open Boat'' embody not only humanity's relationship with nature but with itself. In its portrayal of the indifference of the environment to human beings, the story has been identified as naturalistic, but it also contains elements of symbolism and realism.

As he confronts his own fear and bewilderment in his struggle to stay alive, **the correspondent** rages at his cruel fate. Comparing himself to a mouse—a particularly minuscule and weak image in view of the sea's immensity and power—he notes the injustice of his dilemma. In the end, that the correspondent does survive is attributed to luck, suggesting that human beings are helpless to choose their own fates in a universe that is indifferent to their efforts or suffering.

Similarly, the wounded **captain** survives, despite his weakened condition. Although withdrawn and dejected, the captain feels he must make decisions for the rest of the crew and encourage them onward, although he may secretly believe they will perish. **The cook** has an almost clownish appearance, for he is fat and sloppily dressed. Physically unfit to undertake the task of rowing, he serves as the lookout and seems to take the job quite seriously. The cook's survival is as much a matter of chance as the others'.

The oiler is the only character given a name—Billy—a fact often noted by critics. Despite his strength and determination, he is the only crew member to lose his life to the sea. This circumstance constitutes the story's primary irony and may signify that the assertion of will—whether demonstrated in having a name or in making a heroic effort to swim to shore—is useless in the face of an oblivious universe.

Although at the story's end the surviving characters look out to sea presuming that they understand it, Crane suggests that no one interpretation is adequate to explain the incomprehensibility of existence.

Further Reading

Beer, Thomas. *Stephen Crane: A Study in American Letters.* 1923. Reprint. New York: Octagon Books, 1972.

Benfey, Christopher. "The Courage of Stephen Crane." *New York Review of Books* 36, No. 4 (16 March 1989): 31-4.

Bloom, Harold, ed. *Modern Critical Views: Stephen Crane.* New York: Chelsea House, 1987.

Cady, Edwin H. *Stephen Crane,* rev. ed. Boston: Twayne, 1980.

Dictionary of Literary Biography, Vols. 12, 54, 78. Detroit: Gale.

French, Warren. "Stephen Crane: Moment of Myth." *Prairie Schooner* 55, Nos. 1 & 2 (Summer 1981): 155-67.

Halliburton, David. *The Color of the Sky: A Study of Stephen Crane.* Cambridge: Cambridge University Press, 1989.

Knapp, Bettina L. *Stephen Crane.* New York: Ungar, 1987.

Mitchell, Lee Clark, ed. *New Essays on The Red Badge of Courage.* The American Novel Series. Cambridge: Cambridge University Press, 1986.

Short Story Criticism, Vol. 7. Detroit: Gale.

Solomon, Eric. *Stephen Crane: From Parody to Realism.* Cambridge, Mass.: Harvard University Press, 1966.

Twentieth-Century Literary Criticism, Vols. 11, 17, 32. Detroit: Gale.

Van Doren, Carl, ed. Introduction to *Stephen Crane: Twenty Stories,* pp. v-xvii. Antioch, Tenn.: World Publishing Company, 1945.

Weatherford, Richard M. *Stephen Crane: The Critical Heritage.* The Critical Heritage Series, edited by B.C. Southam. London: Routledge & Kegan Paul, 1973.

Alphonse Daudet
1840-1897
French novelist, short story writer, dramatist, and memoirist.

Sappho (novel, 1884)

Plot: Twenty-one-year-old Jean Gaussin has moved from his home in Provence in the south of France to Paris to study for a diplomatic career. At a costume party he meets Fanny LeGrand, a beautiful and clever woman almost twenty years older than he who has long frequented the city's bohemian district. She is attracted to the handsome young man and accompanies him to his apartment that night. She leaves after two days, and Jean, attaching little importance to the liaison, returns to his studies. Fanny returns, however, and the two begin to spend more and more time together. While staying in Fanny's apartment one night, Jean overhears an argument between his lover and the man whose mistress she had previously been and who is still supporting her; the man begs Fanny to return to him, but she refuses because she has fallen in love with Jean. Jean is horrified to think of Fanny accepting support from another man, and when she suggests that she move into his apartment, he agrees. Jean is pleased with the arrangement until he hears two renowned artists, who are unaware of his relationship with Fanny, discussing her past; each claims that she has been his mistress. They mention relationships she has had with various prominent artists, including an engraver named Flamant who, because he feared that his poverty would cause her to leave him, became a counterfeiter and was eventually caught and sentenced to ten years in prison. It seems Fanny, too, had spent six months in jail, although it was proven that she was not involved in the crime.

All these revelations horrify Jean, and he is also shocked to hear that Fanny is known as Sappho among the intelligentsia, because she once modeled for a sculpture of the ancient Greek poetess. Although repulsed by Fanny's history, Jean is also extremely jealous, and their affair continues. In an effort to end it, Jean returns home but is unable to forget his obsessive love for Fanny. When his family experiences a financial crisis, he writes Fanny to say he can no longer afford to support her. She responds that she has moved out of their apartment and taken a job as manager of a boarding house, and that she will be able to see him only on Sundays. When he returns to Paris, Jean is unhappy with the new arrangement; the two spend much time together, and Jean also fears the corruptive influence of Fanny's employer, a former courtesan. Jean and Fanny subsequently move into a cottage in the country, but Jean is still tormented by jealousy, revulsion, and shame and they argue frequently; in addition, Fanny has adopted an ill-behaved little boy who Jean suspects is her own child from a previous affair. Then Jean meets and begins to court a sweet, naive young girl named Irène Bouchereau, to whom he becomes engaged. Fanny gradually accepts the break-up of her affair with Jean, and soon he hears that she has again taken up with her old lover Flamant, who has recently been released from prison. Consumed by jealousy, Jean rushes back to Fanny and later terminates his engagement to Irène, thus alienating himself from his family. He decides to accept a consular post in a country far from France and plans to take Fanny with him. She does not appear in Marseille as agreed, though, and just before his boat is to leave he receives a letter informing him that she has decided to end their relationship, stay in France, and marry Flamant.

Characters: Daudet's best-known novel, *Sappho* is based on the author's experiences as a young bourgeois entering an unconventional and artistic Parisian realm and struggling with an obsessive love affair. Described by V.S. Pritchett as "one of the masters of the moments of the heart," Daudet employs physical and psychological realism to evoke an atmosphere of profound sensuality and passion.

Jean Gaussin is the handsome young scion of an upright, middle-class Provençal family. Although he is concerned about his family's opinion of him and about his career, these considerations lose their potency as he becomes more embroiled in his affair with Fanny. The bond that develops between the two lovers is overpoweringly physical, and many critics have praised Daudet for his skill in portraying the strong sensual attraction between Jean and Fanny without vulgarity or even much physical detail. Jean is the type of male character often found in Daudet's fiction: weak-willed, gentle, and sensitive, he is virtually enslaved by a domineering woman. At first Jean naively plans to end his relationship with Fanny after a short time, but he is unable to do so. Jean is aware that the liaison is destructive—it so obsesses him that he is unable to attach himself to the sweet, innocent girl who is a more appropriate mate for him—yet he is compelled by his lust and jealousy to continue it. While Fanny's sordid past disgusts him, it also titillates him, a reaction in keeping with his conflicting feelings about the affair. Some scholars speculate that Jean's story might have been Daudet's, except that Daudet left bohemian Paris and married the woman with whom he achieved a happy union.

Fanny LeGrand is thought to be based on Marie Reis, a woman with whom Daudet carried on a lengthy and obsessive love affair when he was a young man. Born poor and illegitimate, Fanny has lived in the bohemian world of sculptors, painters, and writers for many years and has been the mistress of many of them. At thirty-seven, she is experienced, intelligent, sensual, and passionate. These qualities seem to justify her nickname, Sappho, for they are also commonly ascribed to the Greek poetess whose work was distinguished for its lyric power. While Fanny sometimes displays generosity and devotion, as when she saves Jean's life by nursing him through an illness, she also wields power over her lover through her animal magnetism and strong personality. Interestingly, Fanny assumes the role usually played by the male in the traditional illicit romance: she pursues Jean, she seems to be in control of their relationship (since he is unable to escape her influence), and she ultimately decides that they should part. Such a clear-eyed decision might seem out of character for a woman previously so subject to passion, but it may also indicate that she is wiser, stronger, and more mature than Jean. While Daudet's fiction is noted for its sentimentality, his depiction of Fanny has been described as more honest than the stereotypical prostitutes common in the literature of the period.

The other characters in *Sappho* are depicted with much less detail than Jean and Fanny, but they help fill out the two different milieus in which the story takes place. The bohemian characters found in the Parisian setting include Fanny's former lovers, the sculptor **Caoudal** (who created the sculpture of Sappho while she was living with him), the poet **La Gournerie,** and the engraver **Flamant,** with whom she had a child—the wild, uncontrollable little boy **Josaph**—and to whom she returns in the end. **Déchelette** is the wealthy engineer supporting Fanny as the novel opens. Fanny's employer, **Rosa Sanches,** is a courtesan of the bohemian quarter who for many years has been the mistress of the composer **Tatave de Potter.** Rosa and Tatave's affair has completely estranged him from his family, illustrating the damaging effects of such a liaison. While dining with Rosa (somewhat grotesque in her heavy makeup, many jewels, stylish clothing, and advancing age) and her friends, Jean forms a depressing image of the end to which his own affair may come.

Representing Jean's (and Daudet's) southern roots is his **aunt,** who has always been dear to him. Jean realizes how much his passion for Fanny has affected him when he responds to his aunt's tender, maternal caress with the kiss of a lover rather than a nephew; she complains that Paris has corrupted him. **Césaire Gaussin** is Jean's unreliable uncle; while in Paris to retrieve a debt owed to Jean's parents, he gambles away all of the money he collects. He is rescued by Fanny, who borrows the sum from Déchelette. **Irène Bouchereau,** Jean's fiancée, is an innocent, passive girl with a simple charm that proves an inadequate substitute for the sensuality that Fanny offers; Daudet's depiction of this naive young girl has been characterized as flat and sentimental.

Further Reading

Davidson, Arthur F. "Alphonse Daudet." *Macmillan's Magazine* LXXVIII, No. 465 (July 1898): 175-84.

Nineteenth-Century Literature Criticism, Vol. 1. Detroit: Gale.

Pritchett, V. S. "A Love Affair." In *Books in General,* pp. 104-09. London: Chatto & Windus, 1953.

Roche, Alphonse V. *Alphonse Daudet.* Boston: Twayne Publishers, 1976.

Martin R. Delany
1812-1885
African-American novelist, essayist, and journalist.

Blake; or, The Huts of America (novel, 1859)

Plot: Henrico Blacus is the son of a prosperous black Cuban tobacco manufacturer. After running away from home at seventeen and serving as an apprentice aboard a slave ship bound for the United States, he is taken into slavery himself and transported to the Red River region of Louisiana. There he becomes known as Henry Blake and marries another slave, Maggie, who is the illegitimate mulatto daughter of the powerful slave trader Colonel Stephen Franks. Then Maggie is sold to another owner and taken to Cuba. Infuriated and scornful of slave-owning whites who hypocritically proclaim themselves Christians, Blake escapes from the plantation and travels through Louisiana, Arkansas, and Texas, promoting organized rebellion of enslaved blacks against their oppressors. Eventually he returns to the Franks estate and helps some of the slaves there escape to Canada.

At the beginning of the book's second part, Blake sails to Cuba as a manservant with a group of Americans. After locating his wife and reuniting with the family he had left there as a teenager, Blake becomes the leader of an insurgency force dedicated to freeing the country's black population from the tyranny of Spain and the United States (including those southerners who hope to annex Cuba to extend America's slave-owning region). Delany describes in detail the political intrigues and conditions of slavery in Cuba during the 1840s, particularly focusing on its rich multiracial culture. Blake and his associates recruit followers from a variety of backgrounds—from field slaves to servants to middle-class mulattoes—who unite in their determination to overthrow white oppression. The novel was serialized in several newspapers over about three years; since the concluding chapters were never published, it is not known whether or not the story ends with a successful rebellion.

Characters: The son of free black parents, Delany was a dynamic individual who worked as a journalist and publisher before attending Harvard Medical School and becoming a practicing physician. He served as an officer in the Civil War and a justice of the peace in South Carolina, where he also ran unsuccessfully for lieutenant governor. Described by Floyd J. Miller as "the creative offering of an activist rather than the political expression of an artist," *Blake* is one of the first novels written by an African-American; it was also the most radical of those published in the nineteenth century. In promoting an aggressive response to oppression rather than a passive waiting for relief, *Blake* is often described as the antithesis of Harriet Beecher Stowe's famous abolitionist novel, *Uncle Tom's Cabin* (1852), whose protagonist has been accused of undue subservience to whites. Delany's pride in his heritage and belief in black nationalism are expressed in the book's second part, considered an enlightening and authentic portrait of Cuba's political climate, interracial society, and well-established practice of slavery. Apparently too radical even for the dedicated abolitionists of the period, *Blake* anticipates issues important to twentieth-century African-Americans.

Henrico Blacus, or **Henry Blake** (also known at various times as **Henry Holland** and **Gilbert Hopewell**), is an intelligent and apparently charismatic young man who, like Delany, is proud of his African heritage. Delany rejects the image of the tragic mulatto typified by the character of Eliza in *Uncle Tom's Cabin*; instead, Blake affirms the dignity and nobility of his own race. Notably pragmatic, he sees liberation as cultural, economical, and political: he advocates self-reliance, recognizes the power of money as a means to overcome oppression, and distrusts the meek Christianity practiced by many of his fellow blacks. While Uncle Tom was a pious old slave who adhered to the traditional faith taught to him by his white owners, Blake rejects organized religion as an instrument of oppression encouraging blacks to remain passive while so-called Christians keep them enslaved. Although his followers want to make him a spiritual leader, Blake eschews this role and encourages them to follow the "true religion," one apparently rooted in Christianity but lacking its hypocrisy. In advocating the establishment of a separate black nation (in Cuba rather than Liberia, the location more widely discussed during the late nineteenth century) and in referring to whites by such terms as "devils" and "alabasters," Delany has been cited as a precursor to the black radicals of the 1960s, who often promoted separatism and angrily rejected white values. Some critics feel that Delany may have modeled his title character after a fourteen-year-old Jamaican boy named Alexandre Hendrickure, who was kidnapped and brought to Pittsburgh as a slave and was subsequently rescued by Delany and other black residents of that city.

Because *Blake* is a politically motivated work, it is not surprising that its secondary characters are subordinate to the ideas it presents. Nevertheless several of them are interesting and help flesh out both the concepts promoted in *Blake* and the different settings in which it takes place. **Mammy Judy** and **Daddy Joe,** the parents of Blake's wife **Maggie,** react with hopelessness to the news that their daughter has been sold, crying "How long! How long! O Laud how long!" Because they feel they can only wait for justice through some kind of divine intervention, they illustrate Blake's assertion that slave-owners use religion to instill docility. Also representative of a false faith are **Denmark "Veezie"** and **General Gabriel,** two veterans of the failed slave uprising led by Nat Turner in 1831; they have formed their own religion, called the Order of High Conjurers. Blake considers this invented faith as much a psychological trap as the Christianity of the slave-owners. Other figures in the American section of the book include the shrewd, gossipy house servant **Ailcey** and the folk preacher **Andy,** who serves as Blake's confidante and a local organizer for the planned rebellion; both are sympathetically portrayed.

The Cuban section features several notable characters, including **Placido,** the poet and nationalist (based on a real person by the same name who was executed by the Cuban government in 1844). He serves as the director of the civil government that is to be established after the rebellion, while Blake will be the commander-in-chief of the Army of Emancipation. Also significant among the revolutionaries is **Mendi,** a captured African chief who exhibits courage, discipline, and self-reliance and thus illustrates the concept of pride in African heritage. He also represents the vision of a new, powerful Africa where all those of African blood will be united in dignity and equality. The musical trio of **Pino Golias, Seraphina Blacus,** and **Ambrosina Cordora**—who play African banjos and Spanish guitars—demonstrate the cultural blend of Cuban society. It has been noted, however, that Delany's somewhat didactic portrayal of the novel's Creole characters overlooks the suspicion with which many actual Cubans of mixed blood viewed the idea of Africanization. Delany also condemned the racism practiced by those who were themselves of black heritage, which is evident in his depiction of the mulatto slave owner **Albertis,** who cruelly abuses full-blooded blacks.

Further Reading

Bell, Bernard W. *The Afro-American Novel and Its Tradition.* Amherst: University of Massachusetts Press, 1987.

Fleming, Robert E. ''Delany's *Blake.*'' *Negro History Bulletin* 36 (February 1973): 37-40.

Miller, Floyd J. Introduction to *Blake or The Huts of America,* by Martin R. Delany, pp. xi-xxix. Boston: Beacon Press, 1970.

Rollins, Frank A. *Life and Public Services of Martin Robinson Delany.* 1883. Reprint. Salem, N.H.: Ayer Co. Publications, 1970.

Ullman, Victor. *Martin Delany: The Beginning of Black Nationalism.* Boston: Beacon Press, 1971.

Charles Dickens
1812-1870
English novelist, short story writer, dramatist, poet, and essayist.

Oliver Twist (novel, 1838)

Plot: The novel's title character is a destitute boy whose mother died soon after giving birth to him in a workhouse seventy-five miles from London. A locket and ring that were the only clues to the boy's identity were stolen by Old Sally, a beggar who was present at the birth. The child, subsequently named Oliver Twist by Mr. Bumble, an official of the workhouse, spends his dismal childhood at a poor farm whose inmates are habitually mistreated and starved. Its directors are horrified when Oliver asks one day for more gruel, and they offer five pounds to any employer who will take him. The undertaker Mr. Sowerberry hires Oliver as an apprentice; the boy serves as a particularly pathetic-looking mourner at the funerals of children. Sowerberry's other assistant, the bullying Noah Claypole, constantly torments and teases Oliver, who finally strikes out against him. Released by his employer, Oliver starts for London. Just outside the city he meets a sharp-witted street boy named Jack Dawkins, known as the Artful Dodger, who takes Oliver to the headquarters of his gang of pickpockets and other thieves, led by sinister old Fagin. After receiving some lessons in stealing, Oliver goes on his first pickpocketing expedition but is immediately caught. His victim, kind Mr. Brownlee, pities Oliver and takes him home, where the boy's health and spirits improve dramatically. Sent on an errand one day, Oliver encounters Nancy, a female member of Fagin's gang, and is forced to take up again with his old acquaintances.

Oliver unwillingly participates in a burglary with Fagin and Bill Sikes, the gang's second-in-command, and the housebreaker Toby Crackit. The three are discovered, however, and Oliver is wounded while the others escape. He is taken in and tenderly cared for by the intended victims of the burglary, Mrs. Maylie and her adopted daughter Rose. After Oliver tells his new friends his story, they take him to see Brownlee, who has gone to the West Indies. Meanwhile, Fagin has been visited by a man named Monks. Nancy overhears their conversation about Monks's interest in Oliver's parentage and his desire that the boy be made into a criminal. The Maylies take Oliver to the country, where he enjoys a quiet and happy life with his affectionate friends. Mrs. Maylie's son Harry, a dissolute young man, has fallen in love with his foster sister, but Rose refuses to marry him until she has uncovered the secret of her parentage and he has mended his wastrel ways. One night Oliver sees Fagin and an evil-looking young man (Monks) peering through a window of the Maylie home. Monks goes to the work house in which Oliver was born in order to gather information about the boy; he learns that Bumble's new wife, formerly the widow Mrs. Corney, took a pawn ticket from the body of Old Sally when she died and redeemed it for the locket and wedding ring originally stolen from Oliver's mother. Monks buys these items from Mrs. Bumble and throws them into the river. Nancy, who overhears Monks telling Fagin what he has done, evades her lover Bill Sikes and visits Rose Maylie. She tells Rose everything she has overheard and the two agree to meet again. Rose takes Oliver to see the now-returned Brownlee and they are happily reunited.

Meanwhile, Noah Claypole and Charlotte, another servant of the Sowerberry household, have come to London and joined Fagin's gang. Fagin instructs Noah to follow Nancy, whom he suspects of wanting to leave Sikes; Fagin hopes to use Nancy to somehow eliminate Sikes, who is his rival for leadership of the gang. Nancy escapes from her demanding lover again and meets Rose, informing her of the locations of all of the gang's headquarters except that of Sikes. Sikes learns through Noah and Fagin of Nancy's actions—but not of her faithfulness to him—and murders her in anger. He is tormented, however, by the image of her eyes staring at him as she died. Monks is finally captured and confesses that he is the legitimate son of Oliver's father, Edward Leeford, who had been unhappily married and subsequently separated from his wife and had fallen in love with Oliver's mother, Agnes Fremont. When Leeford died suddenly overseas, his will—leaving half of his fortune to his son Edward (Monks) and half to his illegitimate child (Oliver)—had been destroyed by his wife and Monks. Monks had hoped to eliminate any possibility of Oliver claiming his inheritance by ensuring that the boy became a thief. It is also revealed that Rose Maylie is Agnes's younger sister (orphaned and then taken in by Mrs. Maylie) and is thus Oliver's aunt. Fagin and the Artful Dodger are captured, and Fagin is executed for his many crimes. Sikes accidentally hangs himself while trying to escape from the police. Harry Maylie, who has become a minister, marries Rose; Brownlee officially adopts Oliver. The Bumbles lose their positions and eventually become inmates of the work house they had formerly run; Monks meets his death in an American prison.

Characters: *Oliver Twist* is perhaps the most famous novel of Dickens's apprenticeship period, during which he developed the skills and concerns that would continue to distinguish his fiction. The novel's portrayal of the miserable conditions endured by London's poor and the crime, poverty, and cruelty rampant in the city's underworld is riveting, and its characters are vividly—if often melodramatically—depicted.

The novel's title character occupies a well-established position in the popular imagination as the quintessential innocent waif: good-hearted, inherently moral, and victimized by a heartless social system that ignores even his most basic needs. Many critics have noted that **Oliver Twist** is a rather one-sided character in his embodiment of good to the exclusion of any other qualities; indeed, he is often cited as an example of Dickens's excessive sentimentality. Nevertheless, he is widely acknowledged as a genuinely appealing and moving figure. Oliver's orphaned status reflects Dickens's habitual preoccupation with parentless children, a concern that has been attributed to the psychologically scarring circumstances of his own childhood: his father, John Dickens, spent some time in debtor's prison and Dickens seems to have felt during this period a sense of desolation and abandonment that never left him. While Dickens's portrayal of Oliver's lonely, frightful early years is almost universally praised, some scholars have faulted his later development into a more conventional Victorian hero who turns out to be not an authentic member of London's underclass after all but a relatively wealthy young man cheated of his inheritance. In any case, it is through the unforgettable image of Oliver Twist—and particularly his pathetic, terrified request for more gruel—that Dickens condemned the inhumanity of a society whose Poor Laws, legislation intended to alleviate the suffering of the poor, had proved woefully inadequate.

One of the most dominant and malignant figures in Oliver's early childhood is **Mr. Bumble,** who runs the work house that is the only home the orphaned boy knows. Always appearing in a cocked hat and carrying a cane, he is a vain bully who habitually mistreats Oliver and his fellow unfortunates. His habit of naming orphans according to a strict alphabetical system exemplifies his inability to conceive of or treat them as human beings; thus he constitutes a particularly impersonal and uncaring embodiment of authority. He has come to symbolize the simultaneous officiousness and inefficiency of the petty bureaucrat as well. That he and his wife, the sly and domineering woman who was formerly the work house matron known as **Mrs. Corney,** end as paupers in the same work house over which Bumble formerly tyrannized is satisfyingly ironic.

Mr. Sowerberry, the mortician to whom Oliver is apprenticed, is a tall, gaunt, suitably mournful-looking man who, though not unkind, is meek and powerless and dominated by his shrewish wife, **Mrs. Sowerberry.** At the Sowerberry establishment Oliver also must endure the cruel teasing of his fellow apprentice **Noah Claypole,** an overweight bully who is delighted to have someone even lower on the social scale than he to torment. When Noah runs away to London and joins Fagin's gang, his particular assignment is to steal money from children sent by their parents on errands. He is also instrumental in Nancy's eventual murder, for he eavesdrops on her conversation with Rose Maylie and then reports what he has heard to Bill Sikes. The mean-spirited **Charlotte,** Mrs. Sowerberry's servant, is an appropriate mate for Noah.

Some of the most memorable characters in *Oliver Twist* are those the protagonist meets in the grimy, treacherous streets of London. The colorful and precocious **Jack Dawkins,** or the **Artful Dodger,** thrust into premature adulthood by his destitute circumstances, plays his assigned role with relish, dressing and behaving like a miniature man and projecting a breezy professionalism in regard to his pickpocketing vocation. His boisterous sidekick **Charley Bates** displays a similar, if lesser, aplomb. The greasy and sinister old man who leads the gang of street boys and trains them in the art of thievery is **Fagin,** a conniving middle man for stolen goods whose red hair, as well as several references by other characters, identifies him as a distinctly devilish figure. Dickens has been lauded for his masterfully ironic approach to Fagin, who is always described in false terms of respect. Just as the charitable system established to benefit the poor is shown to punish them instead, Fagin represents a reversal of values in his adoption of such socially endorsed virtues as hard work (the boys are punished when they don't steal enough) and competition. Dickens may have based his portrait of Fagin on an actual English criminal convicted in 1830, Isaac Solomons, who, like Fagin, was Jewish and a fence for stolen jewelry and clothing.

Vying with Fagin for control of the gang is the brutal **Bill Sikes,** whose lack of common decency or loyalty is most evident in his forthright murder of Nancy before she has had a chance to explain that she has not betrayed him. Violent and demanding, Sikes is accustomed to manipulating others in his quest for power, so it is ironically appropriate that in the end he is responsible for his own death. The rough street girl and thief **Nancy** is sentimentally—and stereotypically—portrayed as a prostitute with a golden heart, immoral but inherently kind. Though she is courageous enough to risk her own safety to save Oliver, she proves her loyalty to her lover by not divulging the location of his headquarters. Dickens's depiction of Nancy and the other disreputable inhabitants of London's criminal underworld led early reviewers to condemn *Oliver Twist* as sensational, vulgar, and immoral.

Another representative of evil is the sullen, sinister **Monks,** or **Edward Leeford.** Although he is Oliver's stepbrother, he has no affection for the boy and plots to cheat him of his inheritance. Dickens's penchant for coincidence may be detected in the rather unlikely circumstances that draw Monks into the story; for instance, the fact that he recognizes Oliver immediately on the street even though he has never seen him before. Thus Monks has been described as a clumsily contrived figure inserted purely to expedite the plot.

Kind, understanding **Mr. Brownlee** instigates Oliver's transformation into a respectable member of the middle class when he rescues the boy from the evil judge, **Mr. Fang,** at Oliver's trial for pickpocketing. In bestowing both physical well-being and affection upon Oliver, whom he eventually adopts, the benevolent, elderly Brownlee presents a variety of humanity diametrically opposed to that exemplified by such fiends as Bumble and Fagin. Brownlee is often described as a rather flat character typical of the author's gallery of compassionate figures; critic Philip Hobsbaum writes that he is "surely the dullest of Dickens's good rich men." Similarly, **Mrs. Maylie** is a thoroughly gentle and good woman who serves as a surrogate mother to Oliver, nursing him back to health and providing a happy home for him before his eventual reunion with Brownlee. Gentle, pretty **Rose Maylie**—who is revealed to be Oliver's aunt—is also kind to the boy and a figure of faultless virtue. Rose demonstrates her strong principals when she sets several conditions for her marriage to Harry Maylie. Her idealized, virginal depiction may have been inspired by Mary Hogarth, Dickens's adored sister-in-law, who died when she was seventeen. **Harry Maylie** is an irresponsible young man who must mend his ways if he hopes to win Rose's hand in marriage. Although he initially planned to enter politics, he becomes a minister, suggesting Dickens's distrust of the former occupation.

A Christmas Carol (novella, 1843)

Plot: Set in nineteenth-century London, the story centers on the miserly Ebenezer Scrooge, a prosperous but misanthropic owner of a counting house who denies his overworked clerk Bob Cratchit the comfort of even a small fire. On Christmas Eve, Scrooge's nephew Fred visits him to wish him a merry Christmas, but Scrooge responds with his usual comment that Christmas is "humbug." His only interest is money, and he considers Christmas a time when people waste money. Scrooge reluctantly allows Bob to take Christmas Day off, but insists that he come even earlier to work the next day.

Returning to his empty house, Scrooge sees the face of his former, dead partner, Jacob Marley, in the door knocker, but he convinces himself that he has imagined the vision. Just as Scrooge is ready to retire for the evening, all of the bells in the house begin to ring and he hears the sounds of chains clanking and someone coming up the stairs. Through the door walks the ghost of Marley with a chain wrapped around him that is hung with cash boxes, padlocks, keys, and ledgers. He tells the astonished Scrooge that because of the selfish life he had lived, he is condemned to wander restless and remorseful. After informing Scrooge that he will be visited that night by three ghosts who will show him how to avoid a similarly dismal fate, Marley disappears. At the stroke of one, a spirit identified as the Ghost of Christmas Past appears. He delivers Scrooge to some scenes from his childhood: he sees himself at school, lonely and dejected, then being greeted by his beloved sister, who comes to take him home for Christmas; enjoying a festive party at the office of Mr. Fezziwig, where he served as an apprentice; and talking to a lovely young woman who tells him that because he loves money more than her, she is breaking their engagement. The ghost returns Scrooge to his room, where he promptly falls asleep.

Soon, however, the Ghost of Christmas Present—a fat, jolly figure—appears and whisks Scrooge through the city to witness several Christmas celebrations. At the home of Scrooge's clerk, the family is enjoying a meager but happy meal; the youngest Cratchit child, crippled Tiny Tim, is a cheerful presence. Scrooge's nephew is surrounded by a merry group of friends who are laughing and playing games. At both homes, reluctant toasts are raised to Scrooge. The last spirit to appear is the Ghost of Christmas Yet to Come, a frightening apparition who silently beckons Scrooge to follow him. They see a group of ragged people dividing up a dead man's belongings, but Scrooge is afraid to lift the sheet from the face of the body lying on the bed. They look in on the Cratchits and Scrooge learns that Tiny Tim has died. When Scrooge discovers his own grave, he realizes that he is the dead man, alone and friendless, around whom the scavengers had gathered. Scrooge pleads with the spirit for assurance that this fate might be avoided; he promises to change his ways and to honor Christmas properly from this day forward. He wakes up in his own bed, and with a burst of joyful energy runs out into the street. He orders a turkey to be delivered anonymously to the Cratchit family, makes a large donation to the city's poor fund, and enjoys a gay Christmas dinner at his nephew's house. The change in Scrooge's nature is permanent: he gives Cratchit a raise and better working conditions, treats Tiny Tim generously, supports many charities, and is thereafter renowned for knowing how to "keep Christmas well."

Characters: The telling of *A Christmas Carol,* Dickens's best-known work, is now firmly established as a tradition of the Christmas holiday season. This story of a miser's enlightenment as he reviews his life reverberates with good cheer and compassion. The tale's central figure, who has come to symbolize both miserliness and resistance to merriment, is **Ebenezer Scrooge,** a sapless though successful businessman who lives an intentionally austere and friendless life. A determined misanthrope with a hard-hearted approach not just to Christmas but to humanity in general, Scrooge finds no joy in life but the acquisition of wealth. Stingy not only with his money but with his affection as well, he exists as "solitary as an oyster" until he is made to see both the causes and the costs of his isolation. Although Scrooge's character is distinguished by some flashes of grim humor, as when he attributes the appearance of Jacob Marley's ghost to indigestion ("There's more of gravy than of grave about you, whatever you are"), he is utterly disagreeable until the circumstances of his past and the dismal prospect of his future are revealed. It is difficult not to sympathize with the lonely little boy who sits apart from his schoolmates reading books for the escape they offer, or the clerk who partakes with grateful joy of the festivities at Fezziwig's, and even the ambitious young businessman whose fiancee bids him a sad goodbye and who will come to regret his skewed values. By confronting both his own pain and the misery of others—especially those who, like the Cratchits, he might have helped—Scrooge is transformed from a self-pitying to a compassionate man. Several critics have noted that Scrooge's comical and infectious joy as he orders a turkey for the Cratchits and becomes the life of the party at his nephew's Christmas dinner is irresistible—even if his transformation is not entirely convincing.

Bob Cratchit, Scrooge's long-suffering clerk, works long hours in an under-heated office for little pay in order to support his family. He is a good, generous man whose devotion to his family helps alleviate the sting of his deprivation. He exhibits an admirable capacity for compassion and forgiveness when he proposes a toast to his employer, whom the other members of his family have obviously come to despise. **Mrs. Cratchit,** for instance, resists the idea of honoring a man who has contributed to her family's misery, but her basically warm nature and affection for her husband overcome her resentment. Perhaps the most famous member of the Cratchit family is crippled **Tiny Tim,** the pathetic, courageous little boy whose nobility is increased by his physical affliction and who utters those famous concluding words, "God bless us, every one!" Many critics have described Tim as the epitome of Dickens's tendency toward sentimentality, particularly in the scene Scrooge witnesses at the Cratchit home when the Ghost of Christmas Yet to Come takes him there. The other Cratchit children include **Peter, Belinda,** and **Martha.**

The **Ghost of Jacob Marley** is the first spirit to visit Scrooge on the fateful Christmas Eve that changes his life. Draped comically in a ponderous, clanking chain hung with all the accoutrements of his former money-driven life, Marley relates his dismal fate: because he acted with selfish ruthlessness in life, he is doomed to wander thus encumbered for eternity. Thus he serves as an embodiment of Scrooge's own worst qualities, particularly his lack of compassion for his fellow man, as well as a warning of what might await him.

Each of the next three ghosts that appear in Scrooge's bedchamber has its own distinct nature. The **Ghost of Christmas Past** has a childish face, long white hair, and a strong physique, thus combining the vitality of youth with manifestations of old age. He wears a white tunic adorned with both holly and flowers (evoking the imagery of both winter and summer) and projecting from his forehead is a beam of light, presumably to illuminate the dark halls of Scrooge's painful past. His soft, far-away-sounding voice and his fluctuating appearance reflect both the distances and mingled clarity and fogginess of memory. The **Ghost of Christmas Present,** who whirls Scrooge out into the city streets to witness the happy Christmas celebrations occurring in both wealthy and poor households, is a huge, jolly, hearty figure who holds a glowing torch and who personifies the exuberance and merriment of the season. Yet he also shows Scrooge two grotesque little figures that he identifies as the children of man, Ignorance and Want, and reminds Scrooge of the callous indifference he has shown to such matters in the past. The ominous **Ghost of Christmas Yet to Come,** whom Scrooge calls more fearful than any of the others, is shrouded in black and seems to represent death itself. He brings tidings of gloom in the images he reveals of the Cratchit household bereft of Tiny Tim and of Scrooge's own friendless, degrading death. This faceless and silent spirit only stretches out a bony hand to direct Scrooge's observations.

Other significant characters in *A Christmas Carol* include Scrooge's nephew **Fred,** a ruddy-faced, handsome, jovial young man who tries to envelope his misanthropic uncle in his own good cheer. His generosity and warm heart are evident when, like Bob Cratchit, he proposes a toast to Scrooge at his Christmas party and is met with incredulity from his guests. Fred's mother **Fan** is the beloved sister who arrived, in Scrooge's vision of himself as a lonely schoolboy, to take him home; his realization that something of his dead sister lives on in her son forms an important part of his transformation. **Mr. Fezziwig** is the fun-loving, kindhearted old merchant for whom Scrooge worked as a clerk. He is a comical figure, wigged and fat, and the delightful Christmas party he hosts for his employees and friends is one of the book's most memorable scenes. Scrooge is surprised to find himself explaining to the Ghost of Christmas Past that Fezziwig's ability to make others happy was a quality more valuable than money. The equally affectionate and jovial **Mrs. Fezziwig** is described as "one vast substantial smile." Scrooge's fiancee **Belle,** a lovely and virtuous young woman with no dowry to bring to the marriage, releases her lover from his obligation so that he can pursue his "master passion, Gain." Scrooge sees Belle established later in life in a comfortable home with a pleasant husband and many laughing children, a vision of the happiness he himself might have found with her. **Joe, the junk dealer, Mrs. Dilber, the laundress,** as well as **the charwoman** and **the undertaker's man** comprise a gruesomely comic gathering of scavengers who confiscate Scrooge's bedclothes after his death for what little money they will bring.

David Copperfield (serialized novel, 1849-50)

Plot: The title character is born six months after his father's death and spends his early childhood with his kind, childish mother, Clara Copperfield, and their faithful servant Clara

Peggotty. David travels with Peggotty to visit her brother Daniel and his family in Yarmouth, where they live in a seaside house made from a boat. David enjoys playing with Daniel's pretty niece Little Em'ly and sturdy nephew Ham. Returning home, David learns that his mother has married the heartless Mr. Murdstone; soon Murdstone's gloomy and suspicious sister Jane also moves in with the family. When David rebels against his stepfather's cruelty, he is sent to Salem House school, where the brutal headmaster Mr. Creakle makes life miserable for his young charges. The harshness of this period is somewhat alleviated by David's friendships with two schoolmates: likeable Tommy Traddles and aristocratic James Steerforth. When David returns to his home after the death of his mother and her baby, he finds that Peggotty has married the stagecoach driver, Barkis, and moved away. His lonely sojourn at home ends when he goes to work as a clerk in the Murdstone and Grinby wine warehouse, of which his stepfather is part owner. David works long hours, receives little to eat, and endures the company of several unpleasant clerks. He boards, however, in the home of Wilkins Micawber, who becomes his dear friend. Although Micawber's impracticality with money has brought him to the brink of disaster, he is eternally optimistic that something will come along to save him. He finally has to spend some time in debtor's prison, though, and on his release he decides to move his family to Plymouth.

David leaves Murdstone and Grinby and starts for London to seek the aid of his aunt, Miss Betsey Trotwood, who had been present on the night of his birth but had left indignantly when she learned the baby was a boy and thus would not bear her name. The ragged, dirty David is taken in by his gruff but essentially kindhearted aunt, who lives with a feeble-minded but much trusted relative, Mr. Dick. When the Murdstones arrive to retrieve David, Miss Trotwood finds them despicable and decides to raise David herself. She sends him to school in Canterbury, where David boards with Mr. Wickfield (Miss Trotwood's lawyer) and befriends the daughter of the house, gentle and sensible Agnes Wickfield. David is disgusted by Wickfield's clerk, the hypocritically humble and sly Uriah Heep.

After finishing school, David decides to visit Peggotty and her family at Yarmouth. On the way there, he meets his old friend Steerforth and invites him to come along; Steerforth subsequently becomes enamored of the lovely Little Em'ly even though she is now engaged to Ham. David decides to study law and becomes a clerk at the office of Spenlow and Jorkins. Agnes warns David to avoid Steerforth and also expresses suspicions about Heep, who has recently become her mentally weakened father's business partner. David falls in love with his employer's daughter, Dora Spenlow, and they are secretly engaged. He is shocked to hear that Steerforth has run away with Little Em'ly and is further dismayed by the news that his aunt has lost her entire fortune. In order to repay his aunt for her kindness to him, David takes on another part-time job as a secretary to Mr. Strong, his pleasant former headmaster at the Canterbury School, and also studies to become a Parliamentary reporter. Mr. Dick also resolves to help Miss Trotwood and becomes a clerk for David's old friend Traddles, who is now a lawyer. Soon Mr. Spenlow dies, and David learns that he had hardly any money. After David becomes a reporter, he marries Dora, but he soon discovers that she is incapable of managing a household. Micawber has since become Heep's secretary; after initially hiding his knowledge, he finally informs David and the other key characters that Heep had been cheating Wickfield for years and had also caused Miss Trotwood's financial ruin. Heep is forced to make restitution to both injured parties. Micawber decides to take his family to Australia in search of opportunity. Daniel Peggotty and Little Em'ly, who has returned to her family after being deserted by the shiftless Steerforth, emigrate there as well.

Meanwhile, Dora's health had been declining and she finally dies after being compassion-ately nursed by Agnes. David decides to travel abroad for a while, but stops first at Yarmouth to give Ham a letter from Little Em'ly. While he is there, a storm blows up and Ham bravely attempts to rescue the struggling survivor of a shipwreck. He dies in the attempt; it is revealed, ironically, that the man he had tried unsuccessfully to save was Steerforth. After three years on the continent, David returns to England and begins to realize how much he values Agnes's steadfast friendship. Miss Trotwood engineers a meeting between the two at which their mutual love is revealed. They marry and David becomes a successful novelist.

Characters: The autobiographical novel *David Copperfield* is the last of Dickens's apprentice works and his first to be told in the first-person. Its narrative voice is rendered compelling by the author's personal knowledge of the orphaned protagonist's often-harrowing experiences. **David Copperfield** is a sensitive, trusting boy whose early years, spent with his sweet mother and doting nurse Peggotty, are idyllic. The pleasant holiday he spends in Yarmouth with Daniel Peggotty and his family—who live in a cozy house made from a boat that is the stuff of a boy's fantasy—marks the transition from his early innocence to his knowledge of suffering. Returning home to find the evil Mr. Murdstone, and later his shrewish sister Jane, installed there, David enters a period of fear and loneliness that Dickens vividly portrays. David responds fairly passively to Murdstone—at least until, out of sheer terror, he bites his hand—submitting to mistreatment with a bewilderment that makes him even more pathetic. As David matures, however, he develops self-sufficiency and learns to cope with such adult concerns as poverty, overwork, a disappointing marriage, and death. Like his mother, David is softhearted, pliant, even weak, but he also has as a surrogate mother and major influence on his character the firm Miss Trotwood. The long, degrading hours David passes while working at Murdstone and Grinby directly reflect Dickens's own employment, when he was twelve years old, in a shoeblacking factory while his father was in debtor's prison. The memory of this nightmarish experience never left Dickens; as an adult he remarked that he was still occasionally overcome by the feelings of isolation and hopelessness he experienced during that period of his life. David is usually grouped with Dickens's early heroes because he is basically faultless and victimized, and most critics agree that his characterization is more successful in the first half of the book, when he more closely resembles the author who created him, than during the last half, when his eventual evolution into a happily married and successful novelist seems somewhat forced.

David's mother, **Clara Copperfield,** is an understanding, generous, but essentially child-like woman ill-equipped to cope with life's difficulties; significantly, David's first wife Dora is a similar type of woman. The delicate and pretty Clara fails to see evil in anyone, thus Murdstone is able to lure her into a marriage that proves detrimental to her own and her son's happiness. Some scholars have seen in Dickens's portrayal of this kind but weak figure a reflection of Dickens's mixed affection for and resentment of his own mother. It has been noted that **Clara Peggotty**'s sharing the first name of David's mother marks her as an alternative maternal figure, one who contrasts with the other both in appearance and manner. The plump, plain, and rough-skinned Peggotty is very capable of making her way through life and taking care of others. Cheerful and devoted, Peggotty is a constant source of comfort for David, and he feels her absence keenly when, after his mother has died and Peggotty has moved away, he returns to a home devoid of all love. **Mr. Barkis,** who drives the stagecoach between the Copperfield home in Blunderstone and the Peggotty's in Yarmouth, is a good, simple, profoundly bashful man who wins Peggotty's heart with his shy, succinct marriage proposal: ''Barkis is willin'.''

Peggotty also plays the practical role of providing a link with **Daniel Peggotty** and his two wards. Daniel is a fisherman whose converted boat home reflects his fondness for marine pursuits. Generous, kind, and faithful, he represents the idealized, benevolent father; likewise, his compact, comfortable home provides a welcoming sanctuary for his family and friends. His pretty and charming niece **Little Em'ly** is David's first love and also, unfortunately, an instrument of his education. She proves fatally vulnerable to the charms of his friend James Steerforth, whose falseness is not apparent to David until he elopes with Little Em'ly. Stalwart **Ham,** Daniel's nephew and Little Em'ly's fiancee before her elopement, proves his nobility when he sacrifices his own life in an attempt to save that of a stranger. The fact that the stranger is the man who destroyed his hope for a happy marriage provides a bitterly ironic twist as well as an example of Dickens's penchant for coincidence.

Edward Murdstone is one of Dickens's best-known villains. His allegorical name reflects his dark, hard nature; he is a sadistic, miserly, calculating man who not only deprives his wife and stepson of their happiness but threatens David physically. An egotist whose evil deeds are carried out under the guise of humanitarianism, Murdstone has been seen as an embodiment of the kind of hypocritical Victorian morality that justified outright cruelty toward children in the name of character building. He is also directly connected with the institutionalized forms of oppression in the novel, such as at the Salem House school and the Murdstone and Grinby warehouse. Like her brother, the scowling, notably masculine **Jane Murdstone** has dark hair, pronounced eyebrows, and a harsh, rigid, suspicious demeanor. With her black clothing and her steel purse with its clanking chain, she moves in a perpetual aura of gloom.

The cruel headmaster of Salem House school serves as an extension of Murdstone. **Mr. Creakle,** whose name reflects his distinctive voice, was reportedly based on the sadistic headmaster of a school Dickens attended, Wellington House Academy. Ironically unscholarly, he takes pleasure in brutally bullying his charges. When he learns that David has bitten his stepfather's hand, Creakle attaches a placard to the boy's back warning others to beware because "he bites," thus offering proof that he considers his inferiors animals. **Mrs. Creakle** attempts to treat David more kindly but she is a weak woman completely tyrannized by her husband.

David's misery at Salem House is somewhat alleviated by the two friends he meets there. **James Steerforth** is a wealthy, handsome, lighthearted boy who has always been indulged by his aristocratic mother, the proud and austere **Mrs. Steerforth.** Steerforth's charm and willfulness impress David, perhaps because they reflect qualities he feels are missing in his own character. Some critics have noted an implication that Steerforth might have been redeemable under different circumstances, while others consider him the type of aristocratic dandy and seducer common in conventional Victorian fiction. His status as a member of the nobility might also be seen as an indictment of that social class by the middle-class Dickens. By contrast, **Thomas Traddles** is an amiable and loyal friend who is as unhappy at Salem House as David and who draws skeletons as a means of distracting himself from his misery. Thomas grows up to become a judge and proves his constancy and integrity when he helps David and Miss Trotwood with their financial difficulties and hires Mr. Dick as his clerk. He marries the pleasant, cheerful clergyman's daughter, **Miss Sophy Crewler.**

The penniless but eternally optimistic **Wilkins Micawber** is a humorous yet pathetic figure who is always certain that "something will turn up" to extract him from his monetary difficulties. Physically, Micawber resembles the nursery rhyme character Humpty Dumpty: he is stout with a bald, egg-shaped head. The essentially good-hearted, loyal, profoundly unworldly Micawber lives a life of faded gentility until he is finally thrown into debtor's prison. It is widely acknowledged that Dickens modeled Micawber after his own father, a similarly impractical man whose financial naivete or irresponsibility landed him in jail and required his son to go to work. Micawber's relationship with David, however, is more that of a contemporary than that of a father. His grandiloquent, flowery speech, which provides many of the novel's most humorous passages, might be considered his means of creating respectability for himself and of coping with his many troubles. Toward the end of the story, Micawber plays a significant part in the plot when he reveals Uriah Heep's villainy; some critics claim that he becomes a less successful character as his role becomes more practical.

Mrs. Emma Micawber, who claims to come from higher-class circumstances than she currently occupies, tends to react dramatically to crises but recovers remarkably quickly. She frequently proclaims her undying loyalty to her husband and her vow never to desert him. With their children, **Master Wilkins** and **Emma,** the Micawbers provide a source of affection and familial warmth in David's otherwise bleak life.

David's sharp-tongued, eccentric, but basically kind aunt, **Miss Betsey Trotwood,** walks indignantly away from her newborn nephew when she learns he will not bear her name. Nevertheless, she later accepts and nurtures David, ostensibly on the advice of the much-trusted Mr. Dick. With her rigid figure and facial expression and her decisive manner, Miss Trotwood provides a strong contrast to David's soft, sweet mother. She is an important force in his development, resolving when she adopts him to help him grow stronger and more independent. Also unlike Clara Copperfield, Miss Trotwood has an exaggerated distrust of her fellow human beings, yet this wariness does not prevent her from being cheated of her fortune. Her bankruptcy presents David with a valuable lesson in adulthood, for it is he who must help her cope with her difficulties. Miss Trotwood's live-in relative, **Richard Babley,** or **Mr. Dick,** is an amiable though half-witted man whose basic childishness is juxtaposed with his ambitious intention to write a memorial to England's King Charles I. Miss Trotwood considers Mr. Dick an infallible judge of character and she always defers to his opinion, which may suggest merely her own eccentricity or some deeper awareness of his purity. Mr. Dick is considered a primary example of Dickens's attraction to and sympathy for the physically deformed or mentally deficient members of society.

Agnes Wickfield is sensible, gentle, generous, strong, and self-disciplined. Though she loves David, she carefully hides her feelings for him throughout his first marriage and even nurses Dora through her last illness. Agnes's perceptiveness is evident when she warns David that his friend Steerforth is not as honorable as he seems, and she also distrusts Heep. While David's love for Dora is presented as a symptom of his immaturity, the regard he finally develops for the more deserving Agnes marks his arrival at adulthood. Some scholars find Agnes unrealistically virtuous, unpleasantly smug, and overly moralistic, for one of her roles is to remind David of his duty to help others. Agnes's father, **Mr. Wickfield,** is Miss Trotwood's lawyer; although he is a man of high principals, his inherent weakness is evident when he allows himself to be victimized by Heep.

Uriah Heep is another of Dickens's entertainingly wicked villains. His humility and fawning merely mask his conniving, sly nature, for it is eventually revealed that he has embezzled funds from and eventually ruined his employer, Mr. Wickfield, and his client Miss Trotwood. A markedly reptilian figure with a clammy handshake and almost lidless eyes, Heep repulses David, particularly when he expresses his intention to marry Dora. It seems fitting that the generally irresponsible Micawber, who has been hired as Heep's clerk, overcomes his usual lack of resolve to expose his employer's evil deeds.

David falls in love with beautiful **Dora Spenlow** the first time he sees her, a romantic vision that proves faulty when fluttery Dora is incapable of managing her household. In her childishness and impracticality Dora has been said to resemble Dickens's wife Catherine Hogarth, from whom he was eventually separated. In the novel, however, David is released from this obviously inappropriate union by Dora's death. Dora has been characterized as a typically Dickensian heroine, for she is both idealized for her virtues and mocked for her foibles. Some scholars have noted that David seems more irritated by Dora than might be expected given his stated love for her. **Francis Spenlow,** Dora's father, for whom David works as a law clerk, initially opposes the young couple's marriage plans because he has learned of Miss Trotwood's financial ruin. This rigid stance proves ironic when it is revealed, after Spenlow's death, that his own business was in disarray and he has left his daughter penniless.

Also playing a significant role in *David Copperfield* is **Rosa Dartle,** Mrs. Steerforth's companion, who has long harbored a secret and humiliating love for Steerforth and who is thus bitterly gratified when he deserts Little Em'ly. She bears a scar on her lip that is an emblem of Steerforth's angry attack on her when he was a child—a foreboding warning of his behavior as an adult. **Dr. Strong** is the headmaster at Canterbury School, to which Miss Trotwood sends David after he comes to live with her. He provides a strong contrast to Creakle in his kindness and integrity and he represents a genuinely high standard of refinement and scholarship. He assists David after Miss Trotwood's bankruptcy by hiring him to help him compile a dictionary.

Hard Times (novel, 1854)

Plot: Thomas Gradgrind, a resident of the industrial (and fictional) English city of Coketown, runs an experimental school based on the premise that children should learn only facts and that imagination has no role in education. One day, Grandgrind, who had raised his own five children in accordance with this philosophy, discovers his son Tom and daughter Louisa peeking through a circus tent in an attempt to view the merry activities going on inside. With his friend Josiah Bounderby, the wealthy owner of a textile factory and bank, Gradgrind decides that Sissy Jupe, a student at the school and the daughter of a circus clown, was responsible for leading the Gradgrind children astray. Although he has decided to expel Sissy, Gradgrind changes his mind when he learns that her father has deserted her. He allows her to stay at the school and to live with his family. After several years have passed, the unsentimental Louisa agrees to marry Bounderby despite their thirty-year age difference in order to help her beloved but untrustworthy brother Tom, who has become a clerk in Bounderby's bank. Bounderby's housekeeper Mrs. Sparsit resents her dismissal from the household after the marriage and vows to watch Louisa carefully for any signs of misbehavior.

Gradgrind is now a member of Parliament and sends a young political aspirant, James Harthouse, from London to gather information about Coketown for a study of British society. Bounderby tells Harthouse of his rise from a penniless waif to a rich industrialist; though unimpressed by his new acquaintance, Harthouse is taken with Louisa's beauty. He manipulates the weak-natured Tom for information about his sister and decides that her bleak upbringing and unpleasant marriage will make her an easy romantic conquest. He manages to ingratiate himself with Louisa, unaware that Mrs. Sparsit is spying on the couple. When the Bounderby bank is robbed, the humble weaver Stephen Blackpool— whose employer, Bounderby, had recently mistreated him—is suspected, particularly since he could not be found. Meanwhile, Louisa abandons her intention of running away with Harthouse, fleeing instead to her father's house and refusing to return to Bounderby. Bounderby, who has learned of the planned elopement from Mrs. Sparsit, demands Louisa's return, but Gradgrind allows Louisa to make her own decision. Mrs. Sparsit again becomes Bounderby's housekeeper and tries to please him by locating Mrs. Pegler, who had previously been seen in Blackpool's company and thus was wanted for questioning about the robbery. But Mrs. Pegler turns out to be Bounderby's mother, whom he is not at all eager to see because she exposes his real background: he was raised in respectable circumstances and thus is not the rags-to-riches success he claims to be.

While attempting to return to Coketown to prove his innocence, Blackpool falls down a mine shaft. He is accidentally discovered there by Louisa and Sissy; before he dies, he reveals that Tom was the actual culprit. Tom tries to escape but is found by his sister and father, who hide him temporarily in the circus; he is subsequently captured by Bounderby's men, but some of the circus people rescue him again and spirit him safely away aboard a departing boat. None of the other characters meet happy fates: Bounderby dies alone and unhappy, and the Gradgrinds' lives continue to be blighted by their overreliance on facts.

Characters: Although Dickens had included implicit social criticism in many of his previous novels, *Hard Times* was the first in which he presented such condemnation directly. Within his grim, pessimistic portrait of the ugliness of unfettered industrial development and the inhumanity of utilitarianism (a prominent movement of the period), Dickens created characters who embody both positive and negative aspects of humanity's struggle to survive in an increasingly complex world.

Thomas Gradgrind is the founder of a school that emphasizes fact and scientific law over imaginative or fanciful pursuits. Although he is portrayed as a basically kind man (demonstrated, for instance, by his sympathy for the abandoned Sissy), he has overemphasized the practical, declaring that "Facts alone are wanted in life. Plant nothing else, and root out everything else." In doing so, he ruins his children's chances for happiness as adults: Louisa marries a man she does not love and then almost runs away with a cad, and Tom turns to gambling and crime. While the "model" school has presumably prepared its students for life's realities, it has stripped them of the humanity they need to exist happily with themselves and others. After Louisa has returned to him in great misery, Gradgrind admits that though he had meant well, the system he so energetically promoted has done great harm. Gradgrind embodies the views of nineteenth-century utilitarians, who saw human behavior as the self-interested and pre-determined result of external factors and who believed that education should be practical and geared toward the kind of life a student was likely to lead. In *Hard Times,* Dickens makes a plea for humane and intuitive values over pure reason.

Louisa Gradgrind—who with her brother Tom is chastised early in the story for trying to sneak a glance at the circus—is portrayed as a product of her upbringing. She grows into a sensible, practical young woman who lacks not only imagination but the ability to love; thus she sees no reason not to marry Bounderby, particularly since it will benefit her brother. With such inadequate training in the ways of the heart, it is not surprising that she is vulnerable to the false charms of James Harthouse. In the end, however, Louisa lacks the courage (as well as the foolishness, since Harthouse would have made her no more happy than Bounderby) to carry through with her planned rebellion, and she returns shamed and heartbroken to her father's house.

Tom Gradgrind is equally ill-prepared for a useful, happy life. He reacts to the emotional deprivation of his upbringing by pursuing such vices as drinking, gambling, and thievery. When his father wonders how he could have taken this path, Tom reminds him that he himself has said that a certain percentage of the population is bound to turn to crime; thus by becoming part of that percentage he is merely fulfilling a rational law of society. Tom's abdication of personal responsibility reveals the inadequacy of the deterministic view, which held that individuals' fates are inevitably directed by their environments.

The wealthy factory owner and banker **Josiah Bounderby** personifies the dehumanizing force of rapid industrialization as well as the individualism that was a popular Victorian concept. Pompous and power-obsessed, he has created a fictional history of his origin as an orphaned waif and his gradual rise to self-made entrepreneur. In fact, Bounderby was raised by a caring, self-sacrificing mother, **Mrs. Pegler,** from whom he has since imposed a carefully enforced distance—thus exemplifying his isolation from other human beings. He sees other people—whether they are the workers in his factory or his own wife—merely as instruments he can manipulate to achieve what he wants rather than as fellow travelers in life. Portrayed as a particularly melodramatic villain, Bounderby elicits little sympathy from the reader.

James Harthouse is similarly wicked. He is a handsome, suave, cynical political aspirant who uses his shrewd perceptions about human nature to manipulate people for his own gain: he exploits Tom's weakness for drink to gain information about his sister, and he exploits Louisa's loveless upbringing and vulnerability to persuade her to elope with him. Harthouse, however, is more important as an expedient to the plot than as a personality. **Mrs. Sparsit** is another of *Hard Times*'s villains; she is a former member of the aristocracy reduced to working as a housekeeper after her husband's bankruptcy. Jealous and resentful, she spies on Louisa and Harthouse and accidentally draws Bounderby's ire when she brings forth his mother (whom she thinks is involved in the burglary), thereby exposing the truth about his past when she intended to impress him with her diligence.

Among the characters in the novel who stand for the force of good and compassion, **Stephen Blackpool** is perhaps the most poignant. A poor, honest weaver in Bounderby's textile mill, Stephen is victimized by both his difficult and demeaning factory job and his degrading marriage to an alcoholic. Blackpool refuses to take sides in a labor dispute and is subsequently ostracized by his fellow workers and mistreated by his employer. Falsely accused of stealing money from Bounderby's bank, Stephen is nobly returning to face the charges when he is killed. Stephen's death—he falls into an unused but dangerously exposed mine shaft—symbolizes the evils of the industrial system. Many critics have described Stephen as a rather melodramatic portrait of perfection in the saintly patience with which he responds to his victimization. Scholars also fault Dickens for neglecting to illustrate the actual conditions of Stephen's existence as a member of the working class; Dickens's refusal to accept the trade union as a reasonable solution to the workers' dilemma, illustrating his distrust of unionism, has also been condemned. **Mrs. Blackpool,** Stephen's alcoholic wife, is an insubstantial character whose transformation from an attractive and pleasant girl to a harridan is not explained. **Rachel** is the virtuous young woman who works with Stephen in the factory and whose love for him can never be fulfilled.

The circus people are merry and good-hearted representatives of fancy in *Hard Times.* **Cecilia "Sissy" Jupe** is brought into the Gradgrind household as a charity case, but she proves faithful to her heritage as the daughter of a clown (**Signor Jupe**) when she resists the fact-based system of education that Gradgrind tries to impose upon her. Eventually she leaves the Gradgrind home and goes to work in Bounderby's factory. Sensitive, loving, and trusting, she believes the best of everyone (even the father who deserts her). For instance, she shows no fear of the sophisticated Harthouse when she pleads with him to give up his plan of fleeing with Louisa, and she enlists her circus friends to help Tom escape. **Mr. Sleary,** the proprietor of the circus and Sissy's loyal friend, provides a vivid contrast to the novel's representatives of utilitarianism: he is a stout man and a heavy drinker with a profoundly humane heart. Like other "good" characters in *Hard Times,* Sleary is ideally virtuous and inherently innocent. Along with such members of his troupe as **E. W. B. Childers,** who performs as "The Wild Huntsman of the North American Prairies," and **Master Kidderminster,** the young boy with the old man's face, Sleary represents the necessity of imagination and amusement for a balanced and fulfilling life.

The novel's other significant characters include **Mr. M'Choakumchild,** the aptly named headmaster of the model school, and **Bitzer,** its star student, a cold-hearted product of its premise that the social system is based on self-interest. Through **Slackbridge,** the union organizer who is unsuccessful in converting Stephen to his philosophy, Dickens reveals his contempt for trade unions, which he apparently considered as self-interested as the factory owners. Slackbridge may have been based on Mortimer Grimshaw, an English reformer who proposed cooperative ownership of factories by workers.

A Tale of Two Cities (novel, 1859)

Plot: The novel begins in Paris in the mid eighteenth century, several years before the beginning of the French Revolution. Dr. Alexander Manette has been released after an eighteen-year imprisonment in the Bastille, the notorious French jail. His daughter Lucie—whom he has not seen since she was a baby—has traveled to Paris from London with a family friend, Mr. Jarvis Lorry of the Tellson and Company bank, to bring her father home. Mentally traumatized by his ordeal, Dr. Manette is temporarily hidden in a room above a wine shop operated by Monsieur and Madame DeFarge, who are both active in the movement to incite an uprising of the impoverished peasantry against the privileged aristocracy. Madame DeFarge is always seen knitting a long scarf, into which she has worked the names of the aristocrats she despises. Five years later, the Manettes testify at London's Old Bailey court in the treason trial of Charles Darnay, a French language teacher who has been accused by a man named John Barsad of passing secret information between England and France. The Manettes had met Darnay during their voyage back to England after Dr. Manette's release. Darnay is saved from conviction when his lawyer, Mr. Stryver, points out his remarkable resemblance to Sydney Carton, Stryver's associate, thus making positive identification of Darnay as the guilty party impossible. After the trial, both Darnay and Carton call frequently at the home of the Manettes.

Meanwhile, in France, the anger and dissatisfaction of the citizenry is growing. While the Marquis St. Evrémonde (the uncle of Charles Darnay, who has left France and is trying to shed his connections with his noble family) is driving through the countryside toward his estate, his carriage runs over and kills a peasant child. In a subsequent discussion with his uncle, Darnay pleads with him to make amends for the grave wrongs committed by members of the family in the past. The marquis refuses. That night, the marquis is murdered by Gaspard, the father of the dead child. Returning to England, Darnay asks Manette for permission to seek Lucie's hand in marriage; he wants to reveal his real name to his prospective father-in-law, but Manette tells him to wait until the morning of his wedding day to do so. Carton has also fallen in love with Lucie but she refuses his marriage proposal. He tells her never to forget that he will do anything he can to help her or those she loves.

In France, Gaspard is executed for the murder of the marquis while Madame DeFarge knits the story of the Evrémondes' evil deeds into her scarf. The English spy John Barsad tells DeFarge that the marquis's nephew, Charles Darnay, will marry Lucie; DeFarge is troubled by this because Manette's years in the Bastille have made him a heroic figure to the revolutionaries. Lucie and Darnay are married and have a daughter, also named Lucie. Six years after her birth, in 1789, the French Revolution begins with the storming of the Bastille. During the attack, DeFarge retrieves some papers that were hidden in the cell in which Manette had been imprisoned. Darnay learns that a faithful employee of the Evrémondes has been captured by the revolutionary forces; he feels obligated to travel to Paris to try to help the man. Mr. Lorry accompanies Darnay to Paris, planning to check in on his company's French office. Darnay is soon arrested. Manette and Lucie also arrive in Paris, having heard of Darnay's arrest; the doctor hopes that he can enlist the sympathy of his son-in-law's captors by reminding them of his own imprisonment in the Bastille. This plan is successful; Darnay is found not guilty at a trial held fifteen months later. After his release, Darnay is arrested again almost immediately due to an accusation made by an unnamed party. Miss Pross and Jerry Cruncher, the Manette's faithful maid and a helpful employee of Mr. Lorry, happen to meet Miss Pross's lost brother Solomon on a Paris street, though Jerry recognizes the man as John Barsad. Also appearing on the scene is Carton, who forces Barsad to make an unspecified deal with him in exchange for Carton's promising not to reveal him to the French authorities as a former spy for the English. At Darnay's trial, DeFarge names Manette as the accuser and shows the court the papers he took from Manette's cell, which provide an account of why Manette had been imprisoned: he had known about and attempted to expose the rape of a peasant girl and brutal treatment of her brother by the Marquis St. Evrémonde. Darnay is forced to assume responsibility for his ancestor's guilt and is condemned to die. Carton learns that Madame DeFarge is the vengeful sister of the young woman who had been ravished by the marquis. Through Barsad, he gains admission to Darnay's prison cell, where he drugs Darnay and has him taken away; Carton remains and poses as Darnay while the Frenchman escapes safely. Madame DeFarge goes to the Manettes' lodgings with a gun, but she finds only Miss Pross there. The maid tries to prevent Madame DeFarge from learning that the Manettes have left and in the struggle that follows Madame DeFarge is killed and Miss Pross is made permanently deaf by the gun's blast. Lucie and Darnay escape to England, while the self-sacrificing Carton dies at the guillotine.

Characters: Though criticized by many scholars as overly sentimental and melodramatic and overshadowed by Dickens's more accomplished novels, *A Tale of Two Cities* features several memorable characters who help illustrate the novel's theme of human fellowship and love as the only viable means to rectify wrongs in a hopelessly complex and tangled world.

The altruistic **Sydney Carton** is one of the most consistently praised characters in the novel. The once-brilliant but now-dissipated legal assistant to the crafty lawyer Mr. Stryker, Carton was born into privilege but allowed himself to deteriorate through his indulgence in alcohol and other vices. He is aimless, misanthropic, and lacks ideals—until he meets Lucie Manette. Though he realizes that his love for the beautiful, virtuous girl is hopeless, it has a redemptive power, and in the end, it is Carton who saves the life of Lucie's husband, thus making the remarkable sacrifice that is the novel's strongest symbol of the power of love. Some critics fault Dickens for failing to concretely demonstrate the idleness and debauchery to which Carton is supposedly prone, and Carton's sacrifice has been characterized as unconvincingly melodramatic. Nevertheless, this character is clearly presented as Darnay's alter ego: the Frenchman represents the better kind of man Carton could have been, or does finally become, and is thus an example of Dickens's fondness for character pairs who are similar in some ways but represent moral opposites.

The young French nobleman **Charles Darnay,** whose real name is **Charles St. Evrémonde,** is essentially a flat character. Handsome, faithful, and principled, he is more appropriate a choice for Lucie than Carton. Because he has renounced his title and chosen to make his own way in a foreign country as a humble language teacher, Darnay embodies the antiaristocratic sentiment that was an important antecedent to the French Revolution. By contrast, his uncle, the **Marquis St. Evrémonde,** represents the arrogance and brutality that led to the violent reaction of those who felt oppressed and demeaned by the nobility. In this cruel and haughty character, whose pinched nose represents an exaggerated sense of superiority and vanity, Dickens concentrates—some say simplistically—the reasons for the French Revolution.

Dr. Alexander Manette is another of the few characters in *A Tale of Two Cities* that critics praise. Imprisoned in the Bastille for his attempt to expose the Marquis St. Evrémonde's treachery, Manette was permanently altered by his experience. After his initial emergence from eighteen years of solitary confinement, he feels secure only when locked in a small room, and he identifies himself only by the number of his jail cell. Although he gradually recovers under the loving care of his daughter and other faithful friends, Manette reverts in times of stress to the shoemaking that comprised his only link with sanity during his tortuous years in prison. Dickens has been lauded for creating in Manette an interesting portrait of the damage caused by isolation and loneliness. In the vision that appears to Carton in the moments before his death, he sees Manette restored to normalcy, but some critics have questioned the likelihood of such a transformation. **Lucie Manette** is an essentially one-dimensional figure who embodies the typically Dickensian domestic virtues of beauty, devotion, and general goodness combined with practicality.

Jarvis Lorry, a confidential clerk employed by Tellson and Company, proves a kind, faithful friend to the Manettes, though his advice to the doctor to give up the shoemaking equipment to which he returns during his psychotic relapses seems ill-advised. He is a fussy, old-fashioned bachelor whose loyalty is unquestionable. Similarly devoted is the Manette's maidservant, the somewhat absurd but formidable **Miss Pross,** who eventually kills the enraged Madame DeFarge and sacrifices her own hearing in the process. The "resurrection man" **Jerry Cruncher,** who works as a messenger for Tellson and Company and steals corpses for use as anatomical specimens during his spare time, is also a generally positive and helpful figure. He frequently ridicules his pious wife, **Mrs. Cruncher,** who disapproves of his gruesome avocation and continually prays for his reformation. Young **Jerry Cruncher, Jr.** keeps a watchful and intelligent eye on his father's activities.

Mr. Stryver is a shrewd, self-centered, and often bullying attorney; his using an idea that Carton formulated to get Darnay acquitted of treason typifies his habit of taking credit for his associate's legal work. It has been surmised that Dickens based the character on an actual person, Edwin James, a notoriously unscrupulous lawyer whose office the author once visited and who was eventually disbarred for his shifty practices. More outrightly villainous, however, are the characters of **John Barsad** (born **Solomon Pross,** and the brother of Miss Pross), the wily spy and informer whom Carton blackmails into helping him change places with Darnay when the latter is imprisoned in the Bastille, and **Roger Cly,** the spy who first attempts to frame Darnay then fakes his own death, then later joins forces with the French.

The novel's French characters are not skillfully portrayed and their dialogue rings artificial. **Ernest DeFarge,** the proprietor of a wine shop in the Paris suburb of St. Antoine and leader of the local revolutionaries, shows compassion in caring for the much-deteriorated Manette after his release from prison and in attempting (though unsuccessfully) to curb his wife's vengefulness. The cold and ruthless **Madame DeFarge,** one of the book's most memorable figures, lacks her husband's sense of compassion. She vehemently hates the aristocracy not as much for the suffering it has brought to the peasantry in general but for its treachery toward her own family; she has vowed to attain revenge by completely exterminating the Evremondes, including not only Charles but his wife and small daughter. Madame DeFarge is most colorfully characterized by her constant knitting and her prominent position among the other, similarly occupied women—including her fellow radical **The Vengeance**—who sit near the guillotine as France's aristocrats lose their heads.

Other French characters in *A Tale of Two Cities* include **Jacques One, Two, Three,** and **Five,** the assumed names of DeFarge's conspirators (he is known as **Jacques Four**), and **Monsieur Theophile Gabelle,** the Evrémonde's postmaster and rentkeeper, whose appeal for help is answered by Charles Darnay.

Bleak House (novel, 1852-53)

Plot: The case of *Jarndyce* v. *Jarndyce* has languished in the Court of Chancery for many years, subjecting generations of heirs to the disputed Jarndyce fortune to an endless and frustrating wait for their inheritances. Despite his own involvement in the suit, John Jarndyce does not pay it much mind. He has brought his two young cousins, Richard Carstone and Ada Clare, to live with him at Bleak House, his home in Hertfordshire, England, along with a young girl named Esther Summerson who serves as Ada's companion and who becomes Jarndyce's housekeeper. Esther was raised by her austere godmother, Miss Barbary, who told her that her mother had deserted her. Also interested in the case of *Jarndyce* v. *Jarndyce* are Sir Leicester and Lady Honoria Dedlock and their lawyer, Mr. Tulkinghorn, who is one of many involved in the suit. Tulkinghorn becomes suspicious when Lady Dedlock reacts strongly to the sight of some handwriting on a document that he has brought to Chesney Wold, the Dedlocks' home in Lincolnshire. He learns that the document's copyist was a man named Nemo, who lives above Mr. Krook's rag-and-bone (junk) shop. Tulkinghorn goes to see Nemo but finds the man dead of an opium overdose; he suspects that Nemo is not his real name but is unable to discover anything further about him.

Meanwhile, Esther has won the affection of William Guppy, a clerk in the office of Jarndyce's lawyers, Kenge & Carboy; he notices her resemblance to Lady Dedlock. The young surgeon who examines Nemo's body, Allan Woodcourt, calls for an inquest on the death. One of the witnesses is the street sweeper Jo, who reveals that a lady had given him two half-crowns in exchange for guiding her to the cemetery in which Nemo was buried. Through further questioning of other witnesses it is also learned that Mrs. Chadband, the wife of the grandiloquent Reverend Chadband, was formerly the same Mrs. Rachael who had been Miss Barbery's servant when Esther was growing up, and that Esther's last name is actually Hawdon. A French maid, Mademoiselle Hortense, who had previously worked for Lady Dedlock, claims that her former employer was the lady who had given money to Jo. The mystery of Esther's birth is soon unraveled: Lady Dedlock and Nemo, whose real name was Captain Hawdon, had had an affair, of which Esther was the result. Miss Barbary had taken Esther away from her mother after the birth, and Lady Dedlock—who was told that her daughter had died—had eventually married Lord Dedlock.

Lady Dedlock asks Guppy to retrieve from Mr. Krook a packet of Captain Hawdon's letters that she fears might incriminate her. But before he can do so, Krook dies of spontaneous combustion, caused by the liquor-soaked condition of his body, and the letters are assumed lost. Meanwhile, Jarndyce's ward Richard Carstone has attempted to establish himself in various careers, but his obsession with the suit has resulted in his mental and physical deterioration. In love with Richard, Ada marries him secretly in the hope that she will be able to help him by sharing with him her own small fortune. When Esther becomes ill with smallpox and nearly dies, Lady Dedlock visits her and reveals that she is her mother. Esther survives her illness but her face is ravaged; Guppy consequently decides that he no longer loves Esther, while Jarndyce now feels free to declare his love for her and asks her to marry him. She accepts Jarndyce's proposal. Tulkinghorn is murdered, and the police detective Inspector Bucket discovers that the culprit is Mademoiselle Hortense; she had been trying to blackmail the lawyer and killed him when he resisted. In the meantime, Lady Dedlock has disappeared and Esther later finds her dead body near the gate of the graveyard in which Captain Hawdon is buried.

A new Jarndyce will is found in Krook's shop that establishes Richard and Ada as heirs to the legacy; the entire amount, however, has already been consumed in court costs and the young couple and their baby are left penniless. Richard is unable to cope with this resolution of the suit and soon dies; Ada and her son continue to live with Jarndyce. When Jarndyce learns that Esther and Woodcourt have fallen in love, he not only releases Esther from her promise to marry him but presents her with a new home, also named Bleak House, in Yorkshire. Esther and her family remain lifelong friends of Jarndyce and frequent visitors at the original Bleak House.

Characters: Considered by many Dickens's crowning achievement, *Bleak House* depicts with pathos and irony the human costs of a meaningless judicial system that fails to administer true justice. Through this skillfully structured novel that weaves together the lives of a broad spectrum of characters from diverse backgrounds, Dickens elucidates a central theme identified by most scholars: the necessity of social and personal responsibility.

Half of *Bleak House* is narrated by an omniscient and subtly ironic authorial voice; the other is told by **Esther Summerson,** one of Dickens's most frequently studied characters. The daughter of illicit lovers Lady Dedlock and Captain Hawdon (though she herself knows little of her background during the first part of the story), Esther has been raised by a cold, harsh relative but has nevertheless grown into a sympathetic, virtuous, and capable woman who is much loved by all who know her. Her benefactor, John Jarndyce, is so pleased with Esther that he makes her his housekeeper, and she is often identified by the cheerful jingling of the keys that symbolize her domestic responsibilities. Esther was reportedly based on Dickens's esteemed sister-in-law Georgina Hogarth, who ran his household after his wife Catherine proved unequal to such practical duties. Some critics find Esther an overly moralistic, idealized, and artificially modest figure, while others consider her the novel's controlling consciousness. She is an unusually strong heroine for Dickens, though in her mildness she still contrasts his strident female characters. She proves important to the plot as well, for, as Lady Dedlock's illegitimate child, she provides a link between the Jarndyces and the Dedlocks.

John Jarndyce, the elderly scion of the family whose suit has languished for so long in Chancery court, is depicted as admirable, generous, and scrupulous, strongly contrasting the corrupt and tangled legal system that has so ensnared his family. He is the great-nephew of **Tom Jarndyce,** whose frustration with the suit led not only to his naming his home Bleak House but to his suicide. The current Jarndyce is determined to maintain a healthy distance from the destructive force that Chancery represents. A mildly eccentric man who attributes the troubles of life to the blowing of the wicked East Wind, Jarndyce bestows benevolence uniformly upon those around him. Though perhaps misguided in some of his philanthropy, Jarndyce embodies a warm humanity of which Dickens approved (Dickens tended not to favor political solutions to societal ills but condoned instead responsible behavior on the part of individuals). Thus, under Jarndyce's cheerful rule, Bleak House seems ironically named. When Jarndyce perceives the love that exists between Esther and Woodcourt, he gracefully releases her from her promise to marry him, thus demonstrating both his selflessness and his belief that the young lovers' union represents a new beginning for those finally released from the turmoil of the past.

Jarndyce's cousin **Ada Clare** is a lovely, pliant, even-tempered young woman whose generosity and love for Richard Carstone leads her to marry him in order to help him. A rather insubstantial character, Ada is noted for her exaggeratedly sentimental appeal. **Richard Carstone** is a somewhat more compelling figure. Obsessed with the lawsuit that he expects to establish his inheritance, he lives on false hope and is eventually shown to have wasted his life in waiting for a judgment. Unable to commit himself to anything (his attempts to establish a career as a doctor, a lawyer, and a soldier are all unsuccessful), he is both a victim of a destructive system and a person who has failed to take responsibility for his own life.

Lady Honoria Dedlock is also a contradictory character: she is both arrogant and pathetic in her inability to face the truth of her past. Although she was truly in love with the man who fathered her daughter, the rakish Captain Hawdon, she chose not to marry him but to follow a course more certain to lead her to wealth and social status. She married the aristocratic Sir Leicester Dedlock, who sincerely loves her, but has found little satisfaction in the life she chose. When she learns that her daughter is still alive and that her affair with Captain Hawdon has come dangerously close to exposure, she is overcome with shame, fear of her husband's reaction, and guilt over her earlier abandonment of her lover and child. She returns in despair to the place where Hawdon lies, the fetid graveyard in which the city's most destitute citizens are buried, and there, rather melodramatically, she dies. Several critics have pointed to Lady Dedlock's meeting with Jo the street sweeper, whom she pays to help her find Hawdon's grave, as an example of Dickens's penchant for juxtaposing the most exalted and the most lowly members of society in situations which both contrast them and reveal their common humanity.

Lady Dedlock's lover and Esther's father, **Captain Hawdon** or **Nemo,** was a gallant but irresponsible soldier who proved a failure in civilian life. At the time of his death he was a copyist of legal documents and a penniless opium addict reduced to living in a garret above Krook's rag-and-bone shop. He is buried in a pauper's graveyard. Beloved by his associates during his military career as well as by Lady Dedlock (apparently to the end of her own life, as she dies with her body pressed against the gate of the cemetery where he lies buried), Hawdon obviously inspired lasting loyalty among those who knew him. Even the wretched Jo remembers him as a kind man.

Sir Leicester Dedlock is a stiff, ceremonial representative of the rigid old English aristocracy, a social stratum for which the middle-class Dickens had little respect. Pompous, excessively proud of his family's heritage, and suspicious of social reform, he nevertheless exhibits a basic decency when he reacts to the news of his wife's history and her disappearance with concern and unflagging love for her. Dickens uses the Dedlock household to satirize the self-importance and inefficiency of the British government: many of the guests who gather at the estate are politicians who relate with great solemnity the absurd Parliamentary intrigues involving such luminaries as Boodle, Doodle, Foodle, and— most significantly—Noodle. On a sociological level, Dedlock plays a willing part in this entrenched system, while on a personal level he finds his life permanently and tragically altered by the revelation of his beloved wife's past.

The secretive and subtly ominous **Mr. Tulkinghorn,** the Dedlocks' attorney, is an instrumental agent in the plot because it is he who first suspects the existence of a mystery in Lady Dedlock's past and sets out to uncover it. His motive is left ambiguous—he may simply wish to protect his client's honor or he may have his own self-interest at heart. In any case, his fatal mistake is in discounting the element of human emotion that is an integral part of people's behavior. As a vigilant and impersonal representative of the Law, he does not expect to encounter passion in the form of Sir Dedlock's unbending loyalty to his wife, or, more catastrophically, of the volatile Mademoiselle Hortense's desire for revenge.

Cadaverous, withered, white-haired **Mr. Krook** owns the junk shop above which Hawdon lodges. He is a half-mad, grotesque figure who directly parodies the legal system's Lord Chancellor and serves as another example of the corrupt and immoral who prey on unfortunate humanity. The spectacular occasion of Krook's death—his liquor-soaked and grime-encased body spontaneously bursts into flames—provides one of the book's most memorable passages and is usually interpreted as a metaphor for the inevitable self-destruction of the system that has caused so much misery. The novel's matter-of-fact presentation of spontaneous combustion caused something of a stir soon after the book was published; the noted critic George Henry Lewes claimed that there was no scientific evidence that such an occurrence was possible. Significantly, the cat which rides on Krook's shoulder, **Lady Jane,** threatens to devour the pet birds of another of his lodgers, Miss Flite, just as Chancery has devoured Miss Flite's life. Tiny, half-crazy **Miss Flite** is a faithful attendee in court every day despite the hopelessness of ever attaining the judgment for which she waits. She has watched the youth, beauty, and hope that she had once possessed slip away as she ekes out a meager existence and raises her pet birds, which she plans to release when the case is settled (but which perpetually die and are replaced). Poor **Mr. Gridley,** the tragically comic Man from Shropshire, has also been victimized by the legal system: he is repeatedly jailed for contempt of court based on an absurd technicality that he has no power to rectify.

The miserable street sweeper **Jo** (also called **Toughey**), whose occupation was only one step above begging in Victorian London, compellingly exemplifies the deprived condition in which that society's most lowly members lived. Jo is an emanation of the slum in which he lives, Tom-All-Alone's, a stinking, disease-infested, and hope-deserted realm ignored by the insensitive social system that Chancery represents. Muddy and ragged, with his hoarse voice and profound ignorance, Jo challenges the altruism of the most compassionate characters; in exchange for her own kindness to him, Esther contracts smallpox and subsequently forfeits her beauty. Lady Dedlock pays Jo to help her find the graveyard in which Hawdon is buried, and in juxtaposing these two characters Dickens illustrates the gulf between their social classes. In the end, Jo dies of starvation, a tragic byproduct of humanity's neglect.

Dickens lampoons the misguided efforts of charitable institutions as well as the common sin of selfishness through two characters in *Bleak House*. **Mrs. Jellyby,** a plump, determined philanthropist who dreams of establishing a missionary colony in Africa, neglects her own family and the poor who exist in her own neighborhood. Similarly, the overbearing **Mrs. Pardiggle** belies the idea of the charity she espouses by bullying both her own children and the poor she encounters. Dickens's depiction of these two women could also be seen as expressing hostility to nineteenth-century feminism, for they are shown to expend their energies outside of their own homes with grievous consequences to their dependent families. **Mr. Jellyby** is a meek, miserable man who eventually goes bankrupt, while **Caroline "Caddy" Jellyby,** Mrs. Jellyby's daughter, was called by G. K. Chesterton "the greatest, the most human, and the most really dignified of all the heroines of Dickens." Though few other critics have registered such a strong response to Caddy, Dickens is often praised for the pathos and humor of this character whose missionary mother brings her much distress. Caddy's friendship with Esther helps her to grow from a sulky and morose girl to a more amiable and capable woman. Both fond and ashamed of her mother, Caddy has a strong longing for order that she attempts to satisfy by establishing a family of her own with Prince Turveydrop.

The lordly **Mr. Turveydrop,** ironically described as the "Model of Deportment," prides himself on his fancy appearance and falsely gallant manners; his attempt to imitate the ways of royalty demonstrates a self-absorbed form of dandyism that is particularly repellent. His selfishness negatively affects his son **Prince Turveydrop** (named for England's Prince Regent), who is forced to carry on his father's pretenses. The fact that Prince and his wife Caddy produce a feeble, deaf-and-dumb infant has been interpreted as the inevitable result of their own stunted upbringings.

The conniving and indolent dilettante **Harold Skimpole** was reportedly modeled after Leigh Hunt, an English poet and dramatist with a similarly lighthearted demeanor, though Dickens denied that Skimpole's predatory quality was derived from Hunt. Fond of discussing art and music, a sentimental enthusiast of all that is beautiful, Skimpole is at heart selfish and irresponsible and he takes advantage of Jarndyce's trusting nature by allowing the benevolent old man to support him while he himself neglects to play any productive role in society.

Reverend Chadband personifies religious hypocrisy through his self-absorption and conceit; his flowery speech masks the lack of real content in his professed faith. His wife **Mrs. Chadband** is a harsh, gloomy woman who previously, as **Mrs. Rachael,** worked in the household of Esther's aunt. **Miss Barbery,** Lady Dedlock's stern and puritanical sister, was horrified and ashamed by the arrival of the illegitimate Esther, and after separating the mother and child told Esther that her mother was a wicked woman who had deserted her.

Mr. Kenge is one of the partners in the legal firm of Kenge & Carboy, which represents Jarndyce in his suit before Chancery. Nicknamed **Conversation** Kenge because of his fondness for the sound of his own voice, the attorney arranges for Esther to live at Bleak House and thus is her first link with its inhabitants. Kenge's clerk is the sharp-witted young **William Guppy.** He expresses his ardor for Esther in comically legalistic terms, as when he "files a declaration" of love for her, and, after Esther has lost her beauty, he asks her to sign a formal statement verifying that he had never actually agreed to marry her. Guppy's friend and fellow clerk **Tony Jobling,** who calls himself **Weevle,** learns that Krook possesses incriminating documents written by Captain Hawdon while he himself is lodging in Krook's house. Another notable legal character in *Bleak House* is **Mr. Vhole,** the lawyer Richard hires to look after his interests. His name is appropriately suggestive of a burrowing rodent, for he works in an exceedingly dusty office and drags his client deep into the dark maze of the court system.

Allan Woodcourt is the compassionate surgeon with whom Esther falls in love and eventually marries. He is presented as an appropriate mate for the virtuous young woman because he admirably puts his humanitarian convictions into action rather than merely theorizing about them—behavior that is typically the only solution for the alleviation of suffering that Dickens offers. Woodcourt is quick to offer assistance wherever it is needed, and he is said to have become a doctor not for financial gain but for the good it would do his fellow human beings. Several members of the Rouncewell family are also quite positively portrayed. Ironmaster **Mr. Rouncewell,** the son of the Dedlock's housekeeper **Mrs. Rouncewell** (Dickens's grandmother was also a housekeeper in the home of a nobleman), is a self-respecting, productive, hard-working man who represents both the dignity of the working class and a challenge to the superiority of aristocrats like Sir Leicester. His son **George Rouncewell,** an essentially decent former soldier wrongly accused of murdering Tulkinghorn after he had refused to surrender some of Captain Hawdon's papers, has been described as exemplifying Dickens's respect for military men.

The police detective who eventually solves Tulkinghorn's murder, **Inspector Bucket,** is reportedly modeled after an Inspector Fields who once led Dickens on a tour through a London slum. He is basically honorable and, though he relishes his sometimes seedy work, is capable of delicacy and humanity toward others. The fiery **Mademoiselle Hortense,** Lady Dedlock's former servant whom Bucket exposes as Tulkinghorn's murderer, commits the deed after seeking revenge on Lady Dedlock, by whom she feels she has been mistreated. Other characters in *Bleak House* include **Grandfather Smallweed** and the rest of his family, a sordid, goblin-like gang of moneylenders responsible for locating the new Jarndyce will in Krook's shop. Apparently Jewish (the children's names are **Bartholomew** and **Judith,** and Grandfather Smallweed wears a yarmulke-like beanie), they have been identified as illustrating the anti-Semitism critics have detected in Dickens's work. The comically vehement, affectionate, and loyal **Lawrence Boythorn** is Jarndyce's friend and also the Dedlock's neighbor; Esther is recuperating from her illness at his estate when she meets her mother. **Mr. Snagsby** is a seller of legal supplies who helps Tulkinghorn track Captain Hawdon down by identifying the handwriting on a document. A henpecked husband, he is a generally positive character who helps Jo by giving him money rather than the charitable rhetoric offered by more strident philanthropists.

Great Expectations (novel, 1860-61)

Plot: The orphaned Philip Pirrip, who calls himself Pip, was raised by his harsh sister Mrs. Joe and her kind husband Joe Gargery, a blacksmith. While wandering through the marshes near his home one day, Pip encounters a ragged stranger who demands that Pip bring him food and a file to remove the chain that binds his leg. Pip complies with this request. As the frightened boy is making a second delivery of food to the man, Pip sees him struggling with another stranger before they disappear from view. The man Pip had helped is later captured by the police, but, upon seeing Pip, promises to repay him for his aid. Miss Havisham, an eccentric old lady who lives in a huge mansion, asks that Pip come to visit her. All of the clocks in her dark, dusty house are stopped on the hour that the man Miss Havisham planned to marry abandoned her. She still wears her now-yellowed wedding dress, and the moldy wedding cake still stands on a table in her room, inhabited by a colony of spiders. Pip becomes a frequent visitor at the mansion, where he talks with Estella, Miss Havisham's beautiful and haughty young ward. Pip is surprised and pleased when a London lawyer, Mr. Jaggers, offers him the opportunity to go to London to be educated, become a gentleman, and eventually come into an inheritance; Pip assumes that Miss Havisham is financing the venture in order to groom him as a proper husband for Estella. In London, Pip rooms with an agreeable young man named Herbert Pocket, who is a distant relative of Miss Havisham.

In his efforts to become a gentleman, Pip begins to associate with a group of dandified young aristocrats who call themselves the Finches of the Grove, the most prominent of which is a caddish boy named Bentley Drummle. When the still-devoted and affectionate Joe comes to visit him, Pip is embarrassed by his brother-in-law's crude ways and treats him unkindly. Miss Havisham informs Pip that Estella will be moving to London and that she wants Pip to fall in love with the girl, confirming his earlier suspicion about Miss Havisham's motives for helping him. But after her arrival in London, Estella is courted by Drummle. Pip receives an unexpected visit on his twenty-first birthday from the convict whom he had met so long ago in the marshes. The man, whose name is Abel Magwitch, reveals that he has been the boy's benefactor all along, having grown rich after being banished to Australia. He has come back to witness Pip's progress even though his own life is endangered by his illegal return to England. Pip is initially repulsed by Magwitch's coarseness yet realizes how much he owes him; he decides to try to help Magwitch in any way he can. Magwitch, who is using the pseudonym Provis to avoid detection, also reveals that the man with whom he had struggled in the marsh and who still vows to destroy him is the villainous Arthur Compeyson, who, coincidentally, is also the man who abandoned Miss Havisham on her wedding day. Determined to chastise Miss Havisham for allowing him to believe that she was his benefactor, Pip visits her. He learns that Estella is engaged to Drummle and that in fact Miss Havisham had carefully trained her young ward to break the hearts of as many men as possible, vengeance for the cruel desertion she herself had experienced. As a result, Estella had been made into a cold and detached young woman, unable to love or feel compassion. On a final visit to Miss Havisham's house after Estella's wedding, Pip finds the mansion on fire but is unable to save Miss Havisham, who perishes.

Pip eventually learns that Magwitch is Estella's father; her mother was Jaggers' housekeeper Molly. Pip and Herbert scheme to help Magwitch escape to France, but just as they have secured him aboard a boat, Compeyson appears and the two men fight, eventually struggling in the water. Magwitch kills his enemy and is immediately apprehended by the police; he dies in prison, but not before Pip recognizes his pity and love for his benefactor. Pip becomes seriously ill and Joe arrives to nurse him back to health, giving Pip an occasion to realize the value of his old friend's constancy and love. Mrs. Joe has since died—killed by Joe's irate assistant—and Joe has married the Gargery's former servant, good, gentle Biddy. Still despondent over having lost Estella, Pip establishes an importing business with Herbert. Eleven years later he returns to visit Joe and also the spot where Miss Havisham's mansion once stood. He finds the widowed Estella also wandering there; she has become a warmer, more compassionate person over the years. The two leave together, and appear destined for happiness together.

Characters: One of Dickens's most technically brilliant and creatively resonant novels, *Great Expectations* is exceptionally popular with readers. In chronicling the maturation of its likeable young hero, whose "great expectations" prove illusory, the novel promotes generosity, friendship, and love over the shallow virtues of wealth and social status.

Like many of Dickens's protagonists, **Philip Pirrip** or **Pip** is an orphan and thus experiences early in life an overwhelming sense of loneliness and isolation. Tormented by his mean-spirited sister who frequently beats him with "the Tickler" and constantly reminds him that she begrudgingly raised him "by hand," Pip elicits sympathy early on that will be sustained during his later period of less-than-admirable behavior. Dickens is much lauded for having created in Pip a decidedly unheroic hero, a figure who, while basically good, must learn to recognize and conquer serious weaknesses within himself. After his first visit to Miss Havisham, who represents a higher stratum of society than that to which he is accustomed, Pip begins to view his surroundings—and even his beloved friend Joe—with a critical eye. He is thrilled to be offered an escape from the blacksmith shop and a presumably dreary future and eagerly begins the process of becoming a "gentleman." While waiting for the realization of his "great expectations," Pip consorts with the Finches of the Grove, a group of wealthy, indolent young men, and grows disdainful of his humbler friends, even letting Joe see that he is ashamed of his crude speech and manners. Even as he does so, though, Pip is burdened with a secret guilt over his excessive pride and his desertion of such loyal friends as Joe and Biddy. He is also burdened with his hopeless love for the frosty Estella, whose affection, he gradually realizes, he will never win. It is not until Pip learns the truth about his benefactor—that he owes his pampered existence not to Miss Havisham's largesse but to the sacrifices of the wretched Abel Magwitch—that he begins to recognize what constitutes a true gentleman. In learning first to pity and then to love Magwitch (whose gratitude is, ironically, borne out of something the boy did out of fear rather than generosity), Pip also comes to recognize the true worth and integrity of such constant friends as Joe, Biddy, and Herbert. Looking back on his childhood and early manhood, the adult Pip who narrates the novel presents a critical, disillusioned, but not embittered view that is tinged with sadness. It is often noted that that melancholy would have been more appropriately validated if Dickens had not dropped the book's original ending, in which Pip and Estella go their separate ways, and replaced it with one that seems to predict their eventual marriage.

The gentle blacksmith **Joe Gargery** is a simple, considerate, unselfish man who significantly alleviates the general harshness of Pip's childhood. Although he is physically strong, his temper erupts only twice—when his wife and then Pip are threatened—and he tolerates his wife's badgering with almost unearthly patience, admitting to Pip that after witnessing his father's physical abuse of his mother he vowed never to strike a woman. Joe also cares tenderly for Pip when the young man falls ill, and this episode plays an important part in awakening Pip's awareness of his own misguided behavior. An able blacksmith, Joe has been said to represent the dignity of labor; although he realizes that he is uneducated, he takes pride in performing his job well, and his understated self-respect points to the value of following an honest calling even if it is a humble one. Despite his rough manners and ungrammatical speech, traits which embarrass Pip when Joe visits him in London, the blacksmith provides an example of a true, natural gentleman, whose qualifications are based on neither his wealth nor social position but on sterling character. The ways in which the other characters treat Joe provide insight into their own weaknesses: Pip is ashamed of him, Estella makes fun of him, and Jaggers is stunned when Joe refuses to accept money for the loss of Pip from his shop.

Mrs. Georgiana Maria Gargery, or **Mrs. Joe,** Pip's much older sister, is a harsh, vituperative woman who treats her brother cruelly and makes it clear that she resents having had to raise him. She continuously wears an apron stuck with needles and pins, a particularly apt metaphor for her utter lack of any tenderness or warmth and her prickly personality. Mrs. Joe is also cruel to her husband and does not recognize his integrity.

The gentle, loving, soft-spoken, wise, efficient **Biddy** is "the most successful of Dickens's household angels," according to critic Philip Hobsbaum. She reveals her common sense and knowledge of human nature when she marries Joe after Mrs. Joe's demise. Pip, who has previously told Biddy that if it weren't for her lowly station he might be interested in marrying her, eventually recognizes her true worth.

Abel Magwitch, who adopts the alias of **Mr. Provis** after his return to England, is the crusty old convict who finances Pip's ascent to gentlemanliness. With his ragged clothing and fearful leg iron, he frightens young Pip into bringing him some food and a file when they first meet. After promising to repay Pip for helping him, Magwitch is exiled to Australia where he becomes a successful sheep farmer. He determines to make Pip a gentlemen as a way to wreak revenge on the gentlemen who have ridiculed and abused him; as the self-proclaimed "dunghill dog" tells Pip, if he cannot be a gentleman himself he will "own" one. Ironically, the shallow young dandy that Pip becomes is not a gentleman at all. It is Magwitch who subsequently teaches Pip about love, for Pip is at first repulsed by his patron then gradually comes to pity and eventually appreciate him for his sacrifice and devotion. When Magwitch dies, Pip's "great expectations" die along with him, but Pip is a wiser—if sadder—and better person.

One of the most memorable characters in *Great Expectations* is the eccentric, even bizarre **Miss Havisham,** the bitter old lady whose life screeched to a halt on the day she was forsaken by her bridegroom. Still dressed in her now-yellowed wedding gown, she resides in a gloomy, cobweb-strewn room lit by candles and containing a number of half-packed trunks and a moldy wedding cake that houses a thriving colony of spiders, a particularly effective image that mirrors Miss Havisham's deterioration. Early reviewers found Miss Havisham too preposterous a creation to be believed, although scholars have located some actual prototypes upon which she might have been based. As she loved Compeyson passionately and beyond reason, she also passionately and unreasonably seeks revenge for the heartbreak he caused her. That she stopped the clocks on the hour of her abandonment—thereby abdicating responsibility for her own life—and carefully molded Estella into her personal instrument of revenge makes her both wicked and pathetic. In order to avoid the desolation that might result if she confronts reality, Miss Havisham chooses instead to live in a realm of illusion. She and her elegant adopted daughter give Pip his first taste of high society and instill in him a yearning for wealth as well as for the unattainable love that Estella represents. Although he is angry with Miss Havisham when he learns that she has allowed him to believe that she was his benefactor, Pip is moved by the great loneliness of her life, and in the end he feels only compassion for her. That she too has learned compassion is evidenced by her plea for forgiveness on her deathbed and, much to the indignation of her greedier relatives, her leaving her fortune to Mathew Pocket, her only loyal and completely disinterested cousin.

Cold, aloof, and majestically beautiful **Estella** was raised by Miss Havisham to be an effective instrument of destruction: she is trained to destroy men's hearts by causing them to love her and then declining to love them in return. Estella is repeatedly associated with jewel imagery, symbolizing both her role as the crowning gem among Pip's great expectations and her star-like distance and hardness. Although it is eventually revealed that her background is even humbler than Pip's (she is the daughter of the convict Magwitch and the murderess Molly), Estella treats her young, unsophisticated visitor disdainfully. Yet, like Pip, she is actually a mere pretender to a higher social class. Despite her arrogance and insensitivity, it is difficult not to pity Estella for the inability to love that is the logical result of Miss Havisham's warped upbringing. During her marriage to the cruel Bentley Drummle, Estella endures a period of suffering that makes her warmer and more compassionate, thus more mature. It is generally acknowledged that Dickens based Estella, who has been called his most sexually viable female character, on the Irish actress Ellen Ternan, who eventually became his mistress. Pip's helpless attraction to Estella and the mingled hopelessness and intensity of his love for her mirror the emotions reportedly experienced by the author when he fell in love with Ternan. The existence of two different endings to the novel has garnered much critical attention: in the original ending, which Dickens revised on the advice of his fellow novelist Edward Bulwer-Lytton, Estella marries a benevolent doctor after the death of her first husband and she and Pip have one melancholy but friendly meeting years later; in the ending that Dickens decided to use instead, the two walk off hand in hand, apparently destined for marriage. While some critics claim that the latter ending is in keeping with Dickens's general hopefulness, others claim that it represents an unfortunate concession to his audience's desire for a happy ending and is true to neither Pip's nor Estella's character.

The shrewd attorney **Mr. Jaggers,** whom Magwitch hires to help Pip, is an imposing figure who often bites his large forefinger and then points it menacingly. As a criminal lawyer, he is accustomed to associating with extremely unsavory clients; after meeting with them he always washes his hands (and sometimes even his face and mouth) as if to cleanse himself of their corruption. He also carries with him a white handkerchief that starkly contrasts the frequently bloody content of his work. Jaggers is studiously unemotional and concentrates strictly on facts rather than emotions; when one of his clients begins to weep, for instance, he says "I'll have no feelings here. Get out." This detachment is typical of many of Dickens's businessmen characters, for which coldness is apparently a prerequisite for success. Although Jaggers maintains an aura of authority and of secret knowledge, he often claims that he wants to know only that which is necessary to a given case or situation. He controls others by manipulating knowledge, thus he is notably disconcerted when he learns that Pip knows the identity of Estella's father, for that means that someone other than himself has access to a secret. Some scholars consider Jaggers a basically kind and honest figure while others maintain he is wicked; still others claim he is neither good nor bad and that his character is intentionally ambiguous.

Mr. Jaggers's dry, efficient clerk **John Wemmick** provides another example of the forced impersonality that business requires of its practitioners. By day Wemmick is a cold, wooden figure whose frozen expression makes his mouth resemble a mail slot. When he enters his whimsical home, Walworth, which is ingeniously constructed to resemble a castle, complete with moat and drawbridge, he becomes a warm and considerate human being. Unlike some of his other associates, Pip is allowed to enter Wemmick's lair, where he meets the **Aged Parent,** a deaf old man who waits every night for his son to fire a cannon, and **Miss Skiffins,** Wemmick's fiancee. While some scholars have described Wemmick's duality as comic, others consider him unconvincingly quaint. It might also be noted that even in the cozy, humane realm of Walworth, Wemmick's primary concern is with the acquisition of "portable property," a value that derives from the business side of his life.

Herbert Pocket is Pip's cheerful young roommate in London and one of his most loyal friends. Although Pip initially feels superior to Herbert because he knows that his friend has no "great expectations" to which he can look forward, Herbert eventually passes on to Pip a valuable lesson in what constitutes a gentleman: no one who is not a gentleman at heart can be made into one. It is Herbert's kind and tolerant heart that marks him as a superior person, as well as his loyalty to the dandified, obnoxious Pip. In all of his actions, including his industriously establishing a business and marrying the penniless but charming **Clara Barley,** Herbert demonstrates the high quality of his character.

Arthur Compeyson, who jilted Miss Havisham after making off with her money and later betrayed his partner in crime, Magwitch, is the quintessential villain. A swindler and forger, he is also a false gentleman who used his social status to evade punishment: after luring Magwitch into joining him in a criminal act, he successfully accused the lower-class Magwitch of corrupting him.

The journeyman blacksmith who works in Joe's shop, **Dorge Orlick,** is a surly young man who hates Pip for the advantages he feels that the boy has undeservedly received at his expense. He blames Pip for all of his problems, even for his murder of Mrs. Joe (and Pip does feel guilty, particularly since Orlick hit his sister with the leg iron that Pip had helped Magwitch remove), though, in fact, Pip merely provides a focus for Orlick's hatred. Orlick might be seen as Pip's foil, for he too has formed unrealistic expectations about the future which he personally has done nothing to realize. Orlick could also be compared to Magwitch in that he represents a purely evil criminal element, though Pip's benefactor seems more victimized and almost blameless, or to Drummle, because he is a lower-class manifestation of the other's brutality.

Great Expectations features some memorable and much praised comic characters. **Mr. Wopsle** is the parish clerk who dreams of glory on the stage, injecting oratorical flourish into his church readings. He eventually does become an actor, but his appearance as Hamlet is hilariously unsuccessful and he is eventually reduced to playing bit parts, an outcome that might be compared to Pip's loss of his own great expectations. Joe's uncle **Mr. Pumblechook** is a ridiculously pompous corn-dealer with whom Pip spends the night on his way to visit Miss Havisham; upon hearing of Pip's good fortune he immediately pretends to be the boy's benefactor and repeatedly shakes his hand. **Trabb's Boy** is the local ruffian who mocks Pip's elevated status with vigor and relish in his exaggerated imitation of a snob who prances down the street saying ''Don't know yah!'' Mortifying to Pip, this performance might be seen as the only means possible for one of society's lowliest members to assert himself against one of its highest.

Other characters in *Great Expectations* include **Bentley Drummle,** the rich, sulky, and brutal leader of the dandified Finches of the Grove (and thus the ultimate expression of Pip's misguided early notion of a gentleman), who marries and violently mistreats Estella; Miss Havisham's relative **Sarah Pocket,** a withered, sharp-tongued, snobbish woman who resents Pip's ascent to her own elevated social class; **Old Bill Barley,** the father of Herbert's fiancee Clara, a gouty, bedridden, and drunken old man whose habit of surveying a nearby river with a telescope he keeps at his side is a remnant of his former career as a sailor; **Mathew Pocket,** Herbert's father and Pip's tutor, who teaches him only the ''mere rudiments'' of education since as a gentleman he won't need to know much; and **Molly,** Mr. Jaggers's strange, silent housekeeper, who turns out to have been a murderess, Magwitch's mistress, and Estella's mother.

Further Reading

Ackroyd, Peter. *Dickens.* New York: Harper Collins, 1990.

Bloom, Harold, ed. *Charles Dickens.* New York: Chelsea House, 1987.

Chesterton, G. K. *Charles Dickens: A Critical Study.* 1906. Reprint. London: Methuen, 1960.

Collins, Philip. *Charles Dickens.* London: Routledge & Kegan Paul, 1987.

Dictionary of Literary Biography, Vols. 21, 55, 70. Detroit: Gale.

Hobsbaum, Philip. *A Reader's Guide to Charles Dickens.* New York: Farrar, Straus and Giroux, 1972.

House, Humphrey. *The Dickens World.* London: Oxford University Press, 1941.

Irving, John. ''In Defense of Sentimentality.'' *New York Times Book Review* (25 November 1979): 3, 96.

Johnson, Edgar. *Charles Dickens: His Tragedy and His Triumph.* 2 vols. New York: Simon & Schuster, 1952.

Lewes, George Henry. ''Dickens in Relation to Criticism.'' 1872. In *The Dickens Critics,* edited by George H. Ford and Lauriat Lane, Jr., pp. 54-74. Ithaca, N.Y.: Cornell University Press, 1961.

Miller, J. Hillis. *Charles Dickens: The World of His Novels.* Cambridge: Harvard University Press, 1958.

Nelson, Harland S. *Charles Dickens.* Boston: Twayne, 1981.

Nineteenth-Century Literature Criticism, Vols. 3, 8, 18, 26. Detroit: Gale.

Page, Norman. *A Dickens Companion.* New York: Schocken Books, 1984.

Pritchett, V. S. "The Comic World of Dickens." In *The Dickens Critics,* edited by George H. Ford and Lauriat Lane, Jr., pp. 309-24. Ithaca, N.Y.: Cornell University Press, 1961.

Sucksmith, Harvey Peter. *The Narrative Art of Charles Dickens: The Rhetoric of Sympathy and Irony in His Novels.* Oxford: Clarendon Press, 1970.

Wilson, Angus. "The Heroes and Heroines of Dickens." In *Dickens and the Twentieth Century,* edited by John Gross and Gabriel Pearson, pp. 3-11. London: Routledge & Kegan Paul, 1962.

Benjamin Disraeli
1804-1881
English novelist, essayist, poet, and biographer.

Coningsby; or, The New Generation (novel, 1844)

Plot: Young Harry Coningsby grows up under the detached guardianship of his grandfather, Lord Monmouth, a cynical aristocrat. Harry attends Eton preparatory school, where he befriends Oswald Millbank, the son of a Manchester manufacturer. After leaving Eton, Harry travels to the Millbank home on his way to his grandfather's estate. There he tours the Millbanks' factories and meets Oswald's sister Edith; Mr. Millbank explains to Harry his belief that England should be led by a natural aristocracy of competent men rather than by hereditary peers. Returning to Coningsby Castle, Harry learns that Lord Monmouth is backing his friend and fellow member of the Conservative party, Mr. Rigby, in his campaign for reelection to Parliament. Harry also meets the wealthy, learned Sidonia, a Jew with whom he has many stimulating conversations about politics and other topics; Sidonia encourages Harry to develop his potential to become a great leader. During Harry's first year of study at Cambridge University, the Conservative party begins to fall into disfavor, a trend confirmed when Rigby is defeated by a Whig (Liberal) candidate supported by Mr. Millbank. Millbank and Lord Monmouth are longtime enemies, so Monmouth is enraged not only by the election results but by Millbank's purchasing an estate that adjoins Coningsby Castle.

While traveling in Europe, Harry is reacquainted with Edith Millbank and falls in love with her. He hears, however, that Sidonia plans to marry Edith, so he returns to England. When he later finds that Edith and Sidonia are merely friends and have no plans to marry, Harry spends much of his time courting Edith at the Millbank home. But her father opposes the romance, finally revealing that Lord Monmouth had once ended Millbank's engagement to Coningsby's mother, and expresses fear that Edith will be similarly injured. After embarking on further travels, Harry is called home by Lord Monmouth, who wants him to run for Parliament. Not wishing to oppose Millbank's candidate, Harry rejects his grandfather's proposal. Lord Monmouth soon dies, leaving most of his fortune to his illegitimate daughter, Flora, a shy actress to whom Harry has been kind. Harry's precarious finances require him to undertake law studies and curtail his expenses. Then Millbank has a change of heart, withdrawing his own candidate for Parliament and offering to back Harry if he will run. Harry easily defeats his opponent, Rigby. His good fortune continues with his marriage to Edith and his inheritance of Flora's fortune after her death.

Characters: A distinguished British statesman, Disraeli served two separate terms as prime minister to Queen Victoria. He considered fiction an effective way to express his political views, as the trilogy, of which *Coningsby* is the first volume, makes clear. (The other volumes are *Sybil; or, The Two Nations* (1845), which focuses on the Chartist movement, and *Tancred; or, The New Crusade* (1847), which explores the relationship between Christianity and Judaism.) Recognized as the first British political novel, *Coningsby* voices the concerns of the Young England party, of which Disraeli was an important leader. Its members were idealistic Tories (Conservatives) who believed that their nation could be revitalized through a return to a feudalistic society in which an enlightened, paternalistic aristocracy and the Church, rather than the government, looked after the poor. *Coningsby* has been identified as a Bildungsroman (novel of initiation) because it chronicles the title character's development into the kind of dynamic political leader Disraeli felt his country required. While some critics claim that characterization and other literary concerns are subordinate to Disraeli's political intent, most praise his vivid, authentic portrait of the social and political milieu in which he lived.

Harry Coningsby embodies Disraeli's belief in the importance of character and his interest in the intellectual and moral development of a great leader. Harry's potential for achievement is obvious from his early youth, but when he graduates from Eton he is unsure about his future, particularly because of his precarious family situation and finances. As he travels through England, he increases his understanding of his country's problems and needs, and hones his ability to judge between mere social climbers (Rigby and Lucretia) and the wise and virtuous (Sidonia). Harry's movements among the nobility of England allow Disraeli to demonstrate his view of the aristocracy, whom he paints as decadent and irresponsible. Despite the danger of that influence, Harry gradually overcomes his doubts and discovers the values by which to order his own life, as well as those to employ in his eventual leadership role. Some critics have viewed Harry as an autobiographical character despite the differences in Disraeli's circumstances, such as his more advanced age, his notoriety, and the outsider status conferred by his Jewish heritage. Like Harry, Disraeli rose to prominence through diligence, self-confidence, and innate leadership capability. Harry is also thought to have been modeled after another leader of the Young England movement, George Smythe, whose talents were somewhat muted by his frequent uncertainty. While other characters are portrayed somewhat ironically, Disraeli seems thoroughly straight-faced in his presentation of Harry, which renders him priggish to some scholars but also evidences the novel's serious intent.

Sidonia has also been seen as autobiographical, with many characteristics more similar to Disraeli than are Harry's. Extremely intelligent and well-educated, Sidonia has risen to prominence in public life in spite of his society's prejudice against Jews. He is proud of his Jewish heritage and allows Disraeli to illustrate one of the strongest and most prevalent themes of his fiction: the contributions of Jews to human civilization. (This concern becomes most dominant in *Tancred.*) Sidonia provides a model for Harry; he strongly contrasts the young man's aristocratic grandfather. Sidonia furthers this role in Harry's maturation through their long, serious discussions based on Sidonia's views on political and social issues (views that were also Disraeli's) and by encouraging Harry to realize his potential as an important leader. He senses Harry's innate capability and tries to foster the self-confidence that will allow him to achieve greatness.

While Sidonia embodies the intellectual idealism of the Young England party, Harry's grandfather, **Lord Monmouth,** represents the self-centered arrogance of the aristocracy. Supposedly based on Lord Hertford, an actual member of the English nobility, Monmouth is cynical and lacks any sense of responsibility toward his neighbors and tenants. By contrast, **Lord Henry Sidney** (whose estate, Beaumanoir, Harry visits during his travels) rules over his estate with warmth and grace, providing an example of the enlightened aristocrat idealized by the Young England party. Sidney, too, was reputedly modeled after a Young England leader, Lord John Manners, known for his kindness, integrity, and high principles. Also portrayed favorably is **Mr. Millbank**—despite his Whig (Liberal) sympathies, with which Disraeli himself disagreed. Although Millbank is unpolished and volatile, he possesses an innate integrity. Having only recently become wealthy, Millbank expresses fresh, unconventional ideas, such as his belief that England should be ruled not by hereditary peers, but by capable, virtuous men who are well-suited for leadership.

Millbank and Sidonia are positive role models for the young Harry, while **Rigby** serves as a representative of what Harry should avoid. This duplicitous Member of Parliament—who loses his seat first to Millbank's candidate and later to Harry—is a social climber and parasite with no regard for the needs of the people he serves.

Oswald Millbank, Harry's friend at Eton, invites Harry to visit his home in Manchester, allowing Disraeli to show how a well-run factory imitates a feudal system with its hierarchical structure and paternalistic concern for workers. The novel's few female characters include the beautiful, shy, and practically featureless **Edith Millbank**, with whom Harry falls in love and eventually marries; **Lucretia**, a young Italian aristocrat who, in her ambition and greed, angles unsuccessfully for both Harry and Sidonia before marrying Lord Monmouth, to whom she is unfaithful; and **Flora**, Lord Monmouth's illegitimate daughter, a shy, sickly member of an acting troupe who repays Harry's early kindness to her, leaving him the fortune she inherited from her father.

Further Reading

Blake, Robert. *Disraeli.* London: Eyre and Spottiswoode, 1966.

Dictionary of Literary Biography, Vols. 21, 55. Detroit: Gale.

Gordon, Wilhelmina. "Disraeli the Novelist." *Dalhousie Review* 25, No. 2 (July 1945): 212-24.

Nineteenth-Century Literature Criticism, Vol. 2. Detroit: Gale.

O'Kell, Robert. "Disraeli's *Coningsby:* Political Manifesto or Psychological Romance?" *Victorian Studies* XXXIII, No. 1 (Autumn 1979): 57-78.

Pritchett, V. S. "Disraeli." In *The Living Novel and Later Appreciations,* rev. ed., pp. 74-80. New York: Random House, 1964.

Schwarz, Daniel. "Progressive Dubiety: The Discontinuity of Disraeli's Political Trilogy." *Victorian Newsletter* No. 47 (Spring 1975): 12-19.

Swinnerton, Frank. "Disraeli as Novelist." *Yale Review* XVII, No. 2 (January 1928): 283-300.

Thackeray, William Makepeace. "Disraeli's 'Coningsby.'" 1844. Reprint. In *Contributions to the "Morning Chronicle,"* edited by Gordon N. Ray, pp. 39-50. Champaign: University of Illinois Press, 1955.

Fedor Mikhailovich Dostoevsky
1821-1881
Russian novelist, short story writer, and journalist.

"Notes from Underground" (short story, 1864)

Plot: The story is divided into two sections. In the first part, writing from an isolated "cave" he has inhabited for about forty years, the Underground Man presents his negative views of society and the human condition and expresses extreme self-loathing. His rambling diatribe is forceful, condemnatory, and sincere, and it emphasizes free will and the necessity of suffering if one is to achieve authenticity.

The second part of the story focuses on events leading the Underground Man to his self-imposed exile and desolate views. He is an utterly friendless man whose co-workers hated him. When he attends the farewell party for a man he despises, the other guests ignore or insult him. He repeatedly challenges the guest of honor to a duel, even though he lacks the courage to go through with it. Eventually the partygoers go to a brothel, and the Underground Man follows them there, though he arrives after they have departed. He selects a prostitute named Liza as his companion for the evening and speaks at length with her about such topics as sickness, death, remorse, and Liza's occupation. Realizing that Liza is indifferent to him, the Underground Man tries to gain her attention by rhapsodizing sentimentally about family life, expressing the hope that she will eventually be able to escape her degrading profession. This moves Liza to tears, at which point the Underground Man insults her and claims that he has been laughing at her the whole time. Several days later Liza comes to his home and witnesses his violent argument with his servant. The Underground Man is enraged by her bad timing. Liza, however, begs him to rescue her from the demeaning life she has been leading; he treats her spitefully but eventually softens somewhat toward her. They make love, but Liza runs away. After following her for a short while into the snowy night, the Underground Man questions his motives, wondering what point there would be in trying to find her. Utterly confused, he ponders whether it is preferable to pursue "cheap happiness or exalted suffering."

Characters: The psychological and philosophical concerns evident in *Notes from Underground* anticipate Dostoevsky's later works, and the character of the Underground Man is an example of a type that would later be identified as typically Dostoevskian. This powerful, unconventional work examines the idea of free will, which Dostoevsky preferred rationalism and scientific determinism, the other concepts popular in his time.

Unsuccessful at ordinary living, **the Underground Man** has withdrawn from society. He is nasty, petty, and cowardly as well as acutely sensitive to injury. He seems to relish holding grudges against those who hurt him. He subjects himself to abuse from his co-workers because the anguish it causes stimulates him and gives him a reason to hurt others. He derides Liza when she asks him for love and affirmation, because he believes that what she aspires to is an illusion. The Underground Man actually has a great desire for what he calls "the noble and the beautiful," and he dreams of friendship and reconciliation with others, but he is constantly reminded that these ideal can never exist in the real world. Because he quotes frequently from works of literature, some scholars identify the Underground Man as embodying in a bizarre way the romantic sensibility; resistance to the limits of reason is one tenet of romanticism, the literary movement that held sway in the early nineteenth century. The outrageous egoism (often termed "the egoism of suffering") of the Underground Man allows him to express his freedom from the laws of nature and of reason. Critics maintain that Dostoevsky created the Underground Man to illustrate his opposition to the rationalist idea that moral choices are not available to human beings. Dostoevsky believed that people could find their way through the world's despair with the light of Christian faith to guide them. Indeed, his original draft of *Notes from Underground* ends with the Underground Man reading passages from the Bible. These lines were stricken by the censor who edited the manuscript, because he felt it was blasphemous for such a depraved creature to speak lines from the Gospels. If these lines had been retained, the possibility of the Underground Man's redemption would undoubtedly have been more pronounced; as it is, he is left with little hope of escape.

The only other significant character in the story is the prostitute **Liza,** important only in helping to illuminate the Underground Man. Through his emotional manipulation of this girl, the Underground Man sees that ideals are illusions he can use them to impose his will on others. He creates for Liza a glimmer of hope and then snatches it away, enjoying a perverse power over her. For her part, Liza perceives that the seemingly callous Underground Man can actually be hurt emotionally, so she offers him love and the refuge of her simplicity and innocence. Since he believes such values are illusions, the Underground Man rejects Liza.

Crime and Punishment (novel, 1866)

Plot: The novel, set in mid-nineteenth-century St. Petersburg, Russia, centers on a young, impoverished law student named Rodion Raskolnikov. For about a month he has ruminated over the idea of murdering a miserly old pawnbroker—both to rid the world of a negative element and to alleviate his own and his family's deprivation. When he receives a letter from his mother saying that his sister intends to marry a pompous, middle-aged man to help support her family, Raskolnikov finally commits the deed, killing the pawnbroker, Alonya Ivanovna, as well as her innocent sister, Lizaveta, with an ax. He flees with some jewels he finds in their rooms. The next day Raskolnikov is called to the police station and assumes he will be arrested, but they only question him about a debt he owes to his landlady. Raskolnikov faints. When he recovers, he explains that he has been ill, but a clerk is suspicious of his behavior. After hiding the stolen jewels, Raskolnikov is feverishly ill for four days. When he is well again, he learns that Mikolka, the housepainter who lives in the room below the pawnbroker's, has been accused of the murder. Raskolnikov is visited by his sister's fiancé, Piotr Luzhin, who leaves when his future brother-in-law insults him.

Raskolnikov grows more and more troubled by his secret. When his friend Marmeladov, an alcoholic ex-government clerk, is struck by a carriage, Raskolnikov takes the mortally wounded man home. There he meets Marmeladov's eighteen-year-old daughter, Sonia, who has resorted to prostitution to support her family. Raskolnikov gives money to his friend's wife, Katerina Ivanovna, to pay for Marmeladov's funeral. Concerned about Raskolnikov, his mother and sister, Dounia, arrive in St. Petersburg. Raskolnikov neglects them, leaving them in the care of his devoted friend Dmitri Razumihin, who soon falls in love with Dounia. Irresistibly drawn to the police station, Raskolnikov talks to Inspector Porfiry Petrovitch. They discuss Raskolnikov's idea that a superior being, a man of genius, may be justified in committing crimes that an ordinary person could not be allowed to commit. Raskolnikov thinks the detective considers him a suspect in the murder of the two women. Arkady Svidrigailov, the lecherous man Dounia had once worked for as a governess, visits Raskolnikov to deliver a generous sum of money for Dounia, part of it from the estate of Svidrigailov's dead wife and part added by Svidrigailov. The money allows Dounia to break her engagement to the unpleasant Luzhin, whom her brother had long encouraged her to spurn; in the meantime Dounia has fallen in love with Razumihin.

Raskolnikov now tells his family that he can no longer associate with them. He has a long philosophical talk with Sonia, who impresses him with her strong religious convictions.

After another discussion with Porfiry about deeds committed by intelligent criminals and their inevitable compulsion to confess, Raskolnikov assumes that Porfiry is aware of his guilt. He demands that he be arrested, but Porfiry only laughs, and their talk is interrupted when Mikolka confesses to the murder of the two women.

Raskolnikov continues to be tortured by guilt. At a funeral banquet hosted by Katerina Ivanovna, Luzhin accuses Sonia of theft. Eventually it is revealed that Luzhin—because he believes Raskolnikov convinced Dounia to break their engagement—staged the theft in order to humiliate Raskolnikov through Sonia. Later that evening, Raskolnikov admits his guilt to Sonia, explaining that he had hoped to prove himself above the common laws of humanity but that instead he had destroyed himself. Sonia forgives Raskolnikov and urges him to give himself up to the police; he refuses to do so. Svidrigailov overhears their conversation and later confronts Raskolnikov. Porfiry also admits that he knows Raskolnikov murdered the women and encourages him to confess and thus receive a more lenient punishment. Meanwhile, Svidrigailov attempts to seduce Dounia; she tries to shoot him but misses. He allows her to leave his rooms unharmed and even gives her money to aid the impoverished Marmeladov family. Then he kills himself. After struggling with himself, confessing and pleading with his sister for forgiveness, saying farewell to his mother, and meeting Sonia a last time, Raskolnikov admits his guilt to the police. He is given a relatively merciful sentence of eight years at hard labor in Siberia.

In an epilogue, the reader learns that Dounia married Razumihin and that Sonia followed Raskolnikov to Siberia, where she lived in a village near the prison and earned the respect of both townspeople and prisoners for her humility and devotion. It is implied that Raskolnikov eventually found peace and regeneration through Christianity.

Characters: *Crime and Punishment* is one of the most widely read nineteenth-century novels, and Dostoevsky one of the most acclaimed authors in Russian literature. The novel explores the psychological, religious, and moral implications of a crime and its effects on a particular human psyche, thereby touching on universally compelling concerns. Through its main character (whose motives are never clearly defined) as well as its secondary characters (who amplify various aspects of the protagonist's personality), *Crime and Punishment* affirms the complexity of human nature but hints strongly at the possibility of redemption.

The novel's central figure is **Rodion Raskolnikov,** a young intellectual who lives a threadbare, impoverished student's life. As his friend Razumihin points out, Raskolnikov is excessively proud, and he feels humiliated by his circumstances. Before murdering the two women, he wrote an article proposing that certain superior people—such as the French dictator and general Napoleon—are justified in disregarding the traditional legal and moral limits on human behavior because they do so in order to change history. Raskolnikov divided humanity into two lots—people of extraordinary genius and the rest of humanity, whom he compared to "lice." It is possible that Raskolnikov commits the murders as an experiment to determine which category he belongs to—to prove his own superiority—but several other motives are suggested as well. He claims that it cannot be wrong to rid the world of a worthless person such as the pawnbroker, since she does no good for anyone and preys on the poor; this "utilitarian" perspective, which held that the end result justifies the means necessary to achieve it, was promulgated by some nineteenth-century intellectuals. Marxist interpretations of *Crime and Punishment* emphasize that the social conditions in which Raskolnikov lives precipitate his actions, although the Christian affirmation with which the book ends suggests that Dostoevsky would not uphold this view. Or it could be that robbery is Raskolnikov's motive; he does steal his victim's jewels, yet he subsequently buries them and never seems to think of them again.

Raskolnikov himself is unable to understand his own behavior, and his suffering is not only intellectual and spiritual, but also aesthetic, for he is offended by the ugliness of his crime (vividly illustrated by his dream in which a horse is savagely beaten). Critic Philip Rahv noted that Dostoevsky was the first novelist to dramatize "the principle of uncertainty or indeterminacy in the presentation of character," and many other scholars agree that this skillfully depicted uncertainty is a key to the novel's greatness. Raskolnikov resembles other Dostoevskian characters in his dual nature—in fact, his name is derived from the Russian word for "split." On one side is the cold, exacting intellect, and on the other is the warm, imperfect humanity; he is torn between the two sides. After a long period of suffering and punishment both before and after confessing to the murders, Raskolnikov finally achieves redemption through the Christian faith. Yet many scholars find this redemption unconvincing; they claim that Raskolnikov never truly repents his crime and remains proud and isolated to the end. Nevertheless, the character Raskolnikov has generated much critical attention since the novel's publication, and the authentic impact he continues to make on readers attests to Dostoevsky's complex, skillful characterization.

Some readers find **Arkady Svidrigailov** an equally or even more interesting character than Raskolnikov. Svidrigailov has a reputation for cruelty and callousness and is known to have seduced many young girls; he may also have caused the deaths of three people—a girl whom he raped, a servant whom he seduced, and his own wife. His physical appearance mirrors his flagrant sensuality: he has light hair and pale blue eyes set in a mask-like face with strangely red lips and cheeks. Dostoevsky often uses secondary characters to mirror his protagonist, and Svidrigailov is frequently seen as the embodiment of Raskolnikov's destructiveness and yearning for power. Critic R.P. Blackmur calls him Raskolnikov's "other self," and most other scholars concur. Raskolnikov senses his similarity to Svidrigailov even though he is repelled by the man, and Svidrigailov also perceives their likeness. Svidrigailov's decision to kill himself attests to his profound ennui and despair. Dostoevsky has often been praised for creating in Svidrigailov a complex character whose wickedness is tempered with flickers of compassion—he gives both Dounia and the Marmeladovs money they desperately need, and he allows Dounia to escape even after she has tried to kill him. Svidrigailov resembles not so much a gothic villain with a completely evil nature, but a human being whose behavior has destroyed others and, ultimately, himself.

Sonia Marmeladov represents Raskolnikov's capacity for good. Said to be based on Dostoevski's second wife, Anna Snitkina (reportedly a stabilizing influence in his life), Sonia is a fair-haired, thin, pale eighteen-year-old whose gaudy clothing contrasts with her gentle expression and "remarkable blue eyes." Though her family's deprivation has forced Sonia to become a prostitute, her true nature is pure and spiritual. Passive and self-sacrificing, she submits willingly to the humiliation of her occupation. Sonia is the novel's representative of Christianity; it is she who pleads with Raskolnikov to seek redemption through suffering and faith, and her influence ultimately triumphs. Through Sonia, Dostoevsky voices several of the novel's concerns: when Raskolnikov questions the morality of her own choice during their discussion of his guilt, for instance, she asks, "What, then, is to be done?" The difficulty of overcoming despair is a theme frequently explored in Russian literature. She also reads to Raskolnikov the biblical story of Lazarus, thus illustrating both her faith in miracles and her desire to raise Raskolnikov from the dead, as it were. Sonia immediately forgives him when he confesses his crime and in general refuses to judge or condemn other human beings. Some critics have found Sonia colorless and unrealistic, but most consider her a compelling embodiment of faith.

Porfiry, the police inspector Raskolnikov speaks to several times and even confesses to, was described by R.P. Blackmur as a "thirty-five year old roly-poly of the disengaged intellect." Intelligent, perceptive, and intuitive, Porfiry is interested in criminal psychology and motives more than with the technical aspects of hunting down lawbreakers. His interviews with Raskolnikov create an atmosphere of mounting suspense, contributing to the novel's dramatic tension and power. Porfiry has read Raskolnikov's article and discusses it with him, expounding on the criminal's moral need for punishment and thus serving as Dostoevsky's mouthpiece for these ideas. Porfiry's primary role is usually defined as the representative of law and order who draws Raskolnikov to confess.

Sonia's father, **Marmeladov,** is the cause of his family's deprivation, choosing to spend his time drinking rather than trying to improve their situation. Dostoevsky's depiction of the Marmeladovs' poverty has been seen as generally symbolic of suffering and pain in the world; it illustrates specifically how a family may be destroyed through alcoholism, a subject that is known to have interested and troubled Dostoevsky. Marmeladov's bloated face, wild eyes, messy hair, and disorderly clothing signify his degradation. His wordy, self-berating lamentation in the tavern about the course of his downfall and the pain he has inflicted on his higher-born wife and unfortunate children is both comic and pathetic. Marmeladov has been interpreted as yet another double of Raskolnikov, reflecting the isolation, thwarted ambition, and feeling of debasement that typify Raskolnikov. Also like Raskolnikov, Marmeladov has brought harm upon himself and others for no apparent reason.

Marmeladov's wife, **Katerina,** has been driven to despair and even cruelty to her children by her extreme poverty. She also suffers from the chronic cough of tuberculosis. That she blames her husband is obvious, for while he is dying she bitterly rejects the attending priest's suggestion that she forgive Marmeladov, defiantly showing him the blood on her handkerchief as evidence of his guilt. Katerina is the daughter of a military officer and was previously married to a man presumably more prosperous than Marmeladov, but the exalted position from which her husband claims to have dragged her down is probably exaggerated. Nevertheless, her rambling monologue mixing reminiscences of happier times with coughing spells, lamentations about her impoverishment, and admonitions to her children is pathetic, as is the death scene in which she seems to perceive her situation with desperate clarity.

Like other notable characters in Dostoevsky's fiction, including *Crime and Punishment*'s Svidrigailov, **Piotr Luzhin** appears respectable but is actually corrupt. A pompous, self-important government official, he is actually a swindler whose vengefulness is revealed when he tries to frame Sonia for thievery. Dostoevsky is said to have disliked the kind of bourgeois respectability that Luzhin represents. Soviet scholars have characterized Luzhin as the embodiment of capitalism, a greedy schemer who preys on others to improve his own situation.

Raskolnikov's close friend, **Dmitri Razumihin,** is much more sympathetically portrayed. His name derives from the Russian word for ''reason,'' and he serves as a good-hearted, hardworking foil to the tortured, self-involved Raskolnikov. He provides hospitality to Raskolnikov's mother and sister when Raskolnikov neglects them, and he eventually falls in love with Dounia and founds a publishing business that will support them after Raskolnikov is exiled to Siberia. Though Razumihin is fond of his friend and loyal to him, he has no illusions about Raskolnikov and perceives the dual nature of his personality.

Raskolnikov's mother, **Pulcheria,** is an utterly devoted mother whose love for her son withstands her inability to understand him. Her last meeting with Raskolnikov, in which he professes his love for her but does not explain why he is going away, has been praised for its poignancy, particularly because it reveals an unsuspected tenderness in Raskolnikov's nature. Although Pulcheria appears prim, subdued, and not particularly clever, she knows more about her son's life than anyone suspects.

Raskolnikov's sister, **Dounia,** is also devoted to her brother; she is willing to sacrifice her own happiness by marrying Luzhin so that Raskolnikov will not have to suffer deprivation.

Although Dounia is generally passive, she repels Svidrigailov's advances by trying to shoot him (a scene which, incidentally, has been criticized as inappropriately melodramatic); the fact that she misses may indicate an inherent incapacity for murder that her brother does not share.

Raskolnikov describes **Alonya Ivanovna,** the miserly pawnbroker whom he murders, as "a vile, harmful louse ... who bled poor people dry"; she embodies for him all the worst aspects of society. Alonya is a slovenly woman with a pointed nose, greasy hair, and a scrawny neck, and her eyes reveal her wickedness. Dostoevsky supposedly based this character on a pawnbroker he met during a destitute period he spent in Germany. Soviet scholars felt that Alonya, like Luzhin, represents capitalism because of her occupation and avariciousness. The murder scene, in which Raskolnikov kills Alonya and then her sister with an ax, has been praised for its realism, maintaining authenticity and impact without lapsing into melodrama. **Lizaveta,** Alonya's dimwitted sister, is an innocent, pious creature who supports herself by selling old clothes. She is an incidental victim—Raskolnikov kills her only because she is a witness to Alonya's murder, yet he does not seem particularly bothered by her death, presumably because his motive was clear. She serves as a reminder that actions may have unforeseen complications.

Minor characters in *Crime and Punishment* include **Mikolka,** the housepainter who confesses to the murders and whom Porfiry describes as a "fantasist" like Raskolnikov; and **Zametov,** the police clerk who begins to suspect Raskolnikov's complicity in the crime during his first visit to the police station and who informs Porfiry of his suspicion.

The Idiot (novel, 1868-69)

Plot: While returning home on a train to St. Petersburg after spending several years in Switzerland, where he was treated for epilepsy, Prince Lef Myshkin meets Parfen Rogozhin. At the end of their trip, Rogozhin offers to take the impoverished Myshkin to his home and to give him money, but Myshkin wants first to visit some distant relatives, General Epanchin and his family. The general takes an interest in Myshkin and gives him some money, while his wife and daughters appreciate their visitor's naivete, frankness, and simple nobility. They begin to refer to him affectionately as "the Idiot." General Epanchin's secretary, Ganya Ivolgin, who would like to marry the general's youngest daughter, Aglaya, because she is wealthy, invites Myshkin to stay in his family's boarding house. Ganya is having an affair with a beautiful young woman named Nastasya, whose youth and later life have been marred by her seduction by a middle-aged businessman named Totsky. Meeting the aggrieved and vengeful Nastasya, Myshkin senses innocence beneath her rough exterior and treats her with pity and compassion. While drinking one evening, he rashly proposes marriage to Nastasya, informing her that he has inherited some money. She refuses his offer, claiming she wants to spare him the social harm that an alliance with a woman of her kind would bring. Instead she accepts Rogozhin's offer of 100,000 rubles and goes away with him.

Nastasya is derided by the Epanchins and their friends, although Myshkin still treats her kindly. When Nastasya deserts Rogozhin, he blames Myshkin. Myshkin becomes the attempted victim of an extortion scheme concocted by a group of young intellectuals, one of whom feels he is entitled to Myshkin's inheritance. Myshkin proves his innocence, but he earns the scorn of those around him when he offers to help the extortionist. Aglaya falls in love with Myshkin in spite of herself and the two become engaged. Madame Epanchin, who reluctantly sanctions the match, soon hosts a party at which Myshkin is expected to keep quiet and not embarrass the family. He launches into an extended, rambling monologue about his utopian views, however, shocking the guests, then he knocks over an expensive vase. The party ends when Myshkin has an epileptic fit. After his recovery, the Epanchins forgive him. Meanwhile Nastasya has encouraged Aglaya to marry Myshkin. But when the three young people meet at Nastasya's flat, Aglaya and Nastasya argue viciously and Aglaya passionately declares her love for Myshkin. Nastasya faints, and Myshkin rushes to help her. Wildly jealous, Aglaya leaves in a fury.

Myshkin is now barred from the Epanchin home. He plans to marry Nastasya, but on the day of the wedding—even as Myshkin waits at the church—Rogozhin encourages Nastasya to escape with him, and she agrees. Myshkin searches throughout St. Petersburg for Nastasya but is unable to find her, and he finally goes to Rogozhin's apartment even though he knows that Rogozhin hates him enough to kill him. Eventually Myshkin encounters Rogozhin in the street; he takes Myshkin into his apartment and shows him the dead body of Nastasya lying on his bed. In pity and compassion Myshkin spends the night with the feverish Rogozhin. The next day the police arrive, and Rogozhin confesses to the murder. Myshkin is allowed to leave, but these experiences have upset his fragile mental and physical health. He eventually returns to the Swiss sanitarium in a state of permanent disintegration.

Characters: Many readers find *The Idiot* one of Dostoevsky's most moving works, for it features a profoundly admirable protagonist whose goodness and compassion ultimately lead to tragedy for himself and those around him. While focusing on the moral disintegration of modern Europe with its emphasis on materialism, Dostoevsky suggests in *The Idiot* that the answer is not to be found in any earthly utopia but in Christian redemption attainable only through suffering.

Many critics have characterized the central figure of *The Idiot,* **Prince Lev Myshkin** as Dostoevky's ideal man. He is a physically slight person with fair hair and tranquil blue eyes whose naivete is partly due to his long isolation in a Swiss sanitarium. Myshkin is Christlike in his deep humility, compassion, and pity for those who suffer; his refusal to judge others is perhaps best illustrated by his immediate warmth and kindness to Nastasya, who in her role as a "fallen woman" stands for Mary Magdalen, the prostitute befriended by Jesus. Some scholars have detected in Myshkin traces of the "holy fool" of Russian folklore, whose innocence reflected God's special regard for the mentally deficient. Myshkin has also been compared to Don Quixote (the famous seventeenth-century literary character created by Miguel de Cervantes) because he longs to reform his corrupt society. Myshkin envisions a world full of the goodwill that he himself practices, but he is surrounded by violent passions, egoism, and greed, and his utopian dreams are eventually shattered. Myshkin's empathy for others leads him to interfere in their lives, but his friends are hurt by his interference. His kindness toward Nastasya causes violent jealousy in both Aglaya and Roghozhin and results in Aglaya's abandoning him, Nastasya dying, and Roghozhin serving a prison term. He also loses his own mental stability. Myshkin fails to understand the real workings of human nature. His name—"lev" means lion and "myshka" means mouse—reflects the rift between his intentions and their results. Myshkin's epilepsy is often identified as the most dramatic manifestation of his humanity (Dostoevsky himself suffered from epilepsy). Having once left the innocence and neutrality of Switzerland for the complexity of Russian society, Myshkin finally returns to his starting place, his innocence crushed and his sanity stolen.

Dostoevky's tendency to create alter egos or doubles for his central characters is demonstrated in *The Idiot* in **Parfen Roghozhin,** the first of the new acquaintances Myshkin meets after leaving the sanitarium. Roghozhin provides a sharp contrast to Myshkin in his appearance—dark and swarthy with a vigorous, powerful physique—and his passionate nature. Because the two characters are so diametrically opposed, it is not surprising to learn that in early drafts of the novel their attributes were merged into one (Myshkin's) personality. Roghozhin is a sensitive person who finds it impossible to control his emotions. The love he feels for Nastasya is infused with sexual energy and, ultimately, destructiveness, while Myshkin's regard for her is based on pity and is notably asexual. This impulse reaches its inevitable conclusion in Nastasya's death, and Dostoevsky describes Roghozhin as emotionally emptied afterward; he listens to his criminal sentence with bland acceptance. Several critics have noted the painting that hangs in Roghozhin's room—*Christ in the Tomb* by the sixteenth-century German painter Hans Holbein. This depiction of Christ entombed before his resurrection is graphically disturbing and seems to contradict Myshkin's idealized spirituality.

Dostoevsky has been praised for his complex portrayal of **Nastasya Filipovna,** a darkhaired beauty and a tragic figure. The orphan of a military officer, Nastasya was raised by a neighbor, **Totsky,** who began to use the girl for his own sexual purposes as soon as she reached physical maturity. Though she has since left Totsky, Nastasya still lives a life of sexual degradation as Ganya's (and later Roghozhin's) mistress. Her feeling of abasement and despair has led to a thirst for revenge and compels her to debase herself even further— such as when she spurns Myshkin on their wedding day and runs off with Roghozhin. Many scholars have detected in Nastasya's character a tendency toward masochism, for she seems to revel in her degradation. She is an enigmatic figure whose intense, brooding personality has magnified the effect of her dismal history. While Myshkin is seen as a Christ figure, Nastasya is thought to represent Mary Magdalen, the prostitute to whom Jesus offered compassion and forgiveness. Myshkin perceives in her a basic innocence, and he offers her forgiveness and (asexual) love. But Nastasya cannot overcome her feeling that evil surrounds her, and she tells Roghozhin she will go away with him because "there's nothing but ruin anyway." The despair results finally in her death.

Another important female character in *The Idiot* is **Aglaya Epanchin,** the beautiful young daughter of General and Madame Epinchan who falls in love with Myshkin but later rejects him. She is the spoiled darling of her family and has a capricious and changeable but essentially warmhearted, innocent, and idealistic nature. She often acts childishly, but the passionate jealousy she feels when she suspects that Myshkin is in love with Nastasya is an adult emotion previously dormant inside her. At the same time, choosing the somewhat sexless Myshkin over her other suitors may indicate that she fears sexuality. Some critics question whether Myshkin really loves Aglaya; others interpret his feelings for her as evidence of his humanity, for this love is personal, whereas his regard for Nastasya is rooted in compassion for her suffering. Aglaya eventually marries a worthless Polish count and leaves Russia, a depressing fate (in the eyes, at least, of the anti-Catholic Dostoevsky) because the count is Catholic.

Like her daughter, **Madame Lizaveta Epanchin** is capricious, moody, and eccentric. Her stormy exterior masks great sensitivity, however, for she is profoundly hurt by her husband's infidelities and concerned for her children's welfare. Madame Epanchin's own nobility allows her to recognize Myshkin's virtues, and she appreciates him even though she does not consider him an appropriate fiancé for her daughter, perhaps due to Aglaya's changeability. After Myshkin returns to Switzerland, Madame Epanchin visits him there and weeps inconsolably over the deteriorated state in which she finds him. Madame Epanchin is the quintessential Russian woman, loyal and proud; Murray Krieger wrote, "she is always a vigorous force for life, however messily she runs it." **General Epanchin** is a shrewd financier who might be said to embody the power that money wields in nineteenth-century Russian society. He is a suave, easygoing man who tolerates his wife's eccentricities, perhaps because they allow him to justify his liaisons with other women.

Though pervaded by a mood of overwhelming despair, the novel includes some comic moments, provided through the character of **General Ivolgin,** Ganya's father. Once a distinguished man, he is now a drunkard whose stately pretensions cannot hide the fact that he has nearly brought his family to ruin. Ivolgin lies compulsively, and his stories are remarkably creative and elaborate, yet beneath the humor is an undercurrent of tragedy. Another mildly comic character is **Lebedev,** a forty-year-old, red-nosed and pimply-faced clerk who tries to ingratiate himself with his social superiors. Dostoevsky uses him as a mouthpiece for some serious concerns, such as the relationship between art and reality and the deleterious effect of materialism and misdirected "progress" on civilization.

Ganya Ivolgin, General Epanchin's secretary, maintains a smooth appearance and manners but is innately corrupt. He provides an example of modern society's materialism, for he measures worth by money and is eager to gain as much wealth as he can. Called "the very embodiment of an ambitious mediocrity" by Janko Larvin, Ganya might be compared to the mean-spirited businessman Luzhin in *Crime and Punishment.*

Among the group of radical intellectuals who try to cheat Myshkin is **Ippolit Terentyev,** a willful and egotistical young man who is dying of tuberculosis. He resembles Myshkin in his sickliness, but he has responded to it with resentment and rebelliousness against a God cruel enough to let a person of such promise waste away. He hates Myshkin, perhaps because he envies the other man's feeling of connection with the rest of humanity.

The Brothers Karamazov (novel, 1880)

Plot: The story takes place in the mid-nineteenth century in the Russian town of Skotoprigonyvski. Fyodor Karamazov, a successful but corrupt businessman prone to swindling and debauchery, has fathered three sons: Dmitri (by his first wife), and Ivan and Alexey (by his second wife). Upon the deaths of their mothers (whom he mistreated), Karamazov neglected his sons, leaving them in the care of his servant, Grigory. Grigory and his wife Marfa are the adoptive parents of Smerdyakov, an epileptic orphan who is said to be Karamazov's illegitimate son and who eventually works as his servant. As he grew up, Dmitri assumed he would eventually receive a legacy from his dead mother. He joined the army and led a wild, undisciplined life; he has since received only small amounts of money from his father. Ivan attended college and became a professor and writer; he too is impoverished and embittered. Good-natured and likable Alexey, called Alyosha, has entered the local monastery and studies with a respected elder of the Russian Orthodox Church, Father Zosima. When the two eldest sons and their father go to the monastery to meet with Alyosha, a scene erupts during which Karamazov embarrasses the others with his bad behavior. He accuses Dmitri of trying to get money from his father so that he can support his mistress, Grushenka, with whom Karamazov is also in love. Dmitri, who is engaged to the respectable Katerina Ivanovna (the daughter of a colonel), is enraged by his father's accusation. Father Zosima witnesses this tumultuous scene and concludes that the Karamazovs are all outright sensualists. He recommends that, after he dies, Alyosha return to the world outside the monastery. When the two brothers are alone, Dmitri admits to Alyosha that he is indeed in love with Grushenka and that he has given her three thousand rubles that belonged to Katerina. Convinced Katerina is superior to him, he hopes that she will instead fall in love with Ivan. He asks Alyosha to get money from Karamazov so that he can repay his debt to Katerina. But Karamazov, who wants to marry Grushenka himself and fears and despises his two older sons, refuses Alyosha's request.

Alyosha has a long talk with Ivan about their circumstances and also about broader philosophical issues. Ivan says that he and Katerina love each other but that he fears she will never be able to abandon Dmitri, even though Dmitri has rejected her. Ivan describes his feelings about the cruelty of the world and the dual nature of the human psyche, and he shares with Alyosha a parable he has written, called *The Grand Inquisitor.* Father Zosima dies, and because his body decomposes rapidly some of the other monks claim Zosima was not a saint. Following a short period of spiritual doubt, Alyosha feels ready to return to the outside world.

Dmitri is still trying to repay his debt to Katerina but has been unsuccessful in acquiring the money. While jealously searching for Grushenka at Karamazov's house, he seriously wounds Grigory. Dmitri finally locates Grushenka at an inn in a nearby town, where she has gone with a former lover, but she declares that she loves Dmitri only. The police interrupt the subsequent drunken orgy at the inn and charge Dmitri with the murder of Karamazov, who has been found dead and robbed of some money at his home. Dmitri's clothes are bloody and he is in possession of fifteen hundred rubles—which he claims to have saved from the original sum given to him by Katerina—and his frequent angry statements against Karamazov also incriminate him; he is thrown in jail. Ivan visits Smerdyakov in the hospital, where he was placed after experiencing an epileptic seizure following Karamazov's murder, and after three interviews learns that Smerdyakov murdered Karamazov because Ivan had hinted that it would be best for everyone if he was dead. That night, Ivan is feverishly ill and dreams that he is haunted by a devil that exists inside him; Smerdyakov hangs himself the same night.

At the murder trial, the defense lawyer is almost successful in refuting the large amount of evidence against Dmitri, but his case is weakened by Ivan's testimony: he tells the court that Smerdyakov committed the murder and displays the money that Smerdyakov gave him, but he then begins to tell the court about his personal devil; it is obvious that his mind has begun to come unhinged. Then Katerina produces a letter in which Dmitri promises to return her money even if he must kill his father to do it. Dmitri is found guilty and sentenced to a prison term in Siberia. While he is hospitalized for a fever, Katerina visits him and begs his forgiveness for her part in his conviction. At the funeral of a young boy he knows, Alyosha pleads with the mourners to live good lives and to love their fellow human beings. He and Grushenka plan to accompany Dmitri to Siberia.

Characters: *The Brothers Karamazov* is considered Dostoevsky's most mature and accomplished work as well as one of the greatest novels in all literature. In his presentation not only of the conflict between a father and his sons but of complex philosophical and religious concepts, Dostoevsky created a story of great dramatic intensity. The novel demonstrates Dostoevsky's awareness of the difficulties inherent in the search for truth and also shows his faith in "the existence of some higher, absolute, unifying harmony," according to William J. Leatherbarrow.

Provincial landowner **Fyodor Karamazov** is the central figure around whom the action in *The Brothers Karamazov* revolves. Self-centered and self-indulgent, the crude, materialistic, and cunning Karamazov first ruined the lives of his two wives and then neglected his sons, exposing them to his indifference. Now that they are adults, he torments them with his miserliness, his continuing debauchery, his buffoonish behavior, and his obscene jokes; he even competes with Dmitri for Grushenka's love. Any one of Karamazov's sons might have murdered him, and the passionate Dmitri has often contemplated just such a deed, while Ivan projects his resentment of his father onto God. Only Alyosha declines to condemn his father, and Karamazov returns his son's kindness with uncharacteristic affection. Dostoevsky suggests that Alyosha's absorption of Christian values shows that the challenge of faith is not in loving human beings as they might be but as they are, in spite of their weaknesses.

Each of the Karamazov brothers exhibits a different force of personality. The eldest, **Dmitri Karamazov,** represents sensuality, which—as he realizes with fear and disgust—he has inherited from his father. He also resembles Karamazov in appearance: he is slender but muscular, with a sallow complexion, and large, dark eyes. Dmitri lacks self-control in most matters involving his emotions. At the same time, he is essentially good-hearted and even has a kind of naive simplicity; these qualities distinguish him from his more thoroughly corrupt father. Dmitri has been identified as a quintessentially Russian character because of his violent temper and his capacity for strong feeling. Not surprisingly, Dmitri prefers the earthy Grushenka to the neurotic Katya, and when he thinks Grushenka has gone to his father's home, jealousy drives him to the brink of murder. Nevertheless, he resists this impulse and vents his anger instead on the man who has served as his substitute father,

Grigory. The ordeal of false accusation, conviction, and impending imprisonment that Dmitri undergoes has an unusual effect on him, resulting not in embitterment but in a new capacity for introspection. Dmitri submissively accepts his punishment despite his innocence of this particular crime, as if his bad behavior in the past justifies this current judgment.

Ivan Karamazov is the family's intellectual brother. Five years younger than Dmitri, Ivan seems more mature; he does not share his older brother's direct and physical approach to life. Ivan is an educated, intelligent, and essentially aloof person who espouses a rationalistic viewpoint, preferring detached reason to either Dmitri's physicality or Alyosha's spirituality. Although he believes in God's existence, Ivan cannot reconcile himself to the world's cruelty and injustice, so he seeks refuge in the cold but orderly realm of intellect. Yet there is also in Ivan a strain of the Karamazov enthusiasm for living; he admits, "I have a longing for life, and I go on living in spite of logic." The dualism that splits Ivan's nature between skepticism and idealism makes him a particularly Dostoevskian character.

The famous parable *The Legend of the Grand Inquisitor,* which Ivan has written and shares with his brother, comprises a renowned section of the novel that is often studied separately. Dostoevsky voices some of his own religious doubts through the story of Christ's visit to Seville, Spain, during the Spanish Inquisition of the fifteenth and sixteenth centuries. Christ is imprisoned and lectured by the Grand Inquisitor, who informs him that because humanity has proved incapable of living up to the demands of free will and making moral choices, Christ has been replaced by the rigid authority of the church. The story ends ambiguously, with Christ kissing his persecutor and then being allowed to leave.

When Ivan learns that Smerdyakov has murdered Karamazov, he is overwhelmed by guilt and confusion. Smerdyakov was responding to Ivan's statement that "All things are lawful" and was convinced that Ivan implicitly commanded the death. Ivan in turn questions his subconscious motives—did he in fact wish for his father's death, and if so, is he responsible for it? The dream that Ivan has while in the midst of his intellectual torment also demonstrates his dual personality. He argues with the devil, who personifies his own strict rationalism, about good and evil and the existence of God, and all the while the devil teases and derides him. Just as Dmitri is punished in a physical manner, with exile and penile servitude, Ivan's punishment is intellectual. He loses his reason, humiliating himself and hurting Dmitri's case with his appearance at the trial.

Alyosha Karamazov has a spiritual nature and is deeply devoted to the Christian faith. A thoroughly good person—gentle, compassionate, and trustworthy—he is loved by everyone, even his irascible father. A follower of Father Zosima, Alyosha ascribes to the holy man's ethic of universal love and understanding. Critics sometimes compare Alyosha to the angelic Prince Myshkin in *The Idiot,* although Alyosha is a healthy nineteen-year-old while Myshkin suffers from epilepsy. Alyosha is a living example of the kind of loving service to humanity that Father Zosima espouses. The elder recommends that he eventually leave the monastery and find his way through the real and disorderly world outside because he recognizes that Alyosha carries within him the sensual Karamazov blood, which he must confront. But Zosima may also see in Alyosha the potential for an even greater holiness that will be nurtured—as his own was—by experience. Alyosha is aware of his own weaknesses; he blames himself, for instance, for not keeping a close watch on his father and Dmitri, as Father Zosima had asked, and thus inadvertently allowing Karamazov's murder to occur. Alyosha experiences a crisis of faith after Zosima dies and his corpse mortifies, proving that the elder was not a saint. But Alyosha manages to renew his faith and leaves the monastery, as Zosima advised. He becomes engaged to the irresponsible, temperamental **Lise,** apparently as a means of wholeheartedly confronting life (although several scholars have viewed this action as incongruous). Dostoevsky apparently planned a sequel to *The*

Brothers Karamazov that would recount Alyosha's subsequent life, and many critics have speculated on the shape such a novel might have taken.

Karamazov's illegitimate son, **Smerdyakov,** was described by critic William J. Leatherbarrow as "the external projection of all the ugliness and baseness hidden within the brothers Karamazov." Like them, he has been neglected by his father; he is now condemned to life as a servant. He is an unpleasant person—sly, vain, secretive, egotistical, and clever despite his illiteracy. Ivan claims to hate Smerdyakov and yet feels curiously drawn to him, perhaps because they are both detached rationalists. Yet Smerdyakov lacks Ivan's depth and complexity and thus enacts the concept that "All things are lawful" by killing Karamazov. When Smerdyakov sees that Ivan, whom he worships, not only does not approve of his action but is himself subject to doubt and remorse, he kills himself in despair.

Dostoevsky probably based the character of **Father Zosima** on a holy elder of the Russian Orthodox church, Father Ambrosius, who had impressed him an 1878 visit to the Optina Monastery. In a long chapter that some scholars have criticized as superfluous to the main story, Zosima recounts his early career as a military officer, his conversion to Christianity, and his subsequent religious life. He is old and immensely experienced, wise, serene, and compassionate. Zosima claims allegiance to the Church Universal, espousing love and sympathy for all of humanity, and joy in the miracle of life. He recognizes that Alyosha must not seek refuge from the world and from his own nature within the walls of the monastery, so he encourages his young friend to venture out and confront life. Most critics agree that Zosima is a mouthpiece for Dostoevsky's religious views.

Two female characters play significant roles in *The Brothers Karamazov,* though neither is considered to be among Dostoevsky's best creations. **Grushenka** is the woman loved by both Karamazov and Dmitri. She embodies a primitive femininity in her warm earthiness, and she is also cunning and perceptive. She can be loyal and affectionate or spiteful and malicious, and she is an independent woman who follows her own impulses. It is suggested that Grushenka has found a kind of mission or direction by the end of the novel, when she pledges her love to Dmitri and faithfully follows him to Siberia. **Katerina Ivanovna** or **Katya** is a different kind of person altogether, and not just because she comes from an aristocratic, socially respectable background. Prone to theatrical dramatization, Katerina is inherently confused about her own feelings; although she probably loves Ivan she is carried away by the idea of faithfulness to Dmitri, who helped her out of a crisis. Her sentimental declaration of undying love for Dmitri after she has betrayed him in court by producing the incriminating letter is obviously false and typifies her inability to perceive reality clearly.

Other notable minor characters in *The Brothers Karamazov* include Karamazov's longtime servant **Grigory,** charged with the care of his employer's sons. Dmitri derides the ever-loyal Grigory as "faithful to my father as seven hundred poodles." **Kolya Krassotkin,** an appealing schoolboy befriended by Alyosha, is often described as a particularly successful portrait; Richard Curle calls him "one of the most delightful, human boys in literature." Kolya is the outwardly disdainful and conceited but inwardly sensitive leader of a group of boys, and he seems to represent a glimmer of hope for the future of humanity. **Rakitin,** an unscrupulous and smug theological student, has been characterized as the kind of Russian radical Dostoevsky found distasteful. He resembles Ivan in his rationalistic outlook but is essentially shallow. **Peter Miusev** is a Europeanized liberal who likes to imply that he participated directly in a Paris uprising; his impersonal treatment of Dmitri, whose care he undertakes, reveals his actual lack of humanitarian values.

Further Reading

Blackmur, R.P. "'Crime and Punishment': A Study of Dostoevsky's Novel." *The Chimera* I, No. 3 (Winter 1943): 7-29.

Curle, Richard. *Characters of Dostoevsky*. New York: Russell & Russell, 1966.

Holquist, Michael. *Dostoevsky and the Novel*. Princeton: Princeton University Press, 1977.

Jackson, Robert Louis. *The Art of Dostoevsky: Deliriums and Nocturnes*. Princeton: Princeton University Press, 1981.

Jones, Malcolm V. and Garth M. Terry, eds. *New Essays on Dostoevsky*. Cambridge: Cambridge University Press, 1983.

Leatherbarrow, William J. *Fedor Dostoevsky*. Boston: Twayne, 1981.

Murry, J. Middleton. *Fyodor Dostoevsky: A Critical Study*. Martin Secker, 1916.

Nineteenth-Century Literature Criticism, Vols. 2, 7, 21. Detroit: Gale.

Peace, Richard. *Dostoevsky: An Examination of the Major Novels*. Cambridge: Cambridge at the University Press, 1971.

Pisarev, D.I. ''A Contemporary View'' (1867). In *Crime and Punishment and the Critics*, edited and translated by Edward Wasiolek. Belmont, Calif.: Wadsworth, 1969.

Rahv, Philip. ''Dostoevsky in 'Crime and Punishment.''' *Partisan Review* XXVII, No. 3 (Summer 1960): 393-425.

Short Story Criticism, Vol. 2. Detroit: Gale Research.

Yarmolinsky, Avrahm. *Dostoevsky: His Life and Art*, 2nd ed. New Jersey: S.G. Philips, 1965.

Alexandre Dumas (fils)
1824-1895
French dramatist, novelist, poet, and essayist.

Camille; or, The Fate of a Coquette (*La dame aux camélias*; drama, 1852)

Plot: Marguerite Gautier (called Camille because her favorite flower is the white, lightly scented camellia) is a beautiful courtesan (a prostitute with wealthy, prestigious clients) who was once a seamstress; she is now part of the Parisian high-society life. Count Arthur de Varville is in love with her and offers to pay off her substantial gambling debts if she will become his mistress, but she resists his advances. At the home of her friend Prudence, a former courtesan and now a milliner, she meets a young man named Armand Duval. Secretly enamored of Marguerite for two years, he now openly declares his love for her. Though Armand is poor and Marguerite is accustomed to material comforts, she eventually returns the love of the ardent young man. Because Marguerite suffers from a persistent cough and needs rest, the two travel to the countryside, then decide to live there permanently. They move into a cottage and are happy for a short time. Then Armand's father visits Marguerite and pleads with her to end her relationship with his son; he claims that the impending marriage of Armand's sister is threatened by their scandalous affair. Although she loves Armand passionately, Marguerite decides to comply with Monsieur Duval's wishes. She writes Armand a letter claiming that she has tired of their life together and is returning to Count de Varville in Paris. Heartbroken, Armand leaves France.

Marguerite resumes her former life, playing cards with friends and attending the opera, and she is often seen in the company of the count. But her cough has worsened and it appears that she will soon die; she still hopes to see Armand again. She does meet him at the home of her friend Olympe, where he insults both the count and Marguerite, angrily throwing a handful of gold coins at Marguerite, asserting that these are all that she values. De Varville challenges Armand to a duel; the count is wounded, and Armand leaves Paris again. Meanwhile, Monsieur Duval writes to Marguerite, praising her goodness and nobility and promising to reveal to his son the true circumstances of her sacrifice. When Armand learns the reason for Marguerite's deception, he rushes to her side. Now near death and living in a dismal apartment, she is attended only by her maid Nanine and her friend Prudence. Armand declares his eternal love for Marguerite, who claims that she can die peacefully knowing that her sacrifice was worthwhile. She dies in Armand's arms.

Characters: One of the most influential French dramas of the nineteenth century, *Camille* was based on Dumas's popular and controversial 1848 novel by the same name. The plays of the early nineteenth century had been dominated by complex, intriguing, artificial plots devised purely for entertainment, but Dumas's work featured an unusually realistic emphasis on social problems and issues. Dismayed by the decadence of French society, Dumas viewed prostitution and adultery as threats to the traditional family structure. He sought to expose and condemn immorality through his dramas. While not as overtly moralistic as his later works, *Camille* has been faulted for its sentimentality and weak dramatic construction. Nevertheless, audiences continue to respond favorably to this tragic love story (which also provided the basis of Giuseppe Verdi's 1853 opera *La Traviata*).

The role of the beautiful courtesan **Marguerite Gautier** is often cited as one of the most coveted in the theater; Camille has been played memorably by such actresses as Sarah Bernhardt and Greta Garbo. Dumas is said to have modeled Marguerite after a Marie Duplessis, a courtesan he had loved passionately as a young man (also a victim of tuberculosis, she had died at twenty-three). [The author's sympathy for women might also be linked to the fact that his own mother, a seamstress like Marguerite, was not married to his father, novelist Alexandre Dumas *père*; she fought a bitter and unsuccessful battle for custody of her son.] Marguerite's beauty and sensitivity are symbolized by the faintly scented camellia that constantly adorns her dress; all other flowers make her ill. She has been characterized as the epitome of the stereotypical prostitute with a "heart of gold," for she is inherently good, sincere, warm, intelligent, and honest. She seems to have accepted her way of life and makes no excuses for it, and she hesitates to give up material pleasures and the security they afford when the virtually penniless Armand offers his love, but she rejects her old life and gladly gives up many of her possessions in order to support herself and her lover. Ultimately, she relinquishes her claim to Armand in order to save his family's honor and also to enhance his future. On her deathbed, she maintains that this was the right course, claiming in the much-celebrated, extremely emotional final scene, "I lived for love, and I shall die for it." Critics have argued over what Dumas intended by the final scene. Some claim that the ending is in keeping with the romantic notion of the rehabilitated prostitute and that Dumas is excusing Marguerite for her immorality, but most contend that her death signifies the triumph of traditional morality.

Armand Duval is the tender, initially timid young man who loves Marguerite for two years, learning what he can about her from her friends and acquaintances, before revealing his feelings to her. An ardent and devoted lover, he gains Marguerite's respect and regard by treating her well. Though impetuous and unreasonably jealous, he shows his sincerity by his willingness to forego the approval of society and of his family for her sake. Armand's father, **Monsieur Duval,** represents bourgeois morality and the conventional family structure. Other dramas of the period portrayed such figures as ridiculous for adhering to convention, but Dumas echoes Duval's disapproval of his son's alliance. Duval recognizes that

Marguerite sacrifices her own happiness for Armand's sake, and he does feel genuine sympathy for her.

Marguerite's friends and acquaintances include **Count Arthur de Varville,** a young dandy who repeatedly offers to make Marguerite his mistress and submits placidly to her rejections; his patience is finally rewarded when she leaves Armand and returns to Paris. The wealthy, self-confident, aristocratic count provides a strong contrast to the more timid, unsophisticated Armand. **Prudence,** a former courtesan now too old and faded to ply her trade, becomes a milliner. She attaches herself to Marguerite and procures potential lovers for her young friend; it is through Prudence that Marguerite and Armand meet. Her lonely and harsh existence illustrates Dumas's belief that prostitutes must eventually meet cruel fates. **Olympe** is another courtesan who lives a life of temporal pleasures and materialism; it is at her home that Armand insults both his former lover and the Count de Varville. **Monsieur Saint-Gaudens** is another denizen of Parisian high society: a robust old man with a good sense of humor who enjoys life immensely, he provides a contrast to the desperate Prudence, who is unable to grow old gracefully. **Nicholette and Gustave** are the young couple whose happy marriage provides a conventional, respectable foil to the illicit union of Marguerite and Armand. Marguerite's faithful maid **Nanine** remains by her side to the end.

Further Reading

Clark, Roger J. B., ed. Introduction to *La dame aux camélias,* by Alexandre Dumas (fils), pp. 7-48. London: Oxford University Press, 1972.

Maurois, André. *The Titans: A Three-Generation Biography of the Dumas,* translated by Gerard Hopkins. New York: Harper & Brothers, 1957.

Nineteenth-Century Literature Criticism, Vol. 9. Detroit: Gale.

Smith, Hugh Allison, and Robert Bell Michell, eds. Introduction to *La dame aux camélias,* by Alexandre Dumas (fils), pp. iii-xii. New York: Oxford University Press, 1924.

Van de Velde, M.S. "Alexandre Dumas fils and His Plays." *Fortnightly Review* LVIII, No. CCCXLIX (January 1896): 94-103.

Alexandre Dumas (père)

1802-1870

French novelist, dramatist, short story writer, memoirist, historian, essayist, and travel sketch writer.

The Three Musketeers *(Les trois mousquetaires;* novel, 1844)

Plot: The novel takes place in 1625. Young D'Artagnon, a native of the Gascony region of France, is on his way to Paris with the intention of joining the Musketeers of the Guard, who serve King Louis XIII. At an inn in the town of Meung-sur-Loire, D'Artagnon confronts a stranger he thinks is laughing at his pony. The stranger has a scar across his face and is accompanied by a beautiful young woman. Soon after his arrival in Paris, D'Artagnon meets three celebrated musketeers, Athos, Porthos, and Aramis, and challenges each of them to a duel. Their match is interrupted, however, to fight off the guards of Cardinal Richelieu, a powerful government official who is despised by the king. D'Artagnon earns the musketeers' admiration with his bravery and becomes their trusted friend. He must serve a period of apprenticeship in a lesser company before being made a musketeer. Meanwhile he learns a little about his new friends: Athos appears to be a nobleman but is very taciturn and apparently uninterested in women, while Porthos brags about his many amorous conquests, and Aramis claims that he will soon enter a monastery. The four friends have a chance to earn some much-needed money when D'Artagnon's landlord Bonancieux offers him a reward to rescue his wife, Constance, who has been abducted by Richelieu's men because she is thought to have information about the queen's affair with England's Duke of Buckingham. Constance manages to escape and return to her home; when the cardinal's guards attempt to recapture her, D'Artagnon chases them away. He has fallen in love with Constance, but she does not encourage him. When Richelieu learns that the queen has given her lover a set of diamond studs that were originally given to her by the king, he devises a plan to trap the queen: he persuades the king to host a party at which the queen will be pressured to wear the studs. Then Richelieu orders "Milady" or Lady de Winter, the mysterious woman whom D'Artagnon had seen in Meung with the stranger, to go to London and steal two of the studs from Buckingham to be used as proof of the queen's infidelity. Constance overhears the cardinal's plot and elicits D'Artagnon's help to prevent its execution; eager to please his beloved and to help the queen, he agrees to the task. He and the three Musketeers start for London, but along the way they are attacked by the cardinal's henchman. Only D'Artagnon is unwounded and able to escape; he retrieves the studs and returns to Paris, thereby earning the queen's gratitude.

Constance is again seized by the cardinal's agents (including the one D'Artagnon had seen in Meung) and thrown in prison. D'Artagnon and the three musketeers try to rescue her; they spot and follow a woman D'Artagnon recognizes as the one who was with the man he saw at Meung. When they overtake her coach, they learn that she is Lady de Winter. D'Artagnon goes to her room one night and pretends to be her lover de Wardes; she gives him a sapphire ring that Athos later identifies as one he had given to his wife, whom he had deserted when he learned—by discovering a fleur-de-lis tattoo on her shoulder—that she was a former criminal. Thus Athos suspects that Lady de Winter may be his wife, whom he had presumed was dead. D'Artagnon learns that the widowed Lady de Winter is heir to the fortune of her brother-in-law, Lord de Winter, and that she is a spy for Cardinal Richelieu. When he confronts her and admits having posed as de Warde during their earlier liaison, she reacts violently, and in the scuffle that follows her dress shifts off her shoulder, exposing the telltale fleur-de-lis, thus confirming that she is indeed Athos's wife.

The four friends now prepare to fight at the siege of La Rochelle, an important battle in the war between England and France. Richelieu invites D'Artagnon to join his own guards but he refuses. The musketeers learn that Richelieu wants to send Lady de Winter to England to force Buckingham to end the war by threatening to expose his love affair with the queen. In exchange, the cardinal agrees to have the lady's two enemies, Constance and D'Artagnon, killed, and he guarantees her safe passage. Athos soon reveals himself to the terrified Lady de Winter as her former husband, Count de la Fere (whom she thought was dead) and he orders her to leave France. At La Rochelle, D'Artagnon and his three friends perform with remarkable courage and gain the cardinal's respect; he makes D'Artagnon a musketeer. Having been warned about his sister-in-law's real identity, Lord de Winter has Lady de Winter imprisoned when she arrives in England. She is able to trick her jailer into releasing her and then persuades him to stab Buckingham to death. Lady de Winter goes to the French convent where she has had Constance imprisoned and manages to poison her and flee before the musketeers arrive, too late to save Constance. Eventually they do capture Lady de Winter, however, and with Lord de Winter the musketeers try, condemn, and execute her.

Returning to La Rochelle, D'Artagnon is arrested for treason by the stranger he had met at Meung, who is now identified as the Chevalier de Rochefort, the cardinal's trusted associate. D'Artagnon manages to turn the tables on his accusers, however, by showing that the woman who had charged him with treason—Lady de Winter—was herself a criminal and is now dead. Impressed with D'Artagnon's savvy and valor, the cardinal makes him an officer in the musketeers. After the French victory at La Rochelle, the four friends part; after a few more years of military service, Athos goes back to his estate, Porthos marries a wealthy widow, Aramis enters a monastery, and D'Artagnon gains fame through his military career (recounted in the two sequels to *The Three Musketeers*), eventually befriending even his old enemy, the Chevalier de Rochefort.

Characters: This much-loved novel of adventure, romance, and intrigue demonstrates Dumas's considerable storytelling ability with its fast-paced and entertaining plot. Modeled after Gatien de Courtilz de Sandras's *Memoires de Monsieur d'Artagnon,* the novel features a colorful array of historically based characters who, while not depicted with much psychological penetration, capture and maintain the reader's interest.

Young **D'Artagnon** is a native of Gascony, a region of France whose natives are traditionally known for their independence and adventurousness. Described as "Don Quixote at eighteen," D'Artagnon is eager for excitement and ready to fight, when he meets the three valorous musketeers. He impresses them with his bravery and they welcome him into their comradeship, an important step in his eventual formal entry into their elite military unit. Although Dumas based D'Artagnon on a real person, he embellished the character's attributes, making him an idealistic youth longing to defend noble causes, loyal to friends, lovers, and country. French critic Hippolyte Parigot describes D'Artagnon and his three friends as representing the "four cardinal points of French civilization" and sees in D'Artagnon "fierce determination." A rash but shrewd and ambitious swashbuckler, he earns his way not only into the ranks of the musketeers but into the company of literature's most memorable and romantic heroes.

The three musketeers are equally memorable; nineteenth-century commentator Margaret Oliphant called them "as delightfully real as they are impossible." Each is based on an actual person, but Dumas used history as a springboard from which he propelled his narrative into the delightful realm of fancy. The three combine chivalry and valor with somewhat coarse habits and a susceptibility to sexual temptation; although they adhere to a strict code of honor, their own behavior is more pragmatic. They are courageous, energetic, resourceful, and appreciative of each other; the more mundane concerns of existence do not seem to concern them. **Athos,** whose real name is the **Count de la Fere,** has been identified as a stereotypical melancholy aristocrat. He maintains an inherently noble but calm, apparently indifferent demeanor. All of the musketeers are defined by their relations with women, and Athos's history with the other sex has been tragic—his discovery that his wife was a heinous criminal spoiled his desire for female companionship. The physically powerful, boastful, not particularly intelligent **Porthos** is described by Parigot as embodying a "somewhat vainglorious strength." Despite his pomposity, Porthos is an engaging, convivial character whose relations with women are lighthearted; his pleasant fate is to marry the rich widow, **Madame Coquenard. Aramis,** who is actually the **Chevalier d'Herblay,** exudes an "elegance, at once delicate and gay," according to Parigot. Always clothed in black, he is devious and secretive, carrying with him a mysterious suggestion of hidden love affairs; he finally makes good on his promise to enter a monastery.

Cardinal Richelieu, a chief minister in the court of **Louis the XIII,** is a very powerful figure whose monarch hates and fears him. His antagonism toward the queen is rooted in romantic jealousy because she prefers his political enemy, the **Duke of Buckingham;** there is some evidence that the actual Richelieu was interested in **Anne of Austria.** The unhappy queen's affair with the English nobleman is also based in reality, even down to the matter of the diamond studs. The handsome **Duke of Buckingham** was, indeed, a favorite of King Charles I and his assassination closely resembled that portrayed in *The Three Musketeers.*

The beautiful, blonde **Milady** or **Lady de Winter** (who is also known in the story as the **Countess de la Fere** and **Charlotte Beckson**) is a mysterious, enigmatic figure who exemplifies the classic *femme fatale*. Calculating and treacherous, she stops at nothing to gain her ends. Before marrying the Count de la Fere (Athos) she seduced a priest and was a convicted thief, and she proves to be a murderer as well. She attained her title by marrying an English aristocrat, whom she subsequently killed, and she now serves as Richelieu's agent. Although Lady de Winter is modeled after an actual person, Dumas invented her past; the attempt to steal the diamond studs from Buckingham was actually attributed to a second historical figure, the duke's former mistress, Lady Carlisle.

Although the other characters in the novel are only sketchily portrayed, all have integral roles in the plot. **Lord de Winter** is Lady de Winter's brother-in-law; he is able to avenge his brother's death when he and the musketeers put Lady de Winter on trial and have her beheaded by the **Executioner of Lille**—who happens to be the brother of the priest she seduced. **John Felton** is the Puritan jailer who believes Lady de Winter's claim that she was brutally raped by Buckingham and who is subsequently tricked into murdering him; Buckingham's actual assassin was, indeed, named John Felton. **Constance Bonancieux** is the wife of D'Artagnon's landlord and a lady-in-waiting to the queen. Charming and loyal, she serves as a foil to the villainous woman who eventually murders her. Dumas is said to have combined aspects of two members of the real Queen Anne's entourage, Mesdames de Vernet and du Fargis, to create the character of Constance. **De Treville** is the captain of the musketeers. The **Chevalier de Rochefort** is the Cardinal's right-hand man and trusted agent. Each of the musketeers' servants reflects his own prominent quality: D'Artagnon's **Planchet** is shrewd and plucky, Athos's **Grimaud** is very reserved, Porthos's **Musqueton** is handsome, and Aramis's **Bazin** is religious.

The Count of Monte-Cristo (*Le comte de Monte-Cristo;* novel, 1845)

Plot: As the story begins, the young French sailor Edmond Dantès arrives in the harbor of Marseilles at the helm of the *Pharaon,* having taken over when the captain died at sea. The ship's owner, Monsieur Morel, promises to promote Dantès to captain, and he goes joyfully to see his fiancée Mercédès. Through the plotting of two jealous men, however—Monsieur Danglars, who resents Dantès's promotion, and Fernand Mondego, who wishes to marry Mercédès—Dantès is falsely accused of conspiring with the outlawed followers of Napoleon. Dantès's greedy neighbor Caderousse knows about the plot but does not interfere. Deputy prosecutor Monsieur Villefort, eager to hide his own traitorous connections, has Dantès secretly locked away in the dungeon-like Chateau d'If. During the fourteen years Dantès spends there, he befriends a fellow prisoner, the Abbé Faria, who helps him unravel the plot that led to his arrest. Just before dying, the Abbé tells him about a fabulous treasure of gold and jewels hidden on the island of Monte-Cristo. By sewing himself into the burial sack in which his dead friend is to be dumped into the sea, Dantès escapes from the prison and is eventually picked up by a gang of smugglers. He remains with them until their ship comes near the island of Monte-Cristo. Dantès retrieves the treasure and returns to France. Caderousse tells him that Villefort is now attorney general, Danglars a wealthy banker, and Mondego has married Mercédès and become rich and celebrated after fighting in the Greek Revolution; Dantès gives Caderousse a diamond in exchange for this information. He also discovers that Monsieur Morrel, the shipping merchant who had taught him his trade and who had once helped his father, is near bankruptcy, so he anonymously saves his old friend's business.

Dantès now calls himself the Count of Monte-Cristo and participates in Parisian high society. He takes as his companion Haidée, the beautiful and mysterious young woman he had rescued from slavery during his travels. But all the while he is plotting revenge upon those who caused his long and unjust imprisonment. He has already inflamed Caderousse's greed by giving him the diamond, and eventually the tailor is killed when he is discovered attempting to rob Monte-Cristo's home; just before he dies, he learns that the count is actually Edmond Dantès. Monte-Cristo pretends friendship with Danglars while secretly sabotaging his business, and he exposes how Fernand Mondego—now the Count de Morcerf—acquired his wealth (during the Greek revolution of 1823, he betrayed the monarch Pasha Ali, who is also Haidée's father). In order to defend his father's reputation, Morcerf's son, Albert, challenges Monte-Cristo to a duel, but Mercédès begs him to spare her son's life, and the duel ends bloodlessly. Mercédès and Albert then leave Paris, and Morcerf commits suicide. Having ingratiated himself with Villefort's wife, the count convinces her that she should try to acquire the fortune of her stepdaughter, Valentine; he does not realize that Maximilian Morrel, his old friend's son, is in love with the girl. In pursuit of her goal, Madame Villefort poisons Valentine and her grandparents. The count has by now learned of Maximilian's love for the young girl and vows to help him achieve happiness. When Villefort informs his wife that he knows what she has done and plans to expose her, she kills herself and her young son, Edoard, whose interests she had been trying to promote. After learning Monte-Cristo's real identity, Villefort goes insane. Meanwhile, Danglars—whose daughter Eugénie runs away to become a singer—goes bankrupt and leaves France. Finally, Monte-Cristo reveals to Maximilian that he has rescued the comatose Valentine, and the two are reunited on the count's island. After handing over his fortune to the young couple, the count sails away with Haidée and is never heard from again.

Characters: The novel was inspired by the true story, recorded in the *Memoires tires des archives de la police de Paris,* of a man named François Picaud who obtained sudden wealth and then sought revenge against those who had wronged him. While its characters are notably static (they do not change or develop during the course of the story), *The Count of Monte-Cristo* is considered a well-told and engaging story that continues to entertain readers.

Critic Richard S. Stowe describes **Edmond Dantès,** who becomes the **Count of Monte-Cristo,** as "a young man of promise transformed by his experience into a Promethean superman." As the book opens, he is a dutiful, capable nineteen-year-old who has won his colleagues' respect as well as his fiancée's love; he looks forward to his future with joy, never anticipating that his rivals are plotting his downfall. Desolated and confused during his imprisonment, Dantès does not even understand what has happened to him until Abbé Farias is able to piece together an explanation. After escaping from prison and retrieving the fortune, he begins to cultivate a reputation for power, great wealth, and mystery—all qualities that are illustrated during the vivid episode when Franz d'Épinay visits Monte-Cristo's lair on the island from which he took his name. When Monte-Cristo begins to exact his vengeance on his enemies, he does so by indirect methods, allowing them to bring about their own downfalls through their various weaknesses. Several scholars contend that Dumas's portrayal of the protagonist is more effective during the first half of the book, when he is vulnerable and bewildered, than during the second half, when he sets out on a determined course toward revenge; while Edmond Dantès is a sympathetic figure, Monte-Cristo behaves in an excessively petty, cruel, and spiteful manner, which makes him less credible. Through the count's actions, innocent people are hurt (Edouard Villefort dies and Valentine nearly does), and he realizes the potential for evil and harm that lies in his power. His final advice to Maximilian and Valentine to "Wait and hope!" suggests that, having accomplished what he set out to do, he relinquishes his power to a higher force.

Monte-Cristo's four enemies are flatly portrayed figures exemplifying the greed and ambition of both the middle class and the aristocracy. **Gaspard Caderousse** is a tailor and innkeeper whose selfishness causes him to conceal his knowledge of the plot against Dantès. A grasping, avaricious alcoholic, he allows Dantès's father to starve nearly to death for owing Caderousse money. Monte-Cristo knows that he can set the tailor's self-destruction in motion by inflaming his greed with a valuable gem. Caderousse is killed while burglarizing Monte-Cristo's house. **Monsieur Danglars** works for Morrel as the shipowner's accountant, but he covets Dantès's promotion to captain, so he conspires with Mondego to implicate Dantès in treason. While Dantès languishes in jail, Danglars makes his fortune fighting in the war with Spain and marries two wives, one rich and one aristocratic; he eventually becomes a baron and a millionaire banker. His wealth, however, dwindles through Monte-Cristo's covert manipulations, and even his hopes of acquiring money by marrying his daughter, **Eugénie Danglars,** to a rich man are dashed when she runs away with her governess, **Louise D'Armilly,** to become a performer. Danglars is left penniless and finally must flee from France.

Fernand Mondego, later the **Count de Morcerf,** is a Catalan fisherman who becomes wealthy while fighting in the Greek Revolution, when he betrays the **Pasha of Janina** (with whom the French were allied) to the enemy and sells the Pasha's daughter, **Haidée** into slavery. When his past is exposed, his wife and son desert him and he commits suicide. **Viscount Albert de Morcerf** initially befriends the Count of Monte-Cristo when the count rescues him from robbers in Rome. When the count exposes his father's treachery, he is angry at first, but when his mother explains the situation to him, he apologizes to Monte-Cristo, thereby proving that he has more integrity than his father. **Mercédès,** who marries the conniving Fernand Mondego after Dantès suddenly disappears, is a beautiful young Catalan girl at the beginning of the story; she recognizes that Monte-Cristo is Dantès as soon as he reappears after his imprisonment, and she appeals to him to spare her son's life.

Gerard de Villefort is the deputy prosecutor before whom Dantès is brought. He initially sympathizes with the young man, but when he sees that the letter Dantès innocently carries back to France from the Napoleonists at Elba (the island off the coast of Italy to which Napoleon was exiled in 1814) is addressed to his own father, he fears for his position. Thus he allows Dantès to be imprisoned in the Chateau d'If. Then he warns the king of the plot disclosed in the letter, thereby advancing his own career. It is also revealed that he had an affair years earlier with **Madame Hermine Danglars** and she became pregnant; the baby was left to die but, unknown to Villefort, was rescued. With Monte-Cristo's encouragement, **Héloïse de Villefort,** the wife of Gerard de Villefort, begins to covet her stepdaughter Valentine's fortune for her own son, the spoiled and irresponsible **Edouard de Villefort,** and poisons the girl as well as her wealthy grandparents, the **Marquis and Marchioness de Saint-Méran.** Villefort loses his sanity after his wife kills herself and their son rather than face prosecution. It is through the near-death of **Valentine de Villefort,** the beloved of Maximilian Morrel, that Monte-Cristo is forced to wonder if perhaps he has gone too far in his quest for revenge; he is able to revive her. Villefort's elderly father, **Noirtier de Villefort,** is completely paralyzed and must use his eyes to communicate; their intensity reflects his courage and force of character. He is a committed Bonapartist whose political views contrast with those of his royalist son.

Monsieur Morrel, the middle-class merchant and shipowner who employs the young Dantès and makes him captain of the *Pharaon,* is a loyal friend who embodies a natural nobility missing in the novel's aristocratic characters. He is near suicide from desperation over his financial woes, but Monte-Cristo secretly pays his debts and provides him with a new, cargo-loaded ship to replace the lost *Pharaon.* The young soldier **Maximilian Morrel** is also portrayed positively in his loyalty to the count and selfless love for Valentine. The count tests that love by offering his young friend his entire fortune if he will do without Valentine; Maximilian refuses, which proves his virtue and gets him Monte-Cristo's fortune after all, while the count sails off into obscurity.

Abbé Faria is one of the few representatives of morality in the book. Based on an actual Italian cleric who played a part in the experiences of François Picaud, the abbé is a kind, generous, and learned man who shares all that he has with Dantès. In teaching him history, mathematics, chemistry, languages, and other subjects, he gives Dantès a wealth of knowledge that complements the material riches he also bestows on his friend. By discerning what must have happened to lead to Dantès's imprisonment, he also awakens him to a knowledge of evil that influences his later dedication to achieving revenge against his enemies.

Other characters in the novel include **Benedetto,** the unfortunate illegitimate child of Villefort and Madame Danglars, hired by Monte-Cristo to pose as **Count Andrea Cavalcanti,** who is briefly betrothed to Eugénie Danglars and who eventually murders Caderousse; **Franz d'Épinay,** a friend of Albert de Morcerf who visits the tiny island of Monte-Cristo during a hunting expedition (much as Dumas once did, an experience that gave him the idea for the novel) and is invited into the count's fantastic underground cavern, reminiscent of scenes from such exotic oriental tales as "Ali Baba and the Forty Thieves." **Luigi Vampa** is the notorious Italian bandit who kidnaps Albert de Morcerf in the hope of collecting a generous ransom; he is also a friend of Monte-Cristo, who easily secures Albert's release.

Further Reading

Hemmings, F. W. J. *Alexandre Dumas: The King of Romance.* New York: Charles Scribner's Sons, 1979.

Nineteenth-Century Literature Criticism, Vol. 11. Detroit: Gale.

Oliphant, Margaret. "Alexandre Dumas." *Blackwood's Edinburgh Magazine* CXIV, No. DCXCIII (July 1873): 111-30.

Parigot, Hippolyte. Extract in *The Titans: A Three-Generation Biography of the Dumas,* by Andre Maurois, translated by Gerard Hopkins, p. 179. New York: Harper & Brothers, 1957.

Schopp, Claude. *Alexandre Dumas: Genius of Life.* New York: Franklin Watts, 1988.

Maria Edgeworth
1767-1849
Anglo-Irish novelist, short story writer, dramatist, and essayist.

Castle Rackrent: An Hiberian Tale (novel, 1800)

Plot: The story is narrated by Thady Quirk, faithful servant to several generations of the family at Castle Rackrent in Ireland. After the death of Thady's first master, the jovial but hard-drinking Sir Patrick, the estate is inherited by the mean and stingy Sir Murtagh and his penny-pinching wife. During a heated argument with his wife, Sir Murtagh dies of a burst blood vessel, and Lady Murtagh strips the estate of everything valuable and moves to London. Her husband's younger brother, Sir Kit Rackrent, now comes into possession of the property. A rakish, extravagant man, he soon finds that the estate is near ruin and goes to London to find a rich wife whose fortune will save it. He marries a Jewish heiress named Jessica and brings her home, but she refuses to relinquish her valuable jewels and also objects to the presence of pork on the table. Eventually Sir Kit locks Lady Jessica in her room, where she languishes for seven years. When she becomes gravely ill and seems near death, many women in the neighborhood hope to become Sir Kit's next wife. The resulting romantic maneuvers lead to a duel, and Sir Kit is killed, after which Lady Jessica recovers quickly from her illness and returns to London.

The next master of Castle Rackrent is Sir Condy (Connally), a kind and generous master to the servants but a spendthrift who soon has the estate in more financial trouble than ever. He befriends a neighboring family, the Moneygawls; the youngest daughter, Isabella, develops an interest in Sir Condy but her family does not approve of the match. Meanwhile, Sir Condy has fallen in love with Thady's grandniece Judy. He tosses a coin to determine whether Isabella or Judy should become his bride; Isabella wins and the two soon elope. Sir Condy hopes Isabella will bring some money to the marriage, but her family disinherits her for defying their wishes. She and Sir Condy live an extravagant lifestyle despite the general disintegration of the estate and the distressed conditions endured by the servants and tenants. Sir Condy manages to get himself elected to Parliament but is besieged by creditors. Thady's son, Jason, gains power over the estate by helping a neighbor buy up all of its debts; he subsequently begins to act superior toward everyone, including his own father. Isabella decides she can no longer cope with her husband's financial problems and returns to her family. Nevertheless Sir Condy reserves property for his wife in his will. Jason, however, persuades him to sell the land he has promised her and pay off his debts. He does so but leaves the guarantee of a yearly income for Isabella in the will.

While traveling back to her parents' home, Lady Isabella is involved in a carriage accident and is nearly killed. Jason convinces Sir Condy that she will surely die and therefore he should cash in the income he has reserved for her. Sir Condy complies; later, while attempting to drown his sorrows in drink, he dies of a seizure brought on by excessive alcohol consumption. After his death, Jason and Lady Isabella fight in court over the estate. As the novel closes, Thady is not sure how the suit will be resolved.

Characters: The novel satirizes the Irish ruling class of the late-eighteenth and early-nineteenth centuries and illuminates Ireland's common people as well. Considered one of the first regional novels ever written, *Castle Rackrent* depicts Irish speech and mannerisms faithfully and is also innovative in its focus on several generations of one family. A novel of manners intended, as stated in the author's preface, to educate the English about the Irish, *Castle Rackrent* influenced such diverse later writers as Sir Walter Scott, William Makepeace Thackeray, Ivan Turgenev, and James Fenimore Cooper.

Edgeworth apparently modeled the novel's narrator, **Thady Quirk,** after her father's steward, John Langan, whom she had been known to mimic quite accurately. Thady is a loyal, steadfast employee who frequently professes his great pride in the family he serves. Yet the Rackrents' defects and reprehensible history are always evident, making Thady an early example of the unreliable narrator that became a popular literary device in the nineteenth century. Thady's blind partiality to the Rackrents is ironic in view of their real arrogance and irresponsibility. Speaking in an authentic Irish idiom that is one of the novel's distinguishing features, Thady creates an illusion of the Rackrents' noble history (which he shares with the young Sir Condy, thus contributing to his unrealistic outlook) and does not seem to realize that the family's position and privileges are based on money, not inherent worth or nobility. Despite Thady's partiality for the Rackrents, however, he reveals his practical side when his praise of various family members is directly connected with the material gain he receives from them. Some critics consider Thady a villain because he helps his son Jason bring about the Rackrents' downfall. Others view Thady as a passive participant who keeps silent when it will protect his own interests. While some scholars detect in Edgeworth's portrayal of Thady a somewhat superior attitude on her part that she encourages the reader to share, most praise her skillful characterization of the kind of lower class figure that had been portrayed with little depth in the fiction that preceded hers.

Thady's first employer is **Sir Patrick Rackrent** (his original name is **O'Shaughlin**). Friendly and jovial, he is a generous man who loves raucous parties and drinks great quantities of liquor. He dies after being toasted by the guests at one of his festive gatherings. When Sir Patrick's debtors swoop down on his hearse as his body is being transported through the streets, his gathered admirers react angrily; yet the scene foreshadows the financial instability that will continue to plague the family.

Sir Murtagh Rackrent is an entirely different kind of person: he is avaricious and stingy, winning few admirers among the servants and tenants who serve him. A tight-fisted lawyer, Sir Murtagh uses his knowledge of law to bilk others. He forces his tenants to comply with the exact letter of the law and provide him with "duty" food, labor, and other products so he can avoid paying for these things. **Lady Murtagh** is also a penny-pincher; she keeps her larder stocked with items she has acquired from the tenants at no cost to herself. The couple represents the destructiveness and greed of the Irish ruling class which, Edgeworth suggests, exacted a heavy toll on the lower classes obligated to support their aristocratic lifestyle. In fact, the allegorical name "Rackrent" refers directly to the exorbitant rents tenants were forced to pay.

Wild, carefree **Sir Kit Rackrent** is, like his predecessor Sir Patrick, a fun-loving rake who allows his estate to deteriorate through his extravagance. Although his warmth and friendliness make him popular with Thady and the other servants, Sir Kit shows his true lack of concern for them by leaving the management of the estate in the hands of an agent who is subservient to his employer but harsh to his subordinates. Sir Kit views the estate primarily as a source of income that allows him to entertain lavishly and gamble irresponsibly; meanwhile, his property is mortgaged to ambitious Jason Quirk. He dies in a duel brought on by his philandering. **Lady Jessica Rackrent** is a wealthy and uncompromising Jewish heiress whom Sir Patrick meets and marries in London. She proves intractable when asked to give up her diamond-encrusted gold cross (a contradictory possession in view of her religion) and is punished with seven years of confinement, imposed by her husband.

Sir Condy Rackrent is another good-natured spendthrift. He shares with Sir Patrick a view of himself as the quintessential Irish host, and his generosity makes him Thady's favorite of the three masters. He learned to gamble at Thady's knee and also listened raptly to the servant's stories of his family's greatness —both pastimes contribute to his downfall. Sir Condy professes to value honor and responsibility, in keeping with his supposedly noble heritage, but he buys his way into Parliament and later votes "against his conscience but very honorably." After horribly mismanaging his affairs, Sir Condy makes a gesture of connection with his celebrated relative Sir Patrick by staging the same whiskey-drinking feat his forebear was famous for—and the drink kills him. **Lady Isabella Rackrent** marries not for love but to spite her family. After joining enthusiastically in the recklessly lavish lifestyle that brings the estate ever closer to ruin, she flees from her husband and his problems. As the novel ends, her fate—whether she wins or loses possession of the remaining Rackrent property—is uncertain.

Jason Quirk is often said to be the villain of *Castle Rackrent,* for he rises to power by taking advantage of the weakness and irresponsibility of his father's longtime employers. As he points out to Thady, though, he tries to explain the estate's grave situation to Sir Condy and only becomes an opportunist after his warning has been ignored. Although Thady has always encouraged Jason to make his way forward in the world, he is disappointed when his son begins to treat him with scorn. Some critics have seen Jason as representative of a new, defiant middle class that was beginning to emerge in nineteenth-century Ireland. **Judy Quirk,** Thady's niece, is either eminently practical or a fortune-hunter: after her first husband's death, her uncle suggests that she marry Sir Condy, but she points out that it would make more sense to marry the acquisitive Jason.

Further Reading

Butler, Marilyn. *Maria Edgeworth: A Literary Biography.* Oxford: Oxford University Press, 1972.

Flanagan, Thomas. "Maria Edgeworth." In *The Irish Novelists: 1800-1850,* pp. 53-108. New York: Columbia University Press, 1958.

Harden, Elizabeth. *Maria Edgeworth.* Boston: Twayne, 1984.

Myers, M. "The Dilemmas of Gender as Double-Voiced Narrative; or, Maria Edgeworth Mothers the Bildungsroman." In *The Idea of the Novel in the Eighteenth Century,* edited by Robert W. Uphaus, pp. 67-96. East Lansing, Mich.: Colleagues Press, 1988.

Nineteenth-Century Literature Criticism, Vol. 1. Detroit: Gale.

George Eliot
1819-1880

English novelist, short story writer, essayist, poet, editor, and translator.

Adam Bede (novel, 1859)

Plot: The novel is set in the English village of Hayslope in 1799. The hardworking, honest young carpenter Adam Bede is respected by his neighbors, including Captain Arthur Donnithorne, the grandson of a wealthy local landowner. Adam's employer, the builder Jonathan Burge, hopes the young man will eventually become his partner and also marry his daughter Mary. Adam, however, is enamored of Hetty Sorrell, a pretty dairymaid and a niece of Mrs. Poyser, whose husband Martin manages the prosperous Hall Farm. For her part, Hetty fancies the handsome young captain. Adam's dissolute father, Mathias Bede, drowns while on his way home from the village tavern, and his devoted but querulous mother, Lisbeth, becomes even more dependent on her son. Adam's brother, Seth, is in love with a dedicated Methodist preacher named Dinah Morris (another of Mrs. Poyser's nieces), but she rejects his marriage proposal, claiming that her vocation makes marriage impossible. When Captain Donnithorne returns to Hayslope on leave from his army regiment, his grandfather hosts a festive party to celebrate his twenty-first birthday. Almost all of the villagers take part in the occasion, and Adam is invited to sit at Captain Donnithorne's table. Several weeks later he is returning home one night and sees Hetty Sorrel and Captain Donnithorne embracing; Hetty flees after hearing Adam's dog bark. Adam confronts Donnithorne, who claims to have stolen a kiss from the innocent girl; Adam angrily knocks him unconscious. Alarmed, Adam helps Donnithorne recover and then convinces him to write to Hetty and inform her that they must not meet again. Heartbroken at losing her lover, Hetty accepts Adam's subsequent marriage proposal. Adam, now a partner in Burge's business, decides to postpone the wedding until he can build some additional rooms onto his house. Some time later Hetty leaves Hayslope, claiming she is going to visit Dinah, who is preaching in the town of Snowfield. Hetty actually goes to find Donnithorne, but she learns that his regiment has been sent to Ireland. Now far from home and despairing, she wanders around until she is taken in by Sarah Stone, a widow in whose house Hetty gives birth to a child fathered by Donnithorne. The frightened and confused Hetty later leaves her baby in a forest and walks on, returning later—conscience-stricken—to find it gone. She is subsequently arrested, convicted of murder, and condemned to be hanged. Donnithorne learns of Hetty's situation when he returns to Hayslope for his grandfather's funeral. Dinah visits the strangely withdrawn, remote girl in prison and persuades her to explain what really happened: Hetty claims that she had not intended to kill her child and had almost killed herself instead. Just as Hetty is about to be executed, Donnithorne arrives with an official reprieve, and Hetty is instead sent to a penal colony in another country. She dies a few years later while traveling back to England; Donnithorne goes to live in Spain. While staying frequently with the Poysers, Dinah finds herself drawn to Adam but is still dedicated to her preaching. Although she returns for a short time to Snowfield, she and Adam eventually decide to marry and live happily thereafter in Hayslope.

Characters: Adam Bede, a detailed portrait of nineteenth-century English pastoral life, is thought to be based on the memories of the Warwickshire childhood of Mary Ann Evans, who wrote under the pseudonym George Eliot. *Adam Bede* influenced the development of the modern novel through its emphasis on both physical and psychological realism. Employing a narrative voice that ranges from objectivity to authorial asides to stream-of-consciousness description, Eliot renders both the novel's physical setting and its characters' inner conflicts and motivations with care and insight. In depicting the unforeseen changes that disrupt the serene life of a rural community, Eliot highlights the interconnectedness of its inhabitants and heightens the reader's sympathy for their plight.

The title character is a somewhat idealized figure: tall and muscular, **Adam Bede** is a dedicated and honest workman who is widely respected. In falling in love with Hetty Sorrell, however, Adam Bede reveals an inherent weakness. He neither recognize the pretty dairymaid's self-centeredness and lack of depth nor perceives that she does not return his affection. Thus when he comes upon the sight of Donnithorne and Hetty embracing, he can only assume that his aristocratic friend has overpowered the innocent girl and never suspects she is a willing participant in the encounter. Dutiful and morally upright himself, Adam expects the same of others; thus he reacts with little compassion to the indiscretions of his alcoholic father as well as to Donnithorne's behavior with Hetty and, later, to Hetty's arrest and trial. Many scholars have noted in Eliot's fiction her emphasis on developing compassion for others despite their flaws and weaknesses; Adam is one of several important characters in her novels who must learn this lesson. The scene in which Adam shares a meal of bread and wine with Hetty and Dinah before Hetty is to be hanged uses sacramental symbolism to represent the re-establishment of community and the healing power of sympathy. Adam finally faces and accepts the truth about Hetty.

Captain Arthur Donnithorne is an attractive, likeable young man who sees himself as playing a benevolent role in the community of Hayslope, where his birth has entitled him to a prominent position. Despite his good intentions, however, he brings harm not only to Hetty but to the community as a whole by setting in motion a tragic process that will change it permanently. He gives in to the temptation presented by pretty, pliant Hetty, who fantasizes that he will marry her. Although he considers himself a progressive man prepared to help enlighten the current social order, Arthur acts out the traditional story of the lord who seduces and betrays the lowly servant. Refusing to accept individual responsibility and to make difficult choices is repeatedly and clearly condemned in Eliot's work, and Donnithorne represents the novel's most flagrant example of this weakness. Returning to Hayslope in a jubilant mood of self-confidence and well-being, he is jolted back to reality by the news that Hetty has given birth to and apparently murdered his child and is now languishing in a jail cell awaiting execution. His view of himself as benevolent lord of all he surveys is now destroyed, and Arthur's only means of partially repairing the damage he has done is to obtain a reprieve for Hetty that will save her from the gallows. Many critics have described the last-minute reprieve as a markedly melodramatic touch that evokes the fiction of the romantic more than the modern period.

While some scholars characterize **Hetty Sorrell** as a somewhat flat character, others praise Eliot for her penetrating insight into the motives of this self-deluded young girl. Hetty is seventeen years old as the story opens. The blooming, kittenish quality of her appearance and manner is well established through the repeated use of such adjectives as "soft" and "round." But Hetty's nature is not entirely innocent; she is self-centered and vain and has developed a profoundly egotistical core, foreshadowed early in the story when Mrs. Poyser describes her as hard-hearted. Unmoved by the upright and worshipful Adam, Hetty is drawn instead to the handsome, wealthy, but essentially weak Donnithorne. Like her seducer, Hetty is subject to self-delusion, unrealistically imagining herself as the wife of a nobleman when in fact Donnithorne would never consider marrying her. The terror and bewilderment Hetty feels when, pregnant and abandoned, she wanders through an alien and unfriendly landscape for the first time in her life, are compellingly depicted. The cold reserve she presents to the world during her trial is a protective shell that is finally penetrated by Dinah, who visits Hetty in prison and offers her the healing touch of human contact and sympathy. Hetty's last-minute rescue from the gallows has been described as needlessly melodramatic, and her eventual death has been seen as conforming to the tradition of the "fallen woman," who must invariably pay for her sins with her life.

Dinah Morris is Hetty's cousin. A dedicated Methodist preacher, Dinah is firm and serious. Eliot was in her own youth an ardent evangelical Christian; though she later became an agnostic who maintained a Christian ethic, her knowledge of the religious ideals Dinah holds and her respect for her motives is obvious. A profoundly compassionate and unselfish person, Dinah is an outsider who maintains a strong sense of herself that is not dependent on the community's approval and allows her to act as a mediator when that community experiences a crisis. She extends friendship, warmth, and understanding to Hetty in prison, facilitating her confession and helping her achieve peace. Dinah's moral strength has been identified as the kind most prized by Eliot: she has renounced her own happiness to serve others. Her acknowledgment at the story's end of the claims of personal feelings when she decides to marry Adam may be seen as either a concession to the Victorian audience's desire for a happy ending or as Eliot's belief that individual love is as important as social responsibility.

Many other characters bring the community of Hayslope to life. Adam's mother, **Lisbeth Bede,** is devoted but cantankerous; jealous, argumentative, and self-pitying, she is somewhat comic despite the pain she causes her sons. Her husband, **Mathias Bede,** whose death occurs near the beginning of the novel, is an indolent alcoholic who was once a skilled carpenter; Adam's disgust for him provides an early indication of his need to develop compassion for others. **Seth Bede,** Adam's brother, is good and generous but also dreamy and inefficient. He shares Dinah's Methodist faith and wants to marry her, but accepts gracefully her later union with his brother.

While the Bede household is strictly ordered and somewhat antiseptic, that of the Poyser family is warm and energetic. **Mr. Poyser** is the capable manager of Hall Farm and a genial, understanding man who serves as a natural leader among the farmers and tradesmen of Hayslope. He is unshakably loyal to Adam and greatly resents the incident between Hetty and Donnithorne. **Mrs. Poyser** is often identified as one of Eliot's finest comic creations; bustling, efficient, and talkative, she is constantly inserting humorously sententious sayings into her everyday conversations. Though something of a meddler, Mrs. Poyser is loyal and generous, and her comic qualities are not overstated. The Poyser children include the very literal **Marty,** mama's-boy **Tommy,** and spoiled **Charlotte (Totty).**

Reverend Adolphus Irwine has been described as the kind of clergyman most admired and approved by Eliot: sympathetic and honorable though not particularly spiritual, he tries to help his parishioners in practical ways. With his genial, tolerant manner, he is portrayed as more effective in his role than a more dogmatic churchman might be. His mother, **Mrs. Irwine,** is a sophisticated elderly woman whose son dutifully venerates and cares for her. **Bartle Massey,** the local schoolmaster who tutors Adam in the evenings, is an intelligent man who tries to help members of the community achieve greater self-determination through education. His role as an outsider who lives—literally as well as figuratively—on the edge of town is similar to that of Dinah Morris: because his identity exists independently of the community, he can mediate when a crisis develops. For instance, he helps Adam confront and eventually recover from the despair and disillusionment brought on by Hetty's predicament.

Other notable characters in *Adam Bede* include Adam's employer, the builder **Jonathan Burge,** who is very fond of the young man and eventually makes him his partner despite his failure to marry his daughter, **Mary; Bess Cranage** (also called **Chad's Bess** because she is the daughter of blacksmith **Chad Cranage**), who loves fancy clothing and jewelry but is nevertheless periodically converted to the evangelical Methodism of which her father greatly disapproves; and parsimonious **Squire Donnithorne,** Arthur's grandfather and the novel's foremost representative of England's old landowning class.

The Mill on the Floss (novel, 1860)

Plot: Dorlcote Mill, owned by Edward Tulliver, is located on the Floss River near the village of St. Ogg's. Mrs. Tulliver's sisters, Aunt Glegg and Aunt Pullet, disapprove of her husband's ambitions, particularly his plans to educate his son, Tom, so that he can eventually outsmart the lawyers Mr. Tulliver hates. Tom is an honest though somewhat arrogant and intolerant boy who likes farming and the outdoors more than books, while his affectionate sister, Maggie, is sensitive, imaginative, and tomboyish. Her mother and aunts criticize her for her gypsyish ways, while her father indulges her. Tom is sent to study at a school run by Mr. Stelling, who finds him stubborn and ignorant. Soon another student arrives at the school: Philip Wakem, the son of Mr. Tulliver's enemy, the lawyer John Wakem. Though physically handicapped, Philip is highly intelligent and artistic; Tom views him with suspicion and muted hostility. While visiting her brother, Maggie meets and befriends the sensitive Philip, with whom she can discuss the literature and music that interest her. But when Mr. Tulliver becomes involved in a lawsuit and Mr. Wakem is the attorney for the opposition, Tom and Maggie are forbidden to associate with Philip. After losing the suit, Mr. Tulliver also loses all of his property, because he had previously borrowed money to repay a note on the mill held by Aunt Glegg and had used his household goods as collateral. Maggie and Tom have to leave school, and the family's possessions are auctioned off, much to the sorrow of Mrs. Tulliver. Mr. Tulliver subsequently suffers a stroke. Maggie and Tom refuse their aunts' offers of help, and Tom goes to work in a warehouse to try to relieve his family's distress; he makes Maggie promise never to see Philip again. Meanwhile, with the help of his old friend Bob Jakin, a shrewd traveling salesman, Tom begins making secret investments. Mr. Wakem buys the mill and employs the now-recovered Mr. Tulliver as his manager. Tulliver is chagrined with the arrangement but sees no alternative; he has Tom swear on the Bible, and in writing, that he will condemn the Wakems for the rest of his life. Against the wishes of her family, Maggie has been meeting Philip secretly; she demurs, however, when he asks her if she loves him. When Tom learns of their clandestine relationship, he again makes Maggie swear she will no longer see Philip, and he also tells Philip to stay away from his sister. Meanwhile, Tom tells his father he has nearly enough money accumulated to buy the mill back. Excited by this news, Tulliver attacks Wakem and has another stroke that eventually brings on his death.

Maggie becomes a governess. Several years later, while visiting her cousin Lucy Deane, she meets a charming young man named Stephen Guest. Although Stephen had planned to ask for Lucy's hand in marriage, he and Maggie become attracted to each other. At Lucy's home, Maggie also sees Philip, who happens to be a friend of Stephen; her brother again warns her that Philip is still their enemy. Both Stephen and Philip are in love with Maggie and want to marry her, but she refuses Stephen out of respect for Lucy—who does not suspect that her supposed suitor loves her friend—and Philip out of respect for her brother. Tom is finally able to buy the mill, and he orders Maggie to give up her governess position and return home. One day Stephen takes Maggie out in a boat and tries to persuade her to run away with him. She refuses. When they drift too far from shore, they are unable to return and have to spend the night together in the boat. Maggie tries to explain the situation later to her relatives but meets with stony disapproval. Tom wants nothing more to do with her, forbidding her to enter their home again though promising to send her money. Maggie and her mother now live alone together. Both Stephen and Philip write to Maggie, but she determines to remain single if choosing one or the other as her husband will cause pain to either Lucy or Tom. When a great flood occurs in St. Ogg's that autumn, Maggie ventures out in a boat to the mill to find Tom, who is trapped there. He manages to escape through a window into the boat, but the two are drowned when the rushing water dashes them against debris in the river.

Characters: Centered on the changing community of St. Ogg's, where an essentially rural, feudal way of life is becoming more urban and the middle class more dominant, the novel shows how and to what extent Maggie and Tom Tulliver internalize and are limited by the habits and values of their society. Not as picturesque as *Adam Bede, The Mill on the Floss* is more psychologically penetrating and meditative in its depiction of the main characters' quests for fulfillment and unity. The theme of interconnectedness between people that Eliot often stresses and the struggle of the individual against society are evident in Maggie's— and, to some extent, Tom's—attempt to find her way within the narrow course laid out for her by her family and community.

Eliot is often lauded for her portrayal of **Maggie Tulliver,** the novel's central figure. As a child, Maggie is a dreamy, impetuous tomboy whose dark skin and wayward nature give her a gypsyish quality. Although she is intelligent and imaginative, it is her decidedly unbookish brother Tom who is sent off to a prestigious school. Independent yet eager for love and approval, Maggie tries to stifle her own yearnings and mold herself to fit others' expectations, as when she promises Tom that she will no longer be the kind of person who would forget to feed his rabbits, or when she becomes unnaturally submissive and pious after her father's downfall. Although her feelings are strong, her will is relatively weak, and she seems unable to either accept or overcome the restrictions that bind her life. Drawn to Philip Wakem out of pity as well as shared interests, she resists his romantic overtures. Maggie allows herself to be carried along for a while on the tide of her feelings for Stephen, which are much more elemental (in fact, some critics characterize the attraction as strongly sexual) than those she harbors for Philip, even though she knows that her cousin expects to marry him. This self-indulgence is followed by self-renunciation, when she refuses Stephen's marriage proposal on the grounds that Lucy will be hurt, and Philip's because she will not go against her brother's wishes. Instinctively hungry for more than her circumstances offer and unable to muster the strength to overcome them, Maggie's tragic fate is not to live at all. Without ever realizing her vague aspirations toward accomplishment, she dies in the arms of the brother she has both loved and clashed with for so many years and with whom she seems, finally, reconciled.

The young **Tom Tulliver** is a vigorous, practical boy who loves the outdoors and has little use for intellectual pursuits. Although he would like to become a farmer, his father's desire that he pursue a legal career propels him toward school, where he proves a sluggish, indifferent student. Fiercely competitive and willful, Tom is slow to forgive wrongs and judges others harshly. His narrow, self-righteous, even priggish sense of justice makes him essentially unsympathetic to others—even to his adoring sister. In fact, Tom manipulates Maggie to do his bidding, knowing that her love for him gives him power over her, and he fails to perceive her real talents and capabilities. Despite his negative qualities, however, Tom is also hardworking and self-sacrificing, dedicating his energies to alleviating his family's suffering after their financial crisis. His own inclinations, like his sister's, have been thwarted by the demands and restrictions of his family and society, and his chances for happiness seem limited. Tom and Maggie meet the same tragic end, overcome by the flood that might be seen as a symbol of society's power over the individual.

Tom and Maggie's father, **Edward Tulliver**, is an ambitious, closed-minded, hot-tempered man whose obsession with his "rights" and passion for lawsuits leads to his downfall. Tulliver's unreasonable adherence to his own long-held, narrow views—exemplified by his insistence that Tom be educated and by his hatred for the Wakems—results in unhappiness for his children as well as financial disaster. The dull-witted **Mrs. Tulliver** is one of four Dodson sisters, who are described by critic Leslie Stephen as belonging to the "stratum of sheer bovine indifference." Bereft of any original ideas of their own, they refer constantly to their family name as an emblem of unquestionable wisdom and pride. Mrs. Tulliver depends on her two more aggressive sisters for advice and guidance. She has little sympathy for her sensitive daughter and predicts that she will meet a bad end, while she tends to indulge her favorite, Tom. She cherishes most of all her linen, silver, and other household goods and is devastated by their loss; they seem to represent everything of meaning in her life. Ironically, it is Mrs. Tulliver who gives John Wakem the idea of buying the mill when she begs him *not* to do so.

The other Dodson sisters include the pale, sickly **Mrs. Deane**, mother of Lucy and wife of the pompous **Mr. Deane**; wealthy, sentimental **Aunt Pullet**, who weeps at the slightest provocation and who is married to the tiny **Mr. Pullet**, a gentlemen farmer who is constantly sucking on lozenges; and **Aunt Glegg**—wife of the wealthy, retired wool magnate **Mr. Glegg**—a formidable and excessively proud woman who clings to her family's traditions but who remains loyal to Maggie even after the scandal that causes most of her other relations to desert her.

Philip Wakem, the crippled son of Tulliver's enemy, becomes Maggie's friend and, eventually, her suitor. Artistic, intelligent, and scholarly, Philip stirs in Maggie both an empathetic and an intellectual response. Long isolated from others as a result of his handicap, Philip admires Maggie and appreciates her companionship, while she finds in him a friend who can discuss with her the books and music she loves. Philip's disability has resulted in his being better equipped and more resourceful than Maggie in dealing with frustration; he knows, for instance, exactly how to overcome his father's initial resistance to his desire to marry the daughter of his enemy, and before long Wakem has come around to thinking of the match as desirable. A lawyer whom Tulliver hates primarily for having chosen that despised profession, **John Wakem** initially bears no particular animosity toward Tulliver but does eventually gloat over the other man's misfortune.

The handsome, wealthy, rather shallow **Stephen Guest** rouses deeper feelings in Maggie than the empathy she feels for Philip. An ardent lover, Stephen proves somewhat self-indulgent when he allows the situation of the boat ride to evolve so that he and Maggie are forced to spend the night together, thus making their marriage more desirable as a way to avoid public censure. Both personally strong and financially secure, Stephen offers Maggie a measure of stability but would probably not have been able to answer all of her yearnings for a meaningful life (even as the more intellectually appropriate Philip would not have satisfied her need for romantic or sexual satisfaction). Maggie's cousin **Lucy Deane**, to whom Stephen initially planned to become engaged, is a fairly conventional Victorian female character: sweet, pretty, and passive. Always perfectly groomed and utterly docile, Lucy provides a sharp contrast to Maggie's darker appearance and more independent, impetuous nature. Unfailingly supportive and forgiving of her cousin, Lucy eventually marries Stephen.

Other characters in *The Mill on the Floss* include **Bob Jakin**, the childhood friend of Tom and Maggie who is unsophisticated but also a shrewd businessman; he helps Tom make the secret investments that allow him to buy back the mill. Clever and resourceful, Bob helps Maggie after her rift with her brother by giving her a place to stay. **Mr. Stelling** is Tom and Philip's teacher at King's Lorton School; he finds Tom stubborn and ignorant. Mr.

Tulliver's sister, **Mrs. Gritty Moss,** is the impoverished mother of eight children; she has a kind and passionate nature but lacks intelligence.

Silas Marner (novel, 1861)

Plot: Silas Marner is a weaver living in the English village of Raveloe. A former resident of the town of Lantern Yard, he had left after being falsely accused of stealing. He has been a recluse for fifteen years, living alone and carefully hoarding the money he makes from his weaving. The wealthy landowner Squire Cass is the most prominent citizen in Raveloe; his two sons are respectable Godfrey, who is engaged to Nancy Lammeter, and dissolute Dunstan. Without his father's knowledge, Godfrey gives Dunstan a loan from the squire's rent funds to pay off his sizable gambling debts, but Dunstan also gambles away this money. While riding Godfrey's prized horse to a fair to sell it and pay back the debt, Dunstan lames the animal. Desperate and drunk, he comes across Silas's empty cottage and steals his bag of gold. Fleeing the scene, Dunstan falls into a deserted quarry pit and dies. The burglary and Dunstan's disappearance cause much discussion in the neighborhood. Silas continues to isolate himself and is depressed over the loss of his cherished gold. On New Year's Eve a little blonde girl arrives at his cottage, attracted by the light; her destitute mother is dead in the snow nearby. When Silas brings Godfrey and some of the other villagers to the scene, Godfrey recognizes the dead woman as his estranged wife and the child as his daughter, but he tells no one. Silas seems to associate the fair-haired child with his lost gold, and is determined to keep her with him; his neighbor, Dolly Winthrop, convinces the other villagers that he will be a good parent to the little girl. Silas names her Hephzibah—called Eppie—and as she grows, his life changes for the better. His cottage takes on a more cheerful appearance, and he associates more with his neighbors. Eppie often plays with Dolly's little boy Aaron. Silas takes Eppie back to Lantern Yard to show her his birthplace, and he looks unsuccessfully for someone to clear his name of the long-ago crime. Godfrey marries Nancy, but after sixteen years of marriage the two remain childless. When the old quarry pit is drained, Dunstan's skeleton and Silas's stolen bag of gold are found. Godfrey now tells Nancy the truth about his previous marriage and daughter, and Nancy agrees that they should offer to take Eppie into their own home. But given the choice of going to live with her real father or remaining with Silas, Eppie chooses to stay with the man who has loved and cared for her for so many years. Eppie eventually marries Aaron Winthrop.

Characters: This classic moral tale affirms that love represents a wealth superior to gold and that the individual's ties to the community and the connection between the past and the present are vitally important. Eliot is praised for creating a skillfully structured work in which two separate plot strands are woven together in a format that blends elements of myth with realistic detail.

At the beginning of the story, **Silas Marner** embodies all of the traditional qualities of the reclusive miser: he is a shriveled-up, nearsighted, lonely old man who displays affection only for the bag of gold he periodically hauls out to admire. Yet Silas's narrowness and bitter attitude are shown to be rooted in his past. During his life in Lantern Yard, he was a member of a strict religious sect that rejected him as a thief. In reality his supposed friend best friend took advantage of his tendency to suffer from cataleptic fits and framed Silas to escape blame himself. Silas has bitterly suffered this injustice for fifteen years by the time Eppie arrives. He develops a deep love for the little girl that draws him out of his isolation; he learns to trust others and even regains the religious faith he had lost long ago. In learning to trust others and in accepting conflict as a natural part of life, Silas is able to grow and change for the better.

It is Silas's adopted daughter, **Eppie (Hephzibah),** who provides his link to the community, because he needs help and advice in raising her. A pretty blonde and blue-eyed child, Eppie seems to embody the gold that Silas has lost, and indeed she becomes more valuable to him than money. Eppie demonstrates her worthiness when, given the opportunity to change her life, she chooses not the material comfort that her real father can provide but the love and devotion Silas has always offered her.

The principal character in the novel's second plot is **Godfrey Cass,** a wealthy, genial aristocrat who seems to possess everything that Silas lacks but who has actually given up the very thing—Eppie—that helps to make Silas whole. Godfrey is one of several characters in Eliot's fiction who refuse to accept responsibility for their own mistakes and consequently cause suffering to themselves and others. On a drunken spree Godfrey had married and then abandoned a dissolute, lower-class woman; he later learns that he has fathered a child. His childless second marriage contrasts directly with Silas's fatherhood: during the same years that Silas is becoming a fully realized human being, Godfrey is defensive, fearful, and isolated. When he finally does confess the truth about his past to his second wife, she reacts with love and forgiveness.

Godfrey's brother, **Dunstan Cass,** is a dull, drunken, irresponsible spendthrift whose gambling debts lead him to try to blackmail his brother (by threatening to expose Godfrey's secret marriage unless he help him obtain money) and to commit robbery. Although Dunstan is somewhat two-dimensional, his status as a gambler is significant in that Eliot uses this competitive, essentially impersonal practice elsewhere in her fiction as an obstacle to developing sympathy for others. The father of Godfrey and Dunstan, **Squire Cass,** is a prominent landowner with a rigid, inflexible nature who has obviously been unsuccessful in instilling a sense of responsibility or discipline in either of his sons. **Nancy Lammeter** is the pretty, prim woman who marries Godfrey; although she has always seemed to uphold a strict, narrow moral code, she reveals a deep store of courage and sympathy when she reacts to Godfrey's story with calm forgiveness. Through Nancy's unselfishness, Godfrey learns the value of the love that has been present but unappreciated in his life since his marriage.

Another significant character in *Adam Bede* is **Dolly Winthrop,** the wife of the town wheelwright and Silas's frequent visitor. She provides his first contact with the community and is influential in persuading the villagers to allow him to raise Eppie. Described by critic David R. Carroll as "the best-adjusted person in the novel," Dolly expresses how difficult it is to discern the difference between right and wrong and how necessary it is to try to do what's right and to trust that the results will be favorable. In the friendship and plainly spoken wisdom she offers Silas, Dolly communicates the importance of human fellowship. Her charming son, **Aaron Winthrop,** is Eppie's playmate and eventually becomes her sturdy, dependable husband.

Minor characters in the novel include the seemingly pious **William Dane,** Silas's friend in Lantern Yard, who reveals his hypocrisy by stealing money from his church and falsely implicating his innocent friend; and **Molly,** Eppie's mother, a coarse woman and opium addict.

Middlemarch (novel, 1871-1872)

Plot: Set in early nineteenth-century England, the story centers on the inhabitants of the provincial town of Middlemarch. Dorothea Brooke and her sister, Celia, are well-bred young ladies who live with their unmarried uncle, Arthur Brooke. Dorothea is courted by two men: the middle-aged Edward Casaubon, a serious scholar, and the staid Sir James Chettam. Out of admiration and sympathy for Casaubon's intellect, Dorothea accepts his marriage proposal, though neither her sister nor her uncle consider the match desirable. During a visit to the home that will soon be hers, Dorothea meets her fiancé's cousin, Will Ladislaw, who differs from Casaubon in every way. After their marriage, Dorothea and her husband set off for a honeymoon in Italy. Meanwhile, the young, idealistic physician Tertius

Lydgate has fallen in love with beautiful Rosamond Vincy. Lydgate is the director of a new hospital in the town; he hopes to promote his progressive ideas about medicine. Finding himself embroiled in a political dispute over the appointment of a chaplain, he decides to vote with the wealthy, pious banker Nicholas Bulstrode for a clergyman named Mr. Tyke. The Casaubons, meanwhile, encounter Ladislaw in Rome, and Ladislaw quickly recognizes Dorothea's unhappiness with marriage to a cold, pompous man. Ladislaw's initial feeling of pity for Dorothea turns to love. He no longer feels he can accept financial support from Casaubon and returns to England to try to forge his own way in the world.

Rosamond's brother, Fred Vincy, has accumulated substantial debts through irresponsible behavior; he looks forward to the inheritance he expects to receive when his uncle Peter Featherstone dies. He borrows a large sum of money from honest Caleb Garth, that father of Mary, the woman Fred loves; Fred is unable to repay the loan. When Dorothea and Casaubon return to England, they learn that Celia has become engaged to Chettam. Casaubon receives a letter from Ladislaw, in which is enclosed a note to Dorothea; he becomes jealously irate and as a result falls seriously ill. Lydgate recommends that Casaubon put aside his work; he informs Dorothea privately that her husband has a weak heart and must be kept quiet. Mary Garth has been caring for the infirm old Featherstone, whose relatives are anxiously awaiting his death in anticipation of their legacies. He tells Mary he would like to bequeath his fortune to her instead; she refuses to accept the legacy and he becomes enraged, dying soon afterward. His will states that most of his money will go not to his grasping relatives but to a person unknown to the Middlemarch community, Joshua Riggs, who is to take the Featherstone name as his own and then establish some charitable institutions for old men. Rosamond and Lydgate become engaged. With no inheritance forthcoming from his uncle, Fred is told to start studying for the ministry. Casaubon dies suddenly; his will stipulates that Dorothea will forfeit his money and property if she ever marries Ladislaw. Mr. Brooke, who had enlisted Ladislaw's help in publishing a liberal newspaper, breaks off his relations with the young man. Ladislaw knows that Dorothea's family disapproves of him but decides to stay in Middlemarch in order to overcome their suspicions.

Now married, Lydgate and Rosamond embark upon an extravagant lifestyle far beyond their means. Lydgate's attempts to persuade his wife to live more modestly lead to discord, and his medical practice begins to decline as his debts mount. A disreputable newcomer in town, John Raffles, arrives with previously hidden and damaging evidence about the origins of Bulstrode's wealth: once employed as a clerk by Ladislaw's grandfather, who had acquired his money by selling stolen goods, Bulstrode married his employer's widow and then knowingly built his own fortune on money that should have gone to Ladislaw's mother. Blackmailed by Raffles and convinced that Ladislaw will eventually hear the story anyway, Bulstrode offers Ladislaw a bribe to keep quiet about the scandal. Ladislaw is unwilling to be involved in the matter and leaves England, wondering about Dorothea's true feelings for him. Meanwhile Lydgate's financial troubles worsen, but Rosamund convinces him to keep up an appearance of prosperity. When he is on the brink of losing his property, Lydgate asks Bulstrode—who had previously withdrawn his support from the new hospital—for a loan, but the banker suggests he talk to Dorothea instead. Bulstrode reverses his position when Lydgate is called to attend the alcoholic Raffles; fearing that Raffles will disclose the sordid details of his past to the physician, Bulstrode gives Lydgate a loan that allows him to keep his property. After Raffles's death, the circumstances surrounding Bulstrode's loan and Lydgate's attendance on the dying man draw suspicion, and the two are accused of malpractice. Only Dorothea defends Lydgate. Rosamond would like to leave Middlemarch because of the gossip, as would Bulstrode—whose secret is now widely discussed—but he falls ill and must remain confined.

Dorothea wants to help Lydgate and goes to convince Rosamond that the couple should stay in Middlemarch and reestablish Lydgate's good reputation. Finding Ladislaw and Rosamond together and wrongly suspecting that the two are romantically involved, she leaves quickly. Ladislaw confesses to Rosamond that he has loved Dorothea for a long time and bemoans the compromising position in which she has just seen him. Overcoming her personal feelings, Dorothea returns to the Lydgate home the next day to again try to talk to Rosamond, who relays what Ladislaw has told her. Dorothea decides she is willing to sacrifice Casaubon's money for Ladislaw's love. The two are married and move to London. Dorothea's family initially disapproves of the union but forgives them after a son is born and Ladislaw is elected to Parliament. The Lydgates learn to live more harmoniously, and Fred Vincy and Mary Garth are married.

Characters: Widely recognized as Eliot's highest achievement, *Middlemarch* is considered one of the best novels not only of the nineteenth century but of all literature. In her sweeping, insightful depiction of English provincial society, her psychologically penetrating characterizations, and her exploration of such issues as moral choice, vocation, and the struggle to achieve ideals, Eliot has been identified as an important initiator of the modern novel. Her compassionate portrayal of the men and women in the novel and their relationships with each other as well as with their wider society is universally praised.

The novel's central character is **Dorothea Brooke.** Intelligent, sensitive, and idealistic, Dorothea is frustrated by the narrow pettiness of the upper class society to which she belongs. Uninterested in the frivolous pursuits in which young ladies are expected to engage, she would like to devote herself to some noble cause. Eliot injects some gentle mockery into the depiction of Dorothea's idealism, implying that she is not faultless. For instance, Dorothea disapproves of horseback-riding because not everyone is privileged enough to partake of it, yet she enjoys that activity and sometimes indulges in it by rationalizing away her qualms. Marriage was virtually the only fit or desirable means by which a nineteenth-century woman of Dorothea's class could expect to utilize her talents, which were all expected to relate to running a household and raising a family. Dorothea's aspirations and vague desire to improve the world are channeled into her marriage with Edward Casaubon, whom she initially views as charmingly single-minded in his devotion to his obscure scholarly work. Dorothea imagines that she will be an important and respected helpmate to her husband, working alongside him to help him achieve greatness. She believes that marriage to Casaubon will furnish her with purpose and specific duties as well as access to her husband's extensive knowledge. But Dorothea soon learns that her husband is an insecure pedant with little capacity for affection and little appreciation for her help or abilities. Will Ladislaw, whom she meets during her disillusioning Italian honeymoon, appears as a bright, sunny, sensitive contrast to her stiff, pompous husband. He respects Dorothea's intellect and ideals, and she admires his passion and unconventionality. After Casaubon's death, Dorothea is faced with the choice of living a financially secure but solitary life or forfeiting her dead husband's money by marrying the man she loves. While some critics characterize her decision to marry Ladislaw as morally correct and admirable, others see it as a disappointing concession either to the Victorian insistence on a happy ending or to the idea that it is only through marriage that a woman can find fulfillment. The various interpretations of the novel's ending evidence Eliot's skill in creating a morally ambiguous and thus compellingly realistic fictional world. Ultimately Dorothea is unable to fulfil her yearnings or realize her full potential, and this reality—whether it is attributed to the social restrictions that circumscribed women's lives or to the human condition in general—contributes importantly to the novel's depth and impact.

Ladislaw describes Dorothea's husband, **Edward Casaubon,** as a ''whiteblooded pedantic coxcomb.'' Despite his intellectual pretensions, Casaubon is an ineffectual scholar whose supposedly brilliant (and absurdly named) work, ''A Key to All Mythologies,'' is actually trivial and obsolete and will never be finished. He marries Dorothea not out of love but because he desires an assistant; when he realizes that she has discovered the truth about his work, he responds by snubbing and demeaning her. Nevertheless, the reader ultimately pities Casaubon, whose characterization evidences Eliot's skill, compassion, and knowledge of the frustrations and disappointments inherent in the scholarly life. Casaubon is not so much wicked or heartless as he is frightened by his inadequacy as a scholar and his inability to move his project beyond the note-taking stage, and this makes him oversensitive and jealous. He no doubt sees in Will Ladislaw everything he knows he lacks, and he carries his bitterness beyond the grave by forbidding Dorothea to marry Ladislaw. Some critics find Dorothea's willingness to marry Casaubon implausible in the first place, though others consider the union understandable given Dorothea's interests and circumstances.

Will Ladislaw, Dorothea's second husband, is a young man of mixed English and Polish blood—one of his relatives was a fiddler and another was a Jewish pawnbroker—a heritage to which his rashness and unconventionality seem attributed. Imaginative, artistic, ardent, and energetic, Ladislaw shares Dorothea's scorn for the pettiness and narrow vision of Middlemarch society. Introduced in the romantic setting of Italy, Ladislaw immediately impresses Dorothea with his sunny appearance and manner (he is often compared with Apollo, the sun god of Greek mythology). But even more important is his receptivity to Dorothea as a person. He differs from Casaubon in every conceivable way, especially embodying the sexual or romantic element that Dorothea overlooked when she married her first husband. Critics have been divided in their reaction to this idealistic but somewhat undirected young man. Some characterize him as a dilettante who wanders where he wishes with no apparent sense of duty, while others contend that his social detachment and independence are admirable. Eliot's attitude toward Ladislaw is also debated: does she like and approve of him, or is he simply presented as a workable though not necessarily ideal mate for Dorothea? Eventually Ladislaw develops a greater public zeal to complement his sensitivity, and he is elected to Parliament where, presumably, he will do much good with Dorothea by his side every step of the way.

The action of *Middlemarch* revolves around two other couples: Tertius Lydgate and Rosamond Vincy, and Fred Vincy and Mary Garth. **Lydgate** is an idealistic young physician of great energy, intelligence, and ambition. He is eager to promote his progressive ideas regarding health care, and he believes that he can win support for medical reform through sheer determination and the force of his own intellect. Like Dorothea, though, he finds himself limited by his circumstances, and he compounds these restrictions through his own self-indulgence. When he finds that lovely Rosamund is in love with him, he confuses his tender pity for love and marries her. Although he had envisioned life with Rosamund as a calm, orderly antidote to his medical career, he comes to suffer greatly from her selfishness and refusal to temper her spending habits. Similarly, Lydgate goes against his better judgment and allows himself to become entangled with Bulstrode, first by endorsing the banker's candidate for chaplain of the new hospital and later by accepting a loan from him, which injures his practice when he is suspected of malpractice after Raffles's death. In the end, Lydgate achieves success caring for the wealthier inhabitants of Middlemarch, and his marriage settles into a more peaceful mode. But like Dorothea, he has failed to live up to his youthful aspirations, and thus he serves as another example of the difficulty of defining and achieving one's dreams within the context of a restrictive society.

W.D. Howells wrote of Lydgate's wife, the pampered, petulant, willful **Rosamond Vincy,** that "it would be difficult to find a more detestable character, or a truer." Completely self-centered and self-indulgent, Rosamond is incapable of appreciating or even recognizing her husband's aspirations, and she blames him for all of their troubles. Raised in a privileged atmosphere and always indulged by her parents, she believes that it is her right to live elegantly. Despite Rosamond's many negative qualities, however, modern critics point to the subtle aspects of Eliot's portrayal. It is the narrowness of her vision, for instance, that is her greatest defect, rather than any deliberate wickedness. In addition, as a strong-willed and, in her own way, ambitious woman, she can acquire a measure of power only through marriage. She may be no more responsible for the troubles in her marriage than her husband, who thought he was acquiring a pleasant, docile ornament when he married her and found her instead a difficult but very real person. Rosamond briefly shows her vulnerable side when she is lambasted by Ladislaw for being shallow and selfish. Shocked by Ladislaw's attack, Rosamond's defenses are weakened, and she makes an uncharacteristic gesture of generosity toward Dorothea, telling her that Ladislaw had revealed his love for her.

Though spoiled and irresponsible, **Fred Vincy** is not quite as selfish as his sister. He is genial and good-hearted but has some important lessons to learn in thrift and perseverance. In love with level-headed Mary Garth, Fred borrows money from her family and then endangers their security when he is unable to repay the loan. This experience causes Fred to mature, and he abdicates the position of idle landowner to become a property manager and earn his way in the world. His social status may seem diminished, but his moral stature is enhanced, making Fred one of several characters in Eliot's fiction whose personality improves through the acceptance of personal responsibility. **Mary Garth** is just the type of woman Fred needs: plain, honest, and compassionate, she is industrious and fully capable of helping him develop. While she is more conventional and inherently conservative than Dorothea, Eliot seems to approve of her refusal to accept the fortune offered by Featherstone. Mary wants to earn her own happiness in life, rather than accept a windfall from a man whose motives are not particularly admirable.

Like Casaubon, **Nicholas Bulstrode** is a flawed individual for whom the reader nevertheless develops compassion. A wealthy banker who is also evangelically religious, Bulstrode manipulates others with both his money and his piety. Extremely ambitious, he acquired his fortune disreputably but convinces himself that his success is divinely sanctioned. When the truth is revealed, Bulstrode is universally condemned. Yet Eliot depicts the agony of his humiliation with skill and compassion. His rather commonplace wife, **Mrs. Harriet Bulstrode,** gains unexpected moral stature when she reacts to her husband's disgrace with grace and courage, exhorting him to ''look up'' and remaining loyal to him.

Dorothea's sister, **Celia Brooke,** is more conventional and less interesting than her sister: calm, docile, amiable, and unquestioning, she is not interested in ideas. She thus finds an appropriate mate in the equally uncontemplative **Sir James Chettam,** a staid, conservative prototype of the English country gentleman; he and Celia seem relatively well-matched and make a fairly happy marriage. **Arthur Brooke,** Celia and Dorothea's uncle and guardian, is described as a man of ''acquiescent temper, miscellaneous opinions, and uncertain vote.'' Genial but ineffectual, his pseudointellectual, platitudinous rhetoric masks his true purposelessness, and he is often cited as one of Eliot's best comic creations.

A wide variety of minor characters also inhabit the pages of *Middlemarch.* The builder **Caleb Garth,** Mary's father, is a stalwart, honest man who, though not particularly successful, embodies adherence to the work ethic and satisfaction in work for its own sake, both often cited as important themes in Eliot's work. He enjoys a happy marriage to **Susan Garth,** a loyal, devoted wife and mother determined to educate her children, who include athletic **Ben;** bright, competitive **Letty; Alfred,** who hopes to become an engineer; and scholarly **Christy.** Like Caleb and Susan Garth, **Walter Vincy** and his wife **Lucy** have an amiable relationship, but they have not raised their children (Fred and Rosamond) with as much wisdom or true sympathy. Mr. Vincy is a wealthy manufacturer and the mayor of Middlemarch; he is fond of bodily comforts and lighthearted company. Warm, sentimental Mrs. Vincy is the daughter of an innkeeper and very proud of her rise to a loftier station, a trait she seems to have passed on to her daughter.

Peter Featherstone is a rich, churlish old man who seeks to thwart his greedy relatives' designs on his fortune. After Mary Garth refuses to allow him to name her as his heir, he leaves his money to an enigmatic, odd-looking stranger named **Joshua Riggs,** who turns out to be his illegitimate son. A notorious miser during his lifetime, Featherstone orders that almshouses for old men be built with his money after his death—an apparent effort to win favor with God. **Reverend Camden Farebrother** is an amiable clergyman who, like other such clerical characters created by Eliot, is more effective because he lacks spiritual snobbishness. In love with Mary Garth, he loses her to the less deserving Fred Vincy. **Mr. Tyke** is the evangelical clergyman who receives the support of Lydgate and Bulstrode to become chaplain of the new hospital, defeating the kinder, more understanding Reverend Farebrother. **John Raffles** is the blackmailer who comes to town to stir up trouble for Bulstrode; he is the fairly standard, somewhat melodramatic villain who serves primarily to advance the plot. **Mrs. Elinor Cadwallader,** often cited as a particularly humorous character, is the talkative wife of a clergyman and one of Middlemarch's most accomplished gossips.

Further Reading

Barrett, Dorothea. *Vocation and Desire: George Eliot's Heroines.* London: Routledge, 1989.

Beer, Gillian. *George Eliot.* Bloomington: Indiana University Press, 1986.

Chase, Karen. "Mind and Body in 'Middlemarch.'" In *Eros and Psyche: The Representation of Personality in Charlotte Brontë, Charles Dickens, and George Eliot,* pp. 136-62. London: Methuen, 1984.

Bloom, Harold, ed. *George Eliot.* New York: Chelsea House, 1986.

Carroll, David. *George Eliot: The Critical Heritage.* New York: Barnes & Noble, 1971.

Dictionary of Literary Biography, Vols. 21, 35, 55. Detroit: Gale.

Ermath, Elizabeth Deeds. *George Eliot.* Boston: Twayne, 1985.

Gilbert, Sandra M., and Susan Gubar, ed. "Made Keen by Loss: George Eliot's Veiled Vision" and "George Eliot as the Angel of Destruction." In *The Madwoman in the Attic: The Woman Writer and the Nineteenth-Century Literary Imagination,* pp. 443-77, 478-538. New Haven: Yale University Press, 1979.

Hardy, Barbara. *The Novels of George Eliot: A Study in Form.* London: The Athlone Press, 1959.

Howells, W. D. "George Eliot's Rosamond Vincy and Dorothea Brooke." In *Heroines of Fiction,* Vol. II. New York: Harper, 1901.

Nineteenth-Century Literature Criticism, Vols. 4, 13, 23. Detroit: Gale.

Gustave Flaubert
1821-1880
French novelist and short story writer.

Madame Bovary: A Tale of Provincial Life (novel, 1857)

Plot: The first part of the story takes place in the French town of Toste. Charles Bovary is a simple, good-natured man who earns a medical degree and then is persuaded by his mother to marry an ill-tempered, middle-aged widow. After his first wife dies, he marries a young woman with whom he had previously fallen in love: the lovely, refined Emma Roualt, daughter of one of his patients. Although Charles adores his young wife, Emma is disappointed, because her marriage bears no resemblance to the idealized romances she has read about in books. Her husband bores her, especially after she attends an elegant ball that exposes her to a sophisticated, upper-class way of life. She becomes increasingly moody, and her depression causes her health to decline. Charles decides that a change of setting will benefit Emma, who is now pregnant, and they move to the town of Yonville-l'Abbaye. There the Bovarys meet the town's apothecary (pharmacist), the pompous Homais. Renting a room in Homais's house is Léon Dupuis, a clerk, who shares with Emma an interest in literature and music and a disdain for provincial life. Emma soon gives birth to a baby girl, Berthe, but she feels little affection for the child and sends her to a wet-nurse. After a visit with her daughter, Emma is accompanied home by Léon and an attraction begins to grow between them. The relationship remains platonic, however, and eventually Léon goes away to Paris to study law and Emma returns to her idle life, while her debts to the shopkeeper and moneylender Lheureux begin to mount.

A wealthy, cynical young bachelor named Rodolphe Boulanger moves to their town and decides to make Emma his next romantic conquest. He makes advances while the two are attending an agricultural fair and is encouraged by Emma's mild response. Later, with Charles's permission, Rodolphe takes Emma horseback riding and seduces her in the woods. They begin an affair, and the happy, remorseless Emma meets her lover often in the days that follow. Gradually, however, Emma begins to feel somewhat guilty about her infidelity, though she is still convinced her husband is inferior to the glamorous Rodolphe. When Charles botches an operation that might have proved his worth, Emma's disgust for her husband leads to renewed ardor for Rodolphe. Meanwhile she borrows more money from Lheureux to buy clothes and gifts for her lover. She plans to run away with Rodolphe, but he postpones their escape; then he leaves alone, weary of Emma and dismissing her with a letter. As a result Emma becomes seriously ill. Charles attends her faithfully, unaware that his wife has had a lover.

When Emma has recovered, Charles takes her to the larger city of Rouen, where they attend the opera and happen to meet Léon, who is now working as a lawyer. Charles allows Emma to stay another day while he returns home, and Emma and Léon have a tryst during a long drive in a shuttered cab. After Emma's return to Yonville, she persuades Charles to let her go back to Rouen to consult Léon about a legal matter. The three days she spends with her lover are so pleasurable that Emma devises a way to return weekly to the city: she convinces Charles to let her take music lessons in Rouen. Thus she is able to meet Léon every Thursday at a hotel. But Lheureux knows about Emma's affair and uses this knowledge to manipulate her, forcing her to sell some of her husband's property and to sign new notes for the money she has borrowed. She becomes increasingly worried about her debts. Meanwhile Léon's ardor begins to cool. The affair has become tiresome to both, but before they formally break if off, Emma's notes suddenly come due and she must pay them or the Bovarys' household goods will be confiscated. She tries unsuccessfully to borrow funds from Léon and

Rodolphe and is devastated by their refusal to help her. Finally she goes to Homais's drugstore and ingests some arsenic she finds there. After she dies, the heartbroken Charles is ridiculed by his acquaintances and hounded by creditors. He eventually learns the truth about Emma's affairs, and soon dies, an impoverished recluse.

Characters: Considered Flaubert's masterpiece and one of the high points of nineteenth-century French literature, *Madame Bovary* also constitutes a landmark in the development of the modern novel. Written in a precisely detailed style and employing a narrative voice that maintains objectivity yet retains an underlying compassion for the characters, the novel explores with deep psychological insight the clash of ideals and reality. Praised both for his sympathetic penetration of human personality and his technical skill, Flaubert created in *Madame Bovary* one of the most memorable and influential novels in all literature.

The novel's central figure is **Emma Bovary,** a young woman who is unable to tolerate the dreariness of her ordinary life. As a student in a convent school, her imagination and senses are stimulated by the mysticism and rituals of the Catholic faith; she later reads popular novels and fantasizes about a luxurious lifestyle and grand love affairs. Eager to leave her family home and begin life as an adult, she marries the very ordinary Charles Bovary, who adores her but cannot possibly live up to her inflated expectations. Emma's naturally romantic nature is augmented by her intelligence and longing for culture; she is interested in art, music, and poetry and also has an inclination toward religion. Profoundly bored with her quiet provincial life and dull, unimaginative husband, Emma turns to the church for guidance but finds its local representative, Father Bournisien, incapable of administering to or even recognizing her needs. She attempts to find self-fulfillment through love affairs but her two lovers are both inferior men despite the glamour and excitement they initially seem to promise, and they fail her in the end. Her breakup with Rodolphe is particularly devastating, as she is forced for the first time to confront the disparity between dreams and reality. Emma's money problems escalate as the story progresses, and critics have been divided on whether it is despair over her failed romances or fear of financial disaster that finally drives her to suicide; most contend that her financial dilemma is intertwined with or even symbolizes her romantic failures. Flaubert's comment, "La Bovary, c'est moi" (I am Emma Bovary), is frequently discussed by scholars, who note that the author shared with his most famous character a boredom and dissatisfaction with provincial life, a hatred for mediocrity, and a yearning for fulfillment, luxury, and love. Or perhaps Flaubert meant that he—and by extension all other human beings—could identify with Emma as her dreams are shattered by cruel reality. Other interpretations have focused on Flaubert's attitudes toward women, with some critics maintaining that his portrayal of Emma reveals his contempt for the female sex and others claiming that he depicts her with deep compassion, and on the importance of fate in the novel (i.e., Emma's problems may be attributed to her bad luck in choosing a husband, giving birth to a girl instead of a boy, etc.). Some real-life sources for Emma's character have been identified—such as Louise Pradier, a woman of Flaubert's acquaintance whose career (except for the suicide) resembled Emma's; or Delphine Delamarre, an adulteress whose story is recorded in a book written by one of Flaubert's friends—but it is generally agreed that this complex, deluded, vain, fascinating character was primarily the product of her creator's rich imagination.

Emma's husband, **Charles Bovary,** is an important character in the novel, which begins when he is a child and ends with his death. The story opens with Charles a gangly, inept schoolboy teased by other children; thus the reader's sympathy for him is encouraged at an early stage. His domineering mother pushes him into a medical career (Flaubert's father and brother were physicians) and then into marriage to an older, distasteful woman, exposing Charles as weak and malleable but also pathetic. He notices the lovely Emma Roualt when his first wife is still alive, and her death frees him to marry the true object of his affections. But Charles is unable to satisfy Emma's longings and plagues her with his mediocrity, which is conclusively confirmed when he bungles the operation that might have distinguished him. Dull, simple, and foolish, Charles is perfectly satisfied with the bourgeois existence that Emma finds suffocating, but he is also portrayed as an inherently good person who sincerely loves his wife. His idealization of Emma and inability to perceive her unhappiness and her infidelity evidences his stupidity and precipitates the disaster that eventually befalls Emma, but it also stands for something more: despite his grounding in reality (in fact, some critics have characterized him as *representing* reality), Charles too has dreams and ideals that are personified, for him, in Emma. It was his own choice to marry her, and his love continues even after there are good reasons for it to cease. Thus Flaubert illuminates through Charles not only the human weaknesses of stupidity and mediocrity but the deep sympathy for human beings, despite their faults, that pervades his fiction.

Emma's lovers are inadequate figures who fail to answer her need for fulfillment; neither is worthy or capable of the idealized love she craves. Emma initially perceives the intelligent, wealthy **Rodolphe Boulanger** as a romantic, passionate visionary, but he is in fact coarse and cynical, an experienced seducer who knows which platitudes will please the women he pursues. He is seeking in his affair with Emma not love but amusement, and he begins to tire of her almost immediately and starts plotting his escape. Through Rodolphe's conventional response to Emma's effusive attempts to express her feelings for him—he assumes she is simply mouthing insincerities as his other lovers have done—Flaubert illustrates the inadequacy of language to fully relay deep and complex emotions. Despite his literary pretensions, **Léon Dupuis** too is profoundly conventional. It is he who initially inflames Emma's sensual desire and romantic yearnings, so that she is more vulnerable to Rodolphe's advances. When they do become lovers, Léon's mediocrity becomes obvious and tiresome to Emma, and his lack of character is confirmed when he refuses to help her resolve her financial problems.

Often cited as a particularly successful character in *Madame Bovary* is **Homais,** the apothecary of Yonville-l'Abbaye. He is a self-important pedant prone to long-winded, cliché-ridden speeches about trivial concerns. A local correspondent for the Rouen newspaper, Homais is a pompous, moralistic meddler, though he claims to be a progressive free thinker. Frequently described as the type of philistine that both disgusted and fascinated Flaubert, Homais personifies the negative qualities that thrive in the stifling provincial world in which the novel is set. In his position as a pharmacist, Homais competes with trained physicians for the trust of those who need medical help, and his self-interest is served when Charles, encouraged by Homais, operates on the clubfooted patient whose leg must subsequently be amputated. Homais is eventually awarded the prestigious Legion of Honor in an ironic triumph to mediocrity.

Flaubert's depiction of the dry goods merchant and moneylender **Lheureux** is also unflattering. He takes advantage of Emma's weakness in a cold, calculating way so that she falls deeper and deeper in debt, until finally he forecloses on her loans and prepares to seize the Bovarys' household goods. Like Homais, Lheureux illustrates the concept that those who are selfish and insensitive prosper over the weak and idealistic; he is also seen as representing the destructive elements of capitalism that Flaubert feared were becoming too dominant in his society.

While Homais and Lheureux embody, respectively, the menace of a false science and the dangers of commercialism, the priest **Father Bournisien** represents the failure of religion. He encourages Emma to read dry, pious tracts as a substitute for the unhealthy books of romance she prefers, and when she comes to ask for guidance, he is too busy overseeing a noisy group of catechism students to attend to her concerns. Bourisien is an inadequate servant of the religion that is supposed to offer comfort, just as Homais is a false proponent of the science that is also supposed to help humanity. The vigil that Bourisien and Homais keep over Emma's dead body has been interpreted as representing almost comically the nineteenth-century conflict between science and religion.

Significant minor characters in *Madame Bovary* include the Bovarys' daughter, **Berthe,** for whom Emma is unable to muster much affection. Emma yearned for a boy who would accomplish great things in the world, and she is disappointed that her baby is a girl. After the death of her parents, Berthe's dismal fate is to become a worker in a textile mill. Homais's nervous, downtrodden, fourteen-year-old assistant **Justin** is a strikingly poignant character. Hopelessly in love with the beautiful Emma, he allows her into the pharmacy, where she obtains arsenic—making him an unwitting party to her death. The moving scene in which he weeps over her grave in the darkness reveals Flaubert's compassion for even the most seemingly insignificant person. Another character often mentioned by scholars is the **blind beggar.** Emma sees him on her way home from her many trips to Rouen, she throws him her last coin before returning to Yonville and taking arsenic, and she hears him singing outside her window as she lies dying. True to her nature to the very end, Emma had been fantasizing that she is a vision of serenity and beatitude as she faces death, but the beggar's song awakens her to the ugliness of her actual situation. The beggar has been said to symbolize reality and the collapse of Emma's illusions, the devil, and death. Brought to Yonville by Homais, who claims that he can cure the man's blindness, the beggar helps illustrate Homais's penchant for exploiting reality, instead of avoiding it as Emma does.

Further Reading

Bloom, Harold. Introduction to *Madame Bovary,* by Gustave Flaubert. New York: Chelsea House, 1987.

Buck, Stratton. *Gustave Flaubert.* New York: Twayne, 1966.

Gans, Eric. *Madame Bovary: The End of Romance.* Boston: G. K. Hall, 1989.

Kaplan, Louise J. *Female Perversions: The Temptation of Madame Bovary.* New York: Doubleday, 1991.

Maugham, Somerset W. "Flaubert and *Madame Bovary.*" In *The Art of Fiction: An Introduction to Ten Novels and Their Authors,* pp. 163-88. Garden City, N.Y.: Doubleday, 1955.

McCarthy, Mary. "On 'Madame Bovary.'" In *The Writing on the Wall and Other Literary Essays,* pp. 72-94. New York: Harcourt, 1964.

Nabokov, Vladimir. "Gustave Flaubert: *Madame Bovary.*" In *Lectures on Literature,* edited by Fredson Bowers, pp. 125-78. New York: Harcourt Brace Jovanovich, 1980.

Nineteenth-Century Literature Criticism, Vols. 2, 10, 19. Detroit: Gale.

Porter, Lawrence, ed. *Critical Essays on Gustave Flaubert.* Boston: G. K. Hall, 1986.

Theodor Fontane
1819-1898

German novelist, autobiographer, poet, travel writer, and critic.

Effi Briest (novel, 1895)

Plot: Joyful, energetic Effi Briest is sixteen years old when her parents inform her that Baron von Innstetten, an ambitious government official, has asked for her hand in marriage. Though still childishly attached to her family and friends, Effi agrees to marry the much older, rather stiff Innstetten. After their wedding and honeymoon, the couple make their home in the small town of Kessin on the Baltic Sea. They move into a strange old house Effi believes to be haunted by the ghost of a Chinese servant. Innstetten is kind to Effi but not particularly sensitive to her fears or needs, and he spends much of his time away from home. Effi finds the town's gentry stuffy and bigoted, and her only friends are the town's apothecary, Gieshubler, and her good-hearted, straightforward maid, Roswitha, who treats Effi with simple humanity. Effi becomes pregnant and gives birth to a girl, Annie, but nevertheless grows increasingly bored and restless. A new arrival in town, Major von Crampas, provides Effi with some welcome diversion, accompanying her on horseback rides and encouraging her to participate in the community plays he directs. Although Effi does not really love Crampas and realizes the danger he poses to her marriage, she allows herself to be seduced by him. She is uncomfortable with the situation, however, as she fears discovery and hates subterfuge. Thus Effi is relieved when her husband announces that he has been promoted to a new post in Berlin.

Effi finds the lively, bustling city vastly superior to dull Kessin, and for six years she lives contentedly with her husband. Then, while Effi is away from home visiting a spa, Instetten discovers some love letters written by Crampas during the period of his affair with Effi. Though Innstetten claims to feel no jealousy over a matter concluded so long ago and still loves his wife, he considers himself obligated to challenge Crampas to a duel. Having killed Crampas, Instetten banishes Effi from their home. Rejected by her husband, scorned by society, and even abandoned by her parents—who do not wish to appear to condone her infidelity—Effi moves into a small apartment and begins a lonely life, accompanied only by the faithful Roswitha. After some time Effi asks that her daughter visit her, but she is dismayed by Annie's mechanical answers to her questions and concludes that the child has been influenced against her mother. Following this episode, Effi's already declining health takes a turn for the worse, and finally her doctor convinces her parents to take her back into their home. Effi spends her remaining days in relative contentment and peace. Just before she dies, she tells her mother to inform Instetten that he was right to cast her off.

Characters: A prominent man of letters in nineteenth-century Berlin, Fontane is considered a master of the German "Gesellschraftsroman," or social novel, in which he subtly condemns the materialism, narrow-mindedness, and bigotry of both the aristocracy and the middle class. Praised for its psychological depth and realistic detail, *Effi Briest* features a tightly controlled plot and a dispassionate, unobtrusive narrator who delivers no judgment on the events or people described. Fontane has been heralded as a significant contributor to the development of the modern novel, and *Effi Briest* exhibits a psychological approach to character and a belief that human behavior is deterministic (that is, subject to heredity and environment rather than individual will); these qualities also characterize much twentieth-century fiction. The novel explores the consequences of conforming to social convention at the expense of personal happiness and touches on the concepts of individual freedom and the relationships between men and women and between parents and children.

The novel's title character is often compared to two other renowned nineteenth-century heroines, Gustave Flaubert's Emma Bovary and Leo Tolstoy's Anna Karenina; like them, she meets a tragic fate after indulging in an adulterous liaison. Yet **Effi Briest** is more profoundly conventional and more accepting of her punishment than either Emma or Anna. An only child, Effi's early years are happy and carefree. Active and joyful, she dearly loves her home, family, and friends and is in no particular hurry to grow up. Thus she is taken by surprise when, at sixteen, she finds herself engaged to the much older Innstetten—a man her own mother had once considered marrying. The extent to which Effi has absorbed the values of her society is revealed when she explains to a friend, after her engagement, that it is not necessary that she be in love with her husband as long as he has "a title and a situation in society and look[s] presentable." Yet the reality of married life does not conform to Effi's expectations and also contrasts unfavorably with her previous existence. She is frightened by the strange, gloomy house in which the couple lives after their move to Kessin. Her fear of the woeful ghost of a Chinese servant said to haunt the house evidences both her vivid imagination and her basic immaturity; the ghost has also been said to symbolize her conscience (particularly after her affair with Crampas) or her yearning for the exotic, adventure, and excitement. Indeed the energetic Effi feels bored and restless in her new life, and her husband's frequent absences from home and apparent indifference to her feelings as well as the stiffness and bigotry of the Kessin gentry exacerbate her isolation. Not even the birth of a daughter much alleviates Effi's boredom. The arrival of Crampas, who is as carefree and witty as Innstetten is stiff and serious, provides Effi with an escape from dull routine. Although she realizes the danger he poses to her and makes at least some attempt to avoid him, Effi eventually allows Crampas to seduce her. Critics have noted that Effi engages in this illicit liaison not out of passion or because she questions or rejects society's rules but because she longs for adventure, is attracted to a man so different from her husband, or is just irresponsible and frivolous. In any case the affair proves unsatisfactory, for Effi does not love Crampas and resents the clandestine nature of their relationship. Both she and Crampas are relieved when the Briests move to Berlin, where for six years Effi enjoys a much more interesting and satisfying life. Following the discovery of the love letters, Innstetten's duel with Crampas, and her own banishment from her home, Effi begins a cloistered life with only Roswitha for company. Her health declines drastically after her unhappy meeting with Annie, and she returns to her parents' care, content to be sheltered in the same warm home in which she had spent her idyllic childhood. In the end her death is brought on by having spent too long a time gazing at the night sky, wishing for some kind of union with the beautiful heavens. Ironically Effi finally concludes that Innstetten's actions were justified, while he becomes more convinced that he was wrong. Thus Effi may be identified as different from many other adulterous fictional heroines, for she poses no rebellion against society and accepts her role as an extension of her husband. The fact that Fontane used Effi's maiden name in the novel's title seems to highlight her essential youth and innocence, which is sacrificed to the blind, narrow-minded dictates of her society.

Effi's husband, **Baron Geert von Innstetten,** is a formal, highly disciplined government official whose future seems quite promising. He marries the teenaged Effi with no apparent concern about the disparity in their ages or the possibility that Effi will be lonely or dissatisfied, and indeed, the marriage initially appears to be a success. Innstetten treats Effi with kindness and consideration, though he is rather stiff in manner and does not easily express his emotions. His ambition and strong sense of duty result in frequent absences from home as he pursues his career, and he rather callously dismisses such signs of Effi's discontent as her exaggerated fear of the Chinese servant's ghost. Despite his insensitivity, however, Innstetten is not a villain or monster, nor is he as chauvinistic and reactionary as the rest of Kessin's upper class. When he discovers Crampas's love letters to Effi, however, Instetten responds in what he believes is the socially prescribed manner, challenging his wife's lover to a duel. In discussing the matter with his friend Wullersdorf, Instetten admits that he feels no jealousy and claims that he loves his wife, but that life in human society requires compliance with its rules. Some critics view Instetten's willingness to resign himself to convention as evidence of his inherent weakness, since he seems aware that he might just as easily tear up the letters and continue his contented life with Effi. Such inability to resist anachronistic social customs, Fontane suggests, results in unnecessary grief and pain. After Innstetten has dutifully killed Crampas, spurned Effi, and apparently turned his daughter against her mother, he becomes increasingly convinced that his course of action was wrong. Ironically he reaches the high point of his career—receiving the prestigious order of the Red Eagle—just as he has become most disillusioned with his own behavior and life. In an interesting divergence from the traditional pattern of the romantic novel, Innstetten is given a chance to flee his shattered life and accept a government post in Africa, but he decides to stay in Germany and try to salvage what happiness he can from his remaining years. Effi's final description of Innstetten as ''noble as anyone can be who has no real love'' suggests that it is, at least in part, Instetten's shallowness of character that has brought about the story's tragic ending.

Major von Crampas arrives in Kessin to serve as the new commander of its military outpost and quickly takes an active role in the town's social life. Carefree and witty, he is a notorious ladies' man whose disdain for rules, order, and discipline appeals to Effi. The fact that his personality is as different as possible from her husband's may partially explain her attraction to Crampas; in any case his attentions and the activities he introduces (such as community plays in which he encourages Effi to act) provide welcome relief from the dullness of her life. Still, Effi is not in love with Crampas. He is not quite the dashing young hero who inflamed the passions of such heroines as Emma Bovary and Anna Karenina—he is even older than Innstetten, is himself married, and bears a physical deformity that resulted from an injury received during a previous duel. Just before he dies, Crampas gives his killer a glance that serves to highlight for Innstetten the stupidity and inhumanity of what he has just done.

Effi's parents are portrayed as paragons of convention, encouraging their teenaged daughter to marry an older man not for love but for the social prestige she will thus acquire and then rejecting her when she violates society's rules. **Ritterschaftsrat von Briest** is loving but ineffectual, frequently resorting to the phrase ''That is too big a subject,'' which signifies his inability or unwillingness to grapple with troublesome questions. He and his wife do eventually realize that their daughter does not love her husband, but not until the marriage has already taken place. Strict conformists to society's precepts, they feel obliged to publicly condemn Effi's behavior by banning her from their home. Briest finally drops his usual stance when he invites the ailing Effi back home, and his telegrammed ''Komm, Effi'' (''Come back, Effi'') echoes the cries of Effi's girlhood friends as they tried to persuade her to join them at play. **Frau von Briest** is an inherently lively woman whose effort to channel her energies has resulted in a stern, distant demeanor. Once in love with Innstetten herself, she encourages Effi to marry him and thus fulfill her own fantasies of social prestige. Like Effi, Frau von Briest was pressured into marrying a man she did not love, but she has achieved the kind of prosaic but fairly happy marriage that her daughter might also have attained with Innstetten. After Effi's death, Frau von Briest wonders if she and her husband had somehow contributed to their daughter's fate by educating her inadequately or forcing her to marry at too young an age. Her husband responds in his usual, dismissive way: ''That is too big a subject.''

One of few positive forces in Effi's life is her maid, **Roswitha,** who remains faithful to her even after her disgrace. Eminently practical and straightforward, Roswitha calms Effi's fears about such matters as the Chinese servant's ghost and childbirth, serving as a warm, nurturing maternal surrogate for the lonely girl. In her simplicity, humanity, and ability to express her emotions openly and sincerely, Roswitha provides a contrast to the stiff, formal townsfolk of Kessin, among whom Effi feels uncomfortable. As a young woman, Roswitha was involved in an adulterous situation paralleling Effi's, and her father reacted by striking her with a red-hot iron.

Minor characters in *Effi Briest* include Effi's daughter, **Annie,** who reveals during her visit to her mother that she has been influenced against her; Innstetten's friend **Wullersdorf,** with whom he discusses his decision to challenge Crampas to a duel and who admits that their society's "cult of honor . . . is idolatry" but claims that they must nevertheless submit to it; and the kind, eccentric apothecary, **Gieshubler,** one of Effi's few friends in Kessin. The unattractive, cold-hearted spinster **Sidonie von Grasenabb,** the liberal but morally shallow widow **Frau Zwicker,** and the emancipated, self-assured, but religiously conservative **Madame Tripelli** all indicate the limited roles available to women in nineteenth-century society.

Further Reading

Bance, Alan. *Theodor Fontane: The Major Novels.* Cambridge: Cambridge University Press, 1982.

Emmel, Hildegard. "From Heinrich Heine to Thomas Mann." In *History of the German Novel,* translated by Ellen Summerfield, pp. 109-94. Detroit: Wayne State University Press, 1984.

Garland, Henry. *The Berlin Novels of Theodor Fontane.* Oxford: Clarendon Press, 1980.

George, E. F. "Illusions and Illusory Values in Fontane's Works." *Forum for Modern Language Studies* VII, No. 1 (January 1971): 68-75.

Hirsch, Marianne. "Spiritual 'Bildung': The Beautiful Soul as Paradigm." In *The Voyage in Fictions of Female Development,* edited by Elizabeth Abel, Marianne Hirsch, and Elizabeth Langland, pp. 23-48. Hanover, N.H.: University Press of New England, 1983.

Howe, Patricia. "The Child as Metaphor in the Novels of Fontane." In *Oxford German Studies,* Vol. 10, edited by P. F. Ganz, pp. 121-38. Oxford: Willem A. Meeuws, 1979.

Nineteenth-Century Literature Criticism, Vol. 26. Detroit: Gale.

Turner, David. "Theodor Fontane: 'Effi Briest' (1895)." In *The Monster in the Mirror: Studies in Nineteenth-Century Realism,* edited by D. A. Williams, pp. 234-56. Oxford: Oxford University Press, 1978.

Eugène Fromentin
1820-1876
French novelist, critic, travel writer, and essayist.

Dominique (novel, 1863)

Plot: The novel begins with the narrator introducing an acquaintance, shy and unassuming Dominique de Bray, the popular owner of an estate in the town of Villeneuve, where he lives with his wife and children. When Dominique's wealthy friend Olivier d'Orsel tries to kill himself a few days after visiting, Dominique is moved to tell the narrator the story of his earlier life. An orphan, Dominique was raised by an aunt, Madame Ceyssac, in Villeneuve. He was an introspective boy with a great love of nature. His tutor Augustin applied himself to writing plays and eventually moved to Paris to try to establish himself; Dominique moved with his aunt to the town of Ormesson. While attending school, he met the pleasure-loving, perpetually bored Olivier. Dominique became infatuated with Olivier's cousin Madeleine, who was a few years older, and was plunged into despair when she married Monsieur de Nièvres. Their studies completed, Dominique and Olivier moved to Paris, where they often met Augustin. Still tortured by his love for Madeleine, Dominique tried to distract himself with reading, writing, and attending literary lectures, but concluded that his work was mediocre. Augustin, however, advised him to overcome his obsession with Madeleine by applying himself to his work with renewed vigor.

Despite his former tutor's guidance, Dominique's restlessness persisted. He invited Madeleine and her husband to visit his Villeneuve estate and spent several happy months there with them, though he did not reveal his love for Madeleine. When all returned to Paris, Dominique decided that he and Madeleine should admit their love, but when he sensed her discomfort he did not pursue the matter further. Yet the two began to see each other more frequently, meeting secretly as if they actually were adulterous lovers, while Madeleine encouraged Dominique in his writing. Just as their feelings threatened to find physical expression, Dominique began to avoid Madeleine, who was distressed by his rejection. Dominique visited the now happily married Augustin, who seemed content with his lot despite his relative impoverishment. Olivier, meanwhile, had become increasingly depressed and alienated and had rejected the love of Madeleine's sister, Julie. Dominique again determined that he and Madeleine should consummate their love, but she avoided him, so he again plunged himself into intellectual pursuits and published several volumes of poetry as well as some political books. He became convinced, however, that his work was second rate. Two years later, Dominique visited Madeleine at her home, where she had been nursing Julie through an illness, and they experienced several days of mingled happiness and tension that culminated in a passionate embrace. Out of pity for Madeleine's vulnerability, Dominique released her from his arms; she finally told him that she did love him but wanted him to marry and make a life away from her. Dominique returned to his country estate and began a quiet, retired existence. The novel ends with Dominique telling the narrator that he has since found contentment in ordinary pleasures and pursuits.

Characters: Praised for his vividly descriptive yet restrained, graceful style, Fromentin is a respected figure in nineteenth-century French literature. He fused elements of the romanticism that had dominated earlier fiction with a subtle realism that anticipated modern trends, achieving in his most famous work, *Dominique,* an unsentimental, powerful evocation of the sometimes-disappointing search for happiness. Often interpreted as a criticism of romanticism in its suggestion that complete fulfillment is unachievable and that one must make the best of one's circumstances, the novel retains an inherent ambivalence, indicating Fromentin's ties to the romantic tradition.

The title character's maturation is chronicled through the recollections he shares with the narrator, whose comments open and close *Dominique.* At first, **Dominique de Bray** is a respectable husband, father, and estate owner, an introspective middle-aged man who relishes his solitary walks through the countryside. Stimulated by the attempted suicide of his boyhood friend, Olivier, Dominique ventures into what he calls the "dangerous room" of memory. Until the closing narration, the story is told from his subjective perspective. Orphaned, then raised by a pious aunt, Dominique was a sensitive boy, a good student who loved nature and was prone to excessive self-criticism. After meeting Madeleine, he is unaware of his feelings for her, but her marriage shocks him into the realization that he loves her. Not only do his feelings for Madeleine linger, but his professional ambitions are thwarted by his lack of confidence. Dominique's passion for Madeleine is idealized as he knows very little about her as a person; some critics have suggested that her very inaccessibility is what fuels his passion. Until the ball, where he sees Madeleine dressed in more attractive and revealing clothing, Dominique seems to disregard or resist his sexual attraction to her. Now he is inflamed with jealousy and desire, and he attempts to make her confess that she loves him. With her distress, however, he withdraws, illustrating his tormented consciousness and, perhaps, his basic decency.

Two years later, the sexual tension between Dominique and Madeleine comes to a crisis when she collapses into his arms but, again moved with pity for her, Dominique ends the encounter. Dominique rejects that part of him that most resembles Olivier—who is presented as the classic romantic figure—and chooses the path recommended by his sensible tutor, Augustin. He retires to life in the country, abandoning both passion for Madeleine and his literary and political ambitions, finding solace in making himself useful to a few people within a very narrow circle. That Dominique adapts himself to provincial circumstances, relinquishing the desires that filled his youth, has provoked debate among scholars. Some question whether Dominique is content at all and wonder if he is merely trying to persuade himself that he is happy. Others, interpreting *Dominique* as critical of romanticism, claim that Fromentin means to affirm Dominique's choices. These critics contend that the novel's framework supports their position, for it sandwiches Dominique's struggles and love affair between two slices of real life, coloring his final abandonment of self-obsession as markedly positive.

The object of Dominique's love, **Madeleine de Nièvres,** was apparently based on Jenny Léocadie Chessé, for whom a young Fromentin formed an attachment that continued after her marriage. As several critics have noted, the reader learns little about Madeleine's true personality because she is seen entirely through Dominique's perspective. Some facts about Madeleine's life are presented; raised in a convent, she is shy and awkward, and her prettiness is somewhat masked by her drab clothing. She initially resists Dominique's attempts to address their love, pretending she does not grasp the nature of his inquiries. She gradually grows more conflicted and troubled, enduring her suffering silently. Madeleine seems to enjoy the role of older sister, or mother, to Dominique, encouraging him in his literary pursuits, and seems caught between feelings of friendship and love for the man. Madeleine reveals a trace of seductiveness during the scene in which she insists that Dominique join her on a wild ride through the countryside; later she apparently succumbs to his charms when she collapses into his arms. It is Madeleine who finally voices their mutual conclusion: that he must forget her, marry another, and begin anew. Thus Madeleine exhibits her worthiness and practicality, which otherwise remains rather shadowy.

Some critics have seen Fromentin's portrayal of Dominique's friend **Olivier D'Orsel** as one of the novel's strongest indictments of romanticism. A handsome, blonde, somewhat dandified aristocrat, Olivier is said to have pleasing manners and an engaging personality. Although he loves luxury, he is profoundly bored by his surroundings. Even as a young boy, Olivier is precociously morose, disaffected, and blase. While not as dedicated a student as Dominique, he is more worldly and realizes when the time has come for Madeleine to marry, whereas Dominique is shocked when this event occurs. Olivier is often identified as a quintessentially romantic figure in his alienation, his lack of will, his ennui, and his final conviction that life can afford no lasting happiness or satisfaction. His attempted suicide is often cited as an example of what may happen when a romantic youth fails to mature and accept his circumstances. He might have found an ordinary happiness with Julie, who loves him, but instead he seeks escape from life. Some critics complain that Fromentin's effort to portray Olivier as Augustin's opposite resulted in one-dimensional and uninteresting characters.

Augustin is presented as a foil to Olivier as well as to the part of Dominique's personality that resembles Olivier. He assumes the role of Dominique's tutor both literally, during the young man's boyhood, and figuratively, when he attempts to guide him through the crises of adulthood. Kind, honest, and well-educated, Augustin contrasts strongly with Olivier. He forms reasonable ambitions and pursues them with vigor, responding to disappointment not with despair but with courage and faith. Although he initially aspires to be a playwright, he adapts to his failure in that realm by channeling his writing ability into journalism. Augustin has not achieved financial prosperity but has attained a measure of professional and personal contentment. His marriage seems quite happy; while not the romantic ideal of perfect love, it reflects a more universal quality of family harmony and support. Through example and advice, Augustin encourages Dominique to avoid the ennui embodied in Olivier, to overcome his emotions, and to find solace through work. That Dominique does finally achieve contentment by imitating his tutor suggests that Augustin—whom some critics have found lacking in the sensitivity, however destructive, that both Dominique and Olivier possess—is intended as a positive role model.

Other characters in *Dominique* include **Julie,** Madeleine's sister, about whom little other than her love for Olivier and her despair at his rejection is provided; **Madame de Bray,** Dominique's kind, attractive, and capable wife; and **Madame Ceyssac,** Dominique's serious, pious, and old-fashioned aunt, who raised him after he was orphaned.

Further Reading

Barthes, Roland. "Fromentin: 'Dominique.'" In *New Critical Essays,* translated by Richard Howard, pp. 91-104. New York: Hill and Wang, 1980.

Greshoff, G. J. "Fromentin's 'Dominique'—An Analysis." *Essays in Criticism* XI, No. 2 (April 1961): 164-89.

Latiolais, F. M. "'Not Quite a Masterpiece'—Fromentin's *Dominique* Reconsidered." *Mosaic* IV, No. 1 (Fall 1970): 35-48.

Lethbridge, Robert. "Fromentin's 'Dominique' and the Art of Reflection." *Essays in French Literature* No. 16 (November 1979): 43-61.

Martin, Graham Dunstan. "The Ambiguity of Fromentin's *Dominique.*" *Modern Language Review* 77, No. 1 (January 1982): 38-50.

Mickel, Emanuel J., Jr. *Eugène Fromentin.* Boston: Twayne, 1981.

Nineteenth-Century Literature Criticism, Vol. 10. Detroit: Gale Research.

Émile Gaboriau
1835-1873
French novelist and journalist.

Monsieur Lecoq (novel, 1869)

Plot: The mystery presented in *Monsieur Lecoq* revolves around the murder of two men in a Paris wineshop. When the police, headed by inspector Gevrol, arrive at the scene, they find a man with a gun in his hand standing near the bodies. Concluding that the crime resulted from a drunken brawl, Gevrol arrests the man. But young detective Lecoq suspects that the solution to this murder is not so simple. With the help of his experienced old friend, Father Absinthe, he investigates the scene thoroughly, uncovering a number of clues that suggest the suspect had an accomplice. Lecoq presents his case to the presiding judge, Monsieur d'Escorval, who agrees to look into the affair; Gevrol, meanwhile, is disgruntled and jealous because the judge treats Lecoq with respect. Visiting the jail, Lecoq happens to discover the suspect in the act of trying to kill himself. After preventing this, Lecoq learns that a drunken man had shared the accused's cell the previous night, and he suspects that the drunken man may have been the accomplice to the murder. Lecoq is disappointed when Monsieur d'Escorval breaks his leg and is removed from the murder case, but the new judge, Monsieur Segmuller, is also receptive to Lecoq's assertions. Segmuller questions the prisoner, who gives his name as May and speaks nonsensically, claiming that he is a circus performer and that he had shot the two men in self-defense.

Lecoq and Father Absinthe continue their investigation, striving unsuccessfully to trace the owner of a diamond earring they had found at the scene of the crime and the identity of the two women who had been seen there. A mysterious stranger visits May in prison; Father Absinthe follows him but loses his trail. Though he has no conclusive proof, Lecoq suspects that this visitor is the same man who had shared May's cell and who had been his accomplice. Finally Lecoq decides to try to entrap the suspect by allowing him to escape and following him. Leaving the prison, May joins his accomplice and leads Lecoq on an exhaustive chase through the streets of Paris that ends when May disappears over a wall into the grounds of the Duke of Sairmeuse's mansion. The accomplice is arrested but provides no further information, and a search of the Duke's home is equally fruitless. Stumped, Lecoq consults Pére Tabaret, an elderly, eccentric, amateur detective who is considered a sage by the police. After listening to the details of the case, Tabaret explains the mistakes Lecoq has made in trying to unravel the mystery: Monsieur d'Escorval had intentionally injured himself because he was afraid to try the case, and Lecoq did not find May in the Duke's house because May *was* the Duke.

Characters: Gaboriau is often credited with the invention of the detective novel. Though related in some ways to the earlier stories of ratiocination (deductive reasoning) by Edgar Allan Poe, Gaboriau's works established many of the techniques and attributes that characterize later detective fiction, particularly the Sherlock Holmes series by Arthur Conan Doyle. Where Poe had focused primarily on the process of detection, Gaboriau emphasized the detectives themselves as well as the motives and characteristics of the criminals. Gaboriau's stint as secretary to Paul Féval, a popular writer of ''feuilleton'' crime novels (similar to the ''penny dreadfuls'' of England or the dime novels of America), required extensive research into criminal investigation and police procedures, and his novels are, consequently, distinguished by their authenticity. *Monsieur Lecoq* is generally considered the best of Gaboriau's five novels featuring the ambitious and clever young detective, Lecoq, and the savvy, idiosyncratic amateur sleuth, Tabaret.

Monsieur Lecoq is an energetic, dedicated young police detective who must continually struggle against not only the cunning of criminals but the stupidity and stubbornness of his official colleagues to solve crimes. In the first novel of the series, *The Widow Lerouge* (1866), Monsieur Lecoq is described as a reformed criminal, but in *Monsieur Lecoq,* the earlier description is attributed to a misunderstanding, suggesting that Gaboriau had second thoughts about giving Lecoq a disreputable history. Intelligent and resourceful, Lecoq believes in carefully collecting and examining every possible clue, and then making logical deductions. A master of disguise who can mold his extremely mobile face at will, Lecoq is honest but also adept at self-promotion; somewhat vain, he has a definite taste for the dramatic. His personal symbol is the crowing cock, a fitting metaphor for his self-assurance; other qualities that have been identified as notably French are his eye for details and his strong dejection or elation when he experiences failure or success. Many of the methods Lecoq uses to solve crimes have since become standard devices of detective fiction, including the creation of a plaster cast of a footprint, such stage props as the overturned chair, the dirty wine glass or coffee cup, and the half-smoked cigar, the rumpled bed that no one has slept in, and the chiming clock to determine the exact time of a crime. Lecoq is courageous and intuitive but not infallible—hence his turning to Tabaret for help, as he does in this novel—but his imperfection seems to make him more likable. The success of Gaboriau's Lecoq novels is even more impressive when one considers that, at the time of their publication, the French exhibited a strong antipathy to the police, and creating a hero who was a member of the force was risky.

Pére Tabaret, who serves as a special advisor to the police and as Lecoq's tutor in detection, is an elderly, retired pawnbroker with a gift for sleuthing. More prominently featured in the first of the Lecoq novels, *The Widow Lerouge,* Tabaret remains in the background for most of *Monsieur Lecoq,* appearing only at the end to set Lecoq straight about the mystery. In his eccentricity, his amateur status, and his tendency to astonish the hapless police by giving a detailed description of a suspect after only a brief look at a crime scene, Tabaret is frequently viewed as a direct predecessor to Arthur Conan Doyle's Sherlock Holmes. Tabaret certainly helped to establish the conflict between the amateur with a genius for deduction and the less-skilled official that would become a standard device in detective fiction.

The elderly, unimaginative **Gevrol** is the novel's primary representative of official stubbornness and even enmity, as he grows increasingly jealous of and antagonistic toward the clever Lecoq. Although **Pére Absinthe** is also an official colleague of Lecoq, he provides a contrast to Gevrol through his friendly relationship with Lecoq, whom he helps to track down clues. Though steadfast and seasoned, Absinthe plays the role of the less intelligent sidekick to his ingenious friend, and might be compared to Sherlock Holmes's Dr. Watson. **May,** whose murder of two men gives *Monsieur Lecoq* its impetus, is a mysterious figure who speaks nonsensically, claiming to be a circus performer. Tabaret and Lecoq eventually conclude that May is actually the **Duke of Sairmeuse,** a circumstance that evidences the fascination for noble families and their dark secrets that several critics have noted in Gaboriau's fiction; indeed, his mysteries tend to revolve around illicit family scandals rather than the greed that provides the motive in other crime novels.

Other characters in *Monsieur Lecoq* include **Mother Chupin,** the owner of the wineshop in which the murders occur; the mysterious **accomplice,** an ex-convict who helps May "escape"; **Monsieur d'Escorvier,** the presiding judge who demonstrates the difficulty of balancing political allegiance and conscience when he avoids trying May; and **Monsieur Segmuller,** the judge who questions May in a battle of wits that anticipates similar contests in, for instance, the novels of twentieth-century detective novelist Georges Simenon.

Further Reading

Bleiler, E. F. Introduction to *Monsieur Lecoq* by Émile Gaboriau, pp. v-xxviii. Mineola, N.Y.: Dover Publications, 1975.

Cambiaire, Célestin Pierre. "Poe and Émile Gaboriau." In *The Influence of Edgar Allan Poe in France,* pp. 264-80. 1927. Reprint. St. Clair Shores, Mich.: Scholarly Press, 1971.

Murch, A. E. "The Rise of the 'Roman-Policier.'" In *The Development of the Detective Novel,* pp. 115-32. New York: Philosophical Library, 1958.

Nineteenth-Century Literature Criticism, Vol. 14. Detroit: Gale.

Symons, Julian. "Dickens, Collins, Gaboriau: The Pattern Forms." In *Bloody Murder: From the Detective Story to the Crime Novel: A History,* revised ed., pp. 42-56. New York: Viking, 1985.

Williams, Valentine. "Gaboriau: Father of the Detective Novel." *National Review* (London) LXXXII, No. 490 (December 1923): 611-22.

Hamlin Garland

1860-1940

American short story writer, novelist, playwright, essayist, poet, biographer, and critic.

Main-Travelled Roads: Six Mississippi Valley Stories (short stories, 1891)

Plot: The stories are set in the late nineteenth century in what was then termed the "middle border," the region of the United States that included Iowa, Wisconsin, Minnesota, Nebraska, and the Dakotas. "A Branch Road" centers on Will Hannan, who leaves his home on the prairie after a misunderstanding with his sweetheart, Agnes Dingman, and goes to Arizona to make his fortune. He returns seven years later to find that Agnes has married his former rival, Ed Kinney. Exhausted by a life of drudgery as a farm wife and mother, Agnes suffers from failing health, and her blooming beauty has faded. Will feels responsible for Agnes's plight and finally persuades her to leave her husband and, along with her baby, flee with Will to a better life. In "Up the Coulee," Howard McLane returns to his home in Wisconsin after establishing a successful theatrical company in the East. He is overwhelmed by the natural beauty of his birthplace, but gradually he begins to notice the squalor that actually surrounds him. He finds his worn mother and embittered brother, Grant, living on a small, unproductive farm after having been forced to sell their own property. Grant believes that Howard might have prevented their loss, since he is apparently wealthy, and blames him for the misfortune they now endure. The brothers are eventually reconciled, but Grant refuses Howard's offer to buy back the family farm. "Among the Corn Rows" chronicles the journey of young Rob Rodemaker from his prairie farm to his old home in Wisconsin, where he hopes to find a wife to bring back with him. He courts Julia Peterson, the overworked daughter of a tyrannical Norwegian farmer, who has long dreamed of escaping from her dreary life. She agrees to marry Rob, whose need for a wife is primarily practical, and looks on the prospect of marriage with romantic expectations that are bound to be shattered. In "The Return of a Private," a Civil War soldier named Private Edward Smith travels by train to his home in Wisconsin after the war is over. Although he is newly awestruck by the grandeur of the landscape and experiences a tender reunion with his family, he finds his farm in a state of decay. Disillusioned but stoic, Private Smith exchanges the war against the Confederates for the war against nature and the economic hardships faced by the midwestern farmer. The central character of "Under the Lion's Paw" is a farmer named Tim Haskins. A native of the East, Haskins takes his family to Kansas to start a new life. When a plague of grasshoppers devastates their homestead, the Haskins move to Iowa, where they rent a farm from land speculator Jim Butler. Hoping to eventually buy the farm, Haskins and his wife endure many hardships and work diligently to improve it. After three years they have enough money to purchase the farm but Butler, claiming that their hard work has made their property twice as valuable, doubles the price. Frustrated and enraged, Haskins considers murdering Butler but recognizes the dire consequences such an act would have on his family. His only choice is to capitulate to Butler's offer. "Mrs. Ripley's Trip" involves the journey of a worn, wizened farm wife to the eastern home she had left when she moved to the Midwest twenty-three years before. Although she feels guilty for leaving her husband alone even for a short time, she finally makes the trip she has long dreamed about. She returns to the same drudgery she has always had to endure, but she now feels resigned to the circumstances of her life.

Characters: Through the six short stories collected in *Main-Travelled Roads,* Garland chronicles the harsh realities of midwestern American farm life in the nineteenth century and voices the discontent of people whose earlier optimism collapses in the face of natural disasters, an unfavorable economy, and powerful landlords. Garland himself had been raised in Iowa and South Dakota, and when he returned after a long period spent in the East he was shocked by the bleak hardship he found there. Farm families endured grueling, tedious work, harsh weather, and loneliness as they struggled to eke out a living on the prairies of the Midwest. Garland's fictional technique, which he called "veritism," combines objective, realistic description with impressionistic details. He is often associated with such American writers as Stephen Crane, Frank Norris, and Theodore Dreiser, whose naturalistic works present the view that people's lives are shaped by their environment. Despite the generally grim tone that permeates the stories, many critics detect in them a strain of romantic opportunism, a belief that the individual can assert his or her own will to survive, and that such aspects of life as natural beauty, love, and children provide some compensation for its hardships.

"A Branch Road" is one of the most frequently praised stories in *Main-Travelled Roads.* Its longer length allows Garland more development of its setting, plot, themes, and characterizations. In recounting a young man's return to his home and eventual rescue of his former sweetheart from a dismal existence, Garland provides an example of an individual who is able to reverse the seemingly irrevocable dictates of fate. The story features some of Garland's most characteristic techniques, such as the almost lyrical description of nature's splendor and the use of a peculiarly American "return of the native" theme. **Will Hannan** is a stocky, cheerful, ambitious young man—qualities which have also been attributed to the author who created him. Like Garland, he returns to his birthplace to find the loved person he left behind—in Hannan's case, his former sweetheart; in Garland's, his mother—physically depleted and emotionally depressed by the intervening years of hardship. The remorse he feels over his own responsibility for Agnes's plight seems to reflect Garland's sense of guilt when he came back to South Dakota to find his mother worn and lonely. Hannan is a sensitive young man with a romantic attitude toward the natural beauty around him; several critics have likened his observations to those of the exuberant nineteenth-century American poet Walt Whitman. His response to his situation is romantic as well: he paints for Agnes a glorious picture of their life together and persuades her to leave her husband. Although their escape has been seen as immoral by some critics—particularly those of the nineteenth century—others consider it justified by their circumstances.

Through the character of **Agnes Dingman Kinney,** Garland illustrates the toll that midwestern farm life took on the women who worked side by side with their husbands to survive. Once beautiful, Agnes has become faded and exhausted, her health broken, and her dreams of happiness destroyed during her marriage to an insensitive, brutish man. She is burdened with the care of a young child and continually tormented by her husband's irascible parents. Garland's realistic portrayal of the loneliness, hard work, and complete lack of romance experienced by women like Agnes is an important part of his effort to debunk the sanitized myth of the American pastoral. Agnes's husband **Ed Kinney** is portrayed as an tyrannical oaf whose animalistic tendencies lie perilously close to the surface.

"Up the Coulee" is considered a powerful, autobiographical story. Permeated with the sense of guilt that Garland himself felt for leaving his own family when he moved east, the story provides a vivid portrait of the harshness and futility of farm life that contrasts with the natural splendor of the midwestern landscape. Though not a writer, **Howard McLane** has in common with his creator an artistic vocation: he is a successful actor and theatrical director. Upon his arrival in Wisconsin, he feels a profound appreciation for, and even pride in, the landscape of his birthplace and only gradually becomes aware of the difficulties experienced by those who live there. His clean, crisp white shirt provides a symbolic contrast to the mud and squalor that surrounds him. Although he initially feels innately superior—if sympathetic—to those he has left behind, McLane eventually admits to having neglected his family for so long and allowing them to lose their farm. **Grant McLane** is well aware of how dreary his own life is compared to his brother's, and the fancy gifts Howard brings from the East only enrage him more. His embittered, somber outlook is the result not so much of his brother's neglect, however, as of economic and other factors out of his control. He compares himself to a fly caught in a pan of molasses, utterly helpless to extricate itself, an image that describes most of Garland's other characters as well. Another significant character in "Up the Coulee" is **William McTurg,** a local man who drives McLane home in his wagon. McLane misreads McTurg's silence as an appreciative response to the landscape through which he travels, but he is actually too weighed down and exhausted by his troubles to talk.

The character of **Julia Peterson** in "Among the Corn Rows" believes that in marrying she will escape the drudgery she has always experienced. Actually, however, she is at the beginning of what will no doubt be a lonely and difficult married life, and the reader knows from the previous description of Rob's life on the prairie that her romantic expectations of the future must eventually collapse. Her more realistic sweetheart, **Rob Rodemaker,** is a hardworking and well-meaning young man who looks forward to acquiring in his wife a helpmate and companion for the years ahead. These themes are presented against an idyllic rural landscape that highlights the contrast between dreams and reality and the opposing views of nature as nurturing and hostile.

"The Return of a Private" is among Garland's best known stories. It is infused with the disillusionment of the post-Civil War period, when many returning soldiers faced grueling work on farms that had deteriorated during their absence. Scholars have noted that this story features an unusually sentimental tone, relayed through the sad memories of **Private Edward Smith** as he remembers his war companions as well as his happiness when he reunites with his family. Reputedly modeled after the author's father, whose return from the Civil War is recorded in Garland's autobiography, *Son of the Middle Border,* Smith is much older and wearier than before he left his home, handicapped not only by the debilitating fever he contracted during the war but by the heavy mortgage on his farm. His joyful homecoming is a brief, bright moment in what promises to be a hard life ahead, but his feelings for his loved ones give him strength to go on.

Garland's belief in the need for social reforms to help the American farmer is evident in "Under the Lion's Paw," which focuses on the issue of the Single Tax. Garland felt that the tax structure unfairly favored land speculators, and that a "single tax" on all land, whether used or unused, would prevent large tracts of unused land from being monopolized by too-powerful landlords. The story illustrates the practical results of land speculation and the profound fear of homelessness that plagued farmers as they struggled to hold on to their property. **Tim Haskins** makes a grueling effort to purchase the property he lives and toils on and then is coldly cheated by its owner. The story's title refers to Haskins's helpless position; he has no choice but to capitulate to Butler. Enraged by this injustice, Haskins struggles with his violent impulses but finally decides not to murder his enemy. The thought of his innocent, dependent child changes his mind and gives him the determination to go on. Landlord and speculator **Jim Butler** embodies the corporate greed and callousness that Garland condemned as detrimental to the small American farm, but Garland has been faulted for his one-dimensional portrait of this character, who seems unnaturally hateful and sadistic.

In "Mrs. Ripley's Trip," the title character finally achieves the goal of which she has long dreamed: she pays a visit to the eastern home she left twenty-three years before. Like other female characters in Garland's "Middle Border" stories, **Mrs. Ripley** personifies the harsh reality of the farm wife's life. Even so, she achieves a measure of satisfaction by fulfilling her dream, then returns resignedly to her work and isolation. Her husband, **Mr. Ripley,** has also been beaten down by years of hardship, but he is an essentially lighthearted man who finds solace through his fiddle-playing.

Further Reading

Carter, Joseph L. "Hamlin Garland's Liberated Woman." *American Literary Realism* 6, No. 3 (Summer 1973): 255-58.

Dictionary of Literary Biography, Vol. 12, 71, 78. Detroit: Gale.

Gish, Robert. *Hamlin Garland: The Far West.* Boise, Id.: Boise State University, 1976.

Howells, William Dean. "Editor's Study." *Harper's New Monthly Magazine* LXXXIII, No. CCCCXCVI (September 1891): 638-42.

McCullough, Joseph B. *Hamlin Garland.* Boston: Twayne, 1978.

Silet, Charles L., and Robert E. Welch. *The Critical Reception of Hamlin Garland,* 1891-1978. Troy, N.Y.: Whitson, 1985.

Twentieth-Century Literary Criticism, Vol. 3. Detroit: Gale.

Elizabeth Cleghorn Gaskell
1810-1865

English novelist, novella, sketch, and short story writer, biographer, poet, and essayist.

Mary Barton: A Tale of Manchester Life (novel, 1848)

Plot: Set in the economically depressed period of the 1830s and 1840s, the novel centers on John Barton, a mill worker in the northern England city of Manchester, and his daughter Mary, an apprentice seamstress whose mother has died in childbirth early in the book. Out of concern for his fellow workers, many of whom are destitute and even starving, John works as a union organizer. He is repeatedly discouraged, however, by the refusal of the managers and government to help them. His compatriots choose him to murder young Harry Carson, the son of mill owner Henry Carson, as a means of scaring the powerful employers into taking the workers' concerns seriously. John is not aware that Harry is in love with and has tried to seduce his daughter; though tempted briefly by the security offered by Harry, Mary rejects him in favor of her long-faithful suitor, the honest workman Jem Wilson. After Harry is murdered, Jem is accused of the crime, and Mary devotes herself to trying to clear his name. She must bring to court Jem's sailor cousin Will Wilson, who can provide an alibi for the innocent defendant. She travels from Manchester to Liverpool and is finally able to locate him aboard a ship, bringing him back to testify at Jem's trial and saving her lover from conviction. As a result of tension and exhaustion, she falls gravely ill. Upon her recovery, Mary and Jem are married.

The mystery of Harry's murder is not resolved until John is overcome by guilt on his deathbed. Job Legh, a factory worker and self-taught naturalist, brings about a reconciliation between John and the father of his victim. Greatly moved by John's deathbed confession and plea for forgiveness, the formerly vengeful Carson becomes committed to helping the workers improve their lot. Mary and Jem emigrate to Canada to begin a new life.

Characters: *Mary Barton* provides a realistic depiction of working class life in Manchester during a period of great economic hardship in the industrialized north of England. Considered the finest example of Gaskell's "social novels," *Mary Barton* is characterized by its compassionate tone and its understated promotion of a Christian ethic of understanding and reconciliation to solve the rift between workers and managers. While early reviewers faulted Gaskell for portraying the destitute workers too sympathetically, modern critics contend that her stance was actually fairly balanced and moderate, though she obviously believed that workers suffered most in hard economic times. *Mary Barton* has been identified as one of the first nineteenth-century novels to provide a truly authentic, unsentimental portrait of working-class characters and the hardships they endured.

While some scholars have called **Mary Barton** an unremarkable figure whose primary purpose is to provide the conventional love story that Gaskell's nineteenth-century audiences expected, others consider her an interesting heroine who reveals much about the author's attitudes. Described by critic W.A. Craik as a "girl of good impulses and fervent passions [who reaches] maturity by way of many small and one great single test of her fibre," Mary is perceptive, intelligent, and courageous. Raised without a mother in a working-class household, Mary is not ignorant of life's realities, and it is not surprising that she would be tempted to marry the more privileged Harry Carson (who has also appealed to her vanity by appreciating her beauty). Nevertheless, she eventually recognizes the purer motives and more durable qualities of her longtime suitor, Jem Wilson, and she rejects Carson's advances. During the second half of the book, Mary plays a much more prominent role when she works to clear her lover's name, and her character gains strength as her father's deteriorates. Because she takes charge of the situation herself, traveling to Liverpool alone to locate Will Wilson, Mary has been identified as a typical Gaskell heroine who is capable of affecting the course of events and of acquiring a measure of authority in a male-dominated society. By taking action to help a person she loves overcome injustice, Mary herself achieves peace. This is particularly significant in view of the fact that Gaskell wrote *Mary Barton* in part as a way to transcend the grief she felt over the death of her infant son; she makes the claim in the novel that it is those things we cannot fight against or change that most grieve us. Although Mary's breakdown after Jem's trial is over might be seen as somewhat melodramatic, such a collapse is not entirely unknown after a period of great physical and emotional stress. The fact that Mary and Jem leave Manchester after their marriage for a new life in another country has been described as hopeful on the one hand and as a sign of defeat on the other.

John Barton is sometimes identified as the central character of *Mary Barton* because he most clearly personifies the social concerns around which the novel revolves. Yet he differs from similar characters in other "social problem" novels in his complexity and conflicting nature. Increasingly aware of the extreme destitution that many of his fellow workers endure, John first tries to help them through legitimate channels. He is chosen as a delegate by his compatriots to present a petition to Parliament, documenting the workers' misery [a historically accurate occurrence based on the activities of the Chartists during the same period in which the story is set], but John is profoundly disillusioned by the government's indifference. In the Davenport household he finds inadequate sanitation, poor nourishment, and nonexistent medical care, while at the home of the prosperous Carsons the difference in conditions experienced by workers and managers is obvious. Overcome by a sense of irremediable injustice, John is willing to commit a violent act. Early reviewers saw John's outrage and hopelessness as untypical of the working man, even though Gaskell had borrowed details from a real murder that took place in Manchester in 1831 for the novel's plot. While Gaskell certainly does not excuse John for committing murder, neither does she condemn him outright. Too weak to admit, either before or after the trial, that he is the real murderer (even though doing so would clear the name of the innocent Jem), John takes to opium and begins to physically disintegrate. Through his deathbed confession of the murder and his plea for forgiveness, he is reconciled with Henry Carson—a man who, like him, has experienced a great loss—and both are redeemed by the experience.

Representing the managers' side of the economic conflict depicted in *Mary Barton* is **Henry Carson,** a mill owner and leader among the manufacturers of Manchester. Carson was himself once a worker but was able to ascend through the ranks to a position of wealth and power. He is now a stern-mannered man who seems to have forgotten his working-class origins. Although he is initially portrayed as a distasteful character, Gaskell encourages the reader to feel compassion for him after the death of his son. His pain leads to a thirst for vengeance that threatens the life of an innocent man—Jem Wilson—but he is ultimately redeemed by his willingness to forgive Harry's murderer. Thus Gaskell ends the novel on a note of Christian charity and reconciliation, even informing the reader that the mill owner went on to work for the benefit of his employees. Like her husband, **Mrs. Carson** is a former mill worker who now lives a life of privilege and luxury. It is suggested that her indolence and self-indulgence are due to her lack of education, whereas she might have been happier with physical work to occupy her time. Again, Gaskell displays her sympathy for an otherwise unlikable character when she describes Mrs. Carson, as she sits by her son's corpse, unable to accept his death. Young **Harry Carson**'s primary functions are to tempt Mary to choose a life of ease and to provide a likely murder victim. He is reprehensible in his desire to make Mary his mistress rather than his wife and callous in passing around at a managers' meeting a caricature of striking workers, but Gaskell does not suggest that he deserves his fate.

Honest, faithful **Jem Wilson** is rewarded for his virtue with exoneration and marriage to Mary. His murder trial is considered one of the most powerful scenes in the novel. During Mary's breakdown after his trial he tenderly nurses her through her illness, exhibiting his true strength and fineness of character. Although cleared of the murder charges when his cousin **Will Wilson,** a young sailor, provides an alibi, Jem continues to be shunned by the townsfolk. His immigration with Mary to Canada signifies both an escape from the ridicule and hardship of life in Manchester and a hopeful effort to attain a new life.

Several other significant characters flesh out the working class milieu presented in *Mary Barton.* **Job Legh** is a mill operative and also a self-taught scientist who collects and classifies insects in his free time. In his gentleness and fair-mindedness, Job embodies the Christian ethic endorsed by Gaskell. It is he who brings John together with the father of his victim, thus setting the scene for the reconciliation that is an important part of the novel's message. His granddaughter **Margaret Legh,** a blind singer, is also a model of patience and virtue. She shares with her grandfather the qualities of gentleness, prudence, common sense, and resignation to her fate, but she exhibits a certain lack of compassion when she is unable to understand how Mary could be tempted by Harry Carson. Another representative of Christian morality and forbearance is **Old Alice Wilson,** a saintly woman who works as a laundress and also dispenses simple herbal medicines from the damp cellar in which she lives. Although she yearns nostalgically for the country home of her youth, the truth is that her family's dire poverty forced her to leave there, and the pastoral peace she envisions is an illusion. After losing her hearing and her sight, without ever having fulfilled her wish to return to the countryside, but in relative peace, Alice dies. Her death scene is portrayed in a realistic, unromantic way.

Other characters in *Mary Barton* include **the Davenports,** the impoverished family John tries to help when Mr. Davenport is dying of disease and starvation. Their destitution is vividly described. John Barton's sister, **Esther,** serves as an example of the vulnerability of women in the nineteenth century: when she was a pretty, young country girl, she ran off with an Army officer who abandoned her after she had given birth to a baby. She subsequently became an alcoholic and a prostitute, though she attempts to hide her real situation from Mary when she meets her. **Sally Leadbitter** is a mill worker who serves as a go-between for

Harry Carson and Mary; although good-natured on the surface, she is actually vulgar and gossip-hungry. Despite her faults, however, Sally is devoted to her bedridden mother and entertains her with stories about the people she encounters during her work day.

Cranford (novel, 1853)

Plot: The small English village of Cranford is inhabited primarily by older, single women who, because they live on limited incomes, practice an ''elegant economy''; they enjoy each other's company and visit often. Chief among these ladies are the formidable Miss Deborah Jenkyns and her softhearted sister Miss Matty (Matilda) Jenkyns. The arrival of the frank Captain Brown causes something of a stir because—unlike his discreet female neighbors—he freely discusses his financial problems, but he soon wins the women's approval with his kindness and consideration for others. Brown's two daughters live with him, the elder of whom is dying of a terminal illness. When Brown is suddenly killed snatching a child from a train's path, the ladies of Cranford are grief stricken and, following the subsequent death of Brown's older daughter, consider how they might help the younger girl. Happily, her former suitor arrives in town and she accepts his marriage proposal.

After Miss Deborah dies, her submissive sister is forced to make her own decisions for the first time in her life. She is aided by her friends Miss Pole, Mrs. Forrester, Mrs. Jamieson—who has taken over Miss Deborah's dominant role in the village social life—and Miss Mary Smith, who narrates the novel and whose father is Miss Matty's financial adviser. Mary learns that the Jenkyns sisters also have a brother, Peter, who left Cranford years ago after being harshly punished by their father; he is rumored to be living in India. The women are excited to learn that Mrs. Jamieson's aristocratic sister-in-law, Lady Glenmire, will soon be arriving in the neighborhood. They worry about how they will address her, but Mrs. Jamieson lets them know that they are not highborn enough to be introduced to her. When it later turns out that most of the town's more aristocratic citizens are unavailable, Mrs. Jamieson is forced to invite her friends to visit Lady Glenmire. Stung by Mrs. Jamieson's earlier snubbing, the ladies consider rejecting the invitation, but they finally accept. They find Lady Glenmire amiable and unpretentious. Later, when Mrs. Jamieson is away from Cranford for a short period, Lady Glenmire is courted by the town doctor, who holds a decidedly modest social position. Her new friends are delightedly shocked when she decides to marry him; they anticipate Mrs. Jamieson's reaction when she returns. True to form, Mrs. Jamieson refuses to have anything to do with the newly married couple.

Meanwhile Miss Matty experiences a serious financial setback when her bank fails and she is left with inadequate funds. Worried that Mrs. Jamieson will persuade her friends to drop her from their circle, she is relieved when Mrs. Jamieson decrees that Miss Matty's position is secure because her father was a clergyman. Mary Smith obtains her father's advice in managing Miss Matty's curtailed income, and the other women secretly contribute from their own small incomes to help her. In addition, her maid Martha speeds up her marriage with her fiancé so the couple can rent Miss Matty's house and allow her to stay on as a boarder. Another happy occurrence is the arrival of Peter Jenkyns from India. Informed of his sister's crisis, he sells his property and returns to England to share his ample income with her. Peter also reconciles Mrs. Jamieson and the now ordinary Lady Glenmire.

Characters: Originally published serially in Charles Dickens's periodical, *Household Words,* and subsequently expanded to novel length, *Cranford* is one of Gaskell's best known and most respected works. It provides a skillful depiction of an English provincial town (based on the Cheshire village of Knutsford, where Gaskell was raised) and a group of mostly single, mostly elderly women whose lives—despite their age, status, and modest finances—are generally happy and active. Gaskell celebrates the pleasures of friendship and other simple comforts while chronicling a vanishing time and place.

The novel's famous opening sentence describes Cranford as "in possession of the Amazons," referring to the women who dominate its social life. Although it is revealed that the Cranford ladies do rely on men for both worldly advice and material support, from the story's beginning their lives revolve in a primarily feminine sphere. Gaskell has been lauded for her sympathetic portrayal—unusual in Victorian fiction—of unmarried, older women who lead eventful and even joyful lives and whose regard for and support of each other helps them overcome adversity. During the first part of the book (that which was originally published in *Household Words*) the most prominent of the women is **Miss Deborah Jenkyns,** an authoritative person who makes all of the decisions not only for herself but for her sister, Matty. Miss Deborah's death only halfway through the novel has been attributed to the fact that Gaskell did not initially intend to make a novel of her Cranford stories. Likewise, the alarmingly frank, somewhat crude, but generally amiable **Captain Brown** is also eliminated early in the story and thus is not a particularly well-developed character. His older daughter, **Mary,** made sharp-tongued and bitter by her infirmity, provides a note of melodramatic tragedy by dying young of an incurable disease, while her sister, **Jessie,** achieves happiness when her former suitor, **Major Gordon,** rescues her from impoverishment.

The second half of *Cranford* centers on **Miss Matty Jenkyns,** one of Gaskell's best-known characters. At the time of her sister's death she is in her mid-fifties, a gentle, softhearted woman who has always allowed her sister to direct her life. With the help of her loyal friends she learns to make her own decisions. Her decision to invest her money in the Town and Country Bank proves ill-advised, however, when that institution goes out of business, and Miss Matty is left destitute. Her greatest worry is that this new development will cause her to be estranged from her beloved friends, but the usually rigid Mrs. Jamieson allows an exception to be made in deference to the fact that Miss Matty's father was a clergyman. Many years earlier, Miss Matty gave up an opportunity to marry in order to care for her mother. Simple and trusting of others, she brings out the best qualities in those around her. It seems appropriate when her brother arrives in time to bring comfort to the remainder of her life.

Miss Matty's brother, **Peter Jenkyns,** is one of several lost brothers in Gaskell's fiction, a recurrent phenomenon many critics have attributed to the fact that the author's own brother, John, shipped out to India and then disappeared, never to be seen again. In *Cranford,* Peter left home after being severely punished for conducting a prank, in which he dressed himself as a woman and completely hoodwinked his father. Upon his return to Cranford, Peter fits into the society he finds there without disrupting it and, in fact, even improves it: he saves his sister from destitution, restores harmony to her circle of friends by bringing about a reconciliation between Mrs. Jamieson and the former Lady Glenmire, and soon comes to hold the dominant position once held by Miss Deborah. He delights the women with his colorful (indeed, often much embellished) stories of life in India; in fact, Miss Matty is initially concerned about his feelings for Mrs. Jamieson, who is particularly captivated by his tales, but he soon lets his sister know that he has no romantic intentions toward her friend.

Miss Mary Smith is one of the most significant of Miss Matty's friends. The story's narrator, she maintains a certain detachment from the Cranford community—because she is a newcomer there—but is also an accepted part of it. Thus she provides an insider's view of the proceedings but also offers an outsider's objectivity. Although she is generally mild and self-effacing, she directs the reader's journey through Cranford with wisdom, wit, and compassion for others, showing her to be the author's primary representative in the story. Miss Mary's father, **Mr. Smith,** is one of few men who play any significant role in the novel; a rather gruff man of business, he intimidates Miss Matty, whom he finds a bit too naive. The fact that Miss Matty must appeal to her friend's father for financial advice highlights her necessary dependence on men for some aspects of survival.

The inherently conservative and socially pretentious **Mrs. Jamieson** becomes the most dominant of the Cranford ladies after the death of Miss Deborah. She attempts to impose her own rules of propriety and rank on the others when Lady Glenmire arrives, but the absence of suitable gentry to visit her aristocratic relative forces her to allow her women friends to call. She also considers her sister's marriage to Mr. Hoggins unacceptable, but she eventually accedes. **Lady Glenmire,** whom Miss Matty and her friends expect to be quite haughty, surprises them with her amiability and lack of pretension. In marrying the lower-born physician **Mr. Hoggins,** she demonstrates both that advancing age does not necessarily preclude romance and that conventional rules about marrying outside of one's rank can be violated with no ill consequences.

The other members of Miss Matty's circle include **Mrs. Forrester** and **Miss Pole.** The latter declares, "My father was a man, and I know the sex well," humorously underlining the ease with which the women dismiss the male sex. Although she initially advised Miss Matty against investing her money in the Town and Country Bank, it is she who secretly collects funds to help support her friend and who helps Miss Matty establish a tea-selling business. Other characters in *Cranford* include Miss Matty's loyal servant, **Martha,** who arranges for her employer to live in her house as a boarder but does not otherwise alter their relationship, and Martha's husband, **Jem,** with whom Miss Matty is happy to co-exist because he is rarely present—a quality she finds most admirable in a man.

Further Reading

Craik, W. A. *Elizabeth Gaskell and the English Provincial Novel.* London: Methuen, 1975.

Dictionary of Literary Biography, Vol. 21. Detroit: Gale.

Duthie, Enid L. *The Themes of Elizabeth Gaskell.* Totowa, N.J.: Rowman and Littlefield, 1980.

Easson, Angus. *Elizabeth Gaskell.* London: Routledge & Kegan Paul, 1979.

Lansbury, Coral. *Elizabeth Gaskell.* Boston: Twayne, 1984.

Nineteenth-Century Literature Criticism, Vol. 5. Detroit: Gale.

Wright, Edgar. *Mrs. Gaskell: The Basis for Reassessment.* London: Oxford University Press, 1965.

Théophile Gautier
1811-1872

French novelist, novella writer, short story writer, poet, critic, travel writer, and dramatist.

Mademoiselle de Maupin (novel, 1836)

Plot: The novel centers on handsome, worldly, twenty-two-year-old D'Albert, who worships beauty in all its forms. He has conceived of the perfect woman, based on those he has seen in paintings by famous artists, but he has not yet encountered such a creature. Having decided he should have a mistress, he pursues a beautiful and charming young woman whom he calls Rosette, after her pink dress, emphasizing the physical nature of their relationship and D'Albert's refusal to see her as a whole person. The two begin an affair, and Rosette pleases D'Albert with her accommodating sensuality. After five months, however, D'Albert begins to tire of Rosette. Sensing her lover's boredom, Rosette takes him to her country estate. There D'Albert meets another guest, an exceptionally handsome young man named Théodore de Sérannes whose swordplay, horsemanship, and conversational skills are impressive. D'Albert is somewhat alarmed to find himself romantically attracted to Théodore, and he tries to convince himself that the young man is really a woman. Rosette too seems to have fallen in love with Théodore.

To amuse themselves, the assembled guests decide to enact Shakespeare's *As You Like It*. Rosette resists playing Rosalind, the female character who dresses like a man, not wanting to wear men's clothing, so Théodore assumes the part. Seeing his friend's resplendent appearance in a dress, D'Albert becomes convinced that Théodore is a woman. He is correct, for, as she reveals in a letter written to a friend, Théodore is actually Mademoiselle Madelaine de Maupin. Determined to locate her ideal mate, she has disguised herself as a man so that she can circulate freely among them. Her consequent intimate knowledge of the male sex, however, has only disgusted her. She is amused by D'Albert's passion for her and confusion about her true sex. Finally D'Albert writes Mademoiselle de Maupin a letter proclaiming that he believes she is a woman and that he loves her. For several weeks she makes no reply; then one night she appears in his room, willing to give him a night of love. D'Albert has the kind of sensual experience of which he has dreamed, but in the morning Mademoiselle de Maupin is gone. That night, she had also visited Rosette to reveal her true sex, and they too had a sexual encounter. Mademoiselle de Maupin explains in a letter that she has left D'Albert to avoid the suffering that the inevitable end of their love would bring. She vows never to love another man, and she tells Rosette and D'Albert to try to find happiness together.

Characters: Considered an important figure in the transition from romanticism to realism that occurred in the literature of the mid-nineteenth century, Gautier is praised for his evocative, highly descriptive style. *Mademoiselle de Maupin* provides a compelling treatment of the eternal conflict between ideals and reality, conveying in a sometimes wordy, epistolary form the main characters' search for perfection. At its time of publication, the novel was considered shockingly erotic. Infused with images of art, music, and literature (especially in the use of Shakespeare's *As You Like It*), the book voices Gautier's credo of ''art for art's sake''; as stated in the controversial preface, which was written before the novel and not intended to be published with it, he believed that a work of art should be beautiful, not useful, thus the novel lacks concern for conventional morality or virtue.

Composed in epistolary style, much of *Mademoiselle de Maupin* is presented in the form of letters written by **D'Albert** to a friend. Well-educated and artistically inclined, D'Albert enjoyed a pampered childhood, and is already sexually experienced. He is an aesthete who particularly appreciates the female form as represented in the works of Rubens and Titian. In his idealism, expansive speculations, and lack of goals, D'Albert is a typically romantic character. Profoundly bored with the mundane details of life, he dreams of his ideal woman, embodying the attributes of the painted nudes he has admired. He views women as sexual objects, created for his amusement and easily discarded when they have ceased to please. Reflecting on his own behavior, D'Albert admits that he is never satisfied and that he has a dual nature, his conflicts between body and soul usually ending in the body's victory. He also expresses a concept of beauty that originated in classical Greece: the ultimate human form of the hermaphrodite, which harmoniously combines the physical attributes of both men and women. D'Albert finds   sensual pleasure and intellectual stimulation with Rosette, but soon grows tired of her. After meeting Théodore, he is increasingly convinced that she is not only a woman but his *ideal* woman; the truth of this is confirmed during their night of lovemaking. However, D'Albert is denied further contact with Mademoiselle de Maupin, thus leaving the perfection of their encounter intact but also suggesting that he must be satisfied with the less ideal, but still pleasurable reality embodied in Rosette.

The novel's title character is an exquisitely beautiful, independent young woman who, like D'Albert, avidly pursues an ideal. As she explains in letters to a friend, **Mademoiselle Madelaine de Maupin** wanted to find a noble, deserving lover. Her independence and unconventionality are evidenced by her willingness to live as her lover's mistress; she sees no dishonor in such an arrangement and has no desire to marry. In order to study men at close hand and undetected, Madelaine decides to impersonate one herself, becoming **Théodore de Sérannes.** She learns how to ride a horse and use a sword, and begins to spend her time in the company of men, unencumbered by the femininity that would alter their attitude toward her. Far from locating her ideal man, however, Madelaine becomes thoroughly disgusted with them and the way they treat women. Yet she remains physically attracted to the opposite sex despite her distaste for their behavior, as demonstrated by her desire for a drunken youth with whom she shared a bed at an inn. Having attracted D'Albert's attention with her delicate beauty, evident to him even through her disguise, she observes his tormented confusion about her true sex with detached amusement. Although she is not in love with D'Albert, Madelaine concedes that he is less brutal and more appreciative of beauty than other men, and decides to give him a night of love he will never forget. Afterward, she also visits Rosette's room to reveal that Théodore, with whom Rosette is deeply in love, does not really exist. Madelaine has previously expressed an awareness of her bisexual nature, claiming that she wishes to be both femininely catlike and masculinely bold in her sexuality, and her encounter with Rosette also reflects this aspect of her character. Realizing that men often tire of women, and wishing to preserve her experience with D'Albert in its present, perfect form, Madelaine leaves, vowing never to love another man. Based on a remarkable seventeenth-century woman who was an actress, singer, and expert swordsman, frequently dressed as a man, had bisexual affairs, and died at thirty in a convent, Mademoiselle de Maupin has been seen as both an allegorical figure representing ideal beauty and as an essentially human character who must struggle with the clash between ideals and physical reality. Some critics have seen her willingness to fulfill D'Albert's desires as a sign that she has reconciled herself to the demands of imperfect human life and accepted the impossibility of her ideals. Yet her absolute oath never to love another man seems to contradict the idea of accommodation to reality.

D'Albert's other mistress, the beautiful and highly entertaining **Rosette,** is black-haired and sensuous. A twenty-five-year-old widow, she is practical, witty, and charming and seems to bring out the best in those around her—even the bored D'Albert. Rosette is sexually experienced and versatile, and keeps D'Albert satisfied for several months. She is presented entirely through the eyes of D'Albert, not a completely reliable narrator; looking beyond his limited view, the reader may perceive that Rosette is more than a sexual object. Particularly in her response to Théodore, she reveals her capacity for real emotions and suffering. In addition, she embodies what D'Albert calls the "veritable truth" of real life; by combining an engaging, pleasant personality with pleasure in her own body, Rosette might be said to have achieved the union of body and soul that D'Albert has failed to reach.

Isnabel, Théodore's exceptionally pretty page boy, whom he treats with great tenderness, is eventually revealed to be a girl, **Ninon,** whom Mademoiselle de Maupin rescued from a brutal suitor. Mademoiselle de Maupin dresses her as a boy to protect her from further mistreatment and takes joy in depriving coarse men of enjoying her. Isnabel/Ninon's male-female status echoes that of Mademoiselle de Maupin, thus providing another illustration of the hermaphrodite theme.

Further Reading

Brandes, Georg. "Merimée and Gautier." In *Main Currents in Nineteenth-Century Literature: The Romantic School in France,* Vol. 5, pp. 281-306. New York: Boni and Liveright, 1924.

Dillingham, Louise Bulkley. *The Creative Imagination of Théophile Gautier.* Princeton, N.J.: Psychological Review, 1927.

Epstein, Edna Selan. "The Entanglement of Sexuality and Aesthetics in Gautier and Mallarmé." *Nineteenth-Century French Studies* No. 1 (November 1972): 5-20.

Grant, Richard B. *Théophile Gautier.* Boston: Twayne, 1975.

Nineteenth-Century Literature Criticism, Vol. 1. Detroit: Gale.

Palache, John Garber. *Gautier and the Romantics.* New York: Viking, 1926.

Smith, Albert B. *Ideal and Fictional Narratives of Théophile Gautier.* Gainesville: University of Florida Press, 1969.

George Gissing
1857-1903
English novelist, short story writer, critic, and essayist.

The New Grub Street (novel, 1891)

Plot: The story centers on promising young writer Edwin Reardon, whose first book was favorably received but who has since produced little work. His wife, Amy, is the daughter of Edmund Yule, who left his wife and children hardly any money when he died; the two other Yule brothers are John, a prosperous manufacturer, and Alfred, an embittered and generally unsuccessful writer. Edwin's friend Jasper Milvain, a journalist who writes for several publications and knows many important people in the publishing business, believes that Edwin will eventually achieve critical and financial success. Jasper becomes interested in Marian Yule, Alfred's daughter and literary researcher, but Alfred is reluctant to welcome him into their home because the young man has ties with an editor named Fadge for whom Alfred has, over the years, developed a great hatred. Nevertheless Jasper asks Marian to befriend his two sisters, Dora and Maud, who have come to London to live with him after the death of their mother. Marian visits the Milvains frequently and begins to grow fond of Jasper, but, as his sisters realize, he hopes to marry a wealthy woman so that he can pursue his writing career in comfort.

Edwin is burdened with financial worries and finds himself unable to write, while Amy urges him to treat his vocation as a commercial trade and try to make as much money as possible. Their differing views lead to frequent quarrels. Finally Edwin accepts a job as a clerk. Amy considers this situation degrading, and she leaves their home and goes to live with her mother, taking with her their ten-month-old baby, Willie. Meanwhile Jasper admires Marian but hesitates to marry her because she is poor. When both she and her cousin Amy inherit money from their deceased Uncle John, however, Jasper proposes and she accepts. Amy intends to use her legacy to support Edwin in his effort to produce a work of artistic merit. She offers to return to him and share her new wealth, but Edwin is too proud to accept her offer. He subsequently becomes very ill but hides his condition from Amy. The two are briefly reconciled during the illness and subsequent death of their son; Edwin's health also deteriorates and he too finally dies.

When Jasper learns that Marian's inheritance will be smaller than expected, he suddenly suggests that they wait to marry until they can afford it. Then Alfred Yule learns that he will soon be blind, so that Marian will have to support both herself and her parents. Without actually breaking his engagement to Marian, Jasper proposes to another, wealthier woman, but she rejects him. Hoping to force Marian to break their engagement in deference to her family—since her father now depends on her for support—he insists that she marry him immediately. Marian finally realizes the truth about Jasper's motives and parts with him. Her friends secure her a job as a librarian. Jasper writes a favorable review of Edwin's posthumously published works, which wins him Amy's gratitude and friendship. Each comes to see in the other an appropriate partner—Amy answers Jasper's desire for a moneyed mate and Jasper answers Amy's for a husband with social and financial savvy—and they are married. Jasper attains even greater success than he had predicted, and he and Amy achieve a mutually satisfying marriage as well. Jasper eventually ascends to the editorship once held by Fadge.

Characters: Gissing's harshly realistic depiction of literary London in the late nineteenth century has been praised for its authenticity, and Gissing is further lauded for the care and insight he brings to his characterizations. While some aspects of Gissing's work—such as its voluminousness and instances of melodrama—align it with the Victorian period, he also anticipates the twentieth century's pessimism and emphasis on the alienated, unhappy, despairing anti-hero. *The New Grub Street* is infused with the idea that poverty inevitably degrades even the most dedicated and talented, and that both art and relationships are vulnerable to the forces of economics.

Through the novel's central character, **Edwin Reardon,** Gissing explores the role of the artist in society and the difficulty of balancing one's creative ideals with the practical demands of survival. Unlike Jasper Milvain, Edwin has an almost religious reverence for the writing art and aspires to achieve excellence, yet those whose standards are lower are more generously compensated. Edwin is torn between his desire to fulfil his early promise and produce works of real literary merit and the pressing necessity of supporting his family; Amy exacerbates the conflict by encouraging him to take a more commercial approach to writing. As a result Edwin finds himself immobilized by frustration, fear, and helplessness. Forced to support not only a wife with sophisticated tastes and little inclination to curb her excesses but a dependent child, he finally bows to economic pressure and accepts a position as a clerk, and his wife leaves him as a result. An idealist who is easily discouraged, Edwin depends on Amy for inspiration and loses his energy for work as his marriage deteriorates; thus his failure as an artist is inextricably linked with his failure as a husband. His death indicates that commercialism has triumphed over artistic promise. Many critics contend that Edwin represents Gissing's own viewpoint and embodies the frustrations Gissing faced as he struggled to establish himself as a writer and suffered through two unhappy marriages. Unlike the author who depicted him, however, Edwin never ultimately creates anything of transcendent or lasting value.

Although Edwin's wife, **Amy Reardon,** believes in his talent and supports his desire to achieve greatness, she tells him, "Art must be practiced as a trade, at all events in our time. This is the age of trade." She sees no reason why he should not produce works that are commercially viable, and she cannot accept the prospect of enduring poverty for the sake of art. Her matter-of-fact calculation of how many pages Edwin would have to write per day to produce a certain number of novels per year, and her conclusion that this would not comprise a particularly demanding task, are in opposition to Edwin's goals and to the more ethereal worth of literature. She represents public opinion and is a constant reminder to Edwin that his values run counter to his society's. Though she comes into the marriage with no money of her own, Amy has elegant tastes and insists that they live in a flat priced beyond their means; likewise she is disgusted by Edwin's shabby appearance during their attempted reconciliation, despite the fact that he has deprived himself of new clothing in order to send her money. In fact it is because he has been unable to afford a warm coat that Edwin contracts the illness that eventually leads to his death, thereby implicating Amy in his physical as well as his psychological downfall. Several scholars have noted an ambiguous attitude toward women in Gissing's work; he portrays them both as idealized sources of inspiration and as demanding and parasitic, depleting a man's energy as well as his economic viability. Gissing's own life was marred by his first marriage to an alcoholic, working-class woman and his later union with a woman whose psychological stability deteriorated after their marriage.

Gissing presents the novel's primary concerns early in the story through the voice of **Jasper Milvain,** the egotistical and cynical hack writer who serves as Edwin's foil. In describing Edwin to his mother and sisters, Jasper claims that the talented young writer will bring about his own downfall by his high-mindedness and by choosing a genteel, demanding wife. Because Jasper's aim in writing is not to create great art but to make as much money as he can, some critics have characterized him as a villain (the name Jasper was frequently used in Victorian fiction to designate a wicked character), but others dispute that view. Despite his disdain for Edwin's ambitions, he sincerely likes and respects his friend. For his part, Jasper is unencumbered by ideals and freely admits that his superficiality has helped him succeed. He does not understand why writing should be considered a sacred art, a viewpoint not necessarily condemned by Gissing. Jasper admires Marian Yule, but he treats her shabbily and is finally unable to overcome his financial concerns and marry her. Instead he callously proposes to an unattractive but wealthy woman, who spurns him. His eventual union with the equally money-minded Amy is successful (Jasper even comes to love her), and he proves a much more sympathetic and fair-minded editor than his predecessor, Fadge.

Another writer whose dismal fate is chronicled in *The New Grub Street* is **Alfred Yule,** the least successful of the three Yule brothers and an embittered, cranky old man. Alfred has endured a long career of poverty, frustration, humiliation, and disappointment, always dependent on the wavering favor of publishers and editors. He seems to have concentrated his resentment on one editor in particular, Fadge, whom he ardently hates. Yule manipulates his daughter, employing her as a virtual slave to conduct tedious literary research. He also pressures her to give him the money she has inherited so he can establish a magazine of his own, in which he will gain revenge for his many grievances by treating other writers even more harshly than editors have treated him. Yule's solution to the conflict a struggling writer faces when he wants to marry is to choose a working-class wife with lower economic expectations. However, Yule constantly complains about **Mrs. Yule**'s bad grammar, ignorance, and lack of sophistication (although she is more patient and gentle with him than he deserves). Yule's eventual blindness is a particularly horrible fate for a writer, and it also affects the daughter who must now support him.

Marian Yule is the most sympathetic character in the book, an intelligent young woman whose warmth and sensitivity are balanced by moral uprightness. Marian conducts literary research for her father at the British Museum Reading Room (a popular gathering place for London writers and an important setting in the novel). In a frequently noted passage, Marian gazes up at the library's dome and envisions it as a treacherous spider web in which the hapless researchers are trapped like flies—an image that signifies the dreariness and futility of literary life. Like many of the characters in *The New Grub Street,* Marian admits that life is improved by the possession of money, yet ironically money brings no improvements to her life. When the small legacy she receives is almost but not quite enough to keep Jasper interested, she realizes his true nature and breaks their engagement. Then she finds she must support her parents as well—a dismal setback, for, despite the loathing for the British

Museum Reading Room she has developed during her long hours of tedious research, she becomes a librarian.

Harold Biffen is another young writer whose struggles are recounted in *The New Grub Street.* Genuinely talented, he shares Edwin's reverence for the art of writing, and he too has learned of the debilitating effects of poverty. His ambition is to write a highly realistic novel entitled "Mr. Bailey, Grocer" that will feature ordinary characters whose lives are circumscribed by their lack of money. Dedicated and idealistic, he believes that art should not merely entertain but should reflect and illuminate the true circumstances of people's lives; thus many critics have seen in Harold a representative of Gissing's views. The fact that Harold is unmarried is significant, in that he has maintained his courage by avoiding the encumbrances that a woman represents. And when he does fall in love with Amy—hopelessly, because she would never marry a poor writer like him—it brings about his death. After carefully researching the effects of various poisons, Harold kills himself, and once again the impulse toward idealism and creative achievement is destroyed by harsh reality.

Other significant characters in the novel include the notoriously vicious editor **Fadge,** who is never actually seen but who represents the degrading system to which writers must submit; **Dora** and **Maud Milvain,** Jasper's sisters, who are well aware of their brother's selfishness and hence worry about their friend Marian, and who question Jasper about the literary merit of his work as opposed to its monetary value (leading him to admit that it is virtually without merit); and **John Yule,** the robust, sporting, and wealthy uncle of Amy and Marian, who leaves both girls money upon his death.

Further Reading

Coustillas, Pierre, and Colin Partridge, eds. *Gissing: The Critical Heritage.* London: Routledge & Kegan Paul, 1972.

Dictionary of Literary Biography, Vol. 18. Detroit: Gale.

Leavis, Q. D. "Gissing and the English Novel." *Scrutiny* VII, No. 1 (June 1938): 73-81.

Michaux, Jean-Pierre. *George Gissing: Critical Essays.* Totowa, N.J.: Barnes & Noble, 1981.

Selig, Robert L. *George Gissing.* Boston: Twayne, 1983.

Toynton, Evelyn. "The Subversive George Gissing." *American Scholar* 59, No. 1 (Winter 1990): 126-38.

Twentieth-Century Literary Criticism, Vols. 3, 24. Detroit: Gale.

Johann Wolfgang von Goethe
1749-1832

German dramatist, fiction writer, biographer, essayist, critic, and librettist.

The Sorrows of Young Werther (novel, 1774)

Plot: The novel, which takes place in mid-nineteenth-century Germany, is comprised primarily of letters from a young man named Werther to his friend Wilhelm. Escaping from an unhappy love affair and other circumstances, Werther goes to live in a secluded rural area called Walheim. He reports that he finds his surroundings peaceful and calming and that he has given up his former pursuit of painting in favor of reading, solitude, and contemplation of nature. After a significant lapse in correspondence, Wilhelm informs his friend that he has met and fallen in love with Charlotte S., whom he calls Lotte, the beautiful and charming daughter of a neighboring judge. Ignoring the fact that his beloved is engaged to another man, Werther completely abandons himself to his passion. He grows increasingly ardent and is distressed over any separation from Lotte, including her charitable visits to the sick of the community. Wilhelm advises Werther to either declare his intentions to Lotte or stop seeing her, so Werther attempts to give her up. Her fiance, Albert, a respectable and rational young man, arrives on the scene, and Werther concedes that Albert is a fine choice for a husband. Werther sinks deeper into melancholy and despair and finally decides to leave Walheim. Wilhelm secures his friend a diplomatic post in a distant city. Initially Werther's new position occupies his thoughts and time adequately, but he soon grows bored and unhappy and reproaches Wilhelm for saddling him with such a dull, demanding job.

Werther writes to Lotte, and her reply confirms that she and Albert are now married. After resigning his diplomatic post, Werther tries unsuccessfully attempt to enter the army. He then accepts an invitation to spend the summer at the estate of a young prince, but he is too gloomy and restless to remain there long. Werther can no longer resist the impulse to return to Walheim and see Lotte. When he encounters Lotte and her husband, he is shocked by Albert's calm appearance—he had expected his rival to look ecstatic. Both Lotte and Albert express pity and concern for Werther, but there seems to be no solution to his dilemma. At the same time Werther becomes more distraught when he is unable to help a peasant accused of murder. Finally on the advice of her husband, Lotte asks Werther not to come to her home so frequently, and Werther writes that he plans to kill himself. The same narrator who initially introduced the story now finishes it.

Werther went to Lotte's home one evening when Albert was away, frightening her with his wild appearance and incoherence. Lotte eventually ran from Werther and locked herself in her room. The next day Werther borrowed some guns from Albert, claiming that he needed them for a journey he was taking. He shot himself that night and died the next day. On hearing of his death, Lotte became very ill.

Characters: Goethe is widely acknowledged as the greatest of all German writers and one of the most influential authors in all literature. Immensely popular soon after its publication and said to have established Goethe's reputation, *The Sorrows of Young Werther* remains one of his best-known works. Through the protagonist's intense emotionalism, his elevation of intuition and passion over reason, and his self-abandonment to melancholy, despair, and finally suicide, the novel typifies the late eighteenth-century Sturm und Drang (storm and stress) movement with which it is often associated. According to many commentators, *Werther* encapsulated the sentiments and mood of an entire generation of young intellectuals, with many adopting the costume of the novel's hero and some even imitating Werther's final act. Goethe was distressed by this reaction to his work, through which he had apparently intended to purge the intensely romantic side of his own nature and warn against emotional excess.

Most of the relatively simple story presented in *Werther* is told through letters written by its title character to his friend Wilhelm (who never actually appears). Based partly on Goethe's conception of himself as a young man, **Werther** also seems to have been fashioned after Karl Jerusalum, whose suicide was brought on by despair over unrequited love and being socially ostracized. A sensitive, intelligent, and highly sentimental young man, Werther has artistic leanings—though some critics have identified him as a dilettante who merely fancies himself an artist—and spends much of his time in dreamy speculation. Like others of his generation, Werther reveres nature and the rustic life of the peasantry, craves solitude, and resists the binds of social convention. These qualities, along with his elevating feeling above reason and completely abandoning himself to passion, mark Werther as the quintessential romantic. His choppy, emphatic narration reflects his emotionally tempestuous nature and contrasts with the editor/author's calm tone. As the novel begins, Werther has retreated to the peaceful region of Walheim after suffering through an unhappy love affair, and he claims that he desires no company or guidance but is perfectly content to read classical literature, paint, and absorb the rural life around him. After a long gap between letters, however, Werther tells Wilhelm that he has met a charming girl named Charlotte—he calls her Lotte—whose natural, maternal aspect as she cut bread for her younger siblings initially enchanted him. Although (and quite possibly *because*) he knows Lotte is engaged to another man, Werther falls madly in love with her and his former peacefulness vanishes. His passion grows increasingly intense and heedless, and his disregard for how his attentions might compromise or affect Lotte reveals his inherent selfishness. Yet Werther also displays a notable faculty for self-analysis, and he is capable of accurately gauging the fitness of the calm, stolidly middle-class Albert as a husband for Lotte. Gloomy and despondent, Werther accepts a diplomatic post in the hope that it will cure him of his malady. But he is soon dissatisfied and bored with his duties, and he reacts to a social snub with exaggerated annoyance. Werther's return to Walheim and Lotte signifies the beginning of his downfall, for he now sinks irrevocably into an irresponsible, egotistical obsession with his hopeless love. Feeling that no one around him understands or sympathizes with his plight, Werther finally concludes—after frightening Lotte with an open declaration of love and a feverish embrace—that death represents his only possible escape. Werther's melodramatic bent and his lack of concern for others are evident as he contemplates with apparent pleasure the suffering his death will cause Lotte and Albert. As many critics have noted, the impulse toward suicide has been present in Werther's nature all along. His final act was a controversial issue for early reviewers; some felt it was immoral and others deemed it childish and cowardly, while still others who identified with Werther's anguish followed his example and took their own lives. Werther has been identified as an embodiment of the romanticism that dominated literature in the late eighteenth and early nineteenth centuries, and in his intense emotions, reverence for nature, and alienation from others he is considered a precursor to the Byronic (referring to the English romantic poet George Gordon, Lord Byron) heroes of later fiction. Scholars have further characterized Werther as distinctly modern in his penchant for self-examination and in the fact that he is ultimately brought down by destructive forces within his own personality rather than by outside elements. At the same time Werther has been said to represent the frustration and melancholy experienced by many young intellectuals of his times, who felt deprived of any useful activity or outlet for their talents and thus turned their focus in on themselves and their own emotions. Most critics agree that Werther's "sorrows" are finally exposed as barren and destructive, and that through this tormented protagonist Goethe meant to portray the failings of the Sturm und Drang perspective. Yet like other renowned characters in Goethe's work—most notably the title character of his 1832 drama, *Faust*—Werther's passionate striving for the absolute evidences a broad, ardent spirit, and the reader is encouraged to admire Werther and pity his tragic fate while disapproving of his actions.

The other characters in *Werther* are presented almost entirely through the protagonist's perspective, a circumstance that somewhat limits their portrayals but also sheds light on Werther's personality. The object of his obsessive passion is **Charlotte S., or Lotte,** a pretty, kind, charitable, and dutiful girl who seems to appreciate Werther's company but does not share his highly emotional, romantic view of things. Lotte initially attracts Werther's attention and regard when he sees her cutting a large loaf of rye bread for her younger siblings; it is the maternal aspect during this scene that particularly enchants the notably childish Werther. The most intriguing question about Lotte is the extent of her complicity in Werther's passion and consequent responsibility for his suicide. Although she is usually viewed as a basically good, innocent onlooker who merely provides Werther with an object to which he may fasten his ardent love, some critics claim that Lotte is not as blameless as she seems, and a few scholars even contend that she actually encourages Werther. In any case it is generally agreed that Lotte might have put an early end to Werther's attentions but fails to do so, and that she indicates when she is giving Werther the pistols he has asked to borrow that she knows what he plans to do with them but does nothing to prevent his suicide. Often cited as a pivotal scene in *Werther* is that in which Werther visits Lotte while Albert is away and recites the melancholy, turbulent poetry of Ossian, a legendary third-century Gaelic warrior of the Scottish Highlands. The scene makes it clear that while Lotte may share Werther's appreciation for poetry, she is frightened and bewildered by his excessive emotion and has no wish to alter her own situation. Indeed Lotte seems happily married to Albert. The editor's report that she swooned and became very ill upon hearing of Werther's death might indicate either that she did love Werther more deeply than seemed to be the case, or simply that she was overwhelmed by the part she unwillingly played in the tragedy. Goethe is said to have modeled Lotte after Charlotte Buff, a friend's fiancee, one of several unavailable women with whom he fell in love; his feelings for her, however, were apparently not as intense as Werther's for Lotte.

Modeled after Goethe's friend Johann Christian Kestner, **Albert** is the man Lotte has chosen to marry. Rational, clearheaded, and eminently respectable, Albert serves as a foil to the tempestuous, alienated Werther. Even Werther realizes that Albert's steady though stolidly bourgeois temperament ensures that he will be a good, dependable husband to Lotte. Albert reveals his lack of romanticism in his calmness after his marriage to Lotte, which Werther finds incomprehensible, since he feels that if he were in Albert's place he would be transported by happiness. While Albert annoys Werther with his preciseness and hesitance to say anything that isn't completely true, Albert accuses Werther of talking nonsense (a criticism the reader would agree with). It is significant that Goethe made Werther's rival sympathetic rather than repellent and that Lotte seems perfectly happy to marry him, for if Albert had been a villain, Werther's despair and extreme reaction might seem more justified. Critics have suggested that while Werther embodies the tempestuous emotions that formed one part of Goethe's nature (particularly when he was young), Albert may have been drawn from the calmer, more self-sustaining side of his personality that allowed the author to recover from despair. Albert's compliant reaction to Werther's request to borrow his guns has been a subject of critical speculation, implying that both he and Lotte realize Werther's plans yet make no attempt to stop him.

A significant voice in *Werther* is that of **the editor,** who introduces the protagonist's letters and then provides a concluding account of his tragic fate. The editor's dry, detached, analytical tone contrasts strongly with Werther's choppy, emotional effusions and thus establishes a significant distance between author and subject. Although some critics contend that Goethe sympathizes too much with Werther, most feel that he intentionally stands outside of the novel's action and offers neither approval nor censure. The editor does, however, comment that the reader will inevitably admire and pity Werther, whose ardent spirit and heedless abandonment to passion ultimately destroy him.

The plight of **the farmhand,** whose unrequited love for his employer's wife led to his murdering the man hired to replace him after his dismissal, is presented as a clear parallel to Werther's dilemma. Werther seems to identify and sympathize with the accused man and is distressed when he fails to save him from execution. The fact that the farmhand's action is exposed as unjustified—he had no reason to suspect that his victim had succeeded in winning the love he failed to gain—may be interpreted as casting an unfavorable light on Werther's eventual suicide.

Faust I (drama, 1808)

Plot: The opening prologue of the drama takes place in heaven, where God and the Devil, Mephistopheles, are discussing a human being, Faust. Mephistopheles wants to prove to God that he can win the soul of Faust, whose aspirations make him vulnerable to temptation. Claiming that Faust has too much integrity to succumb to the demon's temptation, God agrees to the wager. The title character is first seen in his study. An elderly professor, he has pursued both knowledge and magic and found lasting satisfaction in neither. His frustration leads him to thoughts of suicide, but he decides not to kill himself after taking a walk through the awakening springtime world. A dog follows him back to his study and subsequently turns into Mephistopheles, with whom Faust makes an agreement. The devil will provide him with renewed youth and a lifetime of unlimited experience, but if Faust ever experiences a moment that he wishes would last forever—a moment of pure contentment—he will instantly forfeit his soul. Mephistopheles now guides Faust into the realm of desire and passion. First they visit Auerbach's Cellar (a beer garden), where the devil performs magic tricks for a group of drunken students, then they proceed to the Witches' Kitchen. There Faust sees in a mirror the reflection of a beautiful woman, who mixes him a potion that transforms him into a man of thirty.

The now youthful Faust falls in love with an innocent young woman named Gretchen and, with the help of Mephistopheles, seduces her. After she becomes pregnant, Faust abandons her and also kills her brother, who did not approve of their relationship and tried to interfere. To distract Faust from dwelling on these events, the devil takes Faust to Walpurgis Night, a wild witches' orgy of magic and sex held at the top of a mountain. While cavorting with a naked witch, Faust has a horrifying vision of Gretchen with a red line around her neck. He learns that she is in prison and has been sentenced to death for the murder of their child. Faust visits Gretchen in jail and finds her driven to insanity by her plight; he offers to save her through his magic powers but she is determined to commit herself to God's mercy. Just as Mephistopheles is rejoicing in Gretchen's doom, a voice from heaven proclaims that she is saved.

Faust II (drama, 1832)

Plot: While Part I took place in a personal realm, Part II is set in the "great world" of history, culture, and politics. Faust is the court necromancer (magician) to an emperor who has accepted a sum of false money from Mephistopheles to alleviate his nation's financial difficulties. At a carnival, the emperor asks Faust to conjure up the most beautiful man and woman of all time, and he produces the Greek mythological figures Paris and Helen of Troy. Entranced with the beautiful Helen, Faust tries to escape with her but is knocked unconscious and returned to his laboratory by Mephistopheles. There his assistant, Wagner, has created a spirit called Homunculus who leads Faust back through time to the days of classical antiquity. He locates Helen and enters her mythological life, eventually fathering her child, Euphorion. Full of youthful idealism and yearning for adventure, Euphorion falls from a great height and is killed; the desolate Helen soon follows him.

Returning to his own country, Faust finds it in economic turmoil because of the false money given to the emperor by Mephistopheles. When Faust helps the emperor restore order, he is rewarded with a piece of land that is submerged in the sea. He manages to reclaim the land but, despite his pleasure in seeing it become highly productive, he will not be satisfied until he has also acquired a chapel and several linden trees owned by an old couple. Unwilling to give up their property, the two are killed by Mephistopheles. Faust is visited by the spirit of Care, who blinds him so that he will lose his desire for material things and concern himself only with the spiritual. When Faust dies, he is lifted up and taken away—safely out of

Mephistopheles's grasp—by angels who explain that even though he made many errors during his life, he can be redeemed because he always continued to strive.

Characters: Acclaimed as a preeminent German author as well as a statesman and scientist, Goethe exerted a profound influence on late eighteenth- and early nineteenth-century literature. Written over the course of almost sixty years, the universally praised verse drama *Faust* is considered one of the greatest artifacts of the romantic movement. Based on an old Christian legend that Goethe had seen dramatized in a puppet show during his childhood, *Faust* utilizes a mythological, magic-laced context to explore with broad appeal and compelling results the dilemma of modern man. Part I features an innovative, episodic structure and is centered in a personal, earthly realm while Part II is more meditative, symbolic, and stylized. As a whole, the drama blends classicism and romanticism to present the human pursuit of the ideal, the tension between the physical and the spiritual, and the idea of human life as constantly changing and developing. In the end the effort of striving emerges as a worthy goal in itself—an appropriate response to the confusions, difficulties, and yearning experienced by all human beings.

Goethe's drama made the legendary figure of **Faust** one of the best-known literary characters of all time. The ever-seeking, never-satisfied Faust has come to symbolize the human struggle and yearning for knowledge, achievement, and glory. Critic George Santayana wrote that Faust "cries for air, for nature, for all existence." Faust embodies the dual nature of all human beings in his simultaneous and often conflicting desire for both physical and intellectual experience—a duality that is a dominant theme in the drama. As Part I opens, Faust feels alienated and frustrated, for his study of science has brought him no lasting satisfaction, and the visions he has been able to create through his manipulation of magic have proved similarly inadequate. Lacking faith in a divine, celestial God, Faust reveres only nature and craves earthbound experience. Thus the drama's first section centers on a personal, earthly realm in which Faust's sensual love for Gretchen is the primary focus. Several critics note the significance of Mephistopheles transforming Faust into a man thirty years younger, for Goethe was himself a young man when he wrote Part I and could project more of himself into a younger protagonist. Having exchanged his soul for the freedom and ability to pursue unlimited sensation, Faust cruelly misuses and abandons the innocent Gretchen; his inhumanity seems to reach its nadir when he murders her brother in cold blood. During the Walpurgis Night orgy, however, Faust sees a vision of the suffering Gretchen and subsequently tries to save her. Gretchen, however, seeks and receives redemption only from God, while Faust continues on his own quest under the guidance of Mephistopheles.

Part II is distinguished by a more mature, less emotional tone than Part I, reflecting Goethe's own advancing age as he continued to work on the drama. While Part I was infused with the romanticism that marks the work of Goethe's early career, Part II evokes the images and moods of classical mythology as Faust searches for meaning in aesthetic, political, and civic activities. While serving as court necromancer he creates a vision of Helen of Troy that is so lifelike and beautiful that he wishes to acquire her for himself, thus precipitating his journey into Helen's mythical realm. After Helen's death and his return to his own world, Faust assumes a political role, aiding the emperor in bringing order to the kingdom. His subsequent land reclamation project proves a success but, typically, he is not content with the wealth and accomplishments he has already achieved. His desire for more property leads to the deaths of a kind old couple, thus exposing again his self-centered willfulness. Yet instead of sinking even further into egotism and inhumanity, Faust is blinded by the spirit of Care, who performs this deed so Faust will lose his greed for earthly possessions. His eventual redemption has been interpreted by critics as evidence that, despite the reprehensible things he has done, his life is ultimately deemed meaningful. From this perspective both good and evil are seen as natural aspects of existence, and the effort to continue striving is affirmed. Faust leaves behind him the symbolic sea walls he has built, from which others will continue to benefit but which they too will have to keep renewing. Thus life is presented as a constantly changing, developing process in which, despite its difficulties, human beings should enthusiastically engage.

The name **Mephistopheles,** the demon who tempts Faust to trade his soul for unlimited experience, is drawn from a traditional story, and his red-waistcoated, limping appearance is based on Faust's memory of the devil figure in a puppet show he saw as a child. Despite his origin in such conventional conceptions of the devil, Mephistopheles is portrayed in a distinctly modern, human cast, particularly in his verbal cleverness and frequent use of irony. Extremely old, illusionless, and utterly cold-hearted, Mephistopheles represents the denial of life and morality. In the dichotomies between the soul and the body, light and dark, life and death with which the drama is concerned, Mephistopheles embodies dark, death, earth, and physicality. In Part I he mocks the scientific knowledge that Faust has spent his life pursuing, offering instead a wealth of worldly experience; in Part II, some critics contend, his role becomes more didactic. Mephistopheles is particularly distinguished by his worldly, casual, contemptuous, carelessly witty voice; his comments are frequently laced with a humor that may sometimes even be self-deprecating, and his irony provides not only comic relief but serves as a revealing contrast to Faust's intensity and seriousness. Critics have noted that Mephistopheles's role is not so much to create or encourage evil (though certainly he does so) but to goad him into striving for improvement. Goethe's interest in the duality and organic wholeness of life is evident in his presentation of Mephistopheles as a necessary balance, without whom Faust would remain static.

Innocent, naive, simple **Gretchen** is not a particularly well-rounded character. She serves primarily as a love object for Faust, embodying both the natural, emotional aspect of love as well as its physical or sexual dimension. In her purity and faithfulness Gretchen has been said to represent all that is most sympathetically human. Strictly raised by humble parents, Gretchen is initially dazzled by Faust's worldly, well-traveled aura, which seems quite glamorous to her. Her embarrassment and consequent gratitude for his attentions make her vulnerable to seduction, and indeed she surrenders to Faust with no attempt at self-assertion or resistance. Gretchen's simplicity provides a strong contrast to Faust's sophistication and highlights his guilt and responsibility for her fate. Faust attempts to rescue Gretchen after he has seen a foreboding vision of her, thus indicating that the preoccupation with the physical that had governed his relations with her has been conquered by a spiritual impulse. While languishing in prison, Gretchen has passed through a period of insanity—which, some critics note, evidences a more spirited character than she has previously revealed—but is now determined to seek redemption from God. Though appropriately punished for the sin of killing her child, Gretchen is ultimately received into heaven because her inherent goodness and courage overcome her human weakness.

Another important female character in *Faust* is **Helen of Troy,** the renowned figure from Greek mythology whose beguiling beauty led to the Trojan War. When Faust, who has conjured up her image as a court entertainment, tries to embrace Helen, she vanishes, but he eventually joins her in her own world. Helen has been viewed as an embodiment of the classicism that is, throughout the play, juxtaposed to the romantic; Faust, for example, is an inhabitant of a romantic age who seeks union with the classical Greek ideal that Helen symbolizes. Although Helen has shared with Faust a tender, heartfelt love, she ultimately disappears—thus signifying the inevitable abandonment of classicism in the modern age—and Faust returns to his more physically grounded love with Gretchen.

Faust features a small number of notable minor characters. **Wagner,** Faust's pedantic assistant, has been viewed as a humorous parody of the Enlightenment scholar of the eighteenth century, who promotes and approves of the role of science in improving humanity's lot. **Valentine,** Gretchen's brother, is murdered by Faust when he attempts to defend his victimized sister; the episode reveals the depth to which Faust has descended. **Homunculous** is the mind-reading spirit (created by Wagner in a vial and taking the form of a miniature man) who transports Faust to the classical world so he may join Helen. **Euphorion,** the son born to Helen and Faust, has been viewed as an allegorical figure representing poetry, and he also bears a mythological resemblance to Icarus, who flew too close to the sun on waxen wings and eventually fell to earth. **Philemon** and **Baucis** are the innocent old couple who become victims of Faust's greed when he wishes to acquire their property; in Greek and Roman myth, the two represent hospitality. The allegorical figure of **Care,** who blinds Faust in order to redeem him, awakens him to an awareness of the future and the necessity of striving to improve it.

Further Reading

Brown, Jane K. *Goethe's Faust: The German Tragedy.* Ithaca, N.Y.: Cornell University Press, 1986.

Fuller, Margaret. "Criticism: Goethe." 1841. Reprint. In *The Writings of Margaret Fuller,* edited by Mason Wade, pp. 242-72. New York: Viking Press, 1941.

Gray, Ronald. *Goethe: A Critical Introduction.* Cambridge: Cambridge at the University Press, 1967.

Lewes, George Henry. *The Life of Goethe,* 2nd ed. 1864. Reprint. New York: Ungar, 1965.

Mann, Thomas. "Goethe's 'Faust.'" 1938. Reprint. In *Essays of Three Decades,* translated by H. T. Lowe-Porter, pp. 3-42. New York: Knopf, 1947.

Muenzer, Clark S. *Figures of Identity: Goethe's Novels and the Enigmatic Self.* University Park: Pennsylvania State University Press, 1984.

Nineteenth-Century Literature Criticism, Vols. 4, 22. Detroit: Gale.

Santayana, George. "Goethe's 'Faust.'" In *Three Philosophical Poets: Lucretius, Dante, and Goethe,* pp. 139-99. Cambridge, Mass.: Harvard University Press, 1910.

Swales, Martin. *Goethe: The Sorrows of Young Werther.* Cambridge: Cambridge University Press, 1987.

Nikolai Gogol
1809-1852
Russian novelist, dramatist, short story writer, essayist, critic, and poet.

The Inspector General (*Révizor;* drama, 1836)

Plot: Anton Skovnik-Dmukhanvosky, the mayor of a provincial Russian town, receives a letter from a friend warning him that a government inspector is traveling incognito through the province looking for evidence of corruption and bribery. The mayor calls a meeting at which the notoriously corrupt local dignitaries discuss the improvements they should make to the town. The manager of the hospital, Artemy Zemlyanika, whose philosophy toward the sick is that if they are going to die they will die anyway, decides to give the patients clean nightcaps to wear and a sign over each of their beds naming their diseases in Latin. Judge Ammos Lyapkin-Tyapkin, an ardent sportsman who keeps his guns and other equipment in his courtroom, is told to try to cover up the smell of liquor given off by one of his subordinates. The mayor warns Luka Klopov, who runs the local school, that the odd behavior of some of the teachers will have to be curbed; one of them grimaces weirdly and pulls at his beard under his necktie, while another becomes so excited during his lectures that he jumps onto his desk and throws chairs around. Annoyed by these criticisms, the officials remind the mayor that he himself accepts bribes and once had an army officer's wife whipped by mistake. While they are arguing, postmaster Ivan Shpyokin arrives, and the mayor tells him to open all of the mail in case any information arrives about the inspector's identity or time of arrival; since the postmaster always opens all of the mail anyway, he is happy to oblige.

Next, two local landowners, Pyotr Bobchinsky and Pyotr Dobchinsky, arrive and breathlessly announce that an unidentified guest from St. Petersburg has been staying at the local hotel for two weeks; all of those present surmise that this must be the inspector general and realize with horror that he has already been observing them without their knowledge. Meanwhile the man in question, a dissolute young dandy and lowly copy clerk named Ivan Khlestakov, has run out of money and is wondering how to pay his bill at the inn. When the mayor arrives to see him, Ivan assumes he is about to be arrested, but instead the mayor offers to pay his hotel bill and invites him to stay in his home. Ivan gladly plays along with the mayor's mistake and goes home with him, where he is treated with great respect and admiration. The mayor's wife, Anna, and daughter, Maria, are particularly impressed as he describes himself as an important official, a great writer, and a friend of many famous people. Ivan finally falls into a drunken sleep. The next day all of the town's dignitaries prostrate themselves before him, while some ordinary citizens plead for protection from their corrupt leaders. Ivan responds in an increasingly abrupt manner and borrows money from everyone who visits him. As soon as the officials have left, Ivan's servant, Osip, pleads with him to leave town now before his secret is discovered, and Ivan agrees. But then Maria arrives for a visit, and he flirts with and kisses her; when Maria leaves the room, he turns his charms on her mother. Maria returns and, flustered because he has been caught courting her mother, asks her to marry him; she proudly accepts. Ivan then writes a letter to a friend in which he describes his outrageous adventures and the foolishness of the people he has duped. Promising everyone he will return the next day, he leaves town. As the news of Maria's engagement to Ivan spreads, the mayor and his family are envied by all. However the postmaster suddenly arrives and reads aloud Ivan's letter detailing the hoax he has played on the town and his scorn for its officials. As the astonished group stands pondering their mistake, it is announced that the Inspector General has arrived from St. Petersburg and requests their immediate attendance upon him at the inn.

Characters: *The Inspector General* is regarded as a comedic masterpiece that is as entertaining and thought-provoking for twentieth-century audiences as it was for those of the nineteenth century. Like much of Gogol's work, the play blends social satire with moral allegory in a skillfully structured format. Laced with elements of vaudevillian comedy and populated by characters who are uniformly flawed, *The Inspector General* is a realistic indictment of corrupt bureaucracy, an absurdist commentary on the banality that exists at all levels of society, and a colorful, humorous romp that seems devised purely for amusement.

The young man mistaken for a government inspector, **Ivan Khlestakov,** (whose surname means "whippersnapper"), is one of Gogol's most celebrated characters. He works in St. Petersburg as a menial copy clerk but aspires to the high life of a dandy; when he first appears, he has gambled away all of his money and is unable to pay his hotel bill. The scene in which the mayor arrives in Ivan's room, with the mayor assuming that Ivan is the government inspector and Ivan believing the mayor is about to arrest him, is often cited as a comedic high point of the play. Although he is not particularly clever, Ivan soon catches on to the mistake and begins to play along with it, thus revealing the inherent pliability of his character. Gogol instructed actors to portray Ivan with simplicity and sincerity, and it is his essential vacancy and lack of a coherent personality that allows him to be molded to the fantasies of others. A representative of the big city, Ivan brings to this provincial milieu an air of the superficial refinement and urbanity that the local dignitaries expect, and his behavior—particularly his accepting bribes from all of them—is seen as entirely appropriate to his supposed station. In another much-lauded scene, Ivan expansively describes his glamorous lifestyle and accomplishments, and his extravagant lies (he claims to be a close friend of the great Russian poet Pushkin, for instance) fail to alert his listeners to his deception. Propelled into the situation by circumstance, Ivan accepts his role unquestioningly and even enthusiastically, becoming a fabricator par excellence. Likewise Ivan is unintentionally propelled into flirting with Anna and Maria and then proposing to Maria despite his lack of any real intention to marry her. The hilarious courtship sequence, in which he ardently courts first the daughter and then the mother and then the daughter again, has been characterized as a parody of the traditional love scene that nineteenth-century audiences expected; in also pokes fun at literary convention when Ivan quotes from several well-known writers as he is proclaiming his undying affection for Anna. Ivan has been interpreted as a devilish figure because his presence inspires fear in the townspeople, he proves false, and he is replaced in the end by another inspector, with the possibility that the process will repeat itself indefinitely. The play's conclusion suggests to some scholars that Ivan may in fact be a figment of the mayor's imagination and that reality begins with the arrival of the actual inspector.

The town's mayor is **Anton Skovnik-Dmukhanovsky,** whose name translates to ''Rascal-Puffed Up.'' Although he is well aware of the corruption that runs rife throughout his realm—in fact, he has himself participated in it by taking bribes and by mistakenly ordering an innocent woman flogged—the mayor's efforts to clean up the town involve appearances only. He suggests, for instance, that the court official's liquor-permeated breath be masked with garlic rather than that the man refrain from drinking or be fired. The scene in which the mayor prostrates himself before the man he believes is the government inspector, hoping to make a good impression, is often cited for its comic power. Another humorous scene involving the mayor, when he puts a hatbox on his head instead of a hat, has been described as merely a vaudevillian stunt or as a symptom of his inherent inability to differentiate the true from the false. When the mayor realizes that he has been duped by Ivan, he vehemently berates himself for his blindness, recounting his rise from lowliness to his current elevated position, which he accomplished through ambition, intelligence, and learning how to play the bureaucratic game. As he admits his weaknesses, his character is somewhat humanized. Significantly the mayor turns to the audience near the end of the play and asks, ''What are you laughing at? You're laughing at yourselves.''

The mayor's wife, **Anna,** and daughter, **Maria,** are the only significant female characters in the play. Anna is a vain, pretentious woman whose speech is peppered with vulgarities that reveal her lack of breeding and her shallowness. She allows Ivan to flirt with her, hesitantly reminding him that she is ''to some extent . . . married,'' and never notices how absurd and cliché-ridden his declarations are. After Ivan becomes engaged to her daughter, Anna happily imagines her future as a grand lady of St. Petersburg, and she behaves condescendingly to her envious friends and neighbors. Maria is equally superficial and ignorant, concerned primarily with her appearance and with making an advantageous marriage. She too sees nothing amiss in Ivan's instantaneous ardor and abrupt marriage proposal.

The various corrupt and ridiculous town officials who court Ivan's favor form, according to critic A. de Jonge, ''a kind of dynamic tableau, a chorus of reactions,'' heightening both the play's comic punch and its thematic impact. **Ammos Lyapkin-Tyapkin,** whose name means ''Bungle-Steal'' or ''Slapdash,'' is a judge more devoted to his sporting interests than to the pursuit of justice. He stores his guns and whips in the courtroom and allows a flock of poultry to be kept in a hallway. The excuse he offers for the alcoholic odor of his subordinate—he claims the man has smelt of vodka ever since he was dropped as a baby—is effortlessly accepted by the other dignitaries, thus adding to the absurdity of their discourse. **Luka Klopov** (''bedbug'') is the school official whose eccentric assistants—one has a habit of contorting his face and methodically massaging his chin from beneath his necktie, and another breaks up furniture to illustrate the career of Alexander the Great—have been said to typify the deterioration of the Russian educational system. Slow-witted postmaster **Ivan Shpyokin** gets a great deal of pleasure from reading other people's mail; letters play an important role in *The Inspector General,* and it is the postmaster who brings forth the revealing one written by Khlestakov. **Artemy Zemlyanika** (''strawberry'') is the hospital manager who allows his dirty, ill-clad patients to recover or die as they will and who believes that cleaning them up and labeling their illnesses is an acceptable reform.

Two other memorable characters in the play are the landowners **Pyotr Bobchinsky** and **Pyotr Dobchinsky,** who have been compared to Tweedledum and Tweedledee in Lewis Carroll's classic *Through the Looking Glass.* Together they function as the town gossips, informing the others that a man who is probably the government inspector is in town and interrupting each other frequently in their desire to be the first to announce the news. Short, stocky, fast-talking Bobchinsky eavesdrops on the mayor's initial interview with Ivan and is injured when he accidentally crashes through the door; he appears throughout the rest of the play with a bandage on his nose. He tells Ivan that he would like to be remembered to the great men in St. Petersburg, revealing his yearning for celebrity. Dobchinsky is taller than Bobchinsky and somewhat more serious; he pleads with Ivan to see that his oldest son, born out of wedlock, is legitimatized. While both men seek credit for being the first to recognize Ivan as the inspector general, each reverses this claim when Ivan's true identity is discovered.

Ivan's elderly, taciturn servant, **Osip,** is shrewder than his employer. Plainspoken and down-to-earth, he is the only character who sees the situation clearly from the beginning. Although he disapproves of Ivan's behavior, he participates in the scheme to fool the townsfolk and is instrumental in extricating Ivan before he is discovered. The real **Inspector General,** whose arrival marks the play's conclusion, may be the actual official sent to uncover corruption, but critics have also suggested that he may be either another impostor or—if Khlestakov does indeed represent the devil—simply the next stage in the torment of the sinning townspeople.

"The Overcoat" (short story, 1842)

Plot: The story centers on a lowly government clerk named Akaky Bashmachkin, a short, balding man with bleary eyes and a pockmarked face. Although he has the impressive title of titular counsellor, his job is copying documents, which he does with meticulous care and dedication. He has worked in the same department for years, ridiculed by his peers and unappreciated by his supervisors. Utterly absorbed in his work, Akaky cares little for his appearance and lives a frugal, barren life. His old overcoat—necessary for protection against the cold Russian winter—is threadbare and he takes it to a tailor, Petrovich, for repair. But Petrovich claims that the overcoat is beyond salvaging and offers to make Akaky a new one instead. The sum he names, however, is far beyond the clerk's means, and he leaves the tailor's shop in a gloomy mood. After another unsuccessful attempt to persuade Petrovich to mend his overcoat, Akaky decides that he will save his money for a year in order to pay for a new one. He deprives himself of such basic comforts as tea and candles, and walks on tiptoe to keep his shoes from wearing out too soon. The next year Akaky is able to afford the overcoat, and Petrovich makes it for him. He wears his new garment to work with great pride and wins the admiration of his fellow clerks, who suggest a party to celebrate Akaky's fine acquisition. That night he enjoys strolling through the streets in his warm overcoat, and he drinks several glasses of champagne at the party. On his way home, however, he is accosted by two men who steal his overcoat; a policeman to whom he reports the robbery tells him to talk to an inspector the next day.

Akaky is sick with worry over the loss of his most prized possession. His fellow clerks suggest that he seek the help of a certain Important Personage who could influence the police to step up their work on the case. This official, however, makes an angry show of being bothered by someone as insignificant as Akaky and does not allow him to explain himself. Cowed and depressed, Akaky stumbles home in a blizzard and subsequently becomes very ill. In his delirium he denounces the Important Personage; eventually he dies and is immediately replaced in his job by another clerk. Soon after Akaky's death, reports begin to surface that the ghost of a dead government clerk has appeared to passersby and taken their overcoats from them. One night the Important Personage leaves a party and is going to visit his mistress when he is overtaken by the ghost of Akaky. Frightened, he throws the ghost his overcoat and hurries home. After that, Akaky's spirit is never seen again.

Characters: "The Overcoat" is one of the most significant short stories in modern literature, and its importance in the development of Russian fiction was verified by Fedor Dostoevsky, who said, "We all came out of Gogol's 'Overcoat.'" Considered an important initiator of Russian realism and a master of the "skaz" genre, which features a casual narrative voice and a blending of pertinent information with seemingly inane details, Gogol skillfully infused "The Overcoat" with both incisive humor and pathos. While some critics contend that the story delivers a humanitarian message of sympathy for the downtrodden, others view it as a wry satire that highlights the futility of serving an inept, insensitive bureaucracy.

Akaky Bashmachkin is an underpaid, unappreciated government clerk with a wrinkled, pockmarked face. Myopic and balding, he wears a formerly green uniform that has become rust-colored over the years, and he has only an ancient, threadbare overcoat to protect him from the Russian winter. As many scholars have noted, his name invites mockery: "Akaky" evokes the child's term for feces, "kaka," and his last name is derived from the Russian word for shoe (in a typical digression, the narrator points out that this is rather unusual in view of the fact that Akaky's relatives have always worn boots). Although he bears the impressive-sounding title of titular counsellor, Akaky is a mere copier of documents and in fact desires no more elevated task. He is devoted to his work and even brings it home with him at night; indeed, he has no other interests and hardly even notices what he eats or whether there are bits of straw or food particles clinging to his clothing. The reader pities Akaky when he is forced to forego the most meager comforts in order to afford a new overcoat, yet it seems to provoke a positive transformation in his life: the overcoat brings him a sense of purpose and possibility. He walks with interest through the city streets and interacts with others as he has rarely done before. The loss of the overcoat is devastating, because it destroys Akaky's new-found sense of meaning and resolution, and the realization that he is still as insignificant as ever is underscored by the harsh treatment he receives from the Important Personage. As he lies feverish and near death, he curses "His Excellency" with angry sarcasm. The fact that Akaky can wreak revenge only as a ghost evidences Gogol's characteristic penchant for fantasy and absurdism, and it highlights the helplessness of the ordinary person to attain justice. Early reviewers saw Akaky as an object of pity and a victim of an impersonal bureaucracy, interpreting the story as a commentary on Russian society, but modern critics have focused on "The Overcoat"'s metaphysical aspects, even characterizing Akaky as hiding his own spiritual emptiness behind his overcoat. The story has been variously perceived as depicting the desolation of human beings as they make their way through an indifferent universe, or as a testament to the Christian concept of identification with one's fellow human beings. The latter interpretation is based on the passage in which a new clerk comes to Akaky's office and notices the ridicule he endures from his fellow clerks; Akaky's plaintive request to be left alone is translated by the other clerk as an assertion that "I am thy brother."

Dressed in a uniform adorned with medals, the **Important Personage** (sometimes translated as the **Person of Consequence**) represents the pinnacle of the bureaucratic structure of which Akaky is merely a particularly lowly part. He has only recently been promoted to the rank of general and is both proud of and somewhat uncomfortable in his new position of power. Although his officious title (and the fact that the reader is given no other name for him) seems intended as a form of mockery, his harsh treatment of Akaky is more a way of showing off for a friend who is present during the encounter than a genuine expression of his nature. His character is further humanized by the resemblance of his awkwardness at the party the night he sees Akaky's ghost to Akaky's lack of confidence at the party he attends. Neither is certain how to act in his new role, each is nevertheless feeling jubilant as he leaves the party, and each then undergoes a shocking experience. For the Important Personage, this experience is his frightening encounter with Akaky's ghost, to whom he makes amends for his past unkindness by giving him his own overcoat. Some critics have interpreted the ghost, in fact, as a manifestation of the guilt that the Important Personage feels over having cruelly slighted Akaky; indeed, after his experience his behavior changes for the better, at least to some extent: he treats his subordinates in a less domineering way.

Other characters in "The Overcoat" include **Petrovich,** the one-eyed, pockmarked tailor who makes Akaky's new overcoat; sly and alcoholic, he habitually overprices his work and enjoys Akaky's reaction to the projected cost of the garment. **The mustachioed thief** who steals the overcoat is vividly described as having comically exaggerated fists. While taking the overcoat from Akaky, he exclaims that it belongs to him, and later a policeman mistakes him for the ghost of the dead clerk that has already been sighted several times. This repetition of connection with Akaky establishes the pattern of a vicious circle. The **new, young, unnamed clerk,** who takes a job in Akaky's office and later remembers with horror his fellow workers' tormenting of the downtrodden clerk, calls attention to the inhumanity of which people are capable.

Dead Souls (novel, 1842)

Plot: An agreeable traveler named Pavel Chichikov arrives in a provincial Russian town and soon befriends the local gentry, receiving many invitations to call on various landowners at their country estates. With his coachman, Selifan, and valet, Petrushka, he travels into the countryside to begin his visits. His first host is Manilov, a genial, sentimental man who entertains him royally. While questioning Manilov about his estate, Chichikov learns that a large number of his "souls," or serfs, have died since the last census was taken; Manilov will have to continue to pay taxes on these serfs until the next census. Chichikov offers to buy these "dead souls" and thus help Manilov escape the added tax burden. Manilov accepts Chichikov's claim that such an arrangement is legal, and he agrees to it. Selifan becomes lost while driving to the next estate, so Chichikov unexpectedly spends a night at the home of Madame Korobochkina, an ignorant but efficient widow who also sells him some dead souls. At a nearby inn, Chichikov meets a card shark and braggart named Nozdryov from whom he offers to buy dead souls; Nozdryov, however, questions him about his motives and then challenges him to play cards for the dead souls. The dissolute Nozdryov is eventually arrested for attacking another man. Next Chichikov visits Sobakevich, a bear-like man who haggles over the price of the dead souls that he ultimately sells to his visitor. Likewise the miserly Plyushkin tries to get a high price for his dead souls and also sells Chichikov a number of fugitive serfs. Chichikov returns to town and persuades the town president to legalize the transactions, directing that the names of the dead souls be transferred to his (fictional) estate in the province of Kherson.

Chichikov continues to be a popular guest at various town functions, including a ball where the governor's radiant daughter particularly interests him. But his purchases of so many dead souls draws suspicion, and the townsfolk conjecture about his past and plans: some claim he intends to elope with the governor's daughter, some say he is a forger and spy, and one even suggests that he may be the notorious bandit Captain Kopeykin in disguise. When questioned about Chichikov, Nozdryov swears that he is in fact a spy and forger and plans to elope with the governor's daughter. Chichikov recovers from an illness to find that his formerly warm hosts now regard him with cold distrust, and he leaves the town. Now Chichikov's real history is revealed: his father's death has forced him to make his own way in the world, and he has worked as a clerk and then as a customs officer. After being caught in a smuggling scheme, Chichikov began a new career as a legal agent; in this position he learned that dead souls still on the census lists can be mortgaged for cash, and he set out on his current journey to attain as many as possible. Chichikov now leaves town in his trademark troika (a carriage drawn by three horses).

Part Two of *Dead Souls* begins with Chichikov visiting the young bachelor Alexandr Tyentyelnikov, an intelligent man who has retired from the city to run his country estate by progressive methods; unsuccessful and disillusioned, he lives an apathetic life. Tyentyelnikov is in love with Ulinka, the daughter of his neighbor General Betrishchev, but gives up the courtship after Betrishchev insults him. Chichikov visits the general and manages to win his consent to the marriage, and he also convinces Betrishchev to sell him some dead souls by claiming that his uncle will not bequeath him his estate unless he already has some property. At another estate, Chichikov meets a young man named Platonov who decides to accompany him on his travels. The two travel to the home of Platonov's sister and brother-in-law, Konstantin Skudronzhoglo, who runs his estate in a highly practical and efficient manner. He lends Chichikov money to buy the estate of Khlobuev, an impecunious neighbor who complains that his wealthy aunt will leave him none of her money. Chichikov manages to locate the aunt and forges her will so that he inherits her fortune; he forgets, however, to destroy the original will, and as a result two contradictory wills are found after her death. A government official named Lyenitzyn accuses Chichikov of forging the second will and imprisons him, but Chichikov hires a sly lawyer who gets his client released by uncovering a host of scandals that the town officials are eager to hide. Once again destitute, Chichikov leaves town.

Characters: An often humorous yet faithfully rendered and compelling depiction of life in nineteenth-century Russia, *Dead Souls* blends elements of satire and fantasy with metaphysical musings on such topics as the illusory nature of experience and the destiny of Russia. While the term ''dead souls'' refers literally to the deceased serfs [similar in status to American slaves, Russia's serfs were not liberated until 1861], it also applies to many of the novel's primary characters, who reveal their essential shallowness and lack of ideals as the story progresses. Gogol is praised for successfully and vividly depicting a broad spectrum of Russian people, including the landed gentry, government officials, the middle class, and servants.

Most prominent among the ''dead souls'' who populate the novel is its protagonist, the charming yet conniving **Pavel Chichikov.** Described in an 1882 review in *Literary World* as ''a polished, insinuating scoundrel,'' Chichikov presents a meticulously neat appearance and highly agreeable manner to the world. Beneath this smooth exterior, however, lies a cunning nature. Near the end of the first part of *Dead Souls,* Chichikov's past is delineated: motherless, he was raised by a harsh, ailing father whose most important legacy to his son was a respect for money above all else. Chichikov endured a bleak life of clerical drudgery in the hope of advancing, and in order to speed his ascendance he became involved in bribery; later, as a customs officer, he was caught in a smuggling scheme. Allowed both times to escape punishment, he began a third career as a legal agent and soon discovered the possibility of buying dead souls and mortgaging them for cash. In executing this financial scheme he has been seen as a representative of an increasingly complicated economy and a new, primarily urban class that acquires income by offering not material goods but abstract services. Often cited as an important key to Chichikov's character is his essential ordinariness, which, along with his easy ability to adapt himself to others' ideas, allows him to gain the trust of those he meets. His ambitions are decidedly modest and conservative; he desires not fabulous wealth but a comfortable living and, ironically, he takes great risks to acquire only a small fortune. Several scholars have seen Chichikov's mediocrity as reflective of Gogol's realistic view and his desire that the reader identify with this central character. In Part 2, Chichikov continues his pattern of deception and conniving but he also shows signs of a yearning to reform, and some critics contend that in a third section that Gogol planned but probably never executed, his redemption would have been chronicled.

The individuals encountered by Chichikov in the first part of *Dead Souls* are depicted with both satirical sharpness and meticulous realism, and several are categorized among the most memorable characters in Russian fiction. Chichikov's first host is the blonde, blue-eyed, pleasant **Manilov**. Sentimental and insipid, Manilov is a remnant of the romanticism of an earlier period of Russian history. An incompetent and indolent landlord, his lack of regard for the practical concerns of running his estate is typified by the unupholstered chairs seen in his living room. Manilov is bewildered by the scheme Chichikov proposes but accepts his guarantee of its legality; unlike the other landowners with whom Chichikov deals, Manilov hands over his dead souls for no compensation other than the relief of his tax burden.

Nastasya Korobochkina's surname, which translates as "little box," symbolizes the hoarding instinct that dominates her character. Though essentially ignorant and superstitious, she operates her estate with a canny efficiency; even her hospitality to Chichikov is calculated to cost her little. Suspicious about Chichikov's motives when he proposes purchasing her dead souls and also eager to drive as advantageous a bargain as possible, she suggests—preposterously—that she might be able to find some practical use for them herself. Such illogic is typical of characters throughout Gogol's fiction and exemplifies his use of the ridiculous to illuminate human foibles.

Another memorable character in Part 1 is **Nozdryov**, a dashing, handsome gambler with white teeth and thick black sideburns. A notorious cardshark prone to extravagant lying, Nozdryov is undisciplined and possesses a raucous energy that sometimes erupts into violence. While Chichikov explains his desire to buy dead souls, Nozdryov's mind wanders, and he eventually suggests that they play a game of cards for the souls. Some critics have seen in this character a hint of the eighteenth-century aristocrat typically characterized by recklessness, impudence, and dissipation. Though Nozdryov is initially eager to befriend Chichikov, he is equally quick to betray him by proclaiming that he is a spy and a forger.

The shrewd, lumbering, and brutish landowner **Mihail Sobakevich** is consistently identified by his bear-like quality. He has a confrontational manner and a huge appetite, and even the paintings and furnishings in his house—most notably a large, potbellied bureau—evoke the boorishness that he personifies. Like Madame Korobochkina, Sobakevich behaves as if the dead souls were not abstract entities, describing their skills and virtues to make them seem more valuable when in fact Chichikov is merely buying their names. Sobakevich haggles over the price he will accept, initially demanding one hundred rubles for each dead soul but eventually accepting only two-and-a-half. Sobakevich comments on the lamentable state into which Russian society has fallen, complaining that even he is not as strong and vital as his own father.

Ranked among such classic misers of literature as Molière's Harpagon and Balzac's Felix Grandet, **Plyushkin** is the sordid, avaricious landowner from whom Chichikov buys 120 dead souls as well as 75 fugitives (those who have fled the estate and are still unaccounted for). Once a happy and hospitable man, he began to withdraw from society after his wife died and his children left; now almost completely isolated, he grievously mistreats his serfs. He is the quintessential, raggedly dressed miser in his dread of even the most minute expense, his fear of robbery, and his compulsive hoarding of everything he owns—even the produce he would normally sell. Ironically, his overgrown estate is lush with vegetation while his own soul has dried up.

Other notable characters in the first section of *Dead Souls* include Chichkov's two servants, the dull-witted, frequently drunken coachman, **Selifan** (whose navigational mistake leads them to Madame Korobochkina's estate), and his valet, **Petrushka,** who is distinguished by the strong, unpleasant odor he emits. Selifan is particularly significant because, as the driver of Chichikov's trademark troika, he helps to reinforce the theme of mobility important in *Dead Souls.* **The governor's daughter** is a beautiful young woman who catches Chichikov's eye at a ball he attends before he falls from favor. This young woman is described in terms of her radiance, a possibly symbolic quality that also typifies other idealized female characters in Gogol's fiction (including Ulinka in Part 2 of this novel). In the famous sequence in which the townspeople propose several preposterous possibilities for Chichikov's real identity, the postmaster, **Ivan Andreich,** suggests that Chichikov may in fact be **Captain Kopeykin,** a soldier from the 1812 war who became a Robin Hood-style bandit in revenge for having been denied his pension. The fact that Kopeykin was armless while Chichikov possesses all of his limbs adds to the farcical nature of this sequence.

While the characters in Part 1 are sometimes seen as caricatures designed to illustrate various human failings, those in Part 2 are more rounded and further Gogol's thematic concerns. The thirty-three-year-old bachelor **Andrey Tyentyelnikov,** who plays host to Chichikov, is an educated young man whose earlier life in the city disillusioned him and destroyed his drive to use his intelligence in a productive way. He has retired to the country, intending to apply the sophisticated economic theories he has read about to his estate, but he has been unsuccessful in carrying out his plans. Although he intends to institute a new, mutually respectful, and humane relationship with the peasants who work for him, he is out of touch with the realities of their lives, and they view him with bewilderment rather than respect. In his consequent indolence, apathy, and inability to come to any decision, Tyentyelnikov is often identified as a prototype of Oblomov, the title character of an 1859 novel by Russian realist author Ivan Goncharov. Tyentyelnikov's love for Ulinka promises to rouse him from his stupor, but when he perceives that her father has insulted him he is again plunged into apathy. Chichikov brings about a reconciliation that allows the two young people to resume their engagement.

Beautiful **Ulinka,** the daughter of Tyentyelnikov's neighbor **General Betrishchev** (from whom Chichikov buys a number of dead souls while also winning approval for his friend's marriage), is described as "radiant with life," as if she "had appeared . . . expressly to light up the room." Gogol's consistent use of light imagery to describe Ulinka is similar to his treatment of other female characters in his fiction, where they serve as visions of beauty and truth designed to guide and inspire men. While flawlessly virtuous and a rather flat, idealized female character, Ulinka may also be seen as a symbol of the reconciliation and harmony for which men strive. Also depicted as a figure of classical proportions is Chichikov's young friend **Platonov,** whose name evokes the Greek philosopher Plato. He is physically beautiful and serene but lacks vitality, and Chichikov hopes to take advantage of his innocence.

Another important character in Part 2 is **Konstantin Skudronzhoglo,** a prosperous landowner who is impressed with Chichikov and lends him ten thousand rubles. In contrast to Tyentyelnikov, who returned from the city with sophisticated ideas about how to run an estate, Skudronzhoglo is a man of action. He has achieved his success through hard work, and he enthusiastically advocates the values of honesty and diligence while decrying the laziness, corruption, wastefulness, and snobbery of other Russian landowners, many of whom reside far from the estates that provide their wealth. In his belief in the nobility and healthfulness of the simple country life, Skudronzhoglo anticipates the ideals that would be promoted several years after the publication of *Dead Souls* by the great Russian novelist Leo Tolstoy. He is devoted to his estate and respectful of his serfs, claiming that the "tillers of the soil are the most honorable of all." Through Skudronzhoglo, Gogol presents the notion that the infiltration of sophisticated western European ideas and ways of life has had a detrimental effect on his country, and that Russia should seek salvation through a return to its agrarian roots.

Minor characters in Part 2 include **Khlobuev,** the spendthrift whose rich aunt's fortune Chichikov tries to gain by forging a will; **Lyenitzyn,** the public official who discovers the existence of the two wills and jails Chichikov; and **Murazov,** the shrewd, unscrupulous lawyer who successfully defends Chichikov by revealing his knowledge about scandals involving the town's officials.

Further Reading

Bonnett, Gail. "Deity to Demon: Gogol's Female Characters." *Proceedings: Pacific Northwest Conference on Foreign Languages* XXIII (1972): 253-67.

Fanger, Donald. *The Creation of Nikolai Gogol.* Cambridge, Mass.: Belknap Press, 1979.

"Gogol's 'Dead Souls.'" *Literary World* XVIII, No. 7 (2 April 1887): 101.

Grayson, Jane, and Faith Wizgall, eds. *Nikolay Gogol.* New York: St. Martin's Press, 1988.

Hippisley, Anthony. "Gogol's 'The Overcoat': A Further Interpretation." *Slavic and East European Journal* 20, No. 2 (Summer 1976): 121-29.

Jonge, A. de. "Gogol." In *Nineteenth-Century Russian Literature: Studies of Ten Russian Writers,* edited by John Fennell, pp. 69-129. Berkeley: University of California Press, 1973.

Nineteenth-Century Literature Criticism, Vols. 5, 15, 31. Detroit: Gale.

Peace, Richard. *The Enigma of Gogol: An Examination of the Writings of N. V. Gogol and Their Place in the Russian Literary Tradition.* Cambridge: Cambridge University Press, 1981.

Short Story Criticism, Vol. 4. Detroit: Gale.

Trahan, Elizabeth, ed. *Gogol's "Overcoat": An Anthology of Critical Essays.* Ann Arbor, Mich.: Ardis, 1982.

Ivan Alexandrovich Goncharov
1812-1891

Russian novelist, short story and sketch writer, travel writer, critic, and translator.

Oblomov (novel, 1858)

Plot: The novel takes place in nineteenth-century Russia. Ilya Oblomov is a Russian landowner who has been thoroughly ingrained with the indolence of his class. Brought up in pampered luxury, he is encouraged to do little else but eat and sleep. His childhood friend Andrey Stolz, on the other hand, is raised by his German father to be active, practical, and ambitious, and he becomes a successful businessman. Oblomov manages somehow to finish college and takes a position as a clerk in a government office. He soon decides that the job is too much trouble, however, and he retires to a languorous, completely inactive existence in his St. Petersburg apartment, while a steward manages his country estate. Oblomov's rooms are dirty and disorderly, and he is unable to control his equally slothful—though very loyal—valet, Zahar. Oblomov spends his time in a dressing gown and slippers, never going out and only occasionally receiving visitors.

Oblomov is dismayed to receive a letter from his estate manager (who has habitually cheated his inattentive employer) informing him that, due to the estate's declining profits, Oblomov's income will have to be drastically reduced. His landlord declares that he must leave his apartment. Meanwhile Stolz visits Oblomov and finds him in a unkempt, apathetic state; he learns that his friend's doctor has warned him about the deleterious effects of such an inactive life. In an effort to save Oblomov, Stolz takes him on several excursions around St. Petersburg and tries to encourage him to become interested in the outside world. When Stolz leaves for Europe, Oblomov promises to meet him in Paris in several weeks, but the visit never takes place. Instead Oblomov falls in love with Olga Ilyinsky, a young woman Stolz introduced him to, and the two become engaged. Vivacious and sensitive, Olga initially manages to stimulate her fiance into activity as they plan their wedding and life together, but eventually Oblomov's old torpor overtakes him again. His parasitical friend, Tarantyev, finds him an apartment in a house in the suburb of Vyborg. Indulged by his dull-witted, widowed landlady, Agafya Mateyevna, he retreats into languorous comfort. Though still concerned about the status of his estate, Oblomov is unwilling to travel there to see that it is in order. Olga finally decides that she cannot tolerate Oblomov's idleness, though she still loves him and believes he could have achieved a meaningful life, and she leaves him. Oblomov becomes increasingly sluggish and dependent on his valet and landlady. Still, he is ashamed of himself, referring to his condition as "Oblomovism." Meanwhile the conniving Tarantyev has arranged for a friend to manage Oblomov's estate and skims off much of the income for himself. He also encourages a relationship between Oblomov and his landlady, then attempts to extort money from both by threatening to charge Oblomov with seducing Agafya. Stolz intervenes and prevents Tarantyev from carrying through with this scheme.

After encountering Stolz in France, Olga responds to his romantic overtures and marries him, despite her continuing love for Oblomov. Years later, Stolz looks up his old friend and finds that he is now married to Agafya. Still idle and apathetic, he is close to death because of his unhealthy habits. Oblomov dies in his sleep not long after Stolz's visit, leaving his young son—also named Andrey—in his friend's care.

Characters: *Oblomov* is one of the most acclaimed works of nineteenth-century Russian literature. It has been interpreted both as a realistic, sociological depiction of the torpor of Russia's provincial landowners and as a psychologically penetrating exploration of one individual's nostalgia, disillusionment, and even neurosis. Lauded for its richly detailed description and incisive yet sympathetic rendering of its main character, the novel chronicles a period in Russian history when tradition seemed threatened by innovation and the landed aristocracy was being forced to give way to a rapidly emerging middle class.

Ilya Oblomov is considered one of Russian literature's most important and memorable characters. The term he inspired, "oblomovism," gained common use after the novel's publication as a designation for indolence, apathy, or even the common Russian tendency toward resignation; a famous 1859 review of the novel by Russian critic N. A. Dobrolyubov brought the concept of oblomovism into the forefront of Russian thought. Oblomov is a profoundly lethargic thirty-two-year-old man who, despite his flabby and unkempt appearance, is somehow attractive and likable. The voluminous oriental dressing gown he wears is a particularly effective symbol for his sloth: it envelopes him in its welcoming, comfortable folds. Oblomov is in bed as the story opens and for the next several chapters gets no further than his dressing table. In the much-praised section entitled "Oblomov's Dream"—published separately several years before the novel—Oblomov's early years at his family home, Oblomovka, are described in loving detail. Goncharov's portrayal of Russia's old, patriarchal society reveals his own nostalgia for the daily routines and customs of a bygone time, but it also exposes the roots of Oblomov's personality. Raised in an atmosphere of ease, contentment, and overprotection, Oblomov was encouraged to be idle and to depend on servants for all of his needs—even for such tasks as tying his shoes. Sociological interpretations of the novel have focused on this overreliance on serf labor as contributing to the apathy that ultimately led to the 1917 Communist revolution. Yet critics have seen Oblomov not just as a symbol of aristocratic sloth but as a kind of romantic antihero who scorns society and lives in a world of his own making; as a "Superfluous Man" (a term conceived by Russian novelist Ivan Turgenev) who is alienated and anguished by a world that seems indifferent to him; or as a neurotic whose deeply rooted despair renders him incapable of a normal life. Although Oblomov dreams of great accomplishments and a more active life, he is not quite capable of raising himself out of bed. He barely endures his university education, and finds gainful employment too troublesome. Oblomov's inconclusive love affair with Olga is a particularly poignant episode, because it reveals his latent sensitivity and his potential for true emotion, but he proves inadequate to the demand for action that it presents. His retreat to the apartment at Vyborg and his eventual marriage to the dull, motherly Agafya have been characterized as a regression to childhood, an attempt to return to the womb. It is Oblomov's childlike quality that, while reprehensible in some ways, endears him to the reader. A basically good-natured, gentle, and humane person, he fails to realize his potential for achievement. Critics have seen in him not only some aspects of Goncharov's personality but many universal aspects of human nature.

While many scholars have identified Oblomov as a representative of a traditional Russia, his friend **Andrey Stolz** embodies the forces of western European innovation that were infiltrating Russian culture during the nineteenth century. He is as physically lean and muscular as Oblomov is fat and flabby, and his vitality and ambition contrast with his friend's indolence and apathy. Stolz was raised by a German father from whom he learned the practical value of activity and hard work, while his Russian mother provided a strain of romanticism. Thus Stolz is portrayed as an ideal composite of several cultural influences. In fact, many critics have faulted Goncharov's portrayal of Stolz as overly idealized: because he is too obviously designed to represent the concepts of progressiveness and industriousness, he is an artificial, rather wooden character. Goncharov himself admitted the weakness of this characterization. Nevertheless, scholars are interested in Stolz as evidence of his creator's belief that such westernized values as reason and progressivism could cure Russia's social and economic ills.

Olga Ilyinsky, the young woman who temporarily stimulates Oblomov into action, is vivacious, sensitive, and idealistic. In combining an appreciation of the Russian cultural heritage that Oblomov also cherishes with an inquisitive, forward-looking mind similar to Stolz's, Olga seems to represent a successful reconciliation of the old and the new. When her efforts to cure Oblomov of his apathy are unsuccessful, she takes the difficult but necessary step of leaving him. Although some critics have lauded Goncharov for his perceptive portrayal of an intelligent young woman's psychological development, others claim that Olga is as flat and unbelievable a character as Stolz. Still others contend that the reader's interest in Olga is stimulated during the first part of the book when she is a vital, idealistic young woman but inevitably flags after her marriage to Stolz, when she grows rather dull and conventional.

Oblomov's servant **Zahar** has been seen as his master's alter ego, for he imitates on a lower social level Oblomov's sluggishness and apathy. Although Goncharov's characterization of the fumbling, unkempt valet is often comic, he is not just a one-sided character. While he frequently ignores or even abuses his master, Zahar also idolizes Oblomov. An elderly man who remembers with great fondness and reverence the bygone years of Oblomovka, he serves as a representative of Russia's ultimately doomed patriarchal system. Zahar's cherished grey overcoat and full whiskers have been identified as symbols of past greatness to which the old valet still clings. In his resemblance to Oblomov as well as his unflagging loyalty, Zahar demonstrates the close relationship between master and servant that was an integral part of the patriarchal system. The dismal fate he meets after Oblomov's death, when he becomes a beggar in the streets of St. Petersburg, manifests the failure of the old Russian social structure and another consequence of oblomovism.

Oblomov's parasitical friend, **Tarantyev,** presented as the antithesis to Stolz, is a big, hulking, extremely energetic man who puts his vitality to evil use, cheating Oblomov at every possible opportunity. Tarantyev is a particularly odious product of Russia's growing middle class. Suspicious of foreigners, he hates Stolz for his half-German heritage and considers him his enemy. His inability to establish himself professionally has apparently resulted in disillusionment and corruption, and he now supports himself by fleecing Oblomov—skimming money from the estate's profits, persuading Oblomov to sign a disadvantageous lease, and finally attempting to extort money by inventing a scandal.

Agafya Mateyevna is the maternal, dull-witted widow in whose Vyborg home Oblomov rents an apartment and whom he eventually marries. Agafya is a large, soft woman with a profoundly passive nature that contrasts strongly with Olga's vitality and independence. She loves Oblomov but has no real understanding of any but the most immediate concerns; Oblomov finds a comfort and refuge from reality with her that resembles his early days at Oblomovka. For her own part, Agafya achieves a certain sense of meaning in her own life through her faithful service to her sluggish husband. Their monotonous life together is very realistically portrayed. The son born to their marriage, Andrey Oblomov, will be raised by Stolz after Oblomov's death, and it is suggested that he may achieve success through a blending of his Russian heritage with the European influences that Stolz can provide.

Other characters in *Oblomov* include the visitors who come to see Oblomov during the book's first few chapters, while he is still reclining in bed: the dandified **Volkok;** **Subbinsky,** an overworked official; and **Penkin,** a gossip columnist. By their attendance on Oblomov the three help to establish the innate appeal of his personality. **Mukhoyarov,** Agafya's brother, is Tarantyev's partner in his wicked schemes, even helping him to extort money from his own sister and from Oblomov.

Further Reading

Dobrolyubov, N. A. "What Is Oblomovitis?" 1859. Reprint. In *Belinsky, Chernyshevsky, and Dobrolyubov: Selected Criticism,* edited by Ralph E. Matlaw, pp. 133-75. New York: Dutton, 1962.

Ehre, Milton. *Oblomov and His Creator: The Life and Art of Ivan Goncharov.* Princeton, N.J.: Princeton University Press, 1974.

Freeborn, Richard. "The Novels of Goncharov." In *The Rise of the Russian Novel: Studies in the Russian Novel from "Eugene Onegin" to "War and Peace,"* pp. 135-56. Cambridge: Cambridge University Press, 1973.

Moore, Harry T. Foreword to *Oblomov,* by Ivan Turgenev, translated by Ann Dunnigan, pp. vii-xvii. New York: New American Library, 1963.

Nineteenth-Century Literature Criticism, Vol. 1. Detroit: Gale.

Poggioli, Renato. "On Goncharov and His 'Oblomov.'" In *The Phoenix and the Spider: A Book of Essays about Some Russian Writers and Their View of the Self,* pp. 33-49. Cambridge, Mass.: Harvard University Press, 1957.

Edmond and Jules de Goncourt
1822-1896 and 1830-1870
French novelists, dramatists, historians, biographers, and critics.

Germinie Lacerteux (novel, 1864)

Plot: Orphaned at the age of four, the title character is sent at fourteen to live with an older sister in Paris. She is put to work as a waitress in a café, where she is soon raped and impregnated by a waiter. The baby is stillborn, and Germinie subsequently becomes gravely ill. After her recovery, Germinie holds a succession of domestic jobs and is finally employed as a maid to Mademoiselle de Varandeuil, an elderly spinster whose demanding father never allowed her to marry or even make friends. Germinie proves a devoted, capable servant and also serves as a companion to the lonely old woman. Germinie begins to attend church and becomes devoutly religious, eventually developing a romantic attachment to a young priest who, when he realizes the nature of her feelings, coldly rejects her. Next Germinie grows attached to her sister's niece, whom she informally adopts after the death of the little girl's mother. The child is taken to Africa by another of Germinie's sisters, who manages to extract money from Germinie for her care even though the girl actually died soon after leaving Paris. When a dairy store opens nearby, Germinie befriends its proprietor, Madame Jupillon, and develops a strong affection for the storekeeper's son, who is ten years younger than Germinie. She spends increasing amounts of time with the Jupillons, and Madame Jupillon exploits her friend's interest in her son by allowing her to work in the store for no pay. Young Jupillon also manipulates Germinie's affections, and the two become lovers. Jealous of Jupillon's interest in other women, Germinie provides him with his own apartment, only to be spurned when he takes another mistress. Meanwhile, Germinie becomes pregnant and gives birth to a daughter who dies a few months later.

When young Jupillon is called for military service, Germinie goes into debt to acquire money to pay his way out. Yet her lover does not appreciate her sacrifice and continually ignores her. Eventually Germinie turns to alcohol for solace; though frequently drunk, she successfully hides her vice from Mlle. Varandeuil. When she is about forty years old, Germinie becomes involved with an older housepainter, Gautruche, who serves primarily as an object upon which she may lavish her considerable affection. She refuses his offer of marriage, however, and the two eventually part. Desperate for love, Germinie takes to picking up men on the street. One night she spots Jupillon entering a house; she stands outside in the rain, hoping to see him again, until the next morning. As a result Germinie contracts pleurisy (an inflammatory disease of the respiratory system). She manages to hide her deteriorating condition from her employer for a time but eventually becomes so ill that Mlle. Varandeuil sends her to a hospital, where she soon dies. After Germinie's death, her debtors come to collect the money she owed them, and her employer learns of her servant's secret life. Although initially angry, Mlle. Varandeuil comes to pity Germinie and unsuccessfully attempts to locate her pauper's grave.

Characters: *Germinie Lacerteux* is considered an important forebear of the naturalist fiction that dominated the last quarter of the nineteenth century, and it particularly influenced the most prominent exponent of naturalism, Émile Zola. Known for their *écriture artiste* narrative style, which combines an intensely visual approach with a complex use of language, the Goncourt brothers were innovative chroniclers of their social and literary milieu. *Germinie Lacerteux* evidences their interest in depicting reality in closely observed, even scientific detail. The novel's earliest reviewers found its often harrowing descriptions of lower class life unnecessarily sordid, and even some modern critics charge the aristocratic Goncourts with voyeurism as they explore a world dramatically different from their own. In the much-quoted preface to *Germinie Lacerteux,* the authors defend their subject matter, claiming that the time had come for a novel focusing on working-class characters. The novel is now almost universally praised for its wealth of descriptive detail, its successful balancing of subjectivity and objectivity, and its importance in the transition from romanticism to naturalism in literature.

The Goncourts often based their fictional characters on people they knew, and **Germinie Lacerteux** is the most notable example of this practice. She is modeled after the Goncourt's beloved servant Rose Malingre, who worked for the family from the time of Jules's babyhood until her death. After she died, the brothers learned that Rose lived a secret life of promiscuity and alcoholism and even stole from them to support a disreputable lover. Initially outraged by Rose's duplicity, the Goncourts eventually forgave her and became intrigued by her success in hiding from them the sordid reality of her life. In chronicling Germinie's gradual isolation and disintegration, the Goncourts create circumstances very much like Rose may have had. Germinie's harsh, impoverished childhood—which some critics have accused the authors of relating in a rather mechanical manner—establishes the basis of her later actions, thus anticipating the idea that environment and heredity, rather than free will, determine human experience, which was an important tenet of naturalism. In addition to the neglect and deprivation of her early years, Germinie suffers from an inherent and, according to the Goncourts, exclusively female need to love—a need that is manifested both physically and psychologically. The loss of her first baby (even though conceived during a rape) devastates Germinie, and she spends the rest of her life in a desperate search for someone upon whom to lavish her affection. Soon after going to work for Mademoiselle Varandeuil, Germinie becomes devoutly religious, but this impulse disappears when her romantic interest in her priest is crushed. Critics contend that the Goncourts viewed religion as providing an outlet for women's excessive emotion, and they used Germinie's experience to explain why women were attracted to the Catholic church. The loving care that Germinie next expends on her young niece is also thwarted, when her sister takes the girl away from Paris. That informal and ultimately ill-fated adoption is followed by Germinie's relationship with the Jupillons. As she grows more interested in young Monsieur Jupillon, she ingratiates herself with his mother and allows herself to be exploited as an unpaid worker in her store. Germinie exhibits a poor judgment in her passion for Jupillon, a manipulating scoundrel. Nevertheless her love for the young man and her subsequent jealousy have a powerful physical effect on her, replacing her former indolence with energy. Initially portrayed as a victim of society, Germinie's innate nature now determines the course of her downfall. Torn by her simultaneous hatred and love for Jupillon and wracked with despair over his rejection, Germinie sinks into alcoholism, promiscuity, and debt, all the while continuing to faithfully serve her unsuspecting employer. Germinie's lonely death has generated varied interpretations: while some feel that she is finally redeemed by her suffering, others contend that her death is both gloomily inevitable and pointless. Germinie is one of the first working-class heroines to take center stage in a novel, and the Goncourts have been commended for portraying her as a complex personality rather than a flat stereotype. At the same time, the Goncourts have been accused of misogyny for suggesting that Germinie's weaknesses were inherently connected with her sex and that if she were able to marry and have a family she would have been saved. Indeed they themselves admitted that the revelation about Rose Malingre had permanently and negatively altered their view of the female sex. Nevertheless the brothers achieved in their story of Germinie's disintegration an admirable balance of subjectivity (afforded, no doubt, by their sympathy for Rose Malingre) and the objectivity that their distance from their subject allowed them.

Reportedly based on the Goncourts' aunt, Mademoiselle Cornélie de Courmont, **Mademoiselle Varandeuil** is an elderly, unmarried woman who lives alone in genteel semi-poverty. She welcomes the addition of Germinie to her lonely household, for the young woman proves both an able servant and a pleasant companion. Although the outward circumstances of Mademoiselle Varandeuil's life provide a strong contrast to Germinie's, she too is a victim of social exploitation: her chances for love, marriage, or any life of her own were thwarted by a selfish, tyrannical father she was forced to serve. It is suggested that the old woman's long years of personal anguish made her somewhat unsympathetic to the pain experienced by other people, thus explaining how she could be completely ignorant of Germinie's real life. Like the Goncourt brothers, who were shocked to learn the truth about their servant Rose, Mlle. Varandeuil is initially angered by Germinie's duplicity but eventually comes to forgive and pity her. In the novel's last scene she searches unsuccessfully for Germinie's grave and finally kneels to pray between two headstones marked only with the dates of death of the anonymous bodies beneath them. Mlle. Varandeuil depicts the myopia that allowed the Goncourts themselves to overlook the true life of someone they thought they knew well—though some critics have questioned whether, as a woman, Mlle. Varandeuil could have been as blind to Germinie's problems as the Goncourts were to Rose's.

The Goncourts have been particularly lauded for their detailed descriptions of lower-class existence in nineteenth-century Paris. Among the characters who populate this milieu is **Madame Jupillon,** the sly dairy shop proprietor who takes advantage of Germinie's attraction to her son to exploit her as an unpaid worker. Her syrupy affection for Germinie masks her true hypocrisy. Even more repellent is **Monsieur Jupillon,** ten years younger than Germinie and the object of her heedless, ultimately destructive passion. He is based on a young boxer named Alexandre Colmant, whom Rose Malingre supported by stealing from the Goncourts. Jupillon is cold, calculating, and manipulative, exploiting Germinie's love while it suits his purposes and then cruelly spurning her. His own experience of love is limited to seducing women and then taking pleasure in despising them. **Monsieur Gautruche** is the middle-aged housepainter with whom Germinie becomes involved; although she does not love him, he provides for a time an object upon which to pour her emotions. Gautruche's motives are no more sincere, for he views Germinie more as a potential servant than as a prospective wife.

Further Reading

Duncan, J. Ann. "Self and Others: The Pattern of Neurosis and Conflict in *Germinie Lacerteux.*" *Forum for Modern Language Studies* XIII, No. 3 (July 1977): 204-18.

Grant, Richard B. *The Goncourt Brothers.* Boston: Twayne, 1972.

Jarman, Laura M. *The Goncourt Brothers: Modernists in Abnormal Psychology.* San Bernardino, Calif.: Borgo Press, 1982.

Michot-Dietrich, Hela. "'Blindness to 'Goodness': The Critics' Chauvinism? An Analysis of Four Novels by Zola and the Goncourts." *Modern Fiction Studies* 21, No. 2 (Summer 1975): 215-22.

Nineteenth-Century Literature Criticism, Vol. 7. Detroit: Gale.

Gerald Griffin
1803-1840
Irish novelist, short story writer, dramatist, poet, and essayist.

The Collegians (novel, 1829)

Plot: Set in the (southern) Irish region of Munster in the late eighteenth century, the novel centers on aristocratic Hardress Cregan and middle-class Kyrle Daly, who became friends while attending college together and who have maintained their relationship despite the different social strata they inhabit. One morning Kyrle and his family watch Hardress foolishly sail his yacht into a fishing boat; they do not realize that a young woman is with him. She is sixteen-year-old Eily O'Connor, the daughter of a lowly ropemaker, whom Hardress has secretly married. Fearful that his mother and upper-class friends will object to this unsuitable marriage, Hardress has hidden it and now takes Eily to live with his servant's sister and her family in a remote cottage. He promises Eily that he will soon publicly acknowledge their marriage. Hardress's servant, the hunchbacked Danny Mann, is slavishly devoted to his master. Meanwhile, the virtuous, prudent Kyrle is in love with a beautiful heiress, Anne Chute. He travels to Castle Chute to propose to Anne, but she rejects him, even though she claims to love no one else. That night, Hardress promises to promote Kyrle's suit to Anne, who is coming to stay with the Cregan family. Mrs. Cregan soon realizes that Anne is in love with Hardress, and she contrives to throw the two together frequently. Anne seems like an ideal wife for her son, and she is annoyed with his reluctance to pursue the young woman.

Marooned in an unfamiliar place with a family that does not even realize she is Hardress's wife, Eily becomes increasingly distraught. She begins to feel that the Naughtons (her hosts) resent her presence, and she notices that Hardress has come to treat her coldly. Confronting him, she learns that he now regrets having married her and that he no longer loves her. Hardress's outburst convinces him that he is in love with Anne. When he later discusses his dilemma with his servant, Danny suggests that he could eliminate Eily from the scene. Hardress refuses this offer. He grows increasingly confused as Anne becomes more ardent and as his mother wishes the match to take place; he finally decides to marry Anne despite his obligation to Eily. Meanwhile, Eily visits her uncle, a parish priest, and describes her situation, though she does not reveal her husband's name. Father Edward admonishes Eily to return to the Naughtons' cottage. There she meets Danny, who hands her a letter from Hardress in which he reveals his decision to send her away on a boat bound for Canada. Eily obediently accepts this directive, but Danny, having misinterpreted Hardress's commands, murders the girl. When her body is discovered, Hardress realizes what has happened. Nevertheless, hoping that Danny will never be seen again, he goes ahead with his plan to marry Anne. At the same time, the guilt and fear that torment him cause him to act strangely. Shortly before Hardress is to be married, Danny is captured. Hardress helps him to escape but, enraged when he discovers that Danny has remained in the neighborhood, beats him cruelly. In retaliation, Danny goes to the authorities and confesses to Eily's murder, also implicating Hardress, who is subsequently arrested and sentenced to exile abroad for his part in the crime. Danny is hanged. Finally recognizing Kyrle's true superiority to Hardress, Anne marries him.

Characters: Considered one of the best Irish novels of the romantic period, *The Collegians* provides a comprehensive portrait of eighteenth- and nineteenth-century Irish society through its skillfully rendered peasant, middle class, and aristocratic settings and characters. Griffin's personal knowledge of Irish dialects, folklore, and traditions is evident, as is his strong moral perspective. Many critics note that the novel, which is said to have inspired

Theodore Dreiser's 1925 novel, *An American Tragedy,* illustrates the conflict between Griffin's desire to achieve artistic greatness and his moral principles. As his later, more didactic works and his eventual abandonment of literature for life in a monastery show, Griffin was unable to resolve this conflict. Nevertheless *The Collegians* has retained its value as a compelling chronicle of Irish life and character.

In his first appearance in the novel, **Hardress Cregan** boldly races his yacht as he delivers the wife he had impetuously married a month before to the remote hovel in which he plans to hide her. Thus Hardress is established as a spirited, romantic figure, and his later conversation with Kyrle, in which he advocates the ascendance of the heart over the head or emotion over reason, confirms his stance as Byronic (referring to the famous romantic poet, George Gordon, Lord Byron). Brilliant, headstrong, raised in luxury and too-long spoiled by his indulgent mother, Hardress pursues his desires with abandon and lacks the foresight to guess the consequences of his behavior and the ability to control himself. Captivated by the lovely, naive peasant girl Eily O'Connor despite his aversion to the lower classes, Hardress dashingly whisks her away from her disapproving father and marries her. He soon regrets his action, which ultimately destroys the life of the guileless Eily. His shallowness is demonstrated in how rapidly his love for Eily fades and his passion for the sophisticated Anne Chute develops; his speeches are noted for being overblown and stilted. Though he does not lack admirable qualities, such as his courage, enthusiasm, and intelligence, Hardress is finally punished for his weaknesses, while the unexciting Kyrle is rewarded for kindness and prudence. Griffin ruefully predicted that his audience would no doubt prefer the exciting, dangerous Hardress to his sedate college friend, but there is no doubt that he himself condemns Hardress and in fact intended the book to serve as a warning against such heedless, immoral behavior. He later declined to invent characters as wicked and unredeemed as Hardress for fear of their adverse effect on the public. Griffin's creation of this fairly complex protagonist, who is brought down by "intellectual pride and volatile susceptibility of new impressions," nevertheless evidences the artistic gift that reached its highest expression in *The Collegians.*

Although **Kyrle Daly** is one of the "collegians" referred to in the novel's title, he is not as central or developed a character as Hardress. Through Kyrle and the rest of the Daly family, Griffin depicted middle-class Irish life as prudent, prosperous, and happy, in marked contrast to aristocratic excesses and shallowness. While his friend is clearly a romantic hero, Kyrle bears more resemblance to the kind of temperamentally balanced character affirmed by such pre-romantic authors as Jane Austen. He is shown to adapt to such adversities as Anne's refusal of his marriage proposal and his mother's death with reasoned acceptance, despite his continuing regard for Anne and his real grief over the loss of his mother. He does have deep, even passionate feelings, but his behavior is modulated by self control and regard for·others. Kyrle's intellectual discussions with the fiery Hardress, in which the former advocates reason over passion and claims that elegance of manner does not preclude a wholesome simplicity, are often cited as evidence of Griffin's own inner conflict. In the end, however—and in spite of his prediction that readers would find this character dull in comparison with Hardress—the author clearly sides with Kyrle. In his stoicism, generosity, and integrity, Kyrle embodies his creator's dearly held, inherently Christian moral principles.

Eily O'Connor, the ropemaker's daughter whom Hardress marries and then discards, is a beautiful, trusting young girl possessed of a natural intelligence and dignity that make her inherently superior to other peasant women (such as Poll Naughton), though she lacks the formal education and polished manners of Ann Chute. Hardress is obviously thinking of Eily when, during his discussion with Kyrle, he argues that simplicity is preferable to elegance. Eily's love for Hardress is blind and unreasoning, for she remains loyal to him even after his repudiation of their union, and she meekly acquiesces in his plan to remove her from Ireland. She is portrayed as typically Catholic in her faith in divine providence and in the essentially passive courage with which she accepts the circumstances of her life. The aristocratic **Anne Chute** contrasts with Eily not only in her sophistication and elegance but in her eventual ability to recognize Hardress's weaknesses and to appreciate Kyrle's virtues. It is Hardress's designation of Anne as cold and distant that provokes his argument with Kyrle on whether the head or the heart should determine behavior.

Danny Mann is the hunchbacked servant whose blind devotion to his master leads him to murder Eily when he believes that this is what Hardress desires. His physical handicap was apparently caused by an accident for which the young Hardress was responsible, suggesting that complex ties of blame, guilt, and remorse already exist between the two. Danny is moved to seek revenge on Hardress after his tormented master beats him; he eventually regrets this action. Through this character from the lowest class of Irish society, Griffin demonstrates the tendency of the Irish peasant to be swayed more by warm feelings than by moralistic concerns. In his speech to the judge at his trial, Danny cries out against England's often brutal dominance of Ireland and highlights the fact that the Irish peasantry had to comply with British authority in order to survive.

Another frequently praised peasant character is **Lowry Looby,** who entertains Kyrle en route to Castle Chute with songs and stories, demonstrating the considerable charm and wit of the Irish character and helping to illustrate some Irish customs and superstitions. For instance Looby tells of having encountered a redheaded woman on his way to begin a new job; interpreting this as a bad omen, he returned to his home and consequently lost his job. Looby provides a welcome note of comic relief in an otherwise tragic story. **Myles-na-Coppaleen** is a similarly entertaining and notable peasant character. A mountaineer whose ponies have wandered onto the Chutes' property, he uses his considerable charm and wit to extricate himself from a troublesome situation. **Poll Naughton,** Danny's sister and Eily's hostess while she is waiting for Hardress to acknowledge their marriage, is coarse but canny, immediately guessing Hardress's true nature and skillfully evading the magistrate's questions when interrogated about the murder. Her husband, **Phil Naughton,** also confounds the authorities by speaking only in Gaelic. Other lower-class characters in *The Collegians* include Eily's ropemaker father, **Mihil O'Connor,** who is outraged when she elopes with Hardress; Eily's uncle, **Father Edward,** a parish priest who advises her to accept her situation; and **Dalton,** the faithful huntsman employed by Hardress's father. Asked to give from his deathbed a final hunting cry (signaling the start of a fox hunt), Dalton dies after expending this effort.

Through Hardress's father, **Mr. Cregan,** and his cronies, Griffin illustrates the gracelessness, violence, and drunkenness common in upper-class Irish society. Cregan and his friends, **Hepton Connolly** and **Hyland "Fireball" Creagh,** spend their time in pursuit of sport and liquor; ironically, the faithful Dalton lies dying while his heedless master is merely "dead drunk." Creagh is a notorious duelist who teases the impetuous Hardress into challenging him to a duel immediately after the young man has proclaimed his disapproval of the practice. **Mrs. Cregan** adds to her son's confusion and guilt by pressuring him to pursue Anne Chute, but her influence over him is deep-rooted and destructive: her constant indulgence has contributed to his ultimate downfall. He is cowering in her bedroom when finally captured by the police.

Further Reading

Cronin, John. *Gerald Griffin (1803-1840): A Critical Biography.* Cambridge: Cambridge University Press, 1978.

Davis, Robert. *Gerald Griffin.* Boston: Twayne, 1980.

Davie, Donald. "Gerald Griffin's 'The Collegians.'" *Dublin Magazine* XXVIII, No. 2 (April-June 1953): 23-31.

Flanagan, Thomas. "Gerald Griffin." In *The Irish Novelists: 1800-1850,* pp. 203-51. New York: Columbia University Press, 1959.

Kiely, Benedict. "The Two Masks of Gerald Griffin." *Studies* LXI, No. 243 (Autumn 1972): 241-51.

Nineteenth-Century Literature Criticism, Vol. 7. Detroit: Gale.

Thomas Hardy
1840-1928
English novelist, dramatist, short story writer, poet, and essayist.

Far from the Madding Crowd (novel, 1874)

Plot: Set in the fictional English rural district of Wessex, the novel centers on an honest, well-respected young sheep farmer named Gabriel Oak. He falls in love with beautiful Bathsheba Everdene, who has come to the neighborhood to work for her aunt. Gabriel asks the aunt for Everdene's hand in marriage but his request is refused. Some time later, after his sheep dog chases his flock of sheep over a cliff to their deaths, Gabriel loses his farm and must travel around the countryside looking for work. He stops to help some men extinguish a barn fire, then learns that the barn belongs to Weatherbury Farm and that its owner is Bathsheba, who recently inherited the farm from her uncle. She hires Gabriel to work as her shepherd. Soon after his arrival, he meets a young girl hiding in the woods. She is Fanny Robin, Bathsheba's maid, who had run off to meet a soldier named Sergeant Troy who had promised to marry her. The marriage, however, never occurs.

Bathsheba is a capable if capricious manager, and her farm prospers. On a whim, she sends a valentine to her serious, conservative neighbor, William Boldwood, who has seemed immune to her feminine charms. Although initially disturbed by the valentine, Boldwood falls deeply in love with Bathsheba. He asks her to marry him, but she refuses. Then the dashing Sergeant Troy reappears in the neighborhood and immediately captivates Bathsheba with his wit and good looks. Gabriel tries to warn her about the soldier's weak character—though he does not reveal Fanny's connection with Troy—but Bathsheba refuses to listen, and she and Troy are soon married. Now in charge of Weatherbury Farm, Troy proves an incompetent manager, and Gabriel is forced to oversee most of the work. Troy also drinks heavily and gambles, and his relationship with Bathsheba deteriorates. One day when the two are driving in a cart, they come across a young girl, and Troy talks to her; the girl is the very ill Fanny Robin, and Troy promises to bring her money if she will go on to the next town. Fanny dies soon after reaching the town, and Bathsheba, unaware that her husband was Fanny's lover, has her body brought back to the farm for burial. Opening the coffin she discovers not only Fanny's body but that of her dead child, fathered by Troy. Troy collapses in grief, declaring to Bathsheba that he has loved only Fanny and that he married Bathsheba for her money. Troy leaves, and eventually news that he has been lost at sea reaches Bathsheba.

Although Bathsheba feels that Troy may still be alive, Boldwood is convinced that he is dead and begs Bathsheba to marry him. She promises she will after seven years, when her husband will be considered legally dead. Several years later, Boldwood and Bathsheba are hosting a party to celebrate their engagement when Troy suddenly appears; rescued from drowning, he has since wandered through the countryside as a member of a theatrical troupe. Enraged by the reappearance of his rival, Boldwood shoots and kills Troy. At his murder trial, Boldwood is deemed insane and committed to an asylum. Gabriel again becomes the capable manager of Bathsheba's farm and also takes charge of Boldwood's property; he eventually decides, however, that he should leave Bathsheba's employ. Although she initially agrees with his plan to depart, Bathsheba later visits Gabriel and convinces him to stay, also agreeing to marry him. Together Gabriel and Bathsheba achieve happiness as the owners of prosperous Weatherbury Farm.

Characters: The first of Hardy's five major novels, *Far from the Madding Crowd* features some of the characteristics and themes that are more thoroughly developed in his later works. While the story takes place in a remote rural setting and revolves around a predominantly agricultural community, Hardy reverses the pastoral tradition by depicting nature not as peaceful and benevolent but as overpowering and indifferent to the struggles of human beings. Despite the timelessness and isolation of their natural world (hence the novel's title), the main characters' lives are not immune from violence and tragedy. Nevertheless *Far from the Madding Crowd* is considered the least pessimistic of Hardy's major novels and is lauded for its meticulous representation of a rural England that was fast disappearing.

Honest, uncomplaining **Gabriel Oak** has been identified as the novel's primary stabilizing force. A man of inherent integrity and saintly patience, Gabriel remains loyal to Bathsheba, despite her indifference to him, and finally does win her love. Many critics have noted the significance of Gabriel's occupation, which evokes the image of the gentle, innocuous shepherd found both in the Bible and in classical literature. Like the tree his surname signifies, Gabriel exudes a simple dependability and nobility that make him seem an integral part of the natural world, and he is much more at home both in his physical surroundings and with the humble rural people than the other central characters. In contrast to those who are in various ways removed from the land, such as Troy and Boldwood, Gabriel is abundantly capable of enduring whatever happens to him. Unlike the more tormented characters in Hardy's fiction (Michael Henchard and Jude Fawley are two examples), Gabriel's great misfortune—the loss of his flock of sheep in an absurd incident—results in his developing an indifference to the cruel vagaries of fate. Having lost his small farm, he goes doggedly on to find work where he can and to stand by quietly while the woman he loves marries one inferior man and nearly marries another. In the end, his stoicism is rewarded.

Bathsheba Everdene is the most vividly portrayed figure in *Far from the Madding Crowd* and one of the best known female characters in his fiction. Lovely, vivacious, and unpredictable, Bathsheba is at the beginning of the novel a coquette whose vanity is her dominant quality. Out of vanity she thoughtlessly sends a valentine to Boldwood, thus initiating in his heart a passion that will result in tragedy. Dazzled by Troy's looks and charm and flattered by his attentions, she marries him after refusing to listen to Gabriel's admonitions; some scholars contend that her attraction to Troy reflects her need to be sexually dominated by an intensely masculine partner. In any case, this ill-advised decision leads to both material loss—her husband proves to be a wastrel and an incapable manager— and emotional distress, when she learns that he has never loved her. Bathsheba's discovery that the dead Fanny had given birth to a child fathered by Troy is usually identified as the turning point in the development of her character. Some critics have seen her subsequent sojourn alone in the woods as constituting a reconciliation with the natural world, while others have noted that she actually finds no solace in that essentially hostile setting and instead becomes profoundly aware of her own isolation. Bathsheba reveals an unexpected depth of compassion when she vows to keep Fanny's lock of hair as a memento. By the end of the novel Bathsheba has evolved from a headstrong, capricious girl into a mature, chastened—and perhaps less interesting—woman. Her energy, ability, and independent nature distinguish her from the more conventional heroines of nineteenth-century fiction, and she serves for many readers and scholars as a fine example of Hardy's capacity to portray female characters with sympathy and depth.

Handsome, romantic **Sergeant Francis Troy** is an outsider in the rural world of *Far from the Madding Crowd,* and he proves a corruptive influence. Reputedly the illegitimate offspring of his French mother and her aristocratic lover, Troy is an irresponsible, impulsive rake who marries Bathsheba for her beauty and wealth after he uses Fanny. The scarlet coloring of Troy's military uniform has been said to signify the irrational passion that will ultimately result in tragedy; Hardy typically employed red to symbolize such dark forces as pride, passion, and death. Critics describe the scene in which Troy dazzles Bathsheba with a display of his swordsmanship as erotically charged, yet it remained acceptable to Victorian readers because its sexuality is entirely symbolic. Some critics have seen in Troy's swordplay a demonstration of the masculine dominance to which Bathsheba longs to submit. Although he is almost completely irresponsible, disloyal, and wasteful, Troy sincerely loves Fanny and is genuinely heartbroken at her death. His reappearance years later at the party, during which he is killed by Boldwood, and the story of his sojourn as a second-rate actor have been characterized as somewhat forced and melodramatic.

William Boldwood is the prosperous farmer whose life is changed by the valentine he receives from his beautiful, impulsive neighbor. A conservative, middle-aged bachelor, Boldwood is serious and self-sufficient, and Bathsheba finds him annoyingly indifferent to her charms. In sending the valentine on a whim, with no idea how it might affect her neighbor, she sets in motion a process that leads ultimately to murder, for on the inside Boldwood is as emotional and sensitive as he seems, from the outside, cold and aristocratically detached. He does not perceive the playful intent of the valentine; instead, it causes a disturbance in his psyche that becomes an obsessed love for Bathsheba. After seeing her married and then deserted by another man, Boldwood finally convinces her to accept his proposal. When his happiness is threatened by the reappearance of Troy, he snaps, unable to accept such a loss, and lapses into insanity.

Simple, dutiful, quiet, and pretty **Fanny Robin** suffers most from Troy's self-indulgence and disregard for others. Used and then abandoned by her lover, Fanny never complains and finally dies a lonely and pitiful death, along with the child born of their affair. The rigid morality of the Victorian period forced Hardy to treat Fanny's seduction and pregnancy in the most delicate manner possible in order to avoid censorship, but the fact that he included such a situation testifies to his interest in realistically exploring relationships between men and women. In some ways Fanny anticipates Hardy's more complex and renowned heroine, Tess Durbeyfield. The scene in which rainwater streams onto Fanny's grave from a gargoyle on the church roof, washing away the flowers left there by the grief-stricken Troy, is often cited as a particularly effective symbol of the indifference of the universe to humanity.

An important role is played in *Far from the Madding Crowd* by the residents of the rural community in which it takes place. Often referred to by critics as the "rural chorus"—a device employed by Hardy in several of his major novels—these characters congregate at the local tavern, Warren's Malthouse. Their function is to comment on the events described in the novel, to anticipate events that have not yet occurred, and to provide comic relief. In addition they help to establish the novel's mood and to flesh out its unchanging physical landscape; they form, according to Richard Carpenter, "the substratum . . . against which the fluctuating lives of the main characters are counterpointed." Notable members of the rural chorus include Gabriel's friend, **Jan Coggan,** who works with him on the farm and who reminisces morosely about the "lovely drunks" he has experienced in the past; **Henery Fay,** who insists on spelling his name with an extra e in accordance with his own manner of pronouncing it; and **Joseph Poorgrass,** an aptly named man who is agonizingly timid and easily offended.

The Return of the Native (novel, 1878)

Plot: Set in the neighborhood of Egdon Heath, a wide and gloomy expanse of harsh landscape and weather, the story begins on Guy Fawkes Day—the fifth of November—when, in accordance with pagan tradition, bonfires are lit across the heath. Diggory Venn, an itinerant reddleman (seller of the red dye that is used to mark sheep), is taking Thomasin Yeobright home in his cart. Having refused Diggory's marriage proposal several years earlier, Thomasin recently agreed to marry innkeeper Damon Wildeve and had gone to a nearby town for the wedding. Due to a problem with the license, however, the marriage did not take place, and now Diggory is returning Thomasin to her aunt and guardian, Mrs. Yeobright. Hearing Diggory's story of her niece's thwarted marriage, Mrs. Yeobright is dismayed and concerned. Later that evening, however, Wildeve arrives and promises that he will go through with the marriage. Then he sees a bonfire burning near the home of Eustacia Vye, a beautiful and spirited young girl he has fallen in love with, and he answers her summons despite his intention to break off their affair. During their meeting, which is secretly watched by a young boy named Johnny Nonesuch, the lovers quarrel. Johnny later encounters Diggory and tells him that he has seen Eustacia and Wildeve together. Out of concern for Thomasin, Diggory pleads with Eustacia to end her relationship with Wildeve and let him marry the other girl. Eustacia is unresponsive, so Diggory tells Mrs. Yeobright that he still loves Thomasin and would like to marry her. Mrs. Yeobright, however, feels that Thomasin should marry Wildeve, and she manages to renew Wildeve's interest in her niece by informing him that another man is in love with her.

Mrs. Yeobright's son, Clym, returns home from Paris, where he has been working for a diamond merchant, and a party is held to celebrate his arrival. Curious about this unknown person but not invited to the gathering, Eustacia dresses as one of the players in the traditional "mummers" play and attends the party. Clym is fascinated by this mysterious young woman, and Eustacia, enchanted by his worldliness, fantasizes about escaping the stifling confines of the heath by marrying him. She spurns Wildeve, who immediately marries Thomasin to spite Eustacia. Clym displeases his mother with his decision not to return to France. Instead he plans to open a school and educate the ignorant, superstitious inhabitants of the heath. He invites Eustacia to work as a teacher in the school and soon falls in love with her, although she claims she despises the local people and refuses to have anything to do with educating them. Clym's already troubled relationship with his mother is utterly severed when he marries Eustacia, whom Mrs. Yeobright considers a hussy and blames for her son's decision to stay on Egdon Heath. She later regrets her harshness, though, and commissions her neighbor, Christian Cantle, to deliver equal sums of money to Clym and Thomasin. Christian gambles with Wildeve, however, and loses the money; Diggory later wins the money back and gives it all to Thomasin, not realizing that half had been intended for Clym. Aware that Wildeve won the money from Cantle but not that Diggory had retrieved it, Mrs. Yeobright assumes that Wildeve gave it to Eustacia. She questions Eustacia about the money, and this leads to an angry argument between the women.

Due to his intense studying, Clym damages his eyes and is nearly blind; thus he gives up his plans for the school and becomes a woodcutter. Now despairing of ever leaving the heath with Clym, Eustacia finds her feelings for Wildeve rekindled when she meets him at a local festival. Diggory notices their meeting and begs Mrs. Yeobright to try to save her son's marriage by reconciling with Eustacia. Mrs. Yeobright consequently walks across the heath on a hot, dry day to visit Eustacia. During her long approach to her son's house, she sees first him and then Wildeve go inside. When she finally reaches the house, no one answers her knock, and she assumes that her son has rejected her. Exhausted during her trip home, she stops to rest and is bitten by a snake. Clym, who had been asleep when Mrs. Yeobright arrived, wakes and decides to visit his mother; he soon discovers her dead body on the heath. He learns that Eustacia failed to answer the door because she did not want Mrs. Yeobright to discover her with Wildeve, so Clym blames her for his mother's death. Eustacia moves back into her grandfather's house. Kept from committing suicide by a servant, she desperately agrees to run away with Wildeve, who has recently inherited a large sum of money. She never receives the conciliatory letter that Clym sends her and, on her way to meet Wildeve on the heath, either falls or jumps into a small lake and drowns. Wildeve also drowns in an attempt to rescue her. Diggory eventually marries the widowed Thomasin, while Clym becomes an itinerant preacher.

Characters: Infused with elements of mythology, folklore, and classical tragedy, *The Return of the Native* is nevertheless distinctly modern in its complexity and psychological penetration. Many critics have described Egdon Heath—the somber, unchanging expanse of land upon which the characters live out their destinies—as a kind of character itself, for its implacable face and elemental nature form the backdrop of the story. In *The Return of the Native* Hardy explores his characters' futile attempts to conquer fate and the conflict between the ancient and the modern, the mind and the body, and dreams and reality.

The native referred to in the novel's title is **Clym Yeobright,** an educated, sensitive, and idealistic young man who has been disillusioned by his sojourn as a businessman in Paris. He associates his home with simplicity and friendliness, and he chooses to remain on the heath rather than return to the world of commerce and culture. He plans to establish a school to educate his ignorant and superstitious neighbors, and he ignores his mother's warning that such a goal is futile. Despite his seemingly good intentions, Clym's behavior is selfish and unrealistic, because he seeks not a closer connection with life as it really exists but an escape into abstraction. Likewise he is captivated by Eustacia's beauty and spirit but fails to perceive her deeper needs and aspirations; he expects her to automatically share his hopes and work toward the goal he has established. Thus Clym's eventual blindness—brought on by his obsessive studying—is symbolic of the fact that he has always been blind. His philosophical reaction to his infirmity signifies on the one hand his eagerness to associate himself with the heath (since he becomes a woodcutter) and on the other his desire to divorce himself from reality, to cease to think. Similarly when his mother dies, he focuses not on the complexities of chance, circumstance, and personality that led up to the calamity, but on Eustacia's role in it. Clym's eventual transformation into an itinerant preacher (added to the book after its initial publication, as was the marriage of Diggory and Thomasin) may be seen either as a triumph of the spiritual over the intellectual, with the blinded and bereaved Clym serving as a kind of Christ-figure, or as another manifestation of his characteristic self-righteousness.

Dark, sensual **Eustacia Vye** is one of Hardy's most compelling heroines. Beautiful and passionate, she has the power to captivate men but lacks the power to escape her circumstances. In her pronounced individuality and humanity, Eustacia has been said to represent the human element opposed to the overwhelming natural force of the heath. Though she may be faulted for her selfishness, arrogance, and ambition, Eustacia is nevertheless admirable for her spirit and strength and pitiable for her unfulfilled dreams. Having longed for a great love that would lift her out of her boredom and restlessness and carry her—both literally and figuratively—away from the heath, she is quick to see in Clym her opportunity. Dressed as the Turkish Knight in the traditional, Christmas-time folk drama performed at the party for Clym, she fascinates him with her aura of mystery. After their marriage, Eustacia gradually realizes that Clym's aspirations are different from her own, and his blindness seems to confirm that she will never escape from the heath. She contributes to Mrs. Yeobright's death through her fear and selfishness, but she is mature enough to acknowledge her responsibility. Although she initially agrees to run away with Wildeve, she realizes that he is unworthy of the sacrifice that such an act would entail. Left utterly desolate, she wanders over the heath and finally drowns in one of its small lakes; most scholars agree that her death is a suicide rather than an accident, although Hardy allows for either possibility. In keeping with the novel's mythological aspects, Eustacia has been compared to such goddesses of Greek myth as Artemis, Athena, and Venus as well as the passionate poetess of ancient Greece, Sappho; she might also be considered a Promethean figure in her futile struggle against an indifferent universe.

Eustacia's early interest in **Damon Wildeve,** a former engineer now operating an inn, can probably be attributed to his status as a newcomer to the community. Like Eustacia he is unhappy and dissatisfied, but he is essentially an outsider and Egdon Heath does not have the threatening power over him that it has over those who have always lived in its presence. Wildeve reveals his essential selfishness with his thoughtless behavior toward Thomasin, first carelessly postponing their marriage and then hurriedly marrying her in order to spite Eustacia. He also callously takes advantage of naive Christian Cantle, winning from him the money that was supposed to be delivered to Clym and Thomasin. Though amorous and quick to succumb to his emotions, Wildeve proves incapable of providing the elevated love that Eustacia desires, and she finally rejects his proposal that the two run away together.

Distinguished by the crimson-hued skin that has resulted from his work as a reddleman, **Diggory Venn** is described by Richard Carpenter as an "exotic variant on the staunch yeoman of the Gabriel Oak [in *Far from the Madding Crowd*] type." Playing an ambiguous role in the action, he is a lonely outcast who wanders over the heath with no concrete ties to anyone else, and he frightens the children with his dramatic appearance. At the same time he is essentially decent, patient, and understanding, and his years of quiet loyalty to Thomasin are finally rewarded when they marry. However, this marriage was added by Hardy after the book's first publication; originally, Diggory's fate was to disappear from the heath. Diggory's knowledge of secret meetings and hidden motives and his attempts to alter the course of events might be seen as well-intentioned, but they also make him seem something of a meddler.

Hardy's characterization of simple, faithful **Thomasin Yeobright** has been described as rather weak; she seems to be present primarily to advance the plot. Innocent, gentle, and undemanding, she provides a sharp contrast to Eustacia, particularly in her willing acceptance of her circumstances. Despite the unhappy nature of her marriage to Wildeve, she clings to convention by remaining faithful to him. Her eventual union with Diggory has been said to represent the wisdom of avoiding the two extremes—of passion and of intellect—that Clym and Eustacia represent.

Clym's mother **Mrs. Yeobright** is portrayed as a longtime resident of the heath who seems to have internalized its solitude. She wants her son to experience the wider existence available in the outside world, and she feels that he is misguided in his desire to improve the minds of the rural people. Her resentment of Eustacia is based both on the mistaken belief that she is the reason Clym chooses to stay and on her innate distrust of the spirited young woman. She is a devoted mother, so there may also be an element of jealousy in her attitude toward the woman who has taken her son from her home. Nevertheless she travels across the heath on a hot day with the intention of reconciling her differences with Eustacia. The description of her journey is laced with grotesque natural images, underlining the almost malignant relationship between nature and humanity, and her death is brought about by a combination of physical exhaustion, crushed spirits, and a snakebite. Thus the chain of events that lead up to Mrs. Yeobright's death illustrate the influence of chance in human life.

Other characters in *The Return of the Native* include Eustacia's grandfather, **Captain Vye,** a self-contained former sea captain with little awareness of her true psyche or emotional needs; and **Johnny Nonesuch,** the little boy who witnesses and reports such events as Eustacia's meeting at the bonfire with Wildeve and Mrs. Yeobright's death. The members of the local community form the ''rural chorus'' often found in Hardy's novels; they provide colorful illustrations of folk wisdom and customs, comment on the story's events, and represent the permanence of the heath upon which they live in relative harmony, unlike the main characters. Among the local community members are puckish, ancient **Granfer Cantle** and his elderly son, hapless and unattractive **Christian Cantle,** who loses the money entrusted to him by Mrs. Yeobright to the conniving Wildeve. In the superstitious ritual she practices against Eustacia (who she believes is a witch), Johnny's mother, **Mrs. Nonesuch,** helps to illustrate the endurance of such pagan practices as black masses and voodooism, which, in addition to the Druidical fires at the beginning of the novel, play at least as dominant a role in the community as Christianity. Other members of the rural chorus include **Timothy Fairway, Olly Dowden,** turf-cutter **Sam,** and wood-cutter **Humphrey.**

The Mayor of Casterbridge (novel, 1886)

Plot: The novel, which takes place in the mid-nineteenth century in the fictional English district of Wessex, begins with the arrival of a young farmer named Michael Henchard, his wife, Susan, and their baby, Elizabeth-Jane, in a rural village. Tired and dusty from their travels, the family stops for refreshment at a fair that is taking place there. Henchard becomes drunk and offers to sell his wife and child to the highest bidder; a sailor named Newson accepts the offer, and Susan—disgusted with her husband and unaware that the transaction is not legal—goes away with him. The next day, now sober and ashamed, Henchard searches for his family but is unable to locate them. Much chagrined, he vows to avoid alcohol for twenty years. He settles in the town of Casterbridge and gradually becomes a prosperous grain merchant, also attaining the office of mayor. Henchard becomes involved in a dispute when he sells bad grain; he is ordered to make restitution. He befriends a young Scot named Donald Farfrae who helps him restore his grain, and Henchard subsequently hires Farfrae as his manager. Henchard is surprised when Susan suddenly arrives in Casterbridge, seeking his help; Newson has apparently been lost at sea. Abandoning his romantic ties to another woman, Lucetta LeSueur, Henchard marries Susan. Meanwhile an attraction grows between Farfrae and the now-grown, pretty Elizabeth-Jane. The young Scot becomes more popular in Casterbridge than his well-meaning but impulsive employer, and the jealous Henchard eventually forces him to leave his employ and establish his own business. Henchard forbids Elizabeth-Jane to see Farfrae.

After the death of his wife, Henchard informs Elizabeth-Jane that he, not Newson, is her father. When he opens a letter that Susan had instructed him not to read until his daughter's wedding day, however, he learns that Elizabeth-Jane is in fact Newson's daughter—his own had died while still a baby. Henchard now treats Elizabeth-Jane coolly. Lucetta Le Sueur, made suddenly wealthy when she inherited money from an aunt, arrives in Casterbridge and hires Elizabeth-Jane as her companion so she can see Henchard easily and often; having taking her aunt's name, she is now Lucetta Templeman. When she meets Farfrae, however, Lucetta loses interest in Henchard, and Elizabeth-Jane is chagrined to see that Farfrae is also attracted to Lucetta. Relying on the predictions of a weather prophet, Henchard buys a great deal of grain in order to sell it at a high price when bad weather depletes the harvest. But the bad weather does not occur until late in the harvest, and as a result Henchard is nearly ruined. By contrast Farfrae manages to sell his own grain toward the end of the harvest, after the price has gone up, and becomes wealthy. When the fact that Henchard once sold his wife and child becomes public, Lucetta, who had agreed to marry him because he threatened to expose their affair, leaves town. Upon her return she informs Henchard that she and Farfrae are married—a development which dismays both Henchard and Elizabeth-Jane. Meanwhile Henchard's reputation and fortune have continued to decline, and he is finally forced to go to work for Farfrae as a laborer. He begins to drink heavily. Farfrae becomes mayor of Casterbridge, although Lucetta tries to persuade him to leave the town. Henchard decides to return Lucetta's love letters to her and gives them to a former employee, Jopp, to deliver. However, the vengeful Jopp reads them aloud at the local tavern, thus exposing Lucetta's seedy past. When she learns that this information is common knowledge, Lucetta has a miscarriage and dies. A member of the royal family visits Casterbridge, and a drunken Henchard tries unsuccessfully to join the group of dignitaries assembled to greet the guest.

Newson arrives unexpectedly in Casterbridge; he had not drowned after all. He goes to Henchard to reclaim his daughter, but Henchard lies that Elizabeth-Jane has died. The young woman moves in with the impoverished Henchard, and the two establish a seed-shop. The widowed Farfrae begins to court Elizabeth-Jane again and, to Henchard's disgust, they are engaged. Newson discovers Henchard's lie and returns, quickly replacing Henchard in Elizabeth-Jane's affections. Henchard leaves Casterbridge, but he returns briefly to deliver a goldfinch as a wedding present for his daughter. He dies alone and friendless, cared for by a servant he treated harshly in the past.

Characters: Considered one of the greatest tragic novels of the nineteenth century, *The Mayor of Casterbridge* centers on characters who live in a rapidly changing world. It is marked by an abundance of dramatic incidents—usually attributed to the fact that it was originally serialized and Hardy had to maintain his audience's attention—and by an unforgettable protagonist. While the novel explores the forces within a specific personality in combination with the vagaries of chance and circumstance, it also makes the point that it is impossible to impose one's will on an indifferent universe.

Michael Henchard is the central figure of *The Mayor of Casterbridge* and one of Hardy's most celebrated protagonists. The novel is subtitled "A Man of Character," a reference not to the quality of Henchard's character (as some early reviewers assumed) but to the psychologically penetrating purpose. Critics often point to the "Character is fate" passage as an expression of Hardy's belief in the devastating effect an individual's own weaknesses may have on the course of his life. As the novel opens, Henchard is an unemployed young hay-trusser who considers himself an undeserving victim of bad luck. On a drunken whim he sells his wife and child to another man and then regrets his action. Susceptible to alcohol, his emotions also overpower him. He gives up his drinking habit for the next twenty years and becomes a successful corn merchant official, but Henchard's headstrong, domineering, rash personality remains unchanged. Through a combination of his own irrational behavior, some unfavorable coincidences, and his stubborn adherence to traditional ways (despite the changing circumstances of his environment), Henchard gradually loses his wealth and prominence and is finally reduced to the same lowly status he held at the beginning of the story. His strong, erratic feelings toward Farfrae, which gradually change from admiration and fondness to jealousy and hate, typify his approach to life in general. Though he is eager for companionship and affection, Henchard's self-destructiveness always surfaces to spoil his relationships with others. As his downfall continues, he feels thwarted by unseen forces and wonders if someone is stirring some "unholy brew" in order to blight his life. Despite his impulsiveness and irrationality, though, Henchard is basically honest, fair, and well-meaning, thus lending even more tragedy to his story. While some critics have characterized Henchard's downfall as a kind of divine revenge for his having violated a cosmic moral law when he sold his wife and child, others see it simply as the working out of an amoral, indifferent fate. The death of the goldfinch that Henchard gives to Elizabeth-Jane as a wedding present symbolizes his own demise—in isolation from those who might have loved him and hoping, as he states in his will, that his existence will be remembered by no one. This tragic character has been compared to a variety of other, similar figures of myth and literature, including Prometheus, Oedipus, Faust, Shakespeare's King Lear, Captain

Ahab in Herman Melville's *Moby Dick,* and Lord Jim in Joseph Conrad's novel of the same title. In addition, many critics have noted the novel's evocation of the traditional legend of the "scapegoat king": the leader who must die so that his kingdom may be led into a new age.

Calm, capable **Donald Farfrae** is the opposite of the headstrong, impulsive Henchard. An efficient and intelligent corn expert, he wins Henchard's regard by showing him how to salvage his ruined grain and is soon appointed Henchard's business manager. As his name suggests, Farfrae comes from far away, not only in terms of physical distance but in philosophical outlook. He represents the new age dawning in nineteenth-century England, with the advent of mechanized planting and harvesting techniques that would change the texture of rural life forever. While Henchard operates intuitively, Farfrae bases his decisions on rational, scientific methods, and in the end his approach triumphs over Henchard's. Critics have disagreed on Hardy's attitude toward Farfrae. Some maintain that his exacting, controlled nature is negatively portrayed, suggesting that Hardy disapproved of the changes being wrought upon his beloved countryside; others claim that Hardy's depiction of Farfrae is balanced, and that he neither condemns nor supports the modern trends embodied in this character. Farfrae seems rather cold to some scholars, but he does reveal a sentimental side when he sings a Scottish song in the local tavern. Although he rejects Henchard's overbearing attempts to befriend him, he is scrupulously fair when he starts his own business, refusing to take any customers away from his former employer. Thus Hardy succeeded in depicting Farfrae as a man whose personality—like those of real human beings—is multi-faceted.

Another character who has been the subject of considerable critical attention is **Elizabeth-Jane Henchard Newson,** whom Henchard believes is his own daughter until he learns that Newson is really her father. Unlike Henchard, Elizabeth-Jane is self-restrained and sober. Her rational approach and her intelligence make her a much more appropriate partner for Farfrae than the insubstantial Lucetta Templeton, and their eventual marriage is one of the novel's few bright spots. Throughout the ups and downs of her life, Elizabeth-Jane remains unchangingly stoical and sound, and early reviewers especially admired her for her pronounced virtue. While some critics have found Elizabeth-Jane lacking in compassion because she seems to cast off Henchard quite easily when her real father appears, others note that she is the kind of character who generally thrives in Hardy's fiction. Rather than rebelling against society or railing against fate, she adheres to a strict moral code and always accepts what happens to her with quiet resignation. It is Elizabeth-Jane who states that life is generally dismal with only occasional moments of happiness. She says that she pities those who never achieve the happiness they demand; no matter how much they deserve to be happy, they are unwise to expect it. This resignation allows Elizabeth-Jane to survive in a universe oblivious to the needs and desires of human beings, while her tortured, demanding father is destroyed.

In contrast to Elizabeth-Jane is **Lucetta Templeman,** Henchard's former lover and Farfrae's wife. An attractive though rapidly aging flirt, Lucetta lived a life of easy virtue but seeks to improve her status after receiving an inheritance. She is concerned primarily with appearances and has a strong craving for luxury and glamour; her superficiality and social-climbing have been characterized as symptoms of the new kind of society that was developing in nineteenth-century England, as the middle class gained wealth and assurance. Just as Lucetta has reached, with her marriage to Farfrae, the peak of social eminence, she is assaulted with the sight of the "skimmity" that mocks her former relationship with Henchard. Deeply chagrined by this confrontation with her past, Lucetta has a miscarriage and dies, thus illustrating the power that society's moral code holds over individuals. Although Lucetta is not a likable character, the punishment she receives seems out of proportion to her sins.

Henchard's wife, **Susan Henchard Newson,** is a representative of his past who comes back to haunt him many years after he sells her to another man. She is a simple, passive woman who goes off with Newson partly because she is disgusted with Henchard and partly because she seems to think she has to. In response to those early reviewers who questioned the plausibility of such a transaction, Hardy claimed that wife-selling was a historically authentic practice. Modern critics, however, focus not on the historical accuracy of Henchard's act but on its long-term effect on his life. When Susan reappears, Henchard dutifully marries her, exhibiting both his basic fairness and his tendency to punish himself, since marriage to such a low-born woman will further erode his social standing. Like her husband, Susan is aligned with a rural way of life that was quickly disappearing as the age of industry gathered momentum. Several scholars have commented on the poignancy of the elegy delivered by **Mrs. Cuxsom** after Susan's death, in which her patience and endurance are praised. **Richard Newson,** the jovial sailor who buys Susan from Henchard and later appears to claim his position as Elizabeth-Jane's father, is not a particularly well-developed character. His reappearance is considered by many reviewers a rather clumsy and improbable event, and has been attributed to Hardy's need to keep his serial readers enthralled with many dramatic incidents. The fact that Newson goes away soon after his daughter's wedding has been described as ironic.

As in several of Hardy's other novels, the "rural chorus" plays a significant role in *The Mayor of Casterbridge.* The local characters who congregate at the Three Mariners Inn and in Mixen Lane serve as voices of social commentary, illustrate folk customs and rural ways, and sometimes participate directly in the action. They seem more grim than picturesque in their tendency toward malicious gossip and even cruelty, as when they perform the skimmity ride (in which figures dressed up to resemble Henchard and Lucetta and strapped together back-to-back on a wagon are paraded through town), for it ultimately leads to Lucetta's death. Some of the rural characters include **Jopp,** the surly and vengeful former employee of Henchard, who exposes his affair with Lucetta to the other townsfolk; and **Abel Whittle,** Henchard's simple-minded and long-suffering assistant, who nurses his former employer through his final illness, despite the fact that he was once cruelly humiliated by Henchard. Henchard's calling Whittle a "poor fond fool" reminds many critics of Shakespeare's King Lear, who is attended by his faithful fool during his descent into madness. Another significant character is the **Furmity Woman,** a disreputable old hag often likened to the witches in Shakespeare's *MacBeth.* She serves Henchard the rum-laced beverage that makes him drunk and precipitates the wife-selling incident. When she reappears many years later, Henchard is forced to admit the truth about his past to his friends and neighbors. The furmity woman has been said to represent not only Henchard's secret past but the uncontrollable forces of circumstance and fate that direct his life. A similarly superstitious, malevolent role is played by the **weather prophet,** who wrongly advises Henchard on the best time to purchase grain.

Tess of the D'Urbervilles (novel, 1891)

Plot: Set in rural England in the nineteenth century, the novel begins with the discovery by impoverished, frequently drunken John Durbeyfield that he is descended from the noble D'Urberville family. His wife decides that their daughter Tess should appeal to a nearby wealthy family named D'Urberville to see if they can do anything for her. Tess dutifully visits the family—which has only adopted the name of D'Urberville and has no connection to her own ancestors—and meets their rakish son, Alec. He finds Tess extremely attractive and bothers her with his bold attentions; eventually he arranges for Tess to work in the household. Her family's need later forces her to seek more profitable fieldwork elsewhere. While she is traveling home one evening from an excursion in town with her rowdy workmates, Tess allows Alec to whisk her away on his horse. He seduces her in the woods and she becomes pregnant. Ostracized by her neighbors both before and after the birth of her baby—which she names Sorrow, and which dies after only a few months—Tess finally moves to a dairy farm many miles from her home. There she finds a measure of happiness as a dairymaid among kind, friendly people. One of her new friends is Angel Clare, an idealistic and supposedly progressive-thinking young man who is learning about farming in the hope of becoming a farmer himself. Despite Tess's initial attempts to dissuade Angel from courting her, the two fall in love, and—regardless of Angel's family's disapproval—they marry. Before the wedding Tess tries unsuccessfully to tell Angel about her earlier experience with Alec D'Urberville; on their wedding night, Angel reveals his own illicit romance, so Tess confesses to her seduction and pregnancy. Having idealized Tess as a paragon of innocence and virtue, Angel is unable to cope with this knowledge and insists that they separate. He leaves for Brazil, while Tess—chastised by her mother for needlessly confiding in Angel—is forced to work as a farm laborer to help support her family. While toiling at a farm called Flintcombe-Ash, Tess encounters Alec again. Now an itinerant preacher, he claims to have changed his wicked ways. But soon he is pursuing Tess and trying to seduce her again. Tess writes a tender, remorseful letter to Angel, pleading for his return; she asks his parents to send it on to Brazil. When she receives no reply from Angel, Tess gives in to Alec's pleas and goes to live with him in the resort town of Sandbourne. Having realized that he loves and forgives Tess, Angel returns from Brazil and searches for his wife, finally locating her. Although Tess initially sends Angel away from her door, telling him that his change of heart has come too late, her despair and resentment of Alec overcome her and she stabs him to death. Tess and Angel are reconciled and experience a few days of bliss, knowing that Tess must eventually be captured by the police. At Stonehenge, the lovers are finally overtaken by the authorities. Tess claims that she can accept her fate because she has experienced a short period of happiness with Angel. Some time later, she is executed for the murder of Alec. A sorrowful Angel walks off hand-in-hand with Tess's sister, Liza-Lu.

Characters: The novel is widely acknowledged as Hardy's masterpiece and a classic work of modern fiction. Like all of Hardy's novels, *Tess* is imbued with the deterministic view that man's existence is circumscribed by a combination of social strictures and inherent personality traits. Unusual and controversial at the time of its publication for its sexual frankness and its focus on lower-class, primarily rural characters, the novel comprises a profound indictment of the double standards of Victorian morality as well as an authentic representation of the changes occurring in rural England in the late nineteenth century.

Tess Durbeyfield is one of the most famous figures in nineteenth-century fiction and one of Hardy's most compelling characters. Many critics have identified Tess as a particular favorite of the author who created her. She has been variously seen as Hardy's ideal woman in her combined beauty, strength, and passion; as a victim of circumstance toward whom he felt paternalistic; and as an embodiment of the rural England he so loved and which he believed was rapidly disappearing. The novel's subtitle, "A Pure Woman Faithfully Presented," has been seen as an assertion that Tess is an admirable person destroyed by a society that fails to recognize her inherent virtue. At the beginning of the novel Tess is a naive, innocent young girl who is identified closely with the natural environment in which she lives. Attractive and physically mature, she emanates an unconscious aura of sexuality and—despite her intelligence and sensitivity—relies more on her instincts than her intellect. Her sexual encounter with Alec D'Urberville is one of the novel's most controversial elements: while some critics consider it an outright rape, casting Tess as a victim of male aggression, others see it as a seduction for which Tess must take her share of responsibility. Whether or not Tess is a willing participant in the incident, its ultimately disastrous consequences illustrate the injustice of the Victorian moral code, under which an unmarried young woman who became pregnant was ostracized while the father of her child went completely unpunished.

The unwillingness of the community to accept Tess's child—signified especially by the church's refusal to baptize it—marks a transition in her attitude. Newly aware of the world's injustice, she rejects the organized religion in which she had previously trusted and leaves home. Tess's sojourn in the Valley of the Dairies constitutes a period of regeneration, for she is surrounded by generally benevolent friends and lives in a lush physical landscape that is often noted for its Edenic quality; in fact Tess herself has been described as an Eve-figure because of her naturalness, her passion, and her fall from innocence. Her love for Angel is intense and worshipful, and his rejection devastates her; again she is punished by a rigid moral code. Emotionally desolate and physically exhausted by the backbreaking farm work she undertakes after Angel's departure, Tess is vulnerable to Alec's influence. No longer seeming to care what happens to her, she enters into an illicit relationship with him. When Angel returns for her, Tess strikes out and kills Alec. During the famous scene at Stonehenge, where she and Angel await her inevitable capture, Tess declares that, having experienced a few days of bliss with Angel, she is ready to die. This ending has been interpreted as a triumph, in that Tess has asserted her own will and achieved a higher justice than that meted out by humanity, but it has also been said to signify her acceptance of the emptiness and indifference of the universe. In any case Hardy's portrayal of Tess's beauty, strength, and suffering is universally lauded for its transcendent power.

One of the most prevalent concerns in Hardy's fiction is the conflict between the spiritual and the physical, and in *Tess of the D'Urbervilles,* the spiritual side of this struggle is personified by **Angel Clare.** Unlike Tess, who relies strongly on her instincts, Angel has a more ethereal, intellectual point of view. He is an educated, idealistic young man who claims to disdain the outmoded traditions espoused by such representatives of convention as his pastor father. Although his father wants Angel to follow a ministerial career, Angel decides to become a farmer. He sees Tess as a quintessential representative of the natural world, which he naively envisions as a realm of purity and innocence. He claims to follow a creed of rational skepticism and to spurn social strictures, but when he learns Tess's history, he reveals his true conservatism. He rejects Tess on the basis of her sexual past, despite the fact that he himself has had an illicit affair, thereby reinforcing a contradictory moral code with different standards for women and men. Some critics see Angel as an embodiment of an oppressive, male-dominated society. Nevertheless he is not simply a one-sided character consistently unable to perceive his own wrongheadedness. He sincerely loves Tess, and his eventual realization that he has been wrong to spurn her, followed by his return to England and renewed offer of love, does redeem him somewhat. But his change of heart comes too late to save Tess. Scholars find allegorical significance in Angel's name, referring to his overly ethereal outlook or to the irony that his connection with Tess is ultimately destructive.

If Angel represents the spiritual aspect of the conflict between the spiritual and the physical, **Alec D'Urberville** personifies the physical side. He is a dissolute, dapper, selfish young man who callously seduces—or, as some critics maintain, rapes—a lower-class girl and then abandons her. Though he later claims conversion to evangelical Christianity, he again starts to torment Tess and eventually persuades her to live with him as his mistress. Because of his sophistication, lustfulness, and wicked behavior, Alec is characterized as a stock villain of Victorian melodrama. Despite his rather stereotyped qualities and actions, however, he does exhibit some very human weaknesses, and he is punished for his deeds when Tess murders him. He is said to represent the rapidly advancing middle class of nineteenth-century England; to embody the oppressive male social order that destroys Tess; and, as a devil-figure, to tempt the innocent, Eve-like Tess.

Many scholars have praised Hardy for his faithful depictions of rural life in the earliest days of the industrial revolution. In *Tess* the rural world is portrayed through descriptions of the landscapes and physical settings and through the characters of Tess's family members, neighbors, and co-workers and their relationships with each other. Her indolent, alcoholic father, **Jack Durbeyfield,** initiates the novel's tragic process when he grasps onto the idea that he is of noble Norman ancestry. Claiming that he is too high-born for such a humble pursuit as working for a living, he forces his family into economic desperation that forces Tess to support them. His practical, hard-working wife, **Joan Durbeyfield,** exhibits both ignorance and devotion to her family. While some critics have admired her strength and agreed with her advice to Tess that the secrets of her past should remain hidden, other have seen her sending Tess to the D'Urbervilles as a callous act. At the end of the novel Tess suggests that Angel marry her sister, **Liza-Lu** (Eliza-Louisa), whom Hardy describes as a "spiritualized image of Tess." This possibility might be seen as a faint but positive note of hope in an otherwise dismal world, or as insufficient recompense for the tragedy that has taken place.

Also filling out the rural milieu of *Tess* are **Mr. Tringham,** the elderly pastor and local historian who carelessly informs Tess's father of his noble lineage and who then departs from the story; **Richard Crick,** the kindly owner of Talbothays Farm where Tess is employed as a dairymaid; his hearty and equally kind wife **Christiana Crick**; and **Farmer Groby,** the penny-pinching, harsh owner of Flintcomb-Ash Farm, where Tess leads an exhausting and dismal life. While employed at Talbothays, Tess is befriended by three fellow dairymaids: heavy, red-faced **Marian,** timid **Retty Priddle,** and **Izz Huett,** whom Angel considers taking with him as his mistress when he goes to Brazil (thus further illustrating his adherence to a contradictory moral code). All three dairymaids are in love with the handsome young Angel, but they do not treat Tess spitefully when he chooses her as his beloved.

Other characters in the novel include Angel's parents, the **Reverend James Clare** and his wife. Clare is a sincerely devout, evangelical minister whose theology proves destructively narrow; it is he who influences Alec to change his wicked ways, though the reformation proves shallow. **Mrs. Clare** is basically good but her perspective is as limited as her husband's and she is no more able than he to understand their son. Angel's conventional, snobbish brothers **Felix** and **Cuthbert** disapprove of Tess; the pious charity worker **Mercy Chant** becomes the wife of Cuthbert, though the Clares originally hoped she would marry Angel. **Mrs. Stoke-D'Urberville** is Alec's blind, wealthy, widowed mother, whose nouveau-riche husband adopted an aristocratic name despite his true lack of any noble connections. **Car Darch,** also called the **Queen of Spades,** is a vulgar, jealous woman who once had an affair with Alec.

Jude the Obscure (novel, 1894)

Plot: Eleven-year-old Jude Fawley is greatly disappointed when his beloved teacher, Richard Phillotson, leaves the little English town of Marygreen to attend the university at Christminster. A poor but ardent student, Jude must resign himself to working in his great-aunt Drusilla's bakery. By the age of nineteen, Jude still hopes to become a scholar but becomes an apprentice stonemason restoring old churches. One night while returning home he meets Arabella Donn, who with other young girls is washing pigs' innards in a stream. He is attracted to Arabella, who seduces him and then tricks him into marrying her by telling him that she is pregnant. Although Jude is initially determined to embrace family life and give up his ambitions, marriage soon disillusions him, and he starts to drink, causing Arabella to leave him. Thus unencumbered, Jude moves to Christminster and becomes a stonemason there while applying to the university to commence the education he has long planned. He meets his cousin Sue Bridehead, an intelligent and unconventional young woman, and is much taken with her. Jude resumes his friendship with Phillotson and arranges for Sue to become the teacher's assistant. To Jude's dismay, Phillotson falls in love with Sue and the two become more and more intimate. When he is rejected by all five of the colleges at Christminster because of his economic and social status, Jude lapses into heavy drinking. He loses his job and returns to Marygreen.

Next Jude embarks on a religious career. He moves to Melchester, where Sue is attending a teacher's college, and works as a stonemason there while seeing Sue often, even though she has promised to marry Phillotson when her education is finished. She has unorthodox ideas about religion and tries to persuade Jude to give up studying for the ministry. After Sue's marriage to Phillotson, Jude returns to Christminster, where he continues to pine for her. He discovers Arabella working in a tavern; he also hears that Sue is miserable in her marriage. He finally decides to abandon his religious studies. Jude and Sue meet again at Aunt Drusilla's funeral and realize that they want to be together, so they move to the larger city of Aldbrickham. The amiable Phillotson grants Sue a divorce and loses his teaching position as a result; Jude also divorces Arabella, who wants to marry another man. Because Sue distrusts the conventional bonds of matrimony, she and Jude live together without marrying. But when Arabella suddenly appears and confides that her marriage has not occurred, Sue is jealous and afraid of losing Jude so she promises to marry him. Arabella finally does marry but sends her small boy—fathered by Jude—to live with Jude and Sue; the melancholy child is nicknamed Little Father Time. Because of their unmarried status, Jude and Sue are forced to move from town to town seeking work. After several years they have two children of their own and Sue is pregnant with another. Jude's poor health forces him to give up stonemasonry and become a baker. The family travels to Christminster, a place that still attracts Jude with its aura of learning, despite his failure to achieve the education he has aspired to. When the landlady of a lodging house, fearing that Sue will give birth there, tells her to find a room elsewhere, Sue bitterly remarks to Little Father Time that children should never be born. Returning to their rooms later, Sue and Jude discover that the boy has hanged himself and the two babies. Sue's resulting distress causes her baby to born prematurely, and it too dies.

This horrible experience causes a transformation in Sue's outlook. She concludes that her children's deaths were punishment for her having lived in sin with Jude and that her only alternative is to return to Phillotson, her rightful husband. The two are again married, while Jude drinks heavily. Arabella tricks him into marriage again, and his health deteriorates seriously. Determined to see Sue once more, he travels in a rainstorm to meet her. She consummates her marriage with Phillotson in an effort to atone completely for her sins; when he hears of this, Jude dies in a state of utter despair and misery.

Characters: Considered one of Hardy's most accomplished works, *Jude the Obscure* is his last and gloomiest novel. Hardy said the novel concerned "the tragedy of unfulfilled aims," presenting his views on the dire consequences of overly rigid marriage laws, condemning the academic snobbery of English universities, and providing realistic depictions of relationships between men and women. Hardy portrays life as circumscribed by convention and individual character.

The novel's central figure is an intelligent, sensitive young man who becomes a stonemason (like Hardy's father and grandfather) to support himself but dreams of pursuing academic studies. The novel's themes are delineated through the struggles of **Jude Fawley**— frequently identified as Hardy's most complex character— particularly the conflict between the physical and the spiritual and the gap between goals and opportunities limiting the achievements of human beings. Jude is "obscure" not only because he is socially insignificant and isolated but because he cannot resolve his internal conflicts. He allows himself to be sidetracked from his educational plans by the alluring, intensely physical Arabella. After he has driven her away with his gloominess and drinking, he travels to Christminster, hoping to begin his academic career. There he meets Sue and, although he promises himself he will keep their relationship platonic, he falls in love with her. Jude's inability to get admitted to the university because of his humble social status shows the subversion of the system, which stated originally that it intended to educate those who were promising but poor, when in fact it favors the privileged. This dream shattered, Jude decides to become a minister. Susceptible to Sue's influence, however, he eventually shares her religious skepticism and abandons this goal as well. Critics characterize Jude as a distinctly modern character in his complexity and contradictory motives; he is basically good, but his naivete, tenderheartedness, sensuality, and—to a lesser extent—weakness for drink keep him from progressing. His attraction to Arabella and his sense of duty induce him to marry her immediately when she tells him she is pregnant, while his regard for the unorthodox though essentially cold Sue leads him to abandon his religious studies but face social ostracism when the two live together without getting married, as Sue wishes. In the end Jude is even more alienated from conventional values than Sue claimed to be, for he has seen how her innate allegiance to Christianity has harmed her and how his own life has been limited by circumstance. Yet it is also apparent that Jude's personal weaknesses contribute to his downfall.

Sue Bridehead is another important character in *Jude the Obscure* and one of the most interesting women in Hardy's fiction. When Jude first meets her, she is working as an artist in a religious artifacts warehouse, yet she freely claims she is skeptical about Christianity and instead prefers pagan mythology. It is primarily through her influence that Jude's religious faith deteriorates. Some critics see Sue as a reflection of the "new woman" of the late nineteenth century: intelligent and physically boyish, she represents women's mounting demand for emancipation and equality. Jude is attracted to her ethereal purity, sensitivity, and sharp intellect, and scholars consider her a foil to Arabella—who represents the sensual aspect of love—as well as a projection of forces in Jude's own personality. Despite Sue's professed affinity for paganism, she has an aversion to sex, and this is a major component of her character. She marries Phillotson out of respect for him but finds the prospect of physical relations with him intolerable, and she does not consummate her relationship with Jude until she fears she will lose him. This quality—termed sexual frigidity by some scholars— reflects her inherent narcissism and intellectual vanity and is closely related to her aversion to marriage, which she sees as an unfairly binding contract. Sue's final act is a subject of much critical discussion. In returning to Phillotson, despite her repulsion and because she feels her children's deaths were punishment for living in sin with Jude, Sue adheres to convention, exposing the shallowness of her professed unorthodox beliefs. On the other hand, it also makes her appear a more complex character. Whether Sue is indeed an early feminist attempting to circumvent convention or an inherently average woman whose irrationality and weakness are revealed in the end, she provides an example of Hardy's interest in female characters and ability to portray them effectively.

Arabella Donn represents the more sensual side of Jude's personality. She is portrayed as an attractive and intensely physical but coarse and vulgar woman. When Jude first sees her, she is washing pig's innards, and this imagery seems to follow her throughout the story. With her false dimple and artificial hairpiece and her scheming to trap Jude into marriage, she quickly establishes herself as a disreputable character; Victorian critics found Arabella particularly repulsive (Margaret Oliphant called her "a human pig" and a "fleshly animal"). Notably, Hardy reversed conventional approaches to relationships between men and women by depicting Jude's lawful wife as sensual and his illicit mistress as ethereal and cold. Yet despite her callous lying to twice tempt Jude into marriage, Arabella is not inherently evil, and Hardy—while apparently repulsed by her—does not seem to have intended her as the story's villain. In fact she sometimes exhibits flashes of intelligence or at least common sense, so that she projects a more honest approach to life than Sue. The fact that Arabella is out flirting with other men at a town festival while Jude lies dying emphasizes not only her insensitivity and selfishness but Jude's tragic isolation.

It is schoolteacher **Richard Phillotson** who first inspires Jude with a thirst for learning, and Jude is much distressed when his beloved teacher moves away to pursue his own studies. In addition to encouraging Jude's intellectual pursuits, Phillotson alleviates the orphaned boy's sense of rootlessness and abandonment. After Jude grows up and moves to Christminster, he looks up his old friend and reestablishes their relationship, then is dismayed to see Phillotson falling in love with Sue. Phillotson is inevitably attracted to his bright, sensitive young assistant and marries her despite the disparity in their ages. When Sue requests a divorce, he behaves not with the conventional selfishness that might be expected but with sympathy and generosity. Because of the divorce, however, Phillotson loses his teaching position (a concrete example of the detrimental effects of the strict marriage laws Hardy condemned) and is perhaps spiritually hurt as well, for he seems to grow hardened afterward. Thus he is willing to accept Sue's offer to return to him, even though she is doing so to sacrifice herself rather than because she loves him.

Other significant characters in *Jude the Obscure* include Jude's aunt **Drusilla Fawley,** a bitter old woman who warns him about the family's history of bad luck with marriage; and the **Widow Edlin,** a humble old woman who remains faithful to Jude and Sue despite her bewildered view of their relationship and who strongly disapproves of Sue's decision to return to Phillotson. **Little Father Time,** the son of Jude and Arabella who is taken in by Jude and Sue, is a pathetic, somewhat weird little boy whose nickname refers to his persistently melancholy manner. Although the circumstance of the murder-suicide executed by the child has been criticized for its melodrama and implausibility, it dramatically demonstrates the tragic effect that feelings of rejection, guilt, and despair may have on minor children.

Further Reading

Alexander, Anne. *Thomas Hardy: The "Dream-Country" of His Fiction.* London: Vision, 1987.

Alvarez, A. "Novels: Thomas Hardy's 'Jude the Obscure.'" In *Beyond All This Fiddle: Essays 1955-1967,* pp. 178-87. New York: Random House, 1969.

Cockshut, A. O. J. "The Pessimists." *In Man and Woman: A Study of Love and the Novel, 1740-1940,* pp. 100-35. 1977. Reprint. New York: Oxford University Press, 1978.

Cox, R.G., ed. *Thomas Hardy: The Critical Heritage.* New York: Barnes & Noble, 1970.

Daleski, H.M. "'Tess of the D'Urbervilles': Mastery and Abandon." In *The Divided Heroine: A Recurrent Pattern in Six English Novels,* pp. 69-87. New York: Holmes & Meier Publishers, 1984.

Dave, Jagdish Chandra. *The Human Predicament in Hardy's Novels.* New York: Macmillan Press, 1985.

Kramer, Dale, ed. *Critical Approaches to the Fiction of Thomas Hardy.* New York: Harper & Row, 1979.

Miller, J. Hillis. *Thomas Hardy: Distance and Desire.* Cambridge, Mass.: Harvard University Press, 1970.

Oliphant, Margaret. Review of "Tess of the D'Urbervilles." *Blackwood's Edinburgh Magazine* CLI, No. DCCCCXVII (March 1892): 464-74.

Tennant, Emma. "The Kiss of Life." *New Statesman & Society* 3, No. 132 (21 December 1990): 49-50.

Twentieth-Century Literary Criticism, Vols. 4, 10, 18, 32. Detroit: Gale.

George Washington Harris
1814-1869
American short story writer.

Sut Lovingood's Yarns (short stories, 1867)

Plot: Harris's tales featuring backwoodsman Sut Lovingood appeared in various newspapers from 1854 through 1861; he resumed his story writing after the Civil War, and a volume of yarns narrated by Sut was published in 1867. Stories frequently cited by critics as successful and representative of Harris's craft include: "Sut Lovingood's Daddy, Acting Horse," "Parson John Bullen's Lizards," and "Blown Up with Soda."

Harris's first published tale, "Sut Lovingood's Daddy, Acting Horse" begins with the arrival of Sut at Pat Nash's grocery, where a group of idle, fun-loving mountaineers is gathered. Sut rides up on his decrepit horse, Tearpoke, and, after shaming a few hecklers into silence, relates what happened when his previous horse, Tickeytail, died of cold and starvation. The loss of the horse left Sut's impoverished and voluminous family, including Dad, Mam, seventeen children, and "the Prospect" (Mam is pregnant), wondering how they would raise the crops they needed for the coming year. They hope that some stray horse will wander by. When their usual bad luck prevails, Dad decides to take the horse's place, and Sut and Mam harness him to the plow. Dad enters wholeheartedly into his role, attaching ears made of tree bark to his head and behaving like an ornery horse by trying to kick Mam and bite Sut. With Sut holding the reins, Dad pulls the plow around the field; just as he begins to sweat, however, he runs over a hornets' nest. Hornets immediately cover him, and he strips off his clothing and runs at breakneck speed toward the swimming hole at the nearby creek. Dad jumps off a bluff into the creek while Sut stands on the bluff above, laughing and mocking him. His head bobbing in and out of the water as some hornets continue to sting him and others are drowned, Dad threatens to punish Sut for his derision and lack of concern. Fearful of his father's retribution, Sut stays away from home; the next day he asks a passing stranger what is going on at the Lovingood cabin. The stranger relates that he has seen a man with a hugely swollen head with "jist two black slits" for eyes. Sut concludes the story by explaining that he has not yet returned home, and he raises a whiskey toast to "the durned old fool, an' the hornets too."

The story of "Parson John Bullen's Lizards" is introduced by George, an educated gentleman who knows Sut and often listens tolerantly to his tales. Having seen notices offering an eight-dollar reward for Sut's capture tacked up around the community, George asks Sut to explain why he is being sought by Parson John Bullen. Sut recounts his recent experience at a camp meeting, a religious revival led by a traveling preacher, at Rattlesnake Springs. Parson Bullen caught Sut and a girl making love in the bushes and chastised them loudly; he later told the girl's mother about her scandalous behavior, even though he promised he would not, and she received a whipping. Disgusted with the preacher's hypocrisy, Sut decides to get the better of him. He pretends to be a repentant sinner in order to attain a front-row seat at the meeting. While Bullen is delivering a fiery sermon on how sinners will be tormented after death by "Hell-sarpints," Sut releases eight lizards, which climb up Bullen's pant leg. Convinced that he is being attacked by the very creatures he has just been describing, Bullen panics, stripping off his clothing and leaping into the crowd. Mayhem ensues as the fat, naked preacher scrambles among his mostly female followers, whose reactions include fear, shock, embarrassment, and mirth. Sut himself becomes frightened when he is nearly hit by flying objects, and he flees the scene with the help of his conveniently long legs. He concludes that Bullen has tried unsuccessfully to regain the community's respect and has vowed to seek vengeance against Sut.

In "Blown Up with Soda," Sut begins by describing to George the beautiful Sicily Burns, a saucy and attractive mountain girl who epitomizes for Sut all the charms of the female sex. Having bought some baking soda from a Yankee peddler, Sicily beguiles Sut into drinking two large portions of a baking powder and water mixture. Initially convinced that he is ingesting a love potion, Sut soon feels like he has "swallered a thrashin' masheen in full blast" and hears a strange rumbling coming from his stomach. As Sicily lies on the ground laughing, Sut jumps on his horse and rides toward the home of Dr. Goodman, emitting from his mouth a steady, hissing stream of foam. Sicily yells out that he should "Hole hit down" because it is a cure for puppy love, and the distressed Sut realizes that he has been duped. Sut is apparently a frightening sight, for when he comes upon the "circuit rider" Clapshaw, the traveling preacher's faith fails him and he "tuck a skeer [scare]," jumping into a nearby thicket. Later, Clapshaw tells Sicily that he saw a strange sight resembling a Quaker with a long white beard but which might have been some steam-driven contraption invented to promulgate the Catholic faith. Sut concludes the story by admitting that Sicily did indeed cure him of his infatuation with her, and he proposes that he and George drink to "the durndes' fool in the worl'—jis me!"

Characters: Harris's Sut Lovingood stories are often cited as examples of the southwestern humor that became popular in the United States in the mid-nineteenth century. Told in a lively, colorful, southern vernacular, they feature such elements of the frontier tall tale style as exaggeration, practical jokes, and often violent behavior. Critical response to the stories has been "peculiarly split between hilarity and disgust," as noted by critic Carolyn S. Brown. Early reviewers found Sut excessively vulgar and repellent, and some modern scholars concur; others, however, praise *Sut Lovingood* for its earthy humor and note that Harris's style and characters probably influenced such later writers as Mark Twain and William Faulkner.

Sut Lovingood is one of the most memorable characters to appear before the publication of Mark Twain's classic *The Adventures of Huckleberry Finn.* Illiterate and penniless, Sut was born in squalor to a large family, from whom he claims he inherited his foolishness, living somewhere in the mountains of Tennessee. Frequently referring to himself as a "nat'ral born durn'd fool" and freely acknowledging his gullibility and cowardice, Sut relates in his own distinctive dialect his adventures in the hills and small, country towns of the South. The stories revolve around practical jokes Sut plays on people he considers hypocritical, devious, conceited, or stupid; his victims include "circuit riders" (preachers), sheriffs, Yankees, learned people, women, and blacks. The first story in *Sut Lovingood's Yarns,* "Sut Lovingood's Daddy, Acting Horse," establishes his ungainly appearance: skinny and unkempt, Sut has excessively long legs (which, as he often notes, facilitate his quick escapes), rides a dilapidated horse, and drinks from a flask of whiskey. A practiced and skillful storyteller who needs only a comfortable place to rest and a tolerant audience— almost always including or consisting solely of George—to spin his yarns, Sut conquers life's difficulties by exaggerating and then laughing at them, thereby bringing some relief to his listener, the "poor misfortinit feller" who may otherwise feel he wields little power over his circumstances. In his shiftlessness, sexual promiscuity, contempt for blacks, and defiance of conventional authority, Sut has been viewed as an embodiment of some of the worst elements of the South. Noting that Sut regularly perpetrates physical violence against those who cross him and never acknowledges their pain, some critics find him sadistic and malevolent; in a famous review of the tales, critic Edmund Wilson referred to Sut as "a peasant squatting in his own filth." Others emphasize that the yarns are intentionally exaggerated and the reader should therefore maintain some distance from their brutality. Sut's supporters see him as a boisterous rebel and concur with Franklin J. Meine's assessment of him as a "genuine naive roughneck mountaineer riotously bent on raising hell." Sut has even been characterized as a predecessor to the existential heroes of the twentieth century in his detachment from the ugliness and meaninglessness of life. His disgust for hypocrisy, sometimes cited as one of his few admirable traits, is evident in "Parson Bullen's Lizards," and both his attraction to and distrust of women are illustrated in "Blown Up with Soda." In other stories, Harris uses Sut as a mouthpiece to express his own support for the Confederacy and contempt for such famous northerners as Abraham Lincoln; these satirical pieces are distinguished by their vitriolic tone.

Through **George,** who introduces most of the Lovingood stories, Harris employs the framing technique common in many southwestern comic tales. Although schooled and more sophisticated than the other characters, George seems to be accepted by them. Apparently from the city, thus an outsider to the southern rural society the stories present, he serves as a liaison between that world and the reader. Generally tolerant toward Sut, though occasionally revealing that Sut has told a lie, George remains detached, never moralizing about the often ribald or violent events Sut relates.

Although Sut is the central character in the yarns, several others have been frequently noted and discussed by critics. **Sut's father** is featured in "Sut Lovingood's Daddy, Acting Horse," a tale intended to illustrate the Lovingood family's predilection for foolishness. Sut describes his Dad as "dod-dratted mean, an' lazy, an' ugly, an' savidge, an' durn fool to kill," a luckless, shiftless example of the "poor white trash" among whom Sut has grown up. Dad's enthusiasm in acting like a horse suggests his own proximity to animalistic tendencies. Sut's gleeful reaction to his father's encounter with the nest of hornets is said to evidence his resentment of the misery, ignorance, and degradation that his father has passed on to him; it might also be seen as an expression of the eternal power struggle between parents and children.

Sut is contemptuous of organized, conventional religion and particularly hates "circuit riders," the usually Methodist preachers who traveled through the southern countryside in the nineteenth century organizing religious meetings. Some critics have noted that many of the real-life models for such characters as **Parson Bullen** were, indeed, unintelligent, poorly educated, or even morally corrupt. Known to drink, make, and sell whiskey (and, to Sut's further disgust, not even good whiskey), Bullen further demonstrates his hypocrisy when he breaks his promise not to tell on the girl he caught in the bushes with Sut. The scene in which a panicked, grotesquely fat, naked Parson Bullen flees from his pulpit, his pants full of lizards, is a comic high point of the Sut Lovingood stories. His attempt to recover from humiliation by adapting his preaching to the circumstances—"Nakid I cum into the world, an' nakid I'm a gwine orten hit, ef I'm spard ontil then"—is a dismal failure.

Sut's attitude toward women is simultaneously appreciative and distrustful; deceitful women are a particular target of his satire. A black-haired, spirited beauty with the sensual attractions and underlying conniving of the classic temptress, **Sicily Burns** proves herself as skilled a prankster as Sut when she cures him of his "puppy love" for her. The passage in which Sut praises Sicily's endowments reflects both his frankness about sexuality and the nearly poetic lyricism found in some parts of the tales. Praising Sicily's white skin, smile, and breasts, Sut tells George that she "shows amung wimen like a sunflower among dorg fennil, or a hollyhawk in a patch ove smartweed." Sut not only overcomes his infatuation for Sicily but, in a later story, manages revenge when he disrupts her wedding by releasing a swarm of hornets into the gathering.

Further Reading

Brown, Carolyn S. "Sut Lovingood: A Nat'ral Born Durn'd Yarnspinner." In *The Tall Tale in American Folklore and Literature,* pp. 74-88. Knoxville: University of Tennessee Press, 1987.

Dictionary of Literary Biography, Vols. 3, 11. Detroit: Gale.

Gardiner, Elaine. "Sut Lovingood: Backwoods Existentialist." *Southern Studies* XXII, No. 2 (Summer 1983): 177-89.

Lenz, William E. "Sensuality, Revenge, and Freedom: Women in Sut Lovingood's Yarns." *Studies in American Humor* n.s. 1, No. 3 (February 1983): 173-80.

Meine, Franklin J., ed. Introduction to *Tall Tales of the Southwest: An Anthology of Southwestern Humor, 1830-1860,* pp. xv-xxxii. New York: Knopf, 1930.

Nineteenth-Century Literature Criticism, Vol. 23. Detroit: Gale.

Rickels, Milton. *George Washington Harris.* New York: Twayne, 1966.

Wilson, Edmund. "The Myth of the Old South; Sidney Lanier; The Poetry of the Civil War; 'Sut Lovingood'. In *Patriotic Gore: Studies in the Literature of the American Civil War,* pp. 438-528. Oxford University Press, 1962.

Joel Chandler Harris
1848-1908
American short story writer, novelist, and journalist.

Uncle Remus: His Songs and Sayings; The Folk-Lore of the Old Plantation (short stories, 1881)

Plot: Thirty-four of the tales included in this collection are set in rural Putnam County, Georgia, on a plantation owned by Mars (Master) John and his wife, Miss Sally. All feature the same narrative framework. They begin with Uncle Remus, a kind, elderly former slave, sitting near his fireplace in his cabin located behind the plantation's Big House. He is usually performing some routine task, such as cooking or repairing equipment. The young son of the white plantation owners is seated in rapt attention at Uncle Remus's side. Uncle Remus tells his young friend a story either generated by a direct question from the boy or evolving from the general course of their conversation. As Uncle Remus begins to tell his story, the scene switches to the world of "creeturs," or animals; the action usually takes place on the "big road" where the animals congregate. Typically the animal characters meet and exchange seemingly friendly greetings that mask their underlying animosity. Then they engage in contests or make agreements that are supposed to benefit both, but which always result in the weaker but craftier animal (usually Brer Rabbit, but occasionally Brer Tarrypin) outsmarting the other physically stronger but less resourceful animal (Brer Fox, Brer Wolf, or Brer Bear). The tales end with a return to the cabin and a summarizing comment or words of wisdom from Uncle Remus.

In several stories the devious Brer Fox invites Brer Rabbit to dinner with the intention of eating the hare rather than serving him a meal, but Brer Fox never manages to catch Brer Rabbit. In "The Wonderful Tar-Baby," perhaps the most famous of the Uncle Remus tales, one of Brer Fox's almost-successful schemes is documented. He fashions a "tar baby" out of tar and turpentine and places it in the road, where Brer Rabbit encounters it as he is passing by. He greets the strange figure and tries to engage it in conversation. Finding the tar baby unresponsive, Brer Rabbit grows increasingly frustrated. He yells at the figure to determine if it is deaf and accuses it of being "stuck up." Finally he strikes the tar baby with his hands, which promptly become stuck; then he kicks the figure and his feet are also caught, followed by his head. As Brer Rabbit becomes adhered to the tar baby, writes Harris, "Brer Fox, he lay low." When Brer Rabbit is completely incapacitated, Brer Fox rolls on the ground laughing at his enemy's predicament. Thus Brer Rabbit is forced to accept Brer Fox's dinner invitation. At this point in the story Uncle Remus conducts one of his typical digressions to tell the story of why Brer Possum plays dead, then he resumes the story of the tar baby. Captured by Brer Fox and hopelessly bound to the tar baby, Brer Rabbit adopts a meek, obsequious attitude. He tells Brer Fox to kill him by skinning, drowning, burning, or hanging him, but he begs that he not be thrown into the brier-patch—as if this would be too cruel and horrible a death. Brer Fox falls for Brer Rabbit's ruse and propels the hare into the brier-patch, only to see him land unscathed and gleeful. As Brer Rabbit combs the tar out of his fur, he exclaims in his usual sassy manner that he was "Bred en brawn in a brier-patch!"

Characters: The Uncle Remus tales hold an important place in American literature both because, through memorable, colorful characters and carefully rendered African-American dialect, they chronicle the post-Civil War South and offer a host of allegorical possibilities. Studied by folklorists, psychologists, and sociologists as well as literary critics, the stories have generated a wide variety of interpretations. Some claim they idealize plantation society and encourage black passivity, while others detect an undercurrent of violence and cynicism denoting resentment of white attitudes and oppression of the black population. Although Harris was himself white, he spent his teenage years as a printing apprentice on a Georgia plantation, and the many hours he spent with the black people who also lived there led to an interest in their folklore and speech patterns. Scholars have noted an ambiguity in Harris's comments about the Uncle Remus stories, which appeared in a column he wrote for the *Atlanta Constitution,* for he emphasized both their humorous quality and their serious intent. In any case the stories were enthusiastically received by nineteenth-century audiences in both the northern United States, where they were appreciated for their favorable portrayal of a black character, and the South, where the paternalistic relationship between Uncle Remus and the white boy as well as the idyllic pastoral setting won approval. Twentieth-century critics view the stories not just as entertaining children's tales but as revealing documents of a difficult, transitional period of American history.

When the character of **Uncle Remus** made his first appearance in Harris's *Atlanta Constitution* column, he was an urban black man who supposedly stopped by the journalist's office to offer his comments on the politics of Reconstruction era Atlanta and other topics. In the tales published in *Uncle Remus: His Songs and Sayings,* he is an elderly, rural black man who has lived on a Georgia plantation since the days of slavery. White-haired and bespectacled, Uncle Remus is a tall, strong, still-vigorous man who was once the most versatile and capable of the plantation workers. He continues to play a significant role on the plantation, performing a number of tasks important to its maintenance and management, and he is also respected for his kindness and wisdom. The young white boy whose parents own the plantation adores and reveres Uncle Remus, who in turn treats the child with warm affection, often calling him "Honey." Some critics have seen the relationship between the venerable black man and the lively, curious white boy as a precursor to that portrayed between Huckleberry Finn and Jim in Mark Twain's 1885 novel *The Adventures of Huckleberry Finn.* Despite his gentleness, Uncle Remus does not hesitate to mildly discipline his young friend, advising him to refrain from such misbehavior as tormenting chickens or disobeying his mother, and he sometimes withholds the conclusion of a story as punishment. Through his tales, which draw indirect but clear parallels between the behavior of the animal characters and that of human beings, Uncle Remus subtly endorses the value of hard work, good behavior, and endurance. Critics often comment on the unsentimental or even violent nature of many of Uncle Remus's stories, which feature such occurrences as the scalding to death of a wolf and the serving of a fox's head to his family during a meal. Questioned by the boy about why these gruesome acts must be included in the stories, Uncle Remus explains that such things were not uncommon in the past. This adherence to the sometimes brutal facts of reality has been interpreted as a veiled reference to the hardships endured by African-Americans under slavery; thus Uncle Remus's radiant grin masks the true suffering of his people. Yet Uncle Remus has also been characterized as a stereotypical plantation black man: devoted to his white masters, humble, essentially passive, and perfectly contented with his inferior position and living conditions.

The archetype of the "trickster," who compensates for physical weakness or powerlessness with superior wits, is found in the mythology of many cultures. **Brer Rabbit** is one of the best-known tricksters in American or any other folklore—a mischievous, devious, sharp-witted character who consistently outsmarts his various enemies. Harris claimed that the prototype of this character was probably brought to the United States from Africa by slaves; indeed, several scholars have confirmed that African folklore celebrates the rabbit as the cleverest and most powerful of animals. Because he is a weaker creature who turns the tables on and gains respect from the more physically formidable animals he encounters—such as Brer Fox, Brer Wolf, and Brer Bear—Brer Rabbit has been broadly interpreted as an allegorical embodiment of the human struggle for survival in a sometimes brutal world. That his escapades are related by an African-American ex-slave and take place in a rural southern setting, however, have led some critics to identify Brer Rabbit as a representative of the black population who consistently outmaneuvers those animals who represent white people. While some critics see Harris's portrayal of Brer Rabbit's creativity and endurance as proof of his respect for black people, others contend that the absence of any open conflict between the adversarial animals and the conciliatory tone of the stories manifest instead his conservatism on racial matters. Brer Rabbit's pranks occasionally lead to violence; for instance, Brer Possum is killed after Brer Rabbit steals some butter that several of the animals had agreed to share and frames the possum for the theft. The presence of brutality in the stories may be an allegorical reflection of life in the pre-Civil War South, or it may serve as a subtle reminder that aggression of the kind perpetrated by Brer Rabbit has its perils. "The Wonderful Tar-Baby" provides an excellent example of Brer Rabbit's cleverness, as he uses reverse psychology to convince Brer Fox to release him into the brier-patch, a seemingly hostile environment but one in which he feels entirely comfortable.

Other recurring animals characters in the Uncle Remus tales include **Brer Wolf, Brer Bear, Brer Possum,** and **Brer Tarrypin** (who assumes in four of the stories the trickster role usually played by Brer Rabbit). Also frequently referred to—though never actually seen— are **Miss Meadows and the gals,** a group of vaguely disreputable female characters (possibly modeled after the residents of a brothel) with whom the male animals flirt and for whom they demonstrate their prowess. In "The Wonderful Tar-Baby" and many other tales, **Brer Fox** is Brer Rabbit's adversary. Although he laughs derisively when Brer Rabbit makes his self-defeating attack on the tar baby, the fox is eventually outmaneuvered by his craftier enemy and loses once again his chance to eat Brer Rabbit for dinner. Some critics identify Brer Fox, in his infinite gullibility and exaggerated stupidity, as an allegorical representative of white people who is consistently beaten by the less powerful but cleverer embodiment of black ingenuity, Brer Rabbit.

The six- or seven-year-old, unnamed **white boy** to whom Uncle Remus tells his tales is the high-spirited, curious, alert son of the owners of the plantation on which Uncle Remus lives. He sincerely loves and respects Uncle Remus, visiting him often in his cabin behind the big house to listen to stories about Brer Rabbit and the other "creeturs." Not perfectly behaved, the boy is often chided or even subtly punished (usually through the withholding of stories) by Uncle Remus for such misdeeds as tattling on others, destroying property, teasing animals, or generally annoying his elders. Uncle Remus also cautions him to stay clear of his neighbors, the ''white-trash'' Favers children, to whom he is considered superior. Some critics have characterized the naive boy as a representative of the outside world being initiated into southern culture or, more specifically, African-American folklore. On a broader level he is beginning to learn the difference between right and wrong, and Uncle Remus serves as an affectionate but realistic teacher who does not try to shield him from the brutality and injustice that exist in the real world. The boy's parents are **Mars (Master) John,** a former northerner who served with the Union Army during the Civil War, and **Miss Sally,** a southern woman who captivated and married the Yankee soldier. The story of the couple's romance is related in a later volume of Uncle Remus stories.

Further Reading

Bickley, R. Bruce, Jr., ed. *Critical Essays on Joel Chandler Harris.* Boston: G.K. Hall, 1981.

Dauner, Louise. ''Myth and Humor in the Uncle Remus Fables.'' *American Literature* (May 1948): 129-43.

Dictionary of Literary Biography, Vols. 11, 23, 42, 78, 91. Detroit: Gale.

Rubin, Louis D. ''Uncle Remus and the Ubiquitous Rabbit.'' *Southern Review* NS X (October 1974): 787-804.

Turner, Darwin T. ''Daddy Joel Harris and His Old-Time Darkies.'' *Southern Literary Journal* (Autumn 1968): 20-41.

Twentieth-Century Literary Criticism, Vol. 2. Detroit: Gale.

Wolfe, Bernard. ''Uncle Remus and the Malevolent Rabbit.'' *Commentary* (July 1949): 31-41.

Nathaniel Hawthorne

1804-1864

American novelist, short story writer, and essayist.

''The Minister's Black Veil'' (short story, 1835)

Plot: Seventeenth-century parishioners of a church in the New England town of Milford are shocked when their minister, the Reverend Mr. Hooper, appears at a Sunday morning service wearing a black veil over his face, and speculate on the possible reasons for his strange action. That afternoon, Hooper conducts a funeral service, and one observer claims that the corpse—that of a young woman—shuddered when the minister leaned over the coffin, while others claim they saw Hooper and the spirit of the dead woman walking hand in hand. That evening, the black-veiled minister lends a gloomy presence to the wedding of a fine young Milford couple; when Hooper catches sight of himself in a mirror, he spills his wine and hastily leaves the gathering. The next day, a group of church members visits Hooper to inquire as to the meaning of the black veil, but they learn nothing. Finally Hooper's fiancee Elizabeth confronts him directly. While implying that the veil may represent a secret sin, as some of the townsfolk have surmised, Hooper claims that it is significant primarily as "a type and a symbol." He says that he must always wear the veil, and that even when he is alone with Elizabeth he cannot remove it. The minister asks her to be patient, but she leaves angrily. They never marry. Throughout the rest of his life, Hooper's veil invokes dread, fear, and gloom among his congregation, although its impact as a visual emblem of sin makes him an effective preacher. On his deathbed, with the still faithful and unmarried Elizabeth at his side, Hooper resists the attending clergyman's attempt to remove the veil. Before he dies, the minister claims he can see a black veil on every face around him. Hooper is buried with the veil still covering his face.

Characters: The protagonist of "The Minister's Black Veil" bears some resemblance, as Hawthorne wrote in a footnote to the story, to the actual person of Reverend Mr. Moody of York, Maine, who donned a dark veil after accidentally causing the death of a friend. It is never confirmed whether **Reverend Hooper** has committed a similar—or perhaps more sinful—deed, and that ambiguity lends much to the story's dramatic tension. Like other important Hawthorne characters, Hooper is obsessed with sin and guilt, and he chooses to make manifest his awareness of the human potential for evil. Though he gains in power as a minister, his decision to acknowledge sin and constantly remind those around him of its existence (perhaps hidden in their own hearts) extracts a high cost: he is isolated from the rest of humanity. Scholars have been divided in their interpretation of Hooper's behavior, for the story's intentionally ambivalent tone leaves room for endless speculation. Some characterize him as a selfless servant of God and his fellow man who sacrifices his own happiness to enrich the lives of others. But other critics, including Edgar Allan Poe, have claimed that Hooper's veil does indeed mask some dark sin—probably connected with the dead young woman—and that therefore he deserves his dismal fate. It has also been suggested that the veil signifies Hooper's excessive pride or that he dons it in order to avoid such earthy realities of life as marriage and sex. Hooper is a skillfully drawn manifestation of Hawthorne's interest in the psychological toll that an awareness of evil may take on the human psyche.

Hooper's fiancee **Elizabeth** serves a primarily practical role in the story, for it is to her that Hooper explains—at least as far as he is willing—why he has chosen to wear the black veil. Unlike the other townspeople, she is not frightened by the veil, and she believes that she will be able to help Hooper with whatever struggle or pain he is experiencing. Calmly and directly urging him to remove the veil, Elizabeth suggests that to continue wearing it will encourage the rumors of scandal already circulating about him; but, nothing she says will change Hooper's mind. Finally, Elizabeth does seem to sense the horror of the minister's veil and flees. In the end, however, it is revealed that Elizabeth has remained loyal to Hooper after all, for she has not married and does attend him at his deathbed.

"The Birth Mark" (short story, 1843)

Plot: The story concerns a brilliant scientist, Aylmer, who marries a beautiful woman, Georgiana. Her only flaw is a tiny, hand-shaped birthmark on her cheek that darkens and fades with the flush of blood through her face; Aylmer is repulsed by it. One night he dreams that he attempts to surgically remove the birthmark, but it keeps receding farther into Georgiana until finally it invades her heart. Georgiana has also developed a hatred of the birthmark because she knows how much Aylmer despises it, and she begs him to try to remove it—even if her life is endangered in the process. Aylmer agrees. He secludes his wife in a comfortable, beautifully decorated room while he works with his coarse assistant Aminadab in an adjoining, foul laboratory. While they endeavor to create a potion to destroy Georgiana's imperfection, she occupies herself by reading Aylmer's journal. She learns about the ambitious experiments he has conducted; many were failures, but nevertheless Georgiana's admiration of her husband's aspirations and intellect increases. Finally, Aylmer presents Georgiana with the concoction he has produced. She suspects that it will kill her, but gladly drinks it. The birthmark does indeed fade from Georgiana's cheek, but when it is completely gone, she dies.

Characters: "The Birth Mark" has been characterized as an expression of the nineteenth-century mistrust of science and as a precursor to modern science fiction in its probing of the possibly fatal results of scientific endeavor. The characters in "The Birth Mark" clearly symbolize the opposing forces that are central to the story's theme.

Aylmer is a man of science whose approach to his work contains elements of the abstract and spiritual as well; this combination makes him more akin to the medieval alchemists, who attempted to create gold out of common metals, than to the pragmatic scientists of the twentieth century. He has been described as a Faustian character, one who is dissatisfied with the status quo and who seeks to apply his own intellect toward its improvement. Unable to accept his wife's one imperfection—which to him embodies her "liability to sin, sorrow, decay, and death"—Aylmer endeavors to change her, and instead loses her forever. Describing Aylmer as embodying "the despair that assails the higher [spiritual] nature at finding itself so miserably thwarted by the earthly part," Hawthorne neither overtly condones nor condemns his character's actions. This ambivalence is also reflected in the critics' responses to Aylmer: he has been considered noble and idealistic by some, fiendish and manipulative by others. Yet, in a balanced evaluation of the character's significance, Howard Bruce Franklin asserted that Aylmer is "to be pitied for his folly, abhorred for his heartlessness, and admired for his aspirations."

The near-physically perfect and eager-to-please **Georgiana** is not a particularly well-rounded character, although she does undergo some intellectual growth as she reads her husband's journal and recognizes both the greatness of his mind and the consistent overreaching of his ambitions. That she is so willing to submit to Aylmer's concept of how she should be, even if it means death, has made her seem to some critics an exaggerated portrait of traditional femininity. Georgiana describes herself as neither blind nor coura-geous enough to ignore the birthmark that so repulses her husband, nor is she strong enough to endure the situation hopefully. Instead, she says that she is "of all mortals most fit to die" if that is what it takes to escape her flaw. The birthmark itself has attracted critical attention for its symbolic possibilities. Overtly, it represents mortality, for when it fades Georgiana's life is over. It also gives Georgiana her humanity, providing a balance between heaven and earth which, when upset, brings tragedy. And some scholars further assert that it represents Georgiana's sexuality, the physical manifestation of which repulses Aylmer. Others focus on the birthmark's shape as symbolic of Aylmer's hand directing her to her death.

While Aylmer represents the spiritual aspirations of human nature, his assistant **Aminadab** stands at the other extreme as an embodiment of the purely earthy. His hulking presence, physical strength, unkempt hair, and grimy face make him appear to have been born of dirt. Significantly, he mutters that if Georgiana were his wife, he would not part with her birthmark—indicating his preference for life in its natural, unperfected form. When Georgiana dies, Aminadab's harsh laughter rings with earthly triumph over intellectual illusion. Hawthorne's portrayal of Aminadab as an unsympathetic, repellent figure suggests that the human ideal should lie somewhere between this creature's coarseness and Aylmer's lofty idealism.

"Young Goodman Brown" (short story, 1846)

Plot: The story is set in late-seventeenth-century Salem, Massachusetts. As it opens, the title character is at the door of his house saying goodbye to his pretty wife, Faith. It is early evening, and Young Goodman Brown is about to set off on some mysterious errand. When Faith is unable to dissuade him from going, she sends him away with her blessing. Brown walks into the forest, where he meets—apparently by appointment—an older man who carries a twisted staff. The man, who is gradually revealed to be the devil, reminisces about some of Brown's forebears and their wicked deeds. Brown expresses reluctance to walk any farther and hides when he spots Goody Cloyse, his childhood catechism teacher, coming toward him. She greets Brown's companion and mentions that a ''nice young man'' is to be inducted into their company tonight. Then Brown sees the minister and deacon of his church also making their way toward the evil gathering that will take place deep in the forest. When Brown detects Faith's pink ribbon floating down from a sinister cloud that passes above, Brown knows that she, too, will attend the witches' sabbath. Despairing and convinced of humanity's depravity, Brown rushes toward the meeting place: there is an altar of rock framed by several flaming fir trees, around which all of the town's most pious, upstanding citizens are gathered. At the altar is another initiate, who is revealed to be Faith. The two stand together in a moment of hesitation—on the brink of an evil communion—when Brown calls out to Faith to resist. Suddenly, Brown finds that the whole scene has disappeared and he is alone in the forest. He returns to the village, where all seems normal. For the rest of his life, however, Brown suspects evil at the heart of every person he meets, and spurns even his loving wife. His existence is blighted by his lack of trust in others, his cynicism, and his hopelessness.

Characters: ''Young Goodman Brown'' is generally considered not only Hawthorne's finest short story but one of the best in American fiction. Much of the tale's extensive body of criticism is centered on its title character, **Young Goodman Brown,** whose name suggests he represents Everyman—and is therefore subject to the same yearnings and fears of the average person. It may be that Brown makes his journey to the dark, foreboding forest because he is curious about and even tempted to experience the darker side of life that waits outside the bounds of his Puritan community; his brush with evil, however, has a permanently injurious effect on him. Critics agree that whether the witches' sabbath really does occur or has been dreamed (and arguments have been made for both sides), the impression the experience makes on Brown is very real indeed.

At the beginning of the story Brown appears confident in his ability to choose between good and evil, but once he has stood before the devil's altar with the other damned communicants, he can no longer believe that good always prevails. He becomes a profoundly disillusioned man who sees wickedness everywhere, even in those closest to him. Some critics have interpreted Brown's final distrustful, alienated state as the result of a guilty conscience; he cannot forgive himself or others for hidden sinfulness. Brown is unwilling, as several scholars have noted, to accept the duality of human nature—that a person may be simultaneously innocent and evil. Others have taken a historical approach to ''Young Goodman Brown,'' calling it an illuminating allegory of Calvinist belief in the devil's power and humanity's basic depravity; Brown, then, is seen as a victim of Puritanism, not unlike those who were persecuted as witches in seventeenth-century Salem. He has also been interpreted as symbolizing the American nation as it began to penetrate the dark, unknown wilds of the western frontier. Many modern critics have focused on the story's psychological implications, suggesting, for instance, that Brown's unbalanced condition is caused by his confusion about and dread of the sexuality represented by his wife and by the secret knowledge to be revealed at the witches' sabbath.

Faith Brown serves an overtly allegorical purpose in the story. It is from Faith that Brown departs, presumably only for this one night, in order to keep his appointment with the devil. Explaining to the old man why he is late for their meeting, Brown says, ''Faith kept me back a while.'' She represents the force of good in the world, so that when Brown perceives that she too has been corrupted he cries ''My Faith is gone!'' and rushes in despair toward the witches' gathering. The pink ribbons that adorn Faith's cap have attracted more critical attention than any other symbol in the story. They have been said to signify female sexuality and passion on the one hand, innocence on the other; or they may merely represent the ornament of a sweet, cheerful wife. Whatever their meaning, Faith's pink ribbons are integral to the story's structure. They are mentioned three times: at the beginning, when Brown is leaving Faith behind; near the climax, when Brown sees a pink ribbon floating down from above; and at the end, when a stern, sad Brown is greeted on his return by the beribboned Faith. It is also significant that Faith, married only three months at the time of her husband's crisis, remains devoted to him to the end of his bleak life.

The figure of **the devil** is portrayed in "Young Goodman Brown" as an older—though not ancient—man who carries a twisted, snake-like stick. He seems to vaguely resemble Brown, and it has been suggested that he is a reflection of the darker side of Brown's nature. The devil claims intimacy with Brown's grandfather, who participated in the persecution of the Quakers, and his father, who took part in an attack on an Indian village. (Hawthorne, a native of Salem, had ancestors who committed similar deeds.) **Goody Cloyse, the minister,** and **Deacon Gookin** serve as dramatic examples of the wickedness that may hide in the souls of those who appear most virtuous. The three are distinguished from among the crowd of townsfolk at the gathering because they represent a standard of piety and godliness that is destroyed, for Brown, by his experience.

The Scarlet Letter (novel, 1850)

Plot: Set in mid-seventeenth-century Boston, the novel centers on Hester Prynne, an apparently widowed young woman who brings the wrath of her rigidly Puritan community upon herself when she becomes pregnant and refuses to name the baby's father. Hester is sentenced to stand before the townsfolk on the pillory scaffold for three hours and, for the rest of her life, wear on the bosom of her dress a red cloth "A"—for "adulteress"—that will mark her as a sinner. The young, eloquent Reverend Arthur Dimmesdale is among those who plead in vain with Hester to reveal the guilty man's identity. Hester is visited in jail by a stranger in town, a white-haired physician named Roger Chillingworth. He is Hester's husband; two years before he had sent her ahead of him from England, and he had subsequently been presumed dead. Now he asks Hester not to reveal his identity, and he vows to find the father of her child. Shunned and ridiculed by the townsfolk, Hester lives in a lonely cottage and supports herself through her considerable talent for needlework. Her sole and constant companion is her daughter Pearl, a beautiful but strange child. Meanwhile, Reverend Dimmesdale, who is Pearl's father, is tormented by his hidden guilt and, unable to either confess or forget his crime, his health begins to fail. Chillingworth moves into Dimmesdale's house, ostensibly to provide medical assistance; he soon begins to pry away at the minister's secret. Dimmesdale grows to hate and fear the physician. Meeting Hester by chance at the pillory scaffold one night, Dimmesdale tells her that he is afraid of Chillingworth. He also mounts the scaffold and makes a mock confession of his sin. Chillingworth overhears this exchange. Later Hester reveals Chillingworth's real identity to Dimmesdale, and she and Dimmesdale plan to leave Boston together and make a new life in England. But Chillingworth books passage on the same ship, and Hester realizes they can never escape from him. After delivering a brilliant Election Day sermon, Dimmesdale again ascends the scaffold and declares his guilt—this time before the assembled townspeople. Afterward he collapses and dies. Many of those present later claim they saw a scarlet "A" outlined in the minister's flesh as he tore his shirt apart. It is not long before Chillingworth also dies, leaving money to Pearl that allows her mother to take her to England. Eventually Hester returns to the community (presumably after Pearl has married); she continues to wear the scarlet letter, labors as a seamstress, and performs charity work until her death.

Characters: The characters of *The Scarlet Letter,* though in some ways clearly allegorical, give the novel its psychological realism as well as illuminate its major themes: the consequences of pride, sin, guilt, and retribution and the alienation of the individual from society. **Hester Prynne,** usually identified as the most important character in *The Scarlet*

Letter, was thought to be too prideful and unrepentant by some early critics, who also complained in general about the novel's immoral subject matter. Other nineteenth-century reviewers, however, and many more since, admire her for her strength and perseverance as she not only survives but triumphs over an authoritarian society. And some see in Hester Hawthorne's own ambivalence toward the immorality of her sin—adultery—and the courage she demonstrates in living by her own moral code; though the adulteress is clearly sinful according to traditional mores, by the standards of romanticism—which dominated literary thought at the time of *The Scarlet Letter*'s writing—she has done nothing wrong in following the promptings of her own heart and the laws of nature: it is society which is evil and which persecutes the individual. In any case, Hawthorne seems more concerned with the consequences of Hester's act of passion than with whether it was right or wrong.

Some critics have declared that the **Reverend Arthur Dimmesdale** is the central character of *The Scarlet Letter* because he embodies the conflict between his community's unbending Puritanism—which, by training and profession, he represents—and the claims of human passion. Through him is demonstrated the psychological toll of unconfessed guilt. Nineteenth-century reviewers often disapproved of Dimmesdale not only for the crime he committed but because, like Hester, he seems insufficiently repentant and because he seems to lack the moral courage to confess as well. Later critics have focused on Hawthorne's skillful portrayal of Dimmesdale's internal struggle between the need to unburden himself and his fear of exposure; the physical consequence of that conflict anticipates the modern awareness of the relationship between the body and the emotions. The conflict is made even more tragically ironic when Dimmesdale's sermons, which are infused with a first-hand knowledge of human corruption, bring comfort and inspiration to others but not to himself. Like other important characters in Hawthorne's fiction, Dimmesdale is irreparably damaged and alienated by his perception of the evil that may reside beneath apparent goodness—that resides, indeed, within his own soul.

The significance of Hester's elfin daughter **Pearl** has been a subject of debate since the book's publication. An object of conflicted feeling for her mother, who both loves and fears her bright, capricious child, Pearl is also something of a mystery to the critics. She has been seen as purely symbolic: the living manifestation, like Hester's scarlet "A," of her parents' sin. It is partly through Pearl that Hester demonstrates her strength and independence, for, through her fight for the right to raise the child herself, she demonstrates her perception of Pearl as a blessing rather than a curse. To some readers, Pearl's wild, uncontrollable nature makes her seem more like a fairy or even a witch than a human child. Yet others have described her as representing the primitive beauty and mystery of nature; Anne W. Abbott wrote in 1850 that Pearl was a creation of "perfect and vivid human individuality" and a child "such as many a mother has looked upon with awe, and a feeling of helpless incapacity to rule."

Roger Chillingworth, Hester's wronged husband and Dimmesdale's tormentor, exemplifies the spiritual desolation that results when pride wins out over such emotions as pity, forgiveness, and brotherhood. By harboring in his heart a longing for revenge, Chillingworth is transformed from a basically good person to an evil one. Yet Hawthorne honors the demands of psychological realism by providing a context for Chillingworth's hate: he had married the young Hester out of a very human need for companionship. In the end, however, Chillingworth gains nothing by his victimization of Dimmesdale. In fact, when the object of his torment is gone he "positively withered up, shrivelled away, and almost vanished from mortal sight, like an uprooted weed that lies wilting in the sun."

The House of the Seven Gables (novel, 1851)

Plot: The House of the Seven Gables was built in the seventeenth century by Colonel Pyncheon, a stern Massachusetts Puritan and magistrate who had acquired the property on which it sits by condemning to death the innocent owner of the land he coveted. The victim of his treachery, Matthew Maule, cursed Pyncheon from the scaffold, and Pyncheon died unexpectedly soon after building the house. The main action of the story takes place in the mid-nineteenth century. A wealthy descendent of Colonel Pyncheon has been murdered; Pyncheon's scheming nephew Jaffey, a rich, successful judge who is heir to his uncle's fortune, has caused another nephew, Clifford, to be wrongly imprisoned for the crime. Thirty years later, Clifford's unmarried sister, Hepzibah, who has continued to live in the House of the Seven Gables, sets up a shop in the house to support herself and her brother, who will soon be released from prison. Another family relation, seventeen-year-old Phoebe, comes to live in the house and helps to make the shop profitable. Phoebe falls in love with Mr. Holgrave, a daguerrotypist (photographer) who rents a room in the house, and the two become engaged. Judge Pyncheon is convinced that his returned cousin Clifford, though much altered by his harsh prison term, knows the secret location of a missing deed to a large tract of land owned by the Pyncheons. He threatens to send Clifford to an insane asylum if he withholds the secret. The judge, however, dies suddenly of an apparent stroke. When the judge's only son also dies, the surviving Pyncheons inherit his wealth. Just before they move out of the house, Clifford remembers his childhood discovery of a secret spring that makes a portrait of Colonel Pyncheon move to reveal a hidden recess. There is found the lost deed, which is no longer valid. Holgrave now reveals that his name is actually Maule and that he is a descendent of the wronged Matthew Maule. He and the three happy Pyncheons leave the house, which has finally shed its curse.

Characters: Like *The Scarlet Letter, The House of the Seven Gables* explores the consequences of sin. This novel, however, ends happily with its characters successful in finally shedding the burden of ancestral guilt passed down through many generations of Pyncheons. Critics have noted that the characters are frankly allegorical, representing different aspects of human nature, and that several of them help to bring a comic tone to the story.

Colonel Pyncheon, the originator of the family's evil legacy, is described as a proud, ambitious man who, despite his prominent position in a Puritan society, has a pronounced appetite for such sensual pleasures as rich food and ornate furnishings. Some of his descendants resemble him in this respect: his grandson **Gervayse** betrays his own daughter because of his longing for a more opulent, European-style life, and **Judge Jaffey Pyncheon,** unpleasantly sensual and overweight, bears a striking physical resemblance to his ancestor. And like his ancestor, Jaffey Pyncheon is destined never to live in the House of the Seven Gables—only to die there. In a final, almost ministerial, tongue-lashing, as the judge sits dead in a chair, Hawthorne describes him as a "subtle, worldly, selfish, ironhearted hypocrite."

Clifford Pyncheon is a once-handsome, cheerful man whose essentially dreamy nature has been rendered more childlike by his long prison term. In his deteriorated mental and physical state, he represents the ultimate decay of the Pyncheon family. One critic has noted that Clifford's hunger for beauty, as well as his delight in food, makes him a comic parody of his similarly inclined ancestors. The "rigid and rusty," perpetually scowling **Hepzibah Pyncheon** also cuts a ludicrous figure as she is forced to give up her notion of herself as a fine lady and enter the realm of commerce by opening a store in her home. Hepzibah, like Clifford, is a victim of the past whose pathetic appearance and nature make her more poignant than comic.

Young **Phoebe Pyncheon,** whose presence immediately brightens the dreary household, is consistently portrayed with images of sunshine, flowers, and angels. A cheerful, practical, somewhat shallow girl, she is the only member of the Pyncheon family who is free from its longstanding curse. She has often been described as inherently conservative and the novel's representative of natural, homely values. Under Phoebe's influence, the rather detached Holgrave softens his outlook on traditional values, while Phoebe's perceptions deepen somewhat by the novel's end.

Mr. Holgrave, the house's resident daguerrotypist and self-proclaimed scorner of the past, provides a contrast to the Pyncheons, who are weighted down by their tragic heritage. He is a widely traveled, experienced, modern-thinking young man, but his professed disdain for things dead and gone is belied by his presence in the House of the Seven Gables. For in reality he is the modern forebear of the wronged **Matthew Maule,** and his interest in the intertwined history of his family and the Pyncheons is acute. Hawthorne seems to gently ridicule Holgrave's reformist attitude—at least in so far as Holgrave expects that his own generation will solve all of the world's problems—but approves of the young man's focusing positively on the future rather than dwelling on the past.

The minor character **Uncle Venner,** the elderly handyman who has remained a friend to the Pyncheons despite their ignominious history, provides a comic note with his philosophizing and advice. In the end he's rewarded for his friendship when he is invited to join the other characters at their new country home.

The Blithedale Romance (novel, 1852)

Plot: The story begins one snowy April, when New England poet Miles Coverdale travels to begin a new life at Blithedale, an experimental community of about one hundred people based on a theory of cooperative living. On his arrival he is greeted by the renowned journalist Zenobia, a beautiful, rich, and sophisticated woman who is an ardent proponent of women's rights. That same night another new resident arrives, the zealous reformer Hollingsworth, who brings with him a shabbily dressed, confused-looking young girl named Priscilla, who immediately falls worshipfully at Zenobia's feet. Hollingsworth explains that before leaving town he had been asked by seedy Old Moodie to take Priscilla to Blithedale (Moodie had also approached Coverdale but had been put off by his unaccommodating manner). Coverdale learns that Hollingsworth is a fanatical reformer who seeks to rehabilitate as many criminals as he possibly can; his dream is to build an institution dedicated to their re-education. Coverdale finds Hollingsworth's single-mindedness tiresome, but he notes that Zenobia and Priscilla both seem to be in love with him. Soon Zenobia views the blooming Priscilla as a rival and grows antagonistic toward her despite the obvious fact that the girl idolizes her.

An ominous figure named Professor Westervelt, a professional mesmerist (hypnotist), arrives at the community and Coverdale perceives that he and Zenobia have had a previous relationship, and that now Zenobia seems to hate and fear him. After Westervelt leaves, Zenobia is more ill-tempered and stridently feminist than before, but she continues to adore Hollingsworth. When he expresses the view that women should play a subservient role to men, Zenobia begins checking her speech. It is now clear to Coverdale that Hollingsworth hopes to obtain money from the wealthy Zenobia to build his reform school. When Coverdale refuses to participate in the scheme, Hollingsworth grows hostile toward him. Coverdale leaves Blithedale for a vacation in town and is surprised to encounter Zenobia, Priscilla, and Westervelt together there. His subsequent visit to the two women is extremely tense, and Zenobia warns him not to interfere in their affairs. Coverdale notices that Priscilla seems to be completely under Zenobia's power, and that when Westervelt calls them, both women instantly respond. Finally, Coverdale learns the history of Zenobia and Priscilla from Old Moodie, who explains that he is the father of both. Formerly wealthy but ruined through his own dishonesty, Moodie had abandoned his wife and Zenobia. Eventually he had remarried, and that union produced Priscilla. Though plain and shy compared to her sparkling sister, Priscilla was loved by all for her kind nature. Zenobia had been raised by a wealthy uncle who had left her his fortune; it was rumored that as a headstrong girl she had married a wicked man.

While strolling contemplatively through the city, Coverdale happens upon a performance being given by Westervelt; the mesmerist brings a Veiled Lady onto the stage and claims she will do whatever he asks. Finally, Hollingsworth strides forth and calls out to the woman to remove her veil, which she does. It is Priscilla, and she runs with obvious relief into Hollingsworth's arms. Returning to Blithedale, Coverdale witnesses an alarming encounter between Zenobia, Priscilla, and Hollingsworth during which the reformer tells Zenobia that he loves her half-sister. An aggrieved Zenobia warns Priscilla that Hollingsworth is a heartless cad who has trifled with her affections while coveting her wealth. That night, Zenobia drowns herself in the nearby river. Coverdale leaves Blithedale permanently. Priscilla and Hollingsworth live a quiet life together; Hollingsworth, feeling responsible for Zenobia's death, gives up his philanthropy. Remembering these events of years ago, Coverdale reveals that he had been in love with Priscilla all along.

Characters: The novel's setting was inspired by the author's brief sojourn at the famous nineteenth-century utopian community of Brook Farm in Roxbury, Massachusetts. Hawthorne warned his readers, however, not to assume too close a connection between fact and fiction, and critics are divided on whether *The Blithedale Romance* is an indictment of utopianism or simply an exploration of human psychology played out in an unusual and isolated milieu.

Miles Coverdale, the story's narrator, is a minor New England poet who approaches the Blithedale experiment with skeptical interest. As the only first-person narrator in Hawthorne's novels, Coverdale has generated speculation on whether the views expressed in the novel coincide with Hawthorne's. Coverdale, like his creator, is an artist who is intrigued by the idea of cooperative, communal living but who finally concludes that the blending of artistic pursuits and manual labor are unrealistic. As he is accustomed to an urban existence and partial to such comforts as cigars and wine, it is not particularly surprising that he would not find the rigorous rural life at Blithedale to his liking. But Coverdale's role as an observer of what happens between Zenobia, Hollingsworth, and Priscilla may be more compelling in the end than his reaction to Blithedale and its broad social implications. Coverdale declines any direct participation in the happenings at Blithedale, despite his obvious attraction to both Zenobia and Priscilla. Many critics have described this analytical detachment as egocentric, a view evidenced by his reluctance to help Moodie, his belittling of Priscilla at every opportunity, his spying on Zenobia, and, finally, his self-pity as he looks back on these events with such a melancholy air. Coverdale's surprising confession that he loved Priscilla—delivered in the novel's last sentence—tends to confirm the idea that his hesitancy to involve himself with others has resulted in a lonely, wasted life.

Hawthorne describes the wealthy, beautiful **Zenobia** as "passionate, luxurious, lacking simplicity, not deeply defined." Many critics have praised Hawthorne for his complex depiction of this interesting character; Henry James commented that she is "the nearest approach Hawthorne has made to the creation of a *person.*" Hawthorne's most distinctly sensual character, Zenobia has been said to embody not only earthly sexuality but creative energy, and in her strong-mindedness, pride, and competitiveness with men she repudiates the kind of traditional femininity that the delicate, passive Priscilla represents. The extravagant flower that Zenobia always wears in her hair has been said to represent sensual evil, or it may be a simple sign of her passionate nature or her general rebellion against tradition. Zenobia has reminded many scholars of Hester Prynne in *The Scarlet Letter,* for like Hester she has intelligence, talent, and an aura of past sin—connected, in Zenobia's case, with her mysterious and ambiguous link to Westervelt. Apparently Zenobia was once under Westervelt's control, and it is implied that she has offered her innocent half-sister to the sinister mesmerist in order to remove Priscilla as a rival for Hollingsworth's affection. By falling in love with Hollingsworth, who clearly values Priscilla's conventional womanliness over Zenobia's exotic brilliance, Zenobia contradicts her own nature and inclinations and the only possible result of this alliance is disaster.

Hollingsworth is a former blacksmith who has become an ardent reformer of criminals. Though his commitment to bettering the lives of others suggests a caring nature, Hollingsworth is actually severe, rigid, selfish, dogmatic, proud, and egotistical. He has been compared to the Puritan magistrates found in the seventeenth-century New England communities Hawthorne often depicted: like them, he is possessed by an energy for reform that is revealed as morally blind and without compassion. Because he needs money to build his institution he heartlessly manipulates Zenobia, whose love for him has made her uncharacteristically vulnerable; his desire for control is evident in his rejecting the independent Zenobia for the pliant Priscilla. Several critics have faulted Hawthorne for giving Hollingsworth no sympathetic qualities at all (other than his feeling of responsibility for Zenobia's death) and thus rendering him an unconvincing character.

Frail, delicate **Priscilla** provides a direct contrast to her more substantial half-sister. Priscilla is an ethereal creature who embodies the nineteenth-century ideal of traditional womanhood in her purity and passivity. Her lack of strength and self-determination is exemplified by her susceptibility to Westervelt's manipulation; she herself says, "I am blown about like a leaf . . . I never have any free will." Indeed, Priscilla is rescued from Westervelt's exploitive clutches only to become equally subservient to Hollingsworth, to whom—according to his stated views about the role of women—she can be a supporter but not an equal. Priscilla is most significant in the reactions she arouses in others: Hollingsworth views her with appreciation and protectiveness, Zenobia with jealousy and contempt, Westervelt with coldhearted materialism, and Coverdale—as he finally reveals—with admiration.

Westervelt is the cynical mesmerist who apparently once exploited Zenobia and now seeks to manipulate Priscilla. He is a somewhat melodramatically portrayed character whose gold teeth suggest his falseness and whose general oiliness makes Coverdale's flesh creep. Westervelt introduces to the novel the concept that personality may be controlled hypnotically, a possibility that was of great popular interest in the nineteenth century. Hawthorne's use of mesmerism in *The Blithedale Romance*—with its implications of corruption and decadence—may be compared to his use of witchcraft in earlier novels.

Two additional significant characters in the novel are **Old Moodie** and **Silas Foster**. Old Moodie, the mysterious figure who turns out to be the father of both Zenobia and Priscilla, was a well-to-do man who was ruined by his own graft. Moodie plays a practical role in the plot by providing a link between the two women and by relaying their story to Coverdale. Silas Foster, a member of the Blithedale community, is one of its few residents who is knowledgeable and experienced in rural practices. He is a stereotypical New Englander in his straightforwardness, providing a strong contrast to such veiled figures as Zenobia, Priscilla, and Westervelt. Some critics have seen Foster's role as similar to that of the chorus in classical Greek drama—he is a detached observer of the action who occasionally comments on it but has no emotional stake in the outcome.

The Marble Faun: The Romance of Monte Beni (novel, 1860)

Plot: The novel centers on four artistic friends who live in nineteenth-century Rome. Miriam is an interesting, half-Italian woman whose past is unexplained; Donatello is a carefree young Italian who is in love with her. Hilda is a New England native who produces copies of great works of art, and Kenyon is an American sculptor. The friends notice a strong resemblance between the agile, sunny Donatello and a sculpture of a faun (a mythical creature who is half man, half animal) by Praxiteles, a work dating from the fourth century B.C. While visiting Rome's famous catacombs, Miriam encounters a mysterious Capuchin monk, Brother Antonio, and subsequently uses him as a model for her paintings. However, he begins to follow her everywhere and to torment her with references to her past life. Miriam grows more and more troubled by the man. One night, the four friends go on an excursion to the Tarpeian Rock, from which the ancient Romans pushed criminals to their deaths. Brother Antonio appears, and Donatello follows him and Miriam when they part from the others. A scuffle erupts between Miriam's persecutor and Donatello and—because Miriam's eyes clearly tell him that he should—the young man heaves Brother Antonio over the cliff. Miriam and Donatello are now united not only in love but in their crime. Hilda, however, also witnessed the murder, and is deeply troubled by it; eventually she severs her friendship with Miriam. After the murder, Donatello loses his gayness and is oppressed by guilt. He leaves Rome for his birthplace, Monte Beni, and Kenyon goes to visit him there while Hilda stays in Rome. While staying with Donatello, Kenyon learns of a local legend identifying his friend's family as descendants of the legendary race of fauns. Miriam also travels to Monte Beni and—although Donatello initially refuses to see her—the two are reconciled. Back in Rome, Hilda is detained by the police until they are convinced she was not involved in Brother Antonio's murder. Kenyon, who has been worried about Hilda's disappearance, meets her at the city's festive carnival soon after her release. Just as they are reunited, Donatello is arrested for the murder of Brother Antonio. He is sentenced to a jail term, but Miriam is not charged because it was only her eyes that encouraged Donatello to act. But Miriam's past is finally revealed: her family—though apparently not Miriam herself—had been connected with some dark crime which she had sought to escape by coming to Rome; Brother Antonio had threatened to publicize her real identity. Kenyon and Hilda are married and return to America.

Characters: *The Marble Faun* is unique among Hawthorne's works for its European setting, which is intended to lend the novel both a richly historical underpinning and a distance from American influences. Hawthorne himself had paid an extended visit to Rome, and the novel evidences his ambiguous response to the city, which both attracted and repelled him. *The Marble Faun*'s thematic focuses include the effects of sin and guilt on the human psyche, the development of the human consciousness, the tension between Puritanism and the Roman Catholic faith, the artist's responsibilities and role, and the conflict between Old World values and modern American life and thought. A central thematic focus of the novel is the concept of *felix culpa,* or the "Fortunate Fall"—the idea that sin may actually benefit human beings by deepening their very humanity. Each of *The Marble Faun*'s four main characters is representative of a specific mode of being, and it is through their conversations, actions, and responses to each other that Hawthorne presents the novel's themes.

Hilda is a young New England woman who, instead of creating her own paintings, makes skillful copies of those of the old masters. She is consistently surrounded with images of whiteness and doves, signifying her role as a scion of purity and innocence. She even lives in a room set in a tower overlooking the city, another indicator that she exists on a moral plain high above that of other human beings. Like many of Hawthorne's characters, Hilda is a staunch Puritan, a product of the rigid Calvinism that so shaped the American psyche. Nevertheless, after witnessing the murder of Brother Antonio she is tormented by her perceived complicity in that evil deed and she reveals her knowledge of the crime to a Catholic priest (though assuring him that she does not seek absolution from him, as she believes that can only come from God). Many critics have called attention to the lack of compassion implicit in Hilda's moral stance: instead of extending pity and understanding to

Miriam, Hilda rejects her friend, claiming that her own innocence must not be tainted by the other's guilt. There has been much debate about whether Hawthorne affirms or condemns Hilda's rigid morality, which, along with her exaggerated chastity, some readers find difficult to accept. Yet Hawthorne never clearly indicates that he disapproves, and in fact some scholars contend that Hilda is an idealized symbol of home based on Hawthorne's own beloved wife, Sophia.

Kenyon, also an American, is a promising young sculptor who brings modern values to a place still redolent of antiquity. As Miriam points out, it is appropriate that Kenyon works in marble, for he is as cold as stone himself. He is a detached observer who seems reluctant to interact directly with other people; for example, Miriam is tempted to confide in Kenyon about her secret past but balks when she senses his obvious discomfort at the prospect. However, it is Kenyon who effects the reconciliation between Miriam and Donatello, encouraging the young man to choose involvement in the real world of men and women over guilt-ridden isolation at Monte Beni. In his role as artist and observer, Kenyon is said to be the character closest to Hawthorne's own perspective—particularly in his ultimate union with the idealized Hilda/Sophia, whose viewpoint he finally seems to unquestioningly accept. In his relationship with Hilda, Kenyon might be viewed as seeking escape from the dangerous possibilities and radicalism suggested by Miriam, or as overcoming his isolation from the rest of humanity. Some readers and scholars consider Kenyon—like his fiancee— a colorless figure whose stiffness, prudishness, and timidity render him essentially uninteresting. Nevertheless, in view of the ambiguity that pervades *The Marble Faun,* Kenyon might also represent an American type that Hawthorne means to expose rather than approve.

The beautiful and passionate artist **Miriam** is a European whose heritage includes not only English and Italian but Jewish and even African blood—a background in keeping with her general aura of mystery and exoticism. The crime or sin in Miriam's past, which she has come to Rome to escape and which is symbolized by the red jewel she always wears, is never fully revealed in the novel. It has been suggested that, like the sixteenth-century Roman woman Beatrice Cenci (whose portrait the four friends ponder), she is a victim of incest, or that she is running from a forced marriage with a much older man. Because of this shadowy personal history, and because of her artistic talent and intelligence, Miriam is often compared to another strong female in Hawthorne's fiction, Hester Prynne in *The Scarlet Letter.* From the beginning, Miriam emanates an aura of melancholy and danger, and because it is her meaningful glance that compels Donatello to shove Brother Antonio off the cliff, she may also be seen as Eve-like, in that she lures the Adamic Donatello to sin. Not surprisingly, it is Miriam who articulates the idea of the Fortunate Fall, questioning if the crime that she and Donatello committed together was "a blessing in that strange disguise? Was it a means of education, bringing a simple and imperfect nature to a point of feeling and intelligence, which it could have reached under no other discipline?"

Donatello is the happy-go-lucky Italian whose life is changed by his encounter with Brother Antonio on the Tarpeian Rock. At the beginning of the novel he is a warm, gay, energetic young man who capers about like the mythical faun he so resembles. It is later disclosed that, according to local legend, Donatello is the last remnant of a family indeed descended from the mythical race of fauns. This ambiguity about whether Donatello is human or faun is never clearly resolved and brings an element of fantasy into the novel, accounting at least partially for the subtitle, "The Romance of Monte Beni." Donatello is very much in love with Miriam but—at least until they are united by their common responsibility for the crime—she treats him with somewhat patronizing indulgence. In his innocence, simplicity, and naturalness, Donatello has been interpreted as representing the Biblical Adam as he was before eating the apple of temptation. And the country estate, Monte Beni, from which he has come to Rome and to which he flees, resembles the Garden of Eden in its pastoral, pristine beauty. After the murder, Donatello is overwhelmed with grief and becomes a markedly sadder, more contemplative person. His disgust with his newly discovered capability for evil leads to his initial isolation from others, but he is finally reconnected with humanity by his continuing love for Miriam. Donatello provides the novel's most direct embodiment of the Fortunate Fall, and if *The Marble Faun* proposes that such a fall makes a person wiser and more human, then Donatello is the chief beneficiary of his crime despite the fact that he is punished for it. Several critics have noted a pronounced ambiguity in Hawthorne's attitude toward this character—on the one hand he suggests that Donatello's naturalness is beautiful and innocent, on the other he implies that without an awakening of the kind which does occur Donatello would have degenerated into coarse sensuality later in life.

Brother Antonio is the wildly hirsute, phantomlike monk who haunts Miriam after they meet by chance in the catacombs. During a private conversation with Miriam the monk reminds her of the connection between them, implying strongly that it is rooted in some past evil deed and that they must leave Rome together to face a common destiny of sin. He threatens to expose the truth of her past if she does not comply with his wishes. Scholars have interpreted Brother Antonio in a number of ways, seeing in him an embodiment of the devil, a force of pure malevolence, the shadow of sexuality, or—in keeping with the speculation that Miriam is a victim of incest—her sinning father come to reclaim her. Those critics who feel that *The Marble Faun* is overburdened with mystification usually consider the character of the monk a purely melodramatic device that brings a false mystery to the story. Yet in his preface Hawthorne reminds the reader that the novel is a romance and is not meant to closely imitate real life—thus the darkly ominous Brother Antonio may be no more out of place than the gaily sporting faun/man, Donatello.

Further Reading

Abbott, Anne W. Review of *The Scarlet Letter*. *The North American Review* LXXI, No. CXLVIII (July 1850): 135-48.

Colacurcio, Michael, ed. *New Essays on the Scarlet Letter*. Cambridgeshire: Cambridge University Press, 1985.

Dauber, Kenneth. *Rediscovering Hawthorne*. Princeton: Princeton University Press, 1977.

Dictionary of Literary Biography, Vol. 1, 74. Detroit: Gale.

Fiedler, Leslie A. "The Scarlet Letter: Woman as Faust." In *Love and Death in the American Novel*, pp. 485-519. New York: Criterion Books, 1960.

Harris, Kenneth Marc. *Hypocrisy and Self-Deception in Hawthorne's Fiction*. Charlottesville: University Press of Virginia, 1988.

James, Henry. *Hawthorne*. New York: Harper & Brothers, 1879.

Lee, A. Robert, ed. *Nathaniel Hawthorne: New Critical Essays*. London: Vision Press, 1982.

Martin, Terence. *Nathaniel Hawthorne,* rev. ed. Boston: Twayne, 1983.

Nineteenth Century Literature Criticism, Vols. 2, 10, 17, 23. Detroit: Gale.

Poe, Edgar Allan. "Review of New Books: 'Twice-Told Tales.'"*Graham's Magazine* XX, No. 5 (May 1842): 298-300.

Short Story Criticism, Vol. 3. Detroit: Gale.

O. Henry
1862-1910
American short story writer, humorist, journalist, and poet.

"The Gift of the Magi" (short story, 1906)

Plot: The story begins on Christmas Eve in a shabby city flat, where Della Young is crying because she has only $1.87 with which to buy her beloved husband, Jim, a Christmas present. The impoverished young couple's only treasures are Della's beautiful chestnut hair and the gold watch that once belonged to Jim's father and grandfather. Della suddenly comes to a decision and marches determinedly out of the flat. Entering a hair-goods shop, she sells her hair for twenty dollars. After searching for several hours, Della finally locates a present she considers worthy of her husband: a simple but elegant platinum chain for his watch. Returning home, Della curls her shorn hair and hopes that Jim will love her as well with a new coiffure. When Jim arrives, he looks at Della in stunned silence. Worried about his strange reaction, she explains that she has sold her hair so that she could buy him a Christmas present. Jim embraces Delta and finally explains that he too has a present for her: the expensive tortoiseshell combs she long admired, which would have been perfect for her lovely long hair. Della is nevertheless delighted with her gift and reminds Jim that her hair grows quickly. Then she presents the watch chain, only to learn that Jim sold his gold watch in order to buy the combs. So these "two foolish children," the narrator explains, have sacrificed their greatest treasures for love of each other, thus proving their real nobility.

Characters: William Sydney Porter, who wrote under the pseudonym O. Henry, was one of the most popular and prolific writers of the early twentieth century. Distinguished by their brevity, verbal playfulness, realistic detail, and surprise endings, his short stories are still widely read and have in recent years regained some of the critical acclaim they lost for several decades after Henry's death. "The Gift of the Magi" is possibly Henry's most famous story and occupies a firmly established place in the popular imagination as a Christmas fable affirming the redemptive power of love. While some critics have noted that the story exhibits Henry's characteristic sentimentality, others praise its concise, compassionate rendering of the lives and inherent nobility of two urban American working people.

"The Gift of the Magi" provides a good example of the skillful economy of Henry's prose style, for this very short story contains enough telling details to give the reader a rich picture of its protagonists' lives. By the end of the story it is clear that the love shared by the materially impoverished Youngs and their generosity toward each other make them wealthy, and thus they are equated with the magi or kings who brought gifts to the infant Jesus. **Della Young** is a pretty young woman whose greatest glory is her long chestnut-colored hair, which cascades down past her knees when unfurled. In keeping with the story's biblical allusions, the narrator notes that Della's hair would be envied by the Queen of Sheba (who appears in the books of Kings and Chronicles). Despite the apparent dreariness of her life and the limited income that requires her to live in a humble flat, wear shabby clothing, and do without even modest luxuries, Della is happy in her love for her husband. She wishes to buy him a gift wortny of his nobility and thus sacrifices her most prized possession for his sake. After she has sold her hair to buy the watch chain and is waiting for Jim to come home, she experiences some moments of doubt, wondering if he will find her as pretty with short hair. Indeed, Jim's initial reaction seems to suggest that her fears were well-grounded. Della recovers quickly from her chagrin when she realizes that the coveted combs will be useless without her long hair, and she exhibits an admirable resilience when she reminds Jim that her hair grows quickly.

Della's husband is **James Dillingham Young,** whose vaguely aristocratic middle name, the narrator suggests, was touted more aggressively when he was, at some time in the near past, making more money than he is now. The twenty-two-year-old Jim is thin and serious with a quiet, earnest manner. His most treasured possession is his gold watch, which previously belonged to his father and grandfather. Again the narrator makes a biblical allusion by claiming that the fabulously wealthy King Solomon himself would covet this treasure. Yet by the end of the story it is obvious that Jim values Della more than any material object, for he has sold his watch in order to buy her the combs for which she has longed. He reacts to the revelation that both gifts have been rendered useless with a rueful sense of humor and the same resilience that Della displays. The narrator leaves the young couple to eat their Christmas Eve dinner together, noting that "of all who give gifts these two were the wisest. . . . They are the magi."

The only other character in "The Gift of the Magi" is **Madame Sofronie,** the proprietor of the hair-goods shop to whom Della sells her hair. She is described as "large, too white, chilly" with a rather rough manner; her exotic name contrasts with her commonplace grimness.

"The Furnished Room" (short story, 1906)

Plot: As the story opens, a tired young man arrives at a dilapidated boarding house on the lower west side of Manhattan—the twelfth such establishment he has visited today. The shabby housekeeper takes him to "the third floor back" room, explaining that it was previously occupied by two vaudeville performers and that many of her boarders are "theatrical people." Paying for the room, the young man asks the housekeeper if she has ever encountered a young singer named Eloise Vashner. She replies that she has never heard the name. The young man, apparently a former sweetheart of the girl, has spent the five months since she left home fruitlessly searching for her in music halls and boarding houses throughout the city. The exhausted young man sits in a chair, listening to the various noises of the house and smelling its musty odors. Suddenly, however, he becomes aware of the fragrance of mignonette. This floral scent was Eloise's favorite, and he is convinced that she has been in the room. Unable to locate the source of the odor, he again asks the housekeeper who occupied the room before him. She answers that the former tenants were the vaudeville team Sprowls and Mooney, a married couple. The woman, she claims, was short, stout, and black-haired—nothing like Eloise, who is fair haired with a mole above her left eye. The young man returns to the room to find the scent of mignonette vanished. Making the room completely airtight, he turns on the gas and lies down on the bed. The story's focus now shifts to the housekeeper, Mrs. Purdy, as she drinks beer and talks with her friend Mrs. McCool, explaining how she has rented the "third-floor-back" room to a young man. Her friend is impressed, because a young woman had killed herself in that room only a week ago. Mrs. Purdy admits that she did not reveal this fact to the new tenant. Her companion recollects that the dead girl was very pretty, and Mrs. Purdy says that she might indeed have been attractive except for the mole above her left eyebrow.

Characters: "The Furnished Room" is one of Henry's best known short stories and typifies the author's fiction in its urban setting and working-class characters, its brevity, its wealth of naturalistic detail, and its "twist" ending. While some critics contend that Henry's frequent use of the surprise ending comprises a cheap trick played on the reader, others, such as   Carl Van Doren, defend the technique as evidencing his "unconcern for the timid conventions of realism."

The unnamed **young man** who is the central character of "The Furnished Room" is only sketchily portrayed; the story's emphasis is not on him but on the strong bond of love he represents and on the ironies of fate. Having searched for his sweetheart, **Eloise Vashner,** who left her home five months earlier to seek success as a theatrical singer in New York City, the young man is now physically and emotionally exhausted. As he settles into his dreary room he surveys its decaying, ragged furniture, listens to the sounds made by the house's other tenants, and breathes in its musty odors. The sordid room reflects the coldly impersonal city as well as the possible brutalization of Eloise, and it also manifests the young man's sense of futility. His sudden awareness of the scent of mignonette is so real to him that he jumps up and cries "What, dear?" as if his sweetheart has just entered the room. Whether he really smells the scent or if it is created by his weary and disappointed imagination can never be known. He conducts a thorough and ultimately futile search through the room for the source of the odor, discovering only the trash and discarded keepsakes of previous tenants. Some critics have claimed that the young man's eventual decision to kill himself is insufficiently motivated, for he has no more reason than before to believe his search for Eloise will fail since he does not, technically, know that she has committed suicide. Other critics have suggested that he believes the unexplained mignonette smell in the room comprises her spiritual presence. Thus "he who had loved her best" pursues the same fate she—exactly one week earlier—chose.

The narrator's comparison of the slatternly housekeeper, **Mrs. Purdy,** with an "unwholesome, surfeited worm that had eaten its nut to a hollow shell and now sought to fill the vacancy with edible lodgers" gives both her and the boarding house an unpleasant, predatory aspect. Even more disreputable and animal-like is her "fur-lined" voice. That Mrs. Purdy is indeed sly and dishonest is revealed at the end of the story, when she admits to Mrs. McCool that she did not divulge the room's history to the young man who rented it and ungraciously maintains that the mole over Eloise's left eye deprived the young woman of beauty.

Mrs. McCool, Mrs. Purdy's friend and fellow housekeeper, serves a practical function in the story by providing an occasion for Mrs. Purdy's revelation. Significantly, Mrs. McCool excuses her friend's failure to reveal that a suicide had occurred in the room the previous week by noting that "'tis by renting rooms that we kape alive." Thus Henry displays sympathy for these two impoverished working women and reveals his gift of humanizing even the culpable forms of humanity. Mrs. McCool is more generous than her friend in calling Eloise   a   "pretty slip of a colleen."

"An Unfinished Story" (short story, 1906)

Plot: The story begins with the narrator describing a dream in which he had arrived in heaven for judgment and was asked by an "angel policeman" if he belonged with a nearby group of spirits awaiting judgment. Just as the angel is about to explain who these spirits are, the narrator suspends this account and starts the story. Dulcie is a young woman who works in a department store, earning six dollars a week. As she is leaving her post one evening, she informs her fellow shop girl Sadie that she has accepted a date with a man named Piggy Wiggins; Sadie says she imagines that Dulcie will have "a swell time" with this well-known dandy. Dulcie reaches her shabby little apartment, the furnishings and decor of which the narrator describes in detail. On the mirror are fastened pictures of several famous people, including the renowned General Kitchener of England. The narrator accounts how Dulcie disposes of her meager income, then provides an unflattering description of Piggy Wiggins, who preys on underfed shop girls in order to achieve his own immoral ends. Dulcie arrays herself in what little finery she has—much of it purchased in lieu of food—and is finally ready for her date. When Piggy arrives, however, Dulcie catches a glimpse of the respectable General Kitchener, who seems to admonish her. She tells her landlady to send Piggy away, and spends a lonely, dull evening in her apartment. The narrator suggests that, despite her awareness of Piggy's dishonorable intentions, Dulcie will at some later date succumb to the temptation to exchange her virtue for a luxurious night out with Piggy. The narrator now concludes his dream: the group of spirits awaiting judgment were men who had paid working girls only five or six dollars a week, while the narrator claimed that he was merely an arsonist and murderer.

Characters: Often identified as one of Henry's finest tales, "An Unfinished Story" features the working-class characters upon whom he frequently focused and evidences Henry's interest in social reform. He was well aware of the poverty and potential for exploitation that were part of the urban life he portrayed, and his sympathy for young working women is particularly emphasized here. While Henry's detractors have seen in "An Unfinished Story" the sentimentality and sermonizing they feel weakens his fiction, his admirers praise its realism and compassionate spirit.

The protagonist of "An Unfinished Story" is **Dulcie,** a pretty, apparently innocent young woman who works in a department store, earning only six dollars a week, and lives alone in a tiny, dreary apartment. Her few luxuries are acquired only by depriving herself of food. The narrator mentions that Dulcie has been to Coney Island (the favorite recreational spot for working class New Yorkers) only twice in her life. Despite her poverty Dulcie is well-groomed and seems to maintain a cheerful attitude. She reveals her understanding of the threat Piggy represents when she decides not to go out with him, since it would apparently require her to exchange her virtue for dinner in a grander restaurant than she could ever visit on her own. Thus she exhibits an impressive moral fiber as well as emotional strength, crying only briefly in reaction to her disappointment and facing her evening alone bravely. Yet the narrator suggests that Dulcie's defenses may at a later date be sufficiently worn down to allow Piggy to accomplish his goal. Dulcie idolizes General Kitchener, the immensely popular nineteenth-century leader of the British forces in India and Asia; he seems to represent the conventional morality by which she wants to live, and he might be seen as either a father figure or a substitute lover. At the same time, however, she resents his stern influence and instinctively knows that he would never understand the dullness of her impoverished existence. For now Dulcie makes the right choice, acting in accordance with her conscience, but eventually her longing for a treat—or even for basic nourishment—may cause her to relent.

The narrator claims that when the shop girls gave Dulcie's intended suitor, **Piggy Wiggins,** his nickname "an undeserving stigma was cast upon the noble family of swine." This young man—identified as lower than a pig by the narrator and as a "swell" by Sadie—is a stout, sly dandy with a reputation for spending money freely, exposing the young working girls he preys on to the glamorous life they crave. He is a sexual predator who chooses his victims on the basis of their greatest vulnerabilities, such as hunger. Several critics have noted that Piggy provides one of very few hints of sexual depravity or misbehavior to be found in Henry's fiction.

The only other significant character in the story is **Sadie,** Dulcie's fellow shop girl, whose brief appearance allows Henry to exhibit his knowledge of urban slang. She also performs the practical function of informing the reader that other girls like herself and Dulcie have succumbed to Piggy's charms.

"A Municipal Report" (short story, 1910)

Plot: The story begins with the narrator's arrival in Nashville. The narrator describes in detail his hotel and its surroundings, emphasizing their dullness and lack of activity. In his hotel lobby he meets Major Wentworth Caswell, an effusive Southern gentleman who attempts to befriend the narrator and gets him to buy a round of drinks in the bar. The hotel clerk later informs the narrator that Caswell is a loafer and nuisance with no known means of support. The narrator now explains the reason for his visit to Nashville: he is acting as an agent for a Northern literary journal that wishes to arrange a long-term contract with a particularly talented contributor, Azalea Adair. The next morning the narrator is conveyed to the writer's home by Uncle Caesar, a black cabdriver attired in a ragged, multicolored coat tied with twine and fastened with a large, yellow button made of bone. He seems familiar with the narrator's intended destination and curious about why he wants to go there. Arriving at Miss Adair's dilapidated old mansion, Uncle Caesar convinces the narrator—who explains that he too is a Southerner and thus accustomed to such deviousness—to pay him two dollars instead of the agreed-upon fifty cents. Miss Adair is a thin, white-haired, dignified woman whose quarters are sparsely furnished. The narrator describes her as an impoverished remnant of the old Southern aristocracy, and he again praises the profundity and lyricism of her writing. After answering a knock at her back door, the writer returns in a cheerful mood and sends her servant, a young black girl named Impy, to buy tea and cakes; the narrator notices that she gives the girl the same torn and repatched dollar bill that he had previously given Uncle Caesar. Then sounds are heard that appear to signify a scuffle between Impy and an unseen man, and Miss Adair subsequently withdraws her invitation to tea. The narrator plans to return the next day and arranges to have Uncle Caesar, who now reveals that he was once a slave owned by Miss Adair's father, drive him again.

That evening the narrator has another unpleasant encounter with Major Caswell, who produces the same torn and repaired dollar bill the narrator had seen Miss Adair holding and which he himself had given Uncle Caesar. The next morning, the narrator again travels to Miss Adair's house, and she signs the contract, which the narrator has made more favorable to her than originally planned. During his visit, Miss Adair suddenly faints, and Uncle Caesar quickly brings a doctor to the house who explains that she is suffering from "insufficient nutrition"; he also reveals that she is married to the disreputable Major Caswell, who regularly steals what little money she has, and that Uncle Caesar contributes to her support. Before leaving, the narrator gives Miss Adair a fifty dollar advance. That evening, he sees Uncle Caesar and notices that the cabdriver's coat is now missing its bone button. Several hours later, he learns that Major Caswell has been murdered. As he is viewing the corpse with other curious onlookers, one of its clenched fists opens suddenly and a large yellow button falls to the ground. The narrator retrieves the button before anyone else has seen it. After hearing speculation that Caswell was murdered by "some of these no account niggers" for the fifty dollars he had earlier shown he was carrying but which has since disappeared, the narrator leaves town. As he crosses the Cumberland River, he tosses the button into the water.

Characters: Many critics consider "A Municipal Report" Henry's most accomplished short story. The piece features such typical Henry devices as a surprise ending, verbal play, and allusions to classical literature, but it is further distinguished by an unconventional structure and authorial self-consciousness, anticipating modern fictional techniques. Through characters that are intentionally stereotyped yet still effective, and emphasizing storytelling technique over a plausible story line, Henry explores in "A Municipal Report" the concept that dramatic and significant events may occur in even the most apparently mundane setting.

The narrator is perhaps the most important player in "A Municipal Report," for he gives the tale its unique, innovative structure and depth. His rhetorical virtuosity and frequent digressions call attention to the very act of narration, so that the story itself—while gripping—is subordinate to the storyteller's skill. The narrator is apparently a writer himself who is acting as a kind of agent for a Northern literary journal wishing to acquire Azalea Adair as a regular, contracted contributor. His detailed descriptions of the people and scenes he encounters in Nashville are correlated to the short excerpts from some unnamed, notably dry reference work (identified by several critics as a Rand McNally guide to American cities) that are placed throughout the story to describe such matters as education, industry, trade, and Civil War history. The narrator eventually admits that he is a Southerner himself, though his attitude about his heritage differs significantly from that of the "professional Southerner" Major Caswell. The narrator, by contrast, has a more complex and shame-tinged understanding of the South. Although his tone is generally jocular and ironic, he exhibits his basic decency through his generosity toward Azalea Adair and, most importantly, by concealing Uncle Caesar's role in Caswell's death. Some commentators have connected the narrator's action with Henry's feelings about his own friends' efforts to conceal the fact that he himself had once been jailed for extortion.

The inherently royal aspect of the elderly black cabdriver, **Uncle Caesar,** leads the narrator to nickname him "King Cettiwayo," a reference to a famous Zulu king who resisted British domination during the nineteenth century. A former slave, Uncle Caesar is dressed in a ragged, fantastically colored coat that apparently once belonged to a Confederate officer, thus providing an ironic connection with the South's simultaneously glorious and ignominious past and its failed attempt to preserve the institution of slavery. Fastened with carefully constructed twine toggles, the coat features a large yellow button made of bone, which eventually serves as circumstantial evidence that Uncle Caesar murdered Caswell. Uncle Caesar's manner is alternately obsequious and wise according to the needs of the moment— the former when necessary to deflect attention from white people and the latter when he knows he may relax his defenses (such as when the narrator informs him that he is not the naive northerner Uncle Caesar might have taken him for). The narrator initially seems to ridicule Uncle Caesar's kingliness, describing him in terms that align him with the stereotypically ludicrous, illiterate African-American of popular fiction. Later the narrator learns Uncle Caesar *is* descended from an African monarch, and he understands the depth of this nobility as Uncle Caesar's loyalty to Miss Adair is repeatedly demonstrated. Ultimately he risks his own life to rid her of her cruel, parasitical husband, an act which by the end of "A Municipal Report" seems morally justified.

Azalea Adair Caswell provides the reason for the narrator's visit to Nashville, for her essays and poems have been much admired by the editors of the literary journal he is connected with and they want to contract her as a regular contributor. About fifty years old, she is white-haired and frail and is, when the narrator meets her, dressed in a cheap but scrupulously clean dress. The dilapidated condition of her family mansion and the sparse though neat furnishings of her reception room indicate that she is impoverished; eventually the narrator learns the real extent of her poverty. A remnant of the once proud Southern aristocracy, Miss Adair bravely maintains an appearance of gentility, a poignantly portrayed situation that evidences Henry's penchant for impostures of all kinds. That Miss Adair is a talented writer is suggested by her perceptive, even poetic conversation. The narrator classifies her as a product of the old South whose sheltered life has resulted in an intelligence that is deep rather than broad and who is admirably immune from the concerns of "real life," at least in her approach to her art. For in fact Miss Adair is much afflicted with reality, particularly through the parasitical husband who brings her both emotional and physical pain (the latter in the form of starvation and quite possibly physical abuse). Significantly, this outwardly mild but intellectually intense woman articulates one of the story's central themes when she objects to the narrator's statement that nothing much could happen in such a quiet town. In a voice "like a harpsichord" that enchants the narrator, Miss Adair asks, "Isn't it in the still, quiet places that things do happen?" And she goes on to describe examples from her own circle of friends in which apparently mundane occurrences held immeasurable significance and tragedy for those concerned.

The villain of "A Municipal Report" is **Major Wentworth Caswell,** a shiftless, arrogant boor whom the narrator describes as a "professional Southerner" prone to vainglorious boasts of Civil War bravery and family connections. Caswell represents a stereotype of the disreputable Southern gentleman—a worthless, drunken loafer who maintains a facade of inherited wealth and privilege while actually pilfering from his wife and leaching off strangers whenever possible. The fact that Caswell, the first Nashville resident the narrator encounters, happens to be the husband of the very writer he has come to see may be cited as an example of Henry's use of coincidence. Caswell is a flat character about whom the only good thing that any of his acquaintances can think to say, after his death, is that he was a good speller when he was fourteen years old. It is strongly suggested that he is deserved the death he finally meets at the hands of the noble Uncle Caesar.

Other characters in "A Municipal Report" include twelve-year-old **Impy,** Miss Adair's slovenly, indifferently mannered black servant, who screams loudly when Caswell takes the money she has been given to buy tea and cakes; and **Dr. Merriman,** the physician who informs the narrator that Miss Adair is suffering from "poverty, pride, and starvation," also revealing that she is married to the shiftless Major Caswell and that Uncle Caesar's grandfather was a king in Africa.

Further Reading

Dictionary of Literary Biography, Vols. 12, 78, 79. Detroit: Gale.

Eixenbaum, B. M. *O. Henry and the Theory of the Short Story,* translated by I. R. Titunik. Ann Arbor: University of Michigan, 1968.

Knight, Jesse F. "Some Thoughts on the Urban Romantist." *The Romantist* No. 3 (1979): 33-7.

O'Connor, Richard. *O. Henry: The Legendary Life of William Sydney Porter.* Garden City, N. Y.: Doubleday, 1970.

Pattee, Fred Lewis. "The Journalization of American Literature." *The Unpopular Review* VII, No. 14 (April-June 1917): 374-94.

Pritchett, V. S. "O. Henry." *New Statesman* LIV, No. 1393 (23 November 1957): 697-98.

Short Story Criticism, Vol. 5. Detroit: Gale.

Twentieth-Century Literary Criticism, Vol. 1, 19. Detroit: Gale.

Van Doren, Carl. "O. Henry." *Texas Review* II, No. 3 (January 1917): 248-59.

Victor Marie Hugo
1802-1885
French novelist, dramatist, poet, and critic.

The Hunchback of Notre Dame (*Notre Dame de Paris;* novel, 1831)

Plot: The novel takes place in Paris in 1482, during the reign of King Louis XI. The king's son is to marry a Flemish princess, and the king has invited ambassadors from Flanders (Holland) to visit his court. The day of their arrival coincides with the religious observance of Epiphany as well as the secular Festival of Fools. A poor, incompetent poet named Pierre Gringoire has written a morality play for the amusement of the crowd waiting outside of the Palace of Justice for the royal guests; the play is interrupted and forgotten when the royal procession arrives. Afterward the crowd clamors for the election of a Prince of Fools. The candidates compete by appearing in front of a glass window and making ugly grimaces. The face deemed the most hideous is that of Quasimodo, the grotesque, hunchback bell-ringer of the cathedral of Notre Dame. In addition to his deformed back, he has protruding, broken teeth, a huge nose, bristling red hair, long, dangling arms, and a large wart over one eye. Because he is deaf, he does not understand why he is being carried through the crowd, and he is even pleased. The parade pauses before a gypsy dancing girl named Esmeralda, who is thought by some to be a witch because she performs so enchantingly with her little trained goat, Djali. That night, the penniless Gringoire is walking through the city streets when he witnesses the attempted abduction of Esmeralda by a man wearing a black hood and accompanied by Quasimodo. Esmeralda is rescued by a dashing, handsome member of the order of Royal Archers, Captain Phoebus de Châteaupers, with whom she immediately falls in love.

The hooded man who had tried to abduct Esmeralda is Claude Frollo, the archdeacon of Notre Dame, a formerly pious man whose quest for knowledge and isolation from humanity has led to an interest in black magic and alchemy (the medieval science that sought to create gold from other natural elements). He has developed an overpowering lust for Esmeralda and wishes to make her his own at any cost. He was helped in his unsuccessful kidnapping attempt by Quasimodo, who as a child was abandoned and then taken in by Frollo. After witnessing the near-abduction, Gringoire is himself captured by a band of street thugs and told he will be killed unless one of their women agrees to marry him. His life is saved by Esmeralda, whose promise to wed him will never be fulfilled due to her love for Phoebus. Because he has been seen near Esmeralda and because his master is thought to be a sorcerer, Quasimodo is brought to trial for having suspicious connections; then he is whipped and pilloried before a jeering crowd. Pitying the tortured hunchback, Esmeralda brings him a drink of water and thus wins his undying gratitude and devotion. Frollo, by contrast, witnesses Quasimodo's unjust punishment but merely rides away.

Phoebus employs Esmeralda to entertain his elegant female companions—who believe she is a sorceress because her goat so dutifully does her bidding—and then arranges to meet her in a house of ill repute. On his way to the tryst, Phoebus meets Frollo, who has learned from Gringoire that Esmeralda loves only the young officer. Frollo offers to pay Phoebus to allow him to hide in the room and witness the encounter, and Phoebus agrees to the arrangement. In the dark room, Frollo suddenly springs out of hiding and stabs Phoebus, then escapes. Esmeralda is accused of murdering her lover, convicted of witchcraft, and sentenced to hang. Phoebus, who survived the attack, does nothing to save Esmeralda's life. Before her execution Esmeralda is to do penance on the porch of the cathedral of Notre Dame. When she comes before the archdeacon, he offers to rescue her if she will become his mistress. She refuses. Suddenly Quasimodo appears and daringly carries Esmeralda into the church sanctuary, where no one can touch her. He locks her into his own cell and brings her food, forcibly turning Frollo away when he tries to visit Esmeralda. Misunderstanding Quasimodo's motives, a mob gathers outside the cathedral and demands that Esmeralda be freed. The hunchbacked protector bravely repels several assaults on the cathedral, including one by the king's guard. Meanwhile Frollo persuades Gringoire to go to Esmeralda's cell and convince her to flee with him to safety. She leaves with Gringoire but finds Frollo waiting for her in a boat; he tells her to choose between him and the gallows. She answers that she would rather die than join him. Esmeralda discovers that the insane woman confined in another cell in the cathedral is her own mother, who has been in self-imposed isolation there since the theft of her daughter by gypsies drove her mad. Finally the soldiers arrive and drag Esmeralda from her mother's arms.

Quasimodo spends the night searching for Esmeralda. He eventually arrives on a tower of the cathedral, where he finds a jubilant Frollo; together the two look down upon the Place de la Grève and witness the hanging of the white-draped Esmeralda. Enraged by Frollo's gruesome mirth, Quasimodo heaves the archdeacon over the side of the tower, and Frollo falls to his death. Quasimodo weeps at the loss of the only two people he has ever loved.

Later he disappears from the cathedral and is never seen again. After many years, the entwined skeletons of a woman in a white dress and a deformed man are found in the vault at Montfaucon, where criminals are buried. When the skeletons are touched by human hands, they crumble into dust.

Characters: *The Hunchback of Notre Dame* is one of the first major novels of the French romantic movement and a seminal work in French literature. It combines the social ideas that would continue to interest Hugo—such as the concept of human equality and the plight of the poor—with a tightly structured, exciting plot and compelling characters. Centered on the idea that *ananké* (the Greek word for fate or destiny) determines the course of human lives, the novel explores the ability of human beings to transcend their social and physical limitations to achieve moral greatness. Hugo's depiction of medieval Paris and his skillful rendering of the cathedral itself, which attains such thematic and symbolic importance that many critics have identified it as a character in the story, have been universally praised.

The horribly deformed yet superhumanly strong, virtuous bell-ringer **Quasimodo** is well established in the popular imagination for the spiritual purity that exists beneath his hideous exterior. It is thought that Hugo based this remarkable figure on his memory of a deaf-mute, hunchbacked porter who worked at a Spanish school he attended as a child. With his misshapen back, disproportionately long arms, beaked nose, broken teeth, wart-covered eye, and sparse, bristling red hair, Quasimodo is quintessentially ugly and utterly pitiable. In keeping with the architectural theme that runs through the novel, the hunchback is compared to a building that has been knocked down and then put together again in a confused, distorted manner. Quasimodo himself says that he is neither completely a man nor quite an animal. Though deaf from years of bell-ringing, he has keen eyesight and incredible physical strength, allowing him to perform such deeds as abducting Esmeralda from the porch of the cathedral, fighting off the angry mob of six thousand ruffians, and heaving Frollo over the edge of the tower. Orphaned in his infancy and an object of public repulsion and ridicule, Quasimodo is attached to his protector, Frollo, and unquestioningly does his bidding even when it involves, for instance, kidnapping an innocent girl for evil purposes. Esmeralda's simple act of kindness to him after his unjustified arrest and punishment causes a split in Quasimodo's loyalties: by offering the tormented hunchback a drink of water, she earns his undying devotion. His love for Esmeralda awakens the hidden beauty of his nature, for he is inspired to acts of great courage and selflessness in her service. Unlike the love that Frollo, Phoebus, or even Gringoire feel for the girl, Quasimodo's is spiritual and pure. Its depth is ultimately proven when, in response to Frollo's wicked glee at the sight of Esmeralda's execution, he destroys the man who previously protected him. Quasimodo's skeleton is later found entwined with hers, indicating that he joined her in her grave and died there. Scholars identify the character of Quasimodo closely with the cathedral whose bells it is his duty—and his sole joy in life—to ring. He embodies the element of the grotesque that is as much a part of the building's nature as its beauty, exemplifying Hugo's belief in the coexistence of the grotesque and the sublime and his effort to include both in his writings. Like the cathedral, Quasimodo is both strong and vulnerable, with a rough exterior and virtually impermeable portals guarding a treasure-laden sanctuary.

The corrupt, lustful archdeacon **Claude Frollo** is sometimes identified as the central character of *The Hunchback of Notre Dame,* for he may be even more complex and tragic than Quasimodo. Although he is only thirty-six years old when the story takes place, Frollo is prematurely old in appearance, with thinning, grayed hair and a withered face, and it is suggested that he has always—even as a child—had a melancholy, somber manner. Once morally upright, he engaged in a search for unlimited knowledge that isolated him from others as he spent long hours studying. Frollo turned to the shadowy realm of alchemy and necromancy. In a famous passage he observes a spider web in the window of his room and compares human beings to flies caught in the sticky web of fate; even if they manage to evade the web and move toward the light, he says, they will only be trapped by the glass window that lies on the other side. He claims that he is both the spider (in his lecherous designs on Esmeralda) and the fly, caught in the web of his own desire. Hugo stated that he once saw the Greek word *anankè* carved into a wall of the cathedral of Notre Dame (which he visited many times during his life) and that it was in imagining who might have left such a mark there that inspired his novel. In *The Hunchback of Notre Dame,* Frollo inscribes on his wall the word that designates fate or destiny, indicating his belief that human lives are directed not by free will but by an irresistible fate. Some critics feel Frollo belongs to the Gothic tradition of the demonic monk, or as the evil, coldhearted villain of traditional romance—particularly in his continual association with images of blackness, darkness, and stone—while others see him as a complex character whose resistance to the physical, passionate side of his nature has resulted in an exaggerated lust toward Esmeralda and an overpowering urge to subdue her. His life finally ends in a gruesome fall (some early reviewers objected to the author's realistic description of his death) onto the pavement below the cathedral tower.

If Frollo is a villain out of Gothic fiction, **Esmeralda** might be seen as a traditional romantic heroine. Beautiful, innocent, and virtuous, Esmeralda captivates onlookers with her charming dance and the tricks she has taught her little goat, **Djali,** but her talents also draw suspicion, and she is accused of witchcraft. Her persecution illustrates one of the novel's strongest themes, showing how ignorance and superstition may be institutionalized. Esmeralda resembles Quasimodo in her status as an impoverished orphan, dependent on others for protection, and in her spiritual purity. Some critics consider Esmeralda idealized, while others have found her vulnerability convincing; her blind love for Phoebus, for instance, may be seen as unlikely or as quite typical of a young, impressionable girl. Often identified as a secular version of the Virgin Mary (the patron saint of the cathedral of Notre Dame), she nevertheless provokes lust in several male characters, but she also inspires moral greatness in Quasimodo and maintains to the end her own inherent purity.

Captain Phoebus de Châteaupers, a handsome, dashing member of the order of Royal Archers, quickly captures the heart of the impressionable Esmeralda. His name evokes the Greek god of the sun, Phoebus Apollo, a reference that may be either ironic or linked to the ultimate futility of Frollo's quest for the light of wisdom, for his brilliant appearance masks his true emptiness. He is a dissolute rake and braggart whose interest in Esmeralda is physical; he is even willing to allow Frollo to witness their encounter. His selfishness is further evidenced by his refusal to save Esmeralda from the gallows because he does not want to be associated with witchcraft. Although Phoebus is not punished with death, as Frollo is, he does meet an unhappy fate in his socially advantageous but disastrous marriage.

Pierre Gringoire is the unsuccessful poet whose morality play is interrupted during the celebration that opens the novel, and he narrates the early scenes. Pale and thin, he is also homeless and impoverished. Attacked by the gang Esmeralda associates with, he is nearly killed. She saves his life by agreeing to marry him; although the marriage never takes place, Gringoire is one of four men who are smitten by the lovely Esmeralda. Although he is generally naive or even stupid, Gringoire does manage to get himself released from imprisonment in the Bastille when he impresses a visiting Louis XI with a philosophical argument supporting his release. Spared the horrible death that most of the other major characters meet, Gringoire rescues Esmeralda's goat, Djali, and goes on to a career of writing bad but officially sanctioned plays.

The madwoman who is eventually revealed to be Esmeralda's mother, **Gudule,** has languished in a tiny cell in the cathedral for fifteen years. Her insanity dates back to her daughter's kidnapping; she was so busy bragging about her lovely little girl that she did not notice gypsies stealing the child. A prostitute at the time of her daughter's birth, Gudule now has no other possessions or motivations but her maternal passion. The strength of this emotion is symbolized in the superhuman strength with which she tears down the bars between her cell and Esmeralda's when she learns that the young woman is her daughter. Gudule is destined to lose her a second time.

Another significant though minor character in *The Hunchback of Notre Dame* is **Jacques Coppenole,** one of the Flemish ambassadors who visit King Louis XI. A member of the middle class which was, in the nineteenth century, gradually gaining strength, Coppenole represents the most positive aspects of "le peuple" (the people) in his forthrightness and lack of pretension. Hearing the commotion as the crowd threatens to storm the cathedral, he warns the king that the hour is approaching when the common folk will rise up and demand their rights. Many critics see in this pronouncement the hope for a democracy that had not yet—even at the time of the novel's publication—been achieved in France, but which Hugo believed was inevitable. **Jehan Frollo,** the archdeacon's brother, is a wild and feckless young student who receives a warning from his brother to curb his unruly behavior. Hugo has been praised for his lifelike rendering of **King Louis XI,** the monarch of France who is portrayed as oblivious to his people's suffering. With his Flemish visitors, he visits the cells of the Bastille in which political prisoners languish for years at his capricious orders; he ignores their pitiful cries for mercy and later orders Esmeralda to be taken from the cathedral—which is supposed to provide an impermeable sanctuary to those who seek refuge there—and executed. Several scholars have seen this unpleasant royal figure as symbolizing Hugo's belief that the monarchical form of government was outdated and destructive. **Charmolue,** representing the legal system, visits Frollo to discuss prosecuting Esmeralda for witchcraft; when he witnesses the spider's attack on a fly in the web, he says he wishes to save the fly's life, but Frollo insists that fate must take its course.

Les Misérables (novel, 1862)

Plot: The story begins in France in 1815 with the release of Jean Valjean from prison. Initially sentenced to a five-year term after he stole a loaf of bread to feed his sister's starving family, Valjean has spent nineteen years behind bars because of his frequent escape attempts. While he was in prison he became known for his prodigious physical strength. As he travels through the countryside he is repeatedly refused lodging due to his convict status. He is finally taken in and treated with warm hospitality by the bishop of the town of Digne. Although Jean is affected by the bishop's kindness, the baser instincts fostered during his imprisonment overcome him: he steals some silver from the bishop and flees. Caught by the police, Jean is astonished when the bishop pretends that he had given the silver to his boarder and even adds a pair of candlesticks to the gift. As Jean is leaving, the bishop says that he hopes the valuable items will help Jean live a more virtuous life. Later, Jean steals some coins from a child and then is overwhelmed with remorse. He assumes a new name, Father Madeleine, and establishes himself in a town where he eventually becomes a prosperous owner of a glass factory and so popular with the townsfolk that they elect him mayor. One of the workers in his factory is a beautiful young girl named Fantine, who becomes pregnant by an irresponsible student. Forced by her fellow workers (though without her employer's knowledge) to leave her job, Fantine gives her daughter, Cosette, to innkeepers Madame and Monsieur Thénardier to raise with their own children. She becomes a prostitute to support herself and pay the Thénardiers for Cosette's care.

Meanwhile an extremely diligent police inspector named Javert suspects that Jean is hiding some secret from his past. He sees Jean lift a heavy cart from atop an old man, Fauchevelent, and he remembers that the convict Valjean possessed incredible strength. Javert arrests Fantine for prostitution, and Jean hears of her plight; in addition to her poverty and degradation, she is suffering from tuberculosis. He promises to bring Cosette to her, but before he can leave he learns that an elderly thief has been mistaken for Jean Valjean and will be tried in the town of Arras. Torn by conflicting feelings, Jean finally decides to travel to Arras and admit his true identity. He does so and is soon taken to prison; he escapes, however, after only one day. Meanwhile Fantine has died. After another capture by Javert and another escape, Jean retrieves the now eight-year-old Cosette from the Thénardiers and takes her to the poverty-stricken Gorbeau district of Paris, where the two live contentedly. Javert manages to track them down again, however, and they are forced to flee, finally taking refuge within the walls of a convent where Fauchelevent, the man whose life Jean had previously saved, is working as a gardener. Jean and Cosette spend the next several years at the convent, with Jean posing as Fauchelevent's brother and helping him in his work; Cosette attends the convent school.

When Cosette finishes her education, she and Jean move away from the convent. Meanwhile Thénardier has moved with his family to the Gorbeau neighborhood and now calls himself Jondrette. Living next door is Marius Pontmercy, whose father has told him to do whatever he can to repay the man who saved his life during the Battle of Waterloo; Marius does not realize that his father's rescuer, Thénardier, and Jondrette are the same man. Nevertheless he provides his neighbors with money so they will not be evicted from their home. Marius sees Jean and Cosette out walking one evening and immediately falls in love with the girl. Noticing the young man's interest, however, Jean takes Cosette to live in a different house. Marius overhears the Jondrettes—who had previously asked him for more money—plotting to cheat Jean, who he believes is Cosette's father. He informs Javert of the scheme. Later Marius witnesses an encounter between Jondrette and Jean during which it is revealed that Jondrette is really Thénardier. Marius now feels his loyalties divided between his father's rescuer and his sweetheart's presumed father. Javert arrives just as the thugs Jondrette/Thénardier has hired to help him extort money from Jean are about to kill him; all are arrested except Jean, who escapes. Marius eventually finds Cosette and learns that she and Jean are planning to move to England. Marius asks his grandfather, from whom he is estranged because his liberal views conflict with his grandfather's royalist sentiments, for permission to marry Cosette, but the request is refused. When Marius returns to Jean and Cosette's home, he finds it abandoned. Eponine Thénardier—who, unlike her parents, is honorable and good-hearted person and who is in love with Marius—informs him that his radical friends have instigated an insurrection. Marius follows her to the barricade, where Javert has been captured and detained by the revolutionaries. During the fighting, Eponine saves Marius's life but is killed in the process. Before she dies she gives Marius a note from Cosette that explains where he can find her. Marius writes back to Cosette, claiming that his own impoverishment and his grandfather's opposition makes their marriage impossible and that he expects to be killed during the insurrection. Jean discovers both notes and goes to the barricade; he frees Javert and, finding Marius wounded and unconscious, carries him off. He descends into the extensive Parisian sewer system and, after a long search, finally finds an outlet. Thénardier happens to be waiting outside the locked gate and, not recognizing Jean, accepts money from him to open it. Javert is also there and arrests Jean but agrees to allow him to take Marius to his grandfather's house. While waiting for Jean to do this, however, Javert's exaggerated sense of duty wars with his gratitude to Jean for saving his life. He finally runs into the Seine river and drowns himself.

Marius and Cosette are later married. Jean confesses to them that he is not Cosette's father but an escaped convict who is thought to have drowned. He begs for the privilege of visiting Cosette occasionally, but Marius gradually puts an end to contact between the two. When he eventually learns from Thénardier that it was Jean who rescued him from the barricade, however, Marius and Cosette hurry to Jean's home. They find him on his deathbed, but he dies in the knowledge of their love and he bequeaths to Cosette the candlesticks given to him by the saintly bishop, of whose faith he has spent his life trying to be worthy. His humble grave is marked with a stone that bears no name.

Characters: Variously described as a novel of social concerns, a thrilling detective story, and a dramatic, poignant tale of the struggle between good and evil, *Les Misérables* has maintained its initial popularity and critical acclaim. Infused with the notion that humans are neither thoroughly wicked nor faultless and that redemption is always possible, the novel drew disapproval from early reviewers for suggesting that many social problems originate not so much in people but in society itself. Although modern critics continue to question Hugo's philosophical stance, most agree that *Les Misérables* is a great work that features compelling characters, a chronicling of important concerns and events of the nineteenth century, and an overall tone of deep humanity and compassion.

The central character of *Les Misérables* is **Jean Valjean,** who was initially jailed for stealing bread for his sister and her starving family. His prison term embitters and deforms him. The theft of the loaf of bread has generated varying interpretations from scholars: some see Jean purely as a victim of an unjust social system that punishes him for an altruistic act; others maintain that what he did was a crime and that he exacerbated his situation by his many escape attempts. The character of Jean Valjean is said to be based on an actual figure named Pierre Maurin whose own experiences occurred in 1795—the same year as Jean's theft—before French law was modified to provide for extenuating circumstances. Intelligent and resourceful, Jean also possesses prodigious physical strength, allowing him to save several lives and enabling Javert to identify him. That Jean's personality is warped by his prison experiences is evident when, after a brief inner conflict caused by the bishop's kindness to him, he steals the silver from the bishop and then takes several coins from a little boy. But then the seeds planted by the saintly bishop begin to bear fruit. Jean becomes a successful, productive, and well-liked community member; rescues Cosette from the wicked Thénardiers and lovingly raises her; saves the lives of Fauchelevent and Javert; and, finally, delivers Marius through the sewers of Paris to safety. The famous journey through the sewer tunnels is lauded for its drama and symbolism: descending on a mission of mercy is the test by which Jean ensures his redemption.

In saving Marius's life, Jean makes it possible for the young couple to marry, even though it means forfeiting the relationship he enjoyed with Cosette, an important link in his spiritual rebirth. Throughout his struggles, Jean is inspired by the bishop who treated him with Christian forbearance and love, when he was spurned by everyone else, and who encouraged him to improve his life. At his death, Jean has himself attained considerable moral stature. Critics note that the name Valjean evokes the French verb *valoir* (to be worth), suggesting that Jean must earn the worthiness that he ultimately achieves.

Charles François Bienvenu Myriel, the **Bishop of Digne,** represents the essential goodness that Hugo believed human beings possessed. No mere mouther of pieties, he applies the tenets of Christianity to his daily life, treating everyone with charity, forgiveness, and understanding. His saintly example and his faith in Jean's inherent virtue that inspires the former convict's journey toward redemption. Hugo is said to have been a religious man who disdained organized religion, and the bishop, despite his allegiance to the established church, represents Hugo's unconventional approach to spirituality. Like Hugo, he endorses free education for all citizens, opposes capital punishment, and believes that the human heart is eminently redeemable. When he visits a dying, elderly veteran of the 1793 insurrection, whose principals he had previously disagreed with, he ends by conceding the man's righteousness and asking for his blessing. Some critics feel this episode shows the bishop's instinct for recognizing good and his capacity for humbling himself, while others cite it as a prime example of his implausibly uniform virtue. Nevertheless the bishop is generally considered a credible character whose impact is felt far beyond the few early chapters in which he appears.

Inspector Javert is nearly as renowned a character as Jean Valjean, perhaps due to the dramatized versions of *Les Misérables,* which have tended to cast it as a detective story more than a morality tale. Javert serves as Jean's nemesis throughout the novel, continually threatening to expose his past and bring him under the control of the law. In his exaggerated, nearly fanatical devotion to duty and his lack of compassion, Javert represents a punitive, vengeful form of justice. Hugo suggest that Javert's "respect for authority and hatred of revolt" are rooted in his past, for he was born in a prison. As if to compensate for this fact, he has spent his life in faithful service to law enforcement. When Jean saves Javert by helping him escape from the revolutionaries, Javert's rigid system of behavior is upset, for he realizes that Jean, a criminal who has not yet been officially punished, has performed an act of great kindness and courage. Javert previously would have overlooked such an act and arrested the criminal, but this recognition proves more than he can bear. Unable to resolve his inner conflict, Javert drowns himself in the Seine.

The young lawyer **Marius Pontmercy,** who falls in love with and eventually marries Cosette, is an aristocrat by birth but has rejected his heritage and adopted a liberal, egalitarian view. He is estranged from his grandfather, a crusty old royalist, and lives in poverty in the seedy Gorbeau neighborhood. He is loyal to the memory of his dead father, however, who fought in the Battle of Waterloo and who commissioned him to help the man who saved his life during that conflict, Thénardier. Critics have seen in Marius a reflection of Victor Hugo as a young man, when he held similar enthusiasms and aspirations and also underwent a political conversion to liberalism. In addition Marius's romance with Cosette was apparently modeled after Hugo's with his wife, Adèle Foucher; scholars consider this portrait of naive, exuberant first love particularly convincing. A few critics have found Marius a rather annoying and inconsistent character—particularly in his initial self-righteous rejection of Jean, who, after all, raised Marius's young wife with loving care—but most are impressed with him.

Hugo's portrait of **Cosette** as a graceful, charming, innocent young girl is somewhat idealized and not particularly complex. Nevertheless the description of her lonely, harsh life with the Thénardiers—including her walk through dark, frightening woods to fetch water and her leaving out a wooden shoe for a Santa Claus who never appears—helps to win her the reader's pity and sympathy. Hugo is thought to have based the adult version of Cosette, who is appealing in her innocent, ardent love for Marius, on his own beloved wife, Adèle Foucher. Cosette's mother, **Fantine,** is a beautiful seamstress whose life is tragically altered when she bears an illegitimate child. Cosette's father, the carefree student **Felix Tholomyès,** escapes censure and responsibility, while Fantine is ostracized and feels she must turn her child over to the Thénardiers. Meanwhile, she becomes a prostitute to support herself and pay for Cosette's care. Scholars consider Fantine's circumstances rather conventional—the basically virtuous young woman whose seduction and abandonment lead to her debasement. Early reviewers were reluctant to accept Fantine as virtuous and deemed her immoral, but modern critics are more sympathetic of her plight.

Monsieur Thénardier is the unscrupulous, greedy innkeeper who serves as a cruel stepfather to Cosette in exchange for money from Fantine. He considers himself a free thinker and frequently quotes Voltaire (a highly influential and unorthodox French writer of the seventeenth century), but Thénardier is actually vulgar and narrow-minded, and he never suffers from moral anguish or mental conflict, as do such characters as Jean and Javert. Furthermore, Thénardier is portrayed as a natural criminal rather than one created by adverse social conditions; given a second chance to establish himself overseas, he becomes a slave trader. The ugly and ruthless **Madame Thénardier** is as unpleasant as her husband and contributes equally to the torment of little Cosette, but the Thénardier children differ significantly from their parents. **Eponine Thénardier** is good-hearted and ultimately self-sacrificing, for she gives her own life to save Marius. Portrayed as a victim of her environment and often identified as part of the "flower on a dunghill" tradition of virtuous young women spawned in dismal circumstances, Eponine's hopeless love for Marius makes her even more tragic. Another member of the Thénardier family is one of the most famous characters in *Les Misérables:* **Little Gavroche.** His life in the rough Gorbeau streets has stifled neither his essential goodness nor his high spirits; he is a clever, impudent, likable street urchin. Gavroche dies a heroic death at the barricade with the ardent young revolutionaries he has befriended.

Among the other characters in the novel is **Monsieur Gillenormand,** Marius's stern grandfather, who was described as "a salty, pigheaded, tyrannical old Royalist" by critic Elliott M. Grant. **Monsieur Maboef** is an elderly scholar and churchwarden who, despite his gentle nature and apolitical leanings, is driven by poverty to join the insurrection; he goes to the barricade unarmed to protest oppression, and there he dies. Also killed at the barricade is **Enjolras,** the most notable among the group of young revolutionaries who organize and carry out the insurrection. Enjolras is portrayed as an idealist who dies a noble death fighting to defend his beliefs; he and his friends illustrate the solidarity and enthusiasm that Hugo experienced during his own involvement with an insurrection in 1851. **Father Fauchelevent** was a notary before bankruptcy forced him to become a lowly carter; he is jealous of Jean/Father Madeleine until Jean saves his life, and later he is given an opportunity to help his rescuer when Jean and Cosette climb over the wall into the convent where he works. **Little Gervaise** is the boy Jean steals money from, an episode that signals an important stage in Jean's transformation: he weeps for the first time since leaving prison and then reforms his life.

Further Reading

Baudelaire, Charles. "'Les Misérables.'" 1862. Reprint. In *Baudelaire as a Literary Critic,* pp. 280-89, edited and translated by Lois Boe Hyslop and Francis E. Hyslop, Jr. University Park: Pennsylvania State University Press, 1964.

Bloom, Harold, ed. *Victor Hugo.* New York: Chelsea House, 1987.

Brombert, Victor. *Victor Hugo and the Visionary Novel.* Cambridge, Mass.: Harvard University Press, 1984.

Lewes, G.H. "Victor Hugo's Last Romance." *Blackwood's Magazine* XCII, No. DLXII (August 1862): 172-82.

Nash, Suzanne. "Writing a Building: Hugo's 'Notre Dame de Paris.'" *French Forum* 8, No. 2 (May 1983): 122-23.

Nineteenth-Century Literature Criticism, Vols. 3, 10, 21. Detroit: Gale.

Pritchett, V.S. "Hugo's Impersonations." In *The Living Novel and Later Appreciations,* pp. 353-59. New York: Random House, 1964.

Ward, Patricia. *The Medievalism of Victor Hugo.* University Park: Pennsylvania State University Press, 1975.

Wyldgen, Kathryn E. "Romance and Myth in 'Notre Dame de Paris.'" *French Review* XLIX, No. 3 (February 1976): 319-27.

Henrik Ibsen

1828-1906

Norwegian dramatist

A Doll's House (drama, 1879)

Plot: Set in nineteenth-century Norway, the play begins as Nora Helmer merrily finishes her preparations for Christmas. Her husband, Torvald, has recently been made manager of the bank in which he works, promising an improvement in the family's financial circumstances. Nora has even purchased her favorite treat, macaroons, despite her husband's disapproval of this indulgence. Torvald habitually calls his wife his "lark" or "squirrel," treating her as a frivolous and not particularly intelligent plaything, and Nora responds by acting in the gay, childish manner her husband seems to expect. This playful demeanor belies the depth in Nora's character, for seven years earlier she saved the life of her critically ill husband by secretly borrowing money to take him for a desperately needed rest in Italy. Knowing that Torvald was too proud to borrow money, she forged her dying father's name on the loan she received from Krogstad, Torvald's longtime friend and fellow bank worker. During the intervening years Nora somehow managed to make payments on her loan without her husband's knowledge, while Torvald—who believed the money for the trip had come from his father-in-law—referred to her as his "little spendthrift."

When Nora's old schoolfriend, Christina Linde, arrives in need of a job, Torvald gives her Krogstad's position. Krogstad had hoped to advance his own career through the new manager, but Torvald disapproves of his old friend because Krogstad was once involved in a forgery that he tried to cover up. Learning he is to be dismissed, Krogstad tells Nora that he knows she forged her father's name on the loan; he threatens to expose her and ruin her husband if he is fired. Nora tries unsuccessfully to persuade Torvald to reinstate Krogstad. After receiving his dismissal notice, Krogstad sends Torvald a letter disclosing the details of the forgery. That evening, with Krogstad's letter as yet unread in the mailbox, Nora diverts Torvald and their friend Dr. Rank by practicing the tarantella dance she is to perform at a ball the next night. Desperate, Nora appeals to Christina, whom Krogstad once loved. Christina agrees to try to dissuade Krogstad from carrying out his threat. Nora starts to confide her troubles to Dr. Rank as well, but stops when she perceives that he is in love with her. She manages to make Torvald promise to avoid the mailbox until after the ball.

Christina offers to marry Krogstad and care for his motherless children. Krogstad joyfully accepts her offer and promises to stop his actions against the Helmers. Christina, however, feels that Nora must eventually reveal the truth to her husband, and she instructs Krogstad to leave his letter in the Helmer's mailbox. After Nora and Torvald return from the ball, Torvald reads the letter. Nora assumed her husband would be overcome with grief and would take responsibility for what had happened; she planned to commit suicide. Instead, Torvald is enraged and calls Nora a criminal unfit to raise their children. He tells her that for appearance's sake she may remain in his house, but that he will no longer consider her his wife. When Krogstad's second letter—withdrawing the accusation and promising to take no further action—arrives, Torvald joyfully informs Nora that he is "saved." He resumes his former manner toward her, treating her like his cherished plaything. But Nora is profoundly disillusioned by her husband's hypocrisy and insensitivity. Aware of the inequality and lack of mutual respect in her marriage, Nora decides to leave her home to try to become fully realized rather than a mere reflection of her husband's wishes. Her departure is marked by the slamming of the door of her "doll's house."

Characters: Probably the most famous and acclaimed of Ibsen's works, *A Doll's House* exhibits the qualities that give the playwright his reputation as the father of modern drama. Instead of the artificial premises and plots of the "well-made" plays popular in the early nineteenth century, *A Doll's House* features the realistic setting, emphasis on social problems, and psychologically probing, analytical approach to characterization that made Ibsen an innovator. Some early reviewers condemned the play for endorsing divorce and child abandonment; while modern critics acknowledge the criticism of convention that *A Doll's House* represents, most contend that it promotes not women's rights per se but the self-realization that is vital to the happiness of both men and women.

Pretty, playful, outwardly frivolous **Nora Helmer** is a devoted wife and mother who behaves like the "lark" or "squirrel" her husband considers her. Raised by an indulgent, adoring father who treated her like a precious plaything, Nora simply moved from one doll's house to another when she married Torvald. Although Nora has apparently inherited some measure of her father's irresponsibility, she possesses an underlying seriousness and strength that is little suspected by her husband. Seven years before the action of the play, her love for Torvald prompted her to commit a forgery in order to provide the convalescence he desperately needed, and she has made secret and regular payments on her loan—an accomplishment of which she is quite proud. Nora also carries beneath her cajoling, gay demeanor a vague yearning for "the miracle," which most critics have identified as the ideal, mutually fulfilling love she has not yet achieved with her husband. Along with Krogstad's threat to expose the forgery comes the crisis in Nora's life, for she must finally face the criminality of her act and the possible ruin of her husband. Nora's appearance in costume and performance of the tarantella dance just before the crisis symbolize her final, desperate attempt to evade the truth; afterward she will be dressed in the sober street clothes that represent adult responsibility. Nora's illusions about herself and her husband are shattered when Torvald   displays his selfishness and shallowness; instead of taking the burden of her crime on his own shoulders, as she had expected, he condemns and rejects her. She sees that "the miracle" she has hoped for cannot occur—not, at least, until she achieves autonomy as a person and only if Torvald is also able to change. In an act of great determination and courage, a newly mature Nora walks out of her doll's house and slams its door behind her—a dramatic sound that resonates with thematic meaning—leaving, in the words of critic M. C. Bradbrook, "to embrace an unknown future—to carry the bright flame of her vitality into the dark." Many early reviewers disapproved of Nora abandoning her three children, though later scholars noted that this action, motivated by her conviction that she is unfit to be a mother, highlights her courage. While some critics continue to maintain that Nora's changing from a gay sprite to a serious adult is too rapid and that her departure seems implausible, others note that the seeds of such a transformation were present from the beginning. Proponents of women's rights have been eager to claim Nora as a feminist heroine for her rejection of the degraded position endured by nineteenth-century women, whose lives were severely restricted by both legal binds and social attitudes. Although Ibsen does seem sympathetic to the plight of women, most commentators agree that his primary intent was to explore the development of a fully realized personality and the value of an honest, mutually respectful marital relationship. That he chose a woman through whom to explore these themes evidences his daring as a playwright as well as his deep humanity.

Nora's banker husband, **Torvald Helmer,** is smug and insensitive, too preoccupied with his own concerns to see his charming, playful wife as anything more than an adornment to his household. He treats her condescendingly, imposing upon her a system of petty rules that circumscribe her behavior, and expects her to reflect at all times his own views. In marrying Nora, he has adopted the parental role formerly played by her father, and he alternately indulges and admonishes her. Torvald is often described as the play's representative of convention, for he has accepted unquestioningly the authoritarian role of the nineteenth-century husband. Critics suggest that while Ibsen may not have supported the emancipation of women in general, he does condemn the demeaning treatment they receive from men like Torvald. His extreme reaction to the news of Nora's forgery and Krogstad's plan to ruin him indicates the true shallowness of his feelings for his wife as well as his egotism: he sees the crisis as an affront to himself for which he blames Nora, never considering that she committed the forgery in order to save his life. Nora's decision to leave Torvald shocks and bewilders him, and he can only surmise that she must no longer love him. In fact she has loved not him but an ideal that is now destroyed. Although the long discussion the couple has just before Nora's departure, in which the unfair domination of husbands over wives is emphasized, has been described as somewhat implausible and didactic, it effectively presents Ibsen's belief in the necessity of honesty and mutual respect in marriage. Torvald is left alone in the wake of Nora's determination and idealism, and the question of his own redemption is left ambiguous.

The dissatisfied bookkeeper, **Nils Krogstad,** is Torvald's former schoolmate and longtime friend as well as his subordinate at the bank. At first he seems to be a conventionally sinister figure, an immoral schemer, in his threat to expose his knowledge of Nora's forgery and ruin her husband if she does not help him retain his position. His reconciliation with Christina Linde, however, redeems Krogstad. It is revealed that he was driven to blackmail by his desperate need to support his motherless children, and his noble qualities are further awakened by Christina's love and generosity. Krogstad plays a practical role in the plot by forcing Nora to confront reality. In addition Torvald expresses disgust for Krogstad because he once committed a forgery and cover-up, and states that Krogstad is not morally fit to raise his children, which leads to Nora's doubts of her own fitness as a mother. But Krogstad also serves as a foil to Torvald, whose apparent integrity is revealed to be illusory, just as Krogstad's integrity is established when he withdraws the threat. Krogstad accepts rather than rejects his partner's gift of love, and his relationship with Christina, based on honesty and respect, promises to be as mutually beneficial as the Helmers' is false.

Just as Krogstad serves as a foil to Torvald, **Christina Linde** provides a strong contrast to Nora. Whereas her old schoolfriend is pretty and gay, Christina has a worn appearance and a dull, joyless demeanor caused by the unhappy circumstances of her life. Once in love with Krogstad, she married another, richer man in order to help her demanding family. Now widowed and alone, she is emotionally embittered and financially destitute. She is much more practical and morally diligent than Nora and, convinced that her friend's deception of her husband is wrong, she advises Krogstad to leave his threatening letter in the Helmers' mailbox even after he has decided not to prosecute them. Thus, in what some critics have termed a rather heavy-handed and schoolmarmish way, she forces the action of the play. While Nora looks within herself for fulfillment, Christina reaches out from her loneliness to make contact with Krogstad. Each enters into the union aware of the hardships they may face, and Christina gladly accepts the burden of caring for him and his children. This helps to illustrate the uncertainty and possibly dismal solitude of Nora's position at the end of the play.

Like Krogstad, **Dr. Rank** is a longtime friend of Torvald. He is afflicted with a degenerative spinal disease that he inherited from his syphilitic father; thus he bears a strong resemblance to the character of Oswald Alving in Ibsen's later play, *Ghosts,* and highlights the playwright's interest in the past's impingement on the present—the concept that the sins of the fathers are visited upon the sons. In keeping with his egotistical nature, Torvald is repulsed by the aura of death that Rank seems to carry with him, and consequently their relationship is strained. Rank's sad fate is compounded by his hopeless love for Nora, who, slipping into flirtatious mode, unconsciously torments him by showing him her silk stockings and dancing a seductive tarantella before him. Some critics have seen the doctor as reflecting Nora's predicament, for she too has inherited a negative quality from her father—irresponsibility—and she too faces death when she decides to commit suicide in order to spare Torvald humiliation. Yet Rank's response to the closeness of death is to become embittered and hardened toward others, while Nora's character is ennobled by her willingness to sacrifice her life for another.

Ghosts (drama, 1881)

Plot: The play, which takes place in the Norwegian town of Rosenvold, begins on the tenth anniversary of the death of Mrs. Helen Alving's husband, Captain Alving. Pastor Manders visits Mrs. Alving to discuss the dedication of the orphanage that she founded as a memorial to her dead husband. Mrs. Alving joyfully awaits the arrival of her son, Oswald, a twenty-six-year-old artist who has been living in Paris since he was a young boy and who intends to spend several months with his mother. Oswald has always idealized his father and is unaware that Captain Alving was a philandering drunk. Mrs. Alving once ran away from her husband, in fact, but this scandalized Manders, who had been her girlhood lover, and he persuaded her to return. She endured a long, unhappy marriage. After Oswald's arrival Manders tells Mrs. Alving he does not approve of the young man's bohemian manners and habits. He also reminds her of that time long ago when he provided her with moral guidance. Mrs. Alving decides she must now tell Manders the truth about her husband: after her return to him she discovered not only that he was having an affair with one of their housemaids but that he was afflicted with a venereal disease. Mrs. Alving has not yet had the courage to inform Oswald that he is also infected with this malady.

Mrs. Alving will not be able to avoid the consequences of the past for long, however, for she overhears a flirtatious conversation between her son and Regina, the maid. Although Regina is supposedly the daughter of the dissolute carpenter Jacob Engstrand, she is actually the offspring of Captain Alving's affair with Regina's mother, the maid Johanna. After the death of Johanna, Regina came to live and work in the Alving household. Her father plans to establish a home for seamen—actually a brothel—and tries to entice Regina to join him in the venture. But Regina finds this prospect dreary and instead hopes to fulfill her desire for wealth and status through marriage to Oswald. Oswald too would like to marry Regina. He confides to his mother that he has seen a doctor about the overwhelming fatigue that has stifled his desire to work. He has discovered the nature of his disease, but he blames himself for contracting it and vows to make the most of his remaining life by marrying Regina. Before Mrs. Alving can tell the young people that Captain Alving is the father of both, news arrives that the orphanage is burning. At Manders's recommendation, Mrs. Alving had no insurance on the building, because he felt wealthy benefactors would interpret such an act as a lack of faith in God; thus the orphanage is a total loss. Engstrand insinuates that Manders, who was in the carpentry shop attached to the orphanage with him just before the fire, started the blaze with a dropped candle wick; in fact it was probably Engstrand who caused the fire. Nevertheless Manders fears the damage to his reputation that such an accusation would bring, so he agrees to let Engstrand take the blame for the fire in exchange for money.

Mrs. Alving finally tells Oswald and Regina the truth about their father. Resentful that she has lived as a servant when she ought to have been raised as a daughter and a lady, Regina leaves with Engstrand to help him with his seamen's establishment. Oswald informs his mother that his disease has already begun to affect his mind and will eventually render him completely helpless. Although Mrs. Alving promises to care for her son throughout his trauma, she is not certain she can fulfil his request to give him poison when the time comes. The play ends with Mrs. Alving extinguishing a light and Oswald, in a pronounced childlike state, calling for the sun.

Characters: Innovative in its focus on middle-class characters and distinguished by its exposure of social hypocrisy, *Ghosts* is one of the most renowned works of Ibsen's ''middle period,'' during which his plays were characterized by their realism. *Ghosts* was condemned by early critics for its frank portrayal of venereal disease and cohabitation and for its attack on conventional morality. Often compared to the Greek tragedies in which protagonists are brought down by fate, the play shows how the past may destroy the present, whether through mistaken choices that come back to haunt or through hereditary weakness passed along from generation to generation. Considered the instigator of modern drama, Ibsen broke new ground with his unflinching exploration of human experience and his call for a more humane morality.

Mrs. Helen Alving is often identified as an older version of Nora Helmer from Ibsen's earlier play, *A Doll's House,* which also focused on a woman confined in an unequal, unfulfilling marriage. Many years before the action of this play, Mrs. Alving faced a moral crisis when she discovered her husband's infidelity and considered leaving him. Acquiescing to society's demand for propriety, she accepted her "duty" and remained with her husband, a course of action encouraged by the cowardly, conventional Pastor Manders, whose love she had previously rejected in favor of the more wealthy Captain Alving. Mrs. Alving had endured an outwardly serene but dreadfully unhappy marriage, endeavoring to hide the fact of her husband's philanderings. The community believed **Captain Alving** to be a morally upright man, and Oswald Alving idolizes his dead father. As the play opens Mrs. Alving happily awaits her son's arrival. She believes that she has successfully evaded the claims of the past. That confidence is shattered, however, when she overhears Oswald's flirtation with Regina, the young man's half-sister. Mrs. Alving now realizes that she cannot escape the tragic consequences of what happened long ago. Though she has hidden her information about her son's hereditary disease from him, Oswald informs her that he has discovered his condition. Although Mrs. Alving may be condemned for her lack of courage or for selfishly keeping her son dependent on her by hiding the truth of his past, she is a tragic figure whose weaknesses are recognizably human. In the end Oswald reverts to a childlike state and, ironically, she may choose to reverse her role as a life-giver by aiding her son's suicide. Whether she complies with his request is left for the audience to surmise— a final ambiguity that is often identified as typical in Ibsen's work.

Oswald Alving shares with his father, of whose true profligacy he is initially unaware, an exuberant love of life. A free-spirited artist, he belonged to a Bohemian circle in Paris for several years and advocates unconventional practices, such as cohabitation. (Ibsen's casual reference to the controversial concept of unmarried couples living together was part of what prompted early reviewers to condemn the play.) The rigidly moralistic Manders disapproves of Oswald's radical opinions and behavior, and in turn the young man points out the hypocrisy of many of those who present themselves as respectable. Oswald's enthusiasm for painting has declined due to his increasing fatigue, a symptom that led to his discovery that he suffers from a syphilitic disease. Like other significant characters in Ibsen's works, Oswald pays a high price for his father's sins, though he initially assumes that he himself is responsible for having contracted the ailment. His hereditary disease is the play's strongest "ghost" of the past haunting the present and destroying the future. Some critics note in the predicament of Oswald and other Ibsen characters the influence of Charles Darwin's revolutionary work on evolution, which led many nineteenth-century thinkers to adopt a deterministic view (that lives are directed by heredity rather than by free will). Despite Oswald's determination to live as fully and happily as possible, his future is hopeless: his marriage to the beautiful, vital Regina is impossible because the two are half-siblings, and his illness ultimately deteriorates his mind and personality. He is left in a childlike state, pleading for the "sun" and depending on his mother for release from his suffering.

The play's primary representative of conventional society, **Pastor Manders,** is condemned for his hypocrisy. He was Mrs. Alving's girlhood lover but, on the advice of her domineering aunt, she rejected him for the wealthier Captain Alving. Unhappy in her marriage, Mrs. Alving fled to Manders; though he might then have achieved a happy union with his former sweetheart, he advised her instead to remember her duty and return to her husband. Though he seems to be morally upright, Manders is motivated not by a desire to do what is right but by a fear of disapproval; his exaggerated allegiance to duty masks his inner shallowness. For instance, he advises Mrs. Alving not to take out insurance on the orphanage not because he truly feels this would indicate a lack of faith in God, but because he fears the project's supporters would perceive it as such. He believes the orphanage's benefactors are interested not in the good the institution might do but in the financial benefits they can derive from it. Manders further demonstrates his lack of moral strength by capitulating to Engstrand's blackmailing scheme, preferring to pay off the dishonest carpenter than face being ostracized from his community should he be accused of setting the orphanage on fire.

Jacob Engstrand is the disreputable, greedy, usually drunken carpenter paid to marry the maid Johanna after she became pregnant with Captain Alving's child. Utterly unscrupulous—he is capable not only of blackmail but of engaging his adopted daughter in prostitution—he provides a contrast with Manders in his conscious, deliberate immorality. He might also be compared to Mrs. Alving in his attempt to gain control over his daughter, though his desire to manipulate Regina is motivated by greed. Although it is suggested that Engstrand's crippled condition has somehow resulted in his corruption, the audience is not encouraged to feel sympathy for him. **Regina Engstrand** is a beautiful, spirited girl with the same lust for living found in her half-brother and true father. Ambitious to improve her circumstances, she sees marriage to Oswald as a means to escape from her dismal life, a more attractive alternative than joining her father in establishing a seamen's home. When she learns the truth of her parentage, she reacts with anger and rejects Mrs. Alving, who has always treated her kindly, because she has not been raised in a manner proper to her heritage. Neither is she capable of the selfless love that the ailing Oswald now requires, and she decides to join Engstrand in his venture. Since the seamen's home will actually be a brothel and Regina will become a prostitute, she experiences in the end an obliteration of personality similar to her brother's, becoming another victim of the "ghosts" of the past.

An Enemy of the People (drama, 1883)

Plot: A small Norwegian coastal town has become prosperous through its underground springs, drawing visitors who seek the benefits of the healing waters. The vigorous, rather impetuous Dr. Thomas Stockmann is the chief medical officer in charge of the baths. Acting on his own suspicions, he has the local university investigate whether the baths have been contaminated by pollution from nearby tanneries. The university confirms the contamination—some visitors have already become ill after using the baths—and Stockmann realizes that the pipes leading into the baths will have to be replaced. Two liberal journalists, Hovstad and Billing, are eager to publish Stockmann's findings to expose inefficient local government officials. Despite his reactionary tendencies and conservatism, the printer, Aslaksen, also supports Stockmann's desire to purify the baths. Stockmann sends a copy of his report to Peter, his brother and the town's mayor, so the government may take official action. But Peter declines to act on the report and even asks his brother to suppress the information; he claims that neither the owners of the baths nor the townspeople will be willing to bear the great expense of the repairs. He wants the doctor to issue another report denying the facts revealed in the first one. Stockmann refuses, even when the mayor threatens to fire him. His wife begs him to reconsider his position, while his daughter, Petra, urges him to remain steadfast. Hovstad, Billing, and Aslaksen initially intend to publicize Stockmann's report, but after Peter informs them of the repair costs the town will have to absorb—in addition to closing the baths for two years—they change their position. Learning of this reversal, Stockmann pleads with the journalists and printer to stand by him, but they claim they must support majority opinion, and they refuse to print the article.

Stockmann's loyal friend Captain Horster offers his home as a meeting place for a discussion about the contaminated baths. The attendees are already opposed to Stockmann's plans due to the efforts of the the journalists and the mayor. Aslaksen chairs the meeting, ruling that the baths will not be discussed. Stockmann, however, insists on speaking. He delivers an impassioned speech on the corruption and immorality of the local officials, the stupidity and blindness of majority rule, and the righteousness of the idealistic minority voice. But the crowd is unresponsive, concerned only about the cost of purifying the baths. Stockmann is subsequently ostracized by the community, and both he and Petra, a schoolteacher, lose their jobs. Although she initially urged her husband to be more moderate, Mrs. Stockmann now vows to stand by him. The family's plan to move to America is thwarted when Captain Horster's loyalty to Stockmann costs him his ship. Stockmann learns that his father-in-law, Morten Kiil, has used the money that would have gone to his daughter and grandchildren to buy most of the stock in the baths, now tremendously reduced in price. He accuses Stockmann of disregarding his wife's inheritance in favor of his own crusade, while the townsfolk think Stockmann has discredited the baths only so his own family may profit by buying the stock at a low price. Beset by adversity, Stockmann refuses to give in to his detractors. He plans to establish a school for poor street children and feels he has triumphed in his solitary courage over the ignorance of public opinion.

Characters: *An Enemy of the People,* which strongly condemns social hypocrisy and highlights the ignorance of majority rule, was conceived as a response to the negative reaction to Ibsen's previous plays, *A Doll's House* and *Ghosts.* The pollution that threatens the safety of the town's residents and visitors symbolizes the destructive forces of blind convention that Ibsen, in many of his plays, labored to expose. Usually categorized as the most polemical of the playwright's works, this drama presents a favorable view of idealism and promotes the necessity of taking a moral stance in spite of possible costs.

Dr. Thomas Stockmann is the dedicated, idealistic physician who finds himself isolated and ostracized for wanting to close the baths for repairs. Born into an impoverished family, Stockmann raised himself to his current prominence through his intelligence and energy— as did his highly successful but more conservative brother. It was Dr. Stockmann who first discovered the underground springs that brought the town prosperity, and, ironically, who may bring about its financial downfall. Although Ibsen's portrayal of Stockmann is generally positive, some critics have noted that he is impetuous, impractical, extravagant, and single-minded, allowing for no compromise or mediation. Yet Stockmann's willingness to stand alone against popular opinion makes him admirable. He contrasts strongly with Gregers Werle, a destructively idealistic character in Ibsen's *The Wild Duck* (1884) whose dedication to exposing the truth destroys a family's happiness. Stockmann has been identified as a mouthpiece for Ibsen, who was stridently rebuked for writing about inequality in marriage, infidelity, and venereal disease. Stockmann's impassioned speech condemning the blindness of majority rule and claiming that the most brilliant ideas are always espoused by a minority voice has been seen as a cogent statement of Ibsen's ideals and also as unconvincingly extravagant and willful. Although Stockmann interests some scholars as a positively portrayed idealist, others claim that he is a somewhat weak character who lacks the duality of Ibsen's more compelling protagonists.

The doctor's brother, **Peter Stockmann,** is the town's most powerful official; as mayor he represents the forces of convention against which Dr. Stockmann must struggle. Although he has been informed of the pollution of the baths and the danger of allowing it to remain unchecked, the mayor is concerned only with the cost of the repairs and the public's inevitably negative reaction. He contrasts with his brother not only in his ideas but in his temperament, for he is as rigid, dyspeptic, and conventional as Dr. Stockmann is impetuous, vital, and idealistic. Yet each is equally single-minded and rigid.

At the beginning of the play the journalist **Hovstad** is honest and progressive, dedicated to exposing the hypocrisy and corruption of the town's officials. He lacks the moral courage that Stockmann possesses, however, when he succumbs to public opinion and changes his position on the clean-up of the baths. Because his own material livelihood depends on the good will of his readers, he chooses to align himself with the majority despite his knowledge that Stockmann's position is true. Hovstad's subordinate, **Billings,** also supports Dr. Stockmann at first, but abandons his so-called revolutionary beliefs in favor of self-interest. The printer, **Aslaksen,** is similar in temperament to the reactionary Peter Stockmann, and he initially favors repairing the baths, because he assumes the majority of the townspeople will support such an effort. Active in the temperance movement and an advocate of moderation, Aslaksen finds Dr. Stockmann excessively emotional and extravagant and ultimately turns against him. **Morton Kiil,** Dr. Stockmann's father-in-law, is a wealthy, influential tanner who allows his financial concerns to overshadow his feelings for his daughter and grandchildren, when he uses their inheritance to buy stock in the baths. Yet he hypocritically blames Stockmann for ignoring his family's best interests.

Though she fears what will happen as a result of her husband's radical stand, the loyal (if somewhat weak) **Mrs. Stockmann** eventually supports her husband in his unpopular and isolating position. It is worth noting that the Stockmanns' marriage is one of several in Ibsen's work that are based on mutual respect and support and which contrast with the unequal, destructive unions presented in, for instance, *A Doll's House* and *Ghosts*. **Petra Stockmann,** the doctor's teacher daughter, shares her father's ideals and urges him from the start to hold fast to his beliefs; eventually she also shares his fate when she loses her own job. **Captain Horster** also remains loyal to his friend and proves himself willing to pay a high cost for his ideals when his ship is taken away from him because of his relationship with Stockmann.

The Wild Duck (drama, 1884)

Plot: Gregers Werle is the son of a wealthy, unscrupulous manufacturer. Several years before the action of the play and soon after the death of his mother, Gregers left his father's home in disgust. He knew of Old Werle's affairs with other women and also that Werle's former business partner, Ekdal, had gone to prison for a crime for which Old Werle was probably responsible. Gregers has now returned to his father's home. He invites his old school friend, Hjalmar Ekdal, to a dinner party; Hjalmar is the son of Old Ekdal, who has by now returned from prison in a state of mental and physical deterioration. Apparently out of guilt, Old Werle established Hjalmar in a photography business and also convinced him to marry Gina Hansen, Werle's maid and—though unknown to Hjalmar—his former mistress. Gregers's idealism and awareness of this history leads him to resolve to open Hjalmar's eyes to the truth.

Hjalmar has been living a shabby but contented life with Gina and their fourteen-year-old daughter, Hedvig, whom he adores. Gina takes good care of the family and also runs the photography business while Hjalmar works on an invention he hopes will win back his father's lost wealth. Old Ekdal, who is almost completely insane, keeps a variety of small animals in the attic and spends his time "hunting" there. Visiting the Ekdals, Gregers is shocked by their self-deception and illusions. When he sees Hedvig's favorite possession, a wild duck that had been wounded but now lives in the attic "forest," Gregers decides to take action. He rents a room in the Ekdal house, despite the disapproval of Gina and of their other boarder, the cynical and distrusting Dr. Relling, who feels that Gregers's meddling can come to no good. Gregers learns that his father is the family's primary means of financial support, not their photography business; he also surmises that Hedvig, whose eyesight is failing, is probably the daughter not of Hjalmar but of Werle, who also has weak eyes. He decides to inform Hjalmar that his existence has been completely manipulated by Werle, including his marriage to Werle's former mistress. Hjalmar is mildly upset by this disclosure but takes no more drastic step than vowing to pay Werle back out of the anticipated proceeds from his invention. When he learns, however, that Werle wants to start sending Hedvig money regularly, Hjalmar realizes that she is really not his daughter, and his reaction is extreme. He declares he wants nothing more to do with Hedvig. The girl is confused and grieved by this turn of events. Gregers tells her that she can win back her father's love by sacrificing what is most important to her, the wild duck. He suggests that she have her grandfather shoot the duck. Soon a shot is heard from the attic; Gina and Hjalmar assume that Old Ekdal is hunting again but finally learn that Hedvig has killed herself.

Characters: *The Wild Duck* ushered in the final period of Ibsen's career, during which he concentrated more on symbolism and incisive characterization than on the social realism found in his previous plays. The injured creature for which *The Wild Duck* is named is one of the most renowned and frequently interpreted symbols in literature. In recounting the disillusionment and eventual tragedy of the self-deceiving Ekdal family, Ibsen employs both psychological insight and deep compassion to evoke such themes as the influence of the past on the present, the struggle toward self-realization, and, most importantly, the human need for illusions. Often termed a tragicomedy for its skillful blend of the horrible with the ridiculous, *The Wild Duck* is infused with the irony typical of Greek drama.

Hjalmar Ekdal has a fairly happy, contented life with his wife and daughter. Ostensibly he runs a photographic business, but his wife actually does all of the work while also diligently caring for the family. Hjalmar spends his time "hunting" in the attic with his father or working on the invention that he hopes will restore their lost wealth. The vaguely conceived invention, however, is doomed never to be completed and merely reflects Hjalmar's tendency to delude himself. Although he considers himself superior to those around him, he is lazy, self-indulgent, sentimental, vain, and thoughtless—forgetting, for instance, to bring home favors from the banquet for Hedvig and instead sharing with her only the menu listing the delicacies he had eaten there. Nevertheless Hjalmar's weaknesses are notably human, and some of his egotism and lack of drive may be attributed to his upbringing by two indulgent aunts who convinced him that he was brilliant. He has subsequently failed to realize himself as a person, but he nevertheless enjoys a coddled, comfortable existence and, to his credit, is generally gentle and trusting, particularly with his adoring daughter. Critics have noted that the humor that gives the play its tragicomic reputation is found partly in Ibsen's portrayal of Hjalmar's pretentious, ridiculous posturing before his family. The rather humorless Gregers Werle, for his part, accepts the premise that Hjalmar is noble and gifted. He decides that his friend is like the wild duck, wounded and trapped by deceit, and that knowing the truth about his wife and child will free him. Hjalmar's actual response is less ideal, of course: he melodramatically bemoans his position and makes a theatrical repudiation of Hedvig that she interprets literally; despite his vow to leave his home forever, he makes no effort to do so. The revelation forced upon him by Gregers not only does not help him to achieve personal wholeness but wrecks the measure of happiness he has achieved—temporarily, anyway. For, as Dr. Relling notes, Hjalmar's typically dramatic reaction to Hedvig's death masks the shallowness that will allow him to recover quickly, and soon enough his life will continue much as it was before Greger's interference.

Gregers Werle is the disillusioned idealist whose meddling results in the tragedy of Hedvig's death. His childhood was made unhappy by the constant discord between his parents and their apparent lack of concern for him; his rather morbid, joyless mother instilled in him a strong disgust for his father that has not since abated. Having always lived a lonely, emotionally deprived existence himself, he does not perceive that Hjalmar is fairly contented. Likening himself to the determined hunting dog that once pulled the wounded wild duck from the muck at the bottom of a pond, he decides to enlighten his friend to the truth so that Hjalmar may begin a better, more fully realized existence. Yet his effort to eliminate Hjalmar's illusions has disastrous consequences. His suggestion that Hedvig sacrifice the possession most important to her, the wild duck, in order to win back her father's love forces the girl to confront an impossible dilemma and to choose a tragic solution. Some critics have seen in Gregers's idealistic fervor evidence of a craving for melodrama that will relieve the dullness of his own life and compensate for his own lack of depth; there is also a certain amount of egotism in his readiness to play the role of truth-revealer. Gregers has often been interpreted as a satirical portrait of the role that Ibsen himself had assumed in writing such illusion-destroying plays as *Ghosts* and *An Enemy of the People*. In fact the favorably depicted idealist Dr. Stockmann in *Enemy* is the reversal of Gregers, and some scholars contend that Ibsen meant in *The Wild Duck* to repudiate the kind of extreme idealism he had previously affirmed. Other appraisals of Gregers cast him as well-meaning but misguided in attributing more depth to Hjalmar than he possessess, or as an outright fanatic who needlessly causes the death of a young girl.

Hjalmar's calm, hardworking wife, **Gina Ekdal,** is one of the play's few admirable characters. A simple woman born into a lower social class than her husband, she performs her role as wife and mother with energy and efficiency while also competently running her husband's photographic business. Honest and accepting of life's realities herself, she endures Hjalmar's self-indulgence, delusions, and unconcealed annoyance with her ungrammatical speech and frequent malapropisms. As she explains when Hjalmar demands to know why she never revealed to him her affair with Werle, Gina sincerely loves her husband—a significant achievement given his many faults. In her selfless devotion to making his (and Hedvig's) life more comfortable, Gina has become much more than the "fallen woman" she might have been called when she, after being Werle's mistress and pregnant with his child, married Hjalmar. Although Gregers believes that Hjalmar needs to be rescued from deceit, he has in one way already been rescued by Gina, who has provided a comfortable home life to replace his formerly dissolute, pointless existence. Unlike her husband, Gina reacts to her daughter's death with quiet dignity and determination to carry on.

Fourteen-year-old **Hedvig Ekdal** is a sensitive, somewhat dreamy, shy girl with a winsome charm. Relling calls attention to her distinction from the other characters in the play by commenting that she is "outside of all this." While Hedvig's father and grandfather use the attic to escape reality, she goes there to broaden her experience, exploring the books and keepsakes left by the sea captain who once inhabited the house. An affectionate girl whose fading eyesight not only makes it likely that she is Werle's daughter but adds pathos to her character, she loves her father deeply and believes in his grandiose plans for his invention. Hedvig compares herself to the wounded duck she so loves: like him, she is wounded and lives a confined but contented existence. Also implicit in her identification with the bird is the fact that the origin of neither is clearly established. In the end it is Hedvig's sensitivity that brings about her destruction, for she has identified so strongly with the wild duck that she puts herself in his place and takes her own life rather than his. Her death highlights the narrowness and indifference of the adults around her, who were unable to protect her from harm and even hastened her suicide with their thoughtlessness.

Dr. Relling is the cynical physician who boards in the Ekdal's household. Affecting a cold, dispassionate attitude that masks his inner sense of wasted potential, Relling scorns Gregers's "claims of the ideal." In asserting that human beings require illusions in order to live happily, he voices a viewpoint that many critics believe Ibsen means to affirm in *The Wild Duck,* and one which strongly contrasts with the idealistic revelation of truth promoted by Gregers. Some commentators have even identified Relling as representing Ibsen himself because, like a playwright who creates dramas to entertain audiences, he fosters illusions that bring a measure of comfort to otherwise bleak lives. For instance, Relling rationalizes the tippling of the theology student **Molvik** by claiming that he drinks not because he is an alcoholic but because his "demonic" nature demands it. Relling serves as a general commentator on the other characters' behavior, providing such psychological insights as the observation that Hjalmar will soon recover from the shock of Hedvig's death.

Hjalmar's father, **Old Ekdal,** was once Old Werle's business partner. He was arrested and jailed for illegally cutting timber on state-owned land while Werle—presumably unjustly—escaped prosecution. Having barely survived his debilitating prison term, he is now prone to senile muttering and spends his time either drinking in his room or shooting rabbits and pigeons in the makeshift forest Hjalmar has created in the attic. A former bear-hunter and military officer, Old Ekdal parodies his past through his ludicrous hunting expeditions and his occasional appearances before the family in his old uniform. Like the wild duck, he has been mutilated by existence and is now in retreat from reality, yet he seems content with his deluded life. Gregers compares the old man to the duck in another way: neither was able to adapt to adversity, for the old man became senile, and the duck, immediately after it was shot, behaved self-destructively by trying to attach itself to the bottom of the pond.

Haakon Werle, Gregers's father, is apparently the originator of much of the unhappiness portrayed in *The Wild Duck,* though some critics claim that the charges against him are never clearly substantiated. Formerly Old Ekdal's business partner, he was not prosecuted in the court case that resulted in his friend's imprisonment, and he has since tried to help the Ekdals. He arranged for Hjalmar to establish a business and encouraged him to marry Gina, who was actually his spurned, pregnant mistress at the time, and has continously subsidized their income. Near the end of the play, Werle offers to send money regularly to Hedvig; it is Hjalmar's discovery of this intention, in addition to the fact that both Hedvig and Old Werle have weak eyesight, that confirms for him his daughter's true parentage. As a result of his mother's influence, Gregers sees his father as a complete villain who is responsible for the Ekdal's deluded—and therefore diminished—existence, but in fact Old Werle's machinations have resulted in their relative contentment. Thus, though he may have acquired his current wealth and status by dishonest means, he is a more complex character than his son believes him. Old Werle's housekeeper, **Mrs. Sörby,** to whom he becomes engaged, is a protective, efficent woman with a somewhat disreputable past. She and Werle, however, have been completely honest with each other and this, added to the mutual comfort they take in their relationship, makes it likely that their marriage will be successful. It has been noted that theirs is one of several unions in Ibsen's work whose happiness may be attributed to honesty and forthrightness between partners.

Hedda Gabler (drama, 1890)

Plot: The play begins with the return of Hedda Gabler Tesman and her husband, George Tesman, from their six-month honeymoon. Hedda is the beautiful twenty-nine-year-old daughter of wealthy General Gabler. Her decision to marry Tesman, a dull but promising young scholar, surprised her friends, for she is a vibrant and popular woman who was pursued by several suitors. She chose Tesman for his wealth and social status, but the marriage has disappointed her. Her husband spent most of their honeymoon visiting libraries and gathering material for his studies. Hedda's boredom continues after they return to the expensive villa that George acquired with the help of his Aunt Juliana, who raised him after his parents' deaths. Aunt Juliana unintentionally torments Hedda by noticing and commenting that she is pregnant, a condition that Hedda does not want to face. Hedda finds her only amusement in playing with a set of pistols that her father left her.

George expects to be granted a university professorship, but he learns that he has a rival for the position: Eilert Lovberg, who recently published a much-respected book in George's field of study. Hedda once loved the brilliant Eilert, but she grew tired of his drinking and carousing and spurned him. George learns that Eilert, having reformed his dissolute behavior with the help and encouragement of his employer's wife, Thea Elvsted, has written another important book that is still in manuscript form. The pretty, mild Thea was once Hedda's schoolmate as well as George's sweetheart. Thea and Eilert visit the Tesmans' home one evening, bringing with them Eilert's as-yet-unpublished manuscript, and Hedda is inflamed with jealousy and resentment of Thea because of her positive influence over Eilert. The situation raises a destructive ire in Hedda. She convinces Eilert to attend a bachelor party with her husband and their friend Judge Brack, despite Eilert's inclination to stay behind with Hedda and Thea. The party is rife with debauchery, and Eilert loses control, drinking heavily and ending the evening in the brothel of the notorious Mademoiselle Diana. He returns to the Tesmans' villa without his manuscript, telling Thea that he intentionally destroyed his book but confessing to Hedda that he has lost the manuscript and intends to commit suicide. Concealing from Eilert that she has the lost manuscript, she suggests that he kill himself "beautifully" by using one of her father's pistols. After he leaves, Hedda puts his manuscript into the fire. George is shocked to learn that his wife has burned Eilert's book, but she convinces him that she did so out of love and concern for her husband's career. Meanwhile Eilert returns to Mademoiselle Diana's establishment and is killed not beautifully but ignominiously, in a fight. The ruthless Judge Brack, who has developed a passion for Hedda, tries to blackmail her by informing her that he knows the pistol that killed Eilert belonged to Hedda; he subtly threatens to create a scandal unless she becomes his mistress. Then George resolves to reconstruct Eilert's book from his notes, with help from the devoted Thea. Unable to face either a public scandal or to capitulate to the judge's desire, Hedda uses her father's remaining pistol to kill herself.

Characters: With its emphasis on a particular, distinctive, and complex character rather than on the broad social issues explicated in the plays of Ibsen's middle period, *Hedda Gabler* typifies the third and final stage of Ibsen's career. Innovative for revealing, early in the play, events that occurred in the past, and distinguished by polished, nearly poetic dialogue, the play explores the problem of identity and the contradictory forces that may exist within a single personality.

Hedda Gabler is one of Ibsen's most complex and intriguing characters, and critics praised the psychological penetration he brought to her portrayal. Beautiful, intelligent, and vibrant, the young Hedda was indulged by her father and admired by her friends and suitors, including the brilliant but profligate scholar Eilert Lovberg. Although fascinated by Eilert, Hedda judged him unsuitable as a marriage partner, and she turned him away. Raised in an aristocratic setting, she cherished social status and craved luxury—or perhaps, at twenty-nine, she saw no better option than marrying the dependable but stodgy George Tesman. Hedda quickly learned that George's involvement with his work overshadowed all other concerns, and she soon grew bored, frustrated, and melancholy. As the play opens, the couple returns from a six-month honeymoon to the sumptuous, overly expensive home that George has purchased in order to please his wife. Despite her luxurious surroundings, however, Hedda feels stifled and unhappy, finding pleasure only in playing with the elegant guns given to her by her late father. The arrival of Eilert and Thea sets off a destructive reaction in Hedda. Having realized that her marriage was a mistake, she regards the supportive, productive relationship between Thea and Eilert with jealousy and resentment, so Hedda convinces Eilert to attend Judge Brack's party, conceals and then destroys his lost manuscript, and encourages him to kill himself. She seems to view suicide as a romantic ideal, a dramatic escape from life's tedium, and she suggests that he make a "beautiful" death by using one of her father's guns. Hedda's own suicide—brought on by her husband's new partnership with Thea, Judge Brack's threat, her dreaded pregnancy, and her general misery and disillusionment—is accomplished in the manner she idealizes, with one of her cherished guns. Critics are divided in their response to Hedda's suicide, according to their general view of her character: some feel it is the act of a selfish woman, others contend that it reflects her deep-seated insecurity and lack of a substantial inner life, and still others find it a heroic deed that frees her from the domination of her patriarchal society. Nineteenth-century reviewers responded to Hedda with confusion and dislike, and felt she possessed no positive qualities. Modern critics, however, praise Ibsen for his compelling depiction of a personality with motivations rooted in a complex psyche. Feminist scholars have been particularly interested in Hedda, noting that she is ill-suited to the conventional social role expected of nineteenth-century women.

Hedda's husband, **George Tesman,** is a basically decent but dull, plodding scholar who is an inappropriate partner for his bright, lively wife. Prosaic and utterly devoted to his studies, he is prone to annoying expostulations like "Hmmmm. . .?" and "Eh. . .?" He is a stereotypical absent-minded professor, preoccupied with his discipline, ancient history, and detached from those around him. Although he assumes his role as Hedda's husband in a socially appropriate manner, he is incapable of truly loving her or participating in a mutually satisfactory marriage. Like Hjalmar Ekdal in Ibsen's earlier play *The Wild Duck,* George was raised by two indulgent aunts, and their coddling has apparently resulted in his lack of a strong will. Pedantic and essentially uncreative, he is satisfied at the close of the play to immerse himself in restoring Eilert's work.

Once romantically involved with Hedda, **Eilert Lovberg** is a brilliant young scholar whose propensity for drink and carousing rendered him too difficult a challenge for her. He became a tutor in the Elvsteds' isolated household and thus came under the stabilizing influence of Thea Elvsted, his employer's wife. With her support Eilert has given up drinking and published a much-respected book, and has another scholarly work in manuscript form. Although Eilert and George study similar subject matter, their personalities contrast strongly: whereas George is stolid and prosaic, Eilert is erratic and creative, and George's work is rooted in the past while Eilert's is forward-looking. Eilert's decision to end his life after he has had a drunken relapse and has lost his manuscript reflects his absolutism; he is unable to adapt to circumstances. Hedda idealizes Eilert's dissolution, seeing in it a romantic, bacchanalian boldness and never considering its true destructiveness. Hedda encourages him to commit suicide because she considers this a courageous, picturesque act; not surprisingly Eilert's actual death is crude and vulgar.

Blonde, pretty **Thea Elvsted,** whose curly hair Hedda envied when both were young girls, serves a traditionally female function as a man's stabilizing influence and inspiration. Unhappily married, Thea achieves some satisfaction from her positive influence over Eilert, which Hedda never had and which she envies. The sweet, demure Thea never seems to perceive, however, that Hedda considers her a rival. Though she lacks Hedda's social status, intelligence, and great beauty, Thea is better equipped for survival—perhaps because she adapts to the role her society has assigned her. Like George, she is willing to submerge her own personality into someone else's life's work, and Ibsen infers that the two will forge a bond of their own through restoring Eilert's manuscript.

The Tesmans' sophisticated, coldhearted, cynical, and ruthless friend, **Judge Brack,** serves as a foil to the basic decency of George and the less calculated profligacy of Eilert. His lust for Hedda and knowledge that she gave Eilert her father's gun lead him to try to blackmail her into becoming his mistress, and it is partly out of dread of entering into such an arrangement that Hedda kills herself. Upon hearing of her suicide, Brack says, "People don't do such things!" His declaration has been variously interpreted: it may refer to the pointless or even ludicrous nature of Hedda's action or the surprising courage she shows in escaping from his (and others') domination.

George's **Aunt Julia (Miss Juliana Tesman),** along with her sister, **Rina,** raised her nephew lovingly, though perhaps also stiflingly. A basically good woman, she has found meaning in her life only through caring for others. She quickly guesses that Hedda is pregnant, and her frequent references to this fact annoy Hedda, who does not anticipate the birth of a baby with any happiness and would rather deny her condition. Another minor character in *Hedda Gabler* is **Mademoiselle Diana,** the notorious proprietress of the brothel Eilert visits in a drunken relapse. Significantly both Diana and Hedda possess the red hair that traditionally symbolizes a fiery nature as well as sensuality, but Diana rejects conventional mores and works outside accepted social boundaries.

Further Reading

Allphin, Clela. *Women in the Plays of Henrik Ibsen.* Brooklyn, N.Y.: Revisionist Press, 1974.

Belker, Roslyn. "Prisoners of Convention: Ibsen's 'Other' Women." *Journal of Women's Studies* 1, No. 2 (Spring 1979): 142-58.

Bradbrook, M. C. "'A Doll's House': The Unweaving of the Web." In *Women in Literature, 1779-1982: The Collected Papers of Muriel Bradbrook,* Vol. 2, pp. 81-92. Sussex: Harvester Press, 1982.

Durbach, Errol, ed. *Ibsen and the Theatre: The Dramatist in Production,* pp. 118-30. New York: New York University Press, 1980.

Egan, Michael. *Ibsen: The Critical Heritage.* London: Routledge & Kegan Paul, 1972.

Hardwick, Elizabeth. "Ibsen's Women." In *Seduction and Betrayal: Women and Literature,* pp. 31-83. New York: Random House, 1974.

Lebowitz, Naomi. *Ibsen and the Great World.* Baton Rouge: Louisiana State University Press, 1990.

Lyons, Charles R., ed. *Critical Essays on Henrik Ibsen.* Boston: G. K. Hall, 1987.

Shaw, Bernard. *The Quintessence of Ibsenism.* B. R. Tucker, 1891.

Thomas, David. *Henrik Ibsen.* New York: Macmillan, 1983.

Twentieth-Century Literary Criticism, Vols. 2, 8, 16, 37. Detroit: Gale.

Walkington, J. W. "Women and Power in Henrik Ibsen and Adrienne Rich." *English Journal* 80, No. 3 (March 1991): 64-8.

Washington Irving
1783-1859
American short story writer, essayist, historian, and biographer.

"Rip Van Winkle" (short story, 1819)

Plot: The story begins before the American Revolution, in late-eighteenth-century New York state. In a little town near the Catskill Mountains lives Rip Van Winkle, a good-natured but lazy farmer descended from the Dutch who settled the area with their esteemed leader, Peter Stuyvesant. Although he is popular with the village children and dogs and is always ready to help his neighbors, Rip prefers roaming through the woods, trading stories with other idlers at the village inn, or fishing to working for a living. Consequently his farm has fallen into disrepair, his children are shabbily dressed, and his shrill wife, Dame Van Winkle, continually harangues him. On one of his rambles through the mountains with his dog, Wolf, Rip encounters a magical band of little men, the original crew of the *Half Moon* captained by the legendary explorer Hendrick (Henry) Hudson. The tiny Dutchmen, who are playing a game of ninepins (bowling), offer Rip a drink, and he soon falls asleep. He awakens to find Wolf gone, his gun decayed, and the band of little men nowhere in sight. The landscape looks slightly different too, and when he arrives in the town he finds it changed: his house is empty, a large hotel stands on the sight of the familiar inn, and the townsfolk seem to have adopted a more hurried, brusque manner. Rip meets a young woman whom he eventually recognizes as his daughter, Judith; he also sees a young man who resembles himself exactly and who he realizes is his son, Rip, Jr. After learning that his wife has died, Rip reveals his identity and learns that he has been asleep for twenty years. During his slumber, the American Revolution has taken place and the colony is now the United States, George Washington is president, and many other changes have occurred. Rip, who now sports a long white beard, soon resumes his idle ways, and his storytelling is much appreciated by the townsfolk. They especially enjoy the tale of his encounter with Hendrick Hudson's men, who the older people believe meet every twenty years in the mountains for their game of ninepins.

Characters: Considered the first American writer to gain worldwide esteem, Irving profoundly influenced the art of the American short story by providing an innovative model that combined elements of myth and folklore with a distinctly American setting, simple prose, and characters that have since become archetypes. Adapted from a familiar story from German folklore, "Rip Van Winkle" takes place in the mountains of New York and is infused with the aura of change that so dominated the nation in the years following the American Revolution. Told in a light, humorous, entertaining voice by Irving's famous fictional narrator, the good-natured though somewhat gullible Diedrich Knickerbocker, the story's implicit rebellion against the American values of thrift and industry interests scholars, and its memorable characters continue to delight readers.

In the nearly two hundred years since the story's publication, the lackadaisical Dutch-American **Rip Van Winkle** has become a literary archetype and a universal symbol for time lost and the encroachment of change. He is a good-natured idler whose attempt to embrace a life of leisure is condemned by his harridan wife. While she clearly embodies the American work ethic, Rip has been identified as a kind of subversive renegade rejecting the imperative to be productive. Kind, meek, and proficient as a storyteller, Rip is popular with the village children and a welcome addition to the group of idlers who gather to exchange tall tales at the village inn. His behavior is somewhat contradictory, because he is capable of energetically applying himself to work if it is for the benefit of one of his neighbors rather than for himself or his family. Upon his return to the town from his twenty-year sleep, he finds the world changed: not only has his wife died and his children grown to adulthood, but the American colony has become the United States, and the formerly sleepy hamlet has taken on a more ambitious, forward-looking tone. Rip experiences a mounting crisis of identity that peaks when he sees Rip, Jr.—who is his father's spitting image—but lessens as his innate good nature and sentimentality surface. Although the narrator seems to accept Rip's story as true, Irving planted several strong hints that Rip invented his encounter with the tiny bowlers as a cover for his own voluntary, twenty-year exile from responsibility. If this is indeed what happened, Rip has accomplished a considerable triumph of imagination over the forces of dull industry and ambition. In any case Rip does not seem to regret having been absent during a period of great excitement and upheaval in his country. He settles back into his former indolence and is viewed as a relic of the past whose stories evoke for his listeners the aura of days gone by. Apparently based on a character from a German folktale—a goatherd named Peter Klaus who had a very similar experience—Rip embodies an ethic in marked opposition to that of hard work and thrift promoted by Benjamin Franklin in such works as *Poor Richard's Almanac* and his *Autobiography*. Rip rejects not so much work or activity—he loves to ramble across the countryside, fish, and help his neighbors with projects—as the imperative to make money that was an important function of nineteenth-century American materialism. Rip has also been interpreted as representing Irving himself, who apparently shared his ambiguous attitude toward work and career and who was also disinclined toward business. That Rip is allowed to end his life in the leisurely role of village storyteller may project Irving's own yearning or ambition.

Rip's shrewish, hot-tempered, tyrannical wife, **Dame Van Winkle,** is portrayed as a two-dimensional caricature who serves as the primary obstacle to Rip's contentment. She is described as a termagant, a word that denotes a turbulent, violent nature and one which Irving also applied to several other female characters in his fiction. In her disapproval of Rip's laziness and inability to make or save money, Dame Van Winkle embodies the materialism that Rip implicitly rejects. Her tidiness, thrift, and ambition are the same qualities affirmed in Benjamin Franklin's *Poor Richard's Almanac,* values which formed an important part of the American ethos in the formative years following the revolution. Significantly Rip returns from his sleep to find that the entire town has assumed his wife's outlook, and this change is portrayed as a negative consequence of the upheaval of the late eighteenth century. Cast in the familiar stereotype of the hen-pecking wife who finally gets her just reward—she dies of a fit while haggling over prices with a peddler—Dame Van Winkle has been described as a strongly anti-feminist character. Like other women in Irving's fiction, she is an agent of all that is unpleasant or stifling in civilization, a caricature, according to critic Marvin E. Mengeling, of "all those unpleasant pressures which depreciate and lash out at the impractical and the imaginative."

Rip's daughter, **Judith,** who kindly takes her father into her own home after his return, is diametrically different from her mother. In fact she is the only amiable woman left in the village after Rip's twenty-year hiatus. **Rip Van Winkle, Jr.** resembles his father in both appearance and outlook, making a strong case for the hereditary nature of personality. The pipe-smoking innkeeper, **Nicholas Vedder,** is the most notable of the village patriarchs with whom Rip lounges and exchanges stories, but Vedder runs a successful business and therefore has managed to combine idleness with practicality. The band of diminutive bowlers Rip meets are apparently the ghosts of the Dutch seamen who made up the crew of the *Half Moon,* captained by **Hendrick Hudson** (a Dutch version of the name of the seventeenth-century Englishman Henry Hudson, who explored the area in which the story takes place). Similar dwarf-like figures occur in several German folktales after which "Rip Van Winkle" was modeled. The villagers' belief that the sound of thunder is made by these men playing ninepins is a popular American folk tradition.

"The Legend of Sleepy Hollow" (short story, 1819)

Plot: Ichabod Crane is a grotesquely tall, skinny, impoverished schoolmaster in the Hudson Valley village of Sleepy Hollow, located near Tarrytown, New York. A native of Connecticut, Ichabod depends on the sturdy Dutch settlers who live in the area for his salary, food, and living quarters. Although he considers himself intellectually superior to his neighbors, Ichabod is frustrated by his poverty and tries to alleviate it by performing odd jobs on various farms and by giving singing lessons. One of his students is eighteen-year-old Katrina Van Tassel, the plump, rosy-cheeked daughter of wealthy Farmer Van Tassel. Coveting the vast properties owned by the Van Tassels, Ichabod decides to try to win Katrina's hand in marriage. Her longtime suitor, however, is the strong, cunning Abraham Van Brunt, known as Brom Bones. Learning of Ichabod's designs on Katrina, Brom tries to thwart the schoolmaster through a series of practical jokes. Nevertheless Ichabod is invited to a "quilting frolic" at the Van Tassel home. He dresses in his best clothing and borrows an emaciated horse named Gunpowder in order to ride to the party in style. During the celebration the scheming Brom tells Ichabod the story of the Headless Horsemen, the ghost of a Hessian soldier decapitated by a cannon who sometimes still gallops through the countryside on a phantom horse, carrying his head under his arm. Ichabod is naturally susceptible to tales of the supernatural and immediately believes what Brom tells him. After a disappointing conversation with Katrina he leaves the party and fearfully makes his way home. He soon hears thundering hooves behind him and turns in terror to see the Headless Horseman approaching. The apparition does not burst into flame and disappear, in accordance with the legend, but instead throws its head at Ichabod. The next day Gunpowder returns to the village without his rider and the gawky schoolmaster is never seen again. Some of the residents of Sleepy Hollow believe Ichabod was dragged away into eternity by the Headless Horseman, while others claim that—mortified because Katrina had rejected his marriage proposal and humiliated by his encounter with the supposed ghost— he went to New York City and eventually became a lawyer, politician, and judge. Brom Bones, meanwhile, went on to marry Katrina, and he wears a smug smile whenever the story of Ichabod's meeting with the dead Hessian soldier is mentioned.

Characters: "The Legend of Sleepy Hollow" is one of Irving's best-known works and, like "Rip Van Winkle," holds an important place in the development of the American short story. In portraying a clash between an industrious though poor and unscrupulous Yankee from New England with the wily, prosperous Dutch of New York state, Irving combined elements of Gothic fiction, humor, and a richly portrayed American setting. The result is a colorful story with memorable characters that have retained their appeal to readers.

The gangly schoolmaster, **Ichabod Crane,** is one of the most famous characters in American fiction, one whom most American readers can immediately visualize. Tall and grotesquely skinny, he lives an impoverished life and is dependent on the good will of others, for his salary is meager and his belongings few. A native of Connecticut, Ichabod is a stereotypical Yankee in his propensity to sing hymns to ward off evil spirits, his fondness for the writings of the seventeenth-century Puritan Cotton Mather, and his nasal accent. Although he ridicules the Dutch-Americans among whom he lives and works, considering himself their intellectual superior despite his relative lack of substantial education, he admires their prosperity and particularly appreciates their delicious cuisine. Thus he formulates a plan to acquire as a wife the comely daughter of one of the most wealthy farmers in the area. But Ichabod is an outsider whose worldliness and aura of culture and sophistication are not welcome in the peaceful community of Sleepy Hollow, and he is ultimately cast out. The susceptibility to superstition inherited from his Puritan forebears results in his falling prey to a prank concocted by Brom Bones, who impersonates the Headless Horseman and hurls his pumpkin "head" at Ichabod. Some scholars have interpreted Ichabod as illustrating the plight of the artist or intellectual in materialistic America, and others see him as a caricature of a greedy, scheming Yankee who is bested by the ingenuity of the Dutch. His ultimate success as a lawyer and judge in New York City has been noted by several critics, who suggest that Irving, who himself rejected a career as a lawyer, might have been making through Ichabod the subtle comment that the negative qualities he represents are ultimately rewarded by society. In any case the gaunt, cadaverous schoolmaster who resembles both the bird his surname suggests and the biblical outcast denoted by his first name has earned a permanent place in American literature.

Ichabod's rival for the affection of Katrina Van Tassel is **Abraham Van Brunt,** better known as **Brom Bones.** He is the quintessential local hero: rugged, strong, able, always ready for fun or a fight, and possessed of a raucous sense of humor. Attired in a fur cap trimmed with a dangling fox's tail, skilled as a horseman, and eminently confident, Brom has been seen as a forerunner of the American frontier characters created by such authors as James Fennimore Cooper and Mark Twain. He is endowed with the traditional American quality of common sense, which allows him to capitalize on Ichabod's superstitious nature and win Katrina for himself.

Katrina Van Tassel is a plump, blooming, rosy-cheeked girl who attracts Ichabod's attention when she takes singing lessons from him. Katrina is somewhat coquettish and apparently manipulates Ichabod in order to make Brom jealous. Her father, **Farmer Van Tassel,** owns vast acres of fertile land and a sumptuous home that awaken Ichabod's greed and desire for comfort. Irving's descriptions of Van Tassel's property and of the delicious food offered in his home have been said to celebrate the bountiful American way of life. The **Headless Horseman** is the legendary ghost of a Hessian soldier of the Revolutionary War period who was reputedly decapitated by a cannon and who now rides through the countryside with his head under his arm; in reality, the apparition is the crafty Brom Bones, who throws a pumpkin—in place of a severed head—at the terrified Ichabod as he gallops by on his black horse. The ironically named **Gunpowder** is the nag Ichabod borrows in order to make a dignified arrival at the Van Tassel's party; the horse is as gaunt and shabby as his rider.

"The Devil and Tom Walker" (short story, 1824)

Plot: The story takes place in the colony of Massachusetts in 1727. Tom Walker is a miser who lives in fractious disharmony with his equally miserly wife near a swamp in which the famous pirate Captain Kidd is thought to have buried a cache of treasure. While crossing the swamp one day Tom meets the devil, who appears as a dark-skinned man with a sooty face. "Old Scratch" offers to give Tom the buried treasure in exchange for something that he does not explicitly mention, but which is understood to be Tom's soul. When Tom's wife learns of the offer, she greedily demands that Tom accept the devil's terms, but Tom spitefully refuses to do so. She approaches the devil on her own, hoping to make an advantageous trade with him. She never comes back, and when Tom goes to look for her he finds only her apron hanging from a tree. Inside are bundled a heart and liver—apparently his wife was killed by Old Scratch while trying to drive a hard bargain with him. Tom is happy to be rid of his wife. He gradually grows more eager to acquire the buried treasure and finally strikes a deal with the now somewhat reluctant devil, who insists that the treasure be used in his service. Although Tom rejects the devil's proposal that he become a slave trader, he agrees to work as a moneylender. In Boston Tom becomes wealthy through his unscrupulous business practices. After many years he regrets the bargain he made with the devil and becomes outwardly religious, though he does not alter his behavior. One morning while preparing to foreclose on the mortgage of one of his victims, he is asked to consider the money he has already received from the man. Tom cries that the devil may take him if he has ever earned any profit from their relationship. Old Scratch instantly appears and whisks Tom away on a black horse. Tom is never seen again but his ghost, attired in the white cap and dressing gown he was wearing the morning he disappeared, has been sighted galloping through the swamp on a black horse.

Characters: Unlike the other stories in the collection *Tales of a Traveller,* in which it was originally published, "The Devil and Tom Walker" features an American rather than a European setting. It is considered one of Irving's finest short stories, praised for its skillful blending of supernatural elements with simple narration and its thematic emphasis on the consequences of miserliness and isolation from others. The story is a lightly told but stark allegory warning against greed and hypocrisy.

Tom Walker is one of Irving's least likable characters. A notorious miser, he carries on a combative relationship with his wife; their many conflicts have resulted in his battered appearance. He initially resists the devil's offer because he wants to spite his wife, but after her elimination—which gladdens him—his greed gets the better of him. Irving chose two ignominious professions as Tom's alternatives in his deal with the devil: slave trader or moneylender. Even Tom is not low enough to become a slave trader, but he is willing to follow the usury trade. In Boston, where he soon moves, he gradually grows famous for his wealth as well as his harsh business practices. When he later regrets his bargain with Old Scratch, Tom becomes a regular churchgoer who delights in the tallying of his neighbors' sins, as if their wickedness somehow alleviates his own. His false piety masks his continuing miserliness and lack of regard for others; although he owns an elegant carriage and large mansion, his horses are emaciated and his home unfurnished, and he treats his poor clients inhumanely. A two-dimensional character who merits no sympathy at all from readers, Tom is a recognizably Faustian figure who trades his soul not for knowledge or power but for money. Finally snatched away by the devil, he is apparently doomed to ride a black horse perpetually through the swamp where he once bargained with the devil.

Other characters in the story include **the devil,** or "**Old Scratch,**" who is described as very dark-skinned (though neither black nor Indian) with red eyes, a soot-covered face, and a red sash draped around his body. **Tom's wife** is as miserly and greedy as her husband, and like him is finally destroyed by her greed when she tries to bully the devil into making an advantageous bargain with her. She is often cited as one of Irving's typically anti-feminist women characters in her extreme shrewishness. She is a violent-tempered "termagant," and Tom explains that the experience of having lived with her for so many years is what allows him to approach the devil with little fear.

Further Reading

Antelyes, Peter. *Tales of Adventurous Enterprise: Washington Irving and the Poetics of Western Expansion.* New York: Columbia University Press, 1990.

Bowden, Mary Weatherspoon. *Washington Irving.* Boston: Twayne, 1981.

Brodwin, Stanley, ed. *The Old and New World Romanticism of Washington Irving.* Westport, Conn.: Greenwood Press, 1986.

Dictionary of Literary Biography, Vols. 3, 11, 30, 59, 73, 74. Detroit: Gale.

Fetterley, Judith. "Palpable Designs: Four American Short Stories." In *The Resisting Reader: A Feminist Approach to American Fiction,* pp. 1-45. Bloomington: Indiana University Press, 1978.

Mengeling, Marvin E. "Characterization in 'Rip Van Winkle.'" *English Journal* 53, No. 9 (December 1964): 643-46.

Myers, Andrew. *A Century of Commentary on the Works of Washington Irving: 1860-1974.* Tarrytown, N.Y.: Sleepy Hollow Restorations, 1976.

Nineteenth-Century Literature Criticism, Vols. 2, 19. Detroit: Gale Research.

Roth, Martin. *Comedy and America: The Lost World of Washington Irving.* Port Washington, N. Y.: Kennikat Press, 1976.

Rubin-Dorsky, Jeffrey. *Adrift in the Old World: The Psychological Pilgrimage of Washington Irving.* Chicago: University of Chicago Press, 1988.

Tuttleton, James W., ed. *Washington Irving: The Critical Reaction.* New York: AMS Press, 1990.

Warner, Charles D. *Washington Irving.* New York: Chelsea House, 1981.

Henry James
1843-1916
American novelist and short story writer, critic, and essayist.

Daisy Miller (novel, 1878)

Plot: The novel's action is presented through the perspective of Frederick Winterbourne, a young American who has lived in Europe for many years. While visiting Vevey, Switzerland, with his wealthy aunt, Mrs. Costello, he meets an American girl named Daisy Miller and her younger brother, Randolph. He learns that the two live in Schenectady, New York, and are touring Europe with their mother; they plan to travel to Italy soon. Daisy wants to see a local site, the Castle of Chillon, and Winterbourne promises to take her there. Mrs. Costello, however, refuses to make Daisy's acquaintance, because she finds the nouveau-riche Miller family socially inferior. Although Daisy cancels a scheduled nighttime boat ride with Winterbourne, the two take an unchaperoned excursion to the Castle together as planned. Later both Winterbourne and the Millers go to Rome, where they meet at the home of the American Mrs. Walker. Daisy shocks her hostess by announcing that she is going for a walk with a young Italian man named Giovanelli; Mrs. Walker and her American expatriate friends believe it improper for a young woman to spend time alone with a young man. To lend Daisy's outing more respectability, Winterbourne accompanies her and Giovanelli on their walk. But Mrs. Walker drives up in her carriage and tries to get Daisy to end her outing, also pressuring Winterbourne to persuade Daisy not to walk with Giovanelli, since they consider the Italian an opportunist interested only in Daisy's fortune. But Daisy is impervious to their pleas, and they finally leave her.

Mrs. Walker and the rest of the American expatriate community in Rome thereafter snub Daisy. She is frequently seen with Giovanelli, with whom, they believe, she is carrying on an illicit relationship. Daisy informs Winterbourne that she is not engaged to the Italian, and Winterbourne continues to defend her to his friends, although he is uncertain of her innocence. One night Daisy arranges to meet Giovanelli at the Colosseum, which, despite the great danger of contracting "Roman fever" or malaria at that site, she wishes to view in the moonlight. Winterbourne encounters the couple there and chastises Giovanelli for endangering Daisy's life by bringing her to the Colosseum, but the Italian claims that Daisy had insisted on making the excursion. Daisy soon becomes ill; a week before she dies, she sends word to Winterbourne that she was never engaged to Giovanelli, and asks if he remembers their outing at the Castle of Chillon. In the final scene Winterbourne and Giovanelli stand together at Daisy's grave discussing their young friend. Giovanelli, calling Daisy the most beautiful, amiable, and innocent young lady he has ever met, ruefully admits that she would never have married him. Winterbourne realizes that he and Daisy might have had a romantic relationship if he had been more sensitive and perceptive. He decides that, having lived too long in Europe, he has grown unaccustomed to the different, freer nature of American manners.

Characters: Probably the most popular of Henry James's novels, *Daisy Miller* helped to propel him into prominence as a major force and innovator in literature. His skillful use of point of view and emphasis on the psychological motivations and complexities of individual characters rather than on plot or action are evident in the novel, as are several of the themes that most interested him. James is often credited with initiating the "international novel," which revolves around the experiences of Americans living or traveling in Europe and the consequent clash between American innocence and independence and the rigid conventions of the older, darker culture they encounter abroad. Called a "historian of manners" by critic Van Wyck Brooks, James focuses in *Daisy Miller* not only on the contrast between Old and

New World ways but on the difficulty of separating appearances from reality and on the sexual divisions and inequities in the Victorian social and moral code.

Daisy Miller is often identified as the quintessential American girl of the late nineteenth century. Young, pretty, and vivacious, she is an unsophisticated but generally very charming young woman whose travels through Europe are financed by her wealthy businessman father. Typically American in the freeness of her manners and her occasional rashness and indifference to convention, Daisy approaches her new experiences and encounters with confidence and enthusiasm. The unchaperoned outings and flirting in which Daisy indulges were natural components of youth and courtship in nineteenth-century America, but young women in Europe were more closely sheltered and expected to behave with greater decorum. When Daisy acts in Vevey and Rome as she would at home in Schenectady, she earns the disapproval and finally the rejection of the American expatriate community, which has appropriated (to an exaggerated extent) European values and standards. Because the story is told almost exclusively through the perspective of Frederick Winterbourne, the reader must share with him an uncertainty about Daisy's true nature. His personal biases color his responses to Daisy, whom he wishes to categorize and thus reduce to a type: he believes she must be either truly innocent, a flirt, or outrightly immoral, and after his encounter with her at the Colosseum, he concludes that she is indeed immoral. Daisy's death and the revelations that follow it confirm that she was just what she seemed, an uncomplicated and essentially innocent young girl. While Daisy demonstrates a rather vapid intellect—describing Europe, for example, as "perfectly sweet"—there are indications that she possessed the potential for deeper understanding. Her desire to see the Colosseum in the moonlight, for instance, suggests a yearning for richer experience that links her with Winterbourne, with whom she was apparently in love or at least disposed to love. Several critics have noted the significance of Daisy's name, which refers to a common, plainly pretty American flower and which was also a late-nineteenth-century American slang designation for a young girl. Daisy's death might be interpreted as a grim reminder of the consequences of defying convention or the foolishness of ignoring such well-founded superstitions as avoiding the Colosseum at night, or it may be seen, more simply, as the sad, ironic end to a somewhat shallow but vibrant, innocent girl. Several scholars have identified Daisy as a rehearsal or prototype for the more complex character Isabel Archer in James's later novel *The Portrait of a Lady.* Isabel too is a free-spirited American girl who finds her independent values threatened in a European setting.

Frederick Winterbourne is the novel's wise, often ironic narrator, who views the main characters both critically and sympathetically. A young American who has lived for many years in Europe, he is intelligent and sophisticated and considers himself in possession of a heightened sensibility. He appreciates Daisy's beauty and charm but immediately finds her difficult to categorize. His need to identify Daisy as a "type" based on his own conceptions of female character reveals his basic conventionality and appropriation of his society's code of behavior. Evidence suggests that Winterbourne himself has a mistress in Geneva, and the fact that he can sanction his own illicit behavior while censoring Daisy illustrates the sexual double standard of nineteenth- and even twentieth-century societies. Daisy treats Winterbourne in an open, friendly, lightly flirtatious manner that confuses him and, as several critics have noted, seems to titillate him. Delighted with her willingness to accompany him, unchaperoned, to the Castle of Chillon, he surmises that she must be a coquette. Yet he also defends her innocence to his aunt and Mrs. Walker, asserting to them that she is not corrupt but merely uncultivated. Daisy teases Winterbourne about his reserved, formal manners and speech, labeling him "stiff"; she also applies this adjective to the notion that young women must always be chaperoned. Thus Winterbourne is identified with the rigid social code practiced by the other American expatriates, and after meeting Daisy and Giovanelli at the Colosseum and deciding that Daisy is indeed subject to "lawless passions," he ultimately joins in rejecting her. Nevertheless Winterbourne displays the capacity for deeper understanding, particularly when he stands at Daisy's grave and acknowledges that he has been wrong about her and that he has lost an opportunity for a fulfilling love that might have developed between them. Winterbourne's name reflects the emotional coldness that blinds him from perceiving the truth about Daisy.

Among the group of American expatriates with whom Daisy comes into conflict, the most prominent are Winterbourne's wealthy, widowed aunt, **Mrs. Costello,** and their friend, **Mrs. Walker.** Both women represent and espouse a rigid social code that does not allow for the freer manners of a vivacious, unsophisticated American girl, and both base their moral judgments exclusively on appearances and stereotypes. Although Mrs. Costello acknowledges Daisy's charm and physical beauty, she dismisses her simply on the basis of her lower social standing and later considers her thoroughly vulgar for refusing to comply with conventional standards of behavior. James's portrayal of Mrs. Costello is somewhat comic, particularly in her domination of the subservient Winterbourne and in the notion that it is only her chronic headaches that have kept her from accomplishing anything great. Ironically Mrs. Costello's warning that Winterbourne avoid Daisy lest he make "some great mistake" proves well-founded, for his misjudging her results in his own lost opportunity for love. Mrs. Walker is particularly harsh to Daisy, snubbing her at the party after Daisy refuses to give up her walk with Giovanelli, with the rest of the expatriate community promptly following suit. Although Daisy is outwardly indifferent toward this ostracism, there are subtle hints that it hurts her deeply.

Several scholars contend that parental neglect is a significant theme of *Daisy Miller,* expressed primarily through the failure of the absent-minded **Mrs. Miller** to discipline or supervise her children. This lapse is ultimately portrayed as a failure to protect them as well, as Daisy's complete independence leads to her death. The family's travels are financed by the absent **Mr. Miller,** who is home in Schenectady making money—with a typically American allegiance to hard work and accumulation of wealth. Mrs. Miller's propensity for "pathological gossip" and general gaucheness mark her as inferior, as far as Mrs. Costello is concerned. Daisy's spoiled, obstinate brother, **Randolph,** is utterly unsupervised and apparently incorrigible, maintaining a tyrannical control over the rest of the family with his demands and refusals. He speaks in a comically ungrammatical slang that helps to establish the strongly American identity of the Miller family.

Mr. Giovanelli is one of only two significant European characters in *Daisy Miller.* A handsome young Italian whom Daisy perceives as immensely elegant, he is an opportunist whose primary interest is her money, an interest he has pursued with other American heiresses. His highly attentive, obsequious manner toward Daisy irritates Winterbourne, who wonders with unconscious jealousy how she could possibly mistake Giovanelli for a true gentleman. At Daisy's grave Giovanelli comments with notable simplicity that she was the most beautiful, amiable, and—most significantly—innocent young woman he had ever known, and that she would never have married him. This revelation causes Winterbourne to realize his own mistake. The other Italian character is **Eugenio,** who serves as the Miller family's courier (he makes travel arrangements and serves as their companion) during their tour. Exceedingly well-dressed and well-mannered, he maintains an intimacy with the Millers that the other Americans disapprove of; they comment that Eugenio is treated almost as a member of the family. However Eugenio also objects to Daisy taking an evening boat excursion with Winterbourne.

The Portrait of a Lady (novel, 1881)

Plot: After the death of her father, a young American girl named Isabel Archer receives a visit from her aunt, Lydia Touchett, who then takes Isabel to Europe to expose the bright young girl to a richer culture and wider experience. At Gardencourt, Mrs. Touchett's

English country home, Isabel meets her uncle, Daniel Touchett, her consumptive cousin, Ralph Touchett, and the family's aristocratic friend, Lord Warburton, who becomes immediately interested in her. Isabel's American friend Henrietta Stackpole, a journalist writing a series of articles about Europe for an American newspaper, visits her at Gardencourt. On the same day that Isabel receives a letter from Caspar Goodwood, a wealthy young American who wishes to marry her, Lord Warburton proposes to her. Despite the security and other advantages the match offers, Isabel is eager for more diverse experience, and she rejects the offer. Henrietta, Isabel, and Ralph travel to London, where Isabel receives a visit and another marriage proposal from Goodwood. Rejecting him again, Isabel agrees that he may see her again in two years if he still wishes to marry her. When word arrives that Mr. Touchett is gravely ill, Isabel and Ralph return to Gardencourt; Henrietta stays in London with her new British friend and guide, Mr. Bantling. While Mr. Touchett is dying, Isabel becomes acquainted with Madame Merle, an old friend of Mrs. Touchett and a sophisticated, accomplished, middle-aged widow with no children. Because Ralph has secretly persuaded his father to leave half of Ralph's own fortune to Isabel, she finds herself an heiress after Mr. Touchett's death. Ralph believes that Isabel is capable of great achievements and wants to give her the freedom to do whatever she wishes, while he himself does not expect to live long due to his illness.

Mrs. Touchett sells Gardencourt and takes Isabel to Paris, while Ralph goes to Italy for a rest. Isabel meets the many American expatriates of her aunt's Parisian circle and finds them shamefully indolent. She is reunited with Henrietta and Mr. Bantling, and also spends time with an old friend from a childhood tour of Europe, Edward Rosier. Though something of a dilettante, the wealthy, American-born Rosier is kind and pleasant. Next Isabel and her aunt travel to Florence, Italy, where Mrs. Touchett owns a home and where they again meet Madame Merle. Meanwhile Madame Merle has spoken of Isabel to her friend Gilbert Osmond—another expatriate American who lives in self-imposed exile with his exquisite art collection and his lovely daughter Pansy—informing Osmond that Isabel is wealthy and would make a fine addition to his collection. He courts Isabel and wins her regard; despite the disapproval of her friends, she accepts his marriage proposal. Ralph is especially disappointed for he senses Osmond's selfishness and feels that Isabel's marvelous flight of freedom is over. Goodwood also makes a final, unsuccessful marriage proposal to Isabel.

Now three years later, Isabel is profoundly unhappy and disillusioned in her marriage, having realized that her urbane, tasteful husband regards her as another possession intended merely to reflect his own personality; his basic egoism and meanness are increasingly apparent. Osmond squashes a budding romance between Pansy and Rosier, because he finds the young man insufficiently rich, and he attempts to encourage a match between his daughter and the wealthier, more prestigious Lord Warburton. The Englishman, however, soon realizes that Pansy is in love with Rosier and drops his suit. Meanwhile Ralph's health has steadily declined and he finally returns to Gardencourt. Mrs. Touchett sends word to Isabel that Ralph's seems imminent and he has asked to see her; however Osmond opposes Isabel's plan to go to Gardencourt. His sister, Countess Gemini, who is visiting at the time, perceives the real state of affairs between her brother and sister-and-law, and she decides to tell Isabel the facts about Gilbert's past: nearly twenty years ago he and Madame Merle had been lovers, Pansy is their child, and Gilbert has subsequently passed her off as the child of his first marriage. As a result Isabel decides to travel to England to see Ralph, but she stops first at the convent where Pansy has been sent by Osmond to keep her away from Rosier. There Isabel meets Madame Merle, who instantly realizes that Isabel knows her secret, and she promises she will soon be removing herself from the scene by moving to America. Isabel arrives at Gardencourt in time to speak to Ralph before he dies. After his funeral she again encounters Goodwood, who has heard of her unhappiness and renews his offer of love. Though tempted to yield, Isabel rejects him and returns to Italy, determined to confront her fate.

Characters: Many critics consider *The Portrait of a Lady* James's most accomplished, balanced work, and it is universally acclaimed as an important modern novel. In its intense focus on the developing consciousness of its main character and the often impressionistic quality of its narrative, it anticipates the twentieth-century works created by such authors as James Joyce and Virginia Woolf. Through his incisive, sensitive, psychologically astute portrayal of Isabel Archer, as well as his memorable depictions of several secondary characters, James explores such themes as the importance of wealth in determining the course of a life, the concepts of personal freedom and responsibility, the problem of marriage and the role power plays in relationships, and the dilemma of naive nineteenth-century Americans as they encountered the older, more corrupt culture of Europe. Although James is sometimes faulted for a moral stance that seems divorced from reality and for an erudite verbosity that makes him inaccessible to many readers, *The Portrait of a Lady* has been proclaimed a work of deep human insight, compassion, and universal relevance.

In the preface to *The Portrait of a Lady,* James states that the novel presents his "conception of a young lady confronting her destiny." The portrayal of **Isabel Archer** is formed, like a painting, stroke by stroke as her own self-realizations and those of the people around her contribute to the development of her consciousness. Except for a few isolated episodes, the story is seen from Isabel's point of view, so that the reader's awareness is awakened at much the same pace as hers. As the novel begins, Isabel is a pretty, intelligent, spirited young girl just out of her teens. She has led a sheltered life with a father who provided her with a rather erratic education and only a small inheritance upon which to live after his death. By the time she is discovered and whisked away by her "fairy godmother," Aunt Lydia, she has already conceived an ideal of independence that she plans to pursue, and she travels eagerly to Europe with the intention of embracing a wider experience than what she has known. Intelligent and sensitive, Isabel presumes she is already wise enough to make the right choices, reflecting her grounding in the transcendentalist movement of nineteenth-century New England: possessed of what some have termed a "radical innocence," she faces the world with little concept of evil and a belief in unlimited choice. And her opportunities are broadened by the inheritance she receives, as her benefactor, Ralph Touchett, had hoped they would be. Ironically her ability to pursue an independent, fulfilling destiny is also circumscribed by her wealth, which draws Gilbert Osmond toward her. With a particularly American naivete, Isabel is charmed by her suitor's exile and devotion to culture and beauty; she fails to sense his true egotism or immorality. Seeing herself as his benevolent provider and helpmate as well as a mother for his lovely daughter, Isabel believes that by marrying him she will give him the opportunity to live the privileged life he deserves. Isabel's eventual realization of her mistake and her psychological adjustment to her situation is portrayed through a stream-of-consciousness-style narrative often cited as particularly innovative and influential. The reader witnesses Isabel's growth from a bright, proud, essentially innocent girl to a more experienced, more compelling woman whose inner values—despite her outward circumstances—remain strong and independent. Her return to Italy and her unhappy marriage has been interpreted in a variety of ways: as an empty sacrifice based primarily on pride, an admirable if tragic assertion of selfhood, or evidence of her nobility, redemption, and triumph over moral evil. According to the third of these views, Isabel's return is motivated by her selfless love for Pansy and wish to protect her from Osmond, demonstrating that her consciousness has developed to encompass not just her own concerns but those of others. Isabel is sometimes identified as a more complex, intelligent, and sensitive version of James's earlier heroine, Daisy Miller, but more often she is compared to the author's beloved cousin Minny Temple, a sensitive young woman who died at twenty-four; James is thought to have modeled some of his most successful female characters (including Milly Theale in *The Wings of the Dove* and Maggie Verver in *The Golden Bowl*) after Minny. Most critics agree that James's attitude toward Isabel is ultimately admiring and hopeful, and that Ralph's conviction that there is hope for Isabel's future reflects the author's belief as well. In fact Isabel has been interpreted as a manifestation of James himself, and his success in projecting so much of himself into this female character is considered a major accomplishment.

Isabel's kind and generous cousin, **Ralph Touchett,** is one of several characters in James's fiction who are sensitive and noble but doomed to early death, as if they are too good to live long in an evil world. Upon meeting young Isabel, Ralph immediately recognizes her intelligence and sensitivity, and he empathizes with her yearning for freedom. To give her the means to experience a broader life and to practice the ideal of freedom they both share, he asks his father to give half of his own inheritance to Isabel, for he wants to "put wind in her sails." Although Ralph loves his cousin deeply, he never reveals to her the true extent of his feeling, nor is she fully aware of it until his death. Some critics describe Ralph's effort to conceal his love from Isabel as evidence of his selflessness (for he does not want her to be burdened with a dying husband), but others suspect that it may be due to a fear of sexuality. Although Ralph's intentions in sharing his wealth with Isabel are admirable, they ironically make her eventual unhappiness possible: the money attracts the malignant Osmond to her. More perceptive than Isabel, Ralph quickly sees through both Osmond and Madame Merle, and he makes a gentle but unsuccessful attempt to warn Isabel about them. Ralph has been described as a foil to Osmond: both are cultivated connoisseurs of art, but Ralph values life above art and possesses a sense of humor about himself and others, whereas Osmond is inherently cold, detached, and humorless. Since he possesses the broadest consciousness, Ralph may serve as a surrogate for the author. His last encounter with Isabel, in which he expresses hope for the eventual alleviation of her unhappiness and in which she realizes the extent of his love for her, has been lauded for its tenderness and lack of melodrama.

Isabel's husband, **Gilbert Osmond,** is a voluntary exile from his native country, like many of the people she meets in Europe. Born in America, he was raised in Europe by a misguidedly idealistic mother who appropriated European customs, producing as a result moral shallowness in her son. (The revelation about his illicit relationship with Madame Merle, which comes late in the story, further confirms his corruption.) He lives in seclusion in his exquisitely appointed home, and Isabel initially finds his sheltered, art-centered existence charming. Osmond's exaggerated desire for privacy and his exclusiveness, though based on his repugnance for the ugliness of life and society, initially bear some resemblance to Isabel's sense of superiority and pride, so that in the end he is exposed as a hypocrite. He professes disdain for public opinion, but he actually values nothing more than the world's approval. Concerned with surfaces only, with effect rather than content, he stands in marked contrast to Ralph, who is equally cultivated but sensitive, humane, and morally upright. After their marriage Osmond egotistically attempts to fit Isabel into a prescribed mold and to make her a reflection of himself. Eventually he comes to despise his wife for failing to gratify his ego, and he becomes openly malignant and poisonous in his words and acts.

When Isabel first meets **Madame Merle,** she thinks of the older woman as sophisticated and graceful; accomplished at such traditionally feminine pursuits as letter-writing, painting, needlework, and piano-playing, she adapts herself easily to her social circumstances. Madame Merle is a widow who lives on the generosity of her friends—they pay her expenses in exchange for her agreeable presence in their homes. Ultimately revealed to be morally corrupt, Madame Merle's uncertain, insecure role as an unattached, unoccupied woman underlines the very limited choices available to nineteenth-century women. What power Madame Merle does possess harms Isabel, for she engineers a marriage between her former lover, Osmond, and the wealthy young American woman. Like Osmond, Madame Merle presents an elegant facade that masks her true shallowness. She values not people but things and artificial social relationships. Though she has a sinister quality, Madame Merle seems pathetic in the end, for all her efforts on Osmond's behalf have resulted only in permanent separation from her daughter. During the final encounter between Madame Merle and Isabel, Madame Merle realizes that Isabel knows her secret and that nothing will ever be the same between them. For her part Isabel acknowledges Madame Merle's suffering, but she is nevertheless determined never to see her again.

The opinionated, quintessentially American journalist **Henrietta Stackpole,** who is writing a series of articles on Europe for a New York newspaper (a function also frequently performed by James), serves as a kind of spectator of the novel's action. Her comical name suggests her observations are conducted from a high though rather awkwardly constructed vantage point. Henrietta embodies a particular variety of freedom that counterpoints Isabel's. A single woman with an ardent, restless nature and a great deal of courage, Henrietta ranges alone over Europe and forms her own opinions about what she sees. Even so she is thoroughly conventional and narrow minded, judging the Old World entirely by New World standards and finding it decidedly inferior. She has an unflinching gaze but sees only surfaces, rarely perceiving the underlying human dimensions, as when she first meets Ralph and pigeonholes him as a decadent expatriate. To her credit, however, Henrietta eventually recognizes Ralph's true worth, and she surprises Isabel by agreeing to settle in England with Mr. Bantling, thus demonstrating an uncharacteristic flexibility.

Like Henrietta, Isabel's suitor **Caspar Goodwood** also has a particularly American perspective. Determined, aggressive, and inherently conventional, he offers Isabel the ordinary, stable sort of life young nineteenth-century women were expected to lead. A wealthy young industrialist, he represents the youth, ambition, strength, and lack of inhibition often associated with his native land, and he also exhibits some of its possibly blind self-assurance. His notion of freedom is simpler than Isabel's, and he believes that she will find the independence she idealizes lonely and unsatisfying. Several critics have noted that Caspar also offers Isabel the prospect of a fulfilling sexual relationship that neither of her other suitors seems likely to match. Particularly in her last scene with Caspar—in which his kiss affects her like a flash of "white lightening"—Isabel feels a strong temptation to yield to him, to be possessed by him. Her strength of character and yearning after greater personal fulfillment leads her to resist, however ill-fated her striving may prove.

Lord Warburton is another of the several men in *The Portrait of the Lady* who are captivated by Isabel. A wealthy young aristocrat with a pleasant, manly appearance, he is complaining of boredom and restlessness, when his friend's charming, vibrant young cousin arrives on the scene. He proposes to Isabel after seeing her only three times, modestly offering what he describes as a comfortable existence, though in reality he can give her great wealth and social status. He is kind and thoughtful, and his impressive home, Lockleigh, reminds Isabel of a castle in a fairy tale, but she senses that to marry him would be to sacrifice the wider experience she craves. Because the liberal, reform-minded Lord Warburton enjoys all the privileges of the English aristocracy, he may be seen as somewhat hypocritical, but he demonstrates his honor by withdrawing his suit to Pansy when he realizes she loves Ned Rosier.

If Lord Warburton seems to Isabel like a prince in his castle, surely **Mrs. Lydia Touchett** serves as her fairy godmother. She is often identified as such, as she whisks her niece away from a sheltered, quiet life in America to enchanted Europe. Mrs. Touchett claims complete independence, traveling around the world where and when she wishes with little attachment to her husband, **Daniel Touchett,** (a kind, patient, and decidedly unflamboyant man who complies with his son's wish to split his inheritance with Isabel). Like Henrietta, Mrs. Touchett provides a gloss on the question of freedom, for she is actually rootless and shallow. She claims to lack delusions, but this has narrowed rather than broadened her view, and despite her apparent worldliness, she has never really lived or experienced deeply. Nevertheless Mrs. Touchett is basically honest and forthright and is sincerely interested in

Isabel's well-being; she perceives that Osmond is a poor choice as a husband and warns her niece against him.

Osmond's lovely, angelic young daughter, **Pansy,** convent-bred and carefully sheltered by her father, is not a particularly well-developed character. Even at the age of nineteen, she is a childlike "daddy's girl," never perceiving that her father's intentions are mercenary rather than beneficent. Pansy falls in love with the similarly childlike Ned Rosier, which her father tries to thwart by confining her to a convent again. Osmond's strenuous efforts to marry Pansy to the wealthy Lord Warburton, despite his own personal enmity toward his wife's former suitor, bring in sharp relief the true nature of the mistake Isabel has made in marrying him. Critics suggest that protecting Pansy from her father's malignant influence is what brings Isabel back to Italy; thus she demonstrates her capacity for selfless love and, ultimately, redemption.

Isabel first met **Edward "Ned" Rosier** during a childhood visit to Europe. An American expatriate and a dilettante, he lives on the income from his inheritance and bemoans his native country's dearth of suitable occupations for gentlemen, a condition that necessitates living in Europe. With his rosy cheeks, daintiness, and exquisite taste, Ned makes a somewhat effeminate impression, and his childlike quality gives his passion for Pansy an asexual quality. He is basically kind and thoughtful, however, and he sincerely loves Pansy, but he lacks the wealth that her selfish father requires in a future husband for his daughter.

Osmond's sister, the **Countess Gemini,** has also been corrupted by her confused European upbringing and subsequent experiences. Unlike her brother, however, she is basically honest, and she lacks his exaggerated sense of privacy and exclusiveness. She actually encourages Henrietta to write about her love affairs. While the countess is considered an interestingly eccentric character, her main purpose seems to be to reveal the secrets of Osmond's past to Isabel—a function she performs because she mistrusts the alliance between her brother and Madame Merle and wishes to relieve Isabel's suffering.

"The Beast in the Jungle" (short story, 1903)

Plot: The story centers on John Marcher, an Englishman whose financial security relieves him of the necessity of working. At a party in the home of a mutual friend, he meets a woman named May Bartram. The two realize they already know each other from an occasion several years before in Italy, when Marcher revealed to May that he felt destined for a singular fate. He confides that he still feels something is going to happen to him—something strange and possibly terrible. He and May begin a long relationship that, due to his preoccupation with his destiny, never develops into romance. Although he is apprehensive about his fate, Marcher initially also looks forward to it, for he expects that it will allow him to feel more deeply than others. This anticipation turns to dread, however, as the years pass and nothing happens, and his fate begins to take on a predatory quality. He likens it to a wild animal that crouches in wait for him, and he expects it to spring upon him at any moment. Meanwhile May comforts and supports him, steady in her friendship despite the lack of benefit she derives from it.

As the two grow older, Marcher dimly realizes that May knows more about his fate than he does. She offers to help him become an ordinary man, but he does not grasp her meaning and continues to wait for whatever is going to happen to him. Finally May informs him that his destiny is indeed terrible and has almost overtaken him, but that she cannot show him what it is—he must discover it for himself and then may possibly escape it. May's health, meanwhile, is in a steady decline. Before she dies, she tells Marcher that it is too late for him now, that the beast has already sprung upon him. He still fails to perceive her meaning. After her death Marcher takes a long trip around the world, returning a year later to visit May's grave. Nearby he notices a mourner who is prostrate with grief. The sight brings a realization of what his fate has been all along: he has lived without the love that gives life meaning, thus he has refused to engage in life. Nothing at all has happened to him, and *that* is what has happened. He now sees that May loved him deeply and if he had returned her love, both of them might have been saved. Overcome by despair, he throws himself down on her grave.

Characters: One of the most famous of James's short stories, "The Beast in the Jungle" reflects his interest in the psychological motivations that underlie social behavior. Though the plot moves slowly and is, according to some readers and critics, rather implausible, James succeeds in creating a mood of suspense and terror that culminates in an effective ending. Through the central image of a sense of fate or destiny in the form of a wild beast crouching in a dense jungle, ready to spring on its victim at any moment, James explores the tragedy of the "unlived life," the existence marred by a vague but immobilizing fear of experience. A product of the third and final phase of James's career, the story exhibits characteristics often found in his work of that period, which some identify as verbal and thematic richness and others as excessive verbosity and pretentiousness. Despite its ponderousness, "The Beast in the Jungle" successfully illuminates the psychology of obsession and the difficulty of understanding one's own motivations.

As the story begins, its protagonist is thirty-five years old. Like many other characters in James's fiction, **John Marcher** is supported by some unexplained, independent income and does no real work. Convinced that he is destined for a particular, possibly calamitous fate, Marcher resists his affection for May Bartram because, as he tells himself, it would not be fair to subject her to whatever is going to happen to him. Initially he feels his fate will allow him to have "felt and vibrated" more deeply than other people. This hopeful, if guarded, anticipation turns to dread, however, as the years pass and his destiny has not occurred. He begins to feel doomed rather than singled out. Marcher fails to comprehend the hints of the more perceptive May about what has overtaken his life, and he continues to wait for "the beast" to spring. It is not until a year after her death that he realizes what his fate has been all along: he is "the man of his time, *the* man, to whom nothing on earth was to have happened." He has refused the love that might have existed between him and May, and in so doing has declined to engage in life. Marcher may be compared to the character of Lambert Strether in James's 1903 novel, *The Ambassadors,* who finally asserts the necessity to "have your life," to live fully or otherwise waste one's existence. But Strether retains hope for the future at the end of that novel, whereas Marcher seems destined for a regret-filled, lonely end. Ironically Marcher does not even miss his life while he is waiting for it to happen, but when he realizes the extent of his mistake, he is overcome by despair. The "beast" that haunted him was a product of his own subconscious, and his obsession became a self-fulfilling prophecy. Marcher is possibly the prototype for other, similarly paralyzed figures of twentieth-century literature—such as the title character in T. S. Eliot's 1915 poem "The Love Song of J. Alfred Prufrock"—because he carries within himself the sterility of the modern world. Through Marcher, James illuminates the anguish that results from a person's failure to live, rather than from what actually happens to him or her.

May Bartram, who is thirty years old at the beginning of the story, is the only other person who knows about Marcher's obsession with his anticipated destiny. She is consistently supportive and understanding and in fact loves Marcher despite his inability to reciprocate or respond. Although both characters in "The Beast in the Jungle" have been described as two-dimensional embodiments of ideas, May is said to be somewhat more lifelike and poignant than the story's protagonist. Perhaps this is intentional, for her name suggests a warm, early summer month, while Marcher's name evokes a more wintry season. May's discovery of the true nature of her friend's special fate seems tied to her declining health: the more she unsuccessfully tries to help him discover what is wrong, the more ill she becomes. Ultimately unable to rescue him, she is also the victim of Marcher's fate, as her love goes unrequited and she finally dies without ever having connected with him. In fact, Marcher does not even have the right to attend her deathbed. Critics have speculated that James may have modeled May after his novelist friend Constance Fenimore Woolson, whose love (his biographer Leon Edel suggests) he was unable to return and who eventually committed suicide. Significantly the protagonist of James's 1908 story ''The Jolly Corner,'' who is also tormented by an obsession, finally recovers with the help of a female character who is cast more in the vibrant American mold of Daisy Miller or Isabel Archer than the reserved Englishwoman May Bartram.

The Turn of the Screw (novella, 1898)

Plot: Set in mid-nineteenth-century England, the story centers on a young governess hired to take charge of the niece and nephew of a handsome, charming bachelor. The uncle has instructed her that the children are to be under her sole control and he is not to be bothered about them. When she arrives at Bly, the country estate, the apprehensive governess is relieved to find that ten-year-old Miles and eight-year-old Flora are well-behaved, physically beautiful, delightful children. One evening while walking in the garden, the governess sees a strange man standing on a tower attached to the house. Several days later she sees the same man looking at her through a window, after which he disappears. When the governess tells housekeeper Mrs. Grose about her experiences and describes the man she saw, it seems she has described Peter Quint, the household's former valet, who is now dead. The governess soon sees another apparition, a pale young woman in black identified as the children's former—and also deceased—governess, Miss Jessel. Flora is with her when she sees the ghost, but the little girl claims to see nothing. Mrs. Grose informs the governess that Quint and Miss Jessel had been lovers; although the woman was from a respectable family, Quint was a drunkard and a brute. The governess suspects that the ghosts have come back to lure the children into evil. She is particularly convinced that Miles has already had some secret contact with the ghost of Quint; the boy spent a great deal of time with Quint before his death and apparently knew of the love affair. The governess sees both apparitions again at separate times inside the house. Then one night she discovers that the children have left their beds to range over the lawn, where she believes they communicate with Quint and Miss Jessel.

The children continue to show no sign that they have seen the apparitions, and for a short period they do not appear before the governess, though she feels their presence. Miles announces one day that he would like to go away to school, but the governess feels that he has chosen this course to have more contact with the ghosts. Next she sees Miss Jessel sitting at her desk in the schoolroom and banishes her with an admonition; this prompts her to write a letter requesting help from the children's uncle, even though he wants nothing to do with them. She goes to Miles's bedroom one night and tries to get him to confess to his relations with Quint. While she is talking to him she feels a sudden rush of cold air that extinguishes the candle, even though the window is closed. Miles claims he has blown the candle out. The next day the governess and Mrs. Grose search nearly in vain to locate Flora and finally find her playing by the pond, where Miss Jessel first appeared. The governess can see Miss Jessel standing on the other side, but the little girl refuses to admit seeing the ghost. Flora subsequently becomes feverishly ill and hysterical, angrily and lewdly cursing the governess to Mrs. Grose and demanding to be separated from her; the governess commissions Mrs. Grose to take Flora safely away to London. Then one evening after dinner she confronts Miles again, asking him if he stole the letter she had written to his uncle. She suddenly sees Peter Quint standing at the window looking in, and she pulls Miles close to her so that he cannot see the apparition. He confesses that he did take the letter and that he had already been expelled from a school for mysterious reasons, apparently related to using foul language. The governess's strange manner makes Miles apprehensive, and he asks if Miss

Jessel is nearby. The governess, now nearly hysterical, responds that it is Quint who is present. Miles turns to look, but the ghost has disappeared, and the boy collapses. The governess feels that she has won her struggle with the evil Quint for the soul of her young charge, but Miles is dead.

Characters: "The Turn of the Screw" is one of the most famous and acclaimed ghost stories in all of literature. Since its publication it has generated an astounding volume of critical response and debate. The major controversy over the story lies in whether its ghosts should be interpreted as actual supernatural beings or as figments of the governess's imagination. Much evidence has been presented by both the "apparitionist" and the "hallucinationist" camps, though most contemporary reviewers focus on the story's seemingly intentional ambiguity, which is said to allow and encourage many different levels of interpretation. Whether it is viewed as an outright ghost story pitting good against evil, a religious allegory depicting the corruption and eventual redemption of humanity by a benevolent savior, or the chronicle of a sexually repressed young woman's hallucinations, "The Turn of the Screw" retains its power to interest, puzzle, and frighten both scholars and readers.

The story is introduced by a male narrator named **Douglas** who claims to have known the governess about ten years after the events related in her journal, which her shares with the reader. As a condition of James's stated intention to limit his portrayal of **the governess**'s character, she is never named. The pretty, sensitive, twenty-year-old daughter of a clergyman has lived a rather confined, narrow existence before seeking employment as a governess (a common occupation for young Victorian women of good but not wealthy families) and being hired by the master of Bly. The fact that she is enthralled—even, as many critics claim, in love with—her handsome, charming, bachelor employer is highly significant. She seems well aware of her social inferiority and the fact that such a man would never be interested in her, and she also seems devoted to carrying out to the letter his wish to be left undisturbed. During the years since the story's publication, the governess has served as the center of the critical debate, which has raged in spite of James's claim that he intended to write "a fairy tale, pure and simple." In what has come to be called the "apparitionist" view, the governess is a sane, reliable narrator and a responsible person who takes seriously her duty to protect the children in her charge. The ghosts, then, are not only real but real threats to the innocent Miles and Flora, and the governess must fight for control of their souls. The hallucinationist and the more extreme, Freudian interpretations hold that the governess is at the very least inexperienced, nervous, and emotionally unbalanced enough to hallucinate, and at the most a sexually repressed, neurotic spinster whose desire for her absent master is projected in the apparitions. Proponents of the hallucination theory note that the governess is the daughter of a (possibly insane) clergyman and thus highly susceptible to the idea that evil is a sinister and powerful reality, that she is apprehensive about her new position and suffers from insomnia after arriving, and that she is so eager to believe her own visions that she must continue to build her case, even at the children's expense. While the apparitionists claim that the governess's detailed description of the dead Peter Quint verifies that she has indeed seen his ghost, others claim that Mrs. Grose, to whom she describes the apparition, merely accepts rather than specifically confirms the description. The story has also been viewed as an allegory with strongly religious implications, with the governess serving as a guardian angel or savior and a representative of good who battles with those manifestations of evil, Quint and Miss Jessel, and who, perhaps, goes too far in her desire to conquer them. By any interpretation, the children's fates are tragic, though the apparitionists hold that the governess at least saves Flora and wins her spiritual struggle with Quint over Miles, even though the boy dies, while the hallucinationists contend that the governess propels Flora into a state of delirium and literally scares Miles to death. James infused "The Turn of the Screw" with many bewildering details, leading many critics to conclude that it—and particularly the character of the governess—is meant not only to fascinate and entertain readers but to allow for a variety of readings.

Ten-year-old **Miles** is the primary focus of the governess's attempts to ward off the apparitions she sees. A bright, charming, physically beautiful boy, Miles initially delights the governess with his intelligence and good behavior. She learns from Mrs. Grose, however, that the boy spent a great deal of time with the dissolute Quint while he was employed at Bly and probably knew of the valet's affair with Miss Jessel. There are even vague hints of sexual complicity between the children and the two adults. The governess's gradual perception of a horrible corruption in her outwardly innocent charge is taken literally by the apparitionists as proof of the ghosts' influence, while the hallucinationists hold that she colors perfectly natural, innocuous, or not uncommon behavior—such as Miles's appearance on the lawn in the moonlight or even his expulsion from school—as wicked in order to further her own neurotic view. Many critics have noted an element of sexual attraction in Miles's relationship with the governess, particularly in the scene in which she visits his bedside to persuade him to confess to communication with the ghosts. Like his sister, Miles consistently denies being able to see the apparitions, and the hallucinationists contend that he is the innocent victim of his governess's hysteria, for she finally frightens him to death. The apparitionists hold that Miles's final cry of "Peter Quint—you devil!" indicates either that he is cursing the ghost or, as an already corrupt soul, cursing the governess; in any case, his young constitution is unable to withstand the strain of the encounter. It has been suggested, however, that Miles does not actually die at the end of the story and that the "Douglas" who narrates it, admitting that he knew the governess ten years after this experience and had deep admiration for and even a romantic attachment to her, is actually the adult Miles.

Although **Flora** is not as well developed or significant to the story as her brother, she does add, as James had hoped, another "turn of the screw" to the story's effect. She is also notably angelic in appearance and manner, a lovely, sweet, gentle child whose name fits her well. Scholars consider James's frequent reiteration of the children's great beauty as symbolic of the duality of human nature. And like her brother's, Flora's behavior is interpreted according to the appraiser's stance on the story in general. The apparitionists consider as sinister her claims of not seeing the ghosts, her midnight cavorting with Miles, and her final lewd outburst, while the hallucinationists feel Flora's behavior is consistent with how a confused, defensive, and hysterically frightened child would act. Her foul language in particular may either be evidence of her wickedness or a fairly reasonable reaction to the governess's hysteria. If she is not corrupt, Flora must at least be less vulnerable than her brother, for she escapes with her life (despite her delirium), while Miles is destroyed.

The ghostly character of **Miss Jessel** makes brief appearances in the story, doing little but standing or sitting and looking in a "dishonored and tragic" way at the governess, projecting an "unutterable woe." She is beautiful in spite of her pale, "dreadful" face and "awful eyes," causing the governess to comment that he (her employer) "likes us young and pretty," which Mrs. Grose misinterprets as referring to Quint. Miss Jessel was from a respectable family and was corrupted by the dissolute Quint, whose lower social status made their affair particularly repugnant. Her relations with Quint, though most certainly illicit, are left intentionally vague so that, according to James, the reader may supply the details from his or her own imagination. Both ghosts embody sexual license and corruption—perhaps even of the two children—that would have been especially horrifying to a Victorian audience; horror stories of the nineteenth and even twentieth centuries often blended the erotic with the supernatural. Seeing Miss Jessel in the schoolroom, the governess feels that the ghost is asserting her right to be there, and she immediately renounces the apparition. Some scholars have regarded this moral condemnation as overly defensive, reflecting the governess's deep-seated inferiority and even jealousy. Freudian critics point out Miss Jessel's appearance by the lake (a common Freudian symbol of female sexuality) while nearby Flora attempts to fit the mast of a toy sailboat into its base (mimicking the sexual act) as significant details.

Miss Jessel's ghostly counterpart is the estate's former valet, **Peter Quint,** who during life had a propensity for drink, brutality, and illicit sexuality. The governess's ability to describe him in detail to Mrs. Grose is often cited by the apparitionist critics as evidence of her sanity. The hallucinationist and Freudian critics, however, contend that the description is never actually confirmed by Mrs. Grose and may be based on her memory of her employer, who is never described physically in the story. These critics also often note Quint's first appearance to the governess, when he is standing on a tower—a classic Freudian phallic symbol. Quint had a pale face, thin mouth, and dark eyebrows, as well as curly red hair and whiskers (those who see the story as a religious allegory feel this conveys a distinctly devilish appearance). His clothes seemed too big for him; Mrs. Grose confirms they once belonged to his master. Freudian critics feel this point is evidence of the governess projecting her fantasies about her employer into her vision of Quint. The governess emphasizes that Quint is definitely "not a gentleman," calling attention to the class difference between him and Miss Jessel. Quint's death after spending an evening in a tavern was attributed to a fatal fall on an icy street, but there is a hint that he may have been murdered. One critic even suggests he was killed by a jealous, resentful Mrs. Grose.

It is the good-hearted, talkative, but essentially simple housekeeper, **Mrs. Grose,** who confirms the governess's description of Peter Quint, seemingly verifying the apparitions, even though she herself never sees them. Some reviewers point out, however, that Mrs. Grose merely accepts the governess's description and agrees specifically only to a few, rather generic details. A dutiful employee devoted to the children, Mrs. Grose claims to have unpleasant memories about the period when Quint and Miss Jessel were living at Bly, and this view allows her to believe the governess's claims. But critic Eric Solomon presents the theory that Mrs. Grose killed Quint and tried to drive the governess insane so she could control the children; he calls her the "most clever and desperate of Victorian villainesses." However she is more often viewed as a good though rather slow-witted foil to the more acute, sensitive, and perhaps neurotic governess.

The governess's **employer,** the children's **uncle,** is a significant character in "The Turn of the Screw" despite never appearing in person. The governess obviously worships and idealizes her master, an eligible bachelor she describes as handsome, pleasant, and gallant. The apparitionists say that her feelings about him justify her refusing to bother him and her dealing with the situation by herself, while the hallucinationists and Freudians claim that her repressed sexual desire for her employer initiates her hysterical response. In any case, the uncle displays little concern for the children, which results in the delirious sickness of one child and the death of the other.

Further Reading

Allen, Elizabeth A. *A Woman's Place in the Novels of Henry James.* New York: St. Martin, 1984.

Blackmur, R. P. *Studies in Henry James,* edited by Veronica A. Makowsky. New York: New Directions, 1983.

Bloom, Harold, ed. *Henry James.* New York: Chelsea House, 1987.

Brooks, Cleanth. "The American 'Innocence' in James, Fitzgerald, and Faulkner." In *A Shaping Joy: Studies in the Writer's Craft,* pp. 181-97. London: Methuen, 1971.

Brooks, Van Wyck. *The Pilgrimage of Henry James.* 1925. Reprint. New York: Hippocrene Books, 1972.

Budd, Lewis L., and Edwin H. Cady. *On Henry James: The Best from American Literature,* Chapel Hill, N.C.: Duke University Press, 1990.

Dictionary of Literary Biography, Vols. 12, 71, 74. Detroit: Gale.

Edel, Leon. *Henry James: A Life.* New York: Harper Collins, 1987.

Gale, Robert L. *A Henry James Encyclopedia.* Westport, Conn.: Greenwood Press, 1989.

Long, Robert Emmet. *Henry James: The Early Novels.* Boston: Twayne, 1983.

Lurie, Alison. "A Fine Romance." *New York Review of Books* 38, No. 8 (25 April 1991): 23-4.

McNaughton, William. *Henry James: The Later Novels,* Boston: Twayne Publishers, 1987.

McEwen, Fred B. *A Biographical Dictionary of the Characters in the Fiction of Henry James.* New York: Garland, 1986.

Porte, Joel, ed. *New Essays on the Portrait of a Lady.* Cambridge, England: Cambridge University Press, 1990.

Short Story Criticism, Vol. 8. Detroit: Gale.

Solomon, Eric. "The Return of the Screw." *University Review* XXX, No. 3 (March, 1964): 205-11.

Springer, Mary Doyle. *A Rhetoric of Literary Character: Some Women of Henry James.* Chicago: University of Chicago Press, 1978.

Short Story Criticism, Vol. 8. Detroit: Gale.

Twentieth-Century Literary Criticism, Vols. 2, 11, 24, 40. Detroit: Gale.

Wagenknecht, Edward. *The Tales of Henry James.* New York: Frederick Ungar, 1984.

Geraldine Jewsbury

1812-1880

English novelist, critic, and author of children's stories.

Zoe: The History of Two Lives (novel, 1845)

Plot: The novel's title character is a young woman whose advanced education is rare for a female of her time and milieu. She is determined to make the most of her abilities and to realize her vague ambitions. Raised in England by her uncle, Zoe is faced with the choice of remaining in England, where the questionable legitimacy of her birth limits her options, or going to France and marrying a friend of her father's, guaranteeing her economic stability. Reluctant to become a dependent spinster, Zoe chooses France and marriage. Though she fulfills her conjugal obligations by producing two sons and acting as a gracious hostess in her husband's home, Zoe remains emotionally uncommitted to her marriage. She finds intellectual stimulation through her contact with various learned men. One of these acquaintances is Everhard Burrows, a Catholic priest who attempts to convert Zoe. His disappointment in failing to do so is compounded by his gradual realization that he is in love with Zoe. Distressed by both the cynicism of the older priests he knows and the unquestioning acceptance of the believers he encounters, Everhard experiences a spiritual crisis. After a sensual encounter with Zoe, he leaves the priesthood and goes to Wales to undertake a charitable mission among the destitute. He also works on a philosophical treatise on religious doubt, and continues to adore the distant Zoe. She, meanwhile, has been widowed and, far from pining for Everhard, becomes romantically involved with Count Mirabeau, the French statesman. Their passion is mutual, but Mirabeau has been divorced and French law forbids his remarriage. He proposes that he and Zoe live together unmarried, but Zoe finds this unacceptable and her suitor too demanding; the two finally part.

Everhard, meanwhile, has been forced out of his mission by the more popular, itinerant Wesleyan revivalists, who preach a more firm and evangelistic doctrine than his own. His treatise is published but is lambasted by critics as arrogant and blasphemous. He then goes to Germany, where he writes a well-received philosophical work. Fatally ill, he returns to the French estate where he first met Zoe, but she and her family have moved. By the time Zoe has heard of his illness and arrives to see him, he has slipped into a coma, and dies without seeing her again.

Characters: Jewsbury's outspoken criticism of the Victorian conventions she felt unfairly circumscribed women's lives made her a controversial figure. Well-educated, she believed that traditional education prepared women only for marriage and prevented them from living useful, productive lives. Jewsbury agreed with essayist Thomas Carlyle, whose wife Jane was her close friend, that contentment could only be attained through applying oneself to work and fulfilling one's duties. Even Jane Carlyle, however, was shocked by *Zoe,* which not only featured a highly unconventional female protagonist, but focused on the controversial topic of religious doubt. One of the first of several nineteenth-century novels to deal with this subject, *Zoe* was harshly condemned by early reviewers. While not highly regarded as a literary work, the novel interests modern readers and scholars as a document of Jewsbury's ground-breaking thought on religion and on the limited scope of Victorian women's lives.

Through the novel's title character, Jewsbury illustrates that women too need stimulating employment and outlets for their intelligence and abilities if they are to lead useful lives. Born the illegitimate daughter of an English father and a Greek mother, a heritage that gives her a hint of exoticism, **Zoe** was raised in England by an uncle who gave her a solid education. Beautiful, energetic, and courageous, Zoe is determined to realize her dreams, though she's unsure of how to act on her ambitions. Her essential pragmatism is demonstrated by her decision to avoid the dependency and degradation of spinsterhood, surely her lot if she remained with her uncle, by going to France and marrying a kind but much older man. She views this marriage as an outlet for her energies and as the best of very few options open to her. Although she finds no emotional fulfillment in her marriage, she fulfills her roles as mother and hostess admirably and finds intellectual stimulation through friendships with educated men. For a short time, Everhard seems to offer Zoe a chance for emotional satisfaction; after his withdrawal, she reacts pragmatically, adjusting fairly easily to the loss. Her subsequent relationship with the celebrated Count Mirabeau is mutually passionate. Although Mirabeau is a profoundly intelligent, exciting lover, he is willful and demanding. In asking that Zoe continue her relationship with him and live with him without marriage, Mirabeau seems to want her to submerge her individuality in his life and identity. It may be because she is unwilling to do this, rather than a concern for conventional moral standards, that Zoe refuses to comply with Mirabeau; he, however, concludes that she is more conventional than he had guessed. In the end, Zoe is apparently "composed and chastened,'' suggesting that the extraordinary status she once aspired to has eluded her. Some critics argue that she embodies the stereotypical resignation to limitations that most nineteenth-century women were forced to adopt. Others have detected in Zoe's experiences of romantic passion evidence of Jewsbury's ambivalence toward traditional female roles. Zoe has also been identified as the prototype of the talented but misunderstood and unfulfilled female characters who would be developed more expertly by later nineteenth-century writers such as Charlotte Brontë and George Eliot.

Jewsbury fueled her portrayal of **Everhard Burrows** with what she called her own "religious botherations," doubts that made her question the basis of Christianity. Through Everhard, a Catholic priest in a spiritual crisis exacerbated by his attraction to Zoe, Jewsbury illustrates one of the novel's central concerns. Everhard chooses his vocation during adolescence, when it seems the most desirable of the few bleak alternatives available to him. Initially faithful, he is shocked by the cynicism he encounters at his monastic school, where his questions are dismissed by his elders. Later he is unable to convert Zoe, whose husband is one of his parishioners, to Catholicism and, worse yet, realizes that he is in love with her. Their intense episode of passion, which occurs in a chapel, may help explain the novel's initially negative critical response. Everhard's rigidity is evidenced by his refusal to compromise his ideals after his crisis of belief; he renounces the priesthood as well as his love for Zoe and goes to Wales to immerse himself in social work. He promises himself that he will espouse no religion, but this leads to his being perceived as emotionless, and the Wesleyan revivalists gain popularity and eventually force him to leave. Defeated, he leaves for Germany, where a more healthy climate for doubt and Biblical questioning exists. Thus Jewsbury demonstrates that, unlike Zoe, Everhard has options for fulfillment, traveling where and when he wishes in pursuit of his goals. He does achieve a measure of satisfaction when his later philosophical work is well received in Germany. His love for Zoe, however, is never fulfilled, as he dies before he can see her again.

Count Mirabeau, Zoe's lover, contrasts strongly with Everhard; his love for Zoe is not introspective and self-denying, but openly expressed and willful. Based on the real Count Mirabeau, a leader of the French Revolution and a gifted orator, he is passionate and dazzlingly intelligent, thus stirring Zoe's emotions and stimulating her mind. He is strong as she, but, finally unable to persuade her to be his mistress, he too remains unfulfilled.

Further Reading

Clarke, Norma. *Ambitious Heights: Writing, Friendship, Love: The Jewsbury Sisters, Felicia Hemans, and Jane Welsh Carlyle.* London: Routledge, 1990.

Dictionary of Literary Biography, Vol. 21. Detroit: Gale.

Foster, Shirley. "Introduction: Women and Marriage in Mid-Nineteenth-Century England." In *Victorian Women's Fiction: Marriage, Freedom and the Individual,* pp. 1-39. Croom Helm, 1985.

Hartley, J. M. "Geraldine Jewsbury and the Problems of the Woman Novelist." *Women's Studies International Quarterly* 2, No. 2 (1979): 137-53.

Howe, Susanne. *Geraldine Jewsbury: Her Life and Errors.* London: George Allen & Unwin, 1935.

Nineteenth-Century Literature Criticism, Vol. 22. Detroit: Gale.

Woolf, Virginia. "Geraldine and Jane." In *The Second Common Reader,* pp. 200-17. New York: Harcourt Brace Jovanovich, 1932.

Charles Kingsley
1819-1875

English novelist, dramatist, poet, essayist, children's writer, and songwriter.

Alton Locke (novel, 1850)

Plot: Born into a poor, working-class family, Alton Locke is put to work at an early age in a London tailor's shop. There he meets John Crossthwaite, a radical who rails against the clergy and the upper class for oppressing the poor. He also befriends Saunders "Sandy" Mackaye, a Scottish bookseller who encourages him to educate himself. Alton falls in love with Lillian Winnstay, the daughter of a dean who has taken an interest in him, but he realizes that he has no chance of winning her hand. At Mackaye's suggestion, Alton writes a volume of poems based on his experiences among the London poor. He also follows Crossthwaite's lead and becomes a Chartist—a supporter of the movement to gain more rights for the working class than had been granted under the 1832 Reform Bill. Alton travels from London to Cambridge to visit his cousin George Locke, whom he hopes will help him find a publisher. On the way there, he views the beauties of the countryside for the first time and has a silent encounter with a farm family that impresses him. Visiting his cousin in Cambridge, Alton meets Lord Lyndale, a nobleman who sincerely sympathizes with the plight of working people, and Eleanor Staunton, who asserts that, for reform to occur, workers must reform their behavior and win the respect of the clergy.

Dean Winnstay agrees to publish Alton's poetry if he will remove certain passages that might offend aristocratic readers; Alton reluctantly agrees. He returns to London and becomes a hack writer, producing articles for the popular press in order to support himself. Eleanor and Lord Lyndale are married, and Alton's cousin George, who is pursuing a clerical career, plans to wed Lillian. When Alton's poems are published, he becomes popular with the aristocracy, and Mackaye warns him not to let the gentry exploit him.

Soon Lord Lyndale dies in a fall from a horse. The editor of a Chartist newspaper, Fergus O'Flynn, accuses Alton of deserting the workers' cause, so Alton attends a Chartist meeting and agrees to appear at a rally in the countryside. On his way there, Alton first witnesses the degradation and misery of the rural poor. His subsequent speech at the rally incites so much anger that some of his listeners stage a riot at a nearby farm; though he had tried to stop them, Alton is arrested for his part in the riot and sentenced to three years in jail. Upon release, he participates in the unsuccessful presentation of the Charter to Parliament. The workers have become divided and uneasy, and there are rumors that false signatures have been added to the petition. Distressed by this outcome, Mackaye dies. On the evening of the Charter's failure, Alton encounters Jemmy Downes, an old friend who takes Alton to his squalid home and shows him the bodies of his wife and children, dead from typhoid fever. While the police are investigating the deaths, Jemmy kills himself by jumping into a fetid drainage ditch. Through the exposure, Alton becomes ill and, after experiencing a bizarre dream about biological evolution, wakes to a new life. Under the spiritual guidance of Eleanor, now an active social reformer, he becomes committed to bettering workers' lives through cooperation and self-sacrifice. In accordance with Mackaye's will, Alton and Crossthwaite leave England to spend seven years in America; just before arriving in Texas, Alton dies.

Characters: *Alton Locke* is one of several novels of social reform written in mid-nineteenth-century England; others include Charles Dickens's *Hard Times,* Elizabeth Gaskell's *Mary Barton,* and Charlotte Brontë's *Shirley.* The novel features a vivid portrayal of the conditions suffered by London's poor and reveals Kingsley's belief that violence and division between social classes only impede progress. He stated that his purpose in writing

Alton Locke was to illustrate that members of the working class should not, like the novel's protagonist, attempt to elevate themselves above their social station but should work for reform within their own circumstances. He felt that the upper classes were best suited to govern society, though they often lacked a sense of responsibility and duty. *Alton Locke* interests scholars not for its literary merit (most agree that characterization and plot are subordinated to Kingsley's didactic intent) but as a manifestation of nineteenth-century social concerns.

Through **Alton Locke,** Kingsley dramatizes the hazards of social climbing. He also uses Locke as a mouthpiece to convey the destitution of the urban and rural poor and to condemn the violence of Chartism as a solution to their problems. Born into a poor family, Alton's intelligence surfaces at an early age, which distresses his strict Baptist mother. Having unsuccessfully tried to instill in her son a fear of God and an avoidance of art and literature, which she sees as frivolities, she ejects him from their home when she finds him secretly reading books. Alton's stint in a London tailor's sweatshop allows Kingsley to illustrate how most urban working people toiled under inhumane physical conditions for paltry wages. The proposed Charter seemed to hold out for many of the oppressed the promise of a better life. (Kingsley asserts that the 1832 Reform Bill, designed to improve conditions for all English workers, had benefitted only the commercial class and left laborers' needs still unmet.) Innocent and uneducated, Alton is confronted with a variety of influences, ranging from Crossthwaite's radicalism to Mackaye's more moderate stance, and he lacks the experience to maturely choose his own best course. But he follows Mackaye's advice and attempts to educate himself, also writing a volume of poems based on what he knows best: poverty. After Alton's first journey through the countryside, when he encounters the farm family that symbolizes for him the artificial division between classes, he also means to explore this subject in his poetry, but he will never do so.

After Alton's volume of poetry is published, he becomes the darling of the aristocracy, who view him as an interesting token of a world that fascinates but does not touch them. Locke essentially compromises his principles to gain financial and social status. In an attempt to win back the confidence of his Chartist friends, Alton makes a second trip into the countryside to appear at the rally. Here he notices the wretchedness of the rural poor and confronts with horror the destructive results of a competitive, laissez-faire political system on agricultural life. Nevertheless, he does not condone the violent riot that breaks out after his impassioned speech, but receives a prison sentence for his part in the episode. After his release, Alton must face not only the defeat of the Charter and death of the now disillusioned Mackaye, but the horrifying fate of Jemmy Downes and his family. His visit to their typhoid-ridden home results in his own illness, during which he experiences the strange dream often noted as a particularly interesting part of *Alton Locke*. In the dream, Alton undergoes the process of biological evolution; crawling out of the sea and into the forest, he is gradually transformed into increasingly sophisticated forms of life. Finally he becomes a young ape with the first stirrings of a higher consciousness, but he grows more bestial as he matures. Alton wakes with a new awareness of humanity's still-basically primitive nature. With Eleanor's help, he adopts a Christian philosophy radically different from that which his mother taught him, for it is based on brotherly love, self-sacrifice, and the concept of a loving, merciful God. Realizing that he should never have courted the favor of the wealthy and that Chartists' violence is misguided, Alton concludes that the poor must improve their conditions through peaceful cooperation, aided by the few sympathetic clergy and enlightened members of the upper classes, such as Eleanor, who wish to help them. Now spiritually renewed, Alton is physically ruined by his illness and the long sea journey to America, and dies before reaching Texas.

Two early influences on Alton's life are **John Crossthwaite** and **Saunders "Sandy" Mackaye.** Crossthwaite, Alton's radical coworker in the London tailor's shop who persuades Alton to join the Chartist movement, represents the decent worker who, driven by despair and lack of options, resorts to violence. Mackaye, a Scottish bookseller reputedly based on Thomas Carlyle (a nineteenth-century essayist dedicated to social reform), is an elderly libertarian whose experience with reform movements dates back to the French Revolution. He encourages Alton to educate himself, twice warns him to beware the false friendship of the rich, and warns Alton and Crossthwaite that the Charter contains bogus signatures. In the end, the old radical is dismayed by the corrupt means the workers have used to attain their goal; he realizes before anyone else that the Chartists are doomed to failure.

In Cambridge, Alton becomes better acquainted with his cousin **George Locke,** who introduces him to a more sophisticated circle than he has previously encountered. George embodies, in his lack of conscience, the selfish ambitions of the middle class. He pursues a clerical career, for instance, not out of a wish to serve God or humanity but because he considers it a lucrative and secure occupation. George dies of typhus contracted from coats sewn in Jemmy Downes's disease-infected hovel, emphasizing the concept that class divides people only artificially. His wife **Lillian** also contracts typhus, losing her considerable beauty--a fitting punishment, perhaps, for her lack of compassion.

Aristocrat **Eleanor Staunton** adheres to essayist Carlyle's belief that social reform can only occur if workers learn self restraint, and thus earn the respect of the clergy and nobility. After the death of her philanthropic husband, Lord Lyndale, Eleanor serves humanity by organizing a needleworkers' cooperative, encouraging others of the upper class to join her efforts for reform. While nursing Alton through his illness, she explains that she was once vain and proud but developed a sense of responsibility and a commitment to the Christian values of brotherhood and self-sacrifice. Eleanor represents the concerned members of the nobility who Kingsley felt were best suited to lead his nation into reform. Alton initially dislikes Eleanor and her aristocratic husband, **Lord Lyndale** (he later becomes **Lord Ellerton**), whose exterior coldness masks his real concern for the lower classes. In accordance with his belief that the wealthy have an obligation to help the poor, he takes a paternalistic approach to the reform of his own estates.

Fergus O'Flynn, who writes for the Chartist newspaper *Weekly Warwhoop,* is a disreputable, inflammatory journalist who succeeds in turning his working-class readers against Alton by accusing him of selling out. In fact, it is O'Flynn who exploits the Chartist movement for his own gain; he encourages violent resistance, but is notably absent when conflict occurs. O'Flynn was reputedly modeled after a real person—Fergus O'Connor of the *Morning Star.* **Jemmy Downes** and his ill-fated family graphically illustrate the base conditions endured by the urban poor. Jemmy lives in a hovel built over a sewer; rats have begun to eat his family's corpses; and he kills himself by jumping into a fetid drainage ditch.

Further Reading

Chitty, Susan. *The Beast and the Monk: A Life of Charles Kingsley.* New York: Mason/ Charter, 1975.

Colloms, Brenda. *Charles Kingsley: The Lion of Eversley.* New York: Barnes and Noble, 1975.

Dictionary of Literary Biography, Vols. 21, 32. Detroit: Gale.

Hartley, Allen John. *The Novels of Charles Kingsley: A Christian Social Interpretation.* Folkestone: Hour-Glass Press, 1977.

Kendall, Guy. *Charles Kingsley and His Ideas.* London: Hutchison and Co., 1947.

Uffelman, Larry. *Charles Kingsley.* Boston: Twayne, 1979.

Rudyard Kipling
1865-1936
English short story writer, novelist, poet, essayist, and autobiographer.

"The Man Who Would Be King" (short story, 1888)

Plot: The story takes place in India and Afghanistan in the late nineteenth century. The narrator, a British journalist stationed in India, is returning by train to his office in Jodhpur when he meets two adventurers, Peachey Carnehan and Daniel Dravot, who happen to be posing as correspondents for the same newspaper that employs the narrator. The two vagabonds later visit him in his office, where they tell him of their plan to become kings of a remote country called Kafiristan. They ask him to tell them whatever he knows about the tiny nation, to prepare them for their adventure. Soon after Peachey and Daniel leave the narrator's office, Daniel is seen impersonating a crazy priest and attempting to sell whirligigs (whirling toys) to the natives in the marketplace. Thus begins their journey. Three years later, Peachey returns alone to the journalist's office, a broken, bedraggled shadow of his former self. He explains that he and Daniel did indeed become kings of Kafiristan, while the narrator remained in his sedate office, writing about the experiences of others rather than living an exciting life himself. Instructing the journalist to steady him by looking straight into his eyes, Peachey becomes the story's narrator as he relates what happened to him and his friend. After reaching Kafiristan, the two were able to convince its inhabitants of their royal and even godly status. Daniel was crowned king while Peachey was assigned leadership of the country's army. Daniel gradually developed an enthusiasm for their role that resembled the traditional imperialistic fervor of the British; he predicted that they would make an empire of Kafiristan. His ambition was thwarted, however, when he made a fatal mistake. Despite the pact between Peachey and Daniel to avoid liquor and women, Daniel determined to take a native woman as his wife. He was assigned a Kafiristan woman who, as he was attempting to kiss her, bit him and drew blood, signaling Daniel's mortal status to the natives. After Daniel had asked for and received forgiveness from Peachey for breaking their "contrack," he was forced to walk out onto a bridge over a deep chasm; the bridge's cables were then cut and he fell to his death. Peachey, meanwhile, was tied between two trees and left to die, but when he survived this exposure his captors released him, and he made his way back to Jodhphur. As he finishes his story, Peachey places a shrunken head on the narrator's desk, claiming that it is Daniel's. Then he wanders out into the city, and two days later he dies of sunstroke.

Characters: Kipling is considered one of the finest of all short story writers, and "The Man Who Would Be King" is one of his most effective and respected stories. Characterized by the exotic setting, action, and colorful masculine protagonists found in much of Kipling's fiction, the story is distinguished for its convincing narrative and skillful blending of the serious and the comic, of reality and fantasy. Many critics have seen "The Man Who Would Be King" as an allegory about British imperialism in India, noting that it reveals Kipling's pride in his own people and his country's accomplishments as well as his attraction to Eastern values.

Kipling employs a narrative-within-a-narrative framework to prepare the reader for a tale that might otherwise be too fantastic to accept. The first **narrator** is reassuringly reliable: a journalist who holds a respectable position with a newspaper. This is the same steady, rather stolid role that Peachey and Daniel pretend to hold when the narrator meets them on the train. Unlike Peachey and Daniel, the journalist never experiences adventures himself but only reports on the activities of others, providing a strong contrast to the mythic life that Peachey and Daniel—however briefly—create for themselves. Kipling is said to have modeled the narrator after himself when, as a young man, he worked as a reporter for an Indian newspaper.

Peachey Carnehan is the surviving half of the free-spirited, ambitious duo that sets out to rule Kafiristan. He is a huge-shouldered man whose military experience leads eventually to his commanding and training the remote nation's army. When Daniel decides to take a native wife, Peachey unsuccessfully begs his partner not to break their "contrack." Peachey's physical fortitude is evidenced by his ability to survive the punishment meted out by his captors after he and Daniel are found to be ordinary human beings and Daniel is killed. He also exhibits loyalty to his friend in his willingness to forgive Daniel for his disastrous breach and by retrieving Daniel's head and later producing it—with a certain degree of pride and affection—for the journalist to see.

Peachey and his fellow vagabond, the red-bearded **Daniel Davot,** might almost be a single-though-dual character because, as the story ends, their roles seem to blend. Although it is Daniel who establishes himself as a god and king, it is Peachey who is crucified (i.e., punished by being tied between two trees and left to die) and then resurrected through his later appearance in the journalist's office. The fact that Daniel rather than Peachey is crowned king of Kafiristan attests to the former's greater flamboyance, daring, or charisma. Having demonstrated a capacity for disguise early in the story, when he dresses as a mad priest sells whirligigs in the marketplace, Daniel successfully convinces the villagers that he should be their king. While their downfall might well be inevitable, Daniel precipitates it by breaking their bond and taking a native wife. This action may be due to ambition (for he envisions Kafiristan as a great empire and wishes to produce heirs to carry on his reign) as it was for the more powerful British imperialists in nineteenth-century India; it may also be the result of sexual desire—a subject that, some critics contend, made Kipling uneasy. In any case, its disastrous results demonstrate the necessity of maintaining the illusion of superiority and power over those one wishes to rule. Daniel's shrunken head, which Peachey displays on the journalist's desk, symbolizes the true insubstantiality of human claims as well as the outrageous achievement of the two men, who, after all, did reach the exalted height upon which they had set their sights.

Further Reading

Amis, Kingsley. *Rudyard Kipling and His World.* New York: Charles Scribner's Sons, 1975.

Bloom, Harold, ed. *Rudyard Kipling.* New York: Chelsea House, 1987.

Gilbert, Elliot L. *The Good Kipling: Studies in the Short Story.* Oberlin: Ohio University Press, 1970.

Harrison, James. *Rudyard Kipling.* Boston: G. K. Hall, 1982.

Meyers, Jeffrey. "The Idea of Moral Authority in 'The Man Who Would Be King.'" *Studies in English Literature, 1500-1900* VII, No. 4 (Autumn 1968): 711-23.

Pritchett, V. S. "Kipling's Short Stories." In *The Living Novel and Later Appreciations,* pp. 175-82. New York: Random House, 1964.

Short Story Criticism, Vol. 5. Detroit: Gale.

Twentieth-Century Literary Criticism, Vols. 8, 17. Detroit: Gale.

Joseph Sheridan Le Fanu

1814-1873

Irish novelist, short story writer, poet, journalist, and editor.

"Green Tea" (short story, 1864)

Plot: The narrator is the former secretary of the late Dr. Martin Hesselius, a German physician whose specialty would now be called psychiatry. While sorting through his employer's papers, the narrator discovers a sixty-year-old case history. At that time Dr. Hesselius met a mild-mannered, bachelor clergyman named Reverend Robert Jennings at the home of a mutual friend, Lady Mary Heyduke. She confided to the doctor that Jennings, a respected member of the community, has recently been suffering from an apparent nervous complaint resulting in strange behavior; she also mentioned that Jennings's father reputedly once encountered a ghost. Devoted to the study of ancient religions, Jennings spent many hours in research and writing; he was also interested, as was Hesselius, in "metaphysical medicine." After meeting the doctor, Jennings arranged a consultation with Hesselius, during which he shared his idea that physical illness may not always have a material cause. At a later encounter, Jennings described the condition tormenting him. While riding on a bus one day, he encountered a small, black monkey; when he tried to poke the creature with his umbrella, it proved immaterial. The monkey then repeatedly appeared to Jennings, staring at him with malignant, glowing red eyes. The monkey thwarted Jennings's studies as well as his duties as a clergyman, squatting on his text when he tried to read his sermons. Later, using an evil, hissing voice, the monkey began suggesting that Jennings commit wicked deeds. Wondering if the excessive amount of strong green tea he had habitually consumed while studying could cause this hallucination, Jennings stopped drinking tea. He feared the creature's torment would eventually lead to some dire consequence, but Hesselius assured him the vision resulted from Jennings's depleted physical condition and could not hurt him. Some time later Hesselius was summoned to Jennings's house, only to learn that the clergyman had killed himself. His servant confirmed that, before his suicide, Jennings had complained of the monkey's presence. In concluding the case history, Hesselius regretted not being able to continue his treatment of Jennings, since he had successfully treated many similar cases. He attributed Jennings's condition to hereditary disposition to morbidity and overstimulated nerves.

Characters: "Green Tea" is one of the most renowned stories in Le Fanu's much-praised collection, *In a Glass Darkly.* These skillfully executed tales explore not so much the supernatural as the unseen evil that may lurk within the human psyche. The subtle, gradual revelation of mental breakdown presented in "Green Tea" exemplifies the transition from the sensationalism of earlier gothic fiction to the increasingly psychological emphasis of the modern horror story, a development that Le Fanu is credited with initiating. He has also been lauded for the innovative, sophisticated framing technique he employed in the stories of *In a Glass Darkly.*

The **narrator** of "Green Tea," himself trained as a surgeon, was secretary to **Dr. Martin Hesselius** and greatly revered his former employer. Undertaking the task of organizing the doctor's papers, he presents various case studies, relating them in the voice of Hesselius. A

German physician whose special interest is "metaphysical medicine," Hesselius treats mental disorders in much the same way as the modern psychologist. He propounds the theory that the body is simply the material reflection of a human being's inner, spiritual nature; thus he believes that Jennings's hallucination and eventual suicide were brought on by the morbidity he inherited from his father and overstimulated nerves caused by his intense studying and tea-drinking. Critics are divided on whether Hesselius serves as Le Fanu's mouthpiece or as a long-winded pedant whose conclusions and claims of infallibility must be carefully weighed. Scholars note that, despite his attention to the psychological quirks of human nature, Hesselius is sometimes inept, and they find his claim that he merely needed more time to cure Jennings of his complaint pompous.

Outwardly calm and controlled, the respectable **Reverend Robert Jennings** is inwardly tormented by the repeated appearances of the evil little monkey that seems bent on destroying him. In addition to his clerical duties, Jennings studies pre-Christian religions, spending many hours researching and writing about his topic. He tells Hesselius that he began drinking large quantities of green tea to connect himself with the physical world, since he feared that otherwise his mind might become completely disengaged from reality. He wonders if consuming so much green tea might have produced the hallucination, yet he also says he believes ailments do not always have material causes; regardless, the monkey continues its visits even after he stops drinking the tea. Hesselius believes that Jennings's hereditary background (his father had reputedly seen and conversed with a ghost), his physically depleted state, and his intellectual interests in such topics as primitive religion and mystical Swedenborgianism adequately explain his predicament. The fact that Hesselius is portrayed as a somewhat unreliable narrator, however, has led some scholars to conclude that the author left the real cause of Jennings's malady intentionally ambiguous. Critics have varied in their interpretation of the tale: a few cite the story's title as the definitive clue that Jennings is indeed addicted to green tea; others take a Freudian approach, identifying Jennings as a schizophrenic bachelor whose long-denied sexual desires are made manifest in the monkey; still others suggest that the visions may be Jennings's punishment for some secret sin or that his torment allegorically represents the artist's painful struggle to create. Jennings's devotion to a writing project upon which he works late into the night has its parallels in Le Fanu's life, for at the time of the story's publication, he also kept late writing hours and reportedly drank tea.

Jennings's **monkey** tormentor is one of the most compelling symbols in nineteenth-century literature. Compared with the conventional ghosts of gothic horror stories, the monkey is a notably unusual fiend. Small and black with red, glowing eyes and a hideous, mocking grimace, the creature's presence is discernible even in the dark, when it has a reddish aura or halo. It harasses the mild-mannered bachelor continually, mocking and threatening him in a malicious, hissing voice. Its presence drains his physical energy and prevents him from carrying out his clerical duties. Squatting on Jennings's text when he tries to read his sermons, the monkey has been seen as an embodiment of evil. It might also manifest Jennings's repressed sexuality, since its hideous and hairy appearance make it a classic Freudian symbol of the denial of the sexual drive. Whether the monkey is an other-worldly demon or just a figment of Jennings's imagination is never conclusively determined, though Hesselius feels it is a product of his patient's psyche. Some critics find absurdity in the idea of a gentle, bachelor clergyman sent scampering out of his pulpit by the vision of a tiny, demonic monkey, and they believe this shade of the ridiculous alongside the element of the horrible heighten the story's overall effect.

A minor character in "Green Tea" is **Lady Mary Heyduke,** an aristocrat and a mutual friend of Hesselius and Jennings, at whose house the two men meet and converse. She informs Hesselius of the clergyman's odd behavior and presents the idea that the propensity for seeing ghostly manifestations is a Jennings family trait.

Uncle Silas: A Tale of Bartram-Haugh (novel, 1864)

Plot: The story takes place in the early nineteenth century in the Derbyshire region of England. The narrator is Maud Ruthyn, who recounts events of her early life. She was the daughter of reclusive, eccentric, but kind widower Austin Ruthyn, a devotee of the mystical Swedenborgian religious philosophy. Not far away, at Bartram-Haugh estate, lived Austin's brother, Silas, whom Maud had never met. He was accused but not convicted of murdering a man named Charke, to whom he owed gambling debts and who supposedly committed suicide in a room of Silas's house. Thereafter Silas was scorned by society, and he subsequently withdrew into moody seclusion. When Maud was seventeen her father hired a new governess, the grotesquely large, affected Madame de Rougierre. While under her governess's care, Maud had several frightening encounters with a wicked young man and his rough friends. Madame de Rougierre was fired after she was caught rifling through her employer's papers; Austin's cousin, the cheerful and vivacious Lady Monica Knollys, had previously hinted that the governess had a disreputable past and had warned both Austin and Maud against her. Austin died suddenly, and his will stipulated that Maud, who at twenty-one would inherit her father's estate, should go to live with her uncle, Silas, until she reached her majority. By demonstrating his own willingness to deliver his daughter to his brother, Austin hoped to remove the stain that Silas had brought to his family's honor. Maud duly moved to Bartram-Haugh, where she settled into a fairly comfortable routine once she had formed a warm friendship with her outspoken, rather crude, but good-natured cousin Milly. She rarely saw her strange uncle, who sometimes lapsed into deathlike, opium-induced comas. Maud was surprised and chagrined to learn that the vulgar young man she had previously encountered was Silas's son, Dudley, who Silas maintained was a true gentlemen despite his youthful high spirits. Then Milly was sent away, to Maud's sorrow, to a French convent, and Dudley began to pester Maud with marriage proposals that she repeatedly rejected. When she appealed to Silas for help, he encouraged her to consider marrying his son. Finally Dudley's secret marriage to a barmaid was revealed, and his attentions to Maud ended. Rather incongruously he offered to take Maud to the safe haven of Lady Monica's home for twenty thousand pounds. She refused, and it was later reported that Dudley and his wife had emigrated to Australia.

Silas informed Maud that he was financially ruined and had to send her to France, where he planned to later join her. After an exhausting trip, however, she found herself back at Bartram-Haugh, confined in a room with the repulsive Madame de Rougierre as her jailer. She now realized that her life was in danger. That night the governess drank some drugged wine meant for Maud and fell asleep on Maud's bed. The governess was then murdered by Dudley, who crept in through the window while Maud watched from a hiding place. Maud managed to escape and reach Lady Monica, who subsequently sent her off to France. Two years later, Maud learned of what happened after her departure: Silas died of an opium overdose, Dudley ran away, and Madame de Rougierre was found buried in the courtyard of Bartram-Haugh. It was discovered that the unusual window frame in the room in which Maud was imprisoned—and in which Charke was murdered—allowed entrance from the outside even when locked, explaining not only Dudley's entrance but Charke's murder by Silas. Maud eventually married the upstanding Lord Ilbury, who had been one of her guardians after her father's death, and achieved happiness.

Characters: Although Le Fanu is considered a minor Victorian novelist, he is often cited as an important innovator in the development of the modern horror novel. Recognized as one of Le Fanu's most successful works and sometimes called the first psychological thriller, *Uncle Silas* features many qualities of the typical nineteenth-century gothic horror novel, such as a foreboding mood and setting and elements of the supernatural, and it focuses on the psychology and subconscious motivations of its main characters. Its tightly constructed plot and skillful evocation of mood effectively heightens suspense and horror in the novel, while exploring such themes as the nature of human evil and the deterioration of an aristocratic family.

Silas Ruthyn is the novel's primary embodiment of gloom and, as is ultimately shown, of evil. As a carefree young aristocrat, he had indulged his fondness for gambling and women, becoming debt-ridden and marrying a woman from a much lower social station. When Mr. Charke, to whom he owed a great deal of money, died in Silas's home, it could not be proven that Silas had anything to do with the death, because the room was sealed off from the outside. Although Charke's death was ruled a suicide, Silas was ostracized by society and retreated into moody seclusion. His general aura of otherworldliness is reinforced by his abnormally pale face and large, fiery eyes, which make him appear spectral; he is an opium addict—sometimes falling into deathlike comas—a religious fanatic, and frequently refers to himself as already deceased. Although he treats Maud with civility, she senses something dreadful about him. It is suggested that Silas may once have had the potential for a more virtuous, productive life, but even he is aware that his weaknesses—particularly his craving for money and luxury—and misguided decisions have led him into evil. It is eventually revealed that he *did* kill Charke and also plotted and commissioned the murder of his own niece. Once the head of an aristocratic family, Silas fails through deceit and murder, and with only an inferior son to be his heir, Silas chooses suicide.

Silas's brother, **Austin Ruthyn,** advances the plot by handing over his daughter to the care of his brother. Like Silas, Austin is reclusive and taciturn, but he treats his daughter with kindness. Eccentric and devoted to the study (like several other Le Fanu protagonists) of mystical Swedenborgian philosophy, Austin has a premonition of his own death and alters his will, thus setting in motion the novel's action. By demonstrating to the world his willingness that his daughter be raised by his supposedly evil brother, he wishes to remove the stain that Silas has brought to the family's honor. It is not Silas himself that Austin seeks to vindicate but the Ruthyn name, but both are damaged beyond salvation. Even less rational than relinquishing Maud to Silas is Austin's hiring the grotesquely inappropriate Madame de Rougierre as a governess for his daughter; he only releases her when she is caught going through his papers. This behavior can only be attributed to Austin's general eccentricity and serves as an example of the incongruity often present in Le Fanu's fiction.

Maud Ruthyn, the novel's narrator, recounts her early years from the vantage point of an older, settled woman. She lived a secluded, rather lonely, but generally contented childhood with her dour, eccentric father. Sent by Austin to Bartram-Haugh, where her inheritance makes her a target of evil, Maud initially finds happiness in her relationship with her cousin Milly. After Milly is sent away, however, come the unsought attentions of the vulgar Dudley and, finally, a close brush with death. Although Maud's innocence and naiveté make her a somewhat typical gothic heroine, she is not a uniformly sympathetic character: she can be indecisive, emotionally erratic, and snobbish, and she does not realize the danger she is in until it is too late. But these same qualities also make Maud an effective narrator, for her growing sense of uneasiness and foreboding increase the novel's suspense. Le Fanu's depiction of Maud's confinement in the same room in which Charke was killed, where she witnesses Dudley Ruthyn murdering the sleeping governess, is often cited as particularly effective in creating a mood of psychological terror. Maud's reactions to the other characters help heighten their impact: she is terrified by her spectral Uncle Silas; she feels repulsed and physically threatened by Madame de Rougierre; and Dudley inspires in her anger, repulsion, and fear of sexual violation. Although Maud ultimately escapes the evil that menaces her, the revelation that one of her children later died in childbirth provides a gloss on whether she can achieve complete happiness or contentment.

Dudley Ruthyn is a vulgar, loutish scoundrel who torments Maud with his crude attentions, and he ultimately proves to be a murderer. His preference for instinct over intelligence is evident in his fondness for boxing, his raucous manner and behavior, and his secret marriage to a low-born woman. He possesses a leering sexuality that directly menaces Maud, and his early appearances before her, prior to her move to Bartram-Haugh, help to create the novel's foreboding mood. Dudley embodies the last vestige and final collapse of a formerly dignified aristocratic family, and Silas's attempts to portray his son to Maud as a model English gentleman are notably pathetic; eventually even he must admit the truth about Dudley. Nevertheless, some qualities give Dudley's character more depth: although usually impudent, he is sometimes overcome by shyness; despite his true lack of refinement, he is conceited; his general self-complacency occasionally gives way to uneasiness; and after he has murdered the governess, he is filled with fear and regret and turns angrily on the father who incited him to such a deed.

The terrifying governess, **Madame de Rougierre,** is one of the most memorable characters in *Uncle Silas.* A sly, alcoholic, physically menacing figure, she stands in contrast to the conventional image of the demure, refined governess, and she makes a strongly negative impression on Maud. Her hulking stature, sallow skin, huge mouth, and bald head covered by a false-looking black wig render her physically grotesque, while her exaggerated, psuedo-French manners, awkward gestures, and bizarre vanity add to her unpleasantness. She pretends she is concerned for Maud, then threatens her with physical violence when the girl resists doing her bidding. Madame de Rougierre also presents a subtle sexual threat to Maud with her uninvited intimacy and hints that she is physically attracted to her young charge; indeed the past indiscretions Lady Monica claimed knowledge of were most likely sexual in nature. In the end she seems an almost pathetic figure whose propensity for liquor and lack of real comprehension of the events in which she is involved result in her death. Several critics have noted that in the two short stories upon which *Uncle Silas* is based, it is Maud's cousin who is murdered; the novel's substitution of the malignant governess as Dudley's victim seems more suitable to modern readers, as it no doubt was to Le Fanu's Victorian audience.

Several positively portrayed minor characters provide relief from the tension and evil that infuse *Uncle Silas.* Austin's cousin, **Lady Monica Knollys,** is a good-humored, sensible, energetic woman whose estate provides safe haven for Maud after she escapes from Bartram-Haugh. Lady Monica criticizes Austin for hiring Madame de Rougierre, hinting that she knows of the woman's past wickedness but not revealing any details, and she gives Maud an ominous warning about associating too closely with her governess (some critics suggest this refers to Madame de Rougierre posing a sexual threat to the young girl). Although Maud is initially somewhat frightened and repulsed by her father's trusted friend, the tall, ungainly **Dr. Breyerly** consistently shows his concern for Maud in his visits to Bartram-Haugh, and she eventually realizes that he is one of her most faithful supporters. He criticizes Austin for heedlessly handing his daughter over to Silas's care, though he kindly explains to Maud that her father had taken this step because his long seclusion blinded him to the facts of the situation. Like Breyerly, **Lord Ilbury** is appointed a trustee of Austin's will; he introduces himself to Maud as **Mr. Carysbrook,** claiming to be a tenant of a nearby house, when actually he is checking on her welfare. Maud eventually marries the amiable Lord Ilbury.

The loud, rather coarse **Milly Ruthyn** is as good-hearted as her brother Dudley is wicked, and she proves a fine companion for her cousin, Maud. Though outlandish and uncultivated in her manners, dress, and talk, she offers Maud the warm friendship that both girls have missed during their lonely childhoods. Her departure from Bartram-Haugh to attend a convent school in France marks the onset of danger in Maud's life. Several scholars approved of Le Fanu's choice to break the pattern of the short stories that formed the basis for *Uncle Silas,* in which Dudley murders his sister. In the novel Le Fanu allows Milly to escape her evil home and, eventually, to achieve happiness with her marriage to a clergyman. **Meg Hawkes,** the rough-mannered daughter of the brutal miller **"Pegtop"**

Hawkes (who beats his daughter and also serves as Silas's agent), proves a good friend to Maud, who wins the initially hostile girl's affection by nursing her through a critical illness. Meg influences her sweetheart, **Tom Brice,** who is a servant at Bartram-Haugh, to change his formerly disloyal attitude toward Maud and help her to escape. Tom and Meg later marry and move to a new home abroad.

Other characters in *Uncle Silas* include **Sarah Matilda,** the barmaid Dudley secretly married; Maud's devoted maid, **Mary Quince**; **Mr. Charke,** Silas's murder victim; and **Captain Oakley,** a would-be suitor of Maud's pummeled in a crude fistfight with Dudley.

Further Reading

Barclay, Glen St. John. "Vampires and Ladies: Sheridan Le Fanu." In *Anatomy of Horror: The Masters of Occult Fiction,* pp. 22-38. New York: St. Martin's Press, Inc., 1979.

Begnal, Michael. *Joseph Sheridan Le Fanu.* Lewisburg, Pa.: Bucknell University Press, 1971.

Bleiler, E. F., ed. Introduction to *Ghost Stories and Mysteries* by J. S. Le Fanu, Bleiler, pp. iii-ix. New York: Dover Publications, 1975.

Dictionary of Literary Biography, Vols. 21, 70. Detroit: Gale.

McCormack, W. J. *Sheridan Le Fanu and Victorian England.* Oxford: Clarendon Press, 1980.

Melada, Ivan. *Sheridan Le Fanu.* Boston: Twayne, 1987.

Nineteenth-Century Literature Criticism, Vol. 9. Detroit: Gale.

Peterson, Audrey. *Victorian Masters of Mystery: From Wilkie Collins to Conan Doyle.* New York: Ungar, 1984.

Mikhail Yuryevich Lermontov
1814-1841
Russian novelist, dramatist, short story writer, and poet.

A Hero of Our Time (*Geroi nashego vremeni;* novel, 1840)

Plot: Set in the 1830s in the mountainous Caucasus region of Russia, the novel is comprised of five sections: "Bela," "Maxsim Maxsimich," "Taman," "Princess Mary," and "The Fatalist." The narrator of "Bela" is presumably the author himself. While traveling from Georgia to Russia, he meets an old military officer named Maxsim Maxsimich. A snowstorm forces the two men to spend a night together at an inn. Maxsimich tells the narrator about his friend Grigory Pechorin, a young aristocrat who had come to a remote frontier outpost in the Caucasus several years earlier to serve as a cavalry officer. Pechorin and his comrades had befriended a boy named Azamat, the son of a local chief who subsequently invited his son's acquaintances to a village wedding. Pechorin was attracted to the chief's lovely daughter, Bela, as was a rough bandit named Kazbich who was also present. Noticing the bandit's infatuation, Azamat offered to trade his sister for Kazbich's fine horse. Kazbich refused the offer. Later, however, Pechorin helped Azamat steal the horse from Kazbich and won Bela as his reward. The enraged and vengeful Kazbich killed the chief, who he believed had engineered the deed, and took back his horse. Later he also kidnapped Bela. When Pechorin and Maxsimich pursued Kazbich to rescue the girl, the bandit stabbed her with his knife and rode away. Pechorin seemed grief-stricken over Bela's death, yet he laughed at Maxsimich's attempt to comfort him.

In "Maxsim Maxsimich," the narrator of the first section travels to sleepy Vladikavkaz, where he again encounters Maxsimich. Pechorin's arrival is also anticipated, and Maxsimich is overjoyed at the prospect of seeing his old friend. Pechorin, however, treats Maxsimich coldly; the older officer is bewildered, hurt, and finally sullen. After Pechorin's departure, Maxsimich decides to throw away Pechorin's journal, which he has been carefully guarding. The narrator retrieves the journal and leaves Vladikavkaz the next day. Some time later he learns that Pechorin has died, and he is glad that he may now publish the three stories which comprise the journal. This is why the last three sections of the novel have Pechorin as narrator and action predating the events of the first two.

"Taman" chronicles Pechorin's encounter with a band of smugglers. He arrives in the coastal town of Taman, where a blind boy admits him to a dilapidated cottage to spend the night. Pechorin has a distaste for physically handicapped people, so he is repulsed by the boy and is further disturbed by the absence of any religious icons in the cottage. That night he witnesses a strange encounter between the blind boy, an unidentified woman, and a man named Yanko who arrives by boat. The next day Pechorin meets a beautiful young girl who entices him into joining her for a sail on the ocean. When they have traveled some distance from the shore, the girl tries to force Pechorin from the boat, but he pushes her into the water instead. After making his way back to land, Pechorin spots the girl on the beach talking to Yanko. Then the blind boy arrives, carrying a loaded sack. Finally the girl and Yanko sail away in a boat, leaving the blind boy and the girl's elderly mother to their own fates. Returning to the cottage, Pechorin finds that all of his belongings have been stolen.

The story of "Princess Mary" is set in the town of Pyatigorsk, the town where a spa has been built on the famous Elizabeth spring, attracting many fashionable and sophisticated visitors. There Pechorin meets a previous acquaintance, a pretentious young cadet named Grushnitsky who is recovering from a wound. Both men admire the beautiful and charming Princess Mary, who is staying in the town with her parents. Her apparent preference for Grushnitsky annoys Pechorin and he plans a series of subtle humiliations. Meanwhile Pechorin renews his affair with his former lover, the now-married Vera. He decides to pretend an infatuation with Princess Mary in order to hide his illicit relationship, and soon the princess is in love with him. At a grand ball attended by all of the town's fashionable society, Pechorin raises Grushnitsky's ire by dancing the mazurka with Princess Mary, an honor the cadet had expected to receive. The antagonism between Pechorin and Grushnitsky continues in Kislovodsk, where Pechorin, goes to join Vera and to flee rumors of his impending marriage to Princess Mary. Grushnitsky eventually challenges Pechorin to a duel. Pechorin learns of the cadet's plot to humiliate him by removing the bullets from the guns before the duel. He arranges for Grushnitsky to stand at the edge of cliff during the confrontation and, after ensuring that his own gun is loaded, shoots Grushnitsky, who tumbles into the ravine below. Despite the pleas of Princess Mary's mother, Pechorin refuses to marry the girl and determines to continue his solitary and seemingly futile existence.

In "The Fatalist," Pechorin discusses the concept of predestination with a group of Cossack officers, including Lieutenant Vulich. To prove his own faith in predestination (the idea that one's fate is predetermined and not subject to free will), Vulich raises his pistol to his head and pulls the trigger. The gun does not fire, despite Pechorin's conviction that he has seen the look of death on the man's face. A short time later, however, Vulich is killed by a drunken Cossack. Curious about his own fatalism, Pechorin singlehandedly subdues the murderous Cossack. Pechorin relates these events to Maxsimich, who notes only that Vulich used a notoriously unreliable kind of pistol for his experiment and that his later encounter with the drunken Cossack was unlucky. For his own part, Pechorin suspects that Vulich's death makes predestination more likely, though he remains uncertain of his own belief in the concept and prefers to "doubt everything."

Characters: *A Hero of Our Time* is one of the most important and influential novels in nineteenth-century Russian literature. A psychologically penetrating study of a talented but flawed and frustrated individual, the novel anticipates not only the concerns and narrative techniques of such later Russian authors as Tolstoy and Dostoevsky but the dualistic, disillusioned "anti-heroes" of twentieth-century fiction. Lermontov employed an innovative, nonchronological narrative structure to gradually reveal his central character's personality. The novel is also noted for its poetic prose—particularly in the descriptions of the Caucasian landscape—and for the social criticism evident in its depiction of a particularly frustrating period of Russian history.

Lermontov's portrayal of the disillusioned aristocrat **Grigory Pechorin** was probably influenced by Alexander Pushkin's 1831 novel, *Eugene Onegin,* though most critics consider Lermontov's character more compelling than his predecessor's. Pechorin's personality is revealed in increasing depth as the novel progresses, first through the reminiscences of his good but rather simple-minded friend Maxsimich, then through the more perceptive narrator's observations, and finally through his own self-description and analysis in his journal. Handsome, wealthy, and intelligent, Pechorin shares the dilemma of many aristocratic and talented young men of his period: his only alternatives for employment are to serve his mediocre and tyrannical government, either as a military officer or as a civil servant, or to remain inactive. Pechorin is considered one of the foremost examples of the renowned "superfluous men" of nineteenth-century Russian literature, characters whose talents and potential are wasted and who are consequently overwhelmed by a sense of futility. Although he is only twenty-five, Pechorin has already lost his youthful idealism and sensitivity, and his considerable energies have been channeled into destructive behavior. Selfish and often cruel, he manipulates and exploits others, discarding them when his amusement has ended. Yet Pechorin is not a simple villain but a complex character whose sometimes contradictory behavior reflects his inner conflicts. Although he claims to rely on ideas rather feelings, he reveals his emotion in his appreciation of nature and his grief (though he is unable to express it) over Bela's death, and certainly in his love for Vera. Critics consider Pechorin a particularly modern figure because of his divided personality: despite his egotism, cynicism, and desire to manipulate others, he is capable of tenderness and remorse. He also exhibits a compulsion toward self-analysis, although he is ultimately unable to understand his own motivations or curb his behavior. Pechorin is frequently identified as romantic in his alienation and constant struggle with the world, yet he exhibits an aggressiveness that is not typical of a romantic hero, and he is also more realistically portrayed. Although Pechorin shares with his creator several significant qualities—his wit and cynicism, his exile to the Caucasus, his proclivity for dueling and seducing women— Lermontov claimed that his character was based on neither himself nor anyone else but was intended to embody the destructive forces of his own time. While readers do gain through Pechorin a glance into the stifling world of aristocratic Russia in the nineteenth century, his essentially human weaknesses, yearnings, and inner conflicts give him universal appeal and significance.

The first two sections of *A Hero of Our Time* are narrated by two different voices, a skillfully employed technique that influenced many later novelists. In addition, the narrative is chronologically disordered, as the opening sequences take place *after* the action of the final three sections. **The first narrator,** who is presumably the author himself, relates his encounters with Maxsimich and Pechorin and then presents the journal he retrieved during this episode. He is depicted as a hardy, experienced traveler, an educated and intelligent man whose observations—particularly on the enigmatic Pechorin—can be trusted. In contrast to the less perceptive Maxsimich, the narrator's viewpoint seems more balanced. Several critics have noted that the narrator's lyrical descriptions of the Caucasian landscape reflect Lermontov's poetic powers; in fact, Lermontov and his forerunner Pushkin are considered the two greatest nineteenth-century Russian poets. **Maxim Maxsimich** is the weathered, unsophisticated old soldier who tells in plain, forceful language the story of "Bela" and who passes along Pechorin's journal to the first narrator. Simple and good-hearted, Maxsimich is an honest observer but not quite capable of penetrating the true depths of Pechorin's personality. For instance, he does not comprehend Pechorin's inability to express his grief over Bela's death, nor does he understand Pechorin's observations on predestination and free will after Vulich dies. Though initially attracted by Pechorin's charisma, he is alarmed by his selfish and cruel behavior, and in the end he is dismayed and discouraged by Pechorin's indifference toward him. As the first narrator observes, Maxsimich becomes disillusioned with Pechorin and withdraws into an irritable silence.

The secondary characters who fill out the story of "Bela" are inhabitants of the rough, mountainous Caucasus, where semi-primitive tribes battle for dominance with Russian troops. The beautiful teenaged **Bela** is the daughter of the chief or prince of a tribe friendly with Pechorin's regiment. She is tall and slender and has piercing black eyes, and she immediately attracts the attention of both Kazbich and Pechorin. After her brother gives her to Pechorin in exchange for the prized horse stolen from Kazbich, Bela huddles in frightened despair in the hut of the man who now owns her. Gradually, however, Pechorin charms her into falling in love with him and she becomes gay and playful, delighting everyone with her charming dances. Although Pechorin appreciates Bela's beauty and especially the simplicity that strongly contrasts with the artful sophistication of other women he has known and seduced, he eventually tires of her and spends an increasing amount of his time away from her. Thus she sinks again into loneliness and despair. After Kazbich stabs her, Bela dies a slow and agonizing death with the obviously grieving but emotionally frozen Pechorin at her side. Bela's brother, **Azamat,** is an irresponsible, greedy boy who loves to show off for his soldier friends and who develops an overwhelming desire to own Kazbich's fine horse, and he is willing to trade his sister to either the rough Kazbich or the sophisticated Pechorin to acquire the animal. **Kazbich** is a member of a mountain tribe whose status as a bandit is generally acknowledged though not conclusively proven. He is small but wiry and tough, canny, and bold. His prized possession is a magnificent horse that is envied by all and which once even saved his life; its loss brings out his murderous impulses. Kazbich kills Bela's father because he thinks the old man has incited his son to steal the horse, and later fatally stabs Bela as well.

The characters in the tale of "Taman," the first of three narrated by Pechorin in his journal, have been described as colorful, romantic figures who help lend the story its tone of passion and exoticism. The first member of the smuggling band that Pechorin encounters is the fourteen-year-old **blind boy,** who greets him at the door of the cottage in which he spends the night. Pechorin dislikes physical infirmity, which indicates to him a corresponding spiritual emptiness that may remind him of his own weaknesses. Despite his blindness, the boy arouses Pechorin's suspicions with his strangely knowing air and his ability to maneuver easily through his environment. Next Pechorin meets **the girl** who tricks him into a boat and attempts to drown him. Eighteen years old and possessing an unconventional beauty, she attracts the highly susceptible Pechorin with her gay, spritely, enigmatic manner. The smuggler **Yanko,** apparently the girl's lover, is a bold daredevil who braves rough seas and other hazards to carry on his occupation. Lacking scruples, he leaves the helpless blind boy and the girl's elderly mother behind to pursue his own destiny.

In the "Princess Mary" section of the novel, Lermontov levels some of his most biting criticism against aristocratic Russian society in his portrayal of the pretentious, shallow visitors to the resort town of Pyatigorsk. The most unflattering depiction is that of

Grushnitsky, an egocentric young cadet with whom Pechorin was previously acquainted. He is recovering from a wound of which he is inordinately proud, and he wears an oversized greatcoat to affect a state of disillusionment. Many critics consider Grushnitsky a parody of the Byronic archetype (referring to the English romantic poet Lord Byron), for Grushnitsky tries to present himself as alienated and troubled when in fact he is merely pompous, vain, and shallow. Naive and ridiculous in his exaggerated attentions to Princess Mary, Grushnitsky later schemes to humiliate Pechorin but loses his own life instead. Some scholars have seen Grushnitsky as Pechorin's alter ego: his disillusionment is not genuine, like Pechorin's, and he is thoroughly ordinary, a quality Pechorin rejects. Thus the duel, instigated by the petulant and ridiculous Grushnitsky, is transformed by Pechorin into a deadly serious affair. Scholars feel Lermontov based Grushnitsky on Nikolay Martynov, an elderly military officer he often taunted and who eventually killed him in a duel.

Unlike most of the people around her, **Princess Mary** possesses significant inner resources that make her a fairly unconventional heroine, and her dark, velvety eyes lend her a charismatic aura. Pechorin's impertinent behavior disgusts Princess Mary at first, but after he decides to use her for his own ends he easily charms her into falling in love with him. His account of his early sensitivity and alienated childhood is partly calculated to win her sympathy and esteem, but it also provides a revealing glimpse into his past. Princess Mary exhibits inner strength and maturity when she realizes Pechorin has manipulated her and reacts with anger rather than meek acceptance: her beautiful eyes flashing, she sends him away.

Although Pechorin is never in love with Princess Mary, he does seem to feel a sincere affection for **Vera,** the former lover he meets again in Pyatigorsk and follows to Kislovodsk. She is another of the victims Pechorin overpowers and then discards. After Pechorin ended their initial affair, Vera married a good but dull elderly man. She is still in love with Pechorin and thus immediately resumes her relationship with him, sacrificing her marital stability when her husband discovers the entanglement. Lermontov himself was involved in a number of unhappy love affairs and is said to have based Vera on one of his own lovers, Varya Lopukhina. Another significant character in "Princess Mary" is **Dr. Werner,** a friend of Pechorin who shares his cynicism and sense of alienation. Characterizing Werner as a "tried and noble spirit," Pechorin claims that the two know each other so well that they do not even need to talk; Werner also masks his sensitivity beneath a sarcastic, sneering manner. Playing a practical role in the novel, Werner relays information about Princess Mary to Pechorin and divulges the local gossip concerning her, thus helping Pechorin form his plan to manipulate the girl.

The most significant secondary character in "The Fatalist" is **Lieutenant Vulich,** the rather sketchily portrayed Cossack officer who carries out the experiment in fatalism or predestination. A renowned gambler, Vulich is tall and dark with piercing eyes. He wins Pechorin's admiration when he coolly holds a gun to his head and pulls the trigger. Pechorin believes that he has seen the shadow of death on Vulich's face, and his eventual murder does seem to confirm the idea of predestination. By putting himself in great danger by attempting to subdue the drunken Cossack soldier who has killed Vulich, Pechorin conducts his own experiment with free will and predestination, concluding only that death is inevitable and that "I prefer to doubt everything."

Further Reading

Annensky, Innokenty. "Innokenty Annensky on Mikhail Lermontov," translated by Andrew Field. 1909. Reprint. In *The Complection of Russian Literature: A Cento,* edited by Andrew Field, pp. 57-62. New York: Atheneum, 1971.

Davie, Donald, ed. "Tolstoy, Lermontov, and Others." In *Russian Literature and Modern English Fiction: A Collection of Critical Essays,* pp. 164-99. Chicago: University of Chicago Press, 1975.

Kelly, Laurence. *Lermontov: Tragedy in the Caucasus.* New York: Braziller, 1978.

Lavrin, Janko. *Lermontov.* London: Bowes & Bowes, 1959.

Nabokov, Vladimir. "The Lermontov Mirage." Russian Review 1, No. 1 (November 1941): 31-9.

Nineteenth-Century Literature Criticism, Vol. 5. Detroit: Gale.

Turner, C. J. G. *Pechorin: A Essay on Lermontov's "A Hero of Our Time."* Birmingham, England: University of Birmingham, 1978.

Nikolai Leskov

1831-1895

Russian short story writer, novelist, and journalist.

"The Lady MacBeth of the Mtsensk District" ("Ledi Makbet Mcenskogo uezda"; short story, 1865)

Plot: Katerina Izmaylova is an attractive, passionate young girl who married an aging merchant, Zinovy Izmaylov, out of economic necessity. After five years of marriage the couple still has no children, for which Katerina's husband, relatives, and neighbors blame her, even though Zinovy's first wife was also childless. With no responsibilities, Katerina spends her time aimlessly wandering around her house or sleeping. One day while her husband is away on a business trip, Katerina goes for a walk and hears laughter coming from a barn. Inside, her father-in-law's clerks are teasing the fat cook, Aksinya, by weighing her as they would a sack of flour. Joining the frivolity, Katerina meets Sergey, a handsome, carefree young clerk who she learns was fired from his last job after having an affair with his employer's wife. That night, Sergey appears at Katerina's bedroom door; she makes some weak protests but soon succumbs with long-suppressed passion to his advances. For the next week, Katerina and Sergey spend every night together. Then Katerina's father-in-law, Boris Timofeyevich, catches Sergey leaving her room; realizing what has transpired, he beats the young man and locks him in a storeroom, promising Katerina that both she and Sergey will be punished when her husband returns. Determined to preserve her love affair at any cost, Katerina puts rat poison into some mushrooms her father-in-law eats for dinner, and he soon dies. No one suspects her of murder, for certain mushrooms have been known to kill people, and the two lovers resume their affair.

One night, Katerina dreams that a cat is nuzzling her; later, the same cat reappears in her dreams, but with the head and voice of her dead father-in-law. The same night, Katerina's husband, who has been alerted to her infidelity by his father, arrives home unexpectedly, hoping to spy on her. Katerina hears him in time, however, and Sergey is able to hide. Zinovy immediately accuses his wife of unfaithfulness and threatens to torture her into an admission of guilt. Although she initially denies her liaison, Katerina finally brings Sergey out of hiding and flagrantly kisses him in front of her husband. When Zinovy slaps her, she knocks him to the floor, then clubs him with a heavy candlestick; Sergey joins her in strangling Zinovy to death. They bury him in the cellar, removing all signs of the murder, and Zinovy is later presumed to have disappeared on his way home.

The now-pregnant Katerina decides to take control of her husband's estate, but her plans are thwarted by the arrival of some of Zinovy's relatives, who claim that his young nephew Fedya is heir to the property. Sergey is particularly enraged by this development, claiming that the boy stands between the lovers and ultimate happiness. One evening when everyone but the sickly Fedya has gone to attend a church service, Katerina and Sergey steal into his room and smother him with a pillow. Their deed, however, is witnessed by a group of young men hoping for a glance at the couple's lovemaking. Katerina and Sergey are publicly flogged and sentenced to hard labor in Siberia. During their journey there with a gang of other convicts, Katerina's obsessive love for Sergey continues unabated, but he tires of her attentions. Sergey strikes up relations with two convict women—first the sexually obliging Fiona and then the younger, more coy Sonetka. He and Sonetka now torment and taunt the miserable Katerina. While the convicts are aboard a ferry crossing the turbulent Volga River, Katerina suddenly jumps into the water, pulling Sonetka with her, and prevents the girl from being rescued. Both drown.

Characters: Considered one of the best storytellers in nineteenth-century Russian literature, Leskov is praised for his vivid portrayals of Russian life and characters, which are clearly drawn from personal observations made during his extensive travels through his native land. Leskov is particularly known for his *skaz,* colorful tales featuring a partially unreliable first-person narrator within a wider narrative, but ''The Lady MacBeth,'' one of his most acclaimed stories, is modeled on more traditional lines. Distinguished by its starkly realistic, objective style and propelled by a current of tragic inevitability, this subtly dramatic story presents, according to critic Hugh McLean, ''the most evocative treatment of pure sexuality Leskov ever wrote, and one of the most powerful in all Russian literature.''

Like his fellow Russian writer Ivan Turgenev in his celebrated story ''The Hamlet of the Schigrov District,'' Leskov employs a reference to a Shakespearean character as a universal psychological archetype planted within a distinctly Russian milieu. Shakespeare's Lady MacBeth, a stronger and more forceful personality than her husband, commits murders out of a lust for power—she wants MacBeth to become king so, as queen, she can rule through him. While Lady MacBeth is said to exhibit male qualities trapped in a female body, **Katerina Izmaylova** behaves as she does in pursuit of distinctly female ends. Unreflective and apparently remorseless, she is motivated not by political ambition but by sexual desire. Dissatisfied in her marriage, listless and utterly alone, Katerina is starved for both activity and love, and Sergey's arrival generates a blossoming of life within her. She succumbs completely to sensual passion, developing a heightened awareness of the beauty around her—a recognition in Leskov's description of a sultry summer evening when Katerina and Sergey make love beneath an apple tree. Her obsessive love for the young clerk has a hypnotic quality that seals her tragic fate.

Many of Leskov's stories contain animal symbols, and the vision of the cat that appears twice in ''The Lady MacBeth'' is often cited as an effective device that embodies Katerina's sensuality on its first appearance and her guilt on its second, when it acquires the voice and head of her murdered father-in-law. Although the murders Katerina commits cannot be condoned, she is not thoroughly evil or corrupt and in fact is quite appealing in her vitality, sensuality, and honesty; she does not attempt to rationalize her behavior. Most critics sympathize with Katerina, deeming her a character who might, under more favorable circumstances, have reached heroic heights. The depth of her obsession is indicated by her apathy for the baby she delivers in the prison hospital, and by her contrasting misery when Sergey humiliates her. She responds to this rejection with her usual passion and determination, condemning both herself and her rival to death in the churning river. Originally intended as one of several female character types Leskov planned to sketch from his knowledge of people of the Oka and Volga river regions, Katerina becomes a compelling figure embodying an overpowering sensuality that ultimately proves tragic.

Katerina's lover, **Sergey,** is the fetching young clerk with black, curly hair and a bold, insolent manner. He has a history of seducing women of higher social standing. Leskov so ably depicts the sexual electricity between the two young lovers that the reader is tempted to sympathize with them rather than their victims—at least until they kill the innocent Fedya. When Sergey joins Katerina in strangling her husband, the bond between them becomes one not just of love but of crime, and it is he who hints that they should remove the final obstacle to their happiness, Zinovy's nephew and heir. When Sergey's feelings for Katerina change, he exhibits an unforeseen depth of cruelty as he uses his new lover, Sonetka, to emotionally torture Katerina.

Zinovy Izmaylov, Katerina's much older husband, is a thoroughly unpleasant merchant. His callous manner and inherent meanness, particularly evident when he threatens to torture her into admitting to an illicit love affair, help to evoke sympathy for Katerina, and her passion for the tender, handsome Sergey is more understandable. Her father-in-law, **Boris Timofeyevich,** is also mean-hearted. Crudely moralistic, he threatens Katerina and punishes Sergey when he discovers their alliance, thus provoking Katerina to dispose of him. His reappearance as the dream-cat who walks over Katerina's body and admonishes her implies her guilty conscience.

Zinovy's nephew, **Fedya Lyamin,** is an innocent, sickly young boy; while the first two murders committed by Katerina and Sergey are fueled by their passion for one another, this one is uniquely selfish and reprehensible. Some critics have complained that Fedya's murder is inadequately motivated and is employed as a rash device to bring about the story's denouement.

Other characters in "The Lady MacBeth" include **Aksinya,** the fat, good-natured cook whom the clerks are weighing when Katerina walks past the barn; no stranger to seduction (her own son is illegitimate and she does not even know who his father is), Aksinya warns Katerina about the gay Sergey. **Fiona** is an attractive, languorous convict who willingly obliges the sexual requests of the male prisoners; though she is initially Katerina's rival, having slept with Sergey, she eventually comforts and defends her. Seventeen-year-old **Sonetka,** also a convict, is pretty and coy but jaded and devious. She becomes Sergey's lover and enthusiastically joins him in tormenting Katerina, little guessing that she will eventually be pulled under the waves of the Volga by her rival.

Further Reading

Benjamin, Walter. "The Storyteller: Reflections on the Works of Nikolai Leskov." In *Illuminations,* edited by Hannah Arendt, translated by Harry Zohn, pp. 83-109. New York: Schocken Books, 1969.

Lantz, K. A. *Nikolay Leskov.* Boston: Twayne, 1979.

McLean, Hugh. *Nikolai Leskov: The Man and His Art.* Cambridge, Mass.: Harvard University Press, 1977.

Nineteenth-Century Literature Criticism, Vol. 25. Detroit: Gale.

Pritchett, V. S. Introduction to *Selected Tales* by Nikolai Leskov, translated by David Magershack, pp. vii-xiii. New York: Farrar, Straus and Cudahy, 1961.

Slonim, Marc. "Novelists of the Soil and Patrician Poets." In *Modern Russian Literature: From Chekhov to the Present,* pp. 40-54. Oxford: Oxford University Press, 1953.

Charles Lever
1806-1872
Irish novelist, journalist, and essayist.

Charles O'Malley, the Irish Dragoon (novel, 1841)

Plot: The novel takes place in Ireland and Europe from 1808 to 1812. As it opens, Charles O'Malley is a tall, strong seventeen-year-old, adept at horseback riding and swordsmanship. An orphan, he lives with his uncle Godfrey O'Malley, the elderly owner of a country estate in the western Irish province of Galway. Godfrey hopes to be elected to Parliament and sends his nephew to visit a cousin, Blake, to elicit his support for the election. Upon arrival, Charles learns that Blake is backing another candidate, General Dashwood, who is visiting at the estate with his beautiful daughter Lucy. Charles swiftly falls in love with Lucy, who has won the affection of the general's aide, Captain Hammersley, as well. At dinner one night, Charles is insulted by one of the other guests and, goaded on by his uncle's fiery friend Billy Considine, challenges the man to a duel. His opponent is injured, but Charles escapes unharmed.

Moving to Dublin to attend law school, Charles befriends Frank Webber, a wild young man who introduces him to a life of dining, drinking, and brawling. He frequently encounters Lucy in Dublin society; when he hears her remark casually that only a dragoon (a soldier who fights either on foot or horseback) would be worth loving, he decides to abandon school and join the army. Charles goes with his unit to Portugal to fight Napoleon. There he saves the life of a young woman named Donna Inez, and pursues her until he learns that she knows Lucy. Charles fights bravely at the front and is promoted to lieutenant.

Through continuous valor, Charles becomes a captain, and soon learns that his uncle is ailing and the estate is nearly bankrupt. He returns to Galway but his uncle has already died. Charles decides to stay, and he sells his military commission in order to save the estate. He lives quietly for several years, despairing of ever winning Lucy's heart. When the news arrives that Napoleon has escaped from Elba, Charles rejoins the army and travels to Brussels, Belgium, where the English are massing to fight the French. Lucy is also there with her father; Charles overhears her rejecting Hammersley's marriage proposal but still holds out no hope for requited love. During the ensuing Battle of Waterloo, Charles is captured and his cellmate is General Dashwood, whom the French have condemned to death. When Charles is offered a chance to escape, he sends Dashwood in his place. Finally the English win the battle, and Charles returns to his unit. Lucy has heard of Charles's sacrifice for her father and, having loved him all along, accepts his proposal. The two are married and make their home in Galway, where Charles assumes his role as a country gentleman.

Characters: Lever was one of the most popular authors of mid-nineteenth-century England, and *Charles O'Malley* is his best known novel. Replete with boisterous adventure, the novel typifies Lever's other works in its lighthearted tone, simple plot, anecdotal style, and stereotypical characters. Lever was condemned by most contemporary critics for his lack of originality and for ignoring Ireland's social and political problems, and the writers of the later Irish Literary Renaissance (most notably, poet William Butler Yeats) claimed that he promulgated stereotypes and failed to accurately portray Irish character or life. The lack of literary merit in Lever's works has often been attributed to his financial state, which required that he write books rapidly to support himself. Nevertheless, many modern scholars find *Charles O'Malley* vigorous and often funny, noting that some scenes— particularly those at the beginning of the novel depicting hunts, dinners, and duels—are well-drawn and lively. According to critic Anthony Cronin, Lever depicted a "ramshackle, corrupt, jovial Ireland" that had already disappeared, and he offered no apology for the shortcomings of the Anglo-Irish landlord class upon which he centered his tale.

As the novel opens, **Charles O'Malley** is a strapping seventeen-year-old, and a skilled marksman and horseman who has absorbed his uncle's values of generosity and honor. He proves himself daring but coolheaded as he attempts to best Captain Hammersley, his rival for Lucy's heart, and through his duel with the man who insulted his uncle. When Charles joins the army simply because Lucy has indicated a preference for dragoons, he distinguishes himself and quickly rises through the ranks. Various critics have termed Lever's portrayal of military life as either unrealistic or fairly interesting; although Lever himself did not serve in the military, he had some similarly adventurous experiences, such as an excursion into the American frontier. Though Charles is not a truly original hero, he is a naive, likable figure apparently modeled after such picaresque characters as Tom Jones in Henry Fielding's 1749 novel. A native of the untamed western reaches of Ireland, Charles may have been perceived by English readers as the kind of hard-drinking, hard-riding, reckless commoner found in American frontier literature of the same period.

One of the most notable minor characters is Charles's faithful servant, **Michael "Mickey" Free,** who accompanies his master to war. Merry, lighthearted, and shrewd, Mickey frequently bursts into "songs of very doubtful excellence," as described in a generally negative review by Edgar Allan Poe. Mickey is often cited as an example of the "stage Irishman," the stereotypically boisterous, clownish caricature that became a particular target of critics like Yeats. Another character mentioned by critics is **Major Monsoon,** the self-mocking, life-loving, Falstaffian figure who regales his fellow officers with stories at Brussels. Based on Commissary-General Mayne, who had been stationed at Brussels and whom Lever paid for the privilege of using his anecdotes, Monsoon was described by Poe as "drunken, maudlin, [and] dishonest . . . given to communicativeness and mock morality over his cups, and not over careful in detailing adventures which tell against himself."

Godfrey O'Malley, Charles's uncle and the elderly owner of a Galway country estate, typifies Lever's positive portrayals of the Anglo-Irish landlord class, which some contemporary commentators found unrealistic. While these critics felt that most landlords exploited their tenants, Godfrey's tenants love him. Generous and hospitable, Godfrey displays the stereotypically voluble Irish temperament in his dealings with **General Dashwood,** whom he considers an English interloper. Dashwood responds mildly when Godfrey hotheadedly challenges him to a duel, thereby defusing the situation. Charles assumes that this rift between their parents eliminates his chances of marriage to Lucy, but the situation changes when he saves Dashwood's life.

Lucy Dashwood is a one-dimensional heroine—pretty, demure, and frequently in need of rescue from various perils. In the romantic world of Lever's novels, women require protection and worship and provide the hero with inspiration for his adventures, thus Charles's decision to join the army. In his naivete, he remains doubtful of her affection until the end of the novel, though he never gives her much of a chance to reveal her feelings.

Minor characters include **Captain Hammersley,** General Dashwood's aide and Charles's rival; **William "Billy" Considine,** Godfrey's quick-tempered and jovial friend and co-conspirator, who serves as Charles's second in his duel and later as his advisor; and **Frank Webber,** Charles's companion while he attends law school, who leads him to myriad balls, dinners, and card-parties, drinking, and brawling. Lever claimed he modeled Webber after a bright but idle and mischievous young man he knew during his own tenure at Dublin's Trinity College.

Further Reading

Cronin, Anthony. "Charles Lever: Enter the Stage Anglo-Irishman." In *Heritage Now: Irish Literature in the English Language,* pp. 51-60. New York: St. Martin's Press, 1983.

Dictionary of Literary Biography, Vol. 21. Detroit: Gale.

Lever, Charles. Preface to *Charles O'Malley: The Irish Dragoon.* Vol. 1, pp. vii-xvii. Boston: Little Brown, 1903.

Nineteenth-Century Literature Criticism, Vol. 23. Detroit: Gale.

Poe, Edgar Allan. "Charles James Lever." In *Essays and Reviews,* edited by G. R. Thompson, pp. 311-20. 1842. Reprint. Literary Classics of the U. S., 1984.

Stevenson, Lionel. *Dr. Quicksilver: The Life of Charles Lever.* 1939. Reprint. New York: Russel and Russel, 1969.

George MacDonald
1824-1905

Scottish novelist, short story writer, poet, homilist, essayist, critic, and translator.

Phantastes (novel, 1858)

Plot: The novel centers on twenty-one-year-old Anodos, whose father has recently died. While looking through his father's belongings, Anodos was visited by a tiny female spirit who grew to human size, then rebuked him when he tried to kiss her. She hinted that she might be the spirit of one of his own grandmothers, and promised that Anodos would visit the land of Faerie the next day. As Anodos wakes in his bed and watches while his room is gradually transformed into a forest glen, his adventures begin. He meets a country girl who warns him about the various tree-spirits, some of which are benevolent and some evil. The girl's mother, whom Anodos subsequently visits, particularly warns him about the sinister Ash tree. She allows him to peruse a big book of fairy tales, in which he reads about a knight named Sir Percivale, whose armor became coated with rust after he was seduced by the Alder Maiden, one of the tree-spirits of which Anodos has been warned. Later Anodos enters a mossy cave and discovers the form of a beautiful woman encased in alabaster marble. He sings a song to wake her, but she flees from the cave. Profoundly attracted to the lovely Alabaster Maiden, Anodos follows. He encounters Sir Percivale, who warns him about the Alder Maiden. While singing a sexually suggestive song, Anodos spots a beautiful woman whom he mistakes for his marble lady. Entranced, he spends a night with her, but in the morning she has assumed a horrible, ghoulish form. Realizing that she is the Alder Maiden, he finally manages to escape from her and the ogre-like Ash. Anodos's wanderings lead him to a farm family whose mother and daughter believe in fairies, but whose father and son do not. This encounter depresses Anodos, and he grows even more cynical after entering the cottage of an ogre, where an old woman is reading from a book of dark, despairing philosophy. Opening the door of a mysterious closet, he is engulfed by an ominous Shadow that remains with him through most of his adventures. The Shadow darkens everything it touches, transforming the wondrous into the ordinary and fostering mistrust among people. Anodos's swelling cynicism leads him to break a child's heart by destroying the crystal globe that has delighted her with its music.

Following a stream, Anodos reaches the Marble Palace in the land of Faerie. In the palace library, he becomes a part of each story he reads. He enters the tale of Cosmos, a university student in love with a woman who appears in his mirror. To confirm the reality of their love, Cosmos destroys the mirror to release the woman, knowing that she too may be destroyed. He succeeds and is united with her, though Cosmos dies in the end. In the palace Hall of Statues, Anodos sings to make the Alabaster Maiden appear. She takes shape, standing on a pedestal, but runs away when Anodos tries to embrace her. He follows her through a forbidden door and finds himself in a barren wasteland, through which he wanders in despair. Finally he walks into the sea, experiencing a symbolic death that fills him with joy. Reaching an island, he visits an old woman whose spiritual purity makes her beautiful and who replenishes him both physically and spiritually. She recites "The Ballad of Sir Aglovaile," about a knight whose physical desire for a ghost girl resulted in tragedy. By walking through several doors in the old woman's cottage, Anodos has a variety of adventures; entering the Door of Sighs, he learns that he must lose the Alabaster Maiden to Sir Percivale. Realizing that the knight is more deserving, Anodos accepts his loss. He is subsequently imprisoned in a tower that symbolizes his own pride, but is released through the selfless actions of the now-grown girl, whose crystal globe he had shattered. Anodos begins to perform good deeds of his own while serving as Sir Percivale's squire. In his final act, he attacks the leader of an outwardly religious but actually evil gathering. Anodos is set upon by the leader's followers and killed. Having finally achieved selfless love, Anodos is reborn into the ordinary world, where he takes up his life as lord of his castle. His shadow has been banished by his courage and his devotion to others, and he is ready to live nobly.

Characters: *Phantastes* is a classic of fantasy literature and a precursor to works written by such twentieth century authors as C. S. Lewis and J. R. R. Tolkien, both of whom claimed they were influenced by MacDonald. MacDonald drew his inspiration from the German romantic movement, particularly the works of the mystical poet Novelis, and from John Bunyan's *Pilgrim's Progress*. The episodic and highly symbolic chronicle of a spiritual quest, *Phantastes* reflects the pantheistic religious views held by MacDonald, a minister, who believed that God is present in all things and beings. The novel's protagonist gradually achieves spiritual rebirth as he learns to practice a selfless love for others. Though sometimes faulted for its loose structure and occasional verbosity, *Phantastes* is praised for its imaginative scope and convincing creation of what poet W. H. Auden termed "dream realism."

The novel's protagonist, **Anodos,** provides the only common element in the many episodes that comprise the story. His progress toward moral and spiritual maturity is chronicled as he undergoes his adventures and makes some of the mistakes common to the rogue-heros of picaresque fiction. Critics have provided a number of translations for Anodos's Greek name, including "rising," "a way back," "the way upwards," and "pathless"; in any case, all of these imply a journey. As the novel begins, Anodos is a parentless twenty-one-year-old who has just had an encounter with a strange female spirit. Having recently grappled with the physical desires (in his attraction to the spirit) and material concerns (his arrangements for receiving his inheritance) of ordinary life, Anodos is transported to the land of Faerie, where his spirituality will be developed to overcome these other demands. Anodos learns from the country girl and her mother that he probably has some fairy blood in his veins, perhaps explaining why he can accept his fantastic experiences so easily. When he meets the Alabaster Maiden, animating her through his song, he is filled with enchantment and desire; she represents an ideal of beauty that many critics have identified as notably romantic. Again, though, his physical nature overcomes his spiritual and he tries to embrace her. In accordance with MacDonald's view of sexuality, not as wicked but as sanctified by mutual respect and spiritual connection, Anodos must learn to conquer his selfish instincts, and the Alabaster Maiden eludes him for now. His sensual encounter with the outwardly beautiful but inwardly evil Alder Maiden teaches Anodos about the nature of beauty, which sometimes masks a deeper ugliness. With the arrival of the Shadow as his constant companion, Anodos develops a dark, cynical view. He thinks he needs the Shadow, which has been viewed as his doppelgänger or double, to see things as they are rather than as his imagination wishes them to be. When he destroys the innocent delight of the little girl with the crystal globe, Anodos reveals the darker self he eventually learns to control or vanquish. Anodos' adventures continue to enlighten him, but he still struggles to love unselfishly. After such episodes as his second luckless encounter with the Alabaster Maiden, the joy he feels after his symbolic "death" in the sea, and his conversation with the beautiful old woman, he is filled with pride, particularly because he was able to make the Alabaster Maiden appear with his singing. Eventually, partly motivated by the unselfish example of the now-grown girl with the crystal globe who mercifully saves him from the tower, Anodos sets out to perform good deeds, illustrating MacDonald's belief that theology alone is insufficient, that it must be accompanied by action. Anodos's dream-journey lasts twenty-one days, suggesting that his experiences are an allegorical representation of his maturation process, and teaches him that it is through loving others, rather than through being loved, that happiness is attained.

The **tiny female spirit** who first visits Anodos is a notable example of MacDonald's tendency to cast women as representatives of life's mysteries, and as the media through which men could reach a higher knowledge. Similarly, the **Alabaster Maiden** is an elusive, ideally beautiful female figure whom Anodos unsuccessfully pursues. His singing her to life from the block of marble in which she is initially encased may remind some readers of the classical myth of Pygmalian, the sculptor who falls in love with his own creation. Critics have seen the Alabaster Maiden as an embodiment of the romantic ideal of beauty, a blending of beauty and truth, that is particularly longed for by the artist. Anodos's acceptance of his beloved's eventual union with Sir Percivale signifies his developing maturity, for he recognizes that the noble knight has earned this honor through his good deeds.

Sir Percivale, whose character is derived from the medieval romances of King Arthur and the Knights of the Round Table, helps to unify the novel's plot somewhat by making appearances in several different episodes. Because he was once seduced by the sinister Alder Maiden, his suit of armor is covered with rust that will only disappear if he performs several selfless acts. He does so, periodically rescuing Anodos from danger and proving himself morally superior to the young wanderer, who must learn to imitate Sir Percivale's selflessness.

The magical world of Faerie contains not just good, wondrous visions like the Alabaster Maiden but also evil elements like the **Alder Maiden,** a sinister tree-spirit with great powers of seduction and corruption. Anodos is initially entranced by her beauty, but her transformation into a grotesque creature causes him to ask "How can beauty and ugliness dwell so near?" It is suggested that Anodos's Shadow is a punishment for his sensual encounter with the Alder Maiden. She is in collusion with another wicked, ogre-like tree spirit, the **Ash-Spirit.**

One of the most compelling presences in *Phantastes* is **the Shadow.** It is a frightening apparition, vaguely corpse-like in appearance, that engulfs him and does not leave him until he has learned to act with courage and selflessness. Critics have interpreted the Shadow as a symbol of evil, death, doubt, willfulness, the loss of innocence or virginity, disillusionment, and pessimism. It blackens Anodos's perception of the world, stimulating cynicism and mistrust; in its "common sense" and worldliness it seems to oppose the power of imagination and childlike innocence, qualities that MacDonald considered integral to a healthy Christian spirit.

Other mystical characters in *Phantastes* include **Cosmos,** the storybook figure who proves his love for the princess in his mirror by destroying the mirror to release her, despite the risk of losing her forever; the story reflects, in some ways, Anodos's quest for the Alabaster Maiden, exposing his tendency to view his own beloved as a possession meant only to gratify his desires. The skeptical **farmer and his son,** who refuse, ironically, to believe in fairies even while they live within a fairy world, are also said to represent the forces of rationalism that are opposed to imagination. The island-dwelling, beautiful **old woman,** whom Anodos recognizes as spiritually beautiful, gives him a strong sense of peaceful refuge. She also reinforces the theme of a purer love through selfless devotion when she recites the "Ballad of **Sir Aglovaile,**" in which the title character loses his ghost lover through his desire to possess her physically.

Further Reading

Auden, W. H. "Introduction." In *The Visionary Novels of George MacDonald: Lilith, Phantastes,* edited by Anne Fremantle, pp. v-x. Noonday Press, 1954.

Dictionary of Literary Biography, Vol. 18. Detroit: Gale.

Hein, Rolland. *The Harmony Within: The Spiritual Vision of George MacDonald.* Grand Rapids, Mi.: Christian University Press, 1982.

Jackson, Rosemary. "Victorian Fantasies." In *Fantasy: The Literature of Subversion,* pp. 141-56. London: Methuen, 1981.

Lewis, C. S., ed. Preface to *George MacDonald: An Anthology,* pp. xxi-xxxiv. London: Macmillan, 1947.

Marshall, Cynthia, ed. *Essays on C. S. Lewis and George MacDonald: Truth, Fiction, and the Power of the Imagination.* Wheaton, Il.: Scripture Press, 1990.

Twentieth-Century Literary Criticism, Vol. 9. Detroit: Gale.

Reis, Richard H. *George MacDonald.* Boston: Twayne, 1972.

———. *George MacDonald's Fiction: A Twentieth-Century View.* Eureka, Calif.: Sunrise Books, 1989.

Sendak, Maurice. "The Depths of Fantasy." *Book Week—The Washington Post* (24 July 1966): 14-15.

Joaquim Maria Machado de Assis
1839-1908

Brazilian novelist, short story writer, dramatist, poet, critic, essayist, and journalist.

Epitaph of a Small Winner (*Memórias pósthumas de Braz Cubas;* novel, 1881)

Plot: The novel takes place in late-nineteenth-century Rio de Janeiro, Brazil. The narrator is wealthy, sixty-five-year-old Braz Cubas, who has just died of pneumonia. He wants to recount the story of his life to win fame, glory, and a measure of immortality. Born in 1805, he was raised the pampered son of a rich father who indulged his every whim and excused his misbehavior. At seventeen he had a love affair with Marcella, a beautiful courtesan (a prostitute with wealthy, influential clients), who later refused to accompany him to Spain where, after accumulating a heavy load of debts that his father repaid, he was sent to attend college. After graduating Braz traveled around Europe for several years, financed by his father's wealth. He returned to Brazil when he learned that his mother was dying of cancer; her death plunged him into a period of melancholy. Later he fell in love with a lovely girl named Eugenia. When he learned that she was slightly crippled, however, he rejected her. Braz then capitulated to his father's ambition to make him a legislator, and he began to pursue Vergilia, a wealthy young woman whose social status, his father felt, would benefit his political career. But Vergilia decided to marry the more steady and ambitious Lobo Neves. When they moved away from the city, Braz's political plans came to a halt.

Several years later, after the death of his father, Braz was elated to learn that Vergilia and her husband were returning to Rio de Janeiro; he felt he was still in love with his former sweetheart. Braz encountered the couple at a ball, and he and Vergilia resumed their romance after dancing together. She soon became his mistress, meeting him secretly in the home of her servant, Doña Placida. The affair continued for several years while Lobo— blind to his wife's infidelity—and Braz became good friends. Braz encountered a former schoolmate, Quincas Borba, who was reduced by his extreme poverty to begging; Braz later found that Quincas had stolen his watch. Vergilia eventually became pregnant and felt sure the child was Braz's, although Lobo assumed it was his. All three anticipated the birth with joy, and all were devastated when the baby was born prematurely and died. Some time later Braz received a letter from Quincas explaining that his finances had improved and that he had become a philosopher, espousing a concept he called humanitism. He also sent Braz a watch finer than the one he had stolen. Braz gladly embraced Quincas as a friend, although he regarded Quincas's ideas as crazy. Meanwhile Vergilia and Braz were forced by her husband's growing suspicions to avoid each other, and finally Vergilia and Lobo moved away from Rio de Janeiro. Feeling bored and lonely, Braz again attempted to gain a political position, an effort that proved as unsuccessful as his subsequent venture into newspaper publishing. He eventually became engaged, but his fiancee died in an epidemic. The remaining years of Braz's life passed uneventfully. Not long after the death of his friend Quincas, Braz contracted pneumonia and died after a final visit from Vergilia and a lapse into delirium. In concluding his memoir, he notes that the only profit gained through his existence was his not having fathered any offspring to share the miserable fate of humanity. Thus he is a "small winner" in the ultimately futile game of life.

Characters: *Epitaph of a Small Winner* is the best known and most inventive novel written by Machado, who was considered during his lifetime Brazil's premier man of letters and who is recognized as highly influential in the development of Brazilian fiction. Machado is often compared to the eighteenth-century British novelist Laurence Sterne for his wry humor and whimsical digressions, to the American writer Henry James for his emphasis on characters and ideas over plot, and to various French authors for his psychological realism. Praised for its skillful blend of philosophy and insight with irony and humor, *Epitaph* explores through the narrator's satirical self-reflection the vanity and selfishness of humanity in the face of an indifferent universe and an existence that results only in death. While some critics ascribe Machado's strongly pessimistic tone to his innate insecurity over his part-African heritage and ill health, others feel Machado's own viewpoint may have been more hopeful than that expressed by his protagonist. The novel's ironic tone makes a variety of interpretations possible.

The post-mortem reminiscences of rich Brazilian **Braz Cubas** comprise, he says, a bid for the fame and glory that evaded him during his lifetime. He experienced a pleasant childhood due to his father's wealth and constant indulgence. An indifferent student, he entered into an affair with Marcella primarily for the satisfaction of "owning" a courtesan. His father rescued him from the consequences of his irresponsibility with money, and he received a university education followed by several carefree years of European travel. The death of Braz's mother affected him strongly, but rather than true grief, his reaction is revealed to be self-centered melancholy brought on by his realizing that he too will one day die. Likewise Braz rejected Eugenia, who sincerely loved him, because of her physical infirmity—further evidence of his egotism and inability to form deep connections with others. Neither is his longtime relationship with Vergilia truly substantial, for it eventually deteriorated into a rather tiresome habit and finally faded away entirely. Braz was unsuccessful in his forays into politics and publishing because he lacked the will and tenacity these pursuits required, and even his philanthropic work was motivated not by genuine concern but by the pleasure of feeling superior to others. Always ready to appear an intellectual, he embraced Quincas's philosophy, at least to the extent that it seemed to justify the self-love that he had always practiced; at the same time, he viewed his friend as insane. Braz himself admitted to being superficial, mediocre, shallow, and hypocritical—in fact, his often humorous self-revelations provided the main vehicle for the novel's irony as the narrator described himself in an unflattering but seemingly unremorseful manner. While some critics feel that Braz represents Machado's own view of humanity as foolish, vain, and self-deluded, others see him as a satiric character whose warped personality and profound pessimism are not actually mirrored by Machado. Significantly, Braz lived from 1805 to 1869, a tumultuous and exciting period in Brazilian history, yet public events are barely mentioned in the novel and seem to have made little impression on Braz. Remembering the toy sword he received during his childhood at an event commemorating Napoleon, Braz comments that all men have their cherished "swords" which make the emperor's seem insignificant; thus he highlights the essential self-involvement and blindness of human beings. Having unsuccessfully pursued fulfillment through various romantic and sexual relationships, politics, work, philosophy, and charity, Braz concludes that his life amounts to nothing but that he will at least be credited with having inflicted on no one else the misery of existence. Most readers will probably agree that the world needs no more Brazes, but they may differ in their responses to and interpretations of his bitterly pessimistic outlook.

Braz's old schoolmate, **Quincas Borba,** is a former beggar and pickpocket who became a philosopher when his finances improved, perhaps underlining the fact that intellectual pursuits are to some extent the privilege of those who can afford them. His philosophy of "humanitism" holds that by loving him- or herself first, individual human beings can contribute to the survival of humanity as a whole; he believes that human beings have the power to create happiness for themselves and need not wait for fate to bestow it upon them. Critics often cite this concept as a parody of Frederick Nietzsche, whose concept of the "superman" bears some resemblance to humanitism. It has been suggested that it is Quincas rather than Braz who serves as Machado's mouthpiece.

Vergilia is the beautiful, wealthy woman whose aristocratic status initially attracts the attention of Braz's father, who feels she would make an advantageous wife for his son. Although she chooses another man instead, Vergilia enters immediately into an affair with Braz after her return to Rio de Janeiro. The fact that Braz's early struggle to win her affection failed but that he later won her love with little effort is offered as an example of life's irony and the unreasonableness of human nature. The long relationship between Vergilia and Braz makes up a substantial part of the novel: it is recounted from its passionate beginning through its lapse into tedium to its conclusion brought about by circumstances (Vergilia and her husband move away from Rio de Janeiro). Revealed in the end as essentially shallow, the affair demonstrates Braz's incapacity to truly love another person. Vergilia chooses her husband **Lobo Neves** on the basis of his ambition, but he also proves a convenient partner when he remains unaware for many years that his wife is having an affair with his good friend. Lobo is also portrayed as superstitious, turning down an ill-omened job offer.

Eugenia is Braz's first love, though he rejects her when he discovers she is slightly lame. Due to his superficiality and egoism—or perhaps his fear of confronting anything unpleasant—Braz is unable to accept his sweetheart's flaw. Eugenia has been linked to Machado's black stepmother, Maria Inez, whom he rejected because of her race, which may have caused some lingering feelings of guilt. **Marcella,** the beautiful courtesan with whom the seventeen-year-old Braz becomes involved, is disfigured by smallpox after their parting and earns her former lover's derision when she later meets him. An eminently practical woman, Marcella takes advantage of Braz's interest in her for as long as she can, then opens a small jewelry shop when her disease ruins her looks.

Vergilia's servant, **Doña Placida,** is a poor, unhappy woman manipulated by Braz and Vergilia; they use her home as a location for their romantic encounters. The lovers rationalize that serving as a screen for their illicit affair must be Doña Placida's destined role in life, and Braz later assuages his guilt by establishing a trust fund for her. Another notable character in *Epitaph for a Small Winner* is the allegorical figure of **Nature,** who appears in the delirious dream Braz has shortly before he dies. A grotesque giantess, she has been identified as a parody of characters representing the Eternal Feminine in such works as *The Divine Comedy* by Dante; like Beatrice in that fourteenth-century epic poem, Nature is Braz's guide, ultimately revealing to him the insignificance of human life in an indifferent universe.

Further Reading

Fitz, Earl E. *Machado de Assis.* Boston: Twayne, 1989.

MacAdam, Alfred J. "Machado de Assis: Satire and Madness." In *Modern Latin American Narratives: The Dreams of Reason,* pp. 11-20. Chicago: University of Chicago Press, 1977.

Pritchett, V. S. "Machado de Assis: A Brazilian." In *The Myth Makers: Literary Essays,* pp. 158-63. New York: Random House, 1979.

Sontag, Susan. "Afterlives: The Case of Machado de Assis." *New Yorker* 66, No. 12 (7 May 1990): 102-108.

Twentieth-Century Literary Criticism, Vol. 10. Detroit: Gale.

Wilson, Clotilde. "Machado de Assis, Economist of Lunacy." *Hispania* XXXII, No. 2 (May 1942): 198-201.

Maurice Maeterlinck
1862-1949
Belgian dramatist, short story writer, poet, essayist, and translator.

Pelléas and Mélisande (drama, 1892)

Plot: Arkël is the lord of a manor in medieval Allemonde. His grandson Golaud is out hunting one day when he encounters a beautiful young girl near a spring in the woods. A native of a far-away country, she has become lost; her clothes are torn, and she is weeping piteously. She has misplaced her golden crown, but she has no wish to retrieve it and follows Golaud out of the forest. Although he knows that Arkël wants him to wed the daughter of a rival to increase the prosperity of his impoverished land, Golaud marries Mélisande. When he returns to his home he fears his grandfather will reject his new wife, but his mother,

Geneviève, convinces Arkël to accept the marriage. Meanwhile Golaud's half-brother Pelléas plans to leave the castle to visit a dying friend, but Arkël convinces him to stay until the health of his own seriously ill father improves. After her arrival at the castle, the elfin, childlike Mélisande quickly ingratiates herself with her new family. Pelléas takes her to cool, pleasant Blind Man's Spring, and while the two are talking there Mélisande loses her wedding ring in the pool. At the same moment, though miles away, Golaud is thrown from his horse while hunting. As he is recovering, Mélisande goes to him to tell him that she finds her new home oppressive and wishes to leave. He notices that her ring is missing, but she is afraid to tell him the truth. Instead she claims she lost it in a seaside grotto while looking for shells for Yniold, Golaud's son from his previous marriage. Golaud sends her back to look for the ring, and Pelléas accompanies her to the grotto. The two begin to spend much of their time together. They are often accompanied by little Yniold, who has a premonition one night that Mélisande will soon go away.

One evening Golaud sees Pelléas entwining his hands in Mélisande's long hair and complimenting her beauty. Although Golaud calmly admonishes the two for acting like children, he grows increasingly jealous and agitated. During an excursion into the cavernous, dank vaults beneath the castle to investigate a strange smell, Golaud is tempted to allow his half-brother to fall into a stagnant pool but holds onto his arm instead. As the two emerge into the daylight, Golaud reminds Pelléas that he must treat Mélisande in a proper manner, especially now that she is pregnant. Golaud subsequently questions Yniold about what Pelléas and Mélisande say and do while they are together, but the child tells him nothing of interest; he even uses Yniold to spy on the two but still learns nothing. Since his father has now recovered, Pelléas decides to undertake the journey he had earlier planned. Mélisande agrees to meet him at Blind Man's Spring the night before his departure. Meanwhile Arkël asks Mélisande why she seems so sad, since the recovery of Pelléas's father should have brought happiness to the castle. She denies that she is melancholy, but Arkël subsequently witnesses a violent encounter between Golaud and Mélisande. That night Pelléas and Mélisande meet as lovers by the spring. They dally there too long and are locked out of the castle. When they see an enraged Golaud rushing toward them, they share a final kiss; Golaud immediately kills Pelléas and starts after Mélisande. The next morning the two are found at the castle gate: Mélisande has received only a small, inconsequential wound, and Golaud has made an unsuccessful attempt to kill himself. Mélisande gives birth prematurely to a tiny baby girl and then sinks into a mysterious illness. Meanwhile Golaud still wonders if his half-brother and his wife were really lovers or simply expressing a childish, innocent affection. As she lies dying Mélisande claims that she and Pelléas were indeed innocent, but she is too delirious to answer any of Golaud's questions. After expressing pity for her pathetically small daughter, Mélisande dies.

Characters: Maeterlinck was a major dramatist of the symbolist movement, which developed in France in the last quarter of the nineteenth century. Promulgated by such poets as Arthur Rimbaud, Paul Verlaine, and Stéphane Mallarmé, symbolism rejected the realistic trend in literature in favor of an inward, psychological focus; evocative creation of mood and atmosphere; and the use of symbols or metaphors to represent intangible forces or concepts. Written early in Maeterlinck's career, *Pelléas and Mélisande* is shrouded in unreality and infused with a dark pessimism that would give way in later works to a more optimistic view. Despite its identification as a symbolist work, the play has also been likened to classic seventeenth-century French drama because of its length (five acts), and to the ''well-made'' plays of the nineteenth century because of its artistic unity. *Pelléas and Mélisande* explores the primitive realm of the subconscious through somewhat shadowy characters who seem driven by fate.

When the apparently middle-aged hunter **Golaud** first encounters Mélisande, he has lost his way in the forest, a circumstance that suggests he is at a turning point in his life. He meets the beautiful young girl near a fountain (ever-flowing fountains traditionally symbolize change and rejuvenation). Golaud feels revitalized by his marriage and idealizes his new wife, grateful that she has filled the void in his life. Yet he seems to see her purely as a vision of love and beauty, not as a whole person, and their relationship is thus unbalanced from the beginning. Golaud is portrayed as his half-brother's opposite in many ways: while Pelléas is sensitive and introverted, Golaud is aggressive, extroverted, and powerful (signified by his vocation as a hunter). When he begins to perceive that Pelléas and Mélisande have formed some special connection, he is torn between jealousy and suspicion on the one hand and a belief that they are merely innocent, fond children on the other. Golaud transcends his jealousy when he suppresses his irrational fears, calmly admonishing the lovers to behave themselves and then lecturing Pelléas on treating Mélisande properly. Mélisande's loss of her wedding ring is a symbolically charged event, for Golaud feels its impact miles away when he is thrown from his horse. His bloodied face has been said to signify the emotional wound that his wife's act has inflicted. Golaud's journey into the underground vaults with Pelléas is also highly significant. Although he is tempted to allow his half-brother to fall into a stagnant pool, he clutches his arm to keep him safe, and this struggle embodies the conflict between primitive emotion and morality or reason. In descending to the cave, Golaud makes a symbolic trip down into his own subconscious. Despite his early victories over jealousy, however, Golaud eventually succumbs to his primitive impulses and kills Pelléas, then chases Mélisande and, after wounding her only slightly, tries unsuccessfully to take his own life. Tormented about the two lovers' innocence, Golaud declares that he is not responsible for Mélisande's death, which can be attributed only to the workings of fate. This reference to predestination—the concept that human beings are helpless victims of circumstances rather than shapers of them—may be connected to the deterministic view that dominated literary thought in the late nineteenth and early twentieth centuries.

When she makes her first almost magical appearance, **Mélisande** is a graceful sprite—childlike, naive, and joyful. She comes from a distant land and has lost her way, but she seems happy to dissociate herself from her past (declining, for instance, to retrieve her crown) and make a new life with Golaud. Her elfin presence is welcome at the gloomy castle, and to Golaud represents the beauty, love, youth, and tenderness that had been missing from his life. But Mélisande's role begins to change as her relationship with Pelléas develops, an evolution marked by her losing her wedding ring into the pool at Blind Man's Spring. Some critics believe this act is symbolic of Mélisande's rejecting her marriage and her submissive relationship with Golaud. Mélisande is consistently associated with water imagery, including wells, springs, pools, and fountains, which traditionally represents female sensuality. After her experience at the spring, Mélisande tells Golaud that she feels oppressed by life at the castle, indicating that she has already embarked on her journey toward death. Mélisande's behavior is significantly different with the two men; with Golaud she is innocent and gay, while with Pelléas she is provocative and womanly. Some scholars even feel she assumes the role of the siren found throughout literature, symbolizing the destructive female force that overpowers reason by instinct. When Mélisande and Pelléas walk through the seaside grotto, she expresses fear of its darkness and the possible dangers lurking there, and this experience has been said to evoke a journey through the heart or the subconscious, where either satisfaction or destruction may wait. Mélisande's refusal to come out into the light after she and Pelléas have made love at the fountain is interpreted as symbolizing the connection between the female psyche and darkness. But it is also possible to see Mélisande as an essentially innocent victim of a powerful, primitive, predestined love that can lead only to tragedy. Her pitifully tiny **baby**—too small, in fact, to live long—seems to mimic the defeat, the staunching of a spritely life force, that Mélisande represents.

Pelléas and Mélisande have been compared to many other tragic lovers found throughout literature, from the mythological figures of Tristan and Isolde; to Danté's Paolo and Francesca; to Shakespeare's Othello and Desdemona; to the narrator and subject of Edgar

Allan Poe's poem *Annabel Lee*. Like these famous pairs, Maeterlinck's protagonists are subject to a force that is beautiful and natural but ultimately ill-fated. While Mélisande's role in the relationship is variously described as innocent and siren-like, **Pelléas** is the unwitting victim of a love that ends in his death. Like his half-brother, Pelléas meets Mélisande by a fountain and experiences the new life that such a symbol often represents. He is as passive, introverted, and accommodating as Golaud is aggressive, outgoing, and domineering, and his relationship with Mélisande touches her more deeply than her submissive bond with her husband. During Pelléas's journey into the underground vaults with Golaud, he feels disoriented and stifled while Golaud is confident and surefooted; this discomfort has been said to represent Pelléas's subconscious anxiety over his relationship with his half-brother's wife. It may even be viewed as a premonition of the danger that lurks ahead—a warning he disregards by asking Mélisande to meet him once again at Blind Man's Spring. His attempt to draw her out into the light after they have made love might be seen as symbolizing the contrast between his rational, masculine point of view and her dark, sensuous female psyche.

Arkël is the grandfather of both Golaud and Pelléas and the lord of the castle around which much of the action revolves. The play is set in a time of disease, famine, and rebellion, and Arkël had hoped to alleviate his subjects' suffering by marrying his grandson to the daughter of a prosperous enemy. But Golaud's mother, **Geneviève,** persuades Arkël to accept his son's marriage to Mélisande. Arkël's claim that he must submit to the workings of fate is ironically countered by the fact that he *does* tamper with Pelléas's destiny by convincing him to stay at the castle; the tragedy might have been avoided if the young man had taken the journey he had planned. Arkël is completely won over by the lovely, gentle Mélisande and is quick to sense her sadness as she begins to feel oppressed by life at the castle. Another significant character in *Pelléas and Mélisande* is **Yniold,** Golaud's son by a previous marriage. He accompanies Mélisande and Pelléas everywhere, thus highlighting the essential innocence of their relationship; significantly Golaud is unable to learn through the child anything about what the two lovers do or say. Yniold has a premonition about Mélisande's imminent departure, suggesting that his naiveté allows him to seem more clearly than the adults around him.

Further Reading

Bailly, Auguste. *Maeterlinck.* New York: Haskell House, 1974.

Knapp, Bettina. *Maurice Maeterlinck.* Boston: Twayne, 1975.

Konrad, Linn B. *Modern Drama as Crisis: The Career of Maurice Maeterlinck.* New York: Peter Lang, 1986.

Kosove, Joan Pataky. "Maeterlinck's 'Pelléas and Mélisande.'" *French Review* XL, NO. 6 (May 1967): 781-84.

Rose, Henry. *On Maeterlinck.* New York: Haskell House, 1974.

de Soissons, S. C. "Maeterlinck as a Reformer of the Drama." *Contemporary Review* 86, No. 467 (November 1904): 699-708.

Twentieth-Century Literary Criticism, Vol. 3. Detroit: Gale.

Alessandro Manzoni
1785-1873
Italian novelist, dramatist, poet, essayist, and critic.

The Betrothed (*I promessi sposi;* novel, 1827)

Plot: The novel begins in a seventeenth-century Italian village, where two young peasants, Renzo and Lucia, have become engaged. A corrupt nobleman, Don Rodrigo, wishes to seduce Lucia and manages to frighten the couple's parish priest, Don Abbondio, into refusing to marry them. After Don Rodrigo's henchman try unsuccessfully to kidnap her, Lucia seeks help from a saintly Capuchin monk, Fra Cristoforo. He provides Lucia, her mother, and Renzo with a temporary hiding place, eventually sending the two women to safety with another community of Capuchins and Renzo to a monastery in Milan. After her arrival at the monastery, located in the city of Monza, Lucia is put in the care of Sister Gertrude, a nun whose family had, many years earlier, sent her there against her will. She has subsequently become bitter and corrupt. When Don Rodrigo discovers Lucia's location, he elicits the help of a mysterious, powerful aristocrat called The Unnamed (or L'Innominato) to capture her. Through their knowledge of Sister Gertrude's role in a murder, the Unnamed's men force the nun to send Lucia out of the convent, where they easily kidnap her to their leader's mountain retreat. Meanwhile Renzo never reaches the monastery to which Fra Cristoforo had sent him. After his arrival in Milan he participates in a riot inspired by the famine under which the city's population is suffering. He is arrested by the police and then released by the mob, finally fleeing into Venetian territory. There he works in a silk mill owned by a relative, barely escaping deportation by the Milan police.

After her kidnapping, Lucia's great beauty and innocence bring about a transformation in the Unnamed's previously evil character. He decides not to return her to Don Rodrigo. After speaking to the virtuous and eloquent Cardinal Federigo Boromeo, he gives up his wicked career and converts to Christianity. Then the Unnamed releases Lucia, and the cardinal sends her and her mother to be cared for by a charitable noblewoman who lives in Milan. More than a year later, Renzo has not yet returned to Milan, but he and Lucia exchange letters. She informs her fiancé that she cannot marry him because, during her captivity, she promised the Virgin Mary that if she were allowed to survive, she would never marry. Despite this declaration, Renzo travels to Milan to find Lucia, only to fall prey to the plague infecting much of the population. When he finally recovers, he learns that Lucia has also taken ill and been sent to a *lazaretto,* where a large number of plague victims are housed. There he meets Fra Cristoforo, who is in Milan caring for the sick. Don Rodrigo is also there suffering from the plague, and near death; at the monk's urging, Renzo forgives Don Rodrigo for his transgressions. Finally Renzo finds Lucia, and Fra Cristoforo assures the couple that her earlier betrothal to Renzo makes her vow to the Virgin Mary invalid. Renzo and Lucia return to their village, which has also been ravaged by the plague; Lucia's mother and Don Abbondio, however, have survived. With Don Rodrigo dead, the local manor is now occupied by a new, morally upright lord. After their marriage, the couple moves to the Venetian territory, where Renzo goes to work in a silk mill and the two raise a large family.

Characters: Acclaimed as one of the greatest works of nineteenth-century literature, *The Betrothed* played a particularly important role in the development of the Italian novel. Set in turbulent, troubled seventeenth-century Milan, the novel's historical context has led to frequent comparisons with the works of British author, Sir Walter Scott. Yet *The Betrothed* encompasses a broader spectrum of themes than just the historical and accommodates a variety of interpretations, including those focusing on its religious orientation, its psychologically complex characters, or its presentation of Italian nationalism. The novel is distinguished by its strong focus on how ordinary lives are influenced by divine providence (i.e., an ordering of events that comes from God). Particularly innovative is Manzoni's use of peasants as protagonists and his effort to incorporate a commonly spoken Italian dialect (Tuscan) into the traditionally elevated realm of literature. The novel is said to reflect Manzoni's grounding in both eighteenth-century rationalism and early-nineteenth-century romanticism, as well as his strong commitment to Catholicism. Though some critics describe *The Betrothed* as a work of Catholic propaganda, most affirm the universal appeal of the humanitarian values it presents.

One of the most unusual aspects of *The Betrothed* at the time of its publication was its focus on humble, poor characters, particularly in their role as moral agents. Although Manzoni was himself an aristocrat, it is thought that both his early exposure to romanticism and his later commitment to Catholicism led to his use of common people as paragons of humility and goodness. While several critics have noted that Manzoni keeps his peasant protagonists in a subtle posture of inferiority and emphasizes submission and resignation, most describe them as positively drawn. **Renzo Tramaglino** is the young silk-factory worker who finds his marriage plans thwarted by a wicked nobleman and who endures a dangers and hardships before he is finally united with his fiancée. Manzoni uses Renzo's experiences during the famine riots in Milan and other events to relay and humanize the historical situations around which the novel revolves. His portrayal of this honest, enthusiastic, brave young man reflects his sympathy for the poor, yet Renzo is not just an idealized figure. Although he sincerely loves Lucia and has a generally optimistic and steadfast faith in God, Renzo sometimes behaves rashly or even stupidly, as when he becomes drunk soon after arriving in Milan and gets himself arrested. Renzo is easily excited and rather naive, but he is also inherently quick-witted, good-natured, and compassionate. He demonstrates his strong moral fiber through his determination to find Lucia and, toward the end of the novel, through his willingness to forgive the dying Don Rodrigo for his wicked deeds. Like his fiancée, Renzo retains his faith despite the many difficulties he endures, and fate finally decrees that he be rewarded.

Manzoni's depiction of virtuous **Lucia Mondella,** the other ''betrothed'' of the title, is also said to exemplify the author's compassion for the common people and desire to humanize through them the great events of history. Although she is attractive enough to incite Don Rodrigo's lust, Lucia is thoroughly good and innocent. Modest, shy, and sweet, she is also sensible and steadfastly pious, particularly in her desire to honor the vow of chastity she made after she was captured by the Unnamed. Although some critics see Lucia as an overly idealized and therefore unconvincing vision of faith and morality, others contend that she does exhibit human imperfections, such as her occasionally affected or obstinate manner and her failure to banish her love for Renzo from her heart after she has taken her vow. Lucia seems to catalyze most of the people around her, eliciting strong reactions from them and thus helping to illuminate their characters. In Renzo, of course, she inspires undying devotion and love; in Don Rodrigo, lust and petty pride; in Gertrude, the nun of Monza, fascination and a brief glimmer of hope. Her most important accomplishment, however, is the conversion of the Unnamed. Confronted with Lucia's radiant spirituality, beauty, and innocence, he begins to regard his way of life as evil. Thus she is directly responsible for his change of heart and conversion to Christianity. Like Renzo—though even more chastely and quietly—she maintains her faith through a long period of suffering, and she finally attains the happiness she thought she had renounced.

The tyrannical, lustful **Don Rodrigo** is the lord of the manor connected with Renzo and Lucia's village who thwarts the young couple's marriage plans. He wagers with an equally corrupt friend that he will attain Lucia while she is still a virgin, and this self-centered, capricious vow leads to grievous hardships for her and her fiancé. Although Don Rodrigo is indeed wicked, arrogant, and vain, he exhibits an inherent mediocrity and seems more stupid than truly evil. In fact, his petty meanness and criminality is in contrast with the more powerful evil wielded by the Unnamed, who is Don Rodrigo's obvious superior in every way. The latter's essential weakness is demonstrated by the fact that it is not until he is dying of the plague that he feels remorse; his desire for Renzo's forgiveness nevertheless elicits a certain measure of pity from the reader.

One of the most consistently praised characters in *The Betrothed* is **Don Abbondio,** the parish priest who complies with Don Rodrigo's demand that he refuse to marry Renzo and Lucia. Neither truly good nor utterly villainous, he seems to represent the recognizably human weakness of cowardice. Timid, petty, and fearful by nature, Don Abbondio became a priest not out of devotion to God or a desire to serve humanity but to ensure his own personal safety, because he assumed that as a priest he would be protected from danger. Thus he is supports the status quo even when it is wicked, as exemplified by Don Rodrigo, and he shirks the demands of faith. Manzoni's notably comic portrayal of Don Abbondio both condemns weakness and shows compassion for humanity. In his lax, self-serving approach to his vocation, Don Abbondio serves as a foil to the novel's other clergymen, the highly virtuous, dedicated, and selfless Cardinal Boromeo and Fra Cristoforo.

The saintly Capuchin monk **Fra Cristoforo** serves as one of the novel's strongest examples of Christian morality and goodness. He takes seriously his religious commitment, applying the values of humility, charity, and brotherhood to everything he does. Fra Cristoforo was not, however, always so virtuous: many years earlier, as an impulsive and arrogant young man, he had killed an opponent in a duel fought over some petty point of honor. The experience had a profound, transforming effect on him. Fervently devoted to Christianity, he channels his considerable energy into service to God and humanity. His consistently melancholy manner, however, reflects his continuing awareness of his former wickedness. Fra Cristoforo plays an important role in *The Betrothed* through his efforts to help the innocent young peasant couple, sheltering them from Don Rodrigo in his monastery (even attempting to talk the nobleman out of persecuting them) and then sending them to safety. Later he reappears in Milan, where he has gone to aid the plague sufferers. He eventually dies of the disease himself, but not before he has assured Renzo and Lucia that they may disregard Lucia's chastity vow and reminded them that their hardships and miseries have prepared them for the joy they are now to experience.

Another paragon of Christianity—and particularly of the Catholicism to which Manzoni subscribed—is **Cardinal Federigo Boromeo,** who is based on an actual person. While unrelentingly firm in his own faith, he expresses compassion for human nature in all of its weakness. It is to the eloquent, thoroughly virtuous cardinal that the Unnamed makes his confession and request to become a Christian, and Boromeo warmly accepts and blesses his convert. Some critics consider the cardinal an over-idealized character who, by serving as a model of Christian morality, performs a primarily didactic function in the novel. Others, however, claim that Boromeo's inherent nobility does not make him less convincing. These scholars maintain that Boromeo understands human psychology and that charity is humanity's redeeming hope, thereby personifying the values Manzoni intended *The Betrothed* to present.

Sometimes called the **Nun of Monza, Sister Gertrude** is the nun to whom Lucia and her mother are sent for safe keeping. Often described as one of the most compelling characters in *The Betrothed,* Gertrude is a troubled soul who helps illustrate that evil may be imposed upon an innocent person from outside or that the will may weaken within, leading the individual to capitulate to evil. Born into a noble family that wished to avoid paying a marriage dowry, Gertrude was conditioned from an early age to enter a convent. She had no religious vocation but became a nun to convenience her cold-hearted father. Instead of resisting events, Gertrude silently submitted to them, and as a result she grew bitter and hateful. When she became mother superior at the convent, she exhibited a particularly cruel, stern kind of leadership. She became more corrupt through a sexual relationship and participation in a murder. Frequently compared to the title character of Gustave Flaubert's novel *Madame Bovary* because of her romantic delusions, Gertrude is a complex figure whose corruption is portrayed as resulting from external forces (e.g., her powerful family) as well as her inability to extricate herself from her dilemma or turn it to good purpose.

The most enigmatic character in *The Betrothal* is **the Unnamed (L'Innominato)**, whose mystery and power are signified by his namelessness. Like Don Rodrigo he is an aristocrat, but he has greater intellect and projects more profound evil. Driven to destructiveness by the conviction that life is absurd, he has lived as a dispassionate criminal, immune to the suffering he has created. The Unnamed is continually associated with demonic references and imagery, and some critics describe him as the kind of satanic figure often found in works of the romantic period: a being of monumental corruption whose considerable energies have been channeled into evil. Also a romantic trait is his alienation from society, for he lives in a remote fortress, protected by a private army of henchman. Despite his profound wickedness, though, the Unnamed possesses the deeper awareness that the more petty villain Don Rodrigo lacks. His confrontation with Lucia's purity, radiance, and simple piety sets off a reaction of unexpected emotions in the Unnamed. He begins to doubt himself and to feel overpowering loneliness and dread; Lucia's faith awakens him to the idea that there is a God who judges his deeds and an eternity in which to pay for them. The Unnamed considers with horror the brutalities he has committed, and he is tempted to kill himself. Yet he chooses instead to change his life, to convert to Christianity through Cardinal Boromeo, and to seek the salvation that would otherwise be lost to him. Thus he exercises the free will with which Christians believe human beings are endowed; Sister Gertrude, by contrast, fails to exercise such freedom of choice and so goes unredeemed. Some critics, claiming that the Unnamed's role is primarily didactic, find his conversion too rapid and inadequately motivated, while others consider it a powerful expression of Manzoni's vision and an event that effectively unifies and concludes the novel.

An interesting array of minor characters round out the portrait of Italian life found in *The Betrothed*. Lucia's mother, **Agnese Mondella**, is a colorfully portrayed representative of the common people; strong, affectionate, energetic, and sensible, she provides a more experienced and somewhat less scrupulous counterpart to her daughter. Her frequent use of generally ineffectual proverbs and sayings provides comic relief, and she is almost always able to maintain her optimism even in great hardship. The decent though rather ignorant and pretentious **Donna Prassede** and her highly intellectual, rational, but spiritually shallow husband, **Don Ferrante**, are the aristocratic "couple of much consequence" to whom Cardinal Boromeo sends Lucia and her mother after the Unnamed releases Lucia. **Perpetua** is Don Abbondio's gossipy servant; faithful and protective, she provides contrast to her timid employer with her brashness and strong opinions. **Dr. Azzeccagarbugli** (translated as Tangle-Weaver or Quibble-Weaver) is the lawyer Renzo consults after his marriage to Lucia has been thwarted; although seemingly benevolent, Azzeccagarbugli is actually corrupt, parasitic, cowardly, and subservient to Don Rodrigo, and he quickly discards Renzo when he learns that the young man is not a bandit as he had assumed.

Further Reading

Baricelli, Gian Piero. *Alessandro Manzoni*. Boston: Twayne, 1976.

Caserto, Ernesto G. *Manzoni's Christian Realism*. Florence: Leo S. Olschki Editore, 1977.

Chandler, S. B. "Passion, Reason, and Evil in the Works of Alessandro Manzoni." *Italica* 50, No. 4 (Winter 1973): 551-65.

Foster, Kenelm. "Alessandro Manzoni (1785-1873)." *Italian Quarterly* 17, No. 67 (Fall-Winter 1973): 7-23.

Mateo, Sante, and Larry H. Peer, eds. *The Reasonable Romantic: Essays on Alessandro Manzoni.* New York: Peter Lang, 1986.

Nineteenth-Century Literature Criticism, Vol. 29. Detroit: Gale.

Pritchett, V. S. "Alessandro Manzoni: 'I Promesi Sposi.'" In *A Man of Letters: Selected Essays,* pp. 298-302. New York: Random House, 1985.

Review of "I Promessi Sposi." *London Review* n.s. 21, No. 11 (May 1828): 264-66.

Harriet Martineau
1802-1876

English novelist, short story writer, travel writer, essayist, journalist, historian, and biographer.

Deerbrook (novel, 1839)

Plot: The novel begins as sisters Hester and Margaret Ibbotson, who live in Birmingham, come to visit in the village of Deerbrook. One of the town's prominent gossips, Mrs. Grey, decides that young doctor Edward Hope will surely fall in love with the beautiful Hester. Instead, Hope is smitten with the plainer but more sensitive Margaret. Hester, however, is attracted to Hope, while her sister remains oblivious to the doctor's affections. Determined to make a match, Mrs. Grey convinces Hope that he has led Hester to believe he will propose to her. Chagrined and concerned, Hope decides that it is his duty to marry Hester even though he loves Margaret. Margaret, meanwhile, has fallen in love with the wealthy Philip Enderby, an attorney. His malignant sister, Mrs. Rowland, wishes to thwart the romance because she feels Margaret is not worthy of her brother. Philip is crestfallen to discover that Hope once loved Margaret, who now lives with the newlyweds, and his sister manages to exacerbate his reaction by telling him malicious lies about his intended. Spurned by the angry Philip, Margaret is plunged into a period of despair; her confidante Maria Young, a governess who was also once in love with Philip, tries to comfort her and recommends that she resign herself to unhappiness.

Tormented by guilt over his continuing attraction to Margaret, Hope dutifully suppresses his feelings. After he supports an unpopular candidate in a local election, Hope falls into disfavor with the townsfolk and loses patients; his reputation is also marred by outrageous rumors about his progressive, unconventional medical practices. Their finances depleted, Hope and Hester must release most of their servants and perform their domestic duties themselves. The formerly petulant and jealous Hester is ennobled and inspired by this period of adversity, however, and her relationship with her husband improves. Eventually Hope realizes he sincerely loves Hester. As the novel comes to a close, Philip and Margaret are reconciled and even Mrs. Rowland, chastened by the death of her child, seems likely to mend her ways.

Characters: Although more noted for her influential essays on politics and economics and for her revealing autobiographical writings, Martineau was also a popular novelist. Her best-known work, *Deerbrook* is considered more valuable as an illustration of Martineau's beliefs and as a forebear of later, more accomplished novels than on its own literary merit. Though frequently faulted for its excessive melodrama, flat characters, and poorly sustained narrative, *Deerbrook* anticipates some of the concerns and methods of such renowned authors as Charlotte Brontë, Charles Dickens, and George Eliot. For instance, it features a cross-section of characters and relays the circumstances of their everyday lives in detail, is infused with an aura of moral reflection, and exposes the narrow range of opportunities available to nineteenth-century women.

Dr. Edward Hope's decision to marry not the woman he loves but her sister provides the central impetus of *Deerbrook*. Intelligent, humane, conscientious, and notably passive, Hope allows himself to be propelled into the marriage on a seemingly irresistible tide of duty and social pressure. He endures acute discomfort after the marriage, when his wife's sister moves into his household and he is constantly forced to suppress his affection for her, but he does succeed in repressing that passion. Hope's work and his reputation with the townsfolk distract him from dwelling on his domestic dilemma. Furthermore, his relationship with Hester grows stronger as the two adapt to adversity together. Through forbearance and dedication to duty, Hope finally achieves regeneration and happiness. Many critics have noted that Martineau avoids the sexual implications of Hope's situation, reflecting her own somewhat naive belief that human passion can be overcome if duty necessitates such resistance. Yet the characters' relative lack of passion contradicts the potential volubility of their circumstances, thus rendering the work unconvincing to some scholars. Hope is often identified as a prototype of other doctor characters found in Victorian literature, particularly Tertius Lydgate in George Eliot's *Middlemarch* (1872). Like Lydgate, Hope is a stranger in town who marries the "wrong" woman and whose progressive ideas alienate him from his petty, narrow-minded society. While previous literary portraits of physicians reflected the fairly lowly status they held in society, Martineau helped to spawn a new vision of the doctor as social reformer and philosopher. Hope's interest in innovative methods and research are viewed with distrust by the residents of Deerbrook, and it is falsely rumored that he has indulged in the unsavory practice of grave-robbing to support an obsession with dissecting bodies. Unlike Eliot's Lydgate, who finally leaves the hostile confines of Middlemarch, Hope withstands the forces opposing him, exhibiting strength and stoicism. That he is finally rewarded with an unexpected inheritance seems to some reviewers a too-convenient solution to his economic hardships.

Margaret's friend **Maria Young** is one of the most interesting characters in *Deerbrook*. Once pretty and rich, Maria was crippled in a carriage accident, and was left with little money after her father's death, requiring that she work to support herself. In addition, she lost the regard of the man she still loves, Philip Enderby. Maria now endures the dreary life of the nineteenth-century governess: existing on the fringe of society with no family or real friends of her own, no prospects of marriage, and meager pay. Maria has been identified as the first in a long line of governess characters found in Victorian fiction—the most notable of which is Charlotte Brontë's *Jane Eyre*. Like these governesses, Maria is intelligent and sensitive but forced to suppress her own wishes and feelings. She must also serve as a confidante to a privileged young woman who ultimately marries the man she herself loves. Maria differs from Jane, however, in her attitude toward her situation. She has concluded that happiness is simply not attainable to everyone, and she accepts her dreary life as it is, seeking solace in memory, imagination, and service to others. Some critics have noted autobiographical elements in Maria's character, particularly her physical infirmity, for Martineau was deaf, and understood the disadvantages of such disabilities. In any case, Martineau uses Maria as a mouthpiece for her own views on education, village society, and the hardships endured by governesses. Maria has been seen as an illustration of the predicament of the downtrodden governess and of nineteenth-century women in general, whose ability to employ their intelligence, talents, and interests was highly circumscribed.

While Maria Young is forced to make her way as a single woman, Hester and Margaret follow the path toward love and marriage, one of few choices available to nineteenth-century women. Somewhat less attractive than her sister, **Margaret Ibbotson** is possessed of a profound sensibility and manages to captivate Hope, though she is not aware of his feelings and does not reciprocate them. Despite her sensitivity, Margaret is essentially pragmatic and expresses a distaste for the elaborate artifices of courtship, preferring a serious approach to the realities of marriage and home life. This levelheaded attitude toward marriage is reinforced in later novels by Charlotte Brontë, Charles Dickens, and George Eliot, all of whom warned against the dire consequences of frivolous choices in marriage partners. Margaret's period of anguish when her engagement to Philip is broken and her inability to resign herself to the solitary life of service to others that Maria has accepted may reflect Martineau's belief that many women prefer the satisfactions of domesticity to the single life that Martineau claimed to relish. Many critics have noted that Margaret's moving in with her newly married sister and brother-in-law was a typical Victorian practice; that the sexual tension resulting this arrangement would be defused by her innocence. The husband's fortitude has been difficult for some scholars to accept.

The beautiful **Hester Ibbotson** reflects the expectations of Victorian society in her focus on love and marriage, which seem to her the best route toward happiness. Having fallen in love with Hope, she is forced to conceal her feelings for him, as an admission of passion by Victorian women was considered unseemly. After her marriage, the self-absorbed Hester becomes demanding, jealous, and unbalanced, making Hope even more uncomfortable in his awkward arrangement. Though some critics have faulted Martineau for her rather mechanical portrayal of Hester's behavior, others have praised her depiction of the relationship between Hester and Margaret. Hester is excessively possessive of her sister and wants to be her only friend, accusing Margaret of neglect and unkindness when she feels that she has relied on Maria for companionship. It has been suggested that Martineau based this relationship on her experiences with her own sister, Rachel. When Hope's reputation suffers and the family's finances are depleted, Hester reacts with unsuspected strength; the period of adversity improves her relationship with her husband and helps her mature. The couple forge the kind of tender, mutually supportive friendship that Martineau suggests is an excellent basis for a marriage. Hester demonstrates her new determination when she confronts the wife of the man who has been spreading malicious rumors about Hope, demanding that the rumors be retracted. The hardships and persecution that she and Hope have endured, Hester decides, have ultimately made her wiser and happier.

Gossipy, interfering **Mrs. Grey** readily assumes the role of matchmaker, leading Hope to marry a woman he does not love. Mrs. Grey's meddling is motivated not by maliciousness, however, but by the boredom; Martineau suggests that because village life offers little stimulation to a woman of her energies and social position, she must find vicarious satisfaction through other people's lives. **Mrs. Rowland,** by contrast, is a pointedly, perhaps exaggeratedly, malevolent character whose gossip is intended to injure its subjects. Possessive, shrill, and fanatical, she is vehemently opposed to her brother Philip's engagement to Margaret, and she introduces a rival doctor to Deerbrook in order to force Hope out of town. Her extreme jealousy and meanness seem unmotivated; Philip's suggestion that she suffers from "internal torture" and tends to deny reality imply that she does suffer some psychological problem. After the death of her young daughter, Mrs. Rowland's grief and remorse prove cathartic, for she finally shows signs of emotional growth.

Margaret's fiance, **Philip Enderby,** is intelligent and good-natured. Though basically rational, he allows himself to be blinded by jealousy, reacting angrily to his discovery that Hope once loved Margaret, and refusing to acknowledge Margaret's innocence in the matter. Eventually, however, Enderby does recognize his error and is happily reunited with Margaret, whose security is restored by her marriage to the prosperous young lawyer.

Further Reading

David, Dierdre. *Intellectual Women and Victorian Patriarchy: Harriet Martineau, Elizabeth Barrett Browning, George Eliot.* Ithaca, N.Y.: Cornell University Press, 1987.

Dictionary of Literary Biography, Vols. 21, 55. Detroit: Gale.

Nineteenth-Century Literature Criticism, Vol. 26. Detroit: Gale.

Pichanick, Valerie Kossow. *Harriet Martineau: The Woman and Her Work, 1802-1876.* Ann Arbor: University of Michigan Press, 1980.

Sanders, Valerie. *Reason Over Passion: Harriet Martineau and the Victorian Novel.* Sussex, England: Harvester Press, 1986.

Thomas, Gillian. *Harriet Martineau.* Boston: Twayne, 1985.

Charles Robert Maturin
1780(?)-1824
Irish novelist and dramatist.

Melmoth the Wanderer (novel, 1820)

Plot: The story opens in Ireland in 1816, when Trinity University student John Melmoth leaves Dublin to visit his dying uncle. He finds his wealthy but miserly uncle in a state of great fear and foreboding, though he is unable to fully explain his feelings. When the uncle dies, young John inherits his entire fortune; the will instructs the nephew to destroy a seventeenth-century painting of their ancestor, also named John Melmoth. John destroys the portrait but discovers a tattered manuscript dating from the same period. Written by an Englishman named Stanton, the document explains that the earlier John Melmoth had died in Germany but had been seen many times after his death, thus earning the appellation Melmoth the Wanderer. The story went that after meeting Stanton, Melmoth became angry with him and predicted that the Englishman would be committed to an insane asylum even though he was sane. Stanton was subsequently sent to Bedlam (the famous London asylum) by a disreputable relative, where he suffered greatly from the poor living conditions and the company of the pathologically insane. Finally Melmoth appeared to Stanton and offered to spring him from the asylum in exchange for his soul; Stanton refused and, when eventually released, chronicled his encounters with the Wanderer, leaving the document with the Melmoth family when he visited Ireland. That night young John himself receives a visit from his supposedly dead ancestor. The next evening, while helping with the rescue of some Spanish sailors shipwrecked during a vicious storm, he spots the Wanderer standing on a rocky promontory. One of the Spanish survivors of the shipwreck, Alonzo Monçada, takes refuge with John and reveals that he too encountered the Wanderer in Spain. Monçada was born the illegitimate child of an aristocratic father. In order to dispose of him, some of his relatives forced him to enter a Roman Catholic monastery, even though he had no religious vocation or inclination for monastic life. There he endured a miserable life among the petty, corrupt monks. Finally Monçada's legitimate half-brother learned of his situation and, outraged, tried to have him legally released from the monastery. When this failed, he hired a parricide monk (a man sent to the monastery in lieu of prison after murdering one of his own relatives) to help Monçada escape. The parricide led Monçada through a series of terrifying underground vaults, sharing with him a gruesome story of love that turned to hate and cannibalism; then he delivered the young man not to freedom but to agents of the Spanish Inquisition. Jailed by his captors, Monçada received a visit from Melmoth the Wanderer, who offered to secure his freedom if he would give his soul to the devil. Monçada refused; when he told the Inquisition officials about Melmoth's visit, they sentenced him to be burned alive for consorting with the Devil. Before his execution could take place, however, the prison burned down and Monçada escaped. He found refuge with an elderly Jew named Adonijah, who told him three more stories about Melmoth the Wanderer.

The first concerned a young girl, Immalee, the daughter of a Spanish aristocrat named Don Francisco de Aliaga. Lost in a shipwreck and stranded alone on a tropical island, the girl grew up in a state of complete, natural innocence. She was visited by Melmoth, who offered her complete knowledge of the world in exchange for her soul. Despite her great curiosity and her growing attraction to Melmoth, Immalee resisted his offer. Melmoth fell in love with the girl and asked her to marry him in a satanic ceremony, but she would only consent to wed him in a Christian church. Immalee was eventually rescued by her family and returned to Spain (where she was called Isidore). The Wanderer again visited her, and the two were finally joined in a ceremony that the naive Immalee did not realize was actually satanic. But Melmoth was troubled by fears that he would destroy the life of his lover. He appeared to Don Francisco and told him two stories about the Wanderer that were intended to warn him to protect his daughter. One tale concerned the torments of a man who was tempted to sell his soul in order to feed his starving children; the other involved a young woman whom the Wanderer tempted with the promise of marriage to the man she loved. Despite their suffering, neither of these individuals succumbed to the Wanderer's proposals. Although he realized that the stories were meant as warnings, Don Francisco failed to take any precautions and continued his travels. When he finally returned to Spain, he brought with him a young man to marry his daughter. By this time, however, Immalee was already pregnant with Melmoth's child. When her relationship with the Wanderer was discovered, she was turned over to the Inquisition. She died after giving birth to her child and expressing hope that she and Melmoth would meet in heaven.

Soon after Monçada finishes telling his tale to young John, the Wanderer appears in the room with them. He tells them not to be afraid, as his earthly journeys and exploits are over, and he has come home to die. After his original death, he explains, he had been fated to spend 150 years attempting to win souls for the Devil, but no one had accepted his offer. Left alone at his own request, the Wanderer spends the night in a room from which horrible sounds are heard; in the morning the room is empty, and the Wanderer has apparently jumped or been thrown from a cliff into the sea.

Characters: *Melmoth the Wanderer* is one of the most acclaimed examples of the English gothic novel, a genre distinguished by an emphasis on both physical and psychological horror, mounting suspense, elements of the supernatural, gloomy settings, and complex plots. Widely acknowledged as Maturin's finest work, the novel probes the effect of prolonged emotional pain and suffering on the human psyche. Many critics have identified the circumventing of human goodness and love by corrupt institutions—whether religious, social, or political—as a dominant theme. Employing a pattern of stories within stories that has often been compared to the "Chinese boxes" of incremental sizes that fit snugly into each other, the novel's unusual structure reinforces its major ideas by presenting variations on them that are different but also consistent. A clergyman who is thought to have infused *Melmoth* with didactic intent, Maturin is praised for his skillful evocation of terror and the psychological insight with which he created his characters.

The novel's title character, **John Melmoth** or **Melmoth the Wanderer,** provides a unifying link between the "Chinese boxes" of which it is comprised. An exceptionally curious, rather ruthless seventeenth-century scholar, he sells his own soul to the devil and promises to draw others into damnation in exchange for a longer life and greater knowledge and power. For the 150 years that follow his initial death, however, Melmoth finds his fate joyless, and he is repeatedly unsuccessful in tempting others to share his fate. The part of the novel that involves Immalee is most effective in illuminating the Wanderer's character. Their relationship reveals Melmoth's hitherto unsuspected humanity and ambivalence, for he yearns to love her in an ordinary way but fears she will be damned. He tries several times to push her away, even warning her father that she is in danger. In the end Melmoth succumbs to the darker forces within him, tricking Immalee into participating in a satanic wedding ceremony that proves invalid because she is not conscious of its true nature. As several critics have noted, Maturin emphasizes that Melmoth's primary sin is his inability to believe in the possibility of human good. Obsessed with the perversion he sees around him, he is cynical, hopeless, and blind to the regenerative power of love that Immalee might have shared with him. In addition to the traditional figure of the Devil, Melmoth has been compared to such legendary mythical and literary characters as Adam and Eve, Cain, the Wandering Jew, and Faust. Like the Wandering Jew, Melmoth is bitter, sinister, despairing, and doomed to roam rootless through the world. Like Faust, he has relinquished his soul in exchange for greater knowledge and power. Melmoth has also been identified as Byronic (referring to the English romantic poet, George Gordon, Lord Bryon) for his brooding, alienated, tortured nature; according to Douglas Grant, he is "a damned and fiery intelligence; the eternal outcast." The Wanderer is widely considered the quintessential "hero-villain" of gothic fiction, damned not so much by any inherent evil as an inability to accept human limitations. Villainous in his immoral, insensitive behavior, he is heroic in his courage, strength, and suffering. Unlike the typical gothic hero-villain, however, Melmoth exhibits no traces of sexual sadomasochism, and in fact several scholars have noted that sexuality is missing from the book, even though Immalee bears Melmoth's child.

The opening and closing sequences of *Melmoth the Wanderer* are often referred to as the "frame story" because they provide an enclosing context for the six tales that make up the bulk of the novel. The primary protagonist of the framing sections is young **John Melmoth,** the nineteenth-century ancestor of the novel's title character. John is a student at Trinity University who inherits the considerable fortune and property of his uncle and subsequently learns of the Wanderer. His role in the story is essentially practical, for nothing much happens to him and his importance lies mainly in his inheritance of the portrait, perusal of Stanton's manuscript, and receptivity to Monçada's story. John's sojourn at his uncle's (later his own) country estate allows Maturin to provide a brief but realistic, interesting depiction of Irish life and character through the servants employed there. His portrayal of **John's uncle** is somewhat comic despite the ominous fear that surrounds the old man: a notorious miser who worries as much about the cost of his coffin as about the fate of his soul. With his mysterious exhortation that John destroy the portrait of Melmoth the Wanderer, the uncle helps to establish the novel's mood of mounting suspense.

"The Tale of Stanton," recounted in the manuscript that young John Melmoth discovers, takes place in 1677. **Stanton** is an Englishman who brings the Wanderer's ire upon himself and is consequently doomed by him to enter an insane asylum. Always somewhat unconventional and erratic in his behavior, he raises his unscrupulous relatives' suspicion when he talks about his encounters with Melmoth, and they respond by committing him to Bedlam. Their reaction helps illuminate Maturin's belief that the family is a means of moral support and guidance and dire consequences result when it fails in this function. Stanton's sojourn in the asylum is also significant. The role and nature of madness is a consistent concern throughout *Melmoth,* in which insanity is sometimes seen to provide protection against evil. Some of Stanton's fellow inmates or patients are not pathologically insane or mentally ill but fanatical—zealots whose behavior has become socially inconvenient. Maturin views those who have been driven insane by their own ambition with less sympathy than those whose affliction results from real hardship or misery (such as the woman whose entire family was killed in a fire). Stanton's gradual loss of hope and descent into the same unkempt state displayed by the other inmates effectively illustrates the influence of environment on behavior. The fact that he refuses Melmoth's offer of release from the asylum in exchange for his soul demonstrates the same inner strength that will be found in all of Melmoth's would-be victims, each of whom resists his proposal.

Alonzo Monçada is the young Spaniard who takes refuge with the nineteenth-century John Melmoth after his ship founders off the coast of Ireland. In what is termed "The Tale of the Spaniard," he reveals his own encounter with Melmoth's evil ancestor, thus serving both a practical role in the plot by recounting the Wanderer's exploits in Spain and helping to illuminate one of the novel's central thematic concerns. Born into a noble family, Monçada was illegitimate, and in order to dispose of him his relatives force him against his will to enter a monastery. Maturin's vivid portrayal of the young man's experiences as an unwilling, cloistered Roman Catholic monk is often cited as a particularly powerful section of the novel. Monasticism is often presented as a realm of perversion, cruelty, intrigue, and even Satanism in gothic fiction, and in *Melmoth* this negative image is especially emphasized. Isolated from the rest of society, deprived of their individuality, and compelled to participate in a dull routine of meaningless activities and tasks, the monks' natural human energies and impulses are thwarted. As a result they turn to pettiness, gossip, and tormenting each other in both minor and extremely cruel ways. Initially eager to welcome Monçada because of his wealth, the other monks resent the aloof manner he has adopted in order to steel himself against his unwished-for fate. When they learn of his desire to leave the monastery, Monçada is confined to a small, dark cell and subjected to psychological torture designed to frighten him into staying. Later he is led on a terrifying escape route by the parricide monk, who then turns him over to the agents of the Inquisition. At this point the Wanderer appears, offering to release Monçada from the prison if he will relinquish his soul to the Devil. Despite his misery, the young Spaniard—whose faith, miraculously, is still firm—refuses to join Melmoth in damnation. Maturin was a Protestant clergyman whose Huguenot ancestors had been persecuted for their religious beliefs, and many critics consider his portrayal of monastic life in *Melmoth* a direct and often sermon-like attack on the corruption he felt was endemic to the Catholic church. More generally, though, Maturin sought to convey the ways in which human goodness and love may be destroyed by institutional evil.

The **parricide monk** is the novel's most compelling example of monastic perversion. Having murdered his own father, he was taken into the monastery rather than sent to jail, and he has acquired a measure of power there. While leading Monçada through the dark, dreary vaults beneath the monastery—ostensibly to deliver him to freedom but actually intending to hand him over to the Inquisition—the parricide shares with the younger monk the horrifying story of a young couple he had been charged with punishing, due to their violation of the monastery's rules. The man was a monk and the woman, his wife, had posed as a nun in order to be near her husband. The parricide locked the two into a cell in the subterranean vaults and waited with diabolical glee as hunger gradually destroyed their love. The man finally resorted to cannibalism, sinking his teeth into the shoulder of his loved one. Maturin's vivid description of this episode is often cited as particularly effective in its focus on human corruption and limitations and the debilitating effects of suffering. It also strongly illustrates the evil and sadism of the parricide, who devised the grotesque punishment, then thoroughly enjoyed its enactment. Early reviewers objected to this character because the otherwise diabolical parricide makes some fairly sensible observations, such as his noting the irony that this previously too-spiritual couple had been defeated in the end by a purely physical need. The parricide is eventually punished for his wickedness, when he is literally torn apart by an enraged mob while he is participating in a religious procession. But even the morally upright Monçada, who views the parricide's death, cannot help but participate mentally in the vicious murder, thus further illuminating the bestiality that lurks within human nature.

Adonijah is the gentle, extremely old Jew who shelters Monçada after his escape from the Inquisition prison. He is interested in the exploits of the Wanderer and assigns his Spanish guest the task of translating the three stories that comprise most of the remainder of the novel. Adonijah provides a significant contrast to Melmoth, because he has apparently been *punished* for his desire to attain mysterious knowledge with an exceptionally long life, whereas an extended existence was the *reward* for which Melmoth traded his soul. In addition Adonijah is a representative of a non-Christian faith who practices the compassion that many of the novel's Christians lack.

"The Tale of the Indians," which takes place in the late seventeenth century, features the novel's most significant female character: beautiful, virtuous **Immalee** (called **Isidore** after her return to Spain), the daughter of Don Francisco de Aliaga and the beloved of Melmoth the Wanderer. Shipwrecked as an infant, Immalee grew to adulthood on a deserted tropical island; the nurse who had initially accompanied her had died after several years. Having lived in an idyllic natural setting uninhabited by other human beings, Immalee is completely innocent and pure. In fact she is often identified as an example of the "Noble Savage" common in romantic literature—an archetype based on the premise that the natural state is inherently good and civilization corrupting. While some critics find Immalee's purity implausible and overly sentimental, others claim that she is a compelling figure who represents the lost Edenic ideal of humanity and thus provides a strong contrast to Melmoth, who represents evil. Critic William F. Axton describes Immalee as "the living presence of the undefiled religious impulse in mankind;" indeed, despite her separation from society and ignorance of the world, she refuses to marry Melmoth in any but a Christian ceremony. In his visits to Immalee on her island, the Wanderer offers to give her unlimited knowledge of humanity, which he describes as completely corrupt, and he allows her to look into a kind of telescope through which she views the bizarre, cruel rituals practiced by a variety of religions. This episode has been characterized as amplifying the novel's general theme of religious abuses. Melmoth dazzles Immalee with his eloquent speeches on humanity's many sins and follies, and in turn he is strongly attracted to her beauty and, despite his wicked nature, virtue. The Wanderer's love for Immalee has been described as lending a more human tone to his suffering, for he is compelled both to tempt her into damnation and to save her. That their relationship must inevitably end underlines Melmoth's inability to experience ordinary happiness. Although the two do undergo a satanic marriage ceremony performed by a monk in a deserted monastery, Immalee does not realize the true nature of the ritual and thus is not damned by her participation in it; Melmoth's offer is validated only if *consciously* accepted by his intended victim. Persecuted by cruel agents of the Inquisition, who are ironically blind to her true virtue, Immalee is ultimately redeemed, though her final wish to meet Melmoth in heaven seems implausible.

The last two tales in *Melmoth* are told to Immalee's father, **Don Francisco de Aliaga,** by Melmoth, who encounters the Spanish aristocrat while he is traveling away from home. Although Don Francisco seems to realize that the Wanderer's stories are intended as a warning, he is preoccupied with business of his own and fails, with tragic results, to make any immediate effort to protect his daughter. Set in the mid-seventeenth century, "The Tale of Guzman's Family" concerns a wealthy Catholic named **Guzman** whose sister marries an impoverished Protestant music-master, **Wahlberg.** Although he disapproves of this marriage, Guzman leaves his fortune to the Wahlberg family; the Catholic church, however, hides the will in order to keep the money in its own coffers. Thus the tale provides another illustration of religious abuse. Wahlberg is driven insane by his family's suffering, but in this case—unlike those of some of the asylum inmates in "The Tale of the Spaniard"—his madness is excused because his hardship is undeserved. Wahlberg comes close to accepting Melmoth's offer of relief in exchange for his soul but finally rejects it, even though it might spare him from watching his children slowly starve to death. Wahlberg's wife, **Ines,** remains steadfastly loyal to and uncritical of her husband throughout their troubles; Maturin probably based this courageous, dignified character on his own patient wife, with whom he often endured financial hardship.

"The Lover's Tale," set in England in the 1660s, concerns religious prejudices, material self-interest, and social arrogance. **Elinor and Margaret Mortimer** are cousins; Margaret is the daughter of a wealthy Anglican royalist, while Elinor's father is an Independent (or Puritan) preacher. Another cousin, **John Sandal** (whose mother is the sister of the two girls' fathers), is in love with Elinor and wishes to marry her. **Mrs. Sandal,** however, wants John to marry the wealthy Margaret instead. She lies to John, telling him that Elinor is actually his half-sister. Horrified at the idea of marrying his sibling, John marries Margaret instead. Though devastated, Elinor accepts the situation and suffers in silence. She is visited in her misery by the Wanderer, who offers to arrange for her marriage to John if she will relinquish her soul to the devil. Like all of those Melmoth has tried to tempt, she rejects his proposal, thus revealing her spiritual purity, strength, and superiority in contrast to such corrupt figures as Mrs. Sandal, who sacrifices her son's happiness for material gain.

Further Reading

Axton, William F. Introduction to *Melmoth the Wanderer,* by Charles Robert Maturin, pp. vii-xviii. Lincoln: University of Nebraska Press, 1961.

Grant, Douglas. Introduction to *Melmoth the Wanderer: A Tale,* by Charles Robert Maturin, edited by Douglas Grant, pp. vii-xiv. London: Oxford University Press, 1968.

Kiely, Robert. "'Melmoth the Wanderer': Charles Robert Maturin." In *The Romantic Novel in England,* pp. 189-207. Cambridge, Mass.: Harvard University Press, 1972.

Lougy, Robert E. *Charles Robert Maturin.* Cranbury, N.J.: Bucknell University Press, 1975.

"Maturin—'Melmoth, the Wanderer.'" *Quarterly Review* XXIV, No. XLVIII (January 1821): 303-11.

Nineteenth-Century Literature Criticism, Vol. 6. Detroit: Gale.

Guy de Maupassant
1850-1893

French short story writer, novelist, dramatist, poet, journalist, and travel writer.

"Boule de Suif" (short story, 1880)

Plot: The story—which takes place in France during the Franco-Prussian War (1870-1871)—begins with the passage of bedraggled, defeated French troops through the town of Rouen. Soon a great number of Prussian troops arrive and take control of Rouen. The focus then shifts to a group of residents—three married couples, two nuns, a single man named Cornudet, and a prostitute, Elizabeth Rousset, who is called "Boule de Suif" (ball of fat) because of her plumpness—who have managed to reserve seats in a horse-drawn coach bound for the coastal town of Le Havre. The passengers, representing the various social strata of Rouen's populace, regard Boule de Suif with disdain, but she returns their stares boldly. The trip takes longer than expected and the passengers grow increasingly hungry, but it seems that no one has thought to bring food. Eventually Boule de Suif unpacks a basket of food she has stowed beneath her seat, and she shares it with her fellow travelers.

Soon all are chatting amiably about the Prussian occupation and their contempt for the conquerors. When the coach stops at a town called Tôtes, the passengers take rooms at an inn for the night. During the night, the dissolute Cornudet attempts to seduce Boule de Suif, but she rejects his advances, claiming that to carry on in such a fashion in the presence of France's enemy would be unpatriotic and undignified.

The next day the Prussian officer refuses to let the passengers leave until Boule de Suif agrees to sleep with him. She is indignant at this development, and everyone sympathizes with her initially. As time goes on, however, and the train is still detained in Tôtes, the others grow impatient and try to convince Boule de Suif to accommodate the officer. They speak to her about the rewards of self-sacrifice and the demands of war and patriotism; even the nuns suggest that the sinful act may be justified under the circumstances. Finally Boule de Suif gives in and goes to the officer's room. The other passengers, meanwhile, gleefully celebrate their imminent departure, although a grim Cornudet condemns their actions. The next morning Boule de Suif is the last to board the train. But now the other passengers snub the prostitute disapprovingly and speak only to each other. Boule de Suif spends the remainder of the trip crying softly in a corner of the coach.

Characters: Praised for his observant eye, clear, powerful prose, skillful use of irony, and insightful characterizations, Maupassant is recognized as one of the finest short story writers of all time. Originally published in a collection of anti-war stories by six young writers that was sponsored by such French naturalist writers as Emile Zola, "Boule de Suif" immediately established its author as a major talent. Its historical context lends the story drama and thematic resonance as well as authenticity, for Maupassant himself served in the Franco-Prussian war; the experience is said to have destroyed his youthful idealism and awakened him to the waste and degradation of war. In juxtaposing the socially condemned practice of prostitution with the glorified ideal of patriotism, Maupassant exposes the shallowness and hypocrisy of those who claim to love their country but behave selfishly and hypocritically when confronted with a difficult situation. Initially controversial for its element of eroticism, "Boule de Suif" continues to be lauded as a portrait of a turbulent period of French history and as a universally compelling glimpse into human behavior.

Although the title character's name is actually **Elizabeth Rousset,** she is known by the nickname **Boule de Suif** (variously translated as "ball of fat" or "ball of suet"), reinforcing the concept that she is judged by her appearance and occupation rather than by her real worth. She is short and fat but healthy-looking and attractive, with a ruddy, shiny face, dark eyes, and a sensuous mouth. In the social cross-section the group of passengers comprises, the prostitute occupies the lowest rung. Because hers is a maligned profession, the other, supposedly respectable travelers view her with contempt. Nevertheless she returns their stares challengingly, indicating that she possesses inner dignity and self-esteem. Boule de Suif also reveals her basic kindness and generosity when she shares the sumptuous contents of her food basket with her fellow passengers, which seems to win their approval. During the group's conversation about the Prussian occupation, Boule de Suif mentions that she attacked one of the Prussian soldiers billeted in her home; the others responded less courageously to the Prussian invasion, however, treating their hated conquerors with obsequious friendliness. Boule de Suif further demonstrates her principles when she repels Cornudet's attempt to seduce her, claiming such behavior is inappropriate and unpatriotic in the presence of France's enemy. She indignantly and courageously refuses the Prussian officer's repeated demands for her, and her fellow passengers support her at first. But they soon tire of waiting, and, in order to lift the quarantine on traveling, they now tell Boule de Suif that her compliance with the officer's demand would be a patriotic act. They instill so much confusion and guilt that eventually she capitulates. Their rejection of Boule de Suif afterwards irrevocably establishes their hypocrisy. In her final, pathetic state of isolation and humiliation, Boule de Suif has been said to represent the tragic grandeur of France at the time of the Franco-Prussian war, when, in Maupassant's view, the country was betrayed by her own people. Reportedly modeled after a real prostitute of the author's acquaintance, Adrienne Legay, Boule de Suif exemplifies his compassion for society's most downtrodden and outcast members (and particularly for women). Maupassant portrayed Boule de Suif realistically, not in the stereotypical mold of the prostitute with a heart of gold, but as an imperfect but admirable character of simple honesty, dignity, and inherent morality.

The other passengers of the coach are from various levels of Rouen society. Monsieur and Madame Loiseau represent the merchant class; they are wine sellers who are fleeing their city in the hope of attaining greater profits in Le Havre, or possibly in England. Part of that contingent who behaved in a friendly, even hospitable manner toward the Prussian officers billeted in their homes while ignoring them in public, the Loiseaus have chosen to adapt to rather than resist France's defeat. **Monsieur Loiseau** is pot-bellied and red-faced, with a joviality that masks his true cunning and reputation for crooked business practices. Despite his seeming respectability, he is inherently lascivious, staring at Boule de Suif with ill-disguised lechery and spying on the ''secrets of the corridor'' while staying overnight at the inn. He witnesses Cornudet's attempt to seduce Boule de Suif and shares this knowledge with the others the next morning. **Madame Loiseau** is a tall, imposing, shrill woman who efficiently runs her husband's business. She and the other female travelers portray self-sacrifice as patriotic, citing the examples set by several famous heroines in history, in order to make Boule de Suif's submission seem like her duty. There is a note of sexual excitement or titillation in Madame Loiseau when she speculates that the presence of Boule de Suif is all that prevents the Prussian officer from raping the other women. The other married couples include the pompous, wealthy **Comte Hubert de Bréville** and his reputedly low-born but now imperious wife, the **Comtesse de Bréville,** who represent the aristocracy; and the bourgeois **Monsieur Carré-Lamadon,** a corn mill owner, and his pretty, young wife, **Madame Carré-Lamadon,** whose sexual attraction to the Prussian officer is suggested.

Also notable among the other passengers is the red-bearded **Cornudet,** a well-known proponent of democracy who has squandered his own fortune and now hopes for a government post. The true cowardliness that underlies Cornudet's character is demonstrated by the fact that, after helping fortify Rouen against advancing Prussian troops, he has fled the city rather than participate in the resistance. Dissolute and roguish, he unsuccessfully attempts to seduce Boule de Suif. To his credit Cornudet condemns the others for coercing Boule de Suif into sleeping with the Prussian officer, but he does nothing beyond declaring the immorality of the act. Nor does he comfort the desolated prostitute during the rest of the trip.

The remaining members of the group are **the two nuns:** one is old and pockmarked, the other young and pretty but apparently suffering from tuberculosis. The nuns behave with the piety, submissiveness, and acceptance of suffering expected of religious women, though the older nun is surprisingly aggressive when describing saints whose sinful acts were excused by their pure motives, demonstrating the hypocrisy that may exist even in the most professedly religious. Other characters in ''Boule de Suif'' include **Monsieur Follenvie,** the fat, asthmatic innkeeper who delivers to Boule de Suif the Prussian officer's repeated requests for her sexual favors, and his extremely talkative wife **Madame Follenvie,** who condemns the wastefulness of war. The unnamed **Prussian officer** is portrayed as stereotypically Germanic in his brutality and boorishness; he manipulates the passengers, preventing them from continuing on their way in order to attain the sexual encounter he desires. His conquest of the unwilling Boule de Suif has been described as a metaphor for Prussia's invasion of France.

"Madame Tellier's Establishment" (*La Maison Tellier;* short story, 1881)

Plot: The story begins in the town of Fécamp in the French region of Normandy. There the good-natured, virtuous Madame Tellier operates a popular brothel; its ground floor contains a kind of saloon to accommodate the cruder, more raucous customers, and its upper level is reserved for more sophisticated patrons. The prostitutes Fernande, Raphaelle, and Rosa la Rosse work on the top floor, while Louise and Flora are assigned to the lower level. One day several of the brothel's regular customers arrive to find the house closed; a sign on the door announces that the entire staff has left to attend a first communion. Madame Tellier has taken the women to Virville to visit her brother, Monsieur Rivet, and attend the first communion ceremony and celebration for his daughter, Constance. As the garishly dressed group travels by train through the French countryside, they make a strong impression on their fellow travelers. Arriving at the Rivet home, they participate enthusiastically in preparations for the first communion. The next day the women dress in their finest clothing and attend the religious service, at which they find themselves profoundly moved. The atmosphere evokes memories of more innocent days, and they all weep profusely. The rest of the congregation is touched by the womens' emotion and soon everyone is crying; the priest is convinced that Madame Tellier and her friends have invoked a miracle by bringing the presence of God to the ceremony. At the celebration following the service, a drunken Rivet tries to seduce one of the women but is quickly rebuked by Madame Tellier.

The women return the next day to Fécamp, where they are eagerly welcomed back by the town's men. That night the house is particularly festive and the women accommodating, and everyone drinks champagne in honor of the first communion. In addition, Madame Tellier comes to an amorous agreement with her formerly platonic visitor, a judge named Monsieur Vassi, and she generously pays for most of the cost of the merrymaking.

Characters: Maupassant is regarded as one of the best short story writers of all time, a reputation based on his gift for detailed observation, his skillful prose style, and his incisive characterizations. "Madame Tellier's Establishment" features a juxtaposition of apparently incongruous elements common in Maupassant's fiction—in this case, prostitution and religion. Although this story is similar to the earlier, much respected "Boule de Suif" in its use of prostitutes as characters, "Madame Tellier's Establishment" is farcical in intent and lighthearted in tone. Nevertheless, it provides a revealing glimpse into human nature in a relatively nonjudgmental portrayal. The story is also distinguished for its revealing depiction of the landscape and people of Normandy, the region of France in which Maupassant was born and raised and for which he retained a lasting fondness.

Madame Tellier is the cheerful, popular proprietor of a small-town brothel. Perfectly virtuous herself, she inherited the establishment from an uncle and now runs it with competence and dignity. The brothel serves not just as an oasis for the sexually deprived or hungry but as a gathering place for the town's men, hence their dismay when they find it closed when the women attend a first communion. Madame Tellier is tall and plump with a pale, shiny face and fluffy hair; she appreciates a good joke but has a natural delicacy of manner that belies the nature of her business. Although she considers herself superior to the prostitutes who work for her, she treats them with motherly kindness and skillfully mediates their disputes. As the dominant figure among the group of prostitutes in attendance at the first communion ceremony, she has been said to serve as a foil to the pious priest who leads his congregation in holiness, and he attributes the "miracle" of their emotion to her influence in particular. At the end of the story, the previously celibate Madame Tellier reaches some kind of amorous agreement with Monsieur Vassi, but she will no doubt retain her inherent respectability.

The five prostitutes employed by Madame Tellier are each supposed to embody a different female type, so that all of the brothel's customers may attain their ideal women. **Fernande,**

Raphaelle, and Rosa la Rosse work on the upper floor and service the more respectable customers while Louise and Flora entertain the coarser, rowdier men in the café below. **Fernande** is a big, blonde, freckled country woman with short hair; **Raphaelle** is thin, dark, and Jewish-looking with an aquiline nose; **Louise** portrays the allegorical figure of Liberty by wearing a tricolor sash; and the slightly lame **Flora** dresses like a "comic-opera Spanish woman" and wears spangles in her red hair. **Rosa la Rosse** is chubby and husky-voiced; she sings, talks, and laughs energetically. It is Rosa who initiates the profuse sobbing at the first communion ceremony when she remembers her own childhood and long-lost innocence. She falls asleep with the innocent Constance in her arms, which is frequently cited as a particularly poignant scene highlighting the story's irony. Despite their occupation, all of the women project respectability during their sojourn to Virville and are much admired by those they meet there.

During their enjoyable train ride to attend the first communion, Madame Tellier and the five women make a strong impression on the other passengers with their brightly colored, extravagant clothing and exuberant manner. A **peasant couple** sitting nearby with a basket full of live ducks is particularly awed by the group. A **lingerie salesman** strikes up an immediate acquaintance with the women after boarding the train; having recognized their occupation, he jokes that they must be moving to a "new convent." He is fair-haired and wears many rings and a gold watch chain, and he reduces the women to hysterical giggles with his teasing. He also convinces them to try on the garters in his case and even to buy some for themselves. Eventually he attempts to take sexual liberties with the women but is discouraged by Madame Tellier.

In Virville the group meets Madame's brother, **Monsieur Rivet,** who transports them to his home in a rickety wagon. A comfortable but not wealthy carpenter, he hopes to influence his sister to remember her niece in her will. He is not at all ashamed of Madame Tellier's occupation, although he does not publicize it to his neighbors. Rivet becomes drunk during the celebration and makes a pathetic, unsuccessful attempt to seduce and even rape one of the women, but Madame Tellier throws him out of the room. Rivet's daughter, **Constance,** is a well-behaved, pious little girl who submits to the prostitutes' effusive displays of affection with resignation. When she and Rosa spend the night before the first communion in separate, adjoining rooms, both feel frightened and lonely, and Constance soon joins the affectionate Rosa in her bed. After the first communion, Constance is touchingly awed by the thought that she now carries God inside her. **The priest** who officiates at the ceremony is old and silver-haired. He interprets his congregation's intense emotion as a miracle, claiming that Madame Tellier and her friends have brought the presence of God to the service and that this blessed moment is his reward for a long life of servitude. The priest's response is both poignant and comic, for he has no idea that the women are actually prostitutes.

The regular customers of Madame Tellier's establishment include the most prominent citizens of Fécamp, such as **Monsieur Poulin,** the town's former mayor; **Monsieur Tournevau,** a fish-curer; the tax-collector, **Monsieur Pimpesse;** and **Monsieur Philippe,** the son of a prominent banker. **Monsieur Vasse** is a judge whose platonic relationship with Madame Tellier has, by the end of the story, transformed into something more.

"The Necklace" (*La Parure;* short story, 1884)

Plot: Mathilde Loisel is young and attractive but profoundly depressed and frustrated. Because she possessed no dowry, she was forced to marry a lowly government clerk and now lives in a shabby apartment devoid of the opulence she craves. She feels that she deserves a more easeful, luxurious life, and she is unable to reconcile herself to her ordinary circumstances. She hides dejectedly in her apartment to avoid seeing her former schoolmate, Madame Jeanne Forestier, who is now a wealthy matron. Monsieur Loisel, however, seems satisfied enough with his life, barely noticing the deprivation that torments Mathilde. One day he informs his wife that he is invited to a party at the home of the head of his bureau—a great honor for a junior clerk. Mathilde, however, claims that she cannot possibly attend the party because she has nothing appropriate to wear. Her husband finally agrees to give her the money he had been saving to buy a hunting rifle so that she may purchase a new dress. Once she has the dress, Mathilde bemoans her lack of any jewelry to wear with it; Monsieur Loisel suggests that she borrow a necklace from Madame Forestier. The next day Mathilde explains the situation to her friend, who invites her to choose whatever she likes from a large box of jewelry. Mathilde chooses a beautiful diamond necklace. She is indeed a dazzling success at the party, spending the entire evening dancing and much admired by all of the men present. But after the Loisels return to their home, the necklace is missing. Monsieur Loisel goes out and retraces their journey but finds nothing, and the next day the couple files a police report and places a lost-and-found ad in the local newspaper. Meanwhile they tell Madame Forestier that the clasp on the necklace is being fixed, but soon they realize the necklace will never be found and they will have to replace it. They finally locate an identical-looking necklace; it costs thirty-six thousand francs, so they use Monsieur Loisel's small inheritance and borrow the remaining amount. Mathilde returns the necklace to her friend, who does not even open the box to look at it.

The Loisels spend the next ten years paying back the money they borrowed to replace the necklace, enduring a miserably deprived existence. They must forego a maid, move to a cheaper apartment, and take on extra work in order to repay their debt. Hardship makes Mathilde prematurely old, and she is comforted only by the memory of her triumph at the minister's party. Finally the debt is paid off. When she happens to encounter Madame Forestier, who still looks young and pretty, Mathilde tells her friend the story of the lost necklace and the sacrifices she and her husband made to replace it. Profoundly moved, Madame Forestier informs Mathilde that the necklace she had borrowed was a fake, worth only about five hundred francs.

Characters: "The Necklace" is one of the best known of the nearly three hundred short stories written by Maupassant, who is considered a master of the genre. Like much of his other work, it features rich, detailed description that enhances the impact of the characters and what happens to them, and it is infused with a strongly ironic tone that lends impact to the story's theme. Maupassant exposes in "The Necklace" the shallow social pretensions of the nineteenth-century bourgeoisie, which, in his view, pursued material interests to sometimes cruel and wasteful ends. While some critics believe that the story's main characters are justifiably repaid for their greed and ambition, others maintain that Maupassant portrays them with controlled, objective sympathy. The story's surprise ending has drawn comparisons to the work of the nineteenth-century short story writer, O. Henry, who also frequently employed that device. In "The Necklace," the unexpected finale serves as a point of revelation, at which both the characters as well as the reader see things as they really are.

Mathilde Loisel is a pretty, socially ambitious young homemaker who was forced by her parents' modest circumstances to marry an insignificant government clerk. She spends most of her time either fantasizing about the luxurious life she craves or bemoaning her deprivation, and the knowledge that her friend Madame Forestier enjoys all the privileges of wealth only adds to her misery. Mathilde is nearly immobilized with depression and frustration. Some critics have compared her to Emma Bovary, the famous character created by Maupassant's fellow French author and mentor Gustave Flaubert, in his novel *Madame Bovary*. Emma too felt trapped in her dull, provincial life with a stolid, unromantic husband, and she too dreamed of luxury. While Emma pays for her longings and delusions with her life, however, Mathilde sacrifices her youth and beauty. The memory of the brilliant appearance she made at the minister's party and how all of the men present were attracted to her is her only solace during the desolate years that follow the loss of the necklace, for they leave her shrill-voiced and coarse, with roughened red skin and unattractive clothing, and Madame Forestier does not initially recognize her when they meet. The story ends abruptly with the unexpected revelation that the necklace was a fake, and the reader is left to imagine Mathilde's reaction. Although she and her husband have demonstrated their sense of responsibility and capacity for hard work, their great effort has been in vain. Some critics have seen Mathilde as a negative portrayal of the manipulativeness and superficiality that, they maintain, Maupassant often ascribed to women; others interpret her as a victim of life's random cruelty who, despite her flaws and weaknesses, does not necessarily deserve her fate.

Like Charles Bovary in Flaubert's *Madame Bovary,* **Monsieur Loisel** is dull, complacent, and mediocre. He seems satisfied with his circumstances and never notices the shabbiness of his apartment, the plainness of his meals, or the great unhappiness of his wife. A junior clerk in the Ministry of Public Instruction, he manages to get himself invited to the chief minister's party, indicating that he does yearn to some extent for higher social status. He is accommodating in his willingness to give up the rifle he planned to buy so Mathilde may purchase a new dress for the party, and it is he who suggests that she borrow a necklace from Madame Forestier. At the party Monsieur Loisel demonstrates his basic dullness by falling asleep for several hours while Mathilde dances, along with other husbands whose wives are enjoying themselves. Both he and Mathilde expend a great deal of energy in repaying their debt; Monsieur Loisel is even forced to take on extra work in his free time. At the end of the story the reader is left to imagine the inevitable meeting between the Loisels which must follow, when Mathilde tells her husband that their ten years of effort and deprivation have been wasted.

The only other significant character in "The Necklace" is **Madame Jeanne Forestier,** a wealthy matron who was once Mathilde's schoolmate. She generously offers her friend the use of any jewelry she likes, but she is rather peeved by Mathilde's delay in returning the necklace. When Mathilde meets Madame Forestier again ten years later and admits, with a certain degree of pride, to the sacrifices made to replace the lost necklace, her rich friend—who has remained young-looking and pretty while Mathilde is prematurely aged—clasps her hands sympathetically and explains that the necklace had little worth. Madame Forestier's role in the story is primarily to serve both as a goad to Mathilde, who envies her wealth and status, and as the deliverer of the surprising information with which "The Necklace" ends.

Further Reading

Artinian, Robert Willard, and Artinian Artine. *Maupassant Criticism: A Centennial Bibliography, 1880-1979.* Jefferson, N.C.: McFarland, 1982.

Donaldson-Evans, Mary. *A Woman's Revenge: The Chronology of Dispossession in Maupassant's Fiction.* French Forum, 1986.

Ignotus, Paul. *The Paradox of Maupassant.* London: University of London Press, 1966.

James, Henry. "Guy de Maupassant." In *The House of Fiction: Essays on the Novel,* edited by Leon Edel, pp. 139-67. Rupert Hart-Davis, 1957.

Maugham, Somerset W. Preface to *Complete Short Stories,* Vol. 1, by Guy de Maupassant. In *Selected Prefaces and Introductions of W. Somerset Maugham,* pp. 42-61. London: Heinemann, 1963.

Moger, Angela S. "Narrative Structure in Maupassant: Frames of Desire." *PMLA* 100, No. 3 (May 1985): 315-27.

Short Story Criticism, Vol. 1. Detroit: Gale.

Sullivan, Edward D. *Maupassant: The Short Stories.* Barron's Educational Series, Inc., 1962.

Tolstoy, Leo. *Guy de Maupassant.* 1898. Reprint. New York: Haskell House Publishers, 1974.

Trevor, A. Le V. Harris. *Maupassant in the Hall of Mirrors: Ironies of Repetition in the Work of Guy de Maupassant.* New York: St. Martin, 1991.

Herman Melville

1819-1891

American novelist, short story writer, and poet.

Moby-Dick; or, The White Whale (novel, 1851)

Plot: The story opens with the narrator's famous words: "Call me Ishmael." Ishmael is a schoolteacher who has often gone to sea when he felt restless. Deciding that he will sign up on a whaling expedition, he journeys one December from New York City to the Massachusetts coastal town of New Bedford. He spends a night at the Spouter Inn, where he shares a bed with a tattooed South Sea Islander and harpooner named Queequeg. Although frightened of the man at first, Ishmael grows to admire him and the two become friends, sharing money, a pipe, and the idol that Queequeg worships. Ishmael and Queequeg enlist to serve on the *Pequod,* a whaling ship that sails out of Nantucket. Before leaving they receive ominous warnings about the dangers of sailing with a captain like the *Pequod*'s—a legendary skipper named Ahab. After setting sail, the crew sees nothing of their captain for several days; mates Starbuck and Stubb are in charge. Ahab finally appears on deck, a stern-visaged man with a false leg made of whale bone and a scar on his face that is said to run the whole length of his body. Once the crew has begun its search for schools of whales, Ahab nails a gold coin to the Pequod's mast, declaring that it will be rewarded to the first man who spots the great white whale known as Moby-Dick. This is the ferocious whale that devoured Ahab's leg, and the captain is determined to wreak vengeance on the celebrated creature.

The ship sets out on a course that seems likely to bring them near the great white. They encounter a school of sperm whales—Moby-Dick is not among them—and catch one; the process of stripping the whale and extracting its precious oil is described in great detail. As the *Pequod* continues its search, the crew encounters several other whaling vessels and enquire as to Moby-Dick's whereabouts. One ship's captain, who lost his arm to Moby-Dick, warns Ahab not to pursue the white whale. Starbuck too tries to reason with Ahab, but the captain is determined to pursue his prey.

Queequeg falls ill with a fever and, in keeping with his people's custom, has a coffin made in the shape of a canoe. He recovers, however, and uses the coffin as a sea chest. Fedallah, the leader of a group of five mysterious figures who appeared from out of the ship's shadows at the beginning of the first whale hunt to man Ahab's whaleboat, prophesizes that Ahab's death will follow his own, and that Ahab's will be a death by hemp (rope). The *Pequod* comes across the *Rachel,* whose crew is searching for survivors—including the captain's son—of an encounter with Moby-Dick. Ahab refuses to help in the search and instead sails off toward where the white whale had last been seen. Finally Moby-Dick is sighted—by Ahab, who has remained on watch for days in the hope of spotting him—and an intense three-day battle ensues. On the first day, Moby-Dick cleaves Ahab's whaleboat in two, and its crew is rescued only when the *Pequod* sails directly at the whale to drive it off. On the second day, the harpooners manage to sink three harpoons into Moby-Dick but he twists and turns so that the ropes become tangled; the whale destroys two boats before upsetting Ahab's and dumping its crew into the ocean. Fedallah never emerges from the water. On the third day, the whale is tired and obviously in pain. The crew is shocked when they see the body of Fedallah lashed to Moby-Dick's side by the harpoon ropes. The apparently enraged whale turns on the boats, then rents a huge hole in the *Pequod.* Ahab thrusts his harpoon at the whale, but the rope coils around his neck and drags him into the sea. The *Pequod* sinks, and the only survivor is Ishmael, who clings to Queequeg's buoyant coffin until he is rescued by the passing *Rachel.*

Characters: Although misunderstood and underappreciated when it was first published, *Moby-Dick* is now considered one of the greatest novels in the English language. Indeed, its solid grounding in the American experience and its structure and towering complexity of themes have earned the novel the appellation of "*the* American epic." *Moby-Dick* is part sea adventure story (for which Melville drew on his experiences as a whaling crew member in the Pacific), part treatise on the whaling industry, and part allegorical explication of both individual psychology and humanity's relationship with the universe.

The great white whale **Moby-Dick,** a creature of legendary size, ferociousness, and appearance, has become a subject of great scholarly speculation. On a purely practical level, the *Pequod*'s search for the albino sperm whale with the wrinkled brow and crooked jaw (whose existence might be patterned after Mocha Dick, a whale that supposedly wrought the destruction of the Nantucket whaler *Essex*) provides the novel's context; the epic struggle between Moby-Dick and Captain Ahab serves as the springboard for critical interpretation.

Although the whale is the most dominant symbol in the book, critics are divided as to what he symbolizes. Some feel that he represents evil, and this is also what Ahab claims is concentrated in his gigantic opponent: "I see in him outrageous strength with an insatiable malice sinewing it. That inscrutable thing is chiefly what I hate." Others maintain that the whale is God and it is Ahab who embodies evil in his attempt to conquer a force that is greater than himself. Scholars have also taken an sociophilosophical approach to the whale, perceiving in him the rigid Puritan consciousness of America that was opposed by the more individualistic, liberal thinking—epitomized by Ahab—that was gaining prominence as the nineteenth century progressed. Moby-Dick has even been said to embody a threatening parental figure. But perhaps the most prevalent interpretation of Moby-Dick is expressed by William Ellery Sedgwick, who asserts that the whale "stands for the inscrutable mystery of creation, and he also stands for what man sees in creation of himself." Thus Ahab struggles not so much against the evil that roams through the natural world but against the impossibility of fully comprehending the primitive forces in nature, which in its vastness is—like Moby-Dick—both majestic and horrible, but neither good nor malevolent.

Like the whale he pursues, the dramatic figure of **Captain Ahab** has become a part of America's popular mythology. He is one of the best examples in all literature of a monomaniacal character—one who focuses on a single obsessing interest at the exclusion of all others. Ahab's pursuit of his enemy, Moby-Dick, gives the novel its structure, and his personality dominates the book and helps determine its emotional impact. Ahab is a brilliant man given to bursts of eloquent expression delivered in a notably Shakespearean manner, and it is partly these poetic passages which give the novel its lyrical quality. A tall, powerful-looking man with a proud, regal bearing, on his grim face is a livid scar, which begins above his hairline and disappears under his collar and, supposedly, runs the length of his body. Having lost a leg in an earlier encounter with Moby-Dick—it was this encounter that provoked his desire for revenge—he wears a false leg carved, appropriately, from the jaw bone of a sperm whale. That Ahab is a man tormented by his own thoughts is evidenced by the anguish in his brooding expression; it is this anguish as well as his isolation from the rest of humanity and his doomed, heroic quest that, according to many critics, makes him a tragic figure. Although some scholars have perceived Ahab as wholly evil and hubristic, others consider him a courageous champion of his fellow man who carries the pursuit of knowledge and truth and the desire to triumph over evil to a tragic extreme. "Ahab acknowledges the limitation of man's power to know God through his intellect," writes critic Tyrus Hillway, "yet, instead of submitting to his weakness, he hopes to transcend it by sheer defiance." Some critics have interpreted this defiance as a rejection of religion, seeing in Ahab's blasphemy a profound skepticism about religion on Melville's part. But others assert that Ahab's destruction in the end indicates that Melville, while presenting Ahab as a man whose self-awareness makes his powerlessness to resist his own impulses even more tragic, does not approve of his character's actions. Ahab has often been compared to Shakespeare's similarly tragic King Lear, who also ended as an alienated, isolated madman—though whether Ahab displays the poignant humanity that makes Lear a sympathetic character is disputed; alone in the universe, he battles evil or whatever force Moby-Dick may represent as he attempts, according to Alfred Kazin, to "reassert man's place in nature," and is destroyed in the process.

Much of *Moby-Dick* is narrated by **Ishmael,** whose voice is integral to the book's power. He quickly establishes a comfortable rapport with the reader through his natural, easygoing talk and his gay, humorous attitude. As both a spectator of the action and a participant in it, he displays a remarkable degree of alertness, interest, and enthusiasm for what is happening around him. His primary vocation of schoolmaster is significant because it makes him a skilled purveyor of information and because it gives the knowledge he shares validity. It is often observed that Ishmael sometimes withdraws as the narrator, with Melville switching to an omniscient voice that is generally thought to be more directly his own. Although some scholars have asserted that Melville expresses his own views through Ahab, most contend that Ishmael is actually the author's mouthpiece, reflecting the Calvinistic background, philosophical speculation, and whaling knowledge that characterized Melville's own thought and experience. Ishmael differs from the captain in his openness to a wide variety of interpretations, philosophies, and ways of life. This is particularly exemplified in his growing love and respect for Queequeg, who becomes his only close friend on the voyage, though he was initially prejudiced against the savage-looking harpooner. Many critics contend that it is because Ishmael maintains his connection with humanity and accepts the variety and inscrutability of existence that he survives the encounter with Moby-Dick. He is able to sympathize to some extent with Ahab—he says at one point "a wild, mystical, sympathetical feeling was in me. Ahab's quenchless feud seemed mine"—but he is not willing to make of Moby-Dick the singular symbol of evil he is for Ahab.

Queequeg is one of three veteran harpooners on the *Pequod.* A native of the South Seas kingdom of "Kokovoko," he is a fearless, imposing figure with skin liberally stamped with tattoos. Ishmael recognizes beneath Queequeg's exotic exterior his basic integrity, and the two become fast friends; in fact, several critics—most notably Leslie Fiedler—have called attention to the homosexual implications of their relationship. Queequeg had at one time been converted from his primitive pagan religion to Christianity but was disillusioned by the hypocritical behavior of some of the Christians he encountered; he returned to worshiping Yojo, the little wooden idol he carries with him. Melville himself spent a year living among Polynesians, far away from the Calvinist environment in which he was raised, and some scholars have speculated that his exposure to their more natural way of life as well as the treatment they received from Christian missionaries caused him to question the monolithic precepts of traditional religion. The ultimate symbol of Queequeg's value as a friend is, perhaps, the coffin he builds when he believes he is dying, for it is this canoe-shaped buoyant object that saves Ishmael from drowning.

404

Like Queequeg, the other harpooners help to round out the vision of the *Pequod* as a microcosm of the human community, with representatives from many different segments of society. **Tashtego** is a member of the North American tribe of Gay Head Indians; he is a brawny man of noble bearing who serves as Stubb's harpooner. **Daggoo**, Flask's harpooner, is a huge, coal-black African of great power and dignity.

Another important trio of characters present on the *Pequod* is its three officers. Most significant is **Starbuck**, the first mate, a thirty-year-old native of Nantucket. He is a tall, thin man with a weathered face who is efficient, sensible, and dutiful. With his steadfast, right-minded nature reflecting his Quaker faith, he has been described by many critics as a scion of virtue who stands in direct contrast to the maniacal Ahab. He opposes Ahab's quest from the beginning, viewing the pursuit of Moby-Dick as both impractical and blasphemous. Although he considers killing his captain to keep the ship and crew safe, he is unable in the end to divert Ahab from the ruinous course he has chosen. Starbuck nearly succeeds, however, when he plaintively asks Ahab to remember his wife and child at home, revealing as he does so his own affection for his captain: "Oh, my captain! my captain! noble soul! grand old heart, after all! . . . Away with me! let us fly these deadly waters! let us home!" The second mate, **Stubb**, is an easygoing, pipe-smoking, fearless Cape Codian who doesn't take life too seriously. After the crew catches a whale, he directs the ship's cook to prepare him a whale steak, then insists that the frightened cook give the nearby marauding sharks a lecture on greed. The third mate, **Flask**, is from Martha's Vineyard. He is a short, stout, happy-go-lucky fellow with a ruddy face who thoroughly enjoys the whaling profession. It is he who cruelly jabs a dying whale despite Starbuck's plea that the creature be treated humanely.

Ahab's harpooner, the mysterious **Fedallah**, and his four subordinates, who serve as the special crew for Ahab's whaleboat, do not appear until they set out on their first whale pursuit, though Ishmael and Queequeg see them board the ship in Nantucket. Fedallah is a "Parsee"—a member of the fire-worshipping Zoroastrian religion of India. Tall and dark-skinned with a protruding tooth and a turban wrapped around his head, he rarely speaks except to make cryptic comments like the prophecy he relates to Ahab. Critics generally agree that Fedallah serves as an embodiment of evil; he is Ahab's "bad angel," just as Starbuck is his "good angel." Further, his relationship with Ahab contrasts Ishmael and Queequeg's, for Fedallah brings out the worst in his companion, Queequeg the best. The presence of a mysterious, dark stranger who delivered ominous portents was a common dramatic device in the gothic horror tales popular in the eighteenth century; with Fedallah Melville may have been employing a similar character type.

Other members of the *Pequod*'s crew include **Dough-Boy**, the dull-witted ship's steward who lives in fear of the three harpooners; **Perth**, the old blacksmith who fashions the harpoon with which Ahab hopes to kill Moby-Dick; and **Bulkington**, a suitably named, powerful man who has never been able to remain on shore for very long. **Pip**, the cheerful, Alabama-born black cabin boy, falls overboard during a whale chase and is left in the ocean for some time while the crew continues its pursuit; Pip is rendered permanently insane by this trauma. Ahab feels tender toward the boy, sensing they share a common madness. The black ship's cook, **Fleece**, at Stubb's request, delivers a sermon to the sharks feasting on the dead whale tied to the ship's side: he begs them to curb their greed, but finally concludes that they will not and hopes they will end by eating themselves to death. This speech may be compared to the one delivered by Father Mapple in Nantucket before the *Pequod* leaves port; both advise their listeners to govern their selfish, wicked impulses, but Mapple's is infused with hope and Fleece's with despair.

Father Mapple, a former seagoing man who now preaches from a pulpit shaped like the bow of a ship, delivers the memorable sermon on the Biblical story of Jonah and the whale. Mapple is a skillful, persuasive rhetorician who uses dramatic gestures and language laced with seafaring imagery and terms to capture his audience's imagination. His sermon has been described by Richard Chase as "the high point of American oratory," with a power akin to that displayed by such famous American orators as Daniel Webster and Henry Ward Beecher. In relating the consequences of Jonah's disobeying God, Mapple expresses a major theme of *Moby-Dick.*

Other minor characters in *Moby-Dick* include **Captain Peleg** and **Captain Bildad,** two miserly old Quakers who are part-owners of the *Pequod.* In describing Ahab to Ishmael, Peleg attests to the captain's humanity—he explains that Ahab is a good-hearted man who was made "desperate moody, and savage sometimes" by the loss of his leg. The skippers of two of the nine whaling vessels encountered by the *Pequod* on her journey—**Captain Boomer** of the *Samuel Engerby* and **Captain Gardiner** of the *Rachel*—are both men with good reason to hate Moby-Dick as much as Ahab (Boomer lost his arm to the white whale and Gardiner his son). Yet neither harbors any ill will toward the whale, thus emphasizing the extremity of Ahab's behavior.

"Bartleby the Scrivener" (short story, 1853)

Plot: Set in New York City, the story is narrated by an unnamed, prosperous lawyer with an office on Wall Street who does a steady business in bonds, mortgages, and other documents. The lawyer's staff consists of two scriveners (copyists), nicknamed Turkey and Nippers, and an office boy called Ginger Nut. Each of the scriveners is somewhat eccentric but the lawyer tolerates their behavior. When his own workload increases, the lawyer hires a new scrivener, a solemn young man named Bartleby. At first Bartleby is a model employee, but one day he responds to the lawyer's request that he proofread a copied document by saying, "I would prefer not to." Confused by this behavior, the lawyer takes no disciplinary action. Gradually, however, Bartleby answers all the lawyer's requests with the same phrase and eventually there are no more tasks he is willing to perform. After the lawyer discovers that Bartleby has been spending his evenings and weekends in the office and is apparently homeless, he tells Bartleby that he must either begin to work again or leave his employ. Bartleby still says only, "I would prefer not to." The lawyer becomes increasingly distraught and sees no other solution but to move to a different location. The subsequent tenants force Bartleby to leave the office but he stays in the building. When the lawyer is called in to help with the situation he offers to let his former employee stay in his own home; Bartleby says he would prefer not to.

Finally the former scrivener is arrested for vagrancy and taken to the Tombs, the city's prison. The lawyer visits him there and finds Bartleby standing with his face to the wall of the prison's exercise yard. When the lawyer implies that Bartleby is better off here, he says, "I know where I am." The lawyer arranges for a prison employee to see that Bartleby is well fed, but Bartleby refuses to eat and eventually dies. Later, the lawyer learns that Bartleby may have once worked at the government's Dead Letter Office. The story ends with the narrator's famous words, "Ah, Bartleby! Ah, humanity!"

Characters: Melville's allegorical tale of an individual's passive resistance and another's attempt to understand his behavior has produced a fascinating variety of conjectures about what the characters represent and what, in fact, Melville meant. Perhaps even more than the title character, the narrator has generated a wide spectrum of interpretations. **The lawyer** is respectable and conservative, describing himself as "an eminently *safe* man" who believes that "the easiest way of life is the best." Thus he makes a good living doing unglamorous but profitable legal work. It has been suggested that Melville may have based the character on either his father-in-law, the renowned Massachusetts judge Lemuel Shaw (who seems to have viewed Melville's artistic pursuits as impractical), or his brother Allan, who was a Wall Street lawyer.

Most critics characterize the lawyer as profoundly conventional and materialistic: he cannot understand Bartleby's dilemma because he cannot imagine a life outside of the societal bounds that he unquestioningly accepts. The story's repeated wall imagery—the office is on Wall Street, its windows allow a view only of brick walls, Bartleby stands facing the jail wall—underscores the lawyer's limited view. The narrator's tolerance of the eccentricities first of Turkey and Nippers and then of Bartleby has been seen as both humane and compassionate and as indecisive or self-interested. Many scholars contend that the lawyer is a caricature of society's blindness to the creative and emotional needs of the individual. Thus he provides a good example of Melville's use of an unreliable narrator, and the reader must remain critically conscious of his limited perspective. Others, however, feel that the lawyer is simply an ordinary, truly sympathetic person who does what he can for a troubled acquaintance.

The alienated man who lends his name to the story's title is described as "pallidly neat, pitiably respectable, incurably forlorn!" Because he says "I would prefer not to" rather than "I will not," **Bartleby**'s rebellion is passive rather than aggressive. He is characterized both by the comedy implicit in the extreme courtesy of his disobedience and by the utter pathos of his lonely, isolated situation. The mystery of his behavior—why he chooses to rebel so completely and yet so politely from ordinary existence—is never unraveled in the story, even though the lawyer suggests that a period of employment in the Dead Letter Office may have proved too desolating an experience for Bartleby. The ambiguity of Bartleby's character makes the story more complex and also more open to multiple interpretations. Some scholars describe Bartleby as a frustrated artist who is protesting the world's warped preference for money over art; in fact, many contend that Bartleby is Melville himself. Bartleby's behavior has been understood as the protest of an alienated worker against a boring, demeaning job in a subtly hostile environment. Bartleby has also been seen, in a broader interpretation, as a representative of nonconformity or of the alienated modern man standing up against an ignorant universe of outdated values. The story may be an explication of an actual psychiatric illness such as schizophrenia, in which case, some scholars wonder, was Bartleby mentally ill to begin with or made so by his work situation? Despite its elements of humor, the story's end is tragic, for Bartleby is unable to escape the walls that surround him—whether those walls are society's limits or some barrier inherent in his own personality—and he curls up on the prison floor and dies.

The lawyer's other employees are generally considered incidental figures intended as humorous caricatures of eccentricity. **Turkey** is a short, fat, older man of British origin who works diligently until noon; his lunch apparently features a liberal helping of alcohol because after he returns he is irritable and prone to mistakes. He responds to Bartleby's behavior by offering to give him a black eye, later recommending that the scrivener might be more manageable if he drank some beer. **Nippers** is a sallow-complexioned, whiskered man who is younger than Turkey but equally moody. In the morning, presumably because he suffers from indigestion during those hours, he is nervous and cranky, but he grows mild-mannered and productive in the afternoon. He feels the lawyer should dismiss Bartleby summarily when he refuses to work. The lawyer claims that because his employees' periods of oddness occur at different times he need not take the trouble to replace them. He mildly mocks the scriveners for their lack of ambitiousness and professionalism—suggesting, perhaps, that they share with Bartleby a feeling that their employment is meaningless. **Ginger Nut** is the twelve-year-old office boy who earned his name from the little ginger cakes he likes to eat. His primary duty seems to be to supply the lawyer and scriveners with these same cakes. Ginger Nut's father has placed him in the office in the hope that it will benefit his son's future.

"Benito Cereno" (short story, 1856)

Plot: The story takes place in 1799. The *Bachelor's Delight,* an American ship with Captain Amasa Delano at its helm, is anchored at St. Maria Island off the southern coast of Chile. Noticing a ship in distress at the entrance to the harbor, Delano travels out in a whaleboat to offer assistance. When he boards he finds that the *San Dominick,* a Spanish merchant vessel carrying a cargo of African slaves, is in great disrepair, the crew desperately in need of water and the slaves roaming freely over the ship. The ship's captain, Don Benito Cereno, seems ill and behaves in a notably aloof, almost unpleasant manner. He is attended by his faithful African servant, Babo. Delano sends his whaleboat back for more supplies and tries to talk to Cereno, who maintains his disdainful reserve. After seeming to confer with Babo, Cereno explains that the *San Dominick,* while traveling from Valparaiso to Callao, lost some officers and crew members while battling storms at the notorious Cape Horn. Then the ship had encountered deadly calm seas, which led to an outbreak of illness. All of the other remaining officers and passengers—including Don Alexandro Aranda, who owned the slaves on board—had succumbed to fever. The Spanish captain attributes his own survival to Babo's devotion.

Delano knows that Cereno's account of recent weather conditions is inaccurate but accepts his story. His suspicions are aroused, however, when he notices that Cereno, despite the dilapidated appearance of the ship and crew, is neatly dressed; he also wonders about the six slaves who sit in the rigging holding hatchets (Cereno claims they are cleaning them). Also strange is the periodic appearance of an African named Atufal who is brought before Cereno in chains; when the captain asks if he will beg for pardon, Atufal declines to do so and is led away. Because Cereno and Babo keep moving away from Delano to talk privately and because Cereno asks him about the number of men and weapons there are on the *Bachelor's Delight,* Delano suspects they might be pirates. Nevertheless, he dines with Cereno and Babo—who refuses to leave the captain's side—but is still unable to decide if Cereno's story is true or not.

When the supply boat arrives, Cereno refuses Delano's invitation to visit his ship. Just as Delano is ready to pull away from the *San Dominick,* Cereno jumps into the whaleboat and a knife-wielding Babo jumps after him. Finally realizing that Cereno had been held captive on the ship, Delano rescues the Spanish captain, restrains Babo, and returns to shore. Cereno relates how the slaves had revolted and killed most of the Spanish crew, also committing such atrocities as lashing the skeleton of the murdered Aranda to the ship's masthead. In Lima, Cereno testifies at the trial at which Babo is found guilty of mutiny and sentenced to be hanged. Although he is planning to enter a monastery after the trial, the physically and mentally depleted Cereno dies three months later.

Characters: Through its skillfully maintained aura of mystery and ambiguity, "Benito Cereno" provides a haunting exploration into the evil of which human beings are capable and the different ways in which a knowledge of evil effects the human psyche. The story is based on a true account related by the actual Captain Amasa Delano in an 1817 book about his sea adventures.

Though the story's situation is rooted in reality, Melville seems to have created the character of the American captain. **Captain Amasa Delano** is a good-hearted, principled, and well-meaning Massachusetts native whose belief in the inherent goodness of man makes him slow to suspect evil even when presented with strong evidence. Critics have characterized Delano as the quintessential American figure in his self-confidence, lightheartedness, and naivete; Melville suggests that an outlook such as Delano's, however, is limited, for the captain cannot comprehend the dangerous situation into which he has stumbled. While he is aboard the *San Dominick,* Delano persistently overlooks clues suggesting something suspicious is afoot; he attributes Cereno's unpleasant behavior to illness and misfortune and sees in Babo only an enviably devoted "friend" whom he says, ironically, cannot be called a slave. Cereno realizes that it was ultimately Delano's innocence that saved him, for if he had betrayed suspicion he would surely have been killed; but he is also astounded by Delano's perceiving good in what was actually and intrinsically evil. Unlike Cereno, who is profoundly effected by his experience, Delano seems to consider it merely an interesting incident rather than a significant or educative experience. Melville lets the reader decide if Delano should be lauded for his compassionate, helpful, innocent nature or faulted for his failing to realistically comprehend the world around him.

The Spanish sea captain **Don Benito Cereno** is said to represent a typical eighteenth-century Spanish aristocrat in his elegant appearance and brooding aspect. He exhibits a pride tempered with melancholy and doubt, and some critics have interpreted Cereno as representing the values and conflicts of the "Old World" man as opposed to the shallower concerns and lightheartedness of the American. Though more aware of and troubled by the evil he perceives than Delano, Cereno is passive and dispirited and thus unable to overcome its influence. Cereno's physical illness—he faints several times during his conversation with Delano aboard the *San Dominick*—seems a manifestation of his spiritual suffering, and indeed he will not live for many months after his traumatic experience. When Delano asks Cereno what has cast its shadow over him, he enigmatically answers, "The negro." This response has stimulated much critical debate. Some scholars contend Cereno is referring not to Babo's treachery as to the implications of slavery and the evil that the slave trade has wrought. Others interpret Cereno's phrase less literally, claiming that he is making a broad reference to the darker side of human nature that may be unexpectedly exposed at any time.

The African slave **Babo**—a 30-year-old Senegalese—masterminded the uprising aboard the *San Dominick.* While the slave revolt demonstrated both his intelligence and his ability to direct others, his success in duping Delano proves his cunning. He is probably the most enigmatic figure in the story, for readers who believe Melville is censuring the practice of slavery might consider Babo's actions at least partially justified, while those who consider the tale an exploration of evil might consider this character its most blatant embodiment of humanity's depravity. It is related in the story that after the Africans had stripped Aranda's bones of flesh (possibly through cannibalism) and strapped his skeleton to the masthead, Babo mockingly asked the remaining Spaniards if the color of Aranda's bones proved that he was a white man, thus implying that all men are the same beneath their skin. Some critics have noted that Babo is typical of the dark, primitive, monstrous evil-doers in gothic fiction, while others have compared him to figures in the work of early-twentieth-century writer Joseph Conrad, who often used exotic settings and people to explore humanity's potential for evil.

A minor but significant character in "Benito Cereno" is **Atufal,** the huge African who is periodically brought before Cereno in chains. Because he was a king in his own country, the slaves use him in an intentionally ironic way to remind Cereno of his own subjugation.

Billy Budd, Foretopman (novella, 1924)

Plot: The novella begins in 1797 aboard the British merchant ship *Rights-of-Man,* which is returning to England after a long journey. The vessel is stopped by a British warship, the H.M.S. *Indomitable,* whose crew wishes to impress sailors for service into the British navy (this method of forcibly acquiring sailors was deemed necessary during the war England was then waging against France). The sailor who is chosen to join the *Indomitable*'s crew is Billy Budd, a good-looking, hardworking, peacemaking young man who is much liked by everyone. He does not seem to mind sailing back out to sea on the *Indomitable,* and he settles in well with his new shipmates, with one notable exception: the master-of-arms John Claggert. Budd gradually suspects that Claggert has some grudge against him. The old sailor Dansker confirms that Claggert does indeed hate Budd, but cannot explain why. Claggert tries to hide his enmity, however, carrying out his antagonism toward Budd through his subordinates. A troublemaking crewman offers Budd money to join a group planning to mutiny, but Budd disgustedly rejects the proposal. However, Claggert reports to Captain Vere that Budd has been trying to foment a mutiny. The captain, who believes Budd is innocent, brings both Claggert and Budd to his cabin to discuss the accusation; Budd is so profoundly upset that he is unable to speak. In frustration, he punches Claggert in the face and the man falls down and dies. Though distraught because of his fondness for Budd and his belief in his innocence, Vere feels compelled by the need for strict discipline during wartime to call a drumhead court-martial to try Budd for murder. There is no alternative but for the three-man court to find Budd guilty and condemn him to be hanged from the yardarm the next morning. Everyone aboard the *Indomitable* is grief-stricken but Budd does not seem resentful. As he is about to be hanged, Budd calls out "God bless Captain Vere!" Some time later, Vere is mortally wounded in a battle, and he is heard to murmur the young sailor's name as he lays dying. The yardarm from which Budd's body swung is for years after his death an object of reverence to the sailors, who regard it almost as they would a cross.

Characters: Published several decades after Melville's death, *Billy Budd* features the dramatic ocean setting of most of his other works and centers on a typically Melvillian theme: the conflict between good and evil. The critic Carl Van Doren wrote that in this novel Melville was "no longer asking himself . . . why evil should exist, he asks instead how it moves on its horrid errands and what is to be done about it." Some scholars have focused on the political and historical aspects of *Billy Budd,* interpreting it as an exploration of the extremities of punishment and sacrifice necessary during wartime.

The title character is a remarkably handsome twenty-one-year-old sailor whose good looks are augmented by a loyal, likeable, cheerful nature. Many critics, noting **Billy Budd**'s virtuousness, peacemaking ability, forgiveness of Vere before his death, and the many Biblical references in the book, characterize him as a Christ figure. Symbolically, Budd is "crucified" on the yardarm; that his body never twitches as it swings aloft suggests some kind of divine intervention. Budd has also been said to embody the primitive innocence of Adam, and like that first man he is a victim of evil—personified not by a serpent but by Claggert. Budd's only imperfection is the stammer that afflicts him when he is nervous or upset, and it is this flaw which not only gives him his humanity but brings about his downfall. Budd's essential passivity is exemplified by his easy acceptance when he is impressed onto the *Indomitable* and is most dramatically expressed when he blesses the captain just before he is hanged. Even Budd's one act of violence—striking out at Claggert—could be viewed as passive since it leads directly to his ultimate submission to the authority that rules over him. The fact that Budd, an ideal person, is sacrificed, weighs heavily upon the crew and humanity in general; such sacrifices, Melville implies, are often unavoidable if the greater order of civilization is to be maintained.

Though **Captain Vere**'s tendency toward thoughtfulness and brooding earned him the appellation "Starry" Vere among his men, he is a serious, intellectual man who values directness and honesty. Critics have often described Vere as a balance between Budd's goodness and Claggert's evil, and as such he is a more realistic character than either of them. He develops a great affection for Budd and fully recognizes his virtues, but Vere's commitment to duty and his sense of responsibility will not permit him to save Budd's life. Instead, he feels compelled to act according to the principals established by the authorities he represents, and he interprets those principals as demanding Budd's execution. That Vere is profoundly affected by Budd's death is apparent, for he stands as if paralyzed when Budd calls out his blessing, and the last words the captain speaks before dying are the young man's name. Critics have been divided in their response to Vere. Some feel that Melville condones his action, which is prompted by the necessities of war, thus making Budd an example of the toll that war takes on humanity. Other scholars claim that Vere takes his responsibility too literally, that he acts too quickly when he might have prevented Budd's death. In keeping with the novel's Biblical tone, Vere might be said to resemble Pontius Pilate, who also unwillingly condemned an innocent man, with the important difference that the captain accepts responsibility for what he has done, even meeting privately with Budd to—presumably—discuss his decision.

The villain of *Billy Budd,* **John Claggert,** a tall, thin, thirty-five-year-old with pale skin and dark hair, is the ship's keeper of weapons. Little is known of his early life—adding to the ominous mysteriousness that surrounds his character. Melville portrays Claggert's wickedness as innate and fated rather than informed by any reasonable circumstances. He hates Budd because the young sailor is so good, so beautiful, so innocent. He is subtle in his actions, preferring to antagonize Budd through his subordinates rather than directly, but he is also courageous, for falsely accusing someone of mutiny could cost one his own life. He seems almost as much a victim of the evil inside him as Budd is—certainly he pays the same price for it when he falls down dead after making his deceitful accusation. He observes that he might actually have loved Budd if not for the inescapable hate he bears him; this has caused some critics to see Claggert's resentment as prompted by his own homosexual desire. Several scholars have compared Claggert to the Biblical figure of Judas in his betrayal of the innocent Christ, while others have noted his resemblance to the character of Iago in Shakespeare's *Othello,* whose jealousy leads to evildoing.

Other characters in *Billy Budd* include **the Dansker,** the cynical old sailor who likes Budd so much he calls him "Baby" and who informs him of Claggert's enmity, and **the Afterguardsman,** the troublemaker commissioned by Claggert to entice Budd to join a mutiny.

Further Reading

Branch, Watson, ed. *Melville: The Critical Heritage.* London: Routledge, 1974.

Chase, Richard. *Herman Melville: A Critical Study.* New York: Macmillan, 1949.

Dictionary of Literary Biography, Vols. 3, 74. Detroit: Gale.

Hillway, Tyrus. *Herman Melville,* rev. ed. Boston: Twayne, 1979.

Kazin, Alfred. Introduction to "Moby-Dick; or, The Whale," originally published in 1956. In *Discussions of Moby-Dick,* pp. 52-9, edited by Milton R. Stern. Lexington, Ma.: Heath, 1968.

Melville, Herman, and others. *"Moby-Dick": An Authoritative Text, Reviews and Letters by Melville, Analogues and Sources, Criticism,* edited by Hayford Harrison and Hershel Parker. New York: Norton, 1967.

Nineteenth Century Literature Criticism, Vols. 3, 12, 29. Detroit: Gale.

Pullin, Faith. *New Perspectives on Melville.* Kent, Ohio: Kent State University Press, 1978.

Sedgwick, William Ellery. *Herman Melville: The Tragedy of Mind,* edited by Sarah Cabot Sedgwick. Cambridge, Mass.: Harvard University Press, 1945.

Short Story Criticism, Vol. 1. Detroit: Gale.

Van Doren, Carl. "A Note of Confession." *The Nation* CXXVII, No. 3309 (5 December 1928): 622.

Prosper Mérimée
1803-1870

French short story writer and novella writer, dramatist, poet, critic, historian, and translator.

"Mateo Falcone" (short story, 1829)

Plot: The story takes place in the early nineteenth century on the Mediterranean island of Corsica. Renowned for his marksmanship and sometimes drastic behavior, Mateo Falcone is a relatively prosperous man among the shepherds who populate his area. He has three married daughters and one ten-year-old son, Fortunato, whom he adores and from whom he expects great accomplishments. One day while Mateo and his wife, Giuseppa, are away from home, Fortunato is dozing in the sunshine when he hears a series of gunshots. A ragged, wounded outlaw named Gianetto Sanpierro limps into the yard. He frantically explains that he is fleeing government soldiers and asks Fortunato to hide him; though initially coy, the boy complies when Sanpierro offers him a five-franc piece. Fortunato conceals the outlaw in a bale of hay, places a cat and her kittens on top, and covers with dirt the traces of blood Sanpiero has left on the ground. Soon a band of soldiers arrives, and their leader, Tiodoro Gambo, asks Fortunato if he has seen the outlaw. The boy replies with teasing evasiveness and seems immune to the officer's threats of punishment—and even death—if he does not reveal Sanpierro's location. Finally Gambo offers Fortunato a silver watch as a reward, and the boy is unable to resist the temptation of owning such a magnificent object. He points to the bale of hay, and Sanpierro is quickly captured.

On their return, Mateo and his wife are alarmed to see the soldiers in their yard. Gambo soon explains the situation, praising Fortunato for revealing the outlaw's hiding place. Mateo, however, seems horror-stricken, for, as Sanpierro is being carried away, he calls the Falcone residence "the house of a traitor" and refuses to take back the five-franc piece or accept a drink of milk from Fortunato. After the other men have left, Mateo dashes the silver watch into a thousand pieces and angrily laments his son's act of treachery, which he claims is the first committed by any member of his family. Taking his gun, he marches Fortunato to a shallow ravine, forces him to kneel and say his prayers, and—ignoring the boy's pleas for mercy—shoots him dead. He then returns to his distraught wife and tells her that justice has been done. He instructs her to invite their son-in-law Tiodoro Bianchi to come to live with them.

Characters: Mérimée is recognized as one of France's finest short story writers, and "Mateo Falcone" established his eminence in the genre. The critic Walter Pater called it "perhaps the cruellest story in the world" because of its unflinching, highly effective depiction of family tragedy. In its exotic setting and themes and its restrained prose style, the story displays the blending of romanticism and realism that characterizes all of Mérimée's work. "Mateo Falcone" also exemplifies the author's interest in the strong emotions and traditions of Mediterranean peoples, particularly their dearly held values of honor and hospitality. Like the modern short story writers who would follow him, Mérimée employs a controlled narrative voice, carefully selected details, and an incisive view of human nature to create a story that stands as the best of what American novelist Henry James called his "chiselled and polished little fictions."

The **narrator,** who maintains a notable and ironic distance from the action, explains that he met **Mateo Falcone** several years after the events he relates. He describes Falcone as about fifty years old, small in stature but robust, with curly black hair, tanned skin, and piercing black eyes. A relatively prosperous man in a region populated primarily by humble shepherds, he can afford to hire others to perform most of the hard work on his farm. The narrator provides a pertinent fact about Falcone early in the story, after which he concentrates on describing his act of extreme vengeance: he is known as someone who can be either a good friend or a very dangerous enemy. It is even rumored that he had long ago disposed of a rival for his wife's hand; this hint of his history of brutality helps lend plausibility to his later behavior. In Falcone is concentrated the typically Spanish reverence for hospitality, the violation of which is a grievous breach of honor. When Fortunato betrays the man he had previously sheltered—and who curses the household after his capture— Falcone must rectify the wrong, even by sacrificing his beloved son. His deeply ingrained sense of honor is superior to parental love or even simple human mercy, and the erring young boy dies by his father's hand. Although Falcone seems outwardly untroubled by his act, informing his wife afterward that justice has been done, his true loneliness and, perhaps, sorrow are evidenced by his request that his son-in-law be invited to live with the couple.

Falcone's wife, **Giuseppa,** is portrayed as completely submissive to her husband, thus providing a realistic glimpse into the lives of the women of those times. She is first seen trudging toward her home carrying a heavy burden while her husband carries only his guns, and the narrator ironically comments that it is, in fact, the duty of every good wife to load her husband's gun for him. In this case, hapless Giuseppa will participate through this task in the death of her son. She is obviously anguished when she sees the armed and angry Falcone leading Fortunato away, but is powerless to dissuade him. Instead she hurries into the house and begins to pray to the Virgin Mary, an effort that proves inadequate to save her son.

The ironically named **Fortunato,** ten years old when the story takes place, is a bright young lad who is his father's pride and joy—the beloved son who finally arrived after the births of three daughters. Fortunato is clever in the way he initially treats the bandit (who does not seem to frighten him) and then ingeniously conceals him, placing the cat and kittens atop the hay bale to further disguise the hiding place. Although Fortunato also displays some greediness in desiring first the five-franc piece and then the silver watch, such covetousness is surely more childish than wicked. He does make an attempt to spurn the officer, but he cannot resist the beautiful watch. Fortunato later shows he is sorry and ashamed when he tries to return the five-franc piece to the outlaw and to give him a drink, both of which Sanpierro contemptuously refuses. The story's cruelty is effectively concentrated into Fortunato's piteous, ineffectual plea for mercy, which is followed quickly by his death.

Gianetto Sanpierro is the outlaw whose request for sanctuary precipitates the story's brutal climax. He arrives in a dirty, ragged, wounded state, escaping from government soldiers when attacked. He tried to reach the tall grass of the nearby *maquis* (a thickly overgrown plain) where he would probably be undetectable, but he is too weak to run further. Falcone is initially glad to hear that the outlaw has been captured, for he believes that Sanpierro is responsible for an earlier theft on his own property. Yet when he learns that Fortunato has facilitated the man's capture after agreeing to hide him, he concurs with Sanpierro that the betrayal was the act of a "traitor." Like Falcone, Sanpierro adheres to the ideals of personal honor and hospitality, and he feels nothing but scorn for his betrayer even if he *is* only ten years old.

Despite the fact that he is distantly related to Falcone and therefore might expect a measure of immunity through this family connection, the military officer, **Tiodoro Gamba** is alarmed to see Falcone approaching him with his gun raised, since Falcone's formidability is well known. Gamba immediately begins to placate the other man, explaining the reason for the soldiers' presence. He praises Fortunato for having cooperated with his effort to capture Sanpierro. Gamba is renowned among the lawless as an energetic, much-feared opponent, and he demonstrates his wiliness when he correctly gauges that Fortunato, immune to threats of violence or death, will succumb to the temptation of the glittering silver watch.

Carmen (novella, 1847)

Plot: Set in the early nineteenth century, the story is told by a French narrator, a scholar who met both of the main characters during a research trip to Spain. As it begins, a handsome young soldier named Don José, a native of the Spanish region of Navarre, is assigned to guard duty at a cigarette factory in Seville. Carmen is a beautiful young factory worker who convinces Don José to free her after she has attacked another girl with a knife. A spirited, passionate, capricious gypsy, Carmen soon wins the love of Don José. Although he is punished after deserting his post to be with Carmen, his infatuation only increases. One night while he is in Carmen's apartment, another of her lovers arrives, and a fight erupts between the two rivals. Don José kills the other man, a military officer, and is himself wounded. Admonishing Don José for his stupidity, Carmen tells him he must now flee from prosecution. She persuades him to join a band of smugglers for whom she has often worked as a spy, and she takes him as her *rom,* or husband. Though he applies himself with energy to becoming an outlaw, Don José feels ill-suited to his new life. Unhappy and dissatisfied, he is also troubled by Carmen's many infidelities. He is even more angry and jealous when he learns that the band's one-eyed leader, Garcia, was Carmen's first husband, and eventually he kills the man, even though Garcia would gladly have relinquished any claim to Carmen. Now Don José and another smuggler named Dancaire decide to form a new band, while Carmen goes to Granada and takes up with a bullfighter named Lucas. Tormented by his love for the fickle Carmen, Don José begs her to move with him to America, but she refuses, claiming she wants to remain independent. Don José follows Carmen to Cordoba, where she watches Lucas in a bullfight; distracted by his gypsy admirer, Lucas is severely injured. Don José confronts Carmen and again asks her to be faithful to him and accompany him to America; she responds with a scornful laugh. Finally Don José visits a monastery, asking a monk there to say a mass for someone who will soon die. When he returns to Carmen, she realizes that he intends to kill her but is calmly resigned to her fate. Her declaration that she no longer loves Don José sends him into a rage. He fatally stabs Carmen, then buries her and turns himself in to the police. As he relates the story to the narrator, Don José is in jail awaiting execution for Carmen's murder.

Characters: Considered a highly skilled writer of short fiction, Mérimée gained universal renown with the novella-length *Carmen,* particularly after it was adapted into a popular opera by Georges Bizet in 1875. Like Mérimée's other works, *Carmen* blends the passionate themes and exotic settings of the romantic period with the realism that would become more dominant in the late nineteenth century. *Carmen* reveals the author's fascination with the colorful, passionate people of the Mediterranean and exemplifies the precise, objective, often ironic prose style for which he is consistently lauded. Concentrated on a limited number of vivid characters, the story moves quickly and thrillingly to its tragic yet inevitable dénouement.

Although it is Don José who relates most of the story of *Carmen,* the tale is framed at beginning and end by the narration of an unnamed **narrator.** He is a French scholar who is conducting archeological and historical research in Spain; he relates that he had earlier encountered both Don José and Carmen and then spoke with the former while he was in prison awaiting execution. This narrator's cool, objective, detached tone, which several scholars have likened to the authorial voice common in eighteenth-century literature, not only lends the story authenticity but serves as a counterbalance to the tumultuous passions and violence it encompasses. On the other hand, some commentators find the narrator's presence unnecessary and distracting. In particular, the value of the final chapter, which was added several years after the novella's original publication and which presents a discourse on gypsy customs and language, is often disputed. Because the narrator initially misjudges the essential personalities of both Don José and Carmen, believing the former a dangerous criminal and the latter an innocent young girl, some critics have suggested that he may be a parody of the supposedly objective, learned man or even Mérimée himself.

Don José is a handsome young Basque from the Spanish district of Navarre, the inhabitants of which are known for their passion and volubility. At the beginning of the story he is fairly innocent and honest; for instance, during the prison term he receives for deserting his post to be with Carmen, he refuses to escape by using the file he finds hidden in a loaf of bread that has been sent to him. Although he is by nature kind and relatively unadventurous, his overpowering love for Carmen leads him into a brutal life he never could have imagined or desired. Provoked by jealousy and anger to murder Carmen's officer lover, Don José finds his military career ruined, and he accepts Carmen's judgment that he has no choice but to join the smuggling band. Although he becomes a successful, renowned outlaw, he is unhappy with his criminal life and continually tormented by his fickle lover, whom he seems to love more intensely as she grows more emotionally abusive. In fact it is primarily through Don José's response to Carmen that the reader gauges her power and senses her attraction. While some critics consider Don José a weakling who bends to Carmen's every whim and allows her to destroy his life, most find him a compelling character whose susceptibility to blind passion dooms him to a tragic end. Speaking in a spontaneous, fast-paced manner, he admits his own weakness, and his capacity for self-analysis not only lends his voice emotional impact but increases the reader's sympathy for his plight.

Mérimée's vivid portrait of **Carmen,** the beautiful gypsy girl who entrances and torments Don José, has earned this memorable character almost mythological stature. Although she does in some ways conform to the conventional stereotype of the black-eyed seductress or *femme fatale* who leads men to destruction, Carmen is described by most commentators as a compelling, lifelike figure. Mérimée may have modeled her after an actual acquaintance, a pretty Spanish *gitana* (gypsy) named Carmencita. Carmen reveals both her volatile temper and her cleverness early in the story, when she slashes another girl's forehead during an argument at the Seville cigarette factory where she works, then persuades Don José not to punish her. Bold, passionate, and demanding, Carmen also proves capricious and fickle after embarking on an affair with Don José, tormenting him with her infidelities, and manipulating him to get what she wants. One of Carmen's most important qualities is her strong sense of independence, her insistence on personal freedom. Her inability to commit herself to a single relationship exemplifies her belief that love represents servitude. For this reason she refuses Don José's offer to move with him to America, because she cannot bear to have anyone else direct the course of her life. Combined with Carmen's strong will, however, is a fatalism that is revealed when she calmly accepts the prospect of death at Don José's hands. Having consistently remained true to her own nature while also realizing the power that love holds over people, she sees her violent end as inevitable, and many critics have likewise felt that the story's conclusion is as aesthetically satisfying as it is tragic. Several scholars have noted that despite Mérimée's colorful depiction of Carmen, she is defined primarily by what she does and how she affects others; her own motivations and psyche are left unexplored. This enigmatic quality has led some commentators to conclude that Carmen's role is primarily to help develop the more interesting, rounded character of Don José, while others consider Carmen herself more compelling, even if she is more difficult to understand or analyze. In an extension of the literary archetype of the *femme fatale,* Carmen has also been seen as a castrating female figure who represents the ultimate threat to her lover's life and manhood. In any case, and perhaps primarily through the exposure provided by Bizet's acclaimed opera, Carmen occupies a permanent place in both the popular and the literary imagination.

The other characters in *Carmen* help to facilitate the plot and to fill out the Spanish milieu in which the story is set. Carmen's first husband, **Garcia,** is the one-eyed, brutal, ugly leader of the band of smugglers that Don José is forced to join; it is suggested that his own connection with Carmen is not as irrevocable as Don José's, because he would have been willing to "sell" her to his rival. Don José's murder of Garcia is irrational and unnecessary. **Lucas** is the toreador, or bullfighter, whose affair with Carmen incites Don José's jealousy. Distracted by his lover during his bullfight, Lucas is gored; thus he too is a victim of her deadly seductiveness. That Carmen is unfaithful to Don José with a *macho* toreador has been interpreted as a symbol of her need for virility greater than Don José's. **Dancaire** is the smuggler who joins with Don José in establishing a new gang; the **monk** receives Don José's request to pray for the repose of Carmen's soul.

Further Reading

Bowman, Frank Paul. *Prosper Mérimée: Heroism, Pessimism, and Irony.* Berkeley, Los Angeles: University of California Press, 1962.

George, Albert J. "Prosper Mérimée and the Short Prose Narrative." 1955. Reprint. *Symposium* X, No. 1 (Spring 1956): 25-33.

Gobert, D. L. "Mérimée Revisited." *Symposium* XXVI, No. 2 (Summer 1972): 128-46.

James, Henry. "Mérimée's Last Tales." 1874. Reprint. In *Literary Reviews and Essays: On American, English, and French Literature,* edited by Albert Mordell, pp. 169-72. New York: Twayne, 1957.

Nineteenth-Century Literature Criticism, Vol. 6. Detroit: Gale.

Pater, Walter. "Prosper Mérimée." 1890. Reprint. In *Miscellaneous Studies: A Series of Essays,* pp. 11-37. New York: Johnson Reprint Corporation, 1967.

Raitt, A. W. *Prosper Mérimée.* London: Eyre & Spottiswoode, 1970.

Tilby, Michael. "Languages and Sexuality in Mérimée's 'Carmen.'" *Forum for Modern Language Studies* XV, No. 3 (July 1979): 255-63.

Margaret Oliphant
1828-1897
Scottish novelist, short story writer, biographer, translator, and critic.

Miss Marjoribanks (novel, 1866)

Plot: The novel is set in the nineteenth century in the fictional English town of Carlingford. As it opens, the mother of fifteen-year-old Lucilla Marjoribanks has just died, and Lucilla has been sent home from boarding school to attend the funeral. The strong-minded Lucilla intends to leave school and care for her widowed father, a gruff physician of Scottish heritage, but Dr. Marjoribanks insists that she finish her education. Five years later Lucilla returns to Carlingford, having grown into a statuesque, healthy, self-assured young woman. Announcing to her neighbors that her sole object in life is "to be a comfort to my dear papa," Lucilla sets out to shape and direct her town's social life according to her own design. After befriending her father's initially defensive, extremely talented cook, Nancy, Lucilla has her drawing room refurbished and establishes a tradition of Thursday "evenings"—which, as she carefully explains, are not parties but simple gatherings of friends.

Employing a combination of social grace and outright manipulation, Lucilla attracts a loyal following among her upper-crust social set. Meanwhile she sends her clumsy but devoted, love-struck cousin Tom off to India, assuring him that she has no intention of marrying for at least ten years, when she expects she will have "gone off" (that is, her good looks and youthful bloom will have faded). Nevertheless Lucilla is tempted to consider several suitors, including the handsome Mr. Cavendish, who scandalizes the townsfolk by shifting his attentions from the worthy Lucilla to the selfish, sullen Barbara Lake before he finally leaves town. Archdeacon Beverly is also a promising suitor, until he is found to have a lingering attachment to Mrs. Mortimer, a poor widow Lucilla helped to get a house and a teaching position. Beverly eventually marries Mrs. Mortimer.

The novel's second section begins ten years later, when Lucilla's reign as queen of Carlingford is well established and her daily routine has grown somewhat boring to her. When Mr. Chiltern, Carlingford's elderly member of Parliament, finally dies, thus opening up his seat to a new candidate, Lucilla finds the purpose she has been lacking. She plunges enthusiastically into backing the steady though not particularly brilliant Mr. Ashburton for election to Parliament. Lucilla convinces nearly all her friends to support her candidate when she learns that Cavendish has returned to Carlingford, intending to enter the race himself. Unlike Lucilla, Cavendish proves to have "gone off" considerably in the years since his last appearance, and he fails to win much support from those who formerly admired him. In the middle of the campaign, Dr. Marjoribanks dies suddenly, and Lucilla is both genuinely aggrieved and strangely stimulated by her loss as she tries to imagine her life as an independent single woman. She soon learns, however, that she has been left virtually penniless, and she is forced to contemplate life on her own in a drastically altered light. Meanwhile Ashburton wins the election and, in gratitude and admiration for Lucilla, decides to propose to her. Although Lucilla has anticipated such a scene and has always viewed herself as a particularly appropriate choice as the wife of a Member to Parliament, she finds herself reluctant to accept. In the middle of the proposal scene, her cousin Tom arrives with his usual lack of grace and tact, and Lucilla finally admits that it is Tom she wants to marry. With the surprised blessings of Tom's mother and Lucilla's friends, the two plan their wedding, and Lucilla persuades her future husband to purchase an estate, the affairs and tenants of which she happily intends to manage with her usual skill.

Characters: Prolific and highly popular during her own lifetime, Oliphant was acclaimed for her incisive novels of English and Scottish provincial life and particularly for the strong female characters who populate her fiction. One of five novels in the series known as the "Chronicles of Carlingford," *Miss Marjoribanks* is widely recognized as Oliphant's best work, distinguished by its comic yet insightful presentation of the memorable title character and her friends. The novel is infused with an ironic tone and awareness of life's disappointments that are, generally, missing from Oliphant's other works and which reflect the author's own frustrations and hardships. Simultaneously a celebration of the joys of domesticity and an exposé of wasted female potential, *Miss Marjoribanks* both entertains and provides a telling glimpse into Victorian society.

One of the most memorable female characters in Victorian fiction, **Lucilla Marjoribanks** is an inherently unconventional heroine who manipulates convention and the traditional woman's role to shape her life to her own liking. Big-boned and healthy, with tawny, rather unmanageable hair and a hearty appetite, Lucilla is a physically impressive figure with an equally strong personality. Energetic and clever, Lucilla maintains an ingenuous aura of self-confidence and superiority to those around her—particularly the hapless men who inhabit her circle. She is the quintessentially efficient, practical "managing woman." Although her father sometimes wrongly assumes that her attitude is ironic, Lucilla has, as she freely admits, little sense of humor and always means exactly what she says. Her patient, tolerant, but essentially contemptuous attitude toward men, whom she finds easy to manage and manipulate, has been said to reflect that of her creator, whose father, brothers, and sons all depended on her support at various times in her life. The scope of occupations available to an upper middle-class Victorian woman were severely circumscribed: she could marry and raise a family, stay a "spinster" and live on the fringes of others' families, or, if she had no money, go to a work as a governess or other semi-servant. Full of vitality and capability, Lucilla decides to put off marriage for ten years to devote herself to being "a comfort to my dear papa"—though in actuality her papa needs little comforting—and she immediately goes to work to transform the social life of Carlingford according to her own specifications. Establishing her "Thursday evenings" as an indispensable social institution gives Lucilla a necessary outlet for her energies and a sphere of influence; indeed, she is soon considered the "queen" of Carlingford. Although some critics have found her a colossally smug egotist, others note that her manipulations, even if essentially self-centered, do benefit others and that she is actually quite generous (for she provides her friends with pleasing entertainment and secures a job and pleasant home for impoverished Mrs. Mortimer). Although Lucilla claims that she is not interested in marrying, the possibility is always in the back of her mind, and she shrewdly evaluates such candidates as Mr. Cavendish and Archdeacon Beverly, serenely accepting their departures from her life and comforting herself with the knowledge that her cousin Tom, in any case, is ever her loyal admirer.

After ten years, the now thirty-year-old Lucilla has become bored and restless; her "Thursday evenings" no longer stimulate her. Had she been a man, Lucilla might herself have run for a seat in Parliament; instead, she achieves it vicariously by masterminding Mr. Ashburton's political campaign. Though she claims no knowledge of politics, Lucilla's native canniness is evident as she influences others to vote for Ashburton, who, at her recommendation, declares no positions on any issues in order to offend no one. The death of Dr. Marjoribanks not only puts an end to Lucilla's political activities but causes a major upheaval in her life, and her reaction to this event adds greater depth to her character. Her response is both poignant and realistically practical: though genuinely grief-stricken, she is also intrigued by the possibilities of life on her own. Lucilla reacts to the news of her poverty with notable dignity, exhibiting courage and resilience in her determination to make the best of her bleak situation. For the first time her status as an unmarried woman becomes burdensome rather than freeing. Tom's dramatically awkward, comic return just as Ashburton is proposing to Lucilla proves revelatory, for she finally admits that "it is to be Tom after all"—the honest, loving, and utterly manageable young man will obviously make her an appropriate and supportive husband. Her future life (modeled on traditional lines despite her unconventionality) promises to be full and active, enlivened not only by the demands of her own family but by her management of the estate she persuades Tom to buy. Lucilla is often compared to the title character of Jane Austen's 1816 novel, *Emma,* yet the former heroine's egotism—even if she lacks Emma's capacity for growth and change—has in the end more positive results. Some scholars have, in fact, complained that Lucilla shows no sign of ever altering her behavior; her defenders claim that this makes her not only more comic but more believable. Oliphant's attitude toward her most successful protagonist seems somewhat ambivalent, though generally fond: she satirizes Lucilla mercilessly while also appreciating the abilities that allow her to adapt to and thrive in a restrictive social milieu.

Lucilla's father, the Scottish **Dr. Marjoribanks,** has an unsentimental and unexcitable nature. He reacts to his daughter with amused wonder and sometimes with a little hostility, as when he takes obvious pleasure in informing her that her former suitor, Cavendish, is running for Parliament against her candidate. After Lucilla's installation as mistress of her home and queen of the Carlingford social scene, Dr. Marjoribanks drily accommodates himself to her various schemes, spending most of his own time in the comfort of his secluded library. He wrongly assumes that she practices a "high art"—that there is an element of intentional irony in her manipulations, when actually Lucilla is quite literal-minded and lacks his own sense of humor. Oliphant is often praised for her description of the doctor's death, which is portrayed with understated pathos and unsentimental compassion. The bell which patients have always rung when they needed his help is silent the night of his death. Though no one is made desolate or heartbroken by his loss, "they wept for him honestly." Lucilla sadly remembers his uncharacteristic gesture of affection (patting her shoulder gently) the night before his death, and weeps when she hears that his first response to the news of his bankruptcy was "Poor Lucilla."

Tom Marjoribanks, Lucilla's cousin, is an extremely clumsy, socially inept, but likable young man who has always adored Lucilla but is initially unable to persuade her to marry him. He dutifully goes off to India at her suggestion, where he remains for ten years while she reigns over Carlingford society. Lucilla occasionally thinks of Tom during this period, aware that while others may misunderstand her or fail to show gratitude for her generosity, Tom will always appreciate her, and her knowledge of his steady regard bolsters her self-esteem. Tom arrives back in town with a typical crash, knocking a large bowl to the floor in his eagerness to reach Lucilla, and thus alerting her to his arrival. In his willingness to "throw himself all in a heap at her feet, and make the greatest fool of himself possible for her sake," Tom proves superior to Ashburton and all of Lucilla's previous suitors. His "perfect genius for carrying out a suggestion" as well as his genuine love for Lucilla make him a highly appropriate mate for her, and Lucilla hints that she may one day get him elected to Parliament.

The regular guests at Lucilla's Thursday evening gatherings include a colorful variety of characters and provide a cross-section of Carlingford society. One of Lucilla's most loyal friends is **Mrs. Chiley,** a good-natured, grandmotherly woman who is highly conventional but kind and extremely appreciative of Lucilla's talents. Eager for Lucilla to find an appropriate husband, she is taken aback when her young friend's choice is the awkward Tom Marjoribanks. She and her somewhat gruff but amiable husband, **Mr. Chiley,** have a good, mutually supportive marriage that provides a positive model of that institution; as they grow older, they keep watch on each other's increasing physical infirmities with "a mixture of vexation and sympathy." Another notable neighbor is **Mrs. Woodburn,** a self-styled humorist with a considerable talent for mimicry, with which she keeps her friends both amused and constantly fearful (and justifiably so) that she is mocking them behind their backs. Lucilla's refusal to acknowledge Mrs. Woodburn's comic gift highlights its essential shallowness and cruelty. As the story progresses, the reader learns that Mrs. Woodburn is burdened with responsibility for two inadequate men—her coarse, cranky husband and her irresponsible brother—and that her mimicry is a kind of safety valve for her frustrations.

Barbara Lake, the daughter of a humble drawing master who would not normally be included in that social set, gets invited to Lucilla's Thursday evening gatherings because Lucilla hears her singing and knows that Barbara's fine contralto voice would be a good accompaniment to her own. Sullen and self-centered, Barbara resents rather than appreciates Lucilla's kindness, feeling that she is being patronized. Talented and attractive, with bold black eyes, dark hair, and rosy cheeks, Barbara maintains a defiant posture at the gatherings. Thrilled when Lucilla's suitor, Mr. Cavendish, begins to pay attention to her, she is devastated when he unexpectedly leaves town, and she makes no effort to hide her disappointment. Leaving the care of their large family to her sister, Barbara becomes a governess; after ten years, however, she again meets Cavendish—who has, like her, "gone off" in appearance—and the two are finally married. Plain, considerate **Rose Lake** is her sister's opposite, an unselfish and self-respecting young woman whose desire for a career in art is thwarted when she must devote herself to her family. Apparently talented (she wins a prize for one of her drawings), Rose admits poignantly to Lucilla that she regrets having to give up her "Career," and eventually she loses all of her former confidence in art. Both the unpleasant Barbara and the victimized Rose provide examples of the limited roles available to women in Victorian England.

During the years in which Lucilla is reigning over Carlingford, several men become interested in her. The first is **Mr. Cavendish,** the handsome, wealthy brother of Mrs. Woodburn. Lucilla appreciates his ability to flirt, which she considers an invaluable attribute in social settings, and even feels she would not be averse to marrying him, particularly since he is spoken of as a possible candidate to replace the elderly **Mr. Chiltern** as member to Parliament for Carlingford. Cavendish's reputation is marred, however, by his ill-concealed weakness for Barbara's charms, while Lucilla is much admired for her calm reaction to his abdication. Eventually Lucilla learns that he is not actually "one of the Cavendishes," but inherited his wealth from a wealthy old man he had befriended; Lucilla does not reveal her knowledge of his real origins to anyone, but neither does she again consider marrying him. Cavendish reappears after ten years with the intention of running for Parliament, but his altered appearance and continued attraction to Barbara Lake, whom he finally marries, ensure his defeat.

The self-confident, effusive, generally amiable **Archdeacon Beverly** also seems a likely candidate for Lucilla's affections. But when he unexpectedly meets Mrs. Mortimer, the impoverished widow whom Lucilla has helped, his reaction indicates a previous connection between the two. Lucilla helps resolve a misunderstanding between Beverly, Mrs. Mortimer, and Cavendish (who inherited the money Beverly thought should have gone to Mrs. Mortimer), and the archdeacon and widow are married. Lucilla devotes herself to master-minding the campaign of the steady though not particularly brilliant **Mr. Ashburton,** who hopes to gain the Parliamentary seat of the deceased Mr. Chiltern. The activity provides a temporary outlet for Lucilla's considerable energy, and in the process Ashburton comes to see her as a likely wife. His proposal is interrupted and his campaign for Lucilla's hand defeated by the startling arrival of Tom Marjoribanks. Ashburton's political campaign, however, is victorious.

Other notable characters in *Miss Marjoribanks* include Tom's mother, **Aunt Jemima,** a hypochondriac who finds Dr. Marjoribanks unsympathetic but is fond of her niece. Knowing that her son loves Lucilla, Aunt Jemima is torn between a desire to help him win her heart and a reluctance to have Tom marry such an impoverished woman. Nevertheless she does seem genuinely happy when the two young people are united. She comments that Lucilla's life as a single woman has been enviable in that she has had "all that you wanted, without any of the bother." Lucilla helps **Mrs. Mortimer,** an impoverished widow, establish a fairly satisfactory life by securing her a comfortable home and a schoolteacher's position; surprised to learn of the widow's connection with her own suitor, Archdeacon Beverly, Lucilla reacts graciously to their renewed relationship and marriage. Dr. Marjoribanks's cook, **Nancy,** is a simple woman with a great talent for cooking. Initially hostile toward the idea of another woman entering her realm, Nancy is quickly won over by Lucilla and thus comprises Miss Marjoribanks's first conquest after her return to Carlingford. **Rector Bury** is a strict Evangelical clergyman who unsuccessfully tries to convince Lucilla that she needs a companion to protect her virtue; his pious sister **Miss Bury** is comically shocked by a conversation about people who lack souls that she hears while visiting Lucilla.

Further Reading

Clarke, John Stock. "Mrs. Oliphant: A Case for Reconsideration." *English* XXVIII, No. 131 (Summer 1979): 123-33.

Dictionary of Literary Biography, Vol. 18. Detroit: Gale.

Fitzgerald, Penelope. Introduction to *Miss Marjoribanks* by Margaret Oliphant. New York: Penguin Books, 1989.

Leavis, Q. D. Introduction to *Autobiography and Letters of Mrs. Margaret Oliphant* by Margaret Oliphant, edited by Mrs. Harry Coghill, pp. 9-34. Leicester: Leicester University Press, 1974.

Nineteenth-Century Literature Criticism, Vol. 11. Detroit: Gale.

Terry, R. C. "Queen of Popular Fiction: Mrs. Oliphant." *Victorian Popular Fiction, 1860-80,* pp. 68-101. London: Macmillan, 1983.

Williams, Merryn. *Margaret Oliphant: A Critical Biography.* New York: St. Martin's Press, 1986.

Thomas Love Peacock
1785-1866
English novelist, poet, critic, and essayist.

Headlong Hall (novel, 1816)

Plot: The novel takes place at Headlong Hall, the Welsh country estate of Squire Harry Headlong. Though much occupied with the usual gentlemanly practices of hunting, racing, and drinking, Headlong has a liking for books and has decided that he wants to become "a philosopher and a man of taste." To accomplish this end, he travels to London to make the acquaintance of as many philosophers, writers, and artists as he can. He then invites them to a gathering at Headlong Hall. Four of these guests meet and converse while traveling in a coach toward the estate: Mr. Foster, a "perfectabilian" who believes that humanity is continually improving; Mr. Escot, a "deteriorationist" who believes that humanity is continually declining; Mr. Jenkison, a "status-quo-ite," who ascribes to neither theory; and Dr. Gaster, a clergyman who loves to eat. On their arrival at Headlong Hall they meet the other guests, including poets Mr. Nightshade and Mr. MacLaurel, the literary critics Mr. Gall and Mr. Treacle, Mr. Cranium the phrenologist (who studies the bumps of the skull for clues to human character) and his lovely daughter Cephalis, and Mr. Chromatic, an ardent musician. Sir Patrick O'Prism, a dilettante artist, is visiting with his aunt, Miss Poppyseed, a writer of popular novels, and the celebrated landscape designer, Mr. Marmaduke Milestone. The highly learned Mr. Panscope is also present. The novel's action revolves around the philosophical discourse that occurs between the guests, particularly Foster and Escot, as they argue the merits and pitfalls of progress. These two men and Jenkison travel to the nearby, thriving manufacturing community of Tremedoc, which Foster considers an example of technology's blessings and Escot finds redolent with selfish, material excess.

Back at the estate, Headlong has enthusiastically launched into the plans suggested by Milestone to completely reshape the estate grounds. Unaware that Panscope and Cranium are standing on a nearby tower, Headlong ignites some dynamite to destroy a protruding rock; the resulting explosion so frightens Cranium that he jumps out of the tower and falls into the adjoining lake. Escot, who has fallen in love with Cephalis, happens to be passing by and rescues his beloved's father from drowning. Cranium, however, is still reluctant to deliver his daughter over to Escot and attributes Escot's actions to mere reflex. When Escot subsequently discovers a large skull and gives it to Cranium, erroneously promising him that it belonged to the Welsh hero Cadwallader, the phrenologist weakens. Escot and Cephalis are married by Dr. Gaster, and Headlong, Foster, and O'Prism are also united with various female partners. The guests leave Headlong Hall, hoping to meet again there in the future.

Characters: *Headlong Hall* is the first and most famous example of Peacock's novels of conversation, which revolve around the discussion of moral, political, aesthetic, and social issues of the day. Distinguished by its skillful satire and erudite, classical style, the novel blends comedy with romance and scholarship. The sometimes slapstick humor and fast-paced dialogue evidence Peacock's earlier theatrical experiments; in fact, *Headlong Hall* is partly based on *The Dilettanti* and *The Three Doctors,* two farces he had previously written but never produced. The novel's central theme is the relative merits of progress: whether technological and scientific advances have improved or denigrated life, and whether modern human beings are more or less admirable than their ancestors. The impact of Peacock's friendships with the romantic poet Percy Bysshe Shelley and other prominent nineteenth-century literary figures is illustrated through both the characters and the concerns of *Headlong Hall.*

Squire Harry Headlong, the wealthy scion of an old and venerable Welsh family, hosts the gathering. In accordance with the book's focus on the question of progress, Headlong considers himself considerably more enlightened than his ancestors. Seeming notably sane among his eccentric guests, Headlong does have an obvious foible: his impetuousness. He lives up to the promise of his allegorical name. Headlong's enthusiasm for Milestone's improvements to the estate grounds, and his insistence that they begin posthaste, leads directly to the catastrophe of the explosion, the book's comedic high point. Headlong is never punished for his rashness; the novel's conclusion finds him comfortably married and anticipating future heady gatherings at his idyllic country retreat.

The cast of guests invited to Headlong Hall may be divided into two categories: serious (if sometimes absurd) philosophers, and cranks who are satirically lampooned. Three members of the first category are introduced in the novel's first pages, as they approach the estate in a coach. **Mr. Foster,** the "perfectabilian," whose name is based on the Greek for "one who guards a flame," is commonly thought to have been modeled after Peacock's friend, the romantic poet Percy Bysshe Shelley, who espoused a similar philosophy that was apparently based on the teachings of social and political reformer William Godwin. During a visit to the thriving manufacturing town of Tremedoc, Foster approves of the material, well-distributed prosperity he sees there.

Mr. Escot, the "deteriorationist," whose name is based on a Greek word for "one looking on the dark side," believes that the human race is continually declining and is destined only for further decay. His views are based on the "Natural Man" concept defined by the eighteenth-century French philosopher Jean-Jacques Rousseau, who held that humanity had degenerated from its previous state of primitive goodness. Escot feels that even man's physical stature has declined from that found in the heroic age now gone, and the large skull he uncovers (which he manages to use to his advantage) seems to him a reproach against the puniness of modern human beings. Peacock is thought to have based Escot on himself, for he was known to hold similar views, though Shelley too had absorbed some of the Rousseauistic perspective. During the excursion to Tremedoc, where Foster sees evidence of technology's blessings, Escot complains of the "selfish and ruinous profusion" of the idle luxuries the town's prosperity has made possible. Escot's positive, life-affirming act of rescuing Cranium from the lake is a departure from his usual intellectual detachment, and his wish to marry Cephalis, despite his conviction that humanity is pitifully degenerate, also contradicts his philosophical stance. The fact that Escot does go against his own pessimism in favor of matrimony—and, presumably, a new generation of human beings—suggests that the book's overall tone and attitude toward the question of progress is optimistic.

Mr. Jenkison is the "status quo-ite" who can see the strong and weak arguments on both sides of the issue but refuses to commit himself to either. Thought to be modeled after Thomas Jefferson Hogg, a friend of both Peacock and Shelley who often adopted a skeptical stance, Jenkison is allowed to deliver the novel's last word when he comments that the scales of his "philosophical balance" are "equiponderant"; such a balanced view may represent the position Peacock means, finally, to promote.

Each of the remaining allegorically named characters provide the bulk of the novel's biting satire, for each represents a type of crank or dilettante that Peacock found annoying. The gourmand **Reverend Dr. Gaster,** who sprains his ankle in his haste to reach the breakfast table and who is described by critic James Mulvihill as the "first in a line of venal and foolish clergymen in Peacock's satire," is somewhat distinguished from the others, emerging as rather likable in the end. **Marmaduke Milestone** is based on Humphrey Reston, a famous landscape designer of the day whose approach was highly formalistic and artificial. Milestone sees "great capabilities" in Squire Headlong's estate grounds and is eager to begin "shaving and polishing" them into submission. He believes that "the noble art of picturesque gardening" is the primary accomplishment of the modern age, further illuminating the theme of progress. It is Milestone's effort to improve nature by removing an offending rock that causes the comic cataclysm that propels **Mr. Cranium** from his tower perch. Cranium is a practitioner of phrenology, a pseudo-science popular in the nineteenth-century that involved the interpretation of the skull's bumps to determine character. The pompous Cranium receives his comeuppance when, in a scene that demonstrates Peacock's fondness for burlesque comedy, he is blown out of the tower and bounces laboriously into the water below. Cranium plays the reluctant father in repelling Escot's attempts to win Cephalis, but the acquisition of what he believes is the skull of the hero Cadwallader is too much to resist.

Representing the powerful and politically partisan English literary establishment are the critics, **Mr. Geoffrey Gall** and **Mr. Timothy Treacle,** who may have been modeled after Francis Jeffrey of the Whig (liberal) periodical *The Edinburgh Review* and William Gifford of the Tory (conservative) *Quarterly Review.* Along with the poets, **Mr. Nightshade** and **Mr. MacLaurel** (perhaps parodies of Robert Southey and John Wilson), who seem suspiciously chummy with the critics, these characters suggest the corruption that Peacock believed had infected the literary press. Another literary character is **Miss Philomena Poppyseed,** a talentless, popular novelist apparently based on Amelia Opie, whose works were fashionable at the time. The excessively learned **Mr. Panscope,** who is considered a direct parody of the poet Samuel Taylor Coleridge, is a pedantic scholar who seems to shun intelligible discourse and who frequently refers to the "authority" of the many great authors whose work he has mastered. **Sir Patrick O'Prism** is an artist who discourses on beauty, and **Mr. Cornelius Chromatic** is an amateur violinist.

The most prominent of the few female characters in *Headlong Hall* is the lovely **Cephalis Cranium,** daughter of the phrenologist and beloved of Mr. Escot. The role of most women in Peacock's fiction is to smooth discord between the male characters, sing charmingly, and speak sensibly. Cephalis performs at least one of these functions when she sings "Love and Opportunity," demonstrating the skill that is particularly indicative, in Peacock's heroines, of civilized qualities. Chromatic brings with him his two daughters, **Miss Tenorina** and **Miss Graziosa;** the latter contradicts Milestone's approach to landscape design when she quietly comments that she prefers the natural, untouched countryside to the shaved and polished look he creates. **Caprioletta Headlong,** the squire's sister, oversees the practical aspects of preparing their home for guests and also provides the influence of order and harmony expected of the Peacockian female.

Further Reading

Burns, Bryan. *The Novels of Thomas Love Peacock.* London: Croom Helm, 1985.

Butler, Marilyn. *Peacock Displayed: A Satirist in His Context.* London: Routledge & Kegan Paul, 1979.

Dawson, Carl. *His Fine Wit: A Study of Thomas Love Peacock.* Berkeley: University of California Press, 1970.

Mulvihill, James. *Thomas Love Peacock.* Boston: Twayne, 1987.

Nineteenth-Century Literature Criticism, Vol. 22. Detroit: Gale.

Saintsbury, George. ''Thomas Love Peacock.'' *Macmillan's Magazine* LIII, No. 318 (April 1886): 414-27.

Edgar Allan Poe
1809-1849

American short story writer, novelist, poet, critic, and essayist.

''The Fall of the House of Usher'' (short story, 1839)

Plot: As the story opens the narrator, who is unnamed, has received an unusually frantic, nervous letter from his boyhood friend, Roderick Usher, requesting that he visit him at his family home. As he approaches, the narrator is disturbed by the House of Usher's excessively gloomy, decayed appearance. He finds his friend in a state of mental anguish that Usher identifies as a ''family evil''; exaggeratedly sensitive to all physical stimuli, he is overwhelmed with feelings of morbidity and fear. The narrator notes that the Usher family is comprised of only one line of descent, due, apparently, to a combination of inbreeding and circumstance; its only two surviving members are Roderick Usher and his twin sister, Madeline. Usher's agitated mental state is also partly due to his beloved sister's physical infirmity: she suffers from a mysterious, fatal illness that periodically causes her to become cataleptic (a condition of extreme muscle rigidity and apparent unconsciousness).

Usher reveals to the narrator that he feels his family home exerts a terrible influence over him, as if it were not inanimate but a living manifestation of some great evil. The narrator sees Madeline only for one fleeting moment, and her wraithlike appearance fills him with dread. During his visit, he and Usher pursue a number of activities, all of which contribute to the increasingly morbid atmosphere of the household. Usher plays bizarre dirges on his guitar, creates a strange abstract painting, and composes a poem entitled ''The Haunted Palace.'' His library is stocked with books on the occult and supernatural, and he discusses with the narrator his theory that inanimate objects may be sentient (imbued with life). Usher sinks further into gloom, a mood the narrator also begins to feel. One day Usher informs his guest that Madeline has died. Explaining that her strange illness might invite the intrusions of curious medical investigators, Usher does not bury Madeline immediately in the family plot, which is easily accessible to outsiders. Instead he places her coffin in a tightly sealed vault on a lower floor of the house. Afterward Usher becomes even more agitated than before. His face is paler, his eyes glow wildly, his voice trembles, and he paces continuously. The narrator also feels increasingly nervous and fearful and suffers from insomnia.

One night as a severe storm rages outside, the narrator hears frightening sounds beneath his room, where Madeline's burial vault is located. Usher soon knocks on his door and enters the room. He seems extremely disturbed, so the narrator tries to calm him by reading aloud a romantic tale set in medieval times. He is amazed to hear somewhere in the Usher house the same ripping, grating sounds described in the story he is reading. Usher becomes completely unnerved, muttering unintelligibly then jumping up and screaming that Madeline is outside the door, that she had been alive when he interred her in the vault, and that she has now come for him. The door swings open to reveal the shrouded, bloodied figure of Madeline Usher standing unsteadily in the doorway. She falls on her brother and the two collapse on the floor, both dead. The narrator flees terrified from the house, only to see it disintegrate and fall with a terrible sound into the tarn (small lake or pond) in front of it.

Characters: Edgar Allan Poe is widely regarded as an important architect of the modern short story, and ''The Fall of the House of Usher'' is considered one of his finest. Poe's theory of short fiction held that a story's brevity could heighten its impact by contributing to its artistic unity and intensifying its effect on the reader. His tales exhibit gothic elements in their settings, imagery, and atmosphere. They have romantic components in their melancholy and despairing tone. Yet Poe was also modern in exploring with both technical precision and imaginative flair his characters' psychological conflicts and responses. Like many of Poe's tales, ''Usher'' lends itself to a variety of interpretations: it may be read as a supernatural or horror story, as the chronicle of an individual's psychological collapse, or as a symbol-laden allegory. In any case the story exemplifies Poe's characteristically brilliant creation of atmosphere and insightful depiction of psychological states.

Some of Poe's best short stories employ a basically neutral, somewhat prosaic narrator who relates the experiences of the main characters. These narrators provide the reader a fairly reliable point of view, and they underline the dramatic significance of what occurs. The unnamed **narrator** of ''Usher'' is a childhood friend—a ''boon companion,'' as he himself asserts—of Roderick Usher, who considers him his best and only friend, despite the narrator's claim that no one has ever known the elusive man well. The narrator helps establish the story's enveloping gloom and foreboding when he describes the House of Usher as a decayed and fungi-covered structure which seems almost as much a living being as the tormented people who reside within it. In contrast to the moody usher, the narrator is essentially skeptical about the supernatural, and always tries to find rational explanations for strange occurrences, yet he finds himself more and more effected by the pervasive fear and anxiety preoccupying Usher. The night of the storm he chooses to read aloud to his friend the medieval romance ''The Mad Trist,'' a work unlikely—as several reviewers have noted—to calm a troubled, fearful spirit. Yet in doing so he heightens the story's suspense, for the tale he reads parallels events taking place in the house. The narrator makes a dramatic escape from the House of Usher, then sees it crash into the tarn. This event may be purely supernatural in nature, the final culmination of the evil that has preyed upon the inhabitants; it might also be the allegorical triumph of some universal morality over the accursed Ushers. In either case, the narrator serves as a spectator or witness. But other critics counter that the narrator is an unreliable, subjective participant who actually assists Usher in murdering his sister, or even that the story's concluding events are partly his own hysterical hallucinations and partly the results of a destructive storm.

One of Poe's most successful and memorable fictional creations, **Roderick Usher** represents a type of character appearing in several of the author's subsequent works. Usher's physical description seems to mimic the house with which he is closely aligned: he has a pale, cadaverous face, weblike hair that resembles the fungi hanging from the house, and large, luminous eyes that evoke its dark, mysterious windows. Some critics note the resemblance of Usher to photographs of Poe himself and suggest the similarity was intentional. Usher's manic-depressive mood swings are typically romantic, and some scholars feel the negative aspects are emphasized in the overly introverted, angst-ridden Usher, as they were in many fictional heroes of the period. The narrator reports that Usher has always been aloof and isolated from others, resulting in hypochondria, intolerance to physical stimulation, and abandonment to fear. He complains that the evil influence of the house has invaded his spirit, and this is connected in some unspecified way with his family's cursedness. Many commentators conclude that the Usher's evil is incest, which over generations produced a single line of descent. Usher's mental turmoil results from his resisting the compulsion to marry and produce descendants with his own sister. This line of thinking holds that Usher buries his sister prematurely and then suffers guilt and horror from committing such an act; in his weakened state, the shock of Madeline's return proves fatal. Another interpretation focuses on Usher's identity as a highly sensitive artist whose introversion, isolation, and anguish over his sister's death lead to insanity; a related view holds that the story is an allegory of the self-destructive or conflicting forces within the artistic temperament. A purely supernatural reading of the story casts Usher as the doomed descendent of an evil family who, by demonically stealing his sister's life force brings about their inevitable death and the destruction of the House of Usher.

The enigmatic **Madeline Usher** is Roderick's twin sister, a tall, pale woman who looks wraithlike even before her death, and who appears even more dramatic and horrifying after being entombed. She is afflicted with an unnamed, terminal disease that causes catalepsy, a condition that mimics death by rigidifying the muscles. Although the narrator only sees her momentarily, she fills him with dread. The general ambiguity about Madeline's character is highlighted when the narrator views her body with Usher before the vault is closed, and he comments that there is the "mockery of a faint blush" as well as the suggestion of a smile on her face. At this point the reader might wonder if Madeline is still alive, or—emphasizing the story's supernatural aspect—if she intends to rise again and smiles in mockery at her intended victims. The concept of the twin or double was a common device of gothic fiction that Poe uses effectively in this story, modernizing it with hints of the psychological or even psychosexual relationship between Usher and his sister. The two are said to be so close that they seem to share one consciousness. Many critics cite as particularly important the fact that they are the only surviving Ushers alive, for it introduces the theme of incest. To perpetuate the family line, Roderick and Madeline would have to marry and produce descendants, a concept held universally immoral. The family's history of incestuous relations has apparently brought a curse upon it, and it may be that Roderick intentionally murders his cataleptic sister in order to break the pattern. Madeline has also been viewed as an allegorical figure who returns to punish her brother for his immoral impulses, or as a vampire who wishes to sap his life force. If Madeline was, in fact, alive when Usher buried her, it is doubtful she can have escaped from a coffin that was screwed shut or survived in a tightly locked burial vault for more than a week with no food or water, but some scholars contend that Poe compensates for this lapse by using Madeline to create a mood of escalating terror.

"The Gold Bug" (short story, 1843)

Plot: The story takes place on Sullivan's Island near Charleston, South Carolina, where William Legrand, a descendant of a wealthy old New Orleans family who has lost his fortune, lives with only his Newfoundland dog and his elderly black servant, Jupiter, for company. Legrand is an educated, moody exile from society who spends his time fishing, hunting, and collecting shells and insect specimens. The narrator, an old friend of Legrand, visits him one chilly day in October. As the two sit by the fire, Legrand tells his visitor about an unusual gold-colored beetle he has recently found. He cannot show the narrator the bug, because he has lent it to a soldier at nearby Fort Moultrie who is interested in entomology, so he draws a sketch of it on a scrap of paper that he takes from his pocket. The narrator looks at the drawing in the firelight and sees not a bug but a skull; Legrand seems disturbed by his friend's declaration but simply puts the drawing into a desk drawer and does not mention it again. One month later the narrator receives a visit from Jupiter, who claims that his master has been acting very strangely and that he fears he was bitten by the mysterious gold bug. Jupiter also delivers a letter from Legrand requesting that his friend come to see him immediately. The narrator is alarmed because Jupiter has been commissioned to buy a collection of spades and scythes, and he becomes even more worried about his friend's mental stability when Legrand declares that the gold bug will make him wealthy and that he wants the other two men to accompany him on a night-time expedition.

When the three have hiked into a densely wooded area, Legrand instructs Jupiter to cut a path to a tulip tree and then to climb the tree, taking the gold bug with him. As the narrator stands by, increasingly convinced of his friend's insanity, Legrand tells Jupiter to climb out on the tree's seventh limb and drop the gold bug through the left eye of a skull that he finds resting there. Legrand then makes a series of calculations and the party starts digging, but they unearth nothing. Then Legrand recalls that Jupiter often confuses right and left, and the entire process is repeated with the error corrected. Renewed digging leads to the discovery of a large chest containing gold and gems; a number of human bones are also found buried with the chest. After carrying the chest back to Legrand's house, the men estimate that its contents are worth several million dollars.

Now Legrand explains how he was able to find the treasure. The paper on which he had drawn the sketch of the gold bug was a parchment which Legrand had found, earlier that day, lying near a beached longboat. He had used it to carry the gold bug but had put it into his pocket after lending the insect to his soldier friend. When the narrator held the parchment near the fire, the drawing of a skull appeared, and Legrand subsequently used heat to uncover a number of other symbols. He realized that the parchment contained the directions to the buried treasure of the notorious pirate Captain Kidd. The instructions were in the form of a cipher, or secret code, which he ingeniously unraveled. Thus he located the tulip tree and made exact measurements to find the correct place to dig; he dropped the gold bug through the skull's eye instead of the specified bullet simply to confound the narrator, whose doubts annoyed him and whom he relished mystifying. Legrand speculates that the bones found with the chest belonged to the unfortunate men who helped Kidd bury the treasure and were then murdered to keep from revealing its location.

Characters: In addition to the tales of the macabre for which he is renowned, Edgar Allan Poe also wrote skilled mystery tales. He is generally considered the originator of the modern detective story, and many of his innovative devices and character types became conventions of the genre through the end of the nineteenth century and into the twentieth. Like his popular horror stories, Poe's detective tales feature a gradual buildup of suspense, a skillful creation of atmosphere, and psychological intrigue. ''The Gold Bug'' has been praised for its unique plot and resolution as well as its unusual, authentic setting; Poe himself spent a tour of army duty at the Fort Moultrie mentioned in the story. It differs from other mystery tales because it involves not a crime but a cryptograph, the kind of secret code or puzzle that Poe relished. Although the idea of hidden pirate treasure seems somewhat implausible to modern readers, it provides for an exciting story and is also said to have inspired Robert Louis Stevenson's 1883 novel *Treasure Island.*

Poe is said to have invented the type of the basically reliable but not completely perceptive narrator who serves as a foil to the clever protagonist—employed perhaps most famously by Arthur Conan Doyle in Dr. Watson of the Sherlock Holmes tales. In ''The Gold Bug,'' the unnamed **narrator** is Legrand's old friend who enjoys visiting him on his Sullivan's Island retreat. But he finds his friend's behavior puzzling and begins to question Legrand's sanity. Later Legrand is shown not only to be sane but in possession of brilliant reasoning power, and the narrator's fears prove groundless, even though he is a physician and ought, presumably, to know better. Having identified more with the narrator than with Legrand, the reader is also left feeling a little sheepish, a result that serves as a tribute to Poe's skill.

Because **William Legrand** is a sensitive, moody recluse from society whose manner is alternately enthusiastic and melancholy, he has often been compared to Roderick Usher in Poe's 1839 short story ''The Fall of the House of Usher.'' Legrand's quirks, however, lead to a more positive outcome than Usher's, for he deciphers a complex code and locates a fabulous treasure, thereby restoring the wealth to his formerly prominent New Orleans family. A former aristocrat and an intellectual giant, Legrand resembles C. Auguste Dupin, featured in several of Poe's other mystery stories. Although Legrand's friends initially believe that he is mentally unstable, they are eventually forced to realize that his power of deductive reasoning is impressive. He is convinced that whatever puzzles one human intellect can devise another can unravel, so he solves the cryptogram. Legrand leads the narrator and Jupiter on a midnight excursion they regard as strange, purposely encouraging their inclination to think him insane, but this demonstrates a subtle sense of humor and illustrates the danger of relying only on appearances.

Jupiter is Legrand's devoted black servant, a freed slave whose strong African-American dialect, common to the blacks of Poe's home state of Virginia rather than those of South Carolina, contrasts strongly with the formal speech used by the story's white men. Devoted to his master, Jupiter is treated with both affection and condescension by Legrand, who sometimes shames him so he will do his bidding. Jupiter plays a pivotal role in the story's plot by delivering the letter from Legrand to the narrator, reporting on his master's strange behavior (which he attributes to a bite from the gold bug), accompanying the other men on their excursion, and performing much of the physical work of locating and unearthing the treasure. The first attempt to locate the treasure fails because Jupiter often confuses right and left. Depicted as a person of crude speech and obviously limited intellect, Jupiter is one of several stereotypically portrayed African-Americans found in Poe's fiction.

"The Tell-Tale Heart" (short story, 1843)

Plot: The narrator of the story is an apparent madman who recounts how he murdered an old man because of his pale blue, film-covered eye. On seven successive nights he crept stealthily into the old man's room, making sure that he could not be seen. Then he would open his lantern just enough that a single, narrow beam of light would shine on the "vulture eye" he so hated. Since the eye was never open, however, the narrator was unable to complete his evil deed, because his enemy was not the old man—whom he even claims to have loved—but his hideous eye. On the eighth night the old man awakened and realized that someone was in his room. The narrator remained perfectly still and silent, and for nearly an hour he could sense the old man's mounting terror, which he claims that he himself has often felt. At the same time the narrator exulted in his power. He trained his light on the dreaded eye and became aware of a dull, thudding, repetitious sound he assumed was the beating of the old man's heart. Maddened, he sprang from his hiding place with a scream, pulled the old man to the floor, and threw the bed on top of him. His victim was soon dead, and the narrator then dismembered the corpse, catching all the blood in a tub, which he hid beneath the floor of the old man's room. Soon after he finished his gruesome work, three policemen arrived at the door, explaining that a neighbor heard a suspicious scream during the night. The narrator told the officers that his own bad dream caused him to scream, and that the old man was away from home. He invited them to search the house, then asked them to sit down with him for a chat. He placed his own chair directly over the spot where the old man's remains were. Initially he was sure the police suspected nothing, but as time passed and they showed no intention of leaving, he became increasingly nervous. Then the sound he had heard before, which he believed was the old man's heartbeat, began again. In extreme agitation he paced the room. His feverish talk soon turned to ranting, and, convinced that the policemen knew of his crime, he finally burst out a confession, begging them to tear up the floor boards and discover the dismembered corpse and the "hideous heart" that had tormented him.

Characters: Considered one of the most masterful short story writers of all time, Poe is renowned for his tales of psychological horror. "The Tell-Tale Heart" serves as a prime example of his belief in the power of short fiction, the brevity of which, he asserted, could concentrate its impact on the reader. Narrated by a madman, this story is a chronicle of mental illness and the ways fear and guilt may affect the mind.

The narrator speaks in nervous bursts and broken sentences, repeatedly assuring the reader that he is not insane. The story's famous first line, ''True—nervous—very, very dreadfully nervous I had been and am; but why *will* you say that I am mad?'' is often cited as an example of Poe's inventive, dramatic openings. It immediately suggests the mental instability that the narrator will continue to deny through the remainder of the story. He insists that the carefully planned, stealthy manner in which he murdered the old man and dismembered and hid the corpse was too clever an accomplishment for an insane man. But through Poe's skillful, unnerving depiction of his narrator's psychological state, it becomes increasingly clear that he is completely mad. The narrator's claim that he does not hate the old man but actually loves him has led some critics to suggest that the old man may have been his caretaker. The narrator has no reasonable motive to murder him and even identifies closely with his terror as he crouches in the dark ready to spring upon him. Some critics suggest that the story loses some of the drama because its ''merely insane'' narrator lacks more complex motivations, but most hold that his irrationality lends greater horror to the tale. Like many of Poe's works, ''The Tell-Tale Heart'' exposes the unreasonable, violent, and self-destructive impulses of human nature. As the narrator recounts his overwhelming, compulsive fear of the old man's clouded blue eye and then his maddened belief that he hears his victim's (or perhaps his own) heart beating, the reader is compelled to pity him, despite being revolted by the deed.

The **old man** is seen only through the insane narrator, who reveals little about his victim other than the pale blue, film-shrouded eye that he considers a malignant force. Nevertheless, he seems to be a harmless, mild creature who has probably treated the narrator kindly in the past. The old man has some money and keeps his window shutters locked, suggesting that he may already fear intruders, but the narrator is not interested in robbing him. The terror he feels as he lies in his bed, aware that someone is in the room with him, is very effectively conveyed. Although the old man's specific relationship with the narrator is never stated, some critics feel he has been caring for the insane man. It is possible that he may have anticipated the danger his charge posed and even shared his fear with someone else, which would make the terror the old man exhibited during the long hour before his death even more profound and would also explain the reluctance of the police to leave the narrator after searching the rooms.

''The Purloined Letter'' (short story, 1845)

Plot: The story's narrator is a close associate of C. Auguste Dupin, an amateur detective already famous for solving the murders in the Rue Morgue and the case of Marie Rogêt. The two men are quietly smoking their pipes together at Dupin's apartment when they are visited by Monsieur G——, the prefect of the Paris police force. He explains that an incriminating letter has been stolen from the queen's bedroom by a government official, Minister D——, who was seen taking the letter and who now holds the queen in his power through his knowledge of its contents. During the minister's frequent absences from his home, the police have conducted a thorough and scientific search and have found no trace of the letter. Dupin queries the prefect closely about the extent and nature of the search, and also asks for an exact description of the letter. He suggests that the minister's rooms be searched again, and the despondent Monsieur G—— goes on his way. One month later, the prefect returns to Dupin's home and reports that the letter is still apparently in the possession of Minister D——. Knowing that a large reward has been offered for the return of the letter, Dupin asks the prefect what he would be willing to pay for it; the officer responds with the figure of fifty thousand francs and, at Dupin's request, writes out a check for this amount. Dupin then produces the letter, which the elated prefect carries away with him.

Dupin now explains to the narrator, who had been flabbergasted when his friend brought out the purloined letter, how he came to possess it. He claims that his success lay in his ability to perceptively gauge the minister's intellect and probable behavior. He knew that the minister would never hide the letter where it could easily be found. Instead he would place the letter in plain sight, where it would never even be noticed. Dupin concocted an excuse to visit the minister, whom he knew personally, and surreptitiously scanned the sitting room for clues. He discovered that the missing letter had been subtly placed in an ordinary letter holder on the mantelpiece. By leaving one of his own possessions in the house, he was able to return the next day on the guise of retrieving it. He arranged for a man to fire a gun loaded with blanks at a prearranged time in the street below, and then he easily recovered the queen's letter—leaving a facsimile in its place—while the minister looked out the window.

Characters: Edgar Allan Poe is credited with establishing the genre and many of the conventions of detective fiction, and "The Purloined Letter" is one of his most acclaimed tales of "ratiocination" (the process of logical reasoning). Through the now-familiar types of the brilliant amateur sleuth, accurately gauging a criminal's intellect, and his rather slow-witted, admiring associate, Poe presents a crime that is solved through both deduction and psychological insight. The story differs from other detective stories because the criminal is known at the outset and the mystery involves the location of the stolen object. "The Purloined Letter" generated a significant volume of critical debate, particularly regarding the actual contents of the purloined letter, which are never revealed. French psychoanalyst Jacques Lacan argued that the story is an allegory of illicit sexuality, while philosopher Jacques Derrida maintained that no such definitive interpretation was possible.

The unnamed **narrator** of "The Purloined Letter," like other, similar characters in Poe's fiction, provides a markedly ordinary point of view through which the reader views the action. He also appears in "The Murders in the Rue Morgue" and "The Mystery of Marie Rogêt," cases upon which he and Dupin are ruminating when interrupted by the police prefect. Although the narrator is a decidedly minor participant in the actual events related, he plays a significant role as a foil to the brilliant Dupin. The narrator's rather inferior intellect requires him to ask many questions of his more astute associate, and the reader— though sometimes finding the narrator's questions dull-witted and thus feeling superior to him—also benefits from these explanations. The most important inheritor of this narrative role is probably Arthur Conan Doyle's Dr. Watson, who performs a similar function in the Sherlock Holmes mysteries.

When he created the protagonist of "The Purloined Letter," **C. Auguste Dupin,** Poe established the prototype for a multitude of subsequent detective characters, the most famous of which is undoubtedly Sherlock Holmes. Holmes calls his reasoning process "deduction" and Dupin terms his "analysis," but both involve the application of logic and an understanding of human psychology. A brilliant amateur sleuth, Dupin is a gentleman of leisure who lives in somewhat reduced circumstances, and does no actual work. Among his peculiarities are a reluctance to go about during the daytime and a fondness for smoking a meerschaum pipe (another notable similarity to Holmes). Although generally reclusive, Dupin spends much of his time with the narrator and apparently receives frequent visits from the police, who seek his help on perplexing cases. After placing the purloined letter in the prefect's hands, he describes how he solved the mystery, explaining that the initial investigation conducted by the police displayed a significant weakness. The prefect and his associates assumed that Minister D—— would choose some unexpected, undiscernible place in which to hide the stolen letter, and they applied a great deal of energy to turning his house inside out to find it. Dupin, by contrast, realized that the minister was a man of strong intellect who and would avoid a hiding place that must eventually be discovered. Having correctly anticipated his opponent's thought process, Dupin guesses that Minister D—— has hidden the letter in plain view—that is, in an ordinary letter holder left hanging from his mantelpiece. Early in the story, even before he has unraveled the mystery, Dupin suggests that it is sometimes the simplest possible explanation that is overlooked. During his visit the perfect the police reveals his contempt for writers of poetry, and Dupin admits that he himself is a dabbler at that art. This admission highlights Dupin's success, which results not just from his intelligence and capacity for methodical analysis, but from his imagination and ability to identify with another human psyche.

Monsieur G——, the prefect of the Paris police, plays a practical role in the story by explaining to Dupin the case that has baffled him and his associates and asking for Dupin's help. Dupin's intellectual inferior, he represents the inept authorities whose unimaginative methods prove inadequate for solving complex crimes. The prefect admits he is motivated to recover the letter because he wants to preserve his good reputation and because a huge reward has been offered for it, whereas Dupin (who claims he is well paid for his efforts) says he wishes to do his queen a service. Monsieur G—— approaches the case of the purloined letter by thinking about what he would do in the minister's place rather than by analyzing what kind of man his opponent is and what course he might therefore take. He mentions that Minister D—— has been known to write poetry and must, therefore, be a fool; thus Monsieur G—— demonstrates his inability to solve the crime. In explaining to the narrator the faults of the prefect's approach, Dupin subtly insults Monsieur G——'s intelligence by relating the story of a schoolboy who proved a better reasoner than Monsieur G——. Though not contemptible, the prefect provides an entertainingly dense counterpart to the more perceptive Dupin.

The story's villain is **Minister D——**, a high-ranking official of the French government. While visiting the king and queen one day, he notices a letter in the queen's boudoir and steals it, realizing that it would give him power over her (he left one of his own letters in its place). She is most anxious to recover the letter, and her desire to keep its existence a secret even from the king lends the missing document a hint of sexual indiscretion. Dupin—who has dealt with him before and was once even insulted by him—called Minister D—— an "unprincipled man of genius" who affects laziness but actually possesses a sharp, active mind. He demonstrates his cleverness by hiding the letter exactly where the police would never look for it, and by disguising it simply but effectively to ensure that no eyes will be drawn to it. In fact, the minister has both the imagination of the poet and the intelligence of the mathematician, a combination of qualities that Dupin also possesses. Thus Dupin is able to successfully match his own wits with his opponent's; his exchange of a facsimile for the purloined letter is the identical method used by Minister D—— in the initial theft. Dupin tells the narrator that he might never have emerged alive from the minister's home if he had been caught in the act of recovering the letter, thus establishing his opponent's viciousness and political ambition. Having foiled the minister, Dupin looks forward with relish to his downfall, which must occur when Minister D——, not realizing that he no longer possesses the incriminating letter, acts on the assumption that he does and is unable to produce it at the crucial moment.

"The Cask of Amontillado" (short story, 1846)

Plot: The story is told by an Italian aristocrat named Montresor, who claims he bore a thousand injuries from his fellow nobleman Fortunato, but that he finally received an unforgivable insult that had to be avenged. He waits until the carnival season, when the streets are disorderly with merrymaking, to pursue the perfect revenge. Meeting Fortunato, dressed in the brightly colored and bell-trimmed costume of a jester, he informs him that he has just purchased a quantity of Amontillado wine. He is not sure of the wine's authenticity, however, and admits that he should have asked Fortunato's advice before buying it (Fortunato is a wine connoisseur and takes inflated pride in his skill). Since Fortunato is busy, Montresor continues, he will ask another man, Luchesi, to evaluate the wine. This provokes his companion's ire, and Fortunato insists on sampling the Amontillado. He follows Montresor into the catacombs (an underground system of burial vaults) beneath his house, where the bones of his ancestors vie with his wine casks for space. The two proceed deeper and deeper into the gloomy catacombs, and Montresor repeatedly asks his friend if he would like to turn around, while he offers him swigs of wine. Finally they reach a particular alcove, and when Fortunato steps uncertainly into it, Montresor quickly chains him to iron staples on the wall. He ignores his victim's terrified wails—and even, at one point, matches them with mad screams of his own—and builds a wall of stone and mortar to seal off the recess. Eventually he hears Fortunato begin to laugh grimly, thinking Montresor is playing a practical joke on him. But Montresor puts the last stone in place. Fifty years later, he reports, the wall is still standing.

Characters: "The Cask of Amontillado" is one of the best-known short stories by Poe, considered a master of the genre and a major influence on its development. Although the tale employs the stereotypically gothic setting of dreary, dungeonlike catacombs lined with skeletons, it transcends the boundaries of gothic fiction with its psychological focus. The story also illustrates Poe's belief in "art for art's sake"; that is, a work of fiction need not contain a moral message but may derive value simply by being well-crafted and effective.

Like many of Poe's short stories, this one features a first-person narrator who, in relating his experiences, gives the reader many clues to his psychological makeup. **Montresor** is an Italian aristocrat who declares he has endured a thousand injuries from his fellow nobleman, Fortunato, but a recent insult will not go unavenged. Little else is revealed about Montresor's past or current circumstances, though he must have been fairly young when it took place (since fifty years pass before he relates it). His voice is intelligent, ironic (sometimes to the point of a horrible jocosity), and burning with a cold passion. Montresor's maniacal pride and sadomasochistic tendencies are gradually more apparent, and finally his gruesome intention becomes clear. He makes the reader his confidante, and he assumes the reader appreciates and approves of his clever act; thus Montresor explains how he planned and executed his perfect crime. He waits for a day when the city is preoccupied with the gay pursuits of carnival, ensnares his victim with an appeal to his vanity, and leads him deep into the catacombs while pretending concern that the dampness of the underground passages will adversely effect Fortunato's health. Reaching the fatal alcove, he quickly binds his victim with chains and begins constructing the wall that will trap him there for eternity. Immune to Fortunato's terrified screams, he even matches those wails himself at one point and brandishes his sword; such bizarre behavior evidences his mental instability. Montresor has been labeled a rationalist with no concern for the moral implications of his behavior; a monomaniac who, like the protagonists created by such authors as Nathaniel Hawthorne and Herman Melville, has allowed his hatred to devour his soul and therefore his humanity; and as another example of the abnormal, neurotic personalities frequently found in Poe's works. In any case, the end of the story reveals not only that his crime was never detected, but that he has remained obsessed with it for fifty years.

Through Montresor's victim, the aristocratic **Fortunato,** Poe plays out the theme of premature burial that he uses with terrifying effect elsewhere in his fiction and that seems to have been a particularly dreadful concept for him. Little is learned about Fortunato or what he might have done to provoke Montresor's ire. Although his portrayal is rather negative—he is drunk when he meets his murderer and seems vain and arrogant—there is little evidence that he deserves his gruesome fate. He does not even seem aware that he has offended Montresor. Montresor claims that Fortunato is much respected and feared, but that his one weakness is his excessive pride in his wine connoisseurship; it is this weakness that Montresor brilliantly exploits to lure him into a trap. Both Fortunato's name and his ludicrous jester costume, the bells of which jingle grotesquely in the catacombs, are ironic touches that help to intensify the story's effect. The period in which he waits for Montresor to finish building the wall concentrates the terror and claustrophobia of Fortunato's approaching death. His final, pathetic attempt to ascribe Montresor's actions to a practical joke implies that there is a Lady Fortunato and appreciative friends waiting for him at his palazzo.

Further Reading

Bloom, Harold, ed. *Edgar Allan Poe.* New York: Chelsea House, 1985.

Carlson, Eric W., ed. *The Recognition of Edgar Allan Poe: Selected Criticism since 1829.* Ann Arbor: University of Michigan Press, 1970.

Galloway, David, ed. Introduction to *The Other Poe: Comedies and Satires* by Edgar Allan Poe. New York: Penguin Books, 1983.

Kesterton, David B., ed. *Critics on Poe.* Coral Gables, Fla.: University of Miami Press, 1973.

Knapp, Bettina L. *Edgar Allan Poe.* New York: Frederick Ungar, 1984.

Nineteenth-Century Literature Criticism, Vol. 1,16. Detroit: Gale.

Short Story Criticism, Vol. 1. Detroit: Gale.

Symons, Julian. *The Tell-Tale Heart: The Life and Works of Edgar Allan Poe.* New York: Harper & Row, 1978.

Alexander Pushkin
1799-1837
Russian poet, novelist, dramatist, short story writer, essayist, and critic.

Eugene Onegin (*Yevgeny Onegin;* verse-novel, 1833)

Plot: Set in early nineteenth-century Russia, the novel takes place in and around the cities of St. Petersburg and Moscow. Eugene Onegin is an intelligent young aristocrat and dandy who has grown tired of the frivolous pursuits—drinking and gambling, attending balls, the theater, the opera, and seducing women—that have occupied his young manhood. He is bored and disdainful of his social milieu. Eugene is the heir of a wealthy uncle who dies just as Eugene's deceased father has been declared bankrupt, so the young man moves to his uncle's country estate. Although he for several days enjoys the novelty of pastoral life, his boredom soon returns and is only mildly alleviated by his friendship with an eighteen-year-old neighbor, Vladimir Lensky, a romantic and idealistic young poet who has attended a university in Germany. Vladimir is engaged to a local girl named Olga Larin, and Eugene accompanies his friend to the Larin family's estate. He prefers withdrawn, pensive Tatyana Larin to her pretty, more outgoing sister, Olga, but generally he finds the visit dull. Meanwhile, however, the sensitive and book-reading Tatyana has fallen in love with Eugene, who seems modeled after one of the handsome heroes in her romantic novels. She writes him an impassioned letter stating her feelings. Although Eugene is somewhat affected by the strong emotions evident in Tatyana's letter, he informs her that he does not return her love, that his vast experience with women and disillusioned attitude make him a poor choice for a husband, and that she should try to exercise more self-control. Tatyana accepts this rejection silently. Later that winter Eugene attends a ball at the Larins' home and, annoyed by the tedious the affair and by Tatyana's tearful reaction to his presence, he dances repeatedly with Olga. The jealous Lensky, affronted by what he considers a grievous insult, challenges Eugene to a duel. Although he knows that to fight the duel would be ridiculous, Eugene accepts the challenge because he fears he will be ridiculed if he refuses. He kills Lensky during the confrontation and later leaves his estate for a period of travel. Olga soon marries another man.

Tatyana continues to love Eugene, even after she learns more about his real character by visiting his now-empty house and looking through his books. Worried because her daughter has rejected several suitors, Tatyana's mother takes her to Moscow hoping she will find an appropriate husband there. Tatyana learns to dress and behave in a more sophisticated manner, and soon marries a prestigious though unattractive general. Eugene returns to Moscow several years later and, out of boredom, attends a fashionable ball. There he encounters Tatyana, who has been transformed from a shy, provincial girl to a queenly woman of great poise and subtle beauty and is the center of her social circle. Eugene now finds Tatyana fascinating and falls in love with her. His efforts to speak with and call upon her, however, are met with cool detachment, and his passionate letters go unanswered. Finally Eugene pays Tatyana an unannounced visit and discovers her reading his letters. She refuses to listen to his declarations of love, however, suggesting that he desires not her but the social effect the conquest would have. She claims to be more insulted by his current attempt to seduce her than by his earlier rejection. Tatyana admits that she does still love Eugene, but she vows that she will remain faithful to her husband for the rest of her life.

Characters: Proclaimed as the national poet of Russia, Pushkin is one of his country's most celebrated literary figures, and *Eugene Onegin* is considered his masterpiece. Written in verse and distinguished by its complex, innovative style and narrative method, its meticulous depiction of Russian life, and its psychologically penetrating characterizations, the work was seminal in the development of the Russian novel. Pushkin worked on *Eugene Onegin* over a span of eight years, and the novel reflects his development as a man and poet: while it begins as a fairly lighthearted satire, its depth and significance gradually increase to make it a work of universal impact.

Many critics have noted *Eugene Onegin* resembles *Don Juan,* a narrative poem by the English romantic poet George Gordon, Lord Byron, that was published several years before Pushkin's novel. Tatyana even discovers a copy of *Don Juan* in the library of **Eugene Onegin.** Eugene seems Byronic because of his alienation and disdain for society, but in his cultural setting the Byronic stance is portrayed as selfish, egotistical posturing. He is the first of the "superfluous men" to dominate Russian fiction through the remainder of the nineteenth century. These characters are typically intelligent and sensitive but frustrated and unable to act decisively, due both to their own natures and to the stifling dictates of their society; other examples include Ivan Goncharov's Oblomov and Mikhail Lermontov's Pechorin. Raised in aristocratic luxury, Eugene entered St. Petersburg society at an early age, and by the time he reaches early manhood, he is dissatisfied with the hedonistic life of fancy food, wine, attendance at the opera and ballet, and romantic intrigues. After he comes into an inheritance and moves to a country estate, Eugene is contented with rural life for only a few days, when his overwhelming boredom and sense of purposelessness returns. His tedium is somewhat relieved by his friendship with the likable young poet Vladimir Lensky, but he finds his visit with the Larin family tiresome. When shy, provincial Tatyana—whom he casually preferred to her more outgoing sister—expresses her love for him in a passionate letter, Eugene is mildly touched. Nevertheless he rejects her in a condescending speech that critics have called both cruel and honest; he does reveal some self-awareness as he describes the kind of neglectful husband he would make if he were to marry Tatyana.

Eugene's duel with Lensky is important to the development of his character. Despite his professed disdain for society and his awareness that the duel is absurd and unnecessary, he accepts the challenge because he fears he will otherwise be mocked. Some critics propose that Eugene subconsciously resents the impassioned Lensky for his genuine if misguided passion and his status as a poet; significantly, Eugene does not even wait the proper time before drawing his gun and shooting his friend. He is less ironic and carefree after the duel but continues to feel alienated and disillusioned. Returning to Moscow and drawn irresistibly into the fashionable milieu he claims to disdain, Eugene encounters a transformed Tatyana. Dazzled by her appearance as a sophisticated, celebrated lady of high society, Eugene now falls in love with her. Yet Tatyana remains faithful to her new husband even though she does, in fact, still love Eugene, which lends the novel both structural unity and thematic depth, for it shows a character of greater maturity than Eugene. She suspects his feelings for her have more to do with the effect such a liaison would have publicly than with who she is, and she rejects her first love. While Tatyana is said to embody the traditionally Russian virtues of loyalty and fidelity Eugene has absorbed the western value of independence or, less flatteringly, of rootless wandering and insubstantiality. Scholars note that the similarities between Eugene and Pushkin, who also lived a glamorous life of excess, but whereas the author was able to move beyond the artificiality and wastefulness of that existence, Eugene seems mired in the limitations of his own personality.

When she is first introduced, **Tatyana Larin** is a shy, dreamy, rustic girl with no grasp of social arts or artifice. She has spent her childhood on a remote country estate, steeped in the folklore and traditions of her Russian heritage and also exposed to the romantic, sentimental novels of such eighteenth-century authors as Jean Jacques Rousseau and Samuel Richardson. She naively imagines herself a heroine like those she encountered in fiction, and Eugene seems to her the perfect hero. Reserved and pensive, Tatyana is capable of deep, strong emotion, but, unaccustomed to the art of flirtation, she expresses her feelings simply and openly. She stoically bears Eugene's rejection, suffering in silence despite her grief and humiliation. After she has looked through Eugene's books and read the notes in their margins she learns more about his true character; she recognizes not only his disillusionment but his selfishness, and though she continues to love him, she begins to shed the self-abasement that previously characterized her attitude toward him. No longer interested in romance, Tatyana lets herself be propelled into marriage to an elderly, unattractive man she does not love, which she later acknowledges was probably a mistake. Although she becomes an elegant, sought-after star in her new social realm, Tatyana retains a level-headedness about it, not absorbing shallow social values as Eugene has. Tatyana realizes that Eugene, whom she does still love, is enamored not of her but of the glamour and the risk of notoriety that she now represents. Although her rejection of Eugene on the basis of her loyalty to her husband seems to deny the true inclination of her heart, she demonstrates by it a strength of character and solid, unpriggish virtue that make her more admirable than the novel's protagonist. Many critics have, in fact, identified Tatyana as one of the most significant and compelling female characters in Russian literature. Proclaimed by the Russian novelist Fedor Mikhailovich Dostoyevsky "the apotheosis of the Russian woman," Tatyana projects high personal morality and serves as the novel's moral touchstone.

Eugene's neighbor and friend, **Vladimir Lensky,** is an idealistic, naive, eighteen-year-old poet and student. While attending a German university he was influenced by the romanticism of such nineteenth-century German writers as Friedrich von Schiller and Immanuel Kant. Eugene gets along well with Lensky because the young man is likable and presents an outlook on life that differs amusingly from his own. In addition to forcing the novel's action by providing a link to the Larin family, Lensky serves as a foil to Eugene: his innocent idealism and exalted view of humanity contrast with Eugene's mature cynicism and skeptical outlook. Unlike Eugene, Lensky has substituted imagination for experience and has little understanding of real relationships or emotions. He has formed, for instance, what he believes is a deep, profound passion for the superficial, flighty Olga. In keeping with his romantic nature, he interprets Eugene's flirtation with her as a mortal insult that can only be avenged through a duel, and he is killed over the meaningless incident. Some scholars speculate that Pushkin may have fashioned Lensky as a less talented version of himself as a young poet.

Tatyana's pretty, popular sister, **Olga Larin,** is a lighthearted, cheerful, affectionate girl with little depth of character. Much more socially adept than her sister, she is charming but shallow. Olga's conventionality makes her rather flat and uninteresting, but she contributes to Tatyana's impact by contrasting with her, and she provides an impetus to the duel. Olga's incapacity for the deep passion Lensky desired is demonstrated by her quick recovery from his death, for she marries another man within six months.

Further Reading

Bayley, John. *Pushkin: A Comparative Commentary.* Cambridge: Cambridge at the University Press, 1971.

Bloom, Harold. *Alexander Pushkin.* New York: Chelsea House, 1987.

Clayton, J. Douglas. *Ice and Flame: Aleksandr Pushkin's "Eugene Onegin."* Toronto: University of Toronto Press, 1985.

Dostoyevsky, Fyodor. "On the Unveiling of the Pushkin Memorial." 1880. Reprint. In *Pages from the Journal of an Author,* translated by S. S. Koteliansky and J. Middleton Murry, pp. 47-68. Allen and Unwin, 1916.

Freeborn, Richard. "Eugene Onegin." In *The Rise of the Russian Novel: Studies in the Russian Novel from "Eugene Onegin" to "War and Peace,"* pp. 10-38. Cambridge: Cambridge at the University Press, 1973.

Hoisington, Sona Stephan, ed. *Russian Views of Pushkin's "Eugene Onegin,"* translated by Sona Stephan Hoisington. Bloomington: Indiana University Press, 1988.

Nabokov, Vladimir and Dmitri Nabokov. "Pushkin, or the Real and the Plausible." *New York Review of Books* 35 (31 March 1988): 38.

Nineteenth Century Literature Criticism, Vols. 3, 27. Detroit: Gale.

Pritchett, V. S. "Alexander Pushkin: Founding Father." In *The Myth Makers: Literary Essays,* pp. 77-88. New York: Random House, 1979.

Edmond Rostand
1868-1918
French dramatist and poet.

Cyrano de Bergerac (drama, 1897)

Plot: Set in seventeeth-century France, the drama opens in a theater as an audience waits for the start of a play by the renowned soldier and poet Cyrano de Bergerac. In the audience is Christian de Neuvillette, a young cadet in the Guards who is hopelessly in love with the beautiful Roxane. Also waiting is Ragueneau, a pastry chef and poet whose artist friends often take advantage of his generosity by exchanging their poems for his cakes and buns. The famous actor Montfleury is to star in the play, but Cyrano has pledged to disrupt the performance if Montfleury, whom he hates, takes the stage. Cyrano does appear soon after the play starts, commanding that it end. He then duels with the Comte de Guiche, who has insulted Cyrano's terrifically large nose; as he spars he recites a long poem. Cyrano later confesses to his friend Le Bret that he is in love with Roxane but despairs of ever winning her affection because of his ridiculous appearance. He is overjoyed when he receives a summons to meet Roxane at Ragueneau's shop, where he composes a love poem in her honor while waiting for her. She confesses that she is in love, but Cyrano soon realizes with anguish that he is not the object of her passion. She loves Christian, and asks Cyrano to protect the shy young man from the other, rougher cadets. Later Christian insults Cyrano's nose—a previously unforgivable insult—but Cyrano allows the comment to go unavenged. When Christian tells Cyrano that he is in love with Roxane but lacks the eloquence to win her, Cyrano allows him to use the love poem he has written for her, presenting it to Roxane as his own work. Roxane is charmed by her suitor's apparent wit. Cyrano later finds himself bolstering Christian's reputation by hiding in the shadows and speaking elegant words of love while the inarticulate young man stands before Roxane's balcony.

Roxane receives a letter from another suitor, the Comte de Guiche, announcing that he plans to visit her that evening. She pretends that the letter is an order from the church that she marry Christian, and a wedding is quickly arranged. Roxane asks Cyrano to distract the comte until after the ceremony has taken place. Though heartbroken that his beloved will marry another man, Cyrano delays de Guiche by pretending to be insane, and the two young people are married. The vengeful comte, however, orders both Cyrano and Christian to report to their regiment, which leaves immediately to fight the Spanish at the Siege of Arras. During the long siege, Cyrano repeatedly risks his life to send impassioned love letters from Christian—actually written by himself, of course—to Roxane across enemy lines. Roxane unexpectedly arrives at the camp, drawn, as she tells Christian, by the beauty of his letters. Realizing that Roxane loves not him but the soul of Cyrano, Christian urges his friend to tell her the truth. Christian is soon killed in battle, however, and Cyrano vows that he will never reveal to Roxane her husband's secret. He then plunges back into battle and leads the cadets to victory.

Roxane retires to a convent, and, fifteen years later, is still faithful to the memory of her beloved husband. Cyrano visits her every week, but one day he arrives later than usual. He conceals a bad wound he has recently received when a beam fell from a roof onto his head, apparently dropped by one of his enemies. Roxane begins to recite her husband's last letter to her and Cyrano asks if he may finish it; to her surprise, he knows the letter as well as she does, even though it is now too dark to read it. Roxane realizes that it was Cyrano who wrote the letters and with whom she has actually been in love for so many years. She shares this revelation with Cyrano just before he dies, secure in the knowledge that Roxane recognizes and returns his love.

Characters: Widely acclaimed as a dramatic masterpiece, *Cyrano de Bergerac* is renowned for its unforgettable protagonist and romantic spirit. First produced during a period dominated by the naturalism and symbolism of such playwrights as Henrik Ibsen and Maurice Maeterlinck, *Cyrano* was heralded as a revival of the romantic dramas of an earlier time. The play combines humor, romance, heroism, and exciting action, all relayed in an expert, vivid verse form. Though some critics have faulted the play for insincerity and shallowness, most praise its theatricality and its heroic protagonist who remains loyal to his ideals.

Based on an actual seventeenth-century soldier and poet, **Savinien de Cyrano de Bergerac** is one of literature's most colorful and famous characters. A renowned swordsman and exacting author, he is burdened with an excessively large nose that renders his appearance ludicrous. Nevertheless, Cyrano approaches life with energy and bravado, occasionally even indulging in violent behavior that belies his tender soul. Unable to brook insults to his nose, Cyrano displays his verbal virtuosity when he recites what has come to be known as the ''nose tirade'' while dueling with the Comte de Guiche; in this exquisitely imaginative poem, Cyrano anticipates every possible insult that could be leveled against his nose, thus besting his opponent. But Cyrano's self-mockery masks his true suffering. His unattractive exterior contrasts strongly with his inner nobility, demonstrated in his willingness to help Christian because Roxane, whom he secretly worships, has requested it. Though tortured by his thwarted love, Cyrano enables Christian to make Roxane believe he is a passionate, eloquent lover, when in fact the young man is merely ordinary and inarticulate. In an excruciating test of his loyalty and self-sacrifice, Cyrano actually makes the wedding of Roxane and Christian possible by detaining the comte. He later refuses to disillusion Roxane about her dead husband's true attributes by admitting that he wrote the letters that so moved her—even though Christian urges him to do so. A well-known symbol of Cyrano's personality is his ''panache,'' the white plume he wears that symbolizes his integrity; it is the standard of honor, independence, and self-sacrifice to which he holds himself. He seems to derive satisfaction from acting admirably, allowing no one to discover his true heartache at losing Roxane. At his death, he proudly declares that he has kept his panache aloft, and his love for Roxane has also been affirmed and returned. Critics often describe Cyrano as the quintessential romantic idealist, likening him to the protagonist of Miguel de Cervantes' seventeenth-century novel *Don Quixote*. But it has been repeatedly noted that Cyrano seems to love not so much Roxane but love itself, an idealized emotion preserved when he refuses to reveal his secret to his beloved. Some scholars find Cyrano an essentially shallow, stereotypical character whose sacrifice seems unnecessary and meaningless, while others consider his idealistic struggle against reality convincing and poignant. In any case Cyrano has a permanent place in the public imagination with his oversized nose and noble soul, as evidenced by the many stage and film adaptations of the play since its publication.

The object of Cyrano's idealized affection is **Madeleine Robin**, known as **Roxane.** An attractive, gay young woman, she initially exhibits little spiritual depth, thus, through her grace and beauty, she merely personifies the love that Cyrano feels for her but has not earned it by possessing deeper attributes. Roxane is usually identified as a *précieuse,* referring to the préciosité movement in French literature, which exalted the elaborate refinement and elevation of form over content. Accordingly, Roxane relishes the forms and witty expression of love more than love itself, an attitude comically evident in her frustration when Christian, wooing her without Cyrano's assistance, can think of nothing more eloquent to say than ''I love you.'' However, Roxane grows more mature as the drama progresses. The letters she receives from Christian (written by Cyrano) while he is off fighting the Siege of Arras lead to a gradual deepening of her soul; she develops a finer, more meaningful love for Christian based not on his handsomeness or bravery in battle but on the passionate, pure soul reflected in his letters. Her growth is evident in her stoic reaction to Christian's death: she retreats to a convent, serenely devoted to his memory and unaware that the person who has actually inspired her love visits her every week. Unconsciously influenced by Cyrano's idealism, she has grown from a rather thoughtless, spiritually empty girl to a mature woman. When she finally realizes the truth about Cyrano, she does not hesitate to pledge her devotion to him, and the two are united, if only briefly, in love.

Christian de Neuvillette, Roxane's suitor and Cyrano's rival and friend, is an undistinguished young man from the provinces who is a freshly arrived cadet in the regiment to which Cyrano also belongs. Though handsome and brave, Christian is morbidly shy and inarticulate, and he fears that he will never win the love of the brilliant Roxane. He exhibits courage—or perhaps foolhardiness—when he taunts Cyrano about his nose; he is saved from the consequences of this grievous misdeed only by Cyrano's having promised Roxane that he would look out for her lover. Bereft of any natural wit or poetry, Christian relies on Cyrano's passionate eloquence to impress Roxane; he proves pathetically inadequate at lovemaking when left on his own. His attempt to woo her—during which he can think of nothing more profound than ''I love you''—is a comic scene that makes Christian a more pitiable, likable character. Christian is basically generous, though, when he realizes that Roxane really loves the author of the letters, for he insists before his death that Cyrano reveal the truth to Roxane. Christian's primary role in the drama is to serve as an obstacle to Cyrano's love and to give him an opportunity to display his unselfish loyalty.

Le Bret, Cyrano's close friend and confidant, is also based on an actual historical figure. He is a more realistic, hard-headed foil to Cyrano, frequently cautioning his friend about the possible consequences of his brashness, but he is also loyal and devoted to Cyrano and helps bolster his self-confidence. In his role as companion and sounding board, Le Bret has been compared to Sancho Panza, who performed a similar function for the protagonist of Miguel de Cervantes's *Don Quixote.*

Roxane's aristocratic suitor, the **Comte de Guiche,** who is the commanding officer of Cyrano's and Christian's regiment, is probably the most villainous character in *Cyrano de Bergerac,* vengefully thwarting the young lovers' plans by sending Christian off to battle before they have even consummated their marriage. Rather stereotypical in his arrogance and egotism, he is portrayed as lacking ideals, but he is notoriously brave in battle. Despite the tragic consequences he helps produce, the comte is not uniformly wicked, for he does sincerely admire Cyrano's bravery and even makes a veiled suggestion, during his eulogy for Cyrano, that he feels some remorse for his own underhanded actions.

Another notable character in *Cyrano* is **Ragueneau,** the pastry chef and poet who uses his shop as a kind of proletarian literary salon for his impoverished artist friends. Sincere and passionate about poetry, Ragueneau is somewhat ill-used by the young poets who exchange their work for his goods. Like Cyrano, he is a romantic idealist who maintains his enthusiasm despite the harshness and insensitivity of his scornful, nagging wife. The popular, pompous actor **Montfleury** is scheduled to perform in the play written by Cyrano that is about to be staged as the drama opens. Cyrano halts the play, however, because he considers Montfleury a decadent, insensitive philistine.

Further Reading

Amoia, Alba della Fazia. *Edmond Rostand.* Boston: Twayne, 1978.

Burgess, Anthony. Preface to *Cyrano de Bergerac* by Edmond Rostand, translated by Anthony Burgess, pp. v-xiv. New York: Alfred A. Knopf, 1971.

Eliot, T. S. "Whether Rostand Had Something about Him." *Athenaeum* No. 4656 (25 July 1919): 665-66.

James, Henry. "Edmond Rostand." *The Critic* 29, No. 5 (November 1901): 437-50.

Simon, John. "*Cyrano de Bergerac.*" In *Singularities: Essays on the Theater, 1964-1973,* pp. 17-19. New York: Random House, 1975.

Twentieth-Century Literary Criticism, Vol. 6, 37. Detroit: Gale.

Untermeyer, Louis. Foreword to *Cyrano de Bergerac* by Edmond Rostand, pp. ix-xvii. New York: Heritage Press, 1954.

Williams, Patricia Elliott. "Some Classical Aspects of *Cyrano de Bergerac.*" *Nineteenth-Century French Studies* I, No. 2 (February 1973): 112-24.

Susanna Haswell Rowson

1762-1824

Anglo-American novelist, dramatist, poet, essayist, and editor.

Charlotte: A Tale of Truth (novel, 1791)

Plot: The novel begins in England in 1774. Charlotte Temple, a fifteen-year-old student at a boarding school in Chichester, meets a British army lieutenant named John Montraville. Attracted to the comely young girl and fancying himself in love with her, Montraville eventually persuades the initially reluctant Charlotte to accompany him to America, where he is stationed. Along with Montraville's shifty friend, Belcour, and her own corrupt teacher, Mademoiselle La Rue, Charlotte sails with Montraville to America. After their arrival Montraville falls in love with another woman, Julia, rationalizing his infidelity to Charlotte with Belcour's deceitful declaration that she was unfaithful to him. Pregnant and abandoned by her lover, Charlotte is destitute and alone. She is taken in by the kind Mrs. Beauchamp but dies soon after the birth of her child and the arrival of her father, who sorrowfully takes the baby back to England with him. Both of the novel's villains meet the fates they deserve: Belcour is killed by Montraville in a duel, and Mademoiselle La Rue's life of vice ends in a painful death. Montraville marries Julia but remembers Charlotte and his own role in her fate with sadness and remorse for the rest of his life.

Characters: Considered America's first professional woman writer, Rowson also worked as a governess, actress, and teacher, and she infused her works with her broad knowledge of everyday life. Though dismissed by most early reviewers as mawkish and lacking in literary merit, *Charlotte* was immensely popular with the public through most of the nineteenth century, and it continues to interest modern scholars and readers. Intended, as Rowson stated in the preface, "for the perusal of the young and thoughtless of the fair sex," the novel reflects Rowson's commitment to the guidance and education of young women as well as her flair for the dramatic and dedication to realistic description. *Charlotte* is modeled after the sentimental novels of more accomplished authors, such as Samuel Richardson and Fanny Burney, and features the melodramatic plot that late eighteenth- and early nineteenth-century audiences found so appealing. In blending a strongly didactic, moralistic tone and message with a scandalous, even sensationalist plot, Rowson contributed to the popularizing the novel, which had previously been viewed as immoral. Some critics maintain that *Charlotte*'s sermonizing narrator, who maintains a stance of compassionate scruples, uncritically reinforces the rigid morals and values of her society, but other reviewers consider Rowson a feminist crusader who condemns the victimization of women and affirms the equality of the sexes.

To create the story of **Charlotte Temple,** who is transplanted to America after a childhood in England, Rowson drew on personal knowledge of both milieus. She spent several years of her childhood in America, where her father was stationed as a military officer, and returned there permanently with her husband and their acting company in 1793. Rowson apparently modeled Charlotte after an actual person: Charlotte Stanley, the daughter of an English clergyman who was persuaded to go to America with Rowson's cousin, the already-married John Montrésor, a British army officer. Like her fictional counterpart, the real Charlotte died after giving birth to a child. As the novel begins, Charlotte is an innocent, artless, but tragically deluded young girl whose head is turned by the dashing and ardent Lieutenant Montraville. Despite a fine upbringing by religious, virtuous, and loving parents, Charlotte succumbs to her emotions, allowing Montraville to seduce her. Yet Charlotte's downfall is not colored as entirely her own fault; varying degrees of blame are also shared by Montraville, Belcour, and Mademoiselle La Rue—adults who fail to conduct themselves properly. Thus Rowson does not seem to condemn the "fallen woman," as authors commonly did in late eighteenth- and early nineteenth-century fiction. After Montraville abandons her, the pregnant, solitary Charlotte endures circumstances very like her creator's experience with everyday hardships—particularly poverty—realities Rowson insisted be represented in fiction. The miserable Charlotte lapses into anxious wandering, and finally, after the birth of her baby and just before her death, experiences a complete psychological breakdown. Some critics have characterized Charlotte as a stereotyped female in her excessive weakness and dependence, while others contend that Rowson intended to expose through Charlotte the victimization of women and the need to educate them properly. Actually Charlotte is one of only two female protagonists in Rowson's work in whom sensibility overwhelms practical sense; her other heroines (most notably Rebecca in *Rebecca; or, The Fille de Chambre,* thought to be markedly autobiographical) display much more pluck, resilience, and self-sufficiency. In Charlotte Rowson appealed to her readers' compassion with this tale of innocence destroyed and life smothered, hoping to influence young women to choose the path of virtue and thus avoid the despair and death she believed were the inevitable outcome of vice.

Charlotte's seducer, **John Montraville,** is a British army lieutenant apparently modeled after Rowson's cousin John Montrésor, who had played the seducer's role in the real-life tragedy of Charlotte Stanley. Though he definitely bears a great deal of responsibility for Charlotte's fate, Montraville is not portrayed as completely villainous but as an impulsive young man overcome by physical desire and vanity. Although he initially stifles his own scruples about his behavior toward Charlotte, he does come to feel genuine sorrow and remorse. His past liaison with Charlotte even complicates his relationship with his wife, Julia—who, incidentally, is portrayed as utterly blameless and quite worthy. Just as Charlotte is neither entirely a victim nor entirely guilty, her seducer is not devoid of virtue.

The villains of *Charlotte* are Montraville's deceitful, selfish friend **Belcour,** who convinces him that Charlotte has been unfaithful to him, thus hastening her downfall, and Charlotte's corrupt teacher, **Mademoiselle La Rue.** The fact that this conniving villainess is French is a typical phenomenon in English literature, for the English considered the French more prone to immoral behavior than their own countrymen. Rowson wanted to show how the "profligate of both sexes" may contribute to a young woman's ruin, and she lent a particularly venomous cast to Charlotte's female corrupter, who pointedly rejects the older woman's duty to be a moral guide. Like the Greek goddess Circe, to whom she has been compared, Mademoiselle La Rue uses her evil power of persuasion to convince the doubtful Charlotte to accept Montraville's attentions and then to run away with him. La Rue's dissipated ways finally bring about an end that is, Rowson suggests, deservedly painful.

The evil characters in *Charlotte* are balanced by several figures who serve as exemplars of virtue. Charlotte's parents, **Mr. and Mrs. Temple,** help establish the concept of the family as the center of righteous life—the sanctity of which is undone by Montraville, Belcour, and La Rue. Despite their own devotion to religion and to virtue, the Temples cannot prevent their beloved daughter from going astray, and critics have praised Rowson for her effective depiction of their sorrow at Charlotte's fate. Charlotte's mother, Lucy Temple, represents the contentment women can find in marriage that, some critics claim, Rowson advocates. Another positively portrayed character is **Mrs. Beauchamp,** Charlotte's only friend in America, who takes her in near the end of her life. She too experiences contentment in the conventionally female role of service to others. Kind and generous, she lives in a peaceful, healthy rural setting that contrasts strongly with the dangerous, vice-ridden city. Mrs. Beauchamp's compassion and capacity to forgive the sins of others are evident in her wish that Charlotte might recover and reform, a wish that is never granted.

Further Reading

Dictionary of Literary Biography, Vol. 37. Detroit: Gale.

Kirk, Clara M., and Kirk, Rudolf. Introduction to *Charlotte Temple: A Tale of Truth* by Susanna Rowson, edited by Clara M. and Rudolf Kirk, pp. 11-32. New York: Twayne, 1964.

Martin, Wendy. "Profile: Susanna Rowson, Early American Novelist." *Women's Studies* 2 (1974): 1-8.

Nineteenth-Century Literature Criticism, Vol. 5. Detroit: Gale.

Weil, Dorothy. *In Defense of Women: Susanna Rowson (1792-1824).* University Park: Pennsylvania State University Press, 1976.

George Sand
1804-1876
French novelist, dramatist, and essayist.

Indiana (novel, 1832)

Plot: The novel's protagonist is a young Spanish-French creole woman named Indiana Delmare. Married to a pompous, tyrannical man much older than herself, she is unhappy and dissatisfied with her life. Her only companion is her half-English cousin Rodolphe, called Sir Ralph, a sensitive young man who is also frustrated by his mundane circumstances. Ralph's presence at first made Monsieur Delmare suspicious, but he has become an accepted visitor to the household and a loyal friend to Indiana. One night a neighboring aristocrat named Raymon de Ramière is discovered sneaking onto the estate. Although he claims he has come to see Monsieur Delmare about business, he has actually planned a rendezvous with Indiana's maid, Noun, with whom he has been romantically involved for some time. When he sees Indiana, however, Raymon loses interest in Noun and begins to pursue her mistress. Indiana too grows increasingly attracted to the debonair young man—a notorious lady-killer of high society—but refuses to yield to his sexual advances because she has formed an ideal of pure, spiritual love that precludes physical passion. Finally Raymon rashly enters the Delmare home, determined to make Indiana his lover, but the Delmares are away. Finding Noun in Indiana's room, he makes love to her. They are interrupted by the return of Indiana, and Noun flees, but Indiana discovers Raymon in her room. Much agitated and mystified, she tells him to leave before Monsieur Delmare becomes aware of him.

When Noun discovers she is pregnant with Raymon's child, she despairs of ever marrying her lover and drowns herself. Both Indiana and Raymon are disturbed by the maid's death. Already tired of Indiana, Raymon begins to avoid her; she, however, decides to give in to him sexually. She goes to his home and waits all night for him to return. The two are talking as the sun rises, and a chagrined Indiana hurries home, arousing her husband's suspicions with her arrival. Some time later Delmare's business fails, and he is completely bankrupt. He informs Indiana that they must move to the island of Bourbon to build his fortune again, and she submissively accompanies him. She is very unhappy in her new life, however, and decides to return to France and Raymon. When she reaches Paris, she finds out that Raymon has married a wealthy young woman. Increasingly despondent and hopeless, Indiana determines to kill herself. She happens to meet the equally melancholy Ralph in Paris, and the two make a suicide pact that, at the last minute, they both revoke. Energized by a newly awakened love for the ever-devoted Ralph, Indiana stays with him on Bourbon, where they live together in happy, contented seclusion.

Characters: Amandine Aurore Lucile Dupin Dudevant, who wrote under the pseudonym of George Sand, is one of France's most renowned novelists, celebrated as much for her flamboyant personality and lifestyle as for her writing, which ranged from the quintessentially romantic to the realistic to the pastoral. Sand's early period, from which *Indiana* is drawn, is characterized by her rebellious, feminist approach to love and marriage and her focus—controversial at the time—on eroticism and female sexuality. Critics have often detected autobiographical elements in Sand's works, and *Indiana* is said to reflect Sand's unhappy early marriage to a conventionally domineering husband. Praised for its lyricism, insight, and frank eroticism, the novel exhibits a number of typically romantic elements, including the suicide motif, frequent fainting due to emotional and sexual excitement, melodramatic speeches, an emphasis on individuality, and the prevailing theme that love is divinely inspired and must be obeyed despite the possibly tragic consequences.

Indiana Delmare is a sensitive young woman of Creole (mixed Spanish and French) heritage, born on the island of Bourbon, whose marriage to a jealous, tyrannical older man has brought her only frustration. Bored and dissatisfied, she finds some comfort in her friendship with Ralph, her equally unhappy and quietly adoring cousin. She is both submissive and brave, bearing her husband's domination stoically at first despite her inherently bold spirit; this duality is in keeping with Sand's conception of female nature as both weak and strong. Desperate for any kind of stimulation, Indiana is quickly attracted by the handsome, dashing Raymon. Idealizing love as pure and spiritual, she initially resists Raymon's demands for sex, and both suffer physically as a result: Raymon becomes ill, and Indiana faints frequently. When Monsieur Delmare insists that his wife accompany him to Bourbon, Indiana meekly complies, but her misery in her new life leads to daring action. Defying both the emotional and the legal bonds of marriage in the belief that true love must triumph over superficial moral constraints, Indiana leaves her husband and travels to Paris to join her lover. But she discovers that the shallow Raymon has already married another woman, and she realizes he was unwilling to make the same sacrifice for her that she has made for him; this difference in the capacity of men and women for commitment is frequently found in Sand's fiction. However, Indiana does realize fulfillment in love when she and Ralph unite on Bourbon (after the death of Monsieur Delmare, which some critics have seen as too convenient) to live together, unmarried legally but deeply connected through the new, romantic moral code they have forged together. Like Lélia in Sand's novel of the same title, Indiana has often been described as Byronic (referring to the English poet George Gordon, Lord Byron): sensitive and frustrated, she rebels against the shallow moral constraints of her society and finally lives apart from civilization on a lush tropical island; several scholars liken the island to the settings of romantic author Jean-Jacques Rousseau. Though some critics consider the novel's happy ending implausible and weak, most find Indiana a compelling or even heroic character in her strong-willed defiance of her husband and society and her determination to assert her independence.

Indiana's taciturn, trustworthy, faithful cousin, **Rodolphe Brown**—known by the English version of his name, **Sir Ralph**—is as sensitive and unhappy as she. His rather awkward appearance and unassuming personality mask a passionate soul that will finally find contentment after he and Indiana reject suicide in favor of love. Discovered by Indiana only after much misery and heartache, this love proves more balanced and therefore more meaningful and enduring than her experience with Raymon. The benevolent Ralph has often been described as a father figure who answers Indiana's need for a stable, guiding influence in her life, though their relationship is based on equality and independence from social constraints or stereotypes.

Raymon de Ramière, Indiana's lover, is a worldly aristocrat who is ultimately revealed as cowardly and selfish. Engaged in a love affair with Noun, whose lower social status makes her an unlikely marital choice, Raymon abandons her to pursue the more sophisticated Indiana. The death of the pregnant and despairing Noun affects Raymon only momentarily. He later tires of and abandons Indiana, then marries a wealthy young woman who can advance his status in society. Raymon's conservative political ambitions contrast with the republican egalitarianism represented by Ralph and demonstrate his inherent egotism.

Monsieur Delmare is an elderly military officer, a veteran of France's Napoleonic wars. Pompous, quick-tempered, and tyrannical, he lacks any sympathy for his wife or understanding of her needs. His insensitivity is established early in the story, when he mercilessly bullies her little dog. Although he is at first inordinately suspicious of his young wife's innocent relationship with Ralph, Delmare is hoodwinked by Raymon's charm and never seems to suspect the connection between him and Indiana. This blindness strikes some scholars as implausible, as does his rather too convenient death, which leaves Indiana and Ralph free to forge their own alliance. It is widely thought that Sand based Delmare's character in part on her own husband, Casimir Dudevant, to whom she, at a young age, had been unhappily married.

Like her mistress, Indiana's maid **Noun** is a Spanish creole from the island of Bourbon. Physically robust and passionate, she contrasts strongly with Indiana and thus represents the physical rather than spiritual aspect of female sexuality. Naive despite her sexual aggression, Noun has an affair with a man she cannot possibly marry, and her resulting pregnancy and general despair lead to suicide. Through Noun's plight, Sand illustrates the high cost often paid by women in their relationships with men.

Lélia (novel, 1833)

Plot: Sténio is a young poet in love with the older, more experienced, brilliant Lélia. She introduces her young suitor to her friend Trenmor, who spent five years in prison for stealing to pay off a gambling debt and consequently has become calm and stoical. Lélia contracts cholera and nearly dies; during her illness she is visited by an Irish priest named Magnus who is tormented by his desire for her and who denounces her as a demon. After Lélia's recovery, she attends a ball with Sténio and Trenmor, for which she is dressed as a man. Discussing Lélia with Sténio, Trenmor describes her as a heroic and noble figure, but the younger man notes she is incapable of love. Sténio is increasingly frustrated in his desire to achieve physical union with Lélia, and he has offered to submit to her will in all matters in exchange for her love. At another ball Lélia encounters her sister Pulchérie, a courtesan, whom she has not seen for several years. The two converse on such topics as the role of women, marriage, prostitution, and physical desire. Lélia laments her inability to find satisfaction in sex, explicitly describing her frustration as well as the failure of her experiment in monastic abstinence. Pulchérie suggests that Lélia become a courtesan, asserting that through giving others physical pleasure she may eventually achieve fulfillment herself.

Lélia decides to offer herself to Sténio, but loses her nerve at the last moment and leaves Pulchérie in her place in the bedroom. When Sténio discovers deception, he abandons Lélia for a life of complete debauchery. Lélia writes to him, explaining that she is capable only of spiritual love. After a year Trenmor goes to Pulchérie's establishment to retrieve Sténio, who has become extremely dissipated. Claiming that suffering can purify the soul, Trenmor takes his young friend to a monastery; coincidentally Magnus is a resident of the same monastery. Sténio tries to bolster his religious faith by talking to Magnus, only to learn that the priest is tormented by doubts and that his religion has not weakened his lust. In despair Sténio drowns himself. Lélia is weeping over his body when the completely maddened Magnus attacks and kills her.

Characters: Sand was celebrated perhaps more for her flamboyant lifestyle and love affairs than for her writing, which shocked and fascinated nineteenth-century readers with its frank eroticism and openly feminist precepts. Like the author who created her, the title character of Lélia is an independent, intellectual woman who scorns the prevailing conventions of her society. Mature and experienced, **Lélia** has engaged in many relationships with men, all of them unsatisfying, and her search for truth and identity has also been futile. Though tormented by unfulfilled physical desire, she believes that sex is merely a means for men to dominate women. As a result she dislikes physical passion and yearns for a purely spiritual love. Although the eroticism presented in *Lélia* drew accusations of immorality from early reviewers, modern scholars laud Sand for her convincing portrayal of sexual desire and frustration. Lélia wants to assume the dominant role in a relationship, so she treats the worshipful Sténio like a child; when she fears that he may gain the upper hand, however, she rejects him, sending instead her courtesan sister to bed with him. The contrast between the highly cerebral, physically frigid Lélia and her sensuous, pleasure-loving, emotionally carefree sister has been much noted. Sand explores through their differences the dual nature of female sexuality—the conflict between physical satisfaction and emotional fulfillment. She is widely praised for creating in Lélia a female equivalent of the typical male romantic hero. Like the Byronic figures found in much of the literature of the period, Lélia is talented and sensitive but immobilized by hopelessness, despair, and futility. Her plight might also be seen as Faustian in that she has embarked on an ultimately ill-fated search for knowledge, though the wisdom she seeks is more emotional or spiritual than the intellectual primacy sought by Faust. Lélia exists at a lofty height above ordinary people, but at the same time she experiences a sense of vertigo and fear; she wishes for the kind of dry wisdom that her friend Trenmor possesses, even though he lacks emotional depth. Lélia's dissatisfaction with society is also typical of romantic protagonists, and her situation particularly underlines the servile, misunderstood position that women occupied then. Lélia has driven one admirer to suicide and another to murder, and she seems to welcome her own death at Magnus's hands. Some commentators have seen this ending as a rather disappointing refusal by Sand to confront the implications of Lélia's dilemma. While many critics, particularly those of the nineteenth century, have detected telling similarities between Lélia and her creator, others note that Sand seemed happy in her many love affairs and lived and worked with an enthusiasm and dedication that contrast strongly with Lélia's ennui.

Sténio is a young poet who initially worships the beautiful, talented Lélia from afar. As their relationship develops, he maintains that ideal love blends both the physical and the spiritual, and he insists that Lélia's concept of emotional connection and physical detachment will never fully satisfy her. When Lélia tricks Sténio into sleeping with her sister instead of with her, the formerly gentle, ingenuous, sensitive young man descends into debauchery. He finally drowns himself, a death that has been characterized as typically romantic, and Lélia is weeping over his corpse when she is murdered.

Calm, collected **Trenmor** is Lélia's understanding friend and intellectual equal. As a handsome, spirited young man he had been a notorious gambler. After swindling an old man, Trenmor was sentenced to five years in prison, a punishment he endured with admirable patience and courage. The experience seems to have purified him, for he now lives a quiet, reformed life and maintains an attitude of resignation and philosophical stoicism. Trenmor represents pure reason, and his solitary, emotionless life illustrates the consequences of rejecting passion. Some critics also regard Trenmor as embodying the romantic conception of redemption through suffering, which is a central concern of Fedor Mikhailovich Dostoyevsky's 1866 novel, *Crime and Punishment.*

Lélia's sister, **Pulchérie,** is a courtesan (prostitute with wealthy clients) who embodies the sensuality that Lélia does not possess. She helps illustrate Sand's concept of the dual nature of female sexuality. Pulchérie finds life uncomplicated, accepting her role and enjoying life as it is, and she seems to represent the view that physical pleasure alone is a legitimate form of human fulfillment. Positive in outlook and disposition, Pulchérie is "the only satisfied and complete character" in the novel, according to critic Nancy Rogers.

Magnus is an Irish priest who has lost not only his faith but his sanity due to his irrational, uncontrollable desire to possess Lélia. His belief that she is a kind of devil sent to torment him results in his brutal action when he discovers her weeping over Sténio's corpse. Magnus exhibits an instinctive, fiery passion that clashes tragically with the chaste role he is expected to perform, thus illuminating the romantic themes of rebellion against society and the physical and emotional disintegration that may result from unfulfilled sexual desire. Some critics have seen Magnus's murder of Lélia as an unsatisfying ending to the story.

Further Reading

Crecelius, Kathryn J. *Family Romances: George Sand's Early Novels.* Bloomington: Indiana University Press, 1988.

Datlof, Natalie. *The World of George Sand.* Westport, Conn.: Greenwood Press, 1991.

Dickenson, Donna. *George Sand: A Brave Man, the Most Womanly Woman.* Berg Publications, 1989.

Doumic, René. *George Sand: Some Aspects of Her Life and Writing,* translated by Alys Hallard. 1910. Reprint. Port Washington, N.Y.: Kennikat Press, 1972.

Glasgow, Janis, ed. *George Sand: Collected Essays.* Troy, N.Y.: Whitston, 1986.

Nineteenth Century Literature Criticism, Vol. 2. Detroit: Gale.

Rogers, Nancy. "Psychosexual Identity and the Erotic Imagination in the Early Novels of George Sand." In *Studies in the Literary Imagination* XII, No. 2 (Fall 1979): 19-35.

Thomson, Patricia. *George Sand and the Victorians: Her Influence and Reputation in Nineteenth-Century England.* New York: Columbia University Press, 1977.

Winegarten, Renee. *The Double Life of George Sand: Woman and Writer.* New York: Basic Books, 1978.

Sir Walter Scott
1771-1832

Scottish novelist, short story writer, poet, biographer, historian, critic, and editor.

Waverly; or, 'Tis Sixty Years Since (novel, 1814)

Plot: The novel takes place in Scotland in 1745, centering on the Jacobite rebellion in which followers of Prince Charles Edward Stuart, or "Bonnie Prince Charlie," attempted to restore him to the throne he previously relinquished to King George II. Edward Waverly is a young Englishman whose father, an ambitious Whig politician, has allowed his son to be raised primarily by his uncle, Sir Everard Waverly, a Tory and a Jacobite sympathizer. After a youth spent reading poetry and formulating romantic fantasies, Edward joins the army and is sent to Scotland. There he visits his uncle's friend Baron Bradwardine, also a Jacobite sympathizer, and is much admired by the baron's sweet, mild daughter Rose. When Donald Bean Lean, an outlaw from Scotland's Highlands, steals some of the baron's cows, Edward goes into the hill country to negotiate with an influential clan chieftain, Fergus Mac Ivor. Edward is enthralled with the chivalric traditions of Highland life, impressed with Fergus, and attracted to the spirited Flora Mac Ivor, Fergus's sister. The Mac Ivors are both ardent Jacobites active in the movement to restore the throne to Prince Charles, whom his enemies call ''The Pretender''; Fergus wishes to win Edward to their cause.

Edward's association with the Highlanders causes suspicion among his military superiors, and his inability to return to his unit for a long period, combined with the mutiny of a group of men who had followed him into the army from his family estate, result in Edward being deemed absent without leave. At the same time his father loses his government office. Already angry at these insulting circumstances, Edward is further dismayed when he is arrested while returning to Edinburgh to clear his name; after being rescued by Bean Lean and meeting the Prince, who has now arrived in Scotland from exile in France, Edward is won over to the Jacobite cause. He fights in the battle of Prestonpans, which the Jacobites win, but becomes separated from his comrades during a subsequent clash at Clifton. Fergus is captured, and Edward goes into hiding. With the help of the English officer Colonel Talbot, whose life he had saved at Prestonpans, Edward is pardoned. Fergus, however, is executed. Edward subsequently proposes marriage to Flora, who refuses him and enters a convent. In time Edward becomes interested in Rose, whom he eventually marries. He lives a quiet, comfortable life thereafter, reminded of his earlier adventures by a treasured portrait of himself and Fergus in Highland dress.

Characters: Credited with the invention of the historical novel, Scott was one of the most influential and popular authors of the nineteenth century, though his works are little known by modern readers. *Waverly,* the first in a series of nearly two dozen novels and tales that became known as the ''Waverly novels,'' features one of Scott's most renowned and typical characters as its protagonist. Set during on Scotland's Jacobite rebellion of 1745, when sympathizers of the exiled Prince Charles James Stuart sought to return him to the throne then occupied by King George II of the Hanover family, the novel exemplifies Scott's interest in the conflict between the older, feudal, more heroic way of life and the practical, forward-looking changes that seemed bound to take place. Scott focuses primarily on ordinary characters rather than actual historical figures, revealing their personalities through skillfully rendered dialogue. Though Scott is faulted for his sometimes sloppy style, weak structuring, and overreliance on coincidence, his novels are almost always highly entertaining and provide a vivid, dramatic interpretation of turbulent times and places in history.

Edward Waverly, the novel's title character, serves as a kind of ''historical tourist'' through whom the reader experiences both an unfamiliar setting and culture and a dramatic sequence of events. Although the often self-critical Scott called Waverly ''a sneaking piece of imbecility,'' many scholars find him an interesting and fairly successful character. Neglected by his politically ambitious father, Edward was raised by an uncle who sympathized with the Jacobite cause and who, significantly, left him alone much of the time to read poetry and romantic literature. Thus Edward developed a longing for adventure and a susceptibility to the passionate convictions of others. Arriving in Scotland he is fascinated by the Highland people—from their quaint dialect and costumes, to the comradery they share at the feast hosted by Fergus Mac Ivor, to their ardent devotion to the Jacobite cause. Although he is serving in the army of the English monarch, Edward finds himself swayed by the followers of Bonnie Prince Charlie. Through a combination of wounded vanity due to his wrongful arrest for desertion and his father's dismissal, his appreciation of such heroic figures as Fergus and Flora, and his already romantic outlook, he is eventually won completely over. While fighting several arduous battles with the Jacobites, however, Edward encounters the practical hardships and miseries of war, and he is forced to view rebellion in a more realistic way. In the end he chooses to live a quiet, safe life with the placid Rose, cherishing his Highland costume, weapons, and the portrait of himself with Fergus as souvenirs of his youthful adventure. Although several critics have agreed with Scott's assessment of his protagonist, claiming that the prodigious conversational skills and other assets Edward is supposed to possess are nowhere demonstrated, most identify him as a prominent example of the "passive hero" often found in Scott's fiction. He is decidedly unheroic in his lack of self-awareness and his susceptibility to outside influences (his name suggests his "wavering" between the Jacobites and the Hanoverians); even his final, happy fate is brought about not through his own effort but through his friends' help and his inheriting a fortune. At the same time he is admirably open to new experiences, firm in his loyalties, and often generous. He provides a telling contrast with the more heroic Fergus Mac Ivor, for it is Edward who survives the clash between old and new, between romantic past and practical present.

One of the most memorable characters in *Waverly* is **Fergus Mac Ivor,** the Scottish clan chieftain who entices Edward into joining the Jacobite rebellion. Although he has a reputation for roughness, Fergus impresses Edward with the courtly, polished manners that prove he is well-educated as well as the passion and unpredictability that increase his charisma. Although Fergus initially seems uniformly brave, hospitable, and committed to his cause, his underlying motives are   gradually revealed. The clan traditions that he has revived, such as the feast attended by both chief and peasant, are actually calculated to increase his own personal power. He expects to be granted an earldom for his sacrifices after Prince Charles is restored to the throne, and he is stalwart in his eagerness for his sister to win Edward's heart so that the young Englishman will endorse the Jacobite cause. Fergus contrasts with Edward in nearly every way: he is poor but energetic, dominating, and dark-haired, and he speaks a vibrant colloquial tongue; Edward is wealthy, passive, fair-haired, and prone to rather stiff, formal language. The fact that Fergus is finally killed, however, attests to Scott's reluctant conviction that the new must eventually conquer the old, that change is inevitable and even necessary, though the future promises to be less exciting and romantic than the past. As several critics have noted, Fergus's passions and ambitions are dismissed as "tirrivies" (tantrums) by the young man who accompanies Edward away from Edinburgh, upon the gates of which Fergus's decapitated head has been mounted.

Although equally devoted to the Jacobite cause, Fergus's sister, **Flora Mac Ivor,** differs from her brother in the purity and selflessness of her commitment. She does not approve of his association with the outlaw Donald Bean Lean, nor is she willing to try to attract Edward in order to win him over to their side. In her great beauty, passion, and intelligence, Flora also differs from Edward's other love interest, Rose Bradwardine. She is as powerful and dominating as Rose is meek and subservient, and the fact that Edward does not finally marry her has been identified as a typical outcome in Scott's fiction. Flora rejects Edward's marriage proposal in a rather melodramatic, overblown speech that many critics have described as unconvincing.

One of Edward's most significant new acquaintances after his arrival in Scotland is **Baron Bradwardine,** a nobleman and an old friend of his uncle. The baron, a Jacobite sympathizer, introduces Edward to the forces organized to support Prince Charles and thus participates in Edward's conversion to the cause. Bradwardine received a legal education early in his life, followed by a stint of military service in the French army, and these two influences are much evident in his behavior. His comically pedantic concern with form has led to comparisons with Fluellen in Shakespeare's *Henry V;* his insistence on his hereditary privilege of removing the prince's boots after battle is often cited as a humorous example of his personality. Despite his true impoverishment, the baron has maintained his position as feudal landlord ruling benevolently over the devoted tenants of his village; his power, however, is revealed as anachronistic and soon to be replaced by a new order. Ridiculous as he may be, Bradwardine proves a loyal, gallant, generous friend who is, according to critic John Lauber, "absurd in success . . . but heroic in defeat."

The baron's daughter, **Rose**, is a sweet, simple girl whose placidity and domestic interests mark her the opposite of passionate, politically active Flora Mac Ivor. Although she is immediately attracted to Edward, his recognition that he loves her comes only after he is rejected by Flora. Nevertheless their union is portrayed as a proper outcome. It has been noted that Rose's formal, rather stilted English is somewhat unrealistic, as a young woman in her situation would most likely have spoken the Scots dialect of her native land.

Prince Charles Edward Stuart, called "**the Pretender**" by his enemies and "**Bonnie Prince Charlie**" by his supporters, is the exiled monarch whom the Jacobites wish to restore to the throne in place of King George II. The brevity of the Prince's appearance (he is physically present in only one chapter) reflects Scott's preference for ordinary characters over famous figures. His polished, civil manners and personal charm do much to win Edward over to his cause; indeed, he seems to the young Englishman like a "hero of romance." The war which is fought for his benefit, however, is wasteful and ill-fated.

One of the most colorful of the novel's secondary characters is **Donald Bean Lean**, the rough bandit who precipitates Edward's foray into the Highlands when he steals some of the baron's cows. Edward is initially thrilled to be in pursuit of a thief—though he rues the mundane nature of the stolen property—and imagines Bean Lean as a dashing bandit; he is disappointed with the unimpressiveness of the outlaw's actual appearance. Loyal to Fergus and to the prince, Bean Lean rescues Edward just before he is to be tried for treason, thus contributing to the Englishman's positive estimation of the Highlanders and their cause. **Evan Dhu Maccombich** is another significant Highlander. He too is loyal to Fergus, even rejecting an opportunity to escape execution and choosing instead to die with his leader. He serves as a strong example of the proud, stoic Highland character. Other notable Scots include **Bailie Duncan MacWheeble**, said to be one of Scott's favorite characters; he is the cautious, sly, self-serving manager of the baron's estates and behaves with comical subservience to his master but with arrogance toward his inferiors. **Davie Gellatly**, a singing, storytelling servant employed by Bradwardine, has been compared to Shakespeare's many fools, who help to create atmosphere and illuminate themes through their lighthearted merrymaking.

Other characters in *Waverly* include **Richard Waverly**, Edward's father, an ambitious and loyal Whig who holds a ministerial post in the government of George II until his dismissal; Edward's uncle, **Sir Everard Waverly**, who exposes his nephew to political and social issues and who is himself a Jacobite sympathizer and a marginal participant in an earlier Jacobite rebellion; **Colonel Gardiner**, Edward's superior officer in the English army, who is based on an actual figure killed at the battle of Prestonpans; and **Colonel Talbot**, whom Edward saves from death at Prestonpans and who later demonstrates his generosity by ensuring that the young man is pardoned for his role in the rebellion.

The Heart of Midlothian (novel, 1818)

Plot: Set in Scotland during the first half of the eighteenth century, the novel centers on Jeanie Deans, the daughter of dairy farmer and strict Presbyterian David Deans. Jeanie's sister, Effie, a pretty and carefree girl, becomes pregnant but reveals her condition to no one, and her baby disappears soon after its birth. Even though the child has not been found, Effie—who refuses to divulge the name of her seducer—is arrested for murder under a statute that would excuse her if she could prove that she had shared her secret with someone. Jeanie could save her sister's life by claiming that Effie had told her of the pregnancy, but she refuses to lie, and Effie is condemned to die. She is placed in Tolbooth Prison in Edinburgh. Earlier, a smuggler named Andrew Wilson had been executed after ensuring the escape of his partner, Geordie Robertson. At the execution the Captain of the City Guard, John Porteus, had shot for no reason into the assembled crowd, killing several people. He was condemned to hang for the murders, but his execution had been stayed, and an angry mob led by Robertson had subsequently stormed the prison, captured Porteus, and hanged him themselves. Robertson is now sought by the police for his prominent role in the riot.

While visiting her sister in prison, Jeanie learns that Robertson is the father of Effie's child. The birth had been attended by the witch-like midwife Meg Murdockson, whose daughter, Marge Wildfire, had also been seduced and then abandoned by Robertson. Resentful toward Effie, Meg had probably taken her child away; Effie's innocence, however, seems impossible to prove. Nevertheless Jeanie decides to try to save her sister's life by walking to London and obtaining a pardon from the queen. Although her fiance, Reuben Butler, a schoolmaster whose impoverishment has made their marriage impossible, does not approve of her plan, he helps her by giving her a letter of introduction to the Duke of Argyle, whose ancestor his own grandfather had once helped. Jeanie's journey to London is long and difficult. She is kidnapped and nearly killed by Meg Murdockson, but she escapes and is taken in by the Reverend Mr. Staunton. Jeanie then learns that Staunton's son, George, is actually Geordie Robertson, her sister's seducer. George tells Jeanie that he engineered the Porteus riot primarily to free Effie from prison, but that she had refused to leave with him; several other attempts to help her had also failed. George assures Jeanie that if she is unable to strike a bargain with the Duke, he will turn himself in to the authorities in exchange for Effie's pardon. Arriving in London, Jeanie makes a strongly positive impression on the duke, and he arranges for her to appear before Queen Caroline. The queen also finds Jeanie sincere, determined, and courageous, and she pardons Effie with the stipulation that Effie must stay out of Scotland for fourteen years.

The duke subsequently proves his admiration for Jeanie by putting her father in charge of an experimental farm and also giving Reuben a school to run, thus allowing him to marry Jeanie. Effie, meanwhile, elopes with Staunton and flees Scotland for an unknown destination. The Butlers are busy through the next few years raising three children, although Jeanie thinks often of her absent sister. After George inherits an aristocratic title, he and Effie establish themselves in London, where none of their high-society friends realize he is actually the Geordie Robertson wanted by the authorities. The Stauntons are now wealthy, and Effie sends frequent gifts of money to her sister. Jeanie happens to find a confession written by Meg Murdockson just before the midwife's death, in which she admits giving Effie's baby to a band of outlaws. Despite the danger that he will be arrested, George travels to Scotland to search for his son. He is eventually murdered by an outlaw who turns out to be his and Effie's kidnapped son. Jeanie and Reuben, however, keep the killer's identity a secret from the grieving Effie. After returning to London and living there for several years, Effie finally enters a convent. During the remainder of their quiet, contented lives, Jeanie and Reuben never reveal to anyone the real identities of George Staunton or his murderer.

Characters: Although they are generally neglected by modern readers, Scott's novels were immensely popular in the early nineteenth century and their influence on other authors—including Charles Dickens, Honoré de Balzac, and James Fenimore Cooper—is well documented. Identified by most critics as Scott's best novel, *The Heart of Midlothian* demonstrates his interest in history and the ways in which individuals are shaped and effected by the social, economic, religious, and political forces of their own time. Often called the inventor of the historical novel, Scott based this work on the Porteus Riot, which took place at Edinburgh's Old Tolbooth Prison (commonly referred to as "the heart of Midlothian") in 1736. The novel is innovative in its use of ordinary, lower-class characters who allow Scott to demonstrate his knowledge of Scots dialect, customs, and values and who reveal themselves primarily through skillfully rendered dialogue. Scott was most interested in the conflict between older, more heroic values and the inevitable onslaught of change; *The Heart of Midlothian* also features such themes as the relationship between law and justice, the question of Scotland's national identity, and the influence of Scottish Presbyterianism.

The central character in *The Heart of Midlothian* is **Jeanie Deans,** said to have been Scott's favorite creation. The appearance of this physically plain, decidedly unromantic member of the peasant class as the novel's protagonist was a landmark in English fiction and set the stage for such later works as George Eliot's *Adam Bede* and Thomas Hardy's *Tess of the D'Urbervilles.* Jeanie differs from the conventional heroines of literature not only in her lack of beauty but in her common sense and only marginal literacy (her reading is limited to the Bible and religious tracts). Despite her lowly status and unimpressive appearance, Jeanie possesses ample courage, determination, and moral earnestness to make her an entirely admirable and memorable character. She was apparently modeled after an actual person, Helen Walker, who also succeeded in gaining a pardon from the queen for her condemned sister. Some critics emphasize the fact that Jeanie is a committed Presbyterian, and that her confidence in the workings of providence, her scruples, and her honesty are rooted in her strong religious faith. Effie's arrest and trial confront Jeanie with a compelling moral dilemma that is rare in Scott's fiction and that lends the novel greater depth and seriousness than most of his other works possess. Jeanie proves true to her own conscience, refusing to lie even to save her sister's life. Instead, she acts with great energy, boldness, and courage to obtain a pardon, enduring danger and hardship to reach London and plead her case before the queen. Her sincerity and generosity contrast significantly with George Staunton's false heroics and lack of real willingness to sacrifice himself for Effie. Jeanie's achievement— and particularly her success in impressing both the Duke of Argyle and Queen Caroline with her strength of character—has political as well as personal significance, for she serves as a representative of her fellow Scots and demands that their humanity be recognized. It is possible to interpret Jeanie as a feminist heroine, for she takes the initiative while the novel's male characters play secondary roles, yet at the same time she is always dutiful and obedient toward authority. While a few scholars claim that Jeanie's moral dilemma is attested to but never actually demonstrated, most find her a believable character who played an important role in the development of English literature.

Jeanie's father, **David Deans,** is a dairy farmer and a stern, rigid Presbyterian whose religious principles are severely challenged by Effie's arrest for murder. Although Deans is extremely dogmatic and possesses spiritual pride—or, as Leslie Stephen asserts, "religious pigheadedness''—he is not necessarily hypocritical when he explains that his own scruples against testifying at Effie's trial need not inhibit Jeanie from participating in the procedure. Jeanie interprets this as a signal that she should lie to save her sister's life. Some critics contend Deans abandons his own beliefs and his daughters as well, but others maintain that it merely reflects his love for both daughters and the difficult conflict between conscience and emotion that Effie's arrest has produced. In any case Deans meets a happy fate in the novel's controversial last volume (which many commentators consider superfluous and reflective of Scott's need to fulfill contractual obligations), when he is granted an experimental farm by the Duke of Argyle.

The central legal question of *The Heart of Midlothian* is explicated through the situation of Jeanie's pretty younger sister **Effie Deans,** who bears an illegitimate child and then is not only unwilling to reveal her seducer but unable to produce the baby. She is consequently victimized by a statute decreeing that she may only be excused from child murder charges if she had shared news of her pregnancy with someone else. Chagrined by her condition, which had come about through a lack of the kind of moral vigilance practiced by the rest of the Deans, Effie had concealed her pregnancy from both her family and her employers.

Overcome by fatigue after the delivery, she has no idea what her midwife, Meg Murdockson, does with the baby. Effie exhibits a moral strength when she refuses to name her seducer or later escape from prison with Robertson during the Porteus Riot, which he claims to have engineered primarily for her benefit. In addition, she demonstrates generosity by sending her family money after she becomes wealthy. When Effie is pardoned and released from jail, she marries Staunton and flees Scotland but, despite the social status and wealth she attains after her eventual arrival in London as the wife of a nobleman, Effie's choices do not ultimately lead to happiness. As several critics have noted, both she and Staunton are punished for their moral instability while Jeanie and her husband prosper.

Handsome, reckless **George Staunton** is a young man of respectable family but profligate impulses who seduces and then abandons two young women, impregnating one of them, becomes involved with criminals (during which period he goes by the name of **Geordie Robertson**), leads a riot on Old Tolbooth prison, is eventually forced to leave Scotland, and is ultimately killed by his own son. Though his father is a clergyman, Staunton leads a wild and dissolute life. He claims that the attack he led on the prison was motivated by the injustice of Porteus's stay of execution, but he actually had personal reasons for instigating the riot: he wanted revenge for the death of Wilson, who had generously saved his life, and he hoped to free Effie. Rather self-interested, Staunton offers to exchange his own freedom for Effie's if Jeanie is unable to get a pardon from the queen. Still, the passionate, aggressive Staunton is not presented as a complete villain; some critics even consider him a "hero-villain" whose behavior results from personal weakness rather than inherent evil and who has some admirable qualities. Staunton does eventually marry Effie, who joins him in a life of exile during which they remain childless and fearful of discovery. Significantly the stereotype of the romantic, carefree young adventurer that Staunton might be said to represent is portrayed here as destructive, for he never attains an ordinary life or ordinary happiness and he meets a violent end. While preparing his body for burial, Jeanie discovers that Staunton is wearing a self-torturing "hair shirt," signifying that he has converted to Catholicism in order to expiate his sins; as several critics have noted, Scott considers this a sad pretense that somehow fits Staunton's flamboyant but morally shallow personality.

Jeanie's husband, **Reuben Butler,** is a sensible, educated, but rather pedantic schoolmaster whose extreme poverty makes marriage impossible until he is granted a better position by the Duke of Argyle. Butler plays only a minor role in the action but serves as an example of the passive hero often found in Scott's fiction, contrasting the more aggressive George Staunton. Another young man who is romantically interested in Jeanie is the **Laird of Dumbiedikes,** a taciturn, clumsy nobleman who generously pays for Effie's defense and for Jeanie's trip to London.

It is widely acknowledged that Scott was more successful in portraying lower class or peasant characters than aristocrats, but two upper-class figures in *The Heart of Midlothian* deserve mention. The **Duke of Argyle** is a Scottish statesman who represents his country at the English court of King George II. Jeanie calls him a "native truehearted Scotsman, and not prideful," and his role as Scotland's spokesman in London helps to illuminate the theme of Scottish identity. Honorable and generous, particularly in his ability to recognize Jeanie's worth and his desire to help her even after Effie has been pardoned, the duke maintains a notably benevolent, patriarchal relationship with the novel's more humbly situated characters. Also positively portrayed is England's reigning monarch, **Queen Caroline,** who demonstrates Scott's typical facility with historically based characters. Intelligent, astute, and sensitive, the queen appreciates Jeanie's sincerity and courage. Her decision to pardon Effie, however, seems based not only on the emotional power of Jeanie's appeal but on political considerations; she wishes to remain on good terms with the duke, whose friendship may benefit her someday.

Among the many members of the peasant class who populate the novel are two significant female characters, **Meg Murdockson** and her daughter **Marge Wildfire.** Murdockson, a vicious old lady known among her dissolute acquaintances as "Mother Blood," delivers Effie's baby and, out of vengefulness because Staunton previously seduced her own daughter, hands the child over to a female member of a gang of outlaws. Murdockson continues her efforts to destroy Effie, kidnapping and nearly murdering Jeanie so as to keep her from obtaining a pardon for her sister. Early suggestions about the old woman's evil nature are validated at the end of the story, when she is hanged as a witch. Made insane by Staunton's betrayal, Marge Wildfire is one of several pathetic imbeciles found in Scott's fiction. Her extreme instability contrasts with Jeanie's strength of character and also lends some comic relief to the story, particularly in the scene in which she behaves in a demented way in a church. In addition Scott demonstrates his poetic ability through Marge, who sings the lyrical ballad "Proud Maisie" on her deathbed.

A wide variety of colorful secondary characters fill out the cast of *The Heart of Midlothian.* **John Porteus,** the Captain of the City Guard, is the excitable, callous officer who shoots into the crowd at Wilson's execution, killing several people and inspiring the riot that ensues after his own execution is stayed. Based on an actual historical figure, Porteus serves as an unflattering example of justice miscarried. **Andrew Wilson,** by contrast, is a criminal who demonstrates unexpected generosity when he allows his partner, Geordie Robertson, to escape. **Ratcliffe** is a condemned thief who, during the riot at Old Tolbooth, refuses to leave the prison because he hopes to parlay his obedience into a job as "underturnkey." He does indeed negotiate for the position with a prison official, **Sharpitlaw,** who demonstrates by hiring Ratcliffe how practical compromises are sometimes made to enforce the law. **Bartoline Saddletree** is an exaggeratedly legal-minded friend of the Deans and Effie's employer after she moves to Edinburgh; his pompous, officious manner masks his ignorance. **Mrs. Saddletree,** however, is generous, motherly, and kind to Effie. The **Reverend Mr. Staunton,** George's morally upright father, gives Jeanie shelter during her voyage to London and helps her to reach her destination. **The Whistler** is the only name by which the grown son of Effie and George is known; after having been raised by outlaws, he becomes a criminal himself, unknowingly kills his own father, and flees to America where he is murdered by Indians. **Duncan of Knock** is the quintessentially Scottish, brusque, lively manager of the estate that the duke assigns to David Deans.

Further Reading

Daiches, David. *Sir Walter Scott and His World.* New York: Viking, 1971.

Kerr, James. *Fiction against History: Scott as Storyteller.* Cambridge: Cambridge University Press, 1989.

Lockhart, John G. *Life of Sir Walter Scott.* 1902. Reprint. New York: AMS Press, 1983.

Nineteenth Century Literature Criticism, Vol. 15. Detroit: Gale.

Stephen, Leslie. "Some Words about Sir Walter Scott." *Cornhill Magazine* XXIV, No. 141 (September 1871): 278-93.

Wagenknecht, Edward. *Sir Walter Scott.* New York: Continuum, 1990.

Catharine Maria Sedgwick

1789-1867

American novelist.

Hope Leslie; or, Early Times in the Massachusetts (novel, 1827)

Plot: William Fletcher, the idealistic nephew of a wealthy English gentlemen, moves to the fledgling American colonies in 1760 after a religious dispute with his uncle. Fletcher hoped to marry his cousin Alice, but instead she married Charles Leslie; Fletcher wed an orphan girl, Martha. After several years in Boston, Fletcher joins a group of prominent Puritans planning to establish the town of Springfield, Massachusetts, then located on the edge of the American frontier. The Fletchers are assigned two native American servants, Oneco and Magawisca, son and daughter of a chief of the recently defeated Pequod tribe. When Fletcher learns that Alice's husband has died and that she has arrived in Boston with her two children and needs his help, he travels there to see her. In Boston Fletcher stays with Alice's daughter Hope, sending her sister Faith and the two Indians back to his wilderness home. After their arrival, Indians led by the father of Magawisca and Oneco attack the Fletcher home, killing Martha and her baby and carrying away the Fletchers' son Everill and Faith Leslie as captives. The group travels to an Indian encampment near Stockbridge, Massachusetts. Magawisca intervenes to save the life of Everell, who is about to be executed, and loses her own arm in the process. Everell is subsequently released, but Faith remains with the Pequods.

The energetic, self-reliant Hope Leslie travels to Springfield and explores her new surroundings with relish. During one excursion, her tutor, Master Cradock, is bitten by a rattlesnake, and Hope persuades an Indian woman, Nelema, to save his life with a native American cure. Nelema is arrested by the Puritan authorities, however, and accused of witchcraft. Unable to convince the magistrates of Nelema's innocence and outraged by the unjust sentence, Hope arranges for Nelema's escape from prison. Shocked by Hope's disobedience, Judge Pynchon orders her to submit to the care and influence of straitlaced Margaret Winthrop, wife of Massachusetts governor John Winthrop, and her equally pious, passive, but essentially humane niece, Esther Downing. Seeing that Esther is in love with Everell, Hope sacrifices her own affection for the young man. When Magawisca is arrested for treason, Everell pleads with Esther to help him save the woman who once saved him; ever obedient to authority, however, Esther refuses and thus loses Everell's regard. He applies instead to Hope, who again defies her community's Puritan fathers by helping Magawisca escape. Hope now encounters her long-lost sister, Faith, who has been absorbed into the Pequod tribe and has married Magawisca's brother, Oneco. Although Hope initially assumes that Faith will return to white society, her sister wishes to remain with the Indians, and Hope accepts this decision. Magawisca and Faith retreat with the other Pequods into the western wilderness, while Hope and Everell marry and move to Boston.

Characters: *Hope Leslie* is a historical romance providing a realistically detailed portrait of life among the Puritans and native Americans of seventeenth-century New England. Recognized as Sedgwick's most accomplished work, it is also one of the first novels to utilize a distinctly American setting and characters. Often cited—and sometimes faulted— for its didactic tone, the novel exposed the religious intolerance characterizing colonial America. Sedgwick is frequently compared to the better known James Fennimore Cooper, whose works also depict the tensions and personalities of the nation's westward expansion; while both authors are noted for their positive portrayals of Indians, Sedgwick's female characters are much more rounded and compelling than Cooper's. Though her work was virtually ignored for many decades following her death, Sedgwick is now recognized as a significant contributor to American literature.

Sedgwick is consistently praised for her skillful, markedly unconventional portrayal of the novel's title character. **Hope Leslie** is energetic, courageous, self-reliant, and rebellious and thus bears little resemblance to either the conventional heroine of fiction or the ideal woman projected by her society. Puritan women were expected to be meek, selfless, and unquestioningly obedient to figures of authority. While Margaret Winthrop and Esther Downing fulfill this role to the letter, Hope thinks, speaks, and acts in accordance with the dictates of her own conscience. In her self-reliance and insistence on following her own heart, Hope might be seen either in a feminist light—as a strong, independent woman who challenges the boundaries of a patriarchal order—or, more generally, as a character embodying the values upon which America was founded. Hope's decision to move from the safety and certainty of Boston to the wilderness town of Springfield evidences her unconventionality and adventurousness, as do her reactions to the difficulties she encounters there. She twice confronts an unjust, hypocritical social system—represented by the bigoted magistrates who judge the native American women guilty of breaking Puritan laws—and in both cases Hope responds with courage and strength. Forced to choose between what is legally right and what is morally right, Hope defies authority to help both Nelema and Magawisca escape. However Hope exhibits one quality in accordance with the conventional ideal of womanhood: her capacity for self-sacrifice. She is willful but not selfish, and she demonstrates her concern for others when she abandons Everell so Esther may find happiness with him. Hope's relationship with Magawisca is an important aspect of the novel, for the two women succeed in crossing social and racial boundaries to form a unique friendship. Hope recognizes in Magawisca a kindred spirit whose pantheistic, compassionate religion is similar to her own faith, based on the possibility of redemption and a God who is infinitely merciful. Hope's "pure and disinterested" spirituality, which depends not so much on outward forms as on inner conviction, contrasts strongly with Puritanism, portrayed as hypocritical and chauvinistic. Hope's defiance of Puritanism has also been said to reflect Sedgwick's conversion from rigid, orthodox Congregationalism to Unitarianism. Hope exhibits some traces of ethnocentrism when she is shocked and repulsed by her sister's changed appearance (after Faith has lived with the Pequods for several years and married an Indian man), but she accepts Faith's decision to remain with the tribe. Despite her unconventionality, courage, and tolerance for others, Hope chooses a fairly conventional path in the end, returning to Boston with her Puritan husband. Unlike Faith and Magawisca, Hope is ultimately aligned not with the unplumbed forests of the frontier but with civilization and enlightened progress.

One of the most compelling characters in *Hope Leslie* is **Magawisca,** who is, according to critic Mary Kelley, "the only Indian woman in early American literature invested with substance and strength." Articulate, strong, and loyal, Magawisca parallels Hope in her conscientious thought and behavior. Like some of the native American characters created by Sedgwick's contemporary, James Fennimore Cooper, Magawisca is inherently good and noble. As virtuous and intelligent as any of the novel's white characters, she serves as an effective foil to the intolerance and hypocrisy of the Puritans. Magawisca's courage is demonstrated when she sacrifices her own arm and nearly loses her life to save Everell from execution. Sedgwick interprets history differently than that traditionally accepted by white Americans when she recounts the massacre of Magawisca's tribe by Puritan colonists. Described in Puritan accounts as a righteous victory over brutal savages, Magawisca portrays it as a slaughter of innocent women and children. She assumes a proud, defiant stance at her trial, denying that whites have any authority to rule over her people, thus allowing Sedgwick to introduce the question of native American dispossession. Puritan and other early settlers viewed Indians as godless, but Sedgwick shows Magawisca practicing a pantheistic religion based on reverence for the Great Spirit, whose presence is manifested in the physical world. Magawisca and Hope feel trust and kinship with one another, but Magawisca is essentially identified with the wilderness and in the end retreats into the western forest. Other Indian characters in *Hope Leslie* include Magawisca's father, **Mononotto,** a basically peaceloving chief driven to avenging the massacre of his people; her brother, **Oneco,** whose successful marriage to the white Faith Leslie is used to explore the possibility of union between two disparate cultures; and **Nelema,** who saves Master Cradock's life with a native American cure and is then charged with witchcraft.

Two significant female characters contrast strongly with the rebellious Hope. **Margaret Winthrop,** the wife of Massachusetts governor John Winthrop, is the colony's most respected woman, yet Sedgwick compares her to "a horse easy on the bit" for her unqualified obedience to her husband. A straitlaced model of Puritan womanhood, Margaret is charged with teaching Hope the passivity and compliance with authority that the magistrates have found sorely lacking in her defiant behavior. Assisting Margaret is her niece, **Esther Downing,** a humane, sensitive, and generous young woman portrayed as virtuous but meek and dutiful. She chastises Hope for assuming "too much liberty" and for disobeying the Puritan fathers who hold sway over her own life. When Everell, with whom she is in love, asks her to help him rescue the unfairly imprisoned Magawisca, Esther refuses, claiming that her religion sanctions no subversion of law. Unlike Hope, Esther is incapable of questioning or breaking the Puritan code.

William Fletcher introduces the novel's theme of religious intolerance when a dispute with his uncle forces him to abandon his plans to marry Alice (who later becomes Hope's mother). After he immigrates to America, he discovers with dismay the hypocrisy of the Puritans, who discriminate against those of other faiths despite their own history of experiencing religious persecution. His wife, **Martha Fletcher,** is brutally murdered by Indians, thus depicting native American vengeance balancing the massacre of the Pequods. **Everell Fletcher,** William's son, is a somewhat flat character who, according to some critics, hardly seems to merit the regard of the three women (Hope, Esther, and Magawisca) who fall in love with him. In the end Esther's "slavish obedience" to the letter of the law disappoints him, and he asks Hope to help Magawisca escape.

Hope's sister, **Faith Leslie,** is as passive and modest as Hope is rebellious and forthright. Captured by the Pequods, she is gradually absorbed into the tribe until little is left of her original culture, and she remains permanently with her Indian husband and community. Her union with the devoted Oneco comprises an unusual example of miscegenation (inter-racial marriage) for the nineteenth century, for it is allowed to succeed whereas other such fictional relationships, like that of Cora Munro and Uncas in Cooper's *Last of the Mohicans,* are doomed.

Historically based characters in *Hope Leslie* include **John Winthrop,** who really was the governor of colonial Massachusetts; **Judge Pynchon,** who was among the founders of Springfield, Massachusetts; and **Sir Philip Gardiner** (modeled after Sir Christopher Gardiner), a villainous aristocrat who not only tries to seduce Hope but attempts to deliver the colony into the hands of his Catholic patron. The novel's minor figures include the comical, fashion-obsessed **Aunt Grafton,** who opposes Hope's move to the frontier because it would be "unheard of in England;" **Master Cradock,** Hope's teacher, who nearly dies of a rattlesnake bite before being saved by Nelema, and who participates—albeit reluctantly—in the rescue of Magawisca; and **Jennett,** the bigoted servant who expresses the conventional view of native Americans as "children and heirs of the evil one."

Further Reading

Bell, Michael Davitt. "History and Romance Convention in Catharine Sedgwick's 'Hope Leslie.'" *American Quarterly* XXII, No. 2 (September 1970): 213-21.

Foster, Edward Halsey. *Catharine Maria Sedgwick.* Boston: Twayne, 1974.

Kelley, Mary. Introduction to *Hope Leslie; or, Early Times in the Massachusetts* by Catharine Maria Sedgwick. New Brunswick, N.J.: Rutgers University Press, 1987.

Martineau, Harriet. "Miss Sedgwick's Works." *London and Westminster Review* VI, No. 1 (October 1837 to January 1838): 42-65.

Nineteenth-Century Literature Criticism, Vol. 19. Detroit: Gale.

Review of "Hope Leslie; or, Early Times in the Massachusetts." *Western Monthly Review* 1, No. 5 (September 1827): 289-95.

Welsh, Sister Mary Michael, O. P. *Catharine Maria Sedgwick: Her Position in the Literature and Thought of Her Time Up to 1860.* Washington, D. C.: Catholic University Press, 1937.

Mary Wollstonecraft Godwin Shelley
1797-1851
English novelist.

Frankenstein; or, The New Prometheus (novel, 1818)

Plot: The story is told through the letters of an English explorer, Robert Walton, whose ship becomes icebound in the arctic north. Walton and his crew have seen a northbound dogsled driven by a huge, misshapen man, and later they encounter another wanderer through the ice fields—Victor Frankenstein, who relates his tale to Walton. Born in Geneva and educated at the University of Ingolstadt, Frankenstein was a brilliant student whose research led him to the discovery of an elixir for creating life. Envisioning the genesis of an enlightened, happier new species, he had constructed a man from body parts gathered from graves, butcher shops, and dissecting rooms. On completing his task, however, Frankenstein had misgivings and fled in terror from his gruesome, eight-foot-tall creation.

Later, Frankenstein's young brother William was murdered; the family's servant Justine Moritz was convicted of the crime and condemned to death. Depressed and aware that his monster was probably the real perpetrator, Frankenstein hiked into the Alps, where he encountered his creation. The monster told him that after Frankenstein's departure he had wandered, a vision of terror to all he met, until finally seeking shelter in a dingy hovel attached to a cottage. In secret, the monster had labored to understand the ways of man through observation and reading, but his eventual attempt to befriend the cottage dwellers was cruelly repulsed. He grew to bitterly hate humanity. When he had come upon William playing in a park, the monster had strangled him. Now he vowed to kill again unless Frankenstein constructed a mate for him; he promised to take her into exile deep in the South American jungle. Frankenstein reluctantly agreed, but after beginning his work decided he could not continue with the horrible task. Enraged, the monster vowed revenge; he consequently murdered both Frankenstein's best friend, Henry Clerval, and his bride Elizabeth. Determined to destroy the monster, Frankenstein has chased it across Europe to the arctic. After telling Walton the story, Frankenstein dies. The monster appears in the ship's cabin, declaring that Frankenstein has brought on his own punishment by creating a man forced to exist without love or friendship. Finally, the monster leaps out of the window onto an ice floe and disappears.

Characters: Shelley's novel has made a permanent impression on both the literary and the popular imagination. Through its most vividly portrayed character, the grotesque monster created by Victor Frankenstein, the novel blends qualities of the Gothic horror story popular in the late eighteenth and early nineteenth centuries with elements of the science fiction genre that would develop more fully in the late nineteenth and early twentieth centuries.

Frankenstein's monster is considered Shelley's most successful characterization, embodying several important aspects of the romantic tradition espoused by Shelley's husband, the poet Percy Bysshe Shelley, and his contemporaries. The initially gentle and intelligent nature of the creature, who longs for companionship and who schools himself in the writings of Plutarch and Milton, is warped by humanity's cruelty. His progression from innocence to destructiveness reflects the romantic notion of the Noble Savage—the innocent societal outsider who is tarnished by the world's harsh treatment. The monster's alienation, isolation, and eventual rebellion also corresponds to the romantic concept of the Self, which involves the struggle of individual consciousness against an insensitive universe. The monster is often described as Frankenstein's doppelganger or double, representing the uncontrolled, brutal side of human nature and internal conflicts between good and evil, thought and feeling. Several critics have noted that the common mistake of calling the monster by his creator's name is in one sense no mistake at all, for he is Victor's other self. The monster also serves as a reminder of the potential dangers of scientific inquiry—a theme that became even more compelling with the technological advances of the twentieth century. But perhaps Shelley's monster's most memorable quality is his deep humanity. Critic Harold Bloom has written that Shelley's achievement was making the monster even "more human" than his creator. In recounting to Walton the course of events that led to such horror, the monster says, "Everywhere I see bliss, from which I alone am excluded. I was benevolent and good; misery made me a fiend."

Victor Frankenstein has often been described as a Promethean figure, evoking the character in Greek mythology whose attempt to gain power over the gods brought him a horrible and perpetual punishment. Frankenstein has also been compared to Faust, the legendary character found in various works of literature whose overambitiousness leads to his downfall. Frankenstein displays qualities of the romantic sensibility in that he rebels against society's strictures in daring to create his monster, resulting in his isolation from humanity and his subsequent conflicted state. Realizing his mistake, Frankenstein is unable to act decisively to destroy his creation, and thus flees from it. Some critics have seen Frankenstein's failure to take responsibility for his creation as his true tragedy.

The English explorer **Robert Walton** might be described as playing a practical, storytelling role; his presence in the arctic provides a reasonable excuse for staging the opening and conclusion in that dramatic setting. But Walton also serves as an interesting counterpart to Frankenstein, for he too is on a Faustian voyage of ambition as he attempts to reach an undiscovered land, and to the Frankenstein monster, in his loneliness.

Frankenstein's friend **Henry Clerval,** devoted to "books of chivalry and romance" rather than science, provides a contrast to Frankenstein, and Shelley suggests that the balance of temperaments and interests between the two men made for an ideal relationship. Like Clerval, Frankenstein's murdered brother **William,** and the falsely accused and executed **Justine Moritz,** Frankenstein's bride **Elizabeth** is an innocent victim of the monster's rage. Elizabeth has been said to represent an ideal of domestic purity that is destroyed by the evil hidden in humankind; after the execution of Justine, Elizabeth laments that "men appear to me as monsters thirsting for each other's blood."

Further Reading

Bennett, Betty T., and Charles E. Robinson. *Mary Shelley Reader.* New York: Oxford University Press, 1990.

Bloom, Harold. "'Frankenstein; or, The New Prometheus.'" *Partisan Review* XXXII, No. 4 (Fall 1965): 611-18.

Dictionary of Literary Biography, Vol. 110. Detroit: Gale.

Gilbert, Sandra M., and Susan Gubar. "Horror's Twin: Mary Shelley's Monstrous Eye." In *The Madwoman in the Attic: The Woman Writer and the Nineteenth-Century Literary Imagination,* pp. 213-47. New Haven: Yale University Press, 1979.

Mellor, Anne Kostel. *Mary Shelley: Her Life, Her Fiction, Her Monsters.* New York and London: Routledge, 1988.

Nineteenth Century Literature Criticism, Vol. 14. Detroit: Gale.

Spark, Muriel. *Mary Shelley.* New York: Dutton, 1987.

Sunstein, Emily W. *Mary Shelley: Romance and Reality.* Boston: Little, Brown, 1989.

Madame de Staël
1766-1817
French novelist, playwright, critic, and historian.

Delphine (novel, 1802)

Plot: Narrated in epistolary (letter) form, the novel centers on Delphine d'Albemarle, the widow of a wealthy, much older man. Monsieur d'Albemarle was her tutor during her childhood and had given her a liberal education; consequently she resists both societal and religious convention and supports democratic political reform. Delphine decides to give a generous portion of her fortune to her cousin Mathilde de Vernon, whose mother is her close friend, so that the young girl can marry the aristocratic Léonce de Mondeville. When Delphine meets the handsome, charming Léonce, she falls in love with him; likewise, Léonce develops a passion for Delphine rather than Mathilde. Meanwhile, Delphine's friend Thérèse d'Ervin, who is married to an elderly and extremely jealous man, is having an affair with Monsieur de Serballane. The sympathetic Delphine allows the lovers to meet in her home, then is herself suspected of sexual impropriety when Serballane is seen entering and leaving her house. When d'Ervin discovers his wife and her lover together, he challenges Serballane to a duel; Monsieur d'Ervin is killed. Delphine continues to protect her friend, even though her reputation suffers. Madame de Vernon, determined to bring about her daughter's marriage to Léonce at any cost, lies to Delphine, promising her that she will inform Léonce of Delphine's innocence. Instead, Madame de Vernon tells Léonce that Delphine is involved with Serballane. Ever sensitive to personal honor and public opinion, Léonce agrees to marry Mathilde. At their wedding, a heartbroken Delphine watches from the shadows.

Léonce eventually discovers that Madame de Vernon has deceived him. He and Delphine continue their relationship, but, primarily due to Delphine's fortitude, it remains platonic despite their passionate love. Finally, the now-pregnant Mathilde learns the truth about Delphine and Léonce, and she begs Delphine to leave. Thus Delphine goes to a Swiss convent run by Léonce's aunt, where she feels desperately lonely and hopeless, and is pressured to become a nun. Monsieur de Valorbe, a friend of Delphine's dead husband who had previously tried to win her hand, arrives in Switzerland intending to marry Delphine. He involves her in further scandal, requiring Delphine to take religious vows to clear her name. She soon hears that Mathilde and her baby have died, leaving Léonce free to marry. Léonce's friend, Monsieur Lebensei, tells him not to despair because the French Revolution has abolished the irrevocability of religious vows. Léonce and Delphine subsequently meet again in Germany, but Léonce cannot bear the certainty of public dishonor. He joins the royalist forces fighting the army of the French republican government and is captured and sentenced to death. After an unsuccessful attempt to obtain a pardon for Léonce, Delphine takes poison and dies on the spot on which he is to be executed. Taking pity on Léonce, the soldiers refuse to shoot him, forcing Léonce into taunting them until they kill him. (Note: In a second ending de Staël wrote several years later, the lovers go to Léonce's estate to live but, after realizing that their love cannot withstand the public hostility it generates, Delphine becomes ill and dies, and Léonce joins the army and is killed in battle.)

Characters: More significant as a record of intellectual history than as a literary work, *Delphine* reflects many of the beliefs advocated by Madame de Staël (Anna Louise Germaine Necker) and others of her circle, including a need for broader education for women, political equality, and freedom of religion. Most critics find the novel's style plodding and overly sentimental, claiming that its epistolary form is unsuccessful in conveying such a complex plot. Yet its central theme—the primacy of love and the apparent impossibility of realizing it under the social strictures of the time—typifies the concerns of the emerging romantic period, and the book's social criticism anticipates the fiction of the later nineteenth century.

Through the novel's title character, de Staël illustrates its epigraph: "A man must be able to brave opinion, a woman to submit to it." **Delphine d'Albemarle** is frequently identified as a reflection of de Staël's younger self, a highly intelligent and emotional woman often in conflict with society. Delphine is depicted as a quintessentially superior being: warm, charming, generous, and spirited, she combines deep feelings with a rigorous intellect and physical beauty. Though unconventional, Delphine is spotlessly virtuous, self-controlled, and self-sacrificing. In fact, De Staël has been faulted for idealizing her tragic heroine, whose emotions strike many readers and scholars as overblown and whose motives seem too pure for real life. Educated by the man who would eventually become her husband, Delphine is indoctrinated with his enlightened, liberal views. Consequently, she resists the social, political, and religious convention and dogma that dominate her late-eighteenth-century world. She voices many of the ideas that were precious to her mentor, such as the injustice of her country's divorce laws, which bound unhappy women in marriages to inappropriate husbands (at the time of the book's publication, Napoleon had just signed an agreement with the Pope making these laws even more stringent), and the difficulty of overcoming one's feelings through reason and self-sacrifice. Delphine's intense passion for Léonce typifies the romantic view of love as central to a person's being and happiness; when denied this love, both Delphine and Léonce perish. Independent and wealthy, Delphine is initially able, to some extent at least, to maintain her rebellious stance—such as when she allows her unhappily married friend a place to meet her lover. Delphine's willingness to sacrifice her own good for those she loves is illustrated not only in her silent submission to having her own reputation tarnished for Madame d'Ervin's sake but, most vividly, in her refusal to bring dishonor to Léonce by marrying him. Denied the happiness of marriage and family, Delphine finds some redemption in self-sacrifice, but her end is still tragic. Despite her inherent superiority, Delphine is ultimately unable to escape the binds of her rigid society; though unconventional, she cannot live outside convention. Thus Delphine embodies the stifling restriction of women's roles in the early nineteenth century and reflects a spirit of independence and passion that is, in the end, insufficient to overcome its obstacles.

Léonce Mondeville is the half-Spanish, half-French aristocrat whom Delphine loves and with whom she is tragically unable to achieve happiness. Handsome, charming, and impeccably honorable, Léonce has been seen as an overly idealized character whose virtues are listed but never demonstrated, leaving readers wondering why he was worth Delphine's extravagant sacrifice. Léonce's only fault is his excessive regard for public opinion; in his refusal to tarnish his own honor he becomes the means by which society punishes Delphine for her transgressions. Léonce's insistence that the soldiers kill him after Delphine has taken poison and died before him suggests the depth of his love and his despair. The second ending, in which Delphine dies of illness and Léonce is killed in battle, reflects de Staël's decision not to sanction the suicidal behavior that was becoming a hallmark—and, some said, a fault—of romantic literature.

Madame de Vernon is the villain of *Delphine*. Treacherous and conniving, she pretends to be Delphine's friend while plotting to keep Delphine and Léonce apart so that her own daughter may marry the wealthy nobleman. Her ambitions for herself and Mathilde have overshadowed all moral considerations, thus placing her in strong contrast with the virtuous Delphine. The beautiful **Mathilde de Vernon,** who does marry Léonce and dies after bearing his child, is virtuous and proper, serving as a representative of convention in her meek conformity to the role assigned her. Mathilde's failure to sense the strong current of feeling between her husband and Delphine has been seen as somewhat implausible. **Madame Thérèse d'Ervin** suffers from a plight that de Staël considered unjust: she is irrevocably married to a much older man with whom she is unhappy. The sympathetic Delphine sacrifices her own reputation to help her friend, but Thérèse does not repay her friend in kind. Hypocritically conventional, she lies to Léonce, confirming Madame de Vernon's accusation that Delphine has been having an affair with Serballane. Thérèse's bleak fate—she finally enters a convent—is not much preferable to Delphine's and further illustrates the limited scope of choices available to nineteenth-century women, especially those who became involved in scandals.

Delphine's dilemma is aggravated by **Monsieur de Valorbe,** a friend of her dead husband, who is determined to marry her. He allows his passion to overcome his reason, involving Delphine—whom he proposes to help by marrying and thus legitimizing her—in further scandal. Léonce's liberal, educated friend, **Monsieur Lebensei,** voices de Staël's own religious view, asserting that Protestantism is closer to the true spirit of the Gospels than Catholicism. Unlike Léonce, Lebensei is not tragically bound by public opinion, for he has married a divorced woman and scorns society's disapproval of his situation. Other characters in *Delphine* include **Monsieur de Serballane,** Thérèse's lover, who kills her husband in a duel; and **Mademoiselle d'Albemarle,** the sister of Delphine's dead husband, who warns her about Madame de Vernon's treachery.

Further Reading

Andrews, Wayne. *Germaine: A Portrait of Madame de Staël.* New York; Atheneum, 1963.

Goldsmith, Margaret. *Madame de Staël: Portrait of a Liberal in the Revolutionary Age.* London: Longmans, Green, 1938.

Nineteenth-Century Literature Criticism, Vol. 3. Detroit: Gale.

Posgate, Helen B. *Madame de Staël.* New York: Twayne, 1968.

Saintsbury, George. "Madame de Staël and Chateaubriand." In *A History of the French Novel (to the Close of the 19th Century): From 1800 to 1900,* Vol. II, pp. 1-38. 1917. Reprint. Russell & Russell, 1964.

Smith, Sydney. "Madame de Staël's 'Delphine.'" *Edinburgh Review* II, No. 111 (April 1803): 172-77.

Todd, Janet. "Political Friendship." In *Women's Friendship in Literature*, pp. 191-245. New York: Columbia University Press, 1980.

Weingarten, Renee. *Madame de Stael.* Providence, R.I.: Berg Publications, 1987.

Stendhal
1783-1842

French novelist, novella writer, autobiographer, travel writer, essayist, and critic.

The Red and the Black (*Le rouge et le noir;* novel, 1830)

Plot: The novel takes place in France during the first quarter of the nineteenth century. Julien Sorel, the son of a sawmill owner, is an intelligent, ambitious young man who idolizes Napoleon and feels contemptuous of his provincial home town, Verrières, and his working-class roots. With the help of a kind parish priest, Abbé Chelan, Julien is appointed tutor in the household of Monsieur de Rénal, the town's mayor. Virtuous, inexperienced Madame de Rénal soon falls in love with the handsome Julien, who begins an affair with her out of a sense of duty to himself but eventually comes to sincerely love her. Julien's friend Fouqué encourages him to join him in establishing a timber business, but Julien declines to pursue such a commonplace fate. His love affair with Madame de Rénal, meanwhile, is threatened when Monsieur Valenod, the director of the local poorhouse, who has himself unsuccessfully tried to seduce Madame de Rénal and is jealous of Julien, sends her husband an anonymous letter, informing him that his wife is involved with the family's tutor. The lovers manage to placate Monsieur de Rénal, but Julien is sent away. He enters a seminary to seek distinction and advancement in the church. He finds the seminary unpleasant, however, due to the hypocrisy and meanness of his fellow students, though he befriends Abbé Pirard, whose highly moral views have made him unpopular with the seminary officials. Meanwhile Madame de Rénal has repented her sinful liaison with Julien and become intensely religious; when she happens to encounter him in a church, however, she faints.

After Abbé Piraud is dismissed from the seminary, the Marquis de La Mole—who owes the priest a favor—finds him a new position in Paris and also hires Julien as his secretary. On his way to Paris to begin his new post, Julien stops to visit Madame de Rénal, who initially resists his advances but finally agrees to sleep with him. Julien is nearly discovered in her room by her husband but escapes safely. He quickly impresses the marquis with his intelligence and efficiency and becomes almost more a companion than an employee. Though intrigued by the marquis's brilliant, haughty daughter, Mathilde, Julien finds her aristocratic hangers-on pretentious and boring. Julien and Mathilde begin to spend much of their time together and, despite her snobbery, Mathilde falls in love with the lower-class young man. She yields to Julien's sexual advances but then decides he is too lowly a suitor for her; angry at this snub, Julien decides to try to gain power over her. He starts to court a pious woman who often visits the household, and Mathilde becomes jealous and desperate for his attention, finally throwing herself at him. After some time Mathilde becomes pregnant, a circumstance she greets with joy because she believes Julien will now have to marry her. Although initially furious, the marquis does eventually agree to the marriage and confers upon Julien a title and an army commission. Though indifferent to Mathilde, Julien is delighted with his new prosperity. When the marquis makes inquiries into his future son-in-law's character, however, he receives a letter from Madame de Rénal describing Julien as a shameless, cruel opportunist whose method is to seduce the most influential female in a household in order to achieve his own aims. The marquis withdraws his approval of the marriage, and Julien reacts to this disappointment by traveling to Verrières and shooting Madame de Rénal while she is kneeling in a church. Although she does not die of her wounds, Julien is condemned to die for his crime. His friends frantically attempt to help him but he will do nothing to save his own life, apparently preferring to die. A contrite and again passionate Madame de Rénal visits him in his prison cell and the two reaffirm their love, but he still refuses to appeal his sentence, and she returns to her husband. Julien is annoyed by Mathilde's attempts to change his mind. He faces his death with serenity, and his old friend Fouqué is given his body to bury. The highly romantic Mathilde buries her former lover's head with her own hands, just as had been done for one of her ancestors by the woman who loved him. Devastated by Julien's death, Madame de Rénal herself dies three days later.

Characters: One of the most acclaimed novels of nineteenth-century literature, *The Red and the Black* provides a scathing indictment of the social confusion and hypocrisy of early nineteenth-century French society. Working to some extent within the romantic tradition, Stendhal infused his work with the social and philosophical implications and psychological insight that would characterize the fiction of the modern period. Written in a polished, spare narrative style, the novel features a protagonist whose intensity and capacity for self-examination mirrors his creator's; indeed many critics have noted the autobiographical aspects of Stendhal's works.

Acclaimed as one of the most compelling characters in French literature, the enigmatic **Julien Sorel** is considered the ultimate egotist due to his consuming ambition and preoccupation with himself. Born into a working-class family, the frail, intellectual young man feels only contempt for his vulgar father and provincial hometown. He longs for escape and dreams of achieving greatness like that of his hero, the French emperor Napoleon Bonaparte. During the years of the French Revolution, a young man like Julien would most certainly have tried to realize his goals through military service—the ''red'' of the novel's title refers to the color of the French soldier's uniform jacket—but in the Reformation period of the early nineteenth century, the church (or the ''black'') was considered the best route to success. Accordingly the handsome, intelligent, charming, and highly ambitious Julien decides to beat his hypocritical society at its own game by seeking personal advancement through hypocrisy. Despite his true atheism, he manages to memorize a prodigious portion of the Scriptures, thus affecting a deep piety that impresses kind Abbé Chelan. Soon after his arrival in the Rénal household, where he is to serve as tutor, he realizes that his employer's wife is attracted to him. Adopting the vocabulary of the military realm he might have entered, Julien goes about conquering Madame de Rénal as if she were a fortress. He does so primarily out of opportunism, his ''duty'' to advance himself in the world, but the affair helps to educate him about love, sex, and his power over women. After barely escaping detection by Monsieur de Rénal, Julien enters the seminary, which disheartens him with its ugly appearance and oppressive atmosphere. During this period, however, Julien befriends another priest, Abbé Pirard, who ultimately acquires for him a position as secretary to the Marquis de La Mole. Introduced into Parisian aristocracy, Julien makes the best of his situation by gaining the trust and admiration of his employer. He attracts the attention of Mathilde de La Mole through his haughty silence in the presence of her foppish friends; she finds him enigmatic and is excited by the prospect of a love affair with a member of the working class. Though generally contemptuous of Mathilde and her circle, Julien enjoys wielding power over his lover, and their liaison eventually brings him to the brink of the success he yearns for. After Madame de Rénal scuttles his prospects with an accusatory letter, Julien sets off for Verriére, where he performs the violent act that leads to his own destruction. The rationale behind this murder attempt and Julien's subsequent refusal to save himself from execution has led to much critical debate. Some commentators contend that Julien is motivated by rage, that his passionate anger simply overcomes his ambition or even that he experiences a kind of psychopathic breakdown. Others, however, see the act as Julien's ultimate expression of egotism—as the only way he can practice the self-determination promised by the revolution, a means of dramatically establishing his own, individual greatness. It has also been suggested that Julien sensed that the fate he was on the verge of acquiring (the rift with Mathilde's father, some maintain, could surely have been smoothed over) did not fit his true nature or yearnings and that he sought escape. As Julien awaits his death in his cell at the top of the prison tower, he achieves a notable serenity, reliving the events of the past and even making a last connection with Madame de Rénal, who finally emerges as the true love of his life. Julien's character was based on an actual person, a seminary student and tutor named Antoine Berthet who was executed for murdering his mistress, the wife of his first employer. Critics more often note, however, the similarities between Stendhal and his most famous creation: both demonstrate an aversion to their fathers, a distaste for both provincialism and aristocratic hypocrisy, an enjoyment of amorous intrigue, and a preoccupation with the military. Stendhal, however, turned his own considerable energy and self-examining power to imaginative purposes.

The Red and the Black features two of the most memorable female characters in French fiction. The first of these is **Madame de Rénal,** the beautiful, compassionate, dutiful wife of a provincial mayor. The devoted mother of three children, she has always been faithful to her disagreeable husband despite her lack of love for him. The strong feelings aroused by Julien thus come as a complete surprise to Madame de Rénal. Her confession that she feels for the handsome young tutor the love and obedience that she should rightly give only to God evidences the conflict between piety and passion that will continue to torment her. Madame de Rénal is portrayed as a superior individual trapped among vulgar provincial who are ill-equipped to comprehend the depth of her delicacy, generosity, or sensitivity. Even she herself does not realize her true capacities. Her inexperience makes her vulnerable to the lure of Julien's love, but her lack of self-confidence later causes her to reject it, and she again submits to the rule of the husband and priests who control her. In fact, she writes her accusatory letter to the Marquis de La Mole, denouncing Julien despite her lingering love for him, while under the direction of a priest. In the end Madame de Rénal is tragically destroyed by the conflicting forces of religious fervor and human passion that exist within her; she dies while stretching out her arms to her children, who have been her constant concern throughout her difficulties. An interesting character in her own right, Madame de Rénal also serves the practical purpose of educating Julien about worldly matters and even furthering his position in society when she gives him a much-coveted position in a special honor guard organized for the town's reception of a visiting king. Madame de Rénal may be considered a foil to Mathilde: while the latter is proud, sophisticated, and reserved, the former is humble, adoring, modest, deeply religious, warm, and even somewhat maternal in her love for Julien.

Proud, intelligent **Mathilde de La Mole** is a representative of the conservative aristocratic realm Julien enters after leaving the seminary. Somewhat caustic, willful, and haughty, Mathilde is constantly surrounded by jaded Parisian fops who raise Julien's ire with their pretensions. Though convinced of her own superiority, Mathilde is drawn to the lower-class but enigmatic Julien partly by their shared intellectual interests; both, for instance, admire Voltaire. Their first sexual encounter is the result of an impetuous moment on Mathilde's part, when Julien seems an unconventional distraction, and she subsequently rejects him. The ambitious Julien, however, sets out to re-ignite her ardor by flirting with another woman. This ploy is successful, but eventually Julien feels bored with his lover's fervent solicitude. Mathilde is overjoyed to learn she is pregnant because she feels it will bind Julien to her permanently, and her plans seem likely to be fulfilled until her father receives the letter from Madame de Rénal. During Julien's imprisonment after he has shot his former mistress, Mathilde makes several frantic attempts to free him, but he has no wish to escape his fate and, moreover, is unspeakably bored by her ardent attentions. After Julien's execution, Mathilde demonstrates her romantic impulses when, in imitation of a family legend, she buries her lover's head with her own hands. It is generally thought that Stendhal modeled Mathilde after an actual acquaintance who shared the same first name: Méthilde Dembowski, whom he met in Italy in 1818 and who remained impervious to his advances. As critics have noted, he was able through Julien to conquer the fictional Mathilde, whereas he had been unable to conquer the real one.

As the mayor of a provincial town and the boorish husband of Julien's first lover, **Monsieur de Rénal** is a particularly effective representative of the status-seeking French bourgeoisie. Vulgar and greedy, he is an inappropriate partner for the delicate, sensitive Madame de Rénal, whose attraction to the handsome tutor is thus made more understandable. Monsieur de Rénal's reaction to the news of his wife's infidelity typifies his hypocrisy and small-mindedness: while he would like to make a conventionally masculine expression of vengeance, he fears the ridicule that a public scandal might bring, and he also dreads the loss of his wife's money if they are divorced. Stendhal is thought to have modeled Monsieur de Rénal after his own father, whose ambition and provinciality the author scorned.

Mathilde's father and Julien's second employer, the **Marquis de La Mole,** is a wealthy, gout-ridden aristocrat whose subtlety and educated demeanor mark him as superior to such social climbers as Monsieur de Rénal. He senses Julien's abilities and appreciates his attentions, but in the end his loyalty for his daughter and his own pride take precedence. Despite the fact that Julien is an intelligent, capable young man, the marquis is unwilling to wed his pregnant daughter to a reputed seducer and opportunist. Some critics, however, suggest that the marquis's objection to the match might have been overcome eventually if Julien had not committed his violent act of vengeance.

An important person in Julien's early life is **Abbé Chelan,** the honest local parish priest, who educates Julien and, despite his knowledge of the young man's shortcomings, helps him to advance in the world by securing him a position in the Rénal household. **Abbé Piraud** is also Julien's ally—his only friend, in fact, within the hostile confines of the seminary. Piraud is an irascible but learned, highly moral priest whose Jansenism (a religious doctrine declared heretical by the Pope) makes him unpopular with the seminary's Jesuit officials. (Due to an unpleasant experience with a childhood tutor, Stendhal was vehemently opposed to the Jesuit philosophy.) He recognizes Julien's talent and aids him by making him a tutor and securing him a private room; later, after his own dismissal from the seminary, Piraud's connection with the marquis results in Julien's entrance into Parisian aristocracy.

Other significant minor characters in *The Red and the Black* include Julien's devoted friend, **Fouqué,** who offers him an alternative to the ambitious course that Julien pursues when he suggests that the two go into business together; Fouqué is among those who try unsuccessfully to free Julien from prison. Supposedly modeled after a real person, **Monsieur Valenod** is the corrupt director of the Verriéres poorhouse. Having unsuccessfully attempted to seduce Madame de Rénal himself, he is jealous of Julien and retaliates by sending Monsieur de Rénal an anonymous letter exposing the affair. Valenod succeeds Rénal as the town's mayor. **Count Altamira,** whom Julien meets while employed by the marquis, is a Spanish conspirator in exile from his own country. He briefly inspires Julien to ponder the idea of political activism; unlike Julien, his goals are tangible and selfless, and he has real knowledge of the brutality and killing that Julien tends to glorify.

The Charterhouse of Parma *(La chartreuse de Parme;* novel, 1839)

Plot: Set in early nineteenth-century Italy, the novel centers on Fabrizio del Dongo, the son of a wealthy but miserly marquis. During his childhood Fabrizio often visits his beloved, widowed aunt, Gina Pietranera, who lives in Milan. Although his father detests Napoleon, Fabrizio idolizes the renowned French emperor. At seventeen he leaves home and travels toward Paris disguised as a barometer salesman, determined to join Napoleon's army. While trailing after a French battalion, Fabrizio's ardently professed enthusiasm for Napoleon and his Italian accent cause him to be mistaken for a spy and thrown in prison. Finally the jailer's wife helps him escape, and he travels toward Belgium, where troops are massing. Fabrizio accidentally becomes involved in the battle of Waterloo, although in the confusion of combat he is unsure where he is or what is happening. Back in Italy, meanwhile, Gina has become the mistress of Count Mosca, the kind but cynical prime minister of the state of Parma. The count arranges for Gina to make a marriage of convenience to the Duke of Sansévérina, after which the now financially secure duchess remains Mosca's lover while the duke leaves the country. When Fabrizio returns to his home, he is arrested for using a false passport. His aunt is allowed to transport him in her carriage to Milan, where he is to be imprisoned. On the way there, the party encounters an old man, General Conti, who has also been arrested but forced to walk; Gina invites the general and his pensive daughter, Clélia, to ride in the carriage. Fabrizio is soon released from prison and accompanies Gina, who is growing increasingly fond of her handsome nephew, to Parma. Mosca advises Gina to send Fabrizio to a theological seminary for three years, after which period he will be given an official position.

During his years as a theological student, Fabrizio indulges in many amorous affairs. Suave and worldly, he returns to Parma and is made an alternate for the archbishop. He soon becomes interested in a pretty actress named Marietta Valsera, whose jealous lover he kills during a scuffle. To escape prosecution for the crime, Fabrizio flees to Bologna and, financed by Gina, sets up housekeeping with Marietta. Due to the treachery of several court officials, the prince of Parma is persuaded to try the absent Fabrizio for murder; he is convicted and sentenced to death or hard labor. Meanwhile, in Bologna, Fabrizio has become bored with Marietta and infatuated instead with an opera singer, Fausta, and he follows her back to Parma. He is soon captured and imprisoned. Fabrizio again sees Clélia, whose father is now the director of the jail, and falls in love her. He is perfectly happy to remain in captivity, communicating with his beloved through his window with a system of alphabet cards. Gina, however, is plotting her nephew's escape. She elicits the help of a revolutionary poet named Ferrante, who smuggles in ropes by which Fabrizio escapes from his tower cell. Then Ferrante, following Gina's instructions, assassinates the prince who condemned Fabrizio. Gina and Fabrizio return to Parma, where a new prince has assumed rule, and the now reformed, chaste Fabrizio is eventually made archbishop. He becomes famous for his inspiring sermons. Clélia, meanwhile, has complied with her father's demand that she marry a marquis; in addition, she has made a vow to the Virgin Mary that she will never see Fabrizio again. After hearing him preach, however, Clélia finds herself irresistibly drawn to Fabrizio and the two become lovers. Clélia eventually gives birth to a son fathered by Fabrizio, who kidnaps the baby, named Sandrino, and takes it to his own house. The child dies, and Clélia soon shares the same fate. Devastated by the loss of his lover and child, Fabrizio retires to the Charterhouse of Parma, a monastery, and spends his remaining days in seclusion.

Characters: *The Charterhouse of Parma* and *The Red and the Black,* are Stendhal's two best-known works. The novel provides a panoramic view of Stendhal's beloved Italy in the nineteenth century, featuring both a satirical depiction of political intrigue and compelling characters portrayed with remarkable psychological insight. Distinguished by its ironic tone, *The Charterhouse of Parma* combines adventure, history, and romance, with a special emphasis on the pursuit of love.

Fabrizio del Dongo is a handsome young aristocrat with an eager, romantic spirit. In defiance of his despotic father (he later learns that his real father was a French officer), Fabrizio leaves his dull, provincial town and travels toward France in the hope of joining the army led by his hero, Napoleon. His over ardent enthusiasm for the emperor and his Italian accent lead to his enduring the first of several imprisonments. After his escape he wanders into the great battle of Waterloo, at which the French were routed by the English. Stendhal is often lauded for his highly effective, impressionistic rendering of combat as seen through the eyes of a realistically uncomprehending foot soldier. Fabrizio's youth and naiveté stand out in sharp contrast against a bewildering background of brutality and death. Returning home, Fabrizio is sent by his devoted Aunt Gina to the seminary, during which period he learns through numerous romantic liaisons not piety but worldliness and sensual pleasure. Most women seem to find the handsome, charming Fabrizio irresistible, and he emerges from his three years of study a much more suave and worldly man.

Like Julien Sorel, the protagonist of *The Red and the Black,* Fabrizio accommodates himself to circumstances in order to advance himself, but he is neither as ambitious nor as hypocritical as Julien—nor is he an atheist, even if his beliefs are vague. After returning to Gina's circle, Fabrizio soon perceives that her love for him extends beyond that an aunt normally has for a nephew, yet he knows that she herself is unaware of or unwilling to face her true feelings. Because he feels only gratitude and affection for Gina, Fabrizio worries about the outcome of her emotions and also fears that his own heart is empty, that he is incapable of real love. As a result of his casual affair with Marietta, Fabrizio scuffles with and kills her lover. When he is eventually jailed for murder—the charges inflated by unfriendly forces at court—Fabrizio again encounters the lovely, pensive Clélia, whom he had met earlier but taken little note of. The two young people establish a romance that is initially entirely cerebral, carried on through alphabet signs that each displays at his or her window. For Fabrizio this passion is a revelation—an idealized, dreamlike emotion that convinces him he is, indeed, capable of serious love. Just before Fabrizio's friends help him escape, Clélia slips into his cell and the two physically consummate their relationship. After his escape, however, Clélia's marriage to a nobleman and vow to the Virgin that she will never see Fabrizio again seem to doom their love. Fabrizio gives up his former, voluptuous ways and chastely assumes his role as archbishop, but the inspiring sermons he delivers are actually intended to attract Clélia. Both her vow to the Virgin and Fabrizio's resolution to reform are forgotten as the two renew their love. Fabrizio is so moved by the birth of their son, Sandrino, that he kidnaps the baby and brings him into his own home; likewise his despair at the child's and Clélia's deaths is complete. He finally retires to the monastery that gives the novel its title, suggesting that his worldly adventures have ended. Critics frequently compare Fabrizio to Julien Sorel, who is generally acknowledged as a similar but more interesting character. Lacking Julien's driving ambition and lucidity, Fabrizio is more passive, gentle, and humane. His enthusiasm, impetuosity, and predilection for sensual pleasures have been identified as typically Italian traits; significantly Stendhal lived in Milan and had a deep appreciation and love for Italy. Fabrizio has been called "a young Stendhal with an Italian soul;" he shares with his creator an aversion to his father (in this case his adoptive father) and a susceptibility to amorous entanglements.

Count Mosca, the prime minister of Parma, is a highly skilled diplomat whose sensibility has sometimes been termed Machiavellian (referring to the sixteenth-century Italian statesman who advocated expedient and even duplicitous principles). Intelligent and ambitious, Mosca is a clear-headed cynic who possesses a dry sense of humor and the ability to accurately gauge his own importance. At the same time he is innately humane and generous, but he takes a skeptical, pragmatic approach to life and accepts circumstances as they are. Thus, despite his own morality, he panders to the despotic regime of the prince he serves, as when he stifles a rebellion even though he detests the tyrant being opposed, realizing the futility of the uprising. Though generally self-possessed and fearless, the count finds his hands shaking as he prepares to present himself before the brilliant Gina, and his love for her represents his only real weak spot or occasion for inner turmoil. Mosca loves Gina devotedly despite her failure to return his sentiment; although she admires and respects him, her deepest passion is for Fabrizio. He demonstrates his basic levelheadedness, however, when the raging jealousy he feels upon discovering Gina's feelings for Fabrizio are balanced by his awareness that she herself does not comprehend her own emotions. Mosca's great, tender but never-returned love for Gina and resulting isolation make him something of a tragic figure, but he never becomes pathetic; his inherent strength and flexibility allow him to survive while most of the other characters succumb to the force of fate and their own weaknesses. It is partly through Mosca that Stendhal creates an illuminating portrait of the corruption and hypocrisy of the nineteenth century and the intrigue and pragmatism practiced by its statesman. Although early reviewers believed that Stendhal modeled Mosca after his own enemy, the Austrian statesman and diplomat Prince Metternich, critics have come to see his characterization as more admiring than condemnatory. In fact some have detected in Mosca a reflection of Stendhal's realization of his own strengths and egotism.

The complex, fascinating **Gina, Duchess of Sanséverina,** is Fabrizio's aunt and benefactress. Beautiful, charming, intelligent, and self-assured, Gina was widowed early in life and has devoted much of her attention and energy to promoting her beloved nephew's interests. Spirited and willful, she serves as a foil to the pensive, pious Clélia, and the rivalry between the two for Fabrizio's regard is of primary importance in the novel. Although Gina continually reassures herself that her feelings for Fabrizio are benevolently maternal, their passionate and even sexual nature lurks just beneath the surface, thus infusing their relationship with an incestuous tone. Ironically Fabrizio was actually fathered not by her brother but by a French army officer, yet their longtime tie remains inviolably familial. Gina's encouraging Fabrizio to become a priest might be seen as a subconscious effort to keep him apart from other women, as might her eagerness to see Clélia safely married to someone else. Gina herself forges an amorous arrangement with Mosca, but her feelings for him—despite her faithfulness—are notably unimpassioned. She admires the count for his morality, courtliness, and capabilities and is instinctively drawn to his active approach to life (which resembles her own), but she cannot return his love. Fabrizio's imprisonment fills her with a sense of rage and powerlessness, and she is willing to sacrifice anything to help him escape. Still denying the truth of her feelings for him, Gina claims to admire Fabrizio's simple courage and grace. Some critics have seen her determination to assassinate the prince even after Fabrizio has safely escaped as proof of the extremity of her feelings, for such an action seems unnecessary. After Fabrizio's escape it becomes obvious that he is in love with gentle Clélia and feels only grateful affection for his aunt; nevertheless Gina encourages the marriage between Clélia and the marquis and is inordinately relieved when it takes place, even though it brings her no closer to Fabrizio. In the end Gina marries Mosca, thus— according to some scholars—confronting and accepting not only the futility of her love for Fabrizio but the reality of her advancing age. Described as "Stendhal's most spectacular woman" by critic Howard Clewes, Gina was apparently modeled after Gina Pietragrua, the daughter of a Milanese baker and an early mistress of the author. Although some nineteenth-century reviewers condemned Gina as immoral and corrupt due to her incestuous feelings for Fabrizio, most now consider her a compellingly human character.

Lovely young **Clélia Conti,** the daughter of Fabrizio's jailer, eventually becomes his fervent lover and the mother of his child. Beautiful, innocent, and pious, she serves as an effective foil to the more worldly, willful Gina. Clélia develops an early admiration for Fabrizio during their first meeting, when she and her temporarily downtrodden father are invited to ride to the Milan prison in his carriage. When she meets Fabrizio later, while he is confined to the prison her father now runs, his predicament rouses her pity and she is impressed with his inherent nobility; for his part Fabrizio is drawn by Clélia's beauty and pensive aspect. The two establish a relationship that is initially idealized and entirely cerebral, carried on through a system of alphabet cards displayed through their separate windows. Because Clélia believes that Fabrizio may be poisoned at any moment, she finally manages to slip into his cell, and the two make love. After his escape, however, she is overwhelmed with guilt because her father has been blamed for the lapse in security, and she agrees to his demand that she marry a marquis. At the same time, the ever pious—and even superstitious—Clélia makes a vow to the Virgin Mary that she will never see Fabrizio again. She does comply with the letter of this promise, though not the spirit, when she later resumes her affair with Fabrizio, meeting him only in the dark so that she cannot see his face. Her superstition is further evidenced when she interprets her son's death as punishment for her sins, and she herself soon dies as well. Like Madame de Rénal in Stendhal's other masterpiece, *The Red and the Black,* Clélia is one of the author's inherently superior female characters, portrayed as aloof from and above the hypocrisy of their social milieus. Significantly Fabrizio admires his brilliant, headstrong Aunt Gina but passionately loves the tender, modest Clélia. Some critics have interpreted her character as evidence of Stendhal's apparent yearning for connection with an utterly devoted woman willing to sacrifice everything for love.

Several notable characters help to illustrate the panoramic view of nineteenth-century Italian life presented in *The Charterhouse of Parma.* **Prince Ernesto Ranuccio IV** is the despotic ruler of Parma and the most prominent of the types parodied in the novel. Vain and pompous, he is both cruel and cowardly, proud and insecure. It is he who sends an anonymous letter to Mosca alerting the count to Gina's passion for Fabrizio, and Gina eventually achieves vengeance upon him for this and for imprisoning Fabrizio by arranging his assassination. Stendhal may have modeled the prince after his own enemy, Prince Metternich, the Austrian statesman and diplomat who, like his fictional counterpart in *The Charterhouse of Parma,* insisted that his room be searched every night for murderous liberals. **General Conti,** Clélia's father and Fabrizio's jailer, is wicked and corrupt, participating in a plot to poison Fabrizio that is scuttled when the captive escapes. The **Marquis Crescenzi** is the nobleman Clélia is forced—through her father's insistence and her own guilt—to marry.

Non-aristocratic characters also populate the novel. **Marietta Valsera** is the young, essentially untalented actress Fabrizio feels compelled to conquer despite his lack of any real love for her—perhaps in reaction to his awareness of Gina's feelings for him and his fear of his own heartlessness. After Fabrizio kills Marietta's lover, the jealous scoundrel **Giletti,** the two escape to Bologna, where they live together for a short time in unimpassioned tranquility. **Fausta** is the renowned opera singer who next captivates Fabrizio; he amuses himself by attempting to lure her away from her jealous lover, but he is captured and jailed after following her back to Parma. **Ferrante Palla** is the fervent poet with revolutionary convictions whom Gina employs to assassinate the prince and who briefly captures her regard with his idealism.

Other minor characters in *The Charterhouse of Parma* include **Abbé Blanés,** a priest and amateur astrologer who exerts an early religious influence on Fabrizio and who serves as his surrogate father; **Ludovico,** Gina's brave, trusted servant who helps and protects Fabrizio; and **Sandrino,** the ill-fated son of Fabrizio and Clélia, whom they regard as a manifestation of their love and whose death devastates both.

Further Reading

Alter, Robert, with Cosman, Carol. *A Lion for Love: A Critical Biography of Stendhal.* New York: Basic Books, 1979.

Bloom, Harold, ed. *Stendhal.* New York: Chelsea House, 1989.

Brombert, Victor. *Stendhal: Fiction and the Themes of Freedom.* New York: Random House, 1968.

Chiaromonte, Nicola. "Fabrizio at Waterloo." In *The Paradox of History: Stendhal, Tolstoy, Pasternak, and Others,* revised edition, pp. 1-16. Philadelphia: University of Pennsylvania Press, 1985.

Clewes, Howard. *Stendhal: An Introduction to the Novelist.* A. Barker, 1950.

Day, James T. *Stendhal's Paper Mirror: Patterns of Self-Consciousness in His Novels.* New York: Peter Lang, 1987.

Haig, Stirling. *Stendhal: The Red and the Black.* Cambridge: Cambridge University Press, 1989.

Humphries, Jefferson. *The Red and the Black: Mimetic Desire and the Myth of Celebrity.* Boston: Twayne, 1991.

Maurois, André. "Passionate Love—Heroines of Stendhal." In *Seven Faces of Love,* translated by Haakon M. Chevalier, pp. 11-48. New York: Didier, 1944.

Nineteenth-Century Literature Criticism, Vol. 23. Detroit: Gale.

Talbot, Emile J. *Stendhal and Romantic Esthetics.* Lexington, Ky.: French Forum, 1985.

Robert Louis Stevenson
1850-1894

Scottish novelist, short story writer, dramatist, poet, essayist, and prayer writer.

Treasure Island (novel, 1883)

Plot: Narrated by young Jim Hawkins, the story begins with the arrival of a mysterious old sailor named Bill Bones at the Admiral Benbow, a quiet English seaside inn operated by Jim's father. The old sailor establishes himself at the inn, spending his days watching the sea and his nights singing, drinking, and telling stories in the tavern. He warns Jim to be on the lookout for a dangerous one-legged sailor. Although this figure never appears, another sailor named Black Dog arrives and fights with Bones, frightening the Hawkins family. Not long after this encounter, Jim's father dies. Blind Pew, a deformed sailor, comes to the inn on the day of the funeral and confronts Bones, giving him the dreaded "Black Spot," the pirate's signal of approaching death. Almost immediately the terrified Bones dies of a stroke, and Jim and his mother search his sea chest for the money he owes them. They recover an oilskin packet and escape just before a gang of men bursts into the inn to retrieve Bones's chest; when revenue officers on horseback arrive to disperse the gang, Blind Pew is trampled and killed. Jim delivers the oilskin packet to two adult friends, Dr. Livesey—who had treated his father in his final illness—and Squire Trelawney. They discover that it contains a map disclosing the location of treasure hidden by the brutal pirate Captain Flint.

Inspired by dreams of great wealth, the squire decides to outfit a schooner and search for the treasure; Dr. Livesey also joins the excursion, and Jim is invited to serve as the ship's cabin boy.

The *Hispaniola* sails from Bristol with a crew assembled by the smooth-talking ship's cook, Long John Silver. Soon after their departure, the *Hispaniola*'s captain, John Smollett, expresses his distrust of Silver and the rest of the crew. While inadvertently hidden in an apple barrel, Jim overhears Silver and several other men plotting a mutiny, but before he can share this information with his friends, Treasure Island comes into view. The sailors become disorderly with excitement at the prospect of discovering treasure, and Captain Smollett allows several of them to go ashore with Silver. Jim secretly stows away with this group in order to spy on them, and he witnesses the subsequent murder of a crew member who refuses to go along with the mutiny plans. Jim also meets the island's sole resident, Ben Gunn, a member of Captain Flint's crew who was marooned there three years earlier. When Dr. Livesey learns of the disloyalty of Silver and his followers, he recommends that all the honest men aboard the *Hispaniola* take refuge in an abandoned stockade on the island, where Jim eventually joins them. Silver too arrives there and offers the group safe passage in exchange for the treasure map; Captain Smollett refuses this offer. A gang of pirates then attacks the stockade, and a period of bloody fighting ensues during which all but one of the attackers is killed or wounded. Of the loyal party, only Jim, the squire, Livesey, and Smollett are left. Jim secretly leaves the stockade and rows out to the now apparently abandoned *Hispaniola*, planning to set it adrift. Through a mishap, he ends up aboard the ship and engages in a fight with its sole occupant, the evil pirate Israel Hands. Jim manages to shoot Hands, even though he has a knife lodged in his own shoulder, and secures the ship. He then returns to the stockade, discovering that it is now occupied by the pirates. Jim is captured and nearly killed, but Silver defends him and manages to cajole his angry mates by producing Captain Flint's treasure map. When Dr. Livesey arrives to treat some wounded pirates, Jim explains that Silver saved his life, and the doctor reveals—to Jim's mystification—that he has given the pirate the map. The pirates locate the hiding place of the treasure but find that it has already been taken away. Just as they are about to attack Silver and Jim, Jim's friends arrive with Ben Gunn, and the group manages to overcome the pirates. The mystery of the treasure's location is now explained: soon after his arrival on the island, Gunn discovered the treasure and hid it in the cave in which he lived. When Dr. Livesey learned this from Gunn, he gave Silver the useless map, and Squire Trelawney and the others abandoned the stockade for Gunn's quarters. The group finally leaves Treasure Island aboard the *Hispaniola*. They stop briefly in the West Indies, where Silver manages to escape with a bag of coins. The rest arrive safely in Bristol, sharing the treasure equally.

Characters: *Treasure Island* is one of the best-loved adventure stories in literature; readers young and old still find it fresh and entertaining. While Stevenson came under fire during the years following his death for what some commentators viewed as an emphasis on style over ideas, he is universally praised for his storytelling ability and narrative adeptness. Distinguished by its subtle infusion of realism into the fanciful realm of pure adventure, *Treasure Island* may be viewed as a mythical story peopled by archetypal characters, as a tale centering on the theme of human greed and competition, or as the ultimate (but not complex or deeply significant) boy's daydream.

The narrator of most of *Treasure Island* is **Jim Hawkins,** a young boy whose exact age is never specified. The novel chronicles Jim's journey out of his rather mundane existence into a realm of pirates, intrigue, murder, and hidden treasure, discovering along the way unsuspected strengths within himself. The death of Jim's father frees him to pursue adventure and burdens him with the necessity of supporting his widowed mother, allowing for both fantasy and realism to direct his role in the story. Although Jim is a bright, honest, resourceful boy, he is portrayed as ordinary rather than exceptional and thus provides an example of the decidedly unheroic protagonist often found in Stevenson's literature. In fact Jim has been identified as a less complex predecessor to David Balfour, the hero of *Kidnapped.* Despite his perhaps implausible dexterity with pistols during his encounter with Israel Hands and his subsequent ability to maneuver the ship to safety, Jim is notably human and boyish, demonstrating Stevenson's sympathy for and understanding of young people. Occasionally lonely and fearful, he is susceptible to being impressed by such a dashing character as Long John Silver and to impulsiveness or even foolishness, as evidenced by his bragging to his pirate captors about his success in fighting Hands. Nevertheless Jim displays considerable bravery in such actions as stowing away with Silver's gang when they land on Treasure Island and leaving the stockade alone to set the *Hispaniola* adrift. Although his fight with Hands in the ship's rigging is probably the novel's most unrealistic scene—Jim manages to outfox and kill his opponent even after he is pinned to the mast with a knife through his shoulder—it is also one of its most thrilling and colorful. That the adventure has in part signified Jim's passage to manhood is suggested by his refusal to escape with Dr. Livesey after he has promised Long John Silver that he will return to his captors if he is allowed to speak to his friend alone for a few moments: in standing by his word even at the possible cost of his life, he proves not only that he has gained maturity but that he is on his way to becoming an upright gentleman. In this respect, as well as his lamenting the lives lost during the adventure, he contrasts with the pragmatic, frequently immoral Silver.

The daring, manipulative, and sometimes cruel pirate **Long John Silver** is usually cited as the most compelling character in *Treasure Island* and is said to have been Stevenson's favorite creation. His most notable trait is his inherent ambiguity: he is neither totally admirable nor completely villainous. In fact some critics identify him as a "hero-villain" because he combines such reprehensible qualities as greed, deceit, and brutality with courage, generosity, and even kindness. As several critics have noted, most of Silver's worst behavior occurs at the beginning of the story, and the reader is then gradually exposed to his more positive side. First Bones drops ominous hints about a one-legged sailor, then Jim actually meets the smooth-talking ship's cook and is initially impressed with him. (Silver consistently employs his wit and ability to bluff as a survival tool, whether he is manipulating Jim and his friends or the disreputable pirate gang.) Soon Jim learns that Silver is callously plotting mutiny, and he subsequently witnesses the pirate's cold-blooded murder of an uncooperative crew member. At these early stages Silver appears vain, cruel, and invincible; later, however, he saves Jim's life and even seems to develop a genuine fondness for the boy. In addition, the physical disability that has never prevented him from doing what he wished becomes a handicap as he loses control of his gang, and his vulnerable side is exposed. In the end Silver is neither punished for his wickedness nor rewarded (except for the meager bag of silver) for his better behavior; thus Stevenson allows this character's ambiguity to go unresolved. A character of imagination, bravado, and uninhibited energy, Silver plays an important role in the process of maturation that Jim undergoes during his adventure, contrasting with such morally upright, inherently conservative characters as Squire Trelawney and Dr. Livesey, who also contribute to Jim's development. Yet, in keeping with the novel's focus on greed and the lengths to which people will go to attain wealth, some critics have seen in Silver a similarity with these more conservative figures. The pirate (whose surname evokes the motif of riches) wants the treasure to purchase the social respectability he cannot otherwise achieve, making him the ultimate pragmatist or utilitarian. Scholars have lauded Stevenson for creating in Silver a heroic figure who has little in common with the conventional heroes of literature and who lends *Treasure Island* much of its imaginative appeal.

The two respectable Englishmen Jim accompanies to Treasure Island both provide effective contrasts to daring, anti-conventional Long John Silver. **Squire Trelawney** is a figure of authority and prosperity who finances the adventure, purchasing and outfitting the *Hispaniola* and hiring its crew. Despite his elevated social and financial status and general decency, the squire is motivated by the same impulse as the disreputable pirates: greed. In a telling passage, he describes his dream of literally rolling in money. **Dr. Livesey,** a benevolent physician who treats Jim's dying father and later the wounded mutineers, serves as the narrator for several chapters of *Treasure Island.* He is a paternal influence of stability, maturity, and moral responsibility for the fatherless young boy. Yet he is no less motivated by a hunger for wealth than the other adults in the story, vividly depicted by his rapid pocketing of the oilskin packet Jim recovers from Bones's chest. **Captain John Smollett,** the *Hispaniola*'s captain, is also a figure of respectability. In his dourness and lack of imagination he serves as a foil to Silver, making virtue seem less attractive than pirate bravado.

The strange, fear-inspiring **Bill Bones,** the "retired" sea captain who establishes himself at the placid Admiral Benbow, helps to create an aura of mystery early in the story. He spends his days watching the seacoast for some unexplained arrival and his nights drinking, swearing, and telling stories; he sings the famous ditty about "fifteen men on a dead man's chest" that has since become an established element of the pirate stereotype. His ominous warnings that Jim look out for a dangerous one-legged sailor foreshadow the entrance of Long John Silver into the story. Other notable pirate characters include **Black Dog,** who is chased away from the inn by Bones after their fight; and **Blind Pew,** the deformed and vicious pirate who delivers Bones's ordination of death and who, like Long John Silver, possesses considerable physical strength despite his infirmity. **Ben Gunn,** Ben is a marooned former sailor with the brutal, legendary **Captain Flint,** whose buried treasure the story's characters seek; Gunn plays a practical role in the story through his having hidden the treasure in his own cave, where he provides shelter to Jim and his friends. **Israel Hands** provides an example of a uniformly bad pirate character, as opposed to the good-bad dichotomy found in Silver. Evil and deceptive, he is infinitely more experienced than Jim but is finally outsmarted and defeated by the plucky young boy, demonstrating Jim's inherent superiority.

Jim's parents play small roles at the beginning of the story. His **father** is a weak man finally defeated by his illness. Intimidated by Bones, he never asks for the money the blustery sailor owes him, leaving his wife and son with the task of trying to collect it from the dead sailor's chest. The father's death evokes little pathos, serving primarily to free Jim for his adventure. **Jim's mother,** who is with him when he discovers the oilskin packet, is significant in that his obligation to support her forms part of his motivation for embarking on an adventure that might prove financially lucrative.

Kidnapped (novel, 1886)

Plot: Set in Scotland in 1751, the novel begins in that country's Lowland region but eventually moves into the rugged Highlands. As it opens, David Balfour's father has recently died, leaving him only a letter directing him to seek his inheritance from his uncle, Ebenezer Balfour, from whom the senior Balfour had been estranged. As he approaches Shaws, Ebenezer's estate, David is alarmed when several nearby residents warn him against his uncle, who seems to be extremely unpopular. David soon learns that Ebenezer is indeed mean and miserly, and he suspects that his uncle had long ago cheated his father out of his inheritance. Ebenezer suggests that he and David visit the family's attorney, Mr. Rankeillor, in Queen's Ferry to look into the details of David's legacy. On the way there, however, Ebenezer and Captain Hoseason, the skipper of the *Covenant,* trick David into boarding the ship, and he is made a prisoner; the ship then sets sail for America. After one of the mates murders the ship's cabin boy for a trifling offense, David assumes that function and his situation improves somewhat. One night the ship runs into and destroys a smaller boat, and the crew rescues a man named Alan Breck. A native of the Highlands region and a follower of the Jacobites (the rebellious group which six years earlier attempted to wrest the throne from King George in favor of Bonnie Prince Charlie), Alan is wanted by the authorities. Although Hoseason agrees to return Alan to shore, David overhears the captain plotting with another officer to capture the Highlander. Together David and Alan wage a fight against the ship's crew, killing several men and wounding many others. Alan recounts his part in the 1745 rebellion, which led to his being hunted by the king's men, especially by "The Red Fox," or Colin of Glenure. Although David remains faithful to the king, he and Alan forge a strong friendship and pledge their loyalty to each other.

When the ship strikes a reef and founders, Alan and David are separated, but they meet again in the Highlands. Alan has been blamed for the murder of Colin of Glenure, and the two must flee together from his pursuers. They plan to escape to the Lowlands and find Mr. Rankeillor, who they hope will be able to help them. Setting out through the rugged mountainous terrain with little food or water, they must continually evade their enemies, who include not only the king's soldiers but members of a clan with which Alan's clan is feuding. At one point David feels too fatigued to continue, but Alan spurs him on and, after many hardships, the two reach Mr. Rankeillor. In spite of his initial doubts, the attorney accepts their story. He now reveals to David the truth about his inheritance: as young men, his father and Ebenezer had loved the same woman; when she chose David's father, he pitied the grieving Ebenezer and yielded his own inheritance to his brother. Now David realizes why Ebenezer had been eager to dispose of him—he knew of David's legal right to his legacy and could not bear to part with it. Nevertheless David reaches an agreement with his uncle, frightening him into giving him a significant portion of his rightful income. David pays for Alan's safe passage back into the Highlands, and claims his rightful position as master of Shaws.

Characters: Considered a riveting adventure story with an underpinning of social and psychological realism, *Kidnapped* features a skillful blend of fantasy with history. While the similarly entertaining *Treasure Island* is often called the quintessential boy's daydream, this novel appeals even more to adults with its setting in a place and time of major upheaval, its mix of such thrilling elements as kidnapping and murder with such ordinary problems as hostility within families and drunken sailors, and its focus on the triumph of friendship over seemingly insurmountable philosophical differences. Celebrated for his storytelling ability and lucid prose style, Stevenson is praised for creating in *Kidnapped* a historically authentic novel and characters with very human, universal appeal.

Stevenson's use of a first-person narrator in *Kidnapped* has been said to lend immediacy and believability to the story. Seventeen-year-old **David Balfour,** the son of a schoolmaster, is a native of Scotland's Lowlands, generally characterized as more "civilized" and influenced by its English rulers than the rugged Highland region. David is a Protestant and loyal to King George, whose right to rule Scotland was reinforced six years earlier with the defeat of the Jacobite rebellion. As the novel begins, David's father has just died, and David is faced with the task of fending for himself while, along the way, also discovering his own identity. His upbringing has resulted in his holding very conventional values, and he is by nature prudent and cautious. That he also possesses some youthful curiosity is evidenced by his allowing himself to be lured aboard the *Covenant* and thus kidnapped. David is initially unsure how to respond to the flamboyant Alan Breck, who is not only temperamentally his opposite but, as a Catholic and a Jacobite, holds very different values. Although he approaches Alan warily at first, David soon comes to respect and admire his new acquaintance, and the friendship that grows between the two provides the novel's main thematic focus. During their journey through the Highlands, David receives an education about his country's heritage—which, he comes to realize, had been notably one-sided—and he learns about unsuspected strengths within himself, such as his capacity for loyalty and courage under fire. Through their two distinct personalities, David and Alan are seen to illustrate the duality of human nature—a concept that interested Stevenson and which is found in much of his work. While Alan is often reckless and too quick to respond, David is so conscientious and scrupulous that he finds it difficult to act; each needs the other to balance his own limitations. Like the protagonist of Mark Twain's 1884 novel *The Adventures of Huckleberry Finn,* with which *Kidnapped* is often compared, David befriends an outcast of society, faces a struggle with his conscience, and learns to know, accommodate, and value a person very different from himself. It is the journey taken by David and Alan that is emphasized in *Kidnapped,* and the fact that David ultimately becomes a prosperous Lowlander and the master of Shaws seems less important that the hardships, adventure, and self-discovery he experiences in reaching the final outcome.

The dashing, impetuous Highlander **Alan Breck** provides a strong contrast to his more circumspect friend David Balfour. Alan is an experienced man in his mid-thirties whose Jacobite convictions and natural rebelliousness have made him an outlaw. A Catholic and a supporter of Bonnie Prince Charlie during the Jacobite uprising of 1745, Alan is in flight not only from the English authorities but from feuding Highland factions. He is undeniably brave and through his friendship with David, proves staunchly loyal, but he also exhibits an exaggerated vanity that sometimes make him seem ridiculous. American author Henry James, an ardent admirer of Stevenson's work, described Alan as a "union of courage and swagger . . . a study of the love of glory, carried out with extreme psychological truth." Indeed Alan's posturing might be seen as a necessary defense against the forces that threatened the eighteenth-century Highland identity, and his boasting and flamboyance do not seriously diminish his basic nobility of spirit. Although Alan appears during the sequences aboard the *Covenant* as a fairly conventional figure of romantic fiction, his character acquires complexity during his travels through the Highlands with David. Their friendship develops in spite of their different political orientations and seems to be enhanced rather than weakened by their opposite personalities: Alan is physically tireless, impetuous, and reckless, while the less robust David is cautious and prudent; Alan foolishly loses at cards, while David provides the necessary funds for their journey. Yet both are inherently courageous and both succeed in overcoming their prejudices, pledging their loyalty to each other with obvious sincerity. Alan's status as a political outcast and his role in broadening David's perspective have caused him to be compared with Jim in Mark Twain's 1884 novel, *The Adventures of Huckleberry Finn.* Alan's role might also be interpreted from a historical perspective, for he symbolizes the struggle of Scotland's native people for their land and cultural identity. As a Highlander, Alan illustrates his society's reliance on ancient traditions often expressed in rebellion, feuding, and bloodshed.

David's uncle, **Ebenezer Balfour,** is a mean-spirited, unscrupulous old miser whose unpopularity with his neighbors is revealed to David just before he arrives at Shaws. Ebenezer plays a primarily practical role in the novel in that, out of a selfish desire to keep David from his inheritance, he engineers the kidnapping with which the young man's adventures begin. Some critics consider Ebenezer a rather one-sided villain—so parsimonious, cowardly, and immoral that he would rather see his nephew dead than in possession of money he has long hoarded for himself. Nevertheless the revelation that he was once so distraught with thwarted love for a young woman that he took to his bed lends a shade more depth to his character. The novel's opening and closing sequences both feature Ebenezer, so that he provides, in the words of critic David Daiches, "a pair of wry parentheses" that enclose the more significant and compelling middle part of the story.

Stevenson has been lauded for his portrayal of **Captain Elias Hoseason,** the skipper of the *Covenant,* who conspires with Ebenezer to shanghai David and carry him off as a slave to America. Strangely Hoseason treats his captive with scrupulous decency once the journey is underway, evidencing an inconsistency in his character that has interested many scholars. Likewise he is dutiful in his relations with his mother and in his religious observances, and this strict commitment to duty—even when based on wicked premises—is a trait Stevenson considered common to natives of Scotland's Lowlands. Some critics have compared the half-good, half-bad Hoseason to another famous Stevenson character, Long John Silver in *Treasure Island,* who is also able to assume and shed roles as demanded by various situations, and who exhibits a similar, ultimately unresolved moral ambiguity.

Through several characters encountered by Alan and David during their journey through the Highlands, Stevenson fleshes out the novel's historical context and illuminates David about formerly unknown aspects of his native land. **Colin of Glenure,** or the **Red Fox,** was an actual person, and the 1752 trial of his murderer forms the basis of *Kidnapped's* story. He is chief among the king's soldiers pursuing Alan for participating in the 1745 Jacobite rebellion, thus defending England's right to rule Scotland. Although he is Scottish, Colin serves the English monarch, forcing his countrymen to follow policies they regard as oppressive. **Cluny MacPherson** is a formerly glorified outlaw chieftain now operating card games (in which Alan participates, with disastrous results); **Robin Oig** is the son of the legendary Rob Roy (the dashing Scottish brigand), but does nothing more adventurous himself than playing the bagpipes. **James Stewart,** another historically based character, is the Highland clan leader driven to desperation by his family's destitution and eventually convicted and hanged for the murder of Colin of Glenure.

Other characters in *Kidnapped* include **Mr. Campbell,** the benevolent minister of Essendean, who delivers to David the letter from his father and assures the boy that David may return to him for help if necessary; **Mr. Rankeillor,** the Balfour family's honest, trustworthy attorney, who reveals to David the story behind his inheritance; **Mr. Riach,** the *Covenant's* second mate, who treats David kindly when he is drunk but behaves roughly when sober; **Mr. Shuan,** the ship's first mate and the reverse of Mr. Riach, is gentle when sober but violent when drunk, even beating to death the ship's cabin boy for a minor offense.

The Strange Case of Dr. Jekyll and Mr. Hyde (novel, 1886)

Plot: The novel takes place in late nineteenth-century England. Lawyer Gabriel Utterson and his "man about town " cousin Richard Enfield are taking their customary Sunday walk when they approach a building that is familiar to Enfield. He explains that near this building he recently witnessed the brutal, heedless trampling of a small child by a man named Hyde. Utterson is interested in the story because the will of his friend Dr. Henry Jekyll specifies that Jekyll's entire fortune should go upon his death to an Edward Hyde. Jekyll will not explain who Hyde is or why he wishes to leave his fortune to him, and Utterson suspects that his friend is being blackmailed. About a year later Hyde is sought by the police for the murder of a kindly old man, a well-known member of Parliament named Sir Danvers Carew. Jekyll produces a letter from Hyde promising to disappear forever and apologizes for having compromised his friend. Around the same time a former friend of Jekyll's—and his fellow physician—Dr. Hastie Lanyon, becomes ill and dies. Among his papers is a letter addressed to Utterson; inside is a sealed envelope with the instruction that it must not be opened until after the death of Jekyll.

Utterson is summoned to Jekyll's residence by his friend's servant, Poole, who reports that his master has been confined in his laboratory for a week and has sent Poole on several searches for a particular drug. Poole fears that Jekyll has been killed and that his murderer has remained in the laboratory, impersonating his victim. After a voice that sounds like Hyde's begs them to go away, Utterson and Poole break into the lab and discover Hyde's body; he has killed himself by drinking poison. Jekyll is nowhere in sight. When Utterson finally reads the letters left by Lanyon and Jekyll, he learns the secret of Jekyll and Hyde. Lanyon's letter explains that Hyde had come to his laboratory to retrieve some drugs previously requested by Jekyll. In Lanyon's presence Hyde ingested the drugs and was transformed into Jekyll. Lanyon was so shocked and aggrieved by this experience that he grew ill and died. Jekyll's letter provides a full account of his activities, explaining how he began as a younger man to lead a double life. Morally upright and respectable in public, he indulged in a variety of vices in private, and as a result he became obsessed with the idea of dual personality. Surmising that it might be possible to isolate a man's good and evil natures into two separate beings, he experimented with drugs until he was able to produce Hyde, the physical manifestation of his own wickedness. Hyde was then free to indulge in immoral practices without fear of discovery, while Jekyll would supposedly lead a spotless life of good. Gradually, however, Hyde became more dominant and seemed to be gaining control over Jekyll. After a long period of suppression, Jekyll allowed Hyde to emerge again, and the result had been the murder of Carew. Unable to rid himself of his evil counterpart through experimental drug ingestions, the despairing Jekyll/Hyde finally killed himself.

Characters: The story of Dr. Jekyll and Mr. Hyde is one of the most famous in literature, due in large part to numerous stage and film adaptations. The protagonist's split personality is universally recognized as symbolizing the duality in human nature. Despite the sensationalism and horror with which the novel is infused, the story has compelling moral and psychological underpinnings. Long interested in the concept of dual personality (as evidenced by such characters as Long John Silver in *Treasure Island*), Stevenson employed a highly effective technique of multiple, increasingly revealing narratives to explore the consequences of denying the evil that exists in oneself. The novel serves not only as a skillfully constructed and well-told entertainment but as a warning against intellectual pride and hypocrisy.

It is not until the last section of *Dr. Jekyll and Mr. Hyde* that the protagonist, **Dr. Henry Jekyll,** tells his own story in his own words. Before the reader hears directly from Jekyll, his character and experiences are gradually shown by the other narrators, who reveal that he is a much-respected, kind, upstanding London physician who embodies "the very pink of the proprieties." Though mystified by his unexplained connection with the brutal Edward Hyde, Jekyll's friends do not initially suspect the truth, and when they do discover his secret—first Lanyon, then Utterson and Enfield—they are profoundly affected by the disparity between the conventional man they have known and the creature he actually is. When he begins his own "Full Statement," Jekyll explains he had long lived a double life, maintaining his respectability and gentility in public but indulging in unrestrained vice in private; the nature of this vice is not specified, but appears to be along the lines of cruel and malicious behavior. Jekyll claims that he developed a scientific interest in the idea of dual personality and conjectured that it might be possible to channel the good and evil impulses within himself into two separate individuals. Although he contends that he approached the experiment objectively, surmising that this division would give the good in him broader scope, many critics have detected an inherent hypocrisy in his assertions. Jekyll inadvertently reveals that he is not rejecting the evil within himself by concentrating it in Hyde but instead freeing it from restraint; thus he abandons the responsibility to accept and control both aspects of his personality. It is obvious by the end of Jekyll's narration that he recognizes Hyde as a separate being from himself, and this refusal to accept the truth makes him a tragic figure. Many scholars have described Jekyll as the epitome of the Victorian moral system, which required maintaining external respectability and denying more primitive impulses. A victim of his own weakness and self-deception compounded by an impossibly severe disciplinary code, Jekyll represents the "cry of Victorian man from the depths of his self-imposed underground," according to critic Irving S. Saposnik. Other critics have noted that Jekyll's name might be broken down into "je" (French for "I") and "kill," reinforcing the murderous and suicidal elements of the story.

Through the threatening figure of **Edward Hyde,** who embodies the evil in Jekyll's personality, Stevenson illustrates the theme of the duality of human nature and provides the story's underlying mystery. Hyde's physical description is vague: he is dwarfish and apelike and does not much resemble Jekyll—he even appears to be a younger man, suggesting a kind of father-son relationship between them. In this way he differs from the traditional "doppelganger" (double), frequently employed in literature, who is an exact physical replica of the original. As several critics have noted, Jekyll is not really vicious and violent on his first appearance, though he does heedlessly trample a little girl. Instead, he is amoral and primitive—much like the monster in Mary Shelley's 1818 novel *Frankenstein*—and does not seem to comprehend that what he has done is reprehensible. His transformation into a creature of energetic brutality begins with the almost sadistic reaction of the horrified crowd during the trampling incident: their disgust, and that expressed by Jekyll and others throughout the story, incites Hyde's violent instincts. When he finally murders the elderly Carews, he seems to consciously enjoy his perpetration of an evil act. Hyde has been characterized by some commentators as a character of repressed sexuality, but Stevenson insisted that he was intended not as "a mere voluptuary" but as "the essence of cruelty and malice and selfishness and cowardice." In exhibiting a complete lack of moral restraint, however, Hyde does seem to embody the primitive side of human nature, which—particularly in Victorian society—is often denied in favor of "civilized" behavior. Hyde arouses an exaggerated horrified reaction in various Londoners and thus might be said to embody the dangers (not only within the human personality but in the realms of politics and economics) that threatened the rigidly ordered culture of Victorian England. Jekyll's attempt to isolate those feared and rejected aspects of his own nature is his undoing, and Hyde's gradual ascendance proves the tragic consequences of such an experiment.

The story's first narrator is **Richard Enfield,** who relates to his cousin Gabriel Utterson his earlier encounter with Edward Hyde. Described as a "well-known man about town," Enfield lives an aimless, dissipated lifestyle quite different from the staid Utterson. Yet the two men are in the habit of walking together every Sunday, a rather dull experience that is absolutely necessary for each. In keeping with Stevenson's interest in the duality of human nature, these two men might be said to balance or complement each other's limitations: the self-indulgent Enfield benefits from Utterson's austerity, while Utterson finds relief in Enfield's looser outlook. In any case Enfield introduces the story's main characters and circumstances with a fairly objective and reliable perspective. Generally tolerant toward others, Enfield is utterly repelled by Hyde, who is indifferent to the fact that he has just trampled a little girl, symbolizing the strong effect Hyde produces in people. Likewise Enfield is profoundly disturbed, despite his wide experience and knowledge of the world, by the revelation of Jekyll's secret.

The second narrator is **Gabriel Utterson,** a highly respectable attorney whose interest in Hyde is spurred when Jekyll amends his will to favor the mysterious and increasingly brutal figure. Utterson serves as a foil to his cousin Richard Enfield, with whom he has forged an unlikely friendship, because he is rigidly austere, morally upright, and self-denying. Despite the strictness with which he conducts his own life, Utterson is notably tolerant toward other people and thus serves as a generally reliable, objective narrator. As a lawyer he characterizes correct social behavior, but in his compassion he tempers the idea of justice with that of mercy. Like the other characters Utterson feels overwhelming disgust for Hyde and suspects he is victimizing Jekyll. He remembers that Jekyll indulged in some rather wild behavior in his youth, and he wonders if Hyde also knows about these episodes and is blackmailing Jekyll. Utterson alludes to his own past as not entirely spotless, reinforcing the idea that wickedness may co-exist within even the most irreproachable personality.

Dr. Hastie Lanyon, Jekyll's fellow physician and former friend, is the novel's third narrator. In the letter entrusted to Utterson after Lanyon's death and not opened until after Jekyll's demise, he relates that he was present when Hyde ingested the drugs that transformed him into Jekyll. Lanyon's friendship with Jekyll ruptured ten years earlier, resulting from Lanyon's disapproval of his friend's "fanciful" medical theories. Jekyll himself admits to a longtime interest in blending mysticism or transcendentalism with science, while Lanyon's approach was apparently more practical and conventional. It has been suggested that the bold, boisterous, very modern Lanyon might have been frightened by the suggestion of something threatening or even evil in his Jekyll's work. This view seems confirmed by his extreme reaction when Jekyll's secret is revealed. Terrified by his recognition of the evil that lurks within a seemingly respectable man, he eventually falls sick and dies, another victim Jekyll's tragic experiment.

Sir Danvers Carew is probably the most significant of the minor characters in *Dr. Jekyll and Mr. Hyde.* A kindly old man, he is a renowned member of Parliament. Hyde seems to take delight in brutally beating his unresisting elderly victim to death, an act that marks his transformation from primitive amorality to outright, intentional evil. Other characters in the novel include **Poole,** Jekyll's servant, who plays a primarily practical role in alerting Utterson to his master's strange behavior but who also reinforces through his terrified reaction the universal disgust that Hyde arouses; the same function is performed by the **Edinburgh doctor,** a witness to Hyde's collision with the little girl who, despite his being "about as emotional as a bagpipe," seems to want to murder the infuriatingly heedless Hyde.

Further Reading

Daiches, David. *Stevenson and the Art of Fiction.* Lecture delivered at Yale University on May 18, 1951.

Dictionary of Literary Biography, Vols. 18, 57. Detroit: Gale.

James, Henry. "Robert Louis Stevenson." In *Partial Portraits,* pp. 137-74. New York: Macmillan, 1888.

Maixner, Paul. *Robert Louis Stevenson: The Critical Heritage.* London: Routledge & Kegan Paul, 1981.

Nabokov, Vladimir. "Robert Louis Stevenson: The Strange Case of Dr. Jekyll and Mr. Hyde." In *Lectures on Literature,* edited by Fredson Bowers, pp. 179-206. New York: Harcourt Brace Jovanovich, 1980.

Nineteenth-Century Literature Criticism, Vols. 5, 14. Detroit: Gale.

Pritchett, V. S., ed. Introduction to *Novels & Stories* by Robert Louis Stevenson, pp. vii-xv. The Pilot Press, 1946.

Rankin, Nicholas. *Dead Man's Chest: Travels after Robert Louis Stevenson.* London: Faber & Faber, 1987.

Saposnik, Irving S. *Robert Louis Stevenson.* New York: Twayne, 1974.

Stevenson, Robert Louis. Letter to John Paul Bocock, 1887. *In The True Stevenson: A Study in Clarification,* by George S. Hellman, pp. 129-30. Boston, Mass.: Little, Brown, 1925.

Veeder, William and Gordon Hirsch, eds. *Dr. Jekyll and Mr. Hyde after One Hundred Years.* Chicago: University of Chicago Press, 1988.

Harriet Beecher Stowe
1811-1896
American novelist and essayist.

Uncle Tom's Cabin; or, Life among the Lowly (novel, 1852)

Plot: The novel begins in the mid-nineteenth century on a Kentucky plantation. Mr. Shelby, the plantation owner, is considering selling one of his slaves to a New Orleans slave dealer, Haley, to whom he is in debt. Haley has selected the genial, capable slave Uncle Tom and has also expressed an interest in Harry, the small son of the Shelbys' slave Eliza. Eliza is alarmed by this talk and shares her fears with her husband, George Harris, a slave on another plantation. Embittered by his status as a lowly field hand, the intelligent George vows that he will one day avenge himself on his oppressors. The papers authorizing the sale of Uncle Tom and Harry are soon signed. Eliza flees with her child, jumping across ice floes on the nearby river to reach the Ohio shore. Haley sends two crude slave-catchers, Loker and Marks, to capture her. Uncle Tom, however, resigns himself to his fate. While Eliza eventually reaches safety in the home of Senator Bird and his wife, Uncle Tom is shackled and taken on a boat bound for New Orleans. Before the boat leaves, Tom receives a visit from his former master's son, George Shelby, who promises to buy him back some day. George Harris, meanwhile, escapes from his plantation and is able, due to his light skin, to pass for a Spaniard. He eventually reaches the same Quaker settlement in Ohio where Eliza has found refuge. While traveling toward New Orleans, Uncle Tom saves the life of a little white girl named Evangeline St. Clare, who is called Little Eva. Her grateful father, Augustine St. Clare, purchases Tom and the three return to the family's plantation, where Mrs. St. Clare, a spoiled Southern aristocrat, languishes from imaginary ailments. Because she is supposedly incapable of caring for her daughter, St. Clare brings his cousin, Miss Ophelia, down from Vermont to help him raise the frail little girl. Tom is made head coachman on the plantation, and he and the angelic Little Eva become good friends.

Loker and Marks finally catch up with Eliza and George, and during the ensuing confrontation George injures Loker and Marks flees. Back in Louisiana, the strict, Puritanical Miss Ophelia is shocked by the lavish, easeful lifestyle of the South and by her cousin's indulgent, irresolute ways. She also disapproves of the friendship between Uncle Tom and Little Eva, even though she believes slavery is an evil institution. In order to test his cousin's convictions, St. Clare buys a strange little slave girl named Topsy for Miss Ophelia to educate; the New England spinster struggles against her repulsion for the unruly child. Eva, meanwhile, grows more ill; knowing that she does not have long to live, she asks her father to promise to free his slaves. After her death, St. Clare is preparing to comply with his daughter's wish when he is killed trying to break up a fight. The insensitive Mrs. St. Clare then sells Uncle Tom to a brutal, alcoholic plantation owner named Simon Legree, who habitually catches and tortures runaway slaves. Living conditions on Legree's plantation are harsh, but Tom befriends a slave named Cassy who tells him about her life with their master and of her daughter, who had been sold many years before. Along with another slave, Emmeline, Cassy plots to escape; they trick Legree into thinking they are hiding in a nearby swamp when actually they are still inside the house. Enraged, Legree demands that Tom reveal the missing slaves' hiding place. With the help of his two henchman, Legree beats Tom to the brink of death. Several days later George Shelby arrives to buy Tom back, but Tom soon dies. Cassy and Emmeline, meanwhile, convince the superstitious Legree that there are ghosts in his house, and he reacts by drinking himself into a stupor. George helps the two women escape, and they travel safely to Canada aboard a riverboat. During the voyage they meet Madame de Thoux, who turns out to be George Harris's sister, and Cassy subsequently learns that her daughter Eliza is the same Eliza who married George. These former slaves are finally reunited in Canada, while in Kentucky George Shelby frees all of his father's slaves in honor of Uncle Tom.

Characters: Originally published as a serial in an abolitionist (anti-slavery) journal, *Uncle Tom's Cabin* caused a major stir in a nation already divided over the issue of slavery. It became an immediate and highly controversial bestseller and—some ten years later, during the Civil War—President Lincoln is supposed to have greeted Stowe with the words, "So this is the little lady who made this big war." While often discussed in terms of its historical significance, the novel represents a literary landmark as well in its use of regional dialect and local color in a work of serious (rather than comic) intent. In addition, several of the characters in *Uncle Tom's Cabin* have, despite their stereotypical or sentimental qualities, entered the public imagination as nearly mythic types.

The novel is comprised of two plot lines: the progress of Eliza and her family as they make their way to freedom in the North, and the experiences of **Uncle Tom,** who remains in the South. Tom is a middle-aged slave who has earned the respect of his original owner, Mr. Shelby, with his genial manner and basic intelligence. With his very dark skin and lack of formal learning, Tom provides a contrast to the notably lighter-skinned and articulate Eliza and George, who rebel against their oppression while Tom accepts his. Tom's complacency is, in fact, his most controversial feature, for many commentators have viewed him as embodying a stereotypical servility. His name has even become a part of African-American culture, commonly employed as a pejorative term for a black person who imitates or defers to whites. Tom's simple but firm religious faith is presented as the source of his complacency as well as his inner strength, and he has been characterized as a Christ-figure who bears his suffering passively and influences others for the better by his saintly example. Unlike Eliza and her family, Tom meets a violent end, beaten to death by a brutal master whom he forgives before he dies. His meek Christian forbearance marks him as superior to his oppressors, and his example wins over Legree's two henchman to Christianity. Some modern critics—most notably the renowned African-American novelist James Baldwin—have characterized Uncle Tom as the creation of an innately racist imagination that emasculated and dehumanized him to suit a lofty purpose. Stowe's defenders, however, maintain that Uncle Tom reflects not her racism but her didactic intent; some even suggest that Tom's Christian insistence on "turning the other cheek" resembles the philosophy of passive defiance advocated by such spiritual and social leaders as Mahatma Gandhi and Martin Luther King, Jr. Uncle Tom is thought to have been based partially on an actual person, Josiah Henson, a former fugitive slave who gained notoriety on the abolitionist lecture circuit through his similarity in appearance and manner to Stowe's protagonist, and whose autobiography was one of her acknowledged sources.

Like Uncle Tom, the memorable character of **Evangeline "Little Eva" St. Clare** is often cited as an example of Stowe's tendency toward stereotype and sentimentalism and also of her didactic intent. Eva's appearance is classically angelic—blonde and blue-eyed and always dressed in spotless white—and she embodies the Christian values of charity and brotherhood perfectly . After Tom saves her life, Little Eva idolizes him, and the two forge a friendship despite differences in race and age. That a privileged white Southern girl could achieve mutual respect and friendship with a middle-aged black male slave evidences the kind of love Stowe believed was the only force capable of conquering the evil of slavery. Eva's frailty and impending death were no doubt calculated to increase her appeal to nineteenth-century readers, whose taste for the sentimental is well documented, but modern audiences find her beatific death scene syrupy and implausible.

Little Eva's father, the kind but irresolute **Augustine St. Clare,** is a generally magnanimous but weak character. St. Clare represents the Southern slave-holder at his best; he treats Tom kindly and appreciates his abilities, but he brings misfortune upon his slave, symbolizing that slavery can never be justified or defended. A purposeless, rather frivolous man who enjoys talking and attempting to disarm his listener with frankness, St. Clare's irresponsibility is attributed to several misfortunes. He was only thirteen years old when his mother died, which deprived him of the moral guidance that, according to Stowe, only a mother could provide, and he made an unfortunate marriage to an unworthy and equally incompetent woman. Until his deathbed conversion, which some critics have found unconvincing, St. Clare wavers in his religious faith, and he is similarly undecided on the issue of slavery. His passivity leads to dire consequences for Tom, who after his master's death is sold to the brutal Legree. **Mrs. Marie St. Clare** is presented as a typical Southern aristocrat: spoiled, indolent, and self-centered. A hypochondriac, she forfeits her responsibility to care for her child, thus precipitating the arrival of Miss Ophelia in the household. After her husband's death, Mrs. St. Clare sells Tom to Legree.

Through the character of **Miss Ophelia,** St. Clare's spinster cousin, Stowe demonstrates her knowledge of New England personalities and the Calvinist or Puritan consciousness. A native of Vermont, Miss Ophelia experiences culture shock on her arrival on her cousin's Southern plantation, where order and frugality seem nonexistent and the slaves are given excessive latitude by their indulgent master. In her righteous opposition to the evil institution of slavery but repugnance for the slaves themselves, Miss Ophelia embodies the contradictory idealism that Southerners saw as a typical Northern failing. The confrontation and ensuing struggle between Miss Ophelia and the equally stubborn Topsy, during which the New England lady must overcome her repulsion in order to enact her principles, has been lauded for its realism and comedy. Vivacious, pixie-like **Topsy,** whom St. Clare buys so Miss Ophelia may educate her, is one of the most memorable black characters in *Uncle Tom's Cabin.* She is about Eva's age and provides a strong contrast to the angelic little white girl both in appearance and manner. Shrewd, prematurely skeptical, but ultimately susceptible to positive influence, Topsy was supposedly based on a young black girl named Celeste whom Stowe met when she lived with her family in Cincinnati.

Prominent among the characters in *Uncle Tom's Cabin* who have achieved mythic status is **Simon Legree,** the quintessential villain whose melodramatic name and characteristics have been frequently imitated. The fact that Legree is a Northerner by birth underlines the important concept that Southerners were not alone in blame for the wicked institution of slavery. Legree is an alcoholic, sadistic, thoroughly evil brute who lives in a broken-down, unkempt home with Cassy, the mulatto slave woman he has apparently forced into a sexual relationship. Legree reacts viciously to any provocation, imagined or not, and finally participates with his two henchmen in beating Uncle Tom to death. Although his depravity is never justified, Stowe mentions that he never knew a mother's guiding influence, a force she often promoted as instilling strong moral principles. Legree's only weakness is that he is superstitious, which his slaves exploit, enabling Cassy and Emmeline to escape from him after they convince him his house is haunted. Some critics, however, have found Legree's weakness inadequately established and included merely as a rather transparent expedient to the plot's progress.

The slave **Eliza,** who makes a dramatic escape from the Shelby plantation with her child in her arms, is as resolute and devoted to her family as any white mother could be. Herself the mother of seven children, Stowe intentionally employed the theme of maternal instinct as a means to appeal to her readers. Some critics have also seen in Eliza's flight a subconscious reflection of Stowe's own yearning for revolt. Eliza's journey over the ice floes to the Ohio shore is particularly dramatic, demonstrating the character's desperation, strength, and resourcefulness. Those early reviewers who complained that *Uncle Tom's Cabin* was rife with exaggeration or even fabrication often cited this scene as a prime example, but in *A Key to Uncle Tom's Cabin* (published in 1853), Stowe provided proof that such an incident had actually taken place. Eliza's light-skinned attractiveness has led some scholars to identify her as the stereotypical "beautiful quadroon" common in abolitionist fiction and particularly designed to appeal to white readers. Such disapproving critics as the renowned African-American novelist James Baldwin have characterized both her and her husband as essentially white people called black for convenience.

Like his wife Eliza, **George Harris** is a light-skinned black and even passes as a Spaniard after his escape. Talented (particularly in mechanics), intelligent, and sensitive, George bitterly resents his subjugation. Innately proud despite his lowly status, George knows that he is superior to his masters and vows to achieve vengeance some day. Unlike Uncle Tom, George is unwilling to accept his servitude and resolutely determines to shed it. Fighting with Loker indicates he is also willing to use force to achieve his goal.

Other significant slave characters include **Cassy**, the mulatto woman who has apparently been forced to serve as Legree's mistress. Born a Creole in New Orleans, her slave status was never apparent to her until she was taken to the sordid slave market and sold to the depraved Legree. Resourceful, Cassy executes a successful plot to escape from her master, a trait she shares with Eliza, who is eventually revealed to be her long-lost daughter. Young **Emmeline**, who escapes with Cassy, symbolizes the degrading relationship between slave women and their masters when she is portrayed as the object of Legree's lust. In an implausible coincidence, the two escaped slaves meet **Madame de Thoux** aboard their northbound boat and learn that she is George Harris's sister; through her Cassy also learns that the daughter sold away long ago is the same Eliza now married to George. **Aunt Chloe** is Uncle Tom's wife, left sadly alone in the cabin on Shelby's plantation when Tom is sold to Haley, illustrating the tragic separation of family members common under slavery. **Harry** is the young son of George and Eliza; he performs a gay minstrel act to entertain Mr. Shelby and Haley, thus rousing the latter's interest in buying him.

Uncle Tom's first master is the kindly **Mr. Shelby**, whose financial circumstances force him to sell a slave to Haley. His wife, **Mrs. Shelby**, reveals her humanitarian instincts when she objects to the sale of Tom and Harry and aids Eliza in her escape by intentionally delaying a meal. The couple's son, **George Shelby**, demonstrates his fundamental opposition to slavery through his sincere love for Uncle Tom and determination to buy him back from Legree. Unfortunately, he arrives too late to help Tom but later frees the rest of his father's slaves, dedicating the action to the memory of Uncle Tom. Other benevolent white characters in *Uncle Tom's Cabin* include **Senator and Mrs. Bird,** who offer Eliza refuge after her arrival in Ohio. The noble Mrs. Bird, whom some commentators believe Stowe modeled after herself, embodies a superior moral code that inspires her husband to take a stand against slavery; the two eventually become involved with the efforts of the Underground Railroad to deliver fugitive slaves to safety. **Simeon and Rachel Halliday** are Quakers who aid Eliza and George; they demonstrate their understanding of the true meaning of Christian charity when they provide the brutal Loker with medical care.

The villainous white characters in *Uncle Tom's Cabin* include the New Orleans slave dealer **Haley**, a crude vulgarian and dandy who speaks ungrammatically and swears often and is actually inferior to the noble and articulate Eliza and George, over whom he assumes superiority simply because he is white. Haley does not believe slaves are human beings, asserting they are no better than animals, and he ironically reveals his own shortcomings with every word. The slave-catcher **Loker** is even more inhumane than Haley in his cruelty toward the fugitives he chases. With his grotesque companion **Marks,** Loker tracks Eliza; although he does catch up with her, he is injured in a fight with George, enabling George and Eliza to escape. The cynical anecdotes told by Loker and Marks are self-condemning, revealing through their perverted humor the brutality practiced by the two slave-catchers. **Sambo and Quimbo,** Legree's henchmen, help him beat Uncle Tom to death but are finally converted to Christianity by their victim's saintly forgiveness.

Further Reading

Adams, John R. *Harriet Beecher Stowe.* Boston: Twayne, 1963.

Ammons, Elizabeth, ed. *Critical Essays on Harriet Beecher Stowe.* Boston: G. K. Hall, 1980.

Baldwin, James. "Everybody's Protest Novel." *Partisan Review* 16, No. 6 (June 1949): 578-85.

Crozier, Alice C. *The Novels of Harriet Beecher Stowe.* New York: Oxford University Press, 1969.

Dictionary of Literary Biography, Vols. 1, 12, 42, 74. Detroit: Gale.

Furnas, J. C. *Goodbye to Uncle Tom.* New York: William Sloane Associates, 1956.

Lynn, Kenneth S. Introduction to *Uncle Tom's Cabin; or, Life among the Lowly* by Harriet Beecher Stowe, pp. vii-xxiv. Cambridge, Mass.:

Harvard University Press, 1962.

Nineteenth Century-Literature Criticism, Vol. 3. Detroit: Gale.

"'Uncle Tom's Cabin.'" *Southern Literary Messenger* XVIII, No. 12 (December 1852): 721-31.

Wilson, Edmund. "Harriet Beecher Stowe." In *Patriotic Gore: Studies in the Literature of the American Civil War,* pp. 3-58. New York: Oxford University Press, 1962.

August Strindberg
1849-1912
Swedish dramatist, novelist, short story writer, poet, and essayist.

Miss Julie (*Fröken Julie;* drama, 1888)

Plot: Presented in one continuous act, the play takes place on a country estate in nineteenth-century Sweden. Miss Julie, the daughter of a wealthy count and his lower-born wife, has recently caused a scandal by forcing her fiancé to jump over a whip several times, cutting him in the process. He consequently broke their engagement. It is now Midsummer Eve, a festive holiday celebrated throughout the Swedish countryside. Miss Julie's father is away from home, and she has taken advantage of his absence by joining the servants in their merrymaking. They do not appreciate her intrusion but feel powerless to object. Julie begins to flirt with her father's valet, forcing him to dance with her and following him into the kitchen, where he has gone to be with his fiancée, Kristin, the household's cook. Kristin eventually falls asleep, while Miss Julie and Jean drink and talk together. Each relates a recent dream, and Jean tells Miss Julie about an episode from his childhood during which he secretly admired her from a hiding place. Finally the two go into Jean's room and make love. Afterward they discuss the possibility of running away together; Jean would like to become a hotelier in Como, Italy. While the two drink a bottle of wine that Jean has stolen from the count's cellar, Miss Julie explains that her mother raised her almost as a boy, encouraging her to be independent and to hate men for oppressing women. She decides that she and Jean should leave immediately, and that they should agree to kill themselves if they grow tired of each other. Jean now adopts a practical attitude, suggesting that Miss Julie go away by herself; she duly leaves to make preparations for her departure. Meanwhile Kristin enters the kitchen and soon realizes that Jean has slept with Miss Julie. She blames Miss Julie, condemning her for not keeping to her own social station, and proposes she and Jean should now be married and take jobs elsewhere. Jean allows Kristin to help him dress for church. Then Miss Julie arrives, carrying her pet finch in a cage. Jean informs her that she cannot take the bird with her, and Miss Julie tempts him to kill it. He does so, and she reacts with rage, expressing a wish to see all men dead. Returning to the kitchen, Kristin finds Miss Julie with Jean and informs her that she will not give up her fiancé. Miss Julie tries to persuade Kristin to accompany her and Jean to Como. Meanwhile Jean, who had left the room, comes back with his razor in his hand. Kristin, who has refused to join the other two on their proposed flight, now announces that she is going to church and will order the stableman not to allow any horses to leave until the count returns. When Kristin has gone, Miss Julie asks Jean what he thinks she should do; he gestures toward the razor. Suddenly a bell rings, announcing the count's arrival, and Jean immediately assumes his former subservience as he is ordered to clean his master's boots. Miss Julie, now in a trance-like state, seems elated by the idea of committing suicide to retrieve her honor and escape from her predicament. She takes the razor from Jean and leaves the kitchen.

Characters: Considered Sweden's greatest dramatist and an important forebear of many modern playwrights, including Eugene O'Neill, Strindberg infused *Miss Julie* with the naturalism that characterized his early and middle career. Focusing on the perennial tensions between men and women, servant and master, and life and death, Strindberg employed conversational dialogue and a minimum of artificiality to create a highly realistic yet evocative drama. The play evidences not only Strindberg's defiance of conventional theatrical techniques but his deterministic belief that human lives are shaped by such factors as heredity, environment, and chance rather than by individual will. Strindberg described his convictions and the intentions behind *Miss Julie* in his preface to the play, which has become a famous document of dramatic theory.

The protagonist of *Miss Julie* is the headstrong, unmarried, twenty-five-year-old daughter of a wealthy count. Like many of Strindberg's complex, fragmented characters, **Miss Julie** struggles with conflicting forces within herself: though refined and class-conscious, she is also uncontrolled and rebellious. As she explains during her late-night discussion with Jean, she was raised by a mother who had risen from a working class background to marry a nobleman and who had encouraged her daughter to behave independently and to hate men, as she did. At the same time Miss Julie's aristocratic father—who was frequently humiliated by his wife's infidelities and scorn—had provided a contradictory influence toward respectability and honor. Resentful of women's subservience to men, the confused Miss Julie is disgusted by the physical attraction she feels for the opposite sex, thus perhaps explaining her desire to ridicule and punish her fiancé by forcing him to jump over her whip and then cutting him with it. Her insistence on joining the servants' Midsummer Eve festivities, despite their obvious discomfort with such behavior, and her aggressive flirting with Jean evidence the strange and ultimately destructive impulses that drive her. Critics often cite Miss Julie's dream, which she shares with Jean, as highly symbolic: perched atop a tall tower, she feels both a strong desire to fall down from it and a deep fear of doing so. The dream has been said to embody both her wish to escape her aristocratic heritage and mingle with common people and her fear of lowering herself; the possibility of falling has also been interpreted as a metaphor for sexual release. Miss Julie's flirtatiousness does arouse the working-class Jean and they make love, but when the sexual encounter is over their positions have been reversed. Jean is now dominant, humiliating Miss Julie by calling her a whore and refusing to act tenderly toward her. Like Miss Julie's dream, the death of her pet finch has been noted for its symbolism: a caged, carefully bred creature, it might be said to resemble its mistress. When Jean kills the bird, Miss Julie is filled with rage against the male sex, thus suggesting that the bird's helplessness makes it a symbol of women's subjugation. Miss Julie's dog Diana has also been interpreted as a reflection of her mistress. A sheltered, delicate thoroughbred—named, significantly, for the chaste, boyish Greek goddess of the hunt—Diana mates with the gatekeeper's mongrel, just as Miss Julie couples with her father's valet. Both pets are said to demonstrate not only Miss Julie's appreciation of animals but the influence of animalistic instincts on human nature. In his preface to the play Strindberg suggested that an array of elements contribute to Miss Julie's behavior and eventual suicide, including the hereditary and environmental influences provided by her conflicting parents, the festive, sensual mood of the Midsummer Eve festival, such biological factors as Jean's sexual urgency and her own menstrual cycle, and the vagaries of chance. The fact that Miss Julie is, just before her suicide, in some kind of hypnotic trance adds another dimension to her psychological complexity and also evidences Strindberg's interest (shared with many other nineteenth-century intellectuals) in the subconscious. Her death has been seen as a final, desperate attempt to retrieve the sense of honor that had been destroyed in her encounter with Jean. This interpretation underlines the notion that Miss Julie represents an aristocracy growing weaker as the stronger, proletarian forces represented by Jean begin to dominate society.

Jean, the valet who becomes Miss Julie's lover, embodies the aspiration and vitality that Strindberg apparently saw as contributing to the inevitable rise of the working class. His virility, cleverness, and sense of purpose mark him as a superior being and guarantee his survival, whereas the neurotic, aristocratic, Miss Julie is destroyed. Yet Jean also reveals that his subservience is well-ingrained when, after the count's return, he again adopts his former meekness. It is only in his master's absence that he dares flirt with and then make love to Miss Julie, subsequently humiliating her when he has, through sexual conquest, gained the upper hand. Unlike her, he has no romantic illusions about sex, classifying it as a physical release rather than as an expression of love, and he refuses to express the tenderness Miss Julie expects. Just as critics have deemed Miss Julie's dream symbolic, Jean's is also laden with significance: he is in a deep, dark forest at the foot of a tall tree that he wishes to climb so that he might view the surrounding landscape and steal the golden eggs from a nest at the top. Hard as he tries, however, he can never even climb to the first limb. This dream clearly reflects Jean's social aspiration and sense of frustration, and illustrates the potential for elevation that is a strong theme of the play. Some scholars, however, have also detected in it Jean's apparent reluctance to rise. While he may be viewed as a richly endowed representative of the lower class who signifies the inevitability of their dominance, his lack of motivation and even fear are also discernible. Another significant illustration of Jean's character is found in the anecdote he tells Miss Julie about his childhood encounter with her. Curious and eager to sample the exotic trappings of the wealthy, he had slipped into the fancy outhouse used by the count's family. When it appeared he would be discovered, he escaped through the sewage tunnel, emerging completely covered with excrement. He had then seen and hidden from Miss Julie, who was dressed in a pink dress and white stockings. The contrast between the two at this moment clearly symbolizes the difference in their social positions; in addition, Jean experienced a kind of sexual awakening as he admired the girl whose pristine appearance contrasted with his own filth. Thus his eventual sexual domination of Miss Julie, as well as his killing her pet bird, might be seen as rooted in his past—as, by extension, one of the environmental factors that shape personality. Jean's ambiguous gesture toward his razor after Miss Julie has asked him how she can escape her predicament apparently represents an unspoken suggestion that she kill herself, and the fact that Miss Julie subsequently enters some kind of trance indicates that he has a hypnotic power over her. This circumstance reflects Strindberg's interest in the subconscious, a popular topic of inquiry in the late nineteenth century.

Although Jean's fiancée, **Kristin,** a cook and also member of the lower class, does not seem to share his aspirations. In fact she is particularly peeved by the disregard for class boundaries Miss Julie shows in flirting with Jean. Solid, sober, and realistic, Kristin accepts social distinctions as they are and blames Miss Julie for lowering herself and thus disrupting the servant couple's lives and marriage plans. Five years older than Jean and physically unattractive, she treats him in a maternal, even domineering manner and frequently upbraids him for his various moral lapses. Despite his physical prowess and intelligence, Jean seems to realize that Kristin is well aware of the hidden weaknesses in his character, and he defers to or perhaps even fears her. While Jean and Miss Julie are in the bedroom making love out of the audience's view, Kristin performs a mime that displays Strindberg's defiantly unconventional approach to theatrical technique and anticipates the expressionism of his later plays. Although the mime has generally been considered unsuccessful, the ballet that is simultaneously performed by the reveling servants has been more positively received. The fact that Kristin is a churchgoer has been seen as reflecting the continuing influence of religious faith in the lives of the lower class, whereas the aristocracy had all but abandoned religion. As she leaves Jean and Miss Julie in the kitchen, Kristin mean-spiritedly thwarts any hopes for escape they might have retained by announcing that she will tell the stablemen not to allow any horses to leave until the count returns.

Although he never appears in person, the character of **the count,** Miss Julie's father and Jean's employer, exerts a powerful influence on the play. He is absent during most of the action, but he remains a presence in the minds of both his daughter and his valet, who fear him for different reasons. Miss Julie has been influenced by her father to uphold her dignity and honor as an aristocrat; her sexual encounter with a servant has seriously damaged her honor. For his part Jean's apparent self-assurance belies his true obsequiousness toward authority. As soon as he hears his master's bell and is ordered to clean his boots, he returns to his former subservience. The count is physically present in the play only through those objects which represent him: his gloves, his boots, and particularly the highly evocative bell that elicits a revealing response from Jean.

Further Reading

Brustein, Robert. "August Strindberg." In *The Theatre of Revolt: An Approach to the Modern Drama,* pp. 87-134. Boston: Little, Brown, 1964.

Carlson, Harry G. *Strindberg and the Poetry of Myth.* Berkeley: University of California Press, 1982.

Johnnson, Walter. *August Strindberg.* Boston: Twayne, 1976.

Lally, M. L. K. "Strindberg's 'Miss Julie.'" *Explicator* 48, No. 3 (Spring 1990): 196-99.

Reinert, Otto, ed. *Strindberg: A Collection of Critical Essays.* Englewood Cliffs, N.J.: Prentice-Hall, 1971.

Steene, Birgitta. *The Greatest Fire: A Study of August Strindberg.* Carbondale: Southern Illinois University Press, 1973.

Strindberg, August. "Author's Preface." 1888. Reprint. In *Plays,* 2nd series, translated by Edwin Björkman, pp. 96-112. New York: Scribner's, 1913.

Twentieth-Century Literary Criticism, Vols. 1, 8, 21. Detroit: Gale.

Manuel Tamayo y Baus

1829-1898

Spanish dramatist.

A New Drama (*Un drama nuevo;* drama, 1867)

Plot: Shakespeare, the director of a theater company, is always looking for new plays to present. A young author gives him a play entitled "A New Drama," which interests him so much that he decides to stage it. The play concerns a middle-aged man, Count Octavio, whose adopted son Manfredo and much-younger wife Beatriz have fallen in love. When the jealous Octavio learns of the affair through a love letter given to him by Landolfo, his enemy, he kills Manfredo in a duel. Shakespeare gives the coveted tragic role of Octavio to the ambitious Yorick, who has previously played only comic parts. The company's leading tragic actor, Walton, is incensed that Yorick has been given the best part in the play; Walton takes the role of Landolfo.

Yorick's young wife Alicia and his adopted son Edmundo play Beatriz and Manfredo. Now the play-within-a-play mirrors reality, for Alicia and Edmundo, like the characters they are playing, are in love. The envious Walton knows about their liaison and decides to expose it to Yorick. He does so by switching the stage-prop love letter for a real one that has been exchanged between Alicia and Edmundo. The letter confirms what Yorick has already begun to suspect, and, enraged, he actually kills his son during the scene in which Octavio is to kill Manfredo. At this point, reality overtakes fiction, for the play cannot proceed after one of its actors has died.

Characters: An important nineteenth-century Spanish dramatist, Tamayo was heavily influenced by romanticism and Shakespeare's works. *A New Drama,* Tamayo's best known play, follows the pattern of the Elizabethan revenge tragedy, in which jealousy and honor are central themes. Yet it also features an innovative, play-within-a-play structure that anticipates the work of modern authors, particularly Italian dramatist Luigi Pirandello. The play exhibits Tamayo's skill in moving the action along smoothly and his gift for relaying intense emotion. A mood of duplicity and ambiguity dominates *A New Drama,* so that the boundaries between reality and fiction are constantly shifting.

The most prominent character in *A New Drama* is **Yorick,** the comic actor who assumes the tragic role of **Count Octavio.** Yorick's name also evidences Tamayo's allegiance to Shakespeare, for Yorick is the name of the murdered King of Denmark's dead jester in *Hamlet.* In the play, Hamlet comes upon Yorick's skull and laments his death. Shakespeare's Yorick is said to represent the transitory nature of life and the inevitable uselessness of action, whereas Tamayo casts his Yorick as a symbol of the potential for tragedy in human emotions and relationships. Having long played only comic roles, the ambitious Yorick yearns to become a tragic actor. In pursuit of that aspiration, he flatters the director, Shakespeare, whom he both loves and fears; though scornful of this flattery, Shakespeare allows Yorick to play Octavio. Yorick's ambition proves ill-fated, for it ultimately leads to his murdering his adopted son and the end of the play. He is the classic type of wronged husband, gradually becoming more suspicious and finally overwhelmed by rage. Some critics suggest that Yorick wants to play Octavio because he has already begun to suspect his wife of infidelity and thinks he may learn the truth if he, Alicia, and Edmundo act together in the play; others, however, claim that it is actually his *hubris* (excessive pride or confidence) in aspiring to leave the realm of comedy that brings about his downfall. Indeed, the play's ending is ironic, for Yorick is a clown in the world's eyes but, ultimately, his wife's fool, he becomes a tragic figure.

The name of the director of the theater company, **Shakespeare,** is Tamayo's most direct homage to his favorite playwright. Tamayo's character Shakespeare has been compared to the first-person narrator of a novel, for he serves as the link between the play the audience is watching (or reading) and the play his company members are staging. While he is a part of the action, Shakespeare also crafts that action. He is a dominant personality who receives admiration and deference from everyone around him; some critics have even found him unpleasantly sententious and moralizing.

Alicia, Yorick's wife, plays **Beatriz** in the drama staged by Shakespeare's theater company. She is an integral part of the play's blending of reality and fiction because she is actually in love with her husband's adopted son, just as Beatriz is in love with Manfredo. Alicia is much younger than Yorick, who seems to view her as a kind of trophy and brags about having won her. Throughout most of the play, Alicia and her lover struggle with their guilt; Alicia refers to herself as weak and without virtue and pleads with Edmundo to guide her. It is significant that Alicia refuses to leave with Edmundo when he manages to secure a boat for their escape; perhaps she would have stayed with her husband even if Yorick had not killed Edmundo.

Edmundo is Yorick's adopted son, just as **Manfredo,** the character he plays, bears the same relationship to Octavio. In addition, both Edmundo and his character are in love with their adopted fathers' wives. From the beginning of the play, Edmundo maintains a very reserved manner toward Yorick, foreshadowing the revelation of his guilt. Critics have noted that Edmundo's situation has Oedipal (referring to the protagonist of Sophocles' fifth century B.C. tragedy) overtones, in that Edmundo is attracted to his father's wife; the outcome, however, is the reversal of the Oedipal pattern: this time the son is killed by the father. **Walton** is the theater company's leading tragic actor, and he is unnerved when Yorick lands the compelling part of Octavio. Due to his admiration for Shakespeare, Walton agrees to play **Landolfo,** Octavio's treacherous friend, but he continues to harbor enmity against Yorick. He achieves vengeance when he exchanges the stage prop love letter for a real one, thus setting in motion the play's tragic conclusion.

Further Reading

Crocker, Lester G. "Techniques of Ambiguity in 'Un drama nuevo.'" *Hispania* XXXIX, No. 4 (December 1956): 412-18.

Fitz-Gerald, John Driscoll. Introduction to *A New Drama* by Manual Tamayo y Baus, translated by John Driscoll Fitz-Gerald and Thacher Howland Guild, pp. ix-xxvi. New York: The Hispanic Society of America, 1915.

Flynn, Gerald. *Manuel Tamayo y Baus.* New York: Twayne, 1973.

Nineteenth-Century Literature Criticism, Vol. 1. Detroit: Gale.

Tayler, Neale H. "Manuel Tamayo y Baus: Some Early Romantic Influences." *Hispania* XXXV, No. 4 (November 1952): 395-98.

William Makepeace Thackeray
1811-1863

English novelist, short story, fairy tale, and sketch writer, essayist, poet, critic, and editor.

Vanity Fair: A Novel without a Hero (novel, 1848)

Plot: The story is set in early nineteenth-century England. Rebecca Sharp is an orphan who was taken in as a charity case at the school for young ladies operated by the Pinkerton sisters. There she was befriended by Amelia Sedley, a wealthy and docile girl much more well liked than the saucy Becky. After the girls finish their education and leave the academy, Becky visits Amelia in her family's elegant home before embarking on a career as a governess. She meets and flirts with Amelia's older brother, Joseph "Jos" Sedley, recently returned from military service in India. Jos nearly proposes to Becky, who would like to marry the wealthy young man despite his personal defects, but Amelia's fiancé, George Osborne, disapproves of the match and helps thwart the romance. Becky then leaves the Sedleys to take a governess position with the family of Sir Pitt Crawley, an eccentric and dissolute old man who is charmed by her spirit and wit. Becky also becomes a favorite with Sir Pitt's sister, Miss Crawley, an immensely wealthy spinster with whom her family members all try to ingratiate themselves. Miss Crawley is particularly fond of her nephew Rawdon, a notorious rake and army captain whose gambling debts she good-naturedly pays. Rawdon too becomes Becky's admirer. After Becky accompanies Miss Crawley back to her London home for a long stay, the two young people spend much time together. Soon after the death of his wife, Lady Crawley, Sir Pitt arrives at his sister's home and proposes to Becky, only to learn that she has already secretly married his son Rawdon. Sir Pitt is enraged; despite her previous fondness for Becky, Miss Crawley too condemns the marriage and disowns Rawdon. Becky and Rawdon leave for a honeymoon in Brighton.

Meanwhile Amelia's romance with George is in trouble. Due to some unwise speculations, Amelia's father's business has failed, and George's father now wishes his son to break his engagement. Vain, selfish George, who has never been fully committed to Amelia anyway, feels inclined to comply with his father's demand. But his friend William Dobbin, who has secretly loved Amelia for many years, convinces George that she will die of a broken heart if he does not marry her. Thus the two are married and go to Brighton for their honeymoon, where they meet Rawdon and Becky. The Crawleys are surviving on Rawdon's winnings at the card table and Becky's ability to bluff. Dobbin too arrives in Brighton, informing George that his father has disowned him because of his marriage to Amelia; he also brings the news that Napoleon has escaped from Elba and is expected to invade Belgium. Dobbin, George, and Rawdon, all army officers, immediately leave for Brussels, and Becky and Amelia accompany them there. While the army waits for Napoleon's forces to approach, the young people enjoy a gay life. At various balls Becky dazzles and flirts with a number of men, including the just-married George; Amelia is heartsick at George's obvious infatuation with her friend. When the British army is suddenly ordered to battle at Waterloo, the city is thrust into a state of confusion and fear. To Amelia's great despair, George is killed in the battle, though Rawdon and Dobbin survive. Both Amelia and Becky soon bear sons. Amelia returns to London to live with her now impoverished parents, while Becky and Rawdon spend a brilliant year in Paris. Eventually they too return to London, where Becky ingratiates herself with the nobility and the couple lives an extravagant lifestyle on "nothing a year." Becky becomes particularly friendly with Lord Steyne, a degenerate elderly aristocrat, and is even presented at court. The Rawdon Crawleys are reconciled with Rawdon's staid, pious brother, Pitt (who inherited Miss Crawley's fortune on her death) and his wife Lady Jane; Pitt is captivated by Becky's charms. Little Rawdon, Jr., is sadly neglected by his mother, but his father dotes upon him.

The Sedleys, meanwhile, live in increasingly straitened circumstances, particularly when Jos neglects to send funds from India as he had previously done. Despite her sorrow at parting with her beloved and much-indulged son, Georgy, Amelia decides to send him to his grandfather Osborne to be raised in comfort. In a nearby part of London, Becky and Rawdon have been nearly overtaken by debts. Rawdon is finally arrested and is surprised when Becky seems reluctant to help him. He applies to his brother to pay his way out of jail. When he returns to his home, he finds Becky alone with Lord Steyne, bedecked in diamonds the nobleman has given her. Rawdon leaves his wife and accepts a post as governor of remote Coventry Island, where he eventually dies. As Becky's fortunes have dwindled, Amelia's have taken a turn for the better. Jos returns from India and provides his family with financial relief; Dobbin too returns from India, where he has served for ten years, and proposes to Amelia. She initially refuses, until she encounters Becky when traveling with Jos and Dobbin in Germany and learns that George asked Becky to run away from him the night before he left for Waterloo. Thus Dobbin and Amelia are married, though Dobbin no longer feels the intense, idealized love he once had for Amelia. Meanwhile Becky has been traveling around Europe, dependent on various admirers for support. Meeting the Sedley-Dobbin party in Germany, she manages again to charm Jos and becomes his mistress. Despite Dobbin's warnings, Jos takes out an insurance policy, naming Becky as beneficiary; he dies several months later. With this income, Becky settles into conventional middle class life, doing charity work and known among her new acquaintances as an "injured woman."

Characters: *Vanity Fair* is considered one of the nineteenth century's greatest novels. Praised for his panoramic depiction of English society, Thackeray created for his "novel without a hero" a cast of utterly unforgettable characters whom he compares to puppets that he, as "Master of the Performance," manipulates for the reader's amusement. The novel is also distinguished by its unique narrative voice: personable and often sarcastic, the narrator addresses the reader often, sometimes seeming to be part of the world of Vanity Fair and sometimes its observer. Named for the capital of human corruption found in John Bunyan's seventeenth-century allegory *Pilgrim's Progress,* Vanity Fair serves as a metaphor for the human condition in general. Through the exploits and foibles of his masterfully portrayed protagonists, Thackeray exposes the greed, hypocrisy, and emptiness that are at the heart of much human activity.

Rebecca "Becky" Sharp is not only the central figure of *Vanity Fair* but one of the most famous and controversial characters in English literature. The daughter of a dissolute artist and a French opera-girl, Becky spent her early years in precarious—if sometimes gay and exciting—poverty and was finally taken in as a charity student at the Pinkerton sisters' academy. Educated among the daughters of the wealthy, Becky developed an awareness of the power of money and a determination to acquire it by whatever means she could. The scene in which she defiantly heaves into the dust the copy of Samuel Johnson's *Dictionary* given to her upon her departure from the academy signals the spirited start of her adventures and serves as an early indicator of how she may be expected to behave. Though only a teenager at the beginning of the novel, the energetic and unconventionally attractive Becky possesses ambition and intelligence beyond her years. Her rise from social insignificance to aristocratic prominence is often described as a picaresque journey during which she encounters many obstacles but always seems to successfully surmount them. Having missed two opportunities to attain wealth and respectability by marrying either Jos Sedley or Sir Pitt Crawley, Becky weds the virtually penniless though aristocratic Rawdon Crawley and immediately goes about establishing herself and her husband in society while they live on "nothing a year." Becky survives and thrives through her uncanny ability to cajole and manipulate others, even those who might be expected to dislike her. She gradually ingratiates herself into the high society of Paris and London, even transforming her bohemian upbringing into an asset by calculatedly flaunting her facility with French and her unconventional spirit. The exact nature of Becky's apparently profitable relationship with Lord Steyne is left unspecified—it may or may not involve sexual exchange—as is her responsibility for Jos's death. It is strongly suggested that Becky had every motive (every corrupt motive, that is) to murder Jos, whose only asset when he died was his insurance policy, but the reader must decide if she is capable of such an act. Becky finally becomes solidly middle class, performing charity work and viewed as an "injured woman." Once again she has landed on her feet, though this new arrangement may not necessarily be permanent. As many critics have noted, the reader's awareness of Becky's essential corruption is countered by the admiration she inspires with her courage, resourcefulness, and good nature. In her elevation of money above all else and her extreme self-centeredness, she might be seen as an embodiment of Vanity Fair's empty, loveless values, but she might also be interpreted as a victim of society's inequities who simply does what she must to survive. That most of Becky's victims are at least as objectionable as she prompts readers to applaud when she punctures their "vanities." Her observation that for five thousand pounds a year she could be an honest woman has drawn both agreement and dissent from scholars; some believe she is not completely villainous while others contend she could not tolerate sedate respectability for long. Thackeray's attitude toward his compelling anti-heroine is never stated, but he describes her, near the end of *Vanity Fair,* as a beautiful mermaid whose hideous tail slithers invisibly beneath the waves. Whether she is viewed as a scheming, immoral vixen or a roguish but somehow admirable opportunist, Becky has, in the words of nineteenth-century novelist Anthony Trollope, "made a position for herself in the world of fiction, and is one of our established personages."

Sweet, pretty **Amelia Sedley** provides a contrast to Becky that is established during their first scene together, when Amelia is shocked by Becky defiantly discarding Miss Jemima Pinkerton's gift, and the contrast is reinforced throughout the novel. Brought up in ease and respectability, Amelia has absorbed the conventional values of her society, and her inherent weakness and sentimentality have been allowed to develop in this protected milieu. Encouraged from an early age to admire the wealthy, handsome George Osborne, Amelia sees her young suitor as a faultless, valiant prince. She steadfastly ignores or denies the obvious signs of George's selfishness and lack of any real regard for her. The pathetic aspect of her devotion is initially emphasized, particularly in her touching despair when George is about to leave for Waterloo. Yet as time goes by, Amelia's obsessive worship of her dead husband and blindness to his faults—as well as her indulgence of her son—begin to seem uncomfortably inappropriate (or even, as some scholars contend, neurotic), and her loyalty begins to look like self-centeredness. She bases her love for George on his handsome appearance and overlooks his true caddishness, just as fails to sense the solid worth and gentlemanliness of the less impressive-looking Dobbin. Thackeray depict's Amelia as a supposedly virtuous female character who ostensibly resembles the heroines of conventional literature but whose behavior is exposed as less than admirable, which is consistent with his description of *Vanity Fair* as a "novel without a hero." Thackeray regards Amelia's romantic viewpoint only slightly better than Becky's cold pragmatism, and her self-sacrifice is wasteful and empty. Described as an example of "negative virtue," Amelia's virtues prove shallow; some critics complain that her insipidity makes virtue seem dull while the always fascinating Becky lends excitement to villainy. Amelia does finally marry the noble, long-suffering Dobbin, but the happiness of their union is tempered because her husband is disillusioned with the woman he once worshipped. Despite Dobbin's unflagging kindness, Amelia seems aware of his deeper feelings, for she comments that he seems to love his daughter and his historical work more than her. Thackeray claimed to have based Amelia's character on three people: his mother, his wife, Isabella (who went insane after the birth of their second child), and his close friend, Jane Brookfield. The docile Amelia has been said to indicate both his attraction to and dissatisfaction with such soft, indulgent women, just as his depiction of Becky evidences both appreciation and distaste for more spirited females.

Thackeray described awkward, unattractive, but thoroughly good-hearted **William Dobbin** as the only noble character in *Vanity Fair.* With his big feet, lisp, and general clumsiness he is not at all the conventional hero of fiction, yet he exhibits an integrity and kindness rarely found in the other characters of Vanity Fair. Devoted from childhood to the inherently selfish George Osborne, Dobbin also formed an early and irrevocable attachment to his friend's fiancée. Convinced that George will make Amelia a much more appropriate mate than himself, he never declares his love for Amelia but through the next two decades serves her devotedly, in both large and small ways and with no expectation of recognition. It is Dobbin who, despite his own smoldering passion for Amelia, convinces George that he should resist his inclination to comply with his father's order and marry her. Dobbin's ability to instill a sense of responsibility in others is also evidenced when he encourages Jos to send much-needed and previously neglected financial support to his parents and sister. Dobbin adores the sweet, weak, pretty Amelia even though she seems not only oblivious to his virtues but not particularly grateful for his many kindnesses, and some critics have suggested that his idealized affection for such an undeserving object makes him less admirable as well. In the end, however, Dobbin does realize that he has wasted his life and his considerable store of love on someone who is unworthy of him, and he shares this realization with Amelia after she attacks him for warning her against Becky. He claims he is finished with this futile, unrequited adoration, and even after he marries Amelia—who has finally been enlightened about George's true character and now turns to Dobbin—it is obvious that his feelings for her have changed. Dobbin has achieved what he fervently desired for so many years, yet his marriage is tinged with melancholy. Like the other characters' pursuit of money and social status, his pursuit of ideal love proves essentially shallow.

Although handsome, dashing **George Osborne** is admired by everyone he knows, he is essentially selfish and van. Raised in wealth by an indulgent father, George is pompous and overly proud of his appearance and his status as a military officer. Eager to transcend his father's middle-class background, he pursues friendships with aristocratic soldiers who ridicule him for his toadying; he also thwarts the match between Jos and Becky, since he considers her unworthy of belonging to their family. Yet George lacks personal integrity and any real regard for the devoted Amelia, evidenced by his neglecting her in favor of gambling with his friends and flirting with other women before their marriage, his spendthrift ways soon after they are wed, and his heartless attentions to Becky just before he leaves for Waterloo. In fact he marries Amelia only because Dobbin convinces him that this is his duty; his own inclination is to follow his father's directive and break their engagement. The contents of the note George secretly gives to Becky the night of the ball are not revealed until *Vanity Fair* has nearly ended: it contained a suggestion that the two run away together. Amelia is devastated and enlightened when she finally hears it, though Becky has known all along that George was a cad. Little **Georgy Osborne,** the son of George and Amelia, shows signs of becoming through his mother's and grandfather's pampering as vain and pompous as his father. The much-indulged boy improves, however, when he comes under Dobbin's influence.

Becky's husband, **Rawdon Crawley,** lives the life of a self-indulgent, dissipated early nineteenth-century English aristocrat, whose era of prominence would soon come to an end. At the beginning of *Vanity Fair,* he is a rakish cavalry officer and the favorite of his aunt, Miss Crawley, who is expected to leave her considerable fortune to him. Although generally dull-witted, Crawley is a fairly proficient gambler and takes advantage of such toadies as George Osborne. Rawdon is completely captivated by Becky, whose brilliant manipulations delight him, and he remains worshipful and meek even when she comes to blatantly neglect him. As their marriage progresses, Rawdon becomes both less physically impressive and less essential to Becky's success, and she conducts her social life without him. Rawdon's character is somewhat redeemed by his tenderness toward his son, whom he sincerely loves, thus making up partially for the neglectful attitude of the boy's mother. Although he has always been somewhat aware of Becky's more reprehensible qualities, Rawdon is shocked when she is slow to help him after his arrest for not paying a debt. The scene in which, rescued by Lady Jane, he returns from prison to find his wife draped in diamonds and laughing gaily with Lord Steyne is often cited as one of the novel's most dramatic. Many readers applaud Rawdon's toppling the dissolute old man and scarring him for life, though his subsequent movements evidence the real tragedy of his fate. He eventually accepts a post on a remote tropical island where, separated from his beloved son, he soon dies of yellow fever. The character of **Rawdon Crawley, Jr.,** allows his father to demonstrate a capacity for love and his mother to reveal a lack of any maternal instinct or even basic human warmth. The pathetic little boy initially worships the neglectful and even hostile Becky; as an adult he refuses to see her, and Becky informs her new acquaintances that she is the victim of an ungrateful child.

Despite his portly stature and lack of intelligence, Amelia's brother, **Joseph "Jos" Sedley,** is a conceited dandy. After returning to England from India, where he served for several years as "Collector of Boggley Wollah," Jos refers often and officiously to his exploits abroad, typifying the attitude many Britons adopted when serving in the British colonies. Lazy, selfish, and innately timid, Jos is flattered by Becky's attention when she visits the Sedley home with Amelia after their departure from school. He does not recognize Becky as an adventurer intent on his wealth, but rather he assumes it is his appearance and prestige that impresses her. After behaving in a markedly undignified manner toward Becky while drunk, an embarrassed Jos allows George to talk him out of proposing to her. While some critics view Becky's designs on Jos as implausible because there would be no need for her to settle for such an unpleasant husband, others feel that her attempt to snare him highlights her determination to acquire wealth at any cost. The episode in which Jos, a noncombatant despite his military affectations, stays in Brussels with the womenfolk during the battle of Waterloo, growing ever more terrified by the prospect of a French invasion, is particularly comic and underlines his deep-seated cowardice. His selfishness is demonstrated when he neglects for a long time to send his impoverished family the annuity he has promised them. Sometimes seems pathetic and friendless, when he meets Becky again in Germany, where she has been living a precarious existence after her separation from Rawdon, Jos again succumbs to her charms and she becomes, apparently, his mistress. Later he plaintively admits to the already suspicious Dobbin that he is terrified of Becky, lending credibility to the theory that his death by poison three months later was a murder committed by Becky in order to collect his insurance money.

From the ranks of the Crawley family come some of *Vanity Fair*'s most memorable characters. **Sir Pitt Crawley** is an eccentric, unkempt, miserly old reprobate whose aristocratic stature is in stark contrast to his lack of integrity. Illiterate and boorish, he is much amused by the lively young Becky, whom he hires as governess to his daughters **Rosalind** and **Violet.** As soon as his much-abused, pathetic, sickly wife, **Lady Crawley,** dies, Sir Pitt proposes to Becky, causing her to weep some of the "most genuine tears" of her life because she has already married Rawdon, whose prospects of future wealth are uncertain. Despite his unpleasant nature, Sir Pitt's fate seems rather harsh: he ends as "a whimpering old idiot put in and out of bed and cleaned and fed like a baby," senile and mute and taunted by the servant girls. **Miss Crawley,** Sir Pitt's sister, is an extremely wealthy old spinster whose relatives, as she well knows, cherish her only for her money and constantly jockey for her approval. This scrambling for wealth is one of the novel's strongest examples of the perverted values of Vanity Fair, where love is equated with money. Eccentric, imperious, but essentially lonely, Miss Crawley is immediately drawn to the charming Becky, who she claims is a superior being despite her lowly status. Miss Crawley's supposedly democratic principles are exposed as shallow, however, when she disowns Rawdon for marrying Becky, a mere governess. Miss Crawley projects a carefree, even dissolute worldliness when she is in good health, but when she is ill she is overcome by a great fear of death, after which she anticipates punishment for her lifetime of sins.

Pitt Crawley is Sir Pitt's eldest son, Rawdon's brother, and the eventual recipient of Miss Crawley's fortune. Extremely proper, staid, and tightfisted, Pitt has political ambitions, hoping one day to become a member of Parliament. In fact Becky's ability to convince her brother-in-law that she believes him a born leader of men helps to win his approval and therefore to bring the Rawdon Crawleys back into the family fold. The inherently cold and mediocre though essentially decent Pitt seems for a time to be in love with Becky, but her relationship with Lord Steyne finally awakens him to her true nature. Pitt seems genuinely moved by Rawdon's devastation after his break with Becky, offering him a hand in brotherly friendship. Pitt's wife, the sweet, virtuous **Lady Jane,** is similar in nature to Amelia, and like Amelia, is a foil to Becky. Pretty and amiable, she is favored by Miss Crawley over the domineering Mrs. Bute Crawley and thus is at least partly responsible for her husband's inheriting the old lady's money. Initially rather vacuous, Lady Jane becomes aware of her husband's growing regard for Becky and is distressed by it. Yet, she treats Rawdon very kindly, allowing him to visit her often to talk about his beloved son. When Rawdon writes to Pitt from jail asking for money, Lady Jane immediately goes there herself to free him. Her mother, **Lady Southdown,** is a domineering, pious evangelist who annoys everyone with her moralizing and religious pamphlets.

Sir Pitt's brother, **Bute Crawley,** is a clergyman through circumstance rather than inclination; he would rather hunt and fish than minister to a congregation. He is completely dominated by his wife, **Mrs. Bute Crawley,** who even writes his sermons for him. Mrs. Bute is a sly, determined, ambitious woman who dislikes Becky because she senses in the clever governess an even stronger and more calculating personality than her own. Mrs. Bute is charged with maintaining a genteel household in the face of her husband's many debts, and she hopes to manipulate Miss Crawley into leaving her branch of the family her fortune. Mrs. Bute's rigidity, however, only alienates the dissolute old lady. **James Crawley,** the son of the Bute Crawleys, is a shy, good-looking boy who almost succeeds in charming his elderly aunt and thus guaranteeing her fortune for his family. His weakness for drinking and, comically, his smoking in his room while visiting Miss Crawley put him into disfavor with her.

Unlike the Crawleys, the families of Amelia and George have risen to wealth from the ranks of the middle class. Amelia's father, **John Sedley,** is a prosperous merchant whose desire for even greater wealth results in unwise speculations and bankruptcy. Refusing to settle for a diminished life-style, he embarks on several ill-fated schemes to win back his fortune; by the time he finally dies, he is a broken man. **Mrs. Sedley** is as naturally sweet as her daughter but also has difficulty living with the strain of her new circumstances. Though unflaggingly faithful to her husband, she is increasingly prone to nagging and complaint as her family grows more destitute. George's father, **John Osborne,** like his former friend John Sedley, is a wealthy product of the middle class. Mean-spirited, snobbish, and narrow-minded, he forbids his son to marry Amelia—whom he himself has long encouraged the boy to love— after her father's financial collapse. Despite loving his son and regretting the rift George's marriage causes, he cannot—even after the boy's death at Waterloo—forgive him or accept his wife. He does, however, yearn for contact with his grandson, whose mother finally relinquishes him to the Osbornes' care. In the end Osborne does leave Amelia an annuity and a generous legacy to his grandson. **Jane, Maria,** and **Frances Osborne** are George's sisters, who treat their brother's wife snobbishly but eventually come to adore their nephew.

Thackeray paints a poignant picture of the sterile, lonely life endured by spinster Jane; Maria marries a calculating lawyer named **Frederick Bullock.**

Chief among the unflatteringly portrayed aristocratic characters in *Vanity Fair* is **Lord Steyne,** Becky's elderly admirer. Although he enjoys the numerous privileges of his position, Lord Steyne is jaded and degenerate, thus underlining the shallowness of such social distinctions. Like so many of the story's men, he finds Becky completely charming and admires her gift for connivery. He and Becky apparently achieve some sort of arrangement—with possible sexual implications—and he gives her frequent gifts of money and jewelry. It is suggested that he plotted Rawdon's arrest to facilitate a tryst in any case with Becky; he leaves his encounter with her husband, permanently and ironically scarred by the diamond brooch that Rawdon throws at him. Other aristocratic characters include **Lady Bareacres,** whose name highlights her lack of redeeming virtue; a haughty old lady, she snubs the low-born Becky in Brussels and then is unable to leave when Becky refuses to sell her the horses she has herself acquired. **Lord Southdown,** Lady Jane's brother, is one of the young dandies lured in by Becky to be "shorn" at cards by her husband.

In a novel full of reprehensible characters, one of the less objectionable is **Miss Briggs,** Miss Crawley's faithful companion and later Becky's "sheepdog." Miss Briggs might be viewed as too obsequious and sentimental, thus bringing upon herself the shoddy treatment she receives from others, but her slavish devotion to Miss Briggs and then to Becky might also be seen as essential to her survival. Another particularly memorable character in the novel is **Mrs. Peggy O'Dowd,** wife of the good-natured **Major Michael O'Dowd,** commanding officer of George and Dobbins's regiment. Mrs. O'Dowd is unaffected and extremely garrulous, chatting constantly in an entertaining brogue about her Irish girlhood and relatives. Despite her tendency to annoy her listeners, she treats Amelia with genuine, motherly kindness and seems to have a strong, affectionate relationship with her amiable husband, "Mick." Her rather extravagantly attractive and aggressive sister, **Glorvina Maloney,** makes an unsuccessful play for Dobbin, whose obsession with Amelia makes him impervious to any other woman's charms.

Other notable characters in *Vanity Fair* include the snobbish, devious **Miss Pinkerton,** who with her sister runs the Pinkerton Academy for young ladies. Sentimental **Miss Jemima Pinkerton** is more kind than her sister but also more foolish; the dictionary she generously gives Becky, despite Miss Pinkerton's intention to deprive the girl of this obligatory gift, is thrown back at her. **Miss Swartz** is a very rich, flamboyantly emotional young woman of West Indian Creole heritage who attends the Pinkerton's school and later visits the Osbornes; she is much sought after by families desiring wealthy daughters-in-law for their sons. **Tom Stubble** is the earnest young soldier who serves with Dobbin and George and who brings back news of the battle when he arrives in Brussels, wounded. **Charles Raggles** is the grocer and former gardener who, by carefully saving his money, is finally able to purchase a house on respectable Curzon Street in London; he rents this house to the penniless but celebrated Rawdon Crawleys and is repeatedly cajoled by Becky into extending them credit. **Betsy Horrocks,** the daughter of Sir Pitt's butler, **Horrocks,** is a rather vulgar schemer who, after becoming Sir Pitt's mistress, plots to marry him; after Sir Pitt falls ill, her plans are disrupted by the arrival of Mrs. Bute Crawley.

The History of Henry Esmond, Esq., a Colonel in the Service of Her Majesty Q. Anne (novel, 1852)

Plot: The novel, which takes place in England and the Low Countries (such as Belgium and Holland) during the late seventeenth and early eighteenth centuries, is told in the form of remembrances by the elderly Henry Esmond. As a child, Henry—commonly called Harry—had known only that he had been brought to his home, Castlewood, from some foreign place by Viscount Thomas Castlewood. He had been educated by Father Holt, who, like Harry's guardian, was active in the plot to restore James II, the exiled Stuart king, to the British throne. Thomas was killed in an Irish battle and Father Holt disappeared, so Harry lived for a time by himself at Castlewood. Finally, however, the new viscount and his family arrived. Francis Esmond was rough but kind, and married to a much younger, beautiful woman named Rachel; their two small children were Beatrix and Frank. As he grew Harry became increasingly aware of the tension between the elder Esmonds. After Rachel's face was disfigured by smallpox, her husband seemed to reject her completely. Harry was sent away to school at Cambridge. Upon his return to Castlewood for a vacation, he noticed that Beatrix had grown very beautiful; Beatrix admired her young cousin too, and Rachel's joy in welcoming Henry back into her home was obvious. The relationship between Rachel and her husband, however, had continued to deteriorate. Francis owed a substantial amount in gambling debts to Lord Mohun, who visited Castlewood during Harry's stay. When Francis suspected that Mohun had been paying inappropriate attentions to his wife, he challenged the lord to a duel, which he also believed was the only honorable way to escape his gambling debts. The two men fought in London with Harry in attendance, and the viscount was fatally wounded. On his deathbed he informed Harry that he was not illegitimate, as he previously assumed, but was in fact the son of Thomas Castlewood by an early marriage and the heir to the family title and estate. So that Rachel and her children could retain their positions, however, Harry, decided not to reveal his secret.

Harry was sent to prison for assisting Francis with the duel. Rachel visited him there and severely scolded him, forbidding him to visit Castlewood in the future. On leaving prison Harry joined the army, fighting with the Duke of Marlborough in campaigns against Spain and France in 1702 and in the 1704 battle of Blenheim. Between these two campaigns he became reconciled with Rachel and visited the family at Castlewood; young Frank was now Lord Castlewood. Beatrix treated him with warmth, though her mother warned Harry against falling in love with the temperamental girl. After the 1704 campaign Harry went back to Castlewood and found Beatrix even more bewitching than ever, though he was also attracted to Rachel. Several years later he heard that Beatrix had become engaged to a nobleman, and he despaired of ever winning her love. In Brussels Harry encountered Father Holt, who informed him that his father, Thomas Castlewood, had seduced Harry's mother while traveling through the Low Countries and had, after the birth of her baby, married her because he had been injured in a duel and feared he might die. He had recovered and subsequently deserted Harry's mother to marry an aristocratic woman.

Harry again returned to Castlewood, where Rachel informed him that she knew the secret of his birth. However he still refused to accept the title that was his birthright. Now engaged to the Duke of Hamilton, Beatrix was interested to learn that Harry was the rightful heir to the Castlewood title. Later the duke duelled with Lord Mohun and both were killed. In order to impress the now-available Beatrix, Harry joined the plot to return the young Pretender, the Stuart prince called James III, to the throne on the imminent death of the reigning Queen Anne. Harry managed to smuggle the prince from France, where he had been living in exile, into England, taking him to the Castlewood's London home. The prince was immediately attracted to Beatrix, so her family sent her away London, back to the Castlewood estate. When the queen finally died, the prince could not be located by his supporters. Harry and Frank then discovered that he had gone to Castlewood to be with Beatrix. They renounced him and his cause, and Harry, no longer in love with Beatrix, returned to London, where George I had been made king. Meanwhile the prince returned to France with Beatrix, and Harry proposed to Rachel. The two went to America and established a home and family in Virginia.

Characters: Thackeray called *Henry Esmond* "the very best" he could do, and indeed the novel is acclaimed by many as his most accomplished—if not most popular—work. Unlike

Thackeray's previous novels, *Henry Esmond* was originally published in a single volume rather than serially and consequently features a tighter, more unified structure. In chronicling the protagonist's journey to maturity, Thackeray placed his story within an accurately depicted historical context, and he also seems to have infused it with the irony found in his other fiction, even if it lacks the satirical intent of *Vanity Fair*. The novel's inherent ambiguity and the reliability of its narrator have continued to elicit debate and varying interpretations.

The title character of *Henry Esmond* is also its primary narrator. **Henry Esmond** (called **Harry**), whom Thackeray once described as a handsomer version of himself, relates the events of his youth and young manhood for the benefit of his grandsons. He wishes to spare them the confusion about their origins that he experienced during his own lonely childhood as the ward and—as he initially believed—the illegitimate son of an English viscount. After the death of Thomas Castlewood in Ireland, Harry lived for a time in solitude in his guardian's ancestral home, Castlewood. He felt apprehensive about the arrival of the new viscount, Francis Castlewood, but with his first view of Francis's young wife, Rachel, his fears were allayed. Golden-haired, kind, and virtuous, she became for Harry both beloved mother and adored goddess, and the two spent many hours together. As he grew Harry became increasingly aware that the relationship between Rachel and Francis was unhappy, and this knowledge troubled him. He went away to college, and on his return found Rachel overjoyed with his presence and Beatrix, formerly a child with whom he'd had a brotherly relationship, a blooming and very attractive young woman. Now there were two important women in his life.

After the duel in which he served as the viscount's second and which resulted in death, viscount Harry learned the truth about his own birth and made his first significant sacrifice by refusing to claim his rightful title. He claimed that his concern for Rachel and her children motivated his decision. The dismal period of imprisonment that Harry endured signified his passage to adulthood as well as his break with Rachel, who condemned him for his part in her husband's death. Harry's subsequent military service exposed him to the brutality of war but also educated him about life and distracted him from his disappointment over Rachel's rejection. His involvement in the plot to return the Stuart king to the throne was undertaken not out of any moral or political conviction but to win Beatrix's approval, and it resulted in his disillusionment about several people he had previously revered. He learned that James was not a kingly deity but an ordinary, even weak man, so Harry broke his sword before him and renounced his cause; at the same time he realized that Beatrix no longer enchanted him. He finally returned to Rachel, whom he loved as a real, fallible, but worthy woman, and the two achieved a happy life together. The most frequently discussed aspect of Harry's character is his reliability as a narrator. Some readers and critics accept literally his claims that he is a noble, generous individual whose virtues bring him success. But others claim that there is a great deal of irony in Thackeray's portrayal of Harry: he appears to revel in his self-sacrifices, for instance, and to subtly make himself appear admirable. This ambiguity is particularly notable in his relationship with Rachel, a facet of the book that has been debated ever since its publication. Early reviewers objected to the incestuous implications of the love between Harry and Rachel and indeed, the Oedipal aspect of the story is undeniable (that is, Harry's father-figure is killed—not by him but by a man who has the same first name—and Harry marries his mother-figure). Some critics maintain that the supposedly innocent Harry was always aware of Rachel's feelings for him and even caused the breakup of her marriage, as well as that he never made any sincere effort to win Beatrix's heart but actually enjoyed the knowledge of his power over both women. To establish Harry's unreliability as a narrator, scholars often point to the preface written by his daughter, who reveals that in later life her father was rather unforgiving and self-important and that her parents' marriage, which the elderly Harry describes as blissful, was less than perfect. While the novel may be interpreted as chronicling, in the classic style of the *bildungsroman* (novel of initiation), Harry's arrival at maturity, it may also reveal that he achieved neither deep insight into himself or others or real happiness in his adult life.

Upon her arrival in Harry's life, **Rachel Castlewood** appears to the lonely, twelve-year-old boy as a vision of beauty and kindness. Only eight years older than Harry, she is much younger than her rough, rowdy husband and morally pre-eminent. In fact Rachel's virtue is considered her most notable and her most controversial quality, indicating that it is not so much Francis's misbehavior as Rachel's cold superiority that causes the rift between them. Although she is loving and nurturing toward Harry, Rachel is also possessive and demanding, and after becoming disillusioned with Francis she applies these qualities to Harry. The true nature of her feelings for Harry is seen throughout the story, particularly in her excessively strong displays of emotion—such as her anger when he brings smallpox into the Castlewood home after consorting with a village girl, her joy when he returns home from college, and her fury over his involvement in the duel that killed her husband. Some critics believe her anger at Harry after the duel is a cover for the relief that Francis's death brings. In any case these very human displays help Harry, see and love her not as a goddess but as a woman. Just as Harry may be interpreted as either noble or self-aggrandizing, Rachel may be seen as either a long-suffering martyr who finally achieves happiness or as a demanding shrew who continues to damage others psychologically. Some scholars contend that her long period of self-denial, when she sends her beloved Harry away and later listens to his confessions of love for Beatrix, leads to her redemption and realization as a whole human being. But other critics point out that in the preface her daughter stated that her mother's jealous, demanding nature remained constant through her later life. The controversy over *Henry Esmond*'s incestuous implications has centered on Rachel, whose feelings for Harry are distinctly un-motherly from the time of their first meeting, and early readers and critics considered her shocking and unacceptable as a heroine. It is thought that Thackeray based Rachel on Jane Brookfield, whose suspicious husband forbad her to keep company with the author.

One of the most memorable characters in *Henry Esmond* is the bewitching **Beatrix Castlewood,** the daughter of Francis and Rachel and the object of Harry's passion for several years. Beautiful, spirited, and ambitious, Beatrix is one of Thackeray's self-seeking types, similar in her intelligence and vitality to the even more renowned Rebecca Sharp in *Vanity Fair.* Willful, capricious, and fascinating, Beatrix rejects Harry's love in favor of the wealth and status her aristocratic suitors offer. Yet Beatrix shares with many of the novel's other characters an inherent ambiguity that allows a variety of interpretations. One of these centers on her relationship with her mother, whose virtue she claims she can never match and in whose affection she has never felt secure. She claims that others have always been first in Rachel's heart—whether Francis, Frank, or Harry—that as a result she has turned to selfish and ultimately destructive behavior. Thus she might be seen as a lonely victim of maternal rejection rather than as a heartless coquette manipulating men for material advantage. Beatrix's relationship with Harry has also been debated: some critics detect hints that she is not so evasive as the elderly narrator attempts to paint her, but that Harry himself might have lacked the resolution needed to claim her. In the end Harry loses his fascination for Beatrix and describes her as excessively and unattractively proud and disdainful, but the possibility that the narrator is unreliable leaves the reader to speculate about Beatrix's true nature as well.

Viscount Francis Castlewood is the patriarch of the family that comes to occupy their ancestral estate after the death of Thomas Castlewood. Francis is a loud, rough, but essentially amiable man whom Harry comes to love even as he grows increasingly aware of the discord between Francis and Rachel. Prone to gambling, drinking, and philandering, Francis is blamed for the trouble in his marriage, particularly when he blatantly rejects his wife after her beauty has been marred by smallpox. Nevertheless Francis complains that

Rachel's suffocating possessiveness and her cold, unforgiving nature drove him away. His statements are often used as evidence that Rachel is not the scion of virtue the narrator makes her out to be. Sturdy young **Frank Castlewood,** who acquires the title of viscount after his father's death and in whose favor Harry rejects his own right to the title, is handsome and gay, a good sportsman and swordsman but not the superior being that Harry paints himself. Frank reacts to the revelation about Harry's sacrifice with laudable gratitude and admiration for his benefactor; he never resents that his elevated status has been artificial.

During his early years at Castlewood, Harry was left in the care of **Father Holt,** a Catholic priest who serves as the boy's tutor. Like Thomas Castlewood, Holt is inflamed with the Stuart cause and finally must flee England to escape persecution for his activities. The priest not only provides Harry with the affection he craves but exposes him to a religious zeal that is eventually replaced by the more reasoned Anglicanism propounded by Rachel. The very young Harry considers Father Holt infallible, and his later realization of the priest's weaknesses—his self-deception and his almost comic pretensions to possessing secret knowledge—form part of Harry's maturation process, though he is grateful for the priest's help in establishing his identity. Father Holt tells him the story of his mother's seduction and abandonment by Thomas Castlewood, thus filling a gap in Harry's knowledge of his background.

Several significant historical figures make appearances in *Henry Esmond.* During the military campaigns in France and Spain and in the Battle of Blenheim, Harry encounters the famous commander-in-chief the **Duke of Marlborough.** Harry describes the duke as ruthless and corrupt, though a footnote by his grandsons again brings the narrator's reliability into question, because it reveals that Harry had a personal grudge against him. At the same time this unusual view of Marlborough, normally characterized as a great hero, might be Thackeray's attempt to expose the over-glorification frequently found in military histories, as is Thackeray's depiction of the famous man of letters **Joseph Addison,** whose poem about the Battle of Blenheim made his career. Harry criticizes Addison for portraying war in a sanitized, glorified manner rather than as bloody and brutal; Addison counters that his duty as a poet is to depict and celebrate heroes rather than present reality. One heroic historical figure who is brought down to a human level in *Henry Esmond* is **James,** the Stuart prince whose followers hoped to return him to the throne after the death of Queen Anne. He fell in love with Beatrix and abandoned his duty to his supporters, which marked him as fallible, a weak denizen of what Harry terms a "thankless and shiftless race" (that is, the Stuart family).

Other characters in *Henry Esmond* include **Henry, Lord Mohun,** the dashing, dissolute London rake who tries unsuccessfully to seduce Rachel and incurs Francis's wrath. Mohun shares the same first name as the novel's protagonist, reinforcing its Oedipal theme, since he kills Harry's father-figure. Mohun is later killed in a duel with the **Duke of Hamilton,** Beatrix's wealthy, elderly suitor, who also dies in the confrontation. **Rachel Esmond Warrington,** born to Harry and Rachel after their move to Virginia, narrates the preface in which several significant details help illuminate the plot and suggest ambiguity in the characters of her parents and half-sister. The younger Rachel indicates that she too has suffered from her mother's possessiveness and that her adored father is prone to rigidity and self-importance. Critics note that by placing Rachel's comments at the beginning of the story, Thackeray intends for his reader to be wary of accepting Harry's account at face value.

Further Reading

Bloom, Harold, ed. *William Makepeace Thackeray.* New York: Chelsea House, 1987.

Carey, John. *Thackeray: Prodigal Genius*. London: Faber & Faber, 1977.

Ferris, Ina. *William Makepeace Thackeray*. Boston: Twayne, 1983.

Hardy, Barbara. *The Exposure of Luxury: Radical Themes in Thackeray*. London: Peter Owen, 1972.

McMaster, Juliet. *Thackeray: The Major Novels*. Toronto: University of Toronto Press, 1971.

Olmstead, Charles John. *Thackeray and His Twentieth-Century Critics: An Annotated Bibliography, 1900-1975*. New York: Garland, 1977.

Rawlins, Jack P. *Thackeray's Novels: A Fiction that Is True*. Berkeley and Los Angeles: University of California Press, 1974.

Thackeray, William Makepeace. "Before the Curtain." In *Vanity Fair: A Novel without a Hero*, edited by George Tillotson and Kathleen Tillotson, pp. 5-6. London: Methuen & Co., Limited, 1963.

Trollope, Anthony. *Thackeray*. 1879. Reprint. Detroit: Gale Research, 1968.

Leo Tolstoy
1828-1910
Russian novelist, short story writer, dramatist, essayist, and critic.

War and Peace (*Voina i mir;* novel, 1869)

Plot: The novel opens in 1805, the year in which Russia and Austria joined forces against Napoleon's French troops at the Battle of Austerlizt. Despite the threat that the charismatic French leader represents, life in Russia's aristocratic circles goes on much as before. Young Nikolay Rostov joins the army, earning his family's admiration—especially that of his sister Natasha and his worshipful cousin Sonya—with his strong sense of duty and dashing appearance in his uniform. The Rostov family's friend Pierre Bezuhov, however, is widely disliked by his high society acquaintances. Having returned to St. Petersburg from school in Paris, the large, awkward, bespectacled young man lacks direction and behaves in an irresponsible, sullen manner. The illegitimate son of a wealthy count, Pierre is suddenly made wealthy when his father dies and leaves him a large inheritance, and just as suddenly he is sought after by those who formerly disdained him. He is coerced into marrying the beautiful but corrupt Hélène Kuragina; the match is never happy. Pierre's good friend Prince Andrey Bolkonsky is equally unsatisfied: he finds domestic life with his sweet but somewhat vacuous wife, Princess Lise, stifling and joins the army to escape. When he returns from the Battle of Austerlitz, he learns that Lise has died giving birth to their son, Nikoluschka. Andrey feels no relief in his new freedom and seeks answers to his questions about the meaning of life from his friend Pierre, who has become a member of the brotherhood of Freemasons and an ardent believer in their ideals. Pierre does not realize that his wealth is what makes him attractive to the organization. The always enthusiastic if misguided Pierre decides to free his serfs and modernize his estate, but his lack of business sense leads to a chaotic state of affairs. He leaves with Andrey to visit the Bolkonsky family estate, Bleak Hills.

Meanwhile, Nikolay has fought in several battles waged by the Russian army against Napoleon's advancing forces. Tsar Alexander finally signs a peace treaty with the French leader, who retreats to Spain, but it is an uneasy armistice. Back in Russia, Andrey visits the Rostov family and meets his host's charming daughter Natasha, with whom he soon believes he has fallen in love. Pierre, who has recently become estranged from his wife after fighting a senseless duel over her suspected infidelity, encourages Andrey in pursuing Natasha. Dazzled by her handsome suitor, Natasha accepts his proposal but Andrey's tyrannical father insists that he wait a year before marrying such an inexperienced young girl; neither does Andrey's pious sister Marya approve of the match. Andrey joins the army while Natasha enters the gay social life of Moscow, where she attracts the dishonorable attentions of Hélène's rakish brother Anatole Kuragin. The naive, confused Natasha finally agrees to elope with her insistent suitor, but the plan is discovered by Pierre, who sends Anatole away. In subsequent talks with Natasha, Pierre finds himself attracted to her but keeps his feelings hidden. Andrey, meanwhile, participates in the army's efforts against Napoleon, who has led his troops into Russia and is marching toward Smolensk. Napoleon finds that city burned and deserted, and he pushes on toward Moscow, continually clashing with soldiers under the command of General Kutuzov. During the bloody battle of Borodino, where both the Russian and French forces suffer heavy losses, Andrey is wounded. As the French troops enter Moscow, Andrey is taken with other wounded soldiers to the Rostov estate. Natasha nurses him devotedly and the two reaffirm their love. She and Marya also become close friends while Nikolay, who has also arrived at the estate, begins to find Marya attractive. Andrey finally dies.

While most of the residents have left Moscow, Pierre has decided to stay and attempt to assassinate Napoleon. Instead he is taken prisoner by the French and made to march with them back to Smolensk. The experience drastically alters Pierre's outlook, teaching him responsibility and courage, and his goodnatured personality makes him popular with both his captors and fellow prisoners. When the Russians finally defeat the exhausted, ragged, and demoralized French troops, Pierre is released. He makes his way home to learn of the deaths of Andrey and Hélène; his wife had fallen in and died in St. Petersburg during his absence. Pierre soon recovers from these shocks with a renewed sense of joy in being alive and a humble faith in God. In Moscow, he again encounters the Bolkonsky and Rostov families. Still charmed by Natasha, whose experiences have made her a mature woman, Pierre asks for and receives her hand in marriage. Natasha becomes a humorously domineering but efficient and genial wife to the appreciative Pierre, and the two raise a fine family of four children. Meanwhile, Nikolay marries Marya, and despite his initial misgivings finds with her an unexpected happiness; the couple adopts Andrey's son Nikoluschka.

Characters: The epic *War and Peace* is frequently proclaimed the greatest novel of the nineteenth century; some even consider it the finest novel in all literature. It is said to have moved the genre out of the early-nineteenth-century realm of romanticism into the realistic mode that would dominate fiction well into the twentieth century, and many subsequent authors were heavily influenced by Tolstoy's art and vision. *War and Peace* provides an encyclopedic, panoramic portrait of life in Russia during the Napoleonic era, but its thematic depth and human appeal reach far beyond its immediate context. As the intertwining stories of two families unwind against a historic backdrop, more than five hundred characters bring to life such themes as the artificial versus the natural, the importance of family relationships, the influence of natural law rather than free will on the course of history, and the conflict between reason and passion. Tolstoy is universally praised for his compelling, insightful depictions of the main characters in *War and Peace*— complex individuals whose physical and psychological qualities and conflicts make them both remarkably human and endlessly interesting.

Although there are no conventional heroes in *War and Peace* and no character who may be considered truly central, **Pierre Bezuhov** has been identified as the only figure who is present throughout the course of the novel, and his progress toward maturity is one of several important threads in the novel's complex fabric. As the story opens, the tall, ungainly, rather stout Pierre—who has a habit of peering over the top of his spectacles—has recently completed his university education in Paris and has returned to the high society world of St. Petersburg. The illegitimate son of a count, Pierre lacks direction and a sense of his own identity. In his confusion and dissatisfaction, he engages in a dissolute existence of drinking and gambling. Initially a social pariah whose sullen, argumentative manner alienates him from his acquaintances, Pierre becomes popular with the sudden advent of his inheritance. His failure to perceive that his new friends are drawn only by his wealth is an early indication of the self-deception he will continue to demonstrate. Pierre allows himself to be trapped into marriage with the alluring but corrupt Hélène Kuragin, a match that soon proves ill-advised. With typically unthinking enthusiasm, he next embraces the tenets of the Freemasons—the mystical brotherhood that is actually more interested in his money than in his soul—and agrees to give up his dissipated ways for clean living and philanthropy. Pierre's efforts to improve his country estate—including the very modern practice of freeing his serfs—prove disastrous, however, and he eventually retreats with his friend Andrey to search for some other answer to his yearning for meaning in his life. Pierre's senseless duel with his wife's lover is an expression of the artifical values of his social set and epitomizes his sense of futility. Moscow's invasion by the French provides what Pierre views as an opportunity for self-sacrifice, as he plans to save his homeland by assassinating Napoleon. This grandiose plan, not surprisingly, is scuttled when he is captured and forced to accompany the French army back to Smolensk. Pierre's harrowing experiences as a prisoner of war, during which period he is reduced to the most primitive kind of existence, prove crucial in his development as a mature, more enlightened human being. His essential good nature helps him to survive, and from the peasant Karataev he learns to accept his circumstances with serenity and fortitude and to take joy in simply being alive. Pierre's subsequent marriage to Natasha, who has also undergone a period of change and development, is appropriate because both have exhibited a capacity for growth and an openness to life that makes the success of their partnership seem likely. Tolstoy's epilogue reveals that Pierre later submits humbly and gladly to his wife's domination; this circumstance has been said to evidence the author's conviction that individual concerns are best sublimated to the demands of family life. Pierre is often identified as one of the representatives of Tolstoy's own viewpoint found throughout his fiction, though in *War and Peace* the author's personality seems to be reflected in several different characters. Thus Pierre embodies Tolstoy's passionate, physical side—though perhaps not intellectually rigorous or spiritually deep like Andrey, Pierre possesses a strong hunger for life. The fact that it is Pierre rather than Andrey who survives might be interpreted as indicating their creator's preference for Pierre's more life-affirming qualities.

One of the most popular of all fictional characters, **Natasha Rostova** is particularly beloved by readers of Russian literature. Though not particularly beautiful, her great personal charm and vivacity, capacity for love, and lust for life make her immensely attractive—especially to such men as Boris Dubretsky, Andrey Bolkonsky, and Anatole Kuragin. When she makes her first appearance in the story, Natasha is an enchanting, willful little girl whose parents over-indulge her; later she becomes the eager though naive fiancée of the dashing Andrey. Disappointed by the necessity of waiting a year before she may marry her handsome suitor, Natasha goes to Moscow, where her inexperience and yearning for excitement increase her susceptibility to the dangerous Anatole, who like his sister represents an ultimately destructive sexuality. Natasha is briefly conquered by the lure of the artificial, effectively illustrated by the famous opera scene in which the superficiality of the Moscow aristocracy seems concentrated in the flimsy sets and costumes of the performance. But her good, *natural* instincts ultimately prevail. Rescued from corruption, Natasha goes on to experience a period of suffering that results in her development into a wiser, stronger woman. When Andrey is brought to the Rostov home with the other wounded soldiers, Natasha asks for and receives his forgiveness for her lapse in fidelity, and the two reaffirm their love. With the loving devotion that typifies her nature, Natasha nurses Andrey through his last days. Pierre finally returns from his own life-changing experiences to find that Natasha is no longer the gay, vivacious, frivolous young girl to whom he had previously been attracted, but a mature woman who shines with a deeper, more profound radiance than before. Like Pierre, Natasha has proven capable of change and growth, so it is appropriate that he becomes the partner of her maturity. Tolstoy emphasizes that in marriage, childbearing, and overseeing her household Natasha finds the best outlet for her energies and truest expression of her personality. Almost fanatically devoted to her family, she seems to dominate her husband and serves as the primary anchor of order and stability in their home. Natasha has been interpreted as representing—perhaps more than any other character in *War and Peace*—the instinctively life-affirming, passionate quality that Tolstoy considered quintessentially Russian. In her is concentrated the *natural,* as opposed to the artificiality embodied in such figures as Anatole and Hélène. The aspect of Natasha's characterization that has generated the most controversy is her final incarnation as a rather stout, domineering, conventional matriarch. Some critics have faulted Tolstoy for the limited view of women's roles reflected in Natasha's fate, suggesting that it evidences the author's ambivalent or even hostile attitude toward women. Others, however, claim that Natasha's final role is in keeping with Tolstoy's belief in the sublimation of the self to the greater call of family responsibility. Thus Natasha's staidness at the end of *War and Peace* could be seen either as an unfortunate violation of her exuberant nature or as a necessary and appropriate channeling of her considerable energies.

While Pierre is often said to represent the passionate side of Tolstoy's personality, **Prince Andrey Bolkonsky** seems to embody the more ephemeral impulses of reason and spiritual yearning. At the beginning of *War and Peace,* Andrey is a wealthy, somewhat cynical aristocrat who is bored and dissatisfied in his marriage to Princess Lise, who, though sweet and gay, is his intellectual inferior. As many critics have noted, the reader is given no information about Andrey's earlier life, such as how he came to marry Lise. In order to escape the mundanities and aggravations of domestic life, Andrey joins the army and goes to fight Napoleon at the Battle of Austerlitz. There he experiences the first of several spiritual revelations as he lies wounded on the battlefield: staring up into the wide blue sky, he senses its infinity and the comparative insignificance of human existence. Returning home to find that Lise has died, Andrey fails to enjoy the freedom he had assumed his marriage denied him; bewildered, he turns to his friend Pierre for answers. Although Pierre lacks Andrey's rigorous intellect, he offers warm friendship and shares the quest for meaning and purpose in life. Pierre encourages his friend to pursue Natasha, and for a short time Andrey is diverted and even renewed by his feelings for the vibrant young woman. Yet he accepts their separation with what some scholars have characterized as a too-easy resignation, thus reinforcing the idea that Andrey prefers the course of spiritual searching to the more physical realities of love and marriage. After he has again left home to join the army, Andrey hears the news about Natasha's betrayal and is plunged into bitterness, but he experiences another mystical awakening after he is wounded and is being transported out of Moscow. Reminded again of the insubstantiality and pettiness of human concerns as compared to the infinite reaches of the universe, Andrey is filled with a sense of detachment, well-being, and acceptance of his fate. After his reunion with Natasha, for whom he reaffirms his love, Andrey dies. Andrey is most often identified as a foil to Pierre: although he lacks his friend's lust for life, he possesses a great capacity for spiritual growth and seems to embody the intangible qualities of aspiration and yearning. Although Tolstoy does not casually dismiss or discredit Andrey's perspective, some critics believe that this character's failure to survive signifies the author's preference for Pierre's more passionate, physical approach to life. In keeping with his role as a reflection in part of his creator's personality, Andrey in several instances serves as a mouthpiece for Tolstoy's specific ideas, such as when he explains to Pierre why German and other western European combat strategies will prove unsuccessful when war is waged on Russian soil.

Passionate, energetic young **Count Nikolay Rostov,** Natasha's brother, feels instinctively drawn to the military way of life. Eager to defend his homeland, he joins the cavalry and makes a handsome, dashing appearance in his smart uniform; he is idolized by his sister and by his cousin Sonya, to whom he has been unofficially betrothed since both were children. Frank, energetic, and intelligent, Nikolay is also very impetuous, but this quality will be curbed by his experiences in the war. His unrealistic, glorified expectations of the conflict into which he has propelled himself must eventually crumble as he experiences the realities of combat. His naive admiration for Tsar Alexander—whom he had envisioned as a godly, infallible being—for instance, is diminished when he witnesses the horrible suffering of the wounded soldiers in the hospital at Tilsit while their seemingly immune superiors attempt to forge a peace treaty. Nikolay returns home a more solid, stable man, though he is still more fond of life in the open air (a quality that reflects Tolstoy's own love of the outdoors) than of intense contemplation. Having given up his childhood sweetheart in favor of a more financially advantageous marriage to Marya, Nikolay has misgivings about the appropriateness of the match even though he admires Marya. The marriage, however, proves a success, and Nikolay becomes a gentleman farmer whose peasants respect and admire him as "a proper master." Some critics point to Nikolay's fate as evidence of Tolstoy's clinging, despite his affinity for modern techniques and social theories, to the older, patriarchal system of landowners and serfs.

Princess Marya Bolkonsky is Andrey's sister and, eventually, Nikolay's wife. As *War and Peace* begins, she lives in tiresome subservience to her selfish, tyrannical father, who repeatedly discourages her suitors because he wants her not to marry but to continue to care for him. Obedient and pious, Marya takes solace in religious activities such as the mystical gatherings of peasants, called "God's Folk," that she organizes. Although she seems to have resigned herself to solitude and piety, there are several early indications that her nature is better suited to a different kind of life; for instance, she feels that she is a sinner because she loves her father and her small nephew, who is given into her care after Lise's death, more than God. Marya serves as a foil to Natasha, for she is gentle and humble whereas Natasha is vivacious and willful, and she initially disapproves of her brother's fiancée. During the turbulent crisis of the war and the return of the wounded Andrey, however, the two women are united by diversity and common concerns, and they forge a strong friendship. She even helps to mediate the marriage between Pierre and Natasha, the appropriateness of which she instinctively perceives. Like Natasha, Marya makes a surprisingly suitable marriage, and she too finds fulfillment in managing a home and family. That she is described as being more broadly conscious and wise than her husband has led several critics to note that the novel's wives generally seem stronger and more dominant than their husbands, a circumstance that hints at an interesting ambivalence in Tolstoy's attitude toward women.

One of the most notable representatives of the artificial in *War and Peace* is **Princess Hélène Kuragina,** the beautiful aristocrat who marries Pierre. Repeatedly characterized by her white shoulders and her corrupt, indiscriminately bestowed smile, Hélène possesses a flagrant sexuality that ultimately proves destructive. Her great seductiveness masks the true shallowness of her nature; she marries Pierre only for wealth and social status and carries on her love affairs without interruption or guilt. Concerned only with gratifying her own desires, she lacks any consideration for others. Hélène may be identified as one of the best illustrations of Tolstoy's belief that sexuality is dangerous and potentially fatal; significantly, she refuses to bear children and thus pursues sex only for pleasure, a concept to which

Tolstoy consistently objected. The rumors of an incestuous relationship with her brother further heighten Hélène's aura of moral corruption. Although some critics view her as entirely evil, others note that her apparent realization of the misery she has caused others as well as her final isolation and loneliness prevent her from being a one-dimensional character.

Like his sister Hélène, the rakish **Anatole Kuragin** is a shallow hedonist whose drive to gratify his own desires precludes any consideration for others. Although he is already married to another woman, Anatole is attracted to Natasha and sets out to seduce her, convincing her that he plans to marry her when in fact the ceremony he has arranged will be a sham. In his self-possession, confidence, and intense physicality, Anatole provides a strong contrast to the absent Andrey, so it is perhaps not so surprising that the passionate young Natasha would be taken in by him. One of the novel's foremost representatives of the artificial, which threatens such essentially *natural* characters as Natasha and Pierre, Anatole is closely identified with the city, where superficial values thrive. Significantly, his most notable encounter with Natasha occurs at the opera, a performance that glorifies the idea of masking and artificiality. Another important member of the Kuragin family and representative of the corrupt, hypocritical social realm of St. Petersburg is **Prince Vasily Kuragin,** the father of Anatole and Hélène. The socially adroit, smooth-talking Kuragin is as shallow and corrupt as his children, scheming to increase his own as well as Hélène's wealth and social status by tricking the unsuspecting Pierre into marrying her. Tolstoy's gift for endowing his characters with symbolic physical characteristics is exemplified by the unpleasant facial twitch that occurs only when Kuragin is alone, a tangible expression of his inner corruption.

The structure of *War and Peace* features two family blocks that are presented against a historical backdrop. From the Rostov family come not only the main characters Natasha and Nikolay but several significant minor figures. The Rostovs are depicted as representatives of the natural and also as essentially Russian, both in their rural origins and in their warm familial relations. Critics have noted that Tolstoy's depiction of wealthy landowner **Count Ilya Rostov** is particularly sympathetic. Rostov is carefree, warmhearted, and perhaps somewhat foolish; after the invasion of Moscow and the threatened loss of his property, however, he loses his habitual cheerfulness and grows doubtful and bewildered, weeping pathetically at Andrey's death. Though **Countess Natalya Rostova** has a more anxious, less generous personality than her husband, the two seem happily married. In fact, some scholars have commented on the rather childlike nature of their relationship, which seems immune from both sexual passion and serious conflict. **Countess Vera Rostova,** the family's older daughter, provides a strong contrast to Natasha in her coldness and formality, and indeed, both she and her mother note that she was brought up more strictly than her sister. In fact, Vera's rigidity alienates her from the rest of the family, particularly when she marries the equally stiff Lieutenant Berg. **Count Petya Rostov** is the youngest son, an innocent, gay young man who shares with Natasha and Nikolay a typically Russian love of music. Petya joins the guerilla resistance with great joy and eagerness but is very abruptly killed before he has a chance to fight the French, evidencing the randomness not only of the brutality of war but of fate itself.

Sonya Rostova is the family's poor cousin, brought into the household to serve as a companion for Natasha. She and Nikolay pledged their love for each other when both were children, but Sonya releases him from this early, innocent vow when he wishes to marry the wealthy Marya. In her sweetness and ready compliance, Sonya provides a contrast to Natasha, but she does not ultimately prove as admirable a character as her cousin. Though the reader tends to sympathize with Sonya, she reveals a hint of meanness when she expresses a wish to rescue the Rostov family's possessions rather than aid the wounded men who have been brought to the estate.

Members of the other important family in *War and Peace,* the Bolkonskys, are characterized by their strong intellectual and spiritual capacities but also by their narrowmindedness. The elderly **Prince Nikolay Bolkonsky** is a quarrelsome eccentric whose desire for control over his children's lives leads to their unhappiness. He selfishly prevents Marya from marrying, for instance, and also insists that Andrey wait a year before wedding such a young and inexperienced girl as Natasha. Bolkonsky's strict adherence to routine and habitual suppression of the love he feels for his children are depicted as particularly un-Russian, and the old man's death of a stroke as the French approach suggests that his rigidity has ultimately limited his ability to adapt to his circumstances. Tolstoy is thought to have modeled this character after his own grandfather, who like Bolkonsky was a veteran of the Crimean War. The beautiful, childish **Princess Lise Bolkonskaya**—who is consistently characterized by her fetching upper lip covered in pale, soft down—is an inappropriately frivolous, unintellectual partner for the tormented Andrey. Some critics are frustrated by the fact that no information is offered about the couple's courtship, leaving the motivation for their marriage something of a mystery. Tolstoy has, however, been praised for the poignant scene in which a bewildered Lise dies after giving birth to the couple's son **Nikolushka** (who will later be adopted by Nikolay and Marya).

One of the most notable minor characters in *War and Peace* is the peasant **Platon Karataev,** whom Pierre meets while both are prisoners of the French. Karataev provides an example of Tolstoy's ideal of the Russian peasant: he is simple, goodhearted, and affectionate with a strong faith in God and a stoicism that allows him to accept everything that happens to him. During the long, arduous march toward Smolensk, he performs many acts of kindness for his fellow prisoners and—most important—he helps Pierre to achieve peace of mind. Eventually shot by the French because he is too weak to complete the march, Karataev faces his own death with grace and composure, demonstrating the serenity and acceptance that Pierre will also come to possess. Karataev is characterized by his round face, which is said to manifest his moral wholeness or harmony.

The historical events depicted in *War and Peace* comprise an important part of its impact, and these events are particularly illuminated by two historical personages employed as characters in the novel. **General Michael Kutuzov,** who commanded the Russian army after 1812, is portrayed as an obese, slovenly figure who is unpopular with his fellow officers but who—after initially being ignored because his strategies were considered outdated—is ultimately relied upon to save Russia from Napoleon. Kutuzov employs a quintessentially *natural* "time and patience" strategy to beat Napolean rather than the sophisticated tactics promoted by other commanders; he instinctively relies on the passionate spirit of the Russian people as well as Russia's wild, difficult landscape and climate to conquer the enemy. His belief that the mass of the people rather than one or two great men will alter the course of events exemplifies Tolstoy's theory of history, which features a fatalistic reliance on natural law rather than the free will of individuals. Kutuzov's ultimate victory represents a triumph of the natural over the essentially artificial precepts embodied in **Napoleon Bonaparte,** the French emperor whose colossal pride and belief in his own invincibility lead to his downfall. Napoleon's determination to complete his march to Moscow despite the obvious difficulty of such a task proves disastrous as his troops are finally overcome by hunger, cold, and fatigue. A brilliant strategist who fails to see the futility of invading Russia, Napoleon provides the novel's primary example of Tolstoy's "Great Man" theory of history. He is erroneously convinced that he can control events by the sheer force of his own will, but in fact, says Tolstoy, events are ordered by fate.

An explication of all of the minor characters in *War and Peace* could comprise a volume of its own, but several do bear mentioning. **Dolokhov,** the rake who fights a duel with Pierre after having an affair with Hélène, is a coldly rational, nihilistic (denying allegiance to conventional morality) character sometimes compared to Grigory Pechorin, the protagonist of Mikhail Lermontov's 1840 novel *A Hero of Our Time*. He also cheats Nikolay at cards and assists Anatole in his attempted seduction of Natasha. In battle, he exhibits a vicious enjoyment of killing that is condemned by Tolstoy. Dolokhov is ultimately forgiven by Pierre, whom—as leader of the guerilla resistance to the French—he rescues from captivity. **Boris Drubetskoy** is an ambitious army officer and friend of the Rostov family who unsuccessfully courts Natasha. Always impeccably dressed in accordance with current fashion, he is a shallow social climber who embodies the artificial through his emphasis on surfaces rather than content or meaning. Appropriately, Drubetskoy finally marries the pretentious, wealthy Julie Karagina. Another important representative of St. Petersburg society is **Anna Scherer,** who hosts the fashionable gathering with which *War and Peace* opens. Within her popular "salons" are concentrated the gossip and hypocrisy of the aristocratic world, the artificiality which is reflected in the false expression of enthusiasm she maintains despite her truly jaded outlook. **Lieutenant Alphose Berg,** who marries Vera Rostova, is a satirically portrayed army officer with an exaggeratedly orderly, accurate approach to life. The fact that he dislikes Natasha for the very qualities that make her admirable signifies his untrustworthiness and lack of perception. Other notable characters in *War and Peace* include **Basdayev,** the Freemason who calculatedly persuades Pierre— whose wealth he and his organization covet—to give up his dissolute behavior for clean living and philanthropy; and **Mademoiselle Bourienne,** Marya's shallow and heartless companion, to whom the nearly senile Count Bolkonsky becomes attracted.

Anna Karenina (novel, 1877)

Plot: Set in nineteenth-century Russia, the novel centers on Anna Karenina, who is unhappily married to a cold, ambitious government official named Alexey Karenin. In Moscow, where she has arrived in an effort to resolve a rift between her brother Stiva Oblonsky and his wife Dolly, she meets handsome, dashing Count Vronsky. The two are immediately attracted to each other, though Vronsky is thought to be courting Dolly's sister Kitty. Unlike the more attractive young count, sober Konstantine Levin is truly in love with Kitty, but she rejects his proposal of marriage because she believes that Vronsky will soon ask for her hand. Vronsky has no intention of marrying Kitty; in fact, he is completely enthralled with Anna and follows her to St. Petersburg, where she lives. They begin to attract attention with their frequent public appearances together and Karenin asks Anna to curb her "flirtation;" he is not jealous but fears damage to his reputation. Anna agrees to comply with her husband's wish that she not see Vronsky, but when her beloved is damaged in a racetrack accident she in unable to hide her feelings. Though horrified by Anna's public display of emotion, Karenin nevertheless decides that he will not divorce her. Anna and Vronsky, meanwhile, continue to meet secretly.

After Kitty rejects his proposal, Levin returns to his country estate and throws himself into the management of his farm. He spends a day working in the fields with the peasants and feels that the experience has helped him to understand their viewpoint. His plans for improving his estate include the institution of a cooperative system that will allow the peasants to benefit more directly from their labor. Hearing that Kitty has not married Vronsky after all and that she has been ill, Levin decides to return to Moscow and press his suit with her again. Meanwhile, Anna is pregnant with Vronsky's child. Vronsky insists that she obtain a divorce from her husband so that she may marry him. Karenin, however, dreads the scandal that a divorce would cause and refuses to grant it, informing Anna that he will treat her child as his own and that he will permanently separate her from their son Seryozha if she misbehaves. When Karenin returns home unexpectedly one night and finds Vronsky leaving his house, he decides to divorce Anna, but he is too fearful of a public scandal to take the necessary steps and continues to procrastinate. Anna becomes extremely ill after the birth of her child and Karenin, much affected by her grave condition, allows her to see

Vronsky, who has recently made an unsuccessful suicide attempt. When Anna finally recovers, she and Vronsky travel with their baby daughter to Italy for a short time, eventually returning to Vronsky's estate in Russia. Meanwhile, Levin and Kitty are married and begin to adjust to their life together.

Karenin has still not undergone divorce proceedings but is considered officially separated from his wife, and his acquaintances continue to think well of him. Anna makes several clandestine visits to her beloved son, but she becomes more bitter and despondent after each one. She grows increasingly demanding and jealous toward Vronsky, who responds with patience but begins to avoid her. Finally Anna leaves their home and makes her way to the railway station. Standing on the platform as a train approaches, she remembers having witnessed the death of a man who was run over by a train in the Moscow railway station. She throws herself in front of the train. After Anna's death, the depressed, weary, and fatalistic Vronsky joins the army. On their country estate, Levin and Kitty forge a happy and satisfying life together, though Levin is still tormented by questions about the meaning of life.

Characters: *Anna Karenina* is one of the most acclaimed novels of the nineteenth century and is sometimes even deemed superior to Tolstoy's other masterpiece, *War and Peace,* due to its tighter construction and deeper psychological insight. Often identified as a predecessor to the modern psychological novel, *Anna Karenina* features a highly realistic, detailed portrait both of the Russian society in which it is set and the characteristics and motivations of the inhabitants of that milieu. Through the intertwined stories of three couples, none of whom achieves conventional happiness, Tolstoy explores such themes as the demands and difficulties of moral behavior, the conflict between individual yearning and societal stricture, the destructive force of sexual passion, and the importance of family life.

Anna Karenina is among the most beloved, tragic heroines in literature. Warm, charming, and vital, she is much appreciated by her friends and family, demonstrating her capacity for understanding and her tactfulness when, at the beginning of the novel, she helps to bring about a reconciliation between her brother and his wife. That such a woman would marry a cold, insensitive man like Alexey Karenin has been deemed implausible by some critics, though others feel it illustrates the conflict between ideals and reality that is also experienced by Emma Bovary, the heroine of Gustave Flaubert's 1856 novel *Madame Bovary,* to whom Anna is frequently compared. After Anna's fateful meeting with Vronsky at the Moscow train station, a great and ultimately doomed passion begins to unfold within her. She does not enter lightly into her affair with Vronsky and even attempts to suppress her feelings; her reaction to Vronsky's accident at the racetrack, however, when she believes he has been mortally wounded, signifies the depth of her attachment. Anna's resulting dilemma effectively illustrates her society's harsh penalty for adultery: she is separated from her child and ostracized by her former acquaintances while Vronsky is free to come and go just as he did before his affair with Anna. Ironically, Anna would not have been punished if she had kept her love for Vronsky meaningless and discreet, for adultery is hypocritically tolerated in her social milieu as long as it is kept out of view. Though Anna goes off to live with the man she loves, she achieves not happiness and satisfaction but misery, and her personality loses its lustre and charm as she becomes increasingly jealous, demanding, and petulant. Fearful that she must eventually lose Vronsky's love, and agonizingly torn between her lover and her child, Anna finally chooses to escape. As she travels toward the railway station, she reviews her life in an interior monologue that anticipates the stream-of-consciousness narratives of twentieth-century fiction. Just as a train approaches, she remembers having seen a man crushed to death at the Moscow station the same day she met Vronsky, and she jumps in front of the train. A variety of explanations have been offered for Anna's final emotional breakdown and suicide: she succumbs to a guilty conscience or to weaknesses in her own character; social hypocrisy and unfair divorce laws are to blame; her maternal instincts are fatally violated by her separation from her child; or Vronsky is an inadequate and unworthy partner for her. Critics are divided on whether Anna is meant to be viewed as sinful and thus condemned by Tolstoy or as a relatively innocent victim of society whose admirable qualities exceed her weaknesses. Proponents of the former view interpret the novel's biblical epigraph, "Vengeance is mine; I will repay," as evidence that in committing adultery and therefore violating the sanctity of the family Anna must be punished; indeed, Tolstoy consistently portrayed sexuality as a destructive force. Those who deem Anna a victim, however, fault society for constraining her natural instinct to love and be loved; they hold that the epigraph is a reminder that only God and not mere mortals may judge Anna. Several critics have noted that in early drafts of the novel, Anna was a decidely wicked character but that Tolstoy eventually came to admire and sympathize with her. Despite his stated opposition to women's rights, it seems clear that Tolstoy viewed Anna as a tragic case of wasted potential, and that he meant to show that the humanity reflected in her desire for love makes her worthy of compassion.

In his role as mouthpiece for many of Tolstoy's most dearly held beliefs, **Konstantine Levin** is one of the most important characters in *Anna Karenina;* in addition, he and his wife Kitty provide an alternative to the views of love and marriage provided by Anna and Karenin, Anna and Vronsky, and Stiva and Dolly. Levin is a wealthy landowner who holds democratic opinions about the status of the peasants and the modernization of Russia's patriarchal estate system. Sober, decent, and honest, he hates hypocrisy and shares with his creator a distaste for the artificiality of aristocratic life, government bureaucracy, and the wastefulness of war. Levin feels uncomfortable in the city and frequently behaves in an awkward or even rude manner in social settings; he much prefers the vigorous natural life he leads on his country estate. Always in search of answers to his spiritual yearnings and quest for meaning, Levin finds relief in physical labor, as is demonstrated in the famous harvest scene in which Levin joins his peasants for a day of toil in the fields. Levin's sojourns in the country allow Tolstoy not only to vividly portray the rural Russian landscape and culture but to present his agricultural theories, such as the necessity for modernizing crop cultivation and livestock breeding methods—passages that many critics and readers have found extraneous and boring. Interestingly, Levin's advanced views led to his adoption as a proletarian hero by Soviet critics, who focused on his disapproval of the exploitation of the peasants. Levin's courtship of Kitty, which is initially thwarted by her infatuation with Vronsky, is modeled almost exactly after Tolstoy's experiences with his wife Sonya, as are the early days of their marriage when the two bask in the delight of their mutual love but experience some problems of adjustment. Levin is crucially affected by the birth of his first child and the death of his brother, events which confirm the natural circularity of the life cycle and through which he achieves a tentative measure of acceptance. As he settles into the routine of life on his country estate, Levin finds satisfaction in family and work, but many of his questions are ultimately left unanswered. That his contentment at the end of *Anna Karenina* seems somewhat qualified strikes many scholars as reflective of Tolstoy's psychological state while writing the novel, after which he entered a profound spiritual crisis of his own. While some critics find Levin a rather stiff manifestation of Tolstoy's ideas, most consider him an intriguing and vital character.

Anna's lover is the handsome, dashing **Alexey Vronsky,** a wealthy young army officer who, when Anna first meets him, inhabits a sophisticated, unscrupulous social set and is something of a rake. His connection with Anna begins when both witness the death of a railway worker who is crushed by a train at the Moscow station; Anna later learns that Vronsky has sent some money to the man's widow. Although he initially lives by what Tolstoy portrays as an artificial, immoral social code—trifling, for instance, with the feelings of the innocent and infatuated Kitty—Vronsky proves his basic honesty and honor after he falls in love with Anna. When he learns that she is pregnant, for instance, he encourages her to seek a divorce so that they can be married. The depth of his love for Anna is evident in his suicide attempt when he thinks she is about to die, though his devastation might also be attributed to his humiliation before Karensky when Anna forces him to ask for her husband's forgiveness. While it is true that Vronsky is never particularly ambitious or energetic, he does sacrifice his military career for Anna's sake, taking her to Europe to live and later returning with her to his country estate. He remains loyal, gentle, and tolerant toward her even when her fears, frustration, and jealousy have made her an unpleasant companion. After her death, he is completely drained of his former cheerfulness and self-assurance and becomes morbid and hopeless. Some critics have found Vronsky a decidedly mediocre character whose attractiveness to a vibrant woman like Anna seems unlikely; others, however, contend that even if Vronsky is not Anna's equal, her notably physical passion for him and appreciation for his solicitude lend the match believability. Vronsky's accident with his mare Frou-Frou, in which his mistake in the saddle leads to her broken back, is often seen as symbolic of the ultimate consequence of his love for Anna.

Anna's husband **Alexey Karenin** (who shares, significantly, the same first name as her lover) is an efficient, ambitious, narrowminded government official who lacks any real understanding of his wife's capacities or needs. Cold and self-involved, he seems immune from either love or jealousy, as evidenced by his cool reaction to the rumors about his wife's relationship with Vronsky; his only concern is that his all-important reputation remain spotless. He sees Anna not as an individual but as an extension of himself. After the incident at the racetrack, when he learns of Anna's love for Vronsky, he decides not to divorce her and congratulates himself on his Christian forebearance when in fact he is motivated primarily by the desire to prevent a scandal. He even informs Anna that he will accept Vronsky's child as his own, but he threatens to keep her from her son if she abandons their marriage. Anna's grave illness after the birth of her daughter, however, brings out in Karenin an unexpected capacity for generosity and sympathy. He is willing to do anything he can to help her, even allowing Vronsky to visit her. This manifestation of more admirable impulses in Karenin, albeit only briefly maintained, suggests to some critics that Tolstoy means to show that even such a flawed and seemingly inhuman person as Karenin may possess some moral goodness. In addition, those who feel that Anna must ultimately be punished for committing adultery note that Karenin, despite his repellent qualities, does represent the sanctity of the family and that he is undeniably wronged by his wife. In fact, Karenin was a much more sympathetic and obviously victimized character in earlier drafts of the novel, and it has been suggested that Tolstoy rendered him more distasteful so that he would clearly serve as a representative of corrupt, citified society to contrast with Levin's country-bred naturalness.

Anna's brother, **Prince Stepan "Stiva" Oblonsky,** is a high-ranking government official. Strong, robust, and energetic, he is always cheerful and goodnatured and is well-liked by everyone he knows. Even Konstantine Levin is Stiva's friend, despite his disapproval of Stiva's pragmatic, opportunistic approach to his bureaucratic position. The unreflecting Stiva never questions the precepts by which he lives, and neither is he able to control the philandering which has led to trouble in his marriage. Essentially kind but weak-willed, Oblonsky has engaged in romantic liaisons despite the heartache this causes his wife Dolly, who is devoted to him and their five children. Some critics have suggested that Oblonsky's inclination to pursue illicit sensual pleasure is a trait he shares with his sister. Significantly, however, his adultery goes unpunished by society—and also seems forgiven by Tolstoy— while Anna's destroys her life. **Princess Darya "Dolly" Oblonskaya** is the rather plain, long-suffering wife whose husband's philandering torments her and causes a rift in their relationship. In her fervent devotion to her family, she seems to represent Levin's ideal of the wife and mother; he overhears her speaking about children to a peasant woman with as much interest and animation as he himself discusses farming with his peasant acquaintances. In the end, Dolly forgives Oblonsky's misbehavior, both for their children's sake and because she sincerely loves him. In addition, Tolstoy may have wished to emphasize that the marital bond between the two is irrevocable. Though Dolly might be said to resemble Anna in that she is at the mercy of the men around her, the socially sanctioned position she holds as a wife and mother give her more security.

Dolly's sister, **Princess Catherine "Kitty" Schterbatskaya,** is a lovely, gay, playful girl who wins the admiration of both Vronsky and Levin. Rather naive and frivolous (at least in her first appearances), she is much more attracted to the dashing cavalry officer than to the sober gentlemen farmer, and she refuses Levin's proposal because she expects Vronsky to ask for her hand. When he falls in love with Anna instead and leaves Moscow, Kitty is plunged into a period of despondency that takes a physical toll on her, resulting in her parents taking her to a health resort in Germany to recover. Kitty's natural bouyancy soon returns, and she happily accepts Levin's second proposal. Their courtship and early marriage are closely modeled after the relationship between Tolstoy and his devoted wife Sonya, including such specific incidents as the word game by which Levin proposes, the shirt lost just before the wedding, and Levin's anxiety during the birth of his first child. As the couple's relationship evolves, they seem to achieve an ideal blending of sensuality with mutual respect, tenderness, and strength as a family, whereas Anna and Vronsky's union seems based primarily on physical passion. They reach an important turning point when Kitty insists on accompanying Levin when he leaves to care for his dying brother: initially annoyed by Kitty's presence, Levin eventually finds her help invaluable, signifying the importance of compromise and adaptation in marriage. Like other significant women in Tolstoy's fiction, such as Natasha in *War and Peace,* Kitty reveals unsuspected strength and practicality after her marriage and apparently finds fulfillment in her role as wife and mother.

The numerous, varied minor characters in *Anna Karenina* help to fill out the portrait of nineteenth-century Russian life presented in the novel. The sophisticated, highly artificial world of the Moscow aristocracy is particularly embodied in **Princess Elizabeth "Betsy" Tvershaya,** a heavily powdered, quintessentially superficial society matron who first serves as a liaison between Anna and Vronsky but refuses to see Anna after the affair has become public. In hypocritically rejecting Anna for what she herself has often done in private, Betsy epitomizes aristocratic hypocrisy. Other members of her circle include the beautiful, charming, much-admired **Lisa Merkalova,** and the sharp-tongued, gossiping **Princess Myagkaya.** Another representative of the nobility is Vronsky's domineering, manipulative mother **Countess Vronskaya,** who initially approves of her son's flirtation with the socially prestigious Anna but recoils when the relationship becomes serious. **Veslovsky** is an aristocratic friend of both Levin and the Vronskys; significantly, he seems out of place when he accompanies Levin on an open-air hunt, while he fits easily into the sophisticated life at Vronsky's country estate.

During the lingering illness of his brother **Nicholas,** who suffers from tuberculosis, Levin is forced to confront his own fear of death. Yet the experience also gives him an opportunity to display his nobility when he goes to nurse Nicholas—whose dread, expressed in raging and childishness, is very effectively protrayed—through his final days, and increases his awareness of the full circle of life. Nicholas's lower class mistress, **Mary "Masha" Nikolavna,** is devoted to him despite his petulance and ingratitude; ironically, her selfless love is unsanctioned by society. **Sergius Koznyshev** is Levin's half-brother, an articulate, philosophical novelist who likes to discuss the most popular topics of the day. He has been described as a parody of abstract intellectualism who serves as a foil to his equally contemplative but more realistic brother. Significantly, when Vronsky's mother suggests that the dead Anna has gotten what she deserved, Koznyshev echoes the sentiment expressed in the novel's epigraph, noting that Anna should be judged only by God. Kitty's parents are the cheerful, likable **Prince Alexander Schterbatsky,** who prefers sober Levin to dashing Vronsky as his daughter's suitor, and **Princess Schterbatskaya,** whose ambitiousness makes her eager for Kitty to marry Vronsky but who eventually comes to accept Levin. **Sergey Karenin** is the young son of Alexey and Anna, an uncomprehending little boy distraught by his separation from his beloved mother. Sergey is a major obstacle in the course of Anna's relationship with Vronsky; some critics, in fact, believe that the dilemma of choosing between her child and her lover is the central tragedy of Anna's life and the cause of her suicide.

While Kitty and her parents are visiting a German health resort, they meet a virtuous young woman named **Mademoiselle Varenka,** who selflessly cares for the sick and whose example briefly inspires the grieving Kitty to sacrifice her own comfort and happiness to help others. Her guardian is **Madame Stahl,** who radiates a self-conscious morality and who is apparently an invalid, though it is strongly suggested that her reluctance to stand reflects not infirmity but a dissatisfaction with her unattractive figure. **Mikhailov** is a Russian artist whom Vronsky and Anna meet while they are living in Italy. He voices Tolstoy's view that the role of the artist is to present life realistically rather than to idealize or glamorize it; his painting of Christ appearing before Pilate highlights the theme that only God and not human beings may judge others. Other minor characters in *Anna Karenina* include **Agatha Mikhaylovna,** Levin's trusted housekeeper and confidante; Vronsky's friend **Lieutenant Petritskey,** a heavy drinker and gambler who is always on the verge of being expelled from their regiment; **Petrov,** an invalid artist who becomes infatuated with Kitty during her visit to Germany; and **Annushka,** Anna's faithful maid.

The Death of Ivan Ilyich (*Smert Ivana Ilyicha;* novella, 1886)

Plot: The story takes place in and around St. Petersburg, Russia. As it opens, a group of lawyers discusses the recent death of Ivan Ilyich Golovin, a prominent and respected judge. Each privately considers what the death might mean for his own chance of advancement, and each is relieved that someone else and not himself has died. One of the lawyers, Peter Ivanovich, attends the dead man's funeral, where he acts aggrieved and respectful despite his lack of any real feeling for Ilyich. The widow, Praskovya Golovina, relates her own suffering and asks Ivanovich about the pension she is to receive. Finally Ivanovich hurries with relief to his nightly card game.

An account of Ivan's early and recent life is now offered. He had started out as an intelligent young man who quickly learned how to advance in the world, and by applying himself with conscientiousness and scrupulous observance of the rules he had risen to the position of judge. He had married not for love but for social advantage, and his wife subsequently grew fractious. Unable to cope with the mundane complexities of family life, Ivan had gradually isolated himself from his wife and children—attending scrupulously, however, to his official duties. After being passed over for several promotions, Ivan received an extremely advantageous government appointment that seemed to establish the prominence for which he had long worked. He moved his family to St. Petersburg and bought a home, which he and his wife furnished in accordance with current fashion. Ivan's feeling of serenity and satisfaction, however, was soon shattered. After bumping his side and receiving a bruise while hanging draperies, he began to experience a chronic pain that gradually developed into an illness (usually identified as cancer). Ivan was increasingly tormented by pain that proved impervious to medicine and by a nagging fear that his disease might be fatal. He felt alienated from others and terrified by the prospect of death, with which he had never before reckoned. The physical manifestations of Ivan's illness seemed to make him repulsive to others, but he noticed that the servant Gerasim continued to care for him with kindness and no apparent disgust. Gerasim accepted death as natural and did not fear it, and only he could provide Ivan with any solace. His doctors treated him as impersonally as he had treated the prisoners with whom he had dealt while conducting his official duties. Ivan began to reconsider his life, wondering if his effort to do only what was proper and socially acceptable had been the right way to live and more and more convinced that he had missed something. His wife brought a priest to serve him the last sacrament, but her presence reminded Ivan of the many deceptions of his life and he screamed for her to leave the room. His screaming lasted for three days as he struggled against death and the futility of his past life. When he finally became aware, however, that his young son had come to his side and that his wife was weeping sincere tears for him, Ivan experienced a revelation. He now saw death as a positive force, a kind of release or awakening, and he pitied and forgave his wife and son. He was no longer in pain or afraid of death but aware only of light and joy.

Characters: Written after a long spell in which Tolstoy had produced no novels, *The Death of Ivan Ilyich* is considered a masterpiece of his later period. The novel is distinguished by its incisive portrait of the shallowness of bourgeois life, its unsparingly realistic depiction of illness and death, and its focus on the universal human concern of mortality and the possibility of spiritual renewal. While some critics detect in *The Death of Ivan Ilyich* a nihilisitic (i.e., a rejection of traditional belief and consequent perception of life's meaninglessness) view, others consider the work essentially optimistic in its suggestion that death is an awakening rather than an ending.

Through the novella's protagonist, **Ivan Ilyich Golovin,** Tolstoy explored his own lifelong obsession with death. Unlike his creator's, however, Ivan's existence is "most simple and most ordinary and therefore most terrible." In fact, Tolstoy seems to have intentionally chosen for his central character a quintessentially commonplace individual whose very unremarkability lends his plight poignancy and makes him recognizable to the reader. Ivan is a prominent, respected judge whose conscientiousness and strict adherence to the rules and obedience to authority have allowed him to advance to a prominent position. He is the perfect bureaucrat: correct, impersonal, unquestioning, and essentially mediocre. Ivan's scrupulous observance of the law leaves no room for compassion or humanity when prisoners are brought before him, and he dispenses justice with cold officiousness. He married not for love but for social advantage, and his relationship with his wife is superficial despite the two children that have been born to them. With his strong desire for complete order and decorousness, Ivan finds the mundane realities of family life bothersome and thus focuses primarily on his occupation; his work and home spheres are kept entirely separate. When he finally receives a highly advantageous promotion and moves to St. Petersburg, Ivan feels that he has achieved the serene existence for which he has always yearned. He furnishes his new home according to the accepted standards of his social realm, never realizing that his taste and style are anything but original. It is into this ordered, conventional existence that Ivan's disease suddenly intrudes, gradually gaining control over him despite his typically human desire to consider himself immune from illness and death. Ivan is, indeed, forced to confront the inevitability of his own death, which had previously been the abstraction it is for most human beings. He experiences not only a vividly portrayed physical suffering but an even greater psychological torment as he feels others draw away from him in disgust and wonders what his life has meant. Ivan is now aware of the self-deceptions by which he has lived. His doctors treat him with the same impersonal officiousness that he had once applied from the judicial bench, and the presence of his wife, with whom he has shared no love, aggravates him. Only the kind, simple peasant servant Gerasim brings Ivan any comfort; he does not seem to be repulsed by Ivan but cheerfully attends to even the most unpleasant sickroom tasks. Gerasim's serene acceptance of death initiates the awareness that Ivan finally achieves. This revelation is definitively affirmed just before his death, when he becomes aware that his young son has come to his bedside and kissed his hand, and that his wife, also standing near him, is crying sincere tears. Both his physical pain and his psychological torment evaporate, and he realizes that death is not to be feared but welcomed. He feels love and forgiveness for his family, and his final moments are infused with light and joy as his spirit and soul triumph over his physical self. Some critics find Ivan's final state of redemption unconvincing and indicative primarily of Tolstoy's own yearning to escape the implications of death. Others consider Ivan's spiritual awakening a profoundly uplifting conclusion to a story that warns of the dangers of wasting one's life in superficiality and conformity, while still others contend that Tolstoy's intention was not to preach or present any particular philosophy but to relay a mystical experience that is open to interpretation by each reader.

Tolstoy's admiration for the Russian peasantry is evident in his portrayal of **Gerasim,** the simple, goodnatured servant who brings both physical comfort and emotional solace to Ivan during his illness. In both his healthy, robust physical condition and his lowly social status Gerasim is Ivan's opposite, and he also differs from the other people in Ivan's life in his willingness to spend long periods of time with the sick man. One of the most prominent themes in Tolstoy's fiction is the conflict between the natural—often represented by those who come from or live and work in the country—and the artificial, which is usually concentrated in the highly social world of the city. Just as Ivan has absorbed the superficiality of his milieu, Gerasim displays a close affinity with the natural that is particularly evident in his acceptance of death. Despite his own healthiness, he does not shirk from contact with Ivan and cheerfully carries out such tasks as emptying and cleaning his chamberpot. Gerasim also alleviates Ivan's pain by allowing him to rest his feet on Gerasim's shoulders as he sits before him. In fact, Gerasim is the only person in Ivan's world who seems to sincerely pity him, thus easing somewhat the well-conveyed isolation experienced by Ivan as his illness intrudes upon the feeling of well-being enjoyed by the healthy. Gerasim's pragmatic attitude toward death, which he views as simply a natural part of the life cycle, allows him to behave as he does, and his attitude plays a significant role in Ivan's eventual acceptance of his own death.

Ivan's plump, demanding, nagging wife **Praskoya Golovina** has apparently found little satisfaction in her marriage—a circumstance which might be seen as a natural result not only of her husband's lack of real affection for her but his refusal to accept the mundane responsibilities of family life. Praskoya is first seen at Ivan's funeral, where she seems primarily concerned about her own exhaustion and suffering rather than griefstricken over her husband's demise. Like Ivan's fellow lawyers, she is quick to consider what financial benefit she will gain by his death. Praskoya's appearance at Ivan's sickbed after she has arranged for a priest to visit him sets off the three days of screaming that signify his struggle against death: in her seems concentrated the self-deception that has characterized his life. Despite the general absence of mutual regard in their relationship, however, Ivan finally sees that her tears are sincere. These tears, along with his son's display of affection, introduce a hitherto missing trace of love into Ivan's life. Newly infused with the light and joy of his spiritual triumph over death, Ivan forgives and blesses Praskoya.

Peter Ivanovitch is Ivan's fellow lawyer and a representative of the correct, decorous realm of work to which Ivan has always conformed. It is Ivanovitch who, as the novella opens, announces the news of Ivan's death, thus instigating his colleagues' silent speculations about how they may benefit from the judge's demise. Out of his concern for protocol and wish to appear respectful and concerned, Ivanovitch attends Ivan's funeral, but he is impatient to leave to attend his nightly card game. Many critics have noted the masterful irony of Ivanovitch's comical effort to suppress the squeaking of the metal springs in the hassock upon which he sits while solemnly speaking with the grieving widow. The sorrow that Ivanovitch, his fellow lawyers, and even Praskoya and her children express over Ivan's death is ultimately revealed as masking their relief that he and not themselves have fallen prey to death.

Further Reading

Bayley, John. *Tolstoy and the Novel.* New York: The Viking Press, 1966.

Benson, Ruth Crego. *Women in Tolstoy: The Ideal and the Erotic.* Urbana: University of Illinois Press, 1973.

Berlin, Isaiah. *The Hedgehog and the Fox: An Essay on Tolstoy's View of History.* New York: Simon & Schuster, 1953.

Christian, R. F. *Tolstoy: A Critical Introduction.* Cambridge: Cambridge at the University Press, 1969.

Gibian, George, ed. *War and Peace: The Maude Translation, Backgrounds and Sources, Essays in Criticism.* New York: W. W. Norton, 1966.

Greenwood, E. B. *Tolstoy: The Comprehensive Vision.* New York: St. Martin's Press, 1975.

Gunn, Elizabeth. *A Daring Coiffeur: Reflections on "War and Peace" and "Anna Karenina."* Totowa, N.J.: Rowman and Littlefield, 1971.

Howe, Irving, ed. Introduction to *The Death of Ivan Ilyich* by Leo Tolstoy. In *Classics of Modern Fiction: Eight Short Novels,* pp. 113-21. New York: Harcourt Brace Jovanovich, 1968.

Jones, Malcolm, ed. *New Essays on Tolstoy.* Cambridge: Cambridge University Press, 1978.

Knowles, A. V., ed. *Tolstoy: The Critical Heritage.* London: Routledge & Kegan Paul, 1978.

Lavrin, Janko. *Tolstoy: An Approach.* New York: The Macmillan Co., 1946.

Leavis, F.R. "*Anna Karenina:* Thought and Significance in a Great Creative Work." In *Anna Karenina and Other Essays,* pp. 9-32. London: Chatto & Windus, 1967.

Matlaw, Ralph E., ed. *Tolstoy: A Collection of Critical Essays.* Englewood Cliffs, N.J.: Prentice-Hall, 1967.

Mirsky, D. S. "The Age of Realism: The Novelists (II)." 1926. Reprint. In *A History of Russian Literature Comprising "A History of Russian Literature" and "Contemporary Russian Literature,"* edited by Francis J. Whitfield, pp. 245-90. New York: Knopf, 1949.

Mooney, Harry, Jr. *Tolstoy's Epic Vision: A Study of "War and Peace" and "Anna Karenina".* Tulsa: University of Tulsa, 1968.

Nabokov, Vladimir. "Leo Tolstoy." In *Lectures on Russian Literature,* edited by Fredson Bowers, pp. 137-244. New York: Harcourt Brace Jovanovich, 1981.

Schultze, Sidney. *The Structure of "Anna Karenina."* Ann Arbor, Mich.: Ardis, 1982.

Simmons, Ernest J. *Introduction to Tolstoy's Writings.* Chicago: University of Chicago Press, 1968.

Steiner, George. *Tolstoy or Dostoyevsky: An Essay in the Old Criticism.* New York: Alfred A. Knopf, 1971.

Troyat, Henri. *Tolstoy.* Garden City, N.Y.: Doubleday & Co., 1967.

Twentieth Century Literary Criticism, Vols. 4, 11, 17, 28. Detroit: Gale.

Wasiolek, Edward. *Tolstoy's Major Fiction.* Chicago: The University of Chicago Press, 1978.

Anthony Trollope
1815-1882

English novelist, short story writer, dramatist, autobiographer and essayist.

Barchester Towers (novel, 1857)

Plot: Set in Barchester, a fictional English cathedral town, the novel opens with the death of Bishop Grantly, which leaves available the highest office in the local church hierarchy. Although the bishop's son, Archdeacon Theophilus Grantly, would like to succeed his father, the position is given instead to the mildmannered Dr. Proudie. Mrs. Proudie—whose dominance over her husband is immediately obvious—is an aggressive woman with evangelistic, Low Church (i.e., she believes in the reform or simplification of church ritual) leanings. The bishop's chaplain, Rev. Obadiah Slope, shares Mrs. Proudie's viewpoint and does her bidding. When he preaches a fiery sermon that makes clear his and Mrs. Proudie's position, the established church officials—headed by Dr. Grantly—take offense and a struggle between the Low and High Church parties develops. Meanwhile, the Reverend Septimus Harding, the former warden of Hiram's Hospital (a charitable home for elderly men), who had scrupulously resigned his position after a scandal involving the amount of his compensation, would like to regain the post. Mrs. Proudie objects to this, however, and, through Mr. Slope, makes the wardenship contingent on Harding's accepting a number of extra duties that the elderly, retiring Harding is reluctant to perform.

The new bishop announces that absentee clergyman must now return to the diocese, prompting the arrival in Barchester of Dr. Vesey Stanhope, who had lived in Italy for twelve years, and his family: unmarried Charlotte, the exotic invalid Signora Madeline Stanhope Neroni, and the dilettantish, irresponsible Ethelbert or Bertie. At a reception hosted by the Proudies, Madame Neroni fascinates all of the men present despite her confinement, due to an injury received during her disastrous marriage to an Italian, to a couch.

When the living (position as clergyman) at St. Ewold's, a church in the diocese, becomes available, Dr. Grantly secures it for Rev. Francis Arabin, a scholarly bachelor from Oxford whose conservative orientation would help to bolster the diocese's High Church forces. Meanwhile, Harding's attractive, widowed daughter, Eleanor Bold, the mother of a baby boy (and the sister-in-law of Dr. Grantly), attracts the attention of Mr. Slope, who is primarily interested in her rumored wealth. Both Eleanor's father and Dr. Grantly fear she will marry the Low Church clergyman. Since Harding has declined the position of warden of Hiram Hospital, Mrs. Proudie and Mr. Slope give the job to Mr. Quiverful, the impoverished father of fourteen children and the husband of the determined Mrs. Quiverful. Learning of Slope's role in pushing her father out of the running for the wardenship, Eleanor begins to treat her suitor coldly. At the same time, Bertie Stanhope's sisters, convinced that he will never be able to support himself, encourage him to pursue Eleanor. At a party given by the aristocratic Thorne family, both Slope and Bertie propose to Eleanor; the former receives a slap in the face for his rude approach, while Bertie ruins his chances by admitting that he would be marrying Eleanor for her money. Bertie subsequently leaves Barchester.

When the Dean of Barchester College dies, his post becomes available. Slope is interested in attaining it, but he has lost favor with Mrs. Proudie through his attentions to Signora Neroni, and he is finally sent to another diocese. Arabin—whose love for Eleanor has been detected and sanctioned by the observant Signora Neroni—receives the deanship, which represents a triumph for the High Church viewpoint. Formerly worried that Eleanor would marry the Low Church Mr. Slope, Dr. Grantly is relieved when his sister-in-law accepts Arabin's marriage proposal.

Characters: *Barchester Towers* is the best known of Trollope's "Barchester novels," a series that also includes *The Warden* (1855), *Doctor Thorne* (1858), *Framley Parsonage* (1861), *The Small House at Allington* (1864), and *The Last Chronicle of Barset* (1867). Set in the placid fictional county of Barsetshire (apparently modeled after the lovely English cathedral town of Salisbury), the novels focus on various members of a conservative—though not highly spiritual—ecclesiastical community. Infused with a cheerful comic tone, *Barchester Towers* provides a panoramic view of mid-Victorian society and touches on some of the socioeconomic changes England was experiencing during the latter half of the nineteenth century. Trollope, whose stated goal in characterization was "the creation of human beings in whose existence one is forced to believe," is particularly praised for the vividly portrayed though inherently ordinary individuals who populate the novel.

The aggressive, overbearing **Mrs. Proudie** is often cited as one of Trollope's most successful characters. Arriving in Barchester with her submissive husband, who has just been made bishop, Mrs. Proudie immediately begins to wield her own measure of power to shape the church community as she sees fit. Trollope casts the struggle between the Low and High Church forces as a mock-epic combat that critics sometimes liken to that found in John Milton's famous seventeenth-century poem *Paradise Lost*. An exponent of evangelistic, reform-minded causes, the tyrannical Mrs. Proudie leads the charge against the conservate stronghold maintained by such figures as Dr. Grantly and Reverend Harding. She is humorously compared to such mythic figures as the formidable Roman goddess Juno, the sorceress Medea from Greek mythology, and Achilles, the hero of Homer's *Iliad*. Outspokenly opinionated, Mrs. Proudie seems to resent the efforts of those around her to enjoy life, and she frequently interferes in their affairs and delivers unsolicited moralistic lectures. The scene in which Bertie Stanhope inadvertently tears Mrs. Proudie's dress while moving a couch during a gathering at the Proudie home is often cited as the funniest in the novel; the deeply chagrined Mrs. Proudie is forced to flee from the room. Trollope's unflattering depiction of Mrs. Proudie's determination to gain and manipulate the kind of power that was generally denied to Victorian women might be seen as evidence of his conservatism or even of an antagonism toward women. At the same time, his portrayal of Mrs. Proudie exemplifies the realism and balance he employed in creating all of his characters, however unpleasant or downright wicked they might be. Though strident and narrowminded, there is no doubt that Mrs. Proudie is sincere in her convictions and completely unmindful of popular or fashionable opinion; in addition, she is genuinely moved by Mrs. Quiverful's predicament and wishes to alleviate her family's poverty by ensuring that Mr. Quiverful is granted the wardenship of Hiram Hospital.

Mrs. Proudie's cohort and her husband's chaplain, the **Reverend Obadiah Slope,** is equally hungry for power, though he is more subtle in his manipulations. Praised as a highly effective comic character, Slope stands by Mrs. Proudie's side in the mock-epic battle for dominance of the ecclesiastical community of Barchester. He delivers a fiery sermon on simplifying the too-ritualistic church service, thus ominously revealing his evangelical, Low Church leanings to those conservative, High Church stalwarts, Grantly and Harding, and alerting them to the need for action. Oily, smug, and socially ambitious (and thus sometimes compared to the similar though more melodramatic Uriah Heep in Charles Dickens's 1850 novel *David Copperfield*), Slope projects a London-bred vanity that contrasts with the pastoral quality of Barsetshire, and he might be said to represent the forces of change that threatened England's conservative traditions. Indeed, he coldly announces that "New men. . .are carting away the useless rubbish of past centuries," thus revealing a lack of respect for tradition that Trollope seemed to view as inherently ungentlemanly and reprehensible. In keeping with his creator's penchant for realistic characterization, however, Slope is portrayed as sincerely believing in the Low Church principles he espouses even if his motives in promoting them are more material than spiritual. He ultimately fails to use his alliance with Mrs. Proudie to his own advantage, forfeiting her favor through his susceptibility to Signora Neroni's charms. Slope is also firmly rebuked by Eleanor, whose response to his overly ardent marriage proposal is a literal slap in the face. His scheming checkmated and his ambitions thwarted, Slope is finally forced to retreat from Barchester.

Reverend Theophilus Grantly, the Archdeacon of Barchester and the rector of Plumstead Episcopi, is a prominent character in the first novel in the Barchester series, *The Warden.* Although he maintains the domineering, opinionated, rather pompous personality he exhibited in the earlier book, some critics feel that he is more sympathetically portrayed in *Barchester Towers.* At the beginning of the novel, for instance, Grantly contritely chastises himself for wishing that his gravely ill father might die sooner so that he himself can inherit the position of bishop. An established pillar of the ecclesiastical community, the wealthy, vigorous Grantly represents the conservative, traditional Anglicinism that is threatened by the arrival of the reform-minded Mrs. Proudie and Mr. Slope, and he leads the High Church forces in the mock-epic battle against them. Grantly sincerely believes that the Low Church ideals espoused by those newcomers to Barchester will ultimately destroy his beloved Church of England, and he combats their ruinous influence by such acts as promoting Reverend Harding for the post of Warden of Hiram Hospital and bringing in Reverend Arabin as Dean of Barchester College. Grantly mistakenly fears that his widowed sister-in-law Eleanor will marry the reprehensible Slope, and he vows to bar her from entering his home if she does so. His relief and joy in her marriage to Arabin, who shares his own convictions, are evidenced by his generous wedding gifts to the couple, which might be compared to the victor's dividing the spoils of conquest. Scholars have concluded that Trollope's generally favorable portrayal of Grantly and the final victory of the High Church contingency indicates his preference for this orientation over the evangelical liberalism of Mrs. Proudie.

The mild-mannered **Reverend Septimus Harding** is the central figure in *The Warden,* the first novel in the Barchester series, in which he resigns his post as Warden of Hiram's Hospital (a charitable home for elderly men) after a scandal involving the amount of his compensation. As *Barchester Towers* opens, Harding is interested in regaining his former role, but this desire is opposed by the formidable Mrs. Proudie and her associate, Mr. Slope. They intentionally make his resumption of duties contingent on his accepting a number of other responsibilities that they know the elderly, retiring Harding will be disinclined to perform. The essentially good, humble, and completely guileless Harding serves as a particularly positive embodiment of a placid, traditional world threatened by change. He criticizes Slope's controversial sermon, for instance, on the basis of its condemnatory, discourteous tone, which evidences an ungentlemanliness, he feels, that ill becomes a representative of the church. Trollope seems to approve of Harding's refusal to grasp power at any cost, and he ultimately wins distinction in the reader's eyes by conscientiously declining to pursue personal advancement. He even makes the admirable gesture of introducing the new warden, Mr. Quiverful, to his own fond former charges at the hospital, thus ensuring that his successor will receive the respect he needs to perform effectively. Harding's naive and rather dreamy soul is evidenced by his love for cathedral music and his gently comic habit of sawing away at an imaginary cello; at the end of *Barchester Towers,* he is given a real cello by his triumphant son-in-law, Dr. Grantly.

Though she is cast as the heroine of *Barchester Towers,* Harding's widowed daughter **Eleanor Bold**—whose troubled courtship with the now-dead John Bold is chronicled in the earlier *The Warden*—plays a rather insignificant role in the novel. The confusion and comedy created through her interaction with her three suitors does, however, enliven the action. The unctuous, ambitious Mr. Slope finds Eleanor's rumored wealth her most attractive feature, and the goodnatured, dilettantish Bertie Stanhope openly admits that Eleanor's money has caused his sisters to encourage him to court her. The failings of each of these suitors are glaringly obvious, while the shy scholar Francis Arabin is just as obviously an appropriate partner for Eleanor—as the shrewed Signora Neroni assures her. The heroine vacillating between suitors is a common device in Trollope's fiction, but in *Barchester Towers* he assures the reader ahead of time, in a much-discussed digression, that Eleanor will marry neither Slope or Bertie. Critics often cite this narrative aside as an example of Trollope's authorial intrusions, which some fault as unnecessary and disruptive and others find conducive to intimacy between reader and author.

One of the most memorable female characters in *Barchester Towers* is **Signora Madeline Stanhope Neroni,** the beautiful invalid daughter of the absentee clergyman Dr. Vesey Stanhope, who brings his family back to Barchester after twelve years in Italy. During a brief, ill-fated marriage to an apparently brutal Italian aristocrat, Signora Neroni received a crippling injury that necessitates her remaining in a reclining position. Thus she is confined to her couch—making a regal appearance that provokes comparison to the famous Egyptian queen Cleopatra—from which she fascinates nearly every man she meets. Her dramatic and supposedly violent past seems to add to her attraction, as do her bright eyes and seductive laugh. Signora Neroni is a *femme fatale* who apparently seeks vengeance for the wrong done her by her husband by bewitching and then rejecting every member of the male sex who comes near her. Significantly, she humiliates Slope, who deserves such treatment, but leaves the shy Arabin alone; recognizing both his inherent worth and his attraction to Eleanor, she encourages the young widow to consider him as a possible husband. The siren-like but basically decent and very shrewd Signora Neroni serves to unmask the pretense in those around her by shocking, embarrassing, or disconcerting them. Regretting the fact that she makes no further appearances in the Barchester novels, some critics have suggested that Trollope's Victorian publishers did not approve of her exotic aura of sexuality and thus banished her from subsequent volumes.

Other members of the Stanhope family include **Dr. Vesey Stanhope,** the Canon of Barchester Cathedral, whose self-indulgence and lack of interest in spiritual matters is evidenced by his having spent the last twelve years as an absentee clergyman in Italy while his curates performed his duties at the several churches under his control. **Mrs. Stanhope** is a shallow woman interested only in fashion, while the couple's oldest, unmarried daughter **Charlotte,** efficient and pragmatic, manages their household. Charlotte encourages her brother **Ethelbert "Bertie" Stanhope** to marry the wealthy widow Eleanor Bold because she suspects that he will never be able to support himself otherwise. The goodnatured but hedonistic, indolent Bertie is a dabbler in various realms—including law, art, and religion—who seems incapable of seriously applying or committing himself to anything. Bertie's polite, vacuous talk provides some comic moments in the novel, such as when, during a discussion about religion with one of the town's clergyman, he casually announces, "I was a Jew once myself." Though Bertie is dangerously irresponsible, his amiability and irreverence tempt the reader to like him, and the fact that he undermines his own effort to court Eleanor by frankly admitting his monetary motive makes him somewhat less reprehensible. Trollope seems fond of Bertie, and many readers and scholars have regretted that he makes no more appearances in the Barchester novels. Perhaps, like his sister Madeline, Bertie is too unconventional and morally questionable a character to reside in the placid world of Barsetshire.

Recruited by Dr. Grantly and eventually appointed Dean of Barchester College, the **Reverend Francis Arabin** is brought from the cloistered world of Oxford to bolster the High Church forces of Barsetshire. He is a shy, rather naive academician who represents the solid conservatism of England's religious and scholarly traditions. In his youth, Arabin is said to have considered joining the Catholic church, thus aligning himself with the controversial Oxford Movement, which sought to bring back to the Anglican church practices and rituals that pre-dated the Protestant Reformation. Both Arabin's deanship and his marriage to Eleanor represent triumphs for the conservative forces marshalled under Dr. Grantly, who is overjoyed when his sister-in-law chooses Arabin as her husband rather than Slope. Another significant clergyman in *Barchester Towers* is the meek **Dr. Proudie,** who succeeds Bishop Grantly in the highest office of the Barsetshire eccelesiastical hierarchy. The weak, henpecked Proudie is entirely dominated by his aggressive wife and her shrewd cohort, Dr. Slope, and thus seems an essentially innocent third party to the battle that ensues for control of the church.

Among the minor characters in *Barchester Towers* are **Mr. Quiverful,** the genial clergyman who, like Dr. Proudie, is not as forceful as his wife and thus serves as a fairly innocent third party to the "battle" chronicled in the novel, and the determined **Mrs. Letty Quiverful.** The mother of fourteen children, she is instrumental in securing the post of warden for her husband, effectively employing pathos in describing to Mrs. Proudie the hardships endured by her impoverished family. The latter matriarch responds with compassion and sees that Quiverful receives the wardenship. In their continuous struggle to make ends meet, the Quiverfuls occupy one of several different levels of Barchester society presented in the novel. At the other extreme is **Miss Thorne** and her bachelor brother **Wilfred,** members of the aristocracy who reside at their stately country estate, Ullathorne. Miss Thorne, a highly conservative noblewoman who represents the old order of English society in her vehement opposition to egalitarian reform, hosts the party at which both Slope and Bertie propose to Eleanor. At this gathering, which features a quaint revival of such medieval sports as archery and tilting—again, signifying her clinging to bygone ways—a wide variety of Barchester residents meet and interact. The presence and attempted mingling of such lower-class characters as the socially ambitious, bourgeois Mrs. Lookaloft and Mrs. Greenacre, the wife of a grocer, highlight the blurring of social distinctions that had begun to occur in the Victorian period. Other notable minor characters include **Susan Grantly,** Eleanor's sister and Dr. Grantly's wife; **Mary Bold,** the sister of Eleanor's late husband John and her trusted confidante; and **Dr. Trefoil,** the Dean of Barchester College, whose death of apoplexy leaves his office open.

Can You Forgive Her? (novel, 1869)

Plot: Set in nineteenth century England, the novel revolves around three romantic subplots. Its title refers to Alice Vavasor, a wealthy young woman from an aristocratic family who is initially engaged to her cousin George Vavasor. George wishes to run for Parliament and needs Alice's money to fund his campaign. Although Alice is more attracted to the morally upright John Grey, whom her relations also consider a more appropriate suitor for her, she wishes to make up her own mind, and she finds her cousin's political aspirations exciting. Meanwhile, Lady Glencora Plantaganet (née MacCluskie) has been pushed by her relatives into marrying the respectable but dull Plantaganet Palliser, whom she does not love. Resentful of having been "bought" into marriage and craving tenderness, Lady Glencora still harbors warm feelings for her former suitor, the disreputable, charming Burgo Fitzgerald. The third romance presented in the novel involves Alice's aunt Arabella Greenow, whose wealth gives her the luxury of choosing between two men: comfortably well-off, staid Mr. Cheesacre, a farmer, or dashing Captain Bellfield.

Alice decides to break off her engagement with George and becomes engaged to John Grey, but she goes back to George when he manages to play upon her sense of guilt and unworthiness. Meanwhile, she has become aware of Lady Glencora's unhappiness and shares this discovery with Palliser. Confronted by her husband, Lady Glencora admits to her infatuation with Fitzgerald; the newly enlightened and always noble Palliser decides to take her for an extended vacation in Europe even though it means he will give up a political appointment. During their trip, she becomes pregnant, and the two seem destined for eventual happiness. Alice, meanwhile, finally comes to her senses about the disreputable and even violent George. After struggling with the feeling that she is not worthy of John Grey's love, the two are reunited and married. Arabella chooses the more romantic and exciting of her suitors, the slightly dissipated Bellfield. His political career thwarted by the withdrawal of Alice's funds, an enraged George challenges Grey to a duel but is rebuffed and humiliated. He finally emigrates to America.

Characters: *Can You Forgive Her?* is the first of what have come to be known as the Palliser novels, a series that also includes *Phineas Finn, Phineas Redux,* and *The Prime Minister.* The novel is best known for its introduction of two of Trollope's most acclaimed characters, Plantaganet Palliser and Lady Glencora, and is generally distinguished for its incisive characterizations. Though grounded in the context of politics and various characters' efforts to achieve political office, *Can You Forgive Her?* is primarily a study of human relationships, particularly the institution of marriage. Commentators have especially noted Trollope's apparent awareness of the circumscribed roles assigned to women in the Victorian period evident in the novel.

In his *Autobiography,* Trollope commented that the character of **Plantagenet Palliser** "stands more firmly on the ground than any other personage I have created," a judgment that has been affirmed by many readers and critics. Born into an aristocratic family, Palliser is an intelligent, energetic, and inherently honorable if somewhat dull young man. Instead of pursuing the idle life of the English nobility, Palliser decides to become a Liberal politician. He devotes himself to this path with zeal and perserverence, gaining a reputation not as a brilliant political star but as a hard worker with the potential for future achievement. Armed with wealth, prestige, and high rank, Palliser may choose a wife from among the most desireable young women of his social set. He settles on Lady Glencora MacCulskie, a witty, spirited heiress whose fortune will enhance his political career. Palliser is undeniably good and just in his dealings with his new wife, but he treats her rather coldly and responds humorlessly to her jests. He does not recognize her need for small attentions and tender affection, and as a result her mind and heart begin to wander back to her former lover, Burgo Fitzgerald. Yet Palliser demonstrates his underlying nobility when, after hearing from Lady Glencora herself that she has become infatuated and considered eloping with another man, he sacrifices the promise of a political appointment to take her away from England for some time. He further exhibits his generosity by helping Fitzgerald financially after the couple encounters him in Europe. Some critics note that Palliser's money and status would remain undisturbed during this short lapse in his career, so that it does not comprise a particularly difficult sacrifice; indeed, he will eventually rise to the exalted office of prime minister of England. Palliser's marriage is a subject of much attention and interest throughout the remaining novels in the series. From its beginning as a union of convenience and social propriety it develops through numerous shared difficulties and joys to a successful relationship based on mutual respect, love, and concern. Trollope has been praised for his sensitive portrayal of the complex, imperfect relations between Palliser and Glencora over the years, as they raise three children and Palliser's political career takes shape. Eventually he becomes the Duke of Omnium and, despite the foolish sound of his inherited title, he serves as an example of a true gentleman rather than the kind—found throughout Trollope's fiction—whose aristocratic exterior masks moral laxity and weakness. Trollope is said to have used Palliser as a mouthpiece for his own ideas about politics, society, and morality.

Lady Glencora (MacCulskie) Palliser is considered one of Trollope's most successful and memorable characters. Though perhaps not entirely admirable or virtuous, she wins the reader's affection with her frankness, wit, sensitivity, vivaciousness, and passion. Although she has fallen in love with the charming, disreputable Burgo Fitzgerald, Lady Glencora is pushed by her ambitious relatives into wedding the honorable but dry Plantagenet Palliser, whose political career will be enhanced by marriage to an heiress of her stature. Warmhearted and impulsive, she has a strong craving for love and tenderness that her serious-minded husband fails to satisfy, and she finds herself drawn back to her former lover. Like Alice Vavasor, Lady Glencora exhibits a streak of rebelliousness—at one point she says, "one does get so hampered, right and left, for fear of Mrs. Grundy [the traditional English metaphor for the force of convention]"—and often uses her quick wit as a subtle instrument of defiance as well as a way to make life more exciting. Nevertheless, her yearning is more for love than for the independence Alice craves. Both women must grapple with the demanding precepts of their Victorian society, particularly in regard to the notion that a "pure" woman loves only once in her life. While Alice is tempted to marry a man she does not love, Lady Glencora finds herself married to one man and in love with another. Despite the weakness that her susceptibility to Fitzgerald's charms might evidence, Lady Glencora exhibits a certain amount of courage when she admits to her husband that she has been unhappy and has become infatuated with another man. The subsequent novels in the Palliser series chronicle the Pallisers' marriage as it gathers strength and complexity over many years of both difficulties and happiness. That Lady Glencora is pregnant at the end of *Can You Forgive Her?* might be seen as a symbol promising the deeper union they will eventually achieve. In committing herself to her relationship with Palliser, even though it lacks the wild romance of her love for Fitzgerald, Lady Glencora exhibits an ability to adapt to the circumstances of her life and a capacity to appreciate the richer, more complex reality she thereby acquires.

The novel's title refers to **Alice Vavasor,** the young woman whose vacillation between two suitors finally results in her making the right choice. Based on the character of Margaret de Wynter in Trollope's earlier, unsuccessful play *The Noble Jilt,* Alice is tall and darkhaired with a decidedly ungirlish, rather staid demeanor and a strong sense of self-possession and independence. Her relatives encourage her to marry the respectable John Grey but she resents and resists their interference in her affairs. Although she is actually romantically attracted to John, she imagines that life with him would be dull; in addition, he frequently patronizes her—reacting, for instance, as he might to the petulance of a child when she informs him that she wants to break their engagement. Alice knows that George Vavasor wants her money to finance his political career, but she anticipates an exciting future by his side and thus is initially willing to overlook his suspect motives. Alice's inherent sensitivity and wisdom—evidenced by her alerting Palliser to his wife's unhappiness and thus contributing to the improvement in their relationship—as well as her ability to face and correct her own mistakes finally come to the fore when she realizes that it would be wrong to marry George. The novel's title might more aptly be "Can She Forgive Herself?," for Alice must now convince herself that she is worthy to marry her John. Her contrite, self-doubting attitude might be attributed to the pressures of the Victorian standard of womanhood, which decreed that a "pure" woman loves only once and must love the man she marries. Despite her independent spirit, Alice feels that in contemplating marriage to a man she knew she did not love, she has sinned. She is the kind of heroine that Trollope referred to as "crossgrained": she has acted in defiance of her friends' advice and her own best interest. Although her vacillations between suitors might be seen as evidence of some mental instability, some critics interpret her dilemma as evidencing Trollope's awareness of the too-confined role assigned to Victorian women. Thus opposition to the wishes of her father and other relatives might be seen as her only means of asserting her own will. Alice exhibits both a desire to comply with her society's model of femininity and a vague ambitiousness and yearning for independence (sometimes compared to that of Nora Helmer in Henrik Ibsen's 1879 play *A Doll's House*), a conflict that makes her a particularly compelling character.

Trollope's depiction of the dissolute **George Vavasor,** who spent his youth in idle and wasteful pursuits but later becomes a stockbroker and decides to pursue a political career, was termed a "brilliant, and, coming from the kindly Trollope, surprisingly ruthless portrayal of galloping deterioration" by critic Sir Edward Marsh. Although he does have some talent and is brave and ambitious, George's egotism ultimately brings about his downfall. His handsomeness is both marred and made more romantic by a facial scar he received during a childhood encounter with a burglar whom he killed. This ominous mark, which becomes more prominent and ugly when he is angry, serves as a sign of the inherently violent nature that leads him not only to threaten John Grey's life but to strike his own devoted sister when she will not do his bidding. Eager to ensure the success of his political campaign, George calculatedly takes advantage of the wealthy Alice's confused feelings of guilt and unworthiness to manipulate her into becoming engaged with him a second time. When their engagement is definitively broken and his political career thus destroyed, George reacts with blustering rage and challenges John to a duel. Significantly, though, the days when England's aristocrats indulged in such practices are over; his challenge is rebuffed and he is sent away in humiliation. Unlike Palliser, George lacks the money and status that facilitate political success, and he finally emigrates to America.

Alice's other, ultimately successful suitor is the respectable **John Grey,** whom she actually loves and of whom her relatives approve. Grey is a man of strong character with a moderate but good income; he is well-educated, talented, gentlemanly, noble, generous, clever, and good. To Alice he seems, in fact, perfect, but it is this perfection that bothers her. His attitude toward her is superior and condescending, and she hates to be condescended to. Grey does not initially recognize Alice's separate, independent consciousness, and the idea that she might have other plans than to marry him has never occurred to him. He responds to her breaking their engagement as if she is not quite well, or as if she is a petulant child, but when her seriousness finally becomes clear he is sincerely shaken. Like Palliser, he is forced to confront his own inadequacy in the eyes of the woman in his life, and he emerges from the experience a wiser and more compassionate man. Trollope seems to endorse Grey's decision to run for Parliament, a choice that involves a balancing of private interests and public responsibilities.

Burgo Fitzgerald is a thirty-two-year-old rogue whose irresponsible behavior has led to his estrangement from his father and thus his impoverishment. His unconventionality, charm, and extreme handsomeness make him attractive to women, but his weakness for gambling, drink, and other vices and his inherent selfishness make him a poor choice as a romantic partner. Like George Vavasor, Fitgerald serves as an embodiment of romance and excitement who is ultimately recognized as destructively selfish. Despite his reprehensible qualities, though, Fitgerald is in some ways pitiable and even likeable; for instance, he buys a meal for a prostitute and gives her his last shilling.

Alice's aunt **Arabella Greenow** is a rather vulgar older woman who brings some comic relief to the novel by providing a humorous parallel to her niece's romantic vacillation. Arabella had been a beautiful, flirtatious young woman who nevertheless was still single at thirty-four, when she married a much older man. Though brief, the marriage was apparently quite happy. Now widowed, Arabella is in an admirable state of financial independence that allows her to choose freely from among several suitors—a reversal of the usual position of nineteenth-century women, whose lives depended on their being chosen by suitable and prosperous men. Arabella has the power to select a husband based on her own romantic inclination. Unlike her niece or Lady Glencora, she chooses the more exciting and less respectable of her two suitors, Captain Bellfield, whom she describes as having "a sniff of the rocks and the valleys" about him. While some critics find this third romantic subplot superfluous, others consider Arabella an appealing comic character. Her two suitors are **Mr. Samuel Cheesacre,** a stout, redfaced, bald, bachelor farmer who is quite generous with his money and enjoys boasting about his generosity later; and **Captain Bellfield,** a tall, handsome, dashing military officer with a slight aura of vanity and dissipation that does not alarm Arabella.

Several other female characters provide alternative versions of Victorian womanhood. **Kate Vavasor,** George's sister, finds meaning only in her devotion to her brother and the sacrifices she makes for him. She helps George to draw Alice into an engagement so that his political career may be financed; despite the lack of scruples this scheming reveals, however, Kate's motives are basically unselfish. Her wealthy grandfather, with whom she lives, unexpectedly leaves his property to her when he dies, and her brother's rage at this development causes him to strike out brutally at the one person who has always put his interest before her own. **Euphemia and Iphigenia Palliser,** cousins to Plantagenet, are elderly, unmarried sisters whose lives consist of quiet study and contemplation. Thus they provide an example of the rather dull, sterile life a Victorian woman might expect to lead if she did not marry.

The Way We Live Now (novel, 1875)

Plot: The story takes place in nineteenth-century London. Augustus Melmotte, whose true origins are obscure, moves into the fashionable Grosvenor Square neighborhood with his European-Jewish wife and his daughter Marie. Characterizing himself as a successful financier, he is soon embraced by London's high-society circle. Based on the rumor of his great wealth and ability, he is able to sell shares in a fictional railway company that will supposedly build a railroad from Salt Lake City, Utah to Vera Cruz, Mexico. Melmotte is embraced not just by high society but by the political and religious worlds as well. He hosts a glamorous ball in honor of Marie, who is courted by several suitors interested primarily in the wealth they believe she will inherit. Although her fathers wants her to marry the wealthy, indolent Lord Nidderdale, Marie falls in love with the dissolute Sir Felix Carbury, whose upstanding, kind cousin Roger is his exact opposite. Roger, meanwhile, is in love with Felix's docile sister Henrietta, who fancies not Roger but his rather enigmatic friend Paul Montague. The goodnatured but naive Paul has become involved with Melmotte's railway speculation scheme, and is also being harrassed by Mrs. Hurtle, an American widow with whom he apparently once had an affair. Lady Carbury, the mother of Felix and Henrietta, is a literary dilettante whose ambition is to write commercially successful books, toward which she cajoles several newspaper editors. She also tries to promote the marriage of her beloved, much-indulged son to Marie. Because Marie's parents disapprove of her relationship with Felix, the two agree to elope. Marie makes her way to Liverpool for their rendezvous, as agreed, but Felix has in the meantime gambled away all of the money she gave him and is too drunk to keep their meeting. He is eventually sent out of England by his mother's friends.

After gaining such social and even political prominence that he is actually elected to Parliament, Melmotte begins to be suspected of financial swindling. He has been granted the honor of hosting a dinner for the visiting Emperor of China, but many seats are empty due to the rumors circulating about him. He has, in fact, forged several documents, including one that would allow him to access his daughter's inheritance. Finally rejected and scorned by those who had formerly courted his favor, Melmotte makes a final, drunken attempt to address the House of Commons, after which he kills himself by ingesting prussic acid. Marie eventually marries her father's former business partner, an American businessman named Hamilton K. Fisher, while Melmotte's wife marries his former clerk; both couples emigrate to America. Henrietta and Paul marry, and Roger generously ensures that his estate will be left to their children rather than to Felix. Lady Carbury marries the pragmatic editor, Nicholas Broune.

Characters: *The Way We Live Now* offers a panoramic view of English society in the 1870s, exposing the financial and moral corruption not just of commerce but of literature and even romance. Although early reviewers found the novel insulting or too pessimistic, some modern critics consider it Trollope's masterpiece for its skillful satire and insightful characterizations. Although it does lack the general cheerfulness of Trollope's earlier works, *The Way We Live Now* is not entirely bleak in tone or outcome, and provides an interesting glimpse into life in late-nineteenth-century England.

Augustus Melmotte, whose meteoric rise to and fall from the peak of prominence is chronicled in the novel, embodies the "dishonesty magnificent in its proportions" that Trollope believed had infiltrated the highest levels of society. Literary researchers have determined that Trollope initially conceived Melmotte as a minor character but that he gained importance and complexity as the novel took shape. Although Melmotte claims he was born in England, his origins are obscure: he is assuredly not English but may be Jewish, like his wife; probably, though, he is the son of an Irish-American forger named Melmody. The consummate swindler, Melmotte employs all of his resources of cleverness and ambition to persuade investors to buy shares in a railway company that is supposed to build a railroad from the southwestern United States into Mexico. Whether the railroad will ever actually be built or not is immaterial, for the object is to acquire wealth through the manipulation of public opinion—to convince the public that the railway is a worthwhile investment. Melmotte represents a threat to the traditional values embodied by Roger Carbury because he earns money not through the ownership of land or other tangible resources but through the very modern, very shadowy means of financial speculation. The utter shallowness and moral vacuity of aristocratic society is illustrated through its easy acceptance of Melmotte on the basis of his perceived wealth and prestige. In fact, he is not merely accepted but toadied to by all and is even sought after by representatives of the political (both the liberal and conservative parties) and religious (both Protestant and Catholic churches) worlds. Melmotte's self-confidence, ambitiousness, and sheer audacity propel him to the zenith of his career, which is the dinner he hosts in honor of the visiting Emperor of China. Trollope is thought to have modeled this extravagant occasion after a similar event that took place in London while he was writing the novel: a much-touted and expensive reception and banquet for the Shah of Persia. In *The Way We Live Now,* the public's exaggerated reverence for the very young emperor, who comes from a completely alien culture and speaks no English, provides a parallel for its equally blind allegiance to Melmotte. Although people are initially fighting over tickets to the affair, rumors begin to circulate that Melmotte has forged several documents, and many seats at the dinner are empty. Those who had once eagerly sought Melmotte's favor now quickly abandon him as what had previously been suspected but overlooked comes to the fore. Though deeply chagrined and aware that his brilliant career (which has lasted only two months) is over, Melmotte makes a final attempt to assert himself when he appears, drunk and stumbling, at the House of Commons. Brought down by his deepseated arrogance and belief in his own importance—flaws that have only gradually become evident to the reader due to Trollope's intentionally shadowy portrayal—Melmotte finally commits suicide, thus perhaps proving his faithfulness to his own image by arranging a dramatic exit. Many critics have commented on the touch of grandeur in Melmotte's death, likening it to that of the Roman emperor Ceasar. A number of historical figures have been identified as possible antecedents for Melmotte, including the famous swindlers Charles Lefevre and George Hudson (called "the railway king"); Napoleon III, who was known to have supported widespread speculation; and John Sadleir, who also eventually killed himself with prussic acid and who was apparently the model for the disreputable Mr. Merdle in Charles Dickens's 1857 novel *Little Dorrit.* In fact, several critics have noted the similarities between Melmotte and Merdle, though Trollope claimed he did not read Dickens's novel until after he had written *The Way We Live Now.*

Critics have identified the upright country squire **Roger Carbury** as the novel's standard of virtue. He is an old-fashioned aristocrat who represents the traditional reliance on the solid, enduring value of land rather than on insubstantial, morally tainted financial speculation. Scornful of the hypocrisy and selfishness he sees all around him, Carbury believes that the world he knows and cherishes is threatened by people like Melmotte, whose corruption he immediately perceives. Carbury further evidences his inner nobility on a more personal level, when he reacts graciously to Hetta's failure to return his love; he generous ensures that she and her husband rather than Felix, whom he despises, will inherit his estate. Although Roger has usually been viewed as a positively portrayed character, some scholars feel that his awareness of his own virtue makes him unpleasantly priggish, or even that he could be said to exhibit an overly tenacious, inflexible allegiance to the past. Roger has often been identified as Trollope's mouthpiece in expressing with amusing crankiness the view that civilization is deteriorating rapidly, a position shared most notably by the renowned nineteenth-century writer Thomas Carlyle. Yet it has also been maintained that Trollope believed that despite its flaws, the world was a better place that it had been in the past; thus Roger's anachronistic stance might be seen as too extreme.

Through the aspiring novelist **Lady Matilda Carbury,** Roger's cousin and the mother of Sir Felix and Henrietta, Trollope demonstrates that corruption was not limited to the commercial realm but had infiltrated literature as well. Lady Carbury's goal is not artistic worth but financial gain, and she hopes not to produce a good book but to persuade the right people—i.e., the editors who will review it—to say that it is good so that the public will buy it. Thus she is shown, as the novel opens, writing cajoling letters to three editors requesting that they approach her *Criminal Queens* with indulgence. Lady Carbury is forty-three years old but still very attractive, and she is quite willing to use her coquettish charms to achieve her desired ends. Her eventual marriage to editor Nicholas Broune, in fact, has been interpreted as a kind of prostitution, though such an interpretation might be too extreme. Lady Carbury's devotion to her worthless son, who is constantly taking money from her without the slightest compunction and who cannot even rouse himself to show her some affection, has been seen as somewhat redeeming her otherwise unscrupulous, morally tainted character. Trollope's portrayal of this literary dilettante and her relations with editors was no doubt drawn from his own knowledge of the literary world.

Lady Carbury's beloved son is **Sir Felix Carbury,** a shiftless degenerate who spends his time drinking and gambling with his equally worthless friends at the Beargarden Club and pursuing women—particularly women of inferior social standing. Felix has wasted his own fortune and now draws liberally from his mother's and sister's incomes, thus depriving them of anything nearing the pleasures he regularly indulges in. Despite his good looks and appearance of wealth and status, Felix lacks not only money but principles, loyalty, sincere emotions, or energy. His cynical, egotistical attitude toward his courtship of Marie Melmotte typifies his outlook: he proposes to share his elevated rank with her while she provides the money he needs to maintain his lifestyle. Yet Felix is not even competent enough to accomplish the elopement; he gets drunk and never reaches Liverpool, where he is supposed to meet Marie. Felix's degeneracy is further illustrated by his attempt to seduce the naive country girl, Ruby Ruggles, who is saved at the last minute by her enraged rural lover, John Crumb. After being thrashed by Crumb, Felix is sent away in the company of a chaperoning clergyman. Trollope's contempt for Felix is evident in his description of him as having "the instincts of a horse, not approaching the higher sympathies of a dog."

Marie Melmotte is one of several young women in the novel who must find their way through the dangers of the marital marketplace, a realm that Trollope paints as just as corrupt as the commercial. The illegitimate daughter of the swindling Melmotte, whose wife poses as her mother, Marie is a longtime reader of romantic fiction who craves love and excitement. Although she lacks physical beauty, her wealth attracts the attentions of several suitors. Only one, however, captures her fancy: the outwardly attractive but imminently disreputable Sir Felix Carbury. Though grievously incapable of recognizing the vacuity beneath Felix's pleasing, impressive exterior, Marie does exhibit a certain spiritedness in her determination to have her own way, defying her father's desire that she marry Lord

Nidderdale. With guile and resolution that belie her apparent innocence, Marie proposes that she make her fortune over to Felix and elope with him. She remains faithful to Felix even after his weakness has become obvious, but she is saved from marrying him when his mother and her friends send him away. In the end, Marie marries the only slightly more desireable Hamilton Fisker, her father's former business partner. She might be seen as illustrating the dependent and often humiliating position of Victorian women, whose options were severely circumscribed. The lack of warmth in her relationship with her father, whose passing she does not even mourn, exemplifies the destructive influence of money on family relationships, a significant theme in *The Way We Live Now.*

Henrietta "Hetta" Carbury, the daughter of Lady Carbury and sister of Sir Felix, is another of the novel's marriagable young women. Unlike Marie, however, she lacks the fortune that would attract a multitude of insincere, greedy suitors. Pretty, decorous Hetta provides a strong contrast to her brother in her consideration for others; in fact, she accepts Felix's pillaging of her income with passivity. Although Lady Carbury does love Hetta, she has never indulged her as she has her son, and Hetta has consequently grown into a fine person while Felix is morally bankrupt. Hetta has always been expected to marry the adoring but much older Roger Carbury. Her preference for the enigmatic **Paul Montague** is the only point on which she refuses to yield, and in the end she does marry him. Paul, a friend of Roger's, has an intriguing, ambiguous past: he was once apparently involved with the passionate and possibly dangerous Mrs. Hurtle, who has arrived on the scene in an attempt to win him back. Though goodnatured and essentially honest, Paul exhibits some significant weaknesses. He subverts his own high standards by becoming involved in the shifty railway scheme; his fundamental divergence form the other participants, however, is evident in his eagerness to begin some kind of substantial work with the company. He does not realize that the scheme involves not hard work or producing an actual product but intangible speculation and manipulating public opinion. Paul is finally disentangled from the fictional railway company and is ultimately rewarded with marriage to Hetta. The couple can look forward to inheriting the estate of their generous, forgiving friend Roger Carbury.

Adolphus "Dolly" Longstaffe is perhaps the most prominent among the wealthy, indolent young men who frequent the Beargarden Club, indulging themselves in drink and card games and evading the demands of marriage. The club is a miniature version of the larger, corrupt world within which it exists. None of its members actually work, supporting themselves through gambling and the IOUs they pass among themselves, which are similar to the worthless railway shares circulated by Melmotte and his associates. Dolly is a profoundly foolish, vacuous young man who nevertheless holds the ironic distinction of being one of few who mistrust Melmotte. Though generally apathetic and placid, he is mildly disturbed by his awareness that Melmotte is a swindler, a discovery that eventually leads to the financier's downfall. Dolly's poor relationship with his father is typical of the weak family ties presented in the novel, and he is one of several examples of profligate, disobedient offspring. His father, **Lord Longestaffe,** maintains a proud, superior demeanor but is actually shallow and unscrupulous. His finances depleted by his extravagant lifestyle, he would rather relinquish his country estate to Melmotte to increase his income rather than deny himself any of his accustomed luxuries. Longstaffe's rage at his daughter's engagement to the wealthy Brehgert reveals his deepseated, irrational prejudice against Jews. Ironically, Brehgert is one of very few honorable characters in *The Way We Live Now,* while Longstaffe has no objection to cutting shady deals with Melmotte, and the encounter between the two men effectively illustrates the contrast between the former's dignity and the latter's false hauteur.

Georgiana Longstaffe is perhaps the best example of the novel's "girls who want to get married." Lacking money, beauty, and—increasingly—youth over the several years she has spent on the marriage market, the nearly thirty-year-old Georgiana has had to lower her standards. She finally informs her family that she is engaged to Brehgert, a wealthy Jewish financier. They erupt in extreme anger, outraged that she would consider marrying such an inferior person. While Georgiana might be given credit for rebelling against her shallow father, she exhibits a similar shallowness in her inability to perceive her fiancé's true nobility. Thus when he informs her, with admirable honesty and fairness, that they will not be able to maintain a London home after their marriage, she breaks the engagement. Georgiana provides a contrast to Marie in that she hopes to acquire wealth with her marriage and therefore puts *herself* on the marriage market whereas Marie is plagued with suitors who desire her fortune, but both young women reveal their lack of perceptiveness through the men they choose to marry, and neither is finally successful.

Georgiana's fiancé **Brehgert** is a successful Jewish financier and a widower with two grown children. Inherently decent and fairminded, Brehgert treats Georgiana with scrupulous honest and maintains his dignity even after she rejects him. His nobility contrasts strongly with Lord Longstaffe's shallow haughtiness during their encounter after the engagement has been broken. Some critics have maintained that Trollope's portrayal of Brehgert, who is described as fat and greasy with dyed black hair and beard, reflects his antisemitism. Others, however, contend that by making Brehgert one of the novel's few honest characters he reverses the stereotype of the scheming, disreputable Jew.

Mrs. Winifred Hurtle is the mysterious American woman who has come to England in pursuit of Paul Montague, with whom she apparently was once romantically involved. She provides a strong contrast to Paul's other love interest, Hetta Carbury, in her maturity, passion, and complexity. Mrs. Hurtle has a shadowy reputation for violence: she once shot an attacker and may have also have killed her cruel first husband. She displays several contradictory impulses, such as a feminine desire for revenge that fluctuates with a willingness to accept her pain and allow Paul to go his own way. Significantly, Mrs. Hurtle expresses admiration for Melmotte's courage and ruthlessness—which, as several critics have pointed out, resemble her own. Also notable is the fact that she, like many of the novel's villainous or morally questionable characters, is a foreigner; in fact, she asserts that Americans are inherently rougher than the refined, weak British. Mrs. Hurtle has been interpreted as the stereotypical "other woman" whose fear of aging and possessiveness make her dangerous. She has also been said to embody a resentment of male domination that many Victorian woman might have shared.

Of the novel's remaining minor characters, several are notable. **Lord Nidderdale** is the goodnatured but indolent young man whom Melmotte wishes Marie to marry. Nidderdale's lack of concern over the cheating that has been detected among his cardplaying companions reveals his jaded outlook, as does his matter-of-fact comment that a published statement listing the fortunes of various eligible women would greatly facilitate the maneuvering of young men like himself through the marriage market. Despite his cynicism, however, Nidderdale reveals a trace of decency when he declines to snub Melmotte at the House of Commons and when he remains Marie's friend despite her disinclination to marry him. Like other young people in the novel, Lord Nidderdale pays little attention to his father, the **Marquis of Auld Reekie** (who, interestingly, played a part in Trollope's 1869 novel *Can You Forgive Her?* when he pressured Lady Glencora Plantagenet to marry a man she did not love). **Lord Alfred Grendall** is Melmotte's closest confidante during his rise to power but the first to desert him when the rumors about his swindling begin to circulate. A parasite who pretends to esteem Melmotte merely because he is wealthy and powerful, Grendall points out to his friend that money can secure almost any honor. Like his father, young **Miles Grendall** serves as a toady to Melmotte, providing him the benefit of his own aristocratic prestige in exchange for money. Miles is a regular at the Beargarden Club, where he cheats at cards, and seems to have no redeeming qualities.

Other minor characters in *The Way We Live Now* include **Ruby Ruggles,** the country girl who is nearly seduced by Sir Felix; her sweetheart **John Crumb,** a stalwart farmer retained by Roger Carbury, who follows Ruby to London and thrashes her intended seducer; **Father Barham,** the Catholic priest who solicits Melmotte as a church member and accepts his violent rebuff with calculating placidity; **Nicholas Broune,** the shrewd, opportunistic editor who helps to illustrate that the world of literature is subject to the same immoral code of conduct as the commercial realm, and whose marriage to Lady Carbury thus carries disreputable overtones; and **Hamilton Fisker,** possibly based on a famous and corrupt American speculator named Colonel Fisk, who is Melmotte's partner in the railway scheme and who eventually marries his daughter.

Further Reading

Bareham, Tony, ed. *Anthony Trollope.* New York: Barnes & Noble, 1980.

Bowen, Elizabeth. *Anthony Trollope: A New Judgment.* New York: Oxford University Press, 1946.

Cockshut, A. O. J. *Anthony Trollope: A Critical Study.* 1955. Reprint. New York: New York University Press, 1968.

Dictionary of Literary Biography, Vol. 21. Detroit: Gale.

Edwards, P. D. *Anthony Trollope: His Art and Scope.* St. Lucia: University of Queensland Press, 1977.

Hall, N. John. *Trollope: A Biography.* Oxford: Clarendon Press, 1991.

Harvey, Geoffrey. *The Art of Anthony Trollope.* New York: St. Martin's Press, 1980.

James, Henry. "Anthony Trollope." 1883. Reprint. In *Partial Portraits,* pp. 97-133. London: Macmillan, 1899.

Kincaid, James R. *The Novels of Anthony Trollope.* Oxford: Oxford at the Clarendon Press, 1977.

Kronenberger, Louis. "'Barchester Towers.'" In *The Polished Surface: Essays in the Literature of Worldliness,* pp. 217-32. New York: Knopf, 1969.

MacDonald, Susan Peck. *Anthony Trollope.* Boston: Twayne Publishers, 1987.

McMaster, Juliet. *Trollope's Palliser Novels: Theme and Pattern.* New York: Oxford University Press, 1978.

Nineteenth Century Literature Criticism, Vol. 6. Detroit: Gale.

Pollard, Arthur. *Anthony Trollope.* London: Routledge & Kegan Paul, 1978.

Pritchett, V. S. "Trollope Was Right." In *The Living Novel and Other Appreciations,* rev. ed., pp. 128-40. New York: Random House, 1964.

Roberts, Ruth. *The Moral Trollope.* Athens: Ohio University Press, 1971.

Smalley, Donald, ed. *Trollope: The Critical Heritage.* London: Routledge & Kegan Paul, 1969.

Snow, C. P. *Trollope: His Life and Art.* New York: Charles Scribner's Sons, 1975.

Sutherland, John. Introduction to *The Way We Live Now* by Anthony Trollope, pp. vii-xxviii. Oxford: Oxford University Press, 1982.

Tracy, Robert. *Trollope's Later Novels.* Berkeley: University of California Press, 1978.

Ivan Turgenev
1818-1883
Russian novelist, short story writer, dramatist, poet, and essayist.

"Mumu" (short story, 1852)

Plot: The story, which takes place in Russia before the emancipation of the serfs, centers on a large, strong, deaf-mute house serf named Gerasim. His owner is a tyrannical old woman who treats her serfs like animals. She takes Gerasim with her to live in Moscow, where he misses the hard physical labor he had performed in the country, where he had always previously lived. Gerasim falls in love with another serf, the excrutiatingly shy laundress Tatyana, who is unaware of Gerasim's feelings for her and frightened by his size and apparent ferocity. The meddling old mistress decides that Tatyana should marry another servant, a repellent drunkard named Kapiton Klimov. Just before the couple drives away, Gerasim bids Tatyana farewell and gives her a gift of red scarves, thus making her aware of his love for her. Soon after this leavetaking, Gerasim discovers a small dog struggling to escape from the turbulent waters of a nearby river. Gerasim rescues the spirited creature and names her Mumu. The two quickly become devoted to each other, and the dog seems to fill a place in Gerasim's heart left vacant by the departure of Tatyana. Mumu runs freely about the estate and proves useful as a watchdog. At one point she is stolen by a stranger, but she finds her way back to Gerasim. During an encounter with the mistress, however, Mumu enrages the old lady by baring her teeth at her. The mistress orders Gerasim to drown his little dog. The dutiful though heartbroken Gerasim complies with her wish, holding the completely trustful Mumu over the waves of the river and finally dropping her in. He eventually returns to the country, but he never marries or acquires another dog, living for the rest of his days alone in his humble shack.

Characters: The story, which is perhaps Turgenev's most famous, had its origin in the author's own life. He was raised on a provincial Russian estate and his strong-willed mother frequently mistreated her serfs. Turgenev's outrage at the inhumanity of the Russian feudal system, in which the serfs were considered property and approached as dumb animals, is evident in the story. Yet "Mumu" also has more universal implications in its emphasis on the important role of love in human life.

The central human character in "Mumu" is **Gerasim,** the deaf-mute house serf whose cruel mistress thwarts both of his attempts to attain love and then forces him to drown his cherished pet. Gerasim's large, powerful physique is ironically coupled with an inability to hear or speak, deficits that not only impede communication and social intercourse with others but make him somewhat repellent. The narrator notes that Gerasim might have been attractive to women if not for his infirmities, but as it is he is avoided by all. His size and aura of suppressed energy also elicit fear from those around him and further isolate him. When taken by the mistress to the city, Gerasim feels stifled by the relative inactivity of his city life. He has a strong yearning for love that coexists with a capacity for brutality that is demonstrated whenever he feels that someone has transgressed the boundaries of decency, particularly in regard to Tatyana. Incapable of expressing his love for the servant girl, Gerasim suffers from the knowledge that she only fears him; finally, however, she seems to recognize his feelings as she kisses him goodbye. Gerasim's relationship with the little dog he rescues from drowning provides the story's primary illustration of the human capacity and need for love. His concern and care for her allow him to develop an aspect of himself that had previously been suppressed, and his feelings for Mumu are notably deeper than the embryonic emotion he had felt for Tatyana. There is a tragic irony in the circumstance of Mumu's death: having once saved the dog from drowning, Gerasim is forced to kill her by the same means. His compliance with his mistress's order illustrates the completely dependent relationship between master and serf, an arrangement that denies the dependent party the right to shape his own fate and violates his or her human dignity. At the same time, the incident illustrates Gerasim's simultaneous capacity for brutality and his essential honesty and sense of honor, for he is not only physically able to perform the task but willing to do what he has indicated he would do. In the end, he lives alone, without the comfort of wife or dog, deprived of a meaningful, happy life by his status as a serf. Though portrayed as a markedly ordinary Russian peasant and possessed of very human qualities and weaknesses, Gerasim is in some ways heroic. He has been said to represent the tremendous strength, tempered by abject humility, of the Russian people, particularly in the days before emancipation—an emblem not just of the injustice of serfdom but of a nation's great and perhaps soon-to-be-released energy.

The story's title character is **Mumu,** a small white dog with black spots who exhibits an indomitable spirit on her first appearance, when she struggles to keep herself alive. Rescued by Gerasim, she quickly devotes herself to him and thus becomes the story's main symbol of selfless love and loyalty. Like Gerasim, she has previously experienced isolation, having been unwanted and abandoned by her previous master. She comes to occupy and more than fill the void left by Tatyana's departure. In fact, there are several parallels between Mumu and the girl: both are orphans who have experienced loneliness and hardship, both fear the mistress, and both are loved by Gerasim. Mumu's name has been said to evoke the speechlessness of her rescuer, for the only sound that Gerasim is able to make is a lowing sound similar to that emitted by a cow. Both Mumu, an animal, and Gerasim, a human being, are treated with cruelty by the mistress, who makes no distinction between them and recognizes the merits of neither. Unlike the old, ineffective watchdog Volcek, Mumu ranges freely over the estate and exhibits a life-affirming spirit and purpose by barking out warnings of danger and also by baring her teeth at the old mistress, whom she instinctively despises and fears. The mistress's coldly dictatorial order that the erring dog be drowned represents the cruel tyranny of a heedless master over a dumb, dependent beast; thus Mumu might be seen as a symbol of serfdom's injustice. Yet Mumu's nobility—evident in her spirited nature, her loyalty, and her trust in Gerasim as even as he holds her over the water before dropping her—may also herald the quickly approaching time of emancipation.

The unnamed, dictatorial old **mistress** serves as a particularly reprehensible embodiment of Russia's old feudal system, under which serfs were owned by their masters and frequently treated as animals rather than human beings. Indeed, the mistress views her serfs as mere property, gauging them only in terms of their monetary value, and thus is incapable of recognizing Gerasim's inner nobility. Ironically, she is as isolated from others as Gerasim; her solitude, however, is the result of a nasty temperament that makes everyone want to avoid her. A widow, she has even been deserted by her grown children. Bereft of love in her own life, she meddles in matters of love in other people's when she arranges a match between Tatyana and Kapiton, an action sure to bring unhappiness to both Tatyana and Gerasim. She demonstrates her lack of consideration, kindness, or even simply decency when she orders Gerasim to drown his dog; it would be cruel enough to have the dog killed by someone else, but to force Gerasim to commit the deed seems diabolical. Although the mistress frequently feigns illness in an effort to gain attention, she fails to interest anyone in her condition, and at by the end of the story her manipulations and cruelties have resulted only in an even more bitter solitude. Although Turgenev claimed to have based the mistress on his grandmother, it is widely thought that she was in fact modeled after his mother, whose furious temper and abuse of her serfs was well documented.

The first object of Gerasim's affection is **Tatyana,** a humble laundress with a shy, shrinking nature. Small and fair, Tatyana has—like, significantly, Mumu—been oppressed and mistreated since childhood. An orphan of obscure origin, she was raised by a worthless uncle and is ultimately married to a worthless husband, so that her life promises nothing but misery. Her inability to alter her own fate underlines the helplessness of the serfs, whose servitude makes them vulnerable to such cruel caprice as the mistress's decision to marry Tatyana to Kapiton. Just before she leaves the estate with her new husband, Tatyana receives a gift of red scarves from Gerasim, and she finally recognizes his feelings for her; perhaps this knowledge gives her some comfort–though certainly tinged with regret–as she leaves.

Other characters in the story include **Kapiton Klimov,** the repellent, unreliable, and constantly rationalizing drunkard whom Tatyana is forced to marry; and **Volcek,** the old, weary guard dog who is always chained in the yard but who seems to accept his fate. He never tries to escape and barks only half-heartedly, thus providing a contrast to the spirited and more purposeful Mumu, who ranges freely over the estate and who bravely fights for her life. Volcek might be interpreted as a metaphor for the Russian people, whom Turgenev saw as submissive, silent, and overcome by a sense of futility in the face of their oppression.

"Bezhin Meadow" (short story, 1852)

Plot: The story takes place in the Russian countryside, where the unnamed hunter who narrates all of the "Sportsman's Sketches" has become lost. He encounters a group of five boys who are tending a herd of horses by a river. Joining them at their campfire, he listens to their stories of ghosts and other supernatural beings. First a boy named Iliusha recounts how he was working in a paper mill when an invisible hobgoblin made its presence known by moving the water wheel and other machinery. Finally the spirit sneezed, and Iliusha and the other frightened workers scrambled for hiding places. Now Kostya shares what his father has told him about why Gavrila, a local carpenter, always has such a melancholy expression on his face. While searching in the woods for nuts, Gavrila became lost and encountered a water spite, who insisted that he come to live with her. When he refused, the vengeful spirit cursed him with feeling as griefstricken as she for the rest of his life. While Iliusha is relating a story about a drowned man whose spirit entered a lamb, the dogs begin barking; Pavel goes to investigate and soon returns, concluding that they have smelled something evil, such as a wolf. This leads to talk about wolves and then about the possibility of seeing people one knows who have died and those who will die in the coming year. Several humorous stories are told, one concerning an old woman who broke all of the pots in her kitchen because she thought, due to a solar eclipse, that the Day of Judgment was at hand and that no one should eat on that day; another centers on the panicked reaction of villagers who feared the evil spirit Trishka and thus mistook a man carrying a barrel for someone whose head had been cruelly enlarged.

The boys hear a strange scream in the distance and wonder where it might have come from. They remember a local girl who had gone insane after being submerged in the river for a long time, and a boy named Vassya who had drowned in the same river. Pavel goes to the river to get some water, and when he returns he reports that he has heard Vassya's voice. The boys finally go to sleep. The next morning, the narrator wakes early and says goodbye to Pavel, the only boy awake. He reports that Pavel, whom he particularly liked, was killed later that year after falling from a horse.

Characters: "Bezhin Meadow" is often cited as one of the most accomplished stories in *A Sportsman's Sketches,* a collection of tales narrated by an amiable, observant hunter who travels through the Russian countryside and encounters a wide variety of people and situations. This story reveals Turgenev's interest in Russian folklore and rural life as well as human behavior in general, and also evidences his sympathy for the peasants of his country, whom he felt were oppressed under the system of serfdom. His positive portrayal of the five boys in "Bezhin Meadow" typifies his efforts to depict the creativity, intelligence, dignity, and simple humanity of the Russian peasantry, thus highlighting the injustice of the master-serf relationship.

The **narrator** of "Bezhin Meadow" and the other *Sportsman's Sketches* is apparently a member of the upper class, for he has the leisure to pursue his interest in hunting and travel across the countryside. Goodnatured and well-mannered, he is a quiet observer who takes careful note of his surroundings. His appreciation for the beautiful landscapes and scenes he encounters is evident, and Turgenev has often been praised for his skill in describing the Russian setting in plentiful, authentic detail. The narrator generally allows the boys to hold the reader's attention, though he occasionally makes observations that serve as subtle reminders of his presence. His guidance is therefore understated but still significant; despite his fairly objective presentation of the boys, for instance, he establishes an attitude of sympathy toward them and appreciation for their creativity and pluck. As the story opens, the narrator has lost his way and, with the night approaching, the landscape has taken on a somewhat sinister aspect. Yet through his contact with the boys, who directly confront the fear and mystery of life in their supernatural tales, he ultimately achieves a feeling of confidence and finally rides off into a peaceful morning.

The five boys in "Bezhin Meadow"—**Fedya, Iliusha, Kostya, Pavel,** and **Vanya**—have been charged with caring for a herd of horses as they graze near a river. Gathered around their campfire before going to sleep, they form a small community of their own that is separated from the rest of their society by several factors, including not only their physical isolation but their youth and the "ring of light" from their fire, which forms a kind of magic circle as they share ghost stories. At fourteen, Fedya is the oldest boy and therefore the leader of the group; he gently guides the discussion. Iliusha is the most knowledgable about supernatural matters, particularly since he is the only boy who has had a personal experience with a ghost. His story about the hobgoblin in the paper mill provides a note of humor at its conclusion, when the spirit indulges in the very prosaic act of sneezing. Kostya's story about the eternally melancholy Gavrila has been compared to Nathaniel Hawthorne's 1835 story "Young Goodman Brown," for the protagonists of both tales are doomed, after encounters with supernatural beings, to suffer from a bleak outlook for the rest of their lives.

The most prominent of the story's youthful characters is Pavel, for whom the narrator develops a particular liking, referring to him several times as "a splendid boy" or "a fine boy." Indeed, Pavel exhibits admirable energy and courage when he leaps up after a dog begins barking and follows it into the darkness to locate the source of its fear. He also ventures down to the water soon after the boys have been discussing several frightening events connected with the river. When he returns, he announces solemnly that he has heard the voice of Vassya, a boy who was drowned in the river by thieves. Pavel's statement that "no man can get around his fate" proves significant, for the narrator reports that he died within a year. In addition to giving the story's conclusion a melancholy irony that is typical of Turgenev's fiction, the news of Pavel's death serves as a reminder that the world's evil cannot long be avoided, even within the enchanted circle of the boy's campfire. It may also infer that human beings face the risk of death every day, and that both life and death must be accepted—as Pavel, with his matter-of-fact conclusion about man's fate, had suggested.

"The Hamlet of the Schigrov District" (short story, 1852)

Plot: The narrator is a wandering huntsman who arrives for an overnight visit at the country estate of a wealthy landowner. At dinner, he meets the local wit, Pyotr Lupikhin, who provides humorous accounts of the other guests. The host is preoccupied with awaiting the arrival of a distinguished dignitary, who eventually delivers a pompous, vacuous little speech. That night, the narrator shares a bedroom with a stranger, and since neither is sleepy the two begin to talk. The stranger, whose name is Vasily Vasilyich but who will not reveal his last name, tells the narrator the story of his dissatisfying, thwarted existence and how he came to be overlooked by society. He claims that his greatest fault is his lack of originality, the only quality that allows individuals to achieve meaningful lives. After the death of his father when he was very young, Vasily was raised by a domineering mother and then by a guardian who robbed him of most of his fortune. During his four years at the university, he learned nothing but the pretensions and hypocrisies of young men who belong to intellectual "circles." He then traveled in Europe and lived for some time in Germany, but he derived nothing of value from these experiences. After spending a few months in Moscow, where he felt socially ostracized, he retired to his country estate. He was soon overcome by boredom. Vasily eventually married the daughter of a neighboring army officer. Although he claims that she was a sweet and generous creature, he also admits that her dullness and unexplained melancholy drove him to consider suicide. His wife died four years later during her first pregnancy, having failed to produce a child, and Vasily concludes that she is fortunate to have died. He then attempted to establish himself in a bureaucratic career and as a writer, but neither effort was successful. Retiring again to the country, he had an encounter with the local police captain that proved revelatory: when Vasily criticized a certain official, his acquaintence remarked that men as insignificant as themselves had no right to fault their superiors. At home, Vasily gazed at himself in a mirror and realized that he was indeed a superfluous, unoriginal, worthless person, and he stuck his tongue out at himself with contempt. Vasily concludes the tale by telling the narrator not to wonder about his last name, but to call him "Hamlet;" he claims that there are many like him throughout Russia. Both now fall asleep, and when the narrator wakes the next morning his roommate has already left.

Characters: Published in the acclaimed collection entitled *A Sportsman's Sketches*, the story was written during a time of upheaval and uncertainty in Russia, whose citizens were torn between their desire for isolation and the encroachment of western European influences. Although Turgenev advocated reform, he felt that change must occur slowly, and he was convinced that his country's younger generation was, in any case, too weak to lead the way. The "superfluous man" or Russian Hamlet, as described by Turgenev, was sensitive and intelligent but too overwhelmed by a feeling of futility to act decisively. Along with its subtle irony and pathos and its realistically detailed descriptions, "The Hamlet of the Schigrov District" offers one of Turgenev's most successful examples of this famous character type.

All of the *Sportsman's Sketches* are related by a polite, cultured **narrator** whose objective but discerning voice helps him to maintain a comfortable rapport with the audience. In "The Hamlet of the Schigrov District," he establishes the story's setting and then introduces the reader to several other characters, most notably Lupikhin and Vasily Vasilyich, who are then used as mouthpieces for the tale's satire and themes. Thus he is almost voiceless himself and acts primarily as a sounding board; in keeping with the story's dramatic bent, he might be seen as Vasily/Hamlet's audience, with the small, damp room they share serving as a stage.

The story's central figure is **Vasily Vasilyich,** the narrator's fellow visitor at the country estate of Alexander Mikhailych G. and his roommate for the night they spend there. Vasily is not surprised that the narrator has not previously noticed him among the guests, for he is, he declares, completely unoriginal and consistently overlooked by those around him. Although he is, as he assures the narrator, well-educated and widely traveled, Vasily is stymied by a lack of will and painfully aware of his own inadequacy. His childhood was shaped by a domineering mother and marred by the death of his crippled brother (circumstances which also characterize Turgenev's youth). After his mother's death he was sent to an uncle-guardian who managed to pilfer much of his small fortune. His university career was socially and academically undistinguished. A dreamy youth with a vague longing for beauty and knowledge, Vasily became involved with an intellectual "circle" of like-minded young men whom he now recognizes as self-important hypocrites who knew nothing of real life. His subsequent travels in Europe were equally valueless, for he absorbed none of the cultural influences he encountered there even though he affected an attitude of appreciation. Returning to Moscow, he initially projected himself as sophisticated and glib, but he took offense when he perceived that he had been slandered and eventually crept away to his country estate. Bored by provincial life, Vasily occupied himself by courting and marrying Sofya, the daughter of a neighbor. He claims that she was generous, sweet, and loving but that her pervasive melancholy and her dull, old-maidish habits contributed to his contemplating suicide on several occasions. After his wife's death, Vasily made several unsuccessful attempts to find some useful outlet for his abilities. His encounter with the police captain provided the final blow to his self esteem, and he is now completely consumed with a sense of his own worthlessness and insignificance; he tortures himself by intentionally exposing himself to the contempt and petty slights of others. Vasily refuses to divulge his last name to the narrator, suggesting that he be called Hamlet and claiming that "There are many such Hamlets in every district." This statement has been interpreted as evidencing Turgenev's view that this personality type was common throughout Russia. Vasily shares with the title character of Shakespeare's famous play a penchant for obsessive, melancholy reflection rather than decisive, constructive action. The monologue he delivers to the narrator—with the damp, greenish room as his stage—might be compared to Hamlet's soliloquies. Turgenev's characterization of Vasily is often mentioned in connection with an earlier essay in which he had identified two dominant personality types, the Hamlet and the Don Quixote. The former, Turgenev asserted, was prone to skepticism, hypersensitivity, and resulting inertia, while the latter was a romantic idealist who was enthusiastic but unrealistic. The Hamlet type is also presented in Turgenev's "The Diary of a Superfluous Man," which gave a much-repeated name to the concept of the talented but spineless individual common in Russian literature.

The sarcastic local wit **Pyotr Lupikhin** serves as Turgenev's mouthpiece for his virulent satire of Russian high society. The narrator says that Lupikhin's face also wears an ironic, impudent expression. As he and the narrator survey the assembled guests, Luphikhin makes mocking comments about them, exhibiting an acid wit that can be cruel, as when he remarks that one man's wife is "cracked" within the man's hearing. Significantly, however, Lupikhin admits that he is not so much witty as embittered with life, and speaking his mind freely gives him some relief from his spiritual desolation.

The host of the gathering is **Alexander Mikhailych G.,** whose superficiality is signified by the narrator's declining to mention his last name. A wealthy bachelor with sumptuous tastes, the host represents the small-mindedness of Russia's landowning class, particularly in his exaggerated deference to his guest of honor. Other guests at the dinner include military officers and conservative local dignitaries, all of whom are portrayed as fatuous and hypocritical. The scornful Lupikhin describes **Prince Kozelsky** as "dull-witted. . .as a pair of merchant's horses," notes that a **general** sneaks around the room like a wolf, and comments that a **German businessman** is known to take bribes. The host and his guests spend the long period before dinner anxiously awaiting the arrival of an unnamed **high official.** A stout figure wearing a heavily starched shirt and projecting a smug, haughty manner, the official delivers a particularly fatuous, self-satisfied speech at dinner and seems to view the deference he receives from the others as his due. Another guest at the estate is **Voinitsyn,** a young man who apparently lives with the host and who introduces the narrator to Lupikhin. Voinitsyn has flunked out of college and blames his failure on fate, even though the truth is that he never studied.

Fathers and Sons (*Ottsy i deti;* novel, 1862)

Plot: The novel takes place in Russia in 1859. Provincial landowner Nikolay Kirsanov is eagerly awaiting the arrival of his son Arkady from St. Petersburg, where he has been attending the university for the last three years. Climbing down from the coach along with Arkady is his friend Yevgeny Bazarov, a medical student who is going to stay with the Kirsanovs for a few days before traveling on to his own parents' home. Bazarov has a superior, disdainful demeanor but Arkady appears to idolize him. During the ride to the Kirsanov's country estate, Nikolay anxiously informs his son that he has taken a mistress, Fenichka, who has recently given birth to their son. Arkady relieves his father's fears, assuring him that he does not consider marriage a necessary or even admirable institution. During the young mens' visit, Bazarov's rudeness and aggressively expressed opinions trouble the kindhearted but ineffectual Nikolay and particularly annoy his refined, aristocratic brother Pavel, who lives with the family. Bazarov proclaims himself a nihilist who believes in nothing and recognizes no traditional authority or social convention. Pavel, who was once an army officer and had a tragic affair with a beautiful noblewoman before retiring to country life, frequently disagrees with Bazarov's stridently liberal views. Bazarov trusts only in science and, during his stay with the Kirsanovs, applies himself with energy to his biological studies. Arkady worships his arrogant friend and claims to share his outlook, thus alarming his father and uncle.

In anticipation of the emancipation of the serfs, which has been ordered by law to occur within the next few years, Nikolay has already freed the serfs on his estate and rented each a small plot of land. They have responded with suspicion, however, and frequently cheat Nikolay. Bored with country life, Arkady and Bazarov travel to a nearby city, where they visit their friends Snitikov, a shallow, polished social climber, and Yevdoxia Kukshin, a cigarette-smoking dilettante and "emancipated" woman. They also meet the widowed Madame Anna Odintzov, an intelligent, elegant, but extremely reserved aristocrat. Arkady is attracted to Anna's gentle younger sister Katya, while Bazarov spends much of his time with Anna. Although he professes the view that women are mere instruments of pleasure and claims to disdain marriage and family life, Bazarov finds to his chagrin that he has fallen in love with Anna. When he brashly declares his feelings, however, she coldly rejects him, claiming that she could never love a man from a lower social class than hers. The two young men now travel on to the home of Bazarov's parents, Vasily and Arina, who adore and revere their son. Soon Bazarov feels stifled by their attentions, however, and he and Arkady finally return to the Kirsanov estate.

Bazarov is disappointed to learn that Arkady aspires to a conventional life and marriage with Katya. In an effort to forget Anna and prove to himself that he still considers women mere sexual objects, Bazarov tries to kiss the innocent Fenichka, greatly confusing and upsetting her. Having witnessed this episode, an enraged Pavel challenges Bazarov to a duel. Although Bazarov considers duelling a ridiculous aristocratic practice, he is unable to resist Pavel's challenge. Pavel is wounded during the encounter and Bazarov leaves the Kirsanov estate. Though ashamed at having allowed the nihilistic Bazarov to wound him, Pavel realizes that he has acted snobbishly, and he now encourages Nikolay to marry Fenichka. Eventually he moves to Germany, where he lives the life of an aging dandy. Meanwhile, Bazarov returns to his parents' home and helps his father, a village doctor, with his patients and also conducts his own scientific research. While performing an autopsy on a victim of typhus, Bazarov cuts his finger. He realizes that he will contract the disease unless the wound is cauterized; partly because he neglects his condition, Bazarov does become ill. Anna attends him at his bedside just before his death. His parents are devastated by the loss of their beloved son.

Characters: Along with Leo Tolstoy and Fedor Dostoyevsky, Turgenev is recognized as one of the three most important Russian novelists of the nineteenth century. Considered his masterpiece, *Fathers and Sons* provides a compelling chronicle of Russian society during a period characterized by uncertainty and political division. The novel's first critics responded to it along partisan lines, and Turgenev found himself the unintentional instigator of a controversy: Russia's radical reformers believed *Fathers and Sons* was intended to ridicule them, while more conservative readers felt Turgenev had glorified the radical viewpoint. Modern scholars, however, contend that the novel's artistic depth and broad themes allow it to transcend its immediate political context. The characters in *Fathers and Sons* are portrayed with impressive psychological insight and pathos that lend them universal appeal.

Despite his role as an idealogue who articulates the viewpoint of some of nineteenth-century Russia's most radical reformers, **Yevgeny Bazarov** is a complex character whose human weaknesses lend him depth. Bazarov's spirited defense of *nihilism* helped to bring this term—which Turgenev is often wrongly credited with coining—into common use. The son of a village physician and small landowner, Bazarov has, as the novel opens, just completed his own medical training. A dedicated biologist who claims to trust only in science and the intellect, he rejects the authority and supremacy claimed by the aristocracy and scorns all social, cultural, and political conventions, including such traditional virtues as romantic love and reverence for art. Bazarov is a pragmatist and utilitarian who feels that ''a respectable chemist is twenty times more useful than a poet.'' He considers it his duty to destroy the illusions, superstitions, and sentimentality that impede progress and reform and which he sees as concentrated in the aristocratic Pavel Kirsanov. It is not only Bazarov's opinions that make him so repellent to Pavel, whose views are philosophically opposed to the younger man's, but his sneeringly superior, arrogant, often sarcastic, and stridently uninhibited manner. Bazarov maintains a demeanor of coldly clinical integrity, yet several episodes reveal the existence of impulses and passions within himself. Although he scorns the idea of romantic love as sentimental claptrap and claims to view women as mere instruments of entertainment or physical release, Bazarov discovers that he feels for Anna Odintsov exactly the romantic, idealized love he has always disdained. He impulsively declares his feelings, suggesting not only that he can behave brashly but that he is in fact susceptible to the attractions of marriage and family, and is chagrined when Anna rejects him. Similarly, Bazarov is irresistably drawn into duelling with Pavel even though he considers it a foolish aristocratic practice; the passions of anger and resentment that Pavel has stirred overcome his supposedly cool, intellectual detachment. Bazarov's relationship with his simple, adoring parents provides one of the novel's richest examples of the tenderness and tension that may coexist between parents and children. Although Bazarov loves his father and mother and feels that their lack of pretension makes them inherently superior to such aristocrats as Pavel and Nikolay Kirsanov, he treats them condescendingly and feels stifled by their attentions. These feelings and reactions are not determined by Bazarov's political views or limited to a person of his particular time or place—they are recognizably human and universal. Bazarov's death has generated a variety of interpretations. Critics are divided on whether his neglect of his condition evidences a suicidal tendency, and on what Turgenev meant by the novel's melancholy conclusion. Some claim that the fact that the idealistic Bazarov's demise is brought about through a decidedly trivial, meaningless cause was intended as a mockery of the nihilistic radicals of Turgenev's day or as a sign that the time had not yet come for figures like Bazarov, while others contend that the death is presented as ironically tragic, proof of nature's indifference to human striving. In any case, the death scene itself has been universally praised for its realism and poignancy. The great Russian dramatist Anton Chekhov, himself a physician, claimed that Turgenev's description was so authentic that he felt he might catch Bazarov's infection. Turgenev claimed to have based his most memorable, effective character on an actual Russian doctor whom he had met while traveling in Germany and who had later died. He once said that he agreed with all of Bazarov's views—except his rejection of art—but did not approve of his way of expressing them. Turgenev also admitted that he could not decide whether he loved or hated Bazarov, who, indeed, is both repellent and subtly attractive; though rudely expressed, his views reflect not only personal integrity and idealism but the yearning of many of his compatriots for justice and progress.

The very correct, slightly dandyish **Pavel Kirsanov,** Arkady's uncle, argues frequently with Bazarov during the young mens' visit to the Kirsanov estate. A middleaged aristocrat with refined tastes, Pavel embodies the entrenched values of an older generation of Russian society, a viewpoint that Bazarov finds archaic, far too molded by European influences, and ultimately detrimental to progress. For his part, Pavel is annoyed by the rudeness and arrogance of his nephew's friend; he disagrees with Bazarov's revolutionary ideals and considers him a charlatan and bore. Pavel's studied aura of melancholy is attributed to his troubled past: after a disappointing career in the army, he fell in love with a beautiful noblewoman who subsequently died. He has retired to his brother's country estate, where his wealth allows him to pursue a subdued life of leisure. Pavel seems to represent for Bazarov a reprensible, elitist unconcern for humanity's suffering. Pavel, however, considers nihilists like Bazarov barbarians because they refuse to live by principles. The tension between Bazarov and Pavel finally results in their fighting a duel; Pavel's challenge is motivated not only by his annoyed reaction to Bazarov's manner and opinions but by his exaggerated sense of honor. He has witnessed the younger man's attempt to seduce Fenichka, to whom he himself has felt attracted because she resembles his dead lover, and vows to avenge this transgression. Just as Bazarov feels ashamed of being drawn into duelling despite his scorn for such practices, Pavel is embarrassed by the outcome of the encounter. His stiff formality somewhat shaken by the experience, he advises his brother to marry Fenichka—a blessing for which the couple has long hoped. Although Pavel realizes that his society is bound to change and will not long accommodate men like himself, he still maintains his aristocratic stance, returning eventually to Germany to live as an aging dandy. Critics have detected in Turgenev's portrayal of Pavel evidence of his personal knowledge of aristocratic habits and manners, which he generally condemned but—to a limited extent at least—sympathized with.

Although **Arkady Kirsanov** professes, on returning to his provincial home from three years at the university, to share the revolutionary ideals espoused by his friend Bazarov, he is at heart a more ordinary young man than his friend. His veneration for Bazarov ultimately attests to his being naive, impressionable, and awestruck by his friend's brilliance rather than truly committed to the tenets of nihilism. Arkady is unable to agree with Bazarov that art and poetry are merely useless expressions of sentimentality, inferior to science or other productive pursuits. Further, he develops a purely conventional attachment to Katya and plans an ordinary, comfortable domestic life with her, thus conclusively severing his alliance with Bazarov's nihilistic ideals about women, marriage, and family. Lacking the ruthlessness that Bazarov exhibits and which is evidentally an essential component in the revolutionary stance, Arkady seems destined to become, like his father, a well-meaning though perhaps ineffectual provincial landowner. Some critics have seen the kindhearted Arkady as a reflection of his creator, particularly in his appreciation for art and poetry.

Nikolay Kirsanov, Arkady's warm, gentle, unassuming father, is the owner of five thousand acres of land and about one hundred serfs. A well-meaning liberal, he approves of the government's order that the serfs be emancipated within a few years, and has in fact already freed his own. Taking advantage of his impractical, ineffectual nature, however, the serfs have repeatedly cheated him, and his estate has fallen into disorder. A rather dreamy, tender man who loves music and adores his son, Nikolay has little grasp of practical matters; his problems in managing his estate have made him prematurely old.

Anna Odintsov is a beautiful widow who is a star of her aristocratic social set. Intelligent and well-spoken herself, she is interested in discussing Bazarov's ideas with him, but her reserved, apparently passionless nature prevents her from returning his warmer sentiments.

She is surprised and displeased by his ardent expression of love, which apparently threatens her sense of power and order, and she rejects him. Although she recognizes Bazarov's potential for impressive achievement, she tells him, she could never consider marrying a man from a lower class than her own. Self-possessed, elegant, and proud, Anna's frigidity lessens only once in the story: when she comes to Bazarov's bedside at his request and grants him a final kiss. It is to Anna that Bazarov makes his much-quoted request that she blow on the lamp to ignite it, an action that highlights the contrasting waning of Bazarov's life. His hopeless love for the haughty Anna, an emotion from which he has long considered himself immune, adds poignancy and depth to the novel.

Bazarov's parents, **Vasily and Arina Bazarov,** are simple, unpretentious people who adore and revere their brilliant, arrogant son. Vasily is a former army doctor who now manages his small estate and attends to patients in the village; Arina is uneducated and superstitious but sensible and loving. Turgenev is often praised for his perceptive depiction of the relationship between the Bazarovs and their son, who returns their love but feels somewhat stifled by their attentions. During his first visit home, Vasily and Arina make an effort to leave Yevgeny alone to conduct his scientific research, but they find themselves irresistably drawn toward him and ultimately impede his work. He finally leaves, and they are left wondering if they have indeed driven him away with their solicitousness. When he returns and takes up practicing medicine with his father, Vasily and Arina are happy and relieved; though they sense that he has changed, they are afraid to ask what has happened to him. Turgenev has been universally lauded for his portrayal of the Bazarovs' desolation and loneliness after their son's death. The novel's final scene, in which the couple visits Yevgeny's grave, has been called one of the most moving in all of literature, and it is said that while writing it Turgenev had to turn his head to keep his tears from falling onto the manuscript.

Fenichka Savishna, Nikolay's young mistress, is gentle, quiet, and ingenuous. Although she is of low birth and thus not traditionally worthy to marry her aristocratic lover, she is inherently noble and sincere. Fenichka responds gratefully to Bazarov's attentions to her ill baby, but she is confused and distressed when he kisses her. Pavel witnesses the encounter and is moved to defend her, not only out of regard for her honor but because he has seen something of his dead lover in her and is jealous of Bazarov's attentions to her. Another significant though minor female character in the novel is **Katya Loktiv,** Anna's younger sister, who is gentle, shy, and somewhat fearful of Anna. Though the marriage of Katya and Arkady is portrayed as conventional and bourgeois, their happiness provides a strong contrast to the obvious loneliness of the supposedly heroic, revolutionary stance he has assumed.

Other characters in *Father and Sons* include **Sitnikov,** the polished, absurdly smug friend whom Arkady and Bazarov meet during their visit to the city and who introduces them to Madame Odintsov and her set; and **Yevdoxia Kukshin,** a sloppy, cigarette-smoking parody of the nineteenth-century's "emancipated" woman and a silly, namedropping dilettante who continually espouses the latest trends and ideas.

Further Reading

"A Novel from Russia." *The Nation* IV, No. 102 (13 June 1867): 470-72.

Costlow, Jane T. *Worlds within Worlds: The Novels of Ivan Turgenev.* Princeton, N.J.: Princeton University Press, 1990.

Freeborn, Richard. *Turgenev: The Novelist's Novelist, A Study.* London: Oxford University Press, 1960.

Frost, Edgar L. "Turgenev's 'Mumu' and the Absence of Love." *Slavic and East-European Journal* 31, No. 2 (Summer 1987): 171-86.

Hershkowitz, Harry. *Democratic Ideas in Turgenev's Works.* New York: Columbia University Press, 1932.

James, Henry. "Ivan Turgenieff." In *French Poets and Novelists,* pp. 211-52. Bernhard Tauchnitz, 1883.

Kazin, Alfred. "Turgenev and the Non-Russians." In *The Inmost Leaf: A Selection of Essays,* pp. 89-92. New York: Harcourt Brace Jovanovich, 1955.

Knowles, A. V. *Ivan Turgenev.* Boston: Twayne Publishers, 1988.

Lowe, David A., ed. *Critical Essays on Ivan Turgenev.* Boston: G. K. Hall, 1988.

Lowe, David. *Turgenev's "Fathers and Sons."* Ann Arbor, Mich.: Ardis, 1983.

Maurois, André. "The Art of Turgenev." 1931. Reprint. In *The Art of Writing,* translated by Gerald Hopkins, pp. 295-315. New York: E. P. Dutton & Co., Inc., 1960.

Nineteenth Century Literature Criticism, Vol. 21. Detroit: Gale.

Pritchett, V. S. *The Gentle Barbarian: The Life and Work of Ivan Turgenev.* New York: Random House, 1977.

Ripp, Victor. *Turgenev's Russia: From "Notes of a Hunter"*

to "Fathers and Sons." Ithaca, N.Y.: Cornell University Press, 1980.

Seeley, Frank F. *Turgenev: A Reading of His Fiction.* Cambridge: Cambridge University Press, 1991.

Short Story Criticism, Vol. 7. Detroit: Gale.

Smyrniw, Walter. "Turgenev's Emancipated Women." *The Modern Language Review* 80, No. 1 (January 1985): 97-105.

Turgenev, Ivan. "Apropos of 'Fathers and Sons.'" 1868-69. Reprint. In *Literary Reminiscences and Autobiographical Fragments,* edited by David Magershack, pp. 193-204.

Mark Twain
1835-1910

American novelist, short story writer, dramatist, journalist, essayist, memoirist, and autobiographer.

The Adventures of Tom Sawyer (novel, 1876)

Plot: The novel centers on Tom Sawyer, a mischievous young boy who lives with his Aunt Polly, half-brother Sid, and cousin Mary in St. Petersburg, a small Missouri town on the Mississippi River. Tom envies the carefree life of his friend Huckleberry Finn, the son of the town drunk, who smokes, gambles, swears, spends his time fishing instead of going to school, and sleeps wherever he wishes. Tom falls in love with a new arrival in town, pretty Becky Thatcher. He contrives to sit next to her in class and soon declares his feelings. Becky initially accepts Tom's offer of devotion, but when she learns that he was previously in love with Amy Lawrence, she haughtily spurns him. That same night Tom and Huck creep into the town cemetery, carrying a dead cat they plan to use to test a new cure for warts. There they come upon three disreputable St. Petersburg citizens—the villainous half-breed Injun Joe, Muff Potter, and Doctor Robinson—in the act of robbing a grave; the boys witness a fight between the men that results in Injun Joe murdering Dr. Robinson and making Potter believe he has committed the deed. The terrified Tom and Huck slip away, fearful that Injun Joe will discover and kill them. Dejected over Becky's rejecting him and afraid of Injun Joe, Tom suggests that he, Huck, and their friend Joe Harper run away to Jackson's Island to be pirates. The boys spend an idyllic few days on the island but eventually realize, when they see the townspeople dragging the river, that they have been presumed drowned. Tom makes a surreptitious visit back to his home, where he witnesses a grief-stricken discussion about their beloved boys between Aunt Polly and Joe's mother. After he returns to the island, Tom finds that the other boys are ready to end their adventure, and he convinces them to spy on their own funeral. Once the boys have heard the minister pronounce them good-hearted and sorely missed, they make a dramatic appearance before the startled but relieved mourners.

Tom is now much admired by the other boys, but Becky still ignores him. When he saves her from punishment by confessing to a misdeed that she committed, however, Becky forgives Tom. Meanwhile Muff Potter charged with the murder of Dr. Robinson. Although he is afraid that Injun Joe will seek vengeance against him, Tom decides to reveal his knowledge of the real killer and thus saves Potter from condemnation. Injun Joe manages to escape from the courtroom while Tom is making his statement. Some time later Tom and Huck are hunting for pirate treasure in an abandoned house when, from a hiding place, they see Injun Joe and an accomplice bringing a chest of money up from beneath the house's floorboards. Intrigued, the two boys hope to recover the treasure themselves. Becky's father, Judge Thatcher, hosts a picnic for all of the town's children. A major attraction at the picnic site is a cave on the riverbank, into which Tom and Becky wander. Through a misunderstanding, the adults do not realize until the next day that the two children are still in the cave. Tom and Becky, meanwhile, grow increasingly bewildered and weary as they try to find their way out of their cave; by this time Tom is aware that Injun Joe is also in the cave, though he does not realize that Tom and Becky are there too. After five days Tom locates an exit that is five miles from the cave entrance. He is proclaimed a hero for leading Becky to safety. Later both Injun Joe's body and the chest of money are found in the cave. The twelve thousand dollars in the chest is divided equally between Tom and Huck. Huck is subsequently adopted by the kind Widow Douglas, who hopes to make a respectable boy of him. Huck is reluctant to submit to this civilizing process, but Tom convinces him that he must if he hopes to belong to Tom's new gang of pirates.

Characters: Acknowledged as an American classic, *The Adventures of Tom Sawyer* is a highly entertaining boy's adventure story with an underlying complexity and resonance that attract older readers as well. The novel's plainspoken, distinctly American narrative features a liberal use of vernacular speech and colloquial expressions as well as exaggeration, irreverence, droll cynicism, and deadpan comedy, recognized elements of the tradition of southwest humor. Critics have identified a number of underlying themes in *Tom Sawyer* in addition to the main character's coming-of-age, particularly the contrast between civilization and the wilderness that was a dominant concern of nineteenth-century authors. Based on the childhood recollections of Twain (the pen name for Samuel Langhorne Clemens), who was raised in Hannibal, Missouri, the novel has a strong nostalgic appeal to adults who wish to revisit the exuberant, carefree days of youth.

In the years since the novel's publication, its title character has become a nearly mythic symbol of boyhood and is thought to symbolize American energy and ingenuity. About twelve or thirteen when the story takes place, the lively, imaginative, mischievous **Tom**

Sawyer serves as the ringleader among his admiring friends. An orphan—though the circumstances of his parentlessness are never offered—Tom lives with his sentimental, kindhearted Aunt Polly, his bothersome, well-behaved half-brother Sid, and his sweet cousin Mary. Tom enjoys pulling pranks and getting the better of his aunt, though Sid frequently interferes with his plans by informing on him. His scheme to fool his friends into paying for the privilege of whitewashing the fence comprises one of the best-known episodes in American literature and also effectively illustrates Tom's cleverness. A daydreamer with a strong taste for romantic literature, Tom is something of a show-off and easily dominates those around him through his quick intelligence and ability to talk himself out of the trouble he often finds himself in. Through the course of his adventures, the silliness and irresponsibility Tom exhibits at the beginning of the novel are modified by a developing maturity. By revealing his knowledge of the actual murderer (despite the very real danger this represents) and saving Muff Potter from condemnation, returning from Jackson's Island when he discovers he has been assumed dead, taking responsibility for Becky's misdeed, and, finally, leading Becky through five days of darkness in the cave to safety, Tom demonstrates generosity, conscientiousness, and courage. Unlike his friend Huck Finn an outcast on the fringe of society, Tom is shown to be a integral part of his community and clearly relishes the approval he earns from his fellow townsfolk. The idea that Tom, despite his apparent rebelliousness, in fact embodies a distinctly middle-class propriety is suggested by his admonition to Huck, near the end of the book, that only "respectable" boys may join his new gang. Some critics contend that Tom's ultimate allegiance to social convention made him more appealing to Twain's Victorian audience, whereas the protagonist of his later novel, *The Adventures of Huckleberry Finn,* scandalized them. While several scholars can easily imagine Tom in later life as a successful, perhaps dull conventional businessman, others maintain that he should be viewed as a perpetual and quintessential boy. Tom has been likened to Don Quixote, the unrealistically romantic title character of Miguel de Cervantes' seventeenth-century novel; Tom does have a strong desire not only for adventure but for wealth and "glory." At a time when most juvenile literature featured the inevitable downfall of the "Bad Boy" and the triumph of the "Good Boy," Tom was a charming, likable Bad Boy who was allowed to prosper. He has been said to reflect the romantic yearning and desire to remain a child not only of the author who created him but of all who delightedly follow his adventures.

Tom's friend **Huckleberry Finn,** whose presence dominates the 1884 novel that bears his name, plays a relatively minor role in *Tom Sawyer.* The son of the town drunk, Huck for all intents and purposes is parentless and completely unsupervised, skipping school, fishing, and smoking his pipe. Much admired and envied by the other boys, the self-sufficient Huck wears cast-off clothing, swears freely, and sleeps wherever he wishes. Honest, forthright, and pragmatic, Huck presents a contrast to the romantic Tom that will be even more pronounced in the later novel. In his unschooled naturalism he might represent a frontiersman outside of or in opposition to civilization, whereas Tom is an integral and accepted part of that civilization. Critics who see Tom as a Don Quixote-type character cast Huck in the role of Sancho Panza, the realistic, matter-of-fact right-hand man of the romantic idealist. In the end, Huck is seduced by Tom's promise of entry into his new, "respectable" gang if he will consent to live with, and be civilized by, the Widow Douglas. As readers of *Huckleberry Finn* know, it will not be long before Huck reverts to the role of the independent outcast.

Critics of *Tom Sawyer* notice Twain shows a generally fond, indulgent attitude toward his youthful characters, while the novel's adults are portrayed as dull and conventional. Chief among them is Tom's **Aunt Polly,** who is basically warmhearted but frequently exasperated by her mischievous nephew. Although she naively imagines that she is more crafty than Tom, he frequently outsmarts her, as when he turns her demand that he whitewash the nine-foot fence into a money-making venture for himself. Aunt Polly is piously moralistic and highly sentimental, and Tom knows how to exploit the latter attribute to his own advantage. She provides some comic moments in the novel, such as when she responds to Tom's listlessness by plying him with the quack medicines she has purchased from itinerant peddlers. Apparently based to some extent on Twain's own mother, Aunt Polly provides Tom with the emotional security of knowing she sincerely loves him, but she also challenges his ingenuity as he tries to outwit her.

Sid's status as Tom's half-brother is never explained, but perhaps it is meant to account for the differences in their personalities. While Tom turns the tables on conventional juvenile fiction by being a "Bad Boy" who prospers, Sid is the "Good Boy" who finally gets his comeuppance when Tom   soundly pummels him. A clean, subservient, eager-to-please foil to the mischievous Tom, Sid foreshadows Tom's role in *Huckleberry Finn,* in which Tom is aligned with the respectable world of adults. Quiet, pious, but ever-calculating, Sid is a model child who tells on Tom whenever he can, thus increasing his stature in Aunt Polly's eyes. Twain is said to have fashioned Sid after his own beloved (though much more likable) brother Henry. Tom's cousin **Mary** was also based on a member of Twain's family: his sister Pamela. As well-behaved as Sid but sweet and undesigning, Mary serves as Aunt Polly's emissary in gently trying to persuade Tom to behave, encouraging him, for instance, to wash and dress himself for church.

Blue-eyed, blonde **Becky Thatcher** is an innocent coquette who captures Tom's heart the first time he sees her, causing him to cast off his earlier alliance with Amy Lawrence. But Becky cannot abide the idea that Tom loved anyone else, and she haughtily rejects him. But when Tom takes the punishment for Becky's transgressions, she calls him "noble" and forgives him. The relationship between Tom and Becky is at once a sweetly portrayed, idyllic romance and a comic parody of the silliness of conventional courtship. Supposedly modeled after a girl named Laura Hawkins, who lived across the street from Twain in Hannibal, the pretty and dependent Becky serves as the stereotyped "Good Girl" of juvenile fiction. Her father, **Judge Thatcher,** like Aunt Polly, is a benevolent but dull adult; though pompous, he represents security and authority, particularly in his wise governance of the fortune discovered by Tom and Huck.

Vividly portrayed as evil incarnate, **Injun Joe** is the villain of *Tom Sawyer*: murderous and vindictive, he threatens the novel's hero but finally meets the ignominious end he deserves. Although he is based on the standard villain of popular fiction, Injun Joe is highly effective in evoking nightmarish terror, particularly when Tom discovers he is also present in the cave. Critics point out that "half-breeds," characters of mixed race such as Injun Joe, who is half native American and half white, were traditionally presented as especially unscrupulous, reflecting a popular fear of miscegenation.

Significant minor characters in *Tom Sawyer* include the drunken, disreputable **Muff Potter,** saved from hanging when Tom reveals that the murder was committed by Injun Joe; **Dr. Robinson,** stabbed while attempting to rob a grave; **Joe Harper,** the young boy who accompanies Tom and Huck to Jackson's Island; and the kindhearted, pious **Widow Douglas,** who takes Huck into her home at the end of *Tom Sawyer* with the intention of making him respectable.

The Adventures of Huckleberry Finn (novel, 1884)

Plot: As recounted in the earlier *Adventures of Tom Sawyer,* Huckleberry Finn and his friend Tom Sawyer discovered a treasure of twelve thousand dollars, which was divided equally between them. The Widow Douglas and her sister, Miss Watson, took Huck into their home to make a respectable boy of him. The son of Pap Finn, the town drunkard, Huck was accustomed to complete independence and found it difficult to adjust to going to school, wearing clean clothes, and refraining from smoking and swearing. Huck is finally settling into his new life when he learns that his father—who has been missing for about a year and who, Huck is certain, will want to take his money—has returned to town. Sure enough, Pap Finn confronts Huck at the Widow Douglas's and eventually takes him to his cabin in the woods, where Huck endures frequent beatings. Although Huck likes being free to smoke, swear, and fish whenever he pleases, he finally decides to escape his father's violence and get out on his own. After making it appear that he has been murdered in the cabin, Huck flees to Jackson's Island. There he encounters Jim, Miss Watson's slave, who ran away because he heard Miss Watson was planning to send him further south to be sold. Huck agrees not to turn Jim in. Disguising himself as a girl, Huck ventures back to shore and learns that an award has been offered for the capture of Jim, who is suspected of murdering Huck. The two decide to journey down the Mississippi on a raft toward the town of Cairo, Illinois, then board a steamboat north so that Jim may reach safety in Ohio, a non-slavery state. Jim plans to find a job in the North and eventually buy his wife and children out of slavery. Huck's conscience is bothered because he knows it is wrong to help a runaway slave, but he decides to protect Jim's identity. One foggy night the raft collides with a large boat, and both Jim and Huck dive into the water; Huck reaches shore, but Jim is nowhere in sight.

Huck is taken in by the Grangerford family, whose vicious feud with the neighboring Shepherdsons is so ancient that no one remembers why it started. One day the young slave who has been assigned to Huck leads him to the woods, from which Jim emerges. He has followed Huck to the Grangerfords' and repaired the raft for their departure. That night a horribly bloody battle between the two families erupts, during which Huck and Jim take their leave. Back on the river the two encounter two hustlers who treat them with exaggerated haughtiness, pretending to be a king and a duke. Though not fooled by their claims, they accompany the swindlers as they bilk the citizens of several towns along the river. When the Duke and the King hear that a man named Peter Wilks left a considerable fortune to his three sisters, they pose as the womens' uncles from England and take charge of the inheritance, greatly distressing the sisters. Moved by their plight, Huck ingeniously exposes the impostors, and he and Huck manage to leave without them; the King and the Duke soon rejoin them on the raft, however. During a stop at another town, the Duke turns Jim over to the authorities. Huck undergoes a final struggle with his conscience, concluding that Jim's worth as a friend justifies the "sin" Huck will commit by helping him escape. He goes to the Phelps farm, where Jim is being held. Mrs. Sally Phelps mistakes Huck for her nephew, whose arrival she has been expecting, and when Huck learns that her nephew is Tom Sawyer he easily pretends that he is Tom. When Tom does arrive, he tells Aunt Sally he is Sid. Hearing of Jim's dilemma, Tom concocts a complicated rescue plan that takes three weeks and much maneuvering to arrange. When the attempt finally does take place, Tom is shot in the leg and Jim is recaptured; Tom subsequently reveals that the dying Miss Watson already freed Jim. Aunt Polly arrives, setting straight the two boys' real identities, and Jim is set free. Huck learns that his father is dead; Jim tells of seeing Pap Finn's body in an abandoned house the two had explored. Huck claims that he would rather strike out on his own than be adopted by Aunt Sally, who wants to civilize him as Widow Douglas had once hoped to do.

Characters: Considered Twain's masterpiece, *The Adventures of Huckleberry Finn* is one of the best-loved and most influential works of American literature; twentieth-century author Ernest Hemingway declared "All modern American literature comes from one book by Mark Twain called *Huck Finn*." Initially condemned by some early reviewers for what Victorian readers regarded as improper language and concerns, the novel still provokes controversy but is now universally acclaimed and widely read. Though ostensibly the story of a boy's exciting adventures aboard a raft on the Mississippi River, *Huckleberry Finn* has been seen by many commentators as chronicling an epic journey from bondage to freedom. The raft and river themselves have inspired numerous symbolic interpretations, and the meaning of Huck's and Jim's experiences have been much debated. Twain brilliantly satirizes the foibles of human nature—particularly targeting Southern aristocracy, institutionalized religion, and romantic literature—while exploring the broader themes of freedom versus slavery, corrupt civilization versus the Edenic innocence of nature, brotherhood, and whether it is possible for an individual to transcend the limits of his "training" or social indoctrination. *Huckleberry Finn* is distinctly American in its setting, range of characters, use of regional dialects, and focus on the tension between civilization and wilderness, yet its broad humor and compelling themes lend it universal significance and appeal.

Introduced to readers in Twain's earlier novel, *The Adventures of Tom Sawyer,* **Huckleberry Finn** is the central figure and narrator of the novel that bears his name. He is one of the best-known adolescent characters in literature, and his plainspoken account of his experiences on the Mississippi River comprises an unforgettably comic and resonant vision of American life. Narrated entirely in the vernacular, *Huckleberry Finn* is considered the first novel to sustain a regional dialect from beginning to end. About fourteen years old when the story takes place, Huck has been haphazardly raised by a cruel, neglectful father and subsequently adopted by the kindhearted Widow Douglas and her hypocritically pious sister Miss Watson, who hope to "sivilize" the boy. Though somewhat drawn to the orderly, nurtured life offered by the two women, Huck likes his freedom more. Kidnapped by his drunkard father, who hopes to gain access to Huck's fortune, Huck lapses easily into smoking, swearing, wearing rags, and fishing his days away, troubled only by the frequent beatings he receives from Pap Finn. Like the quintessential outsider he is, Huck eventually forsakes the comfort and restrictions of the Widow Douglas's house for independent solitude elsewhere. Critics have pointed out that Huck's meeting with Jim on Jackson's Island and subsequent trip down the river on the raft marks the story's transition from simple boy's idyll to complex epic. Isolated together on the raft and protected there from the corruption and dangers of civilization, Huck and Jim experience their independence in natural surroundings and develop an appreciation of each other's companionship. Huck exhibits his common sense and resourcefulness when, for instance, he dresses as a girl and ventures to shore to gather information, or when he protects Jim from discovery by pretending that the raft is carrying a victim of smallpox. Although Huck is willing to lie or even steal in order to survive, he always maintains his own integrity and admirable code of ethics. His struggle with his conscience over whether he should turn Jim in to the authorities is the most significant aspect of his journey toward maturity, for he grapples with and overcomes the "training" of his society and takes an independent stance based on his own inherent sense of right and wrong. Taught to view slaves as less than human, Huck has been told it is wrong to help someone who is the property of someone else to run away. He discovers that Jim is a thinking, feeling person— shown in the scene when Jim chides Huck for playing a practical joke on him—and Huck also realizes that Jim is a valuable, devoted friend. This figures in his decision, conveyed by Twain with brilliant irony, to "sin" against society and accept eternal damnation by helping Jim escape. Huck's basic compassion for others is evident not only in how he comes to view Jim but in the pity he feels for the murdered Buck Grangerford, the preyed-upon Wilks sisters, and even the thoroughly disreputable King and Duke after they are tarred, feathered, and ridden out of town on a rail; despite their being scoundrels, he comments that "human beings can be awful cruel." Despite his essential trustworthiness, however, Huck is not always a reliable narrator, and Twain sometimes employs his naiveté to expose folly—as when he fails to sense the irony of Pap's speech about the "govment" or admires the Grangerford's tastelessly decorated home. Perhaps the most controversial aspect of *Huckleberry Finn* is its farcical ending, which features Tom Sawyer's absurd and even harmful scheme to liberate the already free Jim (freed by Miss Watson's deathbed wish). Some critics question whether Huck really achieves the freedom he claims at the end of the story when he suggests he will now "light out" for the frontier. While some commentators defend the final chapters as structurally logical, others contend that they provide a disappointing conclusion in which complacency ultimately prevails. Thus some scholars view Huck's freedom to be illusory, undermining the profundity of his experiences aboard the raft. As an uncultured member from the lowest levels of society, Huck embodies a distinctly American ideal: the effort of the common man, relying not on tradition but on his own ingenuity, to achieve a kind of moral rejuvenation through immersion in the Edenic wilderness. Other critics claim Huck is no pioneer but an alienated vagabond challenging the values of American society. In any case the diverse appeal of this memorable character attests to Twain's great narrative skill and understanding of human nature.

One of the most frequently debated aspects of *Huckleberry Finn* is how it presents the concept of slavery, especially in the case of **Jim,** the runaway slave who accompanies Huck on his journey down the Mississippi. Owned by the falsely pious Miss Watson, Jim flees because he overhears her planning to sell him to a slave trader for eight hundred dollars. Jim plans to seek freedom in a Northern state, then earn enough money to buy his beloved wife and children out of slavery. Jim's conversations with Huck reveal his illiteracy, superstition, and gullibility but also frequently exhibit his loyalty, common sense, and inherent nobility. Like Huck, Jim's origin in a very low level of society has no relation to his worth, and he endures oppression, danger, and hardship with strength and dignity. His quest for freedom parallels that of Huck (who flees not institutionalized bondage but a cruel father and restrictive guardians), demonstrating Twain's condemnation not only of slavery in the pre-Civil War South but of social injustice in general. Initially viewed as a childlike, inferior being by Huck, Jim gains importance and individuality in his friend's eyes as their journey progresses. In the scene in which Huck plays a trick on Jim, making him believe that he dreamed something that actually happened, Jim then chides Huck for treating a loyal friend so shabbily, and this scene is often cited as an important one in illuminating their relationship. Although critic Leslie Fiedler identified their relationship as homosexual, many more contend that Huck finds a substitute father in Jim. Some critics have found Twain's portrayal of Jim racist and demeaning, citing the slave's foolishness, gullibility, and tendency to exaggerate as evidence that he is intended to resemble the African Americans caricatured in the minstrel shows of the late nineteenth and early twentieth centuries. Claiming that as a young boy he could identify with Huck but not with Jim, black novelist Ralph Ellison called Jim "a white man's inadequate portrait of a slave." Yet others have defended Twain's depiction of Jim, asserting that he is one of few adults in the novel who exhibits the virtues of compassion, logic, and self-sacrifice, and that in fact Twain intentionally employed stereotypes in order to expose Southern bigotry. Still other scholars have identified Jim's portrayal as simultaneously ludicrous and admirable, suggesting Twain was ambivalent about African Americans.

Huck's friend **Tom Sawyer,** the central character of the 1876 novel that bears his name, plays a relatively minor role in *Huckleberry Finn.* He appears at the beginning of the novel, when Huck is suffering from the civilizing influence of life with the Widow Douglas and her sister, and at the end, when Tom arrives at the home of his Aunt Sally Phelps and assumes the identity of his brother, Sid. In both instances Tom exhibits the active imagination and flamboyance readers of the earlier novel were familiar with. His appetite for romantic literature—a frequent target of Twain's satire—is as much in evidence in *Huckleberry Finn* as it was in *Tom Sawyer,* though its consequences prove more dire. Although Tom's previous adventures took him to some degree out of his community, by the end he seemed established as an integral, accepted and generally accepting part of the society in which he lived. Huck, who is isolated from society in both books, in this respect and in his common sense and practicality he contrasts with Tom. Tom's reappearance near the end of *Huckleberry Finn* has generated a great deal of controversy in the years since the book's publication. Many critics claim his elaborate, ridiculous plan to free Jim, though it may be an entertaining, farcical parody of conventional romantic literature, mars the novel's overall effect. These commentators maintain that the profound themes evoked by Huck's and Jim's quest, and particularly the issue of slavery, are undermined by the burlesque tone of the final chapters. Other scholars, however, contend that Tom's appearance at the end of the novel makes formal sense, providing the story with a circular structure. In any case Tom is not as flatteringly portrayed in *Huckleberry Finn* as he is in *Tom Sawyer,* for he seems grievously unconcerned about the physical and psychological toll his silly antics might take on Jim, who goes along with the scheme with remarkable patience. Tom's thoughtlessness (some critics even label it cruelty) is compounded by the fact that he knows all along that Miss Watson has already freed Jim. Huck is initially surprised that Tom, whose true convention-ality he seems to sense, is willing to go against the law to help him free Jim; when he later learns the reason for Tom's carefree attitude, he understands "how he *could* help a body set a nigger free with his bringing up." While in the earlier novel Tom's childish romanticism was more fondly portrayed, in *Huckleberry Finn* it is considered arrogant, pretentious, and ultimately hurtful, for the escapade leads to Tom being shot in the leg and Jim being punished for trying to escape. In addition, several critics have noted that the artificial adventures concocted by Tom seem inadequate and false compared to the real and deeply meaningful experiences of Huck and Jim on their journey down the river.

Although he occupies relatively few pages in the novel, Huck's father, **Pap Finn,** makes a strong impression. Unkempt and ragged, he has long, greasy black hair and skin that is "tree-toad white, a fish-belly white." Mean, abusive, and resentful, Pap is an inadequate father whose tyranny over Huck provides the immediate motivation for his flight. His greed aroused by word that Huck acquired a small fortune, Pap appears at the Widow Douglas's and demands that his son give him the money. His monologue on the follies of the "govment" is often cited as brilliantly comic as well as revealing, for this tirade against the existence of a free black man who has become a professor and is even allowed to vote in his own state illuminates his ignorance and inhumanity as well as the attitude of many Southerners toward blacks. Pap begrudges Huck the advantages he has recently acquired, including his education, and accuses his son of "putting on frills" and trying to appear superior to his father. After Pap kidnaps Huck and confines him to the cabin, his heavy drinking leads to a frightening episode of "delirium tremens" that makes him somewhat pathetic, despite the danger he poses to Huck. Several critics have identified Pap's role in the novel as illuminating the conditions of Huck's upbringing, the obstacles against which he must struggle, and his need for the surrogate father some say he finds in Jim. Supposedly based on a well-known drunk in the Missouri town of Hannibal, where Twain grew up, Pap symbolizes the uniquely American type of the alienated, frustrated backwoods squatter. His portrayal shows a darker side of isolation from society.

Two other important figures in Huck's St. Petersburg life are the **Widow Douglas,** who took him in at the end of *Tom Sawyer* with the intention of "sivilizing" him, and her sister **Miss Watson,** who has since come to live with her. The pious, highly respectable widow is essentially kindhearted, hospitable, and generous. In taking responsibility for the virtually parentless Huck, she shows her willingness to give her Christian principles tangible expression. Miss Watson, by contrast, is a strict Calvinist whose concept of Christianity seems harsh and unforgiving. The fact that she owns Jim demonstrates her hypocrisy as well as the type of person Twain had contempt for—those who proclaim their religious convictions while overlooking or even perpetuating injustice and inhumanity. Miss Wat-son's greed and inability to view Jim as a human being are apparent when she succumbs to a slave trader's offer of eight hundred dollars for Jim. On her deathbed Miss Watson has a change of heart and frees her slave, a development that has been viewed as inadequately accounted for. The fact that a slave-holder—and one whose inhumanity had provided the impetus for the story's action—should deliver Jim's freedom disappointed some commen-tators, though others maintained that by it Twain suggests that progress may even come from the most unlikely sources.

The two rapscallions who join Huck and Jim on their journey down the Mississippi and who refer to themselves as **the King** and **the Duke** are among the most memorable characters in *Huckleberry Finn.* Twain uses them to lampoon the pretension to nobility that was one of his favorite satirical targets. The "Duke of Bridgewater," about thirty years old, describes himself as a printer whose royal title was unjustly usurped; he supports himself by bilking hapless small-town residents into buying quack remedies, such as a formula that removes tartar from teeth, as promised, but also the enamel. "King Looey the Seventeenth" is about seventy years old and adept at a variety of scams, including fake temperance revivals. These thoroughly disreputable though clever hustlers have been said to parody the notion of false aristocracy and the equally reprehensible brutishness of America's lower classes, a cross-section of which is described during the group's travels through several riverside communities. Among the schemes devised by the King and the Duke is a theatrical performance, including the balcony scene from "Romeo and Juliet" with the King playing Juliet, which allows Twain to expose the shallowness and excess romanticism; it also features some hilarious manglings of Shakespeare's lyrics. Huck is well aware of these scoundrels' true characters but for a time goes along with them; he exposes them, however, when their scheming threatens the Wilks sisters. Even though the King and Duke are ultimately responsible for Jim's capture, Huck feels sorry for them when they are tarred, feathered, and ridden our of town on a rail, for he is also aware of the cruelty in human nature.

After their raft collides with a larger boat and Huck and Jim are separated, Huck finds refuge on shore with **the Grangerfords,** who fancy themselves aristocrats and through whom Twain satirizes the kind of Southern romantic tradition he abhorred. The true lack of content beneath the family's adherence to established forms is evident in their tastelessly decorated home, their obviously shallow grief for a deceased daughter, and their exaggerated allegiance to etiquette. One of the book's most comic moments is provided by the poem memorializing "Stephen Dowling Bots," written by **Emmeline Grangerford,** who died at fifteen after penning a number of morbidly sentimental poems that Huck, revealing his naiveté, much admires. The most significant aspect of the Grangerfords' lives, however, is their longstanding, senseless feud with the neighboring **Shepherdson** family. Bound by a rigid and clearly false code of "honor" based on a repeated, primitive pattern of retribution, the two families regularly murder each other in cold blood despite the fact that no one remembers why the feud started. When a young Grangerford girl and a Shepherdson boy fall in love and elope—providing a backwoods American version of "Romeo and Juliet"—the result is a vicious battle in which all of the Grangerford males (including Huck's friend Buck) and all but two or three of the Shepherdsons are killed. Horrified by the bloodthirstiness and carnage he has witnessed, the usually stalwart Huck is unable to describe the scene.

The **Reverend Silas and Mrs. Sally Phelps** are Tom Sawyer's aunt and uncle, though Huck is initially unaware of this when he arrives at their farm, where the captured Jim is being held. Learning that he has been mistaken for Tom, Huck easily impersonates his friend while Tom, on his arrival, pretends to be Sid. The Phelpses embody the solidly middle-class values of cleanliness, good manners, and propriety, yet they see nothing wrong with the institution of slavery. Their practice of having their slaves in each evening for Bible readings and prayers provides another example of Twain's distrust of conventional religion. It is Aunt Sally who makes the often-quoted remark, when Huck tells her that no one was hurt in a steamboat accident, though a black person dies "Well, it's lucky; because sometimes people do get killed." Aunt Sally's interest in adopting Huck provokes his final comment that he may have to "light out" for the territories in order to avoid her "sivilizing" influence.

A number of minor characters make brief but memorable appearances in *Huckleberry Finn.* Among the most notable is **Colonel Sherburn,** a well-dressed, self-possessed Southern aristocrat of Bricksville, where Huck and his hustler friends have come to bilk the citizenry.

When his considerable pride was injured by an obnoxious but harmless drunk named **Boggs,** Sherburn coldly kills the man. A mob of Sherburn's fellow townsfolk later arrives at his house with the ostensible intention of lynching him, but he confronts them directly and delivers an acid monologue on the cowardice of the average human being and the mob mentality, scoffing at the idea that such as they are capable of killing him. Sure enough, the sheepish crowd quickly disperses. Another vividly portrayed figure is **Mrs. Judith Loftus,** from whom Huck, ineffectually disguised as a girl, derives information about the reaction to his and Jim's disappearance. Critic Bernard Devoto noted, "In her shrewdness, curiosity, initiative, and brusque humanity one reads an entire history" of the American pioneer woman. Sisters **Mary Jane, Susan,** and **Joanna Wilks** are nearly cheated out of their inheritance by the conniving King and Duke, but Mary Jane so charms Huck with her kindness that he helps the sisters. Two significant characters from *Tom Sawyer* reappear in *Huckleberry Finn*: Tom's sentimental, pious **Aunt Polly,** who arrives at the Phelps farm near the end of the story and reveals the real identities of Tom and Huck; and **Judge Thatcher,** the eminently respectable symbol of justice who safeguards Huck's fortune, managing through legal maneuvers to keep it away from Pap Finn.

A Connecticut Yankee in King Arthur's Court (novel, 1889)

Plot: The novel's protagonist is Hank Morgan, a supervising mechanic in a Hartford, Connecticut, arms factory who, after being struck on the head by a fellow worker, wakes in sixth century England. He is captured by one of the knights of King Arthur's Round Table and taken to the kingdom of Camelot, where he is sentenced to be burned at the stake. In prison Hank remembers that an eclipse of the sun took place on June 21, 528, the scheduled date of his execution. He sends a young page named Clarence to deliver a message predicting that the sun will darken on that day. When the predicted phenomenon duly occurs, Hank is proclaimed more skilled a magician than Merlin, the renowned sorcerer of Arthur's court. Hank proves his prowess again by blowing up Merlin's tower with some primitive explosives, a display that leads to Hank achieving Merlin's exalted position, while the wizard is sent to jail. Disturbed by the primitive inconveniences of life in Camelot and by the illiteracy and degradation of the people, Hank decides to improve the kingdom by implementing the best of American democratic principles and mechanical know-how. Now called "the Boss" by King Arthur's subjects, Hank sets about establishing schools, training mechanics, stringing telephone wires, and instructing Clarence in journalism so Camelot will have a free press. Then Sir Sagramor, goaded by a jealous Merlin, challenges Hank to a duel, and he is sent on a quest to help him prepare for the encounter. He is to aid Alisande, a talkative young girl he nicknames Sandy. Dressed in a cumbersome suit of armor, he sets off on horseback with Sandy, who narrates a long string of stories as they ride through the kingdom. Along the way Hank finds numerous examples of the inhumanities and idiocy of the feudal system. He sends every promising young man he encounters back to Camelot to be educated by Clarence, and he frees many unjustly held prisoners from castle dungeons throughout the land.

Hank has another opportunity to humiliate Merlin when he reaches the Valley of Holiness, where a sacred well has dried up, supposedly from some mysterious wrongdoing. Now freed from prison, Merlin is unable to fix the well with magic, while Hank accomplishes the repair by simply fixing a leak, though he makes the deed look more momentous that it is. Hank persuades King Arthur, who arrives to view the spring newly flowing to dress as a pilgrim and accompany him on a journey through his kingdom. The ever ineffectual Arthur is nonetheless moved by the suffering of his people, which it seems he knew nothing about. Eventually, however, Hank and King Arthur are captured and sold as slaves because they are unable to prove their identities. Taken to London, Hank escapes and calls Clarence on one of the phones he had previously installed, instructing his young friend to send Sir

Launcelot and the other knights to save him and the king. After their rescue, Hank must still fight his duel with Sir Sagramor, who is the unwitting instrument of Merlin. During the contest Hank shoots the knight with his gun and then kills nine other charging knights. Three years pass; Hank has married Sandy and the two have a little girl named Hello-Central. Having already initiated a plethora of nineteenth-century improvements in Camelot, Hank and Clarence plan to establish a republic after King Arthur dies. But when Hank takes his wife and daughter to the seashore so Hello-Central can recuperate from an illness, havoc reigns over the kingdom. On his return Hank learns King Arthur has been killed by Sir Lancelot and the church has reasserted the domination it wielded over the people before Hank's arrival. The population has returned to the ignorant, brutal ways of the feudal system. Hank, Clarence, and the fifty-two young men he trained battle their enemies, protecting their fortress with an electrically charged fence and rigging a large number of guns to fire at one time. However, Hank is injured in the fight, and Merlin, disguised as a nurse, manages to reach him and cast a spell that condemns him to sleep for thirteen hundred years. Hank wakes in the nineteenth century, woefully lamenting the loss of his beloved wife and child.

Characters: In *A Connecticut Yankee in King Arthur's Court* Twain satirized the English traditions of feudalism and knight errantry, which he believed bestowed aristocratic privilege on a few undeserving souls while oppressing the majority of the people. But some scholars maintained that by portraying that nineteenth-century democratic principles and technology failed to bring about the "improvements" intended, Twain was also lampooning the smugness of progress-oriented Victorian culture. The novel features one of the first uses of the concept of time travel, which would be frequently employed in the science fiction of the later nineteenth and twentieth centuries. While *A Connecticut Yankee* is liberally laced with humor, it is also marked by a somberness that critics claimed was the result of the growing pessimism of its author, whose self-described "funereal seriousness" and lack of faith in the possibility of humanity's redeeming itself became more dominant during the final years of his life.

The "Connecticut Yankee" referred to in the book's title is **Hank Morgan,** a foreman in a Colt gun factory in Hartford. An ingenious mechanic, Hank is clever and resourceful, as he demonstrates soon after his arrival in Camelot when he saves his own life by "predicting" an eclipse. His common sense and pragmatism are portrayed as typically American traits, as is the vigor with which he sets about to improve English society. Disgusted with the primitive living conditions and oppression by both church and state endured by the common people, Hank imagines himself as a representative of order, knowledge, and reason who will vanquish the greed and superstition rampant under the feudal system. By instituting a range of modern conveniences and concepts—from telephones to universal education—and by performing feats of ingenuity more impressive than Merlin's magic, Hank plans to bring sixth-century England up to nineteenth-century American standards. Confident that people can be "trained" away from ignorance, superstition, and self-destructive allegiances, Hank is shocked when he returns from a short vacation to find society reverted to its old, oppressive ways. In the end, only the fifty-three boys whose youth made them susceptible to his teachings remain loyal to Hank. While some critics interpreted his final defeat only as necessary to the time-travel plot, most considered it as thematically significant. Twain's apparent ambivalence caused critical debate about whether he meant to portray Hank as a sympathetic character who symbolizes the reforming spirit or as a parody of progress and the smug self-righteousness of the reformer. Hank professes to hold democratic convictions, but he expresses contempt for the English common people, whom he considers helpless "rabbits." Like Merlin, he exploits their ignorance to his own advantage, encouraging them to think his powers are mysterious and great. In fact, and in spite of his intention to institute a republic after Arthur's death, Hank becomes a kind of dictator. Thus it might be argued that Twain is satirizing not only medieval England but modern society and the problematic concept of progress. Hank is frequently compared to another famous Twain character, Huck Finn, due to the similarity not only in their first names but in their humble origins and their pragmatism. Both journey into lands dominated by outmoded aristocratic systems, though only Hank has the opportunity to shape the society he finds there. Hank is also considered an autobiographical character whose reverence for technology, for example, reflects Twain's enthusiasm for and eventual disappointment with the Paige typesetting machine, which he hoped would make his fortune. An idealist who often expressed the need for social reform, Twain grew increasingly bitter toward the end of his life, and the remark Hank makes after the concluding battle—"Imagine such human muck as this"—has been thought to reflect his creator's pessimistic view of human nature.

Clarence, Hank's young page and right-hand man, is educated by Hank and in turn educates fifty-two other young men, all intended to serve as the vanguard of the new republic Hank plans to establish after King Arthur's death. More intelligent than most of his countrymen, Clarence serves as a liaison between the people of sixth-century England and the nineteenth-century Hank. But, he also realizes that Hank cannot succeed in permanently altering people's behavior, and he tells Hank to "unthink" that such a deed is possible. Clarence also performs practical functions, such as when, after a phone call from Hank, he alerts the Knights of the Round Table that Hank and King Arthur have been captured and enslaved, and he informs the reader that Merlin was killed when he ran into an electrified fence.

Just before he wrote *A Connecticut Yankee,* Twain had been reading Sir Thomas Malory's fifteenth-century account of King Arthur and his knights, *Le Morte D'Arthur,* and many of the novel's characters are parodies of figures from the Arthurian legends. One such figure is **Merlin,** the sorcerer whose magic is bested by Hank's nineteenth-century American ingenuity. At the beginning of the story Merlin is made to seem a mere bumbler and bore, putting everyone to sleep with his long tale about Arthur and the Lady of the Lake. After he is repeatedly humiliated by Hank, however, Merlin's enmity toward the energetic intruder grows more dangerous. He begins to spread unflattering rumors about Hank in an effort to subvert his power, and it is he who, at the end of the story, sends Hank back to his own century. Merlin's exploitation of the people's ignorance and susceptibility to superstition makes him a symbol of organized religion, which Twain consistently distrusted and which in *A Connecticut Yankee* he portrayed as particularly repressive.

Twain's unflattering depiction of the beloved characters from the Arthurian tales made him unpopular with the English, who claimed he had neither the knowledge nor the right to criticize their past. The legendary **King Arthur,** for instance, is presented as fairly good-hearted but rather loutish, with no political acumen or particular qualifications to lead his people, thus underlining what Twain viewed as the destructive illogic of a monarchical system. As exalted leader of the land Arthur lives a life of privilege and has no idea of his people's suffering until Hank takes him on a journey through the kingdom. To his credit, Arthur does respond with compassion, especially to a family dying of smallpox, but some critics found this awakening unconvincing. Although **Sir Galahad** and **Sir Launcelot** are made to seem fairly noble, most of the other knights and ladies are colored as ingenuous, coarse, superstitious, and stupid. Notable among them are **Sir Kay,** who captures Hank and brings him to Camelot soon after his waking in the sixth century; and **Sir Sagramor,** induced by Merlin to challenge Hank to a duel and over-credulousness in his foolish faith that Merlin has protected him with an invisible shield.

Alisande, or "Sandy," is the delightful young damsel who accompanies Hank on his quest through the kingdom. Extremely talkative, she narrates a number of tall tales as they ride along, eventually winning Hank's heart. She reveals her susceptibility to superstition, however, when she embraces some pigs that she believes are enchanted, thus shaming Hank and reminding him of humanity's folly. After his return to the nineteenth century, Hank's greatest sorrow is his separation from Sandy and their daughter, **Hello-Central,** named for the original designation for telephone operators.

"The Celebrated Jumping Frog of Calaveras County" (short story, 1865)

Plot: The narrator visits a northern California mining settlement called Angel Camp. An eastern friend suggested that he make the acquaintance of elderly Simon Wheeler and inquire about the Reverend Leonidas W. Smiley. The narrator suspects there is no such person and the inquiry will provoke a long-winded story about someone else entirely. Sure enough, the genial and apparently innocent Wheeler does not remember anyone named Leonidas Smiley but does recall a Jim Smiley, who resided at the camp several years earlier. Smiley's fondness for betting was legendary; he would gamble on anything, whether it was a horse race, a dog fight, or which of two birds sitting on fence would fly away first. Wheeler recounts several of Smiley's most famous wagers, in which he often employed animals of various kinds. He won many bets, for instance, on a broken-down mare who would suddenly accelerate near the end of a race, and he once had a fierce little puppy named Andrew Jackson who beat his opponents by clamping his jaws onto their hind legs (his last opponent lacked hind legs, so he was defeated). But the bulk of the story is devoted to Smiley's frog Daniel Webster, who was trained to jump astoundingly high at the command "Flies, Dan'l, flies." Wheeler assures the narrator that, despite his great talent, the frog was exceedingly modest. One day a stranger arrived in town and asked Smiley what made Daniel Webster so special. He claimed he could see nothing about Smiley's frog that made him any better than others of his species, and he agreed to a contest if Smiley could find a frog for him to bet on. While Smiley went off to hunt for a frog, the stranger poured quail shot into Daniel Webster's mouth. When the jumping contest took place, the other frog hopped away while Smiley's remained stationary, and the stranger left with his prize of forty dollars. Bewildered, Smiley picked up Daniel Webster and noticed he was extremely heavy; when he held the frog upside down, the quail shot poured out of his mouth, and Smiley knew that he had been bilked. Wheeler is now interrupted in his storytelling, and when he later tries to tell the narrator more about Jim Smiley, he is rather rudely rebuked.

Characters: Perhaps the best known of Twain's short stories, "The Celebrated Jumping Frog of Calaveras County" helped propel him to public prominence. The story employs the traditional framing technique of the southwestern tall tale, with an initial narrator introducing the storyteller, then providing a conclusion. Told primarily in the vernacular, the story is a masterful blending of elements of nineteenth-century American folk literature with Twain's distinctive style of deadpan humor and caustic satire. "The Celebrated Jumping Frog" is usually viewed as a parable that illuminates the contrast between the settled traditions and snobbery of the eastern United States and the greater openness of the frontier.

The narrator, who is presumably Mark Twain himself, is an easterner who visits a northern California mining camp. He provides a lead-in to the main story by explaining that a friend of his asked him to look up Simon Wheeler and inquire after a Reverend Leonidas Smiley. The narrator's sense of his own superiority is evident as he mentions his doubt that such a person even exists and suspicion that his friend deliberately sent him to be bored by Wheeler's long-winded stories. Literate, genteel, and politely arrogant, the narrator represents the pretention and hypocrisy of the East. He embodies the competition and hostile individualism that contrast with the West's openness, honesty, and sense of connection or community. The narrator takes Wheeler's simplicity at face value even as the reader senses that the monotonous-toned storyteller is not as naive as he seems and is, in fact, subtly ridiculing the snobbish easterner. At the end, the narrator's carefully maintained attitude of boredom is somewhat ruffled as he curtly dismisses Wheeler. Some critics have suggested that the narrator could be interpreted as a self-mocking character, for Twain was a westerner by birth but had aspirations to literary prominence on the East Coast; thus he may be lampooning his own efforts to project an ultimately shallow gentility and respectability.

Simon Wheeler tells the story of Jim Smiley and his jumping frog in a skillfully achieved deadpan manner, a style that Twain employed throughout his fiction to relay humorous episodes. He felt that a deadpan storyteller who never indicates that what he is saying is funny is essential to the success of a comical story. Fat, bald, and good-natured, Wheeler seems at first a garrulous old codger who likes to sit around telling long-winded stories. He speaks in a monotonous tone and his face never registers anything but innocence and tranquility, so that his listener cannot be certain if he appreciates the humor of the tale. His gentle, sincere manner contrasts sharply and intentionally with the narrator's affectedness, thus marking him as a representative of western values. Beneath Wheeler's simplicity, however, are self-consciousness and sarcasm that the pretentious narrator does not seem to recognize—at least not until the end of the story, when he becomes rather unsettled. Wheeler's name fits him well because he is a remarkably skillful spinner of tales who hides his canniness beneath a genial demeanor. Twain is thought to have based this character on a man he met during his own visit to Angel Camp. He later reported that the man, named Ben Coon, told funny stories with a dull seriousness that indicated he was unaware of their humor.

The subject of Wheeler's story is **Jim Smiley,** a compulsive bettor whose wagers range from the conventional to the absurd; Wheeler reports, for instance, that Smiley might bet on how long it would take a straddle-bug to reach its destination, then follow the bug all the way to Mexico to learn the outcome. Smiley especially like employing animals in his bets, such as the broken-down mare who wins races at the last moment, the puppy named Andrew Jackson who beats his opponents by clamping on to their hind legs, and of course the frog Daniel Webster. Smiley is described as an extraordinarily lucky man, and the names he gives his animals might be seen as a superstitious effort to attract good fortune. His single-minded devotion to gambling, evidenced by the three months he spends training Dan'l to jump higher than other frogs, finally leads to his being duped. As he searches in the swamp for a likely opponent for Daniel Webster, the stranger deviously fills his frog with quail shot. In dropping the defense of guile employed by fellow westerners (such as Wheeler, significantly, as he tells the story to the arrogant narrator), Smiley is beaten at his own game.

Like Wheeler, **the stranger** maintains a placid, innocent exterior that belies his true slyness. Claiming that he sees nothing special about Daniel Webster and would be willing to challenge the frog, he outfoxes Smiley by incapacitating the "celebrated jumping frog" with quail shot. Critics consider the stranger to symbolize frontier common sense, who delivers a lesson in democracy by showing that it is inadvisable, in the West, to make haughty assumptions—either about the talents of your frog or, by extension to Wheeler, the simplicity of a storyteller. But other scholars suggested that the stranger may, in fact, be an easterner who has adapted himself well enough to western ways to be able to turn the situation to his own advantage; he manipulates Smiley, for instance, by pretending to feel like a lonely outsider who is innocently curious about the supposedly talented frog.

Two other noteworthy characters in "The Celebrated Jumping Frog" are Smiley's animal cohorts: the feisty bull-pup **Andrew Jackson** and the frog **Daniel (Dan'l) Webster.** Both evidence Twain's skill for anthropomorphizing animals and may also signify a particularly western urge to treat idols irreverently. Named for the tenacious frontiersman who was president of the United States from 1829 to 1837, Andrew Jackson resembles his namesake in his formidable will and single-mindedness. He apparently shares Smiley's gambling fever, for he lunges wholeheartedly into confrontations as soon as he sees money being laid down. Poor Andrew Jackson is finally defeated by an opponent whose lack of hind legs takes him by surprise. Daniel Webster's jumping feats are stimulated by the mention of flies—presumably his reward if he performs admirably. The frog's namesake was a famous nineteenth-century statesman whose amphibian qualities included a large belly, downsloping face, deep voice, and notably placid demeanor. Webster also underwent several flip-flops in his career, further aligning him with his frog namesake.

"The Man that Corrupted Hadleyburg" (short story, 1899)

Plot: Hadleyburg is a small American town whose inhabitants have always prided themselves on their honesty; their motto is "Lead us not into temptation." A stranger passing through town, however, becomes offended by some unexplained slight or wrong and decides to seek revenge on the townsfolk. He leaves a sack he says contains forty thousand dollars in gold with an elderly couple, Mary and Edward Richards. He asks them to locate someone who once gave him twenty dollars and some advice, requesting that the money be given to whoever can correctly repeat that advice. When the Richardses publicize the offer in the local newspaper, the greed and vanity of the townsfolk are quickly aroused. Everyone believes that the money and advice were given to the stranger by Barclay Goodson, a sincerely honest man who before his death proclaimed the town narrow-minded and stingy, but nineteen prominent citizens nevertheless attempt to claim the money for themselves. Each has received a letter from a Howard L. Stephenson—actually the stranger himself—informing them that the words of advice were: "You are far from being a bad man: go and reform." Each then sends a letter to the Reverend Burgess, who is entrusted with the safekeeping of the sack and will reveal the answer: a letter claiming that this was the advice he had given the stranger. The Richardses are among the nineteen claimants. The real answer, however, is different from that presented by the nineteen citizens and reveals that a joke has been played upon them. The gold in the sack is merely painted lead. Because Richards once did him a favor, however, Burgess omits the couple's letter from the others and they are spared the derision the townsfolk heap on the other eighteen claimants. Believing the Richardses to be as virtuous as they seem, the townsfolk auction off the stranger's sack and give the proceeds to the old couple, who also receive some money from the stranger as an apology. Initially torn between the demands of their conscience to tell the truth about their role in the scam and their desire that others think well of them, the Richardses keep the truth to themselves. Edward is also bothered because years ago, he failed to clear the innocent Burgess when he was suspected of wrongdoing, as he should have, but only warned him to leave town. The Richardses guilt renders them increasingly ill, paranoid, and despairing, and they eventually burn the money, convinced that the stranger devised the joke to torment them. Just before he dies, Edward publicly confessed that he also tried to claim the stranger's money; he also clears Burgess's name, as he failed to do years before. Mary dies soon after. Finally recognizing its own dishonesty, Hadleyburg changes its motto to "Lead us into temptation."

Characters: Two dominant strains have been detected in this story, which is one of Twain's most famous. Some critics consider it a moral satire exposing the consequences of vanity, greed, and hypocrisy, while others claim it reflects the pessimism about human nature marking Twain's later writings. Scholars contend that the cynicism Twain developed during this period of his life was connected to such events as the death of his beloved daughter Susy, the failure of his publishing business, and his disappointment in the Paige typesetting machine, in which he had invested a great deal of money in the hope that it would make his fortune. In an essay written late in his career, "What Is Man?," Twain asserted that people are motivated only by self-interest and tend to lie to themselves about their own motives. This philosophy has been identified as deterministic—that is, that individuals are shaped by environment and heredity rather than by free will. Vainly convinced of their own impeccable honesty, the citizens of Hadleyburg learn that they are susceptible to greed and willing to lie for money. In altering their town motto to "Lead us into temptation," they may either be cynically acknowledging their own shortcomings or expressing the idea that virtue untested by temptation is false.

Just as the story itself might be viewed as either a moral parable or an essentially pessimistic farce, the character of **the stranger** (who signs the letters he sends to the town's nineteen leading citizens **Howard L. Stephenson**) could be viewed as either evil or ultimately helpful. The fact that his practical joke leads indirectly to the deaths of two people who, despite their faults, have done nothing to deserve their fate supports the latter interpretation, and in fact there is something diabolical in the stranger's desire to achieve revenge. Without explaining what has occurred to so offend him, he comments that the action he might have taken—killing two or three people—would have been "a trivial revenge" compared to that which he finally implements. On the other hand, the stranger gives the people of Hadleyburg a valuable opportunity to confront the truth about themselves—that they are not the spotless scions of virtue they pretended to be. Their new motto suggests that they no longer hold an illusion, and perhaps hope to improve themselves in the future.

Elderly **Edward and Mary Richards** are initially portrayed as sweet, loving, and conscientious, but their goodness, as Mary observes, is artificial. First there is the matter of Reverend Burgess: during the clergyman's brush with some unexplained scandal, Edward knew he was innocent but was reluctant to publicly defend him for fear of becoming unpopular himself. To assuage his own conscience, Edward had merely warned Burgess to leave town to save himself, thus earning the clergyman's lasting gratitude. When the stranger leaves the sack, which supposedly contains a fortune in gold, with the Richardses, they are as tempted as the rest of the town's leading citizens to try to gain it for themselves, particularly since they are truly impoverished. When the stranger's practical joke is exposed and the Richardses find themselves sheltered by Burgess from the ridicule showered on the other claimants, Edward makes several attempts to confess their guilt but is instead acclaimed as saintly by the crowd. The Richardses' reluctance to sacrifice this approval finally overcomes the promptings of their consciences, and they accept the money. But they are tormented by this decision for the rest of their lives, and it is suggested that their final illnesses are brought on by the constant guilt and paranoia with which they have struggled. Thus the stranger's joke has a tragic consequence, and if he is a satanic figure the Richardses might be likened to Adam and Eve, punished for their human susceptibility to sin. Those who view the story as a lesson in morality contend that the Richardses deaths signify a divine judgment, while others find the conclusion a sobering reminder that human nature is essentially unredeemable.

Other characters in the story include **Reverend Burgess,** previously disgraced by some mysterious scandal and indebted to Edward for having warned him to leave town; and **Barclay Goodson** (already dead when the story begins), the town cynic and its only truly honest citizen, who had the courage to publicly proclaim Hadleyburg narrow, self-righteous, and stingy.

Further Reading

Anderson, Frederick, ed. *Mark Twain: The Critical Heritage.* New York: Barnes & Noble, 1971.

Bloom, Harold, ed. *Mark Twain.* New York: Chelsea House, 1986.

Brooks, Van Wyck. *The Ordeal of Mark Twain,* pp. 219-41. Rev. ed. 1933. Reprint. New York: AMS Press, 1977.

Budd, Louis J. *Critical Essays on Mark Twain.* Boston: G. K. Hall, 1983.

Ellison, Ralph. "Change the Joke and Slip the Yoke." In *Shadow and Act.* New York: Random House, 1964.

Emerson, Everett. *The Authentic Mark Twain: A Literary Biography of Samuel L. Clemens.* Philadelphia: University of Pennsylvania Press, 1984.

Fiedler, Leslie A. "Come Back to the Raft Ag'in, Huck Honey!" In *The Collected Essays of Leslie Fiedler,* Vol. 1, pp. 142-51. Briarcliff Manor, N.Y.: Stein and Day, 1971.

Furnas, J. C. "The Crowded Raft: 'Huckleberry Finn' and Its Critics." *American Scholar* 54, No. 4 (Autumn 1985): 517-24.

Gerber, John C. *Mark Twain.* Boston: Twayne Publishers, 1988.

Giddings, Robert, ed. *Mark Twain: A Sumptuous Variety.* London: Vision, 1985.

Hemingway, Ernest. "Pursuit and Conversation." In *Green Hills of Africa,* pp. 2-34. New York: Charles Scribner's Sons, 1935.

Leonard, James S., et al. *Satire or Evasion?: Black Perspectives on Huckleberry Finn.* 1991.

Matthews, Brander. "Huckleberry Finn." *Saturday Review* London LIX, No. 1527 (31 January 1885): 153-54.

McMahan, Elizabeth. *Critical Approaches to Mark Twain's Short Stories.* Port Washington, N.Y.: National University Publications, Kennikat Press, 1981.

Seelye, John. "What's in a Name: Sounding the Depths of Tom Sawyer." *Sewanee Review* XC, No. 3 (Summer 1982).

Sloane, David E. E. *Mark Twain as a Literary Comedian.* Baton Rouge: Louisiana State University Press, 1979.

Trilling, Lionel. "*Huckleberry Finn.*" In *The Liberal Imagination: Essays in Literature and Society,* pp. 104-17. New York: Viking Press, 1950.

Warren, Robert Penn. "Mark Twain." *Southern Review* VIII, No. 3 (Summer 1972): 459-92.

Comte de Villiers de l'Isle Adam
1838-1889
French dramatist, novelist, short story writer, and poet.

Axël (drama, 1872)

Plot: The play's first section, "The Religious World," takes place in about 1828 on Christmas Eve in a Flemish convent. The Abbess has confined her niece, Princess Sara de Maupers, there for some time and hopes to make her a nun. Just before the ceremony at which Sara is to take her vows, the Abbess warns the Archdeacon that Sara is rebellious, is interested in the occult, and has probably received a parchment containing a clue from a mysterious figure called Master Janus. During the ceremony, when the Archdeacon asks Sara if she accepts Light, Hope, and Life, she responds in the negative. Subsequently locked away, Sara manages to escape from the convent.

Part Two, "The Tragic World," is set in the Auërsberg's family castle in Germany's Black Forest. Count Axël Auërsberg lives there, frequently conferring with his occult advisor Master Janus; Axël's cousin Commander Kaspar is visiting. The commander wants his cousin to abandon his life of solitude and devotion to the supernatural to become a useful citizen. Herr Zacharias, a steward of the castle, reveals to Kaspar that there is a fortune in gold buried in some nearby caverns. His greed awakened, Kaspar decides to kill Axël and acquire the gold himself; his questions alert Axël to his cousin's duplicity, however, and Kaspar is subsequently killed by Axël in a duel.

In Part Three, "The Occult World," Axël confesses to Janus that his experiences with Kaspar have stirred his long-forgotten desire for gold and made him neglect his occult studies. Although Janus encourages Axël to free himself from such worldly concerns, Axël feels increasingly alienated from occultism; when Janus asks him if he accepts Light, Hope, and Life, like Sara, he says "No." When Sara arrives at the castle, Janus tells the audience that his work is nearly completed.

The play's last section, "The World of Passion," takes place in the caverns beneath Axël's castle. Axël has gone there to commit suicide when he witnesses Sara uncovering the treasure hidden in the caverns. She shoots at Axël but only wounds him; in their subsequent struggle, he notices her beauty, and the two fall instantly in love. Sara suggests that they take the money and leave to pursue their dreams, but Axël feels that, since no future experience could match the moment of ideal love they have already had, they should kill themselves. Sara acquiesces, and the two drink poison and die together.

Characters: Villiers (Jean Marie Mathias Philippe August) is an important French dramatist known for his highly imaginative works, which reveal his intense idealism and anti-materialism. Considered his masterpiece, *Axël* has been called a transitional work that evokes both the romanticism of the early nineteenth century and the symbolism of the early twentieth century. The play focuses on several different approaches to life—including the religious, the materialistic, the ascetic, and the passionate—finally discrediting each as illusory. In the end, Villiers seems to advocate a pessimistic abandonment of life, though some critics have noted his ambiguity on this subject, particularly after his 1885 conversion to Catholicism. The characters in *Axël,* who deliver highly poetic, discursive speeches and take part in little action, are apparently not intended to reflect reality but to embody the ideals the play presents.

The critic Edmund Wilson called *Axël*'s title character a "super-dreamer" who established the type of the later symbolist hero. A wealthy German aristocrat, **Count Axël Auërsberg** is superior in looks, intelligence, and charisma, and he embodies the idealistic attitude Villiers seems to have possessed. He has rejected all worldly concerns and, with the help of Master Janus, devoted himself to studying the occult. He is also a professed enemy of materialism. Axël's victory over Kaspar in the duel represents the triumph of his own idealism over his cousin's monetary, worldly concerns. Soon after the duel, however, Axël becomes increasingly obsessed with the gold that is buried on his estate. (Some critics claim that this abrupt transition from asceticism to materialism is unconvincing, while others maintain that Axël is not intended as a realistic character but as an embodiment of his creator's ideas.) Although he struggles against his material desires, Axël finally repudiates the occultism that had previously sustained him, answering "No" to Janus's query. Yet he also comes to repudiate materialism again, which results in his first decision to commit suicide. After encountering Sara in the cavern and experiencing a moment of pure love, Axël also rejects the passion and possible dream-fulfillment that she offers. His belief that the only way to safeguard happiness—which invariably disappears as reality intrudes—is to escape life altogether, which is in keeping with the illusionist philosophy Villiers held before his conversion to Catholicism. Only infinity, Axël maintains, is not an illusion. His much-quoted declaration, "As for living, our servants will do that for us!," symbolizes not so much aristocratic haughtiness as a scorn for the ordinary, a rejection of the concerns and dilemmas of daily life. Unable to reconcile his longing for perfection with his leaning toward renunciation, Axël chooses suicide. A line added to the play's ending after its initial publication (which seems to condemn suicide as "dreadful") suggests that Villiers did not fully condone Axël's action.

Princess Sara de Maupers is a beautiful, rather stubborn twenty-three-year-old who resists her aunt's attempt to force her into becoming a nun. Sara's scenes with the Abbess and Archdeacon allow Villiers to explore the religious pursuits—in this case, Christian monasticism—that he viewed as one of several, ultimately faulty approaches to life. Beautiful and intelligent, Sara demonstrates her strong determination when she not only refuses to take religious vows but manages to escape from the convent, following the clue she has received from Janus and making her way to Axël's castle, where she hopes to recover the stolen gold. Whereas Axël is essentially passive, choosing renunciation rather than action, Sara embodies a vital life force; she actively seeks experience and relishes her senses. At the same time, she is introspective and narcissistic, qualities that have been identified as characteristic of the heroines of later symbolist dramas. Although she initially wants Axël to join her in seizing the love and power that seem to lie before them, she acquiesces with his desire that they kill themselves, thus escaping the possibility of losing what they have already experienced. This affirmative gesture of unity with her lover might be seen as Sara's final act of passion; by contrast, it is a final act of renunciation for Axël.

The secondary characters in *Axël* revolve around the two protagonists and help to illustrate the play's concerns. **Master Janus** is Axël's occult mentor; he apparently has some mysterious powers, for he has ordained all of the events in which both Axël and Sara become involved and thus shaped their destinies. He serves as Axël's tutor, exhorting him, for instance, to escape "the bonds of the moment" and return to his ascetic studies when Axël has been tempted by worldly concerns. The presence of Janus and occultism in the play exemplifies the preoccupation with the supernatural that characterized both the romantic and the symbolist movements. **Commander Kaspar,** Axël's cousin, is a greedy materialist who epitomizes bourgeois values and who passes on his monetary desires to Axël after their duel; at one point he comments, "I call myself *real life.*" The **Abbess,** who finds Sara grievously prideful and rebellious, tries to break down her niece's resistance through privation and confinement in the convent; she and the **Archdeacon,** who is unsuccessful in persuading Sara to take religious vows, are notably unflattering representatives of the religious way of life. The veteran soldiers **Miklaus, Hartwig,** and **Gotthold,** as well as the steward **Herr Zacharias** help to expedite the play's action through their revealing conversations about Axël and his guests. **Ukko,** Axël's young servant, adds a rare moment of comedy with his flippancy during Kaspar's burial.

Further Reading

Conroy, William Thomas. *Villiers de l'Isle-Adam.* Boston: Twayne, 1978.

Knapp, Bettina. "Adam/Axel/Alchemy." *L'Esprit Créateur* XVIII, No. 2 (Summer 1978): 24-41.

Nineteenth-Century Literature Criticism, Vol. 3. Detroit: Gale.

Rose, Marilyn Gaddis. "'Axel': Play and Hearsay." *Comparative Drama* 2, No. 3 (Fall 1968): 173-84.

Symons, Arthur. "Villiers de L'Isle-Adam." In *The Symbolist Movement in Literature,* pp. 37-58. New York: E. P. Dutton, 1908.

Wilson, Edmund. "Axel and Rimbaud." In *Axel's Castle: A Study in the Imaginative Literature of 1870-1930,* pp. 257-98. New York: Scribner's, 1931.

Yeats, W. B. "A Symbolical Drama in Paris." *Bookman* VI, No. 31 (April 1894): 14-16.

Mrs. Humphry Ward
1851-1920
English novelist, essayist, biographer, translator, and memoirist.

Robert Elsmere (novel, 1888)

Plot: As the novel opens, young Robert Elsmere has recently graduated from Oxford University. He decides to accept a clerical post in England's Surrey region, but before beginning his new position he visits scenic Westmoreland. There he meets and falls in love with Catherine Leyburn, a very religious, virtuous young woman who selflessly cares for her two sisters and widowed mother. Although she initially resists Robert's attentions, Catherine finally submits to her growing fondness for him, and the two are married. They establish their home in Surrey, and Robert begins his pastoral duties, pursuing both practical concerns and intellectual investigations. He frequently visits the home of a local squire, Roger Wendover, a man of considerable intellect and skepticism who invites Robert to peruse his extensive library. The squire's constant questioning of Christian dogma, combined with the influence of Robert's similarly inclined acquaintances Edward Langham and Professor Henry Grey as well as his own historical research, results in a spiritual crisis for Robert. He finds that his doubts about orthodox religion prevent him from serving as an Anglican clergyman. A short period of unbelief causes both Robert and Catherine great pain, for Catherine's faith is still firm and she must reconcile her love for her husband with her religious commitment. In the end, however, Robert discovers a deeper spirituality within himself, and he forges a new faith. He moves his family to the working-class East End of London and establishes the New Brotherhood of Christ, which provides a variety of social, educational, and religious activities for the neighborhood's impoverished residents. Robert gradually attracts a loyal following and develops an almost legendary reputation for piety and good works. Overworked and exhausted, Robert finally dies, while Catherine continues her philanthropic work and even attends services at her husband's "church." Meanwhile, in a subplot to the novel's main action, Catherine's vivacious sister Rose survives an unhappy love affair with the passive, skeptical Langham and goes on to marry the charming but more conventional aristocrat, Lord Flaxman.

Characters: A member of the influential Arnold family (whose members included poet Matthew Arnold), Mary Augusta Humphry Ward wrote many novels of social and religious implication, exhibiting a sharp intellect and a well-developed moral sense. *Robert Elsmere* was her most accomplished and popular work; it was snatched up in impressive numbers by its contemporary audience and its concerns were warmly debated in British, American, and Canadian journals. The novel reflects the pervasiveness of religious doubt and the atmosphere of optimism that characterize the Victorian age. Ward's answer to the nineteenth-century conflict between religion and intellect, *Robert Elsmere* proposes that a synthesis of spirituality and reason is not only possible but socially productive. The book's popularity suggests that Ward's attention to religious doubt and her belief in a new, more active Christianity struck a chord with her first readers, and its concerns—particularly that of the role of religion in marriage—continue to interest modern audiences.

Ward's first experience with spiritual uncertainty came through her father, who converted to Catholicism, returned to the Anglican Church, then reverted again to Catholicism. She herself had been launched on a spiritual quest of sorts through her work as a contributor to the *Dictionary of Christian Biography*; her discovery of the early Christians' excessive credulity and superstitiousness lead her to question the basis of Christian dogma. **Robert Elsmere,** for whose character she apparently drew from her own personality as well as from various clergyman she knew or knew of, is a graduating Oxford University student as the novel begins. During the mid-nineteenth century, Oxford was a hotbed of religious debate and change, particularly through the influential Oxford Movement with its emphasis on a return to "High Church" or traditional practices. A competent though not especially brilliant student, Robert's approach to religion is initially more emotional than intellectual or critical. He is attracted to the devout and dutiful Catherine Leyburn, a native of the remote and ruggedly beautiful north of England partly because she seems to embody the moral simplicity of the conventional church. Assuming his clerical post in Surrey, Robert begins a robust, active new life through such activities as organizing church clubs, helping the poor, and indulging in his favorite hobby, fishing. At the same time, partly through the influence of the skeptical, embittered Squire Wendover, he embarks on a period of intense reading, speculation, and discussion. His study of history (particularly that of the Roman Empire), combined with the intellectual questioning stimulated acquaintances Wendover, Langham, and Grey, leads Robert to a spiritual crisis. Trapped for a brief and painful period in a mire of unbelief, Robert feels he can no longer perform the functions of an Anglican clergyman. His cry of agony, "O God! My wife—my work!," though it might be viewed as rather banal by modern readers accustomed to greater depths of angst, expresses his anguish and disorientation as he faces an uncertain future. This period of doubt, however, soon ends, for Robert discovers a middle ground between his intellect and the deep spirituality that remains within him. He creates a new faith based on the philosophical tenets of Christianity but employing a less literal, more humanistic interpretation of dogma; for instance, Jesus is viewed not as a divine being capable of performing miracles but as a human figure who symbolizes Christian love and charity. In accordance with his conviction that religion should be actively practiced, Robert moves his family to the impoverished East End of London to serve that community through his New Brotherhood of Christ. Critics have noted that in the novel's third volume, which chronicles Robert's life in London, he becomes more a dully saint-like instrument of propaganda than a rounded, compelling character. He attains Moses-like or even Christ-like stature as he devotedly leads his flocks and finally dies a martyr's death. Nevertheless Ward is credited with convincingly infusing Robert with many of her own conflicts and doubts as well as the essential faith and optimism she shared with other nineteenth-century thinkers.

Raised in the ruggedly beautiful landscape of Westmoreland, **Catherine Leyburn** reflects her home region's natural dignity and remoteness from intellectual sophistication. Less educated than her husband, she is an evangelical Christian who unquestioningly accepts orthodox dogma. Virtuous and self-sacrificing, she hesitates to yield to her love for Robert because she feels it is her duty to care for her mother and sisters. Robert's ardor wins her over, however, and the two begin a life of service together in Surrey, with Catherine taking up the role of devoted, loving helpmate to her clergyman husband. Catherine is much aggrieved by Robert's loss of faith, which she does not herself experience, and she struggles valiantly between her love for her husband and her own commitment to traditional religion. Lacking the mental occupation that Robert finds in his intellectual explorations, Catherine is more subject to thoughts of the past as she remembers the Wordsworthian beauty of her home and the simple faith she learned there. Ward seems to approve of Catherine's decision to place her love for Robert ahead of her religion—as Ward's own mother must have done when her husband wavered in his faith. Catherine not only accompanies Robert to London but immerses herself in charitable work there and even attends, albeit uneasily, services of the New Brotherhood. The fact that she continues to attend these services after Robert's death suggests that not even she is immune to the changes wrought as the nineteenth century progressed. Some readers and critics have found Catherine unpleasantly pious and fanatical;

the generally admiring William S. Peterson acknowledged that she is "a saint that has had the misfortune of being born in the wrong century." Ward herself seems ambivalent in her attitude toward Catherine: while admiring the fervor of her religious emotion, she suggests that rigid devotion is anachronistic.

Squire Roger Wendover is a wealthy Surrey landowner who invites Robert to use his extensive library and who involves him in discussions pitting religion against reason. A man of probing intellect, the squire is the novel's rationalist and the polar opposite of the orthodox, devout Catherine; Robert finds himself pressed between these two extremes. Convinced that religious dogma must be subject to the same critical scrutiny as historical precepts, Wendover insists on asking demanding questions that challenge the basis of Robert's faith. Although he does seem to relish the thought of Robert as his disciple, he is more the catalyst than the cause of his young friend's loss of faith, which is rooted in Robert's own historical investigations. The fact that the squire is an embittered man isolated from the concerns of his impoverished tenants has been interpreted as evidence that Ward disapproved of an entirely intellectual life. In fact, asserts William S. Peterson, Ward intended Wendover as "an object lesson in the terrors of modern thought divorced from ethical considerations." Wendover was probably modeled after Mark Pattison, an influential scholar associated with the Oxford Movement who, like the squire, was never to finish his life's work (a biography of the sixteenth-century scholar Scaliger) and who apparently died bitter and frustrated.

The account of **Rose Leyburn**'s romantic difficulties provides the novel with an interesting, entertaining subplot praised by several reviewers. Rose contrasts with her sister Catherine, for she is beautiful, vivacious, and temperamental. Thought to reflect the more artistic, musical side of Ward's own personality, Rose plays the violin and, unlike her sister, identifies more with the outside world than with rugged, remote Westmoreland. Rose is courted by two suitors: the passive, highly intellectual Edward Langham and the shallower but more charming Lord Flaxman, who ultimately wins her. The unhappy end of her affair with Langham has been characterized as a form of punishment for the self-assertiveness she exhibited, and the experience seems to make her morally upright and less frivolous. Nevertheless the lively Rose provides some relief from the rather heavy religious and intellectual preoccupations of the other characters.

In addition to Squire Wendover, two scholars contribute to Robert's questioning of his orthodox religious faith. **Edward Langham** is an Oxford-based intellectual who continually finds himself unable, despite his intentions, to leave that scholarly enclave. His remoteness and passivity in his ill-fated courtship of Rose contrast strongly with Robert's successful conquest of Catherine. Called a portrait of the intellectual who lacks the will to act, Langham is thought to have been modeled after both the title character of Étienne de Senancour's 1804 romantic novel *Obermann,* and the nineteenth-century Swiss author Henri-Frédéric Amiel. **Professor Henry Grey,** though more gentle and compassionate than Squire Wendover, also asks disquieting questions and insists that reason be applied to religion, just as it is to other matters.

Other notable characters in *Robert Elsmere* include the quietly comic **Rector and Mrs. Thornburgh.** Mrs. Thornburgh is a domineering, self-important matchmaker, while her husband periodically emerges from his office to make ironic comments about his wife; the two have been compared to Mr. and Mrs. Bennett in Jane Austen's 1813 novel, *Pride and Prejudice.* **Lord Hugh Flaxman** is the charming, handsome, though rather colorless aristocrat who courts and finally marries Rose Leyburn, a conventional husband for the artistic and temperamental young woman. Sophisticated **Madame de Netteville** is an alluring aristocrat—stereotypically French in her blending of intelligence with moral depravity—who invites Robert to her elegant salons (gatherings of intellectuals, artists, and hangers-on) in the hope of seducing him. This ploy fails, for the virtuous Robert notices only the contrast between this grandiose realm of wealth and privilege and the miserable lives of the poor among whom he works.

Further Reading

Gladstone, William E. "*Robert Elsmere* and the Battle of Belief." *Nineteenth Century* XXIII (May 1888): 766-88.

Jones, Enid Huws. *Mrs. Humphry Ward.* New York: St. Martin's, 1973.

Peterson, William S. *Victorian Heretic: Mrs. Humphry Ward's Robert Elsmere.* England: Leicester University Press, 1976.

"*Robert Elsmere* by Mrs. Humphry Ward." *Quarterly Review* CLXVII (October 1888): 273-302.

Ryals, Clyde de., ed. Introduction to *Robert Elsmere* by Mrs. Humphrey Ward. Lincoln: University of Nebraska Press, 1967.

Smith, Esther Marian Greenwell. *Mrs. Humphry Ward.* Boston: Twayne, 1980.

Sutherland, J. A. *Mrs. Humphry Ward: Eminent Victorian, Pre-Eminent Edwardian.* Oxford: Oxford University Press, 1990.

Frank J. Webb
Birth and death dates unknown
African-American novelist.

The Garies and Their Friends (novel, 1857)

Plot: The novel begins on the Georgia plantation of wealthy, white Mr. Clarence Garie, who lives with a beautiful mulatto (of mixed black and white heritage) woman he bought at a slave auction ten years earlier. Mr. Garie considers Emily his wife and treats her with great respect and solicitude; the two are the parents of young Clarence and Emily, and Mrs. Garie is expecting another baby. She convinces her husband to move the family to Philadelphia, where, she has heard, there is a large, thriving African-American community and where she expects their children will find better opportunities for education and employment. In Philadelphia the Garies reunite with the Ellises, a dark-skinned black family they knew before migrated from Georgia. Mr. Ellis is a fairly successful carpenter; the Ellis children are Esther, Caroline (Caddy), and Charlie, whose best friend is carefree Kinch DeYounge. The Garies purchase a home from the Ellises' friend Mr. Walters, a handsome, dignified black man who has become wealthy through real estate investments. Next door to the Garies reside George Stevens, a bigoted, shifty white lawyer, and his family, including his children George and Lizzie, who are forbidden to play with Clarence and Emily when their mother learns that Mrs. Garie is a mulatto. Mr. Stevens discovers he is related to Mr. Garie and plots to acquire the family fortune. Already involved in clandestine activities to keep Philadelphia's free blacks from owning property, Stevens arranges for a gang of tough Irish immigrants to attack the homes of Walters, Ellis, and Garie. The assault is led by a murderer named McCloskey who owes his freedom to Stevens and thus is easily blackmailed. During the mob's attack, Mr. Garie is killed and Mrs. Garie, forced into a cold woodshed, gives birth prematurely; both she and her baby die of shock and exposure. Meanwhile Walters successfully repels the rioters from his home, but Mr. Ellis is savagely beaten and he is permanently disabled—both physically and mentally—by the attack.

Mr. Garie's will is not found, and Stevens reveals that he is the heir to the Garie fortune. Allowing only a pittance of the money to the Garie children, he moves to New York City to live in luxury. As the years go by, Walters and Esther become increasingly attracted to each other and are eventually married. Having assumed responsibility for the support of his family after his father's misfortune, Charlie becomes a competent engraver and marries Emily Garie. Her brother Clarence, however, is destined for a tragic fate when he tries to "pass" as a white man. His engagement to a white girl is shattered when George Stevens, Jr., reveals that her fiancé is part black. Clarence subsequently grows more miserable and isolated until he finally dies. McCloskey, meanwhile, makes a deathbed confession of the crimes he committed with Stevens, revealing that Stevens was Mr. Garie's murderer and also disclosing the location of Garie's will. Stevens subsequently commits suicide. Emily Garie recovers the fortune that was rightfully hers and her late brother's. Kinch also prospers, for his father's wise investments in real estate—made while he was a humble seller of old clothing—ultimately bring his son great wealth.

Characters: Little is known about the author of *The Garies and Their Friends,* except that he was of African-American heritage, associated with Philadelphia, and knew or was known to Harriet Beecher Stowe, author of *Uncle Tom's Cabin.* Though generally acknowledged as lacking real literary merit, *The Garies* is significant as the third novel published by an American black (the first two were William Wells Brown's *Clotel; or, The President's Daughter* and Harriet E. Wilson's *Our Nig*) and as a record of the lives of free blacks living in the pre-Civil War North. In addition the novel's focus on such issues as interracial marriages, the violence perpetrated by racist lynch mobs, and the concept of "passing" anticipate the concerns of the authors of the celebrated Harlem Renaissance of the 1920s. Though racial prejudice and oppression are dominant themes in the novel, many critics have noted that Webb affirms rather than rejects the dominant values of American society, particularly in his apparent belief that African-Americans may find salvation through the acquisition of wealth. Indeed the novel contains no attack on slavery or even any strong endorsement of the abolitionist movement, though it does expose such problems of free Northern blacks as segregated transportation, the lack of police protection, antagonism from Irish-Americans, and discrimination in apprenticeships and employment. *The Garies* shares with other works of nineteenth-century popular fiction a preponderance of melodrama, a contrived plot, and characters who often seem caricaturist, yet it nevertheless holds an important place in the development of African-American fiction.

The family referred to in the novel's title is headed by **Mr. Clarence Garie,** a wealthy white Southerner who, ten years before the action begins, purchased a beautiful mulatto woman at an auction and subsequently falls in love with her. The owner of a large plantation and the progenitor of a respected family lineage, Garie treats **Emily** as he would a legally and socially sanctioned wife and is scrupulously attentive to her wishes and concerns. Thus he is willing to move the family to Philadelphia so the couple's children may enjoy broader opportunities and, presumably, greater safety from racial prejudice. The move proves disastrous for Mr. Garie, who is killed in a brutal attack by a rioting mob of whites, and Mrs. Garie, who succumbs to shock and exposure as a result of the episode.

The Garies' son, **Clarence,** is often cited as a significant example of the "tragic mulatto" common in late nineteenth- and early twentieth-century American literature. Clarence carries only a small amount of African blood and thus appears to be white; on the advice of an older adviser, he rejects his black heritage and tries to "pass" as a white man. Despite Webb's apparent affirmation of white ways and even the superiority of white physical traits, Clarence's chosen path proves ill-fated. He is portrayed as a sentimental weakling whose hopeless attempt to enter the white world leads only to his isolation from both that realm and the black one he has left behind. He grows increasingly lonely, moody, and misanthropic and finally dies. Characters driven by racial prejudice to the extreme and risky practice of "passing" are common in the works of Harlem Renaissance writers, including James Weldon Johnson and Nella Larsen. Clarence's sister **Emily** is a less notable character, distinguished by the fact that she is the sole member of the Garie family to survive and thrive, as she marries Charlie Ellis and shares with him the family fortune that finally reaches its rightful recipient.

Both the Garies and the dark-skinned Ellis family migrate from Georgia to Philadelphia, but only the thrifty, industrious, and always decorous Ellises overcome their obstacles and attain success. **Mr. Ellis,** whose coal-black complexion places him in stark contrast to such light-skinned blacks as Clarence Garie, is a hard worker who becomes a modestly successful carpenter. Tragically, he is mentally and physically devastated by the brutal attack on his and other black families led by McCloskey, and he is never again his former self. The Ellis children include **Esther,** the eldest daughter and the novel's most admirable female character who eventually marries the equally virtuous Walters; and the energetic, orderly **Caroline,** or **Caddy.** While Caddy reacts with anger to the rioters, calling them "white devils" and assuming God hates them as much as she does, Esther takes a more forgiving approach and is able to recognize at least some good in some of the white people around her. **Charlie Ellis** is initially a carefree young boy but develops maturity and a sense of responsibility after his father's misfortune. Although he has difficulty landing the apprenticeship he needs in order to learn a trade—thus Webb depicts the pervasiveness of prejudice against blacks in the workplace—Charlie becomes a successful engraver and eventually shares the wealth inherited by his wife, Emily.

Two other "good" characters in *The Garies* are Charlie's friend **Kinch DeYounge** and the impressive Mr. Walters, who marries Esther. As a boy, Kinch is mischievous and carefree, prone to impulsive behavior and unconventional garb. His father, a humble seller of old clothing, wisely invests in real estate, which becomes immensely valuable as Philadelphia expands its boundaries. Consequently, by the end of the novel, Kinch is a wealthy man with the means to become a "full-blown dandy." Some modern critics have seen the sometimes undignified, clownish Kinch as a character of "accommodation" designed to conform to white notions of black behavior.

Mr. Walters, a prosperous black realtor, is the novel's standard of male virtue. Always impeccably dressed and dignified in manner, Walters is a handsome man with very dark skin but notably Caucasian features and manners. He has, in fact, been identified as embodying Webb's affirmation of white American culture and values. Nevertheless Walters strongly disagrees with Clarence's attempt to "pass" as white, which he correctly predicts will only lead to unhappiness. Some critics have defended Walters, asserting that his advocacy of wealth as a means of attaining respect is essentially pragmatic. For instance, he responds to the bigotry of a white innkeeper by buying the hotel in which he was refused service and firing the offending man. In addition, Walters advises the Ellises—who wish their son to acquire some work experience—to encourage Charlie not to become a servant but to sell something, such as matches. Walters claims that by this route Charlie may eventually become a merchant and from there achieve the quintessentially American dream of prosperity.

The novel's central villain is **George Stevens,** the Garies' white neighbor in Philadelphia and their primary antagonist. The bigoted Stevens is a shifty lawyer (called "Slippery George" by his associates) who, when he discovers that he is related to Mr. Garie, plots to acquire the Garie family fortune for himself. Since he is already involved in a movement to rob and otherwise torment Philadelphia's free blacks, Stevens easily arranges an attack on the Garies, the Ellises, and Walters and is himself Mr. Garie's murderer. His actions ultimately result in his being named his victim's heir, yet he is never entirely comfortable with his ill-gotten wealth and eventually becomes a reclusive alcoholic, finally killing himself before he is arrested for murder. Other members of the Stevens family include **Mrs. Stevens,** who is horrified to learn that the mother of her children's new playmates is a mulatto; **George, Jr.,** who is even more wicked and sadistic than his father and who exposes Clarence's black heritage to his white fiancée on the eve of their wedding; and **Lizzie,** who, unlike the other members of her family, wishes the Garies well and is happy when Emily recovers their fortune.

Another villainous character in *The Garies* is **McCloskey.** Stevens blackmails this tough, disreputable Irishman into leading a gang of ruffians in an attack against the novel's black characters. Webb employed some well-worn ethnic stereotypes in creating McCloskey, whose crudeness and bigotry are traits shared by other Irish characters in popular nineteenth-century literature. Although McCloskey is a murderer and, later, a blackmailer, he does show some remorse at the end of the novel, when he confesses to his various crimes and discloses the location of Garie's will. Such a deathbed repentance, as several critics have noted, was a common device of melodramatic fiction.

Not all of the white characters in *The Garies* are evil; in fact the novel is sometimes identified as a "goodwill book" in that its author apparently endeavored to balance the bad characters with the good—perhaps in order to avoid offending white audiences. **Mr. Balch** is a respectable white lawyer who represents the Garie children and to whom Stevens makes his melodramatic announcement that he is the heir to the fortune. **Mr. and Mrs. Burrell** are kind, sympathetic white friends to the novel's black characters; Mr. Burrell gives Charlie Ellis a job when other, supposedly liberal whites bowed to pressure and declined to hire him.

Further Reading

Bell, Bernard W. "Frank J. Webb." *The Afro-American Novel and Its Tradition,* pp. 42-45. Amherst: University of Massachusetts Press, 1987.

Berzon, Judith R. *Neither White Nor Black: The Mulatto Character in American Fiction.* New York: New York University Press, 1978.

Bone, Robert. *The Negro Novel in America.* New Haven: Yale University Press, 1958.

Davis, Arthur P. Introduction to *The Garies and Their Friends* by Frank J. Webb, pp. i-ix. New York: Arno Press and the New York Times, 1969.

De Vries, James H. "The Tradition of the Sentimental Novel in *The Garies and Their Friends* by Frank J. Webb." *CLA Journal* 17 (December 1973): 241-49.

Fleming, Robert E. "Humor in the Early Black Novel." *CLA Journal* 17 (December 1973): 256-57, 259-60.

Jackson, Blyden. "Frank J. Webb and Harriet E. Wilson." In *A History of Afro-American Literature,* Vol. 1: *The Long Beginning, 1746-1895,* pp. 343-63. Baton Rouge: Louisiana State University Press, 1989.

Whitlow, Roger. "Frank J. Webb." In *Black American Literature: A Critical History,* rev. ed., pp. 46-48. Chicago: Nelson-Hall, 1976.

Oscar Wilde
1854-1900

Anglo-Irish dramatist, novelist, short story writer, poet, essayist, and critic.

The Picture of Dorian Gray (novel, 1891)

Plot: Set in late nineteenth-century England, the novel begins in the studio of artist Basil Hallward, who is finishing a portrait of a young man as his friend Lord Henry Wotton looks on. Hallward describes his admiration for his subject, Dorian Gray, an extremely handsome youth with a fresh, engaging personality. Although Hallward does not wish the sophisticated Lord Henry to meet his friend, for fear the younger man will be corrupted, Dorian arrives at the studio during Lord Henry's visit. Lord Henry is immediately interested in Dorian. When Hallward presents Dorian with the portrait, Dorian mentions he would give his soul to remain young and unblemished and let the painting grow old and wrinkled. Dorian and Lord Henry begin to spend a great deal of time together, and the older man influences the younger with his theory of the "New Hedonism," emphasizing a detached, aesthetic exploration of new and varied sensations. In keeping with this philosophy, Dorian courts a young actress named Sibyl Vane whose talents have greatly impressed him. After she falls in love with the man she calls "Prince Charming," Sibyl loses her interest in acting and performs listlessly, telling Dorian that acting seems empty compared to the reality of love. To Dorian, however, Sibyl's charm was in her talent, and he coldly spurns her. Returning home after rejecting Sibyl, Dorian notices that his portrait has acquired a subtle look of cruelty, while his own face remains unchanged. Frightened, he decides to break off his relationship with Lord Henry and reconcile with Sibyl, to whom he writes a letter asking forgiveness and proposing marriage. The next morning, however, Lord Henry arrives and informs Dorian that Sibyl has killed herself; he encourages Dorian to view her death only in aesthetic terms.

From this point on Dorian completely abandons himself to sensual gratification, spending the next fifteen years indulging in illicit sexual liaisons, alcohol, and drugs. Dorian gains a reputation for strange vices and for leading others to corruption, and his old friends and acquaintances avoid him. Meanwhile Dorian's youth and physical beauty remain intact while the painting, hidden away in his house, gradually takes on the signs of aging and debauchery. Although Dorian has long been estranged from Hallward, he receives a visit from his old friend on his thirty-eighth birthday. Hallward has heard rumors about Dorian's dissolution and vices, and he tries to convince him to change his ways. Dorian shows Hallward the painting, which appears vastly aged and corrupted, quite unlike the still young and handsome Dorian. Hallward is horrified and urges Dorian to pray for his own redemption. In a sudden fit of anger, Dorian murders Hallward. He then blackmails Alan Campbell, a young chemist he previously corrupted, into completely destroying Hallward's body. One night Dorian is leaving an opium den when he is confronted by James Vane, Sibyl's sailor brother, who has heard a drunken woman address Dorian as "Prince Charming." Although Vane has sworn to kill the man who drove his sister to suicide, Dorian seems too young to be the culprit; Vane subsequently learns that Dorian is, indeed, Prince Charming. He goes to Dorian's estate and is subsequently killed there in a strange accident. Alan Campbell commits suicide. Dorian now decides to destroy the painting that serves as a record of his corruption, and he stabs it with the same knife he used to kill Hallward. Investigating the scream from the locked room, Dorian's servants break in to discover a painting of their young, handsome master and the nearby corpse of a hideous old man, fatally stabbed in the chest. It is only when they see the rings on the man's fingers that they realize he is Dorian Gray.

Characters: Wilde is associated with the late nineteenth-century decadent or "art-for-art's-sake" literary movement, which emphasized aesthetic form and style over ethical concerns and focused on the individual will, imagination, and desire for self-realization. Distinguished by its richly descriptive prose and psychological explorations, *The Picture of Dorian Gray* also employs techniques common in the gothic fiction popular earlier in the century, such as the suggestion of secret crimes, a horrible murder, and a supernaturally endowed portrait. Early reviewers condemned the novel as immoral, and it was used as evidence of Wilde's corruption during his celebrated trial for committing homosexual acts. Since its publication *Dorian Gray* has been viewed as a gothic detective or murder story, a moral fable that condemns excess, a record of a Faustian struggle for fulfillment, and as a document of Wilde's aesthetic ideas. Modern critics tend to focus on the novel's apparent thematic conflict between morality and the "New Hedonism" espoused by Lord Henry—a conflict that, most conclude, reflects an ambivalence within Wilde.

The novel's title character is an exceptionally handsome young man with blue eyes and blonde curls who resembles Adonis, a spectacularly beautiful character in Greek mythology. Little is revealed about **Dorian Gray**'s background except that he is the product of a passionate, tragic, and apparently illicit romantic liaison and that he is an aristocrat. Enchanted by Dorian's looks, engaging personality, and candor, the artist Basil Hallward proclaims him his ideal of youth. Many commentators have, in fact, detected homosexual passion in Hallward's regard for Dorian, though it seems to be platonic and idealized. Lord Henry is similarly enamored of Dorian and encourages the young man to make the most of his youth and beauty by pursuing a life devoted to sensation. With his talk of the "New Hedonism," which promotes self-realization as the ultimate goal in life, Lord Henry begins to initiate Dorian into what will ultimately destroy him. When Dorian sees the portrait Hallward painted of him, he seems to recognize his own beauty for the first time, and he expresses a narcissistic wish to stay perpetually young and unblemished while the painting grows old. Through some force that is never identified, Dorian's wish is fulfilled, but he is destroyed in the process. The first proof that Dorian has come under Lord Henry's influence is his relationship with Sibyl. While some critics contend that Dorian rejects Sibyl because he is inherently homosexual and cannot love a woman, most feel he has absorbed the preference for art over reality, an important component of the New Hedonism. Thus when Sibyl's artistic skill lapses, so does Dorian's regard for her. Lord Henry encourages Dorian to view Sibyl's death with aesthetic detachment, and thus Dorian begins a life of experimentation with sensation. Unlike his mentor, however, Dorian is unable to fully separate himself from reality, and he degenerates into self-gratification and debauchery rather than the refined experience and spectator's role that Lord Henry seems to espouse. Although Dorian's "sins" are unspecified, the fact that he has corrupted a long line of young men suggests that they are homosexual in nature, and some scholars believe these hints of what was then an illegal practice evidence Wilde's exploration of and ambivalence toward his own homosexuality. Dorian also apparently indulges in alcohol and drugs, as evidenced by his visit to an opium den in a particularly disreputable part of the city. Dorian's own death has generated a significant amount of critical debate, for it seems to imply that, as Wilde himself stated, "All excess, as well as all renunciation, brings its own punishment." Wilde also admitted that this moral—a rather Victorian condemnation of self-indulgence—seems to contradict the novel's aesthetic concerns. Dorian is often identified as a Faustian character, referring to the legendary character (made most famous in the early nineteenth-century drama by German writer Johann Wolfgang von Goethe) who exchanged his soul for unlimited knowledge and experience. The mysterious portrait has also been a subject of critical discussion. While some consider it a typical gothic device in its supernatural quality, others claim that it represents Dorian's soul, which he is finally unable to escape. Still others believe the portrait is Dorian's conscience; its increasingly hideous appearance chronicles his corruption and is finally transferred back to him when he attempts to abolish it. In any case the novel's ending strongly suggests that complete self-indulgence leads inevitably to punishment.

Urbane, sophisticated **Lord Henry Wotton** (sometimes called "Harry" by Dorian and Hallward) is an aristocratic dandy who is often identified as Wilde's mouthpiece in the novel. Indeed Wilde once commented that Lord Henry is "what the world thinks of me." He projects a studied languor and is known for his brilliant witticisms twisting or reversing conventional morality; it is he who articulates the "New Hedonism" in which many commentators have identified the same aesthetic principles upheld by Wilde. As Lord Henry explains to Dorian, the goal of the new hedonist is "to realize one's nature perfectly." He advises Dorian to "Live! Live the wonderful life that is in you" by embracing as many different sensual experiences as possible, a process that ideally calls for a separation of the self from the sordid realities of life. Although Lord Henry serves as Dorian's initiator or mentor, he differs significantly from his young friend because he maintains aesthetic distance, remaining an artist or critic rather than a participant, whereas Dorian degenerates into mere self-gratification and subsequently destroys himself. When he first meets Dorian, Lord Henry is roused out of his general indolence and energized by the desire to shape or guide the beautiful young man, and many critics have detected homosexual attraction in his feelings for Dorian. Just before Dorian's death—and after he has murdered Hallward—Lord Henry praises Dorian for having made his life a work of art; obviously he takes some credit for this aesthetic creation yet does not recognize Dorian's forthcoming fate. Lord Henry's more degenerate, sinister qualities and his presence when Dorian expresses his wish to remain young have led to him to be identified as a satanic figure who tempts Dorian into sin. He might be likened to the biblical devil, luring the pure young man into tasting forbidden and ultimately deadly fruit and denying the existence of the soul, or as a Mephistophelean (referring to the legend of Faust, who was tempted by the evil Mephistopheles) figure who offers Dorian intense experience and knowledge in exchange for his soul. Condemned by some as an emotional voyeur who recommends sensual pleasures to others while his own seem purely intellectual, Lord Henry has been said to embody the aristocratic, luxury-craving side of Wilde's personality.

While Lord Henry may represent Wilde's taste for sophisticated languor, **Basil Hallward** embodies Wilde's his devotion to hard work and artistic achievement and his underlying morality. A talented, dedicated, and thoughtful artist, Hallward paints a portrait of Dorian that fully expresses its creator's admiration (or even, as some commentators contend, his sexual passion) for his subject. Hallward considers Dorian the epitome of youth, beauty, and purity and thus does not want to introduce him to the sophisticated and corrupt Lord Henry. Hallward fears he has put too much of himself and his feelings for Dorian into the painting; he feels he has committed a form of idolatry, undermining his belief that art should be idealized and apart from real life. These reflections illuminate one of the novel's primary concerns: the relationship between art and reality. Hallward functions as a strong moral voice and thus serves as a foil to Lord Henry, who elevates instinct and sensuality over ethics or morality. This contrast is particularly evident in Hallward's reaction to Dorian's relationship with Sibyl. When Dorian complains about Sibyl's poor acting, Hallward scolds him for criticizing the woman he loves, noting that "Love is more wonderful than art." Lord Henry, on the other hand, advises Dorian to view his former lover's death with cold detachment. Eighteen years of complete debauchery pass before Dorian is visited by his old friend Hallward, attempting to influence him to reform. Dorian shows him the now hideously deformed painting and accuses Hallward of ruining his life by creating the flattering portrait and introducing him to Lord Henry. Indeed Wilde commented that Hallward did create a "monstrous vanity" in Dorian, thus proving that an excessive admiration for physical beauty may be dangerous. Hallward's murder and Dorian's subsequent efforts to destroy his body add some sensational drama to the novel, as does the fact that Dorian later tries to "kill" the portrait with the same knife he used to stab Hallward.

Sibyl Vane, a talented young actress, is for a brief period Dorian's lover. She initially attracts his attention and admiration when she performs a number of famous dramatic roles, including Juliet in Shakespeare's *Romeo and Juliet,* with great skill and charm. Her beauty, sensitivity, and ability make her stand out sharply against the tawdry, second-rate theatrical company with which she performs. Sibyl first knows Dorian only as "Prince Charming," thus establishing the illusory basis of their relationship, which has come about through Dorian's fascination not with her but with her art. Unlike her lover, Sibyl decides that she has "grown sick of shadows" and turns her attention wholly to her love for Dorian. In choosing life over art, Sibyl denies the tenets of the "New Hedonism," which dictates an aesthetic detachment from the sordid realities of daily existence. Her acting becomes wooden, and Dorian consequently loses his interest in her, stating that "without your art you are nothing." In utter despair Sibyl takes her own life in her lonely dressing room, a circumstance that Lord Henry encourages Dorian to view as merely another interesting sensation to be experienced aesthetically. The episode confirms Lord Henry's influence over Dorian and—as indicated by the cruel look acquired by the portrait—marks the beginning of the younger man's descent into debauchery.

Through the other members of the Vane family, Wilde portrays a world far different than that inhabited by the other characters. Many critics faulted Wilde's depiction of lower-class life, saying he lacked knowledge of such milieus and was unable to describe what is plain and simple with as much skill as he described the luxurious and sophisticated. Sibyl's mother, the unpleasant, downtrodden **Mrs. Vane,** was once an actress who performed in second-rate melodramas. Vulgar and absurdly vain, she is prone to highly theatrical gestures and comments. **James Vane,** Sibyl's brother, is a rough, morose young man who exhibits none of his sister's sensitivity, though he does prove his loyalty to her. He invokes primitive justice in vengeance for Sibyl's death, for he represents conventional society and morality, which Dorian struggles against.

The only other notable character in *Dorian Gray* is **Alan Campbell,** the young chemist Dorian blackmails into completely destroying Hallward's body with fire and chemicals. Campbell is apparently one of the young men Dorian corrupted, possibly through homosexual activity, and he ultimately commits suicide.

The Importance of Being Earnest (drama, 1895)

Plot: Algernon "Algy" Moncrieff is a wealthy young dandy whose aristocratic aunt, Lady Augusta Bracknell, frequently requires his attendance at her boring dinner parties. Thus he invents a fictitious friend named Bunbury whose illnesses regularly require Algy to leave London to visit him. Algy's friend Jack Worthing employs a similar device to escape from his own domestic situation. He is the guardian of young Cecily Cardew, who lives at his country estate with her strict governess, Miss Prism. Jack feels stifled by the correct behavior required in the presence of these two females, so he invents a dissolute brother named Ernest whom Jack must frequently extricate from trouble, necessitating trips to London. While visiting Lady Bracknell, Jack falls in love with her daughter Gwendolen Fairfax, who believes her suitor's name is Ernest. This circumstance pleases her because she particularly admires that name. Lady Bracknell demands to know about the family background of her daughter's sweetheart, but Jack can only tell her that his parentage is a mystery—he was found in a leather satchel at Victoria Station. Snobbish Lady Bracknell refuses to allow Gwendolen to marry Jack unless he can produce at least one parent. Back at his country estate, and planning to announce the death of his "brother" Ernest, Jack finds that Algy has already arrived there and is posing as Ernest. Jack wants Algy to return to London, but Algy has fallen in love with Cecily and is reluctant to leave. Cecily, too, is enamoured of the man she believes is her guardian's brother, particularly since she has always wanted to marry someone named Ernest. Knowing that his marital plans hinge on his being named Ernest, Algy decides to have himself rechristened and enlists the flexible Reverend Chasuble to perform the ceremony; Jack, too, has engaged the clergyman to christen him Ernest.

Gwendolen now arrives at Jack's country house, causing a great deal of confusion because she and Cecily initially believe they are in love with the same man named Ernest. Jack and Algy both appear, however, and their real identities are established. Although they are at first annoyed with their suitors for deceiving them, the two young women decide to forgive them, concluding that style is more important than sincerity in such matters. Lady Bracknell soon appears and is alarmed to learn that her nephew has become engaged to Cecily. She gladly consents to the marriage, however, when she learns that Cecily is a wealthy heiress. Cleverly manipulating his position as Cecily's guardian, Jack refuses to allow her to marry Algy unless he is allowed to marry Gwendolen. The question of his parentage is finally cleared up when it is revealed that Miss Prism, once the nurse to the infant Jack, absentmindedly put the manuscript of a book she was writing into the perambulator while placing the baby in a leather handbag at Victoria Station. Coincidentally Jack's real mother was Lady Bracknell's sister, meaning Jack is therefore Algy's older brother; in addition, his real name is Ernest. Although Jack/Ernest is disappointed to learn that he had been telling the truth all along, Gwendolen is thrilled to be marrying a man named Ernest. Algy and Cecily are happily betrothed, as are Miss Prism and Reverend Chasuble.

Characters: Considered Wilde's most accomplished drama, *The Importance of Being Earnest* is also his best-known work and is still immensely popular with readers and theatergoers. The play is difficult to categorize, for it is simultaneously a farce, a comedy of manners, and a burlesque of literary and social conventions. Distinguished by its lighthearted tone and stylish characters, *Earnest* is particularly praised for its brilliant, polished dialogue, said to resemble the witty conversational style of its author. Some critics characterize the play as purely comic, exemplifying Wilde's aesthetic principle of "art for art's sake" (elevating form over content, style over ethics). However others consider *Earnest* an attack on Victorian solemnity and hypocrisy and detect an underlying morality beneath its comic structure. Thus Wilde's designation of the play as "trivial" may either refer to his aesthetic philosophy or to its ironic social commentary.

Wilde is particularly celebrated for creating the quintessential "dandy," the aristocratic young man who values style rather than moral considerations and who projects a studied elegance, wit, and individuality. **Algernon "Algy" Moncrieff** is often cited as one of Wilde's most successful dandies: fashionable, worldly, and socially prominent, he loves artifice and keeps up a steady tone of pretense and triviality throughout the play. It is notable, however, that despite their sophistication both he and Jack are essentially innocent and childlike; there is no hint of sexual predation in their escapades, and Algernon seems to lust only for food. Algernon's practice of "Bunburyism," a chronically ailing, invented friend who requires his visits, is the height of pretense, employed to allow him to escape for a time from his restrictive immediate surroundings. This deception is particularly significant given the play's setting and context, for the strict moral code of Victorian England made hypocrisy almost required. Wilde employs the name Ernest with brilliant satire, for he found Victorian earnestness and sincerity particularly priggish and hypocritical. Although both Algy and Jack claim to be "Ernest," they are actually its reverse. Thus Jack's announcement at the end of the play that he has learned "the importance of being earnest" rings with resounding irony. Algy's eagerness to be rechristened Ernest in order to secure Cecily's love demonstrates how triviality conquers sincerity in *Earnest:* the conventional principle that a person's character is determined by his or her inner content is reversed as Algy plans to acquire "earnestness" through a mere name change. Algy voices many of the play's most notable witticisms and epigrams, identifying him as Wilde's spokesman, particularly when, in response to Jack's complaint about his triviality, he asserts that no one ever speaks anything but nonsense and that everyone is trivial. Whether Wilde means this to be taken literally, however, may be debated. The fact that Algy does not become Ernest in the end while Jack does has been viewed as a weakness in the plot, though it might also be seen as a deliberate though subtle form of self-parody on Wilde's part.

Algy's friend **John "Jack" Worthing** is another of Wilde's quintessential dandies—elegant, sophisticated, clever, and worldly. Like Algy he flees a restrictive, overly serious and thus typically Victorian home life by frequently employing a deception. Jack invents a fictitious brother Ernest who must often be rescued from various scrapes, thus providing Jack opportunities to travel to London. Despite his sophistication, Jack differs significantly from Algy in his constant worrying and fussing, habits shown to great comic effect in the famous scene in which he and Algy devour a plate of muffins. Algy accuses Jack of the worst sin a dandy can commit—being serious; he suspects, in fact, that Jack is serious "about everything" and this, ironically, is exposed as triviality in that to be serious about everything is to be serious about nothing. The fact that Jack is parentless, having been found in a handbag at Victoria Station when he was an infant, is significant because it allows Wilde to lampoon his society's preoccupation with wealth, social rank, and family lineage. Modern critics have defined the fictional characters of Ernest and Bunbury as evidencing Jack and Algy's search for identity. Jack's quest, cogently expressed when he asks Lady Bracknell to "kindly inform me who I am," is resolved when he learns that he is, indeed, an aristocrat by birth and that his name really is Ernest. Jack's dismay at learning that he has been telling the truth all along provides a good example of the reversed morality presented in the play.

Like their two dandified suitors, **Gwendolen Fairfax** and **Cecily Cardew** are comic characters Wilde uses to satirize Victorian society. Although they are ostensibly proper, refined young ladies, the two actually prove quite self-possessed and hardheaded and help to reinforce the play's system of reversed morality. Bored, elegant Gwendolen Fairfax reflects some of her mother's haughtiness but also exhibits a casual determination to go her own way, despite Lady Bracknell's opinions or plans for her. Described as a "sensible intellectual girl," Gwendolen professes a penchant for reading and scholarly pursuits, causing some critics to view her as a parody of the late nineteenth century's semi-liberated "New Woman." Through Gwendolen's idealization of the name Ernest, Wilde exposes the shallowness beneath high-minded Victorian notions of love and marriage. Discussing with Cecily the revelation of their two Ernests' real identities, Gwendolen complacently states one of the play's major themes: "In matters of grave importance, style, not sincerity, is the main thing." She also reinforces the pattern of reversed conventions when she forgives Jack for having inadvertently told the truth, reassuring him that she expects he will return to lying soon.

Eighteen-year-old **Cecily Cardew** is modeled on the stereotype of the conventional, respectable Victorian girl. Raised in a sheltered country environment, she captivates the jaded, citified Algy with her charm and innocence. Cecily has been bred to project a demure, guileless, and somewhat didactic manner, and her high regard for the name Ernest typifies her moral outlook. Yet like Gwendolen, Cecily is employed to satirize Victorian conventions. Romantic and prone to daydreaming, Cecily informs Algy—whom she believes is her guardian's dissolute brother Ernest—that she fell in love with him long before meeting him and has already recorded the entire course of their romance in her diary, a scene allowing Wilde to lampoon the notion of love at first sight. Cecily introduces several other humorous inversions of romantic conventions, such as when she notes that parting with someone one has known for a long time is much more bearable than parting with someone one has just met. Two other often-cited examples of Cecily's absurdity are her response to Algy's suggestion that she reform him—"I'm afraid I haven't time, this afternoon"—and her comment that she could never wait eighteen years to marry Algy since she finds it impossible to wait even five minutes for anyone.

Considered one of Wilde's most successful comic creations, **Lady Augusta Bracknell** is an elegant, well-dressed, highly self-assured Victorian dowager with a penchant for understatement and literal-mindedness. She is the most conventional figure in the play and represents society, particularly in her reverence for rigid English class structure. Strong-willed, domineering, and narrow-minded, Lady Bracknell disapproves of Jack's parentlessness and refuses to allow her daughter "to marry into a cloakroom, and form an alliance with a parcel" (referring to the handbag infant Jack was found in at Victoria Station). Lady Bracknell absurdly demands that Jack "produce at least one parent, of either sex, before the season is quite over;" ironically, of course, Jack's parentage *is* established by the finale, when he is revealed to be Lady Bracknell's nephew, and she adapts quite easily to this revelation.

Two minor characters in the play help reinforce the absurdity and burlesque reversals of convention. **Miss Letitia Prism**—whose name, as several critics have noted, seems a combination of "prim," "prissy," and "prison"—initially appears to be based on the stereotype of the Victorian spinster governess. Despite her highly proper, morally rigid exterior, however, Miss Prism is as marriage-minded as the younger characters and aggressively pursues Reverend Chasuble as a likely prospect. She is allotted some surprisingly saucy lines, as when she suggests that the Primitive Church's celibacy requirement may be the reason for its extinction. Miss Prism also serves a practical function in *Earnest,* for she proves responsible for the mix-up that has made Jack's parentage a mystery for so many years. Preoccupied with a sensational novel she had written—in which, she explains, "The good ended happily, and the bad unhappily. That is what Fiction means."—Miss Prism had placed her manuscript in a perambulator and baby Jack in a handbag. In keeping with the tone of the play, she is happier about the return of her much-missed handbag than contrite for having lost the baby. In the end Miss Prism is united with **Reverend Frederick Chasuble,** an Anglican clergyman who proves that religion is no more immune from hypocrisy than the rest of society. The reverend is utterly flexible about performing such rites as christening both Algy and Jack with the name Ernest. Similarly Chasuble first consoles Jack on the death of his brother Ernest, then blandly accepts the appearance of Algy posing as Ernest. Critics have interpreted Chasuble as a parody of the High Church movement, which sought to incorporate primitive practices into religious services and which promoted celibacy of the clergy.

Algy's equally dandyish manservant **Lane** is a fine comic character who ably parodies the type of the Victorian butler-confidant who proves sharper than his master. His memorable comments include responding to Algy's request to criticize his piano-playing by saying he had not thought it polite to listen, and describing his limited experience of marriage as "an unfortunate misunderstanding" with a young woman.

Further Reading

Beckson, Karl, ed. *Oscar Wilde: The Critical Heritage.* New York: Barnes & Noble, 1970.

Cohen, Philip K. *The Moral Vision of Oscar Wilde.* Rutherford, N.J.: Fairleigh Dickinson University Press, 1978.

Dictionary of Literary Biography, Vols. 10, 19, 34, 57. Detroit: Gale.

Ellmann, Richard, *Oscar Wilde.* London: Hamish Hamilton, 1987.

Kohl, Norbert. *Oscar Wilde: The Works of a Conformist Rebel.* Cambridge: Cambridge University Press, 1990.

Myers, Jeffrey. "Wilde: 'The Picture of Dorian Gray' (1891)." In *Homosexuality and Literature: 1890-1930*, pp. 20-31. Toronto: McGill-Queen's University Press, 1977.

Powell, Kerry. *Oscar Wilde and the Theatre of the 1890s.* Cambridge: Cambridge University Press, 1990.

Raby, Peter. *Oscar Wilde.* Cambridge: Cambridge University Press, 1991.

Twentieth-Century Literary Criticism, Vols. 1, 8, 23, 41. Detroit: Gale.

Wilde, Oscar. Letter to the editor of the *St. James's Gazette,* 26 June 1890. In *The Artist as Critic: Critical Writings of Oscar Wilde,* edited by Richard Ellmann, pp. 238-41. New York: Random House, 1969.

Harriet E. Wilson
1828(?)-1863(?)
African-American novelist.

Our Nig; or, Sketches from the Life of a Free Black, in a Two-Story White House, North, Showing that Slavery's Shadows Fall Even There (novel, 1859)

Plot: The novel opens with an account of Mag Smith, a beautiful young woman of humble social status whose affair with a wealthy philanderer resulted in pregnancy and abandonment by her lover. Although her baby died soon after birth, Mag is shunned by her family and friends. Lonely and impoverished, she marries a kind black barrel maker named Jim, with whom she lives happily for some years. The couple has two children, one of them a lively, attractive girl named Frado. After Jim's death, Mag becomes involved with his friend and business partner, Seth Shipley. The destitute couple decides to move from the town they are living in, and they leave Frado with the white, upper-class Bellmont family. Frado thus begins a miserable life as an overworked, much-abused indentured servant in the household. Although Mr. Bellmont, his sister Aunt Abby, or Nab, and his children Jane and Jack are generally kind to Frado, Mrs. Bellmont and her daughter Mary treat her with sadistic cruelty and disdain. Frado is allowed three years of schooling and takes to her books with enthusiasm. She is forced to work long, grueling hours in both the house and fields, but nevertheless maintains her vivacious manner and wins friends among the Bellmonts' farmhands as well as her schoolmates. When Frado is nine years old, the Bellmonts' eldest son, James, who lives in Baltimore, comes home for a visit and befriends the persecuted little girl. Frado's troubles increase, however, after James's departure, for she is allotted even more work and continues to endure mistreatment by Mrs. Bellmont. Then James marries Susan, Jane marries and starts her own home, and Jack too leaves to make his way in the West.

When Frado is fourteen, the elder Bellmonts go to Baltimore to visit James, leaving Mary in charge of the household. She is as tyrannical and abusive as her mother, and reacts with escalating cruelty to Frado's declining health. Finally Mr. and Mrs. Bellmont return, and James soon follows, racked by illness. He insists that Frado be treated more humanely and plans to take her back to Baltimore with him after he recovers. His condition worsens, however, and he finally dies after promising to meet Frado again in heaven. When Frado reaches the age of eighteen, her indentureship expires, and she leaves the Bellmont household. With the help of a kind benefactor, Frado becomes a straw sewer (making straw hats) and manages to support herself. She marries a fugitive slave and gives birth to a son; her husband eventually dies of yellow fever, leaving her to make her own way again.

Characters: Since its rediscovery in the early 1980s, *Our Nig* has been hailed as an important work of early African-American fiction. It is not only the first book published in the United States by any black writer but one of the first by a black woman anywhere in the world. Based on the circumstances of Wilson's own life as a free black living in New England in the years before the Civil War, *Our Nig* focuses on the racism practiced by hypocritical Northerners who say they are Christians but treat blacks with cruelty and disdain. In chronicling the protagonist's progression from abandoned child to indentured servant to self-sufficient woman, Wilson combined some aspects of the nineteenth-century slave narrative with the European tradition of the sentimental novel. Critics generally agree that *Our Nig* is a more accomplished work than those by several other notable African-Americans (such as William Wells Brown's *Clotel; or, The President's Daughter* or Martin Delany's *Blake; or, The Huts of America*), and that Wilson was apparently well-read and possessed of creative ability rather than mere didactic intent. In the novel's much-discussed preface, Wilson frankly states that financial destitution has led her to try to earn money through writing; she also indicates, significantly, that in anticipation of a negative reaction from Northern abolitionists and free blacks, whom she does not wish to offend, she has toned down the most brutal details of her story. Wilson has been credited not only with establishing the tradition of the black woman's novel but with playing an important role in the development of African-American literature in general, which was during the latter half of the nineteenth century expanding beyond the limitations of poetry and autobiography into the complex realm of the novel.

The ''Our Nig'' referred to in the novel's title is **Frado,** the mulatto daughter of white Mag Smith and black Jim. In the first published version of the book, the title was followed with ''By 'Our Nig,''' thus indicating not only that the novel was autobiographical but, most significantly and through the use of quotation marks around Our Nig, that Wilson intended to ironically highlight the nickname given to the protagonist by her white masters. The circumstances of Frado's life mirror those of Wilson's. She does not appear in the novel until the second chapter, after her father has died and her mother and her lover are discussing what to do about their impoverished situation. They decide to abandon Frado—an attractive child with expressive eyes and a spirited, innately innocent personality—and leave her with the white, middle-class Bellmonts. Thus Frado begins a life of mistreatment and loneliness as an indentured servant, the constant victim of her mistress's racially motivated cruelty. Although most of the Bellmonts are kind to her, it is notable that one of the kindest, Jack, gives her the derogatory appellation ''Our Nig,'' by which all of the family members address her. Though much overburdened by work in the house and in the fields, Frado remains vivacious and mischievous; her pranks include climbing to the roof of the barn, and putting cigar smoke into her teacher's desk drawer so that he panics when he opens it. She is well-liked by the Bellmonts' field hands and her schoolmates, who forget their initial hostility after they become acquainted with her. Frado's hardships are somewhat alleviated when she is allowed to attend school, where she develops a love of reading that will bring her enrichment and solace (as it did her creator) in the years ahead. Frado also develops good relationships with James Bellmont, who insists during his visits home that she be more humanely treated, and kind Aunt Abby, who takes her to religious meetings and generally serves as a benevolent confidante. Eventually, however, the years of unrelenting work and neglect take a physical toll on Frado, who is much depleted by illness by the time she reaches eighteen and is legally able to leave the Bellmont household. Even before that day arrives, however, Frado establishes a voice of her own and feels the stirrings of independence within herself when she finally stands up to Mrs. Bellmont's abuse, angrily defying her shrewish mistress. Once on her own, Frado becomes a maker of straw hats (just as Wilson did while living in Massachusetts) and is gaining self-sufficiency when she falls in love with and marries a handsome, well-mannered black man named Samuel who is supposedly a fugitive slave. Samuel's eventual desertion of Frado and their child, after admitting that he was never actually a slave, proves that he is the same kind of dissolute lover Wilson found herself attracted to. The novel has no conclusive ending, for Wilson leaves it in the reader's hands to assist Frado (whose identity now merges with her creator's) in her quest for self-reliance by buying the book. Frado is a decidedly sympathetic character who seems deliberately portrayed as strong and spirited rather than weak and helpless in order to highlight the injustice imposed on her from outside. She has been identified as a notable and unique example of the "tragic mulatto" characters found in many nineteenth-century novels— unique because her troubles are due not to her mixed blood per se or to male oppression, but to the racial and class exploitation perpetrated by hypocritical New Englanders.

Mag Smith is Frado's white mother, a once-beautiful woman who endured a difficult childhood and an adulthood marred by poverty and abandonment by her upper-class lover after she became pregnant. Rejected by her family and friends, Mag marries the kind, industrious Jim out of loneliness and destitution, thus violating the strong nineteenth-century taboo against miscegenation (interracial marriage) or, as it was then called, amalgamation. *Our Nig* is, in fact, considered the first American novel to feature a marriage between a white woman and a black man, a union that Wilson herself approaches with some ambivalence. She asks the reader to consider Mag's degraded position, suggesting only desperation could motivate it. Yet she also portrays the marriage of Mag and Jim as happy and fairly prosperous, at least until Jim becomes too ill to work and finally dies. Although Wilson seems to sympathize with her to a certain extent, Mag is faulted for abandoning Frado, and it has been noted that this circumstance reveals a lack of the respect for mothers that was common in fiction by nineteenth-century women authors. **Jim** is a considerate black man whose illiteracy is suggested by the African-American dialect he speaks. He sincerely loves Mag, whose status as his "treasure" is partly based on her being a white woman. Critics have suggested that the relative happiness of Jim's interracial union with Mag may have rankled white readers—even those who were anti-slavery—and thus might account, at least in part, for the lack of attention the book received after its publication.

The inhabitants of the "Two-Story White House" mentioned in the novel's title are the middle-class Bellmonts, the family for whom Frado works as an indentured servant. **John Bellmont** is relatively kind to Frado but generally seems unable or unwilling to restrain his vindictive wife. It is Mr. Bellmont who sends Frado to school for three years, a privilege that serves her well throughout her life. **Aunt Abby,** or **Nab,** is also Frado's friend and even acts as a kind of surrogate mother, providing comfort to her in her misery, influencing her to attend religious meetings, and listening to her confidences. Both the sickly **Jane** and the friendly **Jack** treat Frado well; Jack performs a special favor by retrieving Frado's beloved Fido after Mrs. Bellmont sells the dog. Yet it is the generally sympathetic Jack who coins the derogatory nickname "Our Nig" for Frado, thus highlighting the pervasiveness of racism even within the most supposedly benevolent quarters. **James Bellmont,** the family's oldest son, develops an amiable relationship with Frado, whose lot he continually tries to improve. Handsome and personable, he radiates with an innate gentility, as does **Susan,** the wealthy, worthy young woman he eventually marries. James and Frado have in common a religious inclination, and it has also been suggested that there may be a hint of repressed sexual desire in their friendship.

The novel's villainess is **Mrs. Bellmont,** a shrewish, sadistic bully who delights in making Frado's life miserable. From the time Frado is a small girl, Mrs. Bellmont forces her to work long, grueling hours in the house and fields, beats her frequently, demeans her for being black, and generally subjects her to a brutal form of enslavement. Her cruelty is perhaps best symbolized by her selling Frado's dog, Fido, the girl's only source of comfort after most of the sympathetic members of the Bellmont family have left home. Mrs. Bellmont embodies the racist tendencies that Wilson meant to show were not limited to residents of the South but could be found even among Northerners claiming to be Christians. Wilson makes the point in the novel's preface that Mrs. Bellmont, modeled after the mistress who ruled over her own sojourn as an indentured servant, exhibits ''Southern principles''—an apparent attempt to avoid offending Northern abolitionists. Like her mother, **Mary Bellmont** is thoroughly mean and haughty, insisting that Frado follow behind her at all times and ruling over the household tyrannically while her parents are away. Her sadism is highlighted in the scene in which, enraged by Frado's ill health, she hurls a knife at the miserable girl. Some critics contend that Wilson portrays the oppression of African-Americans as a complex phenomenon; by showing that only these two members of the Bellmont family actually treat Frado inhumanely; others, however, feel that Mrs. Bellmont and her daughter subtly undermine Wilson's message by appearing as the exception rather than the rule.

The man Frado eventually marries, **Samuel,** seems to have been closely modeled after the author's husband, Thomas Wilson. Handsome and well-mannered (the latter quality is attributed to his having once been a house slave), Samuel presents himself as a fugitive slave. He explains his frequent absences from home as necessitated by invitations to deliver lectures on his experiences, but it is eventually revealed that he has merely pretended to have once been a slave in order to make money from sympathetic abolitionists. Like Wilson's husband, Samuel deserts the pregnant Frado once and returns only to abandon her again, the second time permanently. Although he is kind to Frado when he is with her, Samuel lacks the moral fiber and sense of responsibility exhibited by such characters as Frado's father, Jim, and James Bellmont.

Other characters in *Our Nig* include **Seth Shipley,** Jim's friend and business partner, with whom Mag lives after her husband's death; **Henry Reed,** the propertied young man Mrs. Bellmont wishes Jane to marry; and **George Means,** the man Jane marries, with the blessings of her aunt and father.

Further Reading

Bell, Bernard B. ''Harriet E. Wilson.'' In *The Afro-American Novel and Its Tradition,* pp. 45-50. Amherst: University of Massachusetts Press, 1987.

Foreman, P. Gabrielle. ''The Spoken and the Silenced in *Incidents in the Life of a Slave Girl* and *Our Nig.*'' *Callaloo* 13, No. 2 (Spring 1990): 313-24.

Gates, Henry Louis, Jr. Introduction to *Our Nig; or, Sketches from the Life of a Free Black, in a Two-Story House, North. Showing that Slavery's Shadow Falls Even There,* by Harriet E. Wilson. New York: Random House, 1983.

Jackson, Blyden. ''Frank J. Webb and Harriet E. Wilson.'' In *A History of Afro-American Literature,* Vol. 1: *The Long Beginning, 1746-1895,* pp. 343-63. Baton Rouge: Louisiana State University Press.

Russell, Sandi. ''Out of Slavery.'' In *Render Me My Song: African-American Women Writers from Slavery to the Present.* New York: St. Martin's Press, 1990.

José Zorilla y Moral
1817-1893
Spanish dramatist, novelist, and poet.

Don Juan Tenorio (drama, 1844)

Plot: Set in mid-sixteenth century Spain, the play begins in Seville during carnival season. The young nobleman Don Juan Tenorio meets his friend, Don Luis Mejía, in a tavern to learn who has won the wager they made one year earlier. Each had bet that he would be able to commit more wicked deeds than the other during the coming year. Also present at their meeting are Don Gonzalo de Ulloa, the father of the girl Don Juan intends to marry, and his own father, Don Diego Tenorio; both men are masked to avoid detection, and both wish to discover what evil Don Juan has perpetrated. When Don Juan and Don Luis list the men they have killed in duels and the women they have seduced, Don Juan is the winner. However, he has not yet seduced a nun or the beloved of a friend, so he bets Don Luis that he can add these conquests to his list within a week. Don Luis now fears that his friend will attempt to reach his fiancee, Ana de Pantoja, and he takes steps to protect her. Meanwhile, Don Gonzalo vows that Don Juan will never marry his daughter, who has been sequestered in a convent, and Don Diego disowns his son. With the help of his servant, Marcos Ciutti, Don Juan manages to secure a key to Ana's room and to have Don Luis kidnapped and bound. He then persuades Brígida, the servant of his beloved, Ines de Ulloa, to carry a letter to the girl in her convent. Learning that the innocent Ines is already in love with him, though she has never met him, Don Juan decides to take her from the convent. When he appears in her room, she swoons, and Don Juan spirits her away to his own home. While Ines is still unconscious, Don Juan goes to Ana's room and ravishes her. Later he returns to his home, where he meets Don Luis and Don Gonzalo, both enraged; he kills them and escapes. Abandoned by her lover, Ines dies of a broken heart.

Five years later, Don Diego has built a cemetery for his son's victims, with three sculptures commemorating the most notable: Don Gonzalo, Don Luis, and Ines. While Don Juan is visiting the cemetery, the statue of Ines comes to life, entreating him to accept salvation from God, or both she and he will be damned. Don Juan does not believe that this vision is real, and he laughingly invites the statue of Ines's father to join him for dinner that night. At the subsequent banquet, Don Gonzalo appears in the room, demanding that Don Juan beg for God's mercy or face damnation. Don Juan is still skeptical, even when Ines also appears and repeats her previous entreaties. The next morning, Don Juan returns to the cemetery and sees a terrifying vision of hell. Don Gonzalo's statue again commands him to repent but he still refuses; as he is being dragged toward hell, however, Don Juan reaches upward. Ines appears, and the two ascend together to heaven.

Characters: Zorilla is one of Spain's most celebrated dramatists, and *Don Juan Tenorio*, his most famous work, is still traditionally performed on or around All Saint's Day (November 1) in his homeland. Based on the legendary hero of Spanish folk tales, the play is thought to have been modeled after an earlier work by the seventeenth-century dramatist Tirso de Molina, in whose heavily moralistic version Don Juan is punished for his crimes against society. An important difference is that Zorilla portrays the roguish but essentially likable Don Juan as eventually saved by the love of a good woman, thus asserting that sinful humanity may be redeemed through repentance and God's infinite love. Written in about twenty days, *Don Juan Tenorio* is sometimes faulted for its flimsy construction and sentimentality, and Zorilla himself supposedly came to scorn the play. Yet the play's melodic verse and dramatic power are widely acknowledged, and it continues to be one of the best loved works of Spanish literature.

Zorilla's **Don Juan Tenorio** is based on the centuries-old legend of the notorious rake and gallant who duels, charms, and seduces his way through life. The play's title character is, indeed, a wild young aristocrat who seems to expend his considerable energies and ambitions exclusively on vice. Yet he differs from the Don Juan of the folk tales in his essential humanity and generosity. Bold, reckless, and volatile, he kills men and seduces women, but he does occasionally feel melancholy and remorse, and his conversion to Christianity at the end of the play is portrayed as deep and sincere. *Don Juan Tenorio* was written at the height of Spanish romanticism, and its title character is a particularly romantic figure in the almost hallucinatory magnetism he exerts over women. Even the innocent, unworldly Ines de Ulloa is irresistibly drawn to him, and her steadfast love finally saves him. Though initially cynical and disinclined to believe that a sinner like himself can attain salvation, Don Juan ultimately repents and rises to heaven—a conversion that some early critics found unconvincing but that nevertheless vividly illustrates the play's central theme of redemption. Don Juan's audacious presence dominates and energizes the play and evidences Zorilla's dramatic skill.

Described in an 1898 review by Fanny Hale Gardiner as "a picture dear to the hearts of Spaniards of both sexes," **Ines de Ulloa** is a typical romantic heroine in her purity and in her guiding, pacifying influence over the man she loves. Though bred in a convent and presumably completely ignorant of the world, the pious Ines develops a passion for Don Juan even before she meets him. She is both frightened and eager to encounter her daring, passionate lover, and she faints when he finally does appear in her convent cell. After Don Juan abandons her, Ines dies of grief—a particularly romantic concept—and then returns after death, still devoted to the skeptical Don Juan and determined to save him from damnation. The fact that the love of Ines and Don Juan is only consummated after death and, in a spiritual rather than physical manner, has been said to symbolize the triumph of the spirit over the flesh.

Don Diego Tenorio, Don Juan's father, is disgusted by his son's behavior and disowns him, later establishing a cemetery for his victims and commissioning the statues that eventually come to life. Another significant father-figure in the play is **Don Gonzalo de Ulloa,** whose daughter Ines is Don Juan's intended. Like Don Diego, Don Gonzalo is outraged by Don Juan's behavior and vehemently forbids his marriage to Ines. When he comes to Don Juan's house after he has kidnapped Ines from the convent, Don Juan kills him. His statue later comes to life to exhort the sinful young gallant to ask for God's forgiveness and thus achieve eternal life. Don Juan's refusal first to believe that this vision of Don Gonzalo is real, and then to accept his guidance, has been seen as a defiance of the father-figure and, by extension, of God. It is not the paternal Don Gonzalo who finally succeeds in leading Don Juan to redemption but the female, somewhat maternal Ines.

Other characters in *Don Juan Tenorio* include **Don Luis Mejía,** Don Juan's friend and fellow rake, with whom he makes his fateful wager and whose fiancee he seduces; **Ana de Pantoja,** Don Luis's fiancee, who is ravished by Don Juan in fulfillment of his goal of seducing a friend's bride-to-be; **Marcos Ciutti,** Don Juan's servant, who is as villainous as his master and helps him carry out his schemes; and **Brígida,** Ines's servant, who also helps Don Juan by carrying messages between the two lovers and by lying to Ines about the nature of her abduction from the convent.

Further Reading

Brett, Lewis E., ed. "Zorilla." In *Nineteenth Century Spanish Plays,* pp. 283-86. New York, London: D. Appleton-Century Co., 1935.

Feal, Carlos. "Conflicting Names, Conflicting Laws: Zorilla's 'Don Juan Tenorio.'" *PMLA* 96, No. 3 (May 1981): 375-87.

Firmat, Gustavo Pérez. "Carnival in *Don Juan Tenorio.*" *Hispanic Review* 51, No. 3 (Summer 1983): 269-81.

Gardiner, Fanny Hale. "A Spanish Poet-Laureate: José Zorilla." *Poet Lore* X, No. 4 (1898): 506-14.

Nineteenth-Century Literature Criticism, Vol. 6. Detroit: Gale.

Peers, E. Allison. "The Continuance of Romanticism, 1837-1860." In *A History of the Romantic Movement in Spain,* Vol. II, pp. 160-258. Cambridge: Cambridge University Press, 1964.

Ter Horst, Robert. "Ritual Time Regained in Zorilla's *Don Juan Tenorio.*" *Romantic Review* LXX, No. 1 (January 1979): 80-95.

Character and Title Index

581

Fairfax, Mrs. 60
Fairlie, Frederick 121
Fairlie, Laura 120
Fairway, Timothy 274
Falcone, Fortunato 413
Falcone, Giuseppa 413
Falcone, Mateo 413
"The Fall of the House of
   Usher" 424
Fan 155
Fang, Mr. 153
Fanshawe, Ginevra 66
Fantine 316
*Far from the Madding
   Crowd* 268
Farebrother, Reverend
   Camden 214
Farfrae, Donald 276
Faria, Abbé 198
Farmer and his son 376
Farmhand 245
Fathers and Sons 537
Fauchelevent, Father 317
Faust 247
Faust I and II 246
Fausta 469
Fawley, Drusilla 283
Fawley, Jude 281
Fay, Henery 270
Featherstone, Peter 214
Fedallah 405
Fedya 534
Felton, John 196
Ferapont 108
Fere, Count de la
   (Athos) 195
Fere, Countess de la
   (Milady) 195
Fernande 398
Ferrante, Don 386
Ferrars, Edward 18
Ferrars, Mrs. 18
Ferrars, Robert 18
Fezziwig, Mr. and Mrs. 155
Fiers 110
Filipovna, Nastasya 186
Finn, Huckleberry 543, 546
Finn, Pap 548
Fiona 370
Fish Footman 91
Fisker, Hamilton 530
Fitzgerald, Burgo 524
Fitzwilliam, Colonel 22
Five 92
Flamant 147
Flask 405
Flaxman, Lord Hugh 562
Fleece 405

Fleming, Henry (The
   Youth) 140
Fletcher, Everell 456
Fletcher, Martha 456
Fletcher, William 456
Flint, Captain 473
Flite, Miss 168
Flora ("Madame Tellier's
   Establishment") 399
Flora (*Coningsby*) 178
Flora (*The Turn of the
   Screw*) 348
Follenvie, Madame 395
Follenvie, Monsieur 397
Forestier, Madame
   Jeanne 401
Forrester, Captain Roland 51
Forrester, Edith 51
Forrester, Mrs. 236
Fortunato 432
Fosco, Count 120
Fosco, Countess Eleanor 121
Fosdick, Henry 14
Foster, Mr. 422
Foster, Silas 299
Fouqué 465
Frado (Our Nig) 575
Frankenstein, Elizabeth 458
*Frankenstein; or, The New
   Prometheus* 457
Frankenstein, Victor 458
Frankenstein, William 458
Frankenstein's monster 458
Frasquita 4
Fred 155
Free, Michael
   "Mickey" 372
Frigilis 7
Frog Footman 91
Frollo, Claude 311
Frollo, Jehan 313
Furmity Woman 277
"The Furnished Room" 304
Fyodorovna, Nadyezhda 100
G----, Monsieur 431
G., Alexander
   Mikhailych 536
Gabelle, Theophile 165
Gabler, Hedda 329
Gabriel, Brother 87
Gaev, Leonid 109
Galahad, Sir 552
Gall, Geoffrey 423
Gamba, Tiodoro 413
Gambler 142
Gamut, David 130
Garcia 416
Gardiner, Captain 406
Gardiner, Colonel 449

Gardiner, Mr. and Mrs. 22
Gardiner, Sir Philip 456
Gargery, Georgiana Maria
   (Mrs. Joe) 172
Gargery, Joe 172
Garie, Clarence 564
Garie, Clarence, Jr. 564
Garie, Emily (daughter) 564
Garie, Emily 565
*The Garies and Their
   Friends* 563
Garth, Alfred 213
Garth, Ben 213
Garth, Caleb 213
Garth, Christy 213
Garth, Letty 213
Garth, Mary 213
Garth, Susan 213
Gaster, Reverend Dr. 423
Gaussin, Césaire 147
Gaussin, Jean 147
Gautier, Marguerite
   (Camille) 192
Gautruche, Monsieur 264
Gellatly, Davie 449
Gemini, Countess 344
General ("The Hamlet of the
   Schigrov District") 536
General Gabriel 149
Geneviève 382
George 286
Georgiana 292
Gerasim ("Mumu") 531
Gerasim (*The Death of Ivan
   Ilyich*) 515
German businessman 536
Germinie Lacerteux 262
Gertrude, Sister 385
Gevrol 227
The Ghost of Christmas
   Past 155
The Ghost of Christmas
   Present 155
The Ghost of Christmas Yet to
   Come 155
Ghosts 321
Gieshubler 222
"The Gift of the Magi" 303
Giletti 469
Gillenormand, Monsieur 317
Gina, Duchess of
   Sansévérina 468
Ginger Nut 407
Giovanelli, Mr. 339
The Gladiator 48
Glegg, Aunt 207
Glegg, Mr. 207
Glenmire, Lady 236
Glyde, Sir Percival 121